Swimming
ROGER DEAKIN

VINTAGE MINIS

1 3 5 7 9 10 8 6 4 2

Vintage
20 Vauxhall Bridge Road,
London SW1V 2SA

Vintage Classics is part of the Penguin Random House
group of companies whose addresses can be found at
global.penguinrandomhouse.com

Extracts from *Waterlog* copyright © Roger Deakin 1999

Roger Deakin has asserted his right to be identified as the author of this
Work in accordance with the Copyright, Designs and Patents Act 1988

First published in Great Britain by Chatto & Windus in 1999
This short edition published by Vintage in 2017

D.H. Lawrence, 'The Third Thing' by permission of
Laurence Pollinger Ltd and the Estate of Frieda Lawrence
Ravagli; extract from Ted Hughes's address at the memorial
service for Henry Williamson by kind permission of the Estate
of Ted Hughes.

penguin.co.uk/vintage

A CIP catalogue record for this book is available from the British Library

ISBN 9781784872762

Typeset in 9.5/14.5 pt FreightText Pro
by Jouve (UK), Milton Keynes
Printed and bound by Clays Ltd, St Ives plc

Penguin Random House is committed to a sustainable future for
our business, our readers and our planet. This book is made from
Forest Stewardship Council® certified paper.

MIX
Paper from
responsible sources
FSC® C018179
www.fsc.org

Contents

1

The Moat

THE WARM RAIN tumbled from the gutter in one of those midsummer downpours as I hastened across the lawn behind my house in Suffolk and took shelter in the moat. Breaststroking up and down the thirty yards of clear, green water, I nosed along, eyes just at water level. The frog's-eye view of rain on the moat was magnificent. Rain calms water, it freshens it, sinks all the floating pollen, dead bumblebees and other flotsam. Each raindrop exploded in a momentary, bouncing fountain that turned into a bubble and burst. The best moments were when the storm intensified, drowning birdsong, and a haze rose off the water as though the moat itself were rising to meet the lowering sky. Then the rain eased and the reflected heavens were full of tiny dancers: water sprites springing up on tiptoe like bright pins over the surface. It was raining water sprites.

It was at the height of this drenching in the summer of

1996 that the notion of a long swim through Britain began to form itself. I wanted to follow the rain on its meanderings about our land to rejoin the sea, to break out of the frustration of a lifetime doing lengths, of endlessly turning back on myself like a tiger pacing its cage. I began to dream of secret swimming holes and a journey of discovery through what William Morris, in the title to one of his romances, called *The Water of the Wondrous Isles*. My inspiration was John Cheever's classic short story 'The Swimmer', in which the hero, Ned Merrill, decides to swim the eight miles home from a party on Long Island via a series of his neighbours' swimming pools. One sentence in the story stood out and worked on my imagination: 'He seemed to see, with a cartographer's eye, that string of swimming pools, that quasi-subterranean stream that curved across the county.'

I was living by myself, feeling sad at the end of a long love, and, as a freelance film-maker and writer, more or less free to commit myself to a journey if I wanted to. My son, Rufus, was also on an adventure Down Under, working in restaurants and surfing in Byron Bay, and I missed him. At least I could join him in spirit in the water. Like the endless cycle of the rain, I would begin and end the journey in my moat, setting out in spring and swimming through the year. I would keep a log of impressions and events as I went.

My earliest memory of serious swimming is of being woken very early on holiday mornings with my grandparents in Kenilworth by a sudden rain of pebbles at my bedroom window aimed by my Uncle Laddie, who was a local swimming champion and had his own key to the outdoor pool. My cousins and I were reared on mythic tales of his exploits – in races, on high boards, or swimming far out to sea – so it felt an honour to swim with him. Long before the lifeguards arrived, we would unlock the wooden gate and set the straight, black, refracted lines on the bottom of the green pool snaking and shimmying. It was usually icy, but the magic of being first in is what I remember. 'We had the place to ourselves,' we would say with satisfaction afterwards over breakfast. Our communion with the water was all the more delightful for being free of charge. It was my first taste of unofficial swimming.

Years later, driven mad by the heat one sultry summer night, a party of us clambered over the low fence of the old open-air pool at Diss in Norfolk. We joined other silent, informal swimmers who had somehow stolen in, hurdling the dormant turnstiles, and now loomed past us in the water only to disappear again into the darkness like characters from *Under Milk Wood*. Such indelible swims are like dreams, and have the same profound effect on the mind and spirit. In the night sea at Walberswick I have seen bodies fiery with phosphorescent plankton striking through the neon waves like dragons.

The more I thought about it, the more obsessed I became with the idea of a swimming journey. I started to dream ever more exclusively of water. Swimming and dreaming were becoming indistinguishable. I grew convinced that following water, flowing with it, would be a way of getting under the skin of things, of learning something new. I might learn about myself, too. In water, all possibilities seemed infinitely extended. Free of the tyranny of gravity and the weight of the atmosphere, I found myself in the wide-eyed condition described by the Australian poet Les Murray when he said: 'I am only interested in everything.' The enterprise began to feel like some medieval quest. When Merlin turns the future King Arthur into a fish as part of his education in *The Sword in the Stone*, T. H. White says, 'He could do what men always wanted to do, that is, fly. There is practically no difference between flying in the water and flying in the air . . . It was like the dreams people have.'

When you swim, you feel your body for what it mostly is – water – and it begins to move with the water around it. No wonder we feel such sympathy for beached whales; we are beached at birth ourselves. To swim is to experience how it was before you were born. Once in the water, you are immersed in an intensely private world as you were in the womb. These amniotic waters are both utterly safe and yet terrifying, for at birth anything could go wrong, and you are assailed by all kinds of unknown forces over which you have no control. This may account for the anxieties every swimmer experiences from time to time in deep water. A swallow dive off the high board into the void is an image that brings together all the contradictions of birth. The swimmer experiences the terror and the bliss of being born.

So swimming is a rite of passage, a crossing of boundaries: the line of the shore, the bank of the river, the edge of the pool, the surface itself. When you enter the water, something like metamorphosis happens. Leaving behind the land, you go through the looking-glass surface and enter a new world, in which survival, not ambition or desire, is the dominant aim. The lifeguards at the pool or the beach remind you of the thin line between waving and drowning. You see and experience things when you're swimming in a way that is completely different from any other. You are *in* nature, part and parcel of it, in a far more complete and intense way than on dry land, and your sense of the present is overwhelming. In wild water you are on equal terms with the animal world around you: in every sense, on the same level. As a swimmer, I can go right up to a frog in the water and it will show more curiosity than fear. The damselflies and dragonflies that crowd the surface of the moat pointedly ignore me, just taking off for a moment to allow me to go by, then landing again in my wake.

Natural water has always held the magical power to cure. Somehow or other, it transmits its own self-regenerating powers to the swimmer. I can dive in with a long face and what feels like a terminal case of depression, and come out a whistling idiot. There is a feeling of absolute freedom and wildness that comes with the sheer liberation of nakedness

I can dive in with a long face and what feels like a terminal case of depression, and come out a whistling idiot

as well as weightlessness in natural water, and it leads to a deep bond with the bathing-place.

Most of us live in a world where more and more places and things are signposted, labelled, and officially 'interpreted'. There is something about all this that is turning the reality of things into virtual reality. It is the reason why walking, cycling and swimming will always be subversive activities. They allow us to regain a sense of what is old and wild in these islands, by getting off the beaten track and breaking free of the official version of things. A swimming journey would give me access to that part of our world which, like darkness, mist, woods or high mountains, still retains most mystery. It would afford me a different perspective on the rest of landlocked humanity.

My moat, where the journey first suggested itself, and really began, is fed by a vigorous spring eleven feet down, and purified by an entirely natural filtration system far superior to even the most advanced of swimming-pool technology. It is sustained by the plant and animal life you will find in any unpolluted fresh-water pond left to its own devices and given plenty of sunlight. There seems to have been a period, from the later Middle Ages until the seventeenth century, when moats became as fashionable in Suffolk as private pools are today. There are over thirty of them within a four-mile radius of the church in the nearby village of Cotton. Moats are now considered by historians like Oliver Rackham to have functioned as much as status symbols as anything else for the yeoman farmers who dug them. Mine was probably excavated when the house was built in the sixteenth century, and runs along the front and back of the house but not the sides. It had no defensive function except as a stock barrier. It would have yielded useful clay for building and formed a substantial reservoir, but it was certainly never intended for swimming. Its banks plunge straight down and it has no shallow end. At one end, where you climb in or out by a submerged wooden cart-ladder I have staked to the bank, a big willow presides, its pale fibrous roots waving in the water like sea anemones.

The moat is where I have bathed for years, swimming breaststroke for preference. I am no champion, just a competent swimmer with a fair amount of stamina. Part of my intention in setting out on the journey was not to perform any spectacular feats, but to try and learn something of the mystery D. H. Lawrence noticed in his poem 'The Third Thing':

Water is H_2O, hydrogen two parts, oxygen one,
But there is also a third thing, that makes it water
And nobody knows what that is.

Cheever describes being in the water, for Ned Merrill, as 'less a pleasure, it seemed, than the resumption of a natural condition'. My intention was to revert to a similarly feral state. For the best part of a year, the water would become my natural habitat. Otters sometimes set off across country in search of new territory, fresh water, covering as much as twelve miles in a night. I suppose there is part of all of us that envies the otter, the dolphin and the whale, our mammal cousins who are so much better adapted to water than we are, and seem to get so much more enjoyment from life than we do. If I could learn even a fraction of whatever they know, the journey would be richly repaid.

Packing, the night before I left, I felt something of the same apprehension and exhilaration as I imagine the otter might feel about going off into the blue. But, as with Ned Merrill in 'The Swimmer', my impulse to set off was simple enough at heart: 'The day was beautiful and it seemed to him that a long swim might enlarge and celebrate its beauty.'

2

I-Spy at the Seaside

Scilly Isles, 23 April

ST MARY'S ROAD AND TRESCO Flats could easily be somewhere in the East End of London, but they are the names of some of the treacherous waters that have wrecked so many ships on the islands and rocks of the Scillies. I had sailed over from Penzance on the *Scillonian* to St Mary's harbour, and was now bound for the quiet island of Bryher in an open boat with an engine like a rolling kettledrum. We chugged through the calm water of Appletree Bay in the spring sunshine, past the islands of Samson and Tresco, to land at a makeshift planked jetty known as 'Anneka's Quay' after Anneka Rice, who built it (with a little help from the Parachute Regiment) for one of those television programmes in which she performed the impossible before breakfast. Half a dozen of us disembarked along the sandy boardwalk on to the beach path, where I met the postmistress with her red bicycle waiting to hand over the mail. She directed me to a B&B, and in less than twenty minutes I had a room overlooking the bay and was on my way for a swim.

Having crossed the island in a quarter of an hour's walk, I followed a rim of doughnut rocks to the white sands of Great Popplestones Bay. Apart from a solitary sun-worshipper out of sight at the far end of the bay, I was alone. It was still April, and the swimming season could hardly be said to have begun; hence my migration to the reputedly balmy climate of these islands, 'bathed in the warm Gulf Stream', as they put it in the brochure. So far, so good. This was my first sea swim, so I thought I had better grasp the nettle of a skin baptism. I stripped off and ran naked into the water, screaming inwardly with the sudden agony of it. It was scaldingly cold, and the icy water kept on tearing pain through me until I got moving and swam a few frantic strokes as children do on their first visit to the deep end, then scrambled out breathless with cold; a mad moment of masochism. So much for the fabled caress of the gentle Gulf Stream. I climbed straight into my wetsuit and swam comfortably out again into the amazing clear water in a flat calm, crossed the little bay, marvelling at the brightness of everything, and swam back again. The sand was white and fine, and shone up through the water. Small dead crabs floated amongst the thin line of shredded bladderwrack and tiny shells oscillating up the beach. The silence was disturbed only by nature's bagpipes, the incessant gulls. I climbed out onto rocks that glinted gold with quartz and mica, stripped off the wetsuit, and lay down to dry in the sun. Spread out next to me, it looked like another sunbather.

The black rubber Bibendum travelled about with me like my shadow. I knew from the outset that I would have to confront the Wetsuit Question and concede that if I were to swim in all seasons and every variety of open water, I would need to wear one from time to time. So I had myself measured for a tailor-made suit by two friends one night in their kitchen in Suffolk. I stood in my swimming trunks before the fire after dinner while they measured me with a cloth tape from the sewing drawer. The wetsuit couturier had sent a list of the required measurements that could hardly have been more thorough had I been going into space: 'base of throat to top of leg', 'neck to shoulder edge', 'centre back to base of neck', and so on, down to the ankle circumference. When we had finished, someone discovered that the tape had shrunk an inch-and-a-quarter, so we had to re-calculate everything. But the suit fitted like a banana skin when it arrived.

The problem about wearing a wetsuit is sensory deprivation; it is a species of whole-body condom. Of course, there are people who like rubber. They enjoy the feel of it; they may even find it aesthetically pleasing. But there is no getting away from the fact that a wetsuit is an anaesthetic to prevent you experiencing the full force of your physical encounter with cold water, and in that sense it is against nature and something of a killjoy. On the other hand, I tell myself each time I struggle into the rubber, not a drop of water ever actually reaches the skin of the otter. Its outer fur traps air in an insulating layer very like a wetsuit, and the inner fur is so fine and tight together that the water never penetrates it. So if otters are allowed what amounts to a drysuit, I reckoned I could permit myself the occasional, judicious use of the wetsuit to bolster my chances of survival. It can make a long swim in cold water bearable, even comfortable, but it cannot approach the sensuality of swimming in your own skin.

At a triathlon meeting nearly everyone wears a wetsuit, and I always find the best place to witness these events is at the point where the contestants come out of the water and hurry comically towards their bikes, peeling themselves out of wet rubber as they go. It is easy to pull a muscle in the Houdini contortions sometimes necessary to escape from your suit. But some of the most useful equipment for the wild swimmer can be a pair of wetsuit boots and gloves. It is your hands and feet that will drive you out of the water before anything else.

More or less alone on the wild side of this innocent island, I felt myself slipping fast into a 'Coral Island' state of mind. There was exploring to be done. I set off past the Great Pool, a shallow fresh-water tarn outside the modest Hell Bay Hotel, the only hotel on the island, climbed Gweal Hill and found a ruined Bronze-age chambered tomb, then aimed for the shore at Stinking Porth. A pigtailed islander was repairing a low-slung cottage by the bay, and the last washing line in England was proudly flying the family underwear in the breeze. I walked along the top of the shoreline on well-sprung sea pinks. Banks of rocks and earth protected the island along this Atlantic coast, planted by the islanders with agapanthus. Its tough, adventurous roots bind the earth and rocks together and when it flowers in summer it must create a magnificent pale blue hedge along the sea. It was the first of many plants I encountered growing wild on Bryher that I was used to seeing inside conservatories. I snapped, crackled and popped along the line of dried bladderwrack that probably gave Stinking Porth its name, humming to myself and getting lost in a pleasant daze of walking-blues rhythm. I was stopped in my tracks by a dead porpoise at my feet, tangled in sea-weed and oil, baring the hundreds of little saw-teeth serrating its jaw as it began to decompose; the petite, elegant tail curled by the sun as though flipping out of its bonds of black kelp. The greatest excitement of living on islands like these must be the sheer variety and constant surprise of what gets washed up on your local beach or rocks. For one woman, out strolling on the Porth Hellick beach on St Mary's on 22 October 1707, the surprise was Sir Cloudesley Shovel, Admiral of the Fleet, whose flag-ship, HMS *Association*, was wrecked on the Gilstone Rock along with three other ships, and two thousand men were lost. Sir Cloudesley was miraculously still just alive, so she promptly murdered him for his emerald rings.

Spotting the porpoise took me back into the world of the *News Chronicle I-SPY* books, especially No. 1 in the series, *I-SPY at the Seaside*. I still have my original collection of *I-SPY* books, carefully concealed in a secret dossier, improvised from a cigar box, labelled: 'Private and Confidential – *I-SPY* Tribe'. I became an active Redskin around the age of seven, and the details of my sightings are carefully filled in with pencil. 'Going to the sea', says the introduction, 'is always exciting. But it's simply wizard when you are an I-SPY. Such a lot of things to look for – such fun putting them in your record! It's thrilling to see your score mount up.'

Back at the *News Chronicle* Wigwam in London, Big Chief I-SPY awarded points for each entry in your record book. For the rarer things you scored more than for those which were easily spotted. It is interesting to compare how rare or common things were perceived to be in the 1950s, compared to our present-day perceptions. In my *I-SPY Birds*, I find that the linnet and the song thrush score a mere twenty points, level pegging with the starling and the house sparrow. Both birds have suffered big declines in population over the last twenty-five years, and would probably rate more points now. In *I-SPY in the Country*, a grass snake scored a surprisingly low twelve, not much more than a frog, toad or scarecrow at ten, and less than a cattle grid at fifteen. An otter scored a mere twenty, at the same level as a road sign saying, DANGER THIS ROAD IS SUBJECT TO FLOODING, and only marginally more than a thatched pigsty at fifteen. (I have searched high and low for a thatched pigsty and I still haven't seen one.) One of the highest-scoring sightings in *I-SPY at the Seaside* was, in fact, the porpoise or dolphin. Both scored a princely forty, and it was time to open the Tizer if you saw one. The dolphin, according to *I-SPY*, is 'a very fast swimmer, and can move through the water quicker than you can scoot along the road on your cycle'. According to the book, I saw my first porpoise swimming in a school off Portrush on 20/4/54. I spotted my lugworm on 17/9/53 at Eastbourne.

Big Chief I-SPY always ended his messages to us Redskins with the coded message 'Odhu/ntinggo'. If you're a Paleface, I'm afraid you'll have to work it out for yourself. I wish I could help, with my copy of *I-SPY Secret Codes*, but it is Private and Confidential and 'Redskins are enjoined to keep this book in a safe and secret place.'

Masses of wild flowers grew everywhere in this Bronze Age landscape of ancient tracks, hedges, stone walls and tiny bulb fields, nearly all of which were now abandoned, grazed or cut for hay. None of them was more than a half or quarter of an acre and they were full of celandines, bluebells, wild garlic, violets and daisies, as well as leftover daffodils. The islands' traditional flower-growing economy was killed off mainly by the Dutch, who now cultivate everything under glass all the year round. Instead, there is tourism, and the wild flowers abound. Sea cabbage and rock campions line the shore, and pennywort grows from the stone walls. A pair of cows in a paddock munched at their plastic bucket beside five hundred lobster pots and an old Rayburn cooker. The blackbirds were trusting and unafraid.

Down at the southern end of the island I swam in Rushy Bay, a delightful sheltered sandy cove which looks across to Samson. It was completely deserted and I crossed from one side of the bay to the other. The intensity of the sky, the white sand, and the rocks that stood up everywhere out of the sea, had a dream-like quality reminiscent of Salvador Dali. Further out, puffs of light breeze squiffed the sea into little Tintin wavelets with kiss-curl tops. Someone had been here earlier; I found a number of elaborate sand and pebble mazes, one with the caption written with a stick: 'A Scilly Maze'. They too had a distinctly Bronze Age look to them. As I swam out, I pondered the mazes, and a theory John Fowles proposes in the book *Islands* that a pebble maze across the water on St Agnes was originally constructed by Viking visitors, or even a Phoenician sailor two and a half thousand years ago. Such ancient mazes are quite common in Scandinavia, but their ritual significance is a mystery. Fowles thinks it may have been connected with the grave, and escape into reincarnation. He also thinks Shakespeare imagined the maze-like *Tempest* in the Scillies. Drifting ashore again over the seaweed and sand, I wondered how many shipwrecked sailors had landed here, alive or drowned. If there were mermaids anywhere in the world, they must be here.

I walked back past another maze – of tall hedges of escallonia, senecio and pittosporum, a New Zealand immi-grant that does well here in the frost-free conditions and provides belts of shelter from the Atlantic storms for the flower crops. Back in the Fraggle Rock Café for dinner, Les, the proprietor, said she and a gang of her friends originally came to Bryher to live twenty years ago as hippies. They weren't the first. In AD 387, a couple of early Christian bishops called Instantius and Tibericus came to the Scillies and founded a cult of free love well away from the hurly burly of the Dark Ages.

Bryher has a wonderfully relaxed approach to tourism, with little children's stalls outside some of the low garden walls offering painted stones or big pink and purple sea urchin shells for sale for pence left in a Tupperware box. There is an all-pervading sense of a Whole Earth Catalogue culture of improvisation and mixed economics. I recognised it straight away and warmed to it. It reminded me of a time, not long ago, when money was not the main topic of conversation. The Bryher lobster pots, I noticed, are built on a foundation of a steel boot-scraper doormat, with a tented framework of half-inch blue alkathene water-pipe covered in netting, and a funnel entrance improvised from a plastic flowerpot.

The looting of wrecks continues to be an important component of the island economy. There are people who can get you almost anything, depending on the nature of the latest cargo to be washed ashore or upended on the rocks. The current treasure trove was a container ship called *Cita*, wrecked off St Mary's and something of a floating department store for the jubilant islanders. Suddenly every household had a brand-new car battery, plastic toothbrush-holder (a choice of yellow, pink or blue), new stainless-steel sink, several bottles of Jack Daniel's, and a mahogany front door. This information suddenly made sense of the abundance of mahogany front doors lying about in front gardens, slightly frayed at the corners from their adventures at sea, some already installed incongruously in cottage doorways, garden sheds and extension conservatories. All of this, of course, was in strict contravention of the Merchant Shipping Act 1995, Part ix, Section 236, which obliges you to report any cargo you find from a wrecked vessel to the Receiver of Wreck. Forms for the purpose are available from Falmouth, just a two-day journey away on the ferry.

The delight of Bryher is that nowhere on an island a mile and a half long is more than half an hour's walk away. I went over Shipman Head Down to the cliffs above Hell Bay to watch the Atlantic sunset. There were convenient plump cushions of sea pinks on every ledge, and I watched the rocks gradually surfacing like bared teeth as the tide fell. I find sunset more dramatic than dawn because you know the spectacle is going to improve as it reaches a climax. The sun dropped like a billiard ball over the rim of the known world in due splendour, and I was watching from the front row.

I was piped awake early by the oystercatchers next morning, and set off along one of the sandy island paths to Green Bay, facing east towards the island of Tresco. It is more sheltered here, and there were boats pulled up on chocks for repair, and a boatbuilder's shed. Around it, near the shore, was a dazzling semi-natural colony of plants that must have originated in the tropical gardens at Tresco: dark blue aechium (which can grow nearly a foot a week), bright yellow aeolium, banks of blue agapanthus, and creeping masses of the colourful succulent osteospermum.

I went down to the beach for a swim in the Bronze Age fields. The Scilly Isles are the last outcrop of a ridge of volcanic granite that forms the backbone of Cornwall and they were, until about 4,000 years ago, the high points of one big island called Ennor. But the melting of the polar ice caps that began after the last Ice Age meant that Ennor's lowland valleys and fields were gradually submerged by the rising sea.

I donned the wetsuit, mask and snorkel, and swam out into the shallow sandy bay. It was high tide and about thirty yards off the shore I looked down at a pair of stone walls meeting at a right angle, and a circle of stones that must once have been a sheep pen. With seaweed hedges growing from the stones, these are the patterns and remains of the patchwork of old fields that once stretched all the way across the valley to Tresco. They are really just a continuation of the remaining field boundaries on shore. This may be why some stretches of water around the Scillies still have names from Before the Flood that are literally outlandish, like Garden of the Maiden Bower, or Appletree Bay.

As I swam back and forth across the bay, face-down in the clear salt water, searching out the diagonals of more

old field walls, lulled by the rhythm of my own breathing
amplified in the snorkel, I felt myself sinking deeper into
the unconscious world of the sea, deeper into history. I
was going back 4,000 years, soaring above the ancient
landscape like some slow bird, and it reminded me how
like the sea a field can be; how, on a windy day, silver waves
run through young corn, and how a combine harvester can
move through barley like an ungainly sailing vessel. I imagined ploughmen with seagulls in their wake tilling these
fields, and their first flooding by a spring-tide storm, the
crops ruined and the earth poisoned by the salt. The relation between the remaining fields and these that were
submerged is an intimate one. Much of the island topsoil
is composed of centuries of seaweed, forked into carts at
low tide and flung about as a mulch. The molluscs, of
course, were all quite at home on the stones of the sunken
walls, and the winkles could have been so many land snails.

I was struggling out of the wetsuit on the beach when I
noticed a bumblebee fly straight out over the sea towards
Tresco. Three more took the same line of flight and I
tracked them well out along the three-quarter-mile journey to the next island. Tresco has some famous gardens
which would be highly attractive to bees, but Bryher was
hardly short of flowers. Was this, I wondered, some ancient
flight path used by bees 4,000 years ago and somehow
imprinted in the collective bee memory? Or had some
ambitious forager scented flowers on Tresco and blazed
the trail? Along the tidemark were thousands of the most

beautiful miniature shells, all much the same snail design but coloured russet, orange, peach, white, speckled, grey and silver. Each of them might have represented one of the drowned sailors whose spirits crowd the seabed of the Scillies.

Next afternoon I boarded the *Scillonian* and rode the Atlantic swell back to Penzance. A party of men with deep tans, pony-tails and expensive manly footwear with miles of bootlace, dotted themselves about the deck, bagging all the suntraps, and sat with their backs to the funnel or a life-raft, eyes shut, heads back, wearing beatific expressions. (They were met later at Penzance by waving women in jodhpurs and Range Rovers.) I sat against my rucksack, gazed down the snowy wake, and entered my own reverie.

3

Lords of the Fly

Hampshire, 6 May

THE MOMENT I arrived in Stockbridge I scented water. And when I switched off the engine, I heard it. Arriving by car seemed all wrong. I should have been tethering a horse, or handing him over to an ostler. The place has an air of faded gentility, dominated by the rambling Grosvenor Hotel halfway along a main street that must be at least thirty yards wide, like a scene out of the Wild West. Before the 1832 Reform Act, this modest village returned two members of parliament, who had of course paid for the privilege. It was a classic rotten borough. There's an old Georgian rectory with two enormous magnolias either side of the front door, and the most beautiful country garage in all England. It still sells petrol from the original pumps. With perfect timing, a Morris Minor pulled up just as I was admiring the festive red-white-and-blue painted doors and a balcony festooned with geraniums to match, growing in suspended tyres.

The village is a riot of small rivers, a rural Venice. Half a dozen different streams, all purporting to be the authentic Test, flow under the wide main street and emerge to gossip through the hinterland of gardens, paddocks, small-holdings, toolsheds, old stables and outhouses behind the facade of shops and cottages. The gurgling of fast-flowing water is everywhere, and mallards wander the streets at will, like sacred cattle in India. Their ducklings are regularly swept away on the rapids, so there is always the poignant dialogue of orphans and bereaved mothers to strike anguish into the heart of the passing traveller.

How marvellous to find a place that values, uses and enjoys its river like this, instead of tucking it away out of sight, corseted in a concrete pipe. Stockbridge has made the most of the Test in a hundred different ways. And everywhere there are trout, as there are cats in the night streets of Istanbul. Renowned as the finest chalk stream in the world, the Test is a fly-fishing Mecca, home of the august Houghton Fishing Club. The fishing rights along these hallowed banks quietly change hands at over £1 million a mile and a day's sport on the Test can cost as much as £800. If they caught me swimming in their river, these people might cheerfully have me for breakfast, poached, with a little tartar sauce. But there are no greater connoisseurs of fine fresh water than our native brown trout, and I was determined to share with them the delights of the Houghton Club waters.

Five minutes out of the village down a waterside path, I was alone in the meadows on the brink of a wide, cold-water swimming hole, scene of the noisy reunion of the wandering offspring of Mother Test. Slightly to my surprise, there were no fishermen about, so I hurled myself straight in. The water made me gasp. The colder it is the better trout like it, because water's oxygen content rises as the temperature drops. (This is why there is such a super-abundance of marine life in the oceans nearest the poles.) I crossed a gravelly bend, swimming across the current into the confluence, a pool screened with bullrushes along the far bank. Some early swallows swooped low over the water. Squadrons of shadowy trout darted against the pale, stony bed creating bow-waves as they sped away. I turned and glided downstream, brushed by fronds of water crowfoot that gave cover to the trout as well as to the nymphs of the mayflies that would soon emerge to seduce them. No wonder trout love the Test. It is fast, startlingly clear, and alternates between riffling shallows and deeper pools. The bottom is chalky gravel with the odd worn brick. And there's plenty of cover.

Long Pre-Raphaelite tresses of water buttercup belly-danced in the current. I anchored myself on the weed, buoyed by the racing stream, then swam two hundred yards downstream to a peaty bay where the cattle come to drink. One side was kept clear of trees and vegetation to give a clear run to the rods, with all the cover on the opposite bank. A romantic-looking couple in their sixties passed by through the meadow and we exchanged a polite 'good afternoon'. They did their best to look unsurprised. Growing acclimatised, or numbed, I swam on, expecting at any moment to encounter a fly-fisherman knee-deep in waders, wondering what on earth I would say if I did.

THE FOLLOWING MORNING, ten miles to the east in Winchester, I ran into a swarm of reporters outside the Crown Court for the opening of the re-trial of Bruce Grobbelaar, Hans Segers and John Fashanu on charges of fixing the results of football matches for the benefit of some Far-Eastern betting syndicates. Photographers milled about, waiting for Grobbelaar and Co. to arrive. There was excitement in the air, and I couldn't resist slipping into the gallery of Court 3 with the assorted hacks covering the story. At least twelve wigs busied themselves around the court, as well as numbers of clerks, and I mused on the cost of it all. The first trial had collapsed because the jury couldn't reach a verdict. They had found the evidence incomprehensible. Addressing the jury, the judge referred with relish to 'the vast files of papers which are available to us all'. Counsel for the prosecution told them: 'Parts of the story are, dare I say it, quite exciting. Others are extremely turgid.' You could say that again. The interesting bits were the bizarre details about the business lives of these footballers. Fashanu's company, Fash Enterprises, had its offices at Warm Seas House, St John's Wood. Grobbelaar's company was the Mondoro Wildlife Corporation Ltd.,

Mondoro being, the court was helpfully informed, the Shona word meaning 'Lion God'. Nothing like this ever happened in swimming, I naively thought at the time. The furore over the allegedly doped-to-the-gills Chinese team at the Australian games was yet to come. So were similar accusations against the Irish Olympic champion swimmer Michelle Smith and her trainer-husband Erik de Bruin.

I soon adjourned to René's Patisserie for breakfast, and followed that with a reconnaissance of the main object of my visit, the Itchen, one of William Cobbett's favourite rivers. Cobbett loved every inch of the Itchen Valley, from the source at Ropley Dean near Alresford all the way to the sea at Southampton. 'This Vale of Itchen', he writes in *Rural Rides*, 'is worthy of particular attention. There are few spots in England more fertile or more pleasant; and none, I believe, more healthy.' Even by Cobbett's time, Winchester was 'a mere nothing to what it once was' – a place of residence for the Kings of England. But it still has King Arthur's round table in the Guildhall next door to the court where the three errant footballers stood trial. And it still has the Winchester College water meadows, where Izaak Walton must have fished in his later years while staying with his daughter Anne. He died in Winchester in 1683. When I asked my way to the meadows in a bookshop, the proprietor said: 'Let's step outside and I can direct you with more gusto.'

I approached the river through narrow streets lined with college houses and SILENCE – EXAMS notices. The teachers all seemed to live in some splendour, in period town houses like Mill Cottage, approached through a small latched gate and a white wrought-iron footbridge across a mill-race. Roses over the door, a tortoiseshell cat curled by the milk-bottles, and the morning paper half in the letterbox completed the picture. The banks of the little stream, a branch of the Itchen, were decorated at intervals with PRIVATE – NO ACCESS notices. In another of these houses, almost next door to the college porters' lodge, an advertisement on a postcard in the window caught my eye: STONE HOUSE DATING FROM 11TH C. IN CRESPIANO NEAR FIVIZZANO, LA LUNIGIANA, MASSA CARRARA, ITALY. 9–12 ROOMS, 3 FLOORS. 100,000,000 LIRE = £36,000 ETC. This contrasted with another window card I had noticed earlier up in the town: A WHITE HOM MADE TEDDY BEAR WITH WHITE TROUSERS £6.50.

The pathos of this affected me all day. This was a city of such contrasts; the bishop in his palace, the footballers investing huge sums in their offshore enterprises, a gardener in a 'Madness' T-shirt circling on an Atco mower round a mulberry in the college grounds, the invisible students at their exams, the teddy-bear maker coaxing the tailored white trousers over the chubby legs.

Approaching the Itchen along College Walk, I came eventually to the water meadows and two or three piebald horses grazing by the river. I vaulted a low fence, steadying myself on a PRIVATE FISHING notice, and crossed the meadow to a convenient willow, where I changed into bathing trunks and a pair of wetsuit boots for the return journey from my swim, and sank my rucksack and clothes into a patch of nettles. At the chalky, gravel bank I confirmed Cobbett's observation, made on 9 November 1822, that: 'The water in the Itchen is, they say, *famed* for its *clearness*.' I plunged into the river, which was three to four feet deep, with here and there a shallow, sandy bank cushioned by water crowfoot. The current was fast enough to make it slow going if I turned and struck out upstream. But I rode downstream with the river in a leisurely breaststroke, keeping my eyes open for whatever might be round the next bend. I was rewarded with the sight of a water vole crossing over and disappearing into the reed-bed on the far bank. The river swung round in a long arc through the water meadows, and very sweet it was too. Here and there I saw the dark forms of trout, and minnows hung in the sandy riffles. This was very fine swimming, and I continued downstream towards the places once known as Milkhole and Dalmatia, where the Winchester College boys used to swim. The Itchen is fed at intervals by natural springs, which is why there are watercress beds along the valley. At Gunner's Hole, a fabled bathing pool further upstream which I intended to explore in due course, the springs are said to create dangerous undercurrents from time to time, and in the early part of this century a boy was drowned there. What the college now calls 'proper swimming' only began in 1969 when an indoor pool was built.

Breaststroking softly through this famously clear water I was soon dreaming of the strawberry garden at the

family seat of the Ogles at Martyr Worthy upstream, thus
described by Cobbett:

> A beautiful *strawberry garden*, capable of being *watered*
> by a branch of the Itchen which comes close by it, and
> which is, I suppose, brought there on purpose. *Just by*,
> on the greensward, under the shade of very fine
> trees, is an *alcove*, wherein to sit to eat the strawber-
> ries, coming from the little garden just mentioned,
> and met by bowls of cream coming from a little
> *milk-house*, shaded by another clump a little lower
> down the stream. What delight! What a terrestrial
> paradise!

I had climbed out of the river and was strolling back
through the lovely water meadows still far away in my day-
dream, milkmaids plying me with laden bowls of fresh
strawberries and cream, when a *shout* rudely intruded on
my pink and brown study: 'Do you realise this is private
property?' The horses looked up for a moment and
resumed their grazing. I decided to ignore the two irate
figures on the fenced footpath and pressed on with all dignity in my bathing trunks towards the hidden clothes in
the nettle patch. It crossed my mind to make my escape
across the water, but then I thought of Cobbett and what
he would have done, and that settled it. I was going to
stand up for my rights as a free swimmer.

I got changed as languidly as possible, then casually

leapfrogged the fence and sauntered off along the path, whistling softly to myself, as an Englishman is entitled to do. 'Excuse me,' came a voice, 'does that fence mean anything to you?' This was unmistakable school talk, and I turned round to confront two figures straight out of Dickens; a short and portly porter with a beard and Alsatian, and a gangling figure on a bike with binoculars, strawberry-pink with ire, the College River Keeper. I introduced myself and enquired the cause of their disquiet. They said the river was the property of the college, and full of trout for the pleasure of the Old Wykehamists who sometimes fish there. It was definitely not for swimming in by *hoi polloi*.

'But the ladies in the public library told me the whole of Winchester used to swim in the river here right up to the 1970s,' I said.

'That's just the problem,' they replied. 'A few years ago we had six hundred people coming from the town, swimming in the river, eroding the banks and leaving litter behind.'

It sounded like paradise to me.

'But surely,' I said sweetly, 'we should all have access to swim in our rivers just as we should be free to walk in our own countryside. Don't they belong to all of us?'

The River Keeper practically fell off his bike. The porter flushed a deeper strawberry and allowed the Alsatian a little closer to my person. They both looked pityingly at me.

'There's plenty of coast and sea not far away if you want to swim,' ventured the porter.

At this point things suddenly turned nasty. They accused me of scaring away the trout and the porter muttered about calling the police. I said stoutly, and perhaps unwisely, that if I frightened away the fish, which I doubted, perhaps I was doing them a good turn, since if they stayed they would only be murdered by the Old Wykehamists. I told them I swim in the Waveney all the time in Suffolk in a place where bathers and anglers have co-existed happily for at least a century. And anyway, I said, why not designate one stretch of river for bathing and another for the Old Wykehamist fly-fishermen?

'We couldn't possibly do that because the water quality is too dodgy,' said the porter. 'Upstream of here they spray pesticides on the watercress beds and there's a sewage works discharging what should be clean water, but isn't always, into the river.'

I quoted Cobbett to them on the famously clear water. They laughed. There was no sign of the police, but the porter urged me to go away immediately and have a shower with plenty of hot water and soap to wash off all the pollutants in the river. People had been getting skin rashes, he said. Wishful thinking on his part, I fancied.

'But if the water is so evil and polluted, why aren't the trout all dead?' I asked. 'And why have you fenced in this footpath in a straight line miles away from the river instead of letting people enjoy winding along the lovely banks? Isn't that a bit mean?'

'I'm not wasting any more time with this,' he said, and

flounced off, the Alsatian casting hungry looks over its shoulder.

The episode raised some serious issues about swimming in the wild, if you can call Winchester wild. I reflected again on Cobbett, and how upset he was at the hanging of two men in Winchester in the spring of 1822 for resisting the game-keepers of Mr Assheton-Smith at nearby Tidworth. What they did amounted to little more than I had just done, yet I had not, in the end, been marched, dripping, up the hill to join Grobbelaar and Co. in the dock. Things were changing in Winchester, but only slowly. The truth was, I had enjoyed my row with the water bailiffs very much. I already felt invig-orated after a really first-class swim, and now I felt even better after a terrific set-to. But it seemed sad, and a real loss to the city, that the college no longer allowed swimmers in the river, or picnickers on the water meadows. I was left feel-ing very much like the otter, 'trapped but not detained', by one of the Houghton Club keepers in December 1853.

THE MATTER OF ownership of a river is fairly simple. Where a river runs through private land, the riparian owner also owns the river itself. On the question of access, the key legislation is the 1968 Countryside Act, which deliberately defined riverside and woodland as 'open country' in addition to the 'mountain, moor, heathland, cliff, downland and foreshore' originally listed in the 1949 National Parks and Access to the Countryside Act. 'River-side' includes the river as well as the banks in the definition of the Act. So whenever politicians mention 'open country' they are talking about rivers and their banks, as well as all those other kinds of countryside such as mountains and moorland. And when the Labour Party Policy Commission on the Environment promised, in July 1994, 'Labour's commitment to the environment will be backed up with legally enforceable environmental rights: a right of access to common land, open country, mountain and moorland,' they meant rivers and river banks too.

On the very same day as my Winchester fracas, Chris Smith, the Secretary of State for National Heritage, had been saying: 'I look forward, as Heritage Secretary, to working in partnership with the Ramblers' Association to secure access to open country, mountain and moorland for the ordinary people of Britain. Let's make a "right to roam" a reality!' So how about the right to swim? That so many of our rivers should be inaccessible to all but a tiny minority who can afford to pay for fishing 'rights' is surely unjust? I say 'rights' to point up the paradox, that something that *was* once a natural right has been expropriated and turned into a commodity. Fishing rights are only valuable because individuals have eliminated a public benefit – access to their rivers – to create an artificial private gain. The right to walk freely along river banks or to bathe in rivers, should no more be bought and sold than the right to walk up mountains or to swim in the sea from our beaches. At the moment, only where a river is navigable do you have rights of access along its banks.

That so many of our rivers should be inaccessible to all but a tiny minority who can afford to pay for fishing 'rights' is surely unjust?

In a recent survey of public opinion, the Countryside Commission discovered that one in three of all the walks people take in Britain involves water, or waterside, as a valued feature. In April 1967, a government official drawing up the 1968 Countryside Act observed:

> We have received a considerable volume of representations that the present arrangements for securing public access and providing a right of public passage on waterways is inadequate. In our opinion the solution lies in extending the powers to make access agreements or orders to rivers and canals and their banks . . . and we would propose therefore to extend the definition of open country to include these categories.

The flaw in the 1968 Countryside Act turned out to be that it relied on giving local authorities powers, but not *duties*, to create more access to rivers and their banks. Making voluntary agreements with private landowners could still work, if only the local authorities put more energy into it, and if only the landowners didn't have such enormous vested interest in the lucrative fishery. The government now says it will 'seek more access by voluntary means to riverside, woodland and other countryside as appropriate'. There is plenty of scope for such schemes: if all the river banks in Buckinghamshire were opened for public access, it would double the total length of footpaths in that county. Riverside access is extremely popular. Perhaps we should learn from New Zealand, where they have renewed a law originally enacted by a colonial governor at the request of Queen Victoria. 'The Queen's Chain' gives a twenty-two-yard strip of public access along the bank of every river in the land. Across the Channel in Normandy and Brittany, too, people have unlimited access to the rivers.

The Environment Agency, meanwhile, is being influenced by the powerful vested interests of the riparian owners into confusing the natural value of chalk rivers like the Itchen and the Test with their commercial value. It is allowing them to be managed exclusively for the benefit of trout fishery along much of their length. What were once richly varied wild trout rivers have been allowed to become highly manipulated leisure enterprises capable of delivering a more or less guaranteed catch of four or five fish to the people, often tourists, who can pay to fish there. Trout fisheries also persecute the pike, culling coarse fish by electro-fishing, even removing such essentials to the ecology of natural chalk streams as brook lampreys and bullheads. Besides all this, they cut and remove the weed that would otherwise naturally hold up the flow and maintain the depth of water, as well as harbouring the invertebrates that provide vital food in the rivers' ecosystems. On one short stretch of the Test above Whitchurch, the owner deploys over sixty different traps for stoats and weasels along the banks, which tend to be manicured of their natural cover with strimmers to accommodate the fastidious new breed of angler. What is at stake is the very resource that, left alone, would create and sustain the wild trout: the natural chalk stream.

Crayfish were once so abundant in the Itchen that when the river keepers cleared gratings and sluices along Winchester College water meadows, there would be dozens of them amongst the weed. But a few years ago the fish farms upstream introduced the American crayfish. The new arrivals carried a fatal disease, the crayfish plague, to which they, but not our native species, had developed immunity. The result has been the near-extinction of the wild crayfish from the Itchen. They are now reduced to a few isolated populations in side-streams or backwaters, having been replaced by their American cousins.

NOW THAT THE coast was clear again, I sauntered along the footpath across St Stephen's Mead, in search of the once-popular college bathing hole, Gunner's Hole. It was called after the Rev. H. Gunner, one of the college chaplains. There used to be a wide arc of changing sheds following the curve of the river bank, thatched huts on an island, and a system of sluices to regulate the natural flow of the water. Gunner's Hole was about a hundred yards long and twelve yards wide, and the stretch of river was dredged of mud and concreted along its banks towards the end of the nineteenth century. It even had a handrail around the area of 'a high diving erection with four stages and two springboards', as the *Public Schools' Handbook* called it in 1900, continuing enthusiastically: 'Gunner's Hole is now second to none as a bathing place in England. Here, under the shade of the limes, are the best features of a swimming bath and a river rolled into one.'

Sure enough, Gunner's Hole was still there, secluded under the shade of enormous plane trees and poplars, one or two now tumbled over the water. Its motionless surface was entirely covered by a classic duckweed lawn, the fabled disguise of Creeping Jenny, a monster of nursery folklore who would suck children under if they went too close, closing innocently over them to hide all trace of their fate. The massive concrete walls of the pool were in surprisingly good condition, and, on the basis that stolen fruit always tastes sweetest, I climbed through the concrete river inlet sluice to drop in silently at the deep end. Sinking through the opaque green cloak was like breaking the ice. I laboured down the hundred yards of the pool, mowing a path in the lawn which closed behind me as I went. Moorhens scampered off, half-flying over the billiard-baize green. The water beneath was still deep, but no longer the ten feet it used to be below the diving boards. It had silted up to between five and seven feet. Reaching down, I felt soft mud and ancient fallen branches, and sensed giant pike and eels.

Breaststroking back like a fly in soup, I reflected that Gunner's Hole must have been where one of the legendary sea-swimmers of our times evolved his style. Sir James

Lighthill was amongst the great mathematical scientists of the century. He became Lucasian Professor of Mathematics at Cambridge, and later Provost of University College, London. From Winchester he won a scholarship to Trinity College, Cambridge at the age of fifteen, and became a fellow at twenty-one. Lighthill was pre-eminent in the field of wave theory and fluid dynamics, and studied and analysed the pattern of the fierce currents that run round the Channel Islands. He was a strong swimmer, and put his knowledge to the test by becoming one of the first to swim the eighteen miles round Sark in 1973. By careful homework, Lighthill calculated the best course and timing to take advantage of the swirling, ferocious tides and currents. In ensuing years he returned and swam round the island five times. On his sixth island tour, in July 1998, aged seventy-four, he swam all day and was close to completing his nine-hour voyage when he ran into some rough seas. He was seen to stop swimming and died close to the shore. As was his custom, he was alone and had no boat with him. He regarded swimming as 'a most pleasant way to see the scenery', and swam on his back to conserve energy, describing his style as 'a two-arm, two-leg backstroke, thrusting with the arms and legs alternately'. I imagined the young Lighthill swimming up and down Gunner's Hole on summer evenings, perfecting his stroke, observing the complexities of the swimming style of the stickleback, and calculating distances.

There was no longer any sign of the diving boards or the

changing sheds, still marked on the 1953 Ordnance Survey map, but when I swam back to the concrete inlet I caught hold of a bit of the original handrail and climbed over into the fresh, fast water of the main river. In a metaphor for its history, Gunner's Hole used to carry the main stream, and is now a backwater. Dropping into a pool above the main sluice that controls the river level, I shed duckweed in a green confetti ribbon that went licking away on the stream. Standing chest deep, pinioned to the slippery wooden sluice gates whose grain stood out like corduroy, I imagined a future without fish farms or watercress beds, when the river could flow as sweetly as ever it did in Cobbett's day, and there could be bathing again in Gunner's Hole.

4

Tiderips and Moonbeams

Norfolk, 12 June

I SET OFF EARLY in a glowing dawn and drove on empty
roads to the Norfolk coast, where I had arranged to meet
Dudley, an old swimming and sailing companion. I could
think of no better prospect than to enhance the day with
bathing, walking and conversation on one of the best
beaches I know. The journey through the rolling countryside of north Norfolk always feels to me like crossing over
into another land, another state of mind. It is close to
home, yet remote. The sudden lightness of being there,
with such endless miles of level space, feels like a holiday,
even for a few hours. Time passes slowly when you are a
dot on the horizon. There is no anti-depressant quite like
sea-swimming, and Holkham is where I usually go when
I'm feeling sad. Striking out into the enormous expanse of
cold sea, over the vast sands, I immerse myself like the fox

ridding himself of his fleas. I leave my devils on the waves. North Norfolk is one of those places where the weather never seems to bear any relation to the forecasts. The whole of Britain can be covered in cloud, yet as you approach the coast up here, it is braided with a magic band of blue. The Royal Family must have known a thing or two when they chose Sandringham as a country cottage.

You arrive at Holkham beach as you would at Glynde-bourne, Epidaurus or Newmarket races; there is a sense of occasion, as befits a visit to one of our most impressive stretches of wild coastline. Opposite the entrance to the Holkham estate you turn into a dramatic wide boulevard of poplars called Lady Anne's Walk and pay the Viscount Coke's amiable gatekeepers a modest sum to park. We felt we should be showing our passports. Even at this hour there were a couple of parked horseboxes with the ramps down, and a few Volvos with 'A dog is for life not just for Christmas' stickers in the back. This elegant cul-de-sac leads half a mile across the grazing marshes to a narrow gap in the Holkham Meals, the strip of mixed pine and holm-oak wood that runs along the dunes west to Burn-ham Overy Staithe and east to Wells.

Dudley and I set off barefoot over the sandy boardwalk through the wooded dunes and emerged blinking from the shade into the great gleaming theatre of Holkham Bay. A majestic sweep of dunes delineates an endless beach where, at low tide, the sea is only a distant whispering line of white. In the middle of all this are a couple of piratical sand islands that get cut off by the tide and are popular with lovers and picnic parties. Further west towards Burnham the dunes rise into a whale-back ridge reminiscent of the Malverns. There used to be the rusty hulk of an early Austin almost completely buried in the sand, but now I suppose it has sunk for ever, or dissolved. Coming along below the dunes was a string of twenty racehorses and their lads, returning to the horseboxes. It is the sort of thing you expect to see in Ireland, but there are often hoof-prints in the Holkham sand, and you can gallop for miles beside the sea.

We made for the surf across the almost deserted beach and half-waded, half-walked into the sun towards Scolt Head and Burnham Overy Staithe. One of the great joys of Holkham beach is to swim in the lagoons that appear in the sands as the tide goes out. Most are only just deep enough for a wallow, but some are up to four feet deep in places. They can be very warm, and I once stepped on a Dover sole in one. Miles from anywhere, we came upon a waterhole that was especially long and deep, and splashed about in it like two desert travellers in an oasis. Watching the little waves criss-crossing and buffeting each other, Dudley remembered how, as a boy learning to sail in Canada, he would study why this or that current behaved the way it did, or why there was a deep channel in the sand here but not there. Standing knee-deep in the sea and feeling it tug this way and that before we plunged out into deeper water, we agreed that these are indeed serious questions. Swimming into the sun, we struck out against the current. Our coast is being altered by the sea at every tide, and every storm, and nowhere more than here on the east coast. Back there on the beach I had searched for a whale jaw the size of an armchair that was stuck fast in the sand last winter, but was buried now, or washed away. Holkham is compulsive beach-combing. Razor shells are strewn everywhere like bones in a Mad Max film, and the delicate, finely perforated shells of sea urchins are beached like tattooed bums or paper masks.

Three miles on, by the entrance to Burnham Harbour, opposite Scolt Head Island, the channel buzzed with dinghies going in and out. Boats were pulled up on the beaches, and families picnicked in the dunes. I swam alone across to the island and back, dodging the Lasers and Enterprises. I felt the vigorous tug of the tide, and crossed the channel diagonally. If Nelson ever bathed, this would surely have been one of his haunts, close to his native Burnham Thorpe. But it was the policy of the navy to discourage and even forbid sailors to swim. Traditionally, few fishermen were swimmers either, the idea being that if you are going to drown in a shipwreck it is better not to prolong the agony.

We followed the path through Overy Marsh towards Burnham, passing two houseboats moored under Gun Hill. One was based on Noah's original drawings for the ark, with a single window facing west across the marsh. It bore a notice: 'This ark is used by a local artist as a simple working space. You are welcome to see inside when he is here. The only item of value inside is the Vieuw.' From the spelling, we deduced that Noah was Dutch. I could think of worse places to be stranded in the Flood.

A butterfly went past over the sea lavender. I said it was a swallowtail. Dudley thought it was a cabbage white. 'That's the difference between us,' he said. I kept my eyes firmly on the sandy path ahead, hoping to find a lizard out sunbathing. Dudley would probably think it was a stick, but I would know it was a lizard. We were, after all, in one of English Nature's prime reserves. There have been attempts to reintroduce the sand lizard here, but they have an uncooperative way of eating their own young. These dunes are also home to the natterjack toad, who likes to dig himself as much as a foot into the sand in the daytime, emerging at night to roam the flotsam line of the beach, hungrily rummaging the dead seaweed for the *Assiette de Fruits de Mer* of small creatures it contains.

Swimming into Burnham Overy Staithe on the mud-warmed rising tide, we entered a time warp. Sailing people sat about amongst the dinghies with picnic baskets and those Acme Thermos flasks finished in pale green Hammerite that weigh about the same as a milk churn. A woman in rust canvas shorts and plimsolls, with masses of fair curls like Titty in *Swallows and Amazons*, was fishing lifejackets out of a Land Rover Discovery. She told us that the channel through which we had just swum was known affectionately to the locals as Dead Man's Pool. They have a way with metaphor in Burnham, always seeing in the New Year round a bonfire of old boats.

A friend who has spent her springs and summers in Burnham Overy Staithe all her life, once told me, 'I can trace the creeks in the lines of my own hand.' We walked back towards Holkham, navigating through waves of sea lavender on the saltmarsh mud, crazed and frosted with salt, until we reached the dunes again and ascended Gun Hill, where I spotted a common lizard sunbathing obligingly before a clump of marram grass. The view into the hazy distance of this great sweep of utterly wild coast silenced us both for some time. Three miles inland we could make out the elegant wooded landscaping of Holkham Park, with its landmark obelisk and the fine house well sheltered from the sea, looking out instead over a lake. Holm oaks are the distinctive local tree here, planted all over the estate by the pioneering agriculturalist Coke in the eighteenth century. According to one of the Holkham Hall gardeners, the trees first arrived as acorns in a consignment of china from Italy. They had been used as a kind of eighteenth-century bubblewrap, and Coke told his men to fill their pockets with acorns in the mornings and plant them all round the estate. Until Thomas Coke built Holkham Hall in the middle of the eighteenth century, there had been almost no trees here at all, but, as the historian David Dymond discovered, no fewer than 2,123,090 trees were planted on about 720 acres of the park in the twenty years from 1781. It is interesting that although the holm oaks and Scots pines, all planted by Coke, form a useful evergreen screen against the cold winds blowing in across the North Sea straight from the Ural Mountains of Russia, they also hide it from view. It is only relatively recently that we have come to regard a view of the sea as a thing of beauty. For our ancestors, the sea was to be feared and shunned from sight. When Humphry Repton designed Sheringham Hall, or 'Bower', further along this coast, in 1812, he positioned it facing east of south, away from the sea, only three-quarters of a mile away. He thought that 'A view of the sea . . . ought not to be the first consideration.'

A little further on, we were greeted by a sign, courtesy of English Nature, informing us that 'Naturists are requested to keep to the beach. Naturism is not permitted in the woods, or outside designated areas within the dunes.' Curious about the 'designated areas', Dudley and I headed straight off in search of them.

There is nothing quite so good as the feeling of hot sand sifting between your toes as you walk along the tops of dunes. We followed an undulating ridge path through a deserted, silent dunescape. Surely there was nobody about? By and by we came to a little village of driftwood windbreaks built around the natural declivities in the dunes. Still no sign of life. There were stacked-up red, yellow and blue plastic fish trays signalling a desire for privacy and goodness knows what else. Then, one by one, heads began appearing over the parapets of what the poet Kit

Wright has described as 'lust bowls'. Just as suddenly, the heads bobbed out of sight again and the silence continued. It was like the Somme at midday. We were surrounded by dozens of humans in this superheated warren and they had all gone to ground. Nonetheless we felt observed. It was an odd feeling, which we readily exchanged for the freedom of the beach below. 'They're obviously much engrossed in their books,' observed my companion.

Hastening away in the general direction of the distant sea, we encountered another of English Nature's notices: MEMBERS OF THE PUBLIC ARE WARNED THAT THIS PART OF THE BEACH IS UNDER USE BY NATURISTS. The telling use of the words 'warned' and 'under use' made it quite clear that in the well-dressed offices of English Nature a naturist would be regarded with the same degree of alarm as an unexploded mine. Looking back from the beach towards the Somme as casually as we could, naked figures could be seen rising up from time to time out of the bunkers for surveillance purposes. It was like a scene from *Watership Down*. The Unclothed Ones were mostly male and very white, but a few varied in hue from underdone to deep Greek Island tan. Every now and again, in ones or twos, they would make the long trek across the beach to cool off in the sea. There was a distinctly erotic air to the place that some- how lent a restless, urban feeling to the wild and beautiful dunes, and put them out of bounds.

The noticeboards and the frisson of nudity about the dunes bespoke the continuing British confusion about bodies. Well into the nineteenth century, to go swimming was to go naked, especially in the wild. I have a print of a photograph, taken at the bathing-lake in Victoria Park, Hackney, in 1899, in which not a single one of literally hundreds of boys bathing is wearing a stitch, and there is not a girl in sight. Until halfway through the eighteenth century, people still swam in the sea principally for their health, but during the next fifty years they came to the beaches more and more for pleasure. The elaborate bathing machine was simply a recognition by the Victorians of the erotic potentialities underlying sea-bathing. Mention of the seaside was often the occasion for a nudge and a wink. The characteristically English obsession with swimming costumes and near-nudity was the *raison d'être* of McGill's seaside postcards. You find it in the heavy-handed humour of a letter, dated 1930, to the *Swimming Times*, on behalf of 'The Slowbutsure Breast Stroke Swimming Club of Wobbleham Village, Little Loweringham'. It is there, too, in the Amateur Swimming Association's edict, in the same year, that costumes 'must be non-transparent, shall be one piece, devoid of open-work, and reach within three-and-a-half inches from the base of the neck, back and front. In the leg portion, the costume shall be cut in a straight line round the circumference of each leg.' Even as recently as the 1997 World Championships in Australia, when Steve Zellen lost his trunks as he dived in at the start of a race and swam on, he was disqualified. (Arguing his case before the judges, he said he would have stopped had it been a backstroke event.)

English Nature's warnings alerting people to the possibility that a naturist might pass within their field of vision
shared something of the comical quality, it seemed to me,
of the Vatican's precautions, described in this cutting from
the *Telegraph* I found recently on a friend's study wall:

VATICAN OBLIGES SHY SWAMI

Special arrangements of unusual rigour have had to
be made at the Vatican over the weekend for the
Papal audience of Pramukh Swami, an Indian spiritual leader, who has not seen a woman for 46 years. In
order that he should not break this rule inadvertently in the Vatican of all places, women, including
nuns, were kept away from the route as the
63-year-old Hindu monk was brought to the Papal
palace and ushered into the Papal presence on Saturday. The sect's leader is accompanied by nine
other monks and by a group of laymen whose special
task it is to warn him in good time of the approach of
a woman and then guide him with his eyes shut.

It was getting really warm, and, not to be outdone, we
stripped off to wade and swim alternately in the general
direction of Wells, accompanied by a posse of oystercatchers and several sandpipers, who scampered after invisible
delicacies with desperate urgency as the tide went out,
uttering little cries of discovery. We again felt the fierce

undertow that runs along this coast, and the sea bottom was full of sudden dips and channels. Bathing off this beach, you feel the literal meaning behind Larkin's line about misery in 'This Be the Verse': 'It deepens like a coastal shelf.' I thought of the two children, brother and sister, who had drowned a few miles away, at Holme-next-the-Sea a year or so earlier. The family had been picnicking on the wide beach and the children had wandered off to play or paddle in the far-off sea. Their parents suddenly realised they had lost sight of them and began the increasingly desperate search. In line with contemporary fears about paedophiles, much of the anxiety and police attention focused on the possibility of abduction, at the expense of what some might consider the far more obvious danger: the sea. Nobody will ever know what actually happened that day, but it is likely that the children paddled innocently into the warm, inviting shallows, only to stumble into one of those sudden troughs in the sand and find themselves in deep water, clutched by the riptide. In the space of two weeks they were to be carried thirty-four miles round the coast to the beach at Sheringham by the same powerful sea current that sweeps south down the whole east coast of this island, bringing ever more pebbles to the great shingle bank at Blakeney Point.

There were places where the current tugging at our legs almost stopped us wading, and where swimming would not have been a good idea. Whenever we swam, we noticed how much we drifted. Like the currents, waves behave differently all along this beach, and we came to a place where people were vigorously body-surfing into the shallows. I thought of Byron, who 'wantoned' in the breakers in Italy at Lerici. We threw ourselves into the naked buoyant tumbling, and gloried in the abandonment in wave after wave, happy as the bathing pigs of Kythnos we had once discovered.

We had been sailing across the Aegean in a small wooden sloop, heading for the harbour at the northern end of Kythnos, but were blown so far off course by the Meltemi that we almost missed the island altogether. Having just managed to claw our way around its southern tip into the shelter of a providential cove, we rode out an anxious night and awoke to rosy-fingered dawn and a perfect sandy bay. There was not a soul in sight. But the beach was not empty. In the shade of a tin shelter on driftwood stilts, occasionally strolling into the sea for a dip and a roll in the shallows, lolled a dozen ample sows. I hope those pigs still have the beach to themselves.

Heading back for tea at Holkham Hall, we followed the tracks of a pram which had been wheeled a mile across the sands. Amongst the big limes and oaks in the park there were roe deer and sheep, and on the higher fields, an abundance of partridges and hares. The estate is not normally artificially stocked with partridges, so their success must be ascribed to the habitat. There has always been plenty of shooting on these Norfolk estates, but there are miles of good hedges too, the crucial factor for the breeding partridge. I had come across a copy of *The Shooting Man's Bedside Book* by 'BB' staying with some country friends. Holkham featured strongly in the chapter on record bags. It may not make ideal bedside reading for all of us, but on 19 December 1877 a shooting party of eleven killed 1,215 hares, and on 7 November 1905 a party of eight shot 1,671 partridge. It was a neighbouring estate, however, that took the prize for the Record Mixed Bag. At the end of a single day's shooting at Stanford on 31 January 1889, Lord Walsingham's party staggered in with an assortment of pheasants, partridges, red-legged partridges, mallard, gadwall, pochard, goldeneye, teal, swans, cygnet, woodcock, snipe, jack snipe, wood pigeon, herons, coots, moorhens, hares, rabbits, otter, pike and rat. A rare tribute to the biodiversity of north Norfolk.

Henry Williamson, the author of *Tarka the Otter*, loved the abundance and variety of living creatures in this countryside, and for seven years he lived and farmed five miles along the coast at Stiffkey. When Dudley returned home after tea, this is where I went, pitching my tent in a field that was once part of a wartime RAF camp, overlooking thousands of acres of wild saltmarsh, and Cabbage Creek. It is easy to get lost in this watery maze, and find yourself marooned on a rising tide.

From 1937, Williamson farmed 235 acres here, struggling to bring the derelict farmland back into good heart at Old Hall Farm. He recorded his day-to-day adventures in *The Story of a Norfolk Farm*, and in a regular column in the

Evening Standard which ran all through 1944 and '45, under the title 'A Breath of Country Air'. He always left writing the column until the last possible moment, and his two little boys would be waiting in the kitchen, re-tying the laces of their plimsolls ready for the sprint up Stiffkey street to the post van at half past four. The poet of *Tarka* bathed with his children in the warm water of the marsh pools, often by moonlight, after as much as twelve hours' prickly work in the harvest fields.

At dimmit-light, or dimsey, as they called twilight on Tarka's River Taw in Devon (where Williamson lived before and after Stiffkey), I went out over Stiffkey Marshes and swam in the Stiffkey Freshes. A deep pink moon rose up over Blakeney Point, whose bleached pebbles shone from across the water. Although I couldn't see them, I knew there were seals not far away on its outer beaches. A line of small boats rode at their moorings out in Blakeney harbour.

I felt the tide running in as I entered the sea. It advanced at astonishing speed, gaining three or four feet each minute, spilling over the almost level muddy sands in a rolling three-mile meniscus that stretched unbroken all the way west to Wells. The water was warming itself as it inched up the wandering guts and channels where the sun had beaten all day. It was calmed by the sheltering arm of the great shingle bank opposite. I floated out into the freshes, the water beyond the marsh, through bands of seaweed, letting myself drift with the tide along the strand towards the mouth of the Stiffkey River, where there were houseboats, half-hidden in the winding creeks, shuttered, silent and dark against the moon. I listened to the sea percolating into the marsh, sliding up every little meandering mud canyon, between the glidders and uvvers – the mud banks – trickling about the mycelium of creeks, gently rocking the glistening samphire. Even the tiniest channels in the mud or sand mimicked the patterns and movement of a great river.

As I bathed, I imagined Williamson, now an otter himself, swimming at dusk with nine children in one of the marsh pools, with the reflected wing-tip lights and the roar of the warplanes returning to the airfield behind Stiffkey. Then the air would be quiet again, as it was now, except for the cries and splashings of the children, and the marsh birds. The girls' clothes, draped over sea lavender, might well have included blouses or aprons of a fine red cotton, then the fashion in Stiffkey, because the 'mashes' were a popular children's hunting-ground for the much-prized scraps of the red drogue parachute targets, which were towed to and fro all day by aeroplanes, while gunners practised, filling the wide sky with black puffs of smoke.

When Williamson died, it was Ted Hughes who delivered the memorial address at the service of thanksgiving in St Martin-in-the-Fields. Hughes had found and read *Tarka* at the age of eleven and counted it one of the great pieces of good fortune in his life. For the next year he read little else. 'It entered into me,' he said, 'and gave shape and words to my world as no book ever has done since. I recognised even then, I suppose, that it is something of a holy book, a soul-book, written with the life-blood of an unusual poet.' Hughes regarded Williamson as 'one of the truest English poets of his generation', although he never published a word of verse. *Tarka* had taken four years to write, and went through seventeen drafts. Williamson rewrote Chapter Eleven, which begins at the source of five rivers up on Dartmoor, thirty-seven times. He described the writing of those paragraphs to Hughes as 'chipping every word off the breastbone'. The two men became friends when Hughes, not much over thirty, and still spell-bound by the magical book, found himself living in the middle of Devon on the Taw not far from where William-son, now in his sixties and also still under Tarka's spell, was working in a hut on a patch of land he had bought with the prize-money his book had won him long ago. (He had sold the Norfolk farm by the end of 1945, his dreams unrealised.)

I have always admired Williamson, not only for the beauty and ice-clear accuracy of his writing, but for the moral basis of his vision, which sprang from the natural world and his passionate concern to take care of it. In this, he was far ahead of most of his contemporaries. Hughes described Williamson at that service of mourning as 'a North American Indian dreamer among Englishmen'.

When I came out of the water, my shadow fell twenty feet along the shell-strewn shoreline. The moon was rising towards a thin band of mackerel cloud, and terns, duck and wading birds called to one another all over the marsh. Nothing much had changed since Williamson was here, driving his grey Ferguson tractor in a mackintosh tied up with baling twine, building his wooden tide-doors to keep the river from flooding his fields, and trapping eels in his ditches.

5

Borrow & Thoreau

North Wales, 14 June

I WENT TO WALES because the place is stiff with magic, because the Rhinog Mountains are something like a wilderness where I would be free to wander like pipesmoke in a billiard room, and with the kind of apparently random purpose with which the laughing water dashes through the heather, rocks and peat. I went there to be a long way from all the powerful stimuli Wordsworth said prevented us, these days, from doing any proper thinking. My only purpose was to get thoroughly lost; to disappear into the hills and tarns and miss my way home for as long as possible. If I could find a string of swims and dips, each one surpassing the last in aimlessness, so much the better. The great thing about an aimless swim is that everything about it is concentrated in the here and now; none of its essence or intensity can escape into the past or future. The swimmer is content to be borne on his way full of mysteries, doubts and uncertainties. He is a leaf on the stream, free at last from his petty little purposes in life.

I took my Great Uncle Joe's copy of George Borrow's *Wild Wales*, the account of a three-week walk across that country in the summer of 1854. Borrow, who was a great swimmer as well as walker, is in some ways insufferable. He never ceases to pose on the page as he posed in life, and his prose is generally heavier going than even the wildest of Wales. Nonetheless, in his grandiloquent fascination with history and language (he liked to call himself a 'word-master'), and in his genuine curiosity about the lives of country people and gypsies, he is hard to ignore, and wins you round in the end.

Borrow used to swim all over the Norfolk Broads, where he lived, all year round, and in the North Sea when he moved to Great Yarmouth. If he couldn't sleep, or was bored with the company at home, he would walk twenty-five miles to Norwich and, after a rest at his mother's house, tramp back. He was six foot three, with a mane of white hair and massive shoulders, and cut a striking figure in Great Yarmouth in his sombrero and long sheepskin coat, with his servant, Hayim Ben Attar, and his black Arab steed, Sidi Habismilk. In the summer of 1854, Borrow embarked on his Welsh walk carrying only a small leather satchel with 'a white linen shirt, a pair of worsted stockings, a razor and a prayer-book'. Great Uncle Joe had *Wild Wales* with him in Parkhurst prison on the Isle of Wight in 1892, where he was

doing time at the age of twenty on the trumped-up charge
that he was a dangerous anarchist. I have often imagined
the young idealist reading the book in his prison cell,
dreaming of the freedom of the open road and the hills.

The Rhinog Mountains stretch south along the coast for
eighteen miles between Snowdonia and Barmouth Sands.
It was to this trackless quarter that I drove from Stiffkey,
arriving in the dark to camp by the sea on Shell Island,
south of Harlech, where I had arranged to meet my cousin
Adrian in the morning for the first day's walking and high
altitude swimming.

We began by scrambling uphill from the Roman Steps, a
haphazard stair of roughly flat stones that was once a trade
route through the Rhinogs. We were aiming for the *llyns*,
Welsh for tarns, higher up. Connoisseurs of these mountains like Adrian are used to the absence of paths, and after
much toil we eventually hoisted ourselves level with the
lofty Llyn Du. We looked across it to an almost sheer ascent
of some 650 feet to the summit of Rhinog Fawr at 2,347 feet.
A brisk wind coming up the mountainside off the sea ruffled the surface of the tarn, which must have been 350 yards
long and half as wide. The immense shadow of the mountain rendered the water opaque and black. To judge by the
almost vertical plunge of the mountain into the *llyn* on the
far side, it must have been very deep. We were about 1,700
feet above the sea and feeling distinctly cool, even in our
mountain gear. My companion began to shiver, and, lacking
a wetsuit, decided to give this particular treat a miss.

This was a moment I had anticipated with relish. I slipped off a rock into the velvet deeps and swam suspended in what suddenly felt like giddy depth. It was icy. I swam straight out and across the middle of this chasm, gulping air and moving fast towards a sloping ramp of grey fissured rock at the far end of the ruffled tarn, entertaining the usual fantasies about what company I might have below. But it was still a beautiful swim, my feelings of awe intensified by the gothic mist. Adrian, who is Head of PE at a Gloucester comprehensive school, cut a reassuring figure across the water. The rock here is mostly Cambrian, a hundred million years old. The rock and the country are one and the same: Cambrian and Cambria. The two next oldest rocks, the Ordovician and the Silurian, are named after two tribes of ancient Britons who lived on the Welsh borderland.

Halfway across, I turned and swam on my back and confronted the dark presence of the mountain. I thought of the phrase 'deep as England' in Ted Hughes's poem 'Pike'. Wales may be yet deeper. I was a prehistoric creature in my glistening wetsuit, ready to be fossilised unless I kept moving. I scrambled on to the huge, grey, ramped rock at the far end, and slithered higher up it to enjoy the view for a few moments before the wind began to bite. I took a header back in off the rock, my highest dive yet. The imperative to keep moving kept my mind off the chilled water, and I soon acclimatised once I got into the rhythm of the breaststroke, urgent at first, until I began to relax. I doubt I would have had the nerve to attempt the swim had I been alone. It was far colder when I came out; this was no place to stand about with nothing on. Neither of us had any doubt that a warming assault on the summit of Rhinog Fawr should be our next move. The cloud had by now almost cleared, and views were opening up on all sides. Some choc-olate, and we were off on a spiral route up the northern slopes of the mountain to reach the south-western ridge, and the summit. As we clambered up the last few feet of chaotic rock, the cloud was clearing, and there were views across the sea and up the coast to Anglesey, where the sun had come out, and along the other Rhinog mountains stretching south in line towards Barmouth Sands; Rhinog Fach, Y Llethr and Diffwys.

We now descended on a circular route to the next tarn, Gloyw Llyn, which winked at us from below. We followed a stream, at first a tentative rill amongst the rocks and tus-socks, but soon growing into a fully-fledged torrent. Just as we were whingeing about the boggy going, and clamber-ing round a series of minor waterfalls, we came upon a classic swimming hole. It was a verdant pear-shaped pool sheltered by a grassy bank to one side, with steep mossy rock rising out of it on the other, clothed in stunted gorse and tussocks. It felt warmer here, and we had both worked up a sweat. By now the sun was out, shining straight through the lens of water onto the golden peaty pebbles of the bottom. We stripped off and leapt in. It took our breath away. The pool was three or four feet deep with just enough room to swim, as in a treadmill, against the current. Every second was an eternity. Neither of us stayed in for longer than a minute but sprang out on the knife-edge between aching and glowing.

A buzzard circled overhead. It saw two figures bounding downhill over bog moss and cotton grass to the big tarn, Gloyw Llyn, now gilded by the sun. It watched them climb out on to an outcrop of rock, take off all the clothes they had only just put back on, and dive into the lake. As it soared higher into the sun, the bird observed the two pale, naked figures crossing and re-crossing the tarn, and diving far down off the rock several times into the deep, clear water. Then it drifted away across the mountain.

On the way down the mountainside we passed through an ancient grove of stunted oaks, the trees so encrusted with mosses and lichens they looked like old cheeses left in the fridge for too long. The second tarn had been more than twice the size of the first, and nearly as cold, and we still luxuriated in the after-effects of the soft, sweet-tasting water's rigour. It had provided the crowning swim of the day.

We returned to civilisation for dinner at the Victoria Inn at Llanbedr. It was the sort of place where Borrow might well have dined. To my sadness and his, Adrian had to return home that night. I was going to miss his wit as well as his pacemaking. 'Will there be anything else?' asked the waitress as she cleared our table. 'What would you suggest?' we enquired. 'Well, nothing really,' she said.

After supper I went back up the mountain and camped

at the top end of a lake, Llyn Cwm Bychan, on a little sheep-mown peninsula where the river enters it. It had been in such flood a couple of weeks earlier that it would have submerged my tent to a depth of three feet. When it rains hard here, the water simply cascades off the mountains. It would be a perfect spot for an early-morning swim. I lay for a long while by the moonlit lake, imagining Borrow here, reflecting on the convivial pleasures of the day.

I always dream a lot when I am camping, in the sweet repose that comes with exercise and physical fatigue. 'The dreams are getting obsessive and I don't even know if I should own up to them,' I put in my notebook. 'By now I am dreaming almost continuously of rivers, seas, tides and ponds.' Tucked up on my peninsula with the sound of the river vibrating through the turf, I dream I am swimming in a still, black canal overhung by a cobbled wharf with a high roof, like a pagoda. At one end of the wharf there are wooden lock gates in deep water, and beyond the gates is something, I don't know what, that needs retrieving. I am with my dream friend from childhood and the other members of my own version of the Famous Five. We are definitely trespassing. One of us is going to have to creep on to the wharf and plunge down under the lock gates to reach the other side. I am the one who dives and I swim down and down under the looming gates in the green water, but I never know what is on the other side because that is the moment I wake up.

I woke to the beginnings of a fine day and bathed in the

lake off my peninsula, swimming through lingering mias-
mal mists rising off the surface. Thoreau describes Walden
Pond at such a moment: 'As the sun arose, I saw it throwing off its nightly clothing of mist, and here and there, by
degrees, its soft ripples or its smooth reflecting surface
was revealed, while the mists, like ghosts, were stealthily
withdrawing in every direction into the woods, as at the
breaking up of some nocturnal conventicle.' It is a marvellously unconscious evocation of the kind of scene Courbet
loved to paint, of women undressing to bathe.

Searching the map, I had seen some promising upland
streams, a waterfall and a tarn, so I hiked off uphill through
the bracken. There is so much of it in the Rhinogs that the
sheep all carry it around on their coats like camouflaged
soldiers. I watched a ewe standing between two big rocks
the shape of goats' cheeses. They were just far enough
apart to allow the animal in, and I began to understand the
relationship Henry Moore perceived between sheep and
stones. He saw sheep as animate stones, the makers of
their own landscape. By grazing the moors and mountains
they keep the contours – the light and shade – clear, sharp
and well-defined, like balding picture-restorers constantly
at work on every detail. The black oblongs of their pupils
set deep in eyes the colour and texture of frog skin are like
the enormous slate coffin-baths you see in the farmyards
here; seven foot slabs of slate hollowed into baths. Quite
why the farmers made such things is a puzzle, when there
are natural baths and pools in every stream inviting you to

'wash away the night', William Morris's phrase for the morning ablutions of his questing knights in *The Water of the Wondrous Isles*.

I climbed up a *cribin*, or *moel*, a rounded rocky outcrop commanding a view of the valley, and settled down in a warm sheep hollow. Every tree up here has a hollow the size and shape of a sheep, the roots exposed and polished by generations of them hunkering down. I sat perched on the first of a series of tumps rising in succession up a ridge, their rocks rounded by cushions of turf. I was level with the tops of hawthorns, rowans and ashes that grew on the slopes and grassy hillocks. There was birdsong everywhere; the rising notes of pipits, like the turning of a rusty wheel, the mew of the buzzard as it spun into view. Redstarts flew from tree to tree, taking the line a slack rope would take slung between them. Economy in flight is what makes it graceful. Look at the swift, which hardly seems to move its wings at all, or the planing buzzard, ascending a thermal. The redstart flaps its wings just enough to get from A to B and always lands on the upward beat, under full control. Birds always land rising, coming up to a branch or ledge, never down.

I removed my boots and stretched out to enjoy the sun. The hollow-sounding ground was still damp and my glasses, left lying on it, soon steamed up. With my face close to the turf I observed a faint mist rising from clumps of tiny flowers peopled with tiny insects: yellow tormentil, stonecrop, sage, thyme, sorrel, bell heather, foxglove, innumerable grasses, mosses, twayblade and heath bed-straw (now rumpled bedstraw) where I had been lying.

Wandering further on amongst these tumuli, I came upon the entrance of a cave, with a dozen steam genies twisting out of it where hot sun played on its wet, peaty floor, well manured by the sheep that must squeeze in and shelter there. I got my head and shoulders in, and waited for my eyes to grow accustomed to the dark, then used the reflected sunshine in my watch, a tiny sun dancing about the walls, to see how far it stretched into the hill. The cave had filled up with centuries of sheep-shit and ran for at least fifteen or twenty feet in a perfect five-foot arch of slate, with the rotten remains of wood protruding from the walls. I could have entered on all fours, but there was something unappealing about the idea of crawling in wet sheep-shit. Was it a slate mine, a lead mine, or a tomb? There was a stone circle not half a mile away.

I found two more cave entrances close by, both nearly blocked with loose earth, guarded by brambles, thistles and foxgloves. This was *Rogue Male* country, practically unmapped, and unfrequented. I made a mental note that I could go to ground here, as the nameless protagonist of the thriller goes to ground in Dorset, in the event of some future political or personal crisis, living on berries and mutton, and communing with the weasels. Here, too, was a roofless, circular, stone-walled chamber and three more tunnels running into the hill from higher up. They were much easier of access, five feet wide and four feet high, well lined with slates which now dripped on me as I crept in and explored. Practically brushing my cheek, a wagtail flew off a nest of five pale speckled eggs hidden in a sage plant and a hart's-tongue fern near the entrance. I crept in some twenty feet until the shaft ran off to my right in utter darkness and I lost my nerve and retreated gingerly, suddenly fearful of the rock-fall that clearly hadn't ever happened in several hundred years.

There was no sign of these tunnels on the map, and I was content for them to remain a mystery. Indeed, it was infinitely preferable to me that they should not be on the map, and never should be. This was one of those magical places the people of northern Greece call *Agrafa*, 'the unwritten places'. They are the remote and secret places in the Pindos mountains, bordering Albania and Macedonia, that were deliberately left off the map by the inhabitants so as to avoid the imposition of taxes by the occupying Turks. Borrow would certainly have gone and knocked on the nearest farmer's door and demanded to know the full history of the earthworks. No doubt his curiosity was laudable, but it also often seems impertinent and condescending. He would ask total strangers what they thought of their landlord, whether their parents were still living, or about their religion. It says much for the civility of the Welsh country people that they always seemed to give him straight answers.

I had been following a tributary river of the lake uphill and now came to a meeting of the water. I took the left fork and followed a delightful little rushing brook about four feet wide that ran steeply over a series of waterfalls between two and ten feet high. It ran alongside a south-facing stone wall that acted as a sounding board for its song, a continuous chord composed of the deep notes made by the spouting of water into stone hollows and the descants of the shallower rapids. Thus serenaded, I cooled off in a pool below a waterfall, so shaped that I could lie facing the morning sun with the cascade on my shoulders. By angling myself further back, I could get the full, icy force of the water over the back of my head, a sensation more often associated with warm water and the hairdresser's chair, and utterly exhilarating. Behind the curtain of water I saw the secret green lushness of liverwort. The view over the whole bowl of mountains was magnificent, and I hadn't seen a soul all morning. Wedged in the rocks were some old split hazel fencing stakes or wattles, eroded almost to a wafer by the stream. Just the knots and sinews of the wood remained. I retrieved a half-melted chocolate bar I had left to solidify under the water and soon dried off in the warm sun.

My next swim was about a thousand feet up, below the mountain succinctly known as Clip, in the comparatively balmy waters of Llyn Eiddew-mawr overlooking the vast estuary sands of Porthmadog. The tarn must be half a mile long, and it was perfectly clear, with a brown peaty bottom shading into invisible depths. The sun had been shining on the water all day, and I swam across and back very comfortably, having warmed up on the ascent. By now it was tea-time, and I lay on the bank eating nuts, dates and biscuits, wondering if the tarn had ever contained the 'afanc'. This is a creature that reputedly once lived in the Welsh lakes. It was considered by Borrow to have been the crocodile, and by others to have been the beaver. Myth has it that Hu the Mighty, the inventor of husbandry and a leader of the ancient Cymru, drew out the afanc from the water with his team of four oxen and banished it. Certainly there would once have been beavers in Welsh lakes, and, at one time, crocodiles. Musing by just such a lake as this on his walk, Borrow felt sure that if its depths were searched, 'relics of the crocodile and the beaver might be found'. 'Happy were I,' he says, 'if for a brief space I could become a Cingalese, that I might swim out far into that pool, dive down into its deepest part and endeavour to discover any strange things which beneath its surface may lie.' I had swum out far, but I had not dived down. The afanc was possibly some kind of plesiosaur, a fifteen-foot creature resembling a crocodile, one of whose fossil skeletons was discovered in the summer of 1844 at Kettleness on the Yorkshire coast. It is now built into the wall of the Whitby Museum.

I hiked downhill along one of the enormous stone walls, some up to eight feet high, that thread across this rugged country. Their only logic seems to be aesthetic. Only the longer ones appear to do much, like mark a boundary, or keep sheep in or out. These walls are reputed to have been built by French prisoners of war from Waterloo, and enclose wide 'fields' on the hillsides and tops, perhaps sixty or a hundred acres at a time. The work must have been immense. Maintaining them is a life's work too. I couldn't help thinking of the hernia unit at the Harlech General Hospital. It must be a busy place on market day.

I could hear the sound of laughing water across nearly a mile of hillside, and could soon see it too, tumbling, white and sparkling, over a ramp of black rock thirty feet high, like a leaking castle. Feeling like a striptease artist by now, I hung my clothes over a bilberry and climbed up the falls to the top. Water was gushing and surging up through a moraine of massive boulders, then sliding down a forty-five degree slab of rock, black where it was wet, and purple where it was dry. Lying back against the sloping rock I let the water flood over me, then swam against the current in a substantial pool lower down. Water rushed about everywhere here, and amongst the remains of a settlement I found a spring inside a kind of stone temple covered in ferns. I went down to drink from it, and felt its atmosphere and power. The sense of a Delphic presence was so palpable, the Oracle might just have gone for lunch. The cottages had been tiny; no more than eight feet square. The walls of one were still standing, and its hearth, too. On the old track that led away downhill was the most luxuriant bed of wild thyme I have ever seen. None of the ruins were marked on the map at all, which only made discovering them the more thrilling.

I climbed into the river where it ran on through a miniature ravine full of the bright, rich pinks of heather, bracken, stonecrop, thyme, gorse and the little yellow tormentil. I followed it down through a ladder of waterfalls and pools, some of them deep enough to swim, interspersed with straight, high-speed runs between great slabs of rock. Here and there the stream would bend sharply to the left or right and the water would climb up the rock wall and spout into thin air like an eel standing on its tail. Then it merged with another stream, running down an almost parallel ravine, and I slid, scrambled, waded, swam, plunged and surfed through it all until I was delivered into a deep, circling pool. A little further on, a solitary sycamore stood sentinel over a sheep-nibbled lawn of buttercups and daisies by a water- fall and another pool, long and deep, between black slabs of rock, where I swam against the stream and hovered in the clear black water. Here I made my camp, hanging my towel to dry in the sycamore branches. I made delicious tea with the river water, devoured bread, goats' cheese and penny- wort leaves, and fell into a deep sleep, lulled by the song of the waterfall, of Minnehaha, Laughing Water, the bride of Hiawatha, watched over by the dark shapes of menhirs on the hilltops.

I awoke to the croaking of a raven overhead somewhere, dreaming a nonsense of what E. M. Forster in *Howards End* called 'Borrow, Thoreau and sorrow', and squirmed half out of the sleeping bag like a caddis larva, watched by a curious, timid ewe and her lamb. There was a ruined roof- less building by the bank of the waterfall pool and a rounded containing wall with a gate. I realised that this must have been a sheep wash. It would explain the presence of the solitary sycamore providing shade over the lawn where I was encamped, and a gnarled holly overhanging the river as a sign for the shepherds. It might also be the reason why this was the only place I had found daisies and buttercups in the Rhinogs. They belong in the lowland grazing meadows and would have been carried up here as seeds or roots by sheep.

I leapt straight into the pool like a self-dipping sheep. It was six feet deep, and I swam up to the waterfall and hung there again in the bracing stream like a seagull following a boat. Then I waded a little way downstream through the disordered, foaming boulders to the next pool, in a gorge of gleaming, mossy rock crossed by a bridge of six-foot stone slabs slung across the water like the lintels of Stonehenge. It was the wildest natural jacuzzi. Currents jostled me from all directions and I climbed out stunned and galvanised. I made tea on the gas stove and breakfasted on more goats' cheese and bread. Although not quite up to the standards of George Borrow, who sometimes breakfasted on eggs, mutton chops, boiled and pickled salmon, fried trout and potted shrimps, it was made special by the place, with its buttercup lawn shaped into an inverted comma and enclosed by a stone wall that retains the ancient, sloping track running past at a higher level, and tapers from five feet to nothing in a way that a modern architect would completely approve. There were surely never any drawings for this, yet the proportions and sense of harmony with the natural architecture of the water, rocks and trees were very fine. Whoever built it had, as Alexander Pope put it, 'consulted the genius of the place'. It was highly distinctive, like a Greek stage, shaped by years of use and now all the more beautiful for being a ruin and so remote. I had not seen a human soul for thirty-six hours, just sheep and the powerful presence of the Rhinogs, whose peaks that morning were lost in clouds. I could have stayed there for days, walking to the next tarn on the map with an unpronounceable name, and unpronounceably freezing water.

I could have stayed there for days, walking to the next tarn on the map with an unpronounceable name, and unpronounceably freezing water

6

Salmon-runs

Dartmoor, 9 July

DARTMOOR LOOKED DAUNTING, especially on the enormous map, which had taken up the whole of my billiard-table desk in the Map Room in Cambridge. Even on paper, I kept losing my place, running my finger along rivers spawned amidst the thin brown contours of peat-bogs, hills and tors. By the time I actually crossed the moor in the car the following afternoon, I was in a suitably wild, dark mood after sweating in traffic for hours on the way down through Somerset. It was one of several moments when I began seriously to question the whole outlandish project. I had naively imagined bouncing along the lanes of England in some open-topped bus, bursting with friends, their towels and costumes hung out to dry like flags in the breeze, and me at the wheel like Cliff Richard in *Summer Holiday*. Instead, of course, they were all far too busy with their own lives, and my journey was proving a much more solitary, even fugitive affair.

A cold dip in the West Dart River by the stone saddle bridge at Hexworthy came along just in time. I threw myself into a deep pool just upstream, gasping at the shock, and swam down into the stony salmon-haunts below. Surfacing, my spirits began to revive. I was, after all, on my way to visit friends; a family of Dartmoor river-swimmers. The West Dart is spectacular just here, dropping fast over the moor, surging at giant granite slabs ten or twelve feet long. I climbed round into the rapids above the pool and shot down into the eddy in the shadow of the bridge, disturbing a dipper that flew a rock or two away. The water tasted cold and fresh. Watched by a group of Japanese tourists on the bridge, I wallowed, splashed and dived, washing away the journey, feeling a little like an inexpert otter in the zoo, then dried off on warm granite. Half an hour later, the salmon were leaping there.

On Thursday afternoon I went with my friends, under oath of secrecy, to a bathing place where the Dart is joined by an unusually cold moorland torrent. We will call it the Sherberton Stream. Almost from its source in two springs high up beneath the summit of a tor, the torrent rushes headlong downhill, shaded by dense woodland all the way. So the springwater emerges into the Dart as cool as it was underground. The Dart slid like a white glacier into a deep, black pool, through a steep valley of oak and holly woods.

My friend John and I, wearing masks, snorkels and

flippers, dropped straight into deep water off some rocks and swam against the current up into the pool. What we saw there astonished us both. About ten feet down in the clear water, dappled with sunlight, lay dozens of salmon, many of them well over two feet long. They turned and nosed off languidly upstream at our approach, disappearing into the clear green bubbling river, or amongst the shadows of underwater rocks. We followed them upriver, then lost them. Coming back downstream in long, effortless strokes, we were ambushed from the left by the sudden shock of the chilly upland waters of the Sherberton Stream issuing into the pool. The unusually cold water, rich in oxygen, was the special attraction of this place for the salmon. John, who has swum here for over thirty years, had never seen this many fish in the pool. He is a geologist, now in his sixties, and during the 1960s and early '70s, he had his own flourishing Dartmoor tin mine. He still occasionally pans the river for tin or gold, more for pleasure than profit.

Dartmoor has always been rich in minerals. Ashburton and Buckfastleigh once had the biggest tin-mining industry in the world. They were the centre of a huge international trade that stretched all the way to Amsterdam, Byzantium and the Nile, and there is plenty of evidence of it in the river. John showed me the riffles where the mineral stones, sometimes gold or tin, collect in a natural pan. We waded about, looking for obstructions to the flow, like a quartz seam crossing the bed, and searched for tin and gold below them, panning the gravel with saucered hands. The metals are heavier than the rest of the river sediments and sink naturally into these hollows. We found tin nuggets, especially heavy and black, shaped like discarded chewing gum, but no gold. We scooped up haematite, too, named after the blood these dark nuggets of iron-ore resemble. Later on, in a field near the river at his home, John showed me the panning machine he had built in his workshop, a wonderfully Heath-Robinson affair with a rotating perforated steel drum that runs off a belt-drive from his tractor.

John and his family have developed their own river-swimming technique, and each year, before his daughters grew up, John used to take them for a long-distance swim down the river to Totnes. I tried out the novel style nervously the following morning in a fast stretch of the river that runs through fields near their house. John taught me how to swim the rapids, even sliding over the most unlikely shallows, by keeping my head down in the water and breathing through the snorkel. This automatically tilts the rest of your body higher in the water. You wear a wetsuit for protection from bruises, as well as cold, and you look ahead through your mask for fast-approaching rocks, keeping at least one arm outstretched to fend off as necessary. You propel yourself mostly with the flippers.

Seeing a boulder approaching you at high speed, with the irresistible force of the river behind you, is terrifying at first. But by surrendering your body to the current, it is surprising how easily and naturally you are swept down, like the translucent leaves you see dancing underwater in the sunlight. The current urges you along the best course, but you must keep steerage way as you would in a canoe, by swimming faster than the river. You realise why the otter's tail is called its rudder. Your mask seems to magnify things by framing them; and the sounds of the river, and your own breathing, are amplified underwater. You see churned gravel glittering like tinsel, old bricks with their maker's name nearly smoothed out, bright green pebbles, dark rusty haematite, a drowned plastic bag pinioned to a tangle of sticks, water shrimps, bands of bright shining quartz, passing fragments of flimsy waterweed, little bull-heads dodging under stones, and now and again the shadow of a trout. I swept on through a series of long, narrow, natural pools, steep-sided granite tanks that barrelled the river into deafening violence, hurling me down their gullets over dark submerged forms glimpsed skidding away, on past the wrecks of jammed tree-roots into the sudden calm of a deep pool.

Making my way back along the bank in the wetsuit through a field of cattle, carrying my flippers, mask and snorkel, I met the farmer, who said he had fished the Dart for thirty years. He wore tweed, I wore rubber and stood dripping, but he seemed not to notice, or was polite enough not to say anything, and we chatted away by the bank about otters and salmon for some considerable time. Before the war, he said, a favourite evening pastime of the Buckfastleigh citizens was to gather beside their weir and watch the otters playing. He said it was a good year for salmon and otters; there were more of both than he had ever known. He saw otter pads and prints on the sand here night after night and, only a few days before, he had actually seen an otter bitch and a cub; a rare occurrence. The Dart used to be polluted by dieldrin from the sheep-dip chemicals washed out of the wool at a carpet factory in Ashburton. The drastic decline in otters which began in the 1950s and led to their virtual extinction over most of England and Wales is known to have been caused by this very chemical. To make matters worse, the detergent used to wash the wool began over-enriching the river with phosphate and froth, but at last the river seems to be recovering, and the otters with it.

With so much twenty-four-carat water everywhere, there's a tradition of wild swimming in all the towns and villages that fringe the moor. At Throwleigh and South Zeal, they have always bathed and learnt to swim in a remote natural pool in the valley of the Blackaton Brook, which runs between steep banks of gorse and heather from the Raybarrow Pool at the foot of Cawsand Hill. The tiny waterhole was already naturally dammed by boulders, but enterprising swimmers gradually enlarged it by building the rocks higher. I heard about it from Mrs Amy Harvey, then nearly ninety, who had lived on Dartmoor all her life, and swam in this bathing hole throughout her childhood during the 1920s. She had written me a moving letter full of vivid recollections of the place, which is still popular with the village children now.

At Peter Tavy they have their own village swimming hole in the Colley Brook: a secluded mill-pool to which the bathers have added stone steps and a life-belt. I also visited the charming village swimming pool at Chagford, fed by the River Teign, with an outdoor café. It is fringed with trees down one side and – the last thing you expect to see on the edge of Dartmoor – a vigorous hedge of bamboo. The pool is filled from the river by a fast-flowing mill-stream that flows alongside it. These days, the Health and Safety people make them put chlorine in the water, but Pam, who lives in the cottage opposite and is the keyholder, doesn't like to put too much in because it spoils the fresh taste and smell of the clear river water off the moor. Pam's eighty-seven-year-old father-in-law, who helped to dig and build the original pool in 1947, comes down every day in the season and makes tea.

Okehampton used to have a river-fed pool a hundred feet long which was owned by a syndicate of swimmers, but has since been filled in. People who grew up swimming here in the 'ice cold water' remember the strict pre-war caretaker, Mr Wallers. He would open the baths at seven o'clock on a Sunday morning so people could swim before going on to shiver in church or Sunday school. He then closed up for the rest of the day. This is what Dartmoor Puritanism is all about.

Rivers rise everywhere on the moor. In the peat beneath

Great Kneeset, five rivers have their beginnings: the Taw, Tavy, Teign, Torridge and Dart. But of all the Dartmoor rivers, the Erme is the most secretive. It rises in the long shadow of Hartor Tor and flows south through Ivybridge into a farm landscape around Holbeton so hilly that everyone gets an aerial view of their neighbour. Fields, barns and hedgerows are tilted at all angles like the counterpane of an unmade bed.

I had been curious about the Erme ever since first hearing Mike Westbrook's *The Cortège*, a large-scale work for jazz instruments and voices in which one movement, 'Erme Estuary', is a response to the place where he and Kate Westbrook live. It ends with a long, other-worldly solo on the electric guitar. But the estuary was all too real, and none too warm, as I swam across it on the rising tide two days later, seeing it for the first time on a visit to my musical friends. I had crossed to the centre of the wide bay from Coastguard's Beach. A little group of surfers clustered waist deep, waiting for the big grey rollers that surged out of the open sea, breaking on a sandbar. I threw myself in with them and swam inland. I felt the incoming tide lock on to my legs and thrust me in towards the distant woods along the shore. Each time a frond of sea-lettuce lightly brushed me, or glued itself around my arms, I thought it was a jellyfish, and flinched. But I soon grew used to it; seaweed was all around me, sliding down each new wave to drape itself about me. I kept on swimming until I practically dissolved, jostled from behind by the swell. Then, as the tide rose higher, the sandy estuary beach came into focus. The woods reached right over the water, and began accelerating past me. I found I was moving at exhilarating speed, in big striding strokes, like a fell runner on the downhill lap. It was like dream swimming, going so effortlessly fast, and feeling locked in by the current, with no obvious means of escape. I was borne along faster and faster as the rising tide approached the funnel of the river's mouth until it shot me into a muddy, steep-sided mooring channel by some old stone limekilns on the beach. I had to strike out with all my strength to escape the flood and reach the eddy in the shallows. I swam back up to the limekilns and crawled out on to the beach like a turtle, but couldn't resist dropping back into the muscular current for a second ride down the channel.

Earlier, we had all picnicked on Mothecombe Beach together, to the west of the estuary, and Mike and I had swum in the bay. It was a Private Day at the beach, which meant that only bona fide local villagers from Holbeton were allowed access, and then only to one side, leaving the other free for the private enjoyment of the Mildmay-White family, who own it. The whole of the lovely Erme estuary might have been rechristened the Baring Straits, since all the surrounding land was originally purchased in the 1870s by the two cousins who controlled Barings Bank: Edward Baring and Alfred Mildmay-White. Mothecombe is a private beach, and the estate charges the public for access via a man in a small wooden ticket-office at the top of the cliff path. The wild beauty of the coastal estate was evidence of sensitive management.

Mike had come round by the cliff path to our rendezvous at the limekilns, and we stood gazing across the estuary. A dense unbroken canopy of English rainforest flowed down to the water everywhere. It was an almost tropical scene, with six or seven egrets decoratively arranged in an oak, or flying with their long legs outstretched. I had seen them the previous summer on the Arne peninsula in Dorset, where they have even begun to nest. They are now a regular feature of the south coast of England, no longer confined to Spain, Portugal and North Africa. As the tide advanced, we stood listening to the sucking of millions of tiny worms in their mudholes. On the far shore there stood a single boat-house, reflected in the mud, half-hidden in the woods.

As I changed on the beach, we witnessed a scene like a cameo from fifty years ago. A mother, grandmother and a little boy caught crabs in a net baited with chicken from under a rock the grandmother had known as a secret crabbing place from her own childhood. What I found so inspiring about this vignette was the element of continuity that it shared with Mrs Harvey's story of the Blackaton Brook bathing hole. Two generations later, the crabs were still under their rock, and the village children were still swimming in the wild pool.

On the way home, we passed a reed-bed alive with the free improvisation of a sedge warbler ensemble, performing solos like earthy, uninhibited saxophones. Westbrook clearly felt at home with them, quoting the birdbook description of their 'irresponsible song' with approval. We stood on a wooden bridge watching a procession of seaweed carried up by the tide. It created the curious illusion that we and the bridge were moving like a boat through the water, back out to sea.

7

Extinctions

Suffolk, 4 August

NEXT DAY I met an otter in the Waveney. I swam round a bend in my favourite river in Suffolk and there it was, sunning itself on a floating log near the reed-bed. I would have valued a moment face to face, but it was too quick for that. It slipped into the water on the instant, the big paddle tail following through with such stealth that it left hardly a ripple. But I saw its white bib and the unmistakable bulk of the animal, and I knew I had intruded into its territory; knew also that it was underwater somewhere close, sensing my movements. It hadn't paused to puzzle over my unconventional mode of approach. It just went. It didn't miss a beat. We can scarcely be said to have communed, yet I can replay every frame of the brief encounter in slow motion, right down to the just-vacated wet log rolling back into balance, oscillating slightly, and my own emotions, a mixture of elation at a rare moment's audience with the most reclusive animal on the river (Ted Hughes called it 'a king in hiding') and shame at having interrupted its private reverie.

That otters came within a whisker of extinction in England and Wales during the late fifties and early sixties is well known. It happened suddenly and insidiously. But there are hopeful signs that they are now gradually returning to many of their traditional rivers. It has taken thirty years for the powerful poisons that killed them, organo-chloride pesticides like aldrin, dieldrin and DDT, to flush out of our rivers, and for people to realise that otters will only thrive in waters that are left wild and untutored, as well as unpolluted, with plenty of wet woodland, untidy wood stacks, nettles, story-book gnarled trees full of hollows, and as few humans as possible.

I was swimming ten miles from the moat, where the Waveney defines the border between Norfolk and Suffolk. It is a secret river, by turns lazy and agile, dashing over shallow beds of golden gravel, then suddenly quiet, dignified and deep. It winds through water meadows, damp woods and marshes in a wide basin that was once tidal from Yarmouth to Diss, close to its source in the great watershed of Redgrave Fen, where its twin, the Little Ouse, also rises and flows off in the opposite direction, into the Fens. With its secret pools and occasional sandy beaches, the Waveney is full of swimming holes, diving stages improvised from wooden pallets, dangling ropes, and upturned canoes pulled up on the bank. Every two or three miles you come to a weir and a whitewashed watermill.

I swam on beyond the otter pool, under some sort of spell. It struck me that the animal's particular magic does not stem so much from its rarity as its invisibility. It is through their puckish, Dionysian habit of veiling themselves from view that otters come to embody the river spirits themselves. Henry Williamson knew this when he wrote his great mythic poem of Tarka the Otter. In the best traditions of spirits, the otter reveals itself through signs. You hunt for their tracks on sandbars, or for their spraint, the aromatic dung they leave behind to mark their territory, like clues in an Easter-egg hunt, under bridges or on the lowest boughs of willow or alder.

That otters were once plentiful in the Waveney was clear enough until recently if you went to the Harleston Magpie, which used to be a principal meeting place for the Eastern Counties Otter Hounds. Before the pub was altered, there were still otter masks and pads on the walls there, and up the road at the De la Pole Arms in Wingfield they have even installed entire animals, mummified in glass cases. One of my Suffolk friends inherited a red and blue tweed hunting coat that would have been worn by a member of the Eastern Counties Otter Hounds. It must have been hot work, hurrying on foot up and down the river bank, and from pub to pub along the valley, in tweed suits. A student of rural customs, he also once saw an otter pad mounted on a wooden shield with the enigmatic inscription: 'Shanghai Otter Hounds, Wortwell Mill, 1912'. Quite by chance, he stumbled on the explanation in a bookshop the following year, looking through the memoirs of an officer of the Shanghai Police, Maurice Springfield, who, it seemed, had been the Master of the Shanghai Otter Hounds, and bought some of the dogs in Suffolk around 1912 to take back with him to China. He must have been allowed to hunt them with the East Anglian contingent, perhaps by way of a road test, running down the unfortunate otter at Wortwell Mill.

In the autumn of the year before, I had crossed Suffolk to Westleton Village Hall one Saturday morning to attend a training session in animal tracking organised by the Suffolk Wildlife Trust so that we could take part in a survey of the Suffolk rivers for otters, mink and water voles. About forty of us sat in the hall studying slides of their footprints, and learning more about their ways. Small plastic tubs containing otter and mink shit were solemnly passed round. It was a bit like a wine tasting. You waved the poos under your nose, sniffed, then passed on the sample to your neighbour. Our tutor described otter spraint as 'fragrant', with something of the quality of jasmine tea, but perhaps an added nuance of fish oil and new-mown hay. A sample of jasmine tea was also circulated. You need a good nose to be a successful otter detective. We took it on trust from our tutor that otter spraint is also 'tarry and tacky'. Mink, on the other hand, have, or do, 'scats'. Scats look quite like spraint, but smell like burnt rubber or rotten fish. I felt the aesthetics of the matter posed some threat to our scientific objectivity.

That afternoon, we had all gone down to the Eel's Foot at Eastbridge, within sight of the Sizewell B nuclear power station, and walked along the bank of the Minsmere river in a crocodile looking for real live otter spraint. The Minsmere otters, no doubt observing all this from the safety of some hollow tree, would have witnessed the unusual spectacle of forty humans queuing to lie full-length on the bank and sniff small dollops of poo, making appreciative sounds. Someone spotted a bubble and all forty of us froze, bright-eyed and bushy-tailed, but it was just a bubble. I find I have since rather gone off jasmine tea.

THE FOLLOWING AFTERNOON, I swam the length of Benacre Broad at Covehithe a few miles up the coast the other side of Southwold. It is a silty fresh-water lagoon separated from the sea by a low spit of sand and shingle beach, and its days are numbered. The bleached skeleton of a single tree stood defiantly in the middle of the sands. As I swam back in water like cooled tea towards the spit, and the sea beyond, rooks cawed in the dark woods behind me, and a curlew called from the reed-beds. Long Covert, the old bluebell wood beside the broad, is blindly marching into the sea. In spring, bluebells and pink campions grow right up to the pebble strand, which is strewn with the decaying roots and stumps of oaks and sycamores. Meanwhile, the sea was pickling the trees at the edge of the wood to extinction. First it shrivelled their leaves, then it blasted them until the trunks were white and bare. I stepped thirty paces over the beach and swam out into the North Sea.

I had come down the path along the disintegrating cliffs from the magnificent ruined church at Covehithe. Each year, the path moves further inland across the fields because great hunks of England keep falling away in the winter storms. The previous year Roger Middleditch, the beleaguered farmer, had planted carrots. By the time he came to harvest them, they were sticking out of the cliff-top and littering the beach like fish. A year later, his rows of lemming barley grew right up to the cliff and toppled over it. During the winter, Mr Middleditch had lost about twelve metres to the sea. Two years before, he had lost twenty. Since the mid-1970s, when the erosion mysteriously began to accelerate, the waves have taken forty-seven acres of the farm. It was originally nearly 300 acres; now it is 240. Less than four acres of a twenty-one-acre field that led the other way to the sea from the farm in the 1970s now remain. His philosophical words came back to me as I drove away down the lanes towards Dunwich: 'In less than twenty-five years the sea will have reached the church and our farm. The church will go, the farmhouse and buildings will go, Benacre Broad will disappear.'

Richard Mabey, who has often walked the East Anglian beaches, has a sense of the way this shifting coastline may work on the mind: 'I sometimes wondered if the closeness of these unstable edges of the land was part of the secret of Norfolk's appeal to us, a reflection of a half-conscious desire to be as contingent as spindrift ourselves, to stay loose, cast off, be washed up somewhere unexpected.'

THAT EVENING, I visited Suffolk's own lost city of Atlantis, and swam at nightfall over the drowned churches of Dunwich. Pilgrims have been coming here for years to gaze at what no longer is, or to look out to sea in rough weather and listen for the fabled submarine ringing of the bells of fifty sunken churches; perhaps even to pen a line or two like: 'Where frowns the ruin o'er the silent dead.' The tide was almost up, and I swam off the steep bank of shingle by the fishermen's huts. The clattering pebbles, dragged by the swell like castanets, were amplified by the night, and by the cool evening water. The moon was strung on the horizontal vapour trail of a jet plane like a musical note printed on a page.

There never were anything like fifty churches, although a Southwold historian, Thomas Gardner, had said so in 1754 and the exaggeration stuck, along with the underwater pealing of church bells, supposedly swung by the same rampaging sea that had demolished the medieval city and port on the night of 14 January 1328. Hundreds of homes, barns and warehouses in six parishes were eventually inundated. By 1573, only two churches were left standing, and most of what remained except for All Saints' church was destroyed in the great storm of 1740. But one of the church towers still stood perfectly upright on the beach at low tide, until it collapsed in about 1900. So thorough has been the sea's erasure that almost the only historical evidence left is in documentary records. The tempest didn't just take churches, shops and houses, it took hills, a whole hunting forest, and the major harbour on which the city's prosperity was founded. It washed them all away like a sandcastle and blocked the entrance to the harbour with a gigantic shingle bank, closing it forever. The contrast between the clamour of a medieval sea-port city at the peak of prosperity and the empty, silent horizon of today is enough to set the least reflective of souls thinking about the impermanence of things. All that is left of Dunwich now (apart from the car park) is a café, a pub, two fishermen's huts, a row of houses, and a nineteenth-century church. The one medieval building still standing is the ruined twelfth-century chapel of the St James leper hospital, once well outside the city walls. There is something of the myth of Philoctetes about its survival: the outsiders have endured in the end.

The uncomfortable pebble beach shelves steeply, and I was glad to subside into the sea, swimming immediately in deep water, black and treacly after the lightness of the Waveney the day before. Far out past the breakers, shifting like a porpoise in the swell, I had the illusion that the shadowy cliffs were visibly receding. The underlying boulder clay of Suffolk erodes easily, and the layer of shingle that lies on top of it is forever being washed away and moved about by storms and tides to create an undersea topography that changes so much, they have to keep redrawing the navigation charts. I was the only bather in the cool night sea, and everything was very distant. To the north, the lighthouse at Southwold; towards the horizon, a cargo ship and a fishing boat, and to the south at Sizewell, the brash twinkling of the nuclear power station. Moving through the night, suspended in the waves over the extinct city, was like swimming over the submerged Iron Age fields of the Scilly Isles.

8

An Encounter with Naiads

Yorkshire Dales, 13 August

THERE IS A LONG tradition of wild swimming in Yorkshire. Sweating out a shift in the heat and dust underground, coal miners must have cast their thoughts longingly, in summer, towards the abundant cooling rivers and becks of the limestone country of the Dales. In no other industry was communal, ritual bathing such a deeply essential part of life; there were always showers or baths at the head of the pit. Getting into water is still second nature in this part of the world. Hill walking and cycling have always been popular in the north, and the Dales are full of tempting swimming holes to cool one's weary frame. The springs and underground streams burst everywhere from the labyrinthine limestone. Every village has its favourite places, some of them secret and difficult to reach, and often actually called this or that 'hole', like Foss

Hole and Chemist Hole, in the superb River Doe above Ingleton.

The Yorkshire Dales have been shaped and carved by rivers. The Swale, Ure, Nidd, Wharfe, Ribble, Aire, Skirfare and Tees all rise in these hills, with the Lune running south to Lancaster out of Cumbria, and the Eden running north to Carlisle. With such abundance of water, few places are richer in wild flowers than limestone country, and Richard Mabey, an aficionado of the Dales, had intrigued me with a chance remark that set me off on a quest for a particularly remote and enchanting swimming hole above Littondale. His caution that I would probably have to abseil down to it only increased my curiosity. He described a clear tufa pool hidden in a cleft somewhere up a beck, guarded by a limestone canyon on the walk between Arncliffe and Malham. This was too interesting not to pursue, and in any case I couldn't get the place-names he mentioned out of my head: Cowside Beck and Yew Cogar Scar.

At the Falcon Hotel on the village green in Arncliffe, I was awoken early by the screaming of swifts, and a swallow singing in the eves over my open sash-window. It reminded me of home. The little hotel is a haunt of trout anglers on the River Skirfare, a tributary of the Wharfe, and nothing much seemed to have changed since 1950. It was just the sort of place I could imagine T. H. White holing up in for the weekend.

I set out across country towards Malham, climbing up along the top of the steep-sided gorge that contained the beck. The tiny figure of a cyclist laboured up the road on the other side towards Settle – 'a cruel road', they called it in the pub. Everything here carried the signs of use: the path, the sheep-holes worn brown into the hillside, the polished pine handholds of the stile ladders. Massive stone walls plunged almost vertically down the steep sides of the dale to the beck in perfectly straight lines, and the limestone strata showed through the grass like flock in a threadbare sofa.

The sun had come out, and glinted in the Cowside Beck, clearly audible three or four hundred feet below. About two miles further on up the high ridge path I came to a declivity diving towards the increasingly distant bottom of the gorge. There was no path, and the descent was so precipitous that it was impossible to see more than a few yards ahead at a time, but I decided to take the plunge, more or less literally, towards the beck. It was hard to know, even with the help of the map, whether I was heading down towards Yew Cogar Scar, the spectacular cliffs that walled parts of the gorge. They live up to their name with a perpendicular forest of gnarled yews that somehow clings to the rock face. The escarpment I hoped I was going down was Cowside. The descent was so dizzy it was hardly even grazed, so there were tussocks full of ankle-sized pot-holes. A stiff breeze funnelled up the gorge threatening to shake off the gaudy yellow-and-black-striped humbug snails that clung to harebells and yellow bedstraw. I felt for them, hanging on for dear life too, and creeping blindly down. The really amazing thing was that there were trees. Bent old rowan, ash and hawthorn grew from the most daring rocky outcrops, probably the only places where a sapling would have escaped being grazed. Fortunately, I had brought a climbing rope which I looped round a trunk wherever I could, and so slithered my way in stages to the bottom.

By now I was feeling the thrill of the chase, glancing eagerly about in search of hidden pools. I had landed in the canyon bottom just upstream from the cliffs of yew. The first thing I saw was a black rabbit disappearing into a stone wall, then another. Was there a whole colony of them marooned in here? Looking up at the imposing rocks, I could have been in California. I had no idea how I was going to climb out again. I followed the beck upstream, rounding each bend and contour with the warm glow of anticipated pleasure.

At length I came upon a small spinney of ash by the banks, and the promising sound of a waterfall. And there, just below, was the elusive tufa pool and the sparkle of animated water chasing its tail around in it. It was very nearly circular, and rimmed with moss. At one side, natural steps led into its perfectly clear depths, which ran to eight or ten feet by the fall. I stripped and dived in. It was so cold, I might have flung myself into a bed of nettles. Then came the heady rush of the endorphins, or 'endolphins' as a friend once called them, the natural opiates with which the body anaesthetises itself against the cold, and the adrenaline. As the *Oxford Textbook of Medicine* cautiously says, the mood changes they induce 'are difficult to validate scientifically, although feelings of well-being seem to occur'. For swimmers, my friend's inspired malapropism goes straight to the point: you come up feeling like a dolphin. The Cowside Beck dashed towards me like a wind under the trees, and spouted smoothly between two rocks to hurtle into the pool, which I now explored, feeling beneath the bubbling surface with hands and feet, diving under, and swimming against the current to hover in the middle. Immediately uphill, a tributary stream cascaded down a series of waterfalls and saucered pools over mounds of tufa accumulated through the centuries. If it weren't so natural and ancient, it would be easy to mistake tufa for the kind of artificial rocks you see at the Chelsea Flower Show. It is really petrified water that has built up, like the fur in a kettle, from the lime that is carried in the streams. It is voluptuous and spongy and loves to dress itself in fine mosses and algae.

I flopped out on to a rock, up the grassy side, and clambered, dripping, to bathe in a second pool some thirty yards upstream. The boisterous water took my breath away all over again and I returned to the circular pool, where I swam down once more to the bottom under the waterfall and surfaced inside it, coming out with head, hands and feet frozen, feeling wonderful. I thawed them in the gentle, dished, tufa pool, like a warm bath after the frigid beck, its water slipping over the sunlit stone.

I wondered how many walkers must have slid into these tempting waters, remote and hidden though they are. Sunlight reflected back off the rounded white rocks on the bottom, and soft cushions of fine, tight grass and thyme were scattered languidly around the margin, as though for some nocturnal gathering of the nymphs. J. B. Priestley, when he was travelling about these parts in 1933, met a woman who lived in one of the remote Dales farmhouses, 'a solid West Riding countrywoman and not one of your fanciful arts-and-crafts misses', who swore that she saw faeries dancing on the hillside. There are still some places left in England that have unquestioned magic about them. This pool had me enchanted; I could have stayed there quite happily all day and night with the attendant naiads. But a man must take care never to kiss a water sprite. As the English folk-song 'George Collins' relates, it will lead to certain death, and that of any woman he subsequently kisses. The old pagan deities may have fled much of our land, but they have not yet forsaken all their haunts.

Made ravenous by the cold water, I demolished a prosaic sandwich lunch reclining on a cushion of thyme, with my head resting on a clump of moss the size and texture of a British Railways antimacassar, then decided to climb up alongside the tributary gill, through a scree of scattered rock, past the occasional modest waterfall, towards some caves at the top of Cowside. Sleepy dor-beetles crept about in the grass, and Yorkshire rabbits darted out everywhere, more agile than their lazy Suffolk cousins, bouncing between the rocks like bagatelle balls. The head of the steep cleft was a mass of springs spouting extravagantly over a giant sponge of tufa, decked out in mosses, ferns, liverworts and algae. I sat in the cave and ate another cheese sandwich, spiced with sorrel leaves I had gathered on the way up, grateful for the generous hint that sent me to this wild and beautiful spa.

9

A Descent into Hell Gill

Yorkshire/Cumbria border, 18 August

BACK IN BERNIE'S CAFÉ at Ingleton, they had told me to
expect an experience somewhere between potholing,
swimming, surfing and rock-climbing if I ever ventured
down the inside of Hell Gill. To find it, I was going to have
to trek over the wild moorland of Abbotside Common
beyond Wensleydale and Garsdale Head. After an indolent
morning in the wilds of Barbondale, I drove up through
Garsdale, took the road towards Kirkby Stephen, and
parked the car half in Yorkshire, half in Cumbria, astride
the county boundary. To walk up the Hell Gill beck on a
sunny afternoon out of the vale of the River Eden (of
which it is the headwater) was my idea of heaven. There
were foxgloves and trout, and a buzzard sailing lazily aloft.
From here, the Eden runs north through Appleby to Carlisle, and something odd must have happened in the

upheaval of the Ice Age, because Hell Gill is only yards away from the source of the River Ure, which flows the opposite way, to the Humber.

I had packed a rope and wetsuit boots in the rucksack and followed a track over the Settle to Carlisle railway line and uphill past Hell Gill Farm, following the beck to a bridge and a small wood that grows around the precipitous gorge that brought me here. I skirted past it uphill, and there, suddenly, was the entrance to the canyon. The beck just funnelled between four rocks and disappeared into the hillside in a steep, concealed cleft. Even from a few yards away, you wouldn't know it was there, and the hidden character of the beck is one possible origin of its name, from the old Teutonic *Hala*, 'the coverer up, or hider', and the verb *hel*, to hide. Looking down into the chasm, listening to the wild clamour of the hissing water pressing forward over the brink, I felt like a child at the top of the helter-skelter, or some equally dubious fairground ride: not at all sure this was such a good idea.

The Hell Gill gorge is like a pothole whose roof has cracked open sixty feet or more above. It plunges almost vertically down the hillside for four hundred yards in a continuous series of waterfalls dropping into overflowing pools of hollowed limestone. Geologically, the tunnelling of the limestone probably began at the end of the last Ice Age, 11,000 years ago, when the melt-water from above, finding no other way out, flowed down through alternate strata of limestone, shale and sandstone higher up the hill, and, still trapped by the glacier overhead, burst down a weakness in the limestone layer it encountered here, and bored out the gorge by dissolving the rock.

My temporary state of funk took the form of an impromptu exploration of the upstream beck in the afternoon sun. It forms the county boundary here, and with all the energy of the serious procrastinator, I waded and swam my way upstream, criss-crossing from Yorkshire to Cumbria between huge slabs of grey limestone crammed with fossils. Trout lay in the riffles and darted into shadows. I wallowed in a five-foot-deep waterfall pool, and found vast water-slides, twenty- and thirty-foot tablets of the smoothed limestone that was once coral reefs rising out of a tropical seabed 280 million years ago. Here you could bathe all day without meeting a soul, and better still, know in your heart that you would be undisturbed. A hawk had been killing pigeons, butchering them on the rock beside the water here and there. The black stains on the limestone, and stuck feathers, accentuated the desolation of the moor.

Courage up, I returned to the turbulent rim of the gorge and did what I knew might be an unwise thing. I couldn't help it. I began to slide into the mouth of the abyss itself. I found myself in the first of a series of smooth limestone cups four or five feet in diameter and anything between three and five feet deep, stepped at an acute angle down a flooded gulley of hollowed limestone that spiralled into the unknown. In the low light, the smooth, wet walls were a beautiful aquamarine, their shining surface intricately pock-marked like the surface of the moon. All my instincts were to hold on, but to what? The ice and the water had polished everything perfectly. The torrent continually sought to sweep me with it, and so I slithered and climbed down Hell Gill's dim, glistening insides, through a succession of cold baths, in one long primal scream.

There is something atavistic about all swimming, but this was so intensely primitive it was visceral. I felt like Jonah inside the whale. Each time I dropped, or was swept, into a new cauldron, I thought it would be bottomless; the turbulence made the water opaque. Borne down this magical uterus, deafened by the rushing and boiling of the flood, with the sheer rock and just a crack of sky high above me, I felt at once apprehensive and exhilarated. Water was cupped, jugged, saucered, spooned, decanted, stirred and boiled. It was thrown up in a fine spray so you breathed it in, it splashed in your face, it got in your ears, it stung you with its force, it bounced back off every curving surface, it worked unremittingly to sculpt the yielding limestone into the forms of its own well-ordered movement. Beneath the apparent chaos, all this sound and fury conformed to the strict laws of fluid dynamics.

So steep and labyrinthine was the descent that it was impossible to know or see what was to come next. The slippery blue-green wetness and smoothness of everything, and my near-nakedness, only made me more helpless, more like a baby. It was like a dream of being born. Unnamed thunderings like deep, booming heartbeats rose from somewhere below. It was exactly as Frederick Leboyer said in *Birth Without Violence*: 'The horror of being born is the intensity, the immensity of the experience, its variety, its suffocating richness . . . It is a sensory experience so huge, it is beyond our comprehension.'

Everyone I had talked to about this descent had said that once you're in, you must keep on going down, because you can't climb up. I was glad of the rubber boots and the grip of their soles, but the rope was no use at all because every surface was so perfectly smoothed there was nothing to loop it round. I was conscious that I shouldn't really be doing this alone. I had impetuously broken the first rule of potholing or climbing: that you let somebody know where you're heading before you set out. The feeling became acute as I reached a waterfall that sounded as if it dropped to Australia, and might be the source of the thundering Pink Floyd 'Atom Heart Mother' effects. They were becoming louder and more insistent.

Suddenly I found myself beneath an overhang of rock. A rope was bolted in here and there, and stretched off into a gloomy void beyond. It was impossible to see where it led, how deep the pool below might be, or how far down. I had no idea where the next foothold was. The torrent just shot over a rocky lip and disappeared from view, into a gothic emptiness. One option was to plunge blindly towards the waterfall and hope to drop into the pool, which might be deep enough for a safe landing. But the voices of reason shouted above the din that I stood an equal chance of being dashed into a rock face. The dilemma, and the stark solitude of my predicament, set my mind racing feverishly. I considered that for all I knew I might find myself, like the climber in H. G. Wells's story 'The Country of the Blind', marooned in a subterranean land full of people like myself who had strayed optimistically down the Hell Gill chasm and stranded themselves beyond the waterfall. I also recalled that in the story, the sightless majority propose to put out the eyes of the newcomer.

I pondered my position carefully, still thinking fast because every minute I spent immobile I was getting wetter and colder. Normally, you would clip on to an overhead rope, but I had no harness. I had met a pair of potholers down by the road and spoken to them briefly. They were accoutred in harnesses, buckles and steel clips like door-to-door ironmongers, and I now cursed my failure to ask them about Hell Gill. Once over the edge and dangling from the rope there was no going back. I would have to go hand over hand down it with fingers that were by now half-numb. But how far? I didn't fancy being stuck in a freezing beck all night in swimming trunks. On the other hand I had been told it was impossible to climb back up. Was it really? I wondered. I spent what seemed an eternity fighting my reluctance to turn back and accepting a growing conviction of the logic of at least attempting the ascent. The slight fading of the afternoon light filtering down led me to my decision. I would try going up through the cascading water, and, if I failed, then I would just have to risk going down instead. With the help of strung nerves, the rubber boots, and liberal helpings of adrenalin, I managed to heave myself up the narrow chimney from pool to pool, waterfall to waterfall, against the water. It was slow going, making my way up like a salmon, and I resolved to return some day with a companion, a little more local knowledge, and the right kit.

Emerging at last at the mouth of the gorge, I glanced back at it with faint disbelief and greeted the sky. Then, having dressed, I wandered a little way up the beck in the warm evening and fell asleep on the grass like a new-born babe. I was woken with a jolt by the searing rush of a buzzard stooping on an unwary pigeon. There was a silent explosion of pale grey feathers, like a distant shell. I felt a breath of wind in the grass that could have been a white rabbit hurrying by. 'I've had such a curious dream!' I said to myself, and went off for my tea.

10

The Walberswick Shiverers

Suffolk, 25 December

I HAD INVITED a group of friends to come and celebrate my journey's end with a Christmas Day swim in the North Sea. There was little enough good cheer about the weather when we arrived in Walberswick: driving rain and breakers the colour of dirty knickers licking up the beach. We had arranged to meet at eleven o'clock at the Hidden Hut, a clapboard and pebble-dash seaside bungalow with a surprisingly enormous sitting room warmed by a woozing wood stove. My friends Lucy and Madeleine had rented it for the week, and the sweet smell of onion soup already simmering on the hob greeted me as I stepped in out of the horizontal rain to join the gently steaming group in front of the stove. Amongst them were Tim and Meg, serious year-round bathers with a beach hut at Southwold, in a sedate row named after the English monarchs. Theirs is called 'Karl'. Tim broke the news to me that for the first time in years he was going to have to forgo his Christmas North Sea dip because of a touch of flu. Everyone else, however, already had their swimming costumes on under their clothes, ready for a quick change by the sea.

Apart from Tim and Meg, none of us was in the habit of doing this sort of thing, but I had the idea of starting something in Walberswick along the lines of the original Hove Shiverers, who began life in the early 1920s with a handful of winter swimmers, and still meet on Christmas Day. I had been stirred to action by reading one of their early annual reports, written in February 1931, which included the ringing words:

> Ten years ago there were no Shiverers. Ten years ago serious winter swimming was at a standstill in our district, and the Hove baths closed its hospitable doors in the winter evenings. People who worked all day, or children who went to school, if they wished to swim in the evening had no choice but the sea. A few swimmers, newcomers to Hove, looked at the prospect one winter's night and shivered, and that shiver has spread until nearly a thousand now join in the vibration.

With a last glance at the smug little wood stove, we set off for the beach in the slanting, stinging rain driven by a freak wind from the south-west. It was cold, yet there was a hint of mercy in this wind and it lacked the bite of the usual winter draughts that come straight from Russia to bear-hug the Walberswick dunes.

When we arrived on the beach and confronted the sea, the entire swimming party spontaneously bottled out. This was outright mutiny, a wholesale desertion by the Walberswick Shiverers, but what could I do? I was left gamely trying to balance on one leg in the wind and struggle out of a pair of long-johns and into my frozen Speedos. Trunks always seem especially sensitive to the relative humidity of the surrounding atmosphere. Like the seaweed we used to bring home from holiday to hang up by the back door and forecast the weather, costumes breathe in humidity and hold on to it. They never quite dry out, even dangling before the fire all night. The long-johns got stuck round my ankles, and wrestled me on to the wet pebbles just as more well-insulated well-wishers, Virginia and Florence, came into sight along the beach, Virginia in a massive fake ocelot coat, me in goosepimples.

Once in the trunks, I wasted no time getting rainswept, and strode with as much casual determination as I could muster straight into the khaki waves. The sea was not quite as cold as I had feared when I woke up in the night and thought about it, but it was still a case of gritting my teeth and thinking of England for that first moment or two. Having the loyal Shiverers on the beach was a big boost to the morale or, put another way, a big deterrent to copping out. I would, however, have preferred them to be in the water with me. Once fully immersed and striking out for deeper water, I experienced the intoxication of the fiery cold, and found myself splashing about and even body-surfing with manic energy. A dog spotted me and thought it would come and join in the fun. It scampered down to the shore, got one paw wet and instantly retreated. I stayed in far longer than I had intended and even received a modest round of applause when I emerged, to the outstretched towels and concerned piling-on of warm sweaters normally reserved for young children. Very welcome it was too, and my knees glowed bright purple as our party of non-playing swimmers crunched back, still snug in their bathing costumes, towards the beach huts and over the dunes, home to the Hidden Hut and Lucy's onion soup.

ROGER DEAKIN was a writer, filmmaker, traveller and conservationist. During his varied career he worked as an advertising copywriter and an English teacher, was a founding member of Friends of the Earth and a co-founder of the environmental group Common Ground. In 1969 Deakin bought Walnut Tree Farm, a moated Elizabethan farmhouse in Suffolk, where he lived for 38 years, swimming almost daily in the moat.

Deakin's book *Waterlog*, published in 1999 and from which this Mini is extracted, brought him international fame and the affection of readers and swimmers everywhere. The book broke new ground in calling for the right to swim in wild and open water, and as a work of nature writing it remains a classic of its genre. The launch party for the book was held at the Oasis open-air swimming pool in central London.

RECOMMENDED BOOKS BY ROGER DEAKIN:

Waterlog
Wildwood
Notes from Walnut Tree Farm

Enjoy Swimming?

Eating
NIGELLA LAWSON

VINTAGE MINIS

Liberty
VIRGINIA WOOLF

VINTAGE MINIS

Summer
LAURIE LEE

VINTAGE MINIS

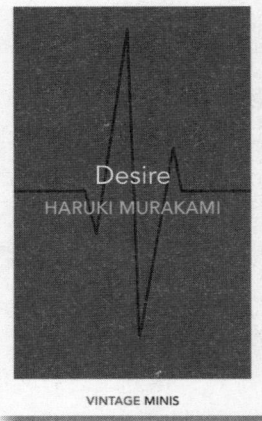

Desire
HARUKI MURAKAMI

VINTAGE MINIS

VINTAGE MINS

The Vintage Minis bring you the world's greatest writers on the experiences that make us human. These stylish, entertaining little books explore the whole spectrum of life – from birth to death, and everything in between. Which means there's something here for everyone, whatever your story.

Desire	Haruki Murakami
Love	Jeanette Winterson
Babies	Anne Enright
Language	Xiaolu Guo
Motherhood	Helen Simpson
Fatherhood	Karl Ove Knausgaard
Summer	Laurie Lee
Jealousy	Marcel Proust
Sisters	Louisa May Alcott
Home	Salman Rushdie
Race	Toni Morrison
Liberty	Virginia Woolf
Swimming	Roger Deakin
Work	Joseph Heller
Depression	William Styron
Drinking	John Cheever
Eating	Nigella Lawson
Psychedelics	Aldous Huxley
Calm	Tim Parks
Death	Julian Barnes

vintageminis.co.uk

1 3 5 7 9 10 8 6 4 2

Vintage
20 Vauxhall Bridge Road,
London SW1V 2SA

Vintage Classics is part of the Penguin Random House
group of companies whose addresses can be found at
global.penguinrandomhouse.com.

Penguin
Random House
UK

First published in Great Britain by Chatto & Windus in 2007
This short edition published by Vintage in 2017

penguin.co.uk/vintage

A CIP catalogue record for this book is available from the British Library

ISBN 9781784872700

Typeset in 9.5/14.5 pt FreightText Pro
by Jouve (UK), Milton Keynes
Printed and bound by Clays Ltd, St Ives plc

Penguin Random House is committed to a sustainable future for
our business, our readers and our planet. This book is made from
Forest Stewardship Council® certified paper.

Language
XIAOLU GUO

VINTAGE MINIS

Before

Sorry of my english

prologue

prologue *n* introduction to a play or book

Now.
Beijing time 12 clock midnight.
London time 5 clock afternoon.
But I at neither time zone. I on airplane. Sitting on 25,000 km above to earth and trying remember all English I learning in school.
I not met you yet. You in future.

Looking outside the massive sky. Thinking air staffs need to set a special time-zone for long-distance airplanes, or passengers like me very confusing about time. When a body floating in air, which country she belonging to?
People's Republic of China passport bending in my pocket.

Passport type	P
Passport No.	G00350124
Name in full	Zhuang Xiao Qiao
Sex	Female
Date of birth	23 JULY 1979
Place of birth	Zhe Jiang, P. R. China

I worry bending passport bring trouble to immigration officer, he might doubting passport is fake and refusing me into the UK, even with noble word on the page:

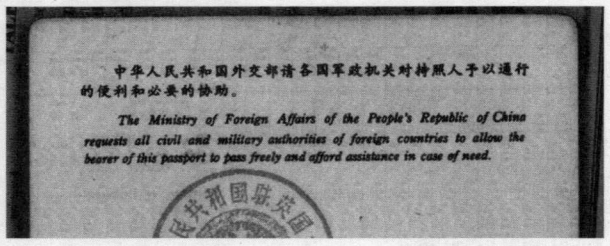

中华人民共和国外交部请各国军政机关对持照人予以通行
的便利和必要的协助。

The Ministry of Foreign Affairs of the People's Republic of China requests all civil and military authorities of foreign countries to allow the bearer of this passport to pass freely and afford assistance in case of need.

China further and further, disappearing behind clouds. Below is ocean. I from desert town. Is the first time my life I see sea. It look like a dream.

As I far away from China, I asking me why I coming to West. Why I must to study English like parents wish? Why I must to get diploma from West? I not knowing what I needing. Sometimes I not even caring what I needing. I not caring if I speaking English or not. Mother only speaking in village dialect and even not speaking official Mandarin, but she becoming rich with my father, from making shoes in our little town. Life OK. Why they want changing my life?

And how I living in strange country West alone? I never been to West. Only Western I seeing is man working in Beijing British Embassy behind tiny window. He stamp visa on brand new passport.

What else I knowing about West? American TV series dubbing into Chinese, showing us big houses in suburb, wife by window cooking and car arriving in front house. Husband back work. Husband say Honey I home, then little childrens running to him, see if he bringing gift.

But that not my life. That nothing to do with my life. I not having life in West. I not having home in West. I scared.

I no speaking English.

I fearing future.

'I no speaking English.
I fearing future'

February

alien

alien adj foreign; repugnant (to); from another world
n foreigner; being from another world

IS UNBELIEVABLE, I arriving London, 'Heathlow Airport'.
Every single name very difficult remembering, because
just not 'London Airport' simple way like we simple way
call 'Beijing Airport'. Everything very confuse way here,
passengers is separating in two queues.

Sign in front of queue say: ALIEN and NON ALIEN.

I am alien, like Hollywood film *Alien*, I live in another
planet, with funny looking and strange language.

I standing in most longly and slowly queue with all
aliens waiting for visa checking. I feel little criminal but I
doing nothing wrong so far. My English so bad. How to do?

In my text book I study back China, it says English
peoples talk like this:

'How are you?'

'*I am very well. How are you?*'

'*I am very well.*'

Question and answer exactly the same!

Old saying in China: '*Birds have their bird language, beasts have their beast talk*' (鸟有鸟语,兽有兽言). English they totally another species.

Immigration officer holding my passport behind his accounter, my heart hanging on high sky. Finally he stamping on my visa. My heart touching down like air plane. Ah. Wo. Ho. Ha. Picking up my luggage, now I a legal foreigner. Because legal foreigner from Communism region, I must re-educate, must match this capitalism freedom and Western democracy.

All I know is: I not understanding what people say to me at all. From now on, I go with *Concise Chinese–English Dictionary* at all times. It is red cover, look just like *Little Red Book*. I carrying important book, even go to the toilet, in case I not knowing the words for some advanced machine and need checking out in dictionary. Dictionary is most important thing from China. *Concise* meaning simple and clean.

hostel

hostel n building providing accommodation at a low cost for a specific group of people such as students, travellers, homeless people, etc

FIRST NIGHT IN 'hostel'. Little *Concise Chinese–English Dictionary* hostel explaining: a place for 'people such as students, travellers and homeless people' to stay. Sometimes my dictionary absolute right. I am student and I am homeless looking for place to stay. How they knowing my situation *precisely*?

Thousands of additional words and phrases reflect scientific and technological innovations, as well as changes in politics, culture, and society. In particular, many new words and expressions as well as new usages and meanings which have entered the Chinese language as a result of China's open-door policy

over the last decade have been included in the
Chinese–English section of the dictionary.

That is sentence in *Preface*. All sentence in preface long
like this, very in-understandable. But I must learning this
stylish English because it high-standard English from
authority. Is parents' command on me: studying how
speak and write English in England, then coming back
China, leaving job in government work unit and making
lots money for their shoes factory by big international
business relations. Parents belief their life is dog's life, but
with money they save from last several years, I make better
life through Western education.

Anyway, *hostel* called 'Nuttington House' in Brown
Street, nearby Edward Road and Baker Street. I write all
the names careful in notebook. No lost. Brown Street seem
really brown with brick buildings everywhere. Prison looking. Sixteen pounds for per bed per day. With sixteen
pounds, I live in top hotel in China with private bathroom.
Now I must learn counting the money and being mean to
myself and others. Gosh.

First night in England is headache.

Pulling large man-made-in-China-suitcase into *hostel*,
second wheel fall off by time I open the door. (First wheel
already fall off when I get suitcase from airport's luggage
bell.) Is typical suitcase produced by any factory in Wen
Zhou, my hometown. My hometown China's biggest

home-products industry town, our government says. Coat hangers, plastic washbasins, clothes, leather belts and nearly-leather bags, computer components etc, we make there. Every family in my town is factory. Big factories export their products to everywhere in the world, just like my parents get order from Japan, Singapore and Israel. But anyway, one over-the-sea trip and I lost all the wheels. I swear I never buy any products made from home town again.

Standing middle of the room, I feeling strange. This is *The West.* By window, there hanging old red curtain with holes. Under feet, old blood-red carpet has suspicions dirty spots. Beddings, they covering by old red blanket too. Everything is dirty blood red.

Room smelling old, rotten. Suddenly my body feeling old too. 'English people respect history, not like us,' teachers say to us in schools. Is true. In China now, all buildings is no more than 10 years old and they already old enough to be demolished.

With my enormous curiosity, walking down to the night street. First night I away home in my entirely twenty-three years life, everything scare me. Is cold, late winter. Windy and chilli. I feeling I can die for all kinds of situation in every second. No safety in this country, I think unsafe feeling come from I knowing nothing about this country. I scared I in a big danger.

I scared by cars because they seems coming from any possible directing. I scared by long hair black man passing because I think he beating me up just like in films. I scared by a dog. Actually chained with old lady but I thinking dog maybe have mad-dog-illness and it suddenly bite me and then I in hospital then I have no money to pay and then I sent back to China.

Walking around like a ghost, I see two rough mans in corner suspicionly smoke and exchange something. Ill-legal, I have to run – maybe they desperate drug addictors robbing my money. Even when I see a beggar sleeping in a sleep bag I am scared. Eyes wide open in darkness staring at me like angry cat. What he doing here? I am taught everybody in West has social security and medical insurance, so, why he needs begging?

I going back quickly to Nuttington House. Red old carpet, red old curtain, red old blanket. Better switch off light.

Night long and lonely, staying nervously in tacky room. London should be like emperor's city. But I cannot feel it. Noise coming from other room. Laughing in drunkenly way. Upstairs TV news speaking intensely nonsense. Often the man shouting like mad in the street. I worry. I worry I getting lost and nobody in China can find me anymore. How I finding important places including Buckingham Palace, or Big Stupid Clock? I looking everywhere but not seeing big posters of David Beckham, Spicy Girls or President Margaret Thatcher. In China we hanging them everywhere. English person not respect their heroes or what?

No sleeping. Switching on the light again. Everything

turning red. Bloody new world. I study little red dictionary. English words made only from twenty-six characters?
Are English a bit lazy or what? We have fifty thousand
characters in Chinese.

Starting at page one:

A

Abacus: (meaning a wooden machine used
                for counting)
Abandon: (meaning to leave or throw away)
Abashed: (meaning to feel embrassed or
                regretful)
Abattoir: (meaning a place to kill the animals)
Abbess: (meaning the boss of woman monk's
                house)
Abbey: (meaning a temple)
Abbot: (meaning the boss of a temple)
Abbreviate: (meaning to write a word quickly)
Abduct: (meaning to tie somebody up and
                take away to somewhere)

Words becoming blurred and no meaning. The first night I
falling into darkness with the jet-lag tiredness.

full english breakfast

1. Builder's Super Platter:
double egg, beans, bacon, sausage, bubble,
mushroom, tomato, 2 toast, tea or coffee included.

2. Vegetarian Breakfast:
double egg, bubble, mushroom, beans, veggie
sausage, hash browns, tea or coffee included.

'TALK DOESN'T COOK *rice*,' say Chinese. Only thing I care in life is eating. And I learning English by food first, of course. Is most practical way.

Getting up early, I have free *Full English Breakfast* from my *hostel*. English so proud they not just say *hotel*, they say *Bed and Breakfast*, because breakfast so importantly to English situation. Even say 'B and B' everyone know what thinking about. Breakfast more important than Bed.

I never seeing a *breakfast* like that. Is big lunch for construction worker! I not believe every morning, my *hostel* offering everybody this meal, lasting three hours, from 7 clock to 10 clock. Food like messy scrumpled eggs, very salty bacons, burned bread, very thick milk, sweet bean in orange sauce, coffee, tea, milk, juice. Church or temple should be like this, giving the generosity to normal people. But 8.30 in the morning I refuse accepting two oily sausage, whatever it made by pork or by vegetables, is just too fat for a little Chinese.

What is this 'baked beans'? White colour beans, in orange sticky sweet sauce. I see some baked bean tins in shop when I arrive to London yesterday. Tin food is very expensive to China. Also we not knowing how to open it. So I never ever try tin food. Here, right in front of me, this baked beans must be very expensive. Delicacy is baked beans. Only problem is, tastes like somebody put beans into mouth but spit out and back into plate.

Sitting on breakfast table, my belly is never so full. Still two pieces of bread and several 'baked tomatoes' on my plate. I can't chew more. Feeling guilty and wasty, I take out little *Concise Chinese–English Dictionary* from my pocket, start study English. My language school not starting yet, so I have to learn by myself first. Old Chinese saying: 'the stupid bird should fly first before other birds start to fly' (笨鸟先飞).

When I am studying the word *Accommodate*, woman come clean table, and tell me I must leave. She must hate me that I eat too much food here. But not my fault.

First morning, I steal white coffee cup from table.

Second morning, I steal glass. So now in my room I can having tea or water. After breakfast I steal breads and boiled eggs for lunch, so I don't spending extra money on food. I even saving bacons for supper. So I saving bit money from my parents and using for cinema or buying books.

Ill-legal. I know. Only in this country three days and I already become thief. I never steal piece of paper in own country. Now I studying hard on English, soon I stealing their language too.

Nobody know my name here. Even they read the spelling of my name: *Zhuang Xiao Qiao*, they have no idea how saying it. When they see my name starts from 'Z', stop trying. I unpronouncable Ms Z.

First three days in this country, wherever I walk, the voice from my parents echo my ears:

'No talking strangers.'

'No talking where you live.'

'No talking how much money you have.'

'And most important thing: no trusting anybody.'

That my past life. Life before in China. The warns speaking in my mother's harsh local dialect, of course, translation into English by *Concise Chinese–English Dictionary*.

properly

proper adj real or genuine; suited to a particular purpose;
correct in behaviour; excessively moral

TODAY MY FIRST time taking taxi. How I find important
place with bus and tube? Is impossibility. Tube map is like
plate of noodles. Bus route is in-understandable. In my
home town everyone take cheap taxi, but in London is very
expensive and taxi is like the Loyal family look down to me.

Driver say: 'Please shut the door properly!'

I already shut the door, but taxi don't moving.

Driver shout me again: 'Shut the door properly!' in a
concisely manner.

I am bit scared. I not understanding what is this
'properly'.

'I beg your pardon?' I ask. 'What is *properly*?'

'Shut the door properly!' Taxi driver turns around his
big head and neck nearly break because of anger.

'Tube map is like plate of noodles'

'But what is "properly", Sir?' I so frightened that I not daring ask it once more again.

Driver coming out from taxi, and walking to door. I think he going kill me.

He opens door again, smashing it back to me hardly.

'Properly!' he shout.

Later, I go in bookshop and check 'properly' in *Collins English Dictionary* ('THE AUTHORITY ON CURRENT ENGLISH'). *Properly* means 'correct behaviour'. I think of my behaviour with the taxi driver ten minutes ago. Why incorrect? I go to accounter buy little *Collins* for my pocket.

My small *Concise Chinese–English Dictionary* not having 'properly' meaning. In China we never think of 'correct behaviour' because every behaviour correct.

I want write these newly learned words everyday, make my own dictionary. So I learn English fast. I write down here and now, in every second and every minute when I hear a new noise from an English's mouth.

fog

fog n mass of condensed water vapour in the lower air, often greatly reducing visibility

'LONDON IS THE Capital of fog.' It saying in middle school textbook. We studying chapter from Charles Dickens's novel *Foggy City Orphan*. Everybody know Oliver Twist living in city with bad fog. Is very popular novel in China.

As soon as I arriving London, I look around the sky but no any fogs. 'Excuse me, where I seeing the fogs?' I ask policeman in street.

'Sorry?' he says.

'I waiting two days already, but no fogs,' I say.

He just look at me, he must no understanding of my English.

When I return Nuttington House from my tourism visiting, reception lady tell me: 'Very cold today, isn't it?' But why she tell me? I know this information, and now is too late, because I finish my tourism visiting, and I wet and freezing.

Today I reading not allowed to stay more than one week in hostel. I not understanding hostel's policy. 'Money can buy everything in capitalism country' we told in China. My parents always saying if you have money you can make the devil push your grind stone.

But here you not staying even if you pay. My parents wrong.

I checking all cheap flats on LOOT in Zone 1 and 2 of London and ringing agents. All agents sound like from Arabic countries and all called Ali. Their English no good too. One Ali charges Marble Arch area; one Ali charges Baker Street area. But I meet different Alis at Oxford Circus tube station, and see those houses. I dare not to move in. Places dirty and dim and smelly. How I live there?

London, by appearance, so noble, respectable, but when I follow these Alis, I find London a refuge camp.

beginner

beginner n person who has just started learning to do something

HOLBORN. FIRST DAY studying my language school. Very very frustrating.

'My name is Margaret Wilkinson, but please call me Margaret,' my grammar teach tells in front blackboard. But I must give respect, not just call Margaret. I will call Mrs Margaret.

'What is grammar? Grammar is the study of the mechanics and dynamics of language,' Mrs Margaret says in the classroom.

I not understanding what she saying. Mrs Margaret have a neatly cut pale blonde hair, with very serious clothes. Top and her bottom always same colour. She not telling her age, but I guessing she from 31 to 56. She wearing womans style shoes, high heel black leather, very possible her shoes are all made in home town Wen Zhou, by my parents. She should know it, one day I tell her. So she not so proud in front of us.

Chinese, we not having grammar. We saying things simple way. No verb-change usage, no tense differences, no gender changes. We bosses of our language. But, English language is boss of English user.

Mrs Margaret teaching us about nouns. I discovering English is very scientific. She saying *nouns* have two types – countable and uncountable.

'You can say *a car*, but not *a rice*,' she says. But to me, *cars* are really uncountable in the street, and we can count the *rice* if we pay great attention to a rice bowl.

Mrs Margaret also explaining nouns is plural and singular.

'Jeans are pairs,' she says. But, everybody know jeans or trousers always one thing, you can't wear many jean or plural trouser. Four years old baby know that. Why waste ink adding 's'? She also saying nouns is three different gender: masculine, feminine, and neuter.

'A table is neuter,' she says.

But, who cares a table is neuter? Everything English so scientific and problematic. Unlucky for me because my science always very bad in school, and I never understanding mathematics. First day, already know I am *loser*.

After lunch breaking, Mrs Margaret introducing us little

about verbs. Gosh, verb is just crazy. Verb has verbs, verb-ed and verb-ing. And verbs has three types of mood too: indicative, imperative, subjunctive. Why so moody? 'Don't be too frustrated. You will all soon be speaking the Queen's English.' Mrs Margaret smiles to me.

pronoun

pronoun n word, such as she or it, used to replace a noun

FIRST WEEK IN language school, I speaking like this:

'Who is her name?'

'It costing I three pounds buying this disgusting sandwich.'

'Sally telling I that her just having coffee.'

'Me having fried rice today.'

'Me watching TV when me in China.'

'Our should do things together with the people.'

Always the same, the people laughing as long as I open my mouth.

'Ms Zh-u-ang, you have to learn when to use *I* as the subject, and when to use *me* as the object!'

Mrs Margaret speaking Queen's English to me.

So *I* have two *me*s? According to Mrs Margaret, one is

subject *I* one is object *I*? But I only one I. Unless Mrs Margaret talking about incarnation or after life.

She also telling me I disorder when speaking English. Chinese we starting sentence from concept of *time* or *place*. Order like this:

Last autumn on the Great Wall we eat barbecue.

So time and space always bigger than little human in our country. Is not like order in English sentence, 'I', or 'Jake' or 'Mary' by front of everything, supposing be most important thing to whole sentence.

English a sexist language. In Chinese no 'gender definition' in sentence. For example, Mrs Margaret says these in class:

'Everyone must do *his* best.'

'If a pupil can't attend the class, he should let *his* teacher know.'

'We need to vote for a *chairman* for the student union.'

Always talking about mans, no womans!

Mrs Margaret later telling verb most difficult thing for our oriental people. Is not only 'difficult', is 'impossibility'! I not understanding why verb can always changing.

One day I find a poetry by William Shakespeare on school's library shelf. I studying hard. I even not stopping for lunch. I open little *Concise Dictionary* more 40 times checking new words. After looking some Shakespeare poetry, I will can return back my China home, teaching everyone about Shakespeare. Even my father know Shake-speare big dude, because our in our local government evening classes they telling everyones Shakespeare most famous person from Britain.

One thing, even Shakespeare write bad English. For example, he says '*Where go thou?*'. If I speak like that Mrs Margaret will tell me wrongly. Also I finding poem of him call '*An Outcry Upon Opportunity*':

> 'Tis thou that execut'st the traitor's treason;
> Thou sett'st the wolf where he the lamb may get

I not understanding at all. What this ''*tis*', '*execut'st*' and '*sett'st*'? Shakespeare can writing that, my spelling not too bad then.

After grammar class, I sit on bus and have deep thought about my new language. Person as dominate subject, is main thing in an English sentence. Does it mean West culture respecting individuals more? In China, you open daily newspaper, title on top is 'OUR HISTORY DECIDE IT IS TIME TO GET RICH' or 'THE GREAT COMMUNIST PARTY HAVE THIRD MEETING' or 'THE 2008 OLYMPICS NEED CITIZENS PLANT MORE GREENS'. Look, no subjects here are mans or womans. Maybe Chinese too shaming putting their name first, because that not modest way to be.

slogan

slogan n catchword or phrase used in politics or advertising

I GO IN bookshop buy the English version of *Little Red Book*. Not easy read but very useful argue with English using Chairman Mao *slogans*. English version is without translator name on cover. Yes, no second name can be shared on Mao's work. Chairman Mao

> **has inherited, defended and developed Marxism-Leninism with genius, creatively and comprehensively and has brought it to a higher and completely new stage.**

The English translators of this book, they are like feather compare with Tai Mountain.

In West, Mao's words work for me, though they not

work in China now. Example, today big confusion in streets. Everywhere people marching to say no to war in Iraq.

'No war for oil!'

'Listen to your people!'

The demon-strators from everywhere in Britain, social-ists, Communists, teachers, students, housewifes, labour workers, Muslim womans covered under the scarf with their children . . . They marching to the Hyde park. I am in march because I not finding way to hostel. So no choice except following. I search Chinese faces in the march team. Very few. Maybe they busy and desperately earning money in those Chinese Takeaways.

People in march seems really happy. Many smiles. They feel happy in sunshine. Like having weekend family picnic. When finish everyone rush drink beers in pubs and ladies gather in tea houses, rub their sore foots.

Can this kind of demon-stration stop war?

From Mao's little red book, I learning in school:

A revolution is not a dinner party, or writing an essay, or painting a picture, or doing embroidery; it cannot be so refined, so leisurely and gentle, so temperate, kind, courteous, restrained and mag-nanimous. A revolution is an insurrection, an act of violence with which one class overthrows another.

Probably Communist love war more than anybody. From Mao's opinion, war able be 'Just' although it is bloody. (But blood happen everyday anyway . . .) He say:

Oppose unjust war with just war, whenever possible.

So if people here want to against war in Iraq, they needing have civil war with their Tony Blair here, or their Bush. If more people bleeding in native country, then those mens not making war in other place.

weather

weather n day-to-day atmospheric conditions of a place
v (cause to) be affected by the weather; come safely through

weather n the state of the atmosphere at a place and time
in terms of temperature, wind, rain, etc

CARRYING MEAT BALL and pork slice from supermarket,
now I am in place calling *Ye Olde English Tea Shop*. What is
this 'Ye'? Why 'Olde' not 'Old'? Wrong spelling.

Tea house like Qing dynasty old style building waiting
for being demolish. Everything looking really old here,
especial wood stick beam in middle of house, supporting
roof. Old carpet under the foot is very complication flower
pattern, like something from emperor mother house.

'Where would you like to sit?', 'What can I get you?', 'A
table for one person?', 'Are you alone?' Smiling waiter ask
so many questions. He making me feel bit lonely. In China

I not have loneliness concept. Always we with family or crowd. But England, always alone, and even waiter always remind you you are alone . . .

Everybody listening the weather at this moment in tea house. All time in London, I hearing weather report from radios. It tells weather situation like emergency typhoon coming. But no emergency coming here. I checking *Concise Chinese–English Dictionary*. It saying all English *under the weather*, and all English is *weather beaten*, means uncomfortable. Is reasonable, of course. England everybody beaten by the weather. Always doubt or choice about weather. Weather it rain or weather it sunshine, you just not know.

Weather report also very difficult understand. The weather man not saying 'rain' or 'sunny' because they speaking in complication and big drama way. He reporting weather like reporting big war: 'Unfortunately . . . Hopefully . . .'. I listen two hours radio I meet twice weather report. Do they think British Empire as big China that it need to report at any time? Or clouds in this country changing every single minute? Yes, look at the clouds now, they are so suspicious! Not like my home town, often several weeks without one piece cloud in sky and weather man has nothing more to say. Some days he just saying 'It is Yin', which mean weather is negative.

confusion

confuse v mix up; perplex, disconcert; make unclear

ENGLISH FOOD VERY confusing. They eating and drinking strange things. I think even Confucius have great confusion if he studying English.

It is already afternoon about 3 o'clock and I so hungry. What can I eat, I asking waiter. He offering 'Afternoon Tea'. What? Eat afternoon tea?

So he showing me blackboard, where is a menu:

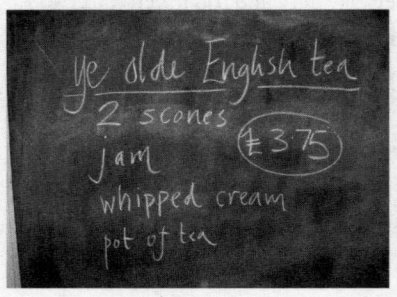

Whatever, I must to eat whatever they have or I faint. Three minutes later my thing arrives: 'scones' hot and thick and dry, cream is unbelieveable, butter is greasy, and jam are three kinds: raspberry, cramberry and strawberry. A white tea pot with a white tea cup.

I confusing again when I look at 'whipped cream' on little blackboard. What is that mean? How people whip the cream? I see a poster somewhere near Chinatown. On poster naked woman only wears leather boots and leather pants, and she whipping naked man kneeling down under legs. So a English chef also whipping in kitchen?

I put scones into mouth, and drink tea like horse. Next door me, I hearing somebody wanting 'frothy coffee'.

A lady with a young man. She say: 'Can I have a frothy coffee, please? And my friend will have a black coffee, with skimmed milk.'

It must be big work making something 'skimmed', and 'frothy', and 'whipped'. Why drinking become so complicating and need so much work?

And water are even more complicating here. Maybe raining everyday here and too much water so English making lots kind water.

I thirsty from eating dry scones.

Waiter asks me: 'What would you like? Still water, or filthy water?'

'What? Filthy water?' I am shocked.

'OK, filthy water.' He leave and fetch bottle of water.

I so curious about strange water. I opening bottle, immediately lots bubbles coming out. How they putting bubbles in water? Must be highly technicaled. I drinking it. Taste bitter, very filthy, not natural at all, like poison.

homesick

homesick adj sad because missing one's home and family

IN MY LANGUAGE school, Mrs Margaret ask me:

'Would you like some tea?'

'No,' I say.

She looking at me, her face suddenly frozen. Then she asking me again:

'Would you like some coffee then?'

'No. I don't want.'

'Are you sure you don't want anything?'

'No. I don't want anything wet,' I saying loudly, precisely.

Mrs Margaret looking very upset.

But why she asking me again and again? I already answer her from first time.

'Oh, dear.' Mrs Margaret sigh heavy. Then she standing up, and starting make her own tea. She drink it in very thirsty way, like angry camel in the desert. I am confusing. Am I make tea for her before she asking me? But how do I know she thirsty if she not telling me directly? All this *manners* very complication. China not have *politeness* in same way.

And how to learn be *polite* if I not getting chance talk people? I am always alone, talking in my notebook, or wandering here and there like invisible ghost. Nobody speak to me and I not dare open my mouth first because when I start talking, I asking the rude questions.

'Excuse me, you know there are some red spots on your face?'

'Are you a bit fatter than me?'

'I don't believe we same age. You look much older than me.'

'I think you are a very normal person. Not a special person.'

'The food you cook is disgusting. Why nobody tell you?'

I already have very famous reputation in my language school. They say: 'You know that Chinese girl . . .' 'Which one?' 'That rude one of course!' I hear it several times. Maybe I need get trained from 'Manners International Etiquette Workshop', which is advertisement I read on Chinese newspaper. It say:

Manners International custom tailors each etiquette program to the specific requirements of each individual, business/corporation, organization, school, Girl Scout Troop, or family.

I think I am exactly that 'individual' needing to be taught there, if fee is not too expensive. Re-education is always important.

Mrs Margaret look at me in sad way. 'You must be very *homesick*,' she says.

Actually not missing family at all, and not missing boring little hometown also. I happy I not needing think about stinking shoes with anyhow the same style on showroom shelfs in parent factory. I glad I not having go work every day at work unit. Only thing I missing is food. Roasted ducks, fresh cut lamb meat in boiling hot pot, and red chilli spicy fish . . . When thinking of food, I feel I make big mistake by leaving China.

This country to me, this a new world. I not having past in this country. No memory being builded here so far, no sadness or happiness so far, only information, hundreds and thousands of information, which confuse me everyday.

Except my English class every morning, I so bored of being alone. I always alone, and talking to myself. When sky become dark, I want grab something warm in this cold country. I want find friend teach me about this strange country. Maybe I want find man can love me. A man in this country save me, take me, adopt me, be my family, be my home. Every night, when I write diary, I feeling troubled. Am I writing in Chinese or in English? I trying express me, but confusing – I see other little me try expressing me in other language.

Maybe I not need feeling lonely, because I always can talk to other 'me'. Is like seeing my two pieces of lips speaking in two languages at same time. Yes, I not lonely, because I with another me. Like Austin Power with his Mini Me.

'I trying express me, but confusing – I see other little me try expressing me in other language'

progressive tenses

(Also called 'Continuous Tenses') Progressive tenses are made with TO BE + – ING. The mose common use of the progressive form is to talk about an action or situation that is already going on at a particular moment we are thinking about. But the 'going to' structure and the present progressive can also be used to talk about the future.

PEOPLE SAY 'I'M going to go to the cinema . . .'

Why there two *go* for one sentence? Why not enough to say one *go* to go?

> *I am going to go to the supermarket to buy some porks?*
> *You are going to go to the Oxford circus to buy clothes?*
> *He is going to go to the park for a walk?*

'I go' is enough to expressing 'I am going to go . . .' Really.

———

This afternoon, I am going to go to cinema watch double bill – *Breakfast at Tiffiny's* and *Some Like it Hot*. Double bill, they letting people pay one time but twice of the bill, how clever the business here! Cinema is my paradise. When a person not having any idea about real life, just walk into cinema choosing a film to see. In China, I seeing some American films, like *Titanic*, and *Rush Hours*, but of course Hollywood stars speaking Mandarin to us, and I can sing soundtrack from *Titanic*, 'My heart goes on and on', only in Chinese translation.

American films strange in London. People at Language School tell me use student card, I can have cheap cinema ticket. Last week I go Prince Charles in Chinatown. They say is cheapest cinema in London. Two films screening: *Moholland Driver*, and *Blue Velvet*. All together is more than 4 hours. Perfect for my lonely night. So I buy tickets and get in.

Gosh what crazy films. I not understanding very much the English speakings, but I understand I must never walk in highway at night alone. The world scary and strange like deep dark dream. Leaving cinema, trembling, I try find bus to home, but some mean kids teasing at each other on bus stop. Shouting and swearing bit like terrorist. Old man drunk in street and walk to me saying words I not under-standing. Maybe he think I prostitute. England is hopeless country, but people having everything here: Queen, Buckingham Place, Loyal Family, oldest and slowest tube, BBC, Channel 4, W. H. Smith, Marx & Spencer, Tesco, Soho, millennium bridge, Tate Modern, Oxford Circus, London Tower, Cider and ale, even Chinatown.

Anyway, after *Breakfast at Tiffany* where posh woman dressing like prostitute and *Some Like It Hot* where mans dressing like womans, I go back my new home which have cheap renting 65 pounds per week. It is ugly place. It smelling pee in every corner of street. Nearby tube station called Tottenham Hale.

House is two floors, lived by Cantonese family: housewife, husband who work as chef in Chinatown, and 16-year-old British-accent son. Is like one child policy still carried on here. The garden is concrete, no any green things. Very often little wild grass growing and come out between the concretes, but housewife pull and kill grass immediately. She is grass killer. The lush next doors trees trying come through rusty iron fence, but nothing getting in this concrete family. This house like factory place in China, just for cheap labours earning money, no life, no green, and no love.

Family speaks Cantonese so I not understanding them. Chinese moon calendar is on wall. Wok, chopsticks, Mah Jong, Chinese cable TV programmes . . . everything inside house is traditional. Not much fun. Outside, view is rough. Old rusty railway leading to maybe more interesting place. Walking along railway I see nearby shopping centre, a McDonalds, a KFC, a Burger King, a petrol station called 'Shell', a sad looking Tottenham Hale tube station.

Every night I coming out Tottenham Hale tube station and walking home shivering. I scared to pass each single dark corner. In this place, crazy mans or sporty kids throwing stones to you or shouting to you without reasons. Also, the robbers robbing the peoples even poorer than them. In China we believe 'rob the rich to feed the poor'. But robbers here have no poetry.

'Dare to struggle and dare to win.' Chairman Mao's words like long time no see friend coming to me. I need somebody protect me, accompany me, but not staring at me in darkness. I longing for smile from man, longing for smile even only remaining several seconds.

March

homosexual

homosexual adj (person) sexually attracted to members of the same sex

I MEET YOU in the cinema. It is film called *Fear Eats Soul*, from German director Rainer Werner Fassbinder. Programme say Fassbinder is *homosexual*. What is it? Now I have this *Collins English Dictionary* – THE AUTHORITY ON CURRENT ENGLISH. It tells me what is *Homosexual*. Strange word, I cannot imagine it.

It is the Ciné-Lumière, near South Kensington. 7 o'clock Monday, raining. Not over ten people, half are old couple with white hair. Then there you are.

You are alone. You sit almost beside me. Two seats between us. Your face quite pale in the dim light, but beautiful. I too am alone in the cinema. I always alone in the cinema before I meet you. I am bit confused whether if cinema make me less lonely or even more lonely.

On the screen, old German woman dancing with young black man in a pub. All the peoples in pub watching. Old woman she has humble smile. She has hard life. Then I see your smile in the dark light. Why I can see your smile while I am watching the film? You turn your face and understand I am looking at you. You smile again, but very gentle, and very little. You look back the screen.

You have warm smile. Is like a baby's smile. Nobody smile to me before like you in this cold country. In the darkness, I am thinking you must be kind man.

It is a film shows impossible love between old white woman and young black man. But nothing to do with 'homosexual'.

After film, we walk to exit. Our bodies so close. Out from cinema, road lights finally light up our faces.

Then, with gentle smile, you ask me:

'Did you like the film?'

I nod head.

Is like the uncomfortable English weather have some sunshine suddenly.

You ask my name. I say name start from Z, 'But please no worry to remember,' I say, 'my name too long pronounce.' You tell me your name, but how I remember English name? Western name are un-rememberable, like all Western look the same. But I want remember you, want remember the difference you with others. I look at your face. Brown eyes, transparent. Thick brown hair, like colour of leafs in autumn. Your voice gentle, but solid. It sound safe.

We walk from South Kensington towards Hyde Park. A long way for feets. What we talk about? I tell you of famous English creamy tea. You say prefer French Patisserie.

'Patty surly?'

'No *patisserie*.'

'How spell?'

'P-a-t-i-s-s-e-r-i-e.' You speak slowly with slowly moving lips, like Mrs Margaret.

'What is it?' I not bring dictionary tonight.

You stop in front very fashionable 'French Patisserie' shop. Still open at late time. Beautiful cakes waiting inside window.

'Which one would you like?' You look at me.

I worried of price.

'I don't know,' I say. How I know about these soft stuffs?

'Then I'll choose one for you.'

You give me a piece of creamy thing.

'What is it?' I hold it on my hand carefully.

'c-h-o-c-o-l-a-t-e e-c-l-a-i-r.'

'OK.'

I bite it, but immediately cream squeeze out, falling on street.

I look at white cream drop on dirty street.

You look at white cream drop on dirty street.

'Oh well, never mind,' you say.

So we talk, and talk, and talk, through Hyde Park, then to West End, then Islington, walk towards my place. Nearly four hours walking. My legs is so sore, and my throat so dry, but I enjoying it. Is first time a person walking beside me through chilly night. Is also first time a person being patience listen my nonsense English, and learning me bad language. You much better than Mrs Margaret. She never let us talk freely.

When I arriving back, is already deep night.

In front of house, you kiss my two cheeks, and watch me go in door.

'Good meeting you,' you say.

Everything happen in very gentle way.

I want go immediately my room think about English man who smile and kiss me like lover, but I see Chinese land-lord sitting on kitchen, watching TV and waiting for me. He is yawning. He worried my late back. At same time wife come down from upstairs bedroom in sleeping robe:

'We were so worried about you! We never come back as late as you do!'

Nervous voice remind me of my mother. My mother always talk to me like that.

I say I OK. Don't worry.

Wife look at me seriously: 'It is dangerous at night and also you are a young girl.'

I take off my guilty shoes.

'Next time if you are late, phone my husband and he can come and pick you up. This is England not China. Men easily get drunk in the pub!'

With last yawn, husband turn off TV. He look cross and tired.

I feel good after I close my bedroom's door. My heart hold a secret to make me warm at night.

The leafs blow outside. The street lights shine on my window. I am thinking I am only person to be awake in the world. I am thinking of China, thinking of old German lady dancing, thinking of your smile. I fall to sleep with sweet feelings inside my body.

guest

guest n person entertained at another's house or at another's expense; invited performer or speaker; customer at a hotel or restaurant

A NEW DAY. You call me. At once I know your voice. You ask if I want visit Kew Gardens.

'Queue Gardens?'

'Meet me at Richmond tube station,' you say. 'R-i-c-h-m-o-n-d.'

Is beautiful weather. What a surprise. And so peaceful in the grassy space. So green. Cherry blossoms is just coming out and you tell me about your favourite snowdrops. We see there is different small gardens with different theme. Africa garden are palm trees. North America garden are rocks. South America garden are cactus. And there is too Asia gardens. I so happy Manager not forgetting Asia gardens.

But I so disappointing after we walk in. Lotuses and bamboos is growing in India garden, plum trees and stone bridge is growing in Japanese garden. Where is my Chinese garden?

'Doesn't look like they've made a Chinese garden,' you say to me.

'But that very unfair,' I say in angry voice. 'Bamboos belongs to China. Panda eats bamboos leafs in China, you must hear, no?'

You laugh. You say you agree. They should move some plants from India and Japan garden to make Chinese garden.

The meadow asking us to lie. We rest beside each other. I never do that with a man. Juice from grass wetting my white shirt. My heart melting. Sky is blue and airplane flying above us, low and clear. I see moving shadows of the plane on the meadow.

'I want see where you live,' I say.

You look in my eyes. 'Be my guest.'

misunderstanding

misunderstand v fail to understand properly

THAT'S HOW ALL start. From a misunderstanding. When you say 'guest' I think you meaning I can stay in your house. A week later, I move out from Chinese landlord.

I not really have anything, only big wheel-missing suitcase. The husband helping me suitcase. The wife opening door. Your white van waiting outside, you with hands on wheel.

Husband puts wheel-missing suitcase on your van, you smile to landlord and turn engine key.

I want ask something to my landlord that I always wanting ask, so I put my head out of window:

'Why you not plant plants in your garden?'

Wife is hesitate: 'Why? It is not easy to grow plants in this country. No sun.'

For last time I look the concrete garden. Is same no

story, same way as before. Like little piece of Gobi desert. What a life! Or maybe all the immigrants here living like that?

White van starting up, I respond to wife:

'Not true. Everywhere green in this country. How you say not easy growing plant here?'

We leave house behind. The couple is waving hands to me.

I say: 'Chinese strange sometimes.'

You smile: 'I don't understand you Chinese at all. But I would like to get to know you.'

We driving in high street. My suitcase lie down obediently at back. Is so easy move house like this in West? I happy I leave my grey and no fun Tottenham Hale, heading to a better area, I think. But streets becoming more and more rough. Lots of black kids shouting outside. Beggars sitting on corner with dogs, smoking, and murmuring.

'Where your house?' I ask.

'Hackney.'

'How is Hackney?'

'Hackney is Hackney,' you say.

bachelor

bachelor n unmarried man; person who holds the lowest university or college degree

YOUR HOUSE IS old house standing lonely between ugly new buildings for poor people. Front, it lemon yellow painted. Both side of house is bricks covered by mosses and jasmine leafs. Through leafs I see house very damp and damaged. Must have lots of stories happened inside this house.

And you are really *bachelor*. Your bed is single bed. Made by several piece of big wood, with wooden boxes underneath. Old bedding sheets cover it. Must be very hard for sleep, like Chinese peasants *kang* bed. In kitchen, teacups is everywhere. Every cup different with other, big or small, half new or broken . . . So everything single, no company, no partner, no pair.

First day I arrive, our conversation like this:

I say: '*I eat. Do you eat?*'

You correct me in proper way: '*I want to eat. Would you like to eat something with me?*'

You ask: '*Would you like some coffee?*'

I say: '*I don't want coffee. I want tea.*'

You change it: '*A cup of tea would be delightful.*'

Then you laughing at my confusing face, and you change your saying: '*I would love a cup of tea, please.*'

I ask: 'How you use word "love" on tea?'

First time you make food for me it is some raw leafs with two boiled eggs. Eggy Salad. Is that all? Is that what English people offer in their homes? In China, cold food for *guest* is bad, only beggars no complain cold food. Maybe you don't know how cook, because you are a *bachelor*.

I sit down on your kitchen table, eat silently. Lampshade is on top of my head, tap is dripping in sink. So quiet. Scarily. I never ate such a quiet food in China. Always with many of family members, everybody shouting and screaming while eating. Here only the noise is from me using the forks and knife. I drop the knife two times so I decide only use one fork in my right hand.

Chewing. Chewing. No conversation.

You look at me eating, patiently.

Finally you ask: '*So, do you like the food?*'

I nod, put another leaf into my mouth. I remember me is bad speak with food full of my mouth. You wait. But patience maybe running out, so you answer your question in my voice: '*Yes, I like the food very much. It is delicious. It is yami.*'

The memory becomes so uncertain.

The memory keeps a portrait about you. An abstract portrait like pictures I saw in Tate Modern, blur details and sketchy lines. I start draw this picture, but my memory about you keep changing, and I have to change the picture.

green fingers

green fingers *Brit. informal* skill in gardening

OUR FIRST NIGHT. First time we make love. First time in my life doing this.

I think you are beautiful. You are beautiful smiles, and beautiful face, and beautiful language. You speak slowly. I almost hear every single word because you speak so slowly, only sometime I not understanding what you mean. But I understanding you more than anybody else I meet in England.

Then you are taking off clothes.

I look at you. Man's body seems ugly. Hair, bones, muscles, skins, more hair. I smell at you. Strong smell. Smell animal. Smell is from your hair, your chest, your neck, your armpit, your skin, your every single little bit in body.

Strong smell and strong soul. I even can feel it and

touch it. And I think your body maybe beautiful also. Is the home of your soul.

I ask how old are you, is first question Chinese people ask to stranger. You say forty-four. Older than me twenty years. Forty-four in my Chinese think is old, is really old. Leaves far behind away from youth. I say age sound old, but you look young. You say thanks, and you don't say more.

I say I think you beautiful, ignoring the age. I think you too beautiful for me, and I don't deserve of you.

Very early morning. You are sleeping, with gentle breathe. I look through bedroom's window. Sky turning dim into bright. I see small dried up old grapes hang under vines by window. Their shapes are become clear and clear in cold spring morning light. Garden is messy and lush. Your clothes and socks hanging in washing line. Your gardening machines everywhere on soil.

You are man, handy and physical. This is man's garden.

You make me feel fragile. Love makes me feel fragile, because I am not beautiful, I never being told I am beautiful. My mother always telling me I am ugly. 'You are ugly peasant girl. You have to know this.' Mother tells this to me for all twenty-three years. Maybe why I not never having boyfriend like other Chinese girls my age. When I badly communicating with others, my mother's words becomes loud in my eardrum. I am ugly peasant girl. I am ugly peasant girl.

'My body is crying for you,' you say.

Most beautiful sentence I heard in my life.

My bad English don't match your beautiful language.

I think I fall in love with you, but my love cannot match your beauty.

And then daytime. Sun puts light through garden to our bed. Birds are singing on roof. I think how sunlight must make people much happier in this dark country, and then I watch you wake up. We see each other naked, without distance. In light of reality. 'Good morning,' you say. 'You look even more lovely than yesterday.' And we make love again in the morning.

fertilise

fertilise v provide (an animal or plant) with sperm or pollen to bring about fertilisation; supply (soil) with nutrients

You TAKE ME to garden. Is very small, maybe ten square metres. One by one, you introduce me all the plants you have put there. Sixteen different plants in a ten square metres garden. In my home town in China, there only one plant in fields: rice.

You know every single plant's name, like they your family and you try tell me but I not remember English names so you write them down:

Potato	Green beans
Daffodil	Wisteria
Lavender	Grape vine
Mint	Bay tree
Spinach	Geranium

Thyme	Beetroot
Dill	Sweet corn
Apple tree	Fig tree

Then I tell you all these plants have very different names and meanings in Chinese. So I write down names in Chinese, and explain every word at you.

Potato   水仙
                    土豆
                    earth bean

Daffodil   水仙
                    fairy maiden from the water

Lavender   熏衣草
                    clothes perfuming weeds

Mint   薄荷
                    light lotus

Spinach   菠菜
                    watery vegetable

Thyme   百里香
                    one hundred miles fragrant

Dill   莳萝
                    the herb of time

Apple tree   苹果树
                    clover fern fruit tree

Green beans   豆子
                    son of beans

Wisteria   紫藤
                    purple vines

Grape vine	葡萄
	crawling plant
Bay tree	月桂树
	moon laurel
Geranium	天竺葵
	sky bamboo flower
Beetroot	甜菜
	sweet vegetable
Sweet corn	玉米
	jade rice
Fig tree	无花果树
	the fruit tree without flowers

You laughing when you hear the names. 'I never knew flutes grew on trees,' you say. It seems I am big comedy to you. I not understand why so funny. 'You can't say your Rs. It's *fruit* not *flute*,' you explain me. 'A *flute* is a musical instrument. But your Chinese name seems just right: a fig tree really is a fruit tree without flowers.'

'How a tree can just have fruit without having flower first?' I ask.

Like teacher, you describe how insect climbs into fruit to fertilise seed.

What 'fertilise'? I need looking in *Concise Chinese–English Dictionary*.

'Fertilise' make me think Chairman Mao. He likes fertiliser. Was big Mao thing increase productivity, increase plants. Maybe that why China, biggest peasants population country, still alive and become stronger after using fertiliser on the soil.

I ask: 'How long a fig tree has figs after insects fertilising it? Like woman have ten months pregnant?'

You look at me, like look at *alien*.

'Why ten months? I thought it took nine months,' you say.

'Chinese we say *shi yue huai tai* (十月怀胎). It means giving the birth after ten months pregnant.'

'That's strange.' You seem like want to laugh again. 'Which day do you start to count the pregnancy in China?' you ask seriously. But how I know? We never being taught this *properly* in school. Too shameful to teach and to study for our Chinese.

Standing under your fruit tree without flowers, I pick up piece of leaf, and put on my palm. A single leaf, but large. I touch the surface and feel hairy.

'Have you read the Bible?' you ask.

'No.' Of course not, not in China.

You fetch a big huge black book from room. You open the pages. 'Actually the fig tree is the oldest of mankind's symbols.' You point at beginning of book:

And the eyes of them both were opened, and they knew that they were naked, and they sewed fig leaves together, and made themselves aprons.

'What is that?' I am curious.

'It is about Adam and Eve. They used fig leaves to cover their naked bodies.'

'They clever. They knowing fig leaves bigger than other leafs,' I say.

You laugh again.

Your gardening machines everywhere in disorder.

Spade	铲子	For cutting the soil
Fork	叉子	For soften the soil
Rake	靶子	For scratching the grass

Suddenly I bit shocked, stop. There are some nudity in your garden.

'What this?' I ask.

'Those are my sculptures,' you say.

Sculptures? A naked man no head, facing to ground of the garden. Body twisted, with enormous hands and enormous feet. Close to ground, between the legs, two beautiful eggs, like two half of apples. In the middle of apples, a penis like little wounded bird. I walk to him and touch. Is made of plaster. I amazed by this body, is huge, looks suffered. I remember picture from Michelangelo's *David* on your bookshelf, a very healthy and balanced body. But yours, yours far different.

Beside this body statue, some other smalls clay sculptures. Ear, big like basin, in brown. Shape of that ear spread like a big flower. Then more ears, different shape, different size. They lie on the grass quietly, listening us.

Under fig tree another penis made from clay, gentle, innocent. Then another one, looks harder, lies down beside honeysuckle roots, in soil colour. Little clay sculptures there, like they live with plants hundred years.

The noisy London being stopped by brick wall. The grey city kept away by this garden. Plants and sculptures on sunshine. Glamorous, like you. Maybe all mans in London green fingers. Maybe this country too cold and too dim, so plants and garden can showing imagination the spring, the sun, the warmth. And plants and garden giving love like womans warm mans life.

When I stand in garden with sixteen different plants, I think of Chinese mans. Chinese city-mans not plant-lover at all. Shameful for Chinese city-mans pour passion onto those leafs. He be considered a loser, no position in society. But you, you different. Who are you?

vegetarian

vegetarian n person who eats no meat or fish
adj suitable for a vegetarian

ONE PROBLEM BETWEEN us and that is food.

Chop Chop, local Chinese restaurant in Hackney. I make you go there even though you say you never go Chinese restaurants.

Restaurant has very plain looking. White plastic table and plastic chairs and white fluorescent lamp. Just like normal government work unit in China. Waiter unhappy when cleans table, not looking anybody. Woman with pony tails behind counter she even more mean. A plastic panda-savings-tin sitting on top of counter. None of them can speak Mandarin.

'No. Sit there. No, no, not this table. Sit at that table.'

Waiter commands like we is his soldiers.

'What you want? . . . We don't have tap water, you have

to order something from the menu . . . We don't do pots of green tea, only cups.'

I hate them. I swear I never been so rude Chinese restaurant in my entirely life. Why Chinese people becoming so mean in the West? I feel bit guilty for horrible service. Because I bring you, and you maybe thinking my culture just like this. Maybe that why some English look down of our Chinese. I am shameful for being a Chinese here.

But we still have to eat. Especially me, starving like the Ghost of Hunger. I always hungry. Even after big meal, later by one or two hours I feel hungry again. My family always very poor until several years ago. We used eat very small, barely had meat. After my parents started shoes factory, and left the poor peasants background behind, changed. But still I think foods all the time.

You not know nothing about Chinese food so I quickly order: duck, pork, fried tofu with beefs.

Meal comes to table, and I digging fastly my chopsticks into dishes like having a snowstorm. But you don't have any action at all. You just look me, like looking a Beijing opera.

'Why you not eat?' I ask, busy chewing my pork in my mouth.

'I am not very hungry,' you say.

'You use chopsticks?' I think maybe that's the reason.

'Yes. Don't worry.' You raise your chopsticks and perform to me.

'But you waste the food. Not like Chinese food?'

'I am a *vegetarian*,' you say picking up little bit rice. 'This menu is a zoo.'

I am surprised. I try find my dictionary. Damn, is not with me this time. I remember film *English Patient* I watch on pirate DVD in China to education me about British people. 'What that word? Word describe a people fall asleep for long long time, like living dying?'

'You mean coma?' You are confused.

'Yes, that is the word! You are not like that, do you?'

You put chopsticks down. Maybe you angry now.

'I presume you are thinking of the *persistent vegetative state*,' you say. '*Vegetarian* means you don't eat meat.'

'Oh, I am sorry,' I say, swallowing big mouthful tofus and beefs.

Now I understand why never buy piece of meat. I thought it is because you poor.

'Why don't eat meat? Meat very nutritious.'

'. . .' You have no comments.

'Also you be depression if you don't eating meat.'

'. . .' You still have no comments.

'My parents beaten me if I don't eating meat or any food on table in a meal. My parents curse me being picky and spoiled. Because others dying without any food to eat.'

'. . .' Still don't say anything.

'How come man is vegetarian? Unless he is monk,' I say.

Still no words from you, but laughing.

You watch me eating all of meal. I try finish the duck,

and the tofu and the beefs. My stomach painful. There are still porks left, and I order to take them away.

While I eating, you write top ten favourite food on a napkin:

lettuce   carrot
           lentils
   broccoli
                      radish
  aubergine   avocado
              pumpkin
  spinach
              asparagus

But, is this list will be the menu in our kitchen for rest of life? Is terrible! What about my meatball, my mutton, my beefs in black bean sauce? Who will be in charge of kitchen?

April

chinese cabbage + english slug

cabbage n vegetable with a large head of green leaves

slug n land snail with no shell; a bullet; a mouthful of an alcoholic

HARDLY DAYS IS absolutely sunny, sunny until sun falling to the west. Sky in England always look suspicious, untrustful, like today's. You see me sad but don't understand why.

Standing in the garden, you ask me: 'Do you want to have your own little plants in this garden? I think it should be a woman's garden as well.'

'Yes. I want. I want plant Chinese cabbages, some water lily, some plum tree, and maybe some bamboos, and maybe some Chinese chives as well . . .'

I immediately image picture of tradition Chinese garden.

'No, honey, it's too small for so many Chinese plants.'

Then, Sunday, we went to Columbia Road Flower Market. It my favourite market. We brought the small little sprouts of Chinese cabbage at home. Eight little sprouts all together.

We plant all these little things. Digging the soil, and putting every single sprout into the hole. You are fast than me. So you finished planting five, and I only putting third one in the little hole.

We watering Chinese cabbage sprouts every morning, loyal and faithful, like every morning we never forgetting brushing our teeth. Seeing tiny sprouts come out, my heart feel happy. Is our love. We plant it.

You say:

'Growing a vegetable and seeing it grow is more interesting than anything else. It's magic. Don't you agree?'

Yes. Is interesting. But in China, is just for peasant. Every person can do this, nothing special for growing food. Why so different here?

Then we see some little leafs come out but are bitten by the slug.

'It's dangerous that the slugs keep eating the small sprouts. They can die really easily,' you tell me.

Carrying with torch, every night, around 11 o'clock, you sneek into garden and check the slug. They are always several slug hidden behind the young leafs. Enjoying the delicious meal under the moonlight. You taking them out from the leafs, one by one. You putting these slug together in one glass bottle. Soon glass bottle becomes a slug-zoo.

'What your favourite words? Give me ten,' I say when we are sitting in garden. I want learn most beautiful English words because you are beautiful. I even not care whether if useful.

A piece of blank paper, a pen.

You writing it down, one by one.

'*Sea, breath, sun, body, seeds, bumble bee, insects.*' You stop: 'How many are there now?'

'Seven,' I say.

'Hm . . . *blood* . . .' you continue.

'Why you like blood?'

'I don't know. I feel blood is beautiful.'

'Really? But blood violence, and pain.'

'No. Not always. Blood gives you life. It makes you strong.' You speaking with surely voice.

You see things from such different perspective from me. I wonder if we change perspective one day.

'And why *breath*, then?'

'Because that's where everything is from and how everything starts.'

You are right.

'So, what else? Last favourite word?' I say.

'Suddenly.'

'*Suddenly*! Why you like *suddenly*? *Suddenly* not even noun.' You a strange brain, I think.

'I want learn most beautiful English words because you are beautiful'

'Well, I just like it,' you say. 'So what are your favorite ten words?'

I write down one by one:

'*Fear, belief, heart, root, challenge, fight, peace, misery, future, solitude . . .*'

'Why *solitude*?'

'Because a song from Louis Armstrong calling "Solitude". It is so beautiful.' I hear song in my ear now.

'Where did you hear that song?' you ask.

'On your shelfs. A CD, from Louis Armstrong.'

'Really? I didn't even know I had that CD.' You frown.

'Yes, is covering the dust, and look very old.'

'So, you've been through all my CDs?'

'Of course,' I say. 'I read your letters and diaries as well.'

'What?'

'And looked your photo.'

'What? You've looked through all my stuff?' You seeming like *suddenly* hear the alien from Mars attack the Earth.

'Not all. Parts that diary are make me sad. I can't sleep at night,' I say.

privacy

privacy n the state of being alone or undisturbed; freedom from interference or public attention

'YOU'VE INVADED MY privacy! You can't do that!' First time, you shout to me, like a lion.

'What privacy? But we living together! No privacy if we are lovers!'

'Of course there is! Everybody has privacy!'

But why people need privacy? Why privacy is important? In China, every family live together, grandparents, parents, daughter, son, and their relatives too. Eat together and share everything, talk about everything. Privacy make people lonely. Privacy make family fallen apart.

When I arguing about privacy, you just listen and not say anything. I know you disagree me, and you not want live inside of my life, because you a 'private' person. A private person doesn't share life.

'When I read your past, when I read those letters you wrote, I think you are *drifter*.'

'What do you mean by that?'

'You know what is drifter, do you? You come and leave, you not care about future.'

'To me, to live life is to live in the present.'

'OK, live in present, and which direction you leading then?'

'What are you talking about?'

'I mean, you don't have plan for tomorrow, for next year?'

'Well, we are talking about different things. I don't think you understand what I am saying. To me the future is about moving on, to some new place. I don't know where I am going. It's like I am riding a horse through the desert, and the horse just carries me somewhere, maybe with an oasis, but I don't know.'

Suddenly the air being frozen. Feeling cold. I not know what to say anymore. You older than me twenty years. You must understand life better than me?

You look at me and you say: 'It's like the way you came into my life. I feel as if I am not naked anymore.'

I feel as if I am not naked anymore. That a beautiful sentence.

I listen, I wait. I feel it something you not finish in your sentence, but you not want say it.

So I help you: 'Ok, I come into your life, but you not know if you wanting carry on this with me all the times.

You will want to break it and see what can make you move
on . . .'

'We will see.' You stop me, and take me into your
arms.

'It's important to be able to live with uncertainty.'

free world

free world esp. US historically non-Communist countries

You say:

'I feel incredibly lucky to be with you. We're going to have loads of exciting adventures together. Our first big adventure will be in west Wales. I'll show you the sea. I'll teach you to swim because it is shameful that a peasant girl cannot swim. I'll show you the dolphins in the sea, and the seals with their babies. I want you to experience the beauty of the peace and quiet in a Welsh cottage. I think you will love it there.'

You also say:

'Then I want to take you to Spain and France. I know that you'll love them. But we'll have to wait for a while. We need to earn some money. I'll have to get more work doing deliveries in the van to boring rich people. Can you put up with me being so boring – or do you think you'll get fed up with me after a while?'

Later you say:

'I feel so good about the love that you and I have with each other because it happened so quickly and spontaneously, like a forest fire.'

And you say:

'I just love the way you are.'

Everything good so far, but from one thing – you don't understand my visa limited situation. I am native Chinese from mainland of China. I am not of *free world*. And I only have student visa for a year here. I not able just leave London English language school and go live somewhere only have trees and sea, although is beautiful. And I can't travel to Spain and France just to fun – I need show these embassy officer my bank account to apply my Europe visa. And my bank statements is never qualify for them. You a free man of free world. I am not free, like you.

May

colony

colony n group of people who settle in a new country but remain under the rule of their homeland; territory occupied by a colony; group of people or animals of the same kind living together

THE WAY YOU make love with me, is totally new experience in my life. Is sex suppose be like this? Penetrating is way for you to enter into my soul. You are so strong. And your strength is overwhelming. For you, I am unprepared. You crush me and press me into your body. Love making is a torture. Love making is a battle. Then I get used it, and I am addicted by it. The way you hold my body is like holding small object, an apple, or a little animal. The force from your arms and your legs and your hip is like force from huge creature living in jungle. The vibrate from your muscle shakes my skins, the beating of your heart also beating my heart.

You are the commander.

You kiss my lips, my eyes, my cheek, my ears, my neck, and my silver necklace. It is like my necklace having a special magic on you. And that magic force you devote yourself to my body. Then you kiss my breasts and you suck them. You are like baby who is thirsty for mother's milk. You lick my belly and my legs and my feet. You possess my whole body. They are your farm. Then you come back to my garden. Your lips are wandering in my cave, and in that warm and wet nature you try find something precious, something you always dream about. You wander alone there and love there and want live there.

My whole body is your colony.

XIAOLU GUO is one of the best Chinese novelists of recent decades. When Xiaolu was born her parents gave her to a childless peasant couple in the mountains. Aged two, and suffering from malnutrition, they sent her to live with her illiterate grandparents in a fishing village on the East China Sea. This is where she grew up. She attended film school in Beijing and then, with a scholarship to study film, moved to Britain in 2002, knowing little more than a few English phrases.

A Concise Chinese-English Dictionary for Lovers, from which this Mini is taken, was written in English just a couple of years after Xiaolu moved to Britain. On her thirtieth birthday, Xiaolu decided to make her isolation in Britain, and her struggle with the English language, an asset and to write a novel about a Chinese immigrant. She kept a detailed diary, filled with the new vocabulary she learned, and this became the basis for the novel. The resulting book was shortlisted for the Orange Prize for Fiction. Xiaolu has written a dozen books in both Chinese and English and has directed a few award-winning fiction and documentary films.

RECOMMENDED BOOKS BY XIAOLU GUO:

A Concise Chinese-English Dictionary for Lovers
I Am China
Once Upon A Time in the East

Still talking about Language?

VINTAGE MINIS

The Vintage Minis bring you the world's greatest writers on the experiences that make us human. These stylish, entertaining little books explore the whole spectrum of life – from birth to death, and everything in between. Which means there's something here for everyone, whatever your story.

vintageminis.co.uk

1 3 5 7 9 10 8 6 4 2

Vintage
20 Vauxhall Bridge Road,
London SW1V 2SA

Vintage Classics is part of the Penguin Random House
group of companies whose addresses can be found at
global.penguinrandomhouse.com.

Little Women was first published in 1868
Good Wives was first published in 1869
This short edition published by Vintage in 2017

penguin.co.uk/vintage

A CIP catalogue record for this book is available from the British Library

ISBN 9781784872755

Typeset in 9.5/14.5 pt FreightText Pro by Jouve (UK), Milton Keynes
Printed and bound by Clays Ltd, St Ives plc

Penguin Random House is committed to a sustainable future for
our business, our readers and our planet. This book is made from
Forest Stewardship Council® certified paper.

Sisters

LOUISA MAY ALCOTT

VINTAGE MINIS

Playing Pilgrims

'CHRISTMAS WON'T BE Christmas without any presents,' grumbled Jo, lying on the rug.

'It's so dreadful to be poor!' sighed Meg, looking down at her old dress.

'I don't think it's fair for some girls to have lots of pretty things, and other girls nothing at all,' added little Amy, with an injured sniff.

'We've got father and mother, and each other, anyhow,' said Beth, contentedly, from her corner.

The four young faces on which the firelight shone brightened at the cheerful words, but darkened again as Jo said sadly,—

'We haven't got father, and shall not have him for a long time.' She didn't say 'perhaps never,' but each silently added it, thinking of father far away, where the fighting was.

Nobody spoke for a minute; then Meg said in an altered tone,—

'You know the reason mother proposed not having any presents this Christmas, was because it's going to be a hard winter for every one; and she thinks we ought not to spend money for pleasure, when our men are suffering so in the army. We can't do much, but we can make our little sacrifices, and ought to do it gladly. But I am afraid I don't;' and Meg shook her head, as she thought regretfully of all the pretty things she wanted.

'But I don't think the little we should spend would do any good. We've each got a dollar, and the army wouldn't be much helped by our giving that. I agree not to expect anything from mother or you, but I do want to buy Undine and Sintram for myself; I've wanted it *so* long,' said Jo, who was a bookworm.

'I planned to spend mine in new music,' said Beth, with a little sigh, which no one heard but the hearth-brush and kettle-holder.

'I shall get a nice box of Faber's drawing pencils; I really need them,' said Amy, decidedly.

'Mother didn't say anything about our money, and she won't wish us to give up everything. Let's each buy what we want, and have a little fun; I'm sure we grub hard enough to earn it,' cried Jo, examining the heels of her boots in a gentlemanly manner.

'I know *I* do,—teaching those dreadful children nearly all day, when I'm longing to enjoy myself at home,' began Meg, in the complaining tone again.

'You don't have half such a hard time as I do,' said Jo. 'How would you like to be shut up for hours with a nervous, fussy old lady, who keeps you trotting, is never satisfied, and worries you till you're ready to fly out of the window or box her ears?'

'It's naughty to fret,—but I do think washing dishes and keeping things tidy is the worst work in the world. It makes me cross; and my hands get so stiff, I can't practise good a bit.' And Beth looked at her rough hands with a sigh that any one could hear that time.

'I don't believe any of you suffer as I do,' cried Amy; 'for you don't have to go to school with impertinent girls, who plague you if you don't know your lessons, and laugh at your dresses, and label your father if he isn't rich, and insult you when your nose isn't nice.'

'If you mean *libel* I'd say so, and not talk about *labels*, as if pa was a pickle-bottle,' advised Jo, laughing.

'I know what I mean, and you needn't be "statirical" about it. It's proper to use good words, and improve your *vocabilary*,' returned Amy, with dignity.

'Don't peck at one another, children. Don't you wish we had the money papa lost when we were little, Jo? Dear me, how happy and good we'd be, if we had no worries,' said Meg, who could remember better times.

'You said the other day you thought we were a deal happier than the King children, for they were fighting and fretting all the time, in spite of their money.'

'So I did, Beth. Well, I guess we are; for though we do

have to work, we make fun for ourselves, and are a pretty jolly set, as Jo would say.'

'Jo does use such slang words,' observed Amy, with a reproving look at the long figure stretched on the rug. Jo immediately sat up, put her hands in her apron pockets, and began to whistle.

'Don't, Jo; it's so boyish.'

'That's why I do it.'

'I detest rude, unlady-like girls.'

'I hate affected, niminy piminy chits.'

'Birds in their little nests agree,' sang Beth, the peacemaker, with such a funny face that both sharp voices softened to a laugh, and the 'pecking' ended for that time.

'Really, girls, you are both to be blamed,' said Meg, beginning to lecture in her elder sisterly fashion. 'You are old enough to leave off boyish tricks, and behave better, Josephine. It didn't matter so much when you were a little girl; but now you are so tall, and turn up your hair, you should remember that you are a young lady.'

'I ain't! and if turning up my hair makes me one, I'll wear it in two tails till I'm twenty,' cried Jo, pulling off her net, and shaking down a chestnut mane. 'I hate to think I've got to grow up and be Miss March, and wear long gowns, and look as prim as a China-aster. It's bad enough to be a girl, any way, when I like boys' games, and work, and manners. I can't get over my disappointment in not being a boy, and it's worse than ever now, for I'm dying to go and fight with

It's bad enough to be a girl, any way, when I like boys' games, and work, and manners

papa, and I can only stay at home and knit like a poky old woman;' and Jo shook the blue army-sock till the needles rattled like castanets, and her ball bounded across the room.

'Poor Jo; it's too bad! But it can't be helped, so you must try to be contented with making your name boyish, and playing brother to us girls,' said Beth, stroking the rough head at her knee with a hand that all the dishwashing and dusting in the world could not make ungentle in its touch.

'As for you, Amy,' continued Meg, 'you are altogether too particular and prim. Your airs are funny now, but you'll grow up an affected little goose if you don't take care. I like your nice manners, and refined ways of speaking, when you don't try to be elegant; but your absurd words are as bad as Jo's slang.'

'If Jo is a tom-boy, and Amy a goose, what am I, please?' asked Beth, ready to share the lecture.

'You're a dear, and nothing else,' answered Meg, warmly; and no one contradicted her, for the 'Mouse' was the pet of the family.

As young readers like to know 'how people look,' we will take this moment to give them a little sketch of the four sisters, who sat knitting away in the twilight, while the December snow fell quietly without, and the fire crackled cheerfully within. It was a comfortable old room, though the carpet was faded and the furniture very plain, for a good picture or two hung on the walls, books filled the recesses, chrysanthemums and Christmas roses bloomed in the windows, and a pleasant atmosphere of home-peace pervaded it.

Margaret, the eldest of the four, was sixteen, and very pretty, being plump and fair, with large eyes, plenty of soft brown hair, a sweet mouth, and white hands, of which she was rather vain. Fifteen-year-old Jo was very tall, thin and brown, and reminded one of a colt; for she never seemed to know what to do with her long limbs, which were very much in her way. She had a decided mouth, a comical nose, and sharp gray eyes, which appeared to see everything, and were by turns fierce, funny, or thoughtful. Her long, thick hair was her one beauty; but it was usually bundled into a net, to be out of her way. Round shoulders had Jo, big hands and feet, a fly-away look to her clothes, and the uncomfortable appearance of a girl who was rapidly shooting up into a woman, and didn't like it. Elizabeth,—or Beth, as every one called her,—was a rosy, smooth-haired, bright-eyed girl of thirteen, with a shy manner, a timid voice, and a peaceful expression, which was seldom disturbed. Her father called her 'Little Tranquillity,' and the name suited her excellently; for she seemed to live in a happy world of her own, only venturing out to meet the few whom she trusted and loved. Amy, though the youngest, was a most important person, in her own opinion at least. A regular snow maiden, with blue eyes, and yellow hair curling on her shoulders; pale and slender, and always carrying herself like a young lady mindful of her manners. What the characters of the four sisters were, we will leave to be found out.

The clock struck six; and, having swept up the hearth, Beth put a pair of slippers down to warm. Somehow the sight of the old shoes had a good effect upon the girls, for mother was coming, and every one brightened to welcome her. Meg stopped lecturing, and lit the lamp, Amy got out of the easy-chair without being asked, and Jo forgot how tired she was as she sat up to hold the slippers nearer to the blaze.

'They are quite worn out; Marmee must have a new pair.'

'I thought I'd get her some with my dollar,' said Beth.

'No, I shall!' cried Amy.

'I'm the oldest,' began Meg, but Jo cut in with a decided—

'I'm the man of the family now papa is away, and I shall provide the slippers, for he told me to take special care of mother while he was gone.'

'I'll tell you what we'll do,' said Beth; 'let's each get her something for Christmas, and not get anything for ourselves.'

'That's like you, dear! What will we get?' exclaimed Jo.

Every one thought soberly for a minute; then Meg announced, as if the idea was suggested by the sight of her own pretty hands, 'I shall give her a nice pair of gloves.'

'Army shoes, best to be had,' cried Jo.

'Some handkerchiefs, all hemmed,' said Beth.

'I'll get a little bottle of Cologne; she likes it, and it won't cost much, so I'll have some left to buy something for me,' added Amy.

'How will we give the things?' asked Meg.

'Put 'em on the table, and bring her in and see her open the bundles. Don't you remember how we used to do on our birthdays?' answered Jo.

'I used to be so frightened when it was my turn to sit in the big chair with a crown on, and see you all come marching round to give the presents, with a kiss. I liked the things and the kisses, but it was dreadful to have you sit looking at me while I opened the bundles,' said Beth, who was toasting her face and the bread for tea, at the same time.

'Let Marmee think we are getting things for ourselves, and then surprise her. We must go shopping tomorrow afternoon, Meg; there is lots to do about the play for Christmas night,' said Jo, marching up and down with her hands behind her back, and her nose in the air.

'I don't mean to act any more after this time; I'm getting too old for such things,' observed Meg, who was as much a child as ever about 'dressing up' frolics.

'You won't stop, I know, as long as you can trail round in a white gown with your hair down, and wear gold-paper jewelry. You are the best actress we've got, and there'll be an end of everything if you quit the boards,' said Jo. 'We ought to rehearse tonight; come here, Amy, and do the fainting scene, for you are as stiff as a poker in that.'

'I can't help it; I never saw any one faint, and I don't

choose to make myself all black and blue, tumbling flat as you do. If I can go down easily, I'll drop; if I can't, I shall fall into a chair and be graceful; I don't care if Hugo does come at me with a pistol,' returned Amy, who was not gifted with dramatic power, but was chosen because she was small enough to be borne out shrieking by the hero of the piece.

'Do it this way; clasp your hands so, and stagger across the room, crying frantically, "Roderigo! save me! save me!"' and away went Jo, with a melodramatic scream which was truly thrilling.

Amy followed, but she poked her hands out stiffly before her, and jerked herself along as if she went by machinery; and her 'Ow!' was more suggestive of pins being run into her than of fear and anguish. Jo gave a despairing groan, and Meg laughed outright, while Beth let her bread burn as she watched the fun, with interest.

'It's no use! do the best you can when the time comes, and if the audience shout, don't blame me. Come on, Meg.'

Then things went smoothly, for Don Pedro defied the world in a speech of two pages without a single break; Hagar, the witch, chanted an awful incantation over her kettleful of simmering toads, with weird effect; Roderigo rent his chains asunder manfully, and Hugo died in agonies of remorse and arsenic, with a wild 'Ha! ha!'

'It's the best we've had yet,' said Meg, as the dead villain sat up and rubbed his elbows.

'I don't see how you can write and act such splendid

things, Jo. You're a regular Shakespeare!' exclaimed Beth, who firmly believed that her sisters were gifted with wonderful genius in all things.

'Not quite,' replied Jo, modestly. 'I do think "The Witch's Curse, an Operatic Tragedy," is rather a nice thing; but I'd like to try Macbeth, if we only had a trapdoor for Banquo. I always wanted to do the killing part. "Is that a dagger that I see before me?"' muttered Jo, rolling her eyes and clutching at the air, as she had seen a famous tragedian do.

'No, it's the toasting fork, with ma's shoe on it instead of the bread. Beth's stage struck!' cried Meg, and the rehearsal ended in a general burst of laughter.

'Glad to find you so merry, my girls,' said a cheery voice at the door, and actors and audience turned to welcome a stout, motherly lady, with a 'can-I-help-you' look about her which was truly delightful. She wasn't a particularly handsome person, but mothers are always lovely to their children, and the girls thought the gray cloak and unfashionable bonnet covered the most splendid woman in the world.

'Well, dearies, how have you got on today? There was so much to do, getting the boxes ready to go tomorrow, that I didn't come home to dinner. Has any one called, Beth? How is your cold, Meg? Jo, you look tired to death. Come and kiss me, baby.'

While making these maternal inquiries Mrs March got her wet things off, her hot slippers on, and sitting down in the easy-chair, drew Amy to her lap, preparing to enjoy the happiest hour of her busy day. The girls flew about, trying to make things comfortable, each in her own way. Meg arranged the tea-table; Jo brought wood and set chairs, dropping, overturning, and clattering everything she touched; Beth trotted to and fro between parlor and kitchen, quiet and busy; while Amy gave directions to every one, as she sat with her hands folded.

As they gathered about the table, Mrs March said, with a particularly happy face, 'I've got a treat for you after supper.'

A quick, bright smile went round like a streak of sunshine. Beth clapped her hands, regardless of the hot biscuit she held, and Jo tossed up her napkin, crying, 'A letter! a letter! Three cheers for father!'

'Yes, a nice long letter. He is well, and thinks he shall get through the cold season better than we feared. He sends all sorts of loving wishes for Christmas, and an especial message to you girls,' said Mrs March, patting her pocket as if she had got a treasure there.

'Hurry up, and get done. Don't stop to quirk your little finger, and prink over your plate, Amy,' cried Jo, choking in her tea, and dropping her bread, butter side down, on the carpet, in her haste to get at the treat.

Beth ate no more, but crept away, to sit in her shadowy corner and brood over the delight to come, till the others were ready.

'I think it was so splendid in father to go as a chaplain

when he was too old to be draughted, and not strong enough for a soldier,' said Meg, warmly.

'Don't I wish I could go as a drummer, a *vivan*—what's its name? or a nurse, so I could be near him and help him,' exclaimed Jo, with a groan.

'It must be very disagreeable to sleep in a tent, and eat all sorts of bad-tasting things, and drink out of a tin mug,' sighed Amy.

'When will he come home, Marmee?' asked Beth, with a little quiver in her voice.

'Not for many months, dear, unless he is sick. He will stay and do his work faithfully as long as he can, and we won't ask for him back a minute sooner than he can be spared. Now come and hear the letter.'

They all drew to the fire, mother in the big chair with Beth at her feet, Meg and Amy perched on either arm of the chair, and Jo leaning on the back, where no one would see any sign of emotion if the letter should happen to be touching.

Very few letters were written in those hard times that were not touching, especially those which fathers sent home. In this one little was said of the hardships endured, the dangers faced, or the homesickness conquered; it was a cheerful, hopeful letter, full of lively descriptions of camp life, marches, and military news; and only at the end did the writer's heart overflow with fatherly love and longing for the little girls at home.

'Give them all my dear love and a kiss. Tell them I think

of them by day, pray for them by night, and find my best comfort in their affection at all times. A year seems very long to wait before I see them, but remind them that while we wait we may all work, so that these hard days need not be wasted. I know they will remember all I said to them, that they will be loving children to you, will do their duty faithfully, fight their bosom enemies bravely, and conquer themselves so beautifully, that when I come back to them I may be fonder and prouder than ever of my little women.'

Everybody sniffed when they came to that part; Jo wasn't ashamed of the great tear that dropped off the end of her nose, and Amy never minded the rumpling of her curls as she hid her face on her mother's shoulder and sobbed out, 'I *am* a selfish pig! but I'll truly try to be better, so he mayn't be disappointed in me by and by.'

'We all will!' cried Meg. 'I think too much of my looks, and hate to work, but won't any more, if I can help it.'

'I'll try and be what he loves to call me, "a little woman," and not be rough and wild; but do my duty here instead of wanting to be somewhere else,' said Jo, thinking that keeping her temper at home was a much harder task than facing a rebel or two down South.

Beth said nothing, but wiped away her tears with the blue army-sock, and began to knit with all her might, losing no time in doing that duty that lay nearest her, while she resolved in her quiet little soul to be all that father hoped to find her when the year brought round the happy coming home.

Mrs March broke the silence that followed Jo's words, by saying in her cheery voice, 'Do you remember how you used to play Pilgrim's Progress when you were little things? Nothing delighted you more than to have me tie my piece-bags on your backs for burdens, give you hats and sticks, and rolls of paper, and let you travel through the house from the cellar, which was the City of Destruction, up, up, to the house-top, where you had all the lovely things you could collect to make a Celestial City.'

'What fun it was, especially going by the lions, fighting Apollyon, and passing through the Valley where the hobgoblins were,' said Jo.

'I liked the place where the bundles fell off and tumbled down stairs,' said Meg.

'My favorite part was when we came out on the flat roof where our flowers and arbors, and pretty things were, and all stood and sung for joy up there in the sunshine,' said Beth, smiling, as if that pleasant moment had come back to her.

'I don't remember much about it, except that I was afraid of the cellar and the dark entry, and always liked the cake and milk we had up at the top. If I wasn't too old for such things, I'd rather like to play it over again,' said Amy, who began to talk of renouncing childish things at the mature age of twelve.

'We never are too old for this, my dear, because it is a play we are playing all the time in one way or another. Our burdens are here, our road is before us, and the longing for goodness and happiness is the guide that leads us through many troubles and mistakes to the peace which is a true Celestial City. Now, my little pilgrims, suppose you begin again, not in play, but in earnest, and see how far on you can get before father comes home.'

'Really, mother? where are our bundles?' asked Amy, who was a very literal young lady.

'Each of you told what your burden was just now, except Beth; I rather think she hasn't got any,' said her mother.

'Yes, I have; mine is dishes and dusters, and envying girls with nice pianos, and being afraid of people.'

Beth's bundle was such a funny one that everybody wanted to laugh; but nobody did, for it would have hurt her feelings very much.

'Let us do it,' said Meg, thoughtfully. 'It is only another name for trying to be good, and the story may help us; for though we do want to be good, it's hard work, and we forget, and don't do our best.'

'We were in the Slough of Despond tonight, and mother came and pulled us out as Help did in the book. We ought to have our roll of directions, like Christian. What shall we do about that?' asked Jo, delighted with the fancy which lent a little romance to the very dull task of doing her duty.

'Look under your pillows, Christmas morning, and you will find your guide-book,' replied Mrs March.

They talked over the new plan while old Hannah cleared the table; then out came the four little workbaskets, and the needles flew as the girls made sheets for Aunt March. It was uninteresting sewing, but tonight no one grumbled. They adopted Jo's plan of dividing the long seams into four parts, and calling the quarters Europe, Asia, Africa and America, and in that way got on capitally, especially when they talked about the different countries as they stitched their way through them.

At nine they stopped work, and sang, as usual, before they went to bed. No one but Beth could get much music out of the old piano; but she had a way of softly touching the yellow keys, and making a pleasant accompaniment to the simple songs they sung. Meg had a voice like a flute, and she and her mother led the little choir. Amy chirped like a cricket, and Jo wandered through the airs at her own sweet will, always coming out at the wrong place with a crook or a quaver that spoilt the most pensive tune. They had always done this from the time they could lisp

'Crinkle, crinkle, 'ittle 'tar,'

and it had become a household custom, for the mother was a born singer. The first sound in the morning was her voice, as she went about the house singing like a lark; and the last sound at night was the same cheery sound, for the girls never grew too old for that familiar lullaby.

Jo Meets Apollyon

'GIRLS, WHERE ARE you going?' asked Amy, coming into their room one Saturday afternoon, and finding them getting ready to go out, with an air of secrecy which excited her curiosity.

'Never mind; little girls shouldn't ask questions,' returned Jo, sharply.

Now if there is anything mortifying to our feelings, when we are young, it is to be told that; and to be bidden to 'run away, dear,' is still more trying to us. Amy bridled up at this insult, and determined to find out the secret, if she teased for an hour. Turning to Meg, who never refused her anything very long, she said, coaxingly, 'Do tell me! I should think you might let me go, too; for Beth is fussing over her dolls, and I haven't got anything to do, and am *so* lonely.'

'I can't, dear, because you aren't invited,' began Meg; but Jo broke in impatiently, 'Now, Meg, be quiet, or you will spoil it all. You can't go, Amy; so don't be a baby, and whine about it.'

'You are going somewhere with Laurie, I know you are; you were whispering and laughing together, on the sofa, last night, and you stopped when I came in. Aren't you going with him?'

'Yes, we are; now do be still, and stop bothering.'

Amy held her tongue, but used her eyes, and saw Meg slip a fan into her pocket.

'I know! I know! you're going to the theatre to see the "Seven Castles!"' she cried; adding, resolutely, 'and I *shall* go, for mother said I might see it; and I've got my rag-money, and it was mean not to tell me in time.'

'Just listen to me a minute, and be a good child,' said Meg, soothingly. 'Mother doesn't wish you to go this week, because your eyes are not well enough yet to bear the light of this fairy piece. Next week you can go with Beth and Hannah, and have a nice time.'

'I don't like that half as well as going with you and Laurie. Please let me; I've been sick with this cold so long, and shut up, I'm dying for some fun. Do, Meg! I'll be ever so good,' pleaded Amy, looking as pathetic as she could.

'Suppose we take her. I don't believe mother would mind, if we bundle her up well,' began Meg.

'If *she* goes I shan't; and if I don't, Laurie won't like it; and it will be very rude, after he invited only us, to go and drag in Amy. I should think she'd hate to poke herself where she isn't wanted,' said Jo, crossly, for she disliked the trouble of overseeing a fidgety child, when she wanted to enjoy herself.

Her tone and manner angered Amy, who began to put her boots on, saying, in her most aggravating way, 'I *shall* go; Meg says I may; and if I pay for myself, Laurie hasn't anything to do with it.'

'You can't sit with us, for our seats are reserved, and you mustn't sit alone; so Laurie will give you his place, and that will spoil our pleasure; or he'll get another seat for you, and that isn't proper, when you weren't asked. You shan't stir a step; so you may just stay where you are,' scolded Jo, crosser than ever, having just pricked her finger in a hurry.

Sitting on the floor, with one boot on, Amy began to cry, and Meg to reason with her, when Laurie called from below, and the two girls hurried down, leaving their sister wailing; for now and then she forgot her grown-up ways, and acted like a spoilt child. Just as the party was setting out, Amy called over the banisters, in a threatening tone, 'You'll be sorry for this, Jo March! see if you ain't.'

'Fiddlesticks!' returned Jo, slamming the door.

They had a charming time, for 'The Seven Castles of Diamond Lake' were as brilliant and wonderful as a heart could wish. But, in spite of the comical red imps, sparkling elves, and gorgeous princes and princesses, Jo's pleasure had a drop of bitterness in it; the fairy queen's yellow curls reminded her of Amy; and between the acts she amused herself with wondering what her sister would do to make her 'sorry for it.' She and Amy had had many lively skir-mishes in the course of their lives, for both had quick tempers, and were apt to be violent when fairly roused. Amy teased Jo, and Jo irritated Amy, and semi-occasional explosions occurred, of which both were much ashamed afterward. Although the oldest, Jo had the least self-control, and had hard times trying to curb the fiery spirit which was continually getting her into trouble; her anger never lasted long, and, having humbly confessed her fault, she sincerely repented, and tried to do better. Her sisters used to say, that they rather liked to get Jo into a fury, because she was such an angel afterward. Poor Jo tried desperately to be good, but her bosom enemy was always ready to flame up and defeat her; and it took years of patient effort to subdue it.

When they got home, they found Amy reading in the parlor. She assumed an injured air as they came in; never lifted her eyes from her book, or asked a single question. Perhaps curiosity might have conquered resentment, if Beth had not been there to inquire, and receive a glowing description of the play. On going up to put away her best hat, Jo's first look was toward the bureau; for, in their last quarrel, Amy had soothed her feelings by turning Jo's top drawer upside down, on the floor. Everything was in its place, however; and after a hasty glance into her various closets, bags and boxes, Jo decided that Amy had forgiven and forgotten her wrongs.

There Jo was mistaken; for next day she made a

discovery which produced a tempest. Meg, Beth and Amy were sitting together, late in the afternoon, when Jo burst into the room, looking excited, and demanding, breathlessly, 'Has any one taken my story?'

Meg and Beth said 'No,' at once, and looked surprised; Amy poked the fire, and said nothing. Jo saw her color rise, and was down upon her in a minute.

'Amy, you've got it!'

'No, I haven't.'

'You know where it is, then!'

'No, I don't.'

'That's a fib!' cried Jo, taking her by the shoulders, and looking fierce enough to frighten a much braver child than Amy.

'It isn't. I haven't got it, don't know where it is now, and don't care.'

'You know something about it, and you'd better tell at once, or I'll make you,' and Jo gave her a slight shake.

'Scold as much as you like, you'll never get your silly old story again,' cried Amy, getting excited in her turn.

'Why not?'

'I burnt it up.'

'What! my little book I was so fond of, and worked over, and meant to finish before father got home? Have you really burnt it?' said Jo, turning very pale, while her eyes kindled and her hands clutched Amy nervously.

'Yes, I did! I told you I'd make you pay for being so cross yesterday, and I have, so—'

Amy got no farther, for Jo's hot temper mastered her, and she shook Amy till her teeth chattered in her head; crying, in a passion of grief and anger,—

'You wicked, wicked girl! I never can write it again, and I'll never forgive you as long as I live.'

Meg flew to rescue Amy, and Beth to pacify Jo, but Jo was quite beside herself; and, with a parting box on her sister's ear, she rushed out of the room up to the old sofa in the garret, and finished her fight alone.

The storm cleared up below, for Mrs March came home, and, having heard the story, soon brought Amy to a sense of the wrong she had done her sister. Jo's book was the pride of her heart, and was regarded by her family as a literary sprout of great promise. It was only half a dozen little fairy tales, but Jo had worked over them patiently, putting her whole heart into her work, hoping to make something good enough to print. She had just copied them with great care, and had destroyed the old manuscript, so that Amy's bonfire had consumed the loving work of several years. It seemed a small loss to others, but to Jo it was a dreadful calamity, and she felt that it never could be made up to her. Beth mourned as for a departed kitten, and Meg refused to defend her pet; Mrs March looked grave and grieved, and Amy felt that no one would love her till she had asked pardon for the act which she now regretted more than any of them.

When the tea-bell rang, Jo appeared, looking so grim

and unapproachable, that it took all Amy's courage to say, meekly,—

'Please forgive me, Jo; I'm very, very sorry.'

'I never shall forgive you,' was Jo's stern answer; and, from that moment, she ignored Amy entirely.

No one spoke of the great trouble,—not even Mrs March,—for all had learned by experience that when Jo was in that mood words were wasted; and the wisest course was to wait till some little accident, or her own generous nature, softened Jo's resentment, and healed the breach. It was not a happy evening; for, though they sewed as usual, while their mother read aloud from Bremer, Scott, or Edgeworth, something was wanting, and the sweet home-peace was disturbed. They felt this most when singing-time came; for Beth could only play, Jo stood dumb as a stone, and Amy broke down, so Meg and mother sung alone. But, in spite of their efforts to be as cheery as larks, the flute-like voices did not seem to chord as well as usual, and all felt out of tune.

As Jo received her good-night kiss, Mrs March whispered, gently,—

'My dear, don't let the sun go down upon your anger; forgive each other, help each other, and begin again tomorrow.'

Jo wanted to lay her head down on that motherly bosom, and cry her grief and anger all away; but tears were an unmanly weakness, and she felt so deeply injured that she

Forgive each other, help each other, and begin again tomorrow

really *couldn't* quite forgive yet. So she winked hard, shook her head, and said, gruffly, because Amy was listening,—

'It was an abominable thing, and she don't deserve to be forgiven.'

With that she marched off to bed, and there was no merry or confidential gossip that night.

Amy was much offended that her overtures of peace had been repulsed, and began to wish she had not humbled herself, to feel more injured than ever, and to plume herself on her superior virtue in a way which was particularly exasperating. Jo still looked like a thunder-cloud, and nothing went well all day. It was bitter cold in the morning; she dropped her precious turn-over in the gutter, Aunt March had an attack of fidgets, Meg was pensive, Beth *would* look grieved and wistful when she got home, and Amy kept making remarks about people who were always talking about being good, and yet wouldn't try, when other people set them a virtuous example.

'Everybody is so hateful, I'll ask Laurie to go skating. He is always kind and jolly, and will put me to rights, I know,' said Jo to herself, and off she went.

Amy heard the clash of skates, and looked out with an impatient exclamation,—

'There! she promised I should go next time, for this is the last ice we shall have. But it's no use to ask such a cross patch to take me.'

'Don't say that; you *were* very naughty, and it is hard to forgive the loss of her precious little book; but I think she might do it now, and I guess she will, if you try her at the right minute,' said Meg. 'Go after them; don't say anything till Jo has got good-natured with Laurie, then take a quiet minute, and just kiss her, or do some kind thing, and I'm sure she'll be friends again, with all her heart.'

'I'll try,' said Amy, for the advice suited her; and, after a flurry to get ready, she ran after the friends, who were just disappearing over the hill.

It was not far to the river, but both were ready before Amy reached them. Jo saw her coming, and turned her back; Laurie did not see, for he was carefully skating along the shore, sounding the ice, for a warm spell had preceded the cold snap.

'I'll go on to the first bend, and see if it's all right, before we begin to race,' Amy heard him say, as he shot away, looking like a young Russian, in his fur-trimmed coat and cap.

Jo heard Amy panting after her run, stamping her feet, and blowing her fingers, as she tried to put her skates on; but Jo never turned, and went slowly zigzagging down the river, taking a bitter, unhappy sort of satisfaction in her sister's troubles. She had cherished her anger till it grew strong, and took possession of her, as evil thoughts and feelings always do, unless cast out at once. As Laurie turned the bend, he shouted back,—

'Keep near the shore; it isn't safe in the middle.'

Jo heard, but Amy was just struggling to her feet, and

did not catch a word. Jo glanced over her shoulder, and the little demon she was harboring said in her ear,—

'No matter whether she heard or not, let her take care of herself.'

Laurie had vanished round the bend; Jo was just at the turn, and Amy, far behind, striking out toward the smoother ice in the middle of the river. For a minute Jo stood still, with a strange feeling at her heart; then she resolved to go on, but something held and turned her round, just in time to see Amy throw up her hands and go down, with the sudden crash of rotten ice, the splash of water, and a cry that made Jo's heart stand still with fear. She tried to call Laurie, but her voice was gone; she tried to rush forward, but her feet seemed to have no strength in them; and, for a second, she could only stand motion-less, staring, with a terror-stricken face, at the little blue hood above the black water. Something rushed swiftly by her, and Laurie's voice cried out,—

'Bring a rail; quick, quick!'

How she did it, she never knew; but for the next few minutes she worked as if possessed, blindly obeying Lau-rie, who was quite self-possessed; and, lying flat, held Amy up by his arm and hockeystick, till Jo dragged a rail from the fence, and together they got the child out, more fright-ened than hurt.

'Now then, we must walk her home as fast as we can; pile our things on her, while I get off these confounded skates,' cried Laurie, wrapping his coat round Amy, and tugging away at the straps, which never seemed so intricate before.

Shivering, dripping, and crying, they got Amy home; and, after an exciting time of it, she fell asleep, rolled in blankets, before a hot fire. During the bustle Jo had scarcely spoken; but flown about, looking pale and wild, with her things half off, her dress torn, and her hands cut and bruised by ice and rails, and refractory buckles. When Amy was comfortably asleep, the house quiet, and Mrs March sitting by the bed, she called Jo to her, and began to bind up the hurt hands.

'Are you sure she is safe?' whispered Jo, looking remorsefully at the golden head, which might have been swept away from her sight forever, under the treacherous ice.

'Quite safe, dear; she is not hurt, and won't even take cold, I think, you were so sensible in covering and getting her home quickly,' replied her mother, cheerfully.

'Laurie did it all; I only let her go. Mother, if she *should* die, it would be my fault;' and Jo dropped down beside the bed, in a passion of penitent tears, telling all that had happened, bitterly condemning her hardness of heart, and sobbing out her gratitude for being spared the heavy punishment which might have come upon her.

'It's my dreadful temper! I try to cure it; I think I have, and then it breaks out worse than ever. Oh, mother! what shall I do! what shall I do!' cried poor Jo, in despair.

'Watch and pray, dear; never get tired of trying; and never think it is impossible to conquer your fault,' said Mrs March, drawing the blowzy head to her shoulder, and kissing the wet cheek so tenderly, that Jo cried harder than ever.

'You don't know; you can't guess how bad it is! It seems as if I could do anything when I'm in a passion; I get so savage, I could hurt any one, and enjoy it. I'm afraid I *shall* do something dreadful some day, and spoil my life, and make everybody hate me. Oh, mother! help me, do help me!'

'I will, my child; I will. Don't cry so bitterly, but remember this day, and resolve, with all your soul, that you will never know another like it. Jo, dear, we all have our temptations, some far greater than yours, and it often takes us all our lives to conquer them. You think your temper is the worst in the world; but mine used to be just like it.'

'Yours, mother? Why, you are never angry!' and, for the moment, Jo forgot remorse in surprise.

'I've been trying to cure it for forty years, and have only succeeded in controlling it. I am angry nearly every day of my life, Jo; but I have learned not to show it; and I still hope to learn not to feel it, though it may take me another forty years to do so.'

The patience and the humility of the face she loved so well, was a better lesson to Jo than the wisest lecture, the sharpest reproof. She felt comforted at once by the sympathy and confidence given her; the knowledge that her mother had a fault like hers, and tried to mend it, made her own easier to bear, and strengthened her resolution to cure it; though forty years seemed rather a long time to watch and pray, to a girl of fifteen.

'Mother, are you angry when you fold your lips tight together, and go out of the room sometimes, when Aunt March scolds, or people worry you?' asked Jo, feeling nearer and dearer to her mother than ever before.

'Yes, I've learned to check the hasty words that rise to my lips; and when I feel that they mean to break out against my will, I just go away a minute, and give myself a little shake, for being so weak and wicked,' answered Mrs March, with a sigh and a smile, as she smoothed and fastened up Jo's dishevelled hair.

'How did you learn to keep still? That is what troubles me—for the sharp words fly out before I know what I'm about; and the more I say the worse I get, till it's a pleasure to hurt people's feelings, and say dreadful things. Tell me how you do it, Marmee dear.'

'My good mother used to help me—'

'As you do us—' interrupted Jo, with a grateful kiss.

'But I lost her when I was a little older than you are, and for years had to struggle on alone, for I was too proud to confess my weakness to any one else. I had a hard time, Jo, and shed a good many bitter tears over my failures; for, in spite of my efforts, I never seemed to get on. Then your father came, and I was so happy that I found it easy to be good. But by and by, when I had four little daughters round me, and we were poor, then the old trouble began again; for I am not patient by nature, and it tried me very much to see my children wanting anything.'

'Poor mother! what helped you then?'

'Your father, Jo. He never loses patience,—never doubts or complains,—but always hopes, and works and waits so cheerfully, that one is ashamed to do otherwise before him. He helped and comforted me, and showed me that I must try to practise all the virtues I would have my little girls possess, for I was their example. It was easier to try for your sakes than for my own; a startled or surprised look from one of you, when I spoke sharply, rebuked me more than any words could have done; and the love, respect, and confidence of my children was the sweetest reward I could receive for my efforts to be the woman I would have them copy.'

'Oh, mother! if I'm ever half as good as you, I shall be satisfied,' cried Jo, much touched.

'I hope you will be a great deal better, dear; but you must keep watch over your "bosom enemy," as father calls it, or it may sadden, if not spoil your life. You have had a warning; remember it, and try with heart and soul to master this quick temper, before it brings you greater sorrow and regret than you have known today.'

'I will try, mother; I truly will. But you must help me, remind me, and keep me from flying out. I used to see father sometimes put his finger on his lips, and look at you with a very kind, but sober face; and you always folded your lips tight, or went away; was he reminding you then?' asked Jo, softly.

'Yes; I asked him to help me so, and he never forgot it, but saved me from many a sharp word by that little gesture and kind look.'

Jo saw that her mother's eyes filled, and her lips trembled, as she spoke; and, fearing that she had said too much, she whispered anxiously, 'Was it wrong to watch you, and to speak of it? I didn't mean to be rude, but it's so comfortable to say all I think to you, and feel so safe and happy here.'

'My Jo, you may say anything to your mother, for it is my greatest happiness and pride to feel that my girls confide in me, and know how much I love them.'

'I thought I'd grieved you.'

'No, dear; but speaking of father reminded me how much I miss him, how much I owe him, and how faithfully I should watch and work to keep his little daughters safe and good for him.'

'Yet you told him to go, mother, and didn't cry when he went, and never complain now, or seem as if you needed any help,' said Jo, wondering.

'I gave my best to the country I love, and kept my tears till he was gone. Why should I complain, when we both have merely done our duty, and will surely be the happier for it in the end? If I don't seem to need help, it is because I have a better friend, even than father, to comfort and sustain me. My child, the troubles and temptations of your life are beginning, and may be many; but you can overcome and outlive them all, if you learn to feel the strength and tenderness of your Heavenly Father as you do that of your earthly one. The more you love and trust Him, the nearer you will feel to Him, and the less you will depend on human power and wisdom. His love and care never tire or change, can never be taken from you, but may become the source of lifelong peace, happiness, and strength. Believe this heartily, and go to God with all your little cares, and hopes, and sins, and sorrows, as freely and confidingly as you come to your mother.'

Jo's only answer was to hold her mother close, and, in the silence which followed, the sincerest prayer she had ever prayed left her heart, without words; for in that sad, yet happy hour, she had learned not only the bitterness of remorse and despair, but the sweetness of self-denial and self-control; and, led by her mother's hand, she had drawn nearer to the Friend who welcomes every child with a love stronger than that of any father, tenderer than that of any mother.

Amy stirred, and sighed in her sleep; and, as if eager to begin at once to mend her fault, Jo looked up with an expression on her face which it had never worn before.

'I let the sun go down on my anger; I wouldn't forgive her, and today, if it hadn't been for Laurie, it might have been too late! How could I be so wicked?' said Jo, half aloud, as she leaned over her sister, softly stroking the wet hair scattered on the pillow.

As if she heard, Amy opened her eyes, and held out her arms, with a smile that went straight to Jo's heart. Neither said a word, but they hugged one another close, in spite of the blankets, and everything was forgiven and forgotten in one hearty kiss.

**Neither said a word,
but they hugged one
another close**

Dark Days

BETH DID HAVE the fever, and was much sicker than any one but Hannah and the doctor suspected. The girls knew nothing about illness, and Mr Laurence was not allowed to see her, so Hannah had everything all her own way, and busy Dr Bangs did his best, but left a good deal to the excellent nurse. Meg stayed at home, lest she should infect the Kings, and kept house, feeling very anxious, and a little guilty, when she wrote letters in which no mention was made of Beth's illness. She could not think it right to deceive her mother, but she had been bidden to mind Hannah, and Hannah wouldn't hear of 'Mrs March bein' told, and worried just for sech a trifle.' Jo devoted herself to Beth day and night; not a hard task, for Beth was very patient, and bore her pain uncomplainingly as long as she could control herself. But there came a time when during the fever fits she began to talk in a hoarse, broken voice, to play on the coverlet, as if on her beloved little piano, and try to sing with a throat so swollen, that there was no music left; a time when she did not know the familiar faces round her, but addressed them by wrong names, and called imploringly for her mother. Then Jo grew frightened, Meg begged to be allowed to write the truth, and even Hannah said she 'would think of it, though there was no danger *yet*.' A letter from Washington added to their trouble, for Mr March had had a relapse, and could not think of coming home for a long while.

How dark the days seemed now, how sad and lonely the house, and how heavy were the hearts of the sisters as they worked and waited, while the shadow of death hovered over the once happy home! Then it was that Margaret, sitting alone with tears dropping often on her work, felt how rich she had been in things more precious than any luxuries money could buy; in love, protection, peace and health, the real blessings of life. Then it was that Jo, living in the darkened room with that suffering little sister always before her eyes, and that pathetic voice sounding in her ears, learned to see the beauty and the sweetness of Beth's nature, to feel how deep and tender a place she filled in all hearts, and to acknowledge the worth of Beth's unselfish ambition, to live for others, and make home happy by the exercise of those simple virtues which all may possess, and which all should love and value more than talent, wealth or beauty. And Amy, in her exile, longed eagerly to be at home, that she might work for Beth, feeling now that no service would be hard or irksome, and remembering, with regretful grief, how many neglected tasks those willing hands had done for her. Laurie haunted the house like a restless ghost, and Mr Laurence locked the grand piano, because he could not bear to be reminded of the young neighbor who used to make the twilight pleasant for him. Every one missed Beth. The milk-man, baker, grocer and butcher inquired how she did; poor Mrs Hummel came to beg pardon for her thoughtlessness, and to get a shroud for Minna; the neighbors sent all sorts of comforts and good wishes, and even those who knew her best, were surprised to find how many friends shy little Beth had made.

Meanwhile she lay on her bed with old Joanna at her side, for even in her wanderings she did not forget her forlorn *protégé*. She longed for her cats, but would not have them brought, lest they should get sick; and, in her quiet hours, she was full of anxiety about Jo. She sent loving messages to Amy, bade them tell her mother that she would write soon; and often begged for pencil and paper to try to say a word, that father might not think she had neglected him. But soon even these intervals of con-sciousness ended, and she lay hour after hour tossing to and fro with incoherent words on her lips, or sank into a heavy sleep which brought her no refreshment. Dr Bangs came twice a day, Hannah sat up at night, Meg kept a tele-gram in her desk all ready to send off at any minute, and Jo never stirred from Beth's side.

The first of December was a wintry day indeed to them,

for a bitter wind blew, snow fell fast, and the year seemed getting ready for its death. When Dr Bangs came that morning, he looked long at Beth, held the hot hand in both his own a minute, and laid it gently down, saying, in a low tone, to Hannah,—

'If Mrs March *can* leave her husband, she'd better be sent for.'

Hannah nodded without speaking, for her lips twitched nervously; Meg dropped down into a chair as the strength seemed to go out of her limbs at the sound of those words, and Jo, after standing with a pale face for a minute, ran to the parlor, snatched up the telegram, and, throwing on her things, rushed out into the storm. She was soon back, and, while noiselessly taking off her cloak, Laurie came in with a letter, saying that Mr March was mending again. Jo read it thankfully, but the heavy weight did not seem lifted off her heart, and her face was so full of misery that Laurie asked, quickly,—

'What is it? is Beth worse?'

'I've sent for mother,' said Jo, tugging at her rubber boots with a tragical expression.

'Good for you, Jo! Did you do it on your own responsibility?' asked Laurie, as he seated her in the hall chair and took off the rebellious boots, seeing how her hands shook.

'No, the doctor told us to.'

'Oh, Jo, it's not so bad as that?' cried Laurie, with a startled face.

'Yes, it is; she don't know us, she don't even talk about

the flocks of green doves, as she calls the vine leaves on the wall; she don't look like my Beth, and there's nobody to help us bear it; mother and father both gone, and God seems so far away I can't find Him.'

As the tears streamed fast down poor Jo's cheeks, she stretched out her hand in a helpless sort of way, as if groping in the dark, and Laurie took it in his, whispering, as well as he could, with a lump in his throat,—

'I'm here, hold on to me, Jo, dear!'

She could not speak, but she did 'hold on,' and the warm grasp of the friendly human hand comforted her sore heart, and seemed to lead her nearer to the Divine arm which alone could uphold her in her trouble. Laurie longed to say something tender and comfortable, but no fitting words came to him, so he stood silent, gently stroking her bent head as her mother used to do. It was the best thing he could have done; far more soothing than the most eloquent words, for Jo felt the unspoken sympathy, and, in the silence, learned the sweet solace which affection administers to sorrow. Soon she dried the tears which had relieved her, and looked up with a grateful face.

'Thank you, Teddy, I'm better now; I don't feel so forlorn, and will try to bear it if it comes.'

'Keep hoping for the best; that will help you lots, Jo. Soon your mother will be here, and then everything will be right.'

'I'm so glad father is better; now she won't feel so bad

about leaving him. Oh, me! it does seem as if all the troubles came in a heap, and I got the heaviest part on my shoulders,' sighed Jo, spreading her wet handkerchief over her knees, to dry.

'Don't Meg pull fair?' asked Laurie, looking indignant.

'Oh, yes; she tries to, but she don't love Bethy as I do; and she won't miss her as I shall. Beth is my conscience, and I *can't* give her up; I can't! I can't!'

Down went Jo's face into the wet handkerchief, and she cried despairingly; for she had kept up bravely till now, and never shed a tear. Laurie drew his hand across his eyes, but could not speak till he had subdued the choky feeling in his throat, and steadied his lips. It might be unmanly, but he couldn't help it, and I am glad of it. Presently, as Jo's sobs quieted, he said, hopefully, 'I don't think she will die; she's so good, and we all love her so much, I don't believe God will take her away yet.'

'The good and dear people always do die,' groaned Jo, but she stopped crying, for her friend's words cheered her up, in spite of her own doubts and fears.

'Poor girl! you're worn out. It isn't like you to be forlorn. Stop a bit; I'll hearten you up in a jiffy.'

Laurie went off two stairs at a time, and Jo laid her wearied head down on Beth's little brown hood, which no one had thought of moving from the table where she left it. It must have possessed some magic, for the submissive spirit of its gentle owner seemed to enter into Jo; and, when Laurie came running down with a glass of wine, she took it

Beth is my conscience, and I *can't* give her up; I can't! I can't!

with a smile, and said, bravely, 'I drink—Health to my Beth! You are a good doctor, Teddy, and *such* a comfortable friend; how can I ever pay you?' she added, as the wine refreshed her body, as the kind words had done her troubled mind.

'I'll send in my bill, by and by; and tonight I'll give you something that will warm the cockles of your heart better than quarts of wine,' said Laurie, beaming at her with a face of suppressed satisfaction at something.

'What is it?' cried Jo, forgetting her woes for a minute, in her wonder.

'I telegraphed to your mother yesterday, and Brooke answered she'd come at once, and she'll be here tonight, and everything will be all right. Aren't you glad I did it?'

Laurie spoke very fast, and turned red and excited all in a minute, for he had kept his plot a secret, for fear of disappointing the girls or harming Beth. Jo grew quite white, flew out of her chair, and the moment he stopped speaking she electrified him by throwing her arms round his neck, and crying out, with a joyful cry, 'Oh, Laurie! oh, mother! I *am* so glad!' She did not weep again, but laughed hysterically, and trembled and clung to her friend as if she was a little bewildered by the sudden news. Laurie, though decidedly amazed, behaved with great presence of mind; he patted her back soothingly, and, finding that she was recovering, followed it up by a bashful kiss or two, which brought Jo round at once. Holding on to the banisters, she put him gently away, saying, breathless, 'Oh, don't! I didn't mean to; it was dreadful of me; but you were such a dear to go and do it in spite of Hannah, that I couldn't help flying at you. Tell me all about it, and don't give me wine again; it makes me act so.'

'I don't mind!' laughed Laurie, as he settled his tie. 'Why, you see I got fidgety, and so did grandpa. We thought Hannah was overdoing the authority business, and your mother ought to know. She'd never forgive us if Beth,—well, if anything happened, you know. So I got grandpa to say it was high time we did something, and off I pelted to the office yesterday, for the doctor looked sober, and Hannah most took my head off when I proposed a telegram. I never *can* bear to be "marmed over;" so that settled my mind, and I did it. Your mother will come, I know, and the late train is in at two, A.M. I shall go for her; and you've only got to bottle up your rapture, and keep Beth quiet, till that blessed lady gets here.'

'Laurie, you're an angel! How shall I ever thank you?'

'Fly at me again; I rather like it,' said Laurie, looking mischievous,—a thing he had not done for a fortnight.

'No, thank you. I'll do it by proxy, when your grandpa comes. Don't tease, but go home and rest, for you'll be up half the night. Bless you, Teddy; bless you!'

Jo had backed into a corner; and, as she finished her speech, she vanished precipitately into the kitchen, where she sat down upon a dresser, and told the assembled cats that she was 'happy, oh, *so* happy!' while Laurie departed, feeling that he had made rather a neat thing of it.

'That's the interferingest chap I ever see; but I forgive him, and do hope Mrs March is coming on right away,' said Hannah, with an air of relief, when Jo told the good news.

Meg had a quiet rapture, and then brooded over the letter, while Jo set the sick room in order, and Hannah 'knocked up a couple of pies in case of company unexpected.' A breath of fresh air seemed to blow through the house, and something better than sunshine brightened the quiet rooms; everything appeared to feel the hopeful change; Beth's bird began to chirp again, and a half-blown rose was discovered on Amy's bush in the window; the fires seemed to burn with unusual cheeriness, and every time the girls met their pale faces broke into smiles as they hugged one another, whispering, encouragingly, 'Mother's coming, dear! mother's coming!' Every one rejoiced but Beth; she lay in that heavy stupor, alike unconscious of hope and joy, doubt and danger. It was a piteous sight,—the once rosy face so changed and vacant, —the once busy hands so weak and wasted,—the once smiling lips quite dumb,—and the once pretty, well-kept hair scattered rough and tangled on the pillow. All day she lay so, only rousing now and then to mutter, 'Water!' with lips so parched they could hardly shape the word; all day Jo and Meg hovered over her, watching, waiting, hoping, and trusting in God and mother; and all day the snow fell, the bitter wind raged, and the hours dragged slowly by. But night came at last; and every time the clock struck the sisters, still sitting on either side of the bed, looked at each other with brightening eyes, for each hour brought help nearer. The doctor had been in to say that some change for better or worse would probably take place about midnight, at which time he would return.

Hannah, quite worn out, lay down on the sofa at the bed's foot, and fell fast asleep; Mr Laurence marched to and fro in the parlor, feeling that he would rather face a rebel battery than Mrs March's anxious countenance as she entered; Laurie lay on the rug, pretending to rest, but staring into the fire with the thoughtful look which made his black eyes beautifully soft and clear.

The girls never forgot that night, for no sleep came to them as they kept their watch, with that dreadful sense of powerlessness which comes to us in hours like those.

'If God spares Beth I never will complain again,' whispered Meg, earnestly.

'If God spares Beth I'll try to love and serve Him all my life,' answered Jo, with equal fervor.

'I wish I had no heart, it aches so,' sighed Meg, after a pause.

'If life is often as hard as this, I don't see how we ever shall get through it,' added her sister, despondently.

Here the clock struck twelve, and both forgot themselves in watching Beth, for they fancied a change passed over her wan face. The house was still as death, and nothing but the wailing of the wind broke the deep hush. Weary Hannah slept on, and no one but the sisters saw the pale shadow which seemed to fall upon the little bed. An hour went by, and nothing happened except Laurie's quiet departure for the station. Another hour,—still no one came; and anxious fears of delay in the storm, or accidents by the way, or, worst of all, a great grief at Washington, haunted the poor girls.

It was past two, when Jo, who stood at the window thinking how dreary the world looked in its winding-sheet of snow, heard a movement by the bed, and, turning quickly, saw Meg kneeling before their mother's easy-chair, with her face hidden. A dreadful fear passed coldly over Jo, as she thought, 'Beth is dead, and Meg is afraid to tell me.'

She was back at her post in an instant, and to her excited eyes a great change seemed to have taken place. The fever flush, and the look of pain, were gone, and the beloved little face looked so pale and peaceful in its utter repose, that Jo felt no desire to weep or lament. Leaning low over this dearest of her sisters, she kissed the damp forehead with her heart on her lips, and softly whispered, 'Good-by, my Beth; good-by!'

As if waked by the stir, Hannah started out of her sleep, hurried to the bed, looked at Beth, felt her hands, listened at her lips, and then, throwing her apron over her head, sat down to rock to and fro, exclaiming, under her breath, 'The fever's turned; she's sleepin' nat'ral; her skin's damp, and she breathes easy. Praise be given! Oh, my goodness me!'

Before the girls could believe the happy truth, the doctor came to confirm it. He was a homely man, but they thought his face quite heavenly when he smiled, and said, with a fatherly look at them, 'Yes, my dears; I think the little girl will pull through this time. Keep the house quiet; let her sleep, and when she wakes give her—'

What they were to give, neither heard; for both crept into the dark hall, and, sitting on the stairs, held each other close, rejoicing with hearts too full for words. When they went back to be kissed and cuddled by faithful Hannah, they found Beth lying, as she used to do, with her cheek pillowed on her hand, the dreadful pallor gone, and breathing quietly, as if just fallen asleep.

'If mother would only come now!' said Jo, as the winter night began to wane.

'See,' said Meg, coming up with a white, half-opened rose, 'I thought this would hardly be ready to lay in Beth's hand tomorrow if she—went away from us. But it has blossomed in the night, and now I mean to put it in my vase here, so that when the darling wakes, the first thing she sees will be the little rose, and mother's face.'

Never had the sun risen so beautifully, and never had the world seemed so lovely, as it did to the heavy eyes of Meg and Jo, as they looked out in the early morning, when their long, sad vigil was done.

'It looks like a fairy world,' said Meg, smiling to herself, as she stood behind the curtain watching the dazzling sight.

'Hark!' cried Jo, starting to her feet.

Yes, there was a sound of bells at the door below, a cry from Hannah, and then Laurie's voice, saying, in a joyful whisper, 'Girls! she's come! she's come!'

The First Wedding

THE JUNE ROSES over the porch were awake bright and early on that morning, rejoicing with all their hearts in the cloudless sunshine, like friendly little neighbors, as they were. Quite flushed with excitement were their ruddy faces, as they swung in the wind, whispering to one another what they had seen; for some peeped in at the dining-room windows, where the feast was spread, some climbed up to nod and smile at the sisters, as they dressed the bride, others waved a welcome to those who came and went on various errands in garden, porch and hall, and all, from the rosiest full-blown flower to the palest baby-bud, offered their tribute of beauty and fragrance to the gentle mistress who had loved and tended them so long.

Meg looked very like a rose herself; for all that was best and sweetest in heart and soul, seemed to bloom into her face that day, making it fair and tender, with a charm more

beautiful than beauty. Neither silk, lace, nor orange flowers would she have. 'I don't want to look strange or fixed
up, today,' she said; 'I don't want a fashionable wedding,
but only those about me whom I love, and to them I wish
to look and be my familiar self.'

So she made her wedding gown herself, sewing into it
the tender hopes and innocent romances of a girlish
heart. Her sisters braided up her pretty hair, and the only
ornaments she wore were the lilies of the valley, which
'her John' liked best of all the flowers that grew.

'You *do* look just like our own dear Meg, only so very
sweet and lovely, that I should hug you if it wouldn't
crumple your dress,' cried Amy, surveying her with
delight, when all was done.

'Then I am satisfied. But please hug and kiss me, every
one, and don't mind my dress; I want a great many crum-
ples of this sort put into it today;' and Meg opened her
arms to her sisters, who clung about her with April faces,
for a minute, feeling that the new love had not changed
the old.

'Now I'm going to tie John's cravat for him, and then to
stay a few minutes with father, quietly in the study;' and
Meg ran down to perform these little ceremonies, and
then to follow her mother wherever she went, conscious
that in spite of the smiles on the motherly face, there was
a secret sorrow hidden in the motherly heart, at the flight
of the first bird from the nest.

As the younger girls stand together, giving the last

touches to their simple toilet, it may be a good time to tell of a few changes which three years have wrought in their appearance; for all are looking their best, just now.

Jo's angles are much softened; she has learned to carry herself with ease, if not grace. The curly crop has been lengthened into a thick coil, more becoming to the small head atop of the tall figure. There is a fresh color in her brown cheeks, a soft shine in her eyes; only gentle words fall from her sharp tongue today.

Beth has grown slender, pale, and more quiet than ever; the beautiful, kind eyes, are larger, and in them lies an expression that saddens one, although it is not sad itself. It is the shadow of pain which touches the young face with such pathetic patience; but Beth seldom complains, and always speaks hopefully of 'being better soon.'

Amy is with truth considered 'the flower of the family'; for at sixteen she has the air and bearing of a full-grown woman—not beautiful, but possessed of that indescribable charm called grace. One saw it in the lines of her figure, the make and motion of her hands, the flow of her dress, the droop of her hair—unconscious, yet harmonious, and as attractive to many as beauty itself. Amy's nose still afflicted her, for it never *would* grow Grecian; so did her mouth, being too wide, and having a decided under-lip. These offending features gave character to her whole face, but she never could see it, and consoled herself with her wonderfully fair complexion, keen blue eyes, and curls, more golden and abundant than ever.

All three wore suits of thin, silvery gray (their best gowns for the summer), with blush roses in hair and bosom; and all three looked just what they were— fresh-faced, happy-hearted girls, pausing a moment in their busy lives to read with wistful eyes the sweetest chapter in the romance of womanhood.

There were to be no ceremonious performances; everything was to be as natural and homelike as possible; so when Aunt March arrived, she was scandalized to see the bride come running to welcome and lead her in, to find the bridegroom fastening up a garland that had fallen down, and to catch a glimpse of the paternal minister marching upstairs with a grave countenance, and a wine bottle under each arm.

'Upon my word, here's a state of things!' cried the old lady, taking the seat of honor prepared for her, and settling the folds of her lavender *moiré* with a great rustle. 'You oughtn't to be seen till the last minute, child.'

'I'm not a show, aunty, and no one is coming to stare at me, to criticize my dress, or count the cost of my luncheon. I'm too happy to care what any one says or thinks, and I'm going to have my little wedding just as I like it. John, dear, here's your hammer,' and away went Meg to help 'that man' in his highly improper employment.

Mr Brooke didn't even say 'Thank you,' but as he stooped for the unromantic tool, he kissed his little bride behind the folding-door, with a look that made Aunt March whisk out her pocket-handkerchief, with a sudden dew in her sharp old eyes.

A crash, a cry, and a laugh from Laurie, accompanied by the indecorous exclamation, 'Jupiter Ammon! Jo's upset the cake again!' caused a momentary flurry, which was hardly over, when a flock of cousins arrived, and 'the party came in,' as Beth used to say when a child.

'Don't let that young giant come near me; he worries me worse than mosquitoes,' whispered the old lady to Amy, as the rooms filled, and Laurie's black head towered above the rest.

'He has promised to be very good today, and he *can* be perfectly elegant if he likes,' returned Amy, gliding away to warn Hercules to beware of the dragon, which warning caused him to haunt the old lady with a devotion that nearly distracted her.

There was no bridal procession, but a sudden silence fell upon the room as Mr March and the young pair took their places under the green arch. Mother and sisters gathered close, as if loath to give Meg up; the fatherly voice broke more than once, which only seemed to make the service more beautiful and solemn; the bridegroom's hand trembled visibly, and no one heard his replies; but Meg looked straight up in her husband's eyes, and said, 'I will!' with such tender trust in her own face and voice, that her mother's heart rejoiced, and Aunt March sniffed audibly.

Jo did *not* cry, though she was very near it once, and was only saved from a demonstration by the consciousness that Laurie was staring fixedly at her, with a comical mixture of merriment and emotion in his wicked black eyes. Beth kept her face hidden on her mother's shoulder, but Amy stood like a graceful statue, with a most becoming ray of sunshine touching her white forehead and the flower in her hair.

It wasn't at all the thing, I'm afraid, but the minute she was fairly married, Meg cried, 'The first kiss for Marmee!' and, turning, gave it with her heart on her lips. During the next fifteen minutes she looked more like a rose than ever, for every one availed themselves of their privileges to the fullest extent, from Mr Laurence to old Hannah, who, adorned with a head-dress fearfully and wonderfully made, fell upon her in the hall, crying, with a sob and a chuckle, 'Bless you, deary, a hundred times! The cake ain't hurt a mite, and everything looks lovely.'

Everybody cleared up after that, and said something brilliant, or tried to, which did just as well, for laughter is ready when hearts are light. There was no display of gifts, for they were already in the little house, nor was there an elaborate breakfast, but a plentiful lunch of cake and fruit, dressed with flowers. Mr Laurence and Aunt March shrugged and smiled at one another when water, lemonade, and coffee were found to be the only sorts of nectar which the three Hebes carried round. No one said anything, however, till Laurie, who insisted on serving the bride, appeared before her with a loaded salver in his hand, and a puzzled expression on his face.

'Has Jo smashed all the bottles by accident?' he

whispered, 'or am I merely laboring under a delusion that I saw some lying about loose this morning?'

'No; your grandfather kindly offered us his best, and Aunt March actually sent some, but father put away a little for Beth, and despatched the rest to the Soldier's Home. You know he thinks that wine should only be used in illness, and mother says that neither she nor her daughters will ever offer it to any young man under her roof.'

Meg spoke seriously, and expected to see Laurie frown or laugh; but he did neither,—for after a quick look at her, he said, in his impetuous way, 'I like that; for I've seen enough harm done to wish other women would think as you do!'

'You are not made wise by experience, I hope?' and there was an anxious accent in Meg's voice.

'No; I give you my word for it. Don't think too well of me, either; this is not one of my temptations. Being brought up where wine is as common as water, and almost as harmless, I don't care for it; but when a pretty girl offers it, one don't like to refuse, you see.'

'But you will, for the sake of others, if not for your own. Come, Laurie, promise, and give me one more reason to call this the happiest day of my life.'

A demand so sudden and so serious, made the young man hesitate a moment, for ridicule is often harder to bear than self-denial. Meg knew that if he gave the promise he would keep it at all costs; and, feeling her power, used it as a woman may for her friend's good. She did not speak, but she looked up at him with a face made very eloquent by happiness, and a smile which said, 'No one can refuse me anything today.' Laurie, certainly, could not; and, with an answering smile, he gave her his hand, saying, heartily, 'I promise, Mrs Brooke!'

'I thank you, very, very much.'

'And I drink "Long life to your resolution," Teddy,' cried Jo, baptizing him with a splash of lemonade, as she waved her glass, and beamed approvingly upon him.

So the toast was drunk, the pledge made, and loyally kept, in spite of many temptations; for, with instinctive wisdom, the girls had seized a happy moment to do their friend a service, for which he thanked them all his life.

After lunch, people strolled about, by twos and threes, through house and garden, enjoying the sunshine without and within. Meg and John happened to be standing together in the middle of the grass-plot, when Laurie was seized with an inspiration which put the finishing touch to this unfashionable wedding.

'All the married people take hands and dance round the new-made husband and wife, as the Germans do, while we bachelors and spinsters prance in couples outside!' cried Laurie, galloping down the path with Amy, with such infectious spirit and skill that every one else followed their example without a murmur. Mr and Mrs March, Aunt and Uncle Carrol, began it; others rapidly joined in; even Sallie Moffat, after a moment's hesitation, threw her train over her arm, and whisked Ned into the ring. But the crowning joke was Mr Laurence and Aunt March; for when the stately old gentleman *chasséed* solemnly up to the old lady, she just tucked her cane under her arm, and hopped briskly away to join hands with the rest, and dance about the bridal pair, while the young folks pervaded the garden, like butterflies on a midsummer day.

Want of breath brought the impromptu ball to a close, and then people began to go.

'I wish you well, my dear; I heartily wish you well; but I think you'll be sorry for it,' said Aunt March to Meg, adding to the bridegroom, as he led her to the carriage, 'You've got a treasure, young man,—see that you deserve it.'

'That is the prettiest wedding I've been to for an age, Ned, and I don't see why, for there wasn't a bit of style about it,' observed Mrs Moffat to her husband, as they drove away.

'Laurie, my lad, if you ever want to indulge in this sort of thing, get one of those little girls to help you, and I shall be perfectly satisfied,' said Mr Laurence, settling himself in his easy-chair to rest, after the excitement of the morning.

'I'll do my best to gratify you, sir,' was Laurie's unusually dutiful reply, as he carefully unpinned the posy Jo had put in his buttonhole.

The little house was not far away, and the only bridal journey Meg had was the quiet walk with John, from the old home to the new. When she came down, looking like a pretty Quakeress, in her dove-colored suit and straw bonnet tied with white, they all gathered about her to say 'good-by,' as tenderly as if she had been going to make the grand tour.

'Don't feel that I am separated from you, Marmee dear, or that I love you any the less for loving John so much,' she said, clinging to her mother, with full eyes, for a moment. 'I shall come every day, father, and expect to keep my old place in all your hearts, though I *am* married. Beth is going to be with me a great deal, and the other girls will drop in now and then to laugh at my housekeeping struggles. Thank you all for my happy wedding-day. Good-by, good-by!'

They stood watching her with faces full of love, and hope, and tender pride, as she walked away, leaning on her husband's arm, with her hands full of flowers, and the June sunshine brightening her happy face,—and so Meg's married life began.

LOUISA MAY ALCOTT was born on 29 November 1832 in Concord, Pennsylvania – one of four girls. Like the sisters in *Little Women* she grew up with plenty of books to read but seldom enough to eat, and went to work when she was very young as a paid companion and teacher. Soon she turned to writing to help provide financial support for her family, mainly sensational thriller stories which were published in magazines and periodicals.

Alcott was a campaigner for women's rights and the abolition of the slave trade, and went to Washington as a nurse during the American Civil War, though the experience permanently damaged her health. *Little Women* was published in 1868 and she followed it with three sequels, *Good Wives* (1869), *Little Men* (1871) and *Jo's Boys* (1886). Louisa died on 6 March 1888.

RECOMMENDED BOOKS BY LOUISA MAY ALCOTT:

Little Women
Good Wives
Little Men
Jo's Boys

There is no friend like a sister, but who comes close?

Fatherhood
KARL OVE KNAUSGAARD

VINTAGE MINIS

Motherhood
HELEN SIMPSON

VINTAGE MINIS

Babies
ANNE ENRIGHT

VINTAGE MINIS

Love
JEANETTE WINTERSON

VINTAGE MINIS

VINTAGE MINIS

The Vintage Minis bring you the world's greatest writers on the experiences that make us human. These stylish, entertaining little books explore the whole spectrum of life – from birth to death, and everything in between. Which means there's something here for everyone, whatever your story.

Desire	Haruki Murakami
Love	Jeanette Winterson
Babies	Anne Enright
Language	Xiaolu Guo
Motherhood	Helen Simpson
Fatherhood	Karl Ove Knausgaard
Summer	Laurie Lee
Jealousy	Marcel Proust
Sisters	Louisa May Alcott
Home	Salman Rushdie
Race	Toni Morrison
Liberty	Virginia Woolf
Swimming	Roger Deakin
Work	Joseph Heller
Depression	William Styron
Drinking	John Cheever
Eating	Nigella Lawson
Psychedelics	Aldous Huxley
Calm	Tim Parks
Death	Julian Barnes

vintageminis.co.uk

1 3 5 7 9 10 8 6 4 2

Vintage
20 Vauxhall Bridge Road,
London SW1V 2SA

Vintage Classics is part of the Penguin Random House
group of companies whose addresses can be found at
global.penguinrandomhouse.com.

Penguin
Random House
UK

Extracts from *Nothing to be Frightened of* copyright © Julian Barnes 2008

Julian Barnes has asserted his right to be identified as
the author of this Work in accordance with the Copyright,
Designs and Patents Act 1988

First published in Great Britain by Jonathan Cape in 2008
This short edition published by Vintage in 2017

Extracts from *Chasing Daylight* by Eugene O'Kelly (© Eugene O'Kelly 2006)
reproduced by kind permission of McGraw-Hill Companies, Inc.

penguin.co.uk/vintage

A CIP catalogue record for this book is available from the British Library

ISBN 9781784872601

Typeset in 9.5/14.5 pt FreightText Pro
by Jouve (UK), Milton Keynes
Printed and bound by Clays Ltd, St Ives plc

Penguin Random House is committed to a sustainable future for
our business, our readers and our planet. This book is made from
Forest Stewardship Council® certified paper.

MIX
Paper from
responsible sources
FSC
www.fsc.org   FSC® C018179

Death

JULIAN BARNES

VINTAGE MINIS

WHEN WE LET THE MIND roam to the circumstances of our own death, there is usually a magnetic pull towards the worst case or the best case. My worst imaginings usually involve enclosure, water, and a period of time in which to endure the certainty of coming extinction. There is, for instance, the overturned-ferry scenario: the air pocket, darkness, slowly rising water, screaming fellow mortals, and the competition for breath. Then there is the solitary version of this: bundled into the boot of a car (perhaps your own) while your captors drive from one cashpoint to another, and then, when your credit card is finally refused, the giddying lurch from river bank or sea cliff, the splash, and the greedy glug of water coming for you. Or the analogous, if more improbable, wildlife version of this: being taken by a crocodile, dragged under water, losing consciousness and then regaining it on a shelf above the waterline in the croc's lair, and realizing that you have just become the waiting contents of the

beast's larder. (And such things happen, in case you doubt.)

The best case, in my fantasizing, used to turn on a medical diagnosis which left me just enough time, and just enough lucidity, in which to write that last book – the one which would contain all my thoughts about death. Although I didn't know if it was going to be fiction or non-fiction, I had the first line planned and noted many years ago: 'Let's get this death thing straight.' But what kind of doctor is going to give you the diagnosis that suits your literary requirements? 'I'm afraid there's good news and bad news.' 'Tell me straight, Doc, I need to know. How long?' 'How long? I'd say about 200 pages. 250 if you're lucky, or work fast.'

No, it isn't going to happen like that, so it's best to get the book done before the diagnosis. Of course, there is a third possibility: you start the book, you are nearly halfway through and then you get the diagnosis! Maybe the narrative is flagging a bit by this stage, so enter the chest pain, the fainting fit, the X-rays, the CAT scan . . . Would that, I wonder, look a little contrived? (The readers' group confers. 'Oh, I always thought he was going to die at the end – well, after the end, didn't you?' 'No, I thought he might be bluffing. I wasn't sure he was even ill. I thought it might be, what do you call it, meta-fiction?')

It probably isn't going to happen this way either. When we imagine our own dying, whether best or worst case, we tend to imagine dying lucidly, dying while aware (all too

aware) of what is going on, able to express ourselves and understand others. How successfully can we imagine dying – and the long lead-up to the event itself – in a state of incoherence and misunderstanding? With the same original pain and fear, of course, but now with an added layer of confusion. Not knowing quite who anybody is, not knowing who is alive or dead, not knowing where you are. (But just as shit-scared anyway.) I remember visiting an elderly and demented friend in hospital. She would turn to me, and in her soft, rather genteel voice which I had once much loved, would say things like, 'I do think you will be remembered as one of the worst criminals in history.' Then a nurse might walk past, and her mood change swiftly. 'Of course,' she would assure me, 'the maids here are frightfully good.' Sometimes I would let such remarks pass (for her sake, for my sake), sometimes (for her sake, for my sake) correct them. 'Actually, they're nurses.' My friend would give a cunning look expressing surprise at my naivety. 'Some of them are,' she conceded. 'But *most* of them are maids.'

My father had a series of strokes which reduced him, over the years, from an erect man of my height, first to a figure hunched over a Zimmer, his head cocked in that awkward angled lift the frame compels, and then to the half-humiliated occupant of a wheelchair. When the social services came to assess his level of incapacity, they explained that he would need, and they would pay for, a handrail to help him from bed to door. My mother

overrode the suggestion: 'Not having that ugly thing in the room.' She maintained that it would spoil the bungalow's decor; but her refusal was, I now suspect, an oblique way of denying what had happened – and what might await her too. One thing she did allow – to my surprise – was an alteration to Dad's armchair. This was the sturdy green high-backed Parker Knoll in which Grandpa used to read his *Daily Express*, and mistake Grandma's stomach for the telephone. Now, its legs were extended with metal sheaths, so that Dad could get in and out more easily.

This slow physical crumbling was paralleled by an erosion of my father's speech: of his articulation, and memory for words. (He had been a French teacher, and now his *langue* was going.) I see again the shuffle-and-push of his slow Zimmer progress from lounge to front door when he came to see me off: a stretch of time which felt endless, and where every conversational topic sounded utterly false. I would pretend to linger, look searchingly at a jug of flowers on the sideboard, or pause to observe again some knick-knack I had always disliked. Eventually, the three of us would make it to the front mat. On one occasion, my father's farewell words were, 'And next time, bring . . . bring . . .' Then he got stuck. I didn't know whether to wait, or, with a pretence of understanding, nod agreeingly. But my mother said firmly, 'Bring who?' – as if my father's mental fallibility were something correctible by the right sort of questioning. 'Bring . . . bring . . .' His expression was now one of furious frustration at his own brain. 'Bring

who?' my mother repeated. By now the answer was so obvious and unnecessary that I wanted to run out of the door, jump in the car and drive away. Suddenly, Dad found a way round his aphasia. 'Bring . . . Julian's wife.' Ah, relief. But not quite. My mother, to my ear not sounding all that sympathetic, said, 'Oh, you mean P.' – thus turning my schoolmaster father into some test-failing schoolboy.

He would stand at the front door, crouched over his frame with its stupid, empty metal basket clipped to the handlebars; his head would be tilted, as if he were trying to prevent the action of gravity on his lower jaw. I would say goodbye and set off the dozen yards or so to my car, whereupon – inevitably – my mother would 'remember' something, come at a trot down the little curve of tarmac (her hurried gait emphasizing my father's immobility) and tap on the window. I would lower it reluctantly, guessing what she was going to say. 'What do you think? He's deteriorated, hasn't he?' I would look past my mother to my father, who knew we were talking about him, and knew that I knew that he knew. 'No,' I would usually reply, out of loyalty to Dad, because the only alternative would have been to bellow, 'He's had a fucking stroke, Ma, what do you expect – volleyball?' But she would judge my diplomatic reply proof of inattention, and as I slowly let out the clutch and inched my way down the tarmac, would hold on to the window and give examples of the deterioration I had failed to observe.

I do not mean that she was unkind to him; but her way

of dealing with my father's condition was to stress her own inconvenience and suffering, while implying that his suffering was a little more his own fault than people realized. 'Of course, when he falls down, he panics,' she would complain. 'Well, I can't lift him, so I have to get someone from the village to help. But he panics because he can't get up.' Black mark. Then there was the matter of my father's pedalling machine, which the hospital physiotherapist had provided. He was supposed to sit in his Parker Knoll and pump away at this shiny little bicycle remnant. Whether mock-cycling in an armchair struck my father as absurd, or whether he simply decided that it wouldn't make the slightest difference to his condition, I don't know. 'He's so stubborn,' my mother would complain.

Of course, when it came to her turn, she was just as stubborn. Her initial stroke was far more immobilizing than Dad's first one: she was largely paralysed down her right side, and her speech was more damaged than his. She showed herself most coherent when in greatest rage at what had happened. With her good hand she would reach across and pick up her stricken arm. 'And of course,' she said, sounding for a moment exactly like her old self, 'this thing's *completely useless*.' This thing had let her down, rather as my father had. And then, exactly like Dad, she treated the physiotherapists with scepticism. 'They're pushing and pulling at me,' she would complain. When I told her they were pushing and pulling at her to help her recover, she replied, satirically, 'Yes, sir.' Yet she was

admirably unflinching, and dismissive of what she saw as false morale-boosting. 'They tell you to do something, and then they say, "Very good." It's so stupid, I *know* it isn't very good.' So she stopped cooperating. Her way of remaining herself was to mock professional optimism and decline the hypothetical recovery.

My niece C. went to visit her. I called to ask how it had gone, and how Ma was. 'Completely bonkers when I got there, but once we started talking about make-up, completely sane.' Suspecting the harshness of youth in my niece's assessment, I asked – perhaps a little stiffly – what form being 'bonkers' had taken. 'Oh, she was very angry with you. She said you'd stood her up three days running for tennis, and left her there on court.' OK, bonkers.

Not that my niece escaped censure. On one occasion she and I sat through twenty mysterious minutes of furious silence and stubborn avoidance of eye contact. Eventually, Ma turned to C. and said, 'You're a *proper monkey*, you are. But you do understand why I had to tear a strip off you, don't you?' Perhaps such dishing-out of fantastical blame gave her the illusion of control over her life. Blame which extended also to my brother, whose absence in France did not excuse or protect him. About two weeks after her first stroke, with her speech largely incomprehensible, we were discussing – or rather, I was telling her – how I would manage things while she was in hospital. I listed the people I could consult, adding that if there was any problem, I could always fall back on my brother's 'fine

brain'. With struggling pauses between each word, our mother succeeded in putting together the flawless sentence: 'His fine brain doesn't think about anything but work.'

Despite months of stubborn non-cooperation in hospital, she recovered some of her speech, though none of her movement. Not being one to fool herself, she announced that she was incapable of returning to live in her bungalow. A staff nurse called Sally came to assess her ability to function in the nursing home C. and I were hoping to get her into. Ma claimed to have already inspected the place and found it 'pukka'; though I suspect that her 'visit' had been fabulated from reading a brochure. She told Staff Nurse Sally that she had decided to take her meals alone in her room: she couldn't eat with the other residents because she lacked the use of her right arm. 'Oh, don't be silly,' said the nurse. 'It doesn't matter.' My mother's reply was commanding: 'When I say it matters, *it matters*.' 'Have you ever been a teacher?' was Sally's canny riposte.

As a young man, I was terrified of flying. The book I would choose to read on a plane would be something I felt appropriate to have found on my corpse. I remember taking *Bouvard et Pécuchet* on a flight from Paris to London, deluding myself that after the inevitable crash a) there would be an identifiable body on which it might be found; b) that Flaubert in French paperback would survive impact

and flames; c) that when recovered, it would still be grasped in my miraculously surviving (if perhaps severed) hand, a stiffened forefinger bookmarking a particularly admired passage, of which posterity would therefore take note. A likely story – and I was naturally too scared during the flight to concentrate on a novel whose ironic truths in any case tend to be withheld from younger readers.

I was largely cured of my fear at Athens airport. I was in my mid-twenties, and had arrived in good time for my flight home – such good time (so eager to leave) that instead of being several hours early, I was a whole day and several hours early. My ticket could not be changed; I had no money to go back into the city and find a hotel; so I camped out at the airport. Again, I can remember the book – the crash companion – I had with me: a volume of Durrell's Alexandria Quartet. To kill time, I went up on to the viewing roof of the terminal building. From there, I watched plane after plane take off, plane after plane land. Some of them probably belonged to dodgy airlines and were crewed by drunks; but none of them crashed. I watched scores of planes not crash. And this visual, rather than statistical, demonstration of the safety of flying convinced me.

Could I try this trick again? If I looked on death more closely and more frequently – took a job as an undertaker's assistant or mortuary clerk – might I again, by the evidence of familiarity, lose my fear? Possibly. But there's a fallacy here, which my brother, as a philosopher, would quickly

point out. The fallacy is this: at Athens airport, I was watching thousands and thousands of passengers *not* die. At an undertaker's or mortuary, I would be confirming my worst suspicion: that the death rate for the human race is not a jot lower than one hundred per cent.

THERE'S ANOTHER FLAW in that 'best-case' death scenario I was describing. Let's assume the doctor says you will live long enough and lucidly enough to complete your final book. Who wouldn't drag the work out as long as possible? Scheherazade never ran out of stories. 'Morphine drip?' 'Oh no, still quite a few chapters to go. The fact is, there's a lot more to say about death than I'd imagined . . .' And so your selfish wish to survive would act to the structural detriment of the book.

Some years ago, a British journalist, John Diamond, was diagnosed with cancer, and turned his condition into a weekly column. Rightly, he maintained the same perky tone that characterized the rest of his work; rightly, he admitted cowardice and panic alongside curiosity and occasional courage. His account sounded completely authentic: this was what living with cancer entailed; nor did being ill make you a different person, or stop you having rows with your wife. Like many other readers, I used to quietly urge him on from week to week. But after a year and more . . . well, a certain narrative expectation inevitably built up. Hey, miracle cure! Hey, I was just having you on! No, neither of those would work as endings. Diamond

had to die; and he duly, correctly (in narrative terms) did. Though – how can I put this? – a stern literary critic might complain that his story lacked compactness towards the end.

I may be dead by the time you are reading this sentence. In which case, any complaints about the book will not be answered. On the other hand, we may both be alive now (you by definition so), but you could die before me. Had you thought of that? Sorry to bring it up, but it is a possibility, at least for a few more years. In which case, my condolences to your nearest and dearest. And either I'll be going to your funeral, or you'll be coming to mine. Such has always been the case, of course; but this grimly unshiftable either/or takes on sharper definition in later years. In the matter of you and me – assuming I'm not already, definitively dead by the time you're reading this – you're more likely, actuarially, to see me out than the other way round. And there's still that other possibility – that I might die in the middle of writing this book. Which would be unsatisfactory for both of us – unless you were about to give up anyway, at exactly the point where the narrative breaks off. I might die in the middle of a sentence, even. Perhaps right in the middle of a wo

Just kidding. Though not entirely so. I've never written a book, except my first, without at some point considering that I might die before it was completed. This is all part of the superstition, the folklore, the mania of the business, the fetishistic fuss. The right pencils, felt-tips, biros,

notebooks, paper, typewriter: necessities which are also objective correlatives for the proper state of mind. This is created by putting aside all that might harmfully impinge, narrowing the focus until only what's important remains: me, you, the world and the book – and how to make it as good as it can possibly be. Reminding myself of mortality (or, more truthfully, mortality reminding me of itself) is a useful and necessary prod.

So is advice from those who have been there before. Instructions, epigrams, dicta pinned up either literally or metaphorically. Both William Styron and Philip Roth have worked beneath the Flaubertian self-reminder: 'Be regular and ordinary in your life, like a bourgeois, so that you may be violent and original in your work.' Perhaps you need to free your mind from the distraction of future critical response? Sibelius would be a help here – 'Always remember that there is no city in Europe which contains a statue to a critic' – though my favourite comes from Ford Madox Ford: 'It is an easy job to say that an elephant, however good, is not a good warthog; for most criticism comes to that.' Many writers could benefit from that line of Jules Renard's: 'One could say of almost all works of literature that they are too long.' Further, and finally, they should expect to be misunderstood. On this, Sibelius again, with the gnomic and ironic instruction: 'Misunderstand me correctly.'

When I first began to write, I laid down for myself the rule – as part of the head-clearing, the focusing, the

psychological primping and tamping – that I should write as if my parents were dead. This was not because I specifically wanted either to use or abuse them; rather, I didn't want to catch myself thinking of what might possibly offend or please them. (And in this, they were not just themselves, they were also standing for friends, colleagues, lovers, let alone warthog-describers.) The strange thing is, that though my parents are many years dead, I now need this rule more than ever.

Dying in the middle of a wo , or three-fifths of the way through a nov . My friend the nov ist Brian Moore used to fear this as well, though for an extra reason: 'Because some bastard will come along and finish it for you.' Here is a novelist's would-you-rather. Would you rather die in the middle of a book, and have some bastard finish it for you, or leave behind a work in progress that not a single bastard in the whole world was remotely interested in finishing? Moore died while at work on a novel about Rimbaud. An irony there: Rimbaud was one writer who made sure he wouldn't die in the middle of a stanza, two-thirds of the way through a *mo* , by abandoning literature half a lifetime before he died.

MY MOTHER, AN only child who became the only woman in a household whose male members had little instinct for dominance, developed a solipsism which did not decrease with age. In widowhood, she became even more of a monologuist than in the days when some polite, loving and

occasionally wry response could be elicited from the Parker Knoll. Inevitably, she became more of a repetitionist too. I was sitting with her one afternoon, my mind half elsewhere, when she took me aback with a new thought. She had been reflecting, she said, on the various forms of decrepitude that might await her, and wondering if she would rather go deaf or go blind. For a moment – naively – I imagined that she was asking my opinion, but she needed no extra input: deafness, she told me, would be her choice. This was how she had argued the matter to herself: 'If I were blind, how would I do my nails?'

Death and dying generate a whole questionnaire of such would-you-rathers. For a start, would you rather know you were dying, or not know? Would you rather watch, or not watch? Aged thirty-eight, Jules Renard noted: 'Please, God, don't make me die too quickly! I shouldn't mind seeing how I die.' He wrote this on 24 January 1902, the second anniversary of the day he had travelled from Paris to Chitry to bury his brother Maurice – a brother transformed in a few silent minutes from a clerk of works complaining about the central heating system to a corpse with his head on a Paris telephone directory. A century later, the medical historian Roy Porter was asked to reflect on death: 'You know, I think it will be interesting to be conscious as one dies, because one must undergo the most extraordinary changes. Thinking, I'm dying now . . . I think I'd like to be fully conscious of it all. Because, you know, you'd just be missing out on something otherwise.' Such

terminal curiosity is in a fine tradition. In 1777, the Swiss physiologist Albrecht von Haller was attended on his deathbed by a brother physician. Haller monitored his own pulse as it weakened, and died in character with the last words: 'My friend, the artery ceases to beat.' The following year, Voltaire similarly clung to his own pulse until the moment he slowly shook his head and, a few minutes later, died. An admirable death – with not a priest in sight. Not that it impressed everyone. Mozart, then in Paris, wrote to his father, 'You probably already know that that godless arch-rogue Voltaire has died like a dog, like a beast – that's his reward!' Like a dog, indeed.

Would you rather fear death or not fear it? That sounds an easy one. But how about this: what if you never gave death a thought, lived your life as if there were no tomorrow (there isn't, by the way), took your pleasure, did your work, loved your family, and then, as you were finally obliged to admit your own mortality, discovered that this new awareness of the full stop at the end of the sentence meant that the whole preceding story now made no sense at all? That if you'd fully realized to begin with that you were going to die, and what that meant, you would have lived according to quite different principles?

And then there is the other way round, perhaps my own: what if you lived to sixty or seventy with half an eye on the ever-filling pit, and then, as death approached, you found that there was, after all, *nothing to be frightened of*? What if you began to feel contentedly part of the great

cycle of nature (please, take my carbon atoms)? What if those easeful metaphors suddenly, or even gradually, began to convince? The Anglo-Saxon poet compared human life to a bird flying from darkness into a brightly lit banqueting hall, and then flying out into the dark on the farther side: perhaps this image will calm one's pang at being human and being mortal. I can't say it works for me yet. It's pretty enough, but the pedantic side of me keeps wanting to point out that any right-thinking bird flying into a warm banqueting hall would perch on the rafters as long as it bloody well could, rather than head straight out again. Moreover, the bird, in its pre- and post-existence on either side of the carousing hall, is at least still *flying*, which is more than can or will be said for us.

When I first came to mortal awareness, it was simple: you were alive, then you were dead, and bid the Deity farewell: Godbye. But who can tell how age will affect us? When I was a young journalist, I interviewed the novelist William Gerhardie. He was then in his eighties, frail and bed-bound; death was not far away. At one point he picked up from his bedside table an anthology about immortality, and showed me a heavily underlined account of an out-of-body experience. This, he explained, was identical to one he had himself undergone as a soldier in the First World War. 'I believe in resurrection,' he said simply. 'I believe in immortality. Do you believe in immortality?' I was awkwardly silent (and failed to remember my own out-of-body experience as a schoolboy). 'No, well, nor

did I at your age,' he went on sympathetically. 'But I do now.'

So perhaps I shall change my mind (though I doubt it). What's more likely is that the choice ahead will blur. Life versus Death becomes, as Montaigne pointed out, Old Age versus Death. What you – I – will be clinging on to is not a few more minutes in a warm baronial hall with the smell of roast chicken and the cheery noise of fife and drum, not a few more days and hours of real living, but a few more days and hours of breathing decrepitude, mind gone, muscles wasted, bladder leaking. And yet – and worse – imagine this failing body now even more fearful of oblivion than when it was healthy and strong and could divert itself from contemplation of that oblivion by physical and mental activity, by social usefulness and the company of friends. A body, the compartments of whose mind now begin shutting down one by one, lucidity gone, speech gone, recognition of friends gone, memory gone, replaced by a fantasy world of proper monkeys and unreliable tennis partners. All that is left – the last bit of the engine still with stoking power – is the compartment that makes us fear death. Yes, that little bit of brain activity will keep going strong, puffing out the panic, sending the chill and the terror coursing through the system. They will give you morphine for your pain – and then, perhaps, a little more than you actually need, and then the necessary excess – but there is nothing they can give you to stop this grim cluster of brain cells scaring you shitless (or, perhaps, the

opposite) until the very end. Then we might find ourselves regretting that we ever thought, with Renard, 'Please, God, don't make me die too quickly.'

The writer and director Jonathan Miller trained as a doctor. Despite having dissected the rigid and handled the waxily pliable from whom the breath of life had only just departed, he was in his forties before, as he put it, 'I began to think, well, hang on – this is something which I'm going to be doing some time.' Interviewed in his mid-fifties, he professed himself still unalarmed by the long-term consequences: 'The fear of just not existing – no, I don't have that at all.' What he admitted to instead was a fear of the deathbed, and what goes with it: agony, delirium, torturing hallucinations, and the lamenting family preparing for his departure. That seems a pretty fair line-up to me, though not as an alternative, merely as an add-on to the proper, grown-up fear of 'just not existing'.

Miller follows Freud in that he 'cannot actually conceive, can't make sense of the notion of total annihilation'. And so, it seems, his capacity for terror is transferred first on to the process and humiliations of dying, and secondly on to various possible states of semi-being or almost-being which might occur around or after death. He fears 'this residual consciousness which is not quite snuffed out', and imagines an out-of-body experience in which he is watching his own funeral: 'or, in fact, not watching it, but being immobilized inside the coffin'. I can picture this new tweak on that old fear of being buried alive, but fail to find it

especially sinister. If there were a residual consciousness watching our own funeral and rippling around inside our coffin, why should it necessarily be one that fears enclosure?

Most of us have thought, or said, of death, 'Well, we shall find out' – while recognizing the near certainty that we shall never 'find out' the negative we expect. A lingering consciousness might be there to give us the answer. It might be a gentle way of saying No. It might hoveringly watch the burial or cremation, farewell this pesky body of ours and the life that has been in it, and (assuming that it is still somehow attached to or representative of the self) allow 'us' to feel that what is happening is appropriate. It might produce a calming sensation, a laying-to-rest, a consolation, a sweet goodnight, an ontological nightcap.

I have a Swedish friend, K., who once, very gently and considerately, whispered to a mutual friend who had been too long dying of cancer, 'It's time to let go.' I have always teased her that I shall know things are really bad for me when I hear this lightly inflected voice in my ear, and those much-rehearsed words of advice. Perhaps the residual consciousness that Miller fears will turn out to be something useful and benevolent, a settling of accounts delivered in a soft Swedish accent.

THAT MEDIEVAL BIRD flies from darkness into a lighted hall and back out again. One of the oh-so-sensible arguments against death-anxiety goes like this: if we don't fear

and hate the eternity of time leading up to our brief moment of illuminated life, why therefore should we feel differently about the second spell of darkness? *Because*, of course, during that first spell of darkness, the universe – or at least, a very, very insignificant part of it – was leading up to the creation of something of decided interest, plaiting its genes appropriately and working its way through a succession of apelike, growling, tool-handling ancestors until such time as it gathered itself and spat out the three generations of schoolteachers who then made . . . me. So that darkness had some purpose – at least, from my solipsistic point of view; whereas the second darkness has absolutely nothing to be said for it.

It could, I suppose, be worse. It almost always can – which is some mild consolation. We might fear the prenatal abyss as well as the post-mortal one. Odd, but not impossible. Nabokov in his autobiography describes a 'chronophobiac' who experienced panic on being shown home movies of the world in the months before he was born: the house he would inhabit, his mother-to-be leaning out of a window, an empty pram awaiting its occupant. Most of us would be unalarmed, indeed cheered, by all this; the chronophobiac saw only a world in which he did not exist, an acreage of himlessness. Nor was it any consolation that such an absence was mobilizing itself irresistibly to produce his future presence. Whether this phobia reduced his level of post-mortal anxiety, or on the other hand doubled it, Nabokov does not relate.

A more sophisticated version of the bird-in-hall argument comes from Richard Dawkins. We are indeed all going to die, and death is absolute and God a delusion, but even so, that makes us the lucky ones. Most 'people' – the vast majority of potential people – don't even get born, and their numbers are greater than all the grains of sand in all the deserts of Araby. 'The set of possible people allowed by our DNA . . . massively exceeds the set of actual people. In the teeth of these stupefying odds it is you and I, in our ordinariness, that are here.' Why do I find this such thin consolation? No, worse than that, such a disconsolation? Because look at all the evolutionary work, all the unrecorded pieces of cosmic luck, all the decision-making, all the generations of family care, all the thissing-and-thatting which have ended up producing me and my uniqueness. My ordinariness, too, and yours, and that of Richard Dawkins, yet a unique ordinariness, a staggeringly against-the-odds ordinariness. This makes it harder, not easier, to give a shrug and say philosophically, Oh well, might never have been here anyway, so may as well get on enjoying this little window of opportunity not granted to others. But then it's also hard, unless you're a biologist, to think of those trillions of unborn, genetically hypothetical others as 'potential people'. I have no difficulty imagining a still-born or aborted baby as a potential person, but all those possible combinations that never came to pass? My human sympathy can only go so far, I'm afraid – the sands of Araby are beyond me.

So I cannot be philosophical. Are philosophers philosophical? Were the Laconians truly laconic, the Spartans
really spartan? Just in comparative terms, I expect. Apart
from my brother, the only philosopher I know well is my
death-haunted friend G., who as a four-year-old beat me to
mortal awareness by a decade. He and I once had a long
exchange about free will. Like everyone, I have always – an
amateur in and of my own life – assumed that I had free
will, and always, to my own mind, behaved as if I did. Professionally, G. explained to me my delusion. He pointed
out that though we might think we are free in acting as we
want, we cannot determine what it is that we want (and if
we deliberately decide to 'want to want' something, there
is the usual problem of regression to a primal 'want'). At
some point your wants must just be givens: the result of
inheritance and upbringing. Therefore, the idea of anyone
having true and ultimate responsibility for their acts is
untenable; at most we can have a temporary, surface
responsibility – and even that, with time, will be shown to
be mistaken. G. might well have quoted to me Einstein's
conclusion that 'a Being endowed with higher insight and
more perfect intelligence, watching man and his doings,
would smile about man's illusion that he was acting
according to his own free will'.

At a certain point, I admitted that I had lost the argument, though carried on behaving in exactly the same way
(which, on reflection, might have been a useful proof of
G.'s point). G. consoled me by remarking that though, in

his philosophical opinion, we cannot possibly have free will, such knowledge doesn't make the slightest practical difference to how we do, or even should, behave. And so I have continued to rely on this delusionary mental construct to help me along the mortal path to that place where no will of mine, free or fettered, will ever operate again.

There is What We Know (or think we know) To Be The Case, there is What We Believe To Be The Case (on the assurance of others whom we trust), and then there is How We Behave. Christian morality still loosely governs Britain, though congregations dwindle and church buildings make their inexorable transition to historic monuments – setting off in some 'a hunger to be serious' – and loft apartments. That sway extends to me too: my sense of morality is influenced by Christian teaching (or, more exactly, pre-Christian tribal behaviour codified by the religion); and the God I don't believe in yet miss is naturally the Christian God of Western Europe and non-fundamentalist America. I don't miss Allah or Buddha, any more than I miss Odin or Zeus. And I miss the New Testament God rather than the Old Testament one. I miss the God that inspired Italian painting and French stained glass, German music and English chapter houses, and those tumbledown heaps of stone on Celtic headlands which were once symbolic beacons in the darkness and the storm. I also realize that this God I am missing, this inspirer of artworks, will seem to some just as much an irrelevant self-indulgence as the much-claimed 'own

personal idea of God'. Further, if any God did exist, He might very well find such decorative celebration of His existence both trivial and vainglorious, a matter for divine indifference if not retribution. He might think Fra Angelico cutesy, and Gothic cathedrals blustering attempts to impress Him by a creation which had quite failed to guess how He preferred to be worshipped.

MY AGNOSTIC AND atheistic friends are indistinguishable from my professedly religious ones in honesty, generosity, integrity and fidelity – or their opposites. Is this a victory for them, I wonder, or for us? When we are young, we think we are inventing the world as we are inventing ourselves; later, we discover how much the past holds us, and always did. I escaped what seemed to me the decent dullness of my family, only to find, as I grow older, that my resemblance to my dead father strikes me more and more. There is the angle I sit at a table, the hang of my jaw, the incipient baldness pattern, and a particular kind of polite laugh I emit when not really amused: these (and doubtless much else that I fail to pick up) are genetic replicas and definitely not expressions of free will. My brother finds the same: he talks more and more like our father, using the same slang and half-finished sentences – he catches himself 'sounding just like him, and even shuffling in my slippers the way he used to'. He has also started to dream about Dad – after sixty years in which neither parent intruded upon his sleep.

Grandma, in her dementia, believed my mother was a

sister of hers who had been dead for fifty years. My mother, in turn, welcomed back all the relatives she had known in childhood, come to express concern for her. In time, our family will come for my brother and for me (only please don't send my mother). But did the past ever really relax its grasp? We live broadly according to the tenets of a religion we no longer believe in. We live as if we are creatures of pure free will when philosophers and evolutionary biologists tell us this is largely a fiction. We live as if the memory were a well-built and efficiently staffed left-luggage office. We live as if the soul – or spirit, or individuality, or personality – were an identifiable and locatable entity rather than a story the brain tells itself. We live as if nature and nurture were equal parents when the evidence suggests that nature has both the whip hand and the whip.

Will such knowledge sink in? How long will it take? Some scientists think we shall never entirely decipher the mysteries of consciousness because all we can use to understand the brain is the brain itself. Perhaps we shall never abandon the illusion of free will because it would take an act of the free will we don't have to abandon our belief in it. We shall go on living as if we are the full arbiters of our every decision. (The various adjustments of grammar and sense that I made to that last sentence, both immediately in the writing and after subsequent time and thought – how can 'I' not believe that 'I' made them? How can I believe that those words, and this parenthesis which follows them, and every elaboration I make within

it, and the occasional misytpings, and the next word, whether completed or abandoned-halfway-through-as-I-have-second-thoughts-about-it and left as a wo , are not emanations of a coherent self making literary decisions by a process of free will? I cannot get my head round this not being the case.)

Perhaps it will be easier for you, or if not you, the generations born after you are dead. Perhaps I – and you – will seem to them like the 'old-type *natural* fouled-up guys' (and gals) of Larkin's poem. Perhaps they will regard as quaint and complacent the half-assumed, half-worked-out morality by which you and I seem to think we live. When religion first began to collapse in Europe – when 'godless arch-rogues' like Voltaire were at work – there was a natural apprehension about where morality was to come from. In a dangerously ungoverned world, every village might produce its Casanova, its Marquis de Sade, its Bluebeard. There were philosophers who, while refuting Christianity to their own satisfaction and that of their intellectual circle, believed that the knowledge should be kept from peasant and potboy, lest the social structure collapse and the servant problem get completely out of hand.

But Europe stumbled on nonetheless. And if the dilemma now seems to pose itself in an even sharper form – what is the meaning of my actions in an empty universe where even more certainties have been undermined? why behave well? why not be selfish and greedy and blame it all on DNA? – the anthropologists and evolutionary

biologists are able to offer comfort (if not to the faithful). Whatever religions may claim, we are set up – genetically programmed – to operate as social beings. Altruism is evolutionary useful (ah! – there's your virtue – another illusion – gone); so whether or not there is a preacher with a promise of heaven and a threat of hellfire, individuals living in societies generally act in much the same way. Religion no more makes people behave better than it makes them behave worse – which might be a disappointment to the aristocratic atheist as much as to the believer.

WHEN I WAS first studying French literature, I was puzzled by the concept of the *acte gratuit*. As I understood it, the notion went like this: in order to assert that we are now in charge of the universe, we must perform a spontaneous action for which there is no apparent motive or justification, and which lies outside conventional morality. The example that I recall, from Gide's *Les Caves du Vatican*, consisted of the gratuitous actor pushing a complete stranger out of a moving train. Pure act, you see (and also, I now realize, a supposed proof of free will). I didn't see – or not enough. I found myself thinking about the unfortunate fellow dashed to death in the middle of the French countryside. Murder – or, perhaps, what bourgeois minds still mired in Christianity chose to call murder – as a means of demonstrating a philosophical point seemed too . . . too theoretical, too French, too repellent. Though my friend G. would say that the gratuitous actor would

have been fooling himself (merely 'wanting to want' something). And I suppose that if his assertion of pure free will was a delusion, then so too was my reaction.

Emperor penguins have been in fashion lately, with cinematic and TV voiceovers urging us to anthropomorphism. How can we resist their loveably incompetent bipedalism? See how they rest lovingly on one another's breasts, shuffle a precious egg between parental feet, share the food search just as we share supermarket duties. Watch how the whole group huddles together against the snowstorm, demonstrating social altruism. Are we like those Antarctic penguins, or are they like us? We go to the supermarket, they slither and wobble across miles of ice to the open sea in search of food. But here is one detail the wildlife programmes omit. When the penguins approach the water's edge, they begin to dawdle and loiter. They have reached food, but also danger; the sea contains fish, but also seals. Their long journey might result not in eating but getting eaten – in which case their offspring back in the penguin-huddle will starve to death and their own gene pool be terminated. So this is what the penguins do: they wait until one of their number, either more hungry or more anxious, gets to where the ice runs out, and is gazing down into the nutritious yet deadly ocean, and then, like a gang of commuters on a station platform, they nudge the imprudent bird into the sea. Hey, just testing! This is what those loveable, anthropomorphizable penguins are 'really like'. And if we are shocked, they are at least behaving

more rationally – more usefully, even more altruistically – than the gratuitous actor of our own species pushing a man from a train.

That penguin doesn't have a would-you-rather. It is plunge or die – sometimes plunge and die. And some of our own would-you-rathers turn out to be equally hypothetical: ways of simplifying the unthinkable, pretending to control the uncontrollable. My mother considered quite seriously whether she would rather go deaf or go blind. Preferring one incapacity in advance seemed a superstitious method of ruling out the other. Except that, as it turned out, the 'choice' never arose. Her stroke affected neither her hearing nor her sight – and yet she never did her nails again in what was left of her life.

My brother hopes for Grandpa's death: felled by a stroke while gardening. He fears the other family examples: Grandma's long-drawn-out senility, Dad's slow confinement and humiliation, Ma's half-self-aware delusions. But there are so many other possibilities to choose from – or to have chosen for us; so many different doors, even if they are all marked Exit. In this respect, death is multiple-choice not would-you-rather, and prodigally democratic in its options.

Stravinsky said: 'Gogol died screaming and Diaghilev died laughing, but Ravel died gradually. That is the worst.' He was right. There have been more violent artistic deaths, ones involving madness, terror, and banal absurdity (Webern shot dead by a GI after politely stepping on to

There are so many other possibilities to choose from – or to have chosen for us; so many different doors, even if they are all marked Exit

the porch to light a cigar), but few as cruel as that of Ravel. Worse, it had a strange prefiguration – a musical pre-echo – in the death of a French composer of the previous generation. Emmanuel Chabrier had succumbed to tertiary syphilis in 1894, the year after the Paris premiere of his only attempt at serious opera, *Gwendoline*. This piece – perhaps the only opera to be set in eighth-century Britain – had taken ten years to be staged; by which time Chabrier's disease was in its final phase, and his mind in never-never land. He sat in his box at the premiere, acknowledging the applause and smiling 'almost without knowing why'. Sometimes, he would forget the opera was his, and murmur to a neighbour, 'It's good, it's really very good.'

This story was well-known among the next generation of French composers. 'Horrible, isn't it?' Ravel used to say. 'To go to a performance of *Gwendoline* and not recognize your own music!' I remember my friend Dodie Smith, in great age, being asked the tender, encouraging question, 'Now, Dodie, you do remember that you used to be a famous playwright?' To which she replied, 'Yes, I *think* so' – in rather the tone I imagine my father using when he said to my mother, 'I think you're my wife.' A milliner might not recognize her own hat, a labourer his own speed bump, a writer her words, a painter his canvas; this is poignant enough. But there is extra pain, for those who witness it, when a composer fails to recognize his own notes.

Ravel died gradually – it took five years – and it was the worst. At first his decline from Pick's disease (a form of cerebral atrophy), though alarming, was non-specific. Words evaded him; motor skills went awry. He would grasp a fork by the wrong end; he became unable to sign his name; he forgot how to swim. When he went out to dinner, the housekeeper used to pin his address inside his coat as a precaution. But then the disease turned malignly particular and targeted Ravel the composer. He went to a recording of his string quartet, sat in the control room, offered various corrections and suggestions. After each movement had been recorded, he was asked if he wanted to listen through again, but declined. So the session went quickly, and the studio was pleased to have it all wrapped up in an afternoon. At the end, Ravel turned to the produ-cer (and our guessing what he is going to say cannot lessen its impact): 'That was really very good. Remind me of the composer's name.' Another day, he went to a concert of his piano music. He sat through it with evident pleasure, but when the hall turned to acclaim him, he thought they were addressing the Italian colleague at his side, and so joined in their applause.

Ravel was taken to two leading French neurosurgeons. Another would-you-rather. The first judged his condition inoperable, and said that nature should be allowed to take its course. The second would have agreed had the patient been anyone but Ravel. However, if there were the slightest chance – for him a few more years, for us a

little more music (which is 'the best way of digesting time' according to Stravinsky) . . . And so the composer's skull was opened up, and the damage seen to be extensive and irreparable. Ten days later, his head still turbanned with hospital windings, Ravel died.

ABOUT TWENTY YEARS ago I was asked if I would be interviewed for a book about death. I declined on writerly grounds: I didn't want to talk away stuff which I might later need myself. I never read the book when it came out: perhaps from a superstitious – or rational – fear that one of its contributors might have better expressed what I was slowly working my way towards. Not long ago, I began cautiously browsing the first chapter, an interview with a certain 'Thomas'. Except that it became instantly clear, after scarcely a page, that this 'Thomas' was none other than my old death-friend and free-will eradicator G.

The primal would-you-rather about death (though again one in which we don't have the choice) is: ignorance or knowledge? Would you prefer to receive *le réveil mortel* or to slumber on in quilted blindness? This might seem an easy one: if in doubt, opt for knowledge. But it's the knowledge that causes the damage. As 'Thomas'/G. puts it: 'People who aren't afraid, I think most of them just don't know what death *means* . . . The standard theory of moral philosophy is that it's a great evil for a person to be suddenly cut off [in the flower of life]; but it seems to me that the evil is knowing it's going to happen. If it happened

without your knowing, it wouldn't matter.' Or at least, it would make us more akin to those penguins: the dupe who toddles to the water's edge and is shouldered in by a non-gratuitous nudge may fear the seal but cannot conceptualize the eternal consequences of the seal.

G. has no difficulty understanding, or believing, that human beings, in all their complexity, simply disappear for ever. It is all part of 'the profligacy of nature', like the micro-engineering of a mosquito. 'I think of it as nature sort of wildly over-shooting, splurging her gifts around; with human beings it's just more of the same kind of profligacy. These extraordinary brains and sensibilities, produced in millions, and then just thrown away, disappearing into eternity. I don't think man's a special case, I think the theory of evolution explains it all. It's a very beautiful theory, come to think of it, a marvellous and inspiring theory, though it has grim consequences for us.'

That's my man! And perhaps a sense of death is like a sense of humour. We all think the one we've got – or haven't got – is just about right, and appropriate to the proper understanding of life. It's everyone else who's out of step. I think my sense of death – which appears exaggerated to some of my friends – is quite proportionate. For me, death is the one appalling fact which defines life; unless you are constantly aware of it, you cannot begin to understand what life is about; unless you know and feel that the days of wine and roses are limited, that the wine

will madeirize and the roses turn brown in their stinking water before all are thrown out for ever – including the jug – there is no context to such pleasures and interests as come your way on the road to the grave. But then I would say that, wouldn't I? My friend G. has a worse case of death, so I find his hauntedness excessive, not to say unhealthy (ah, the 'healthy' attitude to it all – where is that to be found?).

For G. our only defence against death – or rather, against the danger of not being able to think about anything else – lies in 'the acquisition of worthwhile short-term worries'. He also consolingly quotes a study showing that fear of death drops off after the age of sixty. Well, I have got there before him, and can report that I am still waiting for the benefit. Only a couple of nights ago, there came again that alarmed and alarming moment, of being pitchforked back into consciousness, awake, alone, utterly alone, beating pillow with fist and shouting 'Oh no Oh No OH NO' in an endless wail, the horror of the moment – the minutes – overwhelming what might, to an objective witness, appear a shocking display of exhibitionist self-pity. An inarticulate one, too: for what sometimes shames me is the extraordinary lack of descriptive, or responsive, words that come out of my mouth. For God's sake, you're a *writer*, I say to myself. You do *words*. Can't you improve on that? Can't you face down death – well, you won't ever face it down, but can't you at least protest against it – more interestingly than this? We know that extreme physical pain

For me, death is the one appalling fact which defines life

drives out language; it's dispiriting to learn that mental pain does the same.

I once read that Zola was similarly startled from his bed like a projectile, launched from sleep into mortal terror. In my unpublished twenties, I used to think of him fraternally – and also with apprehension: if this stuff is still happening to a world-famous writer in his fifties, then there's not much chance of it getting better for me with the years. The novelist Elizabeth Jane Howard once told me that the three most death-haunted people she had ever known were her ex-husband Kingsley Amis, Philip Larkin and John Betjeman. Tempting to conclude that it might be a writer thing, even a male writer thing. Amis used to maintain – comically, given his biography – that men were more sensitive than women.

I very much doubt it – both the male thing, and the writer thing. I used to believe, when I was 'just' a reader, that writers, because they wrote books where truth was found, because they described the world, because they saw into the human heart, because they grasped both the particular and the general and were able to re-create both in free yet structured forms, because they *understood*, must therefore be more sensitive – also less vain, less selfish – than other people. Then I became a writer, and started meeting other writers, and studied them, and concluded that the only difference between them and other people, the only, single way in which they were better, was that they were better writers. They might indeed be sensitive,

perceptive, wise, generalizing and particularizing – but only at their desks and in their books. When they venture out into the world, they regularly behave as if they have left all their comprehension of human behaviour stuck in their typescripts. It's not just writers either. How wise are philosophers in their private lives?

'Not a whit wiser for being philosophers,' replies my brother. 'Worse, in their semi-public lives, far less wise than many other species of academics.' I remember once laying down Bertrand Russell's autobiography in a moment, not of disbelief, more a kind of appalled belief. This is how he describes the beginning of the end of his first marriage: 'I went out bicycling one afternoon, and suddenly, as I was riding along a country road, I realized that I no longer loved Alys. I had no idea until this moment that my love for her was even lessening.' The only logical response to this, to its implications and manner of expression, would be: keep philosophers off bicycles. Or perhaps, keep philosophers out of marriage. Save them for discussing truth with God. I would want Russell on my side for that.

ON MY SIXTIETH birthday, I have lunch with T., one of my few religious friends. Or do I just mean faith-professing? Anyway, he is Catholic, wears a cross around his neck and, to the alarm of some past girlfriends, has a crucifix on the wall above his bed. Yes, that does sound more like religious

than faith-professing, I know. T. is soon to marry R., who may or may not have the power to remove the crucifix. This being my birthday, I allow myself more interrogatory latitude, so ask why – apart from having been brought up as a Catholic – he believes in his God and his religion. He thinks for a while and replies, 'I believe because I want to believe.' Sounding perhaps a little like my brother, I counter with, 'If you said to me, "I love R. because I want to love R.", I wouldn't be too impressed, and nor would she.' As it is my birthday, T. refrains from throwing his drink over me.

When I return home, I find a small package pushed through the door. My first response is one of mild irritation, as I have specifically requested No Presents, and this particular friend, known for her giftliness, has been warned more than once on the subject. The package contains a lapel badge, battery driven, which flashes '60 TODAY' in blue and red points. What makes it not just acceptable, but the perfect present, turning my irritation into immediate good humour, are the manufacturer's words printed on the cardboard backing: 'WARNING: May Cause Interference With Pacemakers'.

One of the (possibly) 'worthwhile short-term worries' that follows my birthday is an American book tour. The arrival into New York – the transit from airport to city – involves passing one of the vastest cemeteries I have ever seen. I always half-enjoy this ritual memento mori, prob- ably because I have never come to love New York. All the

bustle in that most ever-bustling and narcissistic of cities will come to this; Manhattan mocked by the packed verticality of the headstones. In the past, I have merely noted the extent of the graveyards and the arithmetic of mortality. Now, for the first time, something else strikes me: that there is no one in them. These cemeteries are like the modern countryside: hectares of emptiness extending in every direction. And while you hardly expect a yokel with a scythe, a hedger-and-ditcher or a drystone-waller, the utter absence of human activity that agribusiness has brought to the former meadows and pasture-land and hedgerowed fields is another kind of death: as if the pesticides have killed off all the farm workers as well. Similarly, in these Queens cemeteries, not a body – not a soul – stirs. Of course, it makes sense: the dead ex-bustlers are unvisited because the city's new replacement bustlers are much too busy bustling. But if there is anything more melancholy than a graveyard, it is an unvisited graveyard.

A few days later, on the train down to Washington, somewhere south of Trenton, I pass another cemetery. Though equally empty of the living, this one seems less grim: it straggles companionably alongside the tracks, and doesn't have the same feel of stained finality, of dead-and-doneness. Here, it seems, the dead are not so dead that they are forgotten, not so dead that they will not welcome new neighbours. And there, at the southern end of this unmenacing strip, is a cheery American moment: a sign proclaiming BRISTOL CEMETERY – LOTS AVAILABLE.

It reads as if the pun on 'lots' is intended: come and join us, we have much more space than our rivals.

Lots available. Advertise, even in death – it's the American way. Whereas in Western Europe the old religion is in terminal decline, America remains a Christian country, and it makes sense that the creed still flourishes there. Christianity, which cleared up the old Jewish doctrinal dispute about whether or not there was life after death, which centralized personal immortality as a theological selling-point, is well suited to this can-do, reward-driven society. And since in America all tendencies are taken to the extreme, they have currently installed Extreme Christianity. Old Europe took a more leisurely approach to the final arrival of the Kingdom of Heaven – a long mouldering in the grave before resurrection and judgement, all in God's good time. America, and Extreme Christianity, likes to hurry things along. Why shouldn't product delivery follow promised order sooner rather than later? Hence such fantasies as The Rapture, in which the righteous, while going about their daily business, are instantly taken up into Heaven, there to watch Jesus and the Antichrist duke it out down below on the battleground of planet Earth. The action-man, X-rated, disaster-movie version of the world's end.

Death followed by resurrection: the ultimate 'tragedy with a happy ending'. That phrase is routinely credited to one of those Hollywood directors who are assumed to be the source of all witticism; though I first came across it in

Edith Wharton's autobiography *A Backward Glance*. There she ascribes the quip to her friend the novelist William Dean Howells, who offered it her as consolation after a first-night audience had failed to appreciate a theatrical adaptation of *The House of Mirth*. This would take the phrase back to 1906, before all those movie directors had started making wisecracks.

Wharton's success as a novelist is the more surprising – and the more admirable – given how little her view of life accorded with American hopefulness. She saw small evidence of redemption. She thought life a tragedy – or at best a grim comedy – with a tragic ending. Or, sometimes, just a drama with a dramatic ending. (Her friend Henry James defined life as 'a predicament before death'. And *his* friend Turgenev believed that 'the most interesting part of life is death'.)

Nor was Wharton seduced by the notion that life, whether tragic, comic or dramatic, is necessarily original. Our lack of originality is something we usefully forget as we hunch over our – to us – ever-fascinating lives. My friend M., leaving his wife for a younger woman, used to complain, 'People tell me it's a cliché. But it doesn't feel like a cliché to me.' Yet it was, and is. As all our lives would prove, if we could see them from a greater distance – from the viewpoint, say, of that higher creature imagined by Einstein.

A biographer friend once suggested she take the slightly longer view and write my life. Her husband argued

satirically that this would make a very short work as all my days were the same. 'Got up,' his version went. 'Wrote book. Went out, bought bottle of wine. Came home, cooked dinner. Drank wine.' I immediately endorsed this Brief Life. That will do as well as any other; as true, or as untrue as anything longer. Faulkner said that a writer's obituary should read: 'He wrote books, and then he died.'

SHOSTAKOVICH KNEW THAT making art from and about death was 'tantamount to wiping your sleeve on your nose'. When the sculptor Ilya Slonim did a portrait bust of him, the result failed to please the chairman of the Soviet Committee for the Arts. 'What we need,' the apparatchik told the sculptor (and by extension the composer), 'is an optimistic Shostakovich.' The composer loved repeating this oxymoron.

Apart from being a great brooder on death, he was also – in private, necessarily – a mocker of false hopes, state propaganda and artistic dross. One favourite target was a hit play of the 1930s by the long-forgotten regime creep Vsevolod Vishnevsky, of whom a Russian theatre scholar recently wrote: 'Even by the standards of our literary herbarium, this author was a very poisonous specimen.' Vishnevsky's play was set on board ship during the Bolshevik Revolution, and admirably portrayed the world as the authorities pretended it was. A young female commissar arrives to explain, and impose, the party line on a crew of anarchist sailors and old-school Russian officers.

She is met with indifference, scepticism, and even assault: one of the sailors tries to rape her, whereupon she shoots him dead. Such an example of communist vigour and instant justice helps win over the sailors, who are soon moulded into an effective fighting unit. Deployed against the warmongering, God-worshipping, capitalistic Germans, they are somehow taken prisoner; but rise up heroically against their captors. During the struggle the inspirational commissar is killed, and dies urging the now fully Sovietized sailors, 'Always uphold ... the high traditions ... of the Red Fleet.' Curtain.

It wasn't the cartoonishly obedient plot of Vishnevsky's play that appealed to Shostakovich's sense of humour, but its title: *An Optimistic Tragedy.* Soviet Communism, Hollywood and organized religion were all closer than they knew, dream factories cranking out the same fantasy. 'Tragedy is tragedy', Shostakovich liked to repeat, 'and optimism has nothing to do with it.'

I HAVE SEEN two dead people, and touched one of them; but I've never seen anyone die, and may never do so, unless and until I see myself die. If death ceased to be talked about when it first really began to be feared, and then more so when we started to live longer, it has also gone off the agenda because it has ceased to be there, with us, in the house. Nowadays we make death as invisible as possible, and part of a process – from doctor to hospital to undertaker to crematorium – in which professionals and

bureaucrats tell us what to do, up to the point where we are left to ourselves, survivors standing with a glass in our hands, amateurs learning how to mourn. But not so long ago the dying would have spent their final illness at home, expired among family, been washed and laid out by local women, watched over companionably for a night or two, then coffined up by the local undertaker. Like Jules Renard, we would have set off on foot behind a swaying, horse-drawn hearse for the cemetery, there to watch the coffin being lowered and a fat worm strutting at the grave's edge. We would have been more attending and more attentive. Better for them (though my brother will refer me to hypo-thetical wants of the dead), and probably better for us. The old system made for a statelier progressing from being alive to being dead – and from being dead to being lost from sight. The modern, rushing way is doubtless truer to how we see death nowadays – one minute you're alive, the next you're dead, and truly dead, so let's jump in the car and get it over with. (Whose car shall we take? Not the one she would have wanted.)

Stravinsky went to see Ravel's body before it was placed in the coffin. It was lying on a table draped in black. Every-thing was black and white: black suit, white gloves, white hospital turban still encircling the head, black wrinkles on a very pale face, which had 'an expression of great majesty'. And there the grandeur of death ended. 'I went to the interment,' Stravinsky recorded. 'A lugubrious experience, these civil burials where everything is banned except

protocol.' That was Paris, 1937. When Stravinsky's turn came, thirty-four years later, his body was flown from New York to Rome, then driven to Venice, where black and purple proclamations were posted up everywhere: THE CITY OF VENICE DOES HOMAGE TO THE REMAINS OF THE GREAT MUSICIAN IGOR STRAVINSKY, WHO IN A GESTURE OF EXQUISITE FRIENDSHIP ASKED TO BE BURIED IN THE CITY WHICH HE LOVED ABOVE ALL OTHERS. The Archimandrite of Venice conducted the Greek Orthodox service in the church of SS Giovanni et Paolo, then the coffin was carried past the Colleoni statue, and rowed by four gondoliers in a water-hearse out to the cemetery island of San Michele. There the Archimandrite and Stravinsky's widow dropped earth from their hands on to the coffin as it was lowered into the vault. Francis Steegmuller, the great Flaubert scholar, followed the day's events. He said that as the cortège processed from church to canal, with Venetians hanging from every window, the scene resembled 'one of Carpaccio's pageants'. More, much more than protocol.

Unless and until I see myself die. Would you rather be conscious of your dying, or unconscious of it? (There is a third – and highly popular – option: being deluded into the belief that you are on the way to recovery.) But be careful what you wish for. Roy Porter wanted to be fully conscious: 'Because, you know, you'd just be missing out on something otherwise.' He went on: 'Clearly, one doesn't want excruciating pain and all the rest of it. But I think one

would want to be with the people who mattered to one.' That is what Porter hoped for, and this is what he got. He was fifty-five, had recently taken early retirement, moved to Sussex with his fifth wife, and begun a life of freelance writing. He was bicycling home from his allotment (hard not to imagine the kind of country lane where Bertrand Russell had his marital aperçu) when he was suddenly blasted out by a heart attack, and died alone on the verge. Did he have any time to watch himself die? Did he know he was dying? Was his last thought an expectation that he would wake up in hospital? His final morning had been spent planting peas. And he was taking home a bunch of flowers, which were in a moment transformed into his own roadside tribute.

MY GRANDFATHER SAID that remorse was the worst emotion life could contain. My mother did not understand the remark, and I do not know what events to attach it to.

Death and Remorse 1. When François Renard, ignoring his son's advice to take an enema, took a shotgun instead, and used a walking stick to fire both barrels and produce a 'dark place above the waist, like a small extinguished fire', Jules wrote: 'I do not reproach myself for not having loved him enough. I reproach myself for not having understood him.'

Death and Remorse 2. Ever since I first read it, I have remained haunted by a line from Edmund Wilson's

journals. Wilson died in 1972; the events referred to happened in 1932; I read about them in 1980, the year *The Thirties* was published.

At the beginning of that decade, Wilson had married, as his second wife, one Margaret Canby. She was a stocky, humorous-faced, upper-class woman with 'champagne tastes': Wilson was the first man she had known who had worked for a living. In the previous volume of his journals, *The Twenties*, Wilson had called her 'the best woman drinking companion I had ever known'. There he noted his first intention of marrying her, and also his sensible hesitation: 'Well though we got along, we did not have enough in common.' But marry they did, into an alcoholic companionship marked from the first by infidelity and temporary separations. If Wilson had his doubts about Canby, she had even stronger reservations about him. 'You're a cold fishy leprous person, Bunny Wilson,' she once told him – a remark which Wilson, with typical unsparingness, confided to his diary.

In September 1932 the couple, then married two years, were having one of their separations. Margaret Canby was in California, Wilson in New York. She went to a party in Santa Barbara wearing high heels. As she left, she tripped, fell down a flight of stone steps, broke her skull and died. The event produced, in Wilson's journal, forty-five pages of the most honest and self-flagellant mourning ever written. Wilson starts taking notes as his plane slowly hedge-hops west, as if the enforced literary act will help

block off emotion. Over the next days, these jottings open out into an extraordinary monologue of homage, erotic remembrance, remorse and despair. 'A horrible night but even that seemed sweet in recollection,' he notes at one point. In California, Canby's mother urges him: 'You must believe in immortality, Bunny, you must!' But he doesn't and can't: Margaret is dead and unreturning.

Wilson spares himself, and his putative reader, nothing. He preserves every impaling rebuke Canby delivered. She once told her critical, complaining husband that the epitaph on his tombstone should read: 'You'd better go and fix yourself up.' He also celebrates her: in bed, in drink, in tears, in confusion. He remembers fighting off the flies when they made love on a beach, and iconizes her 'cunning' body with its small limbs. ('Don't say that!' she would protest. 'It makes me sound like a turtle.') He calls to mind the ignorances that charmed him – 'I've found out what that thing over the door is – it's a lentil' – and places them alongside her running complaints: 'I'll crash someday! Why don't you do something about me?' She accused him of treating her as just another luxury item, like Guerlain scent: 'You'd be charmed if I were dead, you know you would.'

The fact that Wilson treated his wife badly, both before and after marriage, and that his grief was contaminated by justified guilt, is what gives this stream of mourning consciousness its power. The animating paradox of Wilson's condition is that he has been released into feeling by the

death of the person who accused him of lack of feeling. And the line that has never left my memory is this: 'After she was dead, I loved her.'

It doesn't matter that Bunny Wilson was a cold, fishy, leprous person. It doesn't matter that their relationship was a mistake and their marriage a disaster. It only matters that Wilson was telling the truth, and that the authentic voice of remorse is sounded in those words: 'After she was dead, I loved her.'

WE MAY ALWAYS choose knowledge over ignorance; we may wish to be conscious of our dying; we may hope for a best-case scenario in which a calm mind observes a gradual decline, perhaps with a Voltairean finger on the ebbing pulse. We may get all this; but even so, we should consider the evidence of Arthur Koestler. In *Dialogue with Death* he recorded his experiences in the Francoist prisons of Malaga and Seville during the Spanish Civil War. Admittedly, there is a difference between young men facing immediate execution by political opponents, and older men and women, most of their lives behind them, contemplating quieter extinctions. But Koestler observed many of those about to die – including, as he was assured, himself – and came to the following conclusions. First, that no one, even in the condemned cell, even hearing the sound of their friends and comrades being shot, can ever truly believe in his own death; indeed, Koestler thought this fact could be expressed quasi-mathematically – 'One's

disbelief in death grows in proportion to its approach.' Secondly, the mind has recourse to various tricks when it finds itself in the presence of death: it produces 'merciful narcotics or ecstatic stimulants' to deceive us. In particular, Koestler thought, it is capable of splitting consciousness in two, so that one half is examining coolly what the other half is experiencing. In this way, 'the consciousness sees to it that its complete annihilation is never experienced'. Two decades previously, in 'Thoughts for the Times on War and Death', Freud had written: 'It is indeed impossible to imagine our own death; and whenever we attempt to do so, we can perceive that we are in fact still present as spectators.'

Koestler also casts doubt on the authenticity of death-bed self-observation, however apparently lucid and rational the mind. 'I don't believe that since the world began a human being has ever died *consciously*. When Socrates, sitting in the midst of his pupils, reached out for the goblet of hemlock, he must have been at least half convinced that he was merely showing off . . . Of course he knew that theoretically the draining of the goblet would prove fatal; but he must have had a feeling that the whole thing was quite different from what his perfervid, humourless pupils imagined it; that there was some clever dodge behind it all known only to himself.'

Koestler ends *Dialogue with Death* with a scene so cinematic, so neat and so implausible that he cannot possibly have made it up. He has been released from prison in

exchange for the wife of a Francoist fighter ace, who is given the job of flying Koestler to the rendezvous. As their plane hovers over a vast white plateau, the black-shirted pilot takes his hand off the joystick and engages his political enemy in a shouted conversation about life and death, Left and Right, courage and cowardice. 'Before we were alive,' the writer bellows at the aviator at one point, 'we were all dead.' The pilot agrees, and asks, 'But why, then, is one afraid of death?' 'I have never been afraid of death,' Koestler replies, 'but only of dying.' 'With me, it's exactly the opposite,' shouts back the man in the black shirt.

Except that they were, presumably, shouting in Spanish. Fear of death or fear of dying, would you rather? Are you with the Communist or the Fascist, the writer or the flyer? Almost everyone fears one to the exclusion of the other; it's as if there isn't enough room for the mind to contain both. If you fear death, you don't fear dying; if you fear dying, you don't fear death. But there's no logical reason why one should block out the other; no reason why the mind, with a little training, cannot stretch to encompass both. As one who wouldn't mind dying as long as I didn't end up dead afterwards, I can certainly make a start on elaborating what my fears about dying might be. I fear being my father as he sat in a chair by his hospital bed and with quite uncharacteristic irateness rebuked me – 'You said you were coming *yesterday*' – before working out from my embarrassment that it was he

who had got things confused. I fear being my mother imagining that she still played tennis. I fear being the friend who, longing for death, would repeatedly confide that he had managed to acquire and swallow enough pills to kill himself, but was now seethingly anxious that his actions might get a nurse into trouble. I fear being the innately courteous literary man I knew who, as senility took hold, began spouting at his wife the most extreme sexual fantasies, as if they were what he had always secretly wanted to do to her. I fear being the octogenarian Somerset Maugham, dropping his trousers behind the sofa and shitting on the rug (even if the moment might happily recall my childhood). I fear being the elderly friend, a man of both refinement and squeamishness, whose eyes showed animal panic when the nurse in the residential home announced in front of visitors that it was time to change his nappy. I fear the nervous laugh I shall give when I don't quite get an allusion or have for-gotten a shared memory, or a familiar face, and then begin to mistrust much of what I think I know, and finally mistrust all of it. I fear the catheter and the stairlift, the oozing body and the wasting brain. I fear the Chabrier/ Ravel fate of not knowing who I have been and what I have made. Perhaps Stravinsky, in extreme old age, had their endings in mind when he used to call out from his room for his wife or a member of the household. 'What is it you need?' they would ask. 'To be reassured of my own existence,' he would reply. And the confirmation might

come in the form of a handclasp, a kiss, or the playing of a favourite record.

Arthur Koestler, in old age, was proud of a conundrum he had formulated: 'Is it better for a writer to be forgotten before he dies, or to die before he is forgotten?' (Jules Renard knew his answer: 'Poil de Carotte and I live together, and I hope that I die before him.') But it is a would-you-rather porous enough to allow a third possibility to sneak in: the writer, before dying, may have lost all memory of having been a writer.

When Dodie Smith was asked if she remembered having been a famous playwright, and replied, 'Yes, I *think* so', she said it in exactly the same way – with a kind of frowning concentration, morally conscious that truth was required – as I had seen her answer dozens of questions over the years. In other words, she at least remained in character. Beyond those nearer fears of mental and physical slippage, this is what we hope and hold to for ourselves. We want people to say, 'He was himself right to the end, you know, even if he couldn't speak/see/hear.' Though science and self-knowledge have led us to doubt what our individuality consists of, we still want to remain in that character which we have perhaps deceived ourselves into believing is ours, and ours alone.

Memory is identity. I have believed this since – oh, since I can remember. You are what you have done; what you have done is in your memory; what you remember defines who you are; when you forget your life you cease to be,

even before your death. I once spent many years failing to save a friend from a long alcoholic decline. I watched her, from close at hand, lose her short-term memory, and then her long-term, and with them most of everything in between. It was a terrifying example of what Lawrence Durrell in a poem called 'the slow disgracing of the mind': the mind's fall from grace. And with that fall – the loss of specific and general memories being patched over by absurd feats of fabulation, as the mind reassured itself and her but no one else – there was a comparable fall for those who knew and loved her. We were trying to hold on to our memories of her – and thus, quite simply, to her – telling ourselves that 'she' was still there, clouded over but occasionally visible in sudden moments of truth and clarity. Protestingly, I would repeat, in an attempt to convince myself as much as those I was addressing, 'She's just the same underneath.' Later I realized that I had always been fooling myself, and the 'underneath' was being – had been – destroyed at the same rate as the visible surface. She had gone, was off in a world that convinced only herself – except that, from her panic, it was clear that such conviction was only occasional. Identity is memory, I told myself; memory is identity.

DYING IN CHARACTER: an instructive case. Eugene O'Kelly was a fifty-three-year-old chairman and CEO of a top American accountancy firm. By his own description, he was a paradigmatic success story: a 'type A' personality

with 20,000 employees under him, a frenetic schedule, children he didn't see enough of, and a devoted wife he referred to as 'my own personal Sherpa'. Here is O'Kelly's account of what he termed 'My Perfect Day':

I have a couple of face-to-face client meetings, my favourite thing of all. I'd meet with at least one member of my inner team. I'd speak on the phone with partners, in New York and in offices around the country, to see how I could help them. I'd put out some fires. Sometimes I'd have a discussion with one of our competitors about how we could work together towards one of our professional common goals. I'd complete lots of items listed in my electronic calendar. And I'd move ahead in at least one of three areas I'd resolved to improve when I was elected to the top spot by the partners of the firm three years earlier: growing our business . . . enhancing quality and reducing risk; and, most vital to me and the long-term health of the firm, making our firm an even better place to work, indeed a great place to work, one that allowed our people to live more balanced lives.

In the spring of 2005, O'Kelly was 'one of 50 CEOs invited to participate at a White House business round-table with President Bush. Was anyone luckier in his job than I?'

But just at that moment, O'Kelly's luck ran out. What he thought was temporary tiredness after an especially tough schedule turned into a slightly drooping cheek muscle, then into a suspicion of Bell's palsy, and then – suddenly, irreversibly – into a diagnosis of inoperable brain cancer. This was one fire that could not be put out. All the most expensive experts could not divert the onrushing truth: three months and barely a day longer.

O'Kelly responds to this news like the 'goal-driven person' and ultimate corporate competitor that he is. 'Just as a successful executive is driven to be as strategic and prepared as possible to "win" at everything, so I was now driven to be as methodical as possible during my last hundred days.' He plans to apply 'the skill set of a CEO' to his predicament. He realizes that he must 'come up with new goals. Fast.' He tries to 'figure out how I as an individual needed to reposition swiftly to adjust to the new circumstances of my life'. He draws up 'the final and most important to-do list of my life'.

Priorities, methods, targets. He gets his business and financial affairs in order. He decides how he is going to 'unwind' his relationships by creating 'perfect moments' and 'perfect days'. He begins 'transition to the next state'. He plans his own funeral. Ever competitive, he wants to make his death 'the best death possible', and after completing his to-do list, concludes: 'Now, I was motivated to "succeed" at death.'

For those who think that any Hundred Days inevitably

leads to Waterloo, the notion of 'succeeding at death' may seem grotesque, even comic. But then everyone's death will be comic to someone. (Do you know what O'Kelly did shortly after learning that he had only three months to live? He wrote a *short story*! As if the world needed another one . . .) And then, with the help of what must inevitably be called a ghost, he put together the book you decide to write – the one about dying – when faced with your final delivery date.

O'Kelly lists and categorizes the friendships he needs to unwind. Even before he gets to his inner circle there are, astonishingly, a thousand names in his book. But with the speed and attack of one used to closing deals, he completes the job in three weeks flat: sometimes with a note or phone call, occasionally with a brief meeting which might perhaps contain a 'perfect moment'. When it comes to unwinding closer friendships there is some sporadic human resistance. One or two friends don't want to be fobbed off with a single farewell, a stroll round the park while shared memories are evoked. But like a true CEO, O'Kelly overrides such clinging sentimentalists. He says firmly, 'I'd like this to be it. I set this up specifically so we could unwind. And we made a perfect moment out of this. Let's take that and go forward. Let's not schedule another one. Trying to improve on a perfect moment never works.'

No, I don't think I'd put it like that either. But then, I doubt I've met anyone quite like O'Kelly. The 'unwinding' he plans for his teenage daughter involves a trip to Prague,

Rome and Venice. 'We would fly by private jet, which would require us to refuel somewhere in the far, far north, and that would give Gina an opportunity to meet and trade with the Inuits.' This is not so much dying in character as dying in caricature. You say goodbye to your daughter, but you also build in for her *an opportunity to trade with the Inuits*? And do you inform the Inuits what their privileged function is to be on this occasion?

Such moments may provoke a satirical and disbelieving gawp. But O'Kelly was surely dying as he had lived, and we should all be so lucky. Whether or not he cheated a little is another matter. The CEO had not previously had much truck with God, because of the tightness of his schedule; though he did use Him as a kind of emergency break-down service. Some years previously, the prospective Inuit-trader had been diagnosed with juvenile arthritis, and her father remembered that 'You could find me in church often that year.' Now, with his own final deal shortly to be closed, O'Kelly again refers things upwards, to the transnational HQ in the sky. He prays, and learns to meditate. He feels supported from 'the other side' and reports that 'there is no pain between this side and the other side'. His wife explains that 'If you conquer fear, you conquer death' – though you don't, of course, end up *not dead*. When O'Kelly expires it is, according to his own personal Sherpa, 'in a state of tranquil acceptance and genuine hope'.

Psychoanalysts tell us that those who are most attached

to their own personalities have the most difficulty in dying. Given O'Kelly's A-typeness, his age, and the swiftness of his end, his behaviour is highly impressive. And perhaps God doesn't mind being addressed only in emergency. It may seem to bystanders that any sensible deity ought to be offended by such spotty, self-interested attention. But He might view things differently. He might, modestly, not want to be a daily, occluding presence in our lives. He might enjoy being a breakdown specialist, an insurance company, a longstop.

O'Kelly didn't want organ music at his funeral; he specified flute and harp. I gave my mother Mozart; she gave my father Bach. We spend time thinking about our funeral music; less about what music we wish to do our dying with. I remember the literary editor Terence Kilmartin, one of my early encouragers, lying on a bed downstairs when he was too weak to climb a stair, listening to late Beethoven string quartets on a portable boom box. Dying popes and emperors could summon their own choirs and instrumentalists to help them sample the glory to come. But modern technology has made popes and emperors of us all; and though you may reject the Christian heaven, you can have the Bach *Magnificat*, Mozart's *Requiem* or Pergolesi's *Stabat Mater* lighting up the inside of your skull as your body fades. Sydney Smith thought of heaven as eating foie gras to the sound of trumpets – which has always felt to me like a clash rather than a concord. Still, you could have the rousing massed brass of Gounod's *St Cecilia Mass*

thundering in your ears while a tube bubbles sugary feed into your arm.

I suspect that if I get any sort of decent dying time, I shall want music rather than books. Will there be space – head-space – for the wonderful trudgery of fiction, the work involved: plot, characters, situation . . . ? No, I think I'm going to need music, fittingly intravenous: straight to the bloodstream, straight to the heart. 'The best means we have of digesting time' will perhaps help us digest the beginnings of death. Music is also associated for me with optimism. I had an instant sense of fellow-feeling when I read that one of the pleasures of Isaiah Berlin's old age was booking concert tickets for months ahead (I often used to spot him, up in the same box at the Festival Hall). Getting the tickets somehow guarantees that you will hear the music, prolongs your life at least until the last echo of the final chords you have paid to hear dies away. Somehow, this wouldn't work with the theatre.

It would, however, depend upon successfully remaining in character. When first considering my best-case death scenario (*x* months, time for 200–250 pages), I took this matter for granted. I assumed that I would remain myself to the end, also instinctively insist on being a writer, keen to describe and define the world even as I was leaving it. But the character may be subjected to sudden jolts, magnifications and distortions in its final stages. A friend of Bruce Chatwin's first realized that the writer must be seriously ill when he paid for lunch, an action hitherto quite

I suspect that if I get any sort of decent dying time, I shall want music rather than books

untypical of him. Who can predict the mind's response to its own short-dated termination?

'WE SHALL PROBABLY die in hospital, you and I.' A foolish thing to write, however statistically probable. The pace, as well as the place, of our dying is fortunately hidden from us. Expect one thing and you will likely get another. On 21 February 1908, Jules Renard wrote: 'Tomorrow I shall be forty-four. It's not much of an age. Forty-five is when you have to start thinking. Forty-four is a year lived upon velvet.' On his actual birthday, he was a little more sombre: 'Forty-four – the sort of age at which you must give up hope of ever doubling your years.'

To admit that you might not make it to eighty-eight seems a modest calculation rather than a declaration of defiance. Even so, by the following year, Renard's health had declined so sharply that he was unable to walk from one end of the Tuileries to the other without sitting down for a chat with the old women selling lilies of the valley. 'I shall have to start taking notes on my old age,' he concluded, and wrote ruefully to a friend, 'I'm forty-five – that wouldn't be old if I were a tree.' Once, he had asked God not to let him die too quickly, as he wouldn't mind observing the process. How much observation did he now think he would need? He made it to forty-six and three months.

When his mother fell backwards into the well, creating 'the soft eddy familiar to those who have drowned an animal', Renard commented, 'Death is not an artist.' Its

virtues are at best artisanal: diligence, stubborn application and a sense of contradictoriness which at times rises
to the level of irony; but it doesn't have enough subtlety, or
ambiguity, and is more repetitive than a Bruckner symphony. True, it has complete flexibility of location, and a
pretty array of encircling customs and superstitions –
though these are our doing, rather than its. Renard noted
one detail certainly unknown to my folklorically impoverished family: 'As death approaches, one smells of fish.'
Now that's something to look out for.

Though why should Death care if we join Renard in
snootily excluding it from the guild of artists? When has it
ever looked for Art's approval? With its co-worker Time, it
just goes about its business, a cheerless commissar reliably
fulfilling a quota of one hundred per cent. Most artists
keep a wary eye on death. Some see it as a hurry-up call;
some optimistically trust that posterity's hindsight will
bring their vindication (though 'Why should people be less
stupid tomorrow than they are today?'); for others, death
is the best career move. Shostakovich, noting that the fear
of death is probably the deepest feeling we have, went on:
'The irony lies in the fact that under the influence of that
fear people create poetry, prose and music; that is, they try
to strengthen their ties with the living and increase their
influence on them.'

Do we create art in order to defeat, or at least defy,
death? To transcend it, to put it in its place? You may take
my body, you may take all the squidgy stuff inside my skull

where lurks whatever lucidity and imagination I possess, but you cannot take away what I have done with them. Is that our subtext and our motivation? Most probably – though *sub specie aeternitatis* (or even the view of a millennium or two) it's pretty daft. '*Les dieux eux-mêmes meurent. | Mais les vers souverains | Demeurent | Plus forts que les airains.*' [The Gods themselves die out, but Poetry, stronger even than bronze, survives everything.] Those proud lines of Gautier's I was once so attached to as a student – everything passes, except art in its robustness; kings die, but sovereign poetry lasts longer than bronze – now read as adolescent consolation. Tastes change; truths become clichés; whole art forms disappear. Even the greatest art's triumph over death is risibly temporary. A novelist might hope for another generation of readers – two or three if lucky – which may feel like a scorning of death; but it's really just scratching on the wall of the condemned cell. We do it to say: I was here too.

WE MAY ALLOW Death, like God, to be an occasional ironist, but shouldn't nevertheless confuse them. The essential difference remains: God might be dead, but Death is well alive.

Death as ironist: the *locus classicus* is the 1000-year-old story I first came across when reading Somerset Maugham. A merchant in Baghdad sends his servant out to buy provisions. In the market the man is jostled by a woman; turning, he recognizes her as Death. He runs home pale

and trembling, and pleads for the loan of his master's horse: he must go at once to Samarra and hide where Death will never find him. The master agrees; the servant rides off. The master himself then goes down to the market, accosts Death and rebukes her for threatening his servant. Oh, replies Death, but I made no threatening gesture – that was just surprise. I was startled to see the fellow in Baghdad this morning, given that I have an appointment with him in Samarra tonight.

And here is a more modern story. Pavel Apostolov was a musicologist, composer for brass band, and lifelong persecutor of Shostakovich. During the Great Patriotic War he had been a colonel commanding a regiment; afterwards, he became a key member of the Central Committee's music section. Shostakovich said of him: 'He rode in on a white horse, and did away with music.' In 1948, Apostolov's committee forced the composer to recant his musical sins, and drove him close to suicide.

Twenty years later, Shostakovich's death-haunted 14th Symphony was given a 'closed premiere' in the Small Hall of the Moscow Conservatoire. This was in effect a private vetting by Soviet musical experts, with no danger of the new work infecting the greater public. Before the concert Shostakovich addressed the audience. The violinist Mark Lubotsky remembered him saying: 'Death is terrifying, there is nothing beyond it. I don't believe in life beyond the grave.' Then he asked the audience to be as quiet as possible because the performance was being recorded.

Lubotsky was sitting next to a female administrator of the Composers' House; beyond her was an elderly, bald man. The symphony had reached its intensely quiet fifth movement when the man jumped up, banged his seat loudly, and rushed out of the hall. The administrator whispered, 'What a bastard! He tried to destroy Shostakovich in 1948, but failed. He still hasn't given up, and he's gone and wrecked the recording on purpose.' It was, of course, Apostolov. What those present didn't realize, however, was that the wrecker was himself being wrecked – by a heart attack which was to prove fatal. The 'sinister symphony of death', as Lubotsky called it, was in fact grimly playing him out.

The Samarra story shows how we used to think of death: as a stalker on the prowl, watching and waiting to strike; a black-clad figure with scythe and hourglass; something out there, personifiable. The Moscow story shows death as it normally is: what we bear within us all the time, in some piece of potentially berserk genetic material, in some flawed organ, in the time-stamped machinery of which we are made up. When we lie on that deathbed, we may well go back to personifying death, and think we are fighting illness as if it were an invader; but we shall really just be fighting ourselves, the bits of us that want to kill the rest of us. Towards the end – if we live long enough – there is often a competition among our declining and decaying parts as to which will get top billing on our death certificate. As Flaubert put it, 'No

sooner do we come into this world than bits of us start dropping off.'

The bit of Jules Renard that did for him was his heart. He was diagnosed with emphysema and arteriosclerosis, and began his last year *au lit et au lait* (bed and milk – two and a half litres a day). He said: 'Now that I am ill, I find I want to make some profound and historic utterances, which my friends will subsequently repeat; but then I get too over-excited.' He teasingly gave his sister responsibility for having his bust erected in the little square in Chitry-les-Mines. He said that writers had a better, truer sense of reality than doctors. He felt his heart was behaving like a buried miner, knocking at irregular intervals to signal that it was still alive. He felt that parts of his brain were being blown away like a dandelion clock. He said: 'Don't worry! Those of us who fear death always try to die as stylishly as possible.' He said: 'Paradise does not exist, but we must nonetheless strive to be worthy of it.' The end came in Paris, on 22 May 1910; he was buried at Chitry four days later, without benefit of clergy, like his father and brother before him. At his writerly request, no words were spoken over his body.

Too many French deaths? Very well, here's a good old British death, that of our national connoisseur of mortal terror, Philip Larkin. In the first decades of his life, Larkin could sometimes persuade himself that extinction, when it eventually came, might prove a mercy. But by his fifties, his biographer tells us, 'The dread of oblivion darkened

everything' – and then, 'As he entered his sixties his fears grew rapidly.' So much for my friend G.'s reassurance that things get better after sixty. In the year that was to contain his death, Larkin wrote to a fellow poet, 'I don't think about death *all* the time, though I don't see why one shouldn't, just as you might expect a man in a condemned cell to think about the drop all the time. Why aren't I screaming?' he wondered, referring back to his poem 'The Old Fools'.

Larkin died in hospital in Hull. A friend, visiting him the day before, said, 'If Philip hadn't been drugged, he would have been raving. He was that frightened.' At 1.24 a.m., a typical deathing hour, he said his last words, to a nurse holding his hand: 'I am going to the inevitable.' Larkin was hardly a Francophile (though more cosmopolitan than he affected); but you could, if you wished, take this as an allusion to, and correction of, Rabelais' supposed deathbed utterance: 'I am going to seek a Great Perhaps.'

Larkin's death can do nothing but chill. Pit-gazing led not to calm, but to increased terror; and though he feared death, he did not die stylishly. Did Renard? Given the discretion of French biography, there are no specific details; however, one friend, Alphonse Daudet's son Léon, wrote that he showed 'wonderful courage' in his last illness. Daudet concluded: 'Good writers, like good soldiers, know how to die, whereas politicians and doctors are afraid of death. Everyone can corroborate this remark by looking around them. Though there are, of course, exceptions.'

Here is the old argument, as phrased by Renard when he was young and in good health: 'Death is sweet; it delivers us from the fear of death.' Is this not a comfort? No, it is a sophistry. Or rather, further proof that it will take more than logic, and rational argument, to defeat death and its terrors.

AFTER WE DIE, the hair and the fingernails continue spookily to grow for a while. We all know that. I've always believed it, or half-believed it, or half-assumed there must be 'something in it': not that we turn into shock-heads with vampiric fingernails as we lie in our coffins, but, well, perhaps a millimetre or two of hair and nail. Yet what 'we all know' is usually wrong, in part if not whole. As the friendly thanatologist Dr Sherwin Nuland points out, the matter is simple and incontrovertible. When we die, we stop breathing; no air, no blood; no blood, no possible growth. There might be a brief flicker of brain activity after the heart ceases to beat; but that's all. Perhaps this particular myth springs from our fear of live burial. Or perhaps it's based on honest misobservation. If the body appears to shrink – indeed, does shrink – after death, then the flesh of the fingers might pull back, giving the illusion of nail growth; while if the face looks smaller, this might have the effect of giving you bigger hair.

Being wrong: my brother in error. After our mother's death, he took our parents' ashes to the Atlantic coast of France, where they had often holidayed. He and his wife

scattered them on the dunes with the help of J., our parents' closest French friend. They read 'Fear no more the heat o' the sun' from *Cymbeline* ('Golden lads and girls all must / As chimney-sweepers, come to dust') and Jacques Prévert's poem *'Les Escargots qui vont à l'enterrement'*; my brother pronounced himself 'strangely moved' by the event. Later, over dinner, conversation turned to our parents' annual visits to that part of France. 'I remember being staggered,' my brother told me, 'when J. described how every night Father had kept them up to the early hours with his anecdotes and lively conversation. I can't remember him ever speaking after they moved to that frightful bungalow, and I had imagined that he had forgotten how to be amusing. But evidently I was quite mistaken.' The best explanation I can offer is that our father's French, being superior to our mother's, enabled him for those few weeks of the year to gain linguistic and social primacy; either that, or our mother, when abroad, might deliberately have become a more conventionally listening wife (however unlikely that sounds).

Being wrong: an error of my own in return. I was breast-fed, my brother bottle-fed: from this I once deduced the bifurcation of our natures. But one of my last visits to my mother produced an uncharacteristic moment of near-intimacy. There had been a report in the newspapers concluding that breastfed children were more intelligent than bottle-fed ones. 'I read that as well,' said Ma, 'and I laughed. Nothing wrong with *my two*, I thought.' And

then – under cross-examination – she confirmed that I had no more been breastfed than my brother. I didn't ask her reason: whether a determination to give us an equal start in life, or a squeamishness at a potentially messy business ('Mucky pup!'). Except that it was still not exactly the same start, for she mentioned that we had been fed on different formulae. She even told me the names on the bottles, which I promptly forgot. A theory of temperament based on different brands of commercial baby-milk? That would be pretty tendentious, even I would admit. And nowadays I don't consider my brother's bringing of tea to our mother's sickbed any less warm-hearted than my own self-indulgent (and perhaps lazy) blanket-snuggling.

And here is a more complicated error, if equally long-term. In the early 1950s one of my father's French *assistants*, P., came to us for a few nights until he could find lodgings, and ended up staying the whole year. He was from Corsica, an easy-going fellow with what seemed to my parents the typically Gallic trait of blowing his month's salary as soon as it arrived. He also had an artistic streak: he used to make railway stations out of cornflakes packets, and once gave my parents – perhaps in lieu of rent – two small landscapes he had painted. They hung on the wall throughout my childhood, and struck me as unimaginably skilful; but then, anything remotely representational would have done so. They had a rather dark, Dutch feel to them: one showed a tumbledown bridge across a river, with foliage cascading from the parapet; the other, a windmill against a rowdy sky

with three white-headdressed women picnicking in the foreground. You could tell they were artistically done because of the thick brushstrokes used in river, sky and meadow. During my childhood and adolescence, these two paintings hung in the sitting room; later, at the 'frightful bungalow', they presided over the dining table. I must have glanced at them regularly for fifty years and more, without ever asking myself, or my parents, where exactly P. had set up his box of oils. France – his native Corsica, perhaps – Holland, England?

When I was house-clearing after my mother's death, I found in a drawer two postcards showing exactly the same two views. My first instinct was to assume that they had been specially printed for P. to advertise his work: he always had a beretful of theoretically money-making schemes. Then I turned them over and realized that they were commercially produced art cards of typically Breton scenes: '*Vieux Moulin à Cléden*' and '*Le Pont fleuri*'. What I had all my life imagined to be competent originality was merely competent copying. And then there was a further twist. The cards were signed 'Yvon' in the bottom right-hand corner, as if by the artist. But 'Yvon' turned out to be the name of the card company. So the pictures had been produced in the first place solely in order to be turned into postcards – whereupon P. had turned them back into the 'original' paintings they had never been. A French theorist would have been delighted by all this. I hastened to tell my brother of our fifty-year error, expecting him to be

equally amused. He wasn't at all: for the simple reason that he had a clear memory of P. painting the pictures, 'and of thinking how much cleverer it was to copy than to make something up out of your own head'.

Such factual corrections are easily made, and may even feel mentally refreshing. It will be harder to face error about perceptions and judgements you have come to look upon as your own achievements. Take death. For most of my sentient life I've known the vivid dread, and also felt fully able – despite what Freud maintained – to imagine my own eternal non-existence. But what if I am quite wrong? Freud's contention, after all, was that our unconscious mind remains doggedly convinced of our immortality – a thesis irrefutable by its very nature. So perhaps what I think of as pit-gazing is only the illusion of truth-examination because deep down I do not – cannot – believe in the pit; and this illusion may even continue until the very end if Koestler is right about our consciousness splitting when we are *in extremis*.

And there's another way of being wrong: what if the dread we feel in advance – which seems to us so absolute – turns out to be as nothing compared to the real thing? What if our void-imaginings are but the palest rehearsal for what we experience in the final hours? And what, further, if the approach of death overwhelms all known language, so that we cannot even report the truth? A sense of having been wrong all the time: well, Flaubert did say that contradiction is the thing that keeps sanity in place.

And beyond death, God. If there were a games-playing God, He would surely get especial ludic pleasure from disappointing those philosophers who had convinced themselves and others of His non-existence. A. J. Ayer assures Somerset Maugham that there is nothing, and nothingness, after death: whereupon they both find themselves players in God's little end-of-the-pier entertainment called Watch the Fury of the Resurrected Atheist. That's a neat would-you-rather for the God-denying philosopher: would you rather there was nothing after death, and you were proved right, or that there was a wonderful surprise, and your professional reputation was destroyed?

'Atheism is aristocratic,' Robespierre declared. The great twentieth-century British embodiment of this was Bertrand Russell – helped, no doubt, by the fact that he *was* aristocratic. In old age, with his unruly white hair, Russell looked, and was treated, like a wise man halfway to god-head: a one-man *Any Questions?* panel in himself. His disbelief never wavered, and friendly provocateurs took to asking him how he would react if, after a lifetime of propagandizing atheism, he turned out to be wrong. What if the pearly gates were neither a metaphor nor a fantasy, and he found himself faced by a deity he had always denied? 'Well,' Russell used to reply, 'I would go up to Him, and I would say, "You didn't give us enough evidence".'

WHEN I REMEMBER my father, I often think of how his nails used to curve over the flesh of his fingertips. In the

weeks after his cremation, I used to imagine, not his face or his bones in the furnace, but those familiar fingernails. Beyond that, I think of the various insults his body showed towards the end. A stroke-damaged brain and tongue; a long scar up his belly which he offered to show me once but I lacked the guts to see; spreading bruises on the backs of his hands from the insertion of drips. Unless we are very lucky, our bodies will reveal the history of our dying. One small revenge might be to die and show no signs of having died. Jules Renard's mother was pulled from the well without a scratch or a scar on her. Not that Death – the ultimate bean counter – would care one way or the other. Any more than it cares whether or not we die in character.

We live, we die, we are remembered, we are forgotten. Not immediately, but in tranches. We remember our parents through most of their adult lives; our grandparents through their last third; beyond that, perhaps, lies a great-grandfather with a scratchy beard and a rank odour. Perhaps he smelt of fish. And beyond that? Photographs, and a little haphazard documentation. In the future generations of ancestors will survive on film and tape and disc, moving, talking, smiling, proving that they too were here. As an adolescent I once hid a tape recorder under the table during dinner in an attempt to prove that, far from it being the 'social event' my mother decreed every meal should be, no one ever said anything remotely interesting and I should therefore be excused conversation and allowed to read a book if I preferred. I did not explain these personal

aims, thinking they would become self-evident once the clatter of cutlery, banalities and non sequiturs was played back. Annoyingly, my mother was enchanted by the tape, declaring that we all sounded just like a Pinter play (to my mind a mixed compliment, in both directions). And then we continued exactly as before; and I never kept the tape, so that my parents' voices are quite extinct in the world and play now only in my head.

I see (and hear) my mother in hospital, wearing a green dress, sitting canted over in a wheelchair by her bed. She was cross with me that day: not over tennis, but because I had been asked to discuss her treatment with the doctor. She resented every manifestation of incapacity, just as she resented the futile optimism of physiotherapists. When asked to name the hands on a watch, she declined; when instructed to open or close her eyes, she remained impassive. The doctors were unable to decide if it was a case of couldn't or wouldn't. My assumption was 'wouldn't' – that she was, in lawyer's terminology, 'mute of malice' – because in my company she was able to articulate whole sentences. Painfully – but then the sentences themselves were often filled with pain. For instance: 'You don't understand how difficult it is for a woman who has always controlled her life to be restricted like this.'

I spent some awkward minutes with her that afternoon, then went to find the doctor. His prognosis was very discouraging. As I returned to the ward, I told myself that my face must not betray his professional judgement that the

next stroke would almost certainly kill her. But my mother was way ahead of me. Turning a corner, I saw, from twenty yards or more across a crowded ward, that she was beadily alert for my return; and as I progressed towards her, refining the semi-lie that I was about to tell, she stuck out her sole working forearm and delivered a thumbs-down sign. It was the most shocking thing I ever saw her do; the most admirable too, and the one occasion when she tore at my heart.

She thought the hospital ought to amputate her 'useless' arm; she thought, for some time, that she was in France, and wondered how I had found her; she thought a Spanish nurse came from her Oxfordshire village, and that all the other nurses came from the various parts of England where she had lived in the previous eighty years. She thought it 'stupid' not to have expired in a single go. When she asked, 'Do you have any trouble comprehending me?' she pronounced each syllable of the verb fastidiously. 'No, Ma,' I replied, 'I understand everything you say, but you don't always get things completely right.' '*Ha*,' she retorted, as if I were some smiley physio. 'That's putting it mildly. I'm quite *loopy*.'

Her mixture of wild confabulation and lucid insight was constantly wrong-footing. In general, she seemed serene about whether she was visited or not, and took to saying, 'You must go now,' which was the complete bloody opposite of how she had been for decades. One day I looked down at her fingernails. You could see how long it was

since she had been able to do them; the heavily lacquered and lovingly shaped nails had continued to grow, pushing on to create an eighth of an inch of clear unvarnished whiteness below the cuticle. The nails she had once imagined herself still tending even if sunk in deafness. I looked upwards from the cuticles: the fingers of her dead arm had now swollen to the size, and to the outer texture, of carrots.

Driving back to London, the setting sun in my mirror, the Haffner Symphony on the radio, I thought: if this is what it's like for someone who has worked with her brain all her life, and can afford decent care, I don't want it. Then wondered if I was deluding myself, and would want it, when it came, on any terms; or whether I would have the courage or the cunning to circumvent it; or whether it just happens, and by happening condemns you to see it through, ragingly, dreadingly. However much you escape your parents in life, they are likely to reclaim you in death – in the manner of your death. The novelist Mary Wesley wrote: 'My family has a propensity – it must be our genes – for dropping dead. Here one minute, gone the next. Neat. I pray that I have inherited this gene. I have no wish to linger, to become a bed-bound bore. A short sharp shock for my loved ones is what I want: nicer for them, lovely for me.'

This is a commonly expressed hope, but one my GP disapproves of. Citing this passage, she calls it 'perhaps another manifestation of the contemporary denial of

death', and an attitude that 'attaches no value to the opportunities provided by a final illness'. I don't think either of my parents would have thought of their final illnesses as providing 'opportunities': for sharing memories, saying farewell, expressing remorse or forgiveness; while the funeral-planning – that's to say, their desire for an inexpensive and virtually mourner-free cremation – had been stated some time before. Would my parents have 'succeeded at death' if they had become emotional, confessional, soppy? Would they have found out that this was what they had always wanted? I rather doubt it. Though I regret my father never told me he loved me, I'm pretty sure that he did or had, and his melancholy silence on this and other key matters at least meant that he died in character.

When my mother was first in hospital, there was a comatose old woman in the next bed. She lay on her back, quite unmoving. One afternoon, with my mother in a fairly loopy state of mind, the woman's husband arrived. He was a small, neat, respectable working man, probably in his late sixties. 'Hello, Dulcie, it's Albert,' he announced in a ward-filling voice, with a rich, pure Oxfordshire accent which should have been recorded before it died out. 'Hello my darling, hello my love, are you going to wake up for me?' He kissed her echoingly. 'It's Albert, darling, are you going to wake up for me?' Then: 'I'll just turn you so I can put your hearing aid in.' A nurse arrived. 'I'm putting her hearing aid in. She didn't wake up for me this morning. Oh, it's fallen out. There, I'm going to turn you some more.

Hello darling, hello Dulcie, hello my beautiful, it's Albert, are you going to wake up for me?' And so on, at intervals, for the next quarter of an hour, with a brief break of, 'You said something, didn't you, I know you said something, what did you say?' Then back to 'Hello darling, it's Albert, are you going to wake up for me?' interspersed with more kissing. It pierced the heart (and the head), and was only bearable by its edge of black comedy. My mother and I naturally pretended that nothing was going on, or if it was, nothing that we could hear; though the fact that my father's name had also been Albert was not, I suspect, lost on her.

The fingernails on my mother's useless arm continued to grow at exactly the same rate as the fingernails on the one with which she gave herself the thumbs-down; then she died and, contrary to popular belief, all ten nails stopped growing immediately. As had my father's, which curled round and over the flesh of his finger-pads. My brother's nails (and teeth) have always been stronger than mine, a detail I used to put down to the fact that he is shorter than me, and therefore his calcium is more concentrated. This may be scientific nonsense (and the answer lie in differing brands of commercial baby-milk). In any case, I have thinned my fingernails over the years by running them between my front teeth, automatically, when I am reading, writing, worrying, correcting this very sentence. Perhaps I should stop and find out if they will grow curvingly over my fingertips as my father comes to reclaim me.

———

MY GRANDFATHER, BERT Scoltock, had only two jokes in his repertoire. The first referred to his and Grandma's wedding day, 4 August 1914, and so came with half a century of repetition (rather than honing): 'We were married the day war broke out,' (heavy pause) 'and it's been *war ever since*!!!' The second was a story drawn out as long as possible, about a chap who went into a café and asked for a sausage roll. He took a bite, then complained that there wasn't any sausage in it. 'You haven't reached it yet,' said the café's proprietor. The fellow took another mouthful and repeated his complaint. 'You've bitten right past it,' came the reply – a punchline my grandfather would then reprise.

My brother agrees that Grandpa was humourless; though when I add 'boring and a little frightening', he dissents. But then Grandpa did favour his first-born grandchild, and taught him how to sharpen a chisel. His was a headmasterly presence in the family, and I can easily summon up his disapproval. For instance: every year, he and Grandma would come over for Christmas. Once, in the early sixties, Grandpa, looking for something to read, went to the bookshelves in my bedroom and, without asking, removed my copy of *Lolita*. I can see the Corgi paperback now, see how my grandfather's woodworking and gardening hands methodically broke the spine as he read. This was something I remember my old school friend Alex Brilliant also used to do – though Alex behaved as if breaking a book's spine showed you were engaging intellectually with its contents; whereas Grandpa's (exactly similar)

behaviour seemed to indicate disrespect for both the novel and its author. At every page – from 'fire of my loins' to 'the age when lads / Play with erector sets' – I expected him to throw it down in disgust. Amazingly, he didn't. He had started, so he would finish: English puritanism kept him doggedly ploughing through this Russian tale of American depravity. As I nervously watched him, I began to feel almost as if I had written the novel, and now stood revealed as a secret nymphet-groper. What *could* he be making of it? Eventually, he handed the book back to me, its spine a vertical mess of whitened cicatrices, with the comment, 'It may be *good literature*, but I thought it was SMUTTY.'

At the time, I smirked to myself, as any aesthete going up to Oxford would. But I did my grandfather a disservice. For he had accurately recognized *Lolita*'s appeal to me then: as a vital combination of literature and smut. (There was such a dearth of sexual information – let alone experience – around that a reworking of Renard obtained: 'It is when faced with sex that we turn most bookish.') I also did Grandpa a disservice by suggesting that he left me nothing in his will. Wrong again. My brother corrects me: 'When Grandpa died, he left me his repro Chippendale desk (which I never liked) and he left you his gold half-hunter watch (which I had always coveted).'

An old press cutting in my archive drawer confirms that the desk was a retirement present in 1949, when Bert Scoltock, then sixty, left Madeley Modern Secondary School

after thirty-six years as a head teacher in various parts of Shropshire. He also received an armchair – quite probably that very Parker Knoll; also, a fountain pen, a cigarette lighter, and a set of gold cufflinks. Girls from the Domestic Science Centre baked him a two-tier cake; while Eric Frost, 'representing a group of boys from the Woodwork Centre', gave him 'a nut bowl and mallet'. I remember this last item well since it was always on display at my grandparents' bungalow, yet never used. When it finally came into my possession, I understood why: it was comically impractical, the mallet firing shell-shrapnel all over the room while reducing the nuts to powder. I always assumed that Grandpa must have made it himself, since almost every wooden object in house and garden, from trug to book trough to grandmother clock case, had been sawn and sanded and chamfered and dowelled by his own hands. He had a great respect for wood, which he took to its final conclusion. Shocked by the notion that coffins crafted from fine oak and elm were reduced to ashes a day or two later, he specified that his own be made from deal.

As for the gold half-hunter, it has been in my top desk drawer for decades. It comes with a gold fob-chain for waistcoat-wear and a leather strap if you prefer to dangle it from lapel buttonhole into top pocket. I open its back: 'Presented to Mr B. Scoltock, by Managers, Teachers, Scholars and Friends, after his leaving after 18 years as head teacher at Bayston Hill C of E School. June 30th 1931.' I had no idea my brother had ever coveted it, so I tell him

that now, after forty-odd years of suffering this sinful emotion, the watch is his. 'As for the half-hunter,' he replies, 'I
think he would have wanted you to keep it.' He *would have
wanted*? My brother is winding me up with this hypothetical
want of the dead. He goes on: 'More to the point, I now want
you to keep it.' Yes, indeed, we can only do what *we* want.

I apply to my brother on the subject of Grandpa and
Remorse. His explanation is this: 'When he used to tell me
stories [about the First World War] they would run up to
the time the boat left for France, and then start back again
in hospital in England. He never said a word to me about
the war. I suppose he was in the trenches. He didn't win any
medals, I'm sure, nor was he wounded (not even a blighty).
So he must have been invalided out for trench feet? Shell
shock? Something less than heroic, in any case. Did he let
his chums down? I once thought I'd try to find out what he
actually did in the war – no doubt there are regimental
records, etc. etc.; but of course I never got round to doing
anything.'

In my archive drawer are Grandpa's birth certificate, his
marriage certificate, and his photo album – a red cloth-bound
book titled 'Scenes from Highways & Byways'. It covers
the period 1912 to 1917, after which, it seems, he laid down
his camera. Here is Grandpa astride a motorbike in 1912,
with Grandma perched on the back; roguishly laying his
head on her bosom the following year, while grasping her
knee with his hand. Here he is on his wedding day, hand
around his bride's shoulder and pipe cocked in front of his

white waistcoat, as Europe prepares to blow itself apart; on his honeymoon (a studio shot which has faded less); and with 'Babs' – as my mother was known before becoming Kathleen Mabel – born ten months after the wedding. There are pictures of him on home leave, first with two stripes up – Prestatyn, August 1916 – and finally three. By this time Sergeant Scoltock is in the Grata Quies hospital outside Bournemouth, where he and the other inmates look remarkably perky as they pose in fancy dress for a concert party. Here is my grandfather in blackface, first with a certain Decker (cross-dressing as a nurse), and then with Fullwood (a Pierrot). And here is a sudden deface-ment, a head-shot of a woman, dated in pencil Sept 1915, but with the name (or perhaps the place) erased, and the face so scarred and gouged that only the lips and the Weetabixy hair remain. An obliteration that makes her more intri-guing than 'Nurse Glynn', or even 'Sgt P. Hyde Killed in Action, Dec 1915'. An obliteration which seems to me a much better symbol of death than the ubiquitous skull. You only get down to bone after rotting through time; and when you do, one skull is much like another. Fine as a long-term symbol, but for the action of death itself, try just such a torn, gouged photograph: it looks both personal and instantly, utterly destructive, a ripping away of the light from the eye and the life from the cheek.

  Formal investigation of my grandfather's war service is initially hampered by not knowing his regiment or date of enlistment. The first Scoltock to turn up is a box-maker

invalided out with a medical statement that reads simply: 'Idiot'. (Oh to have an officially designated Idiot in the family.) But then here comes Private Bert Scoltock of the 17th Battalion, Lancashire Fusiliers, who enlisted on 20 November 1915, and two months later took that boat for France with the 104th Infantry Brigade, 35th Division.

My brother and I are surprised that Grandpa joined up so late. I had always imagined him getting fitted out in khaki just as Grandma was falling pregnant. But this must be a piece of back-imagining from our parents' lives: my father joined up and was sent out to India in 1942, leaving my mother pregnant with what turned out to be my brother. Did Grandpa not volunteer until November 1915 because of his daughter coming into the world? He was, as the inscription on his half-hunter confirms, then head teacher at a Church of England school, so perhaps he was in a reserved profession. Or did such a category not yet exist, given that conscription wasn't introduced until January 1916? Perhaps he saw it coming and preferred to volunteer. If Grandma was already a socialist by this time, he might have wanted to show that, despite having a politically suspicious wife, he was nonetheless patriotic. Did one of those smug women come up to him in the street and offer him a white feather? Did he have a close chum who joined up? Was he suffering from a recently married man's fear of entrapment? Is all this absurdly fanciful? Perhaps trying to trace his statement about remorse back to the First World War is misconceived, since it never came

with any date attached. I once asked my mother why Grandpa never talked about the war. She replied, 'I don't think he thought it was very interesting.'

Grandpa's personal records (like those of many others) were destroyed by enemy action during the Second World War. The brigade diary shows that they reached the Western Front in late January 1916; there was heavy rain; Kitchener inspected them on 11 February 1916. In July, they finally saw action (casualties 19th–27th: 8 officers wounded; Other Ranks, 34 killed, 172 wounded). The following month, the brigade was in Vaux, Montagne, and the front line at Montauban; Grandpa would have been in Dublin Trench, where the brigade complained of being shelled by their own under-aiming artillery; later in Chimpanzee Trench, at the south end of Angle Wood. In September and October they were in the line again (4th Sept–31st Oct, Other Ranks Casualties: 1 killed, 14 wounded – 3 accidental, 3 at duty, 4 rifle grenade, 2 bombed, 1 aerial torpedo, 1 bullet). The brigade commander is listed as a certain 'Captain, Brigade Major B. L. Montgomery (later Alamein)'.

Montgomery of Alamein! We used to watch him on the television – 'ghastly little Monty poncing about in black and white', as my brother put it – explaining how he had won the Second World War. My brother and I used to mimic his inability to pronounce his *r*s. 'I then gave Wommel a wight hook', would be our mock summary of the Desert Campaign. Grandpa never told us he had served under Monty – never even told his own daughter, who

would certainly have mentioned it as part of family history every time we tuned in.

The brigade's diary for 17 November 1916 notes: 'The Army Commander has lately seen a very short-sighted man in a Battalion of Infantry and a deaf man in another. These would be a danger in the front line.' (There's a novel would-you-rather: would you rather be deaf or blind in the First World War?) Another note from Command states: 'The number of courts martial held in the Division during the period 1st Dec. 1916 to date tend to show that the state of discipline in the Division is not what it should be.' Over that period the 17th Lancashire Fusiliers had 1 desertion, 6 Sleeping on Post and 2 'accidental' (presumably self-inflicted) injuries.

There is no evidence – there could be no evidence – that my grandfather featured in these statistics. He was an ordinary soldier who volunteered, was shipped out to France for the middle period of the war, and progressed from private to sergeant. He was invalided out with (as I have always understood it) trench foot or feet, 'a painful condition caused by prolonged immersion in water or mud, marked by swelling, blistering, and some degree of necrosis'. He returned to England at an unspecified date, and was discharged on 13 November 1917, along with twenty others from his regiment, as 'No longer physically fit for service.' He was then twenty-eight, and oddly – I assume mistakenly – listed as a private in the records of discharge. And despite my brother's memory, he did

receive medals, if of the lowliest kind – the kind awarded for simply turning up: the British War Medal, given for entering a theatre of war, and the Victory Medal, given to all eligible personnel who served in an operational theatre. The latter reads, on its reverse, 'The Great War for Civilization 1914–1919.'

And there it all runs out, memory and knowledge. These are the available scraps; nothing more can be known. But since family piety is not my motivation, I am not disappointed. I give my grandfather's service, and its secrets, and his silence, as an example. First, of being wrong: thus I discovered that 'Bert Scoltock, so christened, so called, so cremated', in fact began life, in April 1889, at the register office of Driffield in the County of York, as Bertie; and was still Bertie in the census of 1901. Secondly, as an example of how much you can find out, and where that leaves you. Because what you can't find out, and where that leaves you, is one of the places where the novelist starts. We (by which I mean 'I') need a little, not a lot; a lot is too much. We begin with a silence, a mystery, an absence, a contradiction. If I had discovered that Grandpa had been one of the six Sleeping on Post, and that while he was slumbering the enemy had crept up and slaughtered some of his fellow Fusiliers, and that this had caused him great Remorse, a feeling he had carried to the grave (and if I were to discover all this from a hand-written affidavit – mark that remorsefully shaky signature – while clearing out an old bank-deposit box), I might have been satisfied as a

grandson, but not as a novelist. The story, or the potential story, would have been spoilt. I know a writer who likes to linger on park benches, listening in to conversations; but as soon as his eavesdropping threatens to disclose more than he professionally requires, he moves on. No, the absence, the mystery, they are for us (him and me) to solve.

So in 'Scenes from Highways & Byways', my eye is drawn not to Great Uncle Percy in Blackpool or Nurse Glynn or Sgt P. Hyde Killed in Action Dec 1915 but to the lips and hair and white blouse of 'Sept 1915' and the erasure beside the date. Why was this photograph defaced, and its edges ripped as if by raging fingernails? And further, why was it not either removed from the album entirely, or at least pasted over with another photograph? Here are some possible explanations: 1. It was a picture of Grandma, which Grandpa liked, but which she later took against. However, this wouldn't explain the seeming violence of the attack, which has dug through to the album page below. Unless, 1b., it was done after senility took hold, and Grandma had simply failed to recognize herself. Who is this woman, this interloper, this temptress? And so she scratched herself out. But if so, why this picture rather than any other? And why erase the scrap of information next to the date? 2. If this was another woman, was the gouging done by Grandma? If so, roughly when? Shortly after she was stuck into the album, as a dramatic marital strike? Much later, but in Grandpa's lifetime? Or after Grandpa's

death, as a long-delayed act of revenge? 3. Could this, just possibly, be 'a very nice girl called Mabel', after whom my mother was named? What did Grandma once tell my mother – that there would be no bad men in the world if there were no bad women. 4. Grandpa might have done the gouging and attempted ripping himself. This seems highly unlikely as a) it was his album; b) he was experienced in handicrafts, leatherwork and bookbinding, and would certainly have made a better job of it; and c) photo-mutilation is, I suspect, a predominantly female crime. 5. But in any case, consider the dates. Bert (as he had become by 1914) and Nell were married the day war broke out; their daughter was conceived within a month, and born in June 1915. The mystery photograph is dated September 1915. My grandfather volunteered in November 1915, though conscription was to be introduced anyway within a couple of months. Is this, perhaps, the reason he knew about remorse? And my mother, of course, was an only child.

A Bertie who changed into a Bert; a late volunteer; a mute witness; a sergeant discharged as a private; a defaced photograph; a possible case of remorse. This is where we work, in the interstices of ignorance, the land of contradiction and silence, planning to convince you with the seemingly known, to resolve – or make usefully vivid – the contradiction, and to make the silence eloquent.

MY GRANDFATHER PROPOSES, '"Friday. Worked in garden. Planted potatoes."' My grandmother retorts, 'Nonsense,'

and insists, '"Rained all day. Too wet to work in garden."' He shook his head when his *Daily Express* told him of a Red Plot to Rule the World; she tut-tutted when her *Daily Worker* warned her about US Imperialist Warmongers Sabotaging People's Democracies. We all – their grandson (me), the reader (you), even my last reader (yes, you, you bastard) – are confident that the truth lies somewhere in between. But the novelist (me again) is less interested in the exact nature of that truth, more in the nature of the believers, the manner in which they hold their beliefs, and the texture of the ground between the competing narratives.

Fiction is made by a process which combines total freedom and utter control, which balances precise observation with the free play of the imagination, which uses lies to tell the truth and truth to tell lies. It is both centripetal and centrifugal. It wants to tell all stories, in all their contrariness, contradiction and irresolvability; at the same time it wants to tell the one true story, the one that smelts and refines and resolves all the other stories. The novelist is both bloody back-row cynic and lyric poet, drawing on Wittgenstein's austere insistence – speak only of that which you can truly know – and Stendhal's larky shamelessness.

An anecdote about my brother and me. When we were little, he used to put me on my tricycle, blindfold me, and push me as fast as possible into a wall. I was told this by my niece C., who had it from her father. I have absolutely no memory of it myself, and am not sure what, if anything, to deduce from it. But let me dissuade you from an immediate

conclusion. It sounds to me like the sort of game I would have enjoyed. I can imagine my yelp of pleasure as the front tyre hit the wall. Perhaps I even suggested the game, or pleaded for it to be replayed. Without the kind of psychotherapeutic intervention of which I am suspicious, can I discover whether my non-memory comes from deliberate suppression (trauma! terror! fear of my brother! love of my brother! both!) or the unexceptionality of the event. My elder niece C. first described it to me, at the time she and I were dealing with my mother's final decline. She said that she and her sister were told it 'as a funny story' when they were little. But she did also remember concluding 'that it was not a particularly good way to behave, so perhaps he [her father, my brother] intended it as a cautionary tale of sorts'. If so, what might be the moral? Treat your younger sibling better than I did? Learn that life is like being pushed blindfold into a wall?

I apply to my brother for his version. 'The trike story,' he replies. 'I told it, or versions of it, to C. & C. to make them laugh – which, I fear, it did (I can't recall ever telling them anything with a moral to it . . .).' Now, there's having a philosopher for a father. 'In my memory, it was a game we played in the back garden at Acton. An obstacle course was set up on the lawn – logs, tincans, bricks. The game was to tricycle round the course without serious injury. One of us steered the trike while the other one pushed. (I think the trike had lost its chain; but perhaps the pushing aspect added to the sadistic pleasures of the event.) The

steerer was blindfolded. I'm pretty sure we took it in turns to steer and to push; but I suspect that I pushed you faster than you pushed me. I don't recall any major accident (nor even anyone being pushed into a wall – which in fact would not have been at all easy, given the layout of the garden). I don't recall your being frightened. I seem to think we thought it was fun, and rather naughty.'

My niece's initial summary of the game – my brother blindfolding me before pushing me into a wall – might be a child's shorthand memory, emphasizing what she herself would most have feared; or it might be a subsequent abbreviation or reimagining made in the light of her relationship with her father. What's more surprising is that my own memory is blindfold, especially given the elaborateness of the proceedings. I wonder how my brother and I can have acquired logs and cans and bricks from our very small, neat suburban garden, let alone laid out such a course, without it being known and noted, and permitted or forbidden. But my niece rejects this: 'I'm sure your parents never told me the story; in fact, I thought they never knew about it.'

I apply to her younger sister. She too remembers the obstacle course, the blindfolding, the frequency of the game. 'You were then pushed at breakneck speed through the obstacles and the race ended with you being rammed into the garden wall. It was billed as a Great Bit of Fun for both of you, with an undercurrent of doing something that was certainly disapproved of by Mother; I think not so much because of the damage inflicted on you but the misuse of

garden tools and the soiling of washing hanging up to dry. I don't know why we were told this story (or why I remember it). I think it was the only story about you, in fact about the family at all, except for your grandmother vomiting on a boat into a series of yoghurt pots. I think it was supposed to prove to us that children should do whatever they please, in particular if it is silly and displeasing to adults . . . The story was told in a jokey way and we were certainly supposed to laugh and applaud the daring nature of the whole thing. I don't think we ever questioned the truth of it all.'

You see (again) why (in part) I am a novelist? Three conflicting accounts of the same event, one by a participant, two based on memories of subsequent retellings thirty years ago (and containing detail the original teller might himself have since forgotten); the sudden insertion of new material – 'misuse of garden tools', 'soiling of washing'; the emphasis, in my nieces' versions, on a ritual climax to the game – me being pushed into a wall – that my brother denies; the forgetting of the whole episode by its second participant, despite his serfdom as a log-trundler and brick-gatherer; the absence, from my nieces' versions, of a return match in which I got to push the trike; and most of all, the moral variation between what my brother said he had been intending when he told the story (pure amusement), and what his daughters, separately and differently, concluded he was doing. My informants' replies might almost have been scripted to cast doubt on the reliability of oral history. And I am left with a new proposed

definition of what I do: a novelist is someone who remembers nothing yet records and manipulates different versions of what he doesn't remember.

The novelist in the present instance would need to supply the following: who invented the game; how the trike lost its chain; how the pusher instructed the unseeing driver to steer; whether or not Mother Really Knew; which garden tools were used; how the washing got soiled; what sadistic and/or pre-sexual pleasures might have been involved; and why it was the main, almost the only story a philosopher told about his childhood. Also, if the novel were to be multi-generational, whether the two sisters who first heard it subsequently repeated it to their own daughters (and with what humorous or moral purpose) – whether the story dies out, or is changed again in the mouths and minds of a subsequent generation.

For the young – and especially the young writer – memory and imagination are quite distinct, and of different categories. In a typical first novel, there will be moments of unmediated memory (typically, that unforgettable sexual embarrassment), moments where the imagination has worked to transfigure a memory (perhaps that chapter in which the protagonist learns some lesson about life, whereas in the original the novelist-to-be failed to learn anything), and moments when, to the writer's astonishment, the imagination catches a sudden upcurrent and the weightless, wonderful soaring that is the basis for fiction delightingly happens.

These different kinds of truthfulness will be fully apparent to the young writer, and their joining together a matter of anxiety. For the older writer, memory and the imagination begin to seem less and less distinguishable. This is not because the imagined world is really much closer to the writer's life than he or she cares to admit (a common error among those who anatomize fiction) but for exactly the opposite reason: that memory itself comes to seem much closer to an act of the imagination than ever before. My brother distrusts most memories. I do not mistrust them, rather I trust them as workings of the imagination, as containing imaginative as opposed to naturalistic truth. Ford Madox Ford could be a mighty liar, and a mighty truth-teller, at the same time, and in the same sentence.

CHITRY-LES-MINES LIES SOME twenty miles south of Vézelay. A faded blue tin sign proposes a right turn off the main road to *Maison de Jules Renard*, where the boy grew up amid a silent parental war and, years later, the man broke down the bedroom door to find his suicided father. A second tin sign, and a second right turn, leads you to *Monument de Jules Renard*, whose erection he teasingly entrusted to his sister a few months before he died: 'We were wondering this morning who would see to setting up my bust on the little square in Chitry. We thought straight away that we could count on you . . .' The 'little square', a lime-planted triangle in front of the church, has inevitably become the Place Jules Renard. The writer's bronze bust is

supported by a stone column, at the base of which sits his fictional child alter-ego, a brooding Poil de Carotte, looking melancholy and mature for his age. A stone tree climbs up the other side of the column, bursting into leaf around the writer's shoulders: nature enclosing and protecting him, in death as in life. It is a handsome piece of work, and when unveiled in October 1913 by André Renard – pharmacist, former socialist deputy and distant cousin – it must have seemed the only monument this obscure village would ever require. Its size fits the square, and so renders the First World War memorial, only a few yards away, almost apologetic of its presence, its listed names somehow less important, and less of a loss to Chitry, than its arteriosclerotic chronicler.

There is not a shop, a café or even a grimy petrol pump in this straggly village; the only reason for an outsider to stop here is Jules Renard. Somewhere nearby must be the well, doubtless long since filled in, which claimed Mme Renard nearly a century ago. A tricolore on the building opposite the church identifies the *mairie* where both François Renard and his son performed their civic functions, where Jules was kissed on the lips by a bride he had just joined in matrimony ('It cost me 20 francs'). The tarmacked lane between *mairie* and *église* leads out of the village a few hundred yards to the cemetery, which still lies in open countryside.

It is a July day of canicular heat, and the square, sloping graveyard is as bleak and dusty as a parade round. A list of

names and plot numbers is posted at the gate. Failing to realize that this refers to concessions about to expire, I look at first for the wrong Renard in the wrong plot. The cemetery's only other (living) occupant is a woman with a watering can, moving slowly among her favoured graves. I ask her where the writer might be found. 'He's down there on the left, next to the tap,' is her reply.

The village's most famous inhabitant is indeed tucked away in a corner of the graveyard. I remember that Renard *père* was the first person to be buried here without any religious ceremony. Perhaps that is why the family grave seems positioned a little below the salt, or next to the tap (if the tap was there then). It is a square plot, backed against the boundary wall, and protected by a low, green-painted iron railing; the little gate in the middle sticks from successive repaintings, and requires a certain force. Two stone planters sit just inside this gate. The squat tomb lies horizontally across the rear of the plot, and is surmounted by a large stonework book, open at a double page on which are inscribed the names of those lying beneath.

And here they all are, six of them anyway. The father who didn't speak to his wife for thirty of their forty married years, who laughed at the notion that he might kill himself with a pistol, and used a shotgun instead. The brother who imagined that his mortal enemy was the central heating system in his office, who lay on a couch with the Paris telephone directory propping his inert head, and whose end made Jules angry at 'death and its imbecile tricks'. The

mother, silenced at last after a garrulous life by an 'impenetrable' death. The writer who used them all. The wife who as a widow burnt a third of her husband's *Journal*. The daughter who never married and was buried here in 1945 under her nickname Baïe. This was the last time they opened the deep pit at whose edge Jules had seen a fat worm strutting on the day his brother Maurice was interred.

In the last year of his life, when he knew himself condemned, Jules Renard took to visiting cemeteries. One day he went to see the Goncourt Brothers in their Montmartre tomb. The younger brother had been buried there in 1870; the elder, Edmond, in 1896, after a graveside eulogy from the death-fearing Zola. Renard noted in his *Journal* how the brothers' literary pride was such that they disdained mention of their profession. 'Two names, two sets of dates, they thought that was enough. *Hé! hé!*' Renard comments, in that curious French transcription of a cackle. 'That's not anything you can rely upon.' But did such plainness denote vanity – the assumption that everyone would know who they were – or its very opposite, a proper avoidance of boastfulness? Also, perhaps, a sober awareness that, once released into history, no writer's name is guaranteed?

Looking at the vault, thinking of all the Renards crammed in together – only the writer's sister Amélie and son Fantec escaped – and remembering their history of wrangling, hatred and silence, it strikes me that Goncourt would be justified in returning a *Hé! hé!* back at his younger colleague: for the company he is keeping, for that embarrassing sculptural

cliché of the open stone book, for the naff planters. And then there is the inscription beneath which Renard lies. It begins, unsurprisingly, '*Homme de lettres*', after which you might expect, in a filial echo, '*Maire de Chitry*'. Instead, the writer's subsidiary identification is as a member '*de l'Académie Goncourt*'. It feels like a tiny flicker of revenge for that diary entry: '. . . they thought that was enough'.

I look again at the stone planters. One is quite empty, the other contains a stunted yellow conifer, whose colour seems to mock any idea of keeping the memory green. This grave is no more visited than that of the Goncourts, though the proximity of the tap must bring a little passing traffic. I notice that there is still room on the stone book for a few more entries, so go back to the woman with the watering can and ask if there are any Renard descendants still in the village or its environs. She doesn't think so. I mention that no one has been added to the vault since 1945. 'Ah,' she replies, not entirely apropos, 'I was in Paris then.'

It doesn't matter what they put on your tomb. In the hierarchy of the dead it is visitor numbers that count. Is there anything sadder than an unvisited grave? On the second anniversary of his father's death, a mass was said for him in Chitry; only three old women from the village attended; Jules and his wife took a glazed earthenware wreath to the grave. In his *Journal*, he noted: 'We give the dead metal flowers, the flowers that last.' He went on: 'It is less cruel never to visit the dead than to stop going after a certain time.' Here we are less in the territory of 'What

In the hierarchy of the dead it is visitor numbers that count. Is there anything sadder than an unvisited grave?

they would have wanted' than of 'How would they have reacted had they known?' What will happen to my brother if he gets his wish of a garden grave when his widow is also dead and the house is sold? Who wants a decomposing Aristotle expert turning slowly into mulch?

There is something crueller than leaving the dead unvisited. You may lie in a *concession perpetuelle* for which you have paid, but if no one comes to see you, there is no one to hire a lawyer to defend you when the municipality decides that perpetual doesn't always or necessarily mean perpetual. Then, even here, you will be asked to make way for others, to renounce finally the occupation of space on this earth, to stop saying, 'I was here too.'

So here's another logical inevitability. Just as every writer will have a last reader, so every corpse will have a last visitor. By whom I don't mean the man driving the earth-digger who scoops out your remnants when the graveyard is sold off for suburban housing. I mean that distant descendant; or, in my own case, that gratify-ingly nerdy (or rather, charmingly intelligent) graduate student – still bibliophilic long after reading has been replaced by smarter means of conveying narrative, thought, emotion – who has developed a quaint and lonely (or rather, entirely admirable) attachment to long-forgotten novelists of the distant Print Era. But a last visitor is quite different from a last reader. Grave visiting is not an emulative pastime; you do not swap suggestions like swap-ping stamps. So I shall thank my student in advance for

having made the trip, and not ask what he or she really thinks of my books, or book, or anthologized paragraph, or of this sentence. Perhaps, like Renard when he went to Montmartre to see the Goncourts, my last visitor will have taken to cemetery-tramping after being given a death-warning, a Fayum moment, by the doctor; in which case, my sympathies.

Were I to receive such a diagnosis myself, I doubt I should start visiting the dead. I have done enough of that already, and shall have eternity (or at least, until perpetuity no longer means what it says) in their company. I'd rather spend time with the living; and with music, not books. And in those last days I must try to verify a number of things. Whether I smell of fish, for a start. Whether dread takes over. Whether consciousness splits – and whether I shall be able to recognize it if it does. Whether I feel like forgiveness, memory-invoking, funeral planning. Whether remorse descends, and if it can be dispelled. Whether I am tempted – or deceived – by the idea that a human life is after all a narrative, and contains the proper satisfactions of a decent novel. Whether courage means not scaring others, or something considerably greater and probably out of reach. Whether I have got this death thing straight – or even a little straighter. And whether, in the light of late-arriving information, this book needs an afterword – one in which the *after* is stressed more heavily than usual.

So that's the view from here, now, from what, if I am lucky, if my parents are any sort of guide, might be

three-quarters of the way through my life; though we know
death to be contradictory, and should expect any railway
station, pavement, overheated office or pedestrian crossing to be called Samarra. Premature, I hope, to write:
farewell me. Premature also to scribble that graffito from
the cell wall: I was here too. But not premature to write the
words which, I realize, I have never put in a book before.
Not here, anyway, on the last page:

THE END

Or does that look a little loud? Perhaps better in upper and
lower case:

The End

No, that doesn't look . . . final enough. A last would-you-
rather, but an answerable one.

Note to printer: small caps, please.

THE END

Yes, I think that's more like it. Don't you?

JB
London, 2005–7

© Alan Edwards

JULIAN BARNES is one of Britain's most famous, best-loved writers. His first book was published when he was 34; before then, he was a lexicographer and a TV critic. His work is extremely diverse – he writes novels, stories and non-fiction – but it is the idea of mortality that has most continually preoccupied him.

Nothing To Be Frightened Of (from which this book is taken) puzzles over life's great unimaginable, inevitable conclusion and is also a memoir of Barnes's family. *Levels of Life* is his deeply moving portrait of losing a beloved wife. His most recent novel, *The Noise of Time* and his Booker Prize-wining, *The Sense of an Ending*, also deal with the theme of death.

Barnes has long been a fan of Leicester City Football Club. He lives in London.

RECOMMENDED BOOKS BY JULIAN BARNES:

Levels of Life
The Sense of an Ending
The Noise of Time

How do we cope with Death?

Calm
TIM PARKS

VINTAGE MINIS

Drinking
JOHN CHEEVER

VINTAGE MINIS

Babies
ANNE ENRIGHT

VINTAGE MINIS

Psychedelics
ALDOUS HUXLEY

VINTAGE MINIS

VINTAGE MINIS

The Vintage Minis bring you the world's greatest writers on the experiences that make us human. These stylish, entertaining little books explore the whole spectrum of life – from birth to death, and everything in between. Which means there's something here for everyone, whatever your story.

vintageminis.co.uk

Depression
WILLIAM STYRON

VINTAGE MINIS

Author's note

This book began as a lecture given in Baltimore in May 1989 at a symposium on affective disorders sponsored by the Department of Psychiatry of The Johns Hopkins University School of Medicine. Greatly expanded, the text became an essay published in December of that year in *Vanity Fair*. I had originally intended to begin with a narrative of a trip I made to Paris – a trip which had special significance for me in terms of the development of the depressive illness from which I had suffered. But despite the exceptionally ample amount of space I was given by the magazine, there was an inevitable limit, and I had to discard this part in favor of other matters I wanted to deal with. In the present version, that section has been restored to its place at the beginning. Except for a few relatively minor changes and additions, the rest of the text remains as it originally appeared.

– W. S.

Darkness Visible

For the thing which
I greatly feared is come upon me,
and that which I was afraid of
Is come unto me.
I was not in safety, neither
had I rest, neither was I quiet;
yet trouble came.

– Job

I

IN PARIS ON A CHILLY evening late in October of 1985 I first became fully aware that the struggle with the disorder in my mind – a struggle which had engaged me for several months – might have a fatal outcome. The moment of revelation came as the car in which I was riding moved down a rain-slick street not far from the Champs-Élysées and slid past a dully glowing neon sign that read HÔTEL WASHINGTON. I had not seen that hotel in nearly thirty-five years, since the spring of 1952, when for several nights it had become my initial Parisian roosting place. In the first few months of my *Wanderjahr*, I had come down to Paris by train from Copenhagen, and landed at the Hôtel Washington through the whimsical determination of a New York travel agent. In those days the hotel was one of the many damp, plain hostelries made for tourists, chiefly American, of very modest means who, if they were like me – colliding nervously for the first time with the French and their droll kinks – would always remember how the

exotic bidet, positioned solidly in the drab bedroom, along with the toilet far down the ill-lit hallway, virtually defined the chasm between Gallic and Anglo-Saxon cultures. But I stayed at the Washington for only a short time. Within days I had been urged out of the place by some newly found young American friends who got me installed in an even seedier but more colorful hotel in Montparnasse, hard by Le Dôme and other suitably literary hangouts. (In my mid-twenties, I had just published a first novel and was a celebrity, though one of very low rank since few of the Americans in Paris had heard of my book, let alone read it.) And over the years the Hôtel Washington gradually disappeared from my consciousness.

It reappeared, however, that October night when I passed the gray stone façade in a drizzle, and the recollection of my arrival so many years before started flooding back, causing me to feel that I had come fatally full circle. I recall saying to myself that when I left Paris for New York the next morning it would be a matter of forever. I was shaken by the certainty with which I accepted the idea that I would never see France again, just as I would never recapture a lucidity that was slipping away from me with terrifying speed.

Only days before I had concluded that I was suffering from a serious depressive illness, and was floundering helplessly in my efforts to deal with it. I wasn't cheered by the festive occasion that had brought me to France. Of the many dreadful manifestations of the disease, both physical

and psychological, a sense of self-hatred – or, put less cat-egorically, a failure of self-esteem – is one of the most universally experienced symptoms, and I had suffered more and more from a general feeling of worthlessness as the malady had progressed. My dank joylessness was therefore all the more ironic because I had flown on a rushed four-day trip to Paris in order to accept an award which should have sparklingly restored my ego. Earlier that summer I received word that I had been chosen to receive the Prix Mondial Cino del Duca, given annually to an artist or scientist whose work reflects themes or prin-ciples of a certain "humanism." The prize was established in memory of Cino del Duca, an immigrant from Italy who amassed a fortune just before and after World War II by printing and distributing cheap magazines, principally comic books, though later branching out into publications of quality; he became proprietor of the newspaper *Paris-Jour*. He also produced movies and was a prominent racehorse owner, enjoying the pleasure of having many winners in France and abroad. Aiming for noble cultural satisfactions, he evolved into a renowned philanthropist and along the way established a book-publishing firm that began to produce works of literary merit (by chance, my first novel, *Lie Down in Darkness*, was one of del Duca's offerings, in a translation entitled *Un Lit de Ténèbres*); by the time of his death in 1967 this house, Éditions Mondi-ales, became an important entity of a multifold empire that was rich yet prestigious enough for there to be scant

memory of its comic-book origins when del Duca's widow, Simone, created a foundation whose chief function was the annual bestowal of the eponymous award.

The Prix Mondial Cino del Duca has become greatly respected in France – a nation pleasantly besotted with cultural prizegiving – not only for its eclecticism and the distinction shown in the choice of its recipients but for the openhandedness of the prize itself, which that year amounted to approximately $25,000. Among the winners during the past twenty years have been Konrad Lorenz, Alejo Carpentier, Jean Anouilh, Ignazio Silone, Andrei Sakharov, Jorge Luis Borges and one American, Lewis Mumford. (No women as yet, feminists take note.) As an American, I found it especially hard not to feel honored by inclusion in their company. While the giving and receiving of prizes usually induce from all sources an unhealthy uprising of false modesty, backbiting, self-torture and envy, my own view is that certain awards, though not necessary, can be very nice to receive. The Prix del Duca was to me so straightforwardly nice that any extensive self-examination seemed silly, and so I accepted gratefully, writing in reply that I would honor the reasonable requirement that I be present for the ceremony. At that time I looked forward to a leisurely trip, not a hasty turnaround. Had I been able to foresee my state of mind as the date of the award approached, I would not have accepted at all.

Depression is a disorder of mood, so mysteriously painful and elusive in the way it becomes known to the self – to

the mediating intellect – as to verge close to being beyond description. It thus remains nearly incomprehensible to those who have not experienced it in its extreme mode, although the gloom, "the blues" which people go through occasionally and associate with the general hassle of everyday existence, are of such prevalence that they do give many individuals a hint of the illness in its catastrophic form. But at the time of which I write I had descended far past those familiar, manageable doldrums. In Paris, I am able to see now, I was at a critical stage in the development of the disease, situated at an ominous way station between its unfocused stirrings earlier that summer and the near-violent denouement of December, which sent me into the hospital. I will later attempt to describe the evolution of this malady, from its earliest origins to my eventual hospitalization and recovery, but the Paris trip has retained a notable meaning for me.

On the day of the award ceremony, which was to take place at noon and be followed by a formal luncheon, I woke up at midmorning in my room at the Hôtel Pont-Royal commenting to myself that I felt reasonably sound, and I passed the good word along to my wife, Rose. Aided by the minor tranquilizer Halcion, I had managed to defeat my insomnia and get a few hours' sleep. Thus I was in fair spirits. But such wan cheer was an habitual pretense which I knew meant very little, for I was certain to feel ghastly before nightfall. I had come to a point where I was carefully monitoring each phase of my deteriorating condition.

My acceptance of the illness followed several months of denial during which, at first, I had ascribed the malaise and restlessness and sudden fits of anxiety to withdrawal from alcohol; I had abruptly abandoned whiskey and all other intoxicants that June. During the course of my worsening emotional climate I had read a certain amount on the subject of depression, both in books tailored for the layman and in weightier professional works including the psychiatrists' bible, *DSM* (*The Diagnostic and Statistical Manual of the American Psychiatric Association*). Throughout much of my life I have been compelled, perhaps unwisely, to become an autodidact in medicine, and have accumulated a better-than-average amateur's knowledge about medical matters (to which many of my friends, surely unwisely, have often deferred), and so it came as an astonishment to me that I was close to a total ignoramus about depression, which can be as serious a medical affair as diabetes or cancer. Most likely, as an incipient depressive, I had always subconsciously rejected or ignored the proper knowledge; it cut too close to the psychic bone, and I shoved it aside as an unwelcome addition to my store of information.

At any rate, during the few hours when the depressive state itself eased off long enough to permit the luxury of concentration, I had recently filled this vacuum with fairly extensive reading and I had absorbed many fascinating and troubling facts, which, however, I could not put to practical use. The most honest authorities face up square to the fact that serious depression is not readily treatable.

Unlike, let us say, diabetes, where immediate measures taken to rearrange the body's adaptation to glucose can dramatically reverse a dangerous process and bring it under control, depression in its major stages possesses no quickly available remedy: failure of alleviation is one of the most distressing factors of the disorder as it reveals itself to the victim, and one that helps situate it squarely in the category of grave diseases. Except in those maladies strictly designated as malignant or degenerative, we expect *some* kind of treatment and eventual amelioration, by pills or physical therapy or diet or surgery, with a logical progression from the initial relief of symptoms to final cure. Frighteningly, the layman-sufferer from major depression, taking a peek into some of the many books currently on the market, will find much in the way of theory and symptomatology and very little that legitimately suggests the possibility of quick rescue. Those that do claim an easy way out are glib and most likely fraudulent. There are decent popular works which intelligently point the way toward treatment and cure, demonstrating how certain therapies – psychotherapy or pharmacology, or a combination of these – can indeed restore people to health in all but the most persistent and devastating cases; but the wisest books among them underscore the hard truth that serious depressions do not disappear overnight. All of this emphasizes an essential though difficult reality which I think needs stating at the outset of my own chronicle: the disease of depression remains a great mystery. It has

yielded its secrets to science far more reluctantly than many of the other major ills besetting it. The intense and sometimes comically strident factionalism that exists in present-day psychiatry – the schism between the believers in psychotherapy and the adherents of pharmacology – resembles the medical quarrels of the eighteenth century (to bleed or not to bleed) and almost defines in itself the inexplicable nature of depression and the difficulty of its treatment. As a clinician in the field told me honestly and, I think, with a striking deftness of analogy: "If you compare our knowledge with Columbus's discovery of America, America is yet unknown; we are still down on that little island in the Bahamas."

In my reading I had learned, for example, that in at least one interesting respect my own case was atypical. Most people who begin to suffer from the illness are laid low in the morning, with such malefic effect that they are unable to get out of bed. They feel better only as the day wears on. But my situation was just the reverse. While I was able to rise and function almost normally during the earlier part of the day, I began to sense the onset of the symptoms at midafternoon or a little later – gloom crowding in on me, a sense of dread and alienation and, above all, stifling anxiety. I suspect that it is basically a matter of indifference whether one suffers the most in the morning or the evening: if these states of excruciating near-paralysis are similar, as they probably are, the question of timing would seem to be academic. But it was no doubt the turnabout of

the usual daily onset of symptoms that allowed me that morning in Paris to proceed without mishap, feeling more or less self-possessed, to the gloriously ornate palace on the Right Bank that houses the Foundation Cino del Duca. There, in a rococo salon, I was presented with the award before a small crowd of French cultural figures, and made my speech of acceptance with what I felt was passable aplomb, stating that while I was donating the bulk of my prize money to various organizations fostering French–American goodwill, including the American Hospital in Neuilly, there was a limit to altruism (this spoken jokingly) and so I hoped it would not be taken amiss if I held back a small portion for myself.

What I did not say, and which was no joke, was that the amount I was withholding was to pay for two tickets the next day on the Concorde, so that I might return speedily with Rose to the United States, where just a few days before I had made an appointment to see a psychiatrist. For reasons that I'm sure had to do with a reluctance to accept the reality that my mind was dissolving, I had avoided seeking psychiatric aid during the past weeks, as my distress intensified. But I knew I couldn't delay the confrontation indefinitely, and when I did finally make contact by telephone with a highly recommended therapist, he encouraged me to make the Paris trip, telling me that he would see me as soon as I returned. I very much needed to get back, and fast. Despite the evidence that I was in serious difficulty, I wanted to maintain the rosy

view. A lot of the literature available concerning depression is, as I say, breezily optimistic, spreading assurances that nearly all depressive states will be stabilized or reversed if only the suitable antidepressant can be found; the reader is of course easily swayed by promises of quick remedy. In Paris, even as I delivered my remarks, I had a need for the day to be over, felt a consuming urgency to fly to America and the office of the doctor, who would whisk my malaise away with his miraculous medications. I recollect that moment clearly now, and am hardly able to believe that I possessed such ingenuous hope, or that I could have been so unaware of the trouble and peril that lay ahead.

Simone del Duca, a large dark-haired woman of queenly manner, was understandably incredulous at first, and then enraged, when after the presentation ceremony I told her that I could not join her at lunch upstairs in the great mansion, along with a dozen or so members of the Académie Française, who had chosen me for the prize. My refusal was both emphatic and simpleminded; I told her point-blank that I had arranged instead to have lunch at a restaurant with my French publisher, Françoise Gallimard. Of course this decision on my part was outrageous; it had been announced months before to me and everyone else concerned that a luncheon – moreover, a luncheon in my honor – was part of the day's pageantry. But my behavior was really the result of the illness, which had progressed far enough to produce some of its most famous and

sinister hallmarks: confusion, failure of mental focus and lapse of memory. At a later stage my entire mind would be dominated by anarchic disconnections; as I have said, there was now something that resembled bifurcation of mood: lucidity of sorts in the early hours of the day, gathering murk in the afternoon and evening. It must have been during the previous evening's murky distractedness that I made the luncheon date with Françoise Gallimard, forgetting my del Duca obligations. That decision continued to completely master my thinking, creating in me such obstinate determination that now I was able to blandly insult the worthy Simone del Duca. *"Alors!"* she exclaimed to me, and her face flushed angrily as she whirled in a stately volte-face, *"au . . . re-voir!"* Suddenly I was flabbergasted, stunned with horror at what I had done. I fantasized a table at which sat the hostess and the Académie Française, the guest of honor at La Coupole. I implored Madame's assistant, a bespectacled woman with a clipboard and an ashen, mortified expression, to try to reinstate me: it was all a terrible mistake, a mixup, a *malentendu*. And then I blurted some words that a lifetime of general equilibrium, and a smug belief in the impregnability of my psychic health, had prevented me from believing I could ever utter; I was chilled as I heard myself speak them to this perfect stranger. "I'm sick," I said, *"un problème psychiatrique."*

Madame del Duca was magnanimous in accepting my apology and the lunch went off without further strain,

although I couldn't completely rid myself of the suspicion, as we chatted somewhat stiffly, that my benefactress was still disturbed by my conduct and thought me a weird number. The lunch was a long one, and when it was over I felt myself entering the afternoon shadows with their encroaching anxiety and dread. A television crew from one of the national channels was waiting (I had forgotten about them, too), ready to take me to the newly opened Picasso Museum, where I was supposed to be filmed looking at the exhibits and exchanging comments with Rose. This turned out to be, as I knew it would, not a captivating promenade but a demanding struggle, a major ordeal. By the time we arrived at the museum, having dealt with heavy traffic, it was past four o'clock and my brain had begun to endure its familiar siege: panic and dislocation, and a sense that my thought processes were being engulfed by a toxic and unnameable tide that obliterated any enjoyable response to the living world. This is to say more specifically that instead of pleasure – certainly instead of the pleasure I should be having in this sumptuous showcase of bright genius – I was feeling in my mind a sensation close to, but indescribably different from, actual pain. This leads me to touch again on the elusive nature of such distress. That the word "indescribable" should present itself is not fortuitous, since it has to be emphasized that if the pain were readily describable most of the countless sufferers from this ancient affliction would have been able to confidently depict for their friends and loved ones (even

their physicians) some of the actual dimensions of their torment, and perhaps elicit a comprehension that has been generally lacking; such incomprehension has usually been due not to a failure of sympathy but to the basic inability of healthy people to imagine a form of torment so alien to everyday experience. For myself, the pain is most closely connected to drowning or suffocation – but even these images are off the mark. William James, who battled depression for many years, gave up the search for an adequate portrayal, implying its near-impossibility when he wrote in *The Varieties of Religious Experience*: "It is a positive and active anguish, a sort of psychical neuralgia wholly unknown to normal life."

The pain persisted during my museum tour and reached a crescendo in the next few hours when, back at the hotel, I fell onto the bed and lay gazing at the ceiling, nearly immobilized and in a trance of supreme discomfort. Rational thought was usually absent from my mind at such times, hence *trance*. I can think of no more apposite word for this state of being, a condition of helpless stupor in which cognition was replaced by that "positive and active anguish." And one of the most unendurable aspects of such an interlude was the inability to sleep. It had been my custom of a near-lifetime, like that of vast numbers of people, to settle myself into a soothing nap in the late afternoon, but the disruption of normal sleep patterns is a notoriously devastating feature of depression; to the injurious sleeplessness with which I had been afflicted each

night was added the insult of this afternoon insomnia, diminutive by comparison but all the more horrendous because it struck during the hours of the most intense misery. It had become clear that I would never be granted even a few minutes' relief from my full-time exhaustion. I clearly recall thinking, as I lay there while Rose sat nearby reading, that my afternoons and evenings were becoming almost measurably worse, and that this episode was the worst to date. But I somehow managed to reassemble myself for dinner with – who else? – Françoise Gallimard, co-victim along with Simone del Duca of the frightful lunchtime contretemps. The night was blustery and raw, with a chill wet wind blowing down the avenues, and when Rose and I met Françoise and her son and a friend at La Lorraine, a glittering brasserie not far from L'Étoile, rain was descending from the heavens in torrents. Someone in the group, sensing my state of mind, apologized for the evil night, but I recall thinking that even if this were one of those warmly scented and passionate evenings for which Paris is celebrated I would respond like the zombie I had become. The weather of depression is unmodulated, its light a brownout.

And zombielike, halfway through the dinner, I lost the del Duca prize check for $25,000. Having tucked the check in the inside breast pocket of my jacket, I let my hand stray idly to that place and realized that it was gone. Did I "intend" to lose the money? Recently I had been deeply bothered that I was not deserving of the prize. I believe in

the reality of the accidents we subconsciously perpetrate on ourselves, and so how easy it was for this loss to be not loss but a form of repudiation, offshoot of that self-loathing (depression's premier badge) by which I was persuaded that I could not be worthy of the prize, that I was in fact not worthy of any of the recognition that had come my way in the past few years. Whatever the reason for its disappearance, the check was gone, and its loss dovetailed well with the other failures of the dinner: my failure to have an appetite for the grand *plateau de fruits de mer* placed before me, failure of even forced laughter and, at last, virtually total failure of speech. At this point the ferocious *inwardness* of the pain produced an immense distraction that prevented my articulating words beyond a hoarse murmur; I sensed myself turning wall-eyed, monosyllabic, and also I sensed my French friends becoming uneasily aware of my predicament. It was a scene from a bad operetta by now: all of us near the floor, searching for the vanished money. Just as I signaled that it was time to go, Françoise's son discovered the check, which had somehow slipped out of my pocket and fluttered under an adjoining table, and we went forth into the rainy night. Then, while I was riding in the car, I thought of Albert Camus and Romain Gary.

I sensed myself turning wall-eyed, monosyllabic, and also I sensed my French friends becoming uneasily aware of my predicament

II

WHEN I WAS a young writer there had been a stage where Camus, almost more than any other contemporary literary figure, radically set the tone for my own view of life and history. I read his novel *The Stranger* somewhat later than I should have – I was in my early thirties – but after finishing it I received the stab of recognition that proceeds from reading the work of a writer who has wedded moral passion to a style of great beauty and whose unblinking vision is capable of frightening the soul to its marrow. The cosmic loneliness of Meursault, the hero of that novel, so haunted me that when I set out to write *The Confessions of Nat Turner* I was impelled to use Camus's device of having the story flow from the point of view of a narrator isolated in his jail cell during the hours before his execution. For me there was a spiritual connection between Meursault's frigid solitude and the plight of Nat Turner – his rebel predecessor in history by a hundred years – likewise condemned and abandoned by man and God. Camus's essay

"Reflections on the Guillotine" is a virtually unique document, freighted with terrible and fiery logic; it is difficult to conceive of the most vengeful supporter of the death penalty retaining the same attitude after exposure to scathing truths expressed with such ardor and precision. I know my thinking was forever altered by that work, not only turning me around completely, convincing me of the essential barbarism of capital punishment, but establishing substantial claims on my conscience in regard to matters of responsibility at large. Camus was a great cleanser of my intellect, ridding me of countless sluggish ideas, and through some of the most unsettling pessimism I had ever encountered causing me to be aroused anew by life's enigmatic promise.

The disappointment I always felt at never meeting Camus was compounded by that failure having been such a near miss. I had planned to see him in 1960, when I was traveling to France and had been told in a letter by the writer Romain Gary that he was going to arrange a dinner in Paris where I would meet Camus. The enormously gifted Gary, whom I knew slightly at the time and who later became a cherished friend, had informed me that Camus, whom he saw frequently, had read my *Un Lit de Ténèbres* and had admired it; I was of course greatly flattered and felt that a get-together would be a splendid happening. But before I arrived in France there came the appalling news: Camus had been in an automobile crash, and was dead at the cruelly young age of forty-six. I have almost never felt

so intensely the loss of someone I didn't know. I pondered his death endlessly. Although Camus had not been driving he supposedly knew the driver, who was the son of his publisher, to be a speed demon; so there was an element of recklessness in the accident that bore overtones of the near-suicidal, at least of a death flirtation, and it was inevitable that conjectures concerning the event should revert back to the theme of suicide in the writer's work. One of the century's most famous intellectual pronouncements comes at the beginning of *The Myth of Sisyphus*: "There is but one truly serious philosophical problem, and that is suicide. Judging whether life is or is not worth living amounts to answering the fundamental question of philosophy." Reading this for the first time I was puzzled and continued to be throughout much of the essay, since despite the work's persuasive logic and eloquence there was a lot that eluded me, and I always came back to grapple vainly with the initial hypothesis, unable to deal with the premise that anyone should come close to wishing to kill himself in the first place. A later short novel, *The Fall*, I admired with reservations; the guilt and self-condemnation of the lawyer-narrator, gloomily spinning out his monologue in an Amsterdam bar, seemed a touch clamorous and excessive, but at the time of my reading I was unable to perceive that the lawyer was behaving very much like a man in the throes of clinical depression. Such was my innocence of the very existence of this disease.

Camus, Romain told me, occasionally hinted at his own

deep despondency and had spoken of suicide. Sometimes he spoke in jest, but the jest had the quality of sour wine, upsetting Romain. Yet apparently he made no attempts and so perhaps it was not coincidental that, despite its abiding tone of melancholy, a sense of the triumph of life over death is at the core of *The Myth of Sisyphus* with its austere message: in the absence of hope we must still struggle to survive, and so we do – by the skin of our teeth. It was only after the passing of some years that it seemed credible to me that Camus's statement about suicide, and his general preoccupation with the subject, might have sprung at least as strongly from some persistent distur-bance of mood as from his concerns with ethics and epistemology. Gary again discussed at length his assump-tions about Camus's depression during August of 1978, when I had lent him my guest cottage in Connecticut, and I came down from my summer home on Martha's Vineyard to pay him a weekend visit. As we talked I felt that some of Romain's suppositions about the seriousness of Camus's recurring despair gained weight from the fact that he, too, had begun to suffer from depression, and he freely admitted as much. It was not incapacitating, he insisted, and he had it under control, but he felt it from time to time, this leaden and poisonous mood the color of verdigris, so incongruous in the midst of the lush New England summer. A Russian Jew born in Lithuania, Romain had always seemed possessed of an Eastern European mel-ancholy, so it was hard to tell the difference. Nonetheless,

he was hurting. He said that he was able to perceive a flicker of the desperate state of mind which had been described to him by Camus.

Gary's situation was hardly lightened by the presence of Jean Seberg, his Iowa-born actress wife, from whom he had been divorced and, I thought, long estranged. I learned that she was there because their son, Diego, was at a nearby tennis camp. Their presumed estrangement made me surprised to see her living with Romain, surprised too – no, shocked and saddened – by her appearance: all her once fragile and luminous blond beauty had disappeared into a puffy mask. She moved like a sleepwalker, said little, and had the blank gaze of someone tranquilized (or drugged, or both) nearly to the point of catalepsy. I understood how devoted they still were, and was touched by his solicitude, both tender and paternal. Romain told me that Jean was being treated for the disorder that afflicted him, and mentioned something about antidepressant medications, but none of this registered very strongly, and also meant little. This memory of my relative indifference is important because such indifference demonstrates powerfully the outsider's inability to grasp the essence of the illness. Camus's depression and now Romain Gary's – and certainly Jean's – were abstract ailments to me, in spite of my sympathy, and I hadn't an inkling of its true contours or the nature of the pain so many victims experience as the mind continues in its insidious meltdown.

In Paris that October night I knew that I, too, was in the

process of meltdown. And on the way to the hotel in the car I had a clear revelation. A disruption of the circadian cycle – the metabolic and glandular rhythms that are central to our workday life – seems to be involved in many, if not most, cases of depression; this is why brutal insomnia so often occurs and is most likely why each day's pattern of distress exhibits fairly predictable alternating periods of intensity and relief. The evening's relief for me – an incomplete but noticeable letup, like the change from a torrential downpour to a steady shower – came in the hours after dinnertime and before midnight, when the pain lifted a little and my mind would become lucid enough to focus on matters beyond the immediate upheaval convulsing my system. Naturally I looked forward to this period, for sometimes I felt close to being reasonably sane, and that night in the car I was aware of a semblance of clarity returning, along with the ability to think rational thoughts. Having been able to reminisce about Camus and Romain Gary, however, I found that my continuing thoughts were not very consoling.

The memory of Jean Seberg gripped me with sadness. A little over a year after our encounter in Connecticut she took an overdose of pills and was found dead in a car parked in a cul-de-sac off a Paris avenue, where her body had lain for many days. The following year I sat with Romain at the Brasserie Lipp during a long lunch while he told me that, despite their difficulties, his loss of Jean had so deepened his depression that from time to time he

had been rendered nearly helpless. But even then I was unable to comprehend the nature of his anguish. I remembered that his hands trembled and, though he could hardly be called superannuated – he was in his mid-sixties – his voice had the wheezy sound of very old age that I now realized was, or could be, the voice of depression; in the vortex of my severest pain I had begun to develop that ancient voice myself. I never saw Romain again. Claude Gallimard, Françoise's father, had recollected to me how, in 1980, only a few hours after another lunch where the talk between the two old friends had been composed and casual, even lighthearted, certainly anything but somber, Romain Gary – twice winner of the Prix Goncourt (one of these awards pseudonymous, the result of his having gleefully tricked the critics), hero of the Republic, valorous recipient of the Croix de Guerre, diplomat, bon vivant, womanizer par excellence – went home to his apartment on the rue de Bac and put a bullet through his brain.

It was at some point during the course of these musings that the sign HÔTEL WASHINGTON swam across my vision, bringing back memories of my long-ago arrival in the city, along with the fierce and sudden realization that I would never see Paris again. This certitude astonished me and filled me with a new fright, for while thoughts of death had long been common during my siege, blowing through my mind like icy gusts of wind, they were the formless shapes of doom that I suppose are dreamed of by people in the grip of any severe affliction. The difference now was in

the sure understanding that tomorrow, when the pain descended once more, or the tomorrow after that – certainly on some not-too-distant tomorrow – I would be forced to judge that life was not worth living and thereby answer, for myself at least, the fundamental question of philosophy.

III

To MANY OF US WHO KNEW Abbie Hoffman even slightly, as I did, his death in the spring of 1989 was a sorrowful happening. Just past the age of fifty, he had been too young and apparently too vital for such an ending; a feeling of chagrin and dreadfulness attends the news of nearly anyone's suicide, and Abbie's death seemed to me especially cruel. I had first met him during the wild days and nights of the 1968 Democratic Convention in Chicago, where I had gone to write a piece for the *New York Review of Books*, and I later was one of those who testified in behalf of him and his fellow defendants at the trial, also in Chicago, in 1970. Amid the pious follies and morbid perversions of American life, his antic style was exhilarating, and it was hard not to admire the hell-raising and the brio, the anarchic individualism. I wish I had seen more of him in recent years; his sudden death left me with a particular emptiness, as suicide usually does to everyone. But the event was given a further dimension of poignancy by what one must begin to

regard as a predictable reaction from many: the denial, the refusal to accept the fact of the suicide itself, as if the voluntary act – as opposed to an accident, or death from natural causes – were tinged with a delinquency that somehow lessened the man and his character.

Abbie's brother appeared on television, grief-ravaged and distraught; one could not help feeling compassion as he sought to deflect the idea of suicide, insisting that Abbie, after all, had always been careless with pills and would never have left his family bereft. However, the coroner confirmed that Hoffman had taken the equivalent of 150 phenobarbitals. It's quite natural that the people closest to suicide victims so frequently and feverishly hasten to disclaim the truth; the sense of implication, of personal guilt – the idea that one might have prevented the act if one had taken certain precautions, had somehow behaved differently – is perhaps inevitable. Even so, the sufferer – whether he has actually killed himself or attempted to do so, or merely expressed threats – is often, through denial on the part of others, unjustly made to appear a wrongdoer.

A similar case is that of Randall Jarrell – one of the fine poets and critics of his generation – who on a night in 1965, near Chapel Hill, North Carolina, was struck by a car and killed. Jarrell's presence on that particular stretch of road, at an odd hour of the evening, was puzzling, and since some of the indications were that he had deliberately let the car strike him, the early conclusion was that his death was suicide. *Newsweek*, among other publications, said as

much, but Jarrell's widow protested in a letter to that magazine; there was a hue and cry from many of his friends and
supporters, and a coroner's jury eventually ruled the death
to be accidental. Jarrell had been suffering from extreme
depression and had been hospitalized; only a few months
before his misadventure on the highway and while in the
hospital, he had slashed his wrists.

Anyone who is acquainted with some of the jagged contours of Jarrell's life – including his violent fluctuations of
mood, his fits of black despondency – and who, in addition, has acquired a basic knowledge of the danger signals
of depression, would seriously question the verdict of the
coroner's jury. But the stigma of self-inflicted death is for
some people a hateful blot that demands erasure at all
costs. (More than two decades after his death, in the Summer 1986 issue of *The American Scholar*, a one time student
of Jarrell's, reviewing a collection of the poet's letters,
made the review less a literary or biographical appraisal
than an occasion for continuing to try to exorcise the vile
phantom of suicide.)

Randall Jarrell almost certainly killed himself. He did so
not because he was a coward, nor out of any moral feeble-
ness, but because he was afflicted with a depression that
was so devastating that he could no longer endure the
pain of it.

This general awareness of what depression is really like
was apparent most recently in the matter of Primo Levi,
the remarkable Italian writer and survivor of Auschwitz

who, at the age of sixty-seven, hurled himself down a stairwell in Turin in 1987. Since my own involvement with the illness, I had been more than ordinarily interested in Levi's death, and so, late in 1988, when I read an account in the *New York Times* about a symposium on the writer and his work held at New York University, I was fascinated but, finally, appalled. For, according to the article, many of the participants, worldly writers and scholars, seemed mystified by Levi's suicide, mystified and disappointed. It was as if this man whom they had all so greatly admired, and who had endured so much at the hands of the Nazis – a man of exemplary resilience and courage – had by his suicide demonstrated a frailty, a crumbling of character they were loath to accept. In the face of a terrible absolute – self-destruction – their reaction was helplessness and (the reader could not avoid it) a touch of shame.

My annoyance over all this was so intense that I was prompted to write a short piece for the op-ed page of the *Times*. The argument I put forth was fairly straightforward: the pain of severe depression is quite unimaginable to those who have not suffered it, and it kills in many instances because its anguish can no longer be borne. The prevention of many suicides will continue to be hindered until there is a general awareness of the nature of this pain. Through the healing process of time – and through medical intervention or hospitalization in many cases – most people survive depression, which may be its only blessing; but to the tragic legion who are compelled to destroy

themselves there should be no more reproof attached than to the victims of terminal cancer.

I had set down my thoughts in this *Times* piece rather hurriedly and spontaneously, but the response was equally spontaneous – and enormous. It had taken, I speculated, no particular originality or boldness on my part to speak out frankly about suicide and the impulse toward it, but I had apparently underestimated the number of people for whom the subject had been taboo, a matter of secrecy and shame. The overwhelming reaction made me feel that inadvertently I had helped unlock a closet from which many souls were eager to come out and proclaim that they, too, had experienced the feelings I had described. It is the only time in my life I have felt it worthwhile to have invaded my own privacy, and to make that privacy public. And I thought that, given such momentum, and with my experience in Paris as a detailed example of what occurs during depression, it would be useful to try to chronicle some of my own experiences with the illness and in the process perhaps establish a frame of reference out of which one or more valuable conclusions might be drawn. Such conclusions, it has to be emphasized, must still be based on the events that happened to one man. In setting these reflections down I don't intend my ordeal to stand as a representation of what happens, or might happen, to others. Depression is much too complex in its cause, its symptoms and its treatment for unqualified conclusions to be drawn from the experience of a single individual.

Although as an illness depression manifests certain unvarying characteristics, it also allows for many idiosyncrasies; I've been amazed at some of the freakish phenomena – not reported by other patients – that it has wrought amid the twistings of my mind's labyrinth.

Depression afflicts millions directly, and millions more who are relatives or friends of victims. It has been estimated that as many as one in ten Americans will suffer from the illness. As assertively democratic as a Norman Rockwell poster, it strikes indiscriminately at all ages, races, creeds and classes, though women are at considerably higher risk than men. The occupational list (dressmakers, barge captains, sushi chefs, cabinet members) of its patients is too long and tedious to give here; it is enough to say that very few people escape being a potential victim of the disease, at least in its milder form. Despite depression's eclectic reach, it has been demonstrated with fair convincingness that artistic types (especially poets) are particularly vulnerable to the disorder – which, in its graver, clinical manifestation takes upward of twenty percent of its victims by way of suicide. Just a few of these fallen artists, all modern, make up a sad but scintillant roll call: Hart Crane, Vincent Van Gogh, Virginia Woolf, Arshile Gorky, Cesare Pavese, Romain Gary, Vachel Lindsay, Sylvia Plath, Henry de Montherlant, Mark Rothko, John Berryman, Jack London, Ernest Hemingway, William Inge, Diane Arbus, Tadeusz Borowski, Paul Celan, Anne Sexton, Sergei Esenin, Vladimir Mayakovsky – the list goes on. (The Russian poet Mayakovsky was harshly critical

of his great contemporary Esenin's suicide a few years before, which should stand as a caveat for all who are judgmental about self-destruction.) When one thinks of these doomed and splendidly creative men and women, one is drawn to contemplate their childhoods, where, to the best of anyone's knowledge, the seeds of the illness take strong root; could any of them have had a hint, then, of the psyche's perishability, its exquisite fragility? And why were they destroyed, while others – similarly stricken – struggled through?

IV

WHEN I WAS FIRST AWARE that I had been laid low by the disease, I felt a need, among other things, to register a strong protest against the word "depression." Depression, most people know, used to be termed "melancholia," a word which appears in English as early as the year 1303 and crops up more than once in Chaucer, who in his usage seemed to be aware of its pathological nuances. "Melancholia" would still appear to be a far more apt and evocative word for the blacker forms of the disorder, but it was usurped by a noun with a bland tonality and lacking any magisterial presence, used indifferently to describe an economic decline or a rut in the ground, a true wimp of a word for such a major illness. It may be that the scientist generally held responsible for its currency in modern times, a Johns Hopkins Medical School faculty member justly venerated – the Swiss-born psychiatrist Adolf Meyer – had a tin ear for the finer rhythms of English and therefore was unaware of the semantic damage he had

inflicted by offering "depression" as a descriptive noun for such a dreadful and raging disease. Nonetheless, for over seventy-five years the word has slithered innocuously through the language like a slug, leaving little trace of its intrinsic malevolence and preventing, by its very insipidity, a general awareness of the horrible intensity of the disease when out of control.

As one who has suffered from the malady in extremis yet returned to tell the tale, I would lobby for a truly arresting designation. "Brainstorm," for instance, has unfortunately been preempted to describe, somewhat jocularly, intellectual inspiration. But something along these lines is needed. Told that someone's mood disorder has evolved into a storm – a veritable howling tempest in the brain, which is indeed what a clinical depression resembles like nothing else – even the uninformed layman might display sympathy rather than the standard reaction that "depression" evokes, something akin to "So what?" or "You'll pull out of it" or "We all have bad days." The phrase "nervous breakdown" seems to be on its way out, certainly deservedly so, owing to its insinuation of a vague spinelessness, but we still seem destined to be saddled with "depression" until a better, sturdier name is created.

The depression that engulfed me was not of the manic type – the one accompanied by euphoric highs – which would have most probably presented itself earlier in my life. I was sixty when the illness struck for the first time, in the "unipolar" form, which leads straight down. I shall

never learn what "caused" my depression, as no one will ever learn about their own. To be able to do so will likely forever prove to be an impossibility, so complex are the intermingled factors of abnormal chemistry, behavior and genetics. Plainly, multiple components are involved – perhaps three or four, most probably more, in fathomless permutations. That is why the greatest fallacy about suicide lies in the belief that there is a single immediate answer – or perhaps combined answers – as to why the deed was done.

The inevitable question "Why did he [or she] do it?" usually leads to odd speculations, for the most part fallacies themselves. Reasons were quickly advanced for Abbie Hoffman's death: his reaction to an auto accident he had suffered, the failure of his most recent book, his mother's serious illness. With Randall Jarrell it was a declining career cruelly epitomized by a vicious book review and his consequent anguish. Primo Levi, it was rumored, had been burdened by caring for his paralytic mother, which was more onerous to his spirit than even his experience at Auschwitz. Any one of these factors may have lodged like a thorn in the sides of the three men, and been a torment. Such aggravations may be crucial and cannot be ignored. But most people quietly endure the equivalent of injuries, declining careers, nasty book reviews, family illnesses. A vast majority of the survivors of Auschwitz have borne up fairly well. Bloody and bowed by the outrages of life, most human beings still stagger on down the road, unscathed by

Bloody and bowed by the outrages of life, most human beings still stagger on down the road, unscathed by real depression

real depression. To discover why some people plunge into the downward spiral of depression, one must search beyond the manifest crisis – and then still fail to come up with anything beyond wise conjecture.

The storm which swept me into a hospital in December began as a cloud no bigger than a wine goblet the previous June. And the cloud – the manifest crisis – involved alcohol, a substance I had been abusing for forty years. Like a great many American writers, whose sometimes lethal addiction to alcohol has become so legendary as to provide in itself a stream of studies and books, I used alcohol as the magical conduit to fantasy and euphoria, and to the enhancement of the imagination. There is no need to either rue or apologize for my use of this soothing, often sublime agent, which had contributed greatly to my writing; although I never set down a line while under its influence, I did use it – often in conjunction with music – as a means to let my mind conceive visions that the unaltered, sober brain has no access to. Alcohol was an invaluable senior partner of my intellect, besides being a friend whose ministrations I sought daily – sought also, I now see, as a means to calm the anxiety and incipient dread that I had hidden away for so long somewhere in the dungeons of my spirit.

The trouble was, at the beginning of this particular summer, that I was betrayed. It struck me quite suddenly, almost overnight. I could no longer drink. It was as if my body had risen up in protest, along with my mind, and had conspired to reject this daily mood bath which it had so

long welcomed and, who knows? perhaps even come to need. Many drinkers have experienced this intolerance as they have grown older. I suspect that the crisis was at least partly metabolic – the liver rebelling, as if to say, "No more, no more" – but at any rate I discovered that alcohol in minuscule amounts, even a mouthful of wine, caused me nausea, a desperate and unpleasant wooziness, a sinking sensation and ultimately a distinct revulsion. The comforting friend had abandoned me not gradually and reluctantly, as a true friend might do, but like a shot – and I was left high and certainly dry, and unhelmed.

Neither by will nor by choice had I become an abstainer; the situation was puzzling to me, but it was also traumatic, and I date the onset of my depressive mood from the beginning of this deprivation. Logically, one would be overjoyed that the body had so summarily dismissed a substance that was undermining its health; it was as if my system had generated a form of Antabuse, which should have allowed me to happily go my way, satisfied that a trick of nature had shut me off from a harmful dependence. But, instead, I began to experience a vaguely troubling malaise, a sense of something having gone cockeyed in the domestic universe I'd dwelt in so long, so comfortably. While depression is by no means unknown when people stop drinking, it is usually on a scale that is not menacing. But it should be kept in mind how idiosyncratic the faces of depression can be.

It was not really alarming at first, since the change was

subtle, but I did notice that my surroundings took on a different tone at certain times: the shadows of nightfall seemed more somber, my mornings were less buoyant, walks in the woods became less zestful, and there was a moment during my working hours in the late afternoon when a kind of panic and anxiety overtook me, just for a few minutes, accompanied by a visceral queasiness – such a seizure was at least slightly alarming, after all. As I set down these recollections, I realize that it should have been plain to me that I was already in the grip of the beginning of a mood disorder, but I was ignorant of such a condition at that time.

When I reflected on this curious alteration of my consciousness – and I was baffled enough from time to time to do so – I assumed that it all had to do somehow with my enforced withdrawal from alcohol. And, of course, to a certain extent this was true. But it is my conviction now that alcohol played a perverse trick on me when we said farewell to each other: although, as everyone should know, it is a major depressant, it had never truly depressed me during my drinking career, acting instead as a shield against anxiety. Suddenly vanished, the great ally which for so long had kept my demons at bay was no longer there to prevent those demons from beginning to swarm through the subconscious, and I was emotionally naked, vulnerable as I had never been before. Doubtless depression had hovered near me for years, waiting to swoop down. Now I was in the first stage – premonitory, like a flicker of sheet lightning barely perceived – of depression's black tempest.

I was on Martha's Vineyard, where I've spent a good part of each year since the 1960s, during that exceptionally beautiful summer. But I had begun to respond indifferently to the island's pleasures. I felt a kind of numbness, an enervation, but more particularly an odd fragility – as if my body had actually become frail, hypersensitive and somehow disjointed and clumsy, lacking normal coordination. And soon I was in the throes of a pervasive hypochondria. Nothing felt quite right with my corporeal self; there were twitches and pains, sometimes intermittent, often seemingly constant, that seemed to presage all sorts of dire infirmities. (Given these signs, one can understand how, as far back as the seventeenth century – in the notes of contemporary physicians, and in the perceptions of John Dryden and others – a connection is made between melancholia and hypochondria; the words are often interchangeable, and were so used until the nineteenth century by writers as various as Sir Walter Scott and the Brontës, who also linked melancholy to a preoccupation with bodily ills.) It is easy to see how this condition is part of the psyche's apparatus of defense: unwilling to accept its own gathering deterioration, the mind announces to its indwelling consciousness that it is the body with its perhaps correctable defeats – not the precious and irreplaceable mind – that is going haywire.

In my case, the overall effect was immensely disturbing, augmenting the anxiety that was by now never quite absent from my waking hours and fueling still another strange behavior pattern – a fidgety recklessness that kept

me on the move, somewhat to the perplexity of my family and friends. Once, in late summer, on an airplane trip to New York, I made the reckless mistake of downing a Scotch and soda – my first alcohol in months – which promptly sent me into a tailspin, causing me such a horrified sense of disease and interior doom that the very next day I rushed to a Manhattan internist, who inaugurated a long series of tests. Normally I would have been satisfied, indeed elated, when, after three weeks of high-tech and extremely expensive evaluation, the doctor pronounced me totally fit; and I *was* happy, for a day or two, until there once again began the rhythmic daily erosion of my mood – anxiety, agitation, unfocused dread.

By now I had moved back to my house in Connecticut. It was October, and one of the unforgettable features of this stage of my disorder was the way in which my own farmhouse, my beloved home for thirty years, took on for me at that point when my spirits regularly sank to their nadir an almost palpable quality of ominousness. The fading evening light – akin to that famous "slant of light" of Emily Dickinson's, which spoke to her of death, of chill extraction – had none of its familiar autumnal loveliness, but ensnared me in a suffocating gloom. I wondered how this friendly place, teeming with such memories of (again in her words) "Lads and Girls," of "laughter and ability and Sighing, / And Frocks and Curls," could almost perceptibly seem so hostile and forbidding. Physically, I was not alone. As always Rose was present and listened with unflagging

patience to my complaints. But I felt an immense and aching solitude. I could no longer concentrate during those afternoon hours, which for years had been my working time, and the act of writing itself, becoming more and more difficult and exhausting, stalled, then finally ceased.

There were also dreadful, pouncing seizures of anxiety. One bright day on a walk through the woods with my dog I heard a flock of Canada geese honking high above trees ablaze with foliage; ordinarily a sight and sound that would have exhilarated me, the flight of birds caused me to stop, riveted with fear, and I stood stranded there, helpless, shivering, aware for the first time that I had been stricken by no mere pangs of withdrawal but by a serious illness whose name and actuality I was able finally to acknowledge. Going home, I couldn't rid my mind of the line of Baudelaire's, dredged up from the distant past, that for several days had been skittering around at the edge of my consciousness: "I have felt the wind of the wing of madness."

Our perhaps understandable modern need to dull the sawtooth edges of so many of the afflictions we are heir to has led us to banish the harsh old-fashioned words: madhouse, asylum, insanity, melancholia, lunatic, madness. But never let it be doubted that depression, in its extreme form, is madness. The madness results from an aberrant biochemical process. It has been established with reasonable certainty (after strong resistance from many psychiatrists,

But never let it be doubted that depression, in its extreme form, is madness

and not all that long ago) that such madness is chemically induced amid the neurotransmitters of the brain, probably as the result of systemic stress, which for unknown reasons causes a depletion of the chemicals norepinephrine and serotonin, and the increase of a hormone, cortisol. With all this upheaval in the brain tissues, the alternate drenching and deprivation, it is no wonder that the mind begins to feel aggrieved, stricken, and the muddied thought processes register the distress of an organ in convulsion. Sometimes, though not very often, such a disturbed mind will turn to violent thoughts regarding others. But with their minds turned agonizingly inward, people with depression are usually dangerous only to themselves. The madness of depression is, generally speaking, the antithesis of violence. It is a storm indeed, but a storm of murk. Soon evident are the slowed-down responses, near-paralysis, psychic energy throttled back close to zero. Ultimately, the body is affected and feels sapped, drained.

That fall, as the disorder gradually took full possession of my system, I began to conceive that my mind itself was like one of those outmoded small-town telephone exchanges, being gradually inundated by floodwaters: one by one, the normal circuits began to drown, causing some of the functions of the body and nearly all of those of instinct and intellect to slowly disconnect.

There is a well-known checklist of some of these functions and their failures. Mine conked out fairly close to schedule, many of them following the pattern of

depressive seizures. I particularly remember the lamentable near disappearance of my voice. It underwent a strange transformation, becoming at times quite faint, wheezy and spasmodic – a friend observed later that it was the voice of a ninety-year-old. The libido also made an early exit, as it does in most major illnesses – it is the superfluous need of a body in beleaguered emergency. Many people lose all appetite; mine was relatively normal, but I found myself eating only for subsistence: food, like everything else within the scope of sensation, was utterly without savor. Most distressing of all the instinctual disruptions was that of sleep, along with a complete absence of dreams.

Exhaustion combined with sleeplessness is a rare torture. The two or three hours of sleep I was able to get at night were always at the behest of the Halcion – a matter which deserves particular notice. For some time now many experts in psychopharmacology have warned that the benzodiazepine family of tranquilizers, of which Halcion is one (Valium and Ativan are others), is capable of depressing mood and even precipitating a major depression. Over two years before my siege, an insouciant doctor had prescribed Ativan as a bedtime aid, telling me airily that I could take it as casually as aspirin. The *Physicians' Desk Reference*, the pharmacological bible, reveals that the medicine I had been ingesting was (a) three times the normally prescribed strength, (b) not advisable as a medication for more than a month or so, and (c) to be used with

special caution by people of my age. At the time of which I am speaking I was no longer taking Ativan but had become addicted to Halcion and was consuming large doses. It seems reasonable to think that this was still another contributory factor to the trouble that had come upon me. Certainly, it should be a caution to others.

At any rate, my few hours of sleep were usually terminated at three or four in the morning, when I stared up into yawning darkness, wondering and writhing at the devastation taking place in my mind, and awaiting the dawn, which usually permitted me a feverish, dreamless nap. I'm fairly certain that it was during one of these insomniac trances that there came over me the knowledge – a weird and shocking revelation, like that of some long-beshrouded metaphysical truth – that this condition would cost me my life if it continued on such a course. This must have been just before my trip to Paris. Death, as I have said, was now a daily presence, blowing over me in cold gusts. I had not conceived precisely how my end would come. In short, I was still keeping the idea of suicide at bay. But plainly the possibility was around the corner, and I would soon meet it face to face.

What I had begun to discover is that, mysteriously and in ways that are totally remote from normal experience, the gray drizzle of horror induced by depression takes on the quality of physical pain. But it is not an immediately identifiable pain, like that of a broken limb. It may be more accurate to say that despair, owing to some evil trick

played upon the sick brain by the inhabiting psyche, comes to resemble the diabolical discomfort of being imprisoned in a fiercely overheated room. And because no breeze stirs this caldron, because there is no escape from this smothering confinement, it is entirely natural that the victim begins to think ceaselessly of oblivion.

V

ONE OF THE MEMORABLE MOMENTS in *Madame Bovary* is the scene where the heroine seeks help from the village priest. Guilt-ridden, distraught, miserably depressed, the adulterous Emma – heading toward eventual suicide – stumblingly tries to prod the abbé into helping her find a way out of her misery. But the priest, a simple soul and none too bright, can only pluck at his stained cassock, distractedly shout at his acolytes, and offer Christian platitudes. Emma goes on her quietly frantic way, beyond comfort of God or man.

I felt a bit like Emma Bovary in my relationship with the psychiatrist I shall call Dr. Gold, whom I began to visit immediately after my return from Paris, when the despair had commenced its merciless daily drumming. I had never before consulted a mental therapist for anything, and I felt awkward, also a bit defensive; my pain had become so intense that I considered it quite improbable that conversation with another mortal, even one with professional

expertise in mood disorders, could alleviate the distress. Madame Bovary went to the priest with the same hesitant doubt. Yet our society is so structured that Dr. Gold, or someone like him, is the authority to whom one is forced to turn in crisis, and it is not entirely a bad idea, since Dr. Gold – Yale-trained, highly qualified – at least provides a focal point toward which one can direct one's dying energies, offers consolation if not much hope, and becomes the receptacle for an outpouring of woes during fifty minutes that also provides relief for the victim's wife. Still, while I would never question the potential efficacy of psychotherapy in the beginning manifestations or milder forms of the illness – or possibly even in the aftermath of a serious onslaught – its usefulness at the advanced stage I was in has to be virtually nil. My more specific purpose in consulting Dr. Gold was to obtain help through pharmacology – though this too was, alas, a chimera for a bottomed-out victim such as I had become.

He asked me if I was suicidal, and I reluctantly told him yes. I did not particularize – since there seemed no need to – did not tell him that in truth many of the artifacts of my house had become potential devices for my own destruction: the attic rafters (and an outside maple or two) a means to hang myself, the garage a place to inhale carbon monoxide, the bathtub a vessel to receive the flow from my opened arteries. The kitchen knives in their drawers had but one purpose for me. Death by heart attack seemed particularly inviting, absolving me as it would of

active responsibility, and I had toyed with the idea of self-induced pneumonia – a long, frigid, shirt-sleeved hike through the rainy woods. Nor had I overlooked an ostensible accident, à la Randall Jarrell, by walking in front of a truck on the highway nearby. These thoughts may seem outlandishly macabre – a strained joke – but they are genuine. They are doubtless especially repugnant to healthy Americans, with their faith in self-improvement. Yet in truth such hideous fantasies, which cause well people to shudder, are to the deeply depressed mind what lascivious daydreams are to persons of robust sexuality. Dr. Gold and I began to chat twice weekly, but there was little I could tell him except to try, vainly, to describe my desolation.

Nor could he say much of value to me. His platitudes were not Christian but, almost as ineffective, dicta drawn straight from the pages of *The Diagnostic and Statistical Manual of the American Psychiatric Association* (much of which, as I mentioned earlier, I'd already read), and the solace he offered me was an antidepressant medication called Ludiomil. The pill made me edgy, disagreeably hyperactive, and when the dosage was increased after ten days, it blocked my bladder for hours one night. Upon informing Dr. Gold of this problem, I was told that ten more days must pass for the drug to clear my system before starting anew with a different pill. Ten days to someone stretched on such a torture rack is like ten centuries – and this does not begin to take into account the fact that when a new pill is inaugurated several weeks

must pass before it becomes effective, a development which is far from guaranteed in any case.

This brings up the matter of medication in general. Psychiatry must be given due credit for its continuing struggle to treat depression pharmacologically. The use of lithium to stabilize moods in manic depression is a great medical achievement; the same drug is also being employed effectively as a preventive in many instances of unipolar depression. There can be no doubt that in certain moderate cases and some chronic forms of the disease (the so-called endogenous depressions) medications have proved invaluable, often altering the course of a serious disturbance dramatically. For reasons that are still not clear to me, neither medications nor psychotherapy were able to arrest my plunge toward the depths. If the claims of responsible authorities in the field can be believed – including assertions made by physicians I've come to know personally and to respect – the malign progress of my illness placed me in a distinct minority of patients, severely stricken, whose affliction is beyond control. In any case, I don't want to appear insensitive to the successful treatment ultimately enjoyed by most victims of depression. Especially in its earlier stages, the disease yields favorably to such techniques as cognitive therapy – alone, or in combination with medications – and other continually evolving psychiatric strategies. Most patients, after all, do not need to be hospitalized and do not attempt or actually commit suicide. But until that day when a swiftly acting agent is developed,

one's faith in a pharmacological cure for major depression must remain provisional. The failure of these pills to act positively and quickly – a defect which is now the general case – is somewhat analogous to the failure of nearly all drugs to stem massive bacterial infections in the years before antibiotics became a specific remedy. And it can be just as dangerous.

So I found little of worth to anticipate in my consultations with Dr. Gold. On my visits he and I continued to exchange platitudes, mine haltingly spoken now – since my speech, emulating my way of walking, had slowed to the vocal equivalent of a shuffle – and I'm sure as tiresome as his.

Despite the still-faltering methods of treatment, psychiatry has, on an analytical and philosophical level, contributed a lot to an understanding of the origins of depression. Much obviously remains to be learned (and a great deal will doubtless continue to be a mystery, owing to the disease's idiopathic nature, its constant interchangeability of factors), but certainly one psychological element has been established beyond reasonable doubt, and that is the concept of loss. Loss in all of its manifestations is the touchstone of depression – in the progress of the disease and, most likely, in its origin. At a later date I would gradually be persuaded that devastating loss in childhood figured as a probable genesis of my own disorder; meanwhile, as I monitored my retrograde condition, I felt loss at every hand. The loss of self-esteem is a celebrated symptom, and my own sense of self had all but

disappeared, along with any self-reliance. This loss can quickly degenerate into dependence, and from dependence into infantile dread. One dreads the loss of all things, all people close and dear. There is an acute fear of abandonment. Being alone in the house, even for a moment, caused me exquisite panic and trepidation.

Of the images recollected from that time the most bizarre and discomfiting remains the one of me, age four and a half, tagging through a market after my long-suffering wife; not for an instant could I let out of my sight the endlessly patient soul who had become nanny, mommy, comforter, priestess, and, most important, confidante – a counselor of rocklike centrality to my existence whose wisdom far exceeded that of Dr. Gold. I would hazard the opinion that many disastrous sequels to depression might be averted if the victims received support such as she gave me. But meanwhile my losses mounted and proliferated. There is no doubt that as one nears the penultimate depths of depression – which is to say just before the stage when one begins to act out one's suicide instead of being a mere contemplator of it – the acute sense of loss is connected with a knowledge of life slipping away at accelerated speed. One develops fierce attachments. Ludicrous things – my reading glasses, a handkerchief, a certain writing instrument – became the objects of my demented possessiveness. Each momentary misplacement filled me with a frenzied dismay, each item being the tactile reminder of a world soon to be obliterated.

November wore on, bleak, raw and chill. One Sunday a photographer and his assistants came to take pictures for an article to be published in a national magazine. Of the session I can recall little except the first snowflakes of winter dotting the air outside. I thought I obeyed the photographer's request to smile often. A day or two later the magazine's editor telephoned my wife, asking if I would submit to another session. The reason he advanced was that the pictures of me, even the ones with smiles, were "too full of anguish."

I had now reached that phase of the disorder where all sense of hope had vanished, along with the idea of a futurity; my brain, in thrall to its outlaw hormones, had become less an organ of thought than an instrument registering, minute by minute, varying degrees of its own suffering. The mornings themselves were becoming bad now as I wandered about lethargic, following my synthetic sleep, but afternoons were still the worst, beginning at about three o'clock, when I'd feel the horror, like some poisonous fogbank, roll in upon my mind, forcing me into bed. There I would lie for as long as six hours, stuporous and virtually paralyzed, gazing at the ceiling and waiting for that moment of evening when, mysteriously, the crucifixion would ease up just enough to allow me to force down some food and then, like an automaton, seek an hour or two of sleep again. Why wasn't I in a hospital?

VI

FOR YEARS I HAD KEPT a notebook – not strictly a diary, its entries were erratic and haphazardly written – whose contents I would not have particularly liked to be scrutinized by eyes other than my own. I had hidden it well out of sight in my house. I imply no scandalousness; the observations were far less raunchy, or wicked, or self-revealing, than my desire to keep the notebook private might indicate. Nonetheless, the small volume was one that I fully intended to make use of professionally and then destroy before the distant day when the specter of the nursing home came too near. So as my illness worsened I rather queasily realized that if I once decided to get rid of the notebook that moment would necessarily coincide with my decision to put an end to myself. And one evening during early December this moment came.

That afternoon I had been driven (I could no longer drive) to Dr. Gold's office, where he announced that he had decided to place me on the antidepressant Nardil, an older

medication which had the advantage of not causing the urinary retention of the other two pills he had prescribed. However, there were drawbacks. Nardil would probably not take effect in less than four to six weeks – I could scarcely believe this – and I would have to carefully obey certain dietary restrictions, fortunately rather epicurean (no sausage, no cheese, no pâté de foie gras), in order to avoid a clash of incompatible enzymes that might cause a stroke. Further, Dr. Gold said with a straight face, the pill at optimum dosage could have the side effect of impotence. Until that moment, although I'd had some trouble with his personality, I had not thought him totally lacking in perspicacity; now I was not at all sure. Putting myself in Dr. Gold's shoes, I wondered if he seriously thought that this juiceless and ravaged semi-invalid with the shuffle and the ancient wheeze woke up each morning from his Halcion sleep eager for carnal fun.

There was a quality so comfortless about that day's session that I went home in a particularly wretched state and prepared for the evening. A few guests were coming over for dinner – something which I neither dreaded nor welcomed and which in itself (that is, in my torpid indifference) reveals a fascinating aspect of depression's pathology. This concerns not the familiar threshold of pain but a parallel phenomenon, and that is the probable inability of the psyche to absorb pain beyond predictable limits of time. There is a region in the experience of pain where the certainty of alleviation often permits superhuman

endurance. We learn to live with pain in varying degrees daily, or over longer periods of time, and we are more often than not mercifully free of it. When we endure severe discomfort of a physical nature our conditioning has taught us since childhood to make accommodations to the pain's demands – to accept it, whether pluckily or whimpering and complaining, according to our personal degree of stoicism, but in any case to accept it. Except in intractable terminal pain, there is almost always some form of relief; we look forward to that alleviation, whether it be through sleep or Tylenol or self-hypnosis or a change of posture or, most often, through the body's capacity for healing itself, and we embrace this eventual respite as the natural reward we receive for having been, temporarily, such good sports and doughty sufferers, such optimistic cheerleaders for life at heart.

In depression this faith in deliverance, in ultimate restoration, is absent. The pain is unrelenting, and what makes the condition intolerable is the foreknowledge that no remedy will come – not in a day, an hour, a month, or a minute. If there is mild relief, one knows that it is only temporary; more pain will follow. It is hopelessness even more than pain that crushes the soul. So the decision-making of daily life involves not, as in normal affairs, shifting from one annoying situation to another less annoying – or from discomfort to relative comfort, or from boredom to activity – but moving from pain to pain. One does not abandon, even briefly, one's bed of nails, but is

attached to it wherever one goes. And this results in a striking experience – one which I have called, borrowing military terminology, the situation of the walking wounded. For in virtually any other serious sickness, a patient who felt similar devastation would be lying flat in bed, possibly sedated and hooked up to the tubes and wires of life-support systems, but at the very least in a posture of repose and in an isolated setting. His invalidism would be necessary, unquestioned and honorably attained. However, the sufferer from depression has no such option and therefore finds himself, like a walking casualty of war, thrust into the most intolerable social and family situations. There he must, despite the anguish devouring his brain, present a face approximating the one that is associated with ordinary events and companionship. He must try to utter small talk, and be responsive to questions, and knowingly nod and frown and, God help him, even smile. But it is a fierce trial attempting to speak a few simple words.

That December evening, for example, I could have remained in bed as usual during those worst hours, or agreed to the dinner party my wife had arranged downstairs. But the very idea of a decision was academic. Either course was torture, and I chose the dinner not out of any particular merit but through indifference to what I knew would be indistinguishable ordeals of fogbound horror. At dinner I was barely able to speak, but the quartet of guests, who were all good friends, were aware of my condition and

politely ignored my catatonic muteness. Then, after dinner, sitting in the living room, I experienced a curious inner convulsion that I can describe only as despair beyond despair. It came out of the cold night; I did not think such anguish possible.

While my friends quietly chatted in front of the fire I excused myself and went upstairs, where I retrieved my notebook from its special place. Then I went to the kitchen and with gleaming clarity – the clarity of one who knows he is engaged in a solemn rite – I noted all the trademarked legends on the well-advertised articles which I began assembling for the volume's disposal: the new roll of Viva paper towels I opened to wrap up the book, the Scotch-brand tape I encircled it with, the empty Post Raisin Bran box I put the parcel into before taking it outside and stuffing it deep down within the garbage can, which would be emptied the next morning. Fire would have destroyed it faster, but in garbage there was an annihilation of self appropriate, as always, to melancholia's fecund self-humiliation. I felt my heart pounding wildly, like that of a man facing a firing squad, and knew I had made an irreversible decision.

A phenomenon that a number of people have noted while in deep depression is the sense of being accompanied by a second self – a wraithlike observer who, not sharing the dementia of his double, is able to watch with dispassionate curiosity as his companion struggles against the oncoming disaster, or decides to embrace it. There is a theatrical

quality about all this, and during the next several days, as I went about stolidly preparing for extinction, I couldn't shake off a sense of melodrama – a melodrama in which I, the victim-to-be of self-murder, was both the solitary actor and lone member of the audience. I had not as yet chosen the mode of my departure, but I knew that that step would come next, and soon, as inescapable as nightfall.

I watched myself in mingled terror and fascination as I began to make the necessary preparation: going to see my lawyer in the nearby town – there rewriting my will – and spending part of a couple of afternoons in a muddled attempt to bestow upon posterity a letter of farewell. It turned out that putting together a suicide note, which I felt obsessed with a necessity to compose, was the most difficult task of writing that I had ever tackled. There were too many people to acknowledge, to thank, to bequeath final bouquets. And finally I couldn't manage the sheer dirgelike solemnity of it; there was something I found almost comically offensive in the pomposity of such a comment as "For some time now I have sensed in my work a growing psychosis that is doubtless a reflection of the psychotic strain tainting my life" (this is one of the few lines I recall verbatim), as well as something degrading in the prospect of a testament, which I wished to infuse with at least some dignity and eloquence, reduced to an exhausted stutter of inadequate apologies and self-serving explanations. I should have used as an example the mordant statement of the Italian writer Cesare Pavese,

It turned out that putting together a suicide note was the most difficult task of writing that I had ever tackled

who in parting wrote simply: *No more words. An act. I'll never write again.*

But even a few words came to seem to me too long-winded, and I tore up all my efforts, resolving to go out in silence. Late one bitterly cold night, when I knew that I could not possibly get myself through the following day, I sat in the living room of the house bundled up against the chill; something had happened to the furnace. My wife had gone to bed, and I had forced myself to watch the tape of a movie in which a young actress, who had been in a play of mine, was cast in a small part. At one point in the film, which was set in late-nineteenth-century Boston, the characters moved down the hallway of a music conservatory, beyond the walls of which, from unseen musicians, came a contralto voice, a sudden soaring passage from the Brahms *Alto Rhapsody.*

This sound, which like all music – indeed, like all pleasure – I had been numbly unresponsive to for months, pierced my heart like a dagger, and in a flood of swift recollection I thought of all the joys the house had known: the children who had rushed through its rooms, the festivals, the love and work, the honestly earned slumber, the voices and the nimble commotion, the perennial tribe of cats and dogs and birds, "laughter and ability and Sighing, / And Frocks and Curls." All this I realized was more than I could ever abandon, even as what I had set out so deliberately to do was more than I could inflict on those memories, and upon those, so close to me, with whom the memories were

bound. And just as powerfully I realized I could not commit this desecration on myself. I drew upon some last gleam of sanity to perceive the terrifying dimensions of the mortal predicament I had fallen into. I woke up my wife and soon telephone calls were made. The next day I was admitted to the hospital.

VII

IT WAS DR. GOLD, acting as my attending physician, who was called in to arrange for my hospital admission. Curiously enough, it was he who told me once or twice during our sessions (and after I had rather hesitantly broached the possibility of hospitalization) that I should try to avoid the hospital at all costs, owing to the stigma I might suffer. Such a comment seemed then, as it does now, extremely misguided; I had thought psychiatry had advanced long beyond the point where stigma was attached to any aspect of mental illness, including the hospital. This refuge, while hardly an enjoyable place, is a facility where patients still may go when pills fail, as they did in my case, and where one's treatment might be regarded as a prolonged extension, in a different setting, of the therapy that begins in offices such as Dr. Gold's.

It's impossible to say, of course, what another doctor's approach might have been, whether he too might have discouraged the hospital route. Many psychiatrists, who

simply do not seem to be able to comprehend the nature and depth of the anguish their patients are undergoing, maintain their stubborn allegiance to pharmaceuticals in the belief that eventually the pills will kick in, the patient will respond, and the somber surroundings of the hospital will be avoided. Dr. Gold was such a type, it seems clear, but in my case he was wrong; I'm convinced I should have been in the hospital weeks before. For, in fact, the hospital was my salvation, and it is something of a paradox that in this austere place with its locked and wired doors and desolate green hallways – ambulances screeching night and day ten floors below – I found the repose, the assuagement of the tempest in my brain, that I was unable to find in my quiet farmhouse.

This is partly the result of sequestration, of safety, of being removed to a world in which the urge to pick up a knife and plunge it into one's own breast disappears in the newfound knowledge, quickly apparent even to the depressive's fuzzy brain, that the knife with which he is attempting to cut his dreadful Swiss steak is bendable plastic. But the hospital also offers the mild, oddly gratifying trauma of sudden stabilization – a transfer out of the too familiar surroundings of home, where all is anxiety and discord, into an orderly and benign detention where one's only duty is to try to get well. For me the real healers were seclusion and time.

VIII

THE HOSPITAL WAS A WAY STATION, a purgatory. When I entered the place, my depression appeared so profound that, in the opinion of some of the staff, I was a candidate for ECT, electroconvulsive therapy – shock treatment, as it is better known. In many cases this is an effective remedy – it has undergone improvement and has made a respectable comeback, generally shedding the medieval disrepute into which it was once cast – but it is plainly a drastic procedure one would want to avoid. I avoided it because I began to get well, gradually but steadily. I was amazed to discover that the fantasies of self-destruction all but disappeared within a few days after I checked in, and this again is testimony to the pacifying effect that the hospital can create, its immediate value as a sanctuary where peace can return to the mind.

A final cautionary word, however, should be added concerning Halcion. I'm convinced that this tranquilizer is responsible for at least exaggerating to an intolerable

point the suicidal ideas that had possessed me before entering the hospital. The empirical evidence that persuades me of this evolves from a conversation I had with a staff psychiatrist only hours after going into the institution. When he asked me what I was taking for sleep, and the dosage, I told him .75mg of Halcion; at this his face became somber, and he remarked emphatically that this was three times the normally prescribed hypnotic dose, and an amount especially contraindicated for someone my age. I was switched immediately to Dalmane, another hypnotic which is a somewhat longer-acting cousin, and this proved at least as effective as Halcion in putting me to sleep; but most importantly, I noticed that soon after the switch my suicidal notions dwindled then disappeared.

Much evidence has accumulated recently that indicts Halcion (whose chemical name is triazolam) as a causative factor in producing suicidal obsession and other aberrations of thought in susceptible individuals. Because of such reactions Halcion has been categorically banned in the Netherlands, and it should be at least more carefully monitored here. I don't recall Dr. Gold once questioning the overly hefty dose which he knew I was taking; he presumably had not read the warning data in the *Physicians' Desk Reference*. While my own carelessness was at fault in ingesting such an overdose, I ascribe such carelessness to the bland assurance given me several years before, when I began to take Ativan at the behest of the breezy doctor who told me that I could, without harm, take as many of the pills

as I wished. One cringes when thinking about the damage such promiscuous prescribing of these potentially dangerous tranquilizers may be creating in patients everywhere. In my case Halcion, of course, was not an independent villain – I was headed for the abyss – but I believe that without it I might not have been brought so low.

I stayed in the hospital for nearly seven weeks. Not everyone might respond the way I did; depression, one must constantly insist, presents so many variations and has so many subtle facets – depends, in short, so much on the individual's totality of causation and response – that one person's panacea might be another's trap. But certainly the hospital (and, of course, I am speaking of the many good ones) should be shorn of its menacing reputation, should not so often be considered the method of treatment of last resort. The hospital is hardly a vacation spot; the one in which I was lodged (I was privileged to be in one of the nation's best) possessed every hospital's stupefying dreariness. If in addition there are assembled on one floor, as on mine, fourteen or fifteen middle-aged males and females in the throes of melancholia of a suicidal complexion, then one can assume a fairly laughterless environment. This was not ameliorated for me by the subairline food or by the peek I had into the outside world. *Dynasty* and *Knots Landing* and the *CBS Evening News* unspooling nightly in the bare recreation room, sometimes making me at least aware that the place where I had found refuge was a kinder, gentler madhouse than the one I'd left. In the hospital I

partook of what may be depression's only grudging favor –
its ultimate capitulation. Even those for whom any kind of
therapy is a futile exercise can look forward to the eventual
passing of the storm. If they survive the storm itself, its
fury almost always fades and then disappears. Mysterious
in its coming, mysterious in its going, the affliction runs its
course, and one finds peace.

As I got better I found distraction of sorts in the hospital's routine, with its own institutionalized sitcoms.
Group Therapy, I am told, has some value; I would never
want to derogate any concept shown to be effective for
certain individuals. But Group Therapy did nothing for me
except make me seethe, possibly because it was supervised
by an odiously smug young shrink, with a spade-shaped
dark beard (*der junge Freud?*), who in attempting to get us
to cough up the seeds of our misery was alternately condescending and bullying, and occasionally reduced one or two
of the women patients, so forlorn in their kimonos and
curlers, to what I'm certain he regarded as satisfactory
tears. (I thought the rest of the psychiatric staff exemplary
in their tact and compassion.) Time hangs heavy in the
hospital, and the best I can say for Group Therapy is that
it was a way to occupy the hours.

More or less the same can be said for Art Therapy,
which is organized infantilism. Our class was run by a
delirious young woman with a fixed, indefatigable smile,
who was plainly trained at a school offering courses in
Teaching Art to the Mentally Ill; not even a teacher of very

young retarded children could have been compelled to bestow, without deliberate instruction, such orchestrated chuckles and coos. Unwinding long rolls of slippery mural paper, she would tell us to take our crayons and make drawings illustrative of themes that we ourselves had chosen. For example: My House. In humiliated rage I obeyed, drawing a square, with a door and four cross-eyed windows, a chimney on top issuing forth a curlicue of smoke. She showered me with praise, and as the weeks advanced and my health improved so did my sense of comedy. I began to dabble happily in colored modeling clay, sculpting at first a horrid little green skull with bared teeth, which our teacher pronounced a splendid replica of my depression. I then proceeded through intermediate stages of recuperation to a rosy and cherubic head with a "Have-a-Nice-Day" smile. Coinciding as it did with the time of my release, this creation truly overjoyed my instructress (whom I'd become fond of in spite of myself), since, as she told me, it was emblematic of my recovery and therefore but one more example of the triumph over disease by Art Therapy.

By this time it was early February, and although I was still shaky I knew I had emerged into light. I felt myself no longer a husk but a body with some of the body's sweet juices stirring again. I had my first dream in many months, confused but to this day imperishable, with a flute in it somewhere, and a wild goose, and a dancing girl.

IX

By far the great majority of the people who go through even the severest depression survive it, and live ever afterward at least as happily as their unafflicted counterparts. Save for the awfulness of certain memories it leaves, acute depression inflicts few permanent wounds. There is a Sisyphean torment in the fact that a great number – as many as half – of those who are devastated once will be struck again; depression has the habit of recurrence. But most victims live through even these relapses, often coping better because they have become psychologically tuned by past experience to deal with the ogre. It is of great importance that those who are suffering a siege, perhaps for the first time, be told – be convinced, rather – that the illness will run its course and that they will pull through. A tough job, this; calling "Chin up!" from the safety of the shore to a drowning person is tantamount to insult, but it has been shown over and over again that if the encouragement is dogged enough – and the support

equally committed and passionate – the endangered one can nearly always be saved. Most people in the grip of depression at its ghastliest are, for whatever reason, in a state of unrealistic hopelessness, torn by exaggerated ills and fatal threats that bear no resemblance to actuality. It may require on the part of friends, lovers, family, admirers, an almost religious devotion to persuade the sufferers of life's worth, which is so often in conflict with a sense of their own worthlessness, but such devotion has prevented countless suicides.

During the same summer of my decline, a close friend of mine – a celebrated newspaper columnist – was hospitalized for severe manic depression. By the time I had commenced my autumnal plunge my friend had recovered (largely due to lithium but also to psychotherapy in the aftermath), and we were in touch by telephone nearly every day. His support was untiring and priceless. It was he who kept admonishing me that suicide was "unacceptable" (he had been intensely suicidal), and it was also he who made the prospect of going to the hospital less fearsomely intimidating. I still look back on his concern with immense gratitude. The help he gave me, he later said, had been a continuing therapy for him, thus demonstrating that, if nothing else, the disease engenders lasting fellowship.

After I began to recover in the hospital it occurred to me to wonder – for the first time with any really serious concern – why I had been visited by such a calamity. The psychiatric literature on depression is enormous, with

theory after theory concerning the disease's etiology pro-
liferating as richly as theories about the death of the
dinosaurs or the origin of black holes. The very number of
hypotheses is testimony to the malady's all but impenetrable mystery. As for that initial triggering mechanism – what
I have called the manifest crisis – can I really be satisfied
with the idea that abrupt withdrawal from alcohol started
the plunge downward? What about other possibilities –
the dour fact, for instance, that at about the same time I
was smitten I turned sixty, that hulking milestone of mortality? Or could it be that a vague dissatisfaction with the
way in which my work was going – the onset of inertia
which has possessed me time and time again during my
writing life, and made me crabbed and discontented – had
also haunted me more fiercely during that period than
ever, somehow magnifying the difficulty with alcohol?
Unresolvable questions, perhaps.

These matters in any case interest me less than the
search for earlier origins of the disease. What are the
forgotten or buried events that suggest an ultimate explanation for the evolution of depression and its later flowering
into madness? Until the onslaught of my own illness and
its denouement, I never gave much thought to my work in
terms of its connection with the subconscious – an area of
investigation belonging to literary detectives. But after I
had returned to health and was able to reflect on the past
in the light of my ordeal, I began to see clearly how depression had clung close to the outer edges of my life for many

years. Suicide has been a persistent theme in my books –
three of my major characters killed themselves. In
rereading, for the first time in years, sequences from my
novels – passages where my heroines have lurched down
pathways toward doom – I was stunned to perceive how
accurately I had created the landscape of depression in the
minds of these young women, describing with what could
only be instinct, out of a subconscious already roiled by
disturbances of mood, the psychic imbalance that led
them to destruction. Thus depression, when it finally
came to me, was in fact no stranger, not even a visitor totally unannounced; it had been tapping at my door for
decades.

The morbid condition proceeded, I have come to
believe, from my beginning years – from my father, who
battled the gorgon for much of his lifetime, and had been
hospitalized in my boyhood after a despondent spiraling
downward that in retrospect I saw greatly resembled mine.
The genetic roots of depression seem now to be beyond
controversy. But I'm persuaded that an even more significant factor was the death of my mother when I was thirteen;
this disorder and early sorrow – the death or disappearance
of a parent, especially a mother, before or during puberty –
appears repeatedly in the literature on depression as a
trauma sometimes likely to create nearly irreparable emotional havoc. The danger is especially apparent if the young
person is affected by what has been termed "incomplete
mourning" – has, in effect, been unable to achieve the

catharsis of grief, and so carries within himself through later years an insufferable burden of which rage and guilt, and not only dammed-up sorrow, are a part, and become the potential seeds of self-destruction.

In an illuminating new book on suicide, *Self-Destruction in the Promised Land*, Howard I. Kushner, who is not a psychiatrist but a social historian, argues persuasively in favor of this theory of incomplete mourning and uses Abraham Lincoln as an example. While Lincoln's hectic moods of melancholy are legend, it is much less well known that in his youth he was often in a suicidal turmoil and came close more than once to making an attempt on his own life. The behavior seems directly linked to the death of Lincoln's mother, Nancy Hanks, when he was nine, and to unexpressed grief exacerbated by his sister's death ten years later. Drawing insights from the chronicle of Lincoln's painful success in avoiding suicide, Kushner makes a convincing case not only for the idea of early loss precipitating self-destructive conduct, but also, auspiciously, for that same behavior becoming a strategy through which the person involved comes to grips with his guilt and rage, and triumphs over self-willed death. Such reconciliation may be entwined with the quest for immortality – in Lincoln's case, no less than that of a writer of fiction, to vanquish death through work honored by posterity.

So if this theory of incomplete mourning has validity, and I think it does, and if it is also true that in the nethermost depths of one's suicidal behavior one is still

subconsciously dealing with immense loss while trying to surmount all the effects of its devastation, then my own avoidance of death may have been belated homage to my mother. I do know that in those last hours before I rescued myself, when I listened to the passage from the *Alto Rhapsody* – which I'd heard her sing – she had been very much on my mind.

X

NEAR THE END of an early film of Ingmar Bergman's, *Through a Glass Darkly*, a young woman, experiencing the embrace of what appears to be profound psychotic depression, has a terrifying hallucination. Anticipating the arrival of some transcendental and saving glimpse of God, she sees instead the quivering shape of a monstrous spider that is attempting to violate her sexually. It is an instant of horror and scalding truth. Yet even in this version of Bergman (who has suffered cruelly from depression) there is a sense that all of his accomplished artistry has somehow fallen short of a true rendition of the drowned mind's appalling phantasmagoria. Since antiquity – in the tortured lament of Job, in the choruses of Sophocles and Aeschylus – chroniclers of the human spirit have been wrestling with a vocabulary that might give proper expression to the desolation of melancholia. Through the course of literature and art the theme of depression has run like a durable thread of woe – from Hamlet's soliloquy to the

verses of Emily Dickinson and Gerard Manley Hopkins, from John Donne to Hawthorne and Dostoevski and Poe, Camus and Conrad and Virginia Woolf. In many of Albrecht Dürer's engravings there are harrowing depictions of his own melancholia; the manic wheeling stars of Van Gogh are the precursors of the artist's plunge into dementia and the extinction of self. It is a suffering that often tinges the music of Beethoven, of Schumann and Mahler, and permeates the darker cantatas of Bach. The vast metaphor which most faithfully represents this fathomless ordeal, however, is that of Dante, and his all-too-familiar lines still arrest the imagination with their augury of the unknowable, the black struggle to come:

> *Nel mezzo del cammin di nostra vita*
> *Mi ritrovai per una selva oscura,*
> *Ché la diritta via era smarrita.*

> *In the middle of the journey of our life*
> *I found myself in a dark wood,*
> *For I had lost the right path.*

One can be sure that these words have been more than once employed to conjure the ravages of melancholia, but their somber foreboding has often overshadowed the last lines of the best-known part of that poem, with their evocation of hope. To most of those who have experienced it, the horror of depression is so overwhelming as to be quite

beyond expression, hence the frustrated sense of inadequacy found in the work of even the greatest artists. But in
science and art the search will doubtless go on for a clear
representation of its meaning, which sometimes, for those
who have known it, is a simulacrum of all the evil of our
world: of our everyday discord and chaos, our irrational-
ity, warfare and crime, torture and violence, our impulse
toward death and our flight from it held in the intolerable
equipoise of history. If our lives had no other configuration
but this, we should want, and perhaps deserve, to perish; if
depression had no termination, then suicide would, indeed,
be the only remedy. But one need not sound the false or
inspirational note to stress the truth that depression is not
the soul's annihilation; men and women who have recovered from the disease – and they are countless – bear witness
to what is probably its only saving grace: it is conquerable.

For those who have dwelt in depression's dark wood, and
known its inexplicable agony, their return from the abyss is
not unlike the ascent of the poet, trudging upward and
upward out of hell's black depths and at last emerging into
what he saw as "the shining world." There, whoever has
been restored to health has almost always been restored to
the capacity for serenity and joy, and this may be indemnity
enough for having endured the despair beyond despair.

E quindi uscimmo a riveder le stelle.

And so we came forth, and once again beheld the stars.

WILLIAM STYRON's writing career spanned more than 50 years. He wrote four novels as well as books of essays, stories and this memoir of depression, *Darkness Visible*.

Styron was born in Virginia in 1925. He has said of himself: 'I suppose some of us are cursed with a dark view of life'. His first novel, *Lie Down in Darkness*, published when he was just 26, was about the suicide of a young woman. His two other best-known works are *The Confessions of Nat Turner* which won the Pulitzer Prize in 1967, and *Sophie's Choice* which won the US National Book Award for Fiction in 1980.

Styron's mother died when he was just 14. In an interview for the *Guardian* he said about his mother's death: 'Only over the years has it revealed itself as a wound from which I never fully recovered. At the time, I was rather amazed by the coolness with which I accepted it. It bothered me that I could not weep. I could not mourn. This is what caused my later depression, I'm sure. I can see that it was there all along.'

Styron died from pneumonia in 2006.

RECOMMENDED BOOKS BY WILLIAM STYRON:

Lie Down in Darkness
The Confessions of Nat Turner
Sophie's Choice

In need of an antidote to Depression?

Swimming
ROGER DEAKIN

VINTAGE MINIS

Babies
ANNE ENRIGHT

VINTAGE MINIS

Calm
TIM PARKS

VINTAGE MINIS

Work
JOSEPH HELLER

VINTAGE MINIS

VINTAGE MINIS

The Vintage Minis bring you the world's greatest writers on the experiences that make us human. These stylish, entertaining little books explore the whole spectrum of life – from birth to death, and everything in between. Which means there's something here for everyone, whatever your story.

Desire	Haruki Murakami
Love	Jeanette Winterson
Babies	Anne Enright
Language	Xiaolu Guo
Motherhood	Helen Simpson
Fatherhood	Karl Ove Knausgaard
Summer	Laurie Lee
Jealousy	Marcel Proust
Sisters	Louisa May Alcott
Home	Salman Rushdie
Race	Toni Morrison
Liberty	Virginia Woolf
Swimming	Roger Deakin
Work	Joseph Heller
Depression	William Styron
Drinking	John Cheever
Eating	Nigella Lawson
Psychedelics	Aldous Huxley
Calm	Tim Parks
Death	Julian Barnes

vintageminis.co.uk

1 3 5 7 9 10 8 6 4 2

Vintage
20 Vauxhall Bridge Road,
London SW1V 2SA

Vintage Classics is part of the Penguin Random House
group of companies whose addresses can be found at
global.penguinrandomhouse.com

Penguin
Random House
UK

First published with the title *Min Kamp Andre Bok* in 2009 by
Forlaget Oktober, Oslo
First published in Great Britain by Harvill Secker in 2013
This short edition published by Vintage in 2017

www.vintage-books.co.uk

A CIP catalogue record for this book is available from the British Library

ISBN 9781784872663

Typeset in 9.5/14.5 pt FreightText Pro
by Jouve (UK), Milton Keynes
Printed and bound by Clays Ltd, St Ives plc

Fatherhood

KARL OVE KNAUSGAARD

Translated from the Norwegian by Don Bartlett

VINTAGE MINIS

29 July 2008

THE SUMMER HAS BEEN long, and it still isn't over. I finished the first part of the novel on 26 June, and since then, for more than a month, the nursery school has been closed, and we have had Vanja and Heidi at home with all the extra work that involves. I have never understood the point of holidays, have never felt the need for them and have always just wanted to do more work. But if I must, I must. We had planned to spend the first week at the cabin Linda got us to buy last autumn, intended partly as a place to write, partly as a weekend retreat, but after three days we gave up and returned to town. Putting three infants and two adults on a small allotment, surrounded by people on all sides, with nothing else to do but weed the garden and mow the grass, is not necessarily a good idea, especially if the prevailing atmosphere is disharmonious even before you set out. We had several flaming rows there, presumably to the amusement of the neighbours, and the presence of

hundreds of meticulously cultivated gardens populated by all these old semi-naked people made me feel claustrophobic and irritable. Children are quick to detect these moods and play on them, particularly Vanja, who reacts almost instantly to shifts in vocal pitch and intensity, and if they are obvious she starts to do what she knows we like least, eventually causing us to lose our tempers if she persists. Already brimming with frustration, it is practically impossible for us to defend ourselves, and then we have the full woes: screaming and shouting and misery. The following week we hired a car and drove up to Tjörn, outside Gothenburg, where Linda's friend Mikaela, who is Vanja's godmother, had invited us to stay in her partner's summer house. We asked if she knew what it was like living with three children, and whether she was really sure she wanted us there, but she said she was sure; she had planned to do some baking with the children and take them swimming and go crabbing so that we could have some time to ourselves. We took her up on the offer. We drove to Tjörn, parked outside the summer house, on the fringes of the beautiful Sørland countryside, and in we piled with all the kids, plus bags and baggage. The intention had been to stay there all week, but three days later we packed all our stuff into the car and headed south again, to Mikaela and Erik's obvious relief.

People who don't have children seldom understand what it involves, no matter how mature and intelligent they might otherwise be, at least that was how it was with

me before I had children myself. Mikaela and Erik are careerists: all the time I have known Mikaela she has had nothing but top jobs in the cultural sector, while Erik is the director of some multinational foundation based in Sweden. After Tjörn he had a meeting in Panama, before the two of them were due to leave for a holiday in Provence, that's the way their life is: places I have only ever read about are their stamping grounds. So into that came our family, along with baby wipes and nappies, John crawling all over the place, Heidi and Vanja fighting and screaming, laughing and crying, children who never eat at the table, never do what they are told, at least not when we are visiting other people and really *want* them to behave, because they know what is going on. The more there is at stake for us, the more unruly they become, and even though the summer house was large and spacious it was not large or spacious enough for them to be overlooked. Erik pretended to be unconcerned, he wanted to appear generous and child-friendly, but this was continually contradicted by his body language, his arms pinned to his sides, the way he went round putting things back in their places and that faraway look in his eyes. He was close to the things and the place he had known all his life, but distant from those populating it just now, regarding them more or less in the same way one would regard moles or hedgehogs. I knew how he felt, and I liked him. But I had brought all this along with me, and a real meeting of minds was impossible. He had been educated at Oxford and Cambridge, and had worked

for several years as a broker in the City, but on a walk he and Vanja took up a mountainside near the sea one day he let her climb on her own several metres ahead of him while he stood stock-still admiring the view, without taking into account that she was only four and incapable of assessing the risk, so with Heidi in my arms I had to jog up and take over. When we were sitting in a café half an hour later – me with stiff legs after the sudden sprint – and I asked him to give John bits of a bread roll I placed beside him, as I had to keep an eye on Heidi and Vanja while finding them something to eat, he nodded, said he would, but he didn't put down the newspaper he was reading, did not even look up, and failed to notice that John, who was half a metre away from him, was becoming more and more agitated and at length screamed until his face went scarlet with frustration, since the bread he wanted was right in front of him but out of his reach. The situation infuriated Linda, sitting at the other end of the table – I could see it in her eyes – but she bit her tongue, made no comment, waited until we were outside and on our own, then she said we should go home. Now. Accustomed to her moods, I said she should keep her mouth shut and refrain from making decisions like that when she was in such a foul temper. That riled her even more of course, and that was how things stayed until we got into the car next morning to leave.

The blue cloudless sky and the patchwork, windswept yet wonderful countryside, together with the children's happiness and the fact that we were in a car, and not a train

compartment or on board a plane, which had been the usual mode of travel for the last few years, lightened the atmosphere, but it was not long before we were at it again because we had to eat, and the restaurant we found and stopped at turned out to belong to a yacht club, but, the waiter informed me, if we just crossed the bridge, walked into town, perhaps 500 metres, there was another restaurant, so twenty minutes later we found ourselves on a high, narrow and very busy bridge, grappling with two buggies, hungry, and with only an industrial area in sight. Linda was furious, her eyes were black, we were always getting into situations like this, she hissed, no one else did, we were useless, now we should be eating, the whole family, we could have been really enjoying ourselves, instead we were out here in a gale-force wind with cars whizzing by, suffocating from exhaust fumes on this bloody bridge. Had I ever seen any other families with three children outside in situations like this? The road we followed ended at a metal gate emblazoned with the logo of a security firm. To reach the town, which looked run-down and cheerless, we had to take a detour through the industrial zone for at least fifteen minutes. I would have left her because she was always moaning, she always wanted something else, never did anything to improve things, just moaned, moaned, moaned, could never face up to difficult situations, and if reality did not live up to her expectations, she blamed me in matters large and small. Well, under normal circumstances we would have gone our separate ways, but as

always the practicalities brought us together again: we had one car and two buggies, so you just had to act as if what had been said had not been said after all, push the stained rickety buggies over the bridge and back to the posh yacht club, pack them into the car, strap in the children and drive to the nearest McDonald's, which turned out to be at a petrol station outside Gothenburg city centre, where I sat on a bench eating a sausage while Vanja and Linda ate theirs in the car. John and Heidi were asleep. We scrapped the planned trip to Liseberg Amusement Park, it would only make things worse given the atmosphere between us now; instead, a few hours later, we stopped on impulse at a shoddy so-called 'Fairytale Land', where everything was of the poorest quality, and took the children first to a small 'circus' consisting of a dog jumping through hoops held at knee height, a stout manly-looking lady, probably from somewhere in eastern Europe, who, clad in a bikini, tossed the same hoops in the air and swung them around her hips, tricks which every single girl in my first school mastered, and a fair-haired man of my age with curly-toed shoes, a turban and several spare tyres rolling over his harem trousers, who filled his mouth with petrol and breathed fire four times in the direction of the low ceiling. John and Heidi were staring so hard their eyes were popping out. Vanja had her mind on the lottery stall we had passed, where you could win cuddly toys, and kept pinching me and asking when the performance would finish. Now and then I looked across at Linda. She was sitting with Heidi

on her lap and had tears in her eyes. As we came out and started walking down towards the tiny fairground, each pushing a buggy, past a large swimming pool with a long slide, behind whose top towered an enormous troll, perhaps thirty metres high, I asked her why.

'I don't know,' she said. 'But circuses have always moved me.'

'Why?'

'Well, it's so sad, so small and so cheap. And at the same time so beautiful.'

'Even this one?'

'Yes. Didn't you see Heidi and John? They were absolutely hypnotised.'

'But not Vanja,' I said with a smile. Linda returned the smile.

'What?' Vanja said, turning. 'What did you say, dad?'

'I just said that all you were thinking about at the circus was that cuddly toy you saw.'

Vanja smiled in the way she often did when we talked about something she had done. Happy, but also keen, ready for more.

'What did I do?' she asked.

'You pinched my arm,' I answered. 'And said you wanted to go on the lottery.'

'Why?' she asked.

'How should I know?' I said. 'I suppose you wanted that cuddly toy.'

'Shall we do it now then?' she asked.

'Yes,' I said. 'It's down there.'

I pointed down the tarmac path to the fairground amusements we could make out through the trees.

'Can Heidi have one as well?' she asked.

'If she wants,' Linda said.

'She does,' Vanja said, bending down to Heidi, who was in the buggy. 'Do you want one, Heidi?'

'Yes,' Heidi said.

We had to spend ninety kroner on tickets before each of them held a little cloth mouse in their hands. The sun burned down from the sky; the air beneath the trees was still, all sorts of shrill, plinging sounds from the amusements mixed with 80s disco music from the stalls around us. Vanja wanted candyfloss, so ten minutes later we were sitting at a table outside a kiosk with angry persistent wasps buzzing around us in the boiling-hot sun, which ensured that the sugar stuck to everything it came into contact with – the tabletop, the back of the buggy, arms and hands – to the children's loud disgruntlement; this was not what they envisaged when they saw the container with the swirling sugar in the kiosk. My coffee tasted bitter and was almost undrinkable. A small dirty boy pedalled towards us on his tricycle, straight into Heidi's buggy, then looked at us expectantly. He was dark-haired and dark-eyed, possibly Romanian or Albanian or perhaps Greek. After pushing his tricycle into the buggy a few more times, he positioned himself in such a way that we couldn't get out and he stood there with eyes downcast.

'Shall we go?' I asked.

'Heidi wanted a ride,' Linda said. 'Can't we do that first?'

A powerfully built man with protruding ears, also dark-skinned, came and lifted the boy and bike and carried him to the open space in front of the kiosk, patted him on the head a couple of times and went over to the mechanical octopus he was operating. The arms were fitted with small baskets you could sit in, which rose and fell as they slowly rotated. The boy began to cycle across the entrance area where summer-clad visitors were constantly arriving and leaving.

'Of course,' I said, and got up, took Vanja's and Heidi's candyflosses and threw them in the waste bin, and pushed John, who was tossing his head from side to side to catch all the interesting things going on, across the square to the path leading up to 'Cowboy Town'. But Cowboy Town, which was a pile of sand with three newly built sheds labelled, respectively, MINE, SHERIFF and PRISON, the latter two covered with WANTED DEAD OR ALIVE posters, surrounded on one side by birch trees and a ramp where some youngsters were skateboarding and on the other by a horse-riding area, was closed. Inside the fence, just opposite the mine, the eastern European woman sat on a rock, smoking.

'Ride!' Heidi said, looking around.

'We'll have to go to the donkey ride near the entrance,' Linda said.

John threw his bottle of water to the ground. Vanja crawled under the fence and ran over to the mine. When Heidi saw that she scrambled out of her buggy and followed. I spotted a red and white Coke machine at the rear of the sheriff's office, dredged up the contents of my shorts pocket and studied them: two hairslides, one hairpin with a ladybird motif, a lighter, three stones and two small white shells Vanja had found in Tjörn, a twenty-krone note, two five-krone coins and nine krone coins.

'I'll have a smoke in the meantime,' I said. 'I'll be down there.'

I motioned towards a tree trunk at the far end of the area. John raised both arms.

'Go on, then,' Linda said, lifting him up. 'Are you hungry, John?' she asked. 'Oh, it's so hot. Is there no shade anywhere so that I can sit down with him?'

'Up there,' I said, pointing to the restaurant at the top of the hill. It resembled a train, with the counter in the locomotive and the tables in the carriage. Not a soul was to be seen up there. Chairs were propped against the tables.

'That's what I'll do,' Linda said. 'And feed him. Will you keep an eye on the girls?'

I nodded, went to the Coke machine and bought a can, sat down on the tree trunk, lit a cigarette, looked up at the hastily constructed shed where Vanja and Heidi were running in and out of the doorway.

'It's pitch black in here!' Vanja shouted. 'Come and look!'

I raised my hand and waved, which fortunately appeared to satisfy her. She was still clutching the mouse to her chest with one hand.

Where was Heidi's mouse, by the way?

I allowed my gaze to drift up the hill. And there it lay, right outside the sheriff's office, with its head in the sand. At the restaurant Linda dragged a chair to the wall, sat down and began to breastfeed John, who at first kicked out, then lay quite still. The circus lady was making her way up the hill. A horsefly stung me on the calf. I smacked it with such force that it splattered all over my skin. The cigarette tasted terrible in the heat, but I resolutely inhaled the smoke into my lungs, stared up at the tops of the spruce trees, such an intense green where the sun caught them. Another horsefly landed on my calf. I lashed out at it, got up, threw the cigarette to the ground and walked towards the girls with the half-full still cold can of Coke in my hand.

'Daddy, you go round the back while we're inside and see if you can see us through the cracks, OK?' Vanja said, squinting up at me.

'All right, then,' I said, and walked round the shed. Heard them banging around and giggling inside. Bent my head to one of the cracks and peered in. But the difference between the light outside and the darkness inside was too great for me to see anything.

'Daddy, are you outside?' Vanja shouted.

'Yes,' I said.

'Can you see us?'

'No. Have you become invisible?'

'Yes!'

When they came out I pretended I couldn't see them. Focused my eyes on Vanja and called her name.

'I'm *here*,' she said, waving her arms.

'Vanja?' I shouted. 'Where are you? Come out now. It's not funny any more.'

'I'm here! Here!'

'Vanja?'

'Can't you see me, really? Am I really invisible?'

She sounded boundlessly happy although I sensed a touch of unease in her voice. At that moment John started screaming. I looked up. Linda got up clutching him to her breast. It was unlike John to cry like that.

'Oh, there you are!' I said. 'Have you been there the whole time?'

'Ye-es,' she said.

'Can you hear John crying?'

She nodded and looked up.

'We'll have to go then,' I said. 'Come on.'

I reached out for Heidi's hand.

'Don't want to,' she said. 'Don't want to hold hands.'

'OK,' I said. 'Hop into the buggy then.'

'Don't want buggy,' she said.

'Shall I carry you then?'

'Don't want carry.'

I went down and fetched the buggy. When I returned

she had clambered onto the fence. Vanja was sitting on the ground. At the top of the hill Linda had left the restaurant; she was standing in the road now looking down, waving to us with one hand. John was still screaming.

'I don't want to walk,' Vanja said. 'My legs are tired.'

'You've hardly walked a step all day,' I said. 'How can your legs be tired?'

'Haven't got any legs. You'll have to carry me.'

'No, Vanja, that's rubbish. I can't carry you.'

'Yes, you can.'

'Get in the buggy, Heidi,' I said. 'Then we'll go for a ride.'

'Don't want buggy,' she said.

'I haven't got any leeegs!' Vanja said. She screamed the last word.

I felt the fury rising within me. My impulse was to lift them up and carry them, one pinned under each arm. This would not be the first time I had gone off with them kicking and screaming in my arms, oblivious of passers-by, who always stared with such interest when we had our little scenes, as though I was wearing a monkey mask or something.

But this time I managed to regain my composure.

'Could you get into the buggy, Vanja?' I asked.

'If you lift me,' she said.

'No, you'll have to do it yourself.'

'No,' she said. 'I haven't got any legs.'

If I didn't give way we would be standing here until the next day, for though Vanja lacked patience and gave up as

soon as she met any resistance, she was infinitely stubborn when it was a question of getting her own way.

'OK,' I said, lifting her up into the buggy. 'You win again.'

'Win what?' she asked.

'Nothing,' I said. 'Come on, Heidi. We're going.'

I lifted her off the fence, and after a couple of half-hearted 'No, don't want's we were on our way up the hill, Heidi on my arm, Vanja in the buggy. As we passed, I picked up Heidi's cloth mouse, brushed off the dirt and popped it into the net shopping bag.

'I don't know what's up with him,' Linda said as we arrived at the top. 'He suddenly started crying. Perhaps he's been stung by a wasp or something. Look . . .'

She pulled up his jumper and showed me a small red mark. He squirmed in her grip, his face red and his hair wet from all the screaming.

'Poor little lad,' she said.

'I've been bitten by a horsefly,' I said. 'Perhaps that's what happened. Put him in the buggy though and we can get going. We can't do anything about it now anyway.'

When he was strapped in, he wriggled about and bored his head down, still screaming.

'Let's get into the car,' I said.

'Yes,' Linda replied. 'But I'll have to change him first. There's a nappy changing room down there.'

I nodded, and we began to walk down. Several hours had passed since we arrived, the sun was lower in the sky

and something about the light it cast over the trees
reminded me of summer afternoons at home when we
either drove to the far side of the island with mum and dad
to swim in the sea or walked down to the knoll in the
sound beyond the estate. The memories filled my mind for
a few seconds, not in the form of specific events, more as
atmospheres, smells, sensations. The way the light, which
in the middle of the day was whiter and more neutral,
became fuller later in the afternoon and began to make the
colours darker. Oh, running on the path through the shady
forest on a summer day in the 70s! Diving into the salt
water and swimming across to Gjerstadholmen on the
other side! The sun shining on the sea-smoothed rocks,
turning them almost golden. The stiff dry grass growing in
the hollows between them. The sense of the depths
beneath the surface of the water, so dark as it lay in the
shadow beneath the mountainside. The fish gliding by.
And then the treetops above us, their slender branches
trembling in the sea breeze! The thin bark and the smooth
leg-like tree beneath. The green foliage . . .

'There it is,' Linda said, nodding towards a small octag-
onal wooden construction. 'Will you wait?'

'We'll amble down,' I said.

In the copse inside the fence there were two gnomes
carved in wood. That was how the place justified its status
as Fairytale Land.

'Look, *tompen!*' Heidi shouted. *Tompen,* or in correct
Swedish *tomten,* was a gnome.

She had been fixated on gnomes for quite a time. Well into spring she had pointed to the veranda where the gnome had appeared on Christmas Eve and said '*Tompen*'s coming,' and when she played with one of the presents he had given her she always stated first of all where it had come from. What sort of status he had for her, however, was not easy to say, because when she spotted the gnome outfit in my wardrobe after Christmas she wasn't in the least bit surprised or upset. We hadn't said a word; she just pointed and shouted '*Tompen*' as if that was where he changed his clothes, and when we met the old tramp with the white beard who hung around in the square outside our house she would stand up in the buggy and shout '*Tompen*' at the top of her lungs.

I leaned forward and kissed her chubby cheek.

'No kisses!' she said.

I laughed.

'Can I kiss you then, Vanja?'

'No!' Vanja said.

A meagre though regular stream of people flowed past us, most wearing summery clothes – shorts, T-shirts and sandals – some in jogging pants and trainers, a striking number of them fat, almost none well dressed.

'My daddy in prison!' Heidi shouted with glee.

Vanja turned in the buggy.

'No, daddy's not in prison!' she said.

I laughed again and stopped.

'We'll have to wait for mummy here,' I said.

Your daddy's in prison: that was what kids in the nursery used to say to one another. Heidi had understood it as a great compliment, and often said it when she wanted to boast about me. Last time we were returning from the cabin, according to Linda, she had said it to an elderly lady sitting behind them on the bus. My daddy's in prison. As I hadn't been there, but was standing at the bus stop with John, the comment had been left hanging in the air, unchallenged.

I leaned forward and wiped the sweat off my forehead with my T-shirt sleeve.

'Can I have another ticket, daddy?' Vanja said.

'Nope,' I said. 'You've already won a cuddly toy!'

'Nice daddy, another one?' she said.

I turned and saw Linda walking over. John was sitting upright in the buggy and seemed content under his sun hat.

'Everything OK?' I said.

'Mm. I bathed the sting in cold water. He's tired, though.'

'He'll sleep in the car then,' I said.

'What time do you think it is?'

'Half past three maybe?'

'Home by eight then?'

'Or thereabouts.'

Once again we crossed the tiny fairground, passed the pirate ship, a pathetic wooden façade with gangways behind, where one-legged or one-armed men with headscarves

brandished swords, the llama and ostrich enclosures, the small paved area where some kids rode four-wheelers, and finally arrived at the entrance, where there was a kind of obstacle course, a few logs, that is, and some plank walls with netting in between, a stand with a bungee trampoline and a donkey-riding ring, where we stopped. Linda took Heidi, carried her to the queue and put a helmet on her head, while Vanja and I stood watching by the fence with John.

There were four donkeys in the ring at a time, led by parents. The circuit was no more than thirty metres in length, but most of the animals took a long time to complete it because these were donkeys, not ponies, and donkeys stop when the whim takes them. Desperate parents tugged at the reins with all their strength, but the creatures would not budge. In vain they patted them on their flanks; the accursed donkeys were as motionless as ever. One of the children was crying. The woman taking the tickets kept shouting advice to the parents. Pull as hard as you can! Harder! Just pull, they don't mind! Hard! That's the way, that's it!

'Can you see, Vanja?' I said. 'The donkeys are refusing to move!'

She laughed. I was happy because she was happy. At the same time I was a little concerned about how Linda would cope; she wasn't much more patient than Vanja. But when it was her turn, she managed with aplomb. Whenever the donkey stopped she turned round and stood with her back to its flank while making smacking noises with her lips. In

her youth she had ridden horses, they had formed a large part of her life, so that must have been how she knew what to do.

Heidi was beaming astride the donkey's back. When the donkey no longer responded to her trick Linda pulled so hard on the bridle it was as if there was no room left for any obstinacy.

'You're such a good rider!' I called to Heidi. Looked down at Vanja. 'Do you want a go?'

Vanja firmly shook her head. Straightened her glasses. She had ridden ponies from the age of eighteen months, and the autumn we moved to Malmö, when she was two and a half, she had started at a riding school. It was in the middle of Folkets Park, a sad down-at-heel riding hall with sawdust on the ground, which was a wonderful experience for her, she absorbed everything and wanted to talk about it when the lesson was over. She sat erect on her straggly pony and was led round and round by Linda, or on those occasions I went with her on my own, by one of the eleven- or twelve-year-old girls who seemed to spend their lives there, while an instructor walked about in the middle telling them what to do. It didn't matter that Vanja wouldn't always understand the instructions; the main thing was the experience of the horses and the environment around them. The stable, the cat that had kittens in the hay, the list of who was going to ride which horse that afternoon, the helmet she chose, the moment the horse was led into the hall, the riding itself, the cinnamon bun and the apple

juice she had in the café afterwards. That was the high point of the week. But things changed during the course of the following autumn. They had a new instructor, and Vanja, who looked older than her four years, came face to face with demands she couldn't meet. Even though Linda told the instructor, things didn't get any better and Vanja began to protest when she had to go – she didn't want to go, not at all – and in the end we stopped. Even when she saw Heidi riding the little donkey in the park free of any demands, she didn't want a ride.

Another thing we had signed her up for was a playgroup where the children sometimes sang together, but also did drawings and various other creative activities. The second time she went they were supposed to draw a house, and Vanja had coloured the grass blue. The playgroup leader had gone over to her and said grass wasn't blue but green. Could she do another one? Vanja had torn up her drawing and then shown her annoyance in a way which made the children's parents raise their eyebrows and consider themselves lucky to have the well-brought-up children they had. Vanja is a great many things, but above all she is sensitive, and the fact that this attitude is already hardening – and it is – causes me concern. Seeing her grow up also changes my view of my own upbringing, not so much because of the quality but the quantity, the sheer amount of time you spend with your children, which is immense. So many hours, so many days, such an infinite number of situations that crop up and are lived through. From my own childhood

I remember only a handful of incidents, all of which I regarded as momentous but which I now understand were a few events among many, which completely expunges their meaning, for how can I know that those particular episodes that lodged themselves in my mind were decisive, and not all the others of which I remember nothing?

When I discuss such topics with Geir, with whom I talk on the telephone for an hour every day, he is wont to quote Sven Stolpe, who has written somewhere about Bergman that he would have been Bergman irrespective of where he had grown up, implying, in other words, that you are who you are whatever your surroundings. What shapes you is the way you are towards your family rather than the family itself. When I was growing up I was taught to look for the explanation of all human qualities, actions and phenomena in the environment in which they originated. Biological or genetic determiners, the givens, that is, barely existed as an option, and when they did they were viewed with suspicion. Such an attitude can at first sight appear humanistic, inasmuch as it is intimately bound up with the notion that all people are equal, but upon closer examination it could just as well be an expression of a mechanistic attitude to man, who, born empty, allows his life to be shaped by his surroundings. For a long time I took a purely theoretical standpoint on the issue, which is actually so fundamental that it can be used as a springboard for any debate – if environment is the operative factor, for example, if man at the outset is both equal and malleable

and the good man can be shaped by engineering his surroundings, hence my parents' generation's belief in the
state, the education system and politics, hence their desire
to reject everything that had been and hence their new
truth, which is not found within man's inner being, in his
detached uniqueness, but on the contrary in areas external
to his intrinsic self, in the universal and collective, perhaps
expressed in its clearest form by Dag Solstad, who has
always been the chronicler of his age, in a text from 1969
containing his famous statement 'We won't give the coffee
pot wings': out with spirituality, out with feeling, in with a
new materialism, but it never struck them that the same
attitude could lie behind the demolition of old parts of
town to make way for roads and car parks, which naturally
the intellectual left opposed, and perhaps it has not been
possible to be aware of this until now, when the link
between the idea of equality and capitalism, the welfare
state and liberalism, Marxist materialism and the con-
sumer society is obvious because the biggest equality
creator of all is money, it levels all differences, and if your
character and your fate are entities that can be shaped,
money is the most natural shaper, and this gives rise to the
fascinating phenomenon whereby crowds of people assert
their individuality and originality by shopping in an identical way, while those who once ushered all this in with
their affirmation of equality, their emphasis on material
values and belief in change, are now inveighing against
their own handiwork, which they believe the enemy

created, but like all simple reasoning this is not wholly true
either: life is not a mathematical quantity, it has no theory,
only practice, and though it is tempting to understand a
generation's radical rethink of society as being based on its
view of the relationship between heredity and environment, this temptation is literary and consists more in the
pleasure of speculating, that is of weaving one's thoughts
through the most disparate areas of human activity, than
in the pleasure of proclaiming the truth. The sky is low in
Solstad's books, they show an incredible awareness of the
currents in modern times, from the feeling of alienation in
the 60s, the celebration of political initiatives at the beginning of the 70s, and then, just as the winds of change were
starting to blow, to the distance-taking at the end. These
weathervane-like conditions need be neither a strength
nor a weakness for a writer, but simply a part of his material, a part of his orientation, and in Solstad's case the most
significant feature has always been located elsewhere,
namely in his language, which sparkles with its new
old-fashioned elegance, and radiates a unique lustre, inimitable and full of elan. This language cannot be learned,
this language cannot be bought for money and therein lies
its value. It is not the case that we are born equal and that
the conditions of life make our lives unequal, it is the
opposite, we are born unequal, and the conditions of life
make our lives more equal.

When I think of my three children it is not only their
distinctive faces that appear before me, but also the

quite distinct feeling they radiate. This feeling, which is constant, is what they 'are' for me. And what they 'are' has been present in them ever since the first day I saw them. At that time they could barely do anything, and the little bit they could do, like sucking on a breast, raising their arms as reflex actions, looking at their surroundings, imitating, they could all do that, thus what they 'are' has nothing to do with qualities, has nothing to do with what they can or can't do but is more a kind of light that shines within them.

Their character traits, which slowly began to reveal themselves after only a few weeks, have never changed either, and so different are they inside each of them that it is difficult to imagine the conditions we provide for them, through our behaviour and ways of being, have any decisive significance. John has a mild, friendly temperament, loves his sisters, planes, trains and buses. Heidi is extrovert and talks to everyone she meets; she's obsessed with shoes and clothes, wants to wear only dresses, and is at ease with her little body, such as when she stood naked in front of the swimming pool mirror and said to Linda, Mummy, look what a nice bottom I've got! She hates being reprimanded; if you raise your voice to her she turns away and starts crying. Vanja, on the other hand, gives as good as she gets, has quite a temper, a strong will, is sensitive and gets on easily with people. She has a good memory, knows by heart most of the books we read to her as well as lines in the films we see. She has a sense of humour and is

always making us laugh when we are at home, but when she is outside she is easily affected by what goes on around her, and if the situation is too new or unaccustomed she goes into her shell. Shyness made its appearance when she was around seven months, and manifested itself through her shutting her eyes as if asleep whenever a stranger approached; she simply shut her eyes, as if she were asleep. She still does that on rare occasions; if she is sitting in the car and we bump into a parent from the nursery, for example, her eyes suddenly close. At the nursery in Stockholm, which was directly opposite our flat, after a tentative, fumbling start, she attached herself to a boy of her age called Alexander, and together they ran riot on the playground equipment, so much so that the staff said they sometimes had to protect Alexander from her – he couldn't always handle her intensity. But by and large he brightened up when she came, and was sorry when she left, and since then she has always preferred to play with boys; there is something about their physical and unrestrained side she obviously needs, perhaps because it is uncomplicated and easily gives her a feeling of control.

When we moved to Malmö she went to a new nursery, near the Western Harbour, in the newly built part of town where the most affluent lived, and as Heidi was so small I was the one who had to be responsible for settling her in. Every morning we cycled through the town, past the old shipbuilding yards and out towards the sea, Vanja with her little helmet on her head and her arms around me, me with

my knees at stomach height on the undersized ladies' bike, light-hearted and happy, for everything in the town was still new to me, and the shifts of light in the morning and afternoon sky had still not been dulled by the debilitating gaze of routine. I thought it would be no more than a transitional phase, Vanja telling me first thing every morning, with an occasional tear, that she didn't want to go to the nursery; she would like it after a while, of course she would. But when we arrived she would not budge from my lap, no matter what the three young women who comprised the staff enticed her with. I thought it would be best to throw her in at the deep end, just walk away and leave her to fend for herself, but neither they nor Linda would hear of such brutality, so I sat there on a chair in a corner of the room with Vanja on my lap, surrounded by children at play, with the sun blazing outside, but the weather became gradually more autumnal as the days passed. In the break, for a snack consisting of apple and pear slices served by the staff in the yard, she would only take part if we sat ten metres away from the others, and when I agreed to that, me with an apologetic smile on my face, it was no surprise to me, for this was my way of relating to other people: how had she, only two and a half years old, managed to pick it up? Of course the staff eventually succeeded in coaxing her away from me, and I was able to cycle back to do some writing while she shed heart-rending tears, and after a month had passed I dropped her off and picked her up as normal. But sometimes in the mornings she still said

she didn't want to go, still cried now and then, and when another nursery close to our flat rang to tell us they had a place free we didn't hesitate. It was called Lodjuret and was a parents' cooperative. That meant that all the parents had to put in two weeks' work a year on the staff, as well as filling one of the many administrative or practical posts. How far this nursery was to eat into our lives we had no idea; we talked only of the advantages it would bring: we would get to know Vanja's playmates and, through the duties and meetings, their parents. It was normal, we were told, for the children to go home together, so soon we would have some relief when we needed it. Furthermore, and this was perhaps the weightiest argument, we didn't know anyone in Malmö, not a soul, and this was an easy way to make contacts. And it was true: after a couple of weeks we were invited to one child's birthday party. Vanja was really looking forward to it, not least because she had just got a pair of gold-coloured party shoes she was going to wear, while at the same time not wanting to go, understandably enough, since she still didn't know the others very well. The invitation lay on the shelf in the nursery one Friday afternoon, the party was a week later on the Saturday, and every morning that week Vanja asked if it was Stella's party that day. When we said no, she asked if it was the day after tomorrow; that was about the furthest extent of the future horizon for her. The morning we were at last able to nod and say yes, we were going to Stella's today, she jumped out of bed and headed straight

for the cupboard to put on her golden shoes. A couple of times every hour she asked whether it would soon be time to go, and it could have been an unbearable morning of nagging and scenes, but fortunately there were activities to fill it with. Linda took her to a bookshop to buy a present, afterwards they sat at the kitchen table and made a birthday card. We bathed the girls, combed their hair and put on their white stockings and party dresses. Then Vanja's mood suddenly changed – she didn't want to wear stockings or a dress, there was no question of her going to any party, and she threw the golden shoes at the wall – but after patiently sitting through the few minutes the outburst lasted we managed to get her into everything, including even the white knitted shawl she had been given for Heidi's christening, and when at last the girls were sitting in the buggy in front of us they were again filled with expectation. Vanja was serious and quiet, her golden shoes in one hand and the present in the other, but when she turned to say something to us it was with a smile on her lips. Beside her sat Heidi, excited and happy, for although she didn't understand where we were going, the clothes and preparations must have given her an indication that something unusual was in the offing. The apartment where the party was to take place was a few hundred metres up the street where we lived. It was full of the bustle that marks late Saturday afternoons, the last heavily laden shoppers mingling with kids who have come to the town centre to hang around outside Burger King and

McDonald's, and the stream of traffic passing is no longer purely with a purpose in mind, families on their way to and from multi-storey car parks. Now there are more and more of the low shiny black cars with the bass throbbing through the bodywork driven by immigrant men in their twenties. Outside the supermarket there were so many people that we had to stop for a moment, and when the skinny wizened old lady who usually sat there in her wheelchair at this time of day caught sight of Vanja and Heidi she leaned towards them, rang the bell she had hanging from a stick and beamed a smile that was clearly meant to be engaging but to the girls must have been terrifying. But they said nothing, just looked at her. On the other side of the entrance sat a drug addict of my age, with a cap in his outstretched hand. He had a cat inside a cage next to him, and when Vanja saw it she turned to us.

'When we move to the country I want a cat,' she said.

'Cat!' Heidi said, pointing.

I steered the buggy over the kerb onto the road to pass three people walking so damned slowly, probably thought they owned the pavement, walked a few metres as fast as I could and steered back onto the pavement after we had passed them.

'That could be a long way off, you know, Vanja,' I said.

'You can't keep a cat in an apartment,' she said.

'Exactly,' Linda said.

Vanja looked ahead again. She was squeezing the bag containing the present with both hands.

I looked at Linda.

'What was his name again, Stella's father?'

'My mind's gone blank . . .' she said. 'Oh, it was Erik, wasn't it?'

'That's right,' I said. 'What was his job again?'

'I'm not sure,' she said. 'Something to do with design.'

We went past Gottgruvan and both Vanja and Heidi leaned forward to look through the window. Next door was a pawnbroker's. The shop beside that sold a variety of small statues and jewellery, angels and Buddhas, as well as joss sticks, tea, soap and other New Age knick-knacks. Posters hung in the windows giving information about when yoga gurus and well known clairvoyants were coming to town. On the other side of the street was a clothes shop with cheap brands, Ricco Jeans and Clothing, FASHION FOR THE WHOLE FAMILY, beside it was Taboo, a kind of 'erotic' boutique luring passers-by with dildos and dolls in various negligees and corsets in the window by the door, hidden from the street. Next to it was Bergman Bags and Hats, which must have remained unchanged in terms of interior and range from the day it was founded in the 40s, and Radio City, which had just gone bankrupt but where you could still see a window full of illuminated TV screens, surrounded by a wide selection of electrical goods, with prices written on large almost luminous orange and green bits of cardboard. The rule was that the further you advanced up the street, the cheaper and more dubious the shops became. The same applied to the people frequenting

the area. Unlike in Stockholm, where we had also lived in the centre, the poverty and misery which existed here were visible in the street. I liked that.

'Here it is,' Linda said, stopping by a door. Outside a bingo hall a little further on three pale-skinned women in their fifties stood smoking. Linda's gaze glided down the list of names beside the intercom; she pressed a number. Two buses thundered past one after the other. Then the door buzzed, and we went into the dark hallway, parked the buggy by the wall and went up the two flights of stairs to the flat, me with Heidi in my arms, Linda holding Vanja's hand. The door was open when we arrived. The inside of the flat was dark too. I felt a certain unease walking straight in, I would have preferred to ring, that would have made our arrival more obvious, because now we were standing in the hall without anyone paying us the slightest attention.

I set Heidi down and took off her jacket. Linda was about to do the same with Vanja, but she protested: her boots were to come off first, then she could put on her golden shoes.

There was a room on either side of the hall. In one, children were playing excitedly; in the other some adults were standing around talking. In the hall, which continued deeper into the flat, I saw Erik standing with his back to us chatting to a mother and father from the nursery.

'Hello!' I said.

He didn't turn. I laid Heidi's jacket on top of a coat on a

chair and met Linda's eye. She was looking for somewhere to hang Vanja's jacket.

'Shall we go in then?' she said.

Heidi wrapped her arms round my leg. I lifted her up and took a few steps forward. Erik turned.

'Hi,' he said.

'Hi,' I replied.

'Hi, Vanja!' he said.

Vanja turned away.

'Aren't you going to give Stella her present?' I asked.

'Stella, Vanja's here!' Erik said.

'You do it,' Vanja said.

Stella got up from the group of children on the floor. She smiled.

'Happy birthday, Stella!' I said. 'Vanja's got a present for you.'

I looked down at Vanja. 'Do you want to give it to her?'

'You do it,' she said in a low voice.

I took the present and passed it to Stella.

'It's from Vanja and Heidi,' I said.

'Thank you,' she said, and tore off the paper. When she saw it was a book she put it on the table next to the other presents and went back to the other children.

'Well?' said Erik. 'Everything OK?'

'Yes, fine,' I said. I could feel my shirt sticking to my chest. Was it noticeable? I wondered.

'What a nice apartment,' Linda said. 'Are there three bedrooms?'

'Yes,' Erik said.

He always looked so wily, always looked as though he had got something on the people he spoke to, it was hard to know where you stood with him; that half-smile of his could equally well have been sarcastic or congenial or tentative. If he'd had a pronounced or strong character, that might well have bothered me, but he was dithery in a weak-minded, irresolute kind of way, so whatever he might be thinking didn't worry me in the slightest. My attention was focused on Vanja. She was standing close to Linda and looking down at the floor.

'The others are in the kitchen,' Erik said. 'There's some wine there, if you fancy a glass.'

Heidi had already entered the room, she was standing in front of a shelf with a wooden snail in her hand. It had wheels and a string you could pull.

I nodded to the two parents down the hall.

'Hi,' they said.

What was his name, now? Johan? Or Jacob? And hers? Was it Mia? Oh hell. Of course. Robin, that was it.

'Hi,' I said.

'You all right?' he said.

'Yes,' I said. 'What about you two?'

'Everything's fine, thank you.'

I smiled at them. They smiled back. Vanja let go of Linda and hesitantly entered the room where the children were playing. For a while she stood observing them. Then it was as if she had decided to take the plunge.

KARL OVE KNAUSGAARD   34

'I've got golden shoes!' she said.

She bent forward and took off one shoe, held it up in the air in case anyone wanted to see. But no one did. When she realised that she put it back on.

'Wouldn't you like to play with the children over there?' I suggested. 'Can you see? They've got a big doll's house.'

She went over, sat down beside them but did nothing, just sat watching.

Linda lifted Heidi and carried her to the kitchen. I followed. Everyone said hello, we returned the greeting, sat down at the long table, I was by the window. They were talking about cheap air tickets, how they started out dirt cheap, slowly became more expensive as you had to pay one surcharge after another, until you were left with a ticket that cost as much as those from more expensive airlines. Then the topic moved to buying CO_2 quotas and after that to the newly introduced chartered train journeys. I could definitely have offered an opinion about that, but I didn't – small talk is one of the infinite number of talents I haven't mastered – so I sat nodding at what was said, as usual, smiling when others smiled, while ardently wishing myself miles away. In front of the worktop was Stella's mother, Frida, making some kind of salad dressing. She was no longer with Erik, and even though they were good at working together where Stella was concerned, you could still occasionally notice the tension and irritation between them at committee meetings in the nursery. She was blonde, had high cheekbones and narrow eyes, a long,

slim body, and she knew how to dress, but she was much too pleased with herself, too self-centred for me to find her attractive. I have no problem with uninteresting or unoriginal people – they may have other, more important attributes, such as warmth, consideration, friendliness, a sense of humour or talents such as being able to make a conversation flow to generate an atmosphere of ease around them, the ability to make a family function – but I feel almost physically ill in the presence of boring people who consider themselves especially interesting and who blow their own trumpets.

She placed the dish of what I thought was a dressing but which turned out to be a 'dip' on a board beside a dish of carrot sticks and one of cucumber sticks. At that moment Vanja came into the room. When she had located us she came over and stood close.

'I want to go home,' she said softly.

'We've only just got here!' I said.

'We're going to stay a bit longer,' Linda said. 'And look, now you're all getting some goodies!' Was she referring to the vegetables on the board?

She had to be.

They were crazy in this country.

'I'll go with you,' I said to Vanja. 'Come on.'

'Will you take Heidi as well?' Linda asked.

I nodded, and with Vanja at my heels I carried her into the room where the children were. Frida followed holding the board. She placed it on a little table in the middle of the floor.

'And look, now you're all getting some goodies!' Was she referring to the vegetables on the board? She had to be. They were crazy in this country

'Here's something to eat,' she said. 'Before the cake arrives.'

The children, three girls and a boy, went on playing with the doll's house. In the other room two boys were running around. Erik was in there, by the stereo system with a CD in his hand.

'I've got a bit of Norwegian jazz here,' he said. 'Are you a jazz fan?'

'We-ell . . .' I said.

'Norway has a great jazz scene,' he said.

'Who's that you have there?' I asked.

He showed me the cover. It was a band I had never heard of.

'Great,' I said.

Vanja was standing behind Heidi trying to lift her. Heidi was protesting.

'She says no, Vanja,' I said. 'Put her down.'

As she carried on I went over to them.

'Don't you want a carrot?' I asked.

'No,' Vanja said.

'But there's a dip,' I said. Went over to the table, took a carrot stick and dunked it in the white, presumably cream-based, dip and put it in my mouth.

'Mm,' I said. 'It's good!'

Why couldn't they have given them sausages, ice cream and pop? Lollipops? Jelly? Chocolate pudding?

What a stupid, bloody idiotic country this was. All the young women drank water in such vast quantities it was

coming out of their ears, they thought it was 'beneficial' and 'healthy', but all it did was send the graph of incontinent young people soaring. Children ate wholemeal pasta and wholemeal bread and all sorts of weird coarse-grained rice which their stomachs could not digest properly, but that didn't matter because it was 'beneficial', it was 'healthy', it was 'wholesome'. Oh, they were confusing food with the mind, they thought they could eat their way to being better human beings without understanding that food is one thing and the notions food evokes another. And if you said that, if you said anything of that kind, you were either reactionary or just a Norwegian, in other words ten years behind.

'I don't want any,' Vanja said. 'I'm not hungry.'

'OK, OK,' I said. 'But look here. Have you seen this? It's a train set. Shall we build it?'

She nodded, and we sat down behind the other children. I began to lay railway track in an arc while helping Vanja to fit her pieces. Heidi had moved into the other room, where she walked alongside the bookcase studying everything in it. Whenever the two boys' capers became too boisterous she swivelled round and glared at them.

Erik finally put on a CD and turned up the volume. Piano, bass and a myriad of percussion instruments that a certain type of jazz drummer adores – the kind that bangs stones against each other or uses whatever materials happen to be at hand. For me it sometimes meant nothing, and sometimes I found it ridiculous. I hated it when the audience applauded at jazz concerts.

Erik was nodding to the music, then turned, sent me a wink and went into the kitchen. At that moment the doorbell rang. It was Linus and his son Achilles. Linus had a pinch of *snus* under his top lip, was wearing black trousers, a dark coat and beneath it a white shirt. His fair hair was a touch unkempt, the eyes peering into the flat were honest and naïve.

'Hello!' he said. 'How are you doing?'

'Fine,' I said. 'And you?'

'Yep, jogging along.'

Achilles, who was small with large dark eyes, took off his jacket and shoes while staring at the children behind me. Children are like dogs, they always find their own in crowds. Vanja eyed him as well. He was her favourite, he was the one she had chosen to take over the role of Alexander. But after he had removed his outer clothing he went straight over to the other children, and there was nothing Vanja could do to stop him. Linus slipped into the kitchen, and the glint I thought I detected in his eye could only have been his anticipation of a chance to have a chat.

I got up and looked at Heidi. She was sitting beside the yucca plant under the window, taking earth from the pot and making small piles on the floor. I went over to her, lifted her, scraped what I could back with my hands, and went into the kitchen to find a rag. Vanja followed me. Once there, she climbed onto Linda's lap. In the living room Heidi started to cry. Linda sent me a quizzical look.

'I'll see to her,' I said. 'Just need something to wipe with.'

People were crowded round the worktop, it looked as if a meal was being prepared, and instead of squeezing through, I went to the toilet, unfurled a hefty handful of toilet paper, moistened it under the tap and went back to the living room to clean up. I lifted Heidi, who was still crying, and carried her to the bathroom to wash her hands. She wriggled and squirmed in my grip.

'There, there, sweetheart,' I said. 'Soon be done. Just a bit more, now, OK. There we are!'

As we came out the crying subsided, but she wasn't entirely happy, didn't want to be put down, just wanted to be in my arms. Robin stood in the living room with his arms crossed following the movements of his daughter Theresa, who was only a few months older than Heidi, although she could already speak in long sentences.

'Hi,' he said. 'Writing at the moment, are you?'

'Yes, a bit,' I said.

'Do you write at home?'

'Yes, I've got my own room.'

'Isn't that difficult? I mean, don't you ever feel like watching TV or washing some clothes or something, instead of writing?'

'It's fine. I get less time than if I had an office, but . . .'

'Yes, of course,' he said.

He had quite long blond hair that curled at the nape of his neck, clear blue eyes, a flat nose, broad jawbones. He wasn't strong, nor was he weak. He dressed as if he were in his mid-twenties, even though he was in his late thirties.

What went through his mind I had no idea, I didn't have a clue about what he was thinking, yet there was nothing secretive about him. On the contrary, his face and aura gave the impression of openness. But there was something else nevertheless, I sensed, a shadow of something else. His job was to integrate refugees into the community, he had told me once, and after a few follow-up questions about how many refugees were allowed into the country and so on, I let the matter drop because the opinions and sympathies I had were so far from the norm I assumed he represented that sooner or later they would shine through, whereupon I would come across as the baddie or the idiot, which I saw no reason to encourage.

Vanja, who was sitting on the floor slightly apart from the other children, looked towards us. I put Heidi down, and it was as though Vanja had been waiting for that: she got up at once and came over, took Heidi by the hand and led her to the games shelf, from which she passed her the wooden snail with feelers that whirred when you pulled it along the floor.

'Look, Heidi!' she said, taking it out of her hands and putting it on the floor. 'You pull the string like this. Then it whirrs. See?'

Heidi grabbed the string and pulled. The snail toppled over.

'No, not like that,' Vanja said. 'I'll show you.'

She placed the snail upright and slowly dragged it a few metres.

'I've got a little sister!' she said aloud. Robin had gone to the window, where he stood staring out into the backyard. Stella, who was energetic and presumably extra lively since it was her party, excitedly shouted something which I didn't understand, pointed to one of the two smaller girls, who handed her the doll she was clutching, took out a little buggy, placed the doll in it and began to push it down the hall. Achilles had found his way to Benjamin, a boy eighteen months older than Vanja who usually sat deeply absorbed in something, a drawing or a pile of Lego or a pirate ship with plastic pirates. He was imaginative, independent and well behaved, and was sitting with Achilles now, building the railway track Vanja and I had started. The two smaller girls ran after Stella. Heidi was whimpering. She was probably hungry. I went into the kitchen and sat down beside Linda.

'Will you go and see to them for a bit?' I said. 'I think Heidi's hungry.'

She nodded, patted my shoulder and got up. It took me a few seconds to figure out the subject of the two conversations going on round the table. One was about the car pool, the other about cars, and I inferred that the conversations must have gone off in opposite directions. The darkness outside the windows was dense, the light in the kitchen was frugal, the creases in the Swedish faces around the table were in shadow, and eyes gleamed in the glow from the candles. Erik and Frida and a woman whose name I didn't remember were standing at the worktop with their

backs to us, preparing food. The tenderness I felt for Vanja filled me to the brim, but there was nothing I could do. I glanced at the person speaking, gave a faint smile whenever there was a witticism and sipped at the glass of red wine someone had put in front of me.

Directly facing me was the only person who stood out. His face was large, his cheeks were scarred, features coarse, eyes intense. The hands on the table were large. He was wearing a 50s-style shirt and blue jeans rolled up to the calf. His hair was also typical of the 50s, and he sported side burns. But that was not what made him different; it was his personality, you could sense him sitting there, even though he didn't say much.

Once I had been to a party in Stockholm at which a boxer had been present. He was sitting in the kitchen, his physical presence was tangible, and he filled me with a distinct but unpleasant sensation of inferiority. A sensation that I was inferior to him. Strangely enough, the evening was to prove me right. The party was hosted by one of Linda's friends, Cora, her flat was small, so people were standing around chatting everywhere. Music was blaring from a system in the living room. Outside, the streets were white with snow. Linda was heavily pregnant, this was perhaps the last party we would be able to go to before the child was born and changed everything, so even though she was tired, she wanted to try and stay there for a while. I had a drop of wine and chatted to Thomas, who was a photographer and friend of Geir's; he knew Cora through his partner, Marie, who was

a poet and had been one of Cora's instructors at Biskops-Arnö Folk High School. Linda was sitting on a chair pulled back from the table because of her stomach, she was laughing and happy, and I was probably the only person aware of the slight introversion and faint glow that had come over her during these last few months. After a while she got up and went out, I smiled at her and turned my attention back to Thomas, who was saying something about the genes of redheads, so prevalent here this evening.

Someone was knocking.

'Cora!' I heard. 'Cora!'

Was it Linda?

I got up and went into the hallway.

The knocking was coming from inside the bathroom.

'Is that you, Linda?' I asked.

'Yes,' she said. 'I think the door lock has jammed. Can you get Cora? There must be some sort of knack to it.'

I went into the living room and tapped Cora on the shoulder. She was holding a plate of food in one hand and a glass of red wine in the other.

'Linda's locked in the bathroom,' I said.

'Oh no!' she said, set the glass and the plate down and dashed out.

They conferred for a while through the locked door. Linda tried to follow the instructions she was given, but nothing helped, the door was and remained jammed. Everyone in the flat was aware of the situation now, the mood was both amused and excited, a whole flock of people were

in the hall giving advice to Linda while Cora, flummoxed and anxious, kept saying that Linda was heavily pregnant, we had to do something now. In the end the decision was taken to ring for a locksmith. While we waited for him I stood by the door talking to Linda inside, unpleasantly conscious of the fact that everyone could hear what I said and of my own helplessness. Couldn't I just kick the door in and get her out? Simple and effective?

I had never kicked a door in before. I didn't know how solid it was. Imagine if it didn't budge. How stupid would that look?

The locksmith arrived half an hour later. He laid out a canvas bag of tools on the floor and began to fiddle with the lock. He was small, wore glasses and had the beginnings of a bald patch, said nothing to the circle of people around him, tried one tool after another in vain, the damned lock wouldn't budge. In the end, he gave up, told Cora it was no good, he couldn't get the door open.

'What shall we do then?' Cora asked. 'She's due soon!'

He shrugged.

'You'll have to kick it in,' he said, starting to pack his tools.

Who was going to kick it in?

It had to be me. I was Linda's husband. It was my responsibility.

My heart was pounding.

Should I do it? Take a step back in full view of everyone and kick it with all my might?

What if the door didn't give? What if it swung open and hit Linda?

She would have to take shelter in the corner.

Calmly, I breathed in and out several times. But it didn't help, I was still shaking inside. Attracting attention like this was anathema to me. If there was a risk of failure it was even worse.

Cora looked around.

'We have to kick the door in,' she said. 'Who can do that?'

The locksmith disappeared through the door. If it was going to be me, now was the time to step forward.

But I couldn't bring myself to do it.

'Micke,' Cora said. 'He's a boxer.'

She swivelled to fetch him from the living room.

'I can ask him,' I said. In that way I wouldn't be hiding my humiliation at any rate, I would tell him straight out that I, as Linda's husband, didn't dare to kick in the door, I was asking you, as a boxer and a giant, to do it for me.

He was standing by the window with a beer in his hand chatting to two girls.

'Hello, Micke,' I said.

He looked at me.

'She's still locked in the bathroom. The locksmith couldn't open the door. Could you kick it in, do you think?'

'Of course,' he said, eyeing me for a moment before putting down his beer and going into the hallway. I followed. People moved to the side as he made his way to the door.

'Are you in there?' he asked.

'Yes,' said Linda.

'Stand as far back from the door as you can. I'm going to kick it in.'

'Right,' Linda said.

He waited for a moment. Then he raised his foot and kicked the door with such force that the lock was knocked inwards. Splinters flew.

When Linda came out, some people clapped.

'Poor you,' Cora said. 'I'm so sorry. Subjecting you to that, and then . . .'

Micke turned and went.

'How are you?' I asked.

'Fine,' Linda said. 'But I think maybe we should go home soon.'

'Of course,' I said.

In the living room the music was turned down as two women in their early thirties were about to read their gushing poems. I passed Linda her jacket, put on mine, said goodbye to Cora and Thomas, my shame seared inside me, but the last duty remained, I had to thank Micke for what he had done. I made my way through the poetry audience and stopped by the window in front of him.

'Thank you very much,' I said. 'You rescued her.'

He blew out his cheeks and shrugged his shoulders. 'It was nothing.'

In the taxi on the way home I hardly looked at Linda. I hadn't risen to the task. I had been so cowardly as to let

someone else do the job, and all of that was visible in my eyes. I was a miserable wretch.

When we were in bed she asked what was wrong with me. I said I was ashamed that I hadn't kicked in the door. She looked at me in astonishment. The thought had not even occurred to her. Why should I have done it? I wasn't the type, was I.

The man sitting on the opposite side of the table radiated some of the same vibes the boxer in Stockholm had. It didn't have anything to do with the size of his body or muscle mass, for even though several of the men here had well-trained powerful upper bodies they still made a light-weight impression, their presence in the room was fleeting and insignificant like a casual thought. No, there was something else, and whenever I met it I came off worse, I saw myself as the weak trammelled man I was, who lived his life in the world of words. I sat musing on this while taking occasional peeps at him and listening to the ongoing conversation with half an ear. Now it had turned to various teaching styles, and which schools each of them was considering for their children. After a short inter-mezzo in which Linus talked about a sports day he had attended, the conversation moved to house prices. There was agreement that house prices had soared over recent years, but more in Stockholm than here, and that presumably it was just a question of time before the tide would turn, maybe they would even fall as steeply as they had risen. Then Linus turned to face me.

'What are house prices like in Norway, then?' he asked.

'About the same as here,' I said. 'Oslo's as expensive as Stockholm. It's a bit cheaper in the provinces.'

He kept his eyes fixed on me for a while, in case I might exploit the opening he had given me, but when this proved not to be the case, he turned back and continued chatting. He had done the very same thing at the first general meeting we had attended, though at that time with a kind of critical undertone, because, as he had put it, the meeting was drawing to a close and Linda and I still hadn't said anything, the point was that everyone should have their say, that was the whole idea of a parents' cooperative. I had no idea what to think about the matter under discussion, and it was Linda who, with a faint blush, weighed up the pros and cons on behalf of the family, with the whole assembly staring at her. First on the agenda was whether the nursery should get rid of the cook who was employed there, and instead go for a catering firm, which would be cheaper, and second, if they did that, what kind of food they should opt for: vegetarian or the standard? Lodjuret was actually a vegetarian nursery, that was the principle on which it had been founded in its day, but now only four of the parents were vegetarians, and since the children didn't eat much of the numerous varieties of vegetables that were served up, many parents thought they might as well dispense with the principle. The discussion lasted for several hours and scoured the subject like a trawl net on the seabed. The meat percentage in various types of sausage

was brought up; it was one thing that the sausages bought in shops had the meat percentage printed on the label, but quite another what catering companies did with their sausages, because how could you know how much meat they contained? To me sausages were sausages. I didn't have the slightest idea about the world that was opening before my eyes that evening, least of all that there were people who could delve so deeply into it. Wasn't it nice for the children to have a cook who made food for them in their kitchen? I thought but didn't say, and I was beginning to hope that the whole discussion would pass without our having to say anything, before, that is, Linus fixed his astute and naïve eyes on us.

From the living room came the sound of Heidi crying. Again I thought of Vanja. Usually she solved situations like these by doing exactly the same as the others. If they pulled out a chair, she pulled out a chair, if they sat down, she sat down, if they laughed, she laughed, even if she didn't understand what they were laughing at. If they ran around calling a name, she ran around calling a name. That was her method. But Stella had seen through it. Once I happened to be there and heard her say, You just copy us! You're a parrot! A parrot! That hadn't deterred her from continuing, so far the method had proved too successful for that, but now when Stella herself was holding court it probably did inhibit her. I knew she understood what this was all about. Several times she had said the same to Heidi, that she copied her, she was a parrot.

Stella was eighteen months older than Vanja, who admired her above all else. When she was allowed to tag along, it was at Stella's grace, and she had this hold on all the children in the nursery. She was a beautiful child, she had blonde hair and big eyes, was always nicely, sensibly dressed, and the streak of cruelty she possessed was no worse and no better than that displayed by other children at the top of the hierarchy. That was not why I had problems with her. The problems for me were that she was so aware of the impression she made on adults, and the way in which she exploited this charming innocence. During my compulsory duties at the nursery I had never fallen for it. No matter how sparkling the eyes she clapped on me when she asked for something, my reaction remained one of indifference, which of course confused her, and she redoubled her endeavours to charm me. Once she had stayed with us after nursery to go to the park and sat beside Vanja in the double buggy while I carried Heidi on one arm and pushed them with the other. She jumped out a few hundred metres before the park to run the last stretch, which I reacted sharply to. I called her back and said that she was to sit nicely in the buggy until we arrived, there were cars around, couldn't she see them? She looked at me in surprise, she wasn't used to that tone, and even though I was not satisfied with the way I had resolved the situation, I also thought that a *No!* was not the worst thing that could befall this creature. But she had taken note of it, because when, half an hour later, I swung them round by

their feet to their immense glee, and then knelt down to fight with them, which Vanja loved, especially when she took a run-up and knocked me over onto the grass, Stella, when it was her turn, kicked me on the calf instead, and that was all right once, all right twice, but when she did it a third time I told her, That hurts, that does, just stop it now, Stella, which of course she ignored, now it had become exciting, and she kicked me again, with a loud laugh, and Vanja, who always aped her, also laughed, whereupon I got up, grabbed Stella around the waist and stood her up. 'Listen to me, you little brat,' I felt like saying, and would have done had her mother not been coming to collect her in half an hour. 'Listen, Stella,' I said instead, harshly, with annoyance, looking her in the eye. 'When I say no, I mean no. Do you understand?' She looked down, refusing to answer. I raised her chin. 'Do you understand?' I asked again. She nodded, and I let her go. 'I'm going to sit on that bench over there. You can play on your own until your mother comes.' Vanja sent me a bemused look. But then she laughed and tugged at Stella. For her, scenes like this were everyday occurrences. Fortunately, Stella dropped the matter at once, for I was really skating on thin ice – what on earth would I do if she began to cry or scream? But she went with Vanja over to the big 'train' which was teeming with kids. When her mother came she had two paper cups of latte in her hand. Usually I would have gone as soon as she arrived, but when she passed me a cup of coffee I had no option but to sit down and listen to her chatter on about

her job, while squinting into the low November sun and keeping half an eye on the children.

The week when I'd had nursery duty and in principle had been like any employee ran more or less like clockwork; I had worked a lot in institutions before and soon had all the routines off pat, which the staff were not accustomed to seeing with parents, nor was I a stranger to dressing and undressing children, changing their nappies and even playing if it was required. The children reacted to my presence in different ways, of course. For example, one of them who hung around without any friends, a gangling white-haired boy, wanted to crawl up onto my lap all the time, either to have a story read or just to sit there. I played with another one for half an hour after the others had gone, his mother was late, but he forgot all about that when we played pirate ships. To his great delight, I kept adding new features like sharks and marauding boats and fires. A third boy, on the other hand, the oldest there, immediately discovered one of my weak spots by taking a bunch of keys from my pocket while we were at the table eating. The mere fact that I didn't stop him, even though I was angry, allowed him to follow the scent. First of all, he asked if there was a car key. When I shook my head he asked me why not. I haven't got a car, I said. Why not? he asked. I haven't got a licence, I said. Can't you drive a car? he said. Aren't you an adult, then? he asked. All adults can drive cars, can't they? Then he jingled the keys under my nose. I let him do it, thinking he would soon tire of it,

but he didn't; on the contrary he persisted. I've got your keys, he said. And you can't get them. He kept jingling them under my nose. The other children watched us, the three members of staff as well. I made the mistake of lunging for the keys. He managed to pull them away in time, and laughed and jeered. Ha, ha, you didn't get them! he crowed. Again I tried not to show my annoyance. He started banging the keys on the table. Don't do that, I said. He just smiled cheekily and persisted. One of the nursery staff told him to stop. And he did. But continued to dangle them from his hand. You'll never get them, he said. Then Vanja broke in.

'Give the keys to daddy!' she said.

What kind of situation was this?

I acted as if nothing was happening, leaned over the food again and went on eating. But the little devil continued to tease me. Jingle, jingle. I decided to let him keep them until we had finished eating. Drank some water, feeling my face strangely flushed over such a tiny matter. Was that what Olaf, the head of the nursery, saw? At any rate, he ordered Jocke to hand back the keys. And Jocke did, without any fuss.

All my adult life I have kept a distance from other people, it has been my way of coping because I come so incredibly close to others in my thoughts and feelings they only have to look away dismissively for a storm to break inside me. That closeness naturally informs my relationship with children too, that is what allows me to sit down

and play with them, but as they lack any veneer of courtesy and decency that adults have, this also means they can freely penetrate the outer bulwarks of my personality and then wreak as much havoc as they wish. My only defence, when it all started, was either sheer physical strength, which I was not able to use, or else simply to pretend I wasn't bothered, possibly the best approach, but something I wasn't so adept at, since the children, at least the most forward of them, immediately discovered how uncomfortable I was in their presence.

Oh, how undignified this was!

Everything was suddenly turned on its head. I, who wasn't fond of the nursery Vanja attended, who just wanted it to look after Vanja for me so that I could work in peace for some hours every day without knowing what she was doing or how she was, I who didn't want any closeness in my life, who could not get enough of distance, could not be alone enough, who all of a sudden had to spend a week there as an employee and get involved in everything that happened, but it did not stop there, for when you dropped off your children or picked them up it was normal to sit for a few minutes in the playroom or dining room or wherever they were, and chat to the other parents, perhaps play a little with the children, and every day of the week . . . I usually kept this to the bare minimum, took Vanja and put on her coat before anyone discovered what was going on, but now and then I was trapped in the corridor, a conversation was initiated, and, hey presto, there I was sitting on one of

those low deep sofas making agreement noises about something or other that was of no interest to me whatsoever while the brashest of the children yanked and tugged at me, wanting me to throw them, carry them, swing them round or, in the case of Jocke, who incidentally was the son of the kind book-loving banker Gustav, was content merely to stab me with sharp objects.

Spending Saturday afternoon and evening squeezed between others at a table and eating vegetables with a strained but courteous smile on your face was part of the same obligation.

Erik lifted down a stack of plates from a cupboard above the worktop while Frida counted knives and forks. I took a sip of wine and could feel how hungry I was. Stella stopped in the doorway, her face red and a little sweaty.

'Is it time for the cake now?' she called.

Frida swivelled round.

'Soon, sweetheart. But first we have to eat some proper food.'

Her attention wandered from the child to those sitting around the table.

'The food's ready,' she said. 'Help yourselves. There are the plates and cutlery. And you can take some food for your children too.'

'Ah, that sounds good,' Linus said, getting up. 'What is there?'

I had planned to stay seated until the queue had died down. When I saw what Linus had returned with – beans,

salad, the ever-present couscous and a hot dish I assumed was chickpea casserole – I got up and went into the kitchen.

'Food's in there,' I said to Linda, who was standing with Vanja wrapped around her legs and Heidi in her arms chatting to Mia. 'Shall we swap?'

'Yes, that's good,' Linda said. 'I'm ravenous.'

'Can we go home now, daddy?' Vanja said.

'But we're eating,' I said. 'And afterwards there's cake. Shall I get you some food?'

'Don't want anything,' she said.

'I'll get you something anyway,' I said, and took Heidi by the arm. 'And you come with me.'

'Heidi's had a banana, by the way,' Linda said. 'But she'll probably want some food as well.'

'Come on, Theresa, let's go and get something for you,' Mia said.

I followed them in, lifted Heidi into my arms and stood in the queue. She rested her head against my shoulder, which she only did when she was tired. My shirt stuck to my chest. Every face I saw, every glance I met, every voice I heard, hung like a lead weight on me. When I was asked a question, or asked a question myself, it was as if the words had to be dynamited out. Heidi made it easier, having her there was a kind of protection, both because I had something to occupy myself with and because her presence diverted others' attention. They smiled at her, asked if she was tired and stroked her cheek. A large part of my relationship with Heidi was based on me carrying her. It

was the basis of our relationship. She always wanted to be carried, never wanted to walk, stretched up her arms as soon as she saw me, and smiled with pleasure whenever she was allowed to hang from my arms. And I liked having her close, the little chubby creature with the greedy mouth.

I put some beans, a couple of spoonfuls of chickpea casserole and a dollop of couscous on a plate and carried it into the living room, where all the children were sitting around the low table in the middle, with a helpful parent behind.

'Don't want anything,' Vanja said as soon as I set the plate in front of her.

'That's OK,' I said. 'You don't have to eat if you don't want to. But do you think Heidi wants some?'

I speared some beans on the fork and raised it to her mouth. She pinched her lips together and twisted her head away.

'Come on now,' I said. 'I know you're both hungry.'

'Can we play with the train?' Vanja asked.

I looked at her. Normally she would have stared either at the train set or up at me, begging as often as not, but now she was staring straight ahead.

'Of course we can,' I said. I put Heidi down and went to the corner of the room where I had to press my knees against my body, almost into my chest, to make room between the tiny children's furniture and the toy boxes. I took the railway track apart and passed it piece by piece to Vanja, who tried to reassemble it. When the pieces didn't

fit she forced them together with all her strength. I waited until she was on the point of throwing them down in fury before intervening. Heidi constantly wanted to tear the track up, and my eyes searched for something to give her as a diversion. A puzzle? A cuddly toy? A little plastic pony with large eyelashes and a long pink synthetic mane? She hurled all of them away.

'Daddy, can you help me?' Vanja said.

'Course I can,' I said. 'Look. Let's put a bridge here, so the train can go over and under it. That'll be good, won't it.'

Heidi grabbed one of the bridge pieces.

'Heidi!' Vanja said.

I took it from her, and she began to scream. I took her in my arms and stood up.

'I can't do it!' Vanja said.

'I'll be there in a sec. I'm just going to take Heidi to mummy,' I said, and went to the kitchen carrying Heidi on my hip like an experienced housewife. Linda was chatting with Gustav, the only one of the Lodjuret parents with a good old-fashioned profession, and with whom for some reason she got on well. He was jovial, his face shone, his short always neatly dressed body was robust and stocky, his neck strong, his chin broad, his face chubby but open and cheerful. He liked talking about books he had enjoyed, the latest of which were by Richard Ford.

'They're fantastic,' he would say. 'Have you read them? They're about an estate agent, an ordinary man, yes, and

his life, so recognisable and normal. Ford captures the whole spirit of America! The American mood, the very pulse of the country!'

I liked Gustav, especially his decency, which was thanks to nothing more complicated than his having a basic, honest job, which incidentally none of my friends had, least of all myself. We were the same age, but I thought of him as ten years older from his appearance. He was adult in the way our parents had been when I was growing up.

'I think perhaps Heidi ought to go to sleep soon,' I said. 'She seems tired. And probably hungry too. Will you take her home?'

'Yes, just have to finish eating first, OK?'

'Of course.'

'Now I've held your book in my hand!' Gustav said. 'I was in the bookshop, and there it was. It looked interesting. Was it published by Norstedts?'

'Yes,' I said with a strained smile. 'It was.'

'You didn't buy it then?' Linda asked, not without a teasing tone to her voice.

'No, not this time,' he said, wiping his mouth with a serviette. 'It's about angels, isn't it?'

I nodded. Heidi had slipped from my grasp, and when I lifted her up again I noticed how heavy her nappy was.

'I'll change her before you go,' I said. 'You brought the changing bag, didn't you?'

'Yes, it's in the hall.'

'OK,' I said, and went out to fetch a nappy. In the living

room Vanja and Achilles were running around, jumping from the sofa onto the floor, laughing, getting up and jumping off again. I felt a surge of warmth in my breast. Leaned over and picked up a nappy and a packet of wipes while Heidi clung to me like a little koala bear. There was no changing table in the bathroom, so I laid her on the floor tiles, took off her stockings, tore off the two adhesive tabs on the nappy and threw it in the bin under the sink while Heidi watched me with a serious expression.

'Just wee-wee!' she said. Then she turned her head to the side and stared at the wall, apparently unmoved by my putting on a clean nappy, the way she had done ever since she was a baby.

'There we are,' I said. 'That's you done.'

I grabbed her hands and pulled her up. Then folded her tights, which were slightly damp, and took them to the bag on the buggy, whereupon I dressed her in some jogging pants I found, and then the brown bubble-lined corduroy jacket she had been given for her first birthday by Yngve. Linda came in while I was putting on Heidi's shoes.

'I'll be coming soon too,' I said. We kissed, Linda took the bag in one hand, Heidi in the other, and they left.

Vanja ran at top speed down the hallway, with Achilles in tow, into what must have been the bedroom, from where her overexcited voice could be heard soon afterwards. The thought of going in and sitting at the kitchen table again was not exactly appealing, so I opened the bathroom door, locked it behind me and stood there motionless for a few

minutes. Then washed my face in cold water, dried it carefully on a white towel and met my eyes in the mirror, so
dark and in a face so rigid with frustration I almost started
with alarm at the sight.

No one in the kitchen noticed that I was back. Except
for a stern-looking little woman with short hair and ordinary angular features, who stared for a brief moment at me
from behind her glasses. What did she want now?

Gustav and Linus were discussing pension arrangements, the taciturn man with the 50s shirt had his child, a
wild boy with blond, almost white hair, on his lap, and was
discussing FC Malmö with him, while Frida chatted with
Mia about club evenings she and some friends were going
to start. Meanwhile, Erik and Mathias compared TV screens,
a discussion which Linus wanted to join, I could see that
from his long glances and the shorter ones to Gustav so as
not to appear impolite. The only person not deep in conversation was the woman with cropped hair, and even though
I looked in every direction apart from hers she still leaned
across the table and asked if I was satisfied with the nursery.
I said I was. There was perhaps a bit too much to do there,
I added, but it was definitely worth the investment of time;
you got to know your children's playmates, and that could
only be good, I opined.

She smiled at what I said without any great fervour.
There was something sad about her, some unhappiness.

'What the hell?' Linus said suddenly, thrusting his chair
back. 'What are they *doing* in there?'

He got up and went to the bathroom. The next moment he came out with Vanja and Achilles in front of him. Vanja had put on her broadest smile, Achilles looked rather more guilt-ridden. The sleeves of his small suit jacket were soaked. Vanja's bare arms glistened with moisture.

'They had their hands as far down the toilet as they could get them when I went in,' Linus said. I met Vanja's eyes and couldn't help smiling.

'We'll have to take this off now, young man,' Linus said, leading Achilles into the hall. 'And you make sure you wash your hands properly.'

'The same applies to you, Vanja,' I said, getting up. 'Into the bathroom with you.'

She stretched out her arms over the basin and looked up at me.

'I'm playing with Achilles!' she said.

'I can see that,' I said. 'But you don't have to stick your hands down the loo to do that, do you?'

'No,' she said, and laughed.

I wetted my hands under the tap, soaped them, and washed her arms from the tips of her fingers to her shoulders. Then I dried them before kissing her on the forehead and sending her out again. The apologetic smile I wore when I sat down was unnecessary, no one was interested in pursuing this little episode, not even Linus, who as soon as he returned continued the story about a man he had seen attacked by monkeys in Thailand. His face didn't even break into a smile when the others laughed, but he

seemed to inhale their laughter, as if to give the story renewed vigour, which it did, and only when the next wave of laughter broke did he smile, not much, and not at his own wit, it struck me; it was more like an expression of the satisfaction he felt when his face could bask in the merriment he had evoked. 'Yeah, yeah, yeah,' he said, jabbing his hand in the air. The stern woman, who thus far had been looking out of the window, pulled her chair up and leaned across the table again.

'Isn't it tough to have two children so close in age?' she asked.

'Yes and no,' I answered. 'It is a bit wearing. But it's still better with two than one. The single-child scenario seems a bit sad, if you ask me . . . I've always thought I wanted to have three children. Then there are lots of permutations when they play. And the children are in the majority vis-à-vis the parents . . .'

I smiled. She said nothing. All of a sudden I realised she had an only child.

'But just one can be brilliant too,' I said.

She rested her head on her hand.

'But I wish Gustav had a brother or a sister,' she said. 'It's too much with just us two.'

'Not at all,' I said. 'He'll have loads of pals in the nursery, and that's great.'

'The problem is I haven't got a husband,' she said. 'And so it's not possible.'

What the *fuck* had that got to do with me?

I sent her a look of sympathy and concentrated on preventing my eyes from wandering, which can easily happen in such situations.

'And I can't imagine the men I meet as fathers to my children,' she continued.

'Nonsense,' I said. 'These things sort themselves out.'

'I don't believe they do,' she said. 'But thank you anyway.'

From the corner of my eye I detected a movement. I turned and looked towards the door. Vanja was coming my way. She stopped right next to me.

'I want to go home,' she said. 'Can't we go now?'

'We have to stay for a just a little longer,' I said. 'Soon there'll be cake too. You want some of that, don't you?'

She didn't answer.

'Do you want to sit on my lap?' I asked.

She nodded, and I moved my wine glass and lifted her up.

'You sit with me for a bit, and then we'll go back in. I can stay with you. OK?'

'OK.'

She sat watching the others round the table. I wondered what she was thinking. How did it seem to her?

I observed her. Her blonde hair was already over her shoulders. A small nose, a little mouth, two tiny ears, both with pointed elfin tips. Her blue eyes, which always betrayed her mood, had a slight squint, hence the glasses. At first she had been proud of them. Now they were the

first thing she took off when she was angry. Perhaps because she knew it was important for us that she should wear them?

With us her eyes were lively and cheerful, that is if they didn't lock and become unapproachable when she was having one of her grand bouts of fury. She was hugely dramatic and could rule the whole family with her temperament; she performed large-scale and complicated relational dramas with her toys, loved having stories read to her but watching films even more, and then preferably ones with characters and high drama which she puzzled over and discussed with us, bursting with questions but also the joy of retelling. For a period it was Astrid Lindgren's character Madicken she was mad about, and this caused her to jump off the chairs and lie on the floor with her eyes closed; we had to lift her and think at first that she was dead, then realise she had fainted and had concussion, before carrying her, with eyes closed and arms hanging down, to her bed, where she was to lie for three days, preferably while we hummed the sad theme from this scene in the film. Then she leaped to her feet, ran to the chair and started all over again. At the nursery's Christmas party she was the only one who bowed in response to the applause and who obviously enjoyed the attention. Often the idea of something meant more to her than the thing itself, such as with sweets; she could talk about them for an entire day and look forward to them, but when the sweets were in the bowl in front of her she barely tasted one before spitting it

out. However, she didn't learn from the experience: the next Saturday her expectations of the fantastic sweets were as high again. She wanted so much to go skating, but when we were there, at the rink, with the small skates Linda's mother had bought for her on her feet and the little ice hockey helmet on her head, she shrieked with anger at the realisation that she couldn't keep her balance and probably wouldn't learn to do so any time soon. All the greater therefore was her joy at seeing that she could in fact ski, which happened once when we were on the small patch of snow in my mother's garden trying out equipment she had come by. But then too the idea of skiing and the joy at being able to do it were greater than actually skiing; she could function quite happily without that. She loved to travel with us, loved to see new places and talked about all the things that had happened for several months afterwards. But most of all she loved to play with other children, of course. It was a great experience for her when other children at the nursery came back home with her. The first time Benjamin was due to come she went around the evening before, inspecting her toys, worried stiff that they were not good enough for him. She had just turned three. But when he arrived they got on like a house on fire and all prior concerns went up in a whirl of excitement and euphoria. Benjamin told his parents that Vanja was the nicest girl in the nursery, and when I told her that – she was sitting in bed playing with her Barbies – she reacted with a display of emotion she had never manifested before.

'Do you know what Benjamin said?' I said from the doorway.

'No,' she said, looking up at me with sudden interest.

'He said you were the nicest girl in the nursery.'

I had never seen her filled with such light. She was glowing with happiness. I knew that neither Linda nor I would be able to say anything to make her react like that, and I understood with the immediate clarity of an insight that she was not ours. Her life was utterly her own.

'What did he say?' she answered, she wanted to hear it again.

'He said you were the nicest in the nursery.'

Her smile was shy but happy, and that made me glad too, yet a shadow hung over my happiness, for was it not alarmingly early for others' thoughts and opinions to mean so much to her? Wasn't it best for everything to come from her, for it to be rooted in herself? Another time she surprised me like this was when I was in the nursery. I had gone to pick her up and she ran towards me in the corridor and asked if Stella could go with her to the stables afterwards. I said that things didn't work like that, it had to be planned in advance, we had to speak to her parents first, and Vanja stood watching me say this, obviously disappointed, but when she went to pass on the news to Stella, she didn't use my reasons. I heard her as I was rummaging in the hall for her rain gear.

'It'll be a bit boring for you at the stables,' she said. 'Just watching isn't cool.'

This way of thinking, putting others' reactions before your own, I recognised from myself, and as we walked towards Folkets Park in the rain I wondered about how she had picked that up. Was it just there, around her, invisible but present, like the air she breathed? Or was it genetic?

I never expressed any of these thoughts I had about the children, except to Linda of course, because these complex questions belonged only where they were, in me and between us. In reality, in the world Vanja inhabited everything was simple and found simple expression, and the complexity arose only in the sum of all the parts, of which naturally she knew nothing. And the fact that we talked a lot about them did not help at all in our daily lives, where everything was a mess and constantly on the verge of chaos. In the first of the Swedish 'progress conversations' we had with the nursery staff there was a lot of talk about her not making contact with the teachers, not wanting to sit on their laps or be patted, as well as her shyness. We should work on toughening her up, teaching her to play a more dominant role in games, taking the initiative and talking more, they said. Linda replied that she was tough enough at home, took the lead in all the games, always showed initiative and could talk the hind leg off a donkey. They told us the little she said in the nursery was unclear, her Swedish wasn't correct, her vocabulary was not that large, so they were wondering if we had considered speech therapy. At this juncture in the conversation we were handed a brochure from one of the town's speech therapists. They are

crazy in this country, I thought. A speech therapist? Did everything have to be institutionalised? She's only three!

'No, speech therapy's out of the question,' I said. Until that point Linda had been the one to do all the talking. 'It will sort itself out. I only *started* talking when I was three. Before that I said nothing, apart from single words which were incomprehensible to anyone except my brother.'

They smiled.

'And when I started speaking it came in long, fluent sentences. It all depends on the individual. We are not sending her to a speech therapist.'

'Well, that's up to you,' said Olaf, the head of the nursery. 'But you're welcome to hang on to the brochures and give it some thought.'

'OK then,' I said.

When I was with other people I was bound to them, the nearness I felt was immense, the empathy great. Indeed, so great that their well-being was always more important than my own. I subordinated myself, almost to the verge of self-effacement; some uncontrollable internal mechanism caused me to put their thoughts and opinions before my own. But the moment I was alone others meant nothing to me. It wasn't that I disliked them, or nurtured feelings of loathing for them; on the contrary, I liked most of them, and the ones I didn't actually like I could always see some worth in, some attribute I could identify with, or at least find interesting, something which could occupy my mind for the moment. But liking them was not the same as

caring about them. It was the social situation that bound me, the people within it did not. Between these two perspectives there was no halfway house. There was just the small self-effacing one and the large distance-creating one. And in between them was where my daily life lay. Perhaps that was why I had such a hard time living it. Everyday life, with its duties and routines, was something I endured, not a thing I enjoyed, nor something that was meaningful or made me happy. This had nothing to do with a lack of desire to wash floors or change nappies but rather with something more fundamental: the life around me was not meaningful. I always longed to be away from it, and always had done. So the life I led was not my own. I tried to make it mine, this was my struggle, because of course I wanted it, but I failed, the longing for something else undermined all my efforts.

What was the problem?

Was it the shrill sickly tone I heard everywhere, which I couldn't stand, the one that arose from all the pseudo people and pseudo places, pseudo events and pseudo conflicts our lives passed through, that which we saw but did not participate in, and the distance that modern life in this way had opened up to our own, actually inalienable, here and now? If so, if it was more reality, more involvement I longed for, surely I should be embracing that which I was surrounded by? And not, as was the case, longing to get away from it? Or perhaps it was the prefabricated nature of the days in this world I was reacting to, the rails of

routine we followed, which made everything so predictable that we had to invest in entertainment to feel any hint
of intensity? Every time I went out of the door I knew what
was going to happen, what I was going to do. This was how
it was on the micro level, I go to the supermarket and do
the shopping, I go and sit down at a café with a newspaper,
I fetch my children from the nursery, and this is how it was
on the macro level, from the initial entry into society, the
nursery, to the final exit, the old folks' home. Or was the
revulsion I felt based on the sameness that was spreading
through the world and making everything smaller? If you
travelled through Norway now you saw the same everywhere. The same roads, the same houses, the same petrol
stations, the same shops. As late as in the 60s you could
see how local culture changed as you drove through Gud-
brandsdalen, for example, the strange black timber
buildings, so pure and sombre, which were now encapsu-
lated as small museums in a culture which was no different
from the one you had left or the one you were going to.
And Europe, which was merging more and more into one
large, homogeneous country. The same, the same, everything was the same. Or was it perhaps that the light which
illuminated the world and made everything comprehensible also drained it of meaning? Was it perhaps the forests
that had vanished, the animal species that had become
extinct, the ways of life that would never return?

  Yes, all of this I thought about, all of this filled me with
sorrow and a sense of helplessness, and if there was a

world I turned to in my mind, it was that of the sixteenth and seventeenth centuries, with its enormous forests, its sailing ships and horse-drawn carts, its windmills and castles, its monasteries and small towns, its painters and thinkers, explorers and inventors, priests and alchemists. What would it have been like to live in a world where everything was made from the power of your hands, the wind or the water? What would it have been like to live in a world where the American Indians still lived their lives in peace? Where that life was an actual possibility? Where Africa was unconquered? Where darkness came with the sunset and light with the sunrise? Where there were too few humans and their tools were too rudimentary to have any effect on animal stocks, let alone wipe them out? Where you could not travel from one place to another without exerting yourself, and a comfortable life was something only the rich could afford, where the sea was full of whales, the forests full of bears and wolves, and there were still countries that were so alien no adventure story could do them justice, such as China, to which a voyage not only took several months and was the prerogative of only a tiny minority of sailors and traders, but was also fraught with danger. Admittedly, that world was rough and wretched, filthy and ravaged with sickness, drunken and ignorant, full of pain, low life expectancy and rampant superstition, but it produced the greatest writer, Shakespeare, the greatest painter, Rembrandt, the greatest scientist, Newton, all still unsurpassed in their fields, and

how can it be that this period achieved this wealth? Was it
because death was closer and life was starker as a result?

Who knows?

Be that as it may, we can't go back in time, everything we
undertake is irrevocable, and if we look back what we see is
not life but death. And whoever believes that the conditions and character of the times are responsible for our
maladjustment is either suffering from delusions of grandeur or is simply stupid, and lacks self-knowledge on both
accounts. I loathed so much about the age I lived in, but it
was not that that was the cause of the loss of meaning,
because it was not something that had been constant . . .
The spring I moved to Stockholm and met Linda, for example, the world had suddenly opened, the intensity in it
increased at breakneck speed. I was head over heels in love
and everything was possible, my happiness was at bursting
point all the time and embraced everything. If someone
had spoken to me then about a lack of meaning I would
have laughed out loud, for I was free and the world lay at
my feet, open, packed with meaning, from the gleaming
futuristic trains that streaked across Slussen beneath my
flat, to the sun colouring the nineteenth-century-style
church spires in Ridderholmen red, sinisterly beautiful
sunsets I witnessed every evening for all those months,
from the aroma of freshly picked basil and the taste of ripe
tomatoes to the sound of clacking heels on the cobbled
slope down to the Hilton hotel late one night when we sat
on a bench holding hands and knowing that it would be us

two now and for ever. This state lasted for six months, for six months I was truly happy, truly at home in this world and in myself before slowly it began to lose its lustre, and once more the world moved out of my reach. One year later it happened again, if in quite a different way. That was when Vanja was born. Then it was not the world which opened – we had shut it out, in a kind of total concentration on the miracle taking place in our midst – no, something opened in me. While falling in love had been wild and abandoned, brimming with life and exuberance, this was cautious and muted, filled with endless attention to what was happening. Four weeks, maybe five, it lasted. Whenever I had to do some shopping in town I *ran* down the streets, grabbed whatever we needed, shook with impatience at the counter, and *ran* back with the bags hanging from my hands. I didn't want to miss a minute! The days and nights merged into one, everything was tenderness, everything was gentleness, and if she opened her eyes we rushed towards her. Oh, there you are! But that passed too, we got used to that too, and I began to work, sat in my new office in Dalagatan writing every day while Linda was at home with Vanja and came to see me for lunch, often worried about something but also happy, she was closer to the child and what was happening than me, for I was writing, what had started out as a long essay slowly but surely was growing into a novel, it soon reached a point where it was everything, and writing was all I did, I moved into the office, wrote day and night, sleeping an hour here and

The days and nights merged into one, everything was tenderness, everything was gentleness, and if she opened her eyes we rushed towards her. Oh, there you are!

there. I was filled with an absolutely fantastic feeling, a kind of light burned within me, not hot and consuming but cold and clear and shining. At night I took a cup of coffee with me and sat down on the bench outside the hospital to smoke, the streets around me were quiet, and I could hardly sit still, so great was my happiness. Everything was possible, everything made sense. At two places in the novel I soared higher than I had thought possible, and those two places alone, which I could not believe I had written, and no one else has noticed or said anything about, made the preceding five years of failed writing worth all the effort. They are two of the best moments in my life. By which I mean my whole life. The happiness that filled me and the feeling of invincibility they gave me I have searched for ever since, in vain.

A few weeks after the novel was finished life began as a house husband, and the plan was it would last until next spring while Linda did the last year of her training at the Dramatiska Institut. The novel writing had taken its toll on our relationship. I slept in the office for six weeks, barely seeing Linda and our five-month-old daughter, and when at last it was over she was relieved and happy, and I owed it to her to be there, not just in the same room, physically, but also with all my attention and participation. I couldn't do it. For several months I felt a sorrow at not being where I had been, in the cold clear environment, and my yearning to return was stronger than my pleasure at the life we lived. The fact that the novel was doing well didn't matter. After

every good review I put a cross in the book and waited for
the next, after every conversation with the agent at the
publisher's, when a foreign company had shown some
interest or made an offer, I put a cross in my book and
waited for the next, and I wasn't very interested when it
was eventually nominated for the Nordic Council Literature Prize, for if there was one thing I had learned over the
last six months it was that all writing was about *writing*.
Therein lay all its value. Yet I wanted to have more of what
came in its wake because public attention is a drug, the
need it satisfies is artificial, but once you have had a taste
of it you want more. So there I was, pushing the buggy on
my endless walks on the island of Djurgården in Stockholm
waiting for the telephone to ring and a journalist to ask me
about something, an event organiser to invite me somewhere, a magazine to ask for an article, a publisher to make
an offer, until at last I took the consequences of the disagreeable taste it left in my mouth and began to say no to
everything at the same time as the interest ebbed away and
I was back to the everyday grind. But no matter how hard I
tried, I couldn't get into it, there was always something else
that was more important. Vanja sat there in the buggy looking around while I trudged through the town, first here,
then there, or sat in the sandpit digging with a spade in the
play area in Humlegården, where the tall lean Stockholm
mothers who surrounded us were constantly on their
phones, looking as if they were part of some bloody fashion
show, or she was in her high chair in the kitchen at home

swallowing the food I fed her. All of this bored me out of my mind. I felt stupid walking round indoors chatting to her, because she didn't say anything; there was just my inane voice and her silence, happy babbling or displeased tears, then it was on with her clothes and tramping into town again, to the Moderna Museet in Skeppsholmen, for example, where at least I could see some good art while keeping an eye on her, or to one of the big bookshops in the centre, or to Djurgården or Brunnsviken Lake, which was the closest the town came to nature, unless I took the road out to see Geir, who had his office in the university at that time. Little by little, I mastered everything with regard to small children, there wasn't a single thing I couldn't do with her, we were everywhere, but no matter how well it went, and irrespective of the great tenderness I felt for her, my boredom and apathy were greater. A lot of effort was spent getting her to sleep so that I could read and to making the days pass so that I could cross them off in the calendar. I got to know the most out-of-the-way cafés in town, and there was hardly a park bench I had not sat on at some time or other, with a book in one hand and the buggy in the other. I took Dostoevsky with me, first *Demons*, then *The Brothers Karamazov*. In them I found the light again. But it wasn't the lofty, clear and pure light, as with Hölderlin; with Dostoevsky there were no heights, no mountains, there was no divine perspective, everything was in the human domain, wreathed in this characteristically Dostoevskian wretched, dirty, sick, almost contaminated mood

No matter how well it
went, and irrespective
of the great tenderness I
felt for her, my boredom
and apathy were greater

that was never too far from hysteria. That was where the light was. That was where the divine stirred. But was this the place to go? Was it necessary to go down on bended knee? As usual I didn't think as I read, just engrossed myself in it, and after a few hundred pages, which took several days to read, something suddenly happened: all the details that had been painstakingly built up slowly began to interact, and the intensity was so great that I was carried along, totally enthralled, until Vanja opened her eyes from the depths of the buggy, almost suspicious, it seemed: where have you taken me now?

There was no option but to close the book, lift her up, get out the spoon, the jar of food and the bib if we were indoors, set a course for the nearest café if we were outside, fetch a high chair, put her in it and go over to the counter and ask the staff to warm the food, which they did grudgingly because Stockholm was inundated with babies at that time, there was a baby boom, and since there were so many women in their thirties among the mothers who had worked and led their own lives until then, glamorous magazines for mothers began to appear, with children as a sort of accessory, and one celebrity after another allowed herself to be photographed with and interviewed about her family. What had previously taken place in private was now pumped into the public arena. Everywhere you could read about labour pains, Caesareans and breastfeeding, baby clothes, buggies and holiday tips for parents of small children, published in books written by house husbands or

bitter mothers who felt cheated as they collapsed with exhaustion from working and having children. What had once been normal topics you didn't talk about much were now placed at the forefront of existence and cultivated with a frenzy that ought to make everyone raise their eyebrows, for what could be the meaning of this? In the midst of this lunacy there was me trundling my child around like one of the many fathers who had evidently put fatherhood before all else. When I was in the café feeding Vanja there was always at least one other father there, usually of my age, that is, in his mid-thirties, almost all of whom had shaved heads to hide hair loss. You hardly ever saw a bald patch or a high forehead any longer, and the sight of these fathers always made me feel a little uncomfortable. I found it hard to take the feminised aspect of their actions, even though I did exactly the same and was as feminised as they were. The slight disdain I felt for men pushing buggies was, to put it mildly, a two-edged sword as for the most part I had one in front of me when I saw them. I doubted I was alone in these feelings, I thought I could occasionally discern an uneasy look on some men's faces in the play area, and the restlessness in the bodies, which were prone to snatching a couple of pull-ups on the bars while the children played around them. However, spending a few hours every day in a play area with your child was one thing. There were things that were much worse. Linda had just started to take Vanja to Rhythm Time classes for tiny tots at the Stadsbiblioteket library, and when I took over responsibility she wanted

Vanja to continue. I had an inkling something dreadful was awaiting me, so I said no, it was out of the question, Vanja was with me now, so there would be no Rhythm Time. But Linda continued to mention it off and on, and after a few months my resistance to what the role of the soft man involved was so radically subverted, in addition to which Vanja had grown so much that her day needed a modicum of variety, that one day I said, yes, today we were thinking of going to the Rhythm Time course at the Stadsbiblioteket. Remember to get there in good time, Linda said, it fills up quickly. And so it was that early one afternoon I was pushing Vanja up Sveavägen to Odenplan, where I crossed the road and went through the library doors. For some reason I had never been there before, even though it was one of Stockholm's most beautiful buildings, designed by Asplund some time in the 1920s, the period I liked best of all in the previous century. Vanja was fed, rested and wearing clean clothes, carefully chosen for the occasion. I pushed the buggy into the large completely circular interior, asked a woman behind a counter where the children's section was, followed her instructions into a side room lined with shelves of children's books, where on a door at the back there was a poster about this Rhythm Time class starting here at 2 p.m. Three buggies were already present. On some chairs a little further away sat the owners, three women in heavy jackets and worn faces, all around thirty-five, while what must have been their snot-nosed children were crawling around on the floor between them.

I parked the buggy by theirs, lifted Vanja out, sat down on a little ledge with her on my lap, removed her jacket and shoes and lowered her gently to the floor. Reckoned she could crawl around a bit as well. But she didn't want to, she couldn't remember being here before, so she wanted to stick with me and stretched her arms out. I lifted her back onto my lap. She sat watching the other children with interest.

An attractive young woman holding a guitar walked across the floor. She must have been about twenty-five; she had long blonde hair, a coat reaching down to her knees, high black boots and she stopped in front of me.

'Hi!' she said. 'Haven't seen you here before. Are you coming to the Rhythm Time class?'

'Yes,' I said, looking up at her. She really was attractive.

'Have you signed up?'

'No,' I said. 'Do you have to?'

'Yes, you do. And I'm afraid it's full today.'

Good news.

'What a shame,' I said, getting up.

'As you didn't know,' she said. 'I suppose we can squeeze you in. Just this once. You can sign up afterwards for the next time.'

'Thank you,' I said.

Her smile was so attractive. Then she opened the door and went in. I leaned forward and watched her putting her guitar case on the floor, removing her coat and scarf and hanging them over a chair at the back of the room. She had a light fresh spring-like presence.

I had a hunch where this was going, and I should have got up and left. But I wasn't there for my sake, I was there for Vanja and Linda. So I stayed put. Vanja was eight months old and absolutely bewitched by anything that resembled a performance. And now she was attending one.

More women with buggies came, in dribs and drabs, and soon the room was filled with the sounds of chatting, coughing, laughing, clothes rustling and rummaging through bags. Most seemed to come in twos or threes. For a long time I seemed to be the only person on my own. But just before two a couple more men arrived. From their body language I could see they didn't know each other. One of them, a small guy with a big head, wearing glasses, nodded to me. I could have kicked him. What did he think: that we belonged to the same club? Then it was off with the overalls, the hat and the shoes, out with the feeding bottle and rattle, down on the floor with the child.

The mothers had long since gone into the room where Rhythm Time was due to take place. I waited until last, but at a minute to, I got up and went in with Vanja on my arm. Cushions had been strewn across the floor for us to sit on, while the young woman leading the session sat on a chair in front of us. With the guitar on her lap she scanned the audience smiling. She was wearing a beige cashmere jumper. Her breasts were well formed, her waist was narrow, her legs, one crossed over the other and swinging, were long and still clad in black boots.

I sat down on my cushion. I put Vanja on my lap. She

stared with big eyes at the woman with the guitar, who was now saying a few words of welcome.

'We've got some new faces here today,' she said. 'Perhaps you'd like to introduce yourselves?'

'Monica,' said one.

'Kristina,' said another.

'Lul,' said a third.

Lul? What sort of bloody name was that?

The room went quiet. The attractive young woman looked at me and sent me a smile of encouragement.

'Karl Ove,' I said sombrely.

'Then let's start with our welcome song,' she said, and struck the first chord, which resounded as she was explaining that parents should say the name of their child when she nodded to them, and then everyone should sing the child's name.

She strummed the same chord, and everyone began to sing. The idea behind the song was that everyone should say 'Hi' to their friend and wave a hand. Parents of the children too small to understand took their wrists and waved their hands, which I did too, but when the second verse started I no longer had any excuse for sitting there in silence and had to start singing. My own deep voice sounded like an affliction in the choir of high-pitched women's voices. Twelve times we sang 'Hi' to our friend before all the children had been named and we could move on. The next song was about parts of the body, which, of course, the children should touch when they were mentioned. Forehead, eyes,

ears, nose, mouth, stomach, knee, foot. Forehead, eyes, ears, nose, mouth, stomach, knee, foot. Then we were handed some rattle-like instruments which we were supposed to shake as we sang a new song. I wasn't embarrassed, it wasn't embarrassing sitting there, it was humiliating and degrading. Everything was gentle and friendly and nice, all the movements were tiny, and I sat huddled on a cushion droning along with the mothers and children, a song, to cap it all, led by a woman I would have liked to bed. But sitting there I was rendered completely harmless, without dignity, impotent, there was no difference between me and her, except that she was more attractive, and the levelling, whereby I had forfeited everything that was me, even my size, and that voluntarily, filled me with rage.

'Now it's time for the children to do a bit of dancing!' she said, laying her guitar on the floor. Then she got up and went to a CD player on a chair.

'Everyone stand in a ring, and first we go one way, stamp with our feet, like so,' she said, stamping her attractive foot, 'turn round once and go back the other way.'

I got up, lifted Vanja and stood in the circle that was forming. I looked for the other two men. Both were completely focused on their children.

'OK, OK, Vanja,' I whispered. '"Each to his own," as your great-grandfather used to say.'

She looked up at me. So far she hadn't shown any interest in any of the things the children had to do. She didn't even want to shake the maracas.

'Away we go, then,' said the attractive woman, pressing the CD player. A folk tune poured into the room, and I began to follow the others, each step in time to the music. I held Vanja with a hand under each arm, so that she was dangling, close to my chest. Then what I had to do was stamp my foot, swing her round, after which it was back the other way. Lots of the others enjoyed this, there was laughter and even some squeals of delight. When this was over we had to dance alone with our child. I swayed from side to side with Vanja in my arms thinking that this must be what hell was like, gentle and nice and full of mothers you didn't know from Eve with their babies. When this was finished there was a session with a large blue sail which at first was supposed to be the sea, and we sang a song about waves and everyone swung the sail up and down, making waves, and then it was something the children had to crawl under until we suddenly raised it, this too to the accompaniment of our singing.

When at last she thanked us and said goodbye, I hurried out, dressed Vanja without meeting anyone's eye, just staring down at the floor, while the voices, happier now than before they went in, buzzed around me. I put Vanja in the buggy, strapped her in and pushed her out as fast as I could without drawing attention to myself. Outside on the street I felt like shouting till my lungs burst and smashing something. But I had to make do with putting as many metres between me and this hall of shame in the shortest possible time.

'Vanja, O Vanja,' I said, scurrying down Sveavägen. 'Did you have fun then? It didn't really look like it.'

'Tha tha thaa,' Vanja said.

She didn't smile, but her eyes were happy.

She pointed.

'Ah, a motorbike,' I said. 'What is it with you and motor-bikes, eh?'

When we reached the Konsum shop at the corner of Tegnérgatan I went in to buy something for supper. The feeling of claustrophobia was still there, but the aggression had diminished, it wasn't anger I felt as I pushed the buggy down the aisle between the shelves. The shop evoked memories, it was the one I had used when I had moved to Stockholm three years earlier, when I was staying at the flat Norstedts, the publishers, had put at my disposal a stone's throw further up the street. I had weighed over a hundred kilos at the time and moved in a semi-catatonic darkness, escaping from my former life. It hadn't been much fun. But I had decided to pick myself up, so every evening I went to the Lill-Jansskogen forest to run. I couldn't even manage a hundred metres before my heart was pounding so fast and my lungs were gasping so much that I had to stop. Another hundred metres and my legs were trembling. Then it was back to the hotel-like flat at walking pace for crispbread and soup. One day I had seen a woman in the shop, suddenly she was standing next to me, by the meat counter of all places, and there was some-thing about her, the sheer physicality of her appearance,

which from one moment to the next filled me with almost explosive lust. She was holding her basket in front of her with both hands, her hair was auburn, her pale complexion freckled. I caught a whiff of her body, a faint smell of sweat and soap, and stood staring straight ahead with a thumping heart and constricted throat for maybe fifteen seconds, for that was the time it took her to come alongside me, take a pack of salami from the counter and go on her way. I saw her again when I was about to pay, she was at the other cash desk, and the desire, which had not gone away, welled up in me again. She put her items in her bag, turned and went out of the door. I never saw her again.

From her low position in the buggy Vanja had spotted a dog, which she was pointing a finger at. I never stopped pondering about what she saw when she watched the world around her. What did this endless stream of people, faces, cars, shops and signs mean to her? She did not see it in an undiscriminating way, that at least was certain, for not only did she regularly point at motorbikes, cats, dogs and other babies, she had also constructed a very clear hierarchy with respect to the people around her: first Linda, then me, then grandma and then everyone else, depending on how long they had been near her over the last few days.

'Yes, look, a dog,' I said. I picked up a carton of milk, which I put on the buggy, and a packet of fresh pasta from the adjacent counter. Then I took two packets of serrano ham, a jar of olives, mozzarella cheese, a pot of basil and

some tomatoes. This was food I would never have dreamed of buying in my former life because I had no idea it existed. But now I was here, in the midst of Stockholm's cultural middle classes, and even though this pandering to all things Italian, Spanish, French and the repudiation of all things Swedish appeared stupid to me, and gradually, as the bigger picture emerged, also repugnant, it wasn't worth wasting my energy on. When I missed pork chops and cabbage, beef stew, vegetable soup, dumplings, meatballs, lung mash, fishcakes, mutton and vegetables, smoked sausage ring, whale steaks, sago pudding, semolina, rice pudding and Norwegian porridge, it was as much the 70s I missed as the actual tastes. And since food was not important to me, I might as well make something Linda liked.

I stopped for a few seconds by the newspaper stand wondering whether to buy the two evening papers, the two biggest publications. Reading them was like emptying a bag of rubbish over your head. Now and then I did buy them, when it felt as though a bit more rubbish up there wouldn't make any difference. But not today.

I paid and went into the street again, with the tarmac vaguely reflecting the light from the mild winter sky, and the cars queueing on all sides of the crossing resembling a huge pile-up of logs in a river. To avoid the traffic I went along Tegnérgatan. In the window of the second-hand bookshop, which was one of the ones I kept an eye on, I saw a book by Malaparte that Geir had spoken about with warmth and one by Galileo Galilei in the Atlantis series.

I turned the buggy, nudged the door open with my heel and entered backwards with the buggy following.

'I'd like two of the books in the window,' I said. 'The Galileo Galilei and the Malaparte.'

'Pardon me?' said the shirt-clad man in his fifties who ran the place, as he peered at me over the square-rimmed glasses perched on the tip of his nose.

'In the window,' I said in Swedish. 'Two books. Galilei, Malaparte.'

'The sky and the war, eh?' he said, and turned to pick them out for me.

Vanja had gone to sleep.

Had it been so exhausting at Rhythm Time?

I pulled the little lever under the headrest towards me and lowered her gently into the buggy. She waved a hand in her sleep, and clenched it exactly as she had done just after she had been born. One of the movements that nature had supplied her with but which she had slowly replaced with something of her own. But when she slept it reawakened.

I pushed the buggy to the side so that people could pass, and turned to the shelf of art books as the bookshop owner rang up the prices of the two books on his antiquated cash till. Now that Vanja was asleep I had a few more minutes to myself, and the first book I caught sight of was a photographic book by Per Maning. What luck! I had always liked his photos, especially these ones, the animal series. Cows, pigs, dogs, seals. Somehow he had succeeded in capturing their souls. There was no other way to understand the

looks of these animals in the pictures. Complete presence, at times anguished, at others vacant, and sometimes penetrating. But also enigmatic, like portraits by painters in the seventeenth century.

I put it on the counter.

'That one's just come in,' the owner said. 'Fine book. Are you Norwegian?'

'Yes, I am,' I said. 'I'd like to browse a bit more if that's OK.'

There was an edition of Delacroix's diary, I took it, and then a book about Turner, even though no paintings lost as much by being photographed as his, and Poul Vad's book about Hammershøi, and a magnificent work about orientalism in art.

As I placed them on the counter my mobile rang. Almost no one had my number, so the ringtone, which found its way out of the depths of the side pocket in my parka a touch muffled, aroused no disquiet in me. Quite the contrary. Apart from the brief exchange with the Rhythm Time woman I hadn't spoken to anyone since Linda cycled to school that morning.

'Hello?' Geir said. 'What are you up to?'

'Working on my self-esteem,' I said, turning to the wall. 'And you?'

'Not that, at any rate. I'm just sitting here in the office watching everyone scurry past. So what's been happening?'

'I've just met an attractive woman.'

'And?'

'Chatted to her.'

'Mm?'

'She invited me to hers.'

'Did you say yes?'

'Of course. She even asked what my name was.'

'But?'

'She was the teacher in charge of a Rhythm Time class for babies. So I had to sit there clapping my hands and singing children's songs in front of her, with Vanja on my lap. On a little cushion. With a load of mothers and children.'

Geir burst into laughter.

'I was also given a rattle to shake.'

'Ha ha ha!'

'I was so furious when I left I didn't know what to do with myself,' I said. 'I also had a chance to try out my new waistline. And no one was bothered about the rolls of fat on my stomach.'

'No, they're nice and soft, they are,' Geir said, laughing again. 'Karl Ove, aren't we going out tonight?'

'Are you winding me up?'

'No, I'm serious. I was planning to work here till seven, more or less. So we could meet in town any time after.'

'Impossible.'

'What the hell's the point of you living in Stockholm if we can never meet?'

'You realise you just used a Swedish word, don't you,' I said.

'Can you remember when you first came to Stockholm?' Geir said. 'When you were in the taxi lecturing me about

the expression "hen-pecked" when I didn't want to go to the nightclub with you?'

'There you go. And another. Your Norwegian's gone to pot,' I said.

'For Christ's sake, man. What we're talking about is the expression you used. Hen-pecked. Do you remember?'

'Yes, I'm afraid I do.'

'And?' he said. 'What do you deduce from that?'

'That there are differences,' I said. 'I'm not hen-pecked. I'm a hen-pecker. And you're a woodpecker.'

'Ha ha ha. Tomorrow then?'

'We're eating out with Fredrik and Karin tomorrow night.'

'Fredrik? Is he that idiot of a film producer?'

'I wouldn't express it in that way, but, yes, he is.'

'Oh my God. All right. Sunday? No, that's your day of rest. Monday?'

'OK.'

'There are lots of people in town then, too.'

'Monday at Pelikanen then,' I said. 'By the way, I'm holding a Malaparte book in my hand here.'

'Oh yes? Are you in a second-hand bookshop then? It's good, that one.'

'And Delacroix's diary.'

'That's supposed to be good as well. Thomas has talked about it, I know. Anything else?'

'*Aftenposten* rang yesterday. They wanted to do an interview.'

'You didn't say yes, did you?'

'Yes.'

'You idiot. You said you were going to stop doing them.'

'I know. But the publishers said the journalist was particularly good. And so I thought I would give it one last chance. It *could* turn out all right after all.'

'No, it can't,' Geir said.

'Yes, I know,' I said. 'But never mind. Now I've said yes anyway. Anything new with you?'

'Nothing. Had some bread rolls with the social anthropologists. Then the old institute head popped by with crumbs in his beard and his flies open, wanting to talk. I'm the only one who doesn't give him the heave-ho. So he comes here.'

'The one who was so tough?'

'Yes. And who's now terrified of losing his office. That's all he's got left of course. And so now he's as nice as pie. It's a question of adapting. Tough when he can be, nice when he has to be.'

'I might pop round tomorrow,' I said. 'Have you got any time?'

'Dead right I have. So long as you don't bring Vanja along, that is.'

'Ha ha. Right, but I've got to pay now. See you tomorrow.'

'OK. All the best to Linda and Vanja.'

'And to Christina.'

'See you.'

'Yes, see you.'

I rang off and stuffed the mobile back in my pocket. Vanja was still asleep. The bookshop owner was studying a catalogue. He looked up as I approached the counter.

'That'll be 1,530 kroner,' he said.

I passed him my card. I put the receipt in my back pocket – the only way I could justify these purchases of mine was that they could be written off against tax – I put the two bags of books underneath the buggy, and then I pushed it out of the shop to the sound of the doorbell ringing in my ears.

It was already twenty minutes to four. I had been up since half past four in the morning going through a problematic translation for Damm until half past six, and even though it was tedious work in which all I did was weigh one sentence against the other in the original, it was still a hundred times more interesting and rewarding than what I did during the morning in terms of nappy changing and children's activities, which for me were no longer any more than a means of occupying my time. I wasn't exhausted by this lifestyle, it had nothing to do with expending energy, but as there wasn't even the slightest spark of inspiration in it, it deflated me nonetheless, rather as if I'd had a puncture.

By the crossing at Döbelnsgatan I took a left turn, walked up the hill below Johanneskyrk, which with its red brick walls and green tin roof was similar to Johanneskirk in Bergen and Trefoldighetskirk in Arendal, followed Malmskillnadsgatan for a while, then turned down David

Bagares gata and through the gate to our backyard. Two torches were burning on the pavement outside the café opposite. There was a stench of piss, because people stopped here on their way home from Stureplan at night and pissed through the railings, and a stink of rubbish from the line of dustbins along the wall. In the corner was the pigeon that had taken up residence here when we moved in two years before. At the time it lived in a hole in the wall. When it was bricked up and sharp spikes were cemented into all the flat surfaces higher up, she moved down to ground level. There were rats here too. I saw them occasionally when I went out for a smoke at night, black backs sliding through the bushes and suddenly scuttling across the open illuminated square towards the security of the flower beds on the other side. Now one of the women hairdressers was standing there, talking on her mobile while smoking. She must have been about forty, and I guessed she had grown up as a small-town beauty, at any rate she reminded me of the type you can see in restaurants in Arendal in the summer, women in their forties with hair dyed much too blonde or much too black, skin that was much too brown, eyes much too flirtatious, laughter much too loud. Her voice was raucous, she spoke broad Skåne dialect, and today she was dressed all in white. She nodded on seeing me, and I nodded back. Even though I had barely spoken to her I liked her, she was so different from all the other people I met in Stockholm, who were either on their way up, or were up, or thought they were.

She had no truck, to put it mildly, with their homogeneous style, which not only applied to clothes and objects but also their thoughts and attitudes.

I paused in front of the door and pulled out my key. The smell of detergent and clean clothes streamed out from the vent above the cellar window. I unlocked the door and walked as quietly as I could into the hall. Vanja knew these sounds and the order in which they occurred so well that she almost always woke when we came in here. She did so this time too. With a scream. I let her scream, opened the lift door, pressed the button and regarded myself in the mirror as we went up the two floors. Linda, who must have heard the screams, was waiting for us at the door when we arrived.

'Hi,' she said. 'Have you had a good time? Have you just woken up, sweetheart? Come here then and I'll . . .'

She undid the belt and lifted Vanja up.

'We've been fine,' I said, pushing the empty buggy in while Linda unbuttoned her cardigan and went into the living room to feed her.

'But I'll never set foot in the Rhythm Time session for as long as I draw breath.'

'Was it that bad?' she asked, glancing at me with a fleeting smile before looking down at Vanja and nestling her against her bared breast.

'Bad? It's the worst experience I've ever had. I was furious when I left.'

'I see,' she said, no longer interested.

Her care for Vanja was so different. It was all-embracing. And completely genuine.

I went into the kitchen with the shopping, put the perishables in the fridge, placed the pot of basil on a dish on the windowsill and watered it, fetched the books from under the buggy and put them in the bookcase, sat down in front of the computer and checked my emails. I hadn't looked since the morning. There was an email from Carl-Johan Vallgren, he congratulated me on the nomination, said he was afraid he hadn't read my book yet, and that I just had to ring if I felt like a beer one day. Carl-Johan was someone I really liked, I valued his extravagance – which some found disagreeable, snobbish or stupid – especially after two years in Sweden. But it was impossible for me to have a beer with him. I would just sit there in silence, I knew I would; I had already done it twice. Then there was one from Marta Norheim about an interview in connection with NRK 2's Novel Award, which I had won. And one from my uncle Gunnar, who thanked me for the book and said he was building up his strength to read it, wished me luck with the Nordic championship in literature and concluded with a PS that it was a shame Yngve and Kari Anne were going to divorce. I closed the window without answering.

'Anything interesting?' Linda asked.

'Well. Carl-Johan congratulated me. And then NRK wanted to do an interview in two weeks. Gunnar wrote as well, of all people. He just thanked me for the book.

But that's not bad, considering how angry he was about *Out of the World.*'

'No, it isn't,' Linda said. 'Aren't you going to call Carl-Johan and get him to come over?'

'Are you in such a good mood?' I said.

She pouted at me.

'I'm just trying to be nice,' she said.

'I know that,' I said. 'Sorry. Didn't mean it. OK?'

'That's all right.'

I walked past her and picked up the second volume of *The Brothers Karamazov,* which was lying on the sofa.

'I'm off then,' I said. 'Bye.'

'Enjoy,' she said.

Now I had an hour to myself. It was the sole condition I had made before taking over responsibility for Vanja during the daytime, that I would have an hour on my own in the afternoon, and even though Linda considered it unfair since she'd never had an hour to herself like that, she agreed. The reason she'd never had an hour, I assumed, was that she hadn't thought of it. And the reason she hadn't thought of it was, I also assumed, that she would rather be with us than alone. But that wasn't how I felt. So for an hour every afternoon I sat in a nearby café reading and smoking. I never went to the same café more than four or five times at a stretch because then they started to treat me like a *stammis*, that is, they greeted me when I arrived and wanted to impress me with their knowledge of my predilections, often with a friendly comment about some

topic on everyone's lips. But the whole point for me of living in a big city was that I could be completely alone in it while still surrounded by people on all sides. All with faces I had *never* seen before! The unceasing stream of new faces. For me the very attraction of a big city was immersing myself in that. The Metro swarming with different types and characters. The squares. The pedestrian zones. The cafés. The big malls. Distance, distance, I could never have enough distance. So when a barista began to say hello and smile on catching sight of me and not only brought me a cup of coffee before I asked but also offered me a free croissant, it was time to leave. And it wasn't very hard to find alternatives, we were living in the city centre, and there were hundreds of cafés within a ten-minute radius.

This time I followed Regeringsgatan down towards the centre. It was packed with people. I thought about the attractive woman in the Rhythm Time class as I walked. What had that been all about? I wanted to sleep with her but didn't believe I would get an opportunity, and if I'd had an opportunity I wouldn't have taken it. So why should it be of any importance if I behaved like a woman in front of her?

You can say a lot about my self-image, but it was definitely not shaped in the cool chambers of reason. My intellect may be able to understand it, but it did not have the power to control it. One's self-image not only encompasses the person you are but also the person you want to be, could be or once had been. For the self-image there was

no difference between the actual and the hypothetical. It incorporated all ages, all feelings, all drives. When I pushed the buggy all over town and spent my days taking care of my child it was not the case that I was adding something to my life, that it became richer as a result; on the contrary, something was removed from it, part of myself, the bit relating to masculinity. It was not my intellect which made this clear to me, because my intellect knew I was doing this for a good reason, namely that Linda and I would be on an equal footing with regard to our child, but rather my emotions, which filled me with desperation whenever I squeezed myself into a mould that was so small and so constricted that I could no longer move. The question was which parameter should be operative. If equality and fairness were to be the parameters, well, there was nothing to be said about men sinking everywhere into the thralls of softness and intimacy. Nor about the rounds of applause this was met with, for if equality and fairness were the dominant parameters, change was an undoubted improvement and a measure of progress. But these were not the only parameters. Happiness was one; an intense sense of being alive was another. And it may be that women who followed their careers until they were almost in their forties and then at the last moment had a child, which after a few months the father took care of until a place was found in a nursery so that they could both continue their careers, may have been happier than women in previous generations. It was possible that men who stayed at home and

looked after their infants for six months may have increased their sense of being alive as a result. And women may actually have desired these men with thin arms, large waistlines, shaven heads and black designer glasses who were just as happy discussing the pros and cons of Baby-bjørn carriers and baby slings as whether it was better to cook one's own baby food or buy ready-made ecological purées. They may have desired them with all their hearts and souls. But even if they didn't, it didn't really matter because equality and fairness were the parameters, they trumped everything else a life and a relationship consisted of. It was a choice, and the choice had been made. For me as well. If I had wanted it otherwise I would have had to back out and tell Linda before she became pregnant: listen, I want children, but I don't want to stay at home looking after them, is that fine with you? Which means, of course, that you're the one who will have to do it. Then she could have said, no, it's not fine with me, or, yes, that's fine and our future could have been planned on that basis. But I didn't, I didn't have sufficient foresight, and consequently I had to go by the rules of the game. In the class and culture we belonged to, that meant adopting the same role, previously called the woman's role. I was bound to it like Odysseus to the mast: if I wanted to free myself I could do that, but not without losing everything. As a result I walked around Stockholm's streets, modern and feminised, with a furious nineteenth-century man inside me. The way I was seen changed, as if at the stroke of a magic wand the

I walked around Stockholm's streets, modern and feminised, with a furious nineteenth-century man inside me

instant I laid my hands on the buggy. I had always eyed the women I walked past, the way men always have, actually a mysterious act because it couldn't lead to anything except a returned gaze, and if I did see a really beautiful woman I might even turn round to watch her, discreetly of course, but nevertheless: why, oh why? What function did all these eyes, all these mouths, all these breasts and waists, legs and bottoms serve? Why was it so important to look at them? When a few seconds, or occasionally minutes, later I had forgotten everything about them? Sometimes I had eye contact, and a rush could go through me if the gaze was held a tiny second longer, because it came from a person in a crowd, I knew nothing about her, where she was from, how she lived, nothing, yet we looked at each other, that was what it was about, and then it was over, she was gone and it was erased from memory for ever. When I came along with a buggy no women looked at me, it was as if I didn't exist. One might think it was because I gave such a clear signal that I was taken, but this was just as evident when I was walking hand in hand with Linda, and that had never prevented anyone from looking my way. My God, wasn't I only getting my just deserts, wasn't I being put in my place for walking around ogling women when there was one at home who had given birth to my child?

No, this was not good.

It certainly was not.

Tonje told me once about a man she had met at a restaurant, it was late, he came over to their table, drunk but

harmless, or so they had thought, since he had told them he had come straight from the maternity ward, his partner had given birth to their first baby that day, and now he was on the town celebrating. But then he had started to make advances, he became more and more insistent and in the end suggested they should go back to his . . . Tonje was shaken deep into her soul, full of disgust, though also fascination, I suspected, because how was it possible, what was he thinking of?

I couldn't imagine a greater act of betrayal. But wasn't it what I was doing when I sought the eyes of all these women?

My thoughts inevitably went back to Linda sitting at home and washing and dressing Vanja, their eyes, Vanja's inquisitive or happy or sleepy eyes, Linda's beautiful eyes. I had never ever wanted anyone more than her, and now I had not only her but also her child. Why couldn't I be content with that? Why couldn't I stop writing for a year and be a father to Vanja while Linda completed her training? I loved them; they loved me. So why didn't all the rest stop plaguing and harrying me?

I had to apply myself harder. Forget everything around me and just concentrate on Vanja during the day. Give Linda all she needed. Be a good person. For Christ's sake, being a good person, was that beyond me?

© Sam Barker

KARL OVE KNAUSGAARD is a Norwegian writer. His groundbreaking series of six novels entitled *My Struggle* draws heavily on Knausgaard's own life and have become international bestsellers. The first volume, *A Death in the Family*, focuses on the death of his father. *A Man in Love*, from which this Mini is extracted, follows Knausgaard as he moves to Sweden, falls in love and becomes a father himself.

The series caused huge controversy in Norway because of its unwavering honesty about members of the author's family. As Knausgaard said of the first volume in the *Guardian*: 'The book I had written about myself, which I had seen as an experiment in realistic prose, infinitely dull and uninteresting to others, became a media story for some months in Norway'. The books have also received universal critical acclaim. Jonathan Lethem wrote that Knausgaard is: 'A living hero who landed on greatness by abandoning every typical literary feint, an emperor whose nakedness surpasses royal finery'.

RECOMMENDED BOOKS BY KARL OVE KNAUSGAARD:

A Death in the Family
A Man in Love
Boyhood Island

Where does Fatherhood end up?

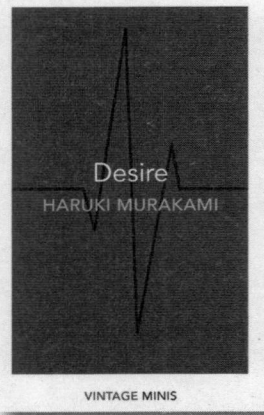

Desire
HARUKI MURAKAMI

VINTAGE MINIS

Babies
ANNE ENRIGHT

VINTAGE MINIS

Eating
NIGELLA LAWSON

VINTAGE MINIS

Language
XIAOLU GUO

VINTAGE MINIS

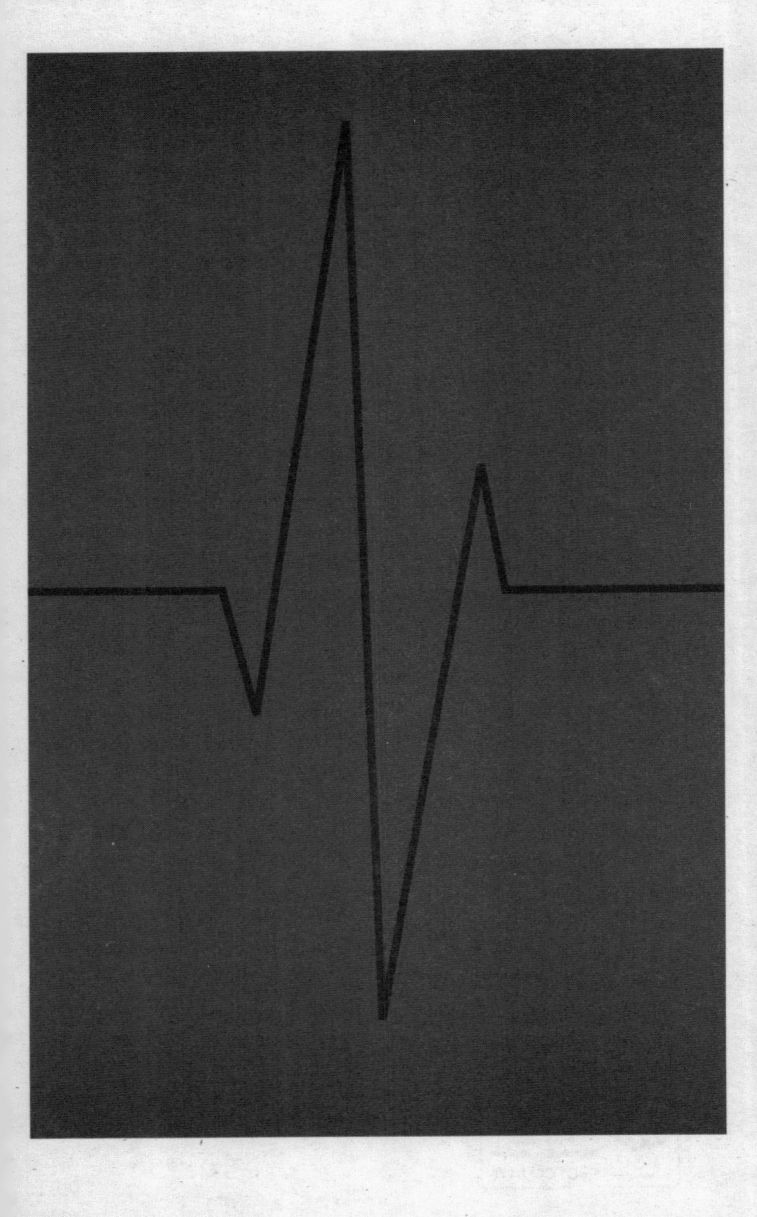

3 5 7 9 10 8 6 4

Vintage
20 Vauxhall Bridge Road,
London SW1V 2SA

Vintage Classics is part of the Penguin Random House
group of companies whose addresses can be found at
global.penguinrandomhouse.com.

 Penguin
Random House
UK

'The Second Bakery Attack' originally appeared in English translation in
Playboy; 'Birthday Girl' in *Harper's*; 'Samsa in Love' in the *New Yorker*

The Elephant Vanishes first published in Great Britain in 1993
by Hamish Hamilton
First published by Vintage in 2003

Blind Woman, Sleeping Willow first published in Great Britain in 2006 by Harvill
Secker
First published by Vintage in 2007

Men Without Women first published in Great Britain in 2017 by Harvill Secker

This short edition published by Vintage in 2017

penguin.co.uk/vintage

A CIP catalogue record for this book is available from the British Library

ISBN 9781784872632

Typeset in 9.5/14.5 pt FreightText Pro
by Jouve (UK), Milton Keynes
Printed and bound by Clays Ltd, St Ives plc

Desire

HARUKI MURAKAMI

Translated from the Japanese by Jay Rubin,
Ted Goossen and Philip Gabriel

The Second Bakery Attack

I'M STILL NOT SURE I made the right choice when I told my wife about the bakery attack. But then, it might not have been a question of right and wrong. Which is to say that wrong choices can produce right results, and vice versa. I myself have adopted the position that, in fact, *we never choose anything at all.* Things happen. Or not.

If you look at it this way, *it just so happens* that I told my wife about the bakery attack. I hadn't been planning to bring it up – I had forgotten all about it – but it wasn't one of those now-that-you-mention-it kind of things, either.

What reminded me of the bakery attack was an unbearable hunger. It hit just before two o'clock in the morning. We had eaten a light supper at six, crawled into bed at nine-thirty, and gone to sleep. For some reason, we woke up at exactly the same moment. A few minutes later, the pangs struck with the force of the tornado in *The Wizard of Oz.* These were tremendous, overpowering hunger pangs.

Our refrigerator contained not a single item that could

be technically categorized as food. We had a bottle of French dressing, six cans of beer, two shriveled onions, a stick of butter, and a box of refrigerator deodorizer. With only two weeks of married life behind us, we had yet to establish a precise conjugal understanding with regard to the rules of dietary behavior. Let alone anything else.

I had a job in a law firm at the time, and she was doing secretarial work at a design school. I was either twenty-eight or twenty-nine – why can't I remember the exact year we married? – and she was two years and eight months younger. Groceries were the last things on our minds.

We both felt too hungry to go back to sleep, but it hurt just to lie there. On the other hand, we were also too hungry to do anything useful. We got out of bed and drifted into the kitchen, ending up across the table from each other. What could have caused such violent hunger pangs?

We took turns opening the refrigerator door and hoping, but no matter how many times we looked inside, the contents never changed. Beer and onions and butter and dressing and deodorizer. It might have been possible to sauté the onions in the butter, but there was no chance those two shriveled onions could fill our empty stomachs. Onions are meant to be eaten with other things. They are not the kind of food you use to satisfy an appetite.

'Would madame care for some French dressing sautéed in deodorizer?'

I expected her to ignore my attempt at humor, and she

did. 'Let's get in the car and look for an all-night restaurant,' I said. 'There must be one on the highway.'

She rejected that suggestion. 'We can't. You're not supposed to go out to eat after midnight.' She was old-fashioned that way.

I breathed once and said, 'I guess not.'

Whenever my wife expressed such an opinion (or thesis) back then, it reverberated in my ears with the authority of a revelation. Maybe that's what happens with newly-weds, I don't know. But when she said this to me, I began to think that this was a special hunger, not one that could be satisfied through the mere expedient of taking it to an all-night restaurant on the highway.

A special kind of hunger. And what might that be?

I can present it here in the form of a cinematic image.

One, I am in a little boat, floating on a quiet sea. *Two*, I look down, and in the water I see the peak of a volcano thrusting up from the ocean floor. *Three*, the peak seems pretty close to the water's surface, but just how close I cannot tell. *Four*, this is because the hypertransparency of the water interferes with the perception of distance.

This is a fairly accurate description of the image that arose in my mind during the two or three seconds between the time my wife said she refused to go to an all-night restaurant and I agreed with my 'I guess not.' Not being Sigmund Freud, I was, of course, unable to analyze with any precision what this image signified, but I knew intuitively that it was a revelation. Which is why – the almost

grotesque intensity of my hunger notwithstanding – I all but automatically agreed with her thesis (or declaration).

We did the only thing we could do: opened the beer. It was a lot better than eating those onions. She didn't like beer much, so we divided the cans, two for her, four for me. While I was drinking the first one, she searched the kitchen shelves like a squirrel in November. Eventually, she turned up a package that had four butter cookies in the bottom. They were leftovers, soft and soggy, but we each ate two, savoring every crumb.

It was no use. Upon this hunger of ours, as vast and boundless as the Sinai Peninsula, the butter cookies and beer left not a trace.

Time oozed through the dark like a lead weight in a fish's gut. I read the print on the aluminum beer cans. I stared at my watch. I looked at the refrigerator door. I turned the pages of yesterday's paper. I used the edge of a postcard to scrape together the cookie crumbs on the tabletop.

'I've never been this hungry in my whole life,' she said. 'I wonder if it has anything to do with being married.'

'Maybe,' I said. 'Or maybe not.'

While she hunted for more fragments of food, I leaned over the edge of my boat and looked down at the peak of the underwater volcano. The clarity of the ocean water all around the boat gave me an unsettled feeling, as if a hollow had opened somewhere behind my solar plexus – a hermetically sealed cavern that had neither entrance nor exit.

Something about this weird sense of absence – this sense of the existential reality of nonexistence – resembled the paralyzing fear you might feel when you climb to the very top of a high steeple. This connection between hunger and acrophobia was a new discovery for me.

Which is when it occurred to me that I had once before had this same kind of experience. My stomach had been just as empty then . . . When? . . . Oh, sure, that was—

'The time of the bakery attack,' I heard myself saying.

'The bakery attack? What are you talking about?'

And so it started.

'I ONCE ATTACKED a bakery. Long time ago. Not a big bakery. Not famous. The bread was nothing special. Not bad, either. One of those ordinary little neighborhood bakeries right in the middle of a block of shops. Some old guy ran it who did everything himself. Baked in the morning, and when he sold out, he closed up for the day.'

'If you were going to attack a bakery, why that one?'

'Well, there was no point in attacking a big bakery. All we wanted was bread, not money. We were attackers, not robbers.'

'We? Who's we?'

'My best friend back then. Ten years ago. We were so broke we couldn't buy toothpaste. Never had enough food. We did some pretty awful things to get our hands on food. The bakery attack was one.'

'I don't get it.' She looked hard at me. Her eyes could

have been searching for a faded star in the morning sky. 'Why didn't you get a job? You could have worked after school. That would have been easier than attacking bakeries.'

'We didn't want to work. We were absolutely clear on that.'

'Well, you're working now, aren't you?'

I nodded and sucked some more beer. Then I rubbed my eyes. A kind of beery mud had oozed into my brain and was struggling with my hunger pangs.

'Times change. People change,' I said. 'Let's go back to bed. We've got to get up early.'

'I'm not sleepy. I want you to tell me about the bakery attack.'

'There's nothing to tell. No action. No excitement.'

'Was it a success?'

I gave up on sleep and ripped open another beer. Once she gets interested in a story, she has to hear it all the way through. That's just the way she is.

'Well, it was kind of a success. And kind of not. We got what we wanted. But as a holdup, it didn't work. The baker gave us the bread before we could take it from him.'

'Free?'

'Not exactly, no. That's the hard part.' I shook my head. 'The baker was a classical-music freak, and when we got there, he was listening to an album of Wagner overtures. So he made us a deal. If we would listen to the record all the way through, we could take as much bread as we

liked. I talked it over with my buddy and we figured, Okay. It wouldn't be work in the purest sense of the word, and it wouldn't hurt anybody. So we put our knives back in our bag, pulled up a couple of chairs, and listened to the overtures to *Tannhäuser* and *The Flying Dutchman*.'

'And after that, you got your bread?'

'Right. Most of what he had in the shop. Stuffed it in our bag and took it home. Kept us fed for maybe four or five days.' I took another sip. Like soundless waves from an undersea earthquake, my sleepiness gave my boat a long, slow rocking.

'Of course, we accomplished our mission. We got the bread. But you couldn't say we had committed a crime. It was more of an exchange. We listened to Wagner with him, and in return, we got our bread. Legally speaking, it was more like a commercial transaction.'

'But listening to Wagner is not work,' she said.

'Oh, no, absolutely not. If the baker had insisted that we wash his dishes or clean his windows or something, we would have turned him down. But he didn't. All he wanted from us was to listen to his Wagner LP from beginning to end. Nobody could have anticipated that. I mean – Wagner? It was like the baker put a curse on us. Now that I think of it, we should have refused. We should have threatened him with our knives and taken the damn bread. Then there wouldn't have been any problem.'

'You had a problem?'

I rubbed my eyes again.

'Sort of. Nothing you could put your finger on. But things started to change after that. It was kind of a turning point. Like, I went back to the university, and I graduated, and I started working for the firm and studying for the bar exam, and I met you and got married. I never did anything like that again. No more bakery attacks.'

'That's it?'

'Yup, that's all there was to it.' I drank the last of the beer. Now all six cans were gone. Six pull-tabs lay in the ashtray like scales from a mermaid.

Of course, it wasn't true that nothing had happened as a result of the bakery attack. There were plenty of things that you could easily have put your finger on, but I didn't want to talk about them with her.

'So, this friend of yours, what's he doing now?'

'I have no idea. Something happened, some nothing kind of thing, and we stopped hanging around together. I haven't seen him since. I don't know what he's doing.'

For a while, she didn't speak. She probably sensed that I wasn't telling her the whole story. But she wasn't ready to press me on it.

'Still,' she said, 'that's why you two broke up, isn't it? The bakery attack was the direct cause.'

'Maybe so. I guess it was more intense than either of us realized. We talked about the relationship of bread to Wagner for days after that. We kept asking ourselves if we had made the right choice. We couldn't decide. Of course, if you look at it sensibly, we *did* make the right choice.

Nobody got hurt. Everybody got what he wanted. The baker – I still can't figure out why he did what he did – but anyway, he succeeded with his Wagner propaganda. And we succeeded in stuffing our faces with bread.

'But even so, we had this feeling that we had made a terrible mistake. And somehow, this mistake has just stayed there, unresolved, casting a dark shadow on our lives. That's why I used the word "curse." It's true. It was like a curse.'

'Do you think you still have it?'

I took the six pull-tabs from the ashtray and arranged them into an aluminum ring the size of a bracelet.

'Who knows? I don't know. I bet the world is full of curses. It's hard to tell which curse makes any one thing go wrong.'

'That's not true.' She looked right at me. 'You can tell, if you think about it. And unless you, yourself, personally break the curse, it'll stick with you like a toothache. It'll torture you till you die. And not just you. Me, too.'

'You?'

'Well, I'm your best friend now, aren't I? Why do you think we're both so hungry? I never, ever, once in my life felt a hunger like this until I married you. Don't you think it's abnormal? Your curse is working on me, too.'

I nodded. Then I broke up the ring of pull-tabs and put them back in the ashtray. I didn't know if she was right, but I did feel she was onto something.

The feeling of starvation was back, stronger than ever,

I never, ever, once in my life felt a hunger like this until I married you

and it was giving me a deep headache. Every twinge of my stomach was being transmitted to the core of my head by a clutch cable, as if my insides were equipped with all kinds of complicated machinery.

I took another look at my undersea volcano. The water was even clearer than before – much clearer. Unless you looked closely, you might not even notice it was there. It felt as though the boat were floating in midair, with absolutely nothing to support it. I could see every little pebble on the bottom. All I had to do was reach out and touch them.

'We've only been living together for two weeks,' she said, 'but all this time I've been feeling some kind of weird presence.' She looked directly into my eyes and brought her hands together on the tabletop, her fingers interlocking. 'Of course, I didn't know it was a curse until now. This explains everything. You're under a curse.'

'What kind of presence?'

'Like there's this heavy, dusty curtain that hasn't been washed for years, hanging down from the ceiling.'

'Maybe it's not a curse. Maybe it's just me,' I said, and smiled.

She did not smile.

'No, it's not you,' she said.

'Okay, suppose you're right. Suppose it is a curse. What can I do about it?'

'Attack another bakery. Right away. Now. It's the only way.'

'Now?'

'Yes. Now. While you're still hungry. You have to finish what you left unfinished.'

'But it's the middle of the night. Would a bakery be open now?'

'We'll find one. Tokyo's a big city. There must be at least one all-night bakery.'

WE GOT INTO my old Corolla and started drifting around the streets of Tokyo at 2:30 a.m., looking for a bakery. There we were, me clutching the steering wheel, she in the navigator's seat, the two of us scanning the street like hungry eagles in search of prey. Stretched out on the backseat, long and stiff as a dead fish, was a Remington automatic shotgun. Its shells rustled dryly in the pocket of my wife's windbreaker. We had two black ski masks in the glove compartment. Why my wife owned a shotgun, I had no idea. Or ski masks. Neither of us had ever skied. But she didn't explain and I didn't ask. Married life is weird, I felt.

Impeccably equipped, we were nevertheless unable to find an all-night bakery. I drove through the empty streets, from Yoyogi to Shinjuku, on to Yotsuya and Aka-saka, Aoyama, Hiroo, Roppongi, Daikanyama, and Shibuya. Late-night Tokyo had all kinds of people and shops, but no bakeries.

Twice we encountered patrol cars. One was huddled at the side of the road, trying to look inconspicuous. The other slowly overtook us and crept past, finally moving off

into the distance. Both times I grew damp under the arms, but my wife's concentration never faltered. She was looking for that bakery. Every time she shifted the angle of her body, the shotgun shells in her pocket rustled like buckwheat husks in an old-fashioned pillow.

'Let's forget it,' I said. 'There aren't any bakeries open at this time of night. You've got to plan for this kind of thing or else—'

'Stop the car!'

I slammed on the brakes.

'This is the place,' she said.

The shops along the street had their shutters rolled down, forming dark, silent walls on either side. A barbershop sign hung in the dark like a twisted, chilling glass eye. There was a bright McDonald's hamburger sign some two hundred yards ahead, but nothing else.

'I don't see any bakery,' I said.

Without a word, she opened the glove compartment and pulled out a roll of cloth-backed tape. Holding this, she stepped out of the car. I got out my side. Kneeling at the front end, she tore off a length of tape and covered the numbers on the license plate. Then she went around to the back and did the same. There was a practiced efficiency to her movements. I stood on the curb staring at her.

'We're going to take that McDonald's,' she said, as coolly as if she were announcing what we would have for dinner.

'McDonald's is not a bakery,' I pointed out to her.

'It's *like* a bakery,' she said. 'Sometimes you have to compromise. Let's go.'

I drove to the McDonald's and parked in the lot. She handed me the blanket-wrapped shotgun.

'I've never fired a gun in my life,' I protested.

'You don't have to fire it. Just hold it. Okay? Do as I say. We walk right in, and as soon as they say "Welcome to McDonald's," we slip on our masks. Got that?'

'Sure, but—'

'Then you shove the gun in their faces and make all the workers and customers get together. Fast. I'll do the rest.'

'But—'

'How many hamburgers do you think we'll need? Thirty?'

'I guess so.' With a sigh, I took the shotgun and rolled back the blanket a little. The thing was as heavy as a sand-bag and as black as a dark night.

'Do we really have to do this?' I asked, half to her and half to myself.

'Of course we do.'

Wearing a McDonald's hat, the girl behind the counter flashed me a McDonald's smile and said, 'Welcome to McDonald's.' I hadn't thought that girls would work at McDonald's late at night, so the sight of her confused me for a second. But only for a second. I caught myself and pulled on the mask. Confronted with this suddenly masked duo, the girl gaped at us.

Obviously, the McDonald's hospitality manual said

nothing about how to deal with a situation like this. She had been starting to form the phrase that comes after 'Welcome to McDonald's,' but her mouth seemed to stiffen and the words wouldn't come out. Even so, like a crescent moon in the dawn sky, the hint of a professional smile lingered at the edges of her lips.

As quickly as I could manage, I unwrapped the shotgun and aimed it in the direction of the tables, but the only customers there were a young couple – students, probably – and they were facedown on the plastic table, sound asleep. Their two heads and two strawberry-milkshake cups were aligned on the table like an avant-garde sculpture. They slept the sleep of the dead. They didn't look likely to obstruct our operation, so I swung my shotgun back toward the counter.

All together, there were three McDonald's workers. The girl at the counter, the manager – a guy with a pale, egg-shaped face, probably in his late twenties – and a student type in the kitchen – a thin shadow of a guy with nothing on his face that you could read as an expression. They stood together behind the register, staring into the muzzle of my shotgun like tourists peering down an Incan well. No one screamed, and no one made a threatening move. The gun was so heavy I had to rest the barrel on top of the cash register, my finger on the trigger.

'I'll give you the money,' said the manager, his voice hoarse. 'They collected it at eleven, so we don't have too much, but you can have everything. We're insured.'

'Lower the front shutter and turn off the sign,' said my wife.

'Wait a minute,' said the manager. 'I can't do that. I'll be held responsible if I close up without permission.'

My wife repeated her order, slowly. He seemed torn.

'You'd better do what she says,' I warned him.

He looked at the muzzle of the gun atop the register, then at my wife, and then back at the gun. He finally resigned himself to the inevitable. He turned off the sign and hit a switch on an electrical panel that lowered the shutter. I kept my eye on him, worried that he might hit a burglar alarm, but apparently McDonald's don't have burglar alarms. Maybe it had never occurred to anybody to attack one.

The front shutter made a huge racket when it closed, like an empty bucket being smashed with a baseball bat, but the couple sleeping at their table was still out cold. Talk about a sound sleep: I hadn't seen anything like that in years.

'Thirty Big Macs. For takeout,' said my wife.

'Let me just give you the money,' pleaded the manager. 'I'll give you more than you need. You can go buy food somewhere else. This is going to mess up my accounts and—'

'You'd better do what she says,' I said again.

The three of them went into the kitchen area together and started making the thirty Big Macs. The student grilled the burgers, the manager put them in buns, and the girl wrapped them up. Nobody said a word.

I leaned against a big refrigerator, aiming the gun toward the griddle. The meat patties were lined up on the griddle like brown polka dots, sizzling. The sweet smell of grilling meat burrowed into every pore of my body like a swarm of microscopic bugs, dissolving into my blood and circulating to the farthest corners, then massing together inside my hermetically sealed hunger cavern, clinging to its pink walls.

A pile of white-wrapped burgers was growing nearby. I wanted to grab and tear into them, but I could not be certain that such an act would be consistent with our objective. I had to wait. In the hot kitchen area, I started sweating under my ski mask.

The McDonald's people sneaked glances at the muzzle of the shotgun. I scratched my ears with the little finger of my left hand. My ears always get itchy when I'm nervous. Jabbing my finger into an ear through the wool, I was making the gun barrel wobble up and down, which seemed to bother them. It couldn't have gone off accidentally, because I had the safety on, but they didn't know that and I wasn't about to tell them.

My wife counted the finished hamburgers and put them into two small shopping bags, fifteen burgers to a bag.

'Why do you have to do this?' the girl asked me. 'Why don't you just take the money and buy something you like? What's the good of eating thirty Big Macs?'

I shook my head.

My wife explained, 'We're sorry, really. But there

weren't any bakeries open. If there had been, we would have attacked a bakery.'

That seemed to satisfy them. At least they didn't ask any more questions. Then my wife ordered two large Cokes from the girl and paid for them.

'We're stealing bread, nothing else,' she said. The girl responded with a complicated head movement, sort of like nodding and sort of like shaking. She was probably trying to do both at the same time. I thought I had some idea how she felt.

My wife then pulled a ball of twine from her pocket – she came equipped – and tied the three to a post as expertly as if she were sewing on buttons. She asked if the cord hurt, or if anyone wanted to go to the toilet, but no one said a word. I wrapped the gun in the blanket, she picked up the shopping bags, and out we went. The customers at the table were still asleep, like a couple of deep-sea fish. What would it have taken to rouse them from a sleep so deep?

We drove for a half hour, found an empty parking lot by a building, and pulled in. There we ate hamburgers and drank our Cokes. I sent six Big Macs down to the cavern of my stomach, and she ate four. That left twenty Big Macs in the back seat. Our hunger – that hunger that had felt as if it could go on forever – vanished as the dawn was break-ing. The first light of the sun dyed the building's filthy walls purple and made a giant SONY BETA ad tower glow with painful intensity. Soon the whine of highway truck tires was joined by the chirping of birds. The American

Armed Forces radio was playing cowboy music. We shared a cigarette. Afterward, she rested her head on my shoulder.

'Still, was it really necessary for us to do this?' I asked.

'Of course it was!' With one deep sigh, she fell asleep against me. She felt as soft and as light as a kitten.

Alone now, I leaned over the edge of my boat and looked down to the bottom of the sea. The volcano was gone. The water's calm surface reflected the blue of the sky. Little waves – like silk pajamas fluttering in a breeze – lapped against the side of the boat. There was nothing else.

I stretched out in the bottom of the boat and closed my eyes, waiting for the rising tide to carry me where I belonged.

—*translated by Jay Rubin*

On Seeing the 100% Perfect Girl One Beautiful April Morning

ONE BEAUTIFUL APRIL MORNING, on a narrow side street in Tokyo's fashionable Harajuku neighborhood, I walk past the 100% perfect girl.

Tell you the truth, she's not that good-looking. She doesn't stand out in any way. Her clothes are nothing special. The back of her hair is still bent out of shape from sleep. She isn't young, either—must be near thirty, not even close to a "girl," properly speaking. But still, I know from fifty yards away: She's the 100% perfect girl for me. The moment I see her, there's a rumbling in my chest, and my mouth is as dry as a desert.

Maybe you have your own particular favorite type of girl—one with slim ankles, say, or big eyes, or graceful fingers, or you're drawn for no good reason to girls who take their time with every meal. I have my own preferences, of course. Sometimes in a restaurant I'll catch myself staring

at the girl at the table next to mine because I like the shape of her nose.

But no one can insist that his 100% perfect girl correspond to some preconceived type. Much as I like noses, I can't recall the shape of hers – or even if she had one. All I can remember for sure is that she was no great beauty. It's weird.

'Yesterday on the street I passed the 100% perfect girl,' I tell someone.

'Yeah?' he says. 'Good-looking?'

'Not really.'

'Your favorite type, then?'

'I don't know. I can't seem to remember anything about her – the shape of her eyes or the size of her breasts.'

'Strange.'

'Yeah. Strange.'

'So anyhow,' he says, already bored, 'what did you do? Talk to her? Follow her?'

'Nah. Just passed her on the street.'

She's walking east to west, and I west to east. It's a really nice April morning.

Wish I could talk to her. Half an hour would be plenty: just ask her about herself, tell her about myself, and – what I'd really like to do – explain to her the complexities of fate that have led to our passing each other on a side street in Harajuku on a beautiful April morning in 1981. This was something sure to be crammed full of warm secrets, like an antique clock built when peace filled the world.

After talking, we'd have lunch somewhere, maybe see a Woody Allen movie, stop by a hotel bar for cocktails. With any kind of luck, we might end up in bed.

Potentiality knocks on the door of my heart.

Now the distance between us has narrowed to fifteen yards.

How can I approach her? What should I say?

'Good morning, miss. Do you think you could spare half an hour for a little conversation?'

Ridiculous. I'd sound like an insurance salesman.

'Pardon me, but would you happen to know if there is an all-night cleaners in the neighborhood?'

No, this is just as ridiculous. I'm not carrying any laundry, for one thing. Who's going to buy a line like that?

Maybe the simple truth would do. 'Good morning. You are the 100% perfect girl for me.'

No, she wouldn't believe it. Or even if she did, she might not want to talk to me. Sorry, she could say, I might be the 100% perfect girl for you, but you're not the 100% perfect boy for me. It could happen. And if I found myself in that situation, I'd probably go to pieces. I'd never recover from the shock. I'm thirty-two, and that's what growing older is all about.

We pass in front of a flower shop. A small, warm air mass touches my skin. The asphalt is damp, and I catch the scent of roses. I can't bring myself to speak to her. She wears a white sweater, and in her right hand she holds a crisp white envelope lacking only a stamp. So: She's

written somebody a letter, maybe spent the whole night writing, to judge from the sleepy look in her eyes. The envelope could contain every secret she's ever had.

I take a few more strides and turn: She's lost in the crowd.

NOW, OF COURSE, I know exactly what I should have said to her. It would have been a long speech, though, far too long for me to have delivered it properly. The ideas I come up with are never very practical.

Oh, well. It would have started 'Once upon a time' and ended 'A sad story, don't you think?'

ONCE UPON A TIME, there lived a boy and a girl. The boy was eighteen and the girl sixteen. He was not unusually handsome, and she was not especially beautiful. They were just an ordinary lonely boy and an ordinary lonely girl, like all the others. But they believed with their whole hearts that somewhere in the world there lived the 100% perfect boy and the 100% perfect girl for them. Yes, they believed in a miracle. And that miracle actually happened.

One day the two came upon each other on the corner of a street.

'This is amazing,' he said. 'I've been looking for you all my life. You may not believe this, but you're the 100% perfect girl for me.'

'And you,' she said to him, 'are the 100% perfect boy

for me, exactly as I'd pictured you in every detail. It's like a dream.'

They sat on a park bench, held hands, and told each other their stories hour after hour. They were not lonely anymore. They had found and been found by their 100% perfect other. What a wonderful thing it is to find and be found by your 100% perfect other. It's a miracle, a cosmic miracle.

As they sat and talked, however, a tiny, tiny sliver of doubt took root in their hearts: Was it really all right for one's dreams to come true so easily?

And so, when there came a momentary lull in their conversation, the boy said to the girl, 'Let's test ourselves – just once. If we really are each other's 100% perfect lovers, then sometime, somewhere, we will meet again without fail. And when that happens, and we know that we are the 100% perfect ones, we'll marry then and there. What do you think?'

'Yes,' she said, 'that is exactly what we should do.'

And so they parted, she to the east, and he to the west.

The test they had agreed upon, however, was utterly unnecessary. They should never have undertaken it, because they really and truly were each other's 100% perfect lovers, and it was a miracle that they had ever met. But it was impossible for them to know this, young as they were. The cold, indifferent waves of fate proceeded to toss them unmercifully.

One winter, both the boy and the girl came down with

the season's terrible influenza, and after drifting for weeks between life and death they lost all memory of their earlier years. When they awoke, their heads were as empty as the young D. H. Lawrence's piggy bank.

They were two bright, determined young people, however, and through their unremitting efforts they were able to acquire once again the knowledge and feeling that qualified them to return as full-fledged members of society. Heaven be praised, they became truly upstanding citizens who knew how to transfer from one subway line to another, who were fully capable of sending a special-delivery letter at the post office. Indeed, they even experienced love again, sometimes as much as 75% or even 85% love.

Time passed with shocking swiftness, and soon the boy was thirty-two, the girl thirty.

One beautiful April morning, in search of a cup of coffee to start the day, the boy was walking from west to east, while the girl, intending to send a special-delivery letter, was walking from east to west, both along the same narrow street in the Harajuku neighborhood of Tokyo. They passed each other in the very center of the street. The faintest gleam of their lost memories glimmered for the briefest moment in their hearts. Each felt a rumbling in the chest. And they knew:

She is the 100% perfect girl for me.

He is the 100% perfect boy for me.

But the glow of their memories was far too weak, and their thoughts no longer had the clarity of fourteen years

earlier. Without a word, they passed each other, disappearing into the crowd. Forever.

A sad story, don't you think?

Yes, that's it, that is what I should have said to her.

—*translated by Jay Rubin*

Birthday Girl

SHE WAITED ON tables as usual that day, her twentieth birthday. She always worked on Fridays, but if things had gone according to plan that particular Friday, she would have had the night off. The other part-time girl had agreed to switch shifts with her as a matter of course: being screamed at by an angry chef while lugging pumpkin gnocchi and seafood *fritto misto* to customers' tables was no way to spend one's twentieth birthday. But the other girl had aggravated a cold and gone to bed with unstoppable diarrhoea and a fever of 104°, so she ended up working after all at short notice.

She found herself trying to comfort the sick girl, who had called to apologise. 'Don't worry about it,' she said. 'I wasn't going to do anything special anyway, even if it is my twentieth birthday.'

And in fact she was not all that disappointed. One reason was the terrible argument she had had a few days earlier with the boyfriend who was supposed to be with

her that night. They had been going together since school. The argument had started from nothing much, but it had taken an unexpected turn for the worse until it became a long and bitter shouting match – one bad enough, she was pretty sure, to have snapped their long-standing ties once and for all. Something inside her had turned rock hard and died. He had not called her since the blow-up, and she was not going to call him.

Her workplace was one of the better-known Italian restaurants in the chic Roppongi district of Tokyo. It had been in business since the late sixties, and while its cuisine was hardly cutting edge, its high reputation was fully justified. It had many regular customers and they were never disappointed. The dining room had a calm, relaxed atmosphere without a hint of pushiness. Rather than a young crowd, the restaurant drew an older clientele that included some famous stage people and writers.

The two full-time waiters worked six days a week. She and the other part-time waitress were students who took turns working three days each. In addition there was one floor manager and, at the desk, a skinny middle-aged woman who supposedly had been there since the restaurant opened – literally sitting in the one place, it seemed, like some gloomy old character from *Little Dorrit*. She had exactly two functions: to accept payment from the customers and to answer the phone. She spoke only when necessary and always wore the same black dress. There was something cold and hard about her: if you set her

afloat on the night-time sea, she would probably sink any boat that happened to ram her.

The floor manager was perhaps in his late forties. Tall and broad-shouldered, his build suggested that he had been a sportsman in his youth, but excess flesh was now beginning to accumulate on his belly and chin. His short, stiff hair was thinning at the crown, and a special ageing bachelor smell clung to him – like newsprint that had been stored in a drawer with cough drops. She had a bachelor uncle who smelled like that.

The manager always wore a black suit, white shirt, and bow tie – not a clip-on bow tie, but the real thing, tied by hand. It was a point of pride for him that he could tie it perfectly without looking in the mirror. He performed his duties adroitly day after day. They consisted of checking the arrival and departure of guests, keeping abreast of the reservation schedule, knowing the names of regular customers, greeting them with a smile, lending a respectful ear to any complaints that might arise, giving expert advice on wines, and overseeing the work of the waiters and the waitresses. It was also his special task to deliver dinner to the room of the restaurant's owner.

'THE OWNER HAD his own room on the sixth floor of the same building where the restaurant was,' she said. 'An apartment, or office or something.'

Somehow she and I had got on to the subject of our twentieth birthdays – what sort of day it had been for each

of us. Most people remember the day they turned twenty. Hers had happened more than ten years earlier.

'He never, ever showed his face in the restaurant, though. The only one who saw him was the manager. It was strictly *his* job to deliver the owner's dinner to him. None of the other employees knew what he looked like.'

'So basically, the owner was getting home delivery from his own restaurant.'

'Correct,' she said. 'Every night at eight, the manager had to bring dinner to the owner's room. It was the restaurant's busiest time, so having the manager disappear just then was always a problem for us, but there was no way around it because that was the way it had always been done. They'd load the dinner on to one of those carts that hotels use for room service, the manager would push it into the lift wearing a respectful look on his face, and fifteen minutes later he'd come back empty-handed. Then, an hour later, he'd go up again and bring down the cart with empty plates and glasses. Every day, like clockwork. I thought it was really odd the first time I saw it happen. It was like some kind of religious ritual, you know? But after a while I got used to it, and never gave it another second thought.'

The owner always had chicken. The recipe and the vegetable sides were a little different every day, but the main dish was always chicken. A young chef once told her that he had tried sending up the same exact roast chicken every day for a week just to see what would happen, but

there was never any complaint. A chef wants to try different ways of preparing things, of course, and each new chef would challenge himself with every technique for chicken that he could think of. They'd make elegant sauces, they'd try chickens from different suppliers, but none of their efforts had any effect: they might just as well have been throwing pebbles into an empty cave. In the end, every one of them gave up and sent the owner some run-of-the-mill chicken dish every day. That's all that was ever asked of them.

Work started as usual on her twentieth birthday, 17 November. It had been raining on and off since the afternoon, and pouring since early evening. At five o'clock the manager gathered the employees together to explain the day's specials. Servers were required to memorise them word for word and not use crib sheets: veal Milanese, pasta topped with sardines and cabbage, chestnut mousse. Sometimes the manager would play the role of a customer and test them with questions. Then came the employees' meal: waiters in *this* restaurant were not going to have growling stomachs as they took their customers' orders!

The restaurant opened its doors at six o'clock, but guests were slow to arrive because of the downpour, and several reservations were simply cancelled. Women didn't want their dresses ruined by the rain. The manager walked around tightlipped, and the waiters killed time polishing the salt and pepper shakers or chatting with the chef about cooking. She surveyed the dining room with just one

couple having their dinner and listened to the harpsichord music flowing discreetly from ceiling speakers. A deep smell of late-autumn rain worked its way from the street.

It was after seven thirty when the manager started feeling sick. He stumbled over to a chair and sat there for a while, pressing his stomach, as if he had just been shot. A greasy sweat clung to his forehead. 'I think I'd better go to the hospital,' he muttered. For him to be taken ill was a wholly uncommon occurrence: he had never missed a day since he started working in the restaurant more than ten years earlier. It was another point of pride for him that he had never been out with illness or injury, but his painful grimace made it clear that he was in a very bad way.

She stepped outside with an umbrella and hailed a taxi. One of the waiters held the manager steady and climbed into the car with him to take him to a nearby hospital. Before ducking into the cab, the manager said to her hoarsely, 'I want you to take a dinner up to room 604 at eight o'clock. All you have to do is ring the bell, say, "Your dinner is here," and leave it.'

'That's room 604, right?' she said.

'At eight o'clock,' he repeated. 'On the dot.' He grimaced again, climbed in, and the taxi took him away.

THE RAIN SHOWED no signs of letting up after the manager had left, and customers arrived at long intervals. No more than one or two tables were occupied at any time, so if the manager and one waiter had to be absent, this was a

good time for it to happen. Things could get so busy that it was not unusual even for the full staff to have trouble coping.

When the owner's meal was ready at eight o'clock, she pushed the room-service trolley into the lift and rode up to the sixth floor. It was the standard meal for him: a half-bottle of red wine with the cork loosened, a thermal pot of coffee, a chicken entrée with steamed vegetables, rolls and butter. The heavy aroma of cooked chicken quickly filled the small lift. It mingled with the smell of the rain. Water droplets dotted the lift floor, suggesting that someone with a wet umbrella had recently been aboard.

She pushed the trolley down the corridor, bringing it to a stop in front of the door marked '604'. She double-checked her memory: 604. That was it. She cleared her throat and pressed the doorbell.

There was no answer. She stood there for a good twenty seconds. Just as she was thinking of pressing the bell again, the door opened inward and a skinny old man appeared. He was shorter than she was, by some four or five inches. He had on a dark suit and a tie. Against his white shirt, the tie stood out distinctly, its brownish-yellow colouring not unlike withered leaves. He made a very clean impression, his clothes perfectly pressed, his white hair smoothed down: he looked as though he were about to go out for the night to some sort of gathering. The deep wrinkles that creased his brow made her think of ravines in an aerial photograph.

'Your dinner, sir,' she said in a husky voice, then quietly cleared her throat again. Her voice grew husky whenever she was tense.

'Dinner?'

'Yes, sir. The manager took sick suddenly. I had to take his place today. Your meal, sir.'

'Oh, I see,' the old man said, almost as if talking to himself, his hand still perched on the doorknob. 'Took sick, eh? You don't say.'

'His stomach started to hurt him all of a sudden. He went to the hospital. He thinks he might have appendicitis.'

'Oh, that's not good,' the old man said, running his fingers along the wrinkles of his forehead. 'Not good at all.'

She cleared her throat again. 'Shall I bring your meal in, sir?' she asked.

'Ah yes, of course,' the old man said. 'Yes, of course, if you wish. That's fine with me.'

If I wish? she thought. What a strange way to put it. What am I supposed to wish?

The old man opened the door the rest of the way, and she wheeled the trolley inside. The floor had short grey carpeting with no area for removing shoes. The first room was a large study, as though the apartment was more a workplace than a residence. The window looked out on to the nearby Tokyo Tower, its steel skeleton outlined in lights. A large desk stood by the window, and beside the desk was a compact sofa and love seat. The old man

pointed to the plastic laminate coffee table in front of the sofa. She arranged his meal on the table: white napkin and silverware, coffee pot and cup, wine and wine glass, bread and butter, and the plate of chicken and vegetables.

'If you would be kind enough to set the dishes in the hall as usual, sir, I'll come to get them in an hour.'

Her words seemed to snap him out of an appreciative contemplation of his dinner. 'Oh yes, of course. I'll put them in the hall. On the trolley. In an hour. If you wish.'

Yes, she replied inwardly, for the moment that is exactly what I wish. 'Is there anything else I can do for you, sir?'

'No, I don't think so,' he said after a moment's consideration. He was wearing black shoes polished to a high sheen. They were small and chic. He's a stylish dresser, she thought. And he stands very straight for his age.

'Well, then, sir, I'll be getting back to work.'

'No, wait just a moment,' he said.

'Sir?'

'Do you think it might be possible for you to give me five minutes of your time, miss? I have something I'd like to say to you.'

He was so polite in his request that it made her blush. 'I . . . think it should be alright,' she said. 'I mean, if it really is just five minutes.' He was her employer, after all. He was paying her by the hour. It was not a question of her giving or his taking her time. And this old man did not look like a person who would do anything bad to her.

'By the way, how old are you?' the old man asked,

standing by the table with arms folded and looking directly into her eyes.

'I'm twenty now,' she said.

'Twenty *now*,' he repeated, narrowing his eyes as if peering through some kind of crack. 'Twenty *now*. As of when?'

'Well, I just turned twenty,' she said. After a moment's hesitation, she added, 'Today is my birthday, sir.'

'I *see*,' he said, rubbing his chin as if this explained a great deal for him. 'Today, is it? Today is your twentieth birthday?'

She nodded.

'Your life in this world began exactly twenty years ago today.'

'Yes, sir,' she said, 'that is so.'

'I see, I see,' he said. 'That's wonderful. Well, then, happy birthday.'

'Thank you very much,' she said, and then it dawned on her that this was the very first time all day that anyone had wished her a happy birthday. Of course, if her parents had called from Oita, she might find a message from them on her answering machine when she got home from work.

'Well, well, this is certainly a cause for celebration,' he said. 'How about a little toast? We can drink this red wine.'

'Thank you, sir, but I couldn't. I'm working now.'

'Oh, what's the harm in a little sip? No one's going to blame you if I say it's alright. Just a token drink to celebrate.'

The old man slid the cork from the bottle and dribbled a little wine into his glass for her. Then he took an ordinary drinking glass from a glass-doored cabinet and poured some wine for himself.

'Happy birthday,' he said. 'May you live a rich and fruitful life, and may there be nothing to cast dark shadows on it.'

They clinked glasses.

May there be nothing to cast dark shadows on it: she silently repeated his remark to herself. Why had he chosen such unusual words for her birthday toast?

'Your twentieth birthday comes only once in a lifetime, young lady. It's an irreplaceable day.'

'Yes, sir, I know,' she said, taking one cautious sip of wine.

'And here, on your special day, you have taken the trouble to deliver my dinner to me like a kind-hearted fairy.'

'Just doing my job, sir.'

'But still,' the old man said with a few quick shakes of the head. 'But still, lovely young miss.'

The old man sat down in the leather chair by his desk and motioned her to the sofa. She lowered herself gingerly on to the edge of the seat, with the wine glass still in her hand. Knees aligned, she tugged at her skirt, clearing her throat again. She saw raindrops tracing lines down the window pane. The room was strangely quiet.

'Today just happens to be your twentieth birthday, and on top of that you have brought me this wonderful

warm meal,' the old man said as if reconfirming the situation. Then he set his glass on the desktop with a little thump. 'This has to be some kind of special convergence, don't you think?'

Not quite convinced, she managed a nod.

'Which is why,' he said, touching the knot of his withered-leaf-coloured necktie, 'I feel it is important for me to give you a birthday present. A special birthday calls for a special commemorative gift.'

Flustered, she shook her head and said, 'No, please, sir, don't give it a second thought. All I did was bring your meal the way they ordered me to.'

The old man raised both hands, palms towards her. 'No, miss, don't *you* give it a second thought. The kind of "present" I have in mind is not something tangible, not something with a price tag. To put it simply –' he placed his hands on the desk and took one long, slow breath – 'what I would like to do for a lovely young fairy such as you is to grant a wish you might have, to make your wish come true. Anything. Anything at all that you wish for – assuming that you *do* have such a wish.'

'A wish?' she asked, her throat dry.

'Something you would like to have happen, miss. If you have a wish – one wish, I'll make it come true. That is the kind of birthday present I can give you. But you had better think about it very carefully because I can grant you only one.' He raised a finger. 'Just one. You can't change your mind afterwards and take it back.'

She was at a loss for words. One wish? Whipped by the wind, raindrops tapped unevenly at the window pane. As long as she remained silent, the old man looked into her eyes, saying nothing. Time marked its irregular pulse in her ears.

'I have to wish for something, and it will be granted?'

Instead of answering her question, the old man – hands still side by side on the desk – just smiled. He did it in the most natural and amiable way.

'Do you *have* a wish, miss – or not?' he asked gently.

'THIS REALLY DID happen,' she said, looking straight at me. 'I'm not making it up.'

'Of course not,' I said. She was not the sort of person to invent some goofy story out of thin air. 'So . . . did you make a wish?'

She went on looking at me for a while, then released a tiny sigh. 'Don't get me wrong,' she said. 'I wasn't taking him one hundred per cent seriously myself. I mean, at twenty you're not exactly living in a fairy-tale world any more. If this was his idea of a joke, though, I had to hand it to him for coming up with it on the spot. He was a dapper old fellow with a twinkle in his eye, so I decided to play along with him. It *was* my twentieth birthday, after all: I reckoned I ought to have *something* not-so-ordinary happen to me that day. It wasn't a question of believing or not believing.'

I nodded without saying anything.

'Do you *have* a wish, miss – or not?' he asked gently

'You can understand how I felt, I'm sure. My twentieth birthday was coming to an end without anything special happening, nobody wishing me a happy birthday, and all I'm doing is carrying tortellini with anchovy sauce to people's tables.'

I nodded again. 'Don't worry,' I said. 'I understand.'

'So I made a wish.'

THE OLD MAN kept his gaze fixed on her, saying nothing, hands still on the desk. Also on the desk were several thick folders that might have been account books, plus writing implements, a calendar and a lamp with a green shade. Lying among them, his small hands looked like another set of desktop furnishings. The rain continued to beat against the window, the lights of Tokyo Tower filtering through the shattered drops.

The wrinkles on the old man's forehead deepened slightly. 'That is your wish?'

'Yes,' she said. 'That is my wish.'

'A bit unusual for a girl your age,' he said. 'I was expecting something different.'

'If it's no good, I'll wish for something else,' she said, clearing her throat. 'I don't mind. I'll think of something else.'

'No, no,' the old man said, raising his hands and waving them like flags. 'There's nothing wrong with it, not at all. It's just a little surprising, miss. Don't you have something else? For example, you want to be prettier, or smarter, or

rich: you're OK with not wishing for something like that – something an ordinary girl would ask for?'

She took some moments to search for the right words. The old man just waited, saying nothing, his hands at rest together on the desk again.

'Of course I'd like to be prettier or smarter or rich. But I really can't imagine what would happen to me if any of those things came true. They might be more than I could handle. I still don't really know what life is all about. I don't know how it *works*.'

'I see,' the old man said, intertwining his fingers and separating them again. 'I see.'

'So, is my wish OK?'

'Of course,' he said. 'Of course. It's no trouble at all for me.'

The old man suddenly fixed his eyes on a spot in the air. The wrinkles of his forehead deepened: they might have been the wrinkles of his brain itself as it concentrated on his thoughts. He seemed to be staring at something – perhaps all-but-invisible bits of down – floating in the air. He opened his arms wide, lifted himself slightly from his chair, and whipped his palms together with a dry smack. Settling in the chair again, he slowly ran his fingertips along the wrinkles of his brow as if to soften them, and then turned to her with a gentle smile.

'That did it,' he said. 'Your wish has been granted.'

'Already?'

'Yes, it was no trouble at all. Your wish has been granted,

lovely miss. Happy birthday. You may go back to work now. Don't worry, I'll put the trolley in the hall.'

She took the lift down to the restaurant. Empty-handed now, she felt almost disturbingly light, as though she were walking on some sort of mysterious fluff.

'Are you OK? You look spaced out,' the younger waiter said to her.

She gave him an ambiguous smile and shook her head. 'Oh, really? No, I'm fine.'

'Tell me about the owner. What's he like?'

'I dunno, I didn't get a very good look at him,' she said, cutting the conversation short.

An hour later she went to bring the trolley down. It was out in the corridor, utensils in place. She lifted the lid to find the chicken and vegetables gone. The wine bottle and coffee pot were empty. The door to room 604 stood there, closed and expressionless. She stared at it for a time, feeling it might open at any moment, but it did not open. She brought the trolley down in the lift and wheeled it in to the dishwasher. The chef looked blankly at the plate: empty as always.

'I NEVER SAW the owner again,' she said. 'Not once. The manager turned out to have just an ordinary stomach ache and went back to delivering the owner's meal again himself the next day. I left the job after New Year's, and I've never been back to the place. I don't know, I just felt it was better not to go near there, kind of like a premonition.'

She toyed with a paper coaster, thinking her own thoughts. 'Sometimes I get the feeling that everything that happened to me on my twentieth birthday was some sort of illusion. It's as though something happened to make me think that things happened that never really happened at all. But I know for sure that they *did* happen. I can still bring back vivid images of every piece of furniture and every knick-knack in room 604. What happened to me in there really happened, and it had an important meaning for me, too.'

The two of us kept silent, drinking our drinks and thinking our separate thoughts.

'Do you mind if I ask you one thing?' I asked. 'Or, more precisely, *two* things.'

'Go ahead,' she said. 'I imagine you're going to ask me what I wished for that time. That's the first thing you want to know.'

'But it looks as though you don't want to talk about that.'

'Does it?'

I nodded.

She put the coaster down and narrowed her eyes as if staring at something in the distance. 'You're not supposed to tell anybody what you wished for, you know.'

'I won't try to drag it out of you,' I said. 'I *would* like to know whether or not it came true, though. And also – whatever the wish itself might have been – whether or not you later came to regret what it was you chose to wish

for. Were you ever sorry you didn't wish for something else?'

'The answer to the first question is yes and also no. I still have a lot of living left to do, probably. I haven't seen how things are going to work out to the end.'

'So it was a wish that takes time to come true?'

'You could say that. Time is going to play an important role.'

'Like in cooking certain dishes?'

She nodded.

I thought about that for a moment, but the only thing that came to mind was the image of a gigantic pie cooking slowly in an oven at low heat.

'And the answer to my second question?'

'What was that again?'

'Whether you ever regretted your choice of what to wish for.'

A moment of silence followed. The eyes she turned on me seemed to lack any depth. The desiccated shadow of a smile flickered at the corners of her mouth, suggesting a kind of hushed sense of resignation.

'I'm married now,' she said. 'To a CPA three years older than me. And I have two children, a boy and a girl. We have an Irish setter. I drive an Audi, and I play tennis with my girlfriends twice a week. That's the life I'm living now.'

'Sounds pretty good to me,' I said.

'Even if the Audi's bumper has two dents?'

'Hey, bumpers are *made* for denting.'

'That would make a great bumper sticker,' she said. '"Bumpers are for denting."'

I looked at her mouth when she said that.

'What I'm trying to tell you is this,' she said more softly, scratching an earlobe. It was a beautifully shaped earlobe. 'No matter what they wish for, no matter how far they go, people can never be anything but themselves. That's all.'

'There's another good bumper sticker,' I said. '"No matter how far they go, people can never be anything but themselves."'

She laughed aloud, with a real show of pleasure, and the shadow was gone.

She rested her elbow on the bar and looked at me. 'Tell me,' she said. 'What would you have wished for if you had been in my position?'

'On the night of my twentieth birthday, you mean?'

'Uh-huh.'

I took some time to think about that, but I couldn't come up with a single wish.

'I can't think of anything,' I confessed. 'I'm too far away now from my twentieth birthday.'

'You really can't think of anything?'

I nodded.

'Not one thing?'

'Not one thing.'

She looked into my eyes again – straight in – and said, 'That's because you've already *made* your wish.'

———

'BUT YOU HAD better think about it very carefully, my lovely young fairy, because I can grant you only one.' In the darkness somewhere, an old man wearing a withered-leaf-coloured tie raises a finger. 'Just one. You can't change your mind afterwards and take it back.'

—*translated by Jay Rubin*

Samsa in Love

HE WOKE TO DISCOVER that he had undergone a meta-morphosis and become Gregor Samsa.

He lay flat on his back on the bed, looking at the ceiling. It took time for his eyes to adjust to the lack of light. The ceiling seemed to be a common, everyday ceiling of the sort one might find anywhere. Once, it had been painted white, or possibly a pale cream. Years of dust and dirt, however, had given it the color of spoiled milk. It had no ornament, no defining characteristic. No argument, no message. It fulfilled its structural role but aspired to nothing further.

There was a tall window on one side of the room, to his left, but its curtain had been removed and thick boards nailed across the frame. An inch or so of space had been left between the horizontal boards, whether on purpose or not wasn't clear; rays of morning sun shone through, casting a row of bright parallel lines on the floor. Why was the window barricaded in such a rough fashion? Was a major

storm or tornado in the offing? Or was it to keep someone from getting in? Or to prevent someone (him, perhaps?) from leaving?

Still on his back, he slowly turned his head and examined the rest of the room. He could see no furniture, apart from the bed on which he lay. No chest of drawers, no desk, no chair. No painting, clock, or mirror on the walls. No lamp or light. Nor could he make out any rug or carpet on the floor. Just bare wood. The walls were covered with wallpaper of a complex design, but it was so old and faded that in the weak light it was next to impossible to make out what the design was.

There was a door to his right, on the wall opposite the window. Its brass knob was discolored in places. It appeared that the room had once served as a normal bedroom. Yet now all vestiges of human life had been stripped away. The only thing that remained was his solitary bed in the center. And it had no bedding. No sheets, no coverlet, no pillow. Just an ancient mattress.

Samsa had no idea where he was, or what he should do. All he knew was that he was now a human whose name was Gregor Samsa. And how did he know *that*? Perhaps someone had whispered it in his ear while he lay sleeping? But who had he been before he became Gregor Samsa? *What* had he been?

The moment he began contemplating that question, however, something like a black column of mosquitoes swirled up in his head. The column grew thicker and

denser as it moved to a softer part of his brain, buzzing all the way. Samsa decided to stop thinking. Trying to think anything through at this point was too great a burden.

In any case, he had to learn how to move his body. He couldn't lie there staring up at the ceiling forever. The posture left him much too vulnerable. He had no chance of surviving an attack – by predatory birds, for example. As a first step, he tried to move his fingers. There were ten of them, long things affixed to his two hands. Each was equipped with a number of joints, which made synchronizing their movements very complicated. To make matters worse, his body felt numb, as though it were immersed in a sticky, heavy liquid, so that it was difficult to send strength to his extremities.

Nevertheless, after repeated attempts and failures, by closing his eyes and focusing his mind he was able to bring his fingers more under control. Little by little, he was learning how to make them work together. As his fingers became operational, the numbness that had enveloped his body withdrew. In its place – like a dark and sinister reef revealed by a retreating tide – came an excruciating pain.

It took Samsa some time to realize that the pain was hunger. This ravenous desire for food was new to him, or at least he had no memory of experiencing anything like it. It was as if he had not had a bite to eat for a week. As if the center of his body were now a cavernous void. His bones creaked; his muscles clenched; his organs twitched.

Unable to withstand the pain any longer, Samsa put his

elbows on the mattress and, bit by bit, pushed himself up. His spine emitted several low and sickening cracks in the process. My goodness, Samsa thought, how long have I been lying here? His body protested each move. But he struggled through, marshaling his strength, until, at last, he managed to sit up.

Samsa looked down in dismay at his naked body. How ill-formed it was! Worse than ill-formed. It possessed no means of self-defense. Smooth white skin (covered by only a perfunctory amount of hair) with fragile blue blood vessels visible through it; a soft, unprotected belly; ludicrous, impossibly shaped genitals; gangly arms and legs (just two of each!); a scrawny, breakable neck; an enormous, misshapen head with a tangle of stiff hair on its crown; two absurd ears, jutting out like a pair of seashells. *Was this thing really him?* Could a body so preposterous, so easy to destroy (no shell for protection, no weapons for attack), survive in the world? Why hadn't he been turned into a fish? Or a sunflower? A fish or a sunflower made sense. More sense, anyway, than this creature, Gregor Samsa. There was no other way to look at it.

Steeling himself, he lowered his legs over the edge of the bed until the soles of his feet touched the floor. The unexpected cold of the bare wood made him gasp. After several failed attempts that sent him crashing to the floor, at last he was able to balance on his two feet. He stood there, bruised and sore, one hand clutching the frame of the bed for support. His head was inordinately heavy and

hard to hold up. Sweat streamed from his armpits, and his genitals shrank from the stress. He had to take several deep breaths before his constricted muscles began to relax.

Once he was used to standing, he had to learn to walk. Walking on two legs amounted to a kind of torture, each movement an exercise in pain. No matter how he looked at it, advancing his right and left legs one after the other was a bizarre proposition that flouted all natural laws, while the precarious distance from his eyes to the ground made him cringe in fear. It took time to learn how to coordinate his hip and knee joints, and even longer to balance their movements. Each time he took a step forward, his knees shook with terror, and he steadied himself against the wall with both hands.

But he knew that he could not remain in this room forever. If he didn't find food, and quickly, his starving belly would consume his own flesh, and he would cease to exist.

HE TOTTERED TOWARD the door, pawing at the wall as he went. The journey seemed to take hours, although he had no way of measuring the time, except by the pain. His movements were awkward, his pace snail-like. He couldn't advance without leaning on something for support. On the street, his best hope would be that people saw him as disabled. Yet, despite the discomfort, with each step he was learning how his joints and muscles worked.

He grasped the doorknob and pulled. It didn't budge. A

push yielded the same result. Next, he turned the knob to the right and pulled. The door opened partway with a slight squeak. It hadn't been locked. He poked his head through the opening and looked out. The hallway was deserted. It was as quiet as the bottom of the ocean. He extended his left leg through the doorway, swung the upper half of his body out, with one hand on the doorframe, and followed with his right leg. He moved slowly down the corridor in his bare feet, hands on the wall.

There were four doors in the hallway, including the one he had just used. All were identical, fashioned of the same dark wood. What, or who, lay beyond them? He longed to open them and find out. Perhaps then he might begin to understand the mysterious circumstances in which he found himself. Or at least discover a clue of some sort. Nevertheless, he passed by each of the doors, making as little noise as possible. The need to fill his belly trumped his curiosity. He had to find something substantial to eat, and quickly.

And now he knew where to find that 'something substantial.'

Just follow the smell, he thought, sniffing. It was the aroma of cooked food, tiny particles that wafted to him through the air. The information gathered by olfactory receptors in his nose was being transmitted to his brain, producing an anticipation so vivid, a craving so violent, that he could feel his innards being slowly twisted, as if by an experienced torturer. Saliva flooded his mouth.

To reach the source of the aroma, however, he would have to go down a steep flight of stairs, seventeen of them. He was having a hard enough time walking on level ground – navigating those steps would be a true nightmare. He grabbed the banister with both hands and began his descent. His skinny ankles felt ready to collapse under his weight, and he almost went tumbling down the steps. When he twisted his body to right himself his bones and muscles shrieked in pain.

And what was on Samsa's mind as he made his way down the staircase? Fish and sunflowers, for the most part. Had I been transformed into a fish or a sunflower, he thought, I could have lived out my life in peace, without our struggling up and down steps like these. Why must I undertake something this perilous and unnatural? It makes no sense – there is no rhyme or reason to it.

When Samsa reached the bottom of the seventeen steps, he pulled himself upright, summoned his remaining strength, and hobbled in the direction of the enticing smell. He crossed the high-ceilinged entrance hall and stepped through the dining room's open doorway. The food was laid out on a large oval table. There were five chairs, but no sign of people. White wisps of steam rose from the serving plates. A glass vase bearing a dozen lilies occupied the center of the table. Four places were set with napkins and cutlery, untouched, by the look of it. It seemed as though people had been sitting down to eat their

breakfast a few minutes earlier, when some sudden and unforeseen event sent them all running off.

What had happened? Where had they gone? Or where had they been taken? Would they return to eat their breakfast?

But Samsa had no time to ponder such questions. Falling into the nearest chair, he grabbed whatever food he could reach with his bare hands and stuffed it into his mouth, quite ignoring the knives, spoons, forks, and napkins. He tore bread into pieces and downed it without jam or butter, gobbled fat boiled sausages whole, devoured hard-boiled eggs with such speed that he almost forgot to peel them, scooped up handfuls of still-warm mashed potatoes, and plucked pickles with his fingers. He chewed it all together, and washed the remnants down with water from a jug. Taste was of no consequence. Bland or delicious, spicy or sour—it was all the same to him. What mattered was filling that empty cavern inside him. He ate with total concentration, as if racing against time. He was so fixated on eating that once, as he was licking his fingers, he sank his teeth into them by mistake. Scraps of food flew everywhere, and when a platter fell to the floor and smashed he paid no attention whatsoever.

By the time Samsa had eaten his fill and sat back to catch his breath, almost nothing was left, and the dining table was an awful sight. It looked as if a flock of quarrelsome crows had flown in through an open window, gorged themselves, and flown away again. The only thing

untouched was the vase of lilies; had there been less food, he might have devoured them as well. That was how hungry he had been.

He sat, dazed, in his chair for a long while. Hands on the table, he gazed at the lilies through half-closed eyes and took long, slow breaths, while the food he had eaten worked its way through his digestive system, from his esophagus to his intestines. A sense of satiety came over him like a rising tide.

He picked up a metal pot and poured coffee into a white ceramic cup. The pungent fragrance recalled something to him. It did not come directly, however; it arrived in stages. It was a strange feeling, as if he were recollecting the present from the future. As if time had somehow been split in two, so that memory and experience revolved within a closed cycle, each following the other. He poured a liberal amount of cream into his coffee, stirred it with his finger, and drank. Although the coffee had cooled, a slight warmth remained. He held it in his mouth before warily allowing it to trickle down his throat. He found that it calmed him to a degree.

All of a sudden, he felt cold. The intensity of his hunger had blotted out his other senses. Now that he was sated, the morning chill on his skin made him tremble. The fire had gone out. None of the heaters seemed to be turned on. On top of that, he was stark naked – even his feet were bare.

Now that he was sated, the morning chill on his skin made him tremble

He knew that he had to find something to wear. He was too cold like this. Moreover, his lack of clothes was bound to be an issue should someone appear. There might be a knock at the door. Or the people who had been about to sit down to breakfast a short while before might return. Who knew how they would react if they found him in this state?

He understood all this. He did not surmise it, or perceive it in an intellectual way; he knew it, pure and simple. Samsa had no idea where such knowledge came from. Perhaps it was related to those revolving memories he was having.

He stood up from his chair and walked out to the front hall. He was still awkward, but at least he could stand and walk on two legs without clinging to something. There was a wrought iron umbrella stand in the hall that held several walking sticks. He pulled out a black one made of oak to help him move around; just grasping its sturdy handle relaxed and encouraged him. And now he would have a weapon to fight back with should birds attack. He went to the window and looked out through the crack in the lace curtains.

The house faced onto a street. It was not a very big street. Nor were many people on it. Nevertheless, he noted that every person who passed was fully clothed. The clothes were of various colors and styles. Most were men, but there were one or two women as well. The men and women wore different garments. Shoes of stiff leather covered their feet. A few sported brightly polished boots.

He could hear the soles of their footwear clack on the cobblestones. Many of the men and women wore hats. They seemed to think nothing of walking on two legs and keeping their genitals covered. Samsa compared his reflection in the hall's full-length mirror with the people walking outside. The man he saw in the mirror was a shabby, frail-looking creature. His belly was smeared with gravy, and bread crumbs clung to his pubic hair like bits of cotton. He swept the filth away with his hand.

Yes, he thought again, I must find something to cover my body.

He looked out at the street once more, checking for birds. But there were no birds in sight.

The ground floor of the house consisted of the hallway, the dining room, a kitchen, and a living room. As far as he could tell, however, none of those rooms held anything resembling clothes. Which meant that the putting on and taking off of clothing must occur somewhere else. Perhaps in a room on the second floor.

Samsa returned to the staircase and began to climb. He was surprised to discover how much easier it was to go up than to go down. Clutching the railing, he was able to make his way up the seventeen steps at a much faster rate and without undue pain or fear, stopping several times along the way (though never for long) to catch his breath.

One might say that luck was with him, for none of the doors on the second floor were locked. All he had to do was turn the knob and push, and each door swung open. There

were four rooms in total, and, apart from the freezing room with the bare floor in which he had woken, all were comfortably furnished. Each had a bed with clean bedding, a dresser, a writing desk, a lamp affixed to the ceiling or the wall, and a rug or a carpet with an intricate pattern. All were tidy and clean. Books were neatly lined up in their cases, and framed oil paintings of landscapes adorned the walls. Each room had a glass vase filled with bright flowers. None had rough boards nailed across the windows. Their windows had lace curtains, through which sunlight poured like a blessing from above. The beds all showed signs of someone's having slept in them. He could see the imprint of heads on pillows.

Samsa found a dressing gown his size in the closet of the largest room. It looked like something he might be able to manage. He hadn't a clue what to do with the other clothes – how to put them on, how to wear them. They were just too complicated: too many buttons, for one thing, and he was unsure how to tell front from back, or top from bottom. Which was supposed to go on the outside, and which underneath? The dressing gown, on the other hand, was simple, practical, and quite free of ornament, the sort of thing he thought he could handle. Its light, soft cloth felt good against his skin, and its color was dark blue. He even turned up a matching pair of slippers.

He pulled the dressing gown over his naked body and, after much trial and error, succeeded in fastening the belt around his waist. He looked in the mirror at himself, clad

now in gown and slippers. This was certainly better than walking around naked. Mastering how to wear clothes would require close observation and considerable time. Until then, this gown was the only answer. It wasn't as warm as it might have been, to be sure, but as long as he remained indoors it would stave off the cold. Best of all, he no longer had to worry that his soft skin would be exposed to vicious birds.

WHEN THE DOORBELL rang, Samsa was dozing in the biggest room (and in the biggest bed) in the house. It was warm under the feather quilts, as cozy as if he were sleeping in an egg. He woke from a dream. He couldn't remember it in detail, but it had been pleasant and cheerful. The bell echoing through the house, however, yanked him back to cold reality.

He dragged himself from the bed, fastened his gown, put on his dark blue slippers, grabbed his black walking stick, and, hand on railing, tottered down the stairs. It was far easier than it had been on the first occasion. Still, the danger of falling was ever present. He could not afford to let down his guard. Keeping a close eye on his feet, he picked his way down the stairs one step at a time, as the doorbell continued to ring. Whoever was pushing the buzzer had to be a most impatient and stubborn person.

Walking stick in his left hand, Samsa approached the front door. He twisted the knob to the right and pulled, and the door swung in.

A little woman was standing outside. A very little woman. It was a wonder she was able to reach the buzzer. When he looked more closely, however, he realized that the issue wasn't her size. It was her back, which was bent forward in a perpetual stoop. This made her appear small even though, in fact, her frame was of normal dimensions. She had fastened her hair with a rubber band to prevent it from spilling over her face. The hair was deep chestnut and very abundant. She was dressed in a battered tweed jacket and a full, loose-fitting skirt that covered her ankles. A striped cotton scarf was wrapped around her neck. She wore no hat. Her shoes were of the tall lace-up variety, and she appeared to be in her early twenties. There was still something of the girl about her. Her eyes were big, her nose small, and her lips twisted a little to one side, like a skinny moon. Her dark eyebrows formed two straight lines across her forehead, giving her a skeptical look.

'Is this the Samsa residence?' the woman said, craning her head up to look at him. Then she twisted her body all over. Much the way the earth twists during a violent earthquake.

He was taken aback at first, but pulled himself together. 'Yes,' he said. Since he was Gregor Samsa, this was likely the Samsa residence. At any rate, there could be no harm in saying so.

Yet the woman seemed to find his answer less than satisfying. A slight frown creased her brow. Perhaps she had picked up a note of confusion in his voice.

'So this is *really* the Samsa residence?' she said in a sharp voice. Like an experienced gatekeeper grilling a shabby visitor.

'I am Gregor Samsa,' Samsa said, in as relaxed a tone as possible. Of this, at least, he was sure.

'I hope you're right,' she said, reaching down for a cloth bag at her feet. It was black, and seemed very heavy. Worn through in places, it had doubtless had a number of owners. 'So let's get started.'

She strode into the house without waiting for a reply. Samsa closed the door behind her. She stood there, looking him up and down. It seemed that his gown and slippers had aroused her suspicions.

'I appear to have woken you,' she said, her voice cold.

'That's perfectly all right,' Samsa replied. He could tell by her dark expression that his clothes were a poor fit for the occasion. 'I must apologize for my appearance,' he went on. 'There are reasons . . .'

The woman ignored this. 'So, then?' she said through pursed lips.

'So, then?' Samsa echoed.

'So, then, where is the lock that's causing the problem?' the woman said.

'The lock?'

'The lock that's broken,' she said. Her irritation had been evident from the beginning. 'You asked us to come and repair it.'

'Ah,' Samsa said. 'The broken lock.'

Samsa ransacked his mind. No sooner had he managed to focus on one thing, however, than that black column of mosquitoes rose up again.

'I haven't heard anything in particular about a lock,' he said. 'My guess is it belongs to one of the doors on the second floor.'

The woman glowered at him. 'Your guess?' she said, peering up at his face. Her voice had grown even icier. An eyebrow arched in disbelief. 'One of the doors?' she went on.

Samsa could feel his face flush. His ignorance regarding the lock struck him as most embarrassing. He cleared his throat to speak, but the words did not come.

'Mr Samsa, are your parents in? I think it's better if I talk to them.'

'They seem to have gone out on an errand,' Samsa said.

'An errand?' she said, appalled. 'In the midst of these *troubles*?'

'I really have no idea. When I woke up this morning, everyone was gone,' Samsa said.

'Good grief,' the young woman said. She heaved a long sigh. 'We did tell them that someone would come at this time today.'

'I'm terribly sorry.'

The woman stood there for a moment. Then, slowly, her arched eyebrow descended, and she looked at the black walking stick in Samsa's left hand. 'Are your legs bothering you, Gregor Samsa?'

'Yes, a little,' he prevaricated.

Once again, the woman writhed suddenly. Samsa had no idea what this action meant or what its purpose was. Yet he was drawn by instinct to the complex sequence of movements.

'Well, what's to be done,' the woman said in a tone of resignation. 'Let's take a look at those doors on the second floor. I came over the bridge and all the way across town through this terrible upheaval to get here. Risked my life, in fact. So it wouldn't make much sense to say, "Oh, really, no one is here? I'll come back later," would it?'

This terrible upheaval? Samsa couldn't grasp what she was talking about. What awful change was taking place? But he decided not to ask for details. Better to avoid exposing his ignorance even further.

Back bent, the young woman took the heavy black bag in her right hand and toiled up the stairs, much like a crawling insect. Samsa labored after her, his hand on the railing. Her creeping gait aroused his sympathy – it reminded him of something.

The woman stood at the top of the steps and surveyed the hallway. 'So,' she said, '*one* of these four doors *probably* has a broken lock, right?'

Samsa's face reddened. 'Yes,' he said. 'One of these. It could be the one at the end of the hall on the left, possibly,' he said, faltering. This was the door to the bare room in which he had woken that morning.

'*It could be,*' the woman said in a voice as lifeless as an

extinguished bonfire. *'Possibly.'* She turned around to examine Samsa's face.

'Somehow or other,' Samsa said.

The woman sighed again. 'Gregor Samsa,' she said dryly. 'You are a true joy to talk to. Such a rich vocabulary, and you always get to the point.' Then her tone changed. 'But no matter. Let's check the door on the left at the end of the hall first.'

The woman went to the door. She turned the knob back and forth and pushed, and it opened inward. The room was as it had been before: only a bed with a bare mattress that was less than clean. This was the mattress he had woken on that morning as Gregor Samsa. It had been no dream. The floor bare and cold. Boards nailed across the window. The woman must have noticed all this, but she showed no sign of surprise. Her demeanor suggested that similar rooms could be found all over the city.

She squatted down, opened the black bag, pulled out a white flannel cloth, and spread it on the floor. Then she took out a number of tools, which she lined up carefully on the cloth, like an inquisitor displaying the sinister instruments of his trade before some poor martyr.

Selecting a wire of medium thickness, she inserted it into the lock and, with a practiced hand, manipulated it from a variety of angles. Her eyes were narrowed in concentration, her ears alert for the slightest sound. Next, she chose a thinner wire and repeated the process. Her face grew somber, and her mouth twisted into a ruthless shape,

like a Chinese sword. She took a large flashlight and, with a black look in her eyes, began to examine the lock in detail.

'Do you have the key for this lock?' she asked Samsa.

'I haven't the slightest idea where the key is,' he answered honestly.

'Ah, Gregor Samsa, sometimes you make me want to die,' she said.

After that, she quite ignored him. She selected a screwdriver from the tools lined up on the cloth and proceeded to remove the lock from the door. Her movements were slow and cautious. She paused from time to time to twist and writhe about as she had before.

While he stood behind her, watching her move in that fashion, Samsa's own body began to respond in a strange way. He was growing hot all over, and his nostrils were flaring. His mouth was so dry that he produced a loud gulp whenever he swallowed. His earlobes itched. And his sexual organ, which had dangled in such a sloppy way until that point, began to stiffen and expand. As it rose, a bulge developed at the front of his gown. He was in the dark, however, as to what that might signify.

Having extracted the lock, the young woman took it to the window to inspect in the sunlight that shone between the boards. She poked it with a thin wire and gave it a hard shake to see how it sounded, her face glum and her lips pursed. Finally, she sighed again and turned to face Samsa.

'The insides are shot,' the woman said. 'It's kaput. This is the one, just like you said.'

'That's good,' Samsa said.

'No, it's not,' the woman said. 'There's no way I can repair it here on the spot. It's a special kind of lock. I'll have to take it back and let my father or one of my older brothers work on it. They may be able to fix it. I'm just an apprentice – I can only handle regular locks.'

'I see,' Samsa said. So this young woman had a father and several brothers. A whole family of locksmiths.

'Actually, one of them was supposed to come today, but because of the commotion going on out there they sent me instead. The city is riddled with checkpoints.' She looked back down at the lock in her hands. 'But how did the lock get broken like this? It's weird. Someone must have gouged out the insides with a special kind of tool. There's no other way to explain it.'

Again she writhed. Her arms rotated as if she were a swimmer practicing a new stroke. He found the action mesmerizing and very exciting.

Samsa made up his mind. 'May I ask you a question?' he said.

'A question?' she said, casting him a dubious glance. 'I can't imagine what, but go ahead.'

'Why do you twist about like that every so often?'

She looked at Samsa with her lips slightly parted. 'Twist about?' She thought for a moment. 'You mean like this?' She demonstrated the motion for him.

'Yes, that's it.'

'My brassiere doesn't fit,' she said dourly. 'That's all.'

'Brassiere?' Samsa said in a dull voice. It was a word he couldn't call up from his memory.

'A brassiere. You know what that is, don't you?' the woman said. 'Or do you find it strange that hunchback women wear brassieres? Do you think it's presumptuous of us?'

'Hunchback?' Samsa said. Yet another word that was sucked into that vast emptiness he carried within. He had no idea what she was talking about. Still, he knew that he should say something.

'No, I don't think so at all,' he mumbled.

'Listen up. We hunchbacks have two breasts, just like other women, and we have to use a brassiere to support them. We can't walk around like cows with our udders swinging.'

'Of course not.' Samsa was lost.

'But brassieres aren't designed for us—they get loose. We're built differently from regular women, right? So we have to twist around every so often to put them back in place. Hunchbacks have more problems than you can imagine. Is that why you've been staring at me from behind? Is that how you get your kicks?'

'No, not at all. I was just curious why you were doing that.'

So, he inferred, a brassiere was an apparatus designed to hold the breasts in place, and a hunchback was a person

with this woman's particular build. There was so much in this world that he had to learn.

'Are you sure you're not making fun of me?' the woman asked.

'I'm not making fun of you.'

The woman cocked her head and looked up at Samsa. She could tell that he was speaking the truth – there didn't seem to be any malice in him. He was just a little weak in the head, that was all. Age about thirty. As well as being lame, he seemed to be intellectually challenged. But he was from a good family, and his manners were impeccable. He was nice-looking, too, but thin as a rail with too-big ears and a pasty complexion.

It was then that she noticed the protuberance pushing out the lower part of his gown.

'What the hell is that?' she said stonily. 'What's that *bulge* doing there?'

Samsa looked down at the front of his gown. His organ was really very swollen. He could surmise from her tone that its condition was somehow inappropriate.

'I get it,' she spat out. 'You're wondering what it would be like to fuck a hunchback, aren't you?'

'Fuck?' he said. One more word he couldn't place.

'You imagine that, since a hunchback is bent at the waist, you can just take her from the rear with no problem, right?' the woman said. 'Believe me, there are lots of perverts like you around, who seem to think that we'll let you

do what you want because we're hunchbacks. Well, think again, buster. We're not that easy!'

'I'm very confused,' Samsa said. 'If I have displeased you in some way, I am truly sorry. I apologize. Please forgive me. I meant no harm. I've been unwell, and there are so many things I don't understand.'

'All right, I get the picture.' She sighed. 'You're a little *slow*, right? But your wiener is in great shape. Those are the breaks, I guess.'

'I'm sorry,' Samsa said again.

'Forget it.' She relented. 'I've got four no-good brothers at home, and since I was a little girl they've shown me everything. They treat it like a big joke. *Mean* buggers, all of them. So I'm not kidding when I say I know the score.'

She squatted to put her tools back in the bag, wrapping the broken lock in the flannel and gently placing it alongside.

'I'm taking the lock home with me,' she said, standing up. 'Tell your parents. We'll either fix it or replace it. If we have to get a new one, though, it may take some time, things being the way they are. Don't forget to tell them, okay? Do you follow me? Will you remember?'

'I'll tell them,' Samsa said.

She walked slowly down the staircase, Samsa trailing behind. They made quite a study in contrasts: she looked as if she were crawling on all fours, while he tilted backward in a most unnatural way. Yet their pace was identical.

Samsa was trying hard to quell his 'bulge,' but the thing just wouldn't return to its former state. Watching her movements from behind as she descended the stairs made his heart pound. Hot, fresh blood coursed through his veins. The stubborn bulge persisted.

'As I told you before, my father or one of my brothers was supposed to come today,' the woman said when they reached the front door. 'But the streets are crawling with soldiers and tanks. There are checkpoints on all the bridges, and people are being rounded up. That's why the men in my family can't go out. Once you get arrested, there's no telling when you'll return. That's why I was sent. All the way across Prague, alone. "No one will notice a hunchbackgirl," they said.'

'Tanks?' Samsa murmured.

'Yeah, lots of them. Tanks with cannons and machine guns. Your cannon is impressive,' she said, pointing at the bulge beneath his gown, 'but these cannons are bigger and harder, and a lot more lethal. Let's hope everyone in your family makes it back safely. You honestly have no clue where they went, do you?'

Samsa shook his head no. He had no idea.

Samsa decided to take the bull by the horns. 'Would it be possible to meet again?' he said.

The young woman craned her head at Samsa. 'Are you saying you want to see me again?'

'Yes. I want to see you one more time.'

'With your thing sticking out like that?'

Samsa looked down again at the bulge. 'I don't know how to explain it, but that has nothing to do with my feelings. It must be some kind of heart problem.'

'No kidding,' she said, impressed. 'A heart problem, you say. That's an interesting way to look at it. Never heard that one before.'

'You see, it's out of my control.'

'And it has nothing to do with fucking?'

'Fucking isn't on my mind. Really.'

'So let me get this straight. When your thing grows big and hard like that, it's not your mind but your heart that's causing it?'

Samsa nodded in assent.

'Swear to God?' the woman said.

'God,' Samsa echoed. Another word he couldn't remember having heard before. He fell silent.

The woman gave a weary shake of her head. She twisted and turned again to adjust her brassiere. 'Forget it. It seems God left Prague a few days ago. Let's forget about Him.'

'So can I see you again?' Samsa asked.

The girl raised an eyebrow. A new look came over her face – her eyes seemed fixed on some distant and misty landscape. 'You really want to see me again?'

Samsa nodded.

'What would we do?'

'We could talk together.'

'About what?' the woman asked.

'About lots of things.'

'Just talk?'

'There is so much I want to ask you,' Samsa said.

'About what?'

'About this world. About you. About me.'

The young woman thought for a moment. 'So it's not all about you shoving *that* in me?'

'No, not at all,' Samsa said without hesitation. 'I feel like there are so many things we need to talk about. Tanks, for example. And God. And brassieres. And locks.'

Another silence fell over the two of them.

'I don't know,' the woman said at last. She shook her head slowly, but the chill in her voice was less noticeable. 'You're better brought up than me. And I doubt your parents would be thrilled to see their precious son involved with a hunchback from the wrong side of town. Even if that son is lame and a little slow. On top of that, our city is overflowing with foreign tanks and troops. Who knows what lies ahead.'

Samsa certainly had no idea what lay ahead. He was in the dark about everything: the future, of course, but the present and the past as well. What was right, and what was wrong? Just learning how to dress was a riddle.

'At any rate, I'll come back this way in a few days,' the hunchbacked young woman said. 'If we can fix it, I'll bring the lock, and if we can't I'll return it to you anyway. You'll be charged for the service call, of course. If you're here, then we can see each other. Whether we'll be able to have that long talk or not I don't know. But if I were you I'd keep

that bulge hidden from your parents. In the real world, you don't get compliments for exposing that kind of thing.'

Samsa nodded. He wasn't at all clear, though, how that kind of thing could be kept out of sight.

'It's strange, isn't it?' the woman said in a pensive voice. 'Everything is blowing up around us, but there are still those who care about a broken lock, and others who are dutiful enough to try to fix it . . . But maybe that's the way it should be. Maybe working on the little things as dutifully and honestly as we can is how we stay sane when the world is falling apart.'

The woman looked up at Samsa's face. She raised one of her eyebrows. 'I don't mean to pry, but what was going on in that room on the second floor? Why did your parents need such a big lock for a room that held nothing but a bed, and why did it bother them so much when the lock got broken? And what about those boards nailed across the window? Was something locked up in there—is that it?'

Samsa shook his head. If someone or something had been shut up in there, it must have been him. But why had that been necessary? He hadn't a clue.

'I guess there's no point in asking you,' the woman said. 'Well, I've got to go. They'll worry about me if I'm late. Pray that I make it across town in one piece. That the soldiers will overlook a poor little hunchbacked girl. That none of them is perverted. We're being fucked over enough as it is.'

'I will pray,' Samsa said. But he had no idea what 'perverted' meant. Or 'pray,' for that matter.

The woman picked up her black bag and, still bent over, headed for the door.

'Will I see you again?' Samsa asked one last time.

'If you think of someone enough, you're sure to meet them again,' she said in parting. This time there was real warmth in her voice.

'Look out for birds,' he called after her. She turned and nodded. Then she walked out to the street.

SAMSA WATCHED THROUGH the crack in the curtains as her hunched form set off across the cobblestones. She moved awkwardly but with surprising speed. He found her every gesture charming. She reminded him of a water strider that had left the water to scamper about on dry land. As far as he could tell, walking the way she did made a lot more sense than wobbling around upright on two legs.

She had not been out of sight long when he noticed that his genitals had returned to their soft and shrunken state. That brief and violent bulge had, at some point, vanished. Now his organ dangled between his legs like an innocent fruit, peaceful and defenseless. His balls rested comfortably in their sac. Readjusting the belt of his gown, he sat down at the dining room table and drank what remained of his cold coffee.

The people who lived here had gone somewhere else. He didn't know who they were, but he imagined that they were his family. Something had happened all of a sudden, and they had left. Perhaps they would never return. What

did 'the world is falling apart' mean? Gregor Samsa had no idea. Foreign troops, checkpoints, tanks – everything was wrapped in mystery.

The only thing he knew for certain was that he wanted to see that hunchbacked girl again. To sit face-to-face and talk to his heart's content. To unravel the riddles of the world with her. He wanted to watch from every angle the way she twisted and writhed when she adjusted her brassiere. If possible, he wanted to run his hands over her body. To touch her soft skin and feel her warmth with his fingertips. To walk side by side with her up and down the staircases of the world.

Just thinking about her made him warm inside. No longer did he wish to be a fish or a sunflower – or anything else, for that matter. For sure, it was a great inconvenience to have to walk on two legs and wear clothes and eat with a knife and fork. There were so many things he didn't know. Yet had he been a fish or a sunflower, and not a human being, he might never have experienced this emotion. So he felt.

Samsa sat there for a long time with his eyes closed. Then, making up his mind, he stood, grabbed his black walking stick, and headed for the stairs. He would return to the second floor and figure out the proper way to dress. For now, at least, that would be his mission.

The world was waiting for him to learn.

—translated by Ted Goossen

A Folklore for My Generation:
A Prehistory of Late-Stage Capitalism

I WAS BORN in 1949, entered high school in 1961 and university in 1967. And reached my long-awaited twentieth birthday – my intro into adulthood – during the height of the boisterous slapstick that was the student movement. Which I suppose qualifies me as a typical child of the sixties. So there I was, during the most vulnerable, most immature, and yet most precious period of life, breathing in everything about this live-for-the-moment decade, high on the wildness of it all. There were doors we had to kick in, right in front of us, and you had better believe we kicked them in! With Jim Morrison, the Beatles and Dylan blasting out the soundtrack to our lives.

There was something special about the sixties. That seems true now, in retrospect, but even when I was caught up in the whirlwind of it happening I was convinced of it. But if you asked me to be more specific, to pinpoint what it was about the sixties that was so special, I don't

think I could do more than stammer out some trite reply. We were merely observers, getting totally absorbed in some exciting movie, our palms all sweaty, only to find that, after the house lights came on and we left the theatre, the thrilling afterglow that coursed through us ultimately meant nothing whatsoever. Maybe something prevented us from learning a valuable lesson from all this? I don't know. I'm far too close to the period to say.

I'm not boasting about the times I lived through. I'm simply trying to convey what it felt like to live through that age, and the fact that there really *was* something special about it. Yet if I were to try to unpack those times and point out something in particular that was exceptional, I don't know if I could. What I'd come up with if I did such a dissection would be these: the momentum and energy of the times, the tremendous spark of promise. More than anything else, the feeling of inevitable irritation as when you look through the wrong end of a telescope. Heroism and villainy, ecstasy and disillusionment, martyrdom and betrayal, outlines and specialised studies, silence and eloquence, people marking time in the most boring way – they were all there, for sure. Any age has all these. The present does, and so will the future. But in Our Age (to use an exaggerated term) these were more colourful, and you could actually *grasp* them. They were literally lined up on a shelf, right before our very eyes.

Nowadays, if you try to grasp the reality of anything, there's always a whole slew of convoluted extras that come

with it: hidden advertising, dubious discount coupons, point cards that stores hand out which you know you should throw away but still hold on to, options that are forced on you before you know what's happening. Back in Our Age, nobody slapped down indecipherable three-volume owner's manuals in front of you. Whatever it was, we just clutched it in our hands and took it straight home – like taking a baby chick home from one of those little night-time stands. Everything was simple, and direct. Cause and effect were good friends back then; thesis and reality hugged each other as if it were the most natural thing in the world. And my guess is that the sixties were the last time that'll ever happen.

A Prehistory of Late-Stage Capitalism – that's my own personal name for that age.

LET ME TELL you a little bit about the young girls back then. And us fellows with our nearly brand new genitals and the wild, joyous, sad sex we had. That's one of my themes here.

Take virginity, for instance – a word that, for some unfathomable reason, always reminds me of a field on a beautiful, sunny spring afternoon. In the sixties, virginity was a much bigger deal than it is today. I'm generalising, of course – I haven't done a survey or anything – but my sense of it is that about 50 per cent of the girls in my generation had lost their virginity by the time they reached twenty. At least among the girls I knew, that seemed to be

the case. Which means that about half of the girls, whether they'd made a conscious choice or not, were still virgins.

It strikes me now that most of the girls in my generation – the moderates, you might dub them – whether virgins or not, agonised over the whole issue of sex. They didn't insist that virginity was such a precious thing, nor did they denounce it as some stupid relic of the past. So what actually happened – sorry, but I'm generalising again – was that they went with the flow. It all depended on the circumstances and the partner. Makes sense to me.

So on either side of this silent majority, you had your liberals and your conservatives – the entire spectrum, from girls who practised sex as a kind of indoor sport, to those who were firm believers in remaining pure till they got married. There were guys, too, who were adamant that whoever they married had to be a virgin.

As in every generation, there were all kinds of people, with all kinds of values. But the big difference between the sixties and the decades before and after was that we were convinced that some day all those differences could be overcome.

Peace!

WHAT FOLLOWS IS the story of a fellow I know, a school classmate in Kobe. He was one of those guys who was an all-round star: good marks, good at sports, a natural leader. He was more clean-cut than handsome, I suppose. He had a nice clear voice, and was a good public speaker, even a

decent singer. He was always elected class representative, and when our class met as a group he was the one who did the final summary. He wasn't full of original opinions, but in class discussion who expects any originality? There're tons of situations when originality is not what's called for. Most situations, in fact. All we wanted was to get out of there as fast as we could, and we could count on him to wind up the discussion in the time allotted. In that sense, he was a handy sort of fellow to have around.

With him, everything went by the book. If somebody was making a racket in the study hall he'd quietly tell them to simmer down. The guy was basically perfect, but it bothered me that I couldn't work out what was going through his head. Sometimes I felt like tearing his head off his neck and giving it a good shake to see what was rattling around inside. He was very popular with the girls, too. Whenever he popped to his feet in class to say something every girl would gaze at him with a dreamy look of admiration. He was also your go-to guy if you were stuck with a maths problem you couldn't solve. We're talking about someone who was twenty-seven times more popular than me.

If you've ever gone to high school, you know the type I mean. There's somebody like him in every class, the kind that keeps things running smoothly. Years spent in school absorbing training manuals for life have taught me many things, and one of the lessons I came away with was this: like it or not, every group has somebody like him.

Personally, I'm not too fond of the type. For whatever

reason, we just don't click. I much prefer imperfect, more memorable types of people. So with this particular fellow, even though we were in the same class for a year, we never spent time together. The first time we ever had a halfway-decent conversation was after we left school, during the summer holiday when we were first-year students at university. We happened to be taking lessons at the same driving school and talked a few times there. We'd have a cup of tea together while we were waiting. Driving school has got to be one of the most boring places on earth, and if you see a familiar face you jump at it. I don't remember what we talked about, but I know I wasn't left with much of an impression one way or the other.

One other thing I did remember about him was his girl-friend. She was in a different class and was one of a handful of girls who were drop-dead gorgeous. Apart from her stunning looks, she got good results, was good at sports, was kind and a natural leader, and was the one who always summed up class discussions. Every class has a girl like her.

To make a long story short, they were perfect for each other. Mister Clean and Miss Clean. Right out of a toothpaste commercial.

They were inseparable. During lunch breaks they sat side by side in a corner of the schoolyard, talking. They went home together, too, taking the same train but getting off at different stops. He was on the football team, she was in the English conversation club, and whoever finished earlier than the other would study in the library, waiting so

they could go home together. It seemed as though they were together every free moment they had. And they were always talking. I don't know how they could keep from running out of things to say, but somehow they managed it.

We – and by 'we' I mean the guys I hung out with – didn't dislike this couple. We never made fun of them or said bad things about them. In fact, we hardly thought about them at all. They were like the weather, something that was just there, that barely registered on our attention meter. We were too much into our own pursuits, the vital thrilling things the times had to offer. For instance? For instance sex, rock'n'roll, Jean-Luc Godard films, political movements, Kenzaburō Ōe's novels. But chiefly sex.

We were ignorant, conceited kids, of course. We had no idea what life was all about. In the real world there was no such thing as Mister Clean and Miss Clean. They only existed on TV. The kind of illusions we had, then, and the kind of illusions this fellow and his girlfriend had, weren't all that different.

This is their story. It's not a very happy one, and looking back on it now it's hard to locate any lesson in it. But anyway, this is their story, and at the same time *our* story. So it's a kind of folklore that I've collected and now, as a sort of bumbling narrator, will pass on to you.

THE STORY HE told me came out after we had knocked around other topics over some wine, so strictly speaking it

might not be altogether true. There are parts I didn't catch, and details I've kind of imagined and woven in. And to protect the real people in it, I've changed some of the facts, though this doesn't have a bearing on the overall story. Still, I think things took place pretty much as set out. I say this because though I might have forgotten some of the details, I distinctly recall the general tone. When you listen to somebody's story and then try to reproduce it in writing, the tone's the main thing. Get the tone right and you have a true story on your hands. Maybe some of the facts aren't quite correct, but that doesn't matter – it actually might elevate the truth factor of the story. Turn this around, and you could say there are stories that are factually accurate yet aren't true at all. Those are the kind of stories you can count on being boring, and even, in some instances, dangerous. You can smell those ones a mile away.

One other thing I need to make clear here is that this former classmate was a lousy storyteller. God might have generously doled out other attributes to the guy, but the ability to relate a story wasn't one of them. (Not that the storyteller's romantic art serves any real purpose in life.) So as he told his story, I could barely stifle a yawn. He'd go off at a tangent, go round in circles, take for ever to remember some of the facts. He'd take a fragment of his story in his hand, frown at it for a while, and once he was convinced he had it right he'd line his facts up one by one on the table. But often this order was wrong. So as a novelist – a story specialist, if you will – I've rearranged these

fragments, carefully gluing them together to form what I hope is a coherent narrative.

We happened to run across each other in Lucca, a town in central Italy. I was renting an apartment in Rome at the time. My wife had to go back to Japan, so I was enjoying a leisurely, solitary train trip, first from Venice to Verona, then on to Mantua and Pisa, with a stopover in Lucca. It was my second time there. Lucca's a quiet, pleasant town, and there's a wonderful restaurant on the outskirts of town where they have superb mushroom dishes.

He'd come to Lucca on business, and we just happened to be staying in the same hotel. Small world.

We had dinner together at the restaurant that night. Both of us were travelling alone, and were bored. The older you get, the more boring travelling alone becomes. It's different when you're younger – whether you're alone or not, travelling can be a gas. But as you age, the fun factor declines. Only the first couple of days are enjoyable. After that, the scenery becomes annoying, and people's voices start to grate. There's no escape, for if you close your eyes to block these out, all kinds of unpleasant memories pop up. It gets to be too much trouble to eat in a restaurant, and you find yourself checking your watch over and over as you wait for buses that never seem to arrive. Trying to make yourself understood in a foreign language becomes a total pain.

That's why, when we spotted each other, we breathed a sigh of relief, just like that time we ran across each other at

driving school. We sat down at a table near the fireplace, ordered a pricey bottle of red wine, had a full-course mushroom dinner: mushroom hors d'oeuvres, mushroom pasta and *arrosto con funghi*.

It turned out he owned a furniture company that imported European furniture, and was in Europe on a buying trip. You could tell his business was doing well. He didn't boast about it or put on any airs – when he handed me his business card he just said he was running a small company – yet he'd clearly done well for himself. His clothes, the way he spoke, his expression, manner, everything about him made this obvious. He was entirely at home with his worldly success, in a pleasant sort of way.

He told me he'd read all my novels. 'Our way of thinking and goals are very different,' he said, 'but I think it's a wonderful thing to be able to tell stories to other people.'

That made sense. 'If you can do a good job of telling the story,' I added.

At first we talked mainly about our impressions of Italy. How the trains never ran on time, how meals took for ever. I don't remember how it came about, exactly, but by the time we were into our second bottle of wine he'd already started telling his story. And I was listening, making the appropriate signs to show I was keeping abreast. I think he must have wanted to get this off his chest for a long time, but for some reason hadn't. If we hadn't been in a nice little restaurant in a pleasant little town in central Italy, sitting before a fireplace, sipping a mellow 1983

Coltibuono, I seriously doubt if he would have told me the tale. But tell it he did.

'I'VE ALWAYS THOUGHT I was a boring person,' he began. 'I've never been the type who could just cut loose and have a good time. It was as if I could always sense a boundary around me and I did my best not to step over the line. As though I was following a well-laid-out highway with signs telling me which were the exits, warning me when a bend was coming up, when not to pass. Follow the directions, I reckoned, and life would turn out OK. People praised me for toeing the line, and when I was little I was sure everybody else was doing the same thing as me. But I soon found out that wasn't the case.'

He held his wine glass up to the fire and gazed at it for a time.

'In that sense, my life, at least the beginning stages, went smoothly. But I had no idea what my life meant, and that kind of vague thought only grew stronger the older I got. What did I want out of life? I had no idea! I was good at maths, at English, sports, you name it. My parents always praised me, my teachers always said I was doing fine, and I knew I could get into a good university with no problem. But I had no idea at all what I was aiming at, what I wanted to do. As far as what subject to study, I hadn't a clue. Should I go in for law, engineering or medicine? I knew I could have done well in any one of them, but noth-ing excited me. So I went along with my parents' and

I could always sense a
boundary around me
and I did my best not
to step over the line

teachers' recommendations and entered the law department at Tokyo University. There was no principle guiding me, really – it's just that everybody said that was the best choice.'

He took another sip of wine. 'Do you remember my girl-friend in school?'

'Was her name Fujisawa?' I said, somehow able to summon up the name. I wasn't entirely sure that was right, but it turned out it was.

He nodded. 'Correct. Yoshiko Fujisawa. Things were good with her, too. I liked her a lot, liked being with her and talking about all kinds of things. I could tell her everything I felt, and she understood me. I could go on for ever when I was with her. It was wonderful. I mean, before her, I never had a friend I could really talk to.'

HE AND YOSHIKO were spiritual twins. It was almost uncanny how similar their backgrounds were. As I've said, they were both attractive, smart, natural-born leaders. Form superstars. Both of them were from affluent families, with parents who didn't get along. Both had mothers who were older than their fathers, and fathers who kept a mistress and stayed away from home as much as they could. Fear of public opinion kept their parents from divorcing. At home, then, their mothers ruled the roost, and expected their children come top in whatever they did. He and Yoshiko were both popular enough, but never had any real friends. They weren't sure why. Maybe it was because

ordinary, imperfect people always choose similarly imperfect people as friends. At any rate, the two of them were
always lonely, always a bit on edge.

Somehow, though, they hooked up and started going
out. They ate lunch together every day, walked home from
school together. Spent every spare moment with each
other, talking. There was always so much to talk about. On
Sundays they studied together. When it was just the two of
them they could relax the most. Each knew exactly how
the other was feeling. They could talk for ever about the
loneliness they'd experienced, the sense of loss, their
fears, their dreams.

They made out once a week, usually in one of the rooms
of their respective houses. It wasn't hard to be alone; what
with their fathers always gone and their mothers running
errands half the time, their homes were practically deserted. They followed two rules during their make-out
sessions: their clothes had to stay on, and they'd only use
their fingers. They'd passionately make out for ten or fifteen minutes, then sit down together at a desk and study
side by side.

'That's enough. Why don't we study now?' she'd say,
smoothing down the hem of her skirt. They got almost
identical marks, so they made a game out of studying,
competing, for instance, to see who could solve maths
problems the quicker. Studying was never a burden; it was
like second nature to them. It was a lot of fun, he told me.
You might think this is stupid, but we really enjoyed

studying. Maybe only people like the two of us could ever understand how much fun it was.

Not that he was totally happy with their relationship. Something was missing. Actual sex, in other words. 'A sense of being one, physically,' is how he put it. I felt we had to take the next step, he said. I thought if we did, we'd be freer in our relationship, and understand each other better. For me that would have been a completely natural development.

But she saw things differently. Her mouth set, she shook her head slightly. 'I love you so much,' she quietly explained, 'but I want to stay a virgin until I get married.' No matter how much he tried to persuade her, she wouldn't listen.

'I love you, I really do,' she said. 'But those are two different things. I'm not going to change my mind. I'm sorry, but you'll just have to put up with it. You will, if you really love me.'

When she put it that way, he told me, I had to respect her wishes. It was a question of how she wanted to live her life and there wasn't anything I could say about that. To me, whether a girl was a virgin or not didn't matter that much. If I got married and found out my bride wasn't a virgin, I wouldn't care. I'm not a very radical type of person, or a dreamy, romantic sort. But I'm not all that conservative, either. I'm more of a realist, I guess. A girl's virginity just isn't that big a deal. It's much more important that a couple really know each other. But that's only

my opinion, and I'm not about to force others to agree. She had her own vision of how her life should be, so I simply had to grin and bear it, and make do with touching her under her clothes. I'm sure you could imagine what this involved.

I can imagine, I said. I have similar memories.

His face reddened a bit and he smiled.

That wasn't so bad, don't get me wrong, but since we never went any further, I never felt relaxed. To me we were always stopping halfway. What I wanted was to be one with her, with nothing coming between us. To possess her, to be possessed. I needed a sign to prove that. Sexual desire was part of it, of course, but that wasn't the main thing. I'm talking about a sense of being one, physically. I'd never once experienced that sense of oneness with a person. I'd always been alone, always feeling tense, stuck behind a wall. I was positive that once we were one, my wall would come crumbling down, and I'd discover who I was, the self I'd only had vague glimpses of.

'But it didn't work out?' I asked him.

'No, it didn't,' he said, and stared for a time at the blazing logs in the fireplace, his eyes strangely dull. 'It never did work out,' he said.

He was seriously thinking of marrying her, and told her so. After we graduate we can get married right away, he told her. We could even get engaged earlier. His words made her very happy, and she beamed a charming smile at him. At the same time, her smile revealed a hint of

weariness, of a wiser, more mature person listening to a young person's immature ideas. I can't marry you, she said. I'm going to marry someone a few years older than me, and you're going to marry someone a few years younger. That's the way things are done. Women mature faster than men, and age more quickly. You don't know anything about the world yet. Even if we were to marry straight out of university, it wouldn't work out. We'd never stay as happy as we are now. Of course I love you – I've never loved anyone else. But those are two different things. ('Those are two different things' being her pet saying.) We're still at school, and we've lived sheltered lives. But the world outside isn't like that. It's a big world out there, and we have to get ready for it.

He understood what she was getting at. Compared to other boys his age, he had his feet firmly on the ground. If someone else had been arguing the same point he probably would have agreed. But this was no abstract generalisation. This was his life they were talking about.

I just don't get it, he told her. I love you so much. I want us to be one. This couldn't be clearer to me, or more important. I don't care if it's unrealistic, that's how much I love you.

She shook her head again, as if to tell him it was out of the question. She stroked his hair and said, 'I wonder what either of us knows about love. Our love has never been tested. We've never had to take responsibility for anything. We're still children.'

He couldn't say a thing. It made him miserable that he couldn't smash down the wall around him now. Until then he'd always seen that wall as protecting him, but now it was a barrier, barring his way. A wave of impotence swept over him. I can't do anything any more, he thought. I'm going to be surrounded by this thick wall for ever, never allowed to venture outside. The rest of my insipid, pointless life.

THEIR RELATIONSHIP REMAINED the same until the two of them left school. They'd meet at the library as always, study together, make out with their clothes on. She didn't seem to mind that they never went all the way. She actually seemed to like things left that way, unconsummated. Everybody else imagined that Mister and Miss Clean were both enjoying an uncomplicated youth. But he continued to struggle with his unresolved feelings.

In the spring of 1967, he entered Tokyo University, while she went to a women's university in Kobe. It was definitely a first-rate college, but with her results she could have got into a much better place, even Tokyo University if she'd wanted to. But she didn't think it was necessary, and didn't take the entrance exam. I don't particularly want to study, or get into the Ministry of Finance, she explained. I'm a girl. I'm different from you. You're going to go far. But I want to take a break, and spend the next four years enjoying myself. After I get married, I won't be able to do that again.

He was frankly disappointed. He'd been hoping they'd both go to Tokyo and start their relationship afresh. He pleaded with her to join him, but again she merely shook her head.

He came back from Tokyo for the summer holiday after his first year, and they went on dates almost every day. (That's the summer he and I ran across each other at driving school.) She drove them all around and they continued the same make-out sessions as before. He started, though, to sense that something in their relationship was changing. Reality was invisibly starting to worm its way between them.

It wasn't that there was some obvious change. Actually, the problem was more a *lack* of change. Nothing about her had changed – the way she spoke, her clothes, the topics she chose to talk about, her opinions – they were all as before. Their relationship was like a pendulum gradually grinding to a halt, and he felt out of sync.

Life in Tokyo was lonely. The city was filthy, the food awful, the people uncouth. He thought about her all the time. At night he'd hole up in his room and write letter after letter to her. She wrote back, though not as often. She wrote about all the details of her life, and he devoured her letters. Her letters were what kept him sane. He started smoking and drinking, and cutting classes.

When the summer holiday finally rolled around, though, and he rushed back to Kobe, a lot of things disappointed him. He'd only been away for three months, yet strangely enough his home town struck him now as dusty and

lifeless. Discussions with his mother were a total bore. The scenery at home which he'd waxed nostalgic over while he was in Tokyo now seemed to him insipid. Kobe, he discovered, was just a self-satisfied backwater town. He didn't want to talk to anybody, and even going to the barber's he'd gone to since he was a child depressed him. When he took his dog for a walk, the seashore was empty and littered with rubbish.

You'd think that going on dates with Yoshiko would have excited him, but it didn't. Every time they said goodbye, he'd go home and brood. He was still in love with her – that was a given. But it wasn't enough. I have to *do* something, he felt. Passion will get by on its own steam for a time, but it doesn't last for ever. If we don't do something drastic our relationship will reach an impasse, and all the passion will be suffocated out of us.

One day, he decided to raise again the issue of sex that they'd frozen out of their conversations. This will be the last time I bring it up, he decided.

'These last three months in Tokyo I've been thinking about you all the time,' he told her. 'I love you, and my feelings won't change, even if we're away from each other. But being apart so long, all kinds of dark thoughts start to take over. You probably don't understand this, but people are weak when they're alone. I've never been so alone like this in my life. It's awful. So I want something that can bring us closer together. I want to know for sure that we're bound together, even if we're apart.'

But his girlfriend turned him down. She sighed and gently kissed him.

'I'm sorry,' she said, 'but I can't give you my virginity. These are two different things. I'll do anything for you, except that. If you love me, please don't bring that up again.'

He raised the question of their getting married.

'There are girls in my class who are engaged already,' she said. 'Two of them, actually. But their fiancés have jobs. That's what getting engaged involves. Marriage involves responsibility. You become independent and accept another person into your life. If you don't take responsibility you can't gain anything.'

'I can take responsibility,' he declared. 'Listen – I'm going to a top university, and I'm getting good course marks. I can get a job later in any company or government office I want. You name the company and I'll get into it as the top candidate. I can do anything, if I put my mind to it. So what's the problem?'

She closed her eyes, leaned back against the car seat, and didn't say anything for a while. 'I'm scared,' she said. She covered her face with her hands and began to cry. 'I'm so very, very scared. Life is frightening. In a few years, I'll have to go out in the real world and that scares me. Why don't you understand? Why can't you try to understand what I'm feeling? Why do you have to torment me like this?'

He held her close. 'As long as I'm here you don't need to

be afraid,' he said. 'I'm scared, too – as much as you are. But if I'm with you, I am not afraid. As long as we pull together, there's nothing to be afraid of.'

She shook her head again. 'You don't understand. I'm not like you. I'm a woman. You don't get it at all.'

IT WAS POINTLESS for him to say anything more. She cried for a long time, and when she was finished she said the following, rather astonishing thing:

'If . . . we ever broke up, I want you to know I'll always think about you. It's true. I'll never forget you, because I really love you. You're the first person I've ever loved and just being with you makes me happy. You know that. But these are two different things. If you need me to promise you, I will. I *will* sleep with you some day. But not right now. After I marry somebody else, I'll sleep with you. I promise.'

'AT THE TIME I had no idea what she was trying to tell me,' he said, staring at the burning logs in the fireplace. The waiter brought over our entrées and lay a few logs on the fire while he was at it. Sparks crackled up. The middle-aged couple at the table next to us was puzzling over which desserts to order. 'What she said was like a riddle. After I got home I gave a lot of thought to what she'd said, but I just couldn't grasp it at all. Do you understand what she meant?'

'Well, I guess she meant she wanted to stay a virgin

until she got married, and since after she was married there was no reason to be a virgin any more, she wouldn't mind having an affair with you. She was just telling you to wait till then.'

'I suppose that's it. That's the only thing I can think of.'

'It's a unique way of thinking,' I said. 'Logical, though.'

A gentle smile played at his lips. 'You're right. It is logical.'

'She gets married a virgin. And once she's somebody's wife she has an affair. Sounds like some classic French novel. Minus any fancy-dress ball or maids running around.'

'But that's the only practical solution she was able to come up with,' he said.

'A damn shame,' I said.

He looked at me for a while, and then slowly nodded. 'You got that right. I'm glad you understand.' He nodded again. 'Now I can see it that way – now that I'm older. Then, though, I couldn't. I was just a kid. I couldn't grasp all the minute fluctuations of the human heart. So pure shock was my only reaction. Honestly, I was completely floored.'

'I could see that,' I said.

We didn't say anything for a while as we ate.

'As I'm sure you can imagine,' he continued, 'we broke up. Neither of us announced that we were breaking up, it just ended naturally. A very quiet break-up. I think we were

too worn out to carry on the relationship. From my perspective, her approach to life was – how should I put it? – not very sincere. No, that's not it . . . What I wanted was for her to have a better life. It disappointed me a little. I didn't want her to get so hung up on virginity or marriage or whatever, but live a more natural, full sort of life.'

'But I don't think she could have acted otherwise,' I said.

He nodded. 'You might be right,' he said, taking a bite of a thick piece of mushroom. 'After a while you become inflexible. You can't bounce back any more. It could have happened to me, too. Ever since we were little, people had been pushing us, expecting us to succeed. And we met their expectations, because we were bright enough to. But your maturity level can't keep pace, and one day you find there's no going back. At least as far as morals goes.'

'That didn't happen to you?' I asked.

'Somehow I was able to overcome it,' he said after giving it some thought. He put his knife and fork down and wiped his mouth with the napkin. 'After we broke up, I started going out with another girl in Tokyo. We lived together for a while. Honestly, she didn't move me as much as Yoshiko did, but I did love her. We really understood each other, and were always up front with each other. She taught me about human beings – how beautiful they can be, the kind of faults they have. I finally made some friends, too, and got interested in politics. I'm not saying my personality changed completely or anything. I

was a very practical person, and I still am. I don't write novels, and you don't import furniture. You know what I mean. In university I learned there were lots of realities in the world. It's a huge world, there are lots of different values coexisting, and there's no need to always be the top student. And then I went out into the world.'

'And you've done very well for yourself.'

'I suppose,' he said, and gave a sheepish sigh. He gazed at me as if we were a pair of accomplices. 'Compared to other people of my generation, I make a good living. So on a practical level, yes, I've been successful.'

He fell silent. Knowing he wanted to say more, I sat there, waiting patiently for him to go on.

'I didn't see Yoshiko for a long time after that,' he continued. 'For a long time. I'd graduated and started work at a trading company. I worked there for five years, part of which took me overseas. I was busy every day. Two years after I graduated, I heard that Yoshiko had got married. My mother gave me the news. I didn't ask who she'd married. When I heard the news, the first thought that struck me was: had she been able to keep her virginity until her marriage. After that I felt a little sad. The next day I felt even sadder. I felt that something important was finally over, like a door closed for ever behind me. That's only to be expected, since I loved her. We'd gone out for four years, and I suppose I was still clinging to the hope that we might get married some day. She'd been a huge part of my youth, so it was only natural that I felt sad. But I decided that as

long as she was happy, I was OK with it. I honestly felt that way. I was a little – worried about her. There was a part of her that was very fragile.'

The waiter came, removed our plates, and wheeled over the dessert trolley. We both turned down dessert and ordered coffee.

'I got married late, when I was thirty-two. So when Yoshiko called me, I was still single. I was twenty-eight, which makes it more than a decade ago. I'd just left the company I'd been working for and had gone out on my own. I was convinced that the imported furniture market was about to take off, so I borrowed money from my father and started up my own little firm. Despite my confidence, though, things didn't go so well at first. Orders were late, goods went unsold, warehouse fees piled up, there were loans to repay. I was frankly worn out, and starting to lose confidence. This was the hardest time I've ever gone through in my life. And it was exactly during that rough spell that Yoshiko phoned me one day. I don't know how she got my number, but one evening around eight, she called. I knew it was her right away. How could I ever forget that voice? It brought back so many memories. I was feeling pretty down then, and it felt wonderful to hear my old girlfriend's voice again.'

He stared at the blazing logs in the fireplace as if trying to summon up a memory. By this time the restaurant was completely full, loud with the sound of people's voices, laughter, plates clinking. Almost all the guests were locals,

it seemed, and they called out to the waiters by first name: *Giuseppe! Paolo!*

'I don't know who she heard it from, but she knew everything about me. How I was still single and had worked abroad. How I'd left my job a year before and started up my own company. She knew it all. Don't worry, she told me, you'll do fine. Just have confidence in yourself. I know you'll be successful. How could you not be? It made me so happy to hear her say that. Her voice was so kind. I can do this, I thought, I *can* make a go of it. Hearing her voice made me regain the confidence I used to have. As long as things stay real, I thought, I know I'm going to make it. I felt as if the world was out there just for me.' He smiled.

'It was my turn then to ask about her life. What kind of person she had married, whether she had children, where she lived. She didn't have any children. Her husband was four years older than her and worked at a TV station. He was a director, she said. He must be very busy, I commented. So busy he doesn't have time to make any children, she replied, and laughed. She lived in Tokyo, in a condo in Shinagawa. I was living in Shiroganedai at the time, so we weren't exactly neighbours but lived pretty close to each other. What a coincidence, I told her. Anyway, that's what we talked about – all the typical things two people who used to go out in school might talk about. Occasionally it felt a bit awkward, but I enjoyed talking to her again. We talked like two old friends who'd said goodbye long ago and who were now walking down two separate paths in

life. It had been a long time since I'd spoken so openly, so
honestly, to anybody, and we talked for a long, long time.
Once we'd said everything there was to say, we were silent.
It was a – how should I put it? – a very deep silence. The
kind of silence where, if you close your eyes, all sorts of
images start to well up in your mind.' He stared for a while
at his hands on the table, then raised his head and looked
at me. 'I wanted to hang up then, if I could have. Thank her
for calling, tell her how much I enjoyed talking to her. You
know what I mean?'

'From a practical standpoint that would have been the
most realistic thing to do,' I agreed.

'But she didn't hang up. And she invited me to her place.
Can you come over? she asked. My husband's on a business trip and I'm by myself and bored. I didn't know what
to say, so I said nothing. Nor did she. There was just that
silence for a while, and then she said this: I haven't forgotten the promise I made to you.'

'I HAVEN'T FORGOTTEN the promise I made to you,' she
said. At first he didn't know what she meant. And then it
all came back – her promise to sleep with him after she got
married. He'd never considered this a real promise, just a
stray thought she'd let slip out in a moment of confusion.

But it hadn't been the result of any confusion on her
part. For her it was a promise, a binding agreement she'd
entered into.

For a moment he didn't know what to think, no idea

what he should do. He glanced around him, completely at a loss, but discovered no signposts to show him the way. Of course he wanted to sleep with her – that goes without saying. After they broke up, he often imagined what it would be like making love to her. Even when he was with other girls, in the dark he pictured holding her. Not that he'd seen her naked – all he knew about her body was what he'd been able to feel with his hand under her clothes.

He knew full well how dangerous it would be for him to sleep with her at this point. How destructive it could finish up being. He also didn't feel like reawakening what he'd already abandoned back there in the dark. This isn't the right thing for me to do, he knew. There's something unreal about it, something incompatible with who I am.

But of course he agreed to see her. This was, after all, a beautiful fairy tale he might experience only once in life. His gorgeous ex-girlfriend, the one he'd spent his precious youth with, was telling him she wanted to sleep with him, asking him to come over to her house right away – and she lived not far away. Plus there was that secret, legendary promise exchanged a long, long time ago in a deep wood.

He sat there for a while, eyes closed, not speaking. He felt as though he had lost the power of speech.

'Are you still there?' she asked.

'I'm here,' he said. 'OK. I'll be over soon. I should be there in less than a half hour. Tell me your address.'

He wrote down the name of her condo and the

apartment number, and her phone number. He quickly shaved, changed clothes and went out to flag down a taxi.

'IF IT'D BEEN you, what would you have done?' he asked me.

I shook my head. I had no idea what to say.

He laughed and stared at his coffee cup. 'I wish I could have got by without answering, too. But I couldn't. I had to make a decision right then and there. To go or not to go, one or the other. There's no in between. I ended up going to her place. As I knocked on her door, I was thinking how nice it would be if she wasn't at home. But she was there, as beautiful as she used to be. Smelling just as wonderful as I remembered. We had a few drinks and talked, listened to some old records. And then what do you think happened?'

I have no idea, I told him.

'A long time ago, when I was a child, there was a fairy tale I read,' he said, staring at the opposite wall the whole time. 'I don't remember how the story went, but the last line has stayed with me. Probably because that was the first time I'd ever read a fairy tale that had such a strange ending. This is how it ended: "And when it was all over, the king and his retainers burst out laughing." Don't you think that's rather a strange ending?'

'I do,' I said.

'I wish I could remember the plot, but I can't. All I can remember is that strange last line. "And when it was all

over, the king and his retainers burst out laughing." What kind of story could it have been?'

We'd finished our coffee by this point.

'We held each other,' he went on, 'but didn't have sex. I didn't take her clothes off. I just touched her with my fingers, just like the old days. I decided that was the best thing to do, and she'd apparently come to the same conclusion. For a long time we sat there, touching each other. That was the only way we could grasp what we were supposed to understand at that time. If this had been long ago, that wouldn't have been the case – we would have had sex, and grown even closer. We might have ended up happy. But we'd already passed that point. That possibility was sealed up, frozen solid. And it would never open up again.'

He turned his empty coffee cup round and round. He did this so long the waiter came over to see if he wanted anything. Finally he let go of the cup, called the waiter back and ordered another espresso.

'I must have stayed at her apartment for about an hour. I don't remember exactly. Any longer and I might have gone a little crazy,' he said and smiled. 'I said goodbye to her and left. This was our final farewell. I knew it, and so did she. The last time I saw her, she was standing in the doorway, arms folded. She seemed about to say something, but didn't. She didn't have to say it out loud – I knew what she was going to say. I felt so empty. So hollow. Sounds struck me as strange, everything looked distorted. I wandered around in a daze, thinking how my life had been

utterly pointless. I wanted to turn round, go back to her place and have her. But I couldn't. There was no way I could do that.'

He closed his eyes and shook his head. He drank his second espresso.

'It's pretty embarrassing to say this, but that night I went out and slept with a prostitute. It was the first time in my life I'd paid for sex. And probably the last.'

I stared at my own coffee cup for a while. And thought of how full of myself I used to be. I wanted to try to explain this to him, but didn't think I could.

'When I tell it like this, it sounds like something that happened to somebody else,' he laughed. He was silent for a time, lost in thought. I didn't say anything, either.

'And when it was all over, the king and his retainers burst out laughing,' he finally said. 'That line always comes to me whenever I remember what happened. It's like a conditioned reflex. It seems to me that very sad things always contain an element of the comical.'

As I SAID at the beginning, there's no real moral or lesson to be learned from all this. But this is something that actually happened to him. Something that happened to all of us. That's why when he told me his story, I couldn't laugh. And even now I can't.

—*translated by Philip Gabriel*

© Elena Seibert

HARUKI MURAKAMI was born in Kyoto in 1949, where his parents both taught Japanese literature. Growing up in post-war Japan, Murakami was drawn to Western influences: Franz Kafka, Raymond Carver, Kurt Vonnegut, as well as the liberating rhythms of jazz music. The notion of writing a novel first came to Murakami at the age of 29, while watching a baseball game in Tokyo's Jingu Stadium. He has since written many novels, as well as short stories and non-fiction, including the books *Norwegian Wood*, *The Wind-Up Bird Chronicle*, *Kafka on the Shore*, *1Q84*, *What I Talk About When I Talk About Running*, *Colorless Tsukuru Tazaki and His Years of Pilgrimage* and *Absolutely on Music*.

Murakami's writing is attuned to the deep undercurrents of human desire, with the hunt for satisfaction often taking a turn for the unexpected. In 'The Second Bakery Attack' a young married couple resort to robbery to gratify their hunger, while in 'Samsa in Love' craving offers a gateway into what it means to be fully human. In 'Birthday Girl' Murakami confronts us with the question: what would be our one wish, if we could have it granted.

Murakami has run a marathon a year for over 20 years. He ran his personal best of 3:27 hours in the New York City Marathon in 1991.

RECOMMENDED BOOKS BY HARUKI MURAKAMI:

Blind Willow, Sleeping Woman
The Elephant Vanishes
Men Without Women

Do you want to indulge in your Desire?

Love
JEANETTE WINTERSON

VINTAGE MINIS

Psychedelics
ALDOUS HUXLEY

VINTAGE MINIS

Eating
NIGELLA LAWSON

VINTAGE MINIS

Summer
LAURIE LEE

VINTAGE MINIS

VINTAGE MINIS

The Vintage Minis bring you the world's greatest writers on the experiences that make us human. These stylish, entertaining little books explore the whole spectrum of life – from birth to death, and everything in between. Which means there's something here for everyone, whatever your story.

Desire	Haruki Murakami
Love	Jeanette Winterson
Babies	Anne Enright
Language	Xiaolu Guo
Motherhood	Helen Simpson
Fatherhood	Karl Ove Knausgaard
Summer	Laurie Lee
Jealousy	Marcel Proust
Sisters	Louisa May Alcott
Home	Salman Rushdie
Race	Toni Morrison
Liberty	Virginia Woolf
Swimming	Roger Deakin
Work	Joseph Heller
Depression	William Styron
Drinking	John Cheever
Eating	Nigella Lawson
Psychedelics	Aldous Huxley
Calm	Tim Parks
Death	Julian Barnes

vintageminis.co.uk

1 3 5 7 9 10 8 6 4 2

Vintage
20 Vauxhall Bridge Road,
London SW1V 2SA

Vintage Classics is part of the Penguin Random House
group of companies whose addresses can be found at
global.penguinrandomhouse.com.

Penguin
Random House
UK

A Room of One's Own first published in the United Kingdom by The Hogarth
Press in 1929
The Waves first published in the United Kingdom by The Hogarth Press in 1931
This version of 'Street Haunting' is taken from *The Essays of Virginia Woolf:
Volume IX*, first published by Chatto & Windus in 1994
This version of 'How Should One Read a Book' is taken from *The Common
Reader: Volume II*, first published by The Hogarth Press in 1932

penguin.co.uk/vintage

A CIP catalogue record for this book is available from the British Library

ISBN 9781784872717

Printed and bound by Clays Ltd, St Ives plc

Penguin Random House is committed to a sustainable future for
our business, our readers and our planet. This book is made from
Forest Stewardship Council® certified paper.

MIX
Paper from
responsible sources
FSC
www.fsc.org   FSC® C018179

Liberty

VIRGINIA WOOLF

VINTAGE MINIS

From the essay *A Room of One's Own*

PERHAPS NOW IT would be better to give up seeking for the truth, and receiving on one's head an avalanche of opinion hot as lava, discoloured as dish-water. It would be better to draw the curtains; to shut out distractions; to light the lamp; to narrow the enquiry and to ask the historian, who records not opinions but facts, to describe under what conditions women lived, not throughout the ages, but in England, say, in the time of Elizabeth.

It is a perennial puzzle why no woman wrote a word of that extraordinary literature when every other man, it seemed, was capable of song or sonnet. What were the conditions in which women lived? I asked myself; for fiction, imaginative work that is, is not dropped like a pebble upon the ground, as science may be; fiction is like a spider's web, attached ever so lightly perhaps, but still attached to life at all four corners. Often the attachment is scarcely perceptible; Shakespeare's plays, for instance, seem to hang there complete by themselves. But when the web is pulled askew, hooked up at the edge, torn in the middle, one remembers that these webs are not spun in mid-air by incorporeal creatures, but are the work of suffering human beings, and are attached to grossly material things, like health and money and the houses we live in.

I went, therefore, to the shelf where the histories stand and took down one of the latest, Professor Trevelyan's *History of England*. Once more I looked up Women, found 'position of' and turned to the pages indicated. 'Wife-beating', I read, 'was a recognized right of man, and was practised without shame by high as well as low . . . Similarly,' the historian goes on, 'the daughter who refused to marry the gentleman of her parents' choice was liable to be locked up, beaten and flung about the room, without any shock being inflicted on public opinion. Marriage was not an affair of personal affection, but of family avarice, particularly in the "chivalrous" upper classes . . . Betrothal often took place while one or both of the parties was in the cradle, and marriage when they were scarcely out of the nurses' charge.' That was about 1470, soon after Chaucer's time. The next reference to the position of women is some two hundred years later, in the time of the Stuarts. 'It was still the exception for women of the upper and middle class to choose their own husbands, and when the husband had been assigned, he was lord and master, so far at least as law and custom could make him. Yet even so,' Professor Trevelyan concludes, 'neither Shakespeare's women nor those of authentic seventeenth-century memoirs, like the Verneys and the Hutchinsons, seem wanting in personality and character.' Certainly, if we consider it, Cleopatra must have had a way with her; Lady Macbeth, one would suppose, had a will of her own; Rosalind, one might conclude, was an attractive girl. Professor Trevelyan is speaking no more than the truth when he remarks that Shakespeare's women do not seem wanting in personality and character. Not being a historian, one might go even further and say that women have burnt like beacons in all the works of all the poets from the beginning of time – Clytemnestra, Antigone, Cleopatra, Lady Macbeth, Phèdre, Cressida, Rosalind, Desdemona, the Duchess of Malfi, among the dramatists; then among the prose writers: Millamant, Clarissa, Becky Sharp, Anna Karenina, Emma Bovary, Madame de Guermantes – the names flock to mind, nor do they recall women 'lacking in personality and character'. Indeed, if woman had no existence save in the fiction written by men, one would imagine her a person of the utmost importance; very various; heroic and mean; splendid and sordid; infinitely beautiful and hideous in the extreme; as great as a man, some think even greater. But this is woman in fiction. In fact, as Professor Trevelyan points out, she was locked up, beaten and flung about the room.

A very queer, composite being thus emerges. Imaginatively she is of the highest importance; practically she is completely insignificant. She pervades poetry from cover to cover; she is all but absent from history. She dominates the lives of kings and conquerors in fiction; in fact she was the slave of any boy whose parents forced a ring upon her finger. Some of the most inspired words, some of the most profound thoughts in literature fall from her lips; in real life she could hardly read, could scarcely spell, and was the property of her husband.

It was certainly an odd monster that one made up by reading the historians first and the poets afterwards – a worm winged like an eagle; the spirit of life and beauty in a kitchen chopping up suet. But these monsters, however amusing to the imagination, have no existence in fact. What one must do to bring her to life was to think poetically and prosaically at one and the same moment, thus keeping in touch with fact – that she is Mrs Martin, aged thirty-six, dressed in blue, wearing a black hat and brown shoes; but not losing sight of fiction either – that she is a vessel in which all sorts of spirits and forces are coursing and flashing perpetually. The moment, however, that one tries this method with the Elizabethan woman, one branch of illumination fails; one is held up by the scarcity of facts. One knows nothing detailed, nothing perfectly true and substantial about her. History scarcely mentions her. And I turned to Professor Trevelyan again to see what history meant to him. I found by looking at his chapter headings that it meant – 'The Manor Court and the Methods of Open-field Agriculture . . . The Cistercians and Sheep-farming . . . The Crusades . . . The University . . . The House of Commons . . . The Hundred Years' War . . .

The Wars of the Roses . . . The Renaissance Scholars . . . The Dissolution of the Monasteries . . . Agrarian and Religious Strife . . . The Origin of English Sea-power . . . The Armada . . .' and so on. Occasionally an individual woman is mentioned, an Elizabeth, or a Mary; a queen or a great lady. But by no possible means could middle-class women with nothing but brains and character at their command have taken part in any one of the great movements which, brought together, constitute the historian's view of the past. Nor shall we find her in any collection of anecdotes. Aubrey hardly mentions her. She never writes her own life and scarcely keeps a diary; there are only a handful of her letters in existence. She left no plays or poems by which we can judge her. What one wants, I thought – and why does not some brilliant student at Newnham or Girton supply it? – is a mass of information; at what age did she marry; how many children had she as a rule; what was her house like, had she a room to herself; did she do the cooking; would she be likely to have a servant? All these facts lie somewhere, presumably, in parish registers and account books; the life of the average Elizabethan woman must be scattered about somewhere, could one collect it and make a book of it. It would be ambitious beyond my daring, I thought, looking about the shelves for books that were not there, to suggest to the students of those famous colleges that they should rewrite history, though I own that it often seems a little queer as it is, unreal, lop-sided; but why should they not add a supplement to history, calling it, of course, by some inconspicuous name so that women might figure there without impropriety? For one often catches a glimpse of them in the lives of the great, whisking away into the background, concealing, I sometimes think, a wink, a laugh, perhaps a tear. And, after all, we have lives enough of Jane Austen; it scarcely seems necessary to consider again the influence of the tragedies of Joanna Baillie upon the poetry of Edgar Allan Poe; as for myself, I should not mind if the homes and haunts of Mary Russell Mitford were closed to the public for a century at least. But what I find deplorable, I continued, looking about the bookshelves again, is that nothing is known about women before the eighteenth century. I have no model in my mind to turn about this way and that. Here am I asking why women did not write poetry in the Elizabethan age, and I am not sure how they were educated; whether they were taught to write; whether they had sitting-rooms to themselves; how many women had children before they were twenty-one; what, in short, they did from eight in the morning till eight at night. They had no money evidently; according to Professor Trevelyan they were married whether they liked it or not before they were out of the nursery, at fifteen or sixteen very likely. It would have been extremely odd, even upon this showing, had one of them suddenly written the plays of Shakespeare, I concluded, and I thought of that old gentleman, who is dead now, but was a bishop, I think, who declared that it was impossible for any woman, past, present, or to come, to have the genius of Shakespeare. He wrote to the papers about it. He also told a lady who applied to him for information that cats do not as a matter of fact go to heaven, though they have, he added, souls of a sort. How much thinking those old gentlemen used to save one! How the borders of ignorance shrank back at their approach! Cats do not go to heaven. Women cannot write the plays of Shakespeare.

Be that as it may, I could not help thinking, as I looked at the works of Shakespeare on the shelf, that the bishop was right at least in this; it would have been impossible, completely and entirely, for any woman to have written the plays of Shakespeare in the age of Shakespeare. Let me imagine, since facts are so hard to come by, what would have happened had Shakespeare had a wonderfully gifted sister, called Judith, let us say. Shakespeare himself went, very probably, – his mother was an heiress – to the grammar school, where he may have learnt Latin – Ovid, Virgil and Horace – and the elements of grammar and logic. He was, it is well known, a wild boy who poached rabbits, perhaps shot a deer, and had, rather sooner than he should have done, to marry a woman in the neighbour-hood, who bore him a child rather quicker than was right. That escapade sent him to seek his fortune in London. He had, it seemed, a taste for the theatre; he began by holding horses at the stage door. Very soon he got work in the the-atre, became a successful actor, and lived at the hub of the universe, meeting everybody, knowing everybody, practising his art on the boards, exercising his wits in the streets, and even getting access to the palace of the queen. Meanwhile his extraordinarily gifted sister, let us suppose, remained at home. She was as adventurous, as imaginative, as agog to see the world as he was. But she was not sent to school. She had no chance of learning grammar and logic, let alone of reading Horace and Virgil. She picked up a book now and then, one of her brother's perhaps, and read a few pages. But then her parents came in and told her to mend the stockings or mind the stew and not moon about with books and papers. They would have spoken sharply but kindly, for they were substantial people who knew the conditions of life for a woman and loved their daughter – indeed, more likely than not she was the apple of her father's eye. Perhaps she scribbled some pages up in an apple loft on the sly, but was careful to hide them or set fire to them. Soon, however, before she was out of her teens, she was to be betrothed to the son of a neighbouring wool-stapler. She cried out that marriage was hateful to her, and for that she was severely beaten by her father. Then he ceased to scold her. He begged her instead not to hurt him, not to shame him in this matter of her marriage. He would give her a chain of beads or a fine petticoat, he said; and there were tears in his eyes. How could she disobey him? How could she break his heart? The force of her own gift alone drove her to it. She made up a small parcel of her belongings, let herself down by a rope one summer's night and took the road to

London. She was not seventeen. The birds that sang in the hedge were not more musical than she was. She had the quickest fancy, a gift like her brother's, for the tune of words. Like him, she had a taste for the theatre. She stood at the stage door; she wanted to act, she said. Men laughed in her face. The manager – a fat, loose-lipped man – guffawed. He bellowed something about poodles dancing and women acting – no woman, he said, could possibly be an actress. He hinted – you can imagine what. She could get no training in her craft. Could she even seek her dinner in a tavern or roam the streets at midnight? Yet her genius was for fiction and lusted to feed abundantly upon the lives of men and women and the study of their ways. At last – for she was very young, oddly like Shakespeare the poet in her face, with the same grey eyes and rounded brows – at last Nick Greene the actor-manager took pity on her; she found herself with child by that gentleman and so – who shall measure the heat and violence of the poet's heart when caught and tangled in a woman's body? – killed herself one winter's night and lies buried at some cross-roads where the omnibuses now stop outside the Elephant and Castle.

That, more or less, is how the story would run, I think, if a woman in Shakespeare's day had had Shakespeare's genius. But for my part, I agree with the deceased bishop, if such he was – it is unthinkable that any woman in Shakespeare's day should have had Shakespeare's genius. For genius like Shakespeare's is not born among labouring, uneducated, servile people. It was not born in England among the Saxons and the Britons. It is not born today among the working classes. How, then, could it have been born among women whose work began, according to Professor Trevelyan, almost before they were out of the nursery, who were forced to it by their parents and held to it by all the power of law and custom? Yet genius of a sort must have existed among women as it must have existed among the working classes. Now and again an Emily Brontë or a Robert Burns blazes out and proves its presence. But certainly it never got itself on to paper. When, however, one reads of a witch being ducked, of a woman possessed by devils, of a wise woman selling herbs, or even of a very remarkable man who had a mother, then I think we are on the track of a lost novelist, a suppressed poet, of some mute and inglorious Jane Austen, some Emily Brontë who dashed her brains out on the moor or mopped and mowed about the highways crazed with the torture that her gift had put her to. Indeed, I would venture to guess that Anon, who wrote so many poems without singing them, was often a woman. It was a woman Edward Fitzgerald, I think, suggested who made the ballads and the folk-songs, crooning them to her children, beguiling her spinning with them, or the length of the winter's night.

This may be true or it may be false – who can say? – but what is true in it, so it seemed to me, reviewing the story of Shakespeare's sister as I had made it, is that any woman born with a great gift in the sixteenth century would certainly have gone crazed, shot herself, or ended her days in some lonely cottage outside the village, half witch, half wizard, feared and mocked at. For it needs little skill in psychology to be sure that a highly gifted girl who had tried to use her gift for poetry would have been so thwarted and hindered by other people, so tortured and pulled asunder by her own contrary instincts, that she must have lost her health and sanity to a certainty. No girl could have walked to London and stood at a stage door and forced her way into the presence of actor-managers without doing herself a violence and suffering an anguish which may have been irrational – for chastity may be a fetish invented by certain societies for unknown reasons – but were none the less inevitable. Chastity had then, it has even now, a religious importance in a woman's life, and has so wrapped itself round with nerves and instincts that to cut it free and bring it to the light of day demands courage of the rarest. To have lived a free life in London in the sixteenth century would have meant for a woman who was poet and playwright a nervous stress and dilemma which might well have killed her. Had she survived, whatever she had written would have been twisted and deformed, issuing from a strained and morbid imagination. And undoubtedly, I thought, looking at the shelf where there are no plays by women, her work would have gone unsigned. That refuge she would have sought certainly. It was the relic of the sense of chastity that dictated anonymity to women even so late as the nineteenth century. Currer Bell, George Eliot, George Sand, all the victims of inner strife as their writings prove, sought ineffectively to veil themselves by using the name of a man. Thus they did homage to the convention, which if not implanted by the other sex was liberally encouraged by them (the chief glory of a woman is not to be talked of, said Pericles, himself a much-talked-of man) that publicity in women is detestable. Anonymity runs in their blood. The desire to be veiled still possesses them. They are not even now as concerned about the health of their fame as men are, and, speaking generally, will pass a tombstone or a signpost without feeling an irresistible desire to cut their names on it, as Alf, Bert or Chas must do in obedience to their instinct, which murmurs if it sees a fine woman go by, or even a dog, Ce chien est à moi. And, of course, it may not be a dog, I thought, remembering Parliament Square, the Sieges Allee and other avenues; it may be a piece of land or a man with curly black hair. It is one of the great advantages of being a woman that one can pass even a very fine negress without wishing to make an Englishwoman of her.

That woman, then, who was born with a gift of poetry in the sixteenth century, was an unhappy woman, a woman at strife against herself. All the conditions of her life, all her own instincts, were hostile to the state of mind which is needed to set free whatever is in the brain. But what is the state of mind that is most propitious to the act of creation? I asked. Can one come by any notion of the state that furthers and makes possible that strange activity? Here I opened the volume containing the Tragedies of Shakespeare. What was Shakespeare's state of mind, for instance, when he wrote *Lear* and *Antony and Cleopatra*? It was certainly the state of mind most favourable to poetry that there has ever existed. But Shakespeare himself said nothing about it. We only know casually and by chance that he 'never blotted a line'. Nothing indeed was ever said by the artist himself about his state of mind until the eighteenth century perhaps. Rousseau perhaps began it. At any rate, by the nineteenth century self-consciousness had developed so far that it was the habit for men of letters to describe their minds in confessions and autobiographies. Their lives also were written, and their letters were printed after their deaths. Thus, though we do not know what Shakespeare went through when he wrote *Lear*, we do know what Carlyle went through when he wrote the *French Revolution*; what Flaubert went through when he wrote *Madame Bovary*; what Keats was going through when he tried to write poetry against the coming death and the indifference of the world.

And one gathers from this enormous modern literature of confession and self-analysis that to write a work of genius is almost always a feat of prodigious difficulty. Everything is against the likelihood that it will come from the writer's mind whole and entire. Generally material circumstances are against it. Dogs will bark; people will interrupt; money must be made; health will break down. Further, accentuating all these difficulties and making them harder to bear is the world's notorious indifference. It does not ask people to write poems and novels and histories; it does not need them. It does not care whether Flaubert finds the right word or whether Carlyle scrupulously verifies this or that fact. Naturally, it will not pay for what it does not want. And so the writer, Keats, Flaubert, Carlyle, suffers, especially in the creative years of youth, every form of distraction and discouragement. A curse, a cry of agony, rises from those books of analysis and confession. 'Mighty poets in their misery dead' – that is the burden of their song. If anything comes through in spite of all this, it is a miracle, and probably no book is born entire and uncrippled as it was conceived.

But for women, I thought, looking at the empty shelves, these difficulties were infinitely more formidable. In the first place, to have a room of her own, let alone a quiet room or a sound-proof room, was out of the question, unless her parents were exceptionally rich or very noble, even up to the beginning of the nineteenth century. Since her pin money, which depended on the goodwill of her father, was only enough to keep her clothed, she was debarred from such alleviations as came even to Keats or Tennyson or Carlyle, all poor men, from a walking tour, a little journey to France, from the separate lodging which, even if it were miserable enough, sheltered them from the claims and tyrannies of their families. Such material difficulties were formidable; but much worse were the immaterial. The indifference of the world which Keats and Flaubert and other men of genius have found so hard to bear was in her case not indifference but hostility. The world did not say to her as it said to them, Write if you choose; it makes no difference to me. The world said with a guffaw, Write? What's the good of your writing? Here the psychologists of Newnham and Girton might come to our help, I thought, looking again at the blank spaces on the shelves. For surely it is time that the effect of discouragement upon the mind of the artist should be measured, as I have seen a dairy company measure the effect of ordinary milk and Grade A milk upon the body of the rat. They set two rats in cages side by side, and of the two one was furtive, timid and small, and the other was glossy, bold and big. Now what food do we feed women as artists upon? I asked, remembering, I suppose, that dinner of prunes and custard. To answer that question I had only to open the evening paper and to read that Lord Birkenhead is of opinion – but really I am not going to trouble to copy out Lord Birkenhead's opinion upon the writing of women. What Dean Inge says I will leave in peace. The Harley Street specialist may be allowed to rouse the echoes of Harley Street with his vociferations without raising a hair on my head. I will quote, however, Mr Oscar Browning, because Mr Oscar Browning was a great figure in Cambridge at one time, and used to examine the students at Girton and Newnham. Mr Oscar Browning was wont to

The world said with a guffaw, Write? What's the good of your writing?

declare 'that the impression left on his mind, after looking over any set of examination papers, was that,
irrespective of the marks he might give, the best woman
was intellectually the inferior of the worst man'. After
saying that Mr Browning went back to his rooms – and it
is this sequel that endears him and makes him a human
figure of some bulk and majesty – he went back to his
rooms and found a stable-boy lying on the sofa – 'a mere
skeleton, his cheeks were cavernous and sallow, his teeth
were black, and he did not appear to have the full use of
his limbs . . . "That's Arthur" [said Mr Browning]. "He's a
dear boy really and most high-minded."' The two pictures
always seem to me to complete each other. And happily in
this age of biography the two pictures often do complete
each other, so that we are able to interpret the opinions of
great men not only by what they say, but by what they do.

But though this is possible now, such opinions coming
from the lips of important people must have been formidable enough even fifty years ago. Let us suppose that a
father from the highest motives did not wish his daughter
to leave home and become writer, painter or scholar. 'See
what Mr Oscar Browning says,' he would say; and there
was not only Mr Oscar Browning; there was the *Saturday
Review*; there was Mr Greg – the 'essentials of a woman's
being', said Mr Greg emphatically, 'are that *they are supported by, and they minister to, men* – there was an enormous
body of masculine opinion to the effect that nothing
could be expected of women intellectually. Even if her

father did not read out loud these opinions, any girl could read them for herself; and the reading, even in the nineteenth century, must have lowered her vitality, and told profoundly upon her work. There would always have been that assertion – you cannot do this, you are incapable of doing that – to protest against, to overcome. Probably for a novelist this germ is no longer of much effect; for there have been women novelists of merit. But for painters it must still have some sting in it; and for musicians, I imagine, is even now active and poisonous in the extreme. The woman composer stands where the actress stood in the time of Shakespeare. Nick Greene, I thought, remembering the story I had made about Shakespeare's sister, said that a woman acting put him in mind of a dog dancing. Johnson repeated the phrase two hundred years later of women preaching. And here, I said, opening a book about music, we have the very words used again in this year of grace, 1928, of women who try to write music. 'Of Mlle. Germaine Tailleferre one can only repeat Dr Johnson's dictum concerning a woman preacher, transposed into terms of music. "Sir, a woman's composing is like a dog's walking on his hind legs. It is not done well, but you are surprised to find it done at all."' So accurately does history repeat itself.

Thus, I concluded, shutting Mr Oscar Browning's life and pushing away the rest, it is fairly evident that even in the nineteenth century a woman was not encouraged to be an artist. On the contrary, she was snubbed, slapped, lectured and exhorted. Her mind must have been strained and her vitality lowered by the need of opposing this, of disproving that. For here again we come within range of that very interesting and obscure masculine complex which has had so much influence upon the woman's movement; that deep-seated desire, not so much that *she* shall be inferior as that *he* shall be superior, which plants him wherever one looks, not only in front of the arts, but barring the way to politics too, even when the risk to himself seems infinitesimal and the suppliant humble and devoted. Even Lady Bessborough, I remembered, with all her passion for politics, must humbly bow herself and write to Lord Granville Leveson-Gower: ' . . . notwithstanding all my violence in politicks and talking so much on that subject, I perfectly agree with you that no woman has any business to meddle with that or any other serious business, farther than giving her opinion (if she is ask'd)'. And so she goes on to spend her enthusiasm where it meets with no obstacle whatsoever, upon that immensely important subject, Lord Granville's maiden speech in the House of Commons. The spectacle is certainly a strange one, I thought. The history of men's opposition to women's emancipation is more interesting perhaps than the story of that emancipation itself. An amusing book might be made of it if some young student at Girton or Newnham would collect examples and deduce a theory, – but she would need thick gloves on her hands, and bars to protect her of solid gold.

But what is amusing now, I recollected, shutting Lady

Bessborough, had to be taken in desperate earnest once. Opinions that one now pastes in a book labelled cock-a-doodle-dum and keeps for reading to select audiences on summer nights once drew tears, I can assure you. Among your grandmothers and great-grandmothers there were many that wept their eyes out. Florence Nightingale shrieked aloud in her agony. Moreover, it is all very well for you, who have got yourselves to college and enjoy sitting-rooms – or is it only bed-sitting-rooms? – of your own to say that genius should disregard such opinions; that genius should be above caring what is said of it. Unfortunately, it is precisely the men or women of genius who mind most what is said of them. Remember Keats. Remember the words he had cut on his tombstone. Think of Tennyson; think – but I need hardly multiply instances of the undeniable, if very fortunate, fact that it is the nature of the artist to mind excessively what is said about him. Literature is strewn with the wreckage of men who have minded beyond reason the opinions of others.

And this susceptibility of theirs is doubly unfortunate, I thought, returning again to my original enquiry into what state of mind is most propitious for creative work, because the mind of an artist, in order to achieve the prodigious effort of freeing whole and entire the work that is in him, must be incandescent, like Shakespeare's mind, I conjectured, looking at the book which lay open at *Antony and Cleopatra*. There must be no obstacle in it, no foreign matter unconsumed.

For though we say that we know nothing about Shakespeare's state of mind, even as we say that, we are saying something about Shakespeare's state of mind. The reason perhaps why we know so little of Shakespeare – compared with Donne or Ben Jonson or Milton – is that his grudges and spites and antipathies are hidden from us. We are not held up by some 'revelation' which reminds us of the writer. All desire to protest, to preach, to proclaim an injury, to pay off a score, to make the world the witness of some hardship or grievance was fired out of him and consumed. Therefore his poetry flows from him free and unimpeded. If ever a human being got his work expressed completely, it was Shakespeare. If ever a mind was incandescent, unimpeded, I thought, turning again to the bookcase, it was Shakespeare's mind.

THAT ONE WOULD find any woman in that state of mind in the sixteenth century was obviously impossible. One has only to think of the Elizabethan tombstones with all those children kneeling with clasped hands; and their early deaths; and to see their houses with their dark, cramped rooms, to realize that no woman could have written poetry then. What one would expect to find would be that rather later perhaps some great lady would take advantage of her comparative freedom and comfort to publish something with her name to it and risk being thought a monster. Men, of course, are not snobs, I continued, carefully eschewing 'the arrant feminism' of Miss Rebecca West; but they appreciate with sympathy for the most part the efforts of a countess to write verse. One would expect to find a lady of title meeting with far greater encouragement than an unknown Miss Austen or a Miss Brontë at that time would have met with. But one would also expect to find that her mind was disturbed by alien emotions like fear and hatred and that her poems showed traces of that disturbance. Here is Lady Winchilsea, for example, I thought, taking down her poems. She was born in the year 1661; she was noble both by birth and by marriage; she was childless; she wrote poetry, and one has only to open her poetry to find her bursting out in indignation against the position of women:

> How we are fallen! fallen by mistaken rules,
> And Education's more than Nature's fools;
> Debarred from all improvements of the mind,
> And to be dull, expected and designed;
> And if someone would soar above the rest,
> With warmer fancy, and ambition pressed,
> So strong the opposing faction still appears,
> The hopes to thrive can ne'er outweigh the fears.

Clearly her mind has by no means 'consumed all impediments and become incandescent'. On the contrary, it is harassed and distracted with hates and grievances. The human race is split up for her into two parties. Men are the 'opposing faction'; men are hated and feared, because they have the power to bar her way to what she wants to do – which is to write.

> Alas! a woman that attempts the pen,
> Such a presumptuous creature is esteemed,

> The fault can by no virtue be redeemed.
> They tell us we mistake our sex and way;
> Good breeding, fashion, dancing, dressing, play,
> Are the accomplishments we should desire;
> To write, or read, or think, or to enquire,
> Would cloud our beauty, and exhaust our time,
> And interrupt the conquests of our prime,
> Whilst the dull manage of a servile house
> Is held by some our utmost art and use.

Indeed she has to encourage herself to write by supposing that what she writes will never be published; to soothe herself with the sad chant:

> To some few friends, and to thy sorrows sing,
> For groves of laurel thou wert never meant:
> Be dark enough thy shades, and be thou there content.

Yet it is clear that could she have freed her mind from hate and fear and not heaped it with bitterness and resentment, the fire was hot within her. Now and again words issue of pure poetry:

> Nor will in fading silks compose,
> Faintly the inimitable rose.

– they are rightly praised by Mr Murry, and Pope, it is thought, remembered and appropriated those others:

Now the jonquille o'ercomes the feeble brain;
We faint beneath the aromatic pain.

It was a thousand pities that the woman who could write like that, whose mind was tuned to nature and reflection, should have been forced to anger and bitterness. But how could she have helped herself? I asked, imagining the sneers and the laughter, the adulation of the toadies, the scepticism of the professional poet. She must have shut herself up in a room in the country to write, and been torn asunder by bitterness and scruples perhaps, though her husband was of the kindest, and their married life perfection. She 'must have', I say, because when one comes to seek out the facts about Lady Winchilsea, one finds, as usual, that almost nothing is known about her. She suffered terribly from melancholy, which we can explain at least to some extent when we find her telling us how in the grip of it she would imagine:

My lines decried, and my employment thought
An useless folly or presumptuous fault:

The employment, which was thus censured, was, as far as one can see, the harmless one of rambling about the fields and dreaming:

My hand delights to trace unusual things,
And deviates from the known and common way,

Nor will in fading silks compose,
Faintly the inimitable rose.

Naturally, if that was her habit and that was her delight,
she could only expect to be laughed at; and, accordingly,
Pope or Gay is said to have satirized her 'as a blue-stocking
with an itch for scribbling'. Also it is thought that she
offended Gay by laughing at him. She said that his *Trivia*
showed that 'he was more proper to walk before a chair
than to ride in one'. But this is all 'dubious gossip' and,
says Mr Murry, 'uninteresting'. But there I do not agree
with him, for I should have liked to have had more even of
dubious gossip so that I might have found out or made up
some image of this melancholy lady, who loved wandering
in the fields and thinking about unusual things and
scorned, so rashly, so unwisely, 'the dull manage of a servile house'. But she became diffuse, Mr Murry says. Her
gift is all grown about with weeds and bound with briars.
It had no chance of showing itself for the fine distinguished gift it was. And so, putting her back on the shelf,
I turned to the other great lady, the Duchess whom Lamb
loved, hare-brained, fantastical Margaret of Newcastle, her
elder, but her contemporary. They were very different, but
alike in this that both were noble and both childless, and
both were married to the best of husbands. In both burnt
the same passion for poetry and both are disfigured and
deformed by the same causes. Open the Duchess and one
finds the same outburst of rage. 'Women live like Bats or

Owls, labour like Beasts, and die like Worms . . .' Margaret too might have been a poet; in our day all that activity would have turned a wheel of some sort. As it was, what could bind, tame or civilize for human use that wild, generous, untutored intelligence? It poured itself out, higgledy-piggledy, in torrents of rhyme and prose, poetry and philosophy which stand congealed in quartos and folios that nobody ever reads. She should have had a microscope put in her hand. She should have been taught to look at the stars and reason scientifically. Her wits were turned with solitude and freedom. No one checked her. No one taught her. The professors fawned on her. At Court they jeered at her. Sir Egerton Brydges complained of her coarseness – 'as flowing from a female of high rank brought up in the Courts'. She shut herself up at Welbeck alone.

What a vision of loneliness and riot the thought of Margaret Cavendish brings to mind! as if some giant cucumber had spread itself over all the roses and carnations in the garden and choked them to death. What a waste that the woman who wrote 'the best bred women are those whose minds are civilest' should have frittered her time away scribbling nonsense and plunging ever deeper into obscurity and folly till the people crowded round her coach when she issued out. Evidently the crazy Duchess became a bogey to frighten clever girls with. Here, I remembered, putting away the Duchess and opening Dorothy Osborne's letters, is Dorothy writing to

Temple about the Duchess's new book. 'Sure the poore woman is a little distracted, shee could never bee soe rediculous else as to venture at writeing book's and in verse too, if I should not sleep this fortnight I should not come to that.'

And so, since no woman of sense and modesty could write books, Dorothy, who was sensitive and melancholy, the very opposite of the Duchess in temper, wrote nothing. Letters did not count. A woman might write letters while she was sitting by her father's sick-bed. She could write them by the fire whilst the men talked without disturbing them. The strange thing is, I thought, turning over the pages of Dorothy's letters, what a gift that untaught and solitary girl had for the framing of a sentence, for the fashioning of a scene. Listen to her running on:

'After dinner wee sitt and talk till Mr B. com's in question and then I am gon. the heat of the day is spent in reading or working and about sixe or seven a Clock, I walke out into a Common that lyes hard by the house where a great many young wenches keep Sheep and Cow's and sitt in the shades singing of Ballads; I goe to them and compare their voyces and Beauty's to some Ancient Shepherdesses that I have read of and finde a vaste difference there, but trust mee I think these are as innocent as those could bee. I talke to them, and finde they want nothing to make them the happiest People in the world, but the knoledge that they are soe. most commonly when we are in the middest of our discourse one looks aboute her and spyes her Cow's goeing into the Corne and then away they all run, as if they had wing's at theire heels. I that am not soe nimble stay behinde, and when I see them driveing home theire Cattle I think tis time for mee to retyre too. when I have supped I goe into the Garden and soe to the syde of a small River that runs by it where I sitt downe and wish you with mee . . .'

One could have sworn that she had the makings of a writer in her. But 'if I should not sleep this fortnight I should not come to that' – one can measure the opposition that was in the air to a woman writing when one finds that even a woman with a great turn for writing has brought herself to believe that to write a book was to be ridiculous, even to show oneself distracted. And so we come, I continued, replacing the single short volume of Dorothy Osborne's letters upon the shelf, to Mrs Behn.

And with Mrs Behn we turn a very important corner on the road. We leave behind, shut up in their parks among their folios, those solitary great ladies who wrote without audience or criticism, for their own delight alone. We come to town and rub shoulders with ordinary people in the streets. Mrs Behn was a middle-class woman with all the plebeian virtues of humour, vitality and courage; a woman forced by the death of her husband and some unfortunate adventures of her own to make her living by her wits. She had to work on equal terms with men. She made, by working very hard, enough to live on. The importance of that fact outweighs anything that she actually wrote, even the splendid 'A Thousand Martyrs I have made', or 'Love in Fantastic Triumph sat', for here begins the freedom of the mind, or rather the possibility that in the course of time the mind will be free to write what it likes. For now that Aphra Behn had done it, girls could go to their parents and say, You need not give me an allowance; I can make money by my pen. Of course the answer for many years to come was, Yes, by living the life of Aphra Behn! Death would be better! and the door was slammed faster than ever. That profoundly interesting subject, the value that men set upon women's chastity and its effect upon their education, here suggests itself for discussion, and might provide an interesting book if any student at Girton or Newnham cared to go into the matter. Lady Dudley, sitting in diamonds among the midges of a Scottish moor, might serve for frontispiece. Lord Dudley, *The Times* said when Lady Dudley died the other day, 'a man of cultivated taste and many accomplishments, was benevolent and bountiful, but whimsically despotic. He insisted upon his wife's wearing full dress, even at the remotest shooting-lodge in the Highlands; he loaded her with gorgeous jewels', and so on, 'he gave her everything – always excepting any measure of responsibility'. Then Lord Dudley had a stroke and she nursed him and ruled his estates with supreme competence for ever after. That whimsical despotism was in the nineteenth century too.

But to return. Aphra Behn proved that money could be

made by writing at the sacrifice, perhaps, of certain agreeable qualities; and so by degrees writing became not merely a sign of folly and a distracted mind, but was of practical importance. A husband might die, or some disaster overtake the family. Hundreds of women began as the eighteenth century drew on to add to their pin money, or to come to the rescue of their families by making translations or writing the innumerable bad novels which have ceased to be recorded even in text-books, but are to be picked up in the fourpenny boxes in the Charing Cross Road. The extreme activity of mind which showed itself in the later eighteenth century among women – the talking, and the meeting, the writing of essays on Shakespeare, the translating of the classics – was founded on the solid fact that women could make money by writing. Money dignifies what is frivolous if unpaid for. It might still be well to sneer at 'blue stockings with an itch for scribbling', but it could not be denied that they could put money in their purses. Thus, towards the end of the eighteenth century a change came about which, if I were rewriting history, I should describe more fully and think of greater importance than the Crusades or the Wars of the Roses. The middle-class woman began to write. For if *Pride and Prejudice* matters, and *Middlemarch* and *Villette* and *Wuthering Heights* matter, then it matters far more than I can prove in an hour's discourse that women generally, and not merely the lonely aristocrat shut up in her country house among her folios and her flatterers, took to writing. Without those forerunners, Jane Austen and the Brontës and George Eliot could no more have written than Shakespeare could have written without Marlowe, or Marlowe without Chaucer, or Chaucer without those forgotten poets who paved the ways and tamed the natural savagery of the tongue. For masterpieces are not single and solitary births; they are the outcome of many years of thinking in common, of thinking by the body of the people, so that the experience of the mass is behind the single voice. Jane Austen should have laid a wreath upon the grave of Fanny Burney, and George Eliot done homage to the robust shade of Eliza Carter – the valiant old woman who tied a bell to her bedstead in order that she might wake early and learn Greek. All women together ought to let flowers fall upon the tomb of Aphra Behn, which is, most scandalously but rather appropriately, in Westminster Abbey, for it was she who earned them the right to speak their minds. It is she – shady and amorous as she was – who makes it not quite fantastic for me to say to you tonight: Earn five hundred a year by your wits.

Here, then, one had reached the early nineteenth century. And here, for the first time, I found several shelves given up entirely to the works of women. But why, I could not help asking, as I ran my eyes over them, were they, with very few exceptions, all novels? The original impulse was to poetry. The 'supreme head of song' was a poetess. Both in France and in England the women poets precede the women novelists. Moreover, I thought, looking at the four famous names, what had George Eliot in common with Emily Brontë? Did not Charlotte Brontë fail entirely to understand Jane Austen? Save for the possibly relevant fact that not one of them had a child, four more incongruous characters could not have met together in a room – so much so that it is tempting to invent a meeting and a dialogue between them. Yet by some strange force they were all compelled when they wrote, to write novels. Had it something to do with being born of the middle class, I asked; and with the fact, which Miss Emily Davies a little later was so strikingly to demonstrate, that the middle-class family in the early nineteenth century was possessed only of a single sitting-room between them? If a woman wrote, she would have to write in the common sitting-room. And, as Miss Nightingale was so vehemently to complain, – 'women never have an half hour . . . that they can call their own' – she was always interrupted. Still it would be easier to write prose and fiction there than to write poetry or a play. Less concentration is required. Jane Austen wrote like that to the end of her days. 'How she was able to effect all this', her nephew writes in his Memoir, 'is surprising, for she had no separate study to repair to, and most of the work must have been done in the general sitting-room, subject to all kinds of casual interruptions. She was careful that her occupation should not be suspected by servants or visitors or any persons beyond her own family party.' Jane Austen hid her manuscripts or covered them with a piece of blotting-paper. Then, again, all the literary training that a woman had in the early nineteenth century was training in the observation of character, in the analysis of emotion. Her sensibility had been educated for centuries by the influences of the common sitting-room. People's feelings were impressed on her; personal relations were always before her eyes. Therefore, when the middle-class woman took to writing, she naturally wrote novels, even though, as seems evident enough, two of the four famous women here named were not by nature novelists. Emily Brontë should have written poetic plays; the overflow of George Eliot's capacious mind should have spread itself when the creative impulse was spent upon history or biography. They wrote novels, however; one may even go further, I said, taking *Pride and Prejudice* from the shelf, and say that they wrote good novels. Without boasting or giving pain to the opposite sex, one may say that *Pride and Prejudice* is a good book. At any rate, one would not have been ashamed to have been caught in the act of writing *Pride and Prejudice*. Yet Jane Austen was glad that a hinge creaked, so that she might hide her manuscript before anyone came in. To Jane Austen there was something discreditable in writing *Pride and Prejudice*. And, I wondered, would *Pride and Prejudice* have been a better novel if Jane Austen had not thought it necessary to hide her manuscript from visitors? I read a page or two to see; but I could not find any signs that her circumstances had harmed her work in the slightest. That, perhaps, was the chief miracle about it. Here was a woman about the year 1800 writing without hate, without bitterness, without fear, without protest, without preaching. That was how Shakespeare wrote, I thought, looking at *Antony and Cleopatra*; and when people compare Shakespeare and Jane Austen, they may mean that the minds of both had consumed all impediments; and for that reason we do not know Jane Austen and we do not know Shakespeare and for that reason Jane Austen pervades every word that she wrote, and so does Shakespeare. If Jane Austen suffered in any way from her circumstances it was in the narrowness of life that was imposed upon her. It was impossible for a woman to go about alone. She never travelled; she never drove through London in an omnibus or had luncheon in a shop by herself. But perhaps it was the nature of Jane Austen not to want what she had not. Her gift and her circumstances matched each other completely. But I doubt whether that was true of Charlotte Brontë, I said, opening *Jane Eyre* and laying it beside *Pride and Prejudice*.

I opened it at chapter twelve and my eye was caught by the phrase 'Anybody may blame me who likes'. What were they blaming Charlotte Brontë for? I wondered. And I read how Jane Eyre used to go up on to the roof when Mrs Fairfax was making jellies and looked over the fields at the distant view. And then she longed – and it was for this that they blamed her – that 'then I longed for a power of vision which might overpass that limit; which might reach the busy world, towns, regions full of life I had heard of but never seen: that then I desired more of practical experience than I possessed; more of intercourse with my kind, of acquaintance with variety of character than was here within my reach. I valued what was good in Mrs Fairfax, and what was good in Adèle; but I believed in the existence of other and more vivid kinds of goodness, and what I believed in I wished to behold.

'Who blames me? Many, no doubt, and I shall be called discontented. I could not help it: the restlessness was in my nature; it agitated me to pain sometimes . . .

'It is vain to say human beings ought to be satisfied with tranquillity: they must have action; and they will make it if they cannot find it. Millions are condemned to a stiller doom than mine, and millions are in silent revolt against their lot. Nobody knows how many rebellions ferment in the masses of life which people earth. Women are supposed to be very calm generally: but women feel just as men feel; they need exercise for their faculties and a field for their efforts as much as their brothers do; they suffer from too rigid a restraint, too absolute a stagnation, precisely as men would suffer; and it is narrow-minded in their more privileged fellow-creatures to say that they ought to confine themselves to making puddings and knitting stockings, to playing on the piano and embroidering bags. It is thoughtless to condemn them, or laugh at them, if they seek to do more or learn more than custom has pronounced necessary for their sex.

'When thus alone I not unfrequently heard Grace Poole's laugh . . .'

That is an awkward break, I thought. It is upsetting to come upon Grace Poole all of a sudden. The continuity is disturbed. One might say, I continued, laying the book down beside *Pride and Prejudice*, that the woman who wrote those pages had more genius in her than Jane Austen; but if one reads them over and marks that jerk in them, that indignation, one sees that she will never get her genius expressed whole and entire. Her books will be deformed and twisted. She will write in a rage where she should write calmly. She will write foolishly where she should write wisely. She will write of herself where she should write of her characters. She is at war with her lot. How could she help but die young, cramped and thwarted?

One could not but play for a moment with the thought of what might have happened if Charlotte Brontë had possessed say three hundred a year – but the foolish woman sold the copyright of her novels outright for fifteen hundred pounds; had somehow possessed more knowledge of the busy world, and towns and regions full of life; more practical experience, and intercourse with her kind and acquaintance with a variety of character. In those words she puts her finger exactly not only upon her own defects as a novelist but upon those of her sex at that time. She knew, no one better, how enormously her genius would have profited if it had not spent itself in solitary visions over distant fields; if experience and intercourse and travel had been granted her. But they were not granted; they were withheld; and we must accept the fact that all those good novels, *Villette*, *Emma*, *Wuthering Heights*, *Middlemarch*, were written by women without more experience of life than could enter the house of a respectable clergyman; written too in the common sitting-room of that respectable house and by women so poor that they could not afford to buy more than a few quires of paper at a time upon which to write *Wuthering Heights* or *Jane Eyre*. One of them, it is true, George Eliot, escaped after much tribulation, but only to a secluded villa in St John's Wood. And there she settled down in the shadow of the world's disapproval. 'I wish it to be understood', she wrote, 'that I should never invite anyone to come and see me who did not ask for the invitation'; for was she not living in sin with a married man and might not the sight of her damage the chastity of Mrs Smith or whoever it might be that chanced to call? One must submit to the social convention, and be 'cut off from what is called the world'. At the same time, on the other side of Europe, there was a young man living freely with this gypsy or with that great lady; going to the wars; picking up unhindered and uncensored all that varied experience of human life which served him so splendidly later when he came to write his books. Had Tolstoy lived at the Priory in seclusion with a married lady 'cut off from what is called the world', however edifying the moral lesson, he could scarcely, I thought, have written *War and Peace*.

But one could perhaps go a little deeper into the question of novel-writing and the effect of sex upon the novelist. If one shuts one's eyes and thinks of the novel as a whole, it would seem to be a creation owning a certain looking-glass likeness to life, though of course with simplifications and distortions innumerable. At any rate, it is a structure leaving a shape on the mind's eye, built now in squares, now pagoda shaped, now throwing out wings and arcades, now solidly compact and domed like the Cathedral of Saint Sofia at Constantinople. This shape, I thought, thinking back over certain famous novels, starts in one the kind of emotion that is appropriate to it. But that emotion at once blends itself with others, for the 'shape' is not made by the relation of stone to stone, but by the relation of human being to human being. Thus a novel starts in us all sorts of antagonistic and opposed emotions. Life conflicts with something that is not life. Hence the difficulty of coming to any agreement about novels, and the immense sway that our private prejudices have upon us. On the one hand, we feel You – John the hero – must live, or I shall be in the depths of despair. On the other, we feel, Alas, John, you must die, because the shape of the book requires it. Life conflicts with something that is not life. Then since life it is in part, we judge it as life. James is the sort of man I most detest, one says. Or, This is a farrago of absurdity. I could never feel anything of the sort myself. The whole structure, it is obvious, thinking back on any famous novel, is one of infinite

complexity, because it is thus made up of so many different judgements, of so many different kinds of emotion.
The wonder is that any book so composed holds together
for more than a year or two, or can possibly mean to the
English reader what it means for the Russian or the
Chinese. But they do hold together occasionally very
remarkably. And what holds them together in these rare
instances of survival (I was thinking of *War and Peace*) is
something that one calls integrity, though it has nothing
to do with paying one's bills or behaving honourably in an
emergency. What one means by integrity, in the case of
the novelist, is the conviction that he gives one that this
is the truth. Yes, one feels, I should never have thought
that this could be so; I have never known people behaving
like that. But you have convinced me that so it is, so it
happens. One holds every phrase, every scene to the light
as one reads – for Nature seems, very oddly, to have provided us with an inner light by which to judge of the
novelist's integrity or disintegrity. Or perhaps it is rather
that Nature, in her most irrational mood, has traced in
invisible ink on the walls of the mind a premonition which
these great artists confirm; a sketch which only needs to
be held to the fire of genius to become visible. When one
so exposes it and sees it come to life one exclaims in rapture, But this is what I have always felt and known and
desired! And one boils over with excitement, and, shutting the book even with a kind of reverence as if it were
something very precious, a stand-by to return to as long

as one lives, one puts it back on the shelf, I said, taking *War and Peace* and putting it back in its place. If, on the other hand, these poor sentences that one takes and tests rouse first a quick and eager response with their bright colouring and their dashing gestures but there they stop: something seems to check them in their development: or if they bring to light only a faint scribble in that corner and a blot over there, and nothing appears whole and entire, then one heaves a sigh of disappointment and says, Another failure. This novel has come to grief somewhere.

And for the most part, of course, novels do come to grief somewhere. The imagination falters under the enormous strain. The insight is confused; it can no longer distinguish between the true and the false, it has no longer the strength to go on with the vast labour that calls at every moment for the use of so many different faculties. But how would all this be affected by the sex of the novelist, I wondered, looking at *Jane Eyre* and the others. Would the fact of her sex in any way interfere with the integrity of a woman novelist – that integrity which I take to be the backbone of the writer? Now, in the passages I have quoted from *Jane Eyre*, it is clear that anger was tampering with the integrity of Charlotte Brontë the novelist. She left her story, to which her entire devotion was due, to attend to some personal grievance. She remembered that she had been starved of her proper due of experience – she had been made to stagnate in a parsonage mending stockings when she wanted to wander free over the world. Her imagination swerved from indignation and we feel it swerve. But there were many more influences than anger tugging at her imagination and deflecting it from its path. Ignorance, for instance. The portrait of Rochester is drawn in the dark. We feel the influence of fear in it; just as we constantly feel an acidity which is the result of oppression, a buried suffering smouldering beneath her passion, a rancour which contracts those books, splendid as they are, with a spasm of pain.

And since a novel has this correspondence to real life, its values are to some extent those of real life. But it is obvious that the values of women differ very often from the values which have been made by the other sex; naturally, this is so. Yet it is the masculine values that prevail. Speaking crudely, football and sport are 'important'; the worship of fashion, the buying of clothes 'trivial'. And these values are inevitably transferred from life to fiction. This is an important book, the critic assumes, because it deals with war. This is an insignificant book because it deals with the feelings of women in a drawing-room. A scene in a battlefield is more important than a scene in a shop – everywhere and much more subtly the difference of value persists. The whole structure, therefore, of the early nineteenth-century novel was raised, if one was a woman, by a mind which was slightly pulled from the straight, and made to alter its clear vision in deference to external authority. One has only to skim those old forgotten novels and listen to the tone of voice in which they are written to divine that the writer was meeting criticism; she was saying this by way of aggression, or that by way of conciliation. She was admitting that she was 'only a woman', or protesting that she was 'as good as a man'. She met that criticism as her temperament dictated, with docility and diffidence, or with anger and emphasis. It does not matter which it was; she was thinking of something other than the thing itself. Down comes her book upon our heads. There was a flaw in the centre of it. And I thought of all the women's novels that lie scattered, like small pock-marked apples in an orchard, about the second-hand book shops of London. It was the flaw in the centre that had rotted them. She had altered her values in deference to the opinion of others.

But how impossible it must have been for them not to budge either to the right or to the left. What genius, what integrity it must have required in face of all that criticism, in the midst of that purely patriarchal society, to hold fast to the thing as they saw it without shrinking. Only Jane Austen did it and Emily Brontë. It is another feather, perhaps the finest, in their caps. They wrote as women write, not as men write. Of all the thousand women who wrote novels then, they alone entirely ignored the perpetual admonitions of the eternal pedagogue – write this, think that. They alone were deaf to that persistent voice, now grumbling, now patronizing, now domineering, now grieved, now shocked, now angry, now avuncular, that voice which cannot let women alone, but must be at them, like some too-conscientious governess, adjuring them, like Sir Egerton Brydges, to be refined; dragging even into the criticism of poetry criticism of sex; admonishing them, if they would be good and win, as I suppose, some shiny prize, to keep within certain limits which the gentleman in question thinks suitable – '. . . female novelists should only aspire to excellence by courageously acknowledging the limitations of their sex'. That puts the matter in a nutshell, and when I tell you, rather to your surprise, that this sentence was written not in August 1828 but in August 1928, you will agree, I think, that however delightful it is to us now, it represents a vast body of opinion – I am not going to stir those old pools; I take only what chance has floated to my feet – that was far more vigorous and far more vocal a century ago. It would have needed a very stalwart young woman in 1828 to disregard all those snubs and chidings and promises of prizes. One must have been something of a firebrand to say to oneself, Oh, but they can't buy literature too. Literature is open to everybody. I refuse to allow you, Beadle though you are, to turn me off the grass. Lock up your libraries if you like; but there is no gate, no lock, no bolt that you can set upon the freedom of my mind.

But whatever effect discouragement and criticism had upon their writing – and I believe that they had a very great effect – that was unimportant compared with the other difficulty which faced them (I was still considering

There is no gate, no lock, no bolt that you can set upon the freedom of my mind

those early nineteenth-century novelists) when they came to set their thoughts on paper – that is that they had no tradition behind them, or one so short and partial that it was of little help. For we think back through our mothers if we are women. It is useless to go to the great men writers for help, however much one may go to them for pleasure. Lamb, Browne, Thackeray, Newman, Sterne, Dickens, De Quincey – whoever it may be – never helped a woman yet, though she may have learnt a few tricks of them and adapted them to her use. The weight, the pace, the stride of a man's mind are too unlike her own for her to lift anything substantial from him successfully. The ape is too distant to be sedulous. Perhaps the first thing she would find, setting pen to paper, was that there was no common sentence ready for her use. All the great novelists like Thackeray and Dickens and Balzac have written a natural prose, swift but not slovenly, expressive but not precious, taking their own tint without ceasing to be common property. They have based it on the sentence that was current at the time. The sentence that was current at the beginning of the nineteenth century ran something like this perhaps: 'The grandeur of their works was an argument with them, not to stop short, but to proceed. They could have no higher excitement or satisfaction than in the exercise of their art and endless generations of truth and beauty. Success prompts to exertion; and habit facilitates success.' That is a man's sentence; behind it one can see Johnson, Gibbon and the rest. It was a sentence that was unsuited for a woman's use. Charlotte Brontë, with all her splendid gift for prose, stumbled and fell with that clumsy weapon in her hands. George Eliot committed atrocities with it that beggar description. Jane Austen looked at it and laughed at it and devised a perfectly natural, shapely sentence proper for her own use and never departed from it. Thus, with less genius for writing than Charlotte Brontë, she got infinitely more said. Indeed, since freedom and fullness of expression are of the essence of the art, such a lack of tradition, such a scarcity and inadequacy of tools, must have told enormously upon the writing of women. Moreover, a book is not made of sentences laid end to end, but of sentences built, if an image helps, into arcades or domes. And this shape too has been made by men out of their own needs for their own uses. There is no reason to think that the form of the epic or of the poetic play suit a woman any more than the sentence suits her. But all the older forms of literature were hardened and set by the time she became a writer. The novel alone was young enough to be soft in her hands – another reason, perhaps, why she wrote novels. Yet who shall say that even now 'the novel' (I give it inverted commas to mark my sense of the words' inadequacy), who shall say that even this most pliable of all forms is rightly shaped for her use? No doubt we shall find her knocking that into shape for herself when she has the free use of her limbs; and providing some new vehicle, not necessarily in verse, for the poetry in her. For it is the poetry that is still denied outlet. And I went on to ponder how a woman nowadays would write a poetic tragedy in five acts. Would she use verse? – would she not use prose rather?

But these are difficult questions which lie in the twilight of the future. I must leave them, if only because they stimulate me to wander from my subject into trackless forests where I shall be lost and, very likely, devoured by wild beasts. I do not want, and I am sure that you do not want me, to broach that very dismal subject, the future of fiction, so that I will only pause here one moment to draw your attention to the great part which must be played in that future so far as women are concerned by physical conditions. The book has somehow to be adapted to the body, and at a venture one would say that women's books should be shorter, more concentrated, than those of men, and framed so that they do not need long hours of steady and uninterrupted work. For interruptions there will always be. Again, the nerves that feed the brain would seem to differ in men and women, and if you are going to make them work their best and hardest, you must find out what treatment suits them – whether these hours of lectures, for instance, which the monks devised, presumably, hundreds of years ago, suit them – what alternations of work and rest they need, interpreting rest not as doing nothing but as doing something but something that is different; and what should that difference be? All this should be discussed and discovered; all this is part of the question of women and fiction. And yet, I continued, approaching the bookcase again, where shall I find that elaborate study of the psychology of women by a woman? If through their incapacity to play football women are not going to be allowed to practise medicine – Happily my thoughts were now given another turn.

I HAD COME at last, in the course of this rambling, to the shelves which hold books by the living; by women and by men; for there are almost as many books written by women now as by men. Or if that is not yet quite true, if the male is still the voluble sex, it is certainly true that women no longer write novels solely. There are Jane Harrison's books on Greek archaeology; Vernon Lee's books on aesthetics; Gertrude Bell's books on Persia. There are books on all sorts of subjects, which a generation ago no woman could have touched. There are poems and plays and criticism; there are histories and biographies, books of travel and books of scholarship and research; there are even a few philosophies and books about science and economics. And though novels predominate, novels themselves may very well have changed from association with books of a different feather. The natural simplicity, the epic age of women's writing, may have gone. Reading and criticism may have given her a wider range, a greater subtlety. The impulse towards autobiography may be spent. She may be beginning to use writing as an art, not as a method of self-expression. Among these new novels one might find an answer to several such questions.

I took down one of them at random. It stood at the very end of the shelf, was called *Life's Adventure*, or some such title, by Mary Carmichael, and was published in this very month of October. It seems to be her first book, I said to myself, but one must read it as if it were the last volume in a fairly long series, continuing all those other books that I have been glancing at – Lady Winchilsea's poems and Aphra Behn's plays and the novels of the four great novelists. For books continue each other, in spite of our habit of judging them separately. And I must also consider her – this unknown woman – as the descendant of all those other women whose circumstances I have been glancing at and see what she inherits of their characteristics and restrictions. So, with a sigh, because novels so often provide an anodyne and not an antidote, glide one into torpid slumbers instead of rousing one with a burning brand, I settled down with a notebook and a pencil to make what I could of Mary Carmichael's first novel, *Life's Adventure*.

To begin with, I ran my eye up and down the page. I am going to get the hang of her sentences first, I said, before I load my memory with blue eyes and brown and the relationship that there may be between Chloe and Roger. There will be time for that when I have decided whether she has a pen in her hand or a pickaxe. So I tried a sentence or two on my tongue. Soon it was obvious that something was not quite in order. The smooth gliding of sentence after sentence was interrupted. Something tore, something scratched; a single word here and there flashed its torch in my eyes. She was 'unhanding' herself as they say in the old plays. She is like a person striking a match that will not light, I thought. But why, I asked her as if she were present, are Jane Austen's sentences not of the right shape for you? Must they all be scrapped because Emma and Mr Woodhouse are dead? Alas, I sighed, that it should be so. For while Jane Austen breaks from melody to melody as Mozart from song to song, to read this writing was like being out at sea in an open boat. Up one went, down one sank. This terseness, this short-windedness, might mean that she was afraid of something; afraid of being called 'sentimental' perhaps; or she remembers that women's writing has been called flowery and so provides a superfluity of thorns; but until I have read a scene with some care, I cannot be sure whether she is being herself or someone else. At any rate, she does not lower one's vitality, I thought, reading more carefully. But she is heaping up too many facts. She will not be able to use half of them in a book of this size. (It was about half the length of *Jane Eyre*.) However, by some means or other she succeeded in getting us all – Roger, Chloe, Olivia, Tony and Mr Bigham – in a canoe up the river. Wait a moment, I said, leaning back in my chair, I must consider the whole thing more carefully before I go any further.

I am almost sure, I said to myself, that Mary Carmichael is playing a trick on us. For I feel as one feels on a
switchback railway when the car, instead of sinking, as
one has been led to expect, swerves up again. Mary is tampering with the expected sequence. First she broke the
sentence; now she has broken the sequence. Very well, she
has every right to do both these things if she does them
not for the sake of breaking, but for the sake of creating.
Which of the two it is I cannot be sure until she has faced
herself with a situation. I will give her every liberty, I said,
to choose what that situation shall be; she shall make it of
tin cans and old kettles if she likes; but she must convince
me that she believes it to be a situation; and then when she
has made it she must face it. She must jump. And, determined to do my duty by her as reader if she would do her
duty by me as writer, I turned the page and read . . . I am
sorry to break off so abruptly. Are there no men present?
Do you promise me that behind that red curtain over
there the figure of Sir Charles Biron is not concealed? We
are all women you assure me? Then I may tell you that the
very next words I read were these – 'Chloe liked Olivia . . .'
Do not start. Do not blush. Let us admit in the privacy of
our own society that these things sometimes happen.
Sometimes women do like women.

'Chloe liked Olivia,' I read. And then it struck me how
immense a change was there. Chloe liked Olivia perhaps
for the first time in literature. Cleopatra did not like Octavia. And how completely *Antony and Cleopatra* would have

been altered had she done so! As it is, I thought, letting my mind, I am afraid, wander a little from *Life's Adventure*, the whole thing is simplified, conventionalized, if one dared say it, absurdly. Cleopatra's only feeling about Octavia is one of jealousy. Is she taller than I am? How does she do her hair? The play, perhaps, required no more. But how interesting it would have been if the relationship between the two women had been more complicated. All these relationships between women, I thought, rapidly recalling the splendid gallery of fictitious women, are too simple. So much has been left out, unattempted. And I tried to remember any case in the course of my reading where two women are represented as friends. There is an attempt at it in *Diana of the Crossways*. They are confidantes, of course, in Racine and the Greek tragedies. They are now and then mothers and daughters. But almost without exception they are shown in their relation to men. It was strange to think that all the great women of fiction were, until Jane Austen's day, not only seen by the other sex, but seen only in relation to the other sex. And how small a part of a woman's life is that; and how little can a man know even of that when he observes it through the black or rosy spectacles which sex puts upon his nose. Hence, perhaps, the peculiar nature of woman in fiction; the astonishing extremes of her beauty and horror; her alternations between heavenly goodness and hellish depravity – for so a lover would see her as his love rose or sank, was prosperous or unhappy. This is not so true of the nineteenth-century novelists, of course. Woman becomes much more various and complicated there. Indeed it was the desire to write about women perhaps that led men by degrees to abandon the poetic drama which, with its violence, could make so little use of them, and to devise the novel as a more fitting receptacle. Even so it remains obvious, even in the writing of Proust, that a man is terribly hampered and partial in his knowledge of women, as a woman in her knowledge of men.

Also, I continued, looking down at the page again, it is becoming evident that women, like men, have other interests besides the perennial interests of domesticity. 'Chloe liked Olivia. They shared a laboratory together . . .' I read on and discovered that these two young women were engaged in mincing liver, which is, it seems, a cure for pernicious anaemia; although one of them was married and had – I think I am right in stating – two small children. Now all that, of course, has had to be left out, and thus the splendid portrait of the fictitious woman is much too simple and much too monotonous. Suppose, for instance, that men were only represented in literature as the lovers of women, and were never the friends of men, soldiers, thinkers, dreamers; how few parts in the plays of Shakespeare could be allotted to them; how literature would suffer! We might perhaps have most of Othello; and a good deal of Antony; but no Caesar, no Brutus, no Hamlet, no Lear, no Jaques – literature would be incredibly impoverished, as indeed literature is impoverished beyond our counting by the doors that have been shut upon women. Married against their will, kept in one room, and to one occupation, how could a dramatist give a full or interesting or truthful account of them? Love was the only possible interpreter. The poet was forced to be passionate or bitter, unless indeed he chose to 'hate women', which meant more often than not that he was unattractive to them.

Now if Chloe likes Olivia and they share a laboratory, which of itself will make their friendship more varied and lasting because it will be less personal; if Mary Carmichael knows how to write, and I was beginning to enjoy some quality in her style; if she has a room to herself, of which I am not quite sure; if she has five hundred a year of her own – but that remains to be proved – then I think that something of great importance has happened.

For if Chloe likes Olivia and Mary Carmichael knows how to express it she will light a torch in that vast chamber where nobody has yet been. It is all half lights and profound shadows like those serpentine caves where one goes with a candle peering up and down, not knowing where one is stepping. And I began to read the book again, and read how Chloe watched Olivia put a jar on a shelf and say how it was time to go home to her children. That is a sight that has never been seen since the world began, I exclaimed. And I watched too, very curiously. For I wanted to see how Mary Carmichael set to work to catch those unrecorded gestures, those unsaid or half-said words, which form themselves, no more palpably than the shadows of moths on the ceiling, when women are alone, unlit by the capricious and coloured light of the other sex. She will need to hold her breath, I said, reading on, if she is to do it; for women are so suspicious of any interest that has not some obvious motive behind it, so terribly accustomed to concealment and suppression, that they are off at the flicker of an eye turned observingly in their direction. The only way for you to do it, I thought, addressing Mary Carmichael as if she were there, would be to talk of something else, looking steadily out of the window, and thus note, not with a pencil in a notebook, but in the shortest of shorthand, in words that are hardly syllabled yet, what happens when Olivia – this organism that has been under the shadow of the rock these million years – feels the light fall on it, and sees coming her way a piece of strange food – knowledge, adventure, art. And she reaches out for it, I thought, again raising my eyes from the page, and has to devise some entirely new combination of her resources, so highly developed for other purposes, so as to absorb the new into the old without disturbing the infinitely intricate and elaborate balance of the whole.

But, alas, I had done what I had determined not to do; I had slipped unthinkingly into praise of my own sex. 'Highly developed' – 'infinitely intricate' – such are undeniably terms of praise, and to praise one's own sex is always suspect, often silly; moreover, in this case, how could one justify it? One could not go to the map and say

Columbus discovered America and Columbus was a woman; or take an apple and remark, Newton discovered the laws of gravitation and Newton was a woman; or look into the sky and say aeroplanes are flying overhead and aeroplanes were invented by women. There is no mark on the wall to measure the precise height of women. There are no yard measures, neatly divided into the fractions of an inch, that one can lay against the qualities of a good mother or the devotion of a daughter, or the fidelity of a sister, or the capacity of a housekeeper. Few women even now have been graded at the universities; the great trials of the professions, army and navy, trade, politics and diplomacy have hardly tested them. They remain even at this moment almost unclassified. But if I want to know all that a human being can tell me about Sir Hawley Butts, for instance, I have only to open Burke or Debrett and I shall find that he took such and such a degree; owns a hall; has an heir; was Secretary to a Board; represented Great Britain in Canada; and has received a certain number of degrees, offices, medals and other distinctions by which his merits are stamped upon him indelibly. Only Providence can know more about Sir Hawley Butts than that.

When, therefore, I say 'highly developed', 'infinitely intricate' of women, I am unable to verify my words either in Whitaker, Debrett or the University Calendar. In this predicament what can I do? And I looked at the bookcase again. There were the biographies: Johnson and Goethe and Carlyle and Sterne and Cowper and Shelley and

Voltaire and Browning and many others. And I began thinking of all those great men who have for one reason or another admired, sought out, lived with, confided in, made love to, written of, trusted in, and shown what can only be described as some need of and dependence upon certain persons of the opposite sex. That all these relationships were absolutely Platonic I would not affirm, and Sir William Joynson Hicks would probably deny. But we should wrong these illustrious men very greatly if we insisted that they got nothing from these alliances but comfort, flattery and the pleasures of the body. What they got, it is obvious, was something that their own sex was unable to supply; and it would not be rash, perhaps, to define it further, without quoting the doubtless rhapsodical words of the poets, as some stimulus, some renewal of creative power which is in the gift only of the opposite sex to bestow. He would open the door of drawing-room or nursery, I thought, and find her among her children perhaps, or with a piece of embroidery on her knee – at any rate, the centre of some different order and system of life, and the contrast between this world and his own, which might be the law courts or the House of Commons, would at once refresh and invigorate; and there would follow, even in the simplest talk, such a natural difference of opinion that the dried ideas in him would be fertilized anew; and the sight of her creating in a different medium from his own would so quicken his creative power that insensibly his sterile mind would begin to plot again, and he would find the phrase or the scene which was lacking when he put on his hat to visit her. Every Johnson has his Thrale, and holds fast to her for some such reasons as these, and when the Thrale marries her Italian music master Johnson goes half mad with rage and disgust, not merely that he will miss his pleasant evenings at Streatham, but that the light of his life will be 'as if gone out'.

And without being Dr Johnson or Goethe or Carlyle or Voltaire, one may feel, though very differently from these great men, the nature of this intricacy and the power of this highly developed creative faculty among women. One goes into the room – but the resources of the English language would be much put to the stretch, and whole flights of words would need to wing their way illegitimately into existence before a woman could say what happens when she goes into a room. The rooms differ so completely; they are calm or thunderous; open on to the sea, or, on the contrary, give on to a prison yard; are hung with washing; or alive with opals and silks; are hard as horsehair or soft as feathers – one has only to go into any room in any street for the whole of that extremely complex force of femininity to fly in one's face. How should it be otherwise? For women have sat indoors all these millions of years, so that by this time the very walls are permeated by their creative force, which has, indeed, so overcharged the capacity of bricks and mortar that it must needs harness itself to pens and brushes and business and politics. But this creative power differs greatly from the creative power of men. And one must conclude that it would be a thousand pities if it were hindered or wasted, for it was won by centuries of the most drastic discipline, and there is nothing to take its place. It would be a thousand pities if women wrote like men, or lived like men, or looked like men, for if two sexes are quite inadequate, considering the vastness and variety of the world, how should we manage with one only? Ought not education to bring out and fortify the differences rather than the similarities? For we have too much like-ness as it is, and if an explorer should come back and bring word of other sexes looking through the branches of other trees at other skies, nothing would be of greater service to humanity; and we should have the immense pleasure into the bargain of watching Professor X rush for his measuring-rods to prove himself 'superior'.

Mary Carmichael, I thought, still hovering at a little distance above the page, will have her work cut out for her merely as an observer. I am afraid indeed that she will be tempted to become, what I think the less interesting branch of the species – the naturalist-novelist, and not the contemplative. There are so many new facts for her to observe. She will not need to limit herself any longer to the respectable houses of the upper middle classes. She will go without kindness or condescension, but in the spirit of fellowship, into those small, scented rooms where sit the courtesan, the harlot and the lady with the pug dog. There they still sit in the rough and ready-made clothes that the male writer has had perforce to clap upon their shoulders. But Mary Carmichael will have out her scissors and fit them close to every hollow and angle. It will be a curious sight, when it comes, to see these women as they are, but we must wait a little, for Mary Carmichael will still be encumbered with that self-consciousness in the presence of 'sin' which is the legacy of our sexual barbarity. She will still wear the shoddy old fetters of class on her feet.

However, the majority of women are neither harlots nor courtesans; nor do they sit clasping pug dogs to dusty velvet all through the summer afternoon. But what do they do then? and there came to my mind's eye one of those long streets somewhere south of the river whose infinite rows are innumerably populated. With the eye of the imagination I saw a very ancient lady crossing the street on the arm of a middle-aged woman, her daughter, perhaps, both so respectably booted and furred that their dressing in the afternoon must be a ritual, and the clothes themselves put away in cupboards with camphor, year after year, throughout the summer months. They cross the road when the lamps are being lit (for the dusk is their favourite hour), as they must have done year after year. The elder is close on eighty; but if one asked her what her life has meant to her, she would say that she remembered the streets lit for the battle of Balaclava, or had heard the guns fire in Hyde Park for the birth of King Edward the Seventh. And if one asked her, longing to pin down the moment with date and season, but what were you doing on the fifth of April 1868, or the second of November 1875, she would look vague and say that she could remember nothing. For all the dinners are cooked; the plates and cups washed; the children sent to school and gone out into the world. Nothing remains of it all. All has vanished. No biography of history has a word to say about it. And the novels, without meaning to, inevitably lie.

All these infinitely obscure lives remain to be recorded, I said, addressing Mary Carmichael as if she were present; and went on in thought through the streets of London feeling in imagination the pressure of dumbness, the accumulation of unrecorded life, whether from the women at the street corners with their arms akimbo, and the rings embedded in their fat swollen fingers, talking with a gesticulation like the swing of Shakespeare's words; or from the violet-sellers and match-sellers and old crones stationed under doorways; or from drifting girls whose faces, like waves in sun and cloud, signal the coming of men and women and the flickering lights of shop windows. All that you will have to explore, I said to Mary Carmichael, holding your torch firm in your hand. Above all, you must illumine your own soul with its profundities and its shallows, and its vanities and its generosities, and say what your beauty means to you or your plainness, and what is your relation to the everchanging and turning world of gloves and shoes and stuffs swaying up and down among the faint scents that come through chemists' bottles down arcades of dress material over a floor of pseudo-marble. For in imagination I had gone into a shop; it was laid with black and white paving; it was hung, astonishingly beautifully, with coloured ribbons. Mary Carmichael might well have a look at that in passing, I thought, for it is a sight that would lend itself to the pen as fittingly as any snowy peak or rocky gorge in the Andes. And there is the girl behind the counter too – I would as soon have her true history as the hundred and fiftieth life of Napoleon or seventieth study of Keats and his use of Miltonic inversion which old Professor Z and his like are now inditing. And then I went on very warily, on the very tips of my toes (so cowardly am I, so afraid of the lash that was once almost laid on my own shoulders), to murmur that she should also learn to laugh, without bitterness, at the vanities – say rather at the peculiarities, for it is a less offensive word – of the other sex. For there is a spot the size of a shilling at the back of the head which one can never see for oneself. It is one of the good offices that sex can discharge for sex – to describe that spot the size of a shilling at the back of the head. Think how much women have profited by the comments of Juvenal; by the criticism of Strindberg. Think with what humanity and brilliancy men, from the earliest ages, have pointed out to women that dark place at the back of the head! And if Mary were very brave and very honest, she would go behind the other sex and tell us what she found there. A true picture of man as a whole can never be painted until a woman has described that spot the size of a shilling. Mr Woodhouse and Mr Casuabon are spots of that size and nature. Not of course that anyone in their senses would counsel her to hold up to scorn and ridicule of set purpose – literature shows the futility of what is written in that spirit. Be truthful, one would say, and the result is bound to be amazingly interesting. Comedy is bound to be enriched. New facts are bound to be discovered.

However, it was high time to lower my eyes to the page again. It would be better, instead of speculating what Mary Carmichael might write and should write, to see what in fact Mary Carmichael did write. So I began to read again. I remembered that I had certain grievances against her. She had broken up Jane Austen's sentence, and thus given me no chance of pluming myself upon my impeccable taste, my fastidious ear. For it was useless to say, 'Yes, yes, this is very nice; but Jane Austen wrote much better than you do', when I had to admit that there was no point of likeness between them. Then she had gone further and broken the sequence – the expected order. Perhaps she had done this unconsciously, merely giving things their natural order, as a woman would, if she wrote like a woman. But the effect was somehow baffling; one could not see a wave heaping itself, a crisis coming round the next corner. Therefore I could not plume myself either upon the depths of my feelings and my profound knowledge of the human heart. For whenever I was about to feel the usual things in the usual places, about love, about death, the annoying creature twitched me away, as if the important point were just a little further on. And thus she made it impossible for me to roll out my sonorous phrases about 'elemental feelings', the 'common stuff of humanity', 'the depths of the human heart', and all those other phrases which support us in our belief that, however clever we may be on top, we are very serious, very profound and very humane underneath. She made me feel, on the contrary, that instead of being serious and profound and humane, one might be – and the thought was far less seductive – merely lazy minded and conventional into the bargain.

But I read on, and noted certain other facts. She was no 'genius' – that was evident. She had nothing like the love of Nature, the fiery imagination, the wild poetry, the brilliant wit, the brooding wisdom of her great predecessors, Lady Winchilsea, Charlotte Brontë, Emily Brontë, Jane Austen and George Eliot; she could not write with the melody and the dignity of Dorothy Osborne – indeed she was no more than a clever girl whose books will no doubt be pulped by the publishers in ten years' time. But, nevertheless, she had certain advantages which women of far greater gift lacked even half a century ago. Men were no longer to her 'the opposing faction'; she need not waste her time railing against them; she need not climb on to the roof and ruin her peace of mind longing for travel, experience and a knowledge of the world and character that were denied her. Fear and hatred were almost gone, or traces of them showed only in a slight exaggeration of the joy of freedom, a tendency to the caustic and satirical, rather than to the romantic, in her treatment of the other sex. Then there could be no doubt that as a novelist she enjoyed some natural advantages of a high order. She had a sensibility that was very wide, eager and free. It responded to an almost imperceptible touch on it. It feasted like a plant newly stood in the air on every sight and sound that came its way. It ranged, too, very subtly and curiously, among almost unknown or unrecorded things; it lighted on small things and showed that perhaps they were not small after all. It brought buried things to light and made one wonder what need there had been to bury them. Awkward though she was and without the unconscious bearing of long descent which makes the least turn of the pen of a Thackeray or a Lamb delightful to the ear, she had – I began to think – mastered the first great lesson; she wrote as a woman, but as a woman who has forgotten that she is a woman, so that her pages were full of that curious sexual quality which comes only when sex is unconscious of itself.

All this was to the good. But no abundance of sensation or fineness of perception would avail unless she could build up out of the fleeting and the personal the lasting edifice which remains unthrown. I had said that I would wait until she faced herself with 'a situation'. And I meant by that until she proved by summoning, beckoning and getting together that she was not a skimmer of surfaces merely, but had looked beneath into the depths. Now is the time, she would say to herself at a certain moment, when without doing anything violent I can show the meaning of all this. And she would begin – how unmistakable that quickening is! – beckoning and summoning, and there would rise up in memory, half forgotten, perhaps quite trivial things in other chapters dropped by the way. And she would make their presence felt while someone sewed or smoked a pipe as naturally as possible, and one would feel, as she went on writing, as if one had gone to the top of the world and seen it laid out, very majestically, beneath.

At any rate, she was making the attempt. And as I watched her lengthening out for the test, I saw, but hoped that she did not see, the bishops and the deans, the doctors and the professors, the patriarchs and the pedagogues all at her shouting warning and advice. You can't do this and you shan't do that! Fellows and scholars only allowed on the grass! Ladies not admitted without a letter of introduction! Aspiring and graceful female novelists this way! So they kept at her like the crowd at a fence on the racecourse, and it was her trial to take her fence without looking to right or to left. If you stop to curse you are lost, I said to her; equally, if you stop to laugh. Hesitate or fumble and you are done for. Think only of the jump, I implored her, as if I had put the whole of my money on her back; and she went over it like a bird. But there was a fence beyond that and a fence beyond that. Whether she had the staying power I was doubtful, for the clapping and the crying were fraying to the nerves. But she did her best. Considering that Mary Carmichael was no genius, but an unknown girl writing her first novel in a bed-sitting-room, without enough of those desirable things, time, money and idleness, she did not do so badly, I thought.

Give her another hundred years, I concluded, reading the last chapter – people's noses and bare shoulders showed naked against a starry sky, for someone had twitched the curtain in the drawing-room – give her a room of her own and five hundred a year, let her speak her mind and leave out half that she now puts in, and she will write a better book one of these days. She will be a poet, I said, putting *Life's Adventure*, by Mary Carmichael, at the end of the shelf, in another hundred years' time.

From the novel *The Waves*

'NOW THE WIND lifts the blind,' said Susan, 'jars, bowls, matting and the shabby arm-chair with the hole in it are now become distinct. The usual faded ribbons sprinkle the wallpaper. The bird chorus is over, only one bird now sings close to the bedroom window. I will pull on my stockings and go quietly past the bedroom doors, and down through the kitchen, out through the garden past the greenhouse into the field. It is still early morning. The mist is on the marshes. The day is stark and stiff as a linen shroud. But it will soften; it will warm. At this hour, this still early hour, I think I am the field, I am the barn, I am the trees; mine are the flocks of birds, and this young hare who leaps, at the last moment when I step almost on him. Mine is the heron that stretches its vast wings lazily; and the cow that creaks as it pushes one foot before another munching; and the wild, swooping swallow; and the faint red in the sky, and the green when the red fades; the silence and the bell; the call of the man fetching cart-horses from the fields—all are mine.

'I cannot be divided, or kept apart. I was sent to school; I was sent to Switzerland to finish my education. I hate linoleum; I hate fir trees and mountains. Let me now fling myself on this flat ground under a pale sky where the clouds pace slowly. The cart grows gradually larger as it comes along the road. The sheep gather in the middle of the field. The birds gather in the middle of the road—they need not fly yet. The wood smoke rises. The starkness of the dawn is going out of it. Now the day stirs. Colour returns. The day waves yellow with all its crops. The earth hangs heavy beneath me.

'But who am I, who lean on this gate and watch my setter nose in a circle? I think sometimes (I am not twenty yet) I am not a woman, but the light that falls on this gate, on this ground. I am the seasons, I think sometimes, January, May, November; the mud, the mist, the dawn. I cannot be tossed about, or float gently, or mix with other people. Yet now, leaning here till the gate prints my arm, I feel the weight that has formed itself in my side. Something has formed, at school, in Switzerland, some hard thing. Not sighs and laughter; not circling and ingenious phrases; not Rhoda's strange communications when she looks past us, over our shoulders; nor Jinny's pirouetting, all of a piece, limbs and body. What I give is fell. I cannot float gently, mixing with other people. I like best the stare of shepherds met in the road; the stare of gipsy women beside a cart in a ditch suckling their children as I shall suckle my children. For soon in the hot midday when the bees hum round the hollyhocks my lover will come. He will stand under the cedar tree. To his one word I shall answer my one word. What has formed in me I shall give him. I shall have children; I shall have maids in aprons; men with pitchforks; a kitchen where they bring the ailing lambs to warm in baskets, where the hams hang and the onions glisten. I shall be like my mother, silent in a blue apron locking up the cupboards.

'Now I am hungry. I will call my setter. I think of crusts and bread and butter and white plates in a sunny room. I will go back across the fields. I will walk along this grass path with strong, even strides, now swerving to avoid the puddle, now leaping lightly to a clump. Beads of wet form on my rough skirt; my shoes become supple and dark. The stiffness has gone from the day; it is shaded with grey, green and umber. The birds no longer settle on the high road.

'I return, like a cat or fox returning, whose fur is grey with rime, whose pads are hardened by the coarse earth. I push through the cabbages, making their leaves squeak and their drops spill. I sit waiting for my father's footsteps as he shuffles down the passage pinching some herb between his fingers. I pour out cup after cup while the unopened flowers hold themselves erect on the table among the pots of jam, the loaves and the butter. We are silent.

'I go then to the cupboard, and take the damp bags of rich sultanas; I lift the heavy flour on to the clean scrubbed kitchen table. I knead; I stretch; I pull, plunging my hands in the warm inwards of the dough. I let the cold water stream fanwise through my fingers. The fire roars; the flies buzz in a circle. All my currants and rices, the silver bags and the blue bags, are locked again in the cupboard. The meat is stood in the oven; the bread rises in a soft dome under the clean towel. I walk in the afternoon down to the river. All the world is breeding. The flies are going from grass to grass. The flowers are thick with pollen. The swans ride the stream in order. The clouds, warm now, sun-spotted, sweep over the hills, leaving gold in the water, and gold on the necks of the swans. Pushing one foot before the other, the cows munch their way across the field. I feel through the grass for the white-domed mushroom; and break its stalk and pick the purple orchid that grows beside it and lay the orchid by the mushroom with the earth at its root, and so home to make the kettle boil for my father among the just reddened roses on the tea-table.

'But evening comes and the lamps are lit. And when evening comes and the lamps are lit they make a yellow fire in the ivy. I sit with my sewing by the table. I think of Jinny; of Rhoda; and hear the rattle of wheels on the pavement as the farm horses plod home; I hear traffic roaring in the evening wind. I look at the quivering leaves in the dark garden and think "They dance in London. Jinny kisses Louis".'

'How strange,' said Jinny, 'that people should sleep, that people should put out the lights and go upstairs. They have taken off their dresses, they have put on white nightgowns. There are no lights in any of these houses. There is a line of chimney-pots against the sky; and a street lamp or two burning, as lamps burn when nobody needs them. The only people in the streets are poor people hurrying. There is no one coming or going in this street; the day is over. A few policemen stand at the corners. Yet night is beginning. I feel myself shining in the dark. Silk is on my knee. My silk legs rub smoothly together. The stones of a necklace lie cold on my throat. My feet feel the pinch of shoes. I sit bolt upright so that my hair may not touch the back of the seat. I am arrayed, I am prepared. This is the momentary pause; the dark moment. The fiddlers have lifted their bows.

'Now the car slides to a stop. A strip of pavement is lighted. The door is opening and shutting. People are arriving; they do not speak; they hasten in. There is the swishing sound of cloaks falling in the hall. This is the prelude, this is the beginning. I glance, I peep, I powder. All is exact, prepared. My hair is swept in one curve. My lips are precisely red. I am ready now to join men and women on the stairs, my peers. I pass them, exposed to their gaze, as they are to mine. Like lightning we look but do not soften or show signs of recognition. Our bodies communicate. This is my calling. This is my world. All is decided and ready; the servants, standing here, and again here, take my name, my fresh, my unknown name, and toss it before me. I enter.

'Here are gilt chairs in the empty, the expectant rooms,

and flowers, stiller, statelier, than flowers that grow, spread green, spread white, against the walls. And on one small table is one bound book. This is what I have dreamt; this is what I have foretold. I am native here. I tread naturally on thick carpets. I slide easily on smooth-polished floors, I now begin to unfurl, in this scent, in this radiance, as a fern when its curled leaves unfurl. I stop. I take stock of this world. I look among the groups of unknown people. Among the lustrous green, pink, pearl-grey women stand upright the bodies of men. They are black and white; they are grooved beneath their clothes with deep rills. I feel again the reflection in the window of the tunnel; it moves. The black-and-white figures of unknown men look at me as I lean forward; as I turn aside to look at a picture, they turn too. Their hands go fluttering to their ties. They touch their waistcoats, their pocket-handkerchiefs. They are very young. They are anxious to make a good impression. I feel a thousand capacities spring up in me. I am arch, gay, languid, melancholy by turns. I am rooted, but I flow. All gold, flowing that way, I say to this one, "Come." Rippling black, I say to that one, "No." One breaks off from his station under the glass cabinet. He approaches. He makes towards me. This is the most exciting moment I have ever known. I flutter. I ripple. I stream like a plant in the river, flowing this way, flowing that way, but rooted, so that he may come to me. "Come," I say, "come." Pale, with dark hair, the one who is coming is melancholy, romantic. And I am arch and fluent

I feel a thousand capacities spring up in me

and capricious; for he is melancholy, he is romantic. He is here; he stands at my side.

'Now with a little jerk, like a limpet broken from a rock, I am broken off: I fall with him; I am carried off. We yield to this slow flood. We go in and out of this hesitating music. Rocks break the current of the dance; it jars, it shivers. In and out, we are swept now into this large figure; it holds us together; we cannot step outside its sinuous, its hesitating, its abrupt, its perfectly encircling walls. Our bodies, his hard, mine flowing, are pressed together within its body; it holds us together; and then lengthening out, in smooth, in sinuous folds, rolls us between it, on and on. Suddenly the music breaks. My blood runs on but my body stands still. The room reels past my eyes. It stops.

'Come, then, let us wander whirling to the gilt chairs. The body is stronger than I thought. I am dizzier than I supposed. I do not care for anything in the world. I do not care for anybody save this man whose name I do not know. Are we not acceptable, moon? Are we not lovely sitting together here, I in my satin; he in black and white? My peers may look at me now. I look straight back at you, men and women. I am one of you. This is my world. Now I take this thin-stemmed glass and sip. Wine has a drastic, an astringent taste. I cannot help wincing as I drink. Scent and flowers, radiance and heat, are distilled here to a fiery, to a yellow liquid. Just behind my shoulder-blades some dry thing, wide-eyed, gently closes, gradually lulls itself to sleep. This is rapture; this is relief. The bar at the back of my throat lowers itself. Words crowd and cluster and push forth one on top of another. It does not matter which. They jostle and mount on each other's shoulders. The single and the solitary mate, tumble and become many. It does not matter what I say. Crowding, like a fluttering bird, one sentence crosses the empty space between us. It settles on his lips. I fill my glass again. I drink. The veils drop between us. I am admitted to the warmth and privacy of another soul. We are together, high up, on some Alpine pass. He stands melancholy on the crest of the road. I stoop. I pick a blue flower and fix it, standing on tiptoe to reach him, in his coat. There! That is my moment of ecstasy. Now it is over.

'Now slackness and indifference invade us. Other people brush past. We have lost consciousness of our bodies uniting under the table. I also like fair-haired men with blue eyes. The door opens. The door goes on opening. Now I think, next time it opens the whole of my life will be changed. Who comes? But it is only a servant, bringing glasses. That is an old man – I should be a child with him. That is a great lady – with her I should dissemble. There are girls of my own age, for whom I feel the drawn swords of an honourable antagonism. For these are my peers. I am a native of this world. Here is my risk, here is my adventure. The door opens. O come, I say to this one, rippling gold from head to heels. "Come", and he comes towards me.'

'Street Haunting: A London Adventure'

No one perhaps has ever felt passionately towards a lead pencil. But there are circumstances in which it can become supremely desirable to possess one; moments when we are set upon having an object, a purpose, an excuse for walking half across London between tea and dinner. As the foxhunter hunts in order to preserve the breed of horses, and the golfer plays in order that open spaces may be preserved from the builders, so when the desire comes upon us to go street rambling the pencil does for a pretext, and getting up we say, 'Really I must buy a pencil,' as if under cover of this excuse we could indulge safely in the greatest pleasure of town life in winter – rambling the streets of London.

The hour should be evening and the season winter, for in winter the champagne brightness of the air and the sociability of the streets are grateful. We are not then taunted as in summer by the longing for shade and solitude and sweet airs from the hayfields. The evening hour, too, gives us the irresponsibility which darkness and lamplight bestow. We are no longer quite ourselves. As we step out of the house on a fine evening between four and six we shed the self our friends know us by and become part of that vast republican army of anonymous trampers, whose society is so agreeable after the solitude of one's own room. For there we sit surrounded by objects which perpetually express the oddity of our own temperaments and enforce the memories of our own experience. That bowl on the mantelpiece, for instance, was bought at Mantua on a windy day. We were leaving the shop when the sinister old woman plucked at our skirts and said she would find herself starving one of these days, but 'Take it!' she cried, and thrust the blue and white china bowl into our hands as if she never wanted to be reminded of her quixotic generosity. So, guiltily, but suspecting nevertheless how badly we had been fleeced, we carried it back to the little hotel where, in the middle of the night, the innkeeper quarrelled so violently with his wife that we all leant out into the courtyard to look, and saw the vines laced about among the pillars and the stars white in the sky. The moment was stabilised, stamped like a coin indelibly, among a million that slipped by imperceptibly. There, too, was the melancholy Englishman, who rose among the coffee cups and the little iron tables and revealed the secrets of his soul – as travellers do. All this – Italy, the windy morning, the vines laced about the pillars, the Englishman and the secrets of his soul – rise up in a cloud from the china bowl on the mantelpiece. And there, as our eyes fall to the floor, is that brown stamp on the carpet. Mr Lloyd George made that. 'The man's a devil!' said Mr Cummings, putting the kettle down with which he was about to fill the teapot so that it burnt a brown ring on the carpet.

But when the door shuts on us, all that vanishes. The shell-like covering which our souls have excreted to house themselves, to make for themselves a shape distinct from others, is broken, and there is left of all these wrinkles and roughness a central oyster of perceptiveness, an enormous eye. How beautiful a street is in winter! It is at once revealed and obscured. Here vaguely one can trace symmetrical straight avenues of doors and windows; here under the lamps are floating islands of pale light through which pass quickly bright men and women, who for all their poverty and shabbiness wear a certain look of unreality, an air of triumph, as if they had given life the slip, so that life, deceived of her prey, blunders on without them. But, after all, we are only gliding smoothly on the surface. The eye is not a miner, not a diver, not a seeker after buried treasure. It floats us smoothly down a stream, resting, pausing, the brain sleeps perhaps as it looks.

How beautiful a London street is then, with its islands of light, and its long groves of darkness, and on one side of it perhaps some tree-sprinkled, grass-grown space where night is folding herself to sleep naturally and, as one passes the iron railing, one hears those little cracklings and stirrings of leaf and twig which seem to suppose the silence of fields all round them, an owl hooting, and far away the rattle of a train in the valley. But this is London, we are reminded; high among the bare trees are hung oblong frames of reddish yellow light – windows; there are points of brilliance burning steady like low stars – lamps; this empty ground which holds the country in it and its peace is only a London square, set about by offices and houses where at this hour fierce lights burn over maps, over documents, over desks where clerks sit turning with wetted forefingers the files of endless correspondences; or more suffusedly the firelight wavers and the lamplight falls upon the privacy of some drawing-room, its easy chairs, its papers, its china, its inlaid table, and the figure of a woman, accurately measuring out the precise number of spoons of tea which – She looks at the door as if she heard a ring downstairs and somebody asking, is she in?

But here we must stop peremptorily. We are in danger of digging deeper than the eye approves; we are impeding our passage down the smooth stream by catching at some branch or root. At any moment, the sleeping army may stir itself and wake in us a thousand violins and trumpets in response; the army of human beings may rouse itself and assert all its oddities and sufferings and sordidities. Let us dally a little longer, be content still with surfaces only – the glossy brilliance of the motor omnibuses; the carnal splendour of the butchers' shops with their yellow flanks and their purple streaks; the blue and red bunches of flowers burning so bravely through the plate glass of the florists' windows.

For the eye has this strange property: it rests only on beauty; like a butterfly it seeks out colour and basks in warmth. On a winter's night like this, when Nature has been at pains to polish and preen itself, it brings back the prettiest trophies, breaks off little lumps of emerald and coral as if the whole earth were made of precious stone. The thing it cannot do (one is speaking of the average unprofessional eye) is to compose these trophies in such a way as to bring out their more obscure angles and relationships. Hence after a prolonged diet of this simple, sugary fare, of beauty pure and uncomposed, we become conscious of satiety. We halt at the door of the boot shop and make some little excuse, which has nothing to do with the real reason for folding up the bright paraphernalia of the streets and withdrawing to some duskier chamber of the being where we may ask, as we raise our left foot obediently upon the stand, 'What, then, is it like to be a dwarf?'

She came in escorted by two women who, being of normal size, looked like benevolent giants beside her. Smiling at the shop girls, they seemed to be at once disclaiming any lot in her deformity and assuring her of their protection. She wore the peevish yet apologetic expression usual on the faces of the deformed. She needed their kindness, yet she resented it. But when the shop girl has been summoned and the giantesses, smiling indulgently, had asked for shoes for 'this lady' and the girl had pushed the little stand in front of her, the dwarf stuck her foot out with an impetuosity which seemed to claim all our attention. Look at that! Look at that! she seemed to demand of us all, as she thrust her foot out, for behold it was the shapely, perfectly proportioned foot of a well-grown woman. It was arched; it was aristocratic. Her whole manner changed as she looked at it resting on the stand. She looked soothed and satisfied. Her manner became full of self-confidence. She sent for shoe after shoe; she tried on pair after pair. She got up and pirouetted before a glass which reflected the foot only in yellow shoes, in fawn shoes, in shoes of lizard skin. She raised her little skirts and displayed her little legs. She was thinking that, after all, feet are the most important part of the whole person; women, she said to herself, have been loved for their feet alone. Seeing nothing but her feet, she imagined perhaps that the rest of her body was of a piece with those beautiful feet. She was shabbily dressed, but she was ready to lavish any money upon her shoes. And as this was the only occasion upon which she was not afraid of being looked at but positively craved attention, she was ready to use any device to prolong the choosing and fitting. Look at my feet, look at my feet, she seemed to be saying, as she took a step this way and then a step that way. The shop girl good-humouredly must have said something flattering, for suddenly her face lit up in an ecstasy. But, after all, the giantesses, benevolent though they were, had their own affairs to see to; she must make up her mind; she must decide which to choose. At length, the pair was chosen and, as she walked out between her guardians, with the parcel swinging from her finger, the ecstasy faded, knowledge returned, the old peevishness, the old apology came back, and by the time she had reached the street again she had become a dwarf.

But she had changed the mood; she had called into being an atmosphere which, as we followed her out into the street, seemed actually to create the humped, the twisted, the deformed. Two bearded men, brothers apparently, stone-blind, supporting themselves by resting a hand on the head of a small boy between them, marched down the street. On they came with the unyielding yet tremulous tread of the blind, which seems to lend to their approach something of the terror and inevitability of the fate that has overtaken them. As they passed, holding straight on, the little convoy seemed to cleave asunder the passers-by with the momentum of its silence, its directness, its disaster. Indeed, the dwarf had started a hobbling grotesque dance to which everybody in the street now conformed: the stout lady tightly swathed in shiny sealskin; the feeble-minded boy sucking the silver knob of his stick; the old man squatted on a doorstep as if, suddenly overcome by the absurdity of the human spectacle, he had sat down to look at it – all joined in the hobble and tap of the dwarf's dance.

In what crevices and crannies, one might ask, did they

lodge, this maimed company of the halt and the blind? Here, perhaps, in the top rooms of these narrow old houses between Holborn and the Strand, where people have such queer names, and pursue so many curious trades, are gold beaters, accordion pleaters, cover buttons, or others who support life, with even greater fantasticality, upon a traffic in cups with saucers, china umbrella handles, and highly coloured pictures of martyred saints. There they lodge, and it seems as if the lady in the sealskin jacket must find life tolerable, passing the time of day with the accordion pleater, or the man who covers buttons; life which is so fantastic cannot be altogether tragic. They do not grudge us, we are musing, our prosperity; when, suddenly, turning the corner, we come upon a bearded Jew, wild, hunger-bitten, glaring out of his misery; or pass the humped body of an old woman flung abandoned on the step of a public building with a cloak over her like the hasty covering thrown over a dead horse or donkey. At such sights, the nerves of the spine seem to stand erect; a sudden flare is brandished in our eyes; a question is asked which is never answered. Often enough these derelicts choose to lie not a stone's throw from theatres, within hearing of barrel organs, almost, as night draws on, within touch of the sequined cloaks and bright legs of diners and dancers. They lie close to those shop windows where commerce offers to a world of old women laid on doorsteps, of blind men, of hobbling dwarfs, sofas which are supported by the gilt necks of proud swans; tables inlaid with baskets of many coloured fruit, sideboards paved with green marble the better to support the weight of boars' heads, gilt baskets, candelabra; and carpets so softened with age that their carnations have almost vanished in a pale green sea.

Passing, glimpsing, everything seems accidentally but miraculously sprinkled with beauty, as if the tide of trade which deposits its burden so punctually and prosaically upon the shores of Oxford Street had this night cast up nothing but treasure. With no thought of buying, the eye is sportive and generous; it creates; it adorns; it enhances. Standing out in the street, one may build up all the chambers of a vast imaginary house and furnish them at one's will with sofa, table, carpet. That rug will do for the hall. That alabaster bowl shall stand on a carved table in the window. Our merrymakings shall be reflected in that thick round mirror. But, having built and furnished the house one is happily under no obligation to possess it; one can dismantle it in the twinkling of an eye, build and furnish another house with other chairs and other glasses. Or let us indulge ourselves at the antique jewellers, among the trays of rings and the hanging necklaces. Let us choose those pearls, for example, and then imagine how, if we put them on, life would be changed. It becomes instantly between two and three in the morning; the lamps are burning very white in the deserted streets of Mayfair. Only motor cars are abroad at this hour, and one has a sense of emptiness, of airiness, of secluded gaiety.

Wearing pearls, wearing silk, one steps out on to a balcony which overlooks the gardens of sleeping Mayfair.
There are a few lights in the bedrooms of great peers
returned from Court, of silk-stockinged footmen, of dow-
agers who have pressed the hands of statesmen. A cat
creeps along the garden wall. Love-making is going on
sibilantly, seductively in the darker places of the room
behind thick green curtains. Strolling sedately as if he
were promenading a terrace beneath which the shires and
counties of England lie sun-bathed, the aged Prime Minister recounts to Lady So-and-So with the curls and the
emeralds the true history of some great crisis in the affairs
of the land. We seem to be riding on the top of the highest
mast of the tallest ship; and yet at the same time we know
that nothing of this sort matters, love is not proved thus,
nor great achievements completed thus; so that we sport
with the moment and preen our feathers in it lightly, as we
stand on the balcony watching the moonlit cat creep
along Princess Mary's garden wall.

But what could be more absurd? It is, in fact, on the
stroke of six; it is a winter's evening; we are walking to the
Strand to buy a pencil. How then are we also on a balcony,
wearing pearls in June? What could be more absurd? Yet
it is Nature's folly, not ours. When she set about her chief
masterpiece, the making of man, she should have thought
of one thing only. Instead, turning her head, looking over
her shoulder, into each one of us she let creep instincts
and desires which are utterly at variance with his main

being, so that we are streaked, variegated, all of a mixture; the colours have run. Is the true self this which stands on the pavement in January, or that which bends over the balcony in June? Am I here, or am I there? Or is the true self neither this nor that, neither here nor there, but something so varied and wandering that it is only when we give the rein to its wishes and let it take its way unimpeded that we are indeed ourselves? Circumstances compel unity; for convenience' sake a man must be a whole. The good citizen when he opens his door in the evening must be banker, golfer, husband, father; not a nomad wandering the desert, a mystic staring at the sky, a debauchee in the slums of San Francisco, a soldier heading a revolution, a pariah howling with scepticism and solitude. When he opens his door, he must run his fingers through his hair and put his umbrella in the stand like the rest.

But here, none too soon, are the second-hand bookshops. Here we find anchorage in these thwarting currents of being; here we balance ourselves after the splendours and miseries of the streets. The very sight of the bookseller's wife with her foot on the fender, sitting beside a good coal fire, screened from the door, is sobering and cheerful. She is never reading, or has only the newspaper; her talk when it leaves bookselling, as it does so gladly, is about hats; she likes a hat to be practical, she says, as well as pretty. Oh no, they don't live at the shop; they live at Brixton; she must have a bit of green to look at. In summer a jar of flowers grown in her own garden is stood on the top of some dusty pile to enliven the shop. Books are everywhere; and always the same sense of adventure fills us. Second-hand books are wild books, homeless books; they have come together in vast flocks of variegated feather, and have a charm which the domesticated volumes of the library lack. Besides, in this random, miscellaneous company we may rub against some complete stranger who will, with luck, turn into the best friend we have in the world. There is always a hope, as we reach down some greyish-white book from an upper shelf, directed by its air of shabbiness and desertion, of meeting here with a man who set out on horseback over a hundred years ago to explore the woollen market in the midlands and Wales; an unknown traveller, who stayed at inns, drank his pint, noted pretty girls and serious customs, wrote it all down stiffly, laboriously for sheer love of it (the book was published at his own expense); was infinitely prosy, busy, and matter-of-fact, and so let flow in without his knowing it the very scent of the hollyhocks and the hay together with such a portrait of himself as gives him forever a seat in the warm corner of the mind's inglenook. One may buy him for eighteen pence now. He is marked three and sixpence, but the bookseller's wife, seeing how shabby the covers are and how long the book has stood there since it was bought at some sale of a gentleman's library in Suffolk, will let it go at that.

Thus, glancing round the bookshop, we make other

such sudden capricious friendships with the unknown and the vanished whose only record is, for example, this little book of poems, so fairly printed, so finely engraved, too, with a portrait of the author. For he was a poet and drowned untimely, and his verse, mild as it is and formal and sententious, sends forth still a frail fluty sound like that of a piano organ played in some back street resignedly by an old Italian organ-grinder in a corduroy jacket. There are travellers, too, row upon row of them, still testifying, indomitable spinsters that they were, to the discomforts that they endured and the sunsets they admired in Greece when Queen Victoria was a girl; a tour in Cornwall with a visit to the tin mines was thought worthy of voluminous record; people went slowly up the Rhine and did portraits of each other in Indian ink, sitting reading on deck beside a coil of rope; they measured the pyramids; were lost to civilisation for years; converted negroes in pestilential swamps. This packing up and going off, exploring deserts and catching fevers, settling in India for a lifetime, penetrating even to China and then returning to lead a parochial life at Edmonton, tumbles and tosses upon the dusty floor like an uneasy sea, so restless the English are, with the waves at their very door. The waters of travel and adventure seem to break upon little islands of serious effort and lifelong industry stood in jagged column upon the bookshop floor. In these piles of puce-bound volumes with gilt monograms on the back, thoughtful clergymen expound the gospels; scholars are to be heard with their hammers and their chisels chipping clear the ancient texts of Euripides and Aeschylus. Thinking, annotating, expounding, goes on at a prodigious rate all round us and over everything, like a punctual, everlasting tide, washes the ancient sea of fiction. Innumerable volumes tell how Arthur loved Laura and they were separated and they were unhappy and then they met and they were happy ever after, as was the way when Victoria ruled these islands.

The number of books in the world is infinite, and one is forced to glimpse and nod and go on after a moment of talk, a flash of understanding, as, in the street outside, one catches a word in passing and from a chance phrase fabricates a lifetime. It is about a woman called Kate that they are talking, how 'I said to her, quite straight last night . . . if you don't think I'm worth a penny stamp, I said . . .' But who Kate is, and to what crisis in their friendship the penny stamp refers, we shall never know; for Kate sinks under the warmth of their volubility; and here, at the street corner, another page of the volume of life is laid open by the sight of two men consulting under the lamp post. They are spelling out the latest wire from Newmarket in the stop press news. Do they think, then, that fortune will ever convert their rags into fur and broad-cloth, sling them with watch chains, and plant diamond pins where there is now a ragged open shirt? But the main stream of walkers at this hour sweeps too fast to let us ask such questions. They are wrapt, in this short passage from work to home, in some narcotic dream, now that they are free from the desk, and have the fresh air on their cheeks. They put on those bright clothes which they must hang up and lock the key upon all the rest of the day, and are great cricketers, famous actresses, soldiers who have saved their country at the hour of need. Dreaming, gesticulating, often muttering a few words aloud, they sweep over the Strand and across Waterloo Bridge whence they will be swung in long rattling trains, still dreaming, to some prim little villa in Barnes or Surbiton where the sight of the clock in the hall and the smell of the supper in the basement puncture the dream.

But we are come to the Strand now, and as we hesitate on the curb, a little rod about the length of one's finger begins to lay its bar across the velocity and abundance of life. 'Really I must – really I must' – that is it. Without investigating the demand, the mind cringes to the accustomed tyrant. One must, one always must, do something or other; it is not allowed one simply to enjoy oneself. Was it not for this reason that, some time ago, we fabricated that excuse, and invented the necessity of buying something? But what was it? Ah, we remember, it was a pencil. Let us go then and buy this pencil. But just as we are turning to obey the command, another self disputes the right of the tyrant to insist. The usual conflict comes about. Spread out behind the rod of duty we see the whole breadth of the River Thames – wide, mournful, peaceful. And we see it through the eyes of somebody who is leaning over the Embankment on a summer evening, without a care in the world. Let us put off buying the pencil; let us go in search of this person (and soon it becomes apparent that this person is ourselves). For if we could stand there where we stood six months ago, should we not be again as we were then – calm, aloof, content? Let us try then. But the river is rougher and greyer than we remembered. The tide is running out to sea. It brings down with it a tug and two barges, whose load of straw is tightly bound down beneath tarpaulin covers. There is too, close by us, a couple leaning over the balustrade murmuring with that curious lack of self-consciousness which lovers have, as if the importance of the affair they are engaged on claims without question the indulgence of the human race. The sights we see and the sounds we hear now have none of the quality of the past; nor have we any share in the serenity of the person who, six months ago, stood precisely where we stand now. His is the happiness of death; ours the insecurity of life. He has no future; the future is even now invading our peace. It is only when we look at the past and take from it the element of uncertainty that we can enjoy perfect peace. As it is, we must turn, we must cross the Strand again, we must find a shop where, even at this hour, they will be ready to sell us a pencil.

It is always an adventure to enter a new room; for the lives and characters of its owners have distilled their atmosphere into it, and directly we enter it we breast some new wave of emotion. Here, without a doubt, in the

It is always an adventure to enter a new room

stationer's shop people had been quarrelling. Their anger
shot through the air. They both stopped; the old woman –
they were husband and wife evidently – retired to a back
room; the old man whose rounded forehead and globular
eyes would have looked well on the frontispiece of some
Elizabethan folio, stayed to serve us. 'A pencil, a pencil,'
he repeated, 'certainly, certainly.' He spoke with the distraction yet effusiveness of one whose emotions have
been roused and checked in full flood. He began opening
box after box and shutting them again. He said that it was
very difficult to find things when they kept so many different articles. He launched into a story about some legal
gentleman who had got into deep waters owing to the
conduct of his wife. He had known him for years; he had
been connected with the Temple for half a century, he
said, as if he wished his wife in the back room to overhear
him. He upset a box of rubber bands. At last, exasperated
by his incompetence, he pushed the swing door open and
called out roughly, 'Where d'you keep the pencils?' as if
his wife had hidden them. The old lady came in. Looking
at nobody, she put her hand with a fine air of righteous
severity upon the right box. There were the pencils. How
then could he do without her? Was she not indispensable
to him? In order to keep them there, standing side by side
in forced neutrality, one had to be particular in one's
choice of pencils; this was too soft, that too hard. They
stood silently looking on. The longer they stood there, the
calmer they grew; their heat was going down, their anger

disappearing. Now, without a word said on either side, the quarrel was made up. The old man who would not have disgraced Ben Jonson's title-page, reached the box back to its proper place, bowed profoundly his good night to us, and they disappeared. She would get out her sewing; he would read his newspaper; the canary would scatter them impartially with seed. The quarrel was over.

During these minutes in which a ghost had been sought for, a quarrel composed, and a pencil bought, the streets had become completely empty. Life had withdrawn to the top floor, and lamps were lit. The pavement was dry and hard; the road was of hammered silver. Walking home through the desolation one could tell oneself the story of the dwarf, of the blind men, of the party in the Mayfair mansion, of the quarrel in the stationer's shop. Into each of these lives one could penetrate a little way, far enough to give oneself the illusion that one is not tethered to a single mind but can put on briefly for a few minutes the bodies and minds of others. One could become a washer-woman, a publican, a street singer. And what greater delight and wonder can there be than to leave the straight lines of personality and deviate into those footpaths that lead beneath brambles and thick tree trunks into the heart of the forest where live those wild beasts, our fellow men?

That is true: to escape is the greatest of pleasures; street haunting in winter the greatest of adventures. Still as we approach our own doorstep again, it is comforting to feel the old possessions, the old prejudices, fold us round, and shelter and enclose the self which has been blown about at so many street corners, which has battered like a moth at the flame of so many inaccessible lanterns. Here again is the usual door; here the chair turned as we left it and the china bowl and the brown ring on the carpet. And here – let us examine it tenderly, let us touch it with reverence – is the only spoil we have retrieved from the treasures of the city, a lead pencil.

'How Should One Read a Book?'

IN THE FIRST place, I want to emphasise the note of interrogation at the end of my title. Even if I could answer the question for myself, the answer would apply only to me and not to you. The only advice, indeed, that one person can give another about reading is to take no advice, to follow your own instincts, to use your own reason, to come to your own conclusions. If this is agreed between us, then I feel at liberty to put forward a few ideas and suggestions because you will not allow them to fetter that independence which is the most important quality that a reader can possess. After all, what laws can be laid down about books? The battle of Waterloo was certainly fought on a certain day; but is *Hamlet* a better play than *Lear*? Nobody can say. Each must decide that question for himself. To admit authorities, however heavily furred and gowned, into our libraries and let them tell us how to read, what to read, what value to place upon what we read, is to destroy the spirit of freedom which is the breath of those sanctuaries. Everywhere else we may be bound by laws and conventions – there we have none.

But to enjoy freedom, if the platitude is pardonable, we have of course to control ourselves. We must not squander our powers, helplessly and ignorantly, squirting half the house in order to water a single rose-bush; we must train them, exactly and powerfully, here on the very spot. This, it may be, is one of the first difficulties that faces us in a library. What is 'the very spot'? There may well seem to be nothing but a conglomeration and huddle of confusion. Poems and novels, histories and memories, dictionaries and blue-books; books written in all languages by men and women of all tempers, races, and ages jostle each other on the shelf. And outside the donkey brays, the women gossip at the pump, the colts gallop across the fields. Where are we to begin? How are we to bring order into this multitudinous chaos and so get the deepest and widest pleasure from what we read?

It is simple enough to say that since books have classes – fiction, biography, poetry – we should separate them and take from each what it is right that each should give us. Yet few people ask from books what books can give us. Most commonly we come to books with blurred and divided minds, asking of fiction that it shall be true, of poetry that it shall be false, of biography that it shall be flattering, of history that it shall enforce our own prejudices. If we could banish all such preconceptions when we read, that would be an admirable beginning. Do not dictate to your author; try to become him. Be his fellow-worker and accomplice. If you hang back, and reserve and criticise at first, you are preventing yourself from getting the fullest possible value from what you read. But if you open your mind as widely as possible, then signs and hints of almost imperceptible fineness, from the twist and turn of the first sentences, will bring you into the presence of a human being unlike any other. Steep yourself in this, acquaint yourself with this, and soon you will find that your author is giving you, or attempting to give you, something far more definite. The thirty-two chapters of a novel – if we consider how to read a novel first – are an attempt to make something as formed and controlled as a building: but words are more impalpable than bricks; reading is a longer and more complicated process than seeing. Perhaps the quickest way to understand the elements of what a novelist is doing is not to read, but to write; to make your own experiment with the dangers and difficulties of words. Recall, then, some event that has left a distinct impression on you – how at the corner of the street, perhaps, you passed two people talking. A tree shook; an electric light danced; the tone of the talk was comic, but also tragic; a whole vision, an entire conception, seemed contained in that moment.

But when you attempt to reconstruct it in words, you will find that it breaks into a thousand conflicting impressions. Some must be subdued; others emphasised; in the process you will lose, probably, all grasp upon the emotion itself. Then turn from your blurred and littered pages to the opening pages of some great novelist – Defoe, Jane Austen, Hardy. Now you will be better able to appreciate their mastery. It is not merely that we are in the presence of a different person – Defoe, Jane Austen, or Thomas Hardy – but that we are living in a different world. Here, in *Robinson Crusoe*, we are trudging a plain high road; one thing happens after another; the fact and the order of the fact is enough. But if the open air and adventure mean everything to Defoe they mean nothing to Jane Austen. Hers is the drawing-room, and people talking, and by the many mirrors of their talk revealing their characters. And if, when we have accustomed ourselves to the drawing-room and its reflections, we turn to Hardy, we are once more spun round. The moors are round us and the stars are above our heads. The other side of the mind is now exposed – the dark side that comes uppermost in solitude, not the light side that shows in company. Our relations are not towards people, but towards Nature and destiny. Yet different as these worlds are, each is consistent with itself. The maker of each is careful to observe the laws of his own perspective, and however great a strain they may put upon us they will never confuse us, as lesser writers so frequently do, by introducing two different kinds of reality into the same book. Thus to go from one great novelist to another – from Jane Austen to Hardy, from Peacock to Trollope, from Scott to Meredith – is to be wrenched and uprooted; to be thrown this way and then that. To read a novel is a difficult and complex art. You must be capable not only of great fineness of perception, but of great boldness of imagination if you are going to make use of all that the novelist – the great artist – gives you.

But a glance at the heterogeneous company on the shelf will show you that writers are very seldom 'great artists'; far more often a book makes no claim to be a work of art at all. These biographies and autobiographies, for example, lives of great men, of men long dead and forgotten, that stand cheek by jowl with the novels and poems, are we to refuse to read them because they are not 'art'? Or shall we read them, but read them in a different way, with a different aim? Shall we read them in the first place to satisfy that curiosity which possesses us sometimes when in the evening we linger in front of a house where the lights are lit and the blinds not yet drawn, and each floor of the house shows us a different section of human life in being? Then we are consumed with curiosity about the lives of these people – the servants gossiping, the gentlemen dining, the girl dressing for a party, the old woman at the window with her knitting. Who are they, what are they, what are their names, their occupations, their thoughts, and adventures?

Biographies and memoirs answer such questions, light up innumerable such houses; they show us people going about their daily affairs, toiling, failing, succeeding, eating, hating, loving, until they die. And sometimes as we watch, the house fades and the iron railings vanish and we are out at sea; we are hunting, sailing, fighting; we are among savages and soldiers; we are taking part in great campaigns. Or if we like to stay here in England, in London, still the scene changes; the street narrows; the house becomes small, cramped, diamond-paned, and malodorous. We see a poet, Donne, driven from such a house because the walls were so thin that when the children cried their voices cut through them. We can follow him, through the paths that lie in the pages of books, to Twickenham; to Lady Bedford's Park, a famous meeting-ground for nobles and poets; and then turn our steps to Wilton, the great house under the downs, and hear Sidney read the *Arcadia* to his sister; and ramble among the very marshes and see the very herons that figure in that famous romance; and then again travel north with that other Lady Pembroke, Anne Clifford, to her wild moors, or plunge into the city and control our merriment at the sight of Gabriel Harvey in his black velvet suit arguing about poetry with Spenser. Nothing is more fascinating than to grope and stumble in the alternate darkness and splendour of Elizabethan London. But there is no staying there. The Temples and the Swifts, the Harleys and the St Johns beckon us on; hour upon hour can be spent disentangling their quarrels and deciphering their characters; and when we tire of them we can stroll on, past a lady in

black wearing diamonds, to Samuel Johnson and Gold-
smith and Garrick; or cross the channel, if we like, and
meet Voltaire and Diderot, Madame du Deffand; and so
back to England and Twickenham – how certain places
repeat themselves and certain names! – where Lady Bedford had her Park once and Pope lived later, to Walpole's
home at Strawberry Hill. But Walpole introduces us to
such a swarm of new acquaintances, there are so many
houses to visit and bells to ring that we may well hesitate
for a moment, on the Miss Berrys' doorstep, for example,
when behold, up comes Thackeray; he is the friend of the
woman whom Walpole loved; so that merely by going
from friend to friend, from garden to garden, from house
to house, we have passed from one end of English literature to another and wake to find ourselves here again in
the present, if we can so differentiate this moment from
all that have gone before. This, then, is one of the ways in
which we can read these lives and letters; we can make
them light up the many windows of the past; we can watch
the famous dead in their familiar habits and fancy sometimes that we are very close and can surprise their secrets,
and sometimes we may pull out a play or a poem that they
have written and see whether it reads differently in the
presence of the author. But this again rouses other questions. How far, we must ask ourselves, is a book influenced
by its writer's life – how far is it safe to let the man interpret the writer? How far shall we resist or give way to the
sympathies and antipathies that the man himself rouses

in us – so sensitive are words, so receptive of the character of the author? These are questions that press upon us when we read lives and letters, and we must answer them for ourselves, for nothing can be more fatal than to be guided by the preferences of others in a matter so personal.

But also we can read such books with another aim, not to throw light on literature, not to become familiar with famous people, but to refresh and exercise our own creative powers. Is there not an open window on the right hand of the bookcase? How delightful to stop reading and look out! How stimulating the scene is, in its unconsciousness, its irrelevance, its perpetual movement – the colts galloping round the field, the woman filling her pail at the well, the donkey throwing back his head and emitting his long, acrid moan. The greater part of any library is nothing but the record of such fleeting moments in the lives of men, women, and donkeys. Every literature, as it grows old, has its rubbish-heap, its record of vanished moments and forgotten lives told in faltering and feeble accents that have perished. But if you give yourself up to the delight of rubbish-reading you will be surprised, indeed you will be overcome, by the relics of human life that have been cast out to moulder. It may be one letter – but what a vision it gives! It may be a few sentences – but what vistas they suggest! Sometimes a whole story will come together with such beautiful humour and pathos and completeness that it seems as if a great novelist had been at work, yet it is only an old actor, Tate Wilkinson, remembering the strange story of Captain Jones; it is only a young subaltern serving under Arthur Wellesley and falling in love with a pretty girl at Lisbon; it is only Maria Allen letting fall her sewing in the empty drawing-room and sighing how she wishes she had taken Dr Burney's good advice and had never eloped with her Rishy. None of this has any value; it is negligible in the extreme; yet how absorbing it is now and again to go through the rubbish-heaps and find rings and scissors and broken noses buried in the huge past and try to piece them together while the colt gallops round the field, the woman fills her pail at the well, and the donkey brays.

But we tire of rubbish-reading in the long run. We tire of searching for what is needed to complete the half-truth which is all that the Wilkinsons, the Bunburys and the Maria Allens are able to offer us. They had not the artist's power of mastering and eliminating; they could not tell the whole truth even about their own lives; they have disfigured the story that might have been so shapely. Facts are all that they can offer us, and facts are a very inferior form of fiction. Thus the desire grows upon us to have done with half-statements and approximations; to cease from searching out the minute shades of human character, to enjoy the greater abstractness, the purer truth of fiction. Thus we create the mood, intense and generalised, unaware of detail, but stressed by some regular, recurrent beat, whose natural expression is poetry;

and that is the time to read poetry when we are almost able to write it.

> Western wind, when wilt thou blow?
> The small rain down can rain.
> Christ, if my love were in my arms,
> And I in my bed again!

The impact of poetry is so hard and direct that for the moment there is no other sensation except that of the poem itself. What profound depths we visit then – how sudden and complete is our immersion! There is nothing here to catch hold of; nothing to stay us in our flight. The illusion of fiction is gradual; its effects are prepared; but who when they read these four lines stops to ask who wrote them, or conjures up the thought of Donne's house or Sidney's secretary; or enmeshes them in the intricacy of the past and the succession of generations? The poet is always our contemporary. Our being for the moment is centred and constricted, as in any violent shock of personal emotion. Afterwards, it is true, the sensation begins to spread in wider rings through our minds; remoter senses are reached; these begin to sound and to comment and we are aware of echoes and reflections. The intensity of poetry covers an immense range of emotion. We have only to compare the force and directness of

> I shall fall like a tree, and find my grave,
>   Only remembering that I grieve,

with the wavering modulation of

> Minutes are numbered by the fall of sands,
> As by an hour glass; the span of time
> Doth waste us to our graves, and we look on it;
> An age of pleasure, revelled out, comes home
> At last, and ends in sorrow; but the life,
> Weary of riot, numbers every sand,
> Wailing in sighs, until the last drop down,
> So to conclude calamity in rest,

or place the meditative calm of

> whether we be young or old,
> Our destiny, our being's heart and home,
> Is with infinitude, and only there;
> With hope it is, hope that can never die,
> Effort, and expectation, and desire,
> And effort evermore about to be,

beside the complete and inexhaustible loveliness of

> The moving Moon went up the sky,
> And nowhere did abide:
> Softly she was going up,
> And a star or two beside –

or the splendid fantasy of

> And the woodland haunter
> Shall not cease to saunter
> When, far down some glade,
> Of the great world's burning,
> One soft flame upturning
> Seems, to his discerning,
> Crocus in the shade,

to bethink us of the varied art of the poet; his power to make us at once actors and spectators; his power to run his hand into characters as if it were a glove, and be Falstaff or Lear; his power to condense, to widen, to state, once and for ever.

'We have only to compare' – with those words the cat is out of the bag, and the true complexity of reading is admitted. The first process, to receive impressions with the utmost understanding, is only half the process of reading; it must be completed, if we are to get the whole pleasure from a book, by another. We must pass judgment upon these multitudinous impressions; we must make of these fleeting shapes one that is hard and lasting. But not directly. Wait for the dust of reading to settle; for the conflict and the questioning to die down; walk, talk, pull the dead petals from a rose, or fall asleep. Then suddenly without our willing it, for it is thus that Nature undertakes these transitions, the book will return, but differently. It will float to the top of the mind as a whole. And the book as a whole is different from the book received currently in separate phrases. Details now fit themselves into their places. We see the shape from start to finish; it is a barn, a pig-sty, or a cathedral. Now then we can compare book with book as we compare building with building. But this act of comparison means that our attitude has changed; we are no longer the friends of the writer, but his judges; and just as we cannot be too sympathetic as friends, so as judges we cannot be too severe. Are they not criminals, books that have wasted our time and sympathy; are they not the most insidious enemies of society, corrupters, defilers, the writers of false books, faked books, books that fill the air with decay and disease? Let us then be severe in our judgments; let us compare each book with the greatest of its kind. There they hang in the mind the shapes of the books we have read solidified by the judgments we have passed on them – *Robinson Crusoe, Emma, The Return of the Native.* Compare the novels with these – even the latest and least of novels has a right to be judged with the best. And so with poetry – when the intoxication of rhythm has died down and the splendour of words has faded, a visionary shape will return to us and this must be compared with *Lear*, with *Phèdre*, with *The Prelude*; or if not with these, with whatever is the best or seems to us to be the best in its own kind. And we may be sure that the newness of new poetry and fiction is its most superficial quality and that we have only to alter slightly, not to recast, the standards by which we have judged the old.

It would be foolish, then, to pretend that the second part of reading, to judge, to compare, is as simple as the first – to open the mind wide to the fast flocking of innumerable impressions. To continue reading without the book before you, to hold one shadow-shape against another, to have read widely enough and with enough understanding to make such comparisons alive and illuminating – that is difficult; it is still more difficult to press further and to say, 'Not only is the book of this sort, but it is of this value; here it fails; here it succeeds; this is bad; that is good'. To carry out this part of a reader's duty needs such imagination, insight, and learning that it is hard to conceive any one mind sufficiently endowed; impossible for the most self-confident to find more than the seeds of such powers in himself. Would it not be wiser, then, to remit this part of reading and to allow the critics, the gowned and furred authorities of the library, to decide the question of the book's absolute value for us? Yet how impossible! We may stress the value of sympathy; we may try to sink our own identity as we read. But we know that we cannot sympathise wholly or immerse ourselves wholly; there is always a demon in us who whispers, 'I hate, I love', and we cannot silence him. Indeed, it is precisely because we hate and we love that our relation with the poets and novelists is so intimate that we find the presence of another person intolerable. And even if the results are abhorrent and our judgments are wrong, still our taste, the nerve of sensation that sends shocks through us, is our chief illuminant; we learn through feeling; we cannot suppress our own idiosyncrasy without impoverishing it. But as time goes on perhaps we can train our taste; perhaps we can make it submit to some control. When it has fed greedily and lavishly upon books of all sorts – poetry, fiction, history, biography – and has stopped reading and looked for long spaces upon the variety, the incongruity of the living world, we shall find that it is changing a little; it is not so greedy, it is more reflective. It will begin to bring us not merely judgments on particular books, but it will tell us that there is a quality common to certain books. Listen, it will say, what shall we call *this*? And it will read us perhaps *Lear* and then perhaps the *Agamemnon* in order to bring out that common quality. Thus, with our taste to guide us, we shall venture beyond the particular book in search of qualities that group books together; we shall give them names and thus frame a rule that brings order into our perceptions. We shall gain a further and a rarer pleasure from that discrimination. But as a rule only lives when it is perpetually broken by contact with the books themselves – nothing is easier and more stultifying than to make rules which exist out of touch with facts, in a vacuum – now at last, in order to steady ourselves in this difficult attempt, it may be well to turn to the very rare writers who are able to enlighten us upon literature as an art. Coleridge and

Dryden and Johnson, in their considered criticism, the poets and novelists themselves in their unconsidered sayings, are often surprisingly relevant; they light up and solidify the vague ideas that have been tumbling in the misty depths of our minds. But they are only able to help us if we come to them laden with questions and suggestions won honestly in the course of our own reading. They can do nothing for us if we herd ourselves under their authority and lie down like sheep in the shade of a hedge. We can only understand their ruling when it comes in conflict with our own and vanquishes it.

If this is so, if to read a book as it should be read calls for the rarest qualities of imagination, insight, and judgment, and you may perhaps conclude that literature is a very complex art and that it is unlikely that we shall be able, even after a lifetime of reading, to make any valuable contribution to its criticism. We must remain readers; we shall not put on the further glory that belongs to those rare beings who are also critics. But still we have our responsibilities as readers and even our importance. The standards we raise and the judgments we pass steal into the air and become part of the atmosphere which writers breathe as they work. An influence is created which tells upon them even if it never finds its way into print. And that influence, if it were well instructed, vigorous and individual and sincere, might be of great value now when criticism is necessarily in abeyance; when books pass in review like the procession of animals in a shooting gallery, and the critic has only one second in which to load and aim and shoot and may well be pardoned if he mistakes rabbits for tigers, eagles for barndoor fowls, or misses altogether and wastes his shot upon some peaceful cow grazing in a further field. If behind the erratic gunfire of the press the author felt that there was another kind of criticism, the opinion of people reading for the love of reading, slowly and unprofessionally, and judging with great sympathy and yet with great severity, might this not improve the quality of his work? And if by our means books were to become stronger, richer, and more varied, that would be an end worth reaching.

Yet who reads to bring about an end, however desirable? Are there not some pursuits that we practise because they are good in themselves, and some pleasures that are final? And is not this among them? I have sometimes dreamt, at least, that when the Day of Judgment dawns and the great conquerors and lawyers and statesmen come to receive their rewards – their crowns, their laurels, their names carved indelibly upon imperishable marble – the Almighty will turn to Peter and will say, not without a certain envy when He sees us coming with our books under our arms, 'Look, these need no reward. We have nothing to give them here. They have loved reading.'

VIRGINIA WOOLF was an astonishingly innovative and creative artist who has exerted a powerful influence over literature and culture since the early twentieth century. Through her novels such as *Mrs Dalloway* (1925), *To the Lighthouse* (1927) and *The Waves* (1931), she created a ground-breaking new narrative structure and style. Alongside her husband Leonard Woolf, she founded The Hogarth Press – its first publications were hand-printed in the Woolfs' dining room, but went on to include works by T. S. Eliot, Vita Sackville-West and Sigmund Freud.

Woolf also maintained an astonishing output of literary criticism, short fiction, journalism and biography, including the playfully subversive *Orlando* (1928) and *A Room of One's Own* (1929) – a passionate argument for equality which resonates to this day. This intense creative productivity was often matched by periods of acute mental struggle. On 28 March 1941, a few months before the publication of her final novel, *Between the Acts*, Virginia Woolf committed suicide.

RECOMMENDED BOOKS BY VIRGINIA WOOLF:

The Waves
Orlando
Selected Essays

How do we use our liberty?

Love
JEANETTE WINTERSON

VINTAGE MINIS

Home
SALMAN RUSHDIE

VINTAGE MINIS

Language
XIAOLU GUO

VINTAGE MINIS

Race
TONI MORRISON

VINTAGE MINIS

VINTAGE MINIS

The Vintage Minis bring you the world's greatest writers on the experiences that make us human. These stylish, entertaining little books explore the whole spectrum of life – from birth to death, and everything in between. Which means there's something here for everyone, whatever your story.

Desire	Haruki Murakami
Love	Jeanette Winterson
Babies	Anne Enright
Language	Xiaolu Guo
Motherhood	Helen Simpson
Fatherhood	Karl Ove Knausgaard
Summer	Laurie Lee
Jealousy	Marcel Proust
Sisters	Louisa May Alcott
Home	Salman Rushdie
Race	Toni Morrison
Liberty	Virginia Woolf
Swimming	Roger Deakin
Work	Joseph Heller
Depression	William Styron
Drinking	John Cheever
Eating	Nigella Lawson
Psychedelics	Aldous Huxley
Calm	Tim Parks
Death	Julian Barnes

vintageminis.co.uk

1 3 5 7 9 10 8 6 4 2

Vintage
20 Vauxhall Bridge Road,
London SW1V 2SA

Vintage Classics is part of the Penguin Random House
group of companies whose addresses can be found at
global.penguinrandomhouse.com.

This short edition published by Vintage in 2017

penguin.co.uk/vintage

A CIP catalogue record for this book is available from the British Library

ISBN 9781784872724

Typeset in 9.5/14.5 pt FreightText Pro
by Jouve (UK), Milton Keynes
Printed and bound by Clays Ltd, St Ives plc

Penguin Random House is committed to a sustainable future for
our business, our readers and our planet. This book is made from
Forest Stewardship Council® certified paper.

Love
JEANETTE WINTERSON

VINTAGE MINIS

Contents

Oranges Are Not The Only Fruit

IN 1658 THE English clergyman Edward Topsell published
a handsome volume of woodcuts called *A History of Four-
Footed Beasts and Serpents.*

Some of the creatures were familiar to townspeople
and countryfolk alike – the dormouse, the cat, the beaver.
Some were fantastical: the sphinx, the lamia, the winged
dragon, the mantichora – a lion with a human face. And the
unicorn, of course.

Other beasts illustrated by woodcut were ones that are
familiar to us now – hippos, rhinos, the Egyptian crocodile,
the giraffe – but in the 17th century, these creatures had
been seen by few – sailors, explorers, convicts, con-men,
who described them for gain and pleasure, talked them
up in taverns and at fairs, whispered about them in
bed late at night, by candlelight, boasted about them for
wagers of money and proof of daring. And we all wanted
to believe it, because the world was still new, and life

was short, and a pair of dragon's wings might come in useful.

So, out of nature and imagination combined, beasts appeared not seen before or since. But they were pictured in a book – and so they came to exist.

What I want does exist if I dare to find it.

That's a line from *Oranges Are Not The Only Fruit*, my first novel, published in 1985 when I was twenty-five.

Oranges is many things: a coming-of-age story, a coming-out story, a little book of fairy tales, a character called Jeanette who is not me and who is me. A story of religious excess, of working-class life in the north of England, of books and of reading.

And love.

Oranges is a quest story. It's the start of a long search for a mythical creature called Love.

I am adopted and that fact has shaped my whole life. At six weeks old I lost the other half of my first love affair – my mother.

So life began with the disappearance of the love object.

My new parents – the Wintersons – found love difficult. They didn't do hugs. My mother was an Old Testament type who believed in fire and brimstone. At the same time the motto of our faith and church was God is Love.

This worked for me because I already had experience of my primary love object being invisible and unreachable.

Solitary by nature and nurture – an only child – I was intense and romantic. School was useless to me, but the library contained all the classics of English literature, and I read them. My roving reading was anchored by Shakespeare at one end and stretched as far as EM Forster at the other end. A few Americans were in there – Henry James, Edith Wharton, Poe, Scott Fitzgerald, Hemingway, Stein. I don't think I read any Europeans back then, other than Gide and Hesse.

Essentially it was 350 years or so of the English imagination, its poetry and prose, that was crucial and formative for me.

And that includes – overshadowing it all, I guess – the King James Bible of 1611, read to me or read by me every single day of my life from babyhood to leaving home at sixteen. That's a lot of Bible.

Literature has only lately been a secular enterprise. Most writers until the 20th century were believers of some kind, or brought up in religious households – the Brontës in their blowy parsonage, John Donne, who gave up sex and writing about it, and became Dean of St Paul's; Laurence Sterne – the amiable author of *Tristram Shandy* – was a vicar. The Romantic poets returned God to Nature. William Blake, like Walt Whitman, saw God in everything.

In the 19th century in England and America, doubt was as potent a force as faith. Not to believe was defiant, and like all defiance contained explosive useful creative energy.

So I felt kinship with the underlying beliefs – or struggles with unbelief, tacit or explicit – of the writers I was reading. Growing up today would be a very different experience. Unbelief is the new normal – there's no energy there. And, outside of secularism, the energy of belief we're used to now manifests as fundamentalism, carrying all the hatred and violence of its competing dogmas, but none of the creative release.

The Bible begins with a grand abandonment. Exit from the Garden of Eden. Paradise lost.

Yahweh is an unstable, angry, rejecting parent with a strange idea of love. Later, in the Christian part of the Jewish story, God will allow his son Jesus to be murdered as a human sacrifice to save mankind, doomed by Yahweh in the first place. God is love? Oy veh.

Or is God so in love with his own story that he can't rewrite it?

To me that felt like a failure of imagination. And the failure of love.

I wanted to do better.

You could call it arrogance or you could call it optimism.

———

So when I wrote *Oranges* I chaptered the sections according to the first eight books of the Bible. Not because I thought I was God, or any kind of authority – in fact, the opposite; the thing didn't have to be written on tablets of stone. There was no rigid rulebook. No last word.

I had understood something – I could change the story.

Could I?

Writing is an attempt to make a world. I was telling myself the story of myself. In *Oranges* I became a fictional character trying to understand love – and coming to understand that, without love, nothing can be understood.

It was first love, awakening love, love as separation, love as sleepless nights and broken hearts. Love as trial by fire. The fearfulness of love. And it was love between women. There wasn't much written about that back then.

Love between women became, for some readers, a way of trying to categorise the book – to lock it into a smaller space than it occupied. I have always been clear – I am a writer whose emotional interest is forwarded towards women, and whose sexual interest usually is. That is important, but it isn't the reason I write, nor does it preoccupy me.

Heterosexual choice is allowed to be the background of a writer's life; its wallpaper. So is maleness. And whiteness. Step out of that and you will be called a feminist writer, a lesbian writer, a gay writer, a woman writer. A black writer. You will never be called a heterosexual writer or a male writer or a white writer. Those signifiers are absorbed into the single word 'writer'.

It is changing. I have been part of the change. And glad to be. It matters to stand up politically for what you believe in. It matters to carry into the mainstream what the mainstream has tried to marginalise.

But writing is more than content. More than the stories we tell. Literature is an engagement with our deepest selves, a shaping of a language to talk about who we are – away from clichés and approximations, away from generalisations and half-truths. And oddly, literature is a way, at last, of not having to talk about anything. The moment that you put the book down. The moment you stare into space. A knowing that is beyond ordinary knowing. Resolution? Or peace? Or illumination? To pass through language back into silence. We start with silence, and we return to silence, but without language to guide us we cannot return there because

Words are the part of silence that can be spoken.

Oranges is about transgressive love – love between young women – and young women who wanted their love to include sex. Why would you not want love to include sex?

Oranges is about absences as well as inclusions; the absence of family love. What do you do if your parents don't know how to love you, and if you don't know how to love your parents?

And overarching the story is God's love – whatever that is. Invisible love – problematic and potent.

And I suppose those demonstrations of love were what I was trying to follow.

Love. Loss. Struggle. Loneliness. Abandonment. Separation. Faithfulness. Rejection. The natural world as an ally. Home as a place to leave behind. The search for meaning.

And could meaning be found through love?

Meaning.
Love.

What do those words mean, comets that they are, their tails stretched with stars? Their tales stretched with stars?

I was trying to trace light that had long left its source.

The story of my life starts there. Or is it here?

LIKE MOST PEOPLE I lived for a long time with my mother and father. My father liked to watch the wrestling. My mother liked to wrestle; it didn't matter what. She was in the white corner and that was that.

She hung out the largest sheets on the windiest days. She wanted the Mormons to knock on the door. At election time in a Labour mill town, my mother put a picture of the Conservative candidate in the window.

My mother had never heard of mixed feelings. There were friends and there were enemies.

Enemies were: The Devil (in his many forms)
                 Next Door
                 Sex (in its many forms)
                 Slugs

Friends were: God
                 Our dog
                 Auntie Madge
                 The Novels of Charlotte Brontë
                 Slug pellets

And me, at first. I had been brought in to join her in a tag match against the Rest of the World. She had a mysterious attitude towards the begetting of children; it wasn't that she couldn't do it, more that she didn't want to do it. She was very bitter about the Virgin Mary getting there first. So she did the next best thing and arranged for a foundling. That was me.

This is both me and not me. *Oranges* isn't autobiography or confessional. Part fiction, part fact is what life is. The stories we tell are all cover versions.

———

MY MOTHER AND I walked on towards the hill that stood at the top of our street. We lived in a town stolen from the valleys, a huddled place full of chimneys and little shops and back-to-back houses with no gardens. The hills surrounded us, and our own pushed out into the Pennines, broken here and there with a farm or a relic from the war. There used to be a lot of old tanks but the council took them away. The town was a fat blot, and the streets spread back from it into the green, steadily upwards. Our house was almost at the top of a long stretchy street. A flag-stone street with a cobbled road. Climb to the top of the hill and look down and you can see everything, just like Jesus on the pinnacle, except it's not very tempting. Over to the right, there's the viaduct, and behind the viaduct, Ellison's Tenement, where we have the fair once a year. I was allowed to go there on condition that I brought back a tub of black peas for my mother. Black peas look like rabbit droppings and they come in a thin gravy made of stock and gypsy mush ... Once when I was collecting the black peas, about to go home, the old woman took hold of my hand. I thought she was going to bite me. She looked at my palm and laughed a bit. 'You'll never marry,' she said, 'not you, and you'll never be still.'

She didn't take any money for the peas, and she told me to run home fast. I ran and ran, trying to understand what she meant. I hadn't thought about getting married anyway. There were two women I knew who didn't have husbands at all; they were old though, as old as my mother. They ran a newspaper shop, and sometimes, on a Wednesday, they gave me a banana bar with my comic. I liked them a lot and I talked about them a lot to my mother. One day, they asked me if I'd like to go to the seaside with them. I ran home, gabbled it out, and was busy emptying my money box to buy a new bucket and spade, when my mother said firmly, and forever, no. I couldn't understand why not, and she wouldn't explain. She didn't even let me go back to say I couldn't go. Then she cancelled my comic and told me to collect it from another shop, further away. I was sorry about that. I never got a banana bar from Grimsby's.

A couple of weeks later I heard her telling Mrs White about it. She said they dealt in unnatural passions. I thought she meant they put chemicals in their sweets.

Does sex begin with a sense of transgression?

> As long as I have known them my mother has gone to
> bed at four and my father has got up at five

Does love survive the loss of physical intimacy?

IT WAS SPRING, the ground still had traces of snow, and I was about to be married. My dress was pure white and I had a golden crown. As I walked up the aisle the crown got heavier and heavier and the dress more and more difficult to walk in. I thought everyone would point at me, but no one noticed.

Somehow I made it to the altar. The priest was very fat and kept getting fatter, like bubblegum you blow. Finally we came to the moment, 'You may kiss the bride.' My new husband turned to me, and here were a number of possibilities. Sometimes he was blind, sometimes a pig, sometimes my mother, sometimes the man from the post office, and once, just a suit of clothes with nothing inside. I told my mother about it, and she said it was because I ate sardines for supper. The next night I ate sausages, but I still had the dream.

There was a woman in our street who told us all she had married a pig. I asked her why she did it, and she said, 'You never know until it's too late.'

Exactly.

No doubt that woman had discovered in life what I had discovered in my dreams. She had unwittingly married a pig.

I kept watch on him after that. It was hard to tell he was a pig. He was clever, but his eyes were close together, and his skin bright pink. I tried to imagine him without his clothes on. Horrid.

Other men I knew weren't much better.

The man who ran the post office was bald and shiny with hands too fat for the sweet jars. He called me poppet, which my mother said was nice. He gave me sweets too, which was an improvement.

One day he had a new sort.

'Sweet hearts for a sweet heart,' he said and laughed. That day I had almost strangled my dog with rage, and been dragged from the house by a desperate mother. Sweet I was not. But I was a little girl, ergo, I was sweet, and here were sweets to prove it. I looked in the bag. Yellow and pink and sky-blue and orange, and all of them heart-shaped and all of them said things like,

Maureen 4 Ken,
Jack 'n' Jill, True.

On the way home I crunched at the *Maureen 4 Ken*s. I was confused. Everyone always said you found the right man.

My mother said it, which was confusing.

My auntie said it, which was even more confusing.

The man in the post office sold it on sweets.

But there was the problem of the woman married to the pig, and the spotty boy who took girls down backs, and my dream.

That afternoon I went to the library. I went the long way, so as to miss the couples. They made funny noises that sounded painful, and the girls were always squashed against the wall. In the library I felt better; words you could trust and look at till you understood them, they couldn't change half way through a sentence like people, so it was easier to spot a lie. I found a book of fairy tales, and read one called 'Beauty and the Beast'.

In this story, a beautiful young woman finds herself the forfeit of a bad bargain made by her father. As a result, she has to marry an ugly beast, or dishonour her family forever. Because she is good, she obeys. On her wedding night she gets into bed with the beast, and feeling pity that everything should be so ugly, gives it a little kiss. Immediately, the beast is transformed into a handsome young prince, and they both live happily ever after.

I wondered if the woman married to a pig had read this story. She must have been awfully disappointed if she had. And what about my Uncle Bill? He was horrible, and hairy, and looking at the picture, transformed princes aren't meant to be hairy at all.

Slowly I closed the book. It was clear that I had stumbled on a terrible conspiracy.

There are women in the world.

There are men in the world.

And there are beasts.

What do you do if you marry a beast?

Kissing them didn't always help. And beasts are crafty. They disguise themselves like you and I.

Like the wolf in 'Little Red Riding Hood'.

Why had no one told me? Did that mean no one else knew?

Did that mean that all over the globe, in all innocence, women were marrying beasts?

I reassured myself as best I could. The minister was a man, but he wore a skirt, so that made him special. There must be others, but were there enough? That was the worry. There were a lot of women, and most of them got married. If they couldn't marry each other, and I didn't think they could, because of having babies, some of them would inevitably have to marry beasts.

My own family had done quite badly, I thought.

If only there was some way of telling, then we could operate a ration system. It wasn't fair that a whole street should be full of beasts.

That night, we had to go to my auntie's to play Beetle. She was in the team at church, and needed to practise. As she dealt the cards, I asked her, 'Why are so many men really beasts?'

She laughed. 'You're too young for that.'

My uncle had overheard. He came over to me, and put his face close.

'You wouldn't love us any other way,' he said, and rubbed his spiky chin against my face. I hated him.

'Leave off, Bill,' my auntie pushed him away. 'Don't worry, love,' she soothed, 'you'll get used to it. When I married, I laughed for a week, cried for a month, and settled down for life. It's different, that's all, they have their little ways.' I looked at my uncle, who was now sunk in the pools coupon.

'You hurt me,' I accused.

'No I didn't,' he grinned. 'It was just a bit of love.'

'That's what you always say,' my auntie retorted, 'now shut up or go out.'

He slunk off. I half expected him to have a tail.

She spread the cards. 'There's time enough for you to get a boy.'

'I don't think I want one.'

'There's what we want,' she said, putting down a jack, 'and there's what we get, remember that.'

'You hurt me.

'No I didn't. It was just a bit of love.'

Was she trying to tell me she knew about the beasts? I got very depressed and started putting the Beetle legs on the wrong way round, and generally making a mess. Eventually my auntie stood up and sighed. 'You might as well go home,' she said.

I went to fetch my mother, who was in the parlour listening to Johnny Cash.

'Come on, we're finished.'

Slowly she put on her coat, and picked up her little Bible, the travel-size one. We set off together down the street.

'I've got to talk to you, have you got time?'

'Yes,' she said, 'let's have an orange.'

I tried to explain my dream, and the beast theory, and how much I hated Uncle Bill. All the time my mother walked along humming 'What a Friend We Have in Jesus', and peeling me an orange. She stopped peeling and I stopped talking about the same time. I had one last question.

'Why did you marry my dad?'

She looked at me closely.

'Don't be silly.'

'I'm not being silly.'

'We had to have something for you, and besides, he's a good man, though I know he's not one to push himself. But don't you worry, you're dedicated to the Lord, I put you down for missionary school as soon as we got you. Remember Jane Eyre and St John Rivers.' A faraway look came into her eye.

I did remember, but what my mother didn't know was

that I now knew she had rewritten the ending. *Jane Eyre* was her favourite non-Bible book, and she read it to me over and over again, when I was very small. I couldn't read it, but I knew where the pages turned. Later, literate and curious, I had decided to read it for myself. A sort of nostalgic pilgrimage. I found out, that dreadful day in a back corner of the library, that Jane doesn't marry St John at all, that she goes back to Mr Rochester. It was like the day I discovered my adoption papers while searching for a pack of playing cards. I have never since played cards, and I have never since read *Jane Eyre*.

We continued our walk in silence. She thought I was satisfied, but I was wondering about her, and wondering where I would go to find out what I wanted to know.

When it was washday I hid in the dustbin to hear what the women said. Nellie came out with her bit of rope and strung it up nail to nail across the back alley. She waved to Doreen who was struggling up the hill with her shopping, offering her a cup of tea and a talk. Each Wednesday Doreen queued up at the butcher's for the special offer mince. It always put her in a bad mood because she was a member of the Labour party and believed in equal shares and equal rights. She started to tell Nellie about the woman in front buying steak. Nellie shook her head which was small and tufted, and said it had been hard for her too since Bert died.

'Bert,' spat Doreen, 'he were dead ten years before they laid him out.' Then she offered Nellie a wine gum.

'Well I don't like to speak ill of the dead,' said Nellie uneasily, 'you never know.'

Doreen snorted and squatted painfully on the back step. Her skirt was too tight, but she always pretended it had shrunk.

'What about speaking ill of the living? My Frank's up to no good.'

Nellie took a deep breath and another wine gum. She asked if it was the woman who served pie and peas in the pub; Doreen didn't know, but now that she thought of it that would explain why he always smelled of gravy when he came home late.

'You should never have married him,' scolded Nellie.

'I didn't know what he was when I married him, did I?' And she told Nellie about the war and how her dad had liked him, and how it seemed sensible. 'I should have guessed though, what kind of a man comes round to court you and ends up drinking with your dad instead? I used to sit all done up playing whist with his mother and one of her friends.'

'Did he not take you anywhere then?'

'Oh yes,' said Doreen, 'we used to go down the dog track every Saturday afternoon.'

The two of them sat in silence for a while then Doreen went on, 'Course the children helped. I ignored him for fifteen years.'

'Still,' Nellie reassured her, 'you're not as bad as Hilda across the road, her one drinks every penny, and she daren't go to the police.'

'If mine touched me I'd have him put away,' said Doreen grimly.

'Would you?'

Doreen paused and scratched in the dirt with her shoe.

'Let's have a smoke,' offered Nellie, 'and you tell me about Jane.'

Jane was Doreen's daughter, just turned seventeen and very studious.

'If she don't get a boyfriend folks will talk. She spends all her time at that Susan's doing her homework, or so she tells me.'

Nellie thought that Jane might be seeing a boy on the quiet, pretending to be at Susan's. Doreen shook her head. 'She's there all right, I check with Susan's mother. If they're not careful folk will think they're like them two at the paper shop.'

'I like them two,' said Nellie firmly, 'and who's to say they do anything?'

'Mrs Fergeson across saw them getting a new bed, a double bed.'

'Well what does that prove? Me and Bert had one bed but we did nothing in it.'

Doreen said that was all very well, but two women were different.

Different from what? I wondered from inside the dustbin.

'Well your Jane can go to university and move away, she's clever.'

'Frank won't put up with that, he wants grandchildren, and if I don't get a move on there'll be no dinner for him and he'll be back with pie and peas in the pub. I don't want to give him an excuse.'

She struggled to her feet as Nellie started to peg out the washing. When it was safe, I crept out of the dustbin, as confused as ever and covered in soot.

It was a good thing I was destined to become a missionary. For some time after this I put aside the problem of men and concentrated on reading the Bible. Eventually, I thought, I'll fall in love like everybody else. Then some years later, quite by mistake, I did.

'By mistake . . .' Does love always happen by chance? That's one of the questions of this first book of mine and many that followed. I still haven't found the answer but the question has become more problematic to me. I like the idea of free will but the ancients knew a thing or two about Fate.

I WOULDN'T HAVE noticed Melanie if I hadn't gone round the other side of the stall to look at the aquarium.

She was boning kippers on a big marble slab. She used a thin stained knife, throwing the gut into a tin bucket. The clean fish she laid on greaseproof paper. Every fourth fish had a sprig of parsley.

'I'd like to do that,' I said.

She smiled and carried on.

'Do you like doing it?'

Still she said nothing, so I slid, as discreetly as a person in a pink plastic mac can, to the other side of the tank. I couldn't see very well because of the hood over my eyes.

'Can I have some fish-bait?' I said.

She looked up, and I noticed that her eyes were a lovely grey, like the cat Next Door.

'I'm not supposed to have friends at work.'

'But I'm not your friend.'

'No, but they'll think you are.'

'Well ... I might as well be then ...'

What follows in *Oranges* is the unfolding of this relationship – how it moves from an unexpected friendship to an unexpected love affair. The girls I am writing about are not savvy, not sophisticated. There was no internet back then. They don't know anyone like themselves. They are both going to church and reading the Bible and they feel happy there, and happy together. And then the thing deepens, because the body can't lie.

WHEN I REACHED MELANIE'S it was getting dark. I had to cut through the churchyard to get to her. Sometimes I'd steal her a bunch of flowers from the new graves. She was always pleased but I never told her where they came from. She asked me if I wanted to stay overnight because her mum was away and she didn't like being in the house on her own. I said I'd ring a neighbour, and after a lot of trouble finally got an agreement from my mother, who had to be fetched from her lettuces. We read the Bible as usual, and we told each other how glad we were that the Lord had brought us together. She stroked my head for a long time, and then we hugged, and it felt like drowning. Then I was frightened but couldn't stop. There was something crawling in my belly. I had an octopus inside me . . .

'Do you think this is Unnatural Passions?'

HERE IS A TABLE set at feast and the guests are arguing about the best recipe for goose. A tremor shakes the chandelier, dropping tiny flakes of plaster into the sherbet. The guests look up, more in interest than alarm. It's cold in here. So cold. The women suffer most. Their shoulders bared and white like hard-boiled eggs. Outside, under the snow, the river sleeps embalmed. These are the elect, and in the hall, an army sleeps on straw.

Outside, a rush of torches.

Laughter drifts through the hall. The elect have always been this way.

Getting old. Dying. Starting again. Not noticing.

Father and Son. Father and Son.

It has always been this way. Nothing can intrude.

Father, Son, and Holy Ghost.

Outside, the rebels storm the Winter Palace.

Love, the naturaliser of everything artificial, and at the same time the ultimate artifice, the elaborate construct, the mind's narrative of the body's desire. Love, the destroyer.

The change in Jeanette (me and not me) is noticed by her mother, who at first concludes that her daughter has fallen for a good-looking lad at church. As the Chief of the Sex Police, Mother feels the time is right for the story of Pierre . . .

'THERE'S A BOY at church I think you're keen on.'

'What?' I said, completely mystified.

She meant Graham, a newish convert, who'd moved over to our town from Stockport. I was teaching him to play the guitar, and trying to make him understand the importance of regular Bible study.

'It's time,' she went on, very solemn, 'that I told you about Pierre and how I nearly came to a bad end.' Then she poured us both a cup of tea and opened a packet of Royal Scot. I was enthralled.

'It's not something I'm proud of, and I'll only say it once.'

My mother had been headstrong, and had got a job teaching in Paris, which was a very daring thing to do at the time. She had lived off the Rue St Germain, eaten croissants and lived a clean life. She wasn't with the Lord then, but she had high standards. Then, one sunny day, without warning, she had been walking towards the river when she met Pierre, or rather Pierre had jumped from his bicycle, offered her his onions, and named her the most beautiful woman he had ever seen.

'Naturally, I was flattered.'

They exchanged addresses, and began to court one another. It was then that my mother experienced a feeling she had never known before: a fizzing and a buzzing and a certain giddiness. Not only with Pierre, but anywhere, at any time.

'Well, I thought it must be love.'

But this puzzled her because Pierre wasn't very clever, and didn't have much to say, except to exclaim how beautiful she was. Perhaps he was handsome? But no, looking in the magazines, she realised he wasn't that either. But the feeling wouldn't go away. Then, on a quiet night, after a quiet supper, Pierre had seized her and begged her to stay with him that night. The fizzing began, and as he clutched her to him, she felt sure she would never love another, and yes she would stay and after that, they would marry.

'Lord forgive me, but I did it.'

My mother stopped, overcome with emotion. I begged her to finish the story, proffering the Royal Scots.

'The worst is still to come.'

I speculated on the worst, while she chewed her biscuit. Perhaps I wasn't a child of God at all, but the daughter of a Frenchman.

A couple of days afterward, my mother had gone to see the doctor in a fit of guilty anxiety. She lay on the couch while the doctor prodded her stomach and chest, asking if she ever felt giddy, or fizzy in the belly. My mother coyly explained that she was in love, and that she often felt strange, but that wasn't the reason for her visit.

'You may well be in love,' said the doctor, 'but you also have a stomach ulcer.'

Imagine my mother's horror. She had given away her all for an ailment. She took the tablets, followed the diet, and refused Pierre's entreaties to visit her. Needless to say, the next time they met, and again by chance, she felt nothing, nothing at all, and shortly fled the country to avoid him.

'Then am I ...?' I began.

'There was no issue,' she said quickly.

For a few moments we sat silent, then:

'So just you take care, what you think is the heart might well be another organ.' It might, Mother, it might, I thought. She got up and told me to go and find something to do. I decided to go and see Melanie, but just as I reached the door she called me back with a word of warning.

'Don't let anyone touch you Down There,' and she pointed to somewhere at the level of her apron pocket.

'No Mother,' I said meekly, and fled.

I TRACED THE OUTLINE of her marvellous bones and the triangle of muscle in her stomach. What is it about intimacy that makes it so disturbing?

Love ends, of course. I mean, the love affair ends badly, because the church calls it a sin and the girls are separated. Melanie believes her love for Jeanette was a perversion, and she's glad to start dating boys, and eventually to marry. For Jeanette, things are more complicated. She can't lie about her feelings.

There's a further relationship with another girl – eventually discovered, and that's it – she's out of house and home, living what kind of a patched-together life she can until she leaves for university.

During her first Christmas holiday she returns to find her mother has bought an electronic organ and built a CB radio to broadcast the gospel to the Heathen – mainly the Heathen living in Manchester.

I MISS GOD. I miss the company of someone loyal. I don't think of God as my betrayer. I miss God who was my friend. I don't know if God exists but I know that if God is your emotional role model, few human relationships will match up. I have an idea that it might be possible. I thought once it had become possible, and that glimpse of something has sent me wandering, trying to find the balance between earth and sky.

I can't settle. I want someone who is fierce and who will love me unto death and know that love is as strong as death and be on my side for ever and ever. I want someone who will destroy and be destroyed by me. There are many forms of love and affection; some people can spend their whole lives together without knowing each other's names. Naming is difficult and time-consuming; it concerns essences and it means power.

On the wild nights, who can call you home? Only the one who knows your name.

Romantic love has been diluted into paperback form and has sold thousands and millions of copies. Somewhere it is still in the original, written on tablets of stone ...

The unknownness of my needs frightens me. I do not know how huge they are or how high they are. I only know that they are not being met ...

One thing I am certain of – I do not want to be betrayed, but that's quite hard to say, casually, at the beginning of a relationship. There are different kinds of infidelity but betrayal is betrayal wherever you find it. By betrayal I mean promising to be on your side, then being on someone else's.

STANDING ON THE SIDE of the hill where it slopes into the quarry, it's possible to see where Melanie used to live. I met her by accident during the second year I didn't live at home. She was pushing a pram. She had been serene to the point of bovine before; now she was nearly vegetable. I kept looking at her wondering how we had ever had a relationship, yet when she first left me I thought I had blood poisoning. I couldn't forget her. Now she seemed to have forgotten everything. I wanted to shake her. Pull off all my clothes in the middle of the street and yell REMEMBER THIS BODY?

Time is a great deadener. People forget, get bored, grow old, go away.

She said that not much had happened between us

anyway, historically speaking. But history is a string full of knots, the best you can do is admire it and maybe knot it up some more. History is a hammock for swinging and a game for playing. A cat's cradle.

She said those sorts of feelings were dead – the feelings she once had for me. There is a seductiveness about dead things. You can ill treat, alter, and recolour what's dead – it won't complain. Then she laughed and said we probably saw what had happened very differently anyway. She laughed again – she said that the way I saw it would make a good story, her version was just the history, the nothing-at-all facts. She said she hoped I hadn't kept any letters, silly to hang onto old things that had no meaning. As though letters and photos made it more real, more dangerous.

I told her I didn't need letters and photos to remember what had happened. Then she looked vague and started to discuss the weather and the roadworks and the soaring price of baby food.

SHE ASKED ME what I was doing and I longed to say I was sacrificing infants on top of Pendle Hill. Anything to make her angry. But she was happy. They had stopped eating meat and she was pregnant again. She had even started writing to my mother.

It was getting dark as I came down the hill, swirls of snow sticking to my face. I thought about the dog and was sad for her death, for my death, for all the inevitable dying that comes with change. There's no choice that doesn't mean a loss. But the dog was buried in the clean earth and the things I had buried were exhuming themselves; clammy fears and dangerous thoughts and the shadows I had put away for a more convenient time. I could not put them away for ever; there is always a day of reckoning. But not all dark places need light. I have to remember that.

I DO HAVE to remember that – all these years later. Not all dark places need light.

The Passion

LOVE AS THE night-haunter, the blood-hunter, the body's rack, antagonist of commonsense.

Love as the space between utility and despair.

Love as the enemy of ease.

When I wrote *The Passion* I was magnificently and recklessly in love with a married woman twenty years older than me. To deal with the feelings this invoked – and I mean invoked (it felt like a kind of conjuring) – I did what writers have always done and transposed the situation.

I went back in time to the Napoleonic Wars and wrote about Henri, a young soldier, about his strange meeting with a woman with webbed feet called Villanelle, about her entanglement with both Henri and a mysterious older woman bored by her marriage. And I set it in Venice, a city I visited for the first time after I had written the book.

———

I saw no reason to go before I was writing the book – or while I was writing it – it was a novel, not a travel guide, and the Venice of the 1800s was gone. I couldn't visit it. What I could do was invent it.

It's not that art imitates life. Creativity releases life from both time and gravity. Events can be reversed, endings change, the weight that bears down on all that we do is lifted.

The Passion is a good story. It's got love, sex, murder, friend-ship, war, politics and characters we care about. TV and movies have brought us into the age of story-telling like never before. Advertising and market-manipulation are all about the story. And no one can resist a story – we're hard-wired to sit round that camp fire and hear what the story-teller has to say.

For me, though, and the texts that interested me, story-telling was a magic carpet to elsewhere. The elsewhere wasn't the story, it was further on – it was where the story might lead.

The last line of *The Passion*, and yes, it does get printed on T-shirts a lot, is this:

I'm telling you stories. Trust me

Why should we trust fictions in a post-truth world?

When I wrote *The Passion* we weren't in a post-truth world – or we thought we weren't. It was the year after deregulation of the markets, the beginning of the economy on steroids that would lead, twenty years later, to the biggest financial crash in history. So everything we were being told, everything we were experiencing, had no truth in it, if truth is lasting, real, dependable, verifiable.

But we didn't know that. Thatcher and Reagan ruled the world. Love your neighbour as yourself had been replaced with Love yourself. The social contract was dead.

Thirty years later, thinking about *The Passion* and about fiction versus lying, I realise all the obvious things about invention as a way of getting at a deeper truth, and lying as a way of avoiding any truth at all or, worse, creating a nightmare world where nothing is as it seems, where nothing can be depended upon – we know human minds can't cope with that, and then we instinctively cling to the 'strong man', who is usually the biggest liar of the lot.

All that is clear enough.

What's less clear is this question of the story itself being a means rather than an end. A map rather than a destination.

And that's what stories have in common with Love.

Love is a means, not an end. Love is a map, not a destination. That's why there is no such thing as 'they all lived happily ever after'.

That's why Act V of the Shakespeare comedies is often so uncomfortable. We know that, in the mirth and resolution, what lies ahead is the start of another play, another journey.

Love is the visible corner of a folded map.

So my commitment to story-telling, like my commitment to love, is a commitment to discomfort, not security. To adventure, not satisfaction. To possibilities, not answers.

And you'll note, because it is so obvious that it needs saying, that lies are always offered as answers.

Brexit. Trump. Border control. Make your own list.

Truth is a questioning place.

Stories are full of questions. What if? What is? Who am I? Who are you? What do I believe? Why do I believe it?

We ask these questions in other ways – of course we do, politically, philosophically, spiritually. We address them head-on.

And that's the difference, I guess, because, as Freud worked out at the start of the 20th century, human beings cannot always, or even optimally, address the big, the dark, the difficult, the shameful, the guilty, the criminal, the crazy head-on. We have to go sideways, downwards, away from without running away. We use a proxy or an avatar. And that's what stories let happen.

———

When we are in love we have the feeling of being understood. The feeling of things being simultaneously settled and disturbed. Hands and voices rummage through us.

We are known while remaining private.
We are held while remaining free.

I'm telling you stories. Trust me

Here, Villanelle, dressed as a boy, meets the mysterious woman for the second time:

NOVEMBER IN VENICE is the beginning of the catarrh season. Catarrh is part of our heritage like St Mark's. Long ago, when the Council of Three ruled in mysterious ways, any traitor or hapless one done away with was usually announced to have died of catarrh. In this way, no one was embarrassed. It's the fog that rolls in from the lagoon and hides one end of the Piazza from another that brings on our hateful congestion. It rains too, mournfully and quietly, and the boatmen sit under sodden rags and stare helplessly into the canals. Such weather drives away the foreigners and that's the only good thing that can be said of it. Even the brilliant water-gate at the Fenice turns grey.

On an afternoon when the Casino didn't want me and I didn't want myself, I went to Florian's to drink and gaze at the Square. It's a fulfilling pastime.

I had been sitting perhaps an hour when I had the feeling of being watched. There was no one near me, but there was someone behind a screen a little way off. I let my mind retreat again. What did it matter? We are always watching or watched. The waiter came over to me with a packet in his hand.

I opened it. It was an earring. It was the pair.

And she stood before me and I realised I was dressed as I had been that night because I was waiting to work. My hand went to my lip.

'You shaved it off,' she said.

I smiled. I couldn't speak.

She invited me to dine with her the following evening and I took her address and accepted.

In the Casino that night I tried to decide what to do. She thought I was a young man. I was not. Should I go to see her as myself and joke about the mistake and leave gracefully? My heart shrivelled at this thought. To lose her again so soon. And what was myself? Was this breeches and boots self any less real than my garters? What was it about me that interested her?

You play, you win. You play, you lose. You play.

I was careful to steal enough to buy a bottle of the best champagne.

Lovers are not at their best when it matters. Mouths dry up, palms sweat, conversation flags and all the time the heart is threatening to fly from the body once and for all. Lovers have been known to have heart attacks. Lovers drink too much from nervousness and cannot perform. They eat too little and faint during their fervently wished consummation. They do not stroke the favoured cat and their face-paint comes loose. This is not all. Whatever you have set store by, your dress, your dinner, your poetry, will go wrong.

Her house was gracious, standing on a quiet waterway, fashionable but not vulgar. The drawing-room, enormous with great windows at either end and a fireplace that would have suited and idle wolfhound. It was simply furnished; an oval table and a *chaise-longue*. A few Chinese ornaments that she liked to collect when the ships came through. She had also a strange assortment of dead insects mounted in cases on the wall. I had never seen such things before and wondered about this enthusiasm.

She stood close to me as she took me through the house, pointing out certain pictures and books. Her hand guided my elbow at the stairs and when we sat down to eat she did not arrange us formally but put me beside her, the bottle in between.

We talked about the opera and the theatre and the visitors and the weather and ourselves. I told her that my real father had been a boatman and she laughed and asked could it be true that we had webbed feet?

'Of course,' I said and she laughed the more at this joke.

We had eaten. The bottle was empty. She said she had married late in life, had not expected to marry at all being stubborn and of independent means. Her husband dealt in rare books and manuscripts form the east. Ancient maps that showed the lairs of griffins and the haunts of whales. Treasure maps that claimed to know the whereabouts of the Holy Grail. He was a quiet and cultured man of whom she was fond.

He was away.

We had eaten, the bottle was empty. There was nothing more that could be said without strain or repetition. I had been with her more than five hours already and it was time to leave. As we stood up and she moved to get something I stretched out my arm, that was all, and she turned back into my arms so that my hands were on her shoulder blades and hers along my spine. We stayed thus for a few moments until I had courage enough to kiss her neck very lightly. She did not pull away. I grew bolder and kissed her mouth, biting a little at the lower lip.

She kissed me.

'I can't make love to you,' she said.

Relief and despair.

'But I can kiss you.'

And so, from the first, we separated our pleasure. She lay on the rug and I lay at right angles to her so that only our lips might meet. Kissing in this way is the strangest of distractions. The greedy body that clamours for satisfaction is forced to content itself with a single sensation and, just as the blind hear more acutely and the deaf can feel the grass grow, so the mouth becomes the focus of love and all things pass through it and are re-defined. It is a sweet and precise torture.

Sexing the Cherry

WHEN JORDAN WAS a baby he sat on top of me much as a fly rests on a hill of dung and I nourished him as a hill of dung nourishes a fly. And when he had eaten his fill he left me.

Jordan ...

I should have named him after a stagnant pond and then I could have kept him, but I named him after a river, and in the flood-tide he slipped away.

Sexing the Cherry is set in the reign of Charles the First, and I suppose it's an historical novel, except that the past is always history, and the past is happening every minute.

I wasn't trying to reproduce a historical period, or ventriloquise the dead. I was using the past as a place to situate what interested me.

I have never believed that to be relevant we have to

write about our own time and place. Literature isn't documentary. Using the past is a way of escaping the clutter of now.

Sexing the Cherry is my third novel, published when I was twenty-nine. It's the story of a giantess called the Dog-Woman, who lives on the banks of the River Thames, breeding hounds. She adopts a boy called Jordan, fished out of the river, and this is their fierce unrequited-love story – love between mother and son – love that never quite joins them together. They are both loners, and in an essential sense they remain alone.

Love is baffling. Love can leave us lonelier than we were without love. Love, like a planet that appears in the sky, dazzling and unreachable.

But loneliness is not the same thing as emotional defeat.

WHEN JORDAN WAS a boy he made paper boats and floated them on the river. From this he learned how the wind affects a sail but he never learned how love affects the heart. His patience was exceeded only by his hope. He spent days and nights with his bits of wood salvaged from chicken crates, and any piece of paper he could steal became a sail. I used to watch him standing in the mud or lying face down, his nose almost in the current, his hand steadying the boat and then letting it go straight into the wind. Letting go hours of himself.

When the time came he did the same with his heart. He didn't believe in shipwreck.

And he came home to me with his boats broken and his face streaked with tears and we sat with our lamp and mended what we could and the next day was the first day all over again. But when he lost his heart there was no one to sit with him. He was alone.

The novel previous to this one, *The Passion*, also has a young man in it, a soldier called Henri, similarly baffled by love. I see no reason to write in your own gender, unless there is a reason to do so. I see no reason to read as your own gender either. Fictional characters are the original avatars for writer and reader alike. In this place of freedom we can choose who we want to be. And we can find a spectrum of feeling, experience, sexuality, even anger or murder, not available in daily life.

But *Sexing the Cherry* belongs to the Dog-Woman. I think she must be a reading of my adoptive mother, Mrs Winterson, who never wanted to be a nobody, and liked dogs. She was also very large – and I am not. So there is size in *Sexing the Cherry*, a novel that is in some ways a fairy tale, and contains twelve little fairy tales. And in fairy tales size is often approximate and unstable. Genies and giants, little people and shape-shifters.

The twelve fairy tales are the stories of the Twelve Dancing Princesses. I liked that story when I was a child, but

I used to wonder about the lives of the girls. Who were they? When I realised I was a writer, I realised I could find out.

Here's one of the stories:

YOU MAY HAVE HEARD of Rapunzel.

Against the wishes of her family, who can best be described by their passion for collecting miniature dolls, she went to live in a tower with an older woman.

Her family were so incensed by her refusal to marry the prince next door that they vilified the couple, calling one a witch and the other a little girl. Not content with names, they ceaselessly tried to break into the tower, so much so that the happy pair had to seal up any entrance that was not on a level with the sky. The lover got in by climbing up Rapunzel's hair, and Rapunzel got in by nailing a wig to the floor and shinning up the tresses flung out of the window. Both of them could have used a ladder, but they were in love.

One day the prince, who had always liked to borrow his mother's frocks, dressed up as Rapunzel's lover and dragged himself into the tower. Once inside he tied her up and waited for the wicked witch to arrive. The moment she leaped through the window, bringing their dinner for the evening, the prince hit her over the head and threw her out again. Then he carried Rapunzel down the rope he had brought with him and forced her to watch while he blinded her broken lover in a field of thorns.

After that they lived happily ever after, of course.

As for me, my body healed, though my eyes never did, and eventually I was found by my sisters, who had come in their various ways to live on this estate.

My own husband?

Oh well, the first time I kissed him he turned into a frog. There he is, just by your foot. His name's Anton.

Back then, British writers like Angela Carter, Michele Roberts and Sara Maitland were breaking into the sealed and locked rooms of fairy stories, and re-telling them, not as PC versions, or feminist versions, necessarily, but claiming the right to re-write, which is part of the feminist proposal. Text, starting with the Bible, has always been a way of claiming knowledge and tradition. Text has been a class-war weapon to keep people in their place. And a gendered weapon too; who is allowed to read? Who is allowed to write? What is the canon? What is literature? And who claims it?

I was conscious of myself as a working-class woman writing. So I was happy to do a pirate raid on the treasure chest of the past. Anyway, it is only when stories are written down that they become codified – myths, legends, fairy tales existed, and still do, in multiple oral versions. The written version is propositional. Isn't it?

So why not propose something different?

———

But to return to the Dog-Woman. She is a lost soul. She will never be found. Her lostness is part of her glory and she glories in it. She is a magnificent misfit. She howls on the banks of the Thames beside her dogs. She barges through life, alternately terrorising and mourning. And in my version of history, she is responsible for the Great Fire of London.

Why not? Just burn it down.

But it is love, not revenge, that occupies her thoughts.

WHAT IS LOVE?

On the morning after our arrival at Wimbledon I awoke in a pool of philosophic thought, though comforted by Jordan's regular breathing and the snorts of my thirty dogs.

I am too huge for love. No one, male or female, has ever dared to approach me. They are afraid to scale mountains.

I wonder about love because the parson says that only God can truly love us and the rest is lust and selfishness.

In church, there are carvings of a man with his member swollen out like a marrow, rutting a woman whose teats swish the ground like a cow before milking. She has her eyes closed and he looks up to Heaven, and neither of them notice the grass is on fire.

The parson had these carvings done especially so that we could contemplate our sin and where it must lead.

There are women too, hot with lust, their mouths sucking at each other, and men grasping one another the way you would a cattle prod.

We file past every Sunday to humble ourselves and stay clean for another week, but I have noticed a bulge here and there where all should be quiet and God-like.

For myself, the love I've known has come from my dogs, who care nothing for how I look, and from Jordan, who says that though I am as wide and muddy as the river that is his namesake, so am I too his kin. As for the rest of this sinning world, they treat me well enough for my knowledge and pass me by when they can.

I breed boarhounds as my father did before me and as I hoped Jordan would do after me. But he would not stay. His head was stuffed with stories of other continents where men have their faces in their chests and some hop on one foot defying the weight of nature.

These hoppers cover a mile at a bound and desire no sustenance other than tree-bark. It is well known that their companions are serpents, the very beast that drove us all from Paradise and makes us still to sin. These beasts are so wily that if they hear the notes of a snake-charmer they lay one ear to the earth and stopper up the other with their tails. Would I could save myself from sin by stoppering up my ears with a tail or any manner of thing.

I am a sinner, not in body but in mind. I know what love sounds like because I have heard it through the wall, but I do not know what it feels like. What can it be like, two bodies slippery as eels on a mud-flat, panting like dogs after a pig?

I fell in love once, if love be that cruelty which takes us

straight to the gates of Paradise only to remind us they are closed for ever.

There was a boy who used to come by with a coatful of things to sell. Beads and ribbons hung on the inside and his pockets were crammed with fruit knives and handkerchiefs and buckles and bright thread. He had a face that made me glad.

I used to get up an hour early and comb my hair, which normally I would do only at Christmas-time in honour of our Saviour. I decked myself in my best clothes like a bullock at a fair, but none of this made him notice me and I felt my heart shrivel to the size of a pea. Whenever he turned his back to leave I always stretched out my hand to hold him a moment, but his shoulder blades were too sharp to touch. I drew his image in the dirt by my bed and named all my mother's chickens after him.

Eventually I decided that true love must be clean love and I boiled myself a cake of soap ...

I hate to wash, for it exposes the skin to contamination. I follow the habit of King James, who only ever washed his fingertips and yet was pure in heart enough to give us the Bible in good English.

I hate to wash, but knowing it to be a symptom of love I was not surprised to find myself creeping towards the pump in the dead of night like a ghoul to a tomb. I had determined to cleanse all of my clothes, my underclothes and myself. I did this in one passage by plying at the pump handle, first with my right arm and washing my left self, then with my left arm and washing my right self. When I was so drenched that to wring any part of me left a puddle at my feet I waited outside the baker's until she began her work and sat myself by the ovens until morning. I had a white coating from the flour, but that served to make my swarthy skin more fair.

In this new state I presented myself to my loved one, who graced me with all of his teeth at once and swore that if only he could reach my mouth he would kiss me there and then. I swept him from his feet and said, 'Kiss me now,' and closed my eyes for the delight. I kept them closed for some five minutes and then, opening them to see what had happened, I saw that he had fainted dead away. I carried him to the pump that had last seen my devotion and doused him good and hard, until he came to, wriggling like a trapped fox, and begged me let him down.

'What is it?' I cried. 'Is it love for me that affects you so?'

'No,' he said. 'It is terror.'

I saw him a few months later in another part of town with a pretty jade on his arm and his face as bright as ever.

Here she is again:

IN THE DARK and in the water I weigh nothing at all. I have no vanity but I would enjoy the consolation of a lover's face. After my only excursion into love I resolved never to make a fool of myself again. I was offered a job in a whore-house but I turned it down on account of my frailty of heart.

Surely such to-ing and fro-ing as must go on night and day weakens the heart and inclines it to love? Not directly, you understand, but indirectly, for lust without romantic matter must be wearisome after a time. I asked a girl at the Spitalfields house about it and she told me she hates her lovers by-the-hour but still longs for someone to come in a coach and feed her on mince pies.

Where do they come from, these insubstantial dreams?

As for Jordan, he has not my common sense and will no doubt follow his dreams to the end of the world and then fall straight off.

I cannot school him in love, having no experience, but I can school him in its lack and perhaps persuade him that there are worse things than loneliness.

A man accosted me on our way to Wimbledon and asked me if I should like to see him.

'I see you well enough, sir,' I replied.

'Not all of me,' said he, and unbuttoned himself to show a thing much like a pea-pod.

'Touch it and it will grow,' he assured me. I did so, and indeed it did grow to look more like a cucumber.

'Wondrous, wondrous, wondrous,' he swooned, though I could see no good reason for swooning.

'Put it in your mouth,' he said. 'Yes, as you would a delicious thing to eat.'

I like to broaden my mind when I can and I did as he suggested, swallowing it up entirely and biting it off with a snap.

As I did so my eager fellow increased his swooning to the point of fainting away, and I, feeling both astonished by his rapture and disgusted by the leathery thing filling up my mouth, spat out what I had not eaten and gave it to one of my dogs.

The whore from Spitalfields had told me that men like to be consumed in the mouth, but it still seems to me a reckless act, for the member must take some time to grow again. None the less their bodies are their own, and I who know nothing of them must take instruction humbly, and if a man asks me to do the same again I'm sure I shall, though for myself I felt nothing.

In copulation, an act where the woman has a more pleasurable part, the member comes away in the great tunnel and creeps into the womb where it splits open after a time like a runner bean and deposits a little mannikin to grow in the rich soil. At least, so I am told by women who have become pregnant and must know their husbands' members as well as I do my own dogs.

When Jordan is older I will tell him what I know about the human body and urge him to be careful of his member. And yet it is not that part of him I fear for; it is his heart. His heart.

Written on the Body

WHY IS THE measure of love loss?

That's the opening line of *Written on the Body*.

What do we do about love? So impossible, so essential, a drug, a lifesaver, the killer, and the cure.

I'm talking here about romantic love, sexual love, only. I say 'only' but you know what I mean.

In *Oranges* I had thought about love between young women, and in *The Passion* between women and between men and women. Now I wondered what would happen if we didn't know, weren't told, the gender of the narrator. How would we read love if it didn't come with the usual signifiers?

There's a beloved – Louise – who is married. Triangles are more interesting than straight lines – for dramatic, if not domestic, purposes. Her lover is not named and we know almost nothing about him or her. What we know is the unfolding story of their love affair.

Written on the body is a secret code only visible in certain light

I am bored by binaries. Are you? I think of male and female as subsets of a totality. Not quite like Plato's hermaphrodites – but forced apart by nurture, not nature, most of us having more of the other in us than social norms allow. What does it mean to love as a man? What does it mean to love as a woman? And does the character of our love change if our own gender, or the gender of our lover, changes?

Why is gender so defining in our culture?

I'm writing this in 2017. A lot has changed since 1992 – but quite a lot hasn't changed at all. Men and women are still judged by different sexual standards. Women who wear trousers are fine. Men who wear skirts or make-up are stared at in the street.

Women have been 'allowed' to express their masculine side – mainly because we want women in the workforce, and work is still, somewhere deep down, associated with what men do. If you don't believe that look at the comments from blue-collar Trump voters wanting 'real' jobs for 'real' men.

Men have fared less well in expressing their feminine side – they are often a little awkward about house-husbanding, taking paternity leave, or even crying. Feminism gives me hope here, because feminism was, and is, an agenda for change for both women and men. And as

Grayson Perry has often said, when talking about his alter ego, Clare, is there really a 'masculine' and a 'feminine' at all?

Younger people are more accepting of bisexuality or intersexuality, and see more flexibility in what we think of as gender norms, but it would be optimistic to say there is no prejudice, no fear, no judgement.

I wanted to undo assumptions. Assumptions about male and female. Assumptions about desire.

Fiction is a set of possibilities. Those possibilities prompt us towards other beginnings, alternative endings, because to some extent we write the book alongside the author, and we often would prefer a different ending. I was aware of this, and so I left the space for it to happen – and, in fact, for the novel to begin again.

Here's the end:

THIS IS WHERE the story starts, in this threadbare room. The walls are exploding. The windows have turned into telescopes. Moon and stars are magnified in this room. The sun hangs over the mantelpiece. I stretch out my hands and reach the corners of the world. The world is bundled up in this room. We can take the world with us when we go and sling the sun under your arm. Hurry now, it's getting late. I don't know if this is a happy ending, but here we are let loose in open fields.

I realise that all my books have second chances in them – some taken and some not. And *Written on the Body* is my first shadow-working of Shakespeare's *The Winter's Tale*.

By which I mean loss and its consequences.

That Louise is miraculously alive and in the room at the end of the story is a direct reference to what happens at the end of *The Winter's Tale*. We always hope we can return the dead. That time can unhappen. That we won't be left alone, staring at the emptiness.

We wish we could undo what we did . . .

None of us lives without loss. Or regret. But none of us need live without imagination. We can learn to see past ourselves.

To write a book without a gendered narrator has caused a few problems. There are problems of translation in those languages that use gendered verbs and nouns – my advice was always to keep switching from masculine to feminine, so that the language itself became a player in the upset of assumption. I don't think too many publishers took that advice. A pity!

And then there were problems from readers – wanting to know, needing to know, which was interesting and revealing. And then, where the book is taught in class, there have been tutors who prefer biography over imagination and assume that because I am a woman the narrator must be a woman. That's just sad!

And there have been gay readers who want this to be a gay love story – and it can be if that is what you want, and I have no problem with that – but it doesn't have to be one.

The great thing about gay culture is how it has challenged heterosexual culture at so many levels. At its simplest, men can now wear pink shirts. At its most profound are questions of sexual identity – the range of sexual expression, the drive not to label anyone according to their sexual choice or destiny.

To judge each other less.

There's a line in the book – 'It's the clichés that cause the trouble. To live beyond cliché is not so easy.'

Fiction helps us to try.

This extract comes early in the novel when the narrator, trying to escape from a rackety past and a nightmare affair with a woman called Bathsheba, has settled with a nice girl who isn't interesting any more. Sex with Louise has already happened.

I PHONED A friend whose advice was to play the sailor and run a wife in every port. If I told Jacqueline I'd ruin everything and for what? If I told Jacqueline I'd hurt her beyond healing and did I have that right? Probably I had nothing more than dog-fever for two weeks and I could get it out of my system and come home to my kennel.

Good sense. Common sense. Good dog.

What does it say in the tea-leaves? Nothing but a capital L.

When Jacqueline came home I kissed her and said, 'I wish you didn't smell of the Zoo.'

She looked surprised. 'I can't help it. Zoos are smelly places.'

She went immediately to run a bath. I gave her a drink thinking how I disliked her clothes and the way she switched on the radio as soon as she got in.

Grimly I began to prepare our dinner. What would we do this evening? I felt like a bandit who hides a gun in his mouth. If I spoke I would reveal everything. Better not to speak. Eat, smile, make space for Jacqueline. Surely that was right?

The phone rang. I skidded to get it, closing the bedroom door behind me.

It was Louise.

'Come over tomorrow,' she said. 'There's something I want to tell you.'

'Louise, if it's to do with today, I can't ... you see, I've decided I can't. That is I couldn't because, well what if, you know ...'

The phone clicked and went dead. I stared at it the way Lauren Bacall does in those films with Humphrey Bogart. What I need now is a car with a running board and a pair of fog lights. I could be with you in ten minutes Louise. The trouble is that all I've got is a Mini belonging to my girlfriend.

We were eating our spaghetti. I thought, As long as I don't say her name I'll be all right. I started a game with myself, counting out on the cynical clock face the extent of my success. What am I? I feel like a kid in the examination room faced with a paper I can't complete. Let the clock go faster. Let me get out of here. At 9 o'clock I told Jacqueline I was exhausted. She reached over and took my hand. I felt nothing. And then there we were in our pyjamas side by side and my lips were sealed and my cheeks must have been swelling out like a gerbil's because my mouth was full of Louise.

I don't have to tell you where I went the next day.

During the night I had a lurid dream about an ex-girlfriend of mine who had been heavily into papier-mâché. It had started as a hobby; and who shall object to a few buckets of flour and water and a roll of chicken wire? I'm a liberal and I believe in free expression. I went to her house one day and poking out of the letter-box just at crotch level was the head of a yellow and green serpent. Not a real one but livid enough with a red tongue and silver foil teeth. I hesitated to ring the bell. Hesitated because to reach the bell meant pushing my private parts right into the head of the snake. I held a little dialogue with myself.

ME: Don't be silly. It's a joke.

I: What do you mean it's a joke? It's lethal.

ME: Those teeth aren't real.

I: They don't have to be real to be painful.

ME: What will she think of you if you stand here all
        night?

I: What does she think of me anyway? What kind of
        a girl aims a snake at your genitals?

ME: A fun-loving girl.

I: Ha Ha.

The door flew open and Amy stood on the mat. She was
wearing a kaftan and a long string of beads. 'It won't hurt
you,' she said. 'It's for the postman. He's been bothering me.'

    'I don't think it's going to frighten him,' I said. 'It's only a
toy snake. It didn't frighten me.'

    'You've nothing to be frightened of,' she said. 'It's got a
rat-trap in the jaw.' She disappeared inside while I stood
hovering on the step holding my bottle of Beaujolais
Nouveau. She returned with a leek and shoved it in the
snake's mouth. There was a terrible clatter and the bottom
half of the leek fell limply on to the mat. 'Bring it in with you,
will you?' she said. 'We're eating it later.'

I awoke sweating and chilled. Jacqueline slept peacefully
beside me, the light was leaking through the old curtains.
Muffled in my dressing gown, I went into the garden, glad of
the wetness suddenly beneath my feet. The air was clean

with a hint of warmth and the sky had pink clawmarks pulled through it. There was an urban pleasure in knowing that I was the only one breathing the air. The relentless in-out-in-out of millions of lungs depresses me. There are too many of us on this planet and it's beginning to show. My neighbour's blinds were down. What were their dreams and nightmares? How different it would be to see them now, slack in the jaw, bodies open. We might be able to say something truthful to one another instead of the usual rolled-up Goodmornings.

I went to look at my sunflowers, growing steadily, sure that the sun would be there for them, fulfilling themselves in the proper way at the proper time. Very few people ever manage what nature manages without effort and mostly without fail. We don't know who we are or how to function, much less how to bloom. Blind nature. Homo sapiens. Who's kidding whom?

So what am I going to do? I asked Robin on the wall. Robins are very faithful creatures who mate with the same mate year by year. I love the brave red shield on their breast and the determined way they follow the spade in search of worms. There am I doing all the digging and there's little Robin making off with the worm. Homo sapiens. Blind Nature.

I don't feel wise. Why is it that human beings are allowed to grow up without the necessary apparatus to make sound ethical decisions?

The facts of my case are not unusual:

1 I have fallen in love with a woman who is married.

2 She has fallen in love with me.

3 I am committed to someone else.

4 How shall I know whether Louise is what I must
   do or must avoid?

The church could tell me, my friends have tried to help me, I could take the stoic course and run from temptation or I could put up sail and tack into this gathering wind.

For the first time in my life, I want to do the right thing more than I want to get my own way. I suppose I owe that to Bathsheba ...

I remember her visiting my house soon after she had returned from a six-week trip to South Africa. Before she had gone, I had given her an ultimatum: Him or me. Her eyes, which very often filled with tears of self-pity, had reproached me for yet another lover's half-nelson. I forced her to it and of course she made the decision for him. All right. Six weeks. I felt like the girl in the story of Rumpelstiltskin who is given a cellar full of straw to weave into gold by the following morning. All I had ever got from Bathsheba were bales of straw but when she was with me I believed that they were promises carved in precious stone. So I had to face up to the waste and the mess and I worked hard to sweep the chaff away. Then she came in, unrepentant, her memory gone as ever, wondering why I hadn't returned her trunk calls or written poste restante.

'I meant what I said.'

She sat in silence for about fifteen minutes while I glued

the legs back on a kitchen chair. Then she asked me if I was seeing anybody else. I said I was, briefly, vaguely, hopefully.

She nodded and turned to go. When she got to the door she said, 'I intended to tell you before we left but I forgot.'

I looked at her, sudden and sharp. I hated that 'we'.

'Yes,' she went on, 'Uriah got NSU from a woman he slept with in New York. He slept with her to punish me of course. But he didn't tell me and the doctor thinks I have it too. I've been taking the antibiotics so it's probably all right. That is, you're probably all right. You ought to check though.'

I came at her with the leg of the chair. I wanted to run it straight across her perfectly made-up face.

'You shit.'

'Don't say that.'

'You told me you weren't having sex with him anymore.'

'I thought it was unfair. I didn't want to shatter what little sexual confidence he might have left.'

'I suppose that's why you've never bothered to tell him that he doesn't know how to make you come.'

She didn't answer. She was crying now. It was like blood in the water to me. I circled her.

'How long is it you've been married? The perfect public marriage. Ten years, twelve? And you don't ask him to put his head between your legs because you think he'll find it distasteful. Let's hear it for sexual confidence.'

'Stop it,' she said, pushing me away. 'I have to go home.'

'It must be seven o'clock. That's your home-time, isn't it?

That's why you used to leave the practice early so that you could get a quick fuck for an hour and a half and then smooth yourself down to say, "Hello, darling," and cook dinner.'

'You let me come,' she said.

'Yes, I did, when you were bleeding, when you were sick, again and again I made you come.'

'I didn't mean that. I meant we did it together. You wanted me there.'

'I wanted you everywhere and the pathetic thing is I still do.'

She looked at me. 'Drive me home, will you?'

Art and Lies

FROM A DISTANCE only the light is visible; a speeding gleaming horizontal angel, trumpet out on a hard bend. The note bells the beauty of the stretching train that pulls the light in a long gold thread. It catches in the wheels, it flashes on the doors that open and close, that open and close, in commuter rhythm.

On the overcoats, briefcases, brooches, the light snags in rough-cut stones that stay unpolished. The man is busy. He hasn't time to see the light that burns his clothes and illuminates his face. The light pouring down his shoulders in biblical excess. His book is a plate of glass.

Art and Lies is a fragmented set of narratives. Three stories, Handel, Picasso, Sappho, but not the composer, not the painter, and somewhat the poet. Nobody finds love or comes near to doing so. Love is unreadable, untranslatable. Love as bafflement. Love as regret.

I don't know why the last line is, 'It was not too late.' I don't feel this book has hope in it.

I think I was lost when I was writing it and this was not a ball of string in the minotaur's labyrinth. I think I was the minotaur.

They are on the same train, Handel, Picasso, Sappho, fleeing a city where anything anyone would want to keep has fled already.

There is a question at the heart of this book:

How shall I live?

I think I was asking myself and getting no answers. But sometimes you have to get lost – both as a writer and as a reader. Sometimes only the question can be asked and the answer is somewhere in the distance – maybe a long way in the distance.

What I know is that life is distance learning. The next thing is out of reach. We reach it. The next thing is out of reach. We reach it.

IT HAPPENED, LATE one afternoon, when David arose from his couch and was walking upon the roof of his house, that he saw from the roof a woman bathing, and the woman was very beautiful. And David sent and inquired about this woman. And one said, 'Is not this Bathsheba, the daughter of Eliam, the wife of Uriah the Hittite?' So David sent messengers and took her; and she came to him and he lay with her. Then she returned to her house. And the woman conceived and she sent and told David, 'I am with child.'

So David sent word to Joab saying, 'Send me Uriah the Hittite.' Then David said to Uriah, 'Go down to your house and wash your feet.' And Uriah went out of the king's house and there followed him a present from the king. But Uriah slept at the door of the king's house with all the servants of his lord and did not go down to his house.

David said, 'Have you not come from a journey? Why did you not go down to your house?'

Uriah said to David, 'The ark, and Israel, and Judah dwell in booths and my lord Joab and the servants of my lord are camping in the open field; shall I then go to my house to eat and to drink and to lie with my wife? As you live and as your soul lives, I will not do this thing.' Then David said to Uriah, 'Remain here today also and tomorrow I will let you depart.' So Uriah remained in Jerusalem that day and the next. And David invited him and he ate in his presence and drank so that he made him drunk; and in the evening he went out to lie on his couch with the servants of his lord but he did not go down to his house. In the morning David wrote a letter to Joab and sent it by the hand of Uriah, 'Set Uriah in the forefront of the hardest fighting and then draw back from him that he may be struck down and die.' And as Joab was besieging the city he assigned Uriah to the place where he knew there were valiant men, and some of the servants of David fell. Uriah the Hittite was slain also.

When the wife of Uriah heard that Uriah her husband was dead she made lamentation for her husband. And when the mourning was over David sent and brought her to his house and she became his wife and bore him a son. But the thing that David had done displeased the Lord.

And the Lord sent Nathan to David. He came to him and said to him, 'There were two men in a certain city, the one rich and the other poor. The rich man had very many flocks and herds but the poor man had nothing but one little ewe lamb which he had bought. And he brought it up and it grew up with him and with his children; it used to eat of his morsel and drink of his cup and lie in his bosom and it was like a daughter to him. Now there came a traveller to the rich man and he was unwilling to take one of his own flock or herd to prepare for the wayfarer, but he took the poor man's lamb and prepared it for the man who had come to him.'

Then David's anger was greatly kindled against the man and he said to Nathan, 'As the Lord lives the man who has done this deserves to die and he shall restore the lamb fourfold, because he did this thing and because he had no pity.'

Nathan said to David, 'You are the man.'

(2 Samuel, 11 and 12:1–7)

'Because he had no pity.' The punishable sin is not lust, not even adultery, the sin is not to do with sex at all. It is a failure of feeling. Not an excess of passion but a lack of compassion.

I am a Sexualist. In flagrante delicto. The end-stop of the universe. Say my name and you say sex. Say my name and you say white sand under a white sky white trammel of my thighs.

Let me net you. Roll up roll up for the naked lady, tuppence a peep. Tup me? Oh no, I do the tupping in this show. I'm the horned god, the thrusting phallus, the spar and mainsail of this giddy vessel. All aboard for the Fantasy Cruise from Mitylene to Merrie England by way of Rome and passing through La Belle France. How long will it take? Not much more than two and a half thousand years of dirty fun and all at my own expense.

Am I making any sense? No? Here's a clue: Very Famous Men have written about me, including Alexander Pope (Englishman 1688–1744 Occupation: Poet) and Charles Baudelaire (Frenchman 1821–67 Occupation: Poet). What more can a girl ask?

I have a lot of questions, not least, WHAT HAVE YOU DONE WITH MY POEMS? When I turn the pages of my manuscripts my fingers crumble the paper, the paper breaks up in burnt folds, the paper colours my palms yellow. I look like a nicotine junkie. I can no longer read my own writing. It isn't surprising that so many of you have chosen to read between the lines when the lines themselves have become more mutilated than a Saturday night whore.

I've had to do that too; go down on the cocks of Very Famous Men, and that has put me in a position to tell you a trade secret: Their dose tastes just the same as anyone else's. I'm no gourmet but I know a bucket of semolina when I've got my head in it. You can lead a whorse to water but you can't make her drink. My advice? Don't swallow it. Spit the little hopefuls down the sink and let them wriggle up the drain. No, I'm not hard-hearted but I have better things to do with my stomach lining. And I have another question: When did he last go down on you?

So many men have got off on me. Large men, small men, bald men, fat men. Men with a hose like a fire-fighter, men with nothing but a confectioner's nozzle. Here they come, poking through the history books, telling you all about me.

I was born on an island. Can you see the marble beach and the glass sea? Both are lies. The white sand damp-veined is warm underfoot. The sea that softly reflects the hull will splinter it soon. What appears is not what is. I love the deception of sand and sea.

'A Deceiver.' 'A notorious seducer of women.' 'A Venom.' 'A God.' 'The Tenth Muse.' It is the job of a poet to name things, blasphemy when the things rise up to name the poet. The praise is no better than the blame. My own words have been lost amongst theirs.

Examine this statement: 'A woman cannot be a poet' Dr Samuel Johnson (Englishman 1709–84 Occupation: Language Fixer and Big Mouth.) What then shall I give up? My poetry or my womanhood? Rest assured I shall have to let go of one if I am to keep hold of the other. In the end the choice has not been mine to make. Others have made it for me.

In the old days I was a great poet but a bad girl. See Plato (Greek 427–347 BC Occupation: Philosopher), then, Ovid came along in the first century AD and tried to clean up my reputation with a proper tragic romance. Me, who could have had any woman in history, fell for a baggy-trousered bus conductor with the kind of below-the-waist equipment funsters put on seaside postcards for a joke. Fuck him? I couldn't even find him. He said I must have bad eyesight, I said it must be because of all those poems I was writing, late at night with only a tallow candle to keep me company. He said I should give it up, it was ruining our sex life.

The World and Other Places

IN THIS NIGHT-SOAKED bed with you it is courage for the day I seek. Courage that when the light comes I will turn towards it. Nothing could be simpler. Nothing could be harder.

In this night-covered world with you I hope to find what I'm looking for; a clue, a map, a bird flying south. And in the morning we will get dressed together and go.

There's a line in Virginia Woolf's essay 'On Being Ill', where she says, 'We do not know our own souls, let alone the souls of others.'

This soul-searching is what writing does/is. Drilling down through the layered accumulations of convention, cliché, fear, neglect, prejudice, hatred, tradition, good and bad, buried dreams and forgotten desires. Is the soul there at all? Yours? Mine? And is there any better way of knowing our own soul than through the souls of others?

———

I believe that fiction, long or short, can work on many levels all at once. The story, of course. The characters. Their lives.

A time that isn't our own – if the text is from the past, or if it is set in the past. Feelings evoked we might not otherwise feel. We expect fiction to deliver other places, other people.

But when we go deeper?

It hasn't been too fashionable to talk about the soul. We live in a material world. Religion is discredited as superstition or, worse, fundamentalism. Spirituality, even when detached from religion, looks a bit hippy, woolly, vague; a comfort-zone for those who can't quite manage life as a biological and chemical accident with miraculous consequences.

Already my language gives me away: miraculous consequences.

If you believe that life has an inside as well as an outside, then how can we recognise and protect that inner life? Develop it?

That has to be the job of art. Nothing works better as a tool for going deeper.

I am a writer because I want to go deeper.

I am on a quest. Is everything a quest story? Probably.

I look at the short fictions and I find the same preoccupations as in my longer work.

There's a story in *The World and Other Places* called 'The

Three Friends'. It's a little fairy story type thing – do you search for riches? Power? Sex?

Or that which cannot be found?

Does that seem like a hopeless quest? A journey for masochists only?

Maybe. But every time I get an answer it leads me to another question. That's all I know. The infinity of space.

The world . . . yes. But what about the other places?

There's a line in *The Powerbook*, 'When I was born I became the visible corner of a folded map.'

That's the journey. That's the unfolding. That's what the stories are.

THE BOAT IN the water . . .

I want to push further; to find the hidden cove, the little bay of delight that fear prevents. Sometimes I want to ride out the storm for no better reason than I need the storm. And if I die, I die. That's the gamble, the game. I cannot protect myself although I can take precautions. Society can protect me least of all. It does it by limiting my freedom. Freedom or protection? What kind of choice is that?

In the boat on the water, these things are clear.

The Powerbook

LOVING YOU IS LIKE lifting a heavy stone. It would be easier not to do it and I'm not sure why I am doing it. It takes all my strength and all my determination and I said I wouldn't love someone again like this.

Is there any sense in loving someone you can only wake up to by chance?

The Powerbook was a millennium novel, published in the wi-fi optimism of a new century.

Writers are all multiple personalities – that's why we're hard to live with – and the internet seemed to offer that playing shape-shifting of character, time, place, that is the core of fiction-making.

So I imagined a story where two people would play with each other online – inventing masks and costumes for themselves – it's a theatrical book. Unfolding their personal stories through a series of make-believe stories. And

Loving you is like lifting a heavy stone. It would be easier not to do it and I'm not sure why I am doing it

meeting in real life, to discover the entanglement of their actual and virtual worlds.

Yes. It's a love story.

THE STORIES WE sit up late to hear are love stories. It seems that we cannot know enough about this riddle of our lives. We go back and back to the same scenes, the same words, trying to scrape out the meaning. Nothing could be more familiar than love. Nothing else eludes us so completely.

In one strange scene a feral self-taught chemist finds his daughter moving among the dim-lit laboratory jars. She finds one labelled with a heart and a dagger. She picks it up, curious, afraid. Suddenly her father's whiskery face is right behind her.

'NEVER TOUCH THAT JAR! Never! If that gets loose, we're finished.'

'What's in it?'

'Love! There's love in that jar ...'

And so I discovered that love is a hazardous liquid.

There's no particular century to that scene. It's gothic but it could be now. I like moving about in time. Only in the outside world are we constrained by time. Our inner lives move freely between past, present and future, and we don't remember chronologically; memories apart in time sit side by side emotionally. As we get older our lives begin to form a pattern, not a straight line.

Fiction has real strengths here. As in the fairy tales, we can fall asleep and a hundred years flies past, or the actions of a lifetime can be compressed into a single day. In fiction, time can accelerate or slow down. That makes it satisfying because everyone knows that, whatever the clock says, an hour with someone you love passes far faster than an hour of boredom in a place you hate.

And I like history. I like writing about the past. The past is not the present as costume drama. Dropping our minds into the past is an underwater experience. We're weightless, floating in an element not our own. The light is blurry, the sights strange. And that experience is both liberating and unsettling.

As writers and readers we can go where we want to. For me, some fast cutting between one time and another – dropping in a story that's out of the main action, for instance – gives a breathing space and a different view.

The Powerbook is packed with stories – it's like having different windows open on your screen.

The writer of these stories, Ali, or Alix – because X marks the spot – will write you anything you like, provided you are prepared to enter the story as yourself and leave it as someone else.

To avoid discovery I stay on the run. To discover things for myself, I stay on the run

And I suppose this book has a motto. I took it from Harold Bloom's translation of the Jewish Blessing:

MORE LIFE INTO A TIME WITHOUT BOUNDARIES

I like that.

The extract below is a real meeting (I think) after a series of virtual encounters:

THE EVENING WAS cooling. She and I had walked without speaking, back over the Pont Neuf, to a little triangle of grass and birch trees set on all sides with small restaurants. I like to eat here. Someone once called it 'the sex of Paris'.

I was angry with myself. The afternoon had been an anticipation – I don't know what for – I do know what for, but I would have been glad and disappointed if nothing had started to happen. If we had gone to the restaurant as planned, and the rest had stayed as a memory whose truth-fulness is not in the detail.

The trouble is that in imagination anything can be per-fect. Downloaded into real life, it was messy. She was messy. I was messy. I blamed myself. I had wanted to be caught.

We slowed down. She spoke.

'You're angry with me.'

'This is the place – Paul's.'

'I said too much too soon.'

'The décor hasn't changed since the 1930s.'

'I don't hold you cheap.'

'The women who serve wear white aprons and won't speak English.'

'I just want to hold you.'

She took me in her arms and I was so angry I could have struck her, and at the bottom of my anger, conducting it, was a copper coil of desire.

'And I want to kiss you.'

A man was exercising two Dalmatians under the trees. Spots ran in front of my eyes.

'Kiss you here and here.'

The man threw them two red tennis balls and the dogs ran for the balls and fetched them back – black and white and red, black and white and red.

This feels like a grainy movie – the black dresses and white aprons of the matrons moving inside the lighted window of Paul's. Your black jeans and white shirt. The night wrapping round you like a sweater. Your arms wrapped round me. Two Dalmatians.

Yes, this is black and white. The outlines are clear. I must turn away. Why don't I?

In my mouth there is a red ball of desire.

'These tiny hairs on your neck ...'

Fetch. My heart returns to me what I turn away. I am my own master but not always master of myself. This woman wants to be ...

'Your lover.'

We went inside. I ordered artichoke vinaigrette and slices of duck with haricots verts. You had pea soup and smoked eel. I could have done with several bottles of wine, but settled for a Paris goblet, at one gulp, from the house carafe.

You tore up the bread with nervous fingers.

'Where were we?'

'It's not where I want to be.'

'It didn't feel like that when I held you.'

'No, you're right.'

'Well then?'

She has beautiful hands, I thought, watching her origami the baguette. Beautiful hands – deft, light, practical, practised. Mine was not the first body and it wouldn't be the last. She popped the bread into her mouth.

'Where shall I start?' I said, ready with my defence.

'Not at the beginning,' she said, feeding me crumbs.

'Why not?'

'We both know the usual reasons, the unwritten rules. No need to repeat them.'

'You really don't care, do you?'

'About you? Yes.'

'About the mess this will make.'

'I'm not a Virgo.'

'I am.'

'Oh God, just my luck. I bet you're obsessed with the laundry.'

'I am, as it happens.'

'Oh yes, I had a Virgo once. He could never leave the washing machine alone. Day and night, wash, wash, wash. I used to call him Lady Macbeth.'

'What are you going to call me?'

'I'll think of something.'

The artichoke arrived and I began to peel it away, fold by fold, layer by layer, dipping it. There is no secret about eating artichoke, or what the act resembles. Nothing else gives itself up so satisfyingly towards its centre. Nothing else promises and rewards. The tiny hairs are part of the pleasure.

What should I have eaten? Beetroot, I suppose.

A friend once warned me never to consider taking as a lover anyone who disliked either artichokes or champagne. That was good advice, but better advice might have been never to order artichokes or champagne with someone who should not be your lover.

At least I had chosen plain red wine.

And then I remembered the afternoon.

She looked at me, smiling, her lips glossy with oil.

'What are you thinking about?'

'This afternoon.'

'We should have gone to bed then.'

'We hardly spoke six sentences to each other.'

'That's the best way. Before the complications start.'

'Don't worry. No start. No complications.'

'Are you always such a moralist?'

'You make me sound like a Jehovah's Witness.'

'You can doorstep me any night.'

'Will you stop it?'

'As you say, we haven't started yet.'

'After supper we go back to the hotel and say goodnight.'

'And tomorrow you will catch the Eurostar to London.'

'And the day after you'll fly Air France to New York.'

'You must be a Jehovah's Witness.'

'Why must I?'

'You're not married but you won't sleep with me.'

'You are married.'

'That's my problem.'

'True ...'

'Well then ...'

'I've done it before and it became my problem.'

'What happened?'
'I fell in love.'

It was a long time ago. It feels like another life until I remember it was my life, like a letter you turn up in your own handwriting, hardly believing what it says.

I loved a woman who was married. She loved me too, and if there had been less love or less marriage I might have escaped. Perhaps no one really does escape.

She wanted me because I was a pool where she drank. I wanted her because she was a lover and a mother all mixed up into one. I wanted her because she was as beautiful as a warm afternoon with the sun on the rocks.

The damage done was colossal.

'You lost her?'
'Of course I did.'
'Have you got over it?'
'It was a love affair, not an assault course.'
'Love is an assault course.'
'Some wounds never heal.'
'I'm sorry.'

She held out her hand. What a strange world it is where you can have as much sex as you like but love is taboo. I'm talking about the real thing, the grand passion, which may not allow affection or convenience or happiness. The truth is that love smashes into your life like an ice floe, and even if your heart is built like the Titanic you go down. That's the size of it, the immensity of it. It's not proper, it's not clean, it's not containable.

She held out her hand. 'You're still angry.'
  'I'm still alive.'
  What to say? That the end of love is a haunting. A haunting of dreams. A haunting of silence. Haunted by ghosts, it is easy to become a ghost. Life ebbs. The pulse is too faint. Nothing stirs you. Some people approve of this and call it healing. It is not healing. A dead body feels no pain.

'But pain is pointless.'
  'Not always.'
  'Then what is the use of suffering? Can you tell me that?'

She thinks I'm holding on to pain. She thinks the pain is a souvenir. Perhaps she thinks that pain is the only way I can feel. As it is, the pain reminds me that my feelings are damaged. The pain doesn't stop me loving – only a false healing could do that – the pain tells me that neither my receptors nor my transmitters are in perfect working order. The pain is not feeling, but it has become an instrument of feeling.

She said, 'Do you still like having sex?'
  'You talk as though I've had an amputation.'
  'I think you have. I think someone has cut out your heart.'

———

I looked at her and my eyes were clear.

'That's not how the story ends.'

She put out her hand. 'I want to rescue you.'
  'From what?'
  'From the past. From pain.'
  'The past is only a way of talking.'
  'Then from pain.'
  'I don't want a wipe-clean life.'
  'Don't be so prickly.'
  'I'm sorry.'
  'What do you want? Tell me.'
  'No compromises.'
  'That's impossible.'
  'Only the impossible is worth the effort.'
  'Are you a fanatic or an idealist?'
  'Why do you need to label me?'
  'I need to understand.'
  'No, you want to explain me to yourself. You're not sure, so you need a label. But I'm not a piece of furniture with the price on the back.'
  'This is a heavy way to get some sex.'

The waitress cleared the plates and brought us some brown and yellow banded ice cream, the same colour as the ceilings and walls. It even had the varnishy look of the

1930s. The cherries round the edges were like Garbo kisses. You speared one and fed it to me.

'Come to bed with me.'

'Now?'

'Yes now. It's all I can offer. It's all I can ask.'

'No difficulties, no complications?'

'None.'

'Except that someone will be waiting for you in Room 29.'

'He'll be drunk and fast asleep.'

'And someone will be waiting for me.'

'Someone special?'

'Just a friend.'

'Well then ...'

'Good manners?'

'I'll leave a message at the night desk.'

She got up and fiddled with some change for the phone. 'Wait ...'

She didn't answer. There she was, at the phone, her face turned away from me.

We went to a small hotel that used to be a spa.

The bathrooms still have steam vents and needle showers, and if you turn the wrong knob while you're cleaning your teeth the whole bedroom will fill up with steam like the set of a Hitchcock movie. From somewhere out of the steam the phone will ring. There will be a footstep on the landing, voices. Meanwhile you'll be stumbling for the window, naked, blinded, with only a toothbrush between yourself and Paris.

The room we took at the Hotel Tonic was on the top floor. It had three beds with candlewick counterpanes and a view over the rooftops of the street. Opposite us, cut into the frame of the window, was a boy dancing alone to a Tina Turner record. We leaned out against the metal safety bars, watching him, watching the cars pull away. You put your hand on the small of my back under my shirt.

This is how we made love.

You kissed my throat.
    The boy was dancing.
    You kissed my collarbone.
    Two taxi drivers were arguing in the street.
    You put your tongue into the channel of my breasts.
    A door slammed underneath us.
    I opened your legs on to my hip.
    Two pigeons were asleep under the red wings of the roof.
    You began to move with me – hands, tongue, body.
    Game-show laughter from the television next door.
    You took my breasts in both hands and I slid you out of your jeans.
    Rattle of bottles on a tray.
    You don't wear knickers.
    A door opened. The tray was set down.
    You keep your breasts in a black mesh cage.

Car headlights reflected in the dressing-table mirror.

Lie down with me.

Get on top of me.

Ease yourself, just there, just there ...

Harry speaks French, he'll pick up the beer.

Push.

Stella or Bud?

Harder.

Do you want nuts?

Make me come. Make me.

Ring her after midnight your time, she said.

Just fuck me.

Got the number?

Fuck me.

The next morning I woke late and turned over to kiss her.
  She had gone. The sheet was still warm but she had gone.

Why Be Happy When You Could Be Normal?

Why Be Happy When You Could Be Normal? was written in a jolt of energy. In two weeks I found I had 15,000 words.

Why?

Is it a memoir? Not really. I think of it as an experiment with experience. None of us recalls our past as though we had carefully filmed it every moment of every day. And what if we had done? What lies beyond the frame? What was happening in our minds? There is always more to say, more to see, more to know.

I had a breakdown between summer 2007 and the end of 2008. In the autumn of 2008 someone I had loved deeply died too early, and at Christmas of that year my father died too. I buried him in a cold Saturnian January, and cancelled an interview with Susie Orbach, a woman I much admired and yet had never met. By May 2009 Susie and I were lovers.

And I had started to hunt for my birth mother – or Bio-Ma, as we called her.

Why?

Clearing out my father's things, I found some paperwork – yellowed, typewritten, as ancient as a codex, or so it felt, but really only from the early 1960s. My adoption. Some details about where I had been, and who I had been before that adoption.

I was no longer in breakdown, and Susie was, and is, a huge part of the healing of my mind. With her, I was able to go through the cellular trauma of looking into a past I had written (*Oranges Are Not The Only Fruit*) in order to own it, understand it, and, yes, to control it.

I knew early, how or why I don't know, that if you can read yourself as a fiction as well as a fact, you will be freer. If you are a story, you can change that story, especially how it ends.

I know this kind of thinking has been hijacked by the neo-liberal agenda of anyone can be a millionaire, a celebrity, a president. And if you are not what or who you want to be, it is your fault. Social justice and global inequality, class, race, background, has nothing to do with it. Utter crap and we know that.

But . . .

For some reason my imagination was strong and I was aligned with myself in crucial ways. For all the fuck-ups and failures, I knew I could write my way out – and I did.

Oranges is fiction. It's not the story of my life and I am not the Jeanette in that story. That is the point. I became my own fiction.

But . . .

Twenty-seven years after writing that book, the cluster of happenings I have described – and one I seem to have left out – forced me back towards the material I knew, and forward towards new material I never thought I wanted, or needed, to face.

As a writer I find I am forced towards discomfort, which is not the same thing as discontent.

The title comes from a Mrs W line, the day she gave me the clear choice of giving up the girl I loved or leaving home. I was sixteen. In our gloomy, cramped terraced house, with its body-count backyard (the kind of place where you bury your victims), and where she had operatically burnt my books in a Gotterdammerung of destruction, she asked me why I was doing this ('this' being in love, fatally, transgressively). I said, 'It makes me happy.' She said, 'WBHWYCBN?'

I wondered then, and have done for a long time since, whether this was a true binary, like black/white, good/evil, day/night, happy/normal?

It was a good question, if a brutal one, for us to end on. It was a gift, though a dark one, though I didn't know it at the time.

She was a violent philosopher.

WHEN LOVE IS UNRELIABLE and you are a child, you assume that it is the nature of love – its quality – to be unreliable. Children do not find fault with their parents until later. In the beginning the love you get is the love that sets.

I did not know that love could have continuity. I did not know that human love could be depended upon. Mrs Winterson's god was the God of the Old Testament and it may be that modelling yourself on a deity who demands absolute love from his 'children' but thinks nothing of drowning them (Noah's Ark), attempting to kill the ones who madden him (Moses), and letting Satan ruin the life of the most blameless of them all (Job), is bad for love.

True, God reforms himself and improves thanks to his relationship with human beings, but Mrs Winterson was not an interactive type; she didn't like human beings and she never did reform or improve. She was always striking me down, and then making a cake to put things right, and very often after a lockout we'd walk down to the fish and chip shop the next night and sit on the bench outside eating from the newspaper and watching people come and go.

For most of my life I have behaved in much the same way because that is what I learned about love. Add to that my own wildness and intensity and love becomes pretty

When love is unreliable and you are a child, you assume that it is the nature of love – its quality – to be unreliable

dangerous. I never did drugs, I did love – the crazy reckless kind, more damage than healing, more heartbreak than health. And I fought and hit out and tried to put it right the next day. And I went away without a word and didn't care.

Love is vivid. I never wanted the pale version. Love is full strength. I never wanted the diluted version. I never shied away from love's hugeness but I had no idea that love could be as reliable as the sun. The daily rising of love.

The Gap of Time

THE GAP OF TIME is a cover version of Shakespeare's *The Winter's Tale*. It was commissioned by the Hogarth Press as part of their Shakespeare celebrations for the 400th anniversary of his death in 2016.

It never occurred to me to work with any other play; not because I don't know them and love them – probably I go back to Shakespeare more than any other writer – but because this one has so many personal connections. Or do I mean personal obsessions?

Time. Second Chances. Forgiveness. Love (always love). And . . .

At the shining centre of the play is an abandoned child. And I am.

As an adopted child, I was always trying to get a reading of myself. Foundling stories of every kind were signs, symbols, symmetries and clues. Often the child left to chance becomes the key to what happens next in the larger drama – but in non-linear time, 'next' can signify backwards as well as forwards. We imagine that the future depends on the past. In *The Winter's Tale* the past depends on the future. Time's arrow shoots both ways until that which is lost is found.

But time's not an arrow, is it?

Time is a boomerang.

The past keeps returning until we nail it.

My version of Shakespeare's story is set now. I didn't want Leontes to be King of Sicilia, but he had to be an Alpha Male who does what he likes, and who is reckless with the lives of others. So I made him a banker called Leo who runs Sicilia, a hedge fund. His wife, MiMi, is a singer, as a nod to the fact that the play itself is full of songs. Polixenes, Leontes's best friend and supposed seducer of Hermione (MiMi), becomes Xeno. Xeno is a gay man. A video-game designer living in New Bohemia, a fictional city in America, based on New Orleans.

In my story the two boys were sent to boarding school together by their divorcing families. This at least gives us a sense of their shared damage and shared experience.

Shakespeare gives us no back story to any of his characters in *The Winter's Tale*. We see a long friendship between two men, a possessive marriage, a jealous husband.

But we see, too, a friendship between Hermione and Polixenes that is intimate and playful. I wanted to preserve that friendship in my version – so I had Xeno sent by Leo to woo MiMi back to him after their first parting.

MiMi and Xeno find there is an attraction. Neither acts on it.

IT WAS AUGUST. THE banks of the Seine had been transformed into a seaside fantasy, part *plage*, part stalls of street food and pop-up bars. The weather was hot. People were easy.

Leo had sent Xeno to ask MiMi to give him another chance.

'I'll mess it up if I see her. You explain.'

'What do you want me to say?'

'I don't know! The long form of "I love you."'

Leo gave Xeno a piece of paper in his bad handwriting. 'This is the long form.'

Xeno looked at it. He nearly laughed, but his friend was so hangdog and anxious that he just nodded while he was reading.

'I've been working on it,' said Leo.

1 Can I live without you? Yes.
2 Do I want to? No.
3 Do I think about you often? Yes.
4 Do I miss you? Yes.
5 Do I think about you when I am with another woman? Yes.
6 Do I think that you are different to other women? Yes.

7 Do I think that I am different to other men? No.

8 Is it about sex? Yes.

9 Is it only about sex? No.

10 Have I felt like this before? Yes and no.

11 Have I felt like this since you? No.

12 Why do I want to marry you? I hate the idea of you marrying someone else.

13 You are beautiful.

So when they had walked awhile and stopped for water at a bar selling *l'eau* in fancy blue bottles, Xeno got out the piece of paper and gave it to MiMi. She started laughing. 'No, listen,' said Xeno, 'he's awkward but he means it. This is his way of being sure.'

MiMi shook her head. 'I don't know.'

'Then say yes,' said Xeno.

'Pourquoi?'

They walked on. They talked about life as flow. About nothingness. About illusion. About love as a theory marred by practice. About love as practice marred by theory. They talked about the impossibility of sex. Was sex different for men? With men? What did it feel like to fall in love? To fall out of love?

'There's a theory,' said Xeno, 'the Gnostics started it as a rival to Christianity right back at the start; this world, ours, was created Fallen, not by God, who is absent, but by a Lucifer-type figure. Some kind of dark angel. We didn't sin, or fall from grace, it wasn't our fault. We were born this way. Everything we do is falling. Even walking is a kind of controlled falling. But that's not the same as failing. And if we know this (gnosis) the pain is easier to bear.'

'The pain of love?'

'What else is there? Love. Lack of love. Loss of love. I never bought into status and power – even fear of death – as independent drivers. The platform we stand on, or fall from, is love.'

'That is romantic for a man who never commits.'

'I like the idea,' said Xeno. 'But I like the idea of living on the moon too. Sadly, it's 293,000 miles away and has no water.'

'But you have come here to see me because you want me to marry Leo.'

'I'm just the messenger.'

They walked to a restaurant in a triangle where some boys were playing boules. A man was exercising two Dalmatians, throwing a red tennis ball. Black and white and red. Black and white and red. The evening was cooling.

They ordered artichokes and haddock. Xeno sat beside MiMi while she talked him through the menu.

'What about you?' MiMi asked Xeno.

'I'm moving to America – the gaming work is there.'

'But you'll be around?'

'I'll always be around.'

What else is there? Love. Lack of love. Loss of love. I never bought into status and power – even fear of death – as independent drivers. The platform we stand on, or fall from, is love

What would it be like if we didn't have a body? If we communicated as spirits do? Then I wouldn't notice the smile of you, the curve of you, *the hair that falls into your eyes*, your arms on the table, brown with faint hairs, *the way you hook your boots on the bar of the chair*, that my eyes are grey and yours are green, *that your eyes are grey and mine are green*, that you have a crooked mouth, that you are petite but your legs are long like a sentence I can't finish, *that your hands are sensitive, and the way you sit close to me to read the menu so that I can explain what things are in French*, and I love your accent, the way you speak English, and never before has anyone said "addock' the way you say it, and it is no longer a smoked fish but a word that sounds like (the word that comes to mind and is dismissed is love). *Do you always leave your top button undone like that? Just one button? So that I can imagine your chest from the animal paw of hair that I can see?* She's not a blonde. No. I think her hair is naturally dark but I like the way she colours it in sections and the way she slips off her shoes under the table. Disconcerting, the way you look at me when we talk. *What were we talking about?*

She ordered a baba au rhum and the waiter brought the St James rum in a bottle and plonked it on the table.

She said, 'Sometimes I'm Hemingway: I I am a Chamberry kir with oysters. Later, for inspiration, a rum St James. It's a brute.'

Xeno sniffed it. Barbecue fuel. But he poured a shot anyway.

She drank her coffee. A couple walked by fighting about the dry-cleaning. You meet someone and you can't wait to get your clothes off. A year later and you're fighting about the dry-cleaning. The imperfections are built into the design.

But then, thought Xeno, beauty isn't beauty because it's perfect.

MiMi was sitting with her knees up, bare legs, her eyes like fireflies.

Xeno smiled: what was number 13 on Leo's list? *You are beautiful.*

They walked hand in hand back to the apartment on Saint Julien le Pauvre.

The staircase was dark. Xeno ran his hand up the seventeenth century iron banister that curved up the building as the narrow staircase rounded the landings like a recurring dream and the doors were closed onto other rooms.

MiMi opened the door into her apartment. The only light came from the street lamps outside. She hadn't closed the long shutters. She went over to the window, standing framed in the window in her blue dress in the yellow light, like a Matisse cut-out of herself.

Xeno came and stood behind her. He didn't shut the front door and he had such a quiet way of moving that she seemed not to hear him. He wondered what she was thinking.

He was directly behind her now. She smelled of limes and mint. She turned. She turned right into Xeno. Up against him. He put his arms round her and she rested her head on his chest.

For a moment they stood like that, then MiMi took his hand and led him to her bed – a big *bateau lit* in the back of the apartment. She lifted her hand and stroked the nape of his neck.

On the landing outside, the electric light, footsteps up the stairs, a woman's heavy French accent complaining about the hot weather. A man grunting in response. The couple climbed slowly on past MiMi's apartment, carrying their groceries, not even glancing in through the open door.

And then Xeno was walking swiftly down the stairs.

Inside *The Winter's Tale* are stories embryonic and untold. On the stage it isn't possible to run those multiple stories. The action and drama must move forward in the two hours or so of theatre.

In a novel it's possible to lift those buried stories into view. The form lends itself to interiority and reflection. We get a glimpse of something and we follow it in our minds.

But the drama still has to happen – and the speed at which *The Winter's Tale* hits us – like an out-of-control truck – was what I wanted for the opening of the novel. So I inverted the structure of the play so that the opening chapter blasts us straight into a car-jack and murder, one stormy night in New Bohemia. And suddenly there's an abandoned baby left in a hospital BabyHatch.

Shakespeare has Perdita, 'the little lost one', raised by a Shepherd and his son the Clown. For me, Shep and Clo are a couple of late-night black guys who instinctively do the right thing at the right time.

For Shakespeare, recognising time as a player is central to so much of his work. There's a time to get things right – or disastrously wrong. Leontes – because he doesn't understand that he doesn't own time – learns the hard way. Shakespeare's late plays are about second chances and forgiveness. As I get older both things matter to me more. I'm an optimist but time is short. Getting things wrong is easier than getting things right. I'm aware of how much we need the generosity and patience of others.

In *The Winter's Tale*, it's the women, Hermione, Perdita and Paulina, who pull the thing to rights. They are an interesting manifestation of the Great Goddess in her triple form as mother, daughter and wise woman. The female principle saves the play from the usual consequences of male rage.

And at last, in Shakespeare, the women stop dying in the fall-out of the hero's soul. Hermione, Perdita and Paulina are alive at the end of *The Winter's Tale*. That's progress.

If there are only four possible endings to any story – comedy, tragedy, revenge and forgiveness – then Shakespeare leaves us where we want to be, as the motionless statue of Hermione steps down to rejoin the flow of time, and to let the past be over.

I altered the ending because I wanted the last word to be Perdita's. If the future exists, the new generation will have to discover it, like a territory not subject to the violent destructiveness of the past.

It has been strange, in the middle of so much global horror, to work with this play. Shakespeare had had it with the 'Great Man' theory of history. The heroes and villains are done. Instead, almost shyly, the women are on stage and the baby – nearly destroyed but saved – has returned.

Here's the very last part of the book:

PERDITA

SOON THIS WILL become our life together and we have to live in the world like everyone else. We have to go to work, have children, make homes, make dinner, make love, and the world is low on goodness these days so our lives may come to nothing. We will have dreams but will they come true?

Maybe we'll forget that we were the site where the miracle happened. The place of pilgrimage that fell into disuse, overgrown with weeds, run-down and neglected. Maybe we won't stay together. Maybe life is too hard anyway. Maybe love is just for the movies.

Maybe we'll hurt each other so much that we will deny that what happened happened. We'll find an alibi to prove that we were never there. Those people didn't exist.

Maybe, one night, when the weather is bad and you are holding my wrists too tight, I'll take a torch and go for a walk in the rain, my collar up against the wind, and the stars not there in the dark, and a bird startles out of the hedge, and there's the gleam of puddles under battery-light, and further off the sound of the main road, but here the sound of the night and my footsteps and my breathing.

Maybe then I will remember that, although history repeats itself and we always fall, and I am a carrier of history whose brief excursion into time leaves no mark, yet I have known something worth knowing, wild and unlikely and against every rote.

Like a pocket of air in an upturned boat.

Love. The size of it. The scale of it. Unimaginable. Vast. Your love for me. My love for you. Our love for one another. Real. Yes. Though I find my way by flashlight in the dark, I am witness and evidence of what I know; this love.

The atom and jot of my span.

Christmas Days

WHY ARE THE REAL things, the important things, so easily mislaid under the things that hardly matter at all?

When I was having a breakdown I came home one night to a cold, empty house and I was too depressed to cook or light the fire. And too broken to sleep.

Christmas was coming and so I decided to tell myself a story.

I learned this years ago, as a child, when my mother, Mrs Winterson, used to shut me in the coal-shed as a punishment.

There are only two things you can do when locked in a coal-shed: count coal, a limited activity, or tell yourself a story. And so I escaped my confinement as many have done before me – by vanishing into my imagination.

———

That Christmas, then, I thought I would re-tell the Nativity story from the point of view of the Donkey. Nothing special about that, except that I was the Donkey, feeling small, overlooked, unlikely, carrying my own body weight and too much more. In the story the Donkey auditions with all the animals for the job of carrying the Christ Child. Down to the last three, he has to beat the Lion: '*If He is to be the King of the World, He should be carried by the King of the Beasts.*' And the Unicorn: '*If He is to be the Mystery of the World, He should be carried by the most mysterious of us all.*'

The Donkey says, '*If He is to bear the Burdens of the World, He had better be carried by me . . .*'

Later in the story, the angels are sitting on the wormy, shattered roof of the stable, their feet dangling over the rim of time. A foot touches the Donkey's nose, and it turns golden.

I had need of a golden nose.

The twelve stories in the collection are mixed up with twelve recipes. These recipes, like Ruth Rendell's Red Cabbage or Kamila Shamsie's Turkey Biriyani, are all food cooked with friends, or personal rituals, like My New Year's Day Steak Sandwich.

I put in everything I like. Christmas doesn't have to be a commercial hijack, but the only way to prevent that is to make it personal and meaningful.

Our lives are losing both the personal and the

meaningful. Every occasion to return those values matters. And Christmas is celebrated all over the world by people of faith and people of no faith. It is potentially a time for coming together, as well as a time for reflection.

And, in these dark days of nationalism and unthinking hatreds, community and reflection give us a different world view. One planet. One people. Many different lives.

The book is a celebration of Christmas and a history of Christmas. Here are the myths and facts of Christmas: did you know it was the Coca-Cola Company that gave Santa a makeover in 1931, and turned his green robes red?

Did you know that Puritans in England and New England succeeded in banning Christmas for years because it was too pagan?

You did? Well, just enjoy the stories, then: ghost stories, magical interventions, SnowMamas, speaking frogs and froglissimos, funny stories, spooky stories and love stories, of course. Because everything comes back to love.

TIME IS A BOOMERANG, not an arrow.

I was adopted by Pentecostals and stamped Missionary. Christmas was important in the missionary calendar. From the beginning of November, either we were preparing packages to send to the Foreign Field or we were preparing packages to deliver to those in Hot Places returning to the Home Front.

It might have been because my parents had been in

WWII. It might have been because we lived in End Time, waiting for Armageddon. Whatever the reason, there was a drill to Christmas, from making the mincemeat for the mince pies to singing carols to, or rather at, the unsaved of Accrington. Still, Mrs Winterson loved Christmas. It was the one time of the year when she went out into the world looking as though the world was more than a vale of tears.

She was an unhappy woman, and so this happy time in our house was precious. I am sure I love Christmas because she did.

On December 21st every year my mother went out in her hat and coat while my father and I strung up the paper chains, made by me, from the corners of the parlour cornice to the centre light bulb.

Eventually my mother returned, in what seemed to be a hailstorm, though maybe that was her personal weather. She carried a goose, half-in, half-out of her shopping bag, its slack head hung sideways like a dream nobody can remember. She passed it to me – goose and dream – and I plucked the feathers into a bucket. We kept the feathers to restuff whatever needed restuffing, and we saved the thick goose fat drained from the bird for roasting potatoes through the winter. Apart from Mrs W, who had a thyroid problem, everyone we knew was as thin as a ferret. We needed goose fat.

After I had left home, and later gone to university at Oxford, I went back to the old house, that first Christmas-time. My mother had given me the ultimatum to leave home long since, when I fell in love with a girl, and in a religious house like ours I might as well have married a goat. We hadn't spoken since that time. I had lived in a Mini for a bit, lodged with a teacher and eventually left town.

During my first term at Oxford I received a postcard — one of those postcards that says POST CARD in blue letters at the top. Underneath, in her immaculate copperplate handwriting, was the message: ARE YOU COMING HOME THIS CHRISTMAS? LOVE MOTHER.

As I reached our little terraced house at the top of the street I could hear the mostly musical sounds of what is best described as a bossa-nova version of 'In the Bleak Midwinter'. My mother had thrown out the old upright piano and got herself an electronic organ with double keyboard, orchestra stops, drum and bass.

She hadn't seen me for two years. Nothing was said. We spent the next hour admiring the effects of snare drum and trumpet solo on 'Hark! The Herald Angels Sing'.

My Oxford friend from St Lucia was due to visit me at home, which was brave of her, but when I had tried to explain about my family she thought I was exaggerating.

At first the visit was a great success. Mrs W considered a black friend as a missionary endeavour all of its own. She went round to the retired missionaries from the church and asked, 'What do they eat?' Pineapples, came the answer.

When Vicky arrived my mother gave her a wool blanket

she had knitted so that Vicky would not be cold. 'They feel the cold,' she told me.

Mrs Winterson was an obsessive and she had been knitting for Jesus all year. The Christmas tree had knitted decorations on it, and the dog was imprisoned inside a Christmas coat of red wool with white snowflakes. There was a knitted Nativity scene, and the shepherds were wearing little scarves because this was Bethlehem on the bus route to Accrington.

My dad opened the door dressed in a knitted waistcoat and matching knitted tie. The whole house had been re-knitted.

Mrs W was in a merry mood. 'Would you like some gammon and pineapple, Vicky? Cheese on toast with pineapple? Pineapples and cream? Pineapple upside-down cake? Pineapple fritters?'

Eventually, after a few days of this fare, Vicky said, 'I don't like pineapple.'

Mrs W's mood changed at once. She didn't speak to us for the rest of the day and she crushed up a papier-mâché robin. The next morning, at breakfast, the table was set with a pyramid of unopened tins of pineapple chunks and a Victorian postcard of two cats on their hind legs dressed up like Mr and Mrs. The caption said NOBODY LOVES US.

That night, when Vicky went to bed, she found that her pillow had been taken out of its pillowcase, and the pillowcase stuffed with warning leaflets about the Apocalypse.

She wondered whether to go home, but I'd seen worse and I thought things might improve.

On Christmas Eve we had a group of carol singers round from the church. Mrs W did seem happier. She had forced me and Vicky to wrap several half-cabbages in tinfoil and spear them with cocktail sticks of Cheddar cheese, topped with the rejected pineapple chunks.

She called these things sputniks. It was something to do with the Cold War. Tinfoil? Antennae? The scaremongering that the KGB had listening devices hidden in cheese?

Never mind. The offending pineapples had found a purpose and we were all singing carols quite happily when there was a knock at the door. It turned out to be the Salvation Army singing carols too.

This was reasonable. It was Christmas-time. But Mrs Winterson was having none of it. She opened the front door and shouted, 'Jesus is here. Go away.'

Slam.

When I went away after that Christmas I never went back. I never saw Mrs W again – she was soon too furious about my debut novel, *Oranges Are Not The Only Fruit*. Quote: 'It's the first time I've had to order a book in a false name.'

She died in 1990.

As you get older you remember the dead at Christmas. The Celts, during their midwinter festival of Samhain, expected the dead to join the living. Many cultures would understand that; not ours.

That is a pity. And a loss. If time is a boomerang and not an arrow, then the past is always returning and repeating. Memory, as a creative act, allows us to reawaken the dead, or sometimes to lay them to rest, as at last we understand our past.

Last Christmas I was alone in my kitchen, the fire lit – I love having a fire in the kitchen. I was pouring myself a drink when Judy Garland came on the radio singing 'Have Yourself a Merry Little Christmas'. I remembered how Mrs W had played that song on the piano. It was one of those moments we all know, of sadness and sweetness mixed together. Regret? Yes, I think so, for everything we got wrong. But recognition too, because she was a remarkable woman. She deserved a miracle to get her out of her trapped life of no hope, no money, no possibility of change.

Fortunately, she got the miracle. Unfortunately, the miracle was me. I was the Golden Ticket. I could have taken her anywhere. She could have been free . . .

The Christmas story of the Christ Child is complex. Here's what it tells us about miracles:

Miracles are never convenient (the baby's going to be born whether or not there's a hotel room – and there isn't).

Miracles are not what we expect (an obscure man and woman find themselves parenting the Saviour of the World).

Miracles detonate the existing situation – and the blow-up and the back-blast mean some people get hurt.

What is a miracle? A miracle is an intervention — it breaks through the space-time continuum. A miracle is an intervention that cannot be accounted for purely rationally. Chance and fate are in the mix. A miracle is a benign intervention, yes, but miracles are like the genie in the bottle — let them out and there's a riot. You'll get your Three Wishes, but a whole lot else besides.

Mrs W wanted a baby. She couldn't have one. Along comes me — but as she often said, 'The Devil led us to the wrong crib.' Satan as a faulty star.

That's the fairy-tale element of the story.

Sometimes the thing we long for, the thing we need, the miracle we want, is right there in front of us, and we can't see it, or we run the other way, or, saddest of all, we just don't know what to do with it. Think how many people get the success they want, the partner they want, the money they want, et cetera, and turn it into dust and ashes — like the fairy gold no one can spend.

So at Christmas I think about the Christmas story, and all the Christmas stories since. As a writer I know that we get along badly without space in our lives for imagination and reflection. Religious festivals were designed to be time outside of time. Time where ordinary time was subject to significant time. What we remember. What we invent.

So light a candle to the dead.

And light a candle to miracles, however unlikely, and pray that you recognise yours.

And light a candle to the living; the world of friendship and family that means so much.

And light a candle to the future; that it may happen and not be swallowed up by darkness.

And light a candle to love.

Lucky Love.

Afterword

LOVE – THAT moves the sun and the other stars? As Dante put it?

Love is as strong as death – as the Bible puts it.

Or this: 'When my love swears that she is made of truth/I do believe her, though I know she lies.' (WS. SONNET 138)

So many versions of love. So many love songs. So much that is romantic. Or sentimental.

I am still looking for clues. Still trying to understand what should be obvious, and isn't: how to love.

How to love?

Experience. Heartbreak. But hearts are made to be broken. It's integral to the design.

Writing is the best way I know to talk about the most difficult thing I know: Love.

THE DOOR OF the house opens. It's you, coming out of the house, coming towards me, smiling, pleased. It's you, and it's me, and I knew it would end like this, that you would be there, had always been there; it was just a matter of time.

Everything is imprinted forever with what it once was.

JEANETTE WINTERSON OBE was born in Manchester. Adopted by Pentecostal parents, she was raised to be a missionary. This did and didn't work out.

Discovering early the power of books, she left home at 16 to live in a Mini and get on with her education. After graduating from Oxford University she worked for a while in the theatre and published her first novel at 25. *Oranges Are Not The Only Fruit* is based on her own upbringing but using herself as a fictional character. She scripted the novel into a BAFTA-winning BBC drama. 27 years later she revisited that material in the bestselling memoir *Why Be Happy When You Could Be Normal?* She has written 10 novels for adults, as well as children's books, non-fiction and screenplays. She writes regularly for the *Guardian*. She lives in the Cotswolds in a wood and in Spitalfields, London.

She believes that art is for everyone and it is her mission to prove it.

RECOMMENDED BOOKS BY JEANETTE WINTERSON:

Oranges Are Not The Only Fruit
Why Be Happy When You Could Be Normal?
Christmas Days

BOOKS BY JEANETTE WINTERSON

Novels
Oranges Are Not The Only Fruit
The Passion
Sexing the Cherry
Written on the Body
Art and Lies
Gut Symmetries
The Powerbook
Lighthousekeeping
The Stone Gods
The Gap of Time

Comic Book
Boating for Beginners

Short Stories
The World and Other Places
Midsummer Nights (ed.)
Christmas Days

Novellas
Weight (Myth)
The Daylight Gate (Horror)

Non-fiction
Art Objects: Essays in Ecstasy and Effrontery

Memoir
Why Be Happy When You Could Be Normal?

Collaboration
LAND (with Antony Gormley and Clare Richardson)

Children's Books
Tanglewreck
The Lion, the Unicorn and Me
The King of Capri
The Battle of the Sun

How do we express Love?

Eating
NIGELLA LAWSON

VINTAGE MINIS

Jealousy
MARCEL PROUST

VINTAGE MINIS

Babies
ANNE ENRIGHT

VINTAGE MINIS

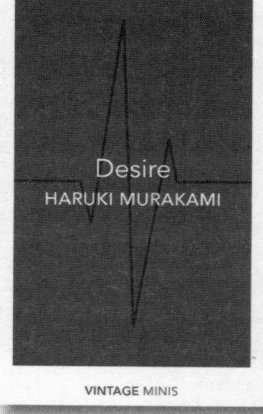

Desire
HARUKI MURAKAMI

VINTAGE MINIS

VINTAGE MINIS

The Vintage Minis bring you the world's greatest writers on the
experiences that make us human. These stylish, entertaining little
books explore the whole spectrum of life – from birth to death,
and everything in between. Which means there's something
here for everyone, whatever your story.

Desire	Haruki Murakami
Love	Jeanette Winterson
Babies	Anne Enright
Language	Xiaolu Guo
Motherhood	Helen Simpson
Fatherhood	Karl Ove Knausgaard
Summer	Laurie Lee
Jealousy	Marcel Proust
Sisters	Louisa May Alcott
Home	Salman Rushdie
Race	Toni Morrison
Liberty	Virginia Woolf
Swimming	Roger Deakin
Work	Joseph Heller
Depression	William Styron
Drinking	John Cheever
Eating	Nigella Lawson
Psychedelics	Aldous Huxley
Calm	Tim Parks
Death	Julian Barnes

vintageminis.co.uk

1 3 5 7 9 10 8 6 4 2

Vintage
20 Vauxhall Bridge Road,
London SW1V 2SA

Vintage Classics is part of the Penguin Random House
group of companies whose addresses can be found at
global.penguinrandomhouse.com

Penguin
Random House
UK

First published in Great Britain in 1974 by Jonathan Cape
First published by Vintage in 1995
A portion of this book first appeared in *Esquire*
This short edition published by Vintage in 2017

penguin.co.uk/vintage

A CIP catalogue record for this book is available from the British Library

ISBN 9781784872786

Typeset in 9.5/14.5 pt FreightText Pro
by Jouve (UK), Milton Keynes
Printed and bound by Clays Ltd, St Ives plc

Penguin Random House is committed to a sustainable future for
our business, our readers and our planet. This book is made from
Forest Stewardship Council® certified paper.

Work

JOSEPH HELLER

VINTAGE MINIS

The office in which I work

IN THE OFFICE in which I work there are five people of whom I am afraid. Each of these five people is afraid of four people (excluding overlaps), for a total of twenty, and each of these twenty people is afraid of six people, making a total of one hundred and twenty people who are feared by at least one person. Each of these one hundred and twenty people is afraid of the other one hundred and nineteen, and all of these one hundred and forty-five people are afraid of the twelve men at the top who helped found and build the company and now own and direct it.

All these twelve men are elderly now and drained by time and success of energy and ambition. Many have spent their whole lives here. They seem friendly, slow, and content when I come upon them in the halls (they seem dead) and are always courteous and mute when they ride with others in the public elevators. They no longer work hard. They hold meetings, make promotions, and allow their names to be used on announcements that are prepared and issued by somebody else. Nobody is sure anymore who really runs the company (not even the people who are credited with running it), but the company does run. Sometimes these twelve men at the top work for the government for a little while. They don't seem interested in doing much more. Two of them know what I do and recognize me, because I have helped them in the past, and they have been kind enough to remember me, although not, I'm sure, by name. They inevitably smile when they see me and say: 'How are you?' (I inevitably nod and respond: 'Fine.') Since I have little contact with these twelve men at the top and see them seldom, I am not really afraid of them. But most of the people I am afraid of in the company are.

Just about everybody in the company is afraid of somebody else in the company, and I sometimes think I am a cowering boy back in the automobile casualty insurance company for which I used to work very long ago, sorting and filing automobile accident reports after Mrs Yerger was placed in charge of the file room and kept threatening daily to fire us all. She was a positive, large woman of overbearing confidence and nasty amiability who never doubted the wisdom of her biases. A witty older girl named Virginia sat under a big Western Union clock in that office and traded dirty jokes with me ('My name's Virginia—Virgin for short, but not for long, ha, ha.'); she was peppy and direct, always laughing and teasing (with me, anyway), and I was too young and dumb then to see that she wasn't just joking. (Good God—she used to ask me to get a room for us somewhere, and I didn't even know how! She was extremely pretty, I think now, although I'm not sure I thought so then, but I did like her, and she got me hot. Her father had killed himself a few years before.) Much went on there in that company too that I didn't know about. (Virginia herself had told me that one of the married claims adjusters had taken her out in his car one night, turned insistent, and threatened to rape her or put her out near a cemetery, until she pretended to start to cry.) I was afraid to open doors in that company too, I remember, even when I had been sent for by one of the lawyers or adjusters to bring in an important file or a sandwich. I was never sure whether to knock or walk right in, to tap deferentially or rap loudly enough to be heard at once and command admission. Either way, I would often encounter expressions of annoyance and impatience (or feel I did. I had arrived too soon or arrived too late).

Mrs Yerger bullied us all. In a little while, nearly all of the file clerks quit, a few of the older ones to go into the army or navy, the rest of us for better jobs. I left for a job that turned out to be worse. It took nerve to give notice I was quitting, and it always has. (I rehearsed my resignation speech for days, building up the courage to deliver it, and formulated earnest, self-righteous answers to accusing questions about my reasons for leaving that neither Mrs Yerger nor anyone else even bothered to ask.) I have this thing about authority, about walking right up to it and looking it squarely in the eye, about speaking right out to it bravely and defiantly, even when I know I am right and safe. (I can never make myself believe I *am* safe.) I just don't trust it.

That was my first job after graduating (or being graduated *from*) high school. I was seventeen then—that 'older,' witty, flirting girl under the Western Union clock, Virginia, was only twenty-one (too young now by at least a year or two, even for me)—and in every job I've had since, I've always been afraid I was about to be fired. Actually, I have never been fired from a job; instead, I receive generous raises and rapid promotions, because I am usually very alert (at the beginning) and grasp things quickly. But this feeling of failure, this depressing sense of imminent catastrophe and public shame, persists even here, where I do good work steadily and try to make no enemies. It's just that I find it impossible to know exactly what is going on behind the closed doors of all the offices on all the floors occupied by all the people in this and all the other companies in the whole world who might say or do something, intentionally or circumstantially, that could bring me to ruin. I even torture myself at times with the ominous speculation that the CIA, FBI, or Internal Revenue Service has been investigating me surreptitiously for years and is about to close in and arrest me, for no other reason than that I have some secret liberal sympathies and usually vote Democratic.

I have a feeling that someone nearby is soon going to find out something about me that will mean the end, although I can't imagine what that something is.

———

IN THE NORMAL course of a business day, I fear Green and Green fears me. I am afraid of Jack Green because my department is part of his department and Jack Green is my boss; Green is afraid of me because most of the work in my department is done for the Sales Department, which is more important than his department, and I am much closer to Andy Kagle and the other people in the Sales Department than he is.

Green distrusts me fitfully. He makes it clear to me every now and then that he wishes to see everything coming out of my department before it is shown to other departments. I know he does not really mean this: he is too busy with his own work to pay that much attention to all of mine, and I will bypass him on most of our assignments rather than take up his time and delay their delivery to people who have (or think they have) an immediate need for them. Most of the work we do in my department is, in the long run, trivial. But Green always grows alarmed when someone from another department praises something that has come from my department. He turns scarlet with rage and embarrassment if he has not seen or heard of it. (He is no less splenetic if he *has* seen it and fails to remember it.)

The men in the Sales Department like me (or pretend to). They don't like Green. He knows this. They complain about him to me and make uncomplimentary remarks, and he knows this too. He pretends he doesn't. He feigns indifference, since he doesn't really like the men in the Sales

Department. I don't really like them, either (but I pretend I do). Generally, Green makes no effort to get along with the men in the Sales Department and is pointedly aloof and disdainful. He worries, though, about the enmity he creates there. Green worries painfully that someday soon the Corporate-Operations Department will take my department away from his department and give it to the Sales Department. Green has been worrying about this for eighteen years.

IN MY DEPARTMENT, there are six people who are afraid of me, and one small secretary who is afraid of all of us. I have one other person working for me who is not afraid of anyone, not even me, and I would fire him quickly, but I'm afraid of him.

THE THOUGHT OCCURS to me often that there must be mail clerks, office boys and girls, stock boys, messengers, and assistants of all kinds and ages who are afraid of *everyone* in the company; and there is one typist in our department who is going crazy slowly and has all of *us* afraid of *her*.

Her name is Martha. Our biggest fear is that she will go crazy on a weekday between nine and five. We hope she'll go crazy on a weekend, when we aren't with her. We should get her out of the company now, while there is still time. But we won't. Somebody should fire her; nobody will. Even Green, who actually enjoys firing people, recoils from the responsibility of making the move that might bring about her shattering collapse, although he cannot stand her, detests the way she looks, and is infuriated by every reminder that she still exists in his department. (It was he who hired her after a cursory interview, on the strong recommendation of the woman in the Personnel Department who is in charge of finding typists and sending them up.) Like the rest of us, he tries to pretend she isn't there.

We watch her and wait, and pussyfoot past, and wonder to ourselves how much more time must elapse before she comes on schedule to that last, decisive second in which she finally does go insane—shrieking or numb, clawing wildly or serene, comprehending intelligently that she has now gone mad and must therefore be taken away, or terrified, ignorant, and confused.

Oddly, she is much happier at her job than the rest of us. Her mind wanders from her work to more satisfying places, and she smiles and whispers contentedly to herself as she gazes out over her typewriter roller at the blank wall only a foot or two in front of her face, forgetting what or where she is and the page she is supposed to be copying. We walk away from her if we can, or turn our backs and try not to notice. We each hope somebody else will do or say something to make her stop smiling and chatting to herself each time she starts. When we cannot, in all decency, delay any longer doing it ourselves, we bring her back to our office and her work with gentle reminders that contain no implication of criticism or reproach. We feel she would be surprised and distraught if she knew what she was doing and that she was probably going mad. Other times she is unbearably nervous, unbearable to watch and be with. Everyone is very careful with her and very considerate. Green has complained about her often to the head of Personnel, who does not want to fire her either and has contacted her family in Iowa. Her mother has married again and doesn't want her back. Martha has bad skin. Everyone resents her and wishes she would go away.

THE COMPANY IS benevolent. The people, for the most part, are nice, and the atmosphere, for the most part, is convivial. The decor of the offices, particularly in the reception rooms and anterooms, is bright and colorful. There is lots of orange and lots of sea green. There are lots of office parties. We get all legal holidays off and take days off with pay whenever we need them. We have many three- and four-day weekends. (I can't face these long weekends anymore and don't know how I survive them. I may have to take up skiing.)

Every two weeks we are paid with machine-processed checks manufactured out of stiff paper (they are not thick enough to be called cardboard) that are patterned precisely with neat, rectangular holes and words of formal, official warning in small, black, block letters that the checks must not be spindled, torn, defaced, stapled, or mutilated in any other way. (They must only be cashed.) If not for these words, it would never occur to me to do anything else with my check but deposit it. Now, though, I am occasionally intrigued. What would happen, I speculate gloomily every two weeks or so as I tear open the blank, buff pay envelope and stare dully at the holes and numbers and words on my punched-card paycheck as though hoping disappointedly for some large, unrectifiable mistake in my favor, if I did spindle, fold, tear, deface, staple, and mutilate it? (It's my paycheck, isn't it? Or is it?) What would happen if, deliberately, calmly, with malice aforethought and obvious premeditation, I disobeyed?

I know what would happen: nothing. Nothing would happen. And the knowledge depresses me. Some girl downstairs I never saw before (probably with a bad skin also) would simply touch a few keys on some kind of steel key punch that would set things right again, and it would be as though I had not disobeyed at all. My act of rebellion would be absorbed like rain on an ocean and leave no trace. I would not cause a ripple.

I suppose it is just about impossible for someone like me to rebel anymore and produce any kind of lasting effect. I have lost the power to upset things that I had as a child; I can no longer change my environment or even disturb it seriously. They would simply fire and forget me as soon as I tried. They would file me away. That's what will happen to Martha the typist when she finally goes crazy. She'll be fired and forgotten. She'll be filed away. She'll be given sick pay, vacation pay, and severance pay. She'll be given money from the pension fund and money from

I suppose it is just about impossible for someone like me to rebel anymore

the profit-sharing fund, and then all traces of her will be hidden safely out of sight inside some old green cabinet for dead records in another room on another floor or in a dusty warehouse somewhere that nobody visits more than once or twice a year and few people in the company even know exists; not unlike the old green cabinets of dead records in all those accident folders in the storage room on the floor below the main offices of the automobile casualty insurance company for which I used to work when I was just a kid. When she goes crazy, her case will be closed.

I had never imagined so many dead records as I saw in that storage room (and there were thousands and thousands of even deader records at the warehouse I had to go to once or twice a year when a question arose concerning a record that had been dead a really long time). I remember them accurately, I remember the garish look of the data in grotesquely blue ink on the outside of each folder: a number, a name, an address, a date, and an abbreviated indication of whether the accident involved damage to property only (PD) or damage to people (PI, for personal injury). Often, I would bring sandwiches from home (baloney, cooked chopped meat with lots of ketchup, or tuna fish or canned salmon and tomato) and eat them in the storage room downstairs on my lunch hour, and if I ate there alone, I would read the New York *Mirror* (a newspaper now also dead) and then try to entertain myself by going through some old accident folders picked from the file cabinets at random. I was searching for action, tragedy, the high drama of detective work and courtroom suspense, but it was no use. They were dead. None of the names or appraisals or medical statements or investigations or eye-witness reports brought anything back to life. (The *Mirror* was better, and even its up-to-the-minute true stories of family and national misfortunes read just like the comic strips.) What impressed me most was the sheer immensity of all those dead records, the abounding quantity of all those drab old sagging cardboard file cabinets rising like joined, ageless towers from the floor almost to the ceiling, that vast, unending sequence of unconnected acci-dents that had been happening to people and cars long before I came to work there, were happening then, and are happening still.

There was a girl in that company too who went crazy while I was there. She was filed away. And in the company I worked for before this one, there was a man, a middle-minor executive, who went crazy and jumped out of a hotel win-dow and killed himself; he left a note saying he was sorry he was jumping out of the hotel window and killing himself, that he would have shot himself instead but didn't know how to obtain a gun or use one. He was picked up off the ground by the police (probably) and filed away.

I think that maybe in every company today there is always at least one person who is going crazy slowly.

THE COMPANY IS having another banner year. It continues to grow, and in many respects we are the leader in the field.

According to our latest Annual Report, it is bigger and better this year than it was last year.

We have twenty-nine offices now, twelve in this country, two in Canada, four in Latin America, and eleven overseas. We used to have one in Cuba, but that was lost. We average three suicides a year: two men, usually on the middle-executive level, kill themselves every twelve months, almost always by gunshot, and one girl, usually unmarried, separated, or divorced, who generally does the job with sleeping pills. Salaries are high, vacations are long.

People in the company like to live well and are unusually susceptible to nervous breakdowns. They have good tastes and enjoy high standards of living. We are well-educated and far above average in abilities and intelligence. Everybody spends. Nobody saves. Nervous breakdowns are more difficult to keep track of than suicides because they are harder to recognize and easier to hush up. (A suicide, after all, is a suicide: there's something final about it. It's the last thing a person does. But who knows with certainty when a person is breaking down?) But nervous breakdowns do occur regularly in all age and occupational groups and among all kinds of people—thin people and fat people, tall people and short people, good people and bad people. In the few years I have been in charge of my department, one girl and one man here have each been out for extended absences because they broke down. Both have been fixed and are now back working for me, and not many people outside my department know why they were gone. (One of them, the man, hasn't been fixed too well, I think, and will probably break down again soon. He is already turning into a problem again, with me and with everyone else he talks to. He talks too much.)

In an average year, four people I know about in the company will die of natural causes and two-and-a-half more (two men one year, three the next) will go on sick leave for ailments that will eventually turn out to be cancer. Approximately two people will be killed in accidents every year, one in an auto, the other by fire or drowning. Nobody in the company has yet been killed in an airplane crash, and this is highly mysterious to me, for we travel a lot by air to visit other offices or call on customers, prospects, and suppliers in other cities and countries. When regular, full-time employees do go on sick leave, they are usually paid their full salary for as long as the illness lasts (even though it may last a lifetime. Ha, ha), for the company excels in this matter of employee benefits. Everybody is divorced (not me, though). Everyone drinks and takes two hours or more for lunch. The men all flirt. The women all respond, except for a few who are very religious or very dull, or a few very young ones who are out in the world for the first time and don't understand yet how things are.

Most of us like working here, even though we are afraid, and do not long to leave for jobs with other companies. We make money and have fun. We read books and go to plays. And somehow the time passes.

———

THIS FISCAL PERIOD, I am flirting with Jane. Jane is new in the Art Department and not quite sure whether I mean it or not. She is just a few years out of college, where she majored in fine arts, and still finds things in the city daring, sophisticated, and intellectual. She goes to the movies a lot. She has not, I think, slept with a married man yet.

Jane is assistant head of the Art Department in Green's department. There are only three people in the Art Department. She has, like the rest of us, much time in which to brood and fantasize and make personal phone calls and kid around with whoever in the company (me) wants to kid around with her. She has a tall, slim figure that's pretty good and a clogged duct in one eye that makes it dribble with tears. She wears loose lamb's-wool sweaters that hug the long points of her small breasts beautifully. (Often, my fingertips would love to hug and roll those same long points of her small breasts just as beautifully, but I know from practice that my desire would not remain with her breasts for long. They make a convenient starting place.) Her good figure, prominent nipples, and clogged tear duct give me easy openings for suggestive wisecracks that cover the same ground as those I used to exchange with that older girl Virginia under that big Western Union clock in the automobile casualty insurance company (the company is still in business after all these years, at the same place, and probably the clock too is still there, running, although the office building is now slated to come down), except that now I am the older, more experienced (and more jaded) one and can control and direct things pretty much the way I choose. I have the feeling now that I can do whatever I want to with Jane, especially on days when she's had two vodka martinis for lunch instead of one (I, personally, hate vodka martinis and mistrust the mettle of people who drink them) or three whiskey sours instead of two. I could, if I wished, take her out for *three* vodka martinis after work one day and then up to Red Parker's apartment nearby, and the rest, I'd bet, would be as easy as pie (and possibly no more thrilling). I can make Jane laugh whenever I want to, and this, I know, can be worth more than half the game if I ever decide I seriously do want to play, but *I'm* not sure either whether I mean it or not.

Probably, I should be ashamed of myself, because she's only a decent young girl of twenty-four. Possibly I should be proud of myself, because she is, after all, a decent and very attractive young girl of only twenty-four whom I can probably lay whenever I want to. (I have her scheduled vaguely somewhere ahead, probably in the weeks before the convention, when I will be using everybody in the Art Department a great deal.) I don't really know how I am supposed to feel. I do know that girls in their early twenties are easy and sweet. (Girls in their late twenties are easier but sad, and that isn't so sweet.) They are easy, I think, because they are sweet, and they are sweet, I think, because they are dumb.

On days when *I've* had two martinis for lunch, Jane's breasts and legs can drive me almost wild as she parks her slender ass against the wall of one of the narrow corridors in the back offices near the Art Department when I stop to kid with her. Jane smiles a lot and is very innocent (she thinks I'm a very nice man, for example), although she is not, of course, without some sex experience, about which she boasts laughingly when I taunt her with being a virgin and denies laughingly when I taunt her with being a whore. I make teasing, rather mechanical and juvenile jokes (I've made them all before to other girls and ladies in one variation or another) about her eye or sweater or the good or bad life I pretend she is leading as I lean down almost slavering toward the front of her skirt (I don't know how she can bear me in these disgusting moments—but she can) and gaze lecherously over the long stretch of her thighs underneath, even though I know already I would probably find her legs a little thin when I had her undressed and would probably describe her as a bit too skinny if I ever spoke about her afterward to anyone.

I think I really do like Jane a lot. She is cheerful, open, trusting, optimistic—and I don't meet many of *those* anymore. Till now, I've decided to do nothing with her except continue the lascivious banter between us that tickles and amuses and encourages us both. Maybe her face and her figure are a little too good. I used to like girls who were tall and heavy, and slightly coarse, and maybe I still do, but I seem to be doing most of my sleeping these days with girls who are slim and pretty and mostly young. My wife is tall and slim and used to be very pretty when she was young.

———

THE PEOPLE IN the company who are most afraid of most
people are the salesmen. They live and work under pressure that is extraordinary. (I would not be able to stand it.)
When things are bad, they are worse for the salesmen; when
things are good, they are not much better.

They are always on trial, always on the verge of failure,
collectively and individually. They strain, even the most
secure and self-assured of them, to look good on paper;
and there is much paper for them to look good on. Each
week, for example, a record of the sales results of the
preceding week for each sales office and for the Sales
Department as a whole for each division of the company is
kept and compared to the sales results for the corresponding week of the year before; the figures are photocopied on
the latest photocopying machines and distributed throughout the company to all the people and departments whose
work is related to selling. In addition to this, the sales
record for each sales office for each quarter of each year
for each division of the company and for the company as a
whole is tabulated and compared to the sales record for
the corresponding quarter of the year before; along with
this, cumulative quarterly sales totals are also kept, and all
these quarterly sales totals are photocopied and distributed too. In addition to this, quarterly and cumulative
sales totals are compared with quarterly and cumulative sales totals* (*estimated) of other companies in the same
field, and these figures are photocopied and distributed
too. The figures are tabulated in stacks and layers of

parallel lines and columns for snap comparisons and judgments by anyone whose eyes fall upon them. The result of
all this photocopying and distributing is that there is
almost continuous public scrutiny and discussion throughout the company of how well or poorly the salesmen in
each sales office of each division of the company are doing
at any given time.

When salesmen are doing well, there is pressure upon
them to begin doing better, for fear they may start doing
worse. When they are doing poorly, they are doing terribly.
When a salesman lands a large order or brings in an important new account, his elation is brief, for there is danger he
might lose that large order or important new account to a
salesman from a competing company (or from a competing division of this company, which shows how complex
and orderly the company has become) the next time
around. It might even be canceled before it is filled, in
which case no one is certain if anything was gained or
lost. So there is crisis and alarm even in their triumphs.

Nevertheless, the salesmen love their work and would
not choose any other kind. They are a vigorous, fun-loving
bunch when they are not suffering abdominal cramps or
brooding miserably about the future; on the other hand,
they often turn cranky without warning and complain and
bicker a lot. Some sulk, some bully; some bully and then
sulk. All of them drink heavily until they get hepatitis or
heart attacks or are warned away from heavy drinking for
some other reason, and all of them, sooner or later, begin

to feel they are being picked on and blamed unfairly. Each of them can name at least one superior in the company who he feels has a grudge against him and is determined to wreck his career.

The salesmen work hard and earn big salaries, with large personal expense accounts that they squander generously on other people in and out of the company, including me. They own good houses in good communities and play good games of golf on good private golf courses. The company encourages this. The company, in fact, will pay for their country club membership and all charges they incur there, if the club they get into is a good one. The company seeks and rewards salesmen who make a good impression on the golf course.

Unmarried men are not wanted in the Sales Department, not even widowers, for the company has learned from experience that it is difficult and dangerous for unmarried salesmen to mix socially with prominent executives and their wives or participate with them in responsible civic affairs. (Too many of the wives of these prominent and very successful men are no more satisfied with their marital situation than are their husbands.) If a salesman's wife dies and he is not ready to remarry, he is usually moved into an administrative position after several months of mourning. Bachelors are never hired for the sales force, and salesmen who get divorced, or whose wives die, know they had better remarry or begin looking ahead toward a different job.

(Red Parker has been a widower too long and is getting into trouble for that and for his excessive drinking. He is having too good a time.)

Strangely enough, the salesmen, who are aggressive, egotistical, and individualistic by nature, react very well to the constant pressure and rigid supervision to which they are subjected. They are stimulated and motivated by discipline and direction. They thrive on explicit guidance toward clear objectives. (This may be one reason golf appeals to them.) For the most part, they are cheerful, confident, and gregarious when they are not irritable, anxious, and depressed. There must be something in the makeup of a man that enables him not only to *be* a salesman, but to *want* to be one. Ours actually *enjoy* selling, although there seem to be many among them who suffer from colitis, hernia, hemorrhoids, and chronic diarrhea (I have one hemorrhoid, and that one comes and goes as it pleases and is no bother to me at all, now that I've been to a doctor and made sure it isn't cancer), not to mention the frequent breakdowns from tension and overwork that occur in the Sales Department as well as in other departments, and the occasional suicide that pops up among the salesmen about once every two years.

The salesmen are proud of their position and of the status and importance they enjoy within the company, for the function of my department, and of most other departments, is to help the salesmen sell. The company exists to sell. That's the reason we were hired, and the reason we are paid.

———

THE PEOPLE IN the company who are least afraid are the few in our small Market Research Department, who believe in nothing and are concerned with collecting, organizing, interpreting, and reorganizing statistical information about the public, the market, the country, and the world. For one thing, their salaries are small, and they know they will not have much trouble finding jobs paying just as little in other companies if they lose their jobs here. Their budget, too, is small, for they are no longer permitted to undertake large projects.

Most of the information we use now is obtained free from trade associations, the U.S. Census Bureau, the Department of Commerce, the U.S. Chamber of Commerce, the National Association of Manufacturers, and the Pentagon, and there is no way of knowing anymore whether the information on which we base our own information for distribution is true or false. But that doesn't seem to matter; all that does matter is that the information comes from a reputable source. People in the Market Research Department are never held to blame for conditions they discover outside the company that place us at a competitive disadvantage. What is, is—and they are not expected to change reality but merely to find it if they can and suggest ingenious ways of disguising it. To a great extent, that is the nature of my own work, and all of us under Green work closely with the Sales Department and the Public Relations Department in converting whole truths into half truths and half truths into whole ones.

I am very good with these techniques of deception, although I am not always able anymore to deceive myself (if I were, I would not know that, would I? Ha, ha). In fact, I am continually astonished by people in the company who do fall victim to their own (our own) propaganda. There are so many now who actually believe that what we do is really important. This happens not only to salesmen, who repeat their various sales pitches aloud so often that they acquire the logic and authority of a mumbo-jumbo creed, but to the shrewd, capable executives in top management, who have access to all data and ought to know better. It happens to people on my own level and lower. It happens to just about everybody in the company who graduated from a good business school with honors: these are uniformly the most competent and conscientious people in the company, and also the most gullible and naïve. Every time we launch a new advertising campaign, for example, people inside the company are the first ones to be taken in by it. Every time we introduce a new product, or an old product with a different cover, color, and name that we present as new, people inside the company are the first to rush to buy it—even when it's no good.

When salesmen and company spokesmen begin believing their own arguments, the result is not always bad, for they develop an outlook of loyalty, zeal, and conviction that is often remarkably persuasive in itself. It produces that kind of dedication and fanaticism that makes good citizens and good employees. When it happens to a person in my own department, however, the result can be disastrous, for he begins relying too heavily on what he now thinks is the truth and loses his talent for devising good lies. He is no longer convincing. It's exactly what happened to Holloway, the man in my own department who broke down (and is probably going to break down again soon).

'But it's true, don't you see?' he would argue softly to the salesmen, the secretaries, and even to me, with a knowing and indulgent smile, as though what he was saying ought to have been as obvious to everyone as it was to him. 'We *are* the best.' (The point he missed is that it didn't matter whether it was true or not; what mattered was what people *thought* was true.)

He is beginning to smile and argue that way again and to spend more time talking to us than we want to spend listening to him. My own wish when he is buttonholing me or bending the ear of someone else in my department is that he would hurry up and have his nervous breakdown already, if he is going to have one anyway, and get it—and himself—out of the way. He is the only one who talks to Martha, our typist who is going crazy, and she is the only one who listens to him without restlessness and irritation. She listens to him with great intensity because she is paying no attention to him at all.

Everyone grew impatient with him. And he lost his power to understand (as he is losing this power again) why the salesmen, who would come to him for solid proof to support their exaggerations and misrepresentations, turned skeptical, began to avoid him, and refused to depend on him any longer or even take him to lunch. He actually expected them to get by with only the 'truth.'

It's a wise person, I guess, who knows he's dumb, and an honest person who knows he's a liar. And it's a dumb person, I guess, who's convinced he is wise, I conclude to myself (wisely), as we wise grown-ups here at the company go gliding in and out all day long, scaring each other at our desks and cubicles and water coolers and trying to evade the people who frighten us. We come to work, have lunch, and go home. We goose-step in and goose-step out, change our partners and wander all about, sashay around for a pat on the head, and promenade home till we all drop dead. Really, I ask myself every now and then, depending on how well or poorly things are going with Green at the office or at home with my wife, or with my retarded son, or with my other son, or my daughter, or the colored maid, or the nurse for my retarded son, is this *all* there is for me to do? Is this really the *most* I can get from the few years left in this one life of mine?

And the answer I get, of course, is always . . . *Yes!*

Because I have my job, draw my pay, get my laughs, and seem to be able to get one girl or another to go to bed with me just about every time I want; because I am envied and looked up to by neighbors and coworkers with smaller salaries, less personality, drab wives; and because I really do seem to have everything I want, although I often wish I were working for someone other than Green, who likes me

We goose-step in and goose-step out, change our partners and wander all about, sashay around for a pat on the head, and promenade home till we all drop dead and likes my work but wouldn't let me make a speech at the company convention in Puerto Rico last year, or at the company convention in Florida the year before—and who knows I hate him for that and will probably never forgive him or ever forget it.

(I have dreams, unpleasant dreams, that relate, I think, to my wanting to speak at a company convention, and they are always dreams that involve bitter frustration and humiliation and insurmountable difficulty in getting from one location to another.)

GREEN NOW THINKS I am conspiring to undermine him. He is wrong. For one thing, I don't have the initiative; for another, I don't have the nerve; and for still another thing, I guess I really like and admire Green in many respects (even though I also hate and resent him in many others), and I know I am probably safer working for him than I would be working for anyone else—even for Andy Kagle in the Sales Department if they did decide to move me and my department from Green's department to Kagle's department.

In many ways and on many occasions Green and I are friends and allies and do helpful, sometimes considerate things for each other. Often, I protect and defend him when he is late or forgetful with work of his own, and I frequently give him credit for good work from my department that he does not deserve. But I never tell him I do this; and I never let him know when I hear anything favorable about him.

I enjoy seeing Green apprehensive. I'm pleased he distrusts me (it does wonders for my self-esteem), and I do no more than necessary to reassure him.

And I am the best friend he has here.

So I SCARE Green, and Green scares White, and White scares Black, and Black scares Brown and Green, and Brown scares me and Green and Andy Kagle, and all of this is absolutely true, because Horace White really is afraid of conversation with Jack Green, and Johnny Brown, who bulldozes everyone around him with his strong shoulders, practical mind, and tough, outspoken mouth, is afraid of Lester Black, who protects him.

I know it's true, because I worked this whole color wheel out one dull, wet afternoon on one of those organizational charts I am always constructing when I grow bored with my work. I am currently occupied (as one of my private projects) with trying to organize a self-sufficient community out of people in the company whose names are the same as occupations, tools, or natural resources, for we have many Millers, Bakers, Taylors, Carpenters, Fields, Farmers, Hammers, Nichols (puns are permitted in my Utopia, else how could we get by?), and Butchers listed in the internal telephone directory; possibly we'd be a much better organization if all of us were doing the kind of work our names suggest, although I'm not sure where I'd fit in snugly there, either, because my name means nothing that I know of and I don't know where it came from.

Digging out valuable information of no importance distracts and amuses me. There are eleven Greens in the company (counting Greenes), eight Whites, four Browns, and four Blacks. There is one Slocum . . . me. For a while, there were two Slocums; there was a Mary Slocum in our Chicago office, a short, sexy piece just out of secretarial school with a wiggling ass and a nice big bust, but she quit to get married and was soon pregnant and disappeared. Here and there in the company colored men, Negroes, in immaculate white or blue shirts and very firmly knotted ties are starting to appear; none are important yet, and nobody knows positively why they have come here or what they really want. All of us (almost all of us) are ostentatiously polite to them and pretend to see no difference. In private, the salesmen make jokes about them.

('Know what they said about the first Negro astronaut?'
'What?'

'The jig is up.')

I am bored with my work very often now. Everything routine that comes in I pass along to somebody else. This makes my boredom worse. It's a real problem to decide whether it's more boring to do something boring than to pass along everything boring that comes in to somebody else and then have nothing to do at all.

Actually, I enjoy my work when the assignments are large and urgent and somewhat frightening and will come to the attention of many people. I get scared, and am unable to sleep at night, but I usually perform at my best under this stimulating kind of pressure and enjoy my job the most. I handle all of these important projects myself, and I rejoice with tremendous pride and vanity in the compliments I receive when I do them well (as I always do). But between such peaks of challenge and elation there is monotony and despair. (And I find, too, that once I've succeeded in impressing somebody, I'm not much excited about impressing that same person again; there is a large, emotional letdown after I survive each crisis, a kind of empty, tragic disappointment, and last year's threat, opportunity, and inspiration are often this year's inescapable tedium. I frequently feel I'm being taken advantage of merely because I'm asked to do the work I'm paid to do.)

On days when I'm especially melancholy, I begin constructing tables of organization from standpoints of plain malevolence, dividing, subdividing, and classifying people in the company on the basis of envy, hope, fear, ambition, frustration, rivalry, hatred, or disappointment. I call these charts my Happiness Charts. These exercises in malice never fail to boost my spirits—but only for a while. I rank pretty high when the company is analyzed this way, because I'm not envious or disappointed, and I have no expectations. At the very top, of course, are those people, mostly young and without dependents, to whom the company is not yet an institution of any sacred merit (or even an institution especially worth preserving) but still only a place to work, and who regard their present association with it as something temporary. To them, it's all just a job, from president to porter, and pretty much the same job at that. I put these people at the top because if you asked any one of them if he would choose to spend the rest of his life working for the company, he would give you a resounding *No!*, regardless of what inducements were offered. I was that high once. If you asked me that same question today, I would also give you a resounding *No!* and add:

'I think I'd rather die now.'

But I am making no plans to leave.

I have the feeling now that there is no place left for me to go.

NEAR THE VERY bottom of my Happiness Charts I put those people who are striving so hard to get to the top. I am better off (or think I am) than they because, first, I have no enemies or rivals (that I know of) and am almost convinced I can hold my job here for as long as I want to and, second, because there is no other job in the company I want that I can realistically hope to get. I wouldn't want Green's job; I couldn't handle it if I had it and would be afraid to take it if it were offered. There is too much to do. I'm glad it won't be (I'm sure it won't be).

I am one of those many people, therefore, most of whom are much older than I, who are without ambition already and have no hope, although I do want to continue receiving my raise in salary each year, and a good cash bonus at Christmastime, and I do want very much to be allowed to take my place on the rostrum at the next company convention in Puerto Rico (if it will be Puerto Rico again this year), along with the rest of the managers in Green's department and make my three-minute report to the company of the work we have done in my department and the projects we are planning for the year ahead.

It was downright humiliating to be the only one of Green's managers left out. The omission was conspicuous, the rebuff intentionally public, and for the following four days, while others had a great, robust time golfing and boozing it up, I was the object of expressions of pity and solemn, perfunctory commiseration from many people I hate and wanted to hit or scream at. It was jealousy and pure, petty spite that made Green decide abruptly to push me off the schedule after we were already in Puerto Rico and the convention had gotten off to such a promising start, and after I had worked so long and nervously (I even rehearsed at home just about every night—to the wonder and consternation of my family) on my speech for the three-minute segment of the program allotted to me and had prepared a very good and witty demonstration of eighteen color slides.

'Stop sulking,' Green commanded me curtly, wearing that smile of breezy and complacent innocence he likes to affect when he knows he is cutting deep. 'You're a rotten speaker anyway, and you'll probably be much happier working the slide machines and movie projectors and seeing that the slides of the others don't get all mixed up.'

'I want to do it, Jack,' I told him, trying to keep my voice strong and steady. (What I really wanted to do was burst into tears, and I was afraid I would.) 'I've never made a speech at a convention before.'

'And you aren't going to make one now.'

'This is a good talk I've got here.'

'It's dull and self-conscious and of no interest to anyone.'

'I've prepared some fine slides.'

'You aren't going to use them,' he told me.

'You did the same thing to me in Florida last year.'

'And I may do it again to you next year.'

'It isn't fair.'

'It probably isn't.'

I waited. He added nothing. He is so much better at this sort of ego-baiting than I am. It was my turn to speak, and he had left me nothing to say.

'Well,' I offered, shrugging and looking away.

'I don't care if it's fair or not,' he continued then. 'We're discussing an important company convention, not a college commencement exercise. I've got to use what little time they give us on the program as effectively as possible.'

'It's only three minutes,' I begged.

'I can use those three minutes better than you can.' He laughed suddenly, in the friendliest, most inoffensive fashion, as though nothing of consequence had just happened, letting me know in that arrogantly firm and rude manner of his that the argument was over. 'You must understand,

Bob,' he bantered (while I thought he might actually throw an arm around my shoulder. He never touches me), 'that this ambition of yours to make a little speech is nothing more than a shallow, middle-class vanity. I'm as shallow as you are, and as middle class as the best of them. So I'm going to take your three minutes away from you and cover you and your department in my own speech.'

You bastard, I thought. 'You're the boss,' I said.

'That's right,' he retorted coldly. 'I am. And you've already received more than enough attention here for an employee of mine. I want to make certain that nobody in this company gets the idea you're working for Andy Kagle and not for me. Or that you're doing a better job in your position than I'm doing in mine. Do you get what I mean?'

I certainly did, then. Green was reasserting his owner-ship of me publicly by demonstrating his right to treat me with contempt. And in his own long (rather self-conscious and pedantic) speech to the convention, he 'covered' me and my department in a single aside:

'And Bob Slocum and his people will help, when you feel you really need them, provided your requests are not unreasonable.'

And that was all, even though the two projects I had prepared for the coming year were the real high spots of the whole convention. Everyone was enthusiastic about them, even executives from other divisions of the com-pany, who were there as guests and observers: several asked to meet me and expressed the wish for work of similar kind and quality in their own areas of the company. I could have had a grand, triumphant time that week if not for Green (Green's?) kicking me off the schedule. The salesmen, who would have to use these projects in connection with their own work, congratulated me over and over again and never stopped slapping my back as they drank their whiskey in the evening and their Bloody Marys at breakfast in the morning (although some were already implying that they would want to discuss some modifications with me for their own purposes when the convention was over and we were back in New York). And even Arthur Baron, who is boss of us all in this division, drifted over to me on the terrace of the hotel during one of the twilight cocktail parties to tell me that both my projects were the best of their kind he had ever seen and would probably be very useful.

Arthur Baron, who is tactful and soft-spoken, addressed his comments to Green, who was standing beside me on the terrace because he does not like to be seen standing alone. (I was Green's roosting place for the moment, while he took his bearings; and I knew he would walk from me to someone more important as soon as he spied an opportunity. At crowded social or business gatherings, Green never leaves one person unless he has someone else to move to.) Green laughed quickly and gave all credit for the work to me; then he promptly diminished its importance by declaring he had not even seen any of it until that same afternoon (which was not true, since his criticism and suggestions all through the previous ten weeks had helped enormously, and nothing had been included without his inspection and approval). Green went on to observe, with another pleasant laugh, that the excellent response to something prepared by me without his knowledge or assistance all went to prove what a superb administrator he was. (All I was able to get in to Arthur Baron was a mumbled:

'Thanks. I'm glad.')

'The only legitimate goal of a good administrator,' Green continued affably, smiling directly at Arthur Baron and excluding me from his attention entirely, 'is to make himself superfluous as quickly as possible, and then have no work of his own to do until he's promoted to vice-president or retires. Don't you agree?'

Arthur Baron chuckled softly in reply and said nothing. He turned from Green to me, squeezed my shoulder, and moved away. Green beamed hopefully after him, then turned somber and began to worry (I guessed) that his hint to Arthur Baron about a vice-presidency had been too broad. He was already regretting it. Green knows he often pushes too hard—even at the exact moment he is pushing too hard—but he simply cannot control himself. (He is out of his own control.)

(I am in it.) I am dependent on Green. It was Green who hired and promoted me and Green who recommends me for the generous raises and good cash bonuses I receive each year.

'You were a third-rate assistant when you came to work for me,' he likes to joke when we are getting along comfortably with each other, 'and I turned you into a third-rate manager.'

I am grateful to Green for promoting me, even though he makes fun of me often and hurts my feelings.

GREEN IS A clever tactician with long experience at office politics. He is a talented, articulate, intelligent man of fifty-six and has been with the company more than thirty years. He was a young man when he came here; he will soon be old. He has longed from the beginning to become a vice-president and now knows that he will never succeed.

He continues to yearn, and he continues to strive and scheme, sometimes cunningly, other times desperately, abjectly, ineptly, because he can neither admit nor deny to himself for very long that he has already failed. Green fawns compulsively and labors clumsily to curry favor in every contact he has with someone in top management or someone near top management. He knows he does this and is ashamed and remorseful afterward for having demeaned himself in vain; he is willing to demean himself, but not in vain. Often, he will turn perverse afterward and deliberately offend somebody important in order to restore what dignity and self-respect he feels he has lost as a man. He is a baby.

Green is a clever tactician at office politics whose major mistake has always been to overestimate the value of office politics in getting ahead. He has refused to recognize that promotion to high place in the company has invariably been based on certain abilities and accomplishments. He has never really understood why so many people of less intelligence, taste, knowledge, and imagination have gone so much further than he has and *have* become vice-presidents. He does not see that they work hard continuously and that they believe in the company, that they do well and meticulously whatever they are asked to do, that they do *everything* they are asked to do, and that they do *only* what they are asked to do—and that this is what the company wants. Green will not grant that these people are all luminously well-qualified for the higher positions into which they are moved.

At least they *appear* to be well-qualified for their new positions at the time the promotions are made. Periodically, errors occur: forecasts miscarry and people fail; a man tires, weakens in will, or buckles under new responsibilities at the office or new problems at home and ceases to operate as anticipated, and we have another minor malfunction in Personnel. We have another nervous breakdown or another executive (the envy of rivals and subordinates) who resigns (in quiet disgrace) for a job with another company or is pushed aside to allow someone else to move through or retires early or puts a bullet through his head. Periodically, I would imagine, we have single instances of all: a man breaks down, is pushed aside, resigns or retires, and then puts a bullet through his head, although I am unable to think of anyone offhand who has succeeded in traversing this full gamut of defeat. The company survives all mishaps.

While other men in high position work hard and believe in the company, Green worries hard and still tries to believe in himself. He has a vacillating infatuation for Mildred, a young, divorced girl in his department who helps coordinate production, and he surprises her often in the office, or at the banks of elevators, by kissing her suddenly and noisily on the mouth, always though with a flippant, loud remark to denote indifference and only, I suspect, when someone else is there to see. Other times he will stride past her without notice or make some terse criticism of her work or the appearance of her desk, humbling and wounding her cruelly without provocation. And she, of course, adores him in return and is scared stiff. That is, I think, the way Green wants all people to feel about him, adoring and scared stiff.

He is, I think, as big a coward as I am; yet, he is the only person in the company with enough courage to behave badly. I envy that: I am cordial and considerate to many people I detest (I am cordial and considerate to just about *everybody*, I think, except former girl friends and the members of my family); I trade jokes convivially with several salesmen who annoy the hell out of me and make me waste much of my time with their frantic and contradictory requests; I get drunk with others who bore and irritate me and join them at orgiastic parties with secretaries, waitresses, salesgirls, housewives, nurses, models from Oklahoma, and airline stewardesses from Pennsylvania and Texas; I have two men in my department I'd like to fire and one girl, and there are days when I would truly like to be rid of them all; but I try not to show how I feel, and I'll probably never do anything about any of them, except keep hoping sullenly that they'll disappear on their own; I'm glad that Martha, our crazy typist, isn't going crazy in my department, because I know that I wouldn't have the nerve or competence to do anything about her before she finally falls apart; there's a fellow executive in the Merchandising Department I have lunch with once or twice a month who I sincerely wish would drop dead. (Once a year we have him to dinner, always with a lot of other people, and once each spring he has us to lunch on his God-damned boat.) I know so many people I want to be mean to, but I just don't have the character.

Green, on the other hand, is notorious for being frank and unkind (he is frank, I suspect, *just* to be unkind). He would rather make a bad impression than no impression. He tries extremely hard to be inconsiderate to people on his own level and lower. He creates tension, terror, and uneasiness in an organization that values harmony, dreads disagreements, conceals failure, and disguises conflict and personal dislike. He is aggressive and defensive. He attacks others and is sorry for himself.

People in the company, for example, do their best to minimize friction (we are encouraged to revolve around each other eight hours a day like self-lubricating ball bearings, careful not to jar or scrape) and to avoid quarreling with each other openly. It is considered much better form to wage our battles sneakily behind each other's back than to confront each other directly with any semblance of complaint. (The secret attack can be denied, lied about, or reduced in significance, but the open dispute is witnessed and has to be dealt with by somebody who finds the whole situation deplorable.) We are all on a congenial, first-name basis, especially with people we loathe (the more we loathe them, the more congenial we try to be), and our wives and children are always inquired about familiarly by their first names, even by people who have never met them or met them only once. The right to this pose of comfortable intimacy does not extend downward to secretaries, typists, or mail boys, or more than two levels upward through the executive hierarchy. I can call Jack Green Jack and Andy Kagle Andy and even Arthur Baron Art, but I would not call anyone higher than Arthur Baron anything but mister. That would be not only dangerous but rude, and I am always hesitant about being rude (to anyone but the members of my family) even when it isn't dangerous. Even Jane in the Art Department still calls me Mr Slocum respectfully when we meet (sometimes by telephone appointment when I am feeling especially frivolous) and kid around in one of the back corridors, and Jane and I have gone pretty far with each other by now in conversation. I used to encourage the girls I was after to call me by my first name, but I've learned from experience that it's always better, and safer, and more effective, to preserve the distinction between executive and subordinate, employer and employee, even in bed. (*Especially* in bed.)

People in the company are almost never fired; if they grow inadequate or obsolete ahead of schedule, they are encouraged to retire early or are eased aside into hollow, insignificant, newly created positions with fake functions and no authority, where they are sheepish and unhappy for as long as they remain; nearly always, they must occupy a small and less convenient office, sometimes one with another person already in it; or, if they are still young, they are simply encouraged directly (though with courtesy) to find better jobs with other companies and then resign. Even the wide-awake young branch manager with the brilliant future who got drunk and sick one afternoon and threw up into the hotel swimming pool during the company convention in Florida two years ago wasn't fired, although everyone knew he would not be permitted to remain. He knew it, too. Probably nothing was ever said to him. But he knew it. And four weeks after the convention ended, he found a better job with another company and resigned.

Green, on the other hand, does fire people, at least two or three people every year, and makes no secret of it; in fact, he makes it a point to let everyone know immediately after he *has* fired someone. Often, he will fire someone for no better reason than to cause discussion about himself or

It's always better, and safer, and more effective, to preserve the distinction between executive and subordinate, employer and employee, even in bed. (*Especially* in bed.)

to wake the rest of us up for a while. Most of us who won't ever amount to anything really big here, including Green, do tend to sink into lethargy and coast along sluggishly on the energy and new ideas that helped us make it safely through the year before. That's one of the reasons we won't ever amount to anything much. Most of the men who do make it toward the top are persistent hard workers if they are nothing else (and they are frequently nothing else. Ha, ha).

Sometimes the people Green fires are people he likes personally whose work is good enough (that may, in fact, be just the reason he does fire them—that he has no reason). Then he will grow compassionate and become seriously concerned with their plight (as though he were not the one who created it). He will begin an earnest effort to find other jobs for them somewhere else in the company. He is usually not successful, for his zest for catty advantage quickly replaces his original (and uncharacteristic) good intention, and his approach turns malicious and self-defeating.

'He'd be perfect for you,' is one method Green likes to use in recommending someone in his department to someone who is the head of another department. 'He just isn't good enough for me.'

Once he has made this point in enough places, he soon forgets about the people he has fired, and they go away.

He is charming (ha, ha). At the important company planning sessions that are held out of town every three months

at some luxurious resort hotel or plush country club with a
well-known golf course, division and department heads
(I am told) normally do not argue or complain or express
dissatisfaction aloud with each other's work or viewpoint.
But Green does: Green criticizes, ridicules, and disparages
impatiently, and he always protests vehemently against any
cuts in his own budget or any new curtailments of his activities. Then he is sorry. Green rocks the boat impetuously,
and is fearful afterward that he is going to sink. He is better
read than most people in the company and affects a suave,
intellectual superiority that makes even Arthur Baron
slightly uncomfortable and makes Andy Kagle and everyone
else in the Sales Department feel crude and graceless. (I am
much better educated than Green is and, I think, more intelligent, but he is glib and forward, and I am not.) News of
Green's repartee and audacious bad behavior at these planning sessions (Green does not even play golf) usually
trickles down to us (mainly through Green himself) and
we are often proud to be working for him; but I know he
is tormented each time by the fear that this time he has
at last gone too far. Green worries that none of the important people in the company really like him, and he's
right; he is wrong, though, when he surmises it is only
because they envy him. (He really isn't likable.) And then
there are the many other worries that I know assail Green
because the company is large and mainly Protestant.

Green, for example, is afraid of Phillip Reeves, a timid,
underpaid young employee in Green's own department,

and this amuses me greatly because I know that Phillip Reeves, who is Protestant, English, and went to Yale, is afraid of Green; each complains to me about the other. Reeves confides in me because he thinks I am capable, honest, and unpretentious; he knows I drink and lie and whore around a lot, and he therefore feels he can trust me.

'I'm absolutely terrified every time I have to go into his office,' Reeves complains to me about Green. 'He'll make some sarcastic remark as soon as I walk in, and I won't be able to think of a single intelligent thing to say in reply. I freeze. It's as though I'm paralyzed and struck dumb. It's all I can do to nod or shake my head or mumble answers to his questions, and I stand there almost speechless with an idiotic smile on my face while he goes on and on making caustic remarks. I can't say that I blame him. Afterwards I hate myself for being so stupid and tongue-tied.'

'I'm absolutely terrified every time I have to speak to him in my office,' Green complains to me about Phillip Reeves. 'It's those good manners of his, I guess, and that vulgar good breeding. I can cope with good manners and I can cope with good breeding, but I can't cope with good manners *and* good breeding. They throw me off stride, and it's like listening to some total, idiotic stranger running off at the mouth as I hear what I'm saying and realize what I'm doing. I'll make some innocent joke to him when he walks in, just to try to put us both at ease, and he'll just draw to a stop and stare back at me with that icy, superior smile frozen on his face. I can't get a response out of him. I become so rattled that I begin making one asinine remark after another in an effort to be friendly, but he just stands there in supercilious contempt and waits for me to finish. He must despise me by now, and I can't say that I blame him. God knows he does nothing to put *me* at ease, I can tell you that. Afterwards, I hate myself for being so stupid and weak. I wonder why I don't fire him. Because it would be an admission of defeat, that's why, even though his work *is* lousy.'

I do not tell either of them about the other (although I do try to cheer Reeves up). Neither would believe me, and it would do no good. They've got the whammy on each other—it's as plain as that—and nothing can change the whammy that springs up between one person and another and usually lasts a lifetime.

Green's got the whammy on me.

'I think they've decided to fire *me*,' Green blurts out to me unexpectedly. 'Kagle's the one they should get rid of, but I think that he and Horace White have finally persuaded them. Your pal. You hear things. Go find out from Kagle or Brown or someone else just what's going on. Or I'll fire *you*.'

I don't think Green really intends to fire me (but I'm never that confident about it for very long. I'm not secure about it at all on days when I know he is in a bad mood and I see his door shut for long periods of time). I know Green likes me, although we are not close, and confides in me, and I know he likes my work and the way I run my department for him. And I know Green is afraid of Andy Kagle, who likes me also and might try to protect me, and of Arthur Baron, who also likes me (I think he likes me: Arthur Baron always treats everybody as though he likes them—him—even people I know he doesn't like, so how can one be sure?) and might not let Green fire me. Kagle has sworn, in fact, that he *would* protect me if Green ever decides he does want to get rid of me, and that he would take me right into his own department at a much higher salary, just to spite Green, so I seem to be perfectly safe, until I go to Kagle to find out what I can about Green and hear him say, as soon as I walk into his office:

'I think they've finally decided to fire me!'

AND WHERE WOULD I be if that happened?

Andy Kagle, as head of our Sales Department, has a very powerful position with the company and is now afraid of losing it.

He may be right. His name is all wrong. (Half wrong. Andrew is all right, but Kagle?) So are his clothes. He shows poor judgment in colors and styles, as well as in fabrics, and his suits and coats and shirts do not fit him well enough. He moves to madras and paisley months after others have gone to linen or hopsack or returned to worsted and seersucker. He wears terrible brown shoes with *fleur-de-lis* perforations. He wears anklets (and I want to scream or kick him when I see his shin). Kagle is a stocky man of less than middle height and was born with a malformation of the hip and leg (which also doesn't help his image much); he walks with a slight limp.

Kagle has ability and experience, but they don't count anymore. What does count is that he has no tone. His manners are not good. He lacks wit (his wisecracks are bad, and so are the jokes he tells) and did not go to college, and he does not mix smoothly enough with people who did go to college. He knows he is awkward. He is not a hearty extrovert; he is a nervous extrovert, the worst kind (especially to other nervous extroverts), and so he may be doomed.

Kagle is one of those poor fellows who started at the bottom and worked his way up, and it shows. He is a self-made man and unable to hide it. He knows he doesn't fit, but he doesn't know when he doesn't or why, or how to alter himself so that he will fit in as well as he should. Gauche is what he is, and gauche is what he knows he is (although he is so gauche he doesn't even know what the word *gauche* means, but Green does, and so do I). He has a good record as head of sales, but that hardly matters. (Nothing damages us much anymore.) He thinks it counts. He really thinks that what he does is more important than what he is, but I know he's wrong and that the beautiful Countess Consuelo Crespi (if there is such a thing) will always matter more than Albert Einstein, Madame Curie, Thomas Alva Edison, Andy Kagle, and me.

Kagle is a church-going Lutheran with a strong anti-Catholic bias that he confides to me in smirking, bitter undertones when we are alone. He begins small meetings at which Catholic salesmen are present with joking references to the Pope in an effort to radiate an attitude of camaraderie. The jokes are bad, and nobody laughs. I have advised him to stop. He says he will. He doesn't. He seems compelled.

Kagle is not comfortable with people on his own level or higher. He tends to sweat on his forehead and upper lip, and to bubble in the corners of his mouth. He feels he doesn't belong with them. He is not much at ease with people who work for him. He tries to pass himself off as one of them. This is a gross (and gauche) mistake, for his salesmen and branch managers don't want him to identify with them. To them, he is management; and they know that they are nearly wholly at his mercy, with the exception of the several salesmen below him from very good families above him who do mingle smoothly with higher executives in the company who have *him* at *their* mercy, making him feel trapped and squeezed in between.

Kagle relies on Johnny Brown, whom he fears and distrusts, to keep the salesmen in line (to be the bad guy for him). And Brown does this job efficiently and with great relish. (Brown is related to Black, by his marriage to Black's niece.) Brown's success in scaring the salesmen merely strengthens Kagle's insecurity and weakens his sense of control. Kagle is convinced that Brown is after his job, but he lacks the courage to confront Brown, transfer him, or fire him. Kagle (wisely) avoids a showdown with Brown, who is blunt and belligerent with almost everybody, especially in the afternoon if he's been drinking at lunch. Kagle would rather go out of town on an unnecessary business trip than have a showdown here with anybody about anything, and he usually manufactures excuses for travel whenever his problems here or at home with his wife and children build toward a crisis he wants other people to settle. He hopes they'll be over by the time he returns, and they usually are.

With the exception of Brown (whom Kagle hates, fears, and distrusts, and can do nothing about), Kagle tries to like everyone who works for him and to have everyone like him. He is reluctant to discipline his salesmen or reprimand them, even when he (or Brown) catches them cheating on their expense accounts or lying about their sales calls or business trips. (Kagle lies about his own business trips and, like the rest of us, probably cheats at least a little on his expense accounts.) He is unwilling to get rid of people, even those who turn drunkard, like Red Parker, or useless in other ways. This is one of the criticisms heard about him frequently. (It is occasionally made against him by the same people other people want him to get rid of.) He won't, for example, retire Ed Phelps, who wants to hang on. ('I'd throw half those lying sons of bitches right out on their ass,' Brown enjoys bragging out loud to me and Kagle about Kagle's sales force, as though challenging

Kagle to do the same. 'And I'd put the other half of those lazy bastards on notice.')

Kagle wants desperately to be popular with all the 'lying sons of bitches' and 'lazy bastards' who work for him, even the clerks, receptionists, and typists, and goes out of his way to make conversation with them; as a result, they despise him. The more they despise him, the better he tries to be to them; the better he is to them, the more they despise him. There are days when his despair is so heavy that he seems almost incapable of stirring from his office or allowing anyone (but me) in to see him. He keeps his door shut for long periods of time, skips lunch entirely rather than allow even his secretary to deliver it, and does everything he can by telephone.

Kagle is comfortable with me (even on his very bad days), and I am comfortable with him. Sometimes he sends for me just to have me confirm or deny rumors he has heard (or made up) and help dispel his anxieties and shame. I do not test or threaten him; I pose no problem; on the contrary, he knows I aid him (or try to) in handling the problems created by others. Kagle trusts me and knows he is safe with me. Kagle doesn't scare me any longer. (In fact, I feel that I could scare him whenever I chose to, that he is weak in relation to me and that I am strong in relation to him, and I have this hideous urge every now and then while he is confiding in me to shock him suddenly and send him reeling forever with some brutal, unexpected insult, or to kick his crippled leg. It's a weird mixture of injured rage and cruel loathing that starts to rise within me and has to be suppressed, and I don't know where it comes from or how long I will be able to master it.) Kagle has lost faith in himself; this could be damaging, for people here, like people everywhere, have little pity for failures, and no affection.

I have pity for Kagle (as though I have already delivered my insult or kicked him in his deformed leg viciously—I know it will happen sooner or later, the wish is sometimes so strong), as I have pity for myself. I am sorry for him because he is basically a decent person, if not especially dazzling or admirable. I do worry and sympathize with him often, because he has been good to me from the day I came to work here for Green, and is good to me still. He makes my job easier. He relies on my judgment, takes my word, and backs me up in disputes I have with his salesmen. Many of his salesmen, particularly the new ones, hold me in some kind of awe because they sense I operate under his protection. (A number of the old ones who are not doing well hold me to blame, I'm sure, for having helped bring them to ruin.) Invariably in these disagreements with his salesmen, I am right and they are wrong. I am patient, practical, rational, while they are emotional and insistent. It is easy for me to be practical and rational in these situations because I am not the least bit endangered by the business problems that threaten *them*.

Kagle often comments jokingly to Arthur Baron and other important people, sometimes even in my presence, that I would be much better in Green's job than Green is;

Kagle does this with a gleam of mischief if I am there, because I have begged him not to. I am not certain if Kagle really believes I would be better than Green or is merely making an amiable gesture that he thinks will honor me and get back to Green to irritate and concern him. Because Andy Kagle is good to me and doesn't scare me any longer, I despise him a little bit too.

I TRY MY best to conceal it (although I am often surprised to discover a harder edge to my sarcasms and admonitions than I intended. There is something cankered and terrifying inside me that wishes to burst out and demolish him, lame and imperfect as he is). I try my best to help and protect him in just about every way I can. I am the one who even offers regularly to carry censures and instructions from him to Johnny Brown that he shrinks from delivering himself, although I will never risk anything with Brown after lunch if I can possibly avoid it. Along with everyone else who knows Brown, I endeavor to steer clear of him after lunch (unless I need him on my side in an argument with someone else), when he is apt to be red-eyed and irritable with drink and in a contrary, bellicose mood. Brown in a bad temper with whiskey working inside him always gives the clear impression that he is eager for a fist fight. And there is no doubt that with his deep chest, sturdy shoulders, and thick, powerful hands, he can handle himself in one. And there is also no doubt that Brown is usually right.

The current (and recurrent) antagonism between Kagle and Brown is over call reports again. The salesmen are reluctant to fill out these small printed pink, blue, and white forms (pink for prospects, blue for active, and white for formerly active; that is, accounts that have lapsed and are therefore prospects again, though not necessarily lively ones) describing with some hope and detail the sales calls they have made (or allege they have made). The salesmen are reluctant to come to grips with any kind of paperwork more elaborate than writing out order forms; they especially hate to fill out their expense account reports and fall weeks, sometimes months, behind. The salesmen know beforehand that most of the information they will have to supply in their call reports will be false. Brown maintains that call reports are a waste of everybody's time, and he is reluctant to compel the salesmen to fill them out. Kagle is afraid of Brown, and he is reluctant to compel Brown to compel the salesmen to fill them out.

But Arthur Baron wants the call reports. Arthur Baron has no other way of keeping familiar with what the salesmen are up to (or say they are) and a no more reliable source of knowledge on which to base his own decisions and reports, even though he is certainly aware that most of the knowledge on which he bases his decisions and prepares his own reports is composed of lies.

I try to keep out of it and expel an air of innocence and sympathetic understanding to all concerned. I would rather sit here in my office writing, doodling, flirting on the telephone with Jane, or talking to a good girl named Penny I've known a long time, or classifying people in the company and constructing my Happiness Charts, than get mixed up in this one. I don't care about the call reports and don't have to. The matter is trivial; yet, it seems to be one of those trivial matters that might destroy a person or two, and I don't see how I can gain favor with one person in this situation without losing favor with another. So, prudently, I contrive to keep as far away from it as I can, although I *will* manage to mention every now and then to a salesman I happen to be with on some other business that Kagle, Brown, or Arthur Baron has been asking about his call reports and that it is extremely urgent they be handed in as soon as possible for prompt study and evaluation. (I don't manage to mention—and never would—that I think they're a waste of everybody's time but mine.)

In this and other small ways I do what I can to be of help to Kagle (and Brown) (and Arthur Baron). I give him advice and I bring him gossip and news and portents from other parts of the company that I think will be of value or concern to him.

'What do you hear?' he wants to know.

'About what?'

'You know.'

'What do you mean?'

'Jesus Christ,' he complains, 'you used to be truthful with me. Now I can't even trust you, either.'

'What are you talking about?'

'I hear that I'm out and Brown's in, and that you probably know all about it. I was tipped off in Denver.'

'You're full of shit.'

'I like your honesty.'

'I like yours.'

Kagle grins mechanically, sardonically, and moves with his slight limp across the carpet of his office to close the door. I smile back at him and settle smugly into his brown leather armchair. I always feel very secure and very superior when I'm sitting inside someone's office with the door closed and other people, perhaps Kagle or Green or Brown, are doing all the worrying on the outside about what's going on inside. Kagle has a large, lush corner office in which he seems out of place. He looks nervous and tries to smile as he comes back and sits down behind his desk.

'Seriously, you hear everything,' he says to me. 'Haven't you heard anything?'

'About what?'

'About me.'

'No.'

'The grapevine says I'm finished. They're going to listen to Green and Horace White and get rid of me. Brown's got the job.'

'Who told you that?'

'I can't name names. But I was tipped off by people in Denver who passed it along to me in strictest confidence. It's true. You can take my word for it.'

'You're full of shit again.'

'No, I'm not.'

'There's nobody in our Denver office who would know something like that or tip you off about it if they did.'

'Only about the Denver part. The rest is true.'

'You tell terrible lies,' I say. 'You tell the worst lies of anybody in the whole business. I don't see how you ever made it as a salesman.'

Kagle grins for an instant to acknowledge my humor and then turns glum again.

'Brown tells you things,' he says. 'Hasn't he given any hints?'

'No.' I shake my head. (Everybody seems to think I know everything. 'You know everything,' Brown said to me. 'What's going on?' 'I didn't even know there was anything going on,' I answered. Jane asked: 'What's going on? Are they really getting rid of the whole Art Department?' 'I wouldn't *let* them get rid of you, honey,' I answered. 'Even if I had to pay your salary myself.')

I shake my head again. 'And it's probably not true. They'd never put Brown in. He fights with everybody.'

'Then you *have* heard something,' Kagle exclaims.

'No, I haven't.'

'Who would they put in?'

'Nobody. Andy, why don't you stop all this horseshit and buckle down to your job if you're so really worried? If you're really so worried, why don't you start doing the things you're supposed to do?'

'What am I supposed to do?'

'The things you're supposed to do. Stop trying to be such a good guy to all the people who work for you. You ain't succeeding, and nobody wants you to be. You're a member of management now. Your sales force is your enemy, not your buddy, and you're supposed to be theirs and drive them like slaves. Brown is right.'

'I don't like Brown.'

'He knows his business. Make Ed Phelps retire.'

'No.'

'That's what Horace White wants you to do.'

'Phelps is an old man now. He wants to stay.'

'That's why you have to force him out.'

'His son was divorced last year. His daughter-in-law just took his granddaughter away to Seattle. He might never see the little girl again.'

'That's all very sad.'

'How much does it cost the company to keep him on, even if he doesn't do anything?'

'Very little.'

'Then why should I make him retire?'

(Kagle is right, here, and I like him enormously for his determination to let Phelps stay. Phelps is old and will soon be dead, anyway, or too sick to continue.)

'Because he's past the official retirement age. And Horace White wants you to.'

'I don't like Horace White,' Kagle observes softly, irrelevantly. 'And he doesn't like me.'

'He knows his business also,' I point out.

'How can I tell it to Ed Phelps?' Kagle wants to know. 'What could I say to him? Will you do it for me? It's not so easy, is it?'

'Get Brown to do it,' I suggest.

'No.'

'It's part of *your* job, not mine.'

'But it's not so easy, is it?'

'That's why they pay you so much.'

'I don't get so much,' he digresses almost automatically, 'what with taxes and all.'

'Yes, you do. And stop traveling all the time. Nobody likes that. What the hell were you doing in Denver all this week when there's nothing going on there and you're supposed to be here organizing the next convention and working on your sales projections?'

'I've got Ed Phelps working on the convention.'

'A lot he'll do.'

'And my sales projections are always wrong.'

'So what? At least they're done.'

'What else?'

'Play more golf. Talk to Red Parker and buy a blue blazer. Buy better suits. Wear a jacket in the office and keep your shirt collar buttoned and your necktie up tight around your neck where it belongs. Jesus, look at you right now. You're supposed to be a distinguished white-collar executive.'

'Don't take the name of the Lord in vain,' he jokes.

'Don't you.'

'I've got a good sales record,' he argues.

'Have you got a good sports jacket?' I demand.

'Jesus Christ, what does a good sports jacket matter?'

'More than your good sales record. Nobody wears jackets with round leather patches on the elbows to the office, unless it's on a weekend. Get black shoes for your blue and gray suits. And stop driving into the city in your station wagon.'

'Okay,' he gives in with a gloomy, chastised smile and exhales a long, low whistle of mock surprise and resignation. 'You win.' He gets up slowly and moves toward the coat rack in the corner of his office for his jacket. 'I promise. I'll get a blue blazer.'

It will be too big—I can see it in advance—and hang over his shoulders and sag sloppily around his chest, and he will probably get his worsted blue blazer just about the time the rest of us have switched to mohair or shantung or back to madras, plaids, and seersucker. It is already too late for him, I suspect; I suspect it is no longer in his power (if it ever was in his power) to change himself to everyone's satisfaction. For the moment, though (while I am still with him), he makes an effort: he buttons his shirt collar, and slides tight to his neck the knot of his tie, and puts on his jacket. It is a terrible jacket of coarse, imitation tweed, with oval suede patches at the elbows.

'Better?' he wants to know.

'Not much.'

'I'll throw out these brown shoes.'

'That will help.'

It is already too late for him, I suspect; I suspect it is no longer in his power (if it ever was in his power) to change himself to everyone's satisfaction

'How's Green treating you these days?' he asks casually.

'Pretty good,' I reply. 'Why?'

'If you were in my department,' he offers with a cagey, more confident air, and the beginnings of a mischievous smile, 'I would let you make as many speeches as you want to at the next convention. The salesmen are always very interested in the work you're doing for them and what you have to say.'

'So long,' I answer. 'I'll see you around.'

We both laugh, because we each know what the other wants and where the fears and sore spots are. Kagle knows I want to keep my job and be allowed to make a speech at the next company convention. (God dammit—it would be an honor and an act of recognition, even if it is only three minutes, and I've earned it and I want it, and that's all!) And I know that Kagle wants my help in defending himself against Green (and Brown) (and Black) (and White) (and Arthur Baron, as well).

'You'll let me know if you do hear anything, won't you?' he asks, as we walk to the door.

'Of course I will,' I assure him.

'But don't ask questions,' he cautions with a dark, moody snicker. 'You might give them the idea.'

We laugh.

AND WE ARE both still chuckling when Kagle opens the door of his office and we find my secretary outside talking to his secretary.

'Oh, Mr Slocum,' she sings out cheerily, because that is her way, and I wish I were rid of her. 'Mr Baron wants to see you right away.'

Kagle pulls me to the side. 'What does he want?' he asks with alarm.

'How should I know?'

'Go see him.'

'What did you think I was going to do?'

'And come and tell me if he says anything about getting rid of me.'

'Sure.'

'You will, won't you?'

'Of course I will. For Christ sakes, Andy, can't you trust me?'

'Where are *you* going?' Green wants to know, as I pass him in the corridor on my way to Arthur Baron's office.

'Arthur Baron wants to see me.'

Green skids to a stop with a horrified glare; and it's all I can do not to laugh in his face.

'What does he want with *you*?' Green wants to know.

'I haven't any idea.'

'You'd better go see him.'

'I thought of doing that.'

'Don't be so God-damned sarcastic,' Green snaps back at me angrily, and I lower my eyes, abashed and humbled by his vehemence. 'I'm not even sure I trust *you*, either.'

'I'm sorry, Jack,' I mumble. 'I didn't intend that to sound rude.'

'You come see me as soon as you've finished talking to him,' he orders. 'I want to know what he says. I want to know if I'm being fired or not.'

'What was Kagle talking to you about?' Brown asks when I bump into him.

'He wanted to know what you were up to while he was away in Denver.'

'I was correcting his mistakes and protecting his God-damned job, that was what I was up to,' Brown retorts.

'That's just what I told him.'

'You're a liar,' Brown tells me pleasantly.

'Johnny, that's what they pay me for.'

'But everybody knows it . . .'

'So?'

' . . . so I guess it doesn't matter.'

'A diplomat, Johnny. Not a liar.'

'Yeah, a diplomat,' Brown agrees with a gruff and hearty laugh. 'You lying son of a bitch.'

'I was just coming to see you,' Jane says to me. 'I want to show you this layout.'

I stare brazenly at her tits. 'I can see your layout.' She starts to giggle and blush deliciously, but I turn serious. 'Not now, Jane. I have to go see Arthur Baron.'

'Oh, hello, Mr Slocum,' Arthur Baron's secretary says to me. 'How are you?'

'You look fine today.'

The door to Arthur Baron's office is closed, and I don't know how to cope with it, whether to turn the knob and go right in or knock diffidently and wait to be asked. But Arthur Baron's twenty-eight-year-old secretary, who is fond of me and having trouble with her husband (he's probably queer), nods encouragingly and motions me to go right through. I turn the knob gingerly and open the door. Arthur Baron sits alone at his desk and greets me with a smile. He rises and comes forward slowly to shake my hand. He is always very cordial to me (and everyone) and always very gentle and considerate. Yet I am always afraid of him. He's got the whammy on me, I guess (just as everyone I've ever worked for in my whole life has had the whammy on me), and I guess he always will.

'Hello, Bob,' he says.

'Hi, Art.'

'Come in.' He closes the door noiselessly.

'Sure.'

'How are you, Bob?'

'Fine, Art. You?'

'I want you to begin preparing yourself,' he tells me, 'to replace Andy Kagle.'

'KAGLE?' I ask.

'Yes.'

'Not Green?'

'No.' Arthur Baron smiles, knowledgeable and reassuring. 'We don't really think you're ready for Green's job yet.'

There is polite irony here, for we both know that Kagle's job is bigger and more important than Green's, and that

Green would be subordinate to Kagle if Kagle were of stronger character. The proposition stuns me, and for a few bewildered seconds I have absolutely no idea what to say or do or what expression to keep on my face. Arthur Baron watches me steadily and waits.

'I've never done any real selling,' I say finally, very meekly.

'We won't want you to do any,' he replies. 'We want you to manage. You're loyal and intelligent and you've got good character and good work habits. You seem to have a good understanding of policy and strategy, and you get along well with all kinds of people. You're diplomatic. You're perceptive and sensitive, and you seem to be a good administrator. Is that enough to encourage you?'

'Kagle's a good man, Art,' I say.

'He's a good salesman, Bob,' Arthur Baron replies, emphasizing the distinction. 'And you'll probably be allowed to keep him on as a salesman if we decide to make the change and you decide you want to.'

'I know I'd want to.'

'We'll probably let you keep him as an assistant even, or as a consultant on special projects with people he'd be good with. But he hasn't been a good manager, and we don't think he's going to be able to get better. Kagle doesn't go along with the rest of us on too many things, and that's very important in his job. He lies a lot. Horace White wants me to get rid of him just because he does tell lies to us. He still travels too much, although I've told him I want him to spend more time here. He dresses terribly. He still wears brown shoes. That shouldn't count, I know, but it does count, and he ought to know that by now. He doesn't send in my call reports.'

'Most of the stuff on the call reports isn't true.'

'I know that. But I have to have them anyway for my own work.'

'Brown is in charge of that,' I have to point out.

'He doesn't control Brown.'

'That isn't easy.'

'He's afraid of him.'

'So am I,' I admit.

'And so am I,' he admits. 'But I would control him or get rid of him if he worked for me. Would you?'

'Brown is married to Black's niece.'

'I wouldn't let that matter. We wouldn't let Black interfere if it came to doing something about Brown.'

'Would you let me fire him?'

'If you decided you really wanted to, although we'd prefer to transfer him. Kagle could have had him fired, but by now Brown has a better grasp of specifics than he has. Kagle never wants to fire anybody, even the ones who are drunks or dishonest or useless in other ways. He won't fire Parker or retire Phelps, and he doesn't cooperate with Green. And he still discriminates in the people he hires, although he's been warned about that, too.'

'It's a very big job,' I say.

'We think you might be able to handle it.'

'If I couldn't?'

'Let's not think about that now.'

'I have to,' I say with a grin.

He grins back sympathetically. 'We'd find another good job for you somewhere else in the company if you found you wanted to stay here, unless you did something disgraceful or dishonest, and I'm sure that wouldn't happen. You don't have to decide now. This is just an idea of mine, and it's anything but definite, so please keep it secret. But we are trying to look ahead, and we'd like to know what we're going to do by convention time. So give it some serious thought, will you, and let me know if you would take it if we did decide to move Kagle out and give it to you. You don't have to take it if you don't want to—I promise you that—and you won't be penalized if you don't.' He smiles again as he stands up and continues in a lighter tone. 'You'll still get your raise this year and a good cash bonus. But we think you should. And you might just as well begin preparing yourself while you make up your mind.'

'What should I do?'

'Keep close to Kagle and the salesmen and try to find out even more about everything that's happening. Decide what realistic goals to establish and what changes you would have to make to achieve them if we did put you in charge.'

'I like Andy Kagle.'

'So do I.'

'He's been very good to me.'

'It isn't your fault. We'd move him out anyway. He'll probably be happier working for you on special projects. Will you think about it?'

'Of course.'

'Good. You'll keep this quiet, won't you?'

'Sure.'

'Thank you, Bob.'

'Thank you, Art.'

'WHAT DID ARTHUR BARON want?' Green demands, the instant I'm out in the corridor.

'Nothing,' I answer.

'Did he say anything?'

'No.'

'Anything about me, I mean.'

'No.'

'Well, what did he say? He must have wanted to see you about something.'

'He wants me to put some jokes in a speech his son has to make at school.'

'Is that all?' Green snorts with contempt, satisfied. 'I could do that,' he sneers. 'Better than you.'

Up yours, I think in reply, because I know I could squash him to the ground and make him crawl like a caterpillar if I ever do find myself in Kagle's job. But he does believe me, doesn't he?

'What did Arthur Baron want?' Johnny Brown asks.

'He wants me to put some jokes in a speech his son has to make at school.'

'You're still a liar.'

'A diplomat, Johnny.'

'But I'll find out.'

'Should I start looking for another job?' asks Jane.

'I've got a job you can do, right here at hand.'

'You're terrible, Mr Slocum,' she laughs, her color rising with embarrassment and pleasure. She is aglow, tempting. 'You're worse than a boy.'

'I'm better than a boy. Come into my office now and I'll show you. What boy that you go with has an office with a couch like mine and pills in the file cabinet?'

'I'd like to,' she says (and for a second I am in terror that she will). 'But Mr Kagle is waiting for you there.'

'What did Arthur Baron want?' Kagle asks as soon as I step inside my office and find him lurking anxiously in a corner there.

I close the door before I turn to look at him. He is shabby again, and I am dismayed and angry. The collar of his shirt is unbuttoned, and the knot of his tie is inches down. (For a moment, I have an impulse to seize his shirt front furiously in both fists and begin shaking some sense into him; and at exactly the same time, I have another impulse to kick him as hard as I can in the ankle or shin of his crippled leg.) His forehead is wet with beads of perspiration, and his mouth is glossy with a suggestion of spittle, and dry with the powdered white smudge of what was probably an antacid tablet.

'Nothing,' I tell him.

'Didn't he say anything?'

'No. Nothing important.'

'About me?'

'Not a word.'

'You mean that?'

'I swear.'

'Well, I'll be damned,' Kagle marvels with relief. 'What did he talk about? Tell me. He must have wanted to see you about something.'

'He wants me to put some jokes in a speech his son has to make at school.'

'Really?'

'Yeah.'

'And he didn't say anything about me, anything at all?'

'No.'

'Or the call reports or the trip to Denver?'

'No.'

'Ha! In that case, I may be safe, you know. I might even make vice-president this year. What did he talk about?'

'Just his son. And the speech. And the jokes.'

'I'm probably imagining the whole thing,' he exclaims exultantly. 'You know, maybe I can use those same jokes someday if one of *my* kids is ever asked to make a speech at school.' He frowns, his face clouding suddenly with a distant distress. 'Both my kids are no good,' he reminds himself aloud abstractedly. 'Especially the boy.'

Kagle trusts me also. And I'm not so sure I want him to.

'Andy,' I call out to him suddenly. 'Why don't you play it safe? Why don't you behave? Why don't you start doing everything everybody wants you to do?'

He is startled. 'Why?' he cries. 'What's the matter?'

'To keep your job, that's why, if it's not too late. Why don't you start trying to go along? Stop telling lies to Horace White. Don't travel so much. Transfer Parker to another office if you can't get him to stop drinking and retire Ed Phelps.'

'Did somebody say something?'

'No.'

'Then how do you know all that?' he demands. 'Who told you?'

'You did,' I bark back at him with exasperation and disgust. 'You've been telling me about all those things over and over again for months. So why don't you start doing something about them instead of worrying about them all the time and taking chances? Settle down, will you? Control Brown and cooperate with Green, and why don't you hire a Negro and a Jew?'

Kagle scowls grimly and broods in heavy silence for several seconds. I wait, wondering how much is sinking in.

'What would I do with a coon?' he asks finally, as though thinking aloud, his mind wandering.

'I don't know.'

'I could use a Jew.'

'Don't be too sure.'

'We sell to Jews.'

'They might not like it.'

'But what would I do with a coon?'

'You would begin,' I advise, 'by finding something else to call him.'

'Like what?'

'A Black. Call him a Black.'

'That's funny.'

'Yeah.'

'I've always called them coons,' Kagle says. 'I was brought up to call niggers coons.'

'I was brought up to call Negroes coons.'

'What should I do?' he asks. 'Tell me what to do.'

'Grow up, Andy,' I tell him earnestly, trying with all my heart now to help him. 'You're a middle-aged man with two kids and a big job in a pretty big company. There's a lot that's expected of you. It's time to mature. It's time to take it seriously and start doing all the things you should be doing. You know what they are. You keep telling me what they are.'

Kagle nods pensively. His brow furrows as he ponders my advice without any hint of levity. I am getting through to him. I watch him tensely as I wait for his reply. Kagle, you bastard, I want to scream at him desperately as he meditates solemnly, I am trying to help you. Say something wise. For once in your mixed-up life, come to an intelligent conclusion. It's almost as though he hears me, for he makes up his mind finally and his face brightens. He stares up at me with a slight smile and then, while I hang on his words hopefully, says:

'Let's go get laid.'

————

THE COMPANY HAS a policy about getting laid. It's okay.

And everybody seems to know that (although it's not spelled out in any of the personnel manuals). Talking about getting laid is even more okay than doing it, but doing it is okay too, although talking about getting laid with your own wife is never okay. (Imagine: 'Boy, what a crazy bang I got from my wife last night!' That wouldn't be nice, not with gentlemen you associate with in business who might know her.) But getting laid with somebody else's wife is very okay, and so is talking about it, provided the husband is not with the company or somebody anybody knows and likes. The company is in favor of getting laid if it is done with a dash of élan, humor, vulgarity, and skill, without emotion, with girls who are young and pretty or women who are older and foreign or glamorous in some other way, without too much noise and with at least some token gesture toward discretion, and without scandal, notoriety, or any of the other serious complications of romance. Falling in love, for example, is *not* usually okay, although marrying someone else right after a divorce is, and neither is 'having an affair,' at least not for a man.

Getting laid (or talking about getting laid) is an important component of each of the company conventions and a decisive consideration in the selection of a convention site; and the salesmen who succeed in getting laid there soonest are likely to turn out to be the social heroes of the convention, though not necessarily the envy. (That will depend on the quality of whom they find to get laid with.)

Getting laid at conventions is usually done in groups of three or four (two decide to go out and try and take along one or two others). Just about everybody in the company gets laid (or seems to), or at least talks as though he does (or did). In fact, it has become virtually *comme il faut* at company conventions for even the very top and very old, impotent men in the company—in fact, *especially* those— to allude slyly and boastfully to their own and each other's sexual misconduct in their welcoming addresses, acknowledgments, introductions, and informal preambles to speeches on graver subjects. Getting laid is a joking matter on all levels of the company, even with people like Green and Horace White. But it's not a matter for Andy Kagle to joke about now.

'Andy, I'm serious,' I say.

'So,' he says, 'am I.'

I CLOSE THE door of my office after Kagle leaves, sealing myself inside and shutting everybody else out, and try to decide what to do about my conversation with Arthur Baron. I cancel my lunch appointment and put my feet up on my desk.

I've got bad feet. I've got a jawbone that's deteriorating and someday soon I'm going to have to have all my teeth pulled. It will hurt. I've got an unhappy wife to support and two unhappy children to take care of. (I've got that other child with irremediable brain damage who is neither happy nor unhappy, and I don't know what will happen to him after we're dead.) I've got eight unhappy people working for me who have problems and unhappy dependents of their own. I've got anxiety; I suppress hysteria. I've got politics on my mind, summer race riots, drugs, violence, and teen-age sex. There are perverts and deviates everywhere who might corrupt or strangle any one of my children. I've got crime in my streets. I've got old age to face. My boy, though only nine, is already worried because he does not know what he wants to be when he grows up. My daughter tells lies. I've got the decline of American civilization and the guilt and ineptitude of the whole government of the United States to carry around on these poor shoulders of mine.

And I find I am being groomed for a better job.

And I find—God help me—that I want it.

JOSEPH HELLER WAS one of the twentieth century's best known satirists. He was a pilot with the US Air Corps during the Second World War, and later worked as a copywriter in an advertising agency. His debut novel, *Catch-22*, based on his experiences with the Air Corps, catapulted him to international literary fame and established Heller as a writer capable of voicing the madness of modern life.

Something Happened (from which this book is taken) offers a piercingly sharp satire on suburban and corporate America. Narrated by discontented company executive Bob Slocum, the novel offers a grim portrait of the limits to which we let work push, and ultimately, mould us.

Alongside *Catch-22*, *Something Happened* has been hailed as Joseph Heller's 'other masterpiece'. Heller died in 1999.

RECOMMENDED BOOKS BY JOSEPH HELLER:

Something Happened
Catch-22
God Knows

How to wind down after Work?

Drinking
JOHN CHEEVER

VINTAGE MINIS

Swimming
ROGER DEAKIN

VINTAGE MINIS

Liberty
VIRGINIA WOOLF

VINTAGE MINIS

Death
JULIAN BARNES

VINTAGE MINIS

VINTAGE MINIS

The Vintage Minis bring you the world's greatest writers on the experiences that make us human. These stylish, entertaining little books explore the whole spectrum of life – from birth to death, and everything in between. Which means there's something here for everyone, whatever your story.

vintageminis.co.uk

1 3 5 7 9 10 8 6 4 2

Vintage
20 Vauxhall Bridge Road,
London SW1V 2SA

Vintage Classics is part of the Penguin Random House
group of companies whose addresses can be found at
global.penguinrandomhouse.com.

 Penguin
Random House
UK

First published in Great Britain by Jonathan Cape in 2004
This short edition published by Vintage in 2017

penguin.co.uk/vintage

A CIP catalogue record for this book is available from the British Library

ISBN 9781784872588

Typeset in 9.5/14.5 pt FreightText Pro
by Jouve (UK), Milton Keynes
Printed and bound by Clays Ltd, St Ives plc

Penguin Random House is committed to a sustainable future for
our business, our readers and our planet. This book is made from
Forest Stewardship Council® certified paper.

Babies
ANNE ENRIGHT

VINTAGE MINIS

Contents

Apologies All Round

SPEECH IS A selfish act, and mothers should probably remain silent. When one of these essays, about pregnancy, appeared in the *Guardian* magazine there was a ferocious response on the letters page. Who does she think she is? and Why should we be obliged to read about her insides? and Shouldn't she be writing about the sorrow of miscarriage instead?

So I'd like to say sorry to everyone in advance. Sorry. Sorry. Sorry. Sorry.

I'd like to apologise to all those people who find the whole idea of talking about things as opposed to just getting on with them mildly indecent, or provoking – I do know what they mean. Also to those who like to read about the dreadful things that happen to other people, when nothing particularly dreadful has happened to me, or my children, so far, touch wood, *Deo gratias*. Also to those readers who would prefer me not to think so much (because mothers just shouldn't), and to those thinkers who will realise that in the last few years I have not had time to research, or check a reference – the only books I have finished, since I had children, being the ones I wrote myself (not quite true, but it's a nice thing to say). And, of course, people who don't have children are just as good and fine and real as those who do, I would hate to imply otherwise. Also, sorry about my insides: I was reared with the idea that, for a woman, anatomy is destiny, so I have always paid close attention to what the body is and what it actually does. Call it a hobby.

'MARRIED WOMAN HAS CHILDREN IN THE SUBURBS' – it's not exactly a call to arms, and I do genuinely apologise for being so ordinary, in the worst sense. Here I am, all fortunate, living a 1950s ideal of baby powder and burps, except that, in the twenty-first century we know that talc is linked, bizarrely, to ovarian cancer, so there is no baby powder in this house, and we also know that the hand that rocks the cradle also pays for the cradle, or a fair amount of it, and that, for many people, babies are a luxury that they cannot yet afford. But even for the twenty-first century I am doing well: I have flexible working hours, no commuting, I have a partner who took six weeks off for the birth of his first baby and three months for the second (unpaid, unpaid, unpaid). He also does the breakfasts. And the baths. So you might well say, 'Oh, it's all right for her,' as I do when I read women writing about the problems they have with their nannies or other domestic staff. More usually, though, when I read women writing about having children, it is not their circumstances that annoy me so much as their tone. I think, 'What a wretch, would someone please call the social services.' It is the way they are both smug and astonished. It is the way we think we have done something amazing, when we have done no more than most other people on the planet – except we, in our over-educated way, have to brag about it.

Most of these pieces were started after my first child, a daughter, was born. I played around with them in the two years before I became pregnant again, and they were finished soon after the birth of my son, so though the baby is a 'she', both children are in there, somewhere. The reason I kept writing about my babies, even when they were asleep in the room, was that I could not think about anything else. This might account for any wildness of tone. The pieces were typed fast. They were written to the sound of a baby's sleeping breath. Some were assembled, later, from notes, but I have tried to keep the flavour of the original scraps.

Anyway, these are the material facts (for which I also apologise). I met my husband, Martin, a long time ago, we married I can't remember when, and after eighteen years of this and that we knuckled down to having children. It was not an impulse decision.

After our first child was born I worked while she slept, for the first year, and also in the evenings when her father came home. When she was one, she went to a nursery for (count them) six and a half hours per day, three of which were spent having a nap. When she was two and a half, she got a baby brother, and I worked while he slept. And so on. I would really like a rest, now.

Finally, and quietly, I have to apologise to my family and hope that they will forgive me for loving them in this formal, public, plundering way. Starting with my own mother – whose voice comes through my own, from time to time – and working down the generations. Like all women who write about their children, I have a wonderful partner – except in my case it is true. I also have to apologise to my children for writing about their baby selves; either too much, or not enough, or whatever changing way this book takes them, over the years.

My only excuse is that I think it is important. I wanted to say what it was like.

The Glass Wall

I SPENT MOST of my thirties facing a glass wall. On the other side of this wall were women with babies – 'mothers', you might call them. On my side were women who simply *were*. It didn't seem possible that I would ever move through the glass – I couldn't even imagine what it was like in there. All I could see were scattered reflections of myself; while on the other side real women moved with great slowness, like distantly sighted whales.

I always assumed I would have children, but only dimly – I never thought about when. I was reared in the seventies, by a woman who had been reared in the thirties, and we were both agreed that getting pregnant was the worst thing that could happen to a girl. My mother thought it would ruin my marriage prospects and I thought it would ruin my career prospects (same thing, really, by the different lights of our times). And when do you stop being a girl? By 'career' I meant something more than salary. I could not get pregnant, I thought, until I had 'gotten somewhere', until I 'knew who I was', until I was, in some way, more thoroughly myself.

These things are important: they do happen, but they often happen late, and you can hardly tell people to stop dithering. I look at women in their thirties with their noses pressed up against the glass, and all I can tell them (wave!) is that life in here on the other side is just the same – only much better, and more difficult.

I see them wondering, Does he love me and do I love him? and Will I have to give up smoking? and What about my job? and I don't want to be that fat woman in the supermarket, and What if it is autistic and Don't they cry all the time? and I want to say, 'It's fine.' More than that, when I first had a child, I was so delighted, I wanted to say, 'Do whatever it takes.' Children seemed to be such an absolute good, independent of the relationship that made them, that I wanted to say, 'Buy one if you have to,' or, 'Hurry.'

I was wrong, of course. Besides, most women are more interested in sexual love than they are in the maternal variety, they want a man more than they want children, or at least they want it *first*. Still, it is good to keep in mind the fact that, in a world where sexual partners can come and go, children remain. They are our enduring love.

It is good to keep in mind the fact that, in a world where sexual partners can come and go, children remain. They are our enduring love

Dream-Time

ONE FRIDAY IN October I started falling in love with everyone, and I stayed in love for two weeks, with everyone. This was awkward. It was a moony, teenage sort of love. I waited for the phone to ring. I was shy, almost anguished. I missed appointments, even with the people I loved, which was everyone, and so stayed at home and saw no one, my mind full of impossible thoughts.

I did manage to go to a school reunion (where I loved them all) and to the opening night of a play (where I made some wonderful new friends), but mostly I mooched, and wrote letters to celebrate the fact that I had just finished a book and that life was, perhaps unbearably, good.

Towards the end of this peculiar fortnight, I had a dream full of the usual suspects: people from my past who spoke to me in an unsettling, unresolved way. I have this dream, with variations, all the time, but this night it was interrupted by a woman I barely knew twenty years ago who floated in through a window, dressed in pink. She smiled an angelic smile, as if to say, 'None of this matters any more,' and then she patted her stomach, very gently. I started awake with the thought that I was pregnant; then I turned over to go back to sleep, saying to myself that the moment had come: it was time to stop the shilly-shally, the hit-and-miss, we had to get this conception thing going, properly, finally, and have the baby that was waiting for us, after all these years.

Soon after, I went to Berlin for a reading, half-dreading who I might be obliged to fall in love with there – but sometime in the middle of the weekend, I hit a wall. I couldn't say why this was. I didn't tell my hosts that I knew German and disliked the half-understood conversations they held in front of me, before turning to talk English with a smile. I walked the streets, planning a story about a woman who falls in love all the time, and another story that was full of mistranslation and sly insinuation, in which a woman meets a foreign couple and cannot quite tell what is going on.

My hostess said that she loved the passage in my book about a dream in which the ceiling is full of dangling penises. I have never written such a passage, nor anything like it, but she insisted: she was even quite insulted, as though I were accusing *her* of having my own porno-graphic thoughts. What could I say? I said I would check. But I noticed, in myself, a terrible physical weight, as if I could not carry my life around any more, I could not even lift it off the chair. I thought that perhaps I should stop writing books: something, at any rate, had to change. I walked from Schönhauser Allee to Unter den Linden, looking at the afternoon moon over Berlin, thinking that when it was full my period would come and then maybe everything would right itself again.

On the way back, I stopped over in London and got very drunk. The hangover seemed to last a week. I felt terrible. I dosed myself with miso soup and seaweed. I was insane for miso soup and seaweed. I still thought my life must change. I went on the Internet and typed in 'ovulation' on the search engine, then turned to my husband, Martin, saying, 'I think this beer is off. Is there something wrong with this beer?'

We bought the pregnancy test from a girl with romantic thoughts behind the cash register in Boots. Martin says I was delighted when it proved positive, but I was not delighted, I was shocked and delighted maybe, but I was mostly deeply shocked.

If Kafka had been a woman, then Gregor Samsa would not have turned into an insect, he would not have had to. Gregor would be Gretel and she would wake up one morning pregnant. She would try to roll over and discover she was stuck on her back. She would wave her little hands uselessly in the air.

It seems to me that I spent the next six weeks on the sofa listening to repeats of radio dramas, but my computer files record the fact that I worked, and that I also surfed the Net. I was looking for information on what happens when you get drunk in the very early stages of pregnancy, but the women on the Internet all wanted to lock expectant mothers up for drinking Diet Coke. In the chat rooms and on the notice-boards all the pregnant women talked about their pets: the cat who just knew, the dog who got upset. There was also a lot of stuff about miscarriages.

Martin took me up the mountains to keep me fit and I nearly puked into the bog. I got stuck on one tussock and could not jump to the next. The life inside me was too delicate, and impossible and small. No jumping, no running, no sex, no driving, no drink, no laughs, no household cleaning, no possibility, however vague or unwanted, of amorous adventures, no trips to India, no cheerful leaps from one tussock to the next in the god-damn bog. I made the jump anyway and went over on my ankle. Darkness started to fall.

The next weekend he brought me to Prague, as a surprise. There are two things in my life that I have never turned down, one is a drink and the other is an aeroplane ticket. Already, friends were starting to look askance when I stuck to water; now I sat in the departures lounge and did not want to board the plane. This intense reluctance, this exhaustion, was pregnancy. It was nine in the morning. People were running to the gates, buying newspapers, checking their boarding passes and drinking prophylactic shots of whiskey. I looked at the world around me and listened to my own blood. There was a deep note humming through me, so low that no one else could hear. It was in every part of me, swelling in my face and hands, and it felt like joy.

The weeks when you are generally, as opposed to locally, pregnant are a mess. I put on weight in odd places. I went to the kitchen in the middle of the night to see what nameless but really specific thing I was starving for. I sat down on the floor in front of the open fridge and cried. The aisles of the supermarket were filled with other possibly pregnant women – paralysed in front of the breakfast cereals, stroking packets of organic lentils, picking up, and setting down again, a six-pack of Petits Filous. Starvation is no joke, especially when you have been eating all day. I had, in my life, managed to have every neurosis except the one about food, and now my body was having it for me.

At ten weeks I went to the obstetrician, as if she could somehow fix what was wrong with me. We talked about postnatal depression (could I be having it already?). We talked about amniocentesis, but not much. She did not seem to realise that the child I had inside me would have to be deformed. She led me up a terrazzo staircase that smelt of school, and brought me into a dark room. 'Right,' she said, flicking on the light. 'Let's have a look.' I was expecting stirrups, but instead I got an ultrasound. The baby was like a little bean sprout. It flicked and jumped, as though annoyed to be disturbed. She lingered, with her sonic pen, as though this sight amazed her every time. It was all too much to bear. I said, 'It looks a bit disgusting,' and she said, 'Don't be silly,' as though she knew I was just shamming.

All of a sudden I was going to have a baby. The fact of my pregnancy was as real and constant to me as a concrete block in the middle of the room, but I still did not know what it meant. A baby. A baby! I had to realise this many times: first with a premonition, then with a shock. I had to realise it slowly, and I had to realise the joy. After the ultrasound, it came to me all in a clatter and I walked home, roaring it out in my head. That night we went out to tell my parents. My mother said very little but, every time I looked at her, she looked five years younger, and then five years younger again. She was fundamentally, *metabolically* pleased. She was pleased all the way through, as I was pregnant all the way through.

I spent the next six months remembering and forgetting again, catching up with what my body already knew. The world senses this gap. It seemed like everyone was trying to persuade me into this baby, as though they had made a great investment in me, and didn't trust me to take care of it. Out of badness, I did my best to drink (and failed) and took an occasional cigarette. This made one woman, a practical stranger, burst into tears. I wondered what her mother was like.

A pregnant woman is public property. I began to feel like a bus with 'Mammy' on the front – and the whole world was clambering on. Four women in a restaurant

cheered when I ordered dessert. A friend went into a prolonged rage with me, for no reason at all. Everyone's
unconscious was very close to their mouth. Whatever my
pregnant body triggered was not social, or political, it was
animal and ancient and quite helpless. It was also most
unfair. Another friend showed me a pair of baby's shoes
and said, 'Look, look!' He said that in prison, they show
little shoes to child molesters to make them realise how
small and vulnerable their victims were. He did not seem
to notice that he had put pregnant women and child
molesters in the same category, as if we both needed to be
told what we were.

Perhaps he was right. A pregnant woman does not know
what she is. She has been overtaken. She feels sick but she
is not sick, she lives underwater, where there are no words.
The world goes funny on her; it is accusing when she is
delighted, and applauds when she feels like shit.

People without children went, without exception, a little mad. People who had children succumbed to a
cherishing nostalgia. I began to enter into the romance of
their lives, and see them as they must have been, newly
married perhaps, and in love; dreaming of the future that
they were living now. Pregnancy is a non-place, a suspen-
sion, a holiday from our fallible and compromised selves.
There is no other time in a woman's life when she is so
supported and praised and helped and loved. Though perhaps it is not 'she' who gets all the attention, but 'they';
this peculiar, mutant, double self – motherandchild.

I looked in the mirror. I had a body out of Rouault, big thick slabs of flesh, painted on stained glass. I was an amazement to myself, a work of engineering, my front cantilevered out from the solid buttress of my backside. Every night now, there was a ritual of wonder as we measured the bump. From week to week I felt my body shift into different cycles, like some slow-motion, flesh-based washing machine. 'Oh. Something else is happening now.' In the middle of January I surfaced, quite suddenly. I realised that the strenuous work was done, the baby was somehow 'made', all it had to do now was grow.

I have no idea why the first stages of pregnancy, when the child is so tiny, should be the most exhausting. I suppose you are growing your own cells before you start on theirs. Your blood volume goes up by 30 per cent, so your bone marrow is working, your very bone marrow is tired. It is as if you planted a seed and then had to build a field to grow it in. When that was over, everything, for me, was pure delight. If someone sold the hormones you get in the second trimester of pregnancy, I would become a junkie. I cycled everywhere, walked at a clip, fell asleep between one heartbeat and the next. I started dreaming again, vivid, intense, learning dreams. I was breast-feeding a blue-eyed girl and it was easy. I was in labour and it was easy – the child that slithered out was small and as hot as a childhood dream of wetting the bed; she was the precise temperature of flesh. Some of the dreams were funny, many were completely filthy. I had 30 per cent more blood

If someone sold the hormones you get in the second trimester of pregnancy, I would become a junkie

in my body and, as far as I could tell, it was all going to the one place. Another thing the books don't tell you.

The child was still hiding. The days ticked inexorably past. I did not feel like an animal, I felt like a clock, one made of blood and bone, that you could neither hurry nor delay. At four and a half months, right on cue, it started to chime. Butterflies. A kick.

The child leapt in my womb. Actually, the child leaps in the womb all day long, but it takes time for the womb to realise it. You wait for the first kick but, like the first smile, the early versions are all 'just wind'. The first definite kick (which coincided with the discovery of the first, definite pile, a shock severe enough to send a surge of adrenalin through any child) was wonderful. My body had been blind, and I barely comprehending; I had begun to long for a sign, a little something in return. The first kick is the child talking back to you, a kind of softening up. I began to have ideas about this baby, even conversations with it, some of which, to my great embarrassment, took place out loud.

'Hello, sweetheart.'

Sugar made the child jump, as well as hunger. Music made it stop, a listening stillness. I began to time my digestion: ten minutes after chocolate, a kick; fifteen minutes after pasta; half an hour after meat. I was bounced awake at five every morning and got up for a bowl of cereal – already feeding this little tyrant, getting in training for the real event. Early afternoon was a cancan, also nine o'clock at night. I went to New York and the child stayed on Irish time, which was very odd. In the middle of the day I would go back to my hotel room for a rest and a chat. My belly made peculiar company. We watched *My Dinner with Andre* together, and ate big handfuls of nuts.

What did I know? I knew this child liked music, but maybe all children do. I thought it was an independent type, wriggling already, as though to get away. I began to identify whatever part of its body was squirming under my hand. One day a shoulder bone scything up from the depths, another day a little jutting heel. My indifference to the world grew vast. I liked things from a distance. I was in the middle of the sweetest, quietest romance.

In our first antenatal class the midwife said, 'Is there a pelvis over there on the floor behind you, could you pass it here?' And when some hapless male picked up the bit of dead person they used for demonstration purposes, she said, 'Don't be afraid of it. It's not a chalice.' I thought this was very Irish. Secretly, I thought that perhaps my pelvis *was* a chalice. I also thought that it might be beginning to crack. She passed around a vial of amniotic fluid (of unspecified age, it would have been nice to know if it was fresh) and on the other side of the room, a woman bent forward on to her belly, in an awkward, pregnant attempt at a faint. The midwife turned to a diagram – we had to have the window opened for air. She told us about perineal massage. I had never heard of anything so peculiar and unlikely in my life. I was surrounded by strangers, half of them men and all of them catatonic with shock. It might have been the way she lay down on a mat with her legs up in the air (she was in her late fifties), or it might just have been the fact that all of us realised that there was a fundamental problem, here, of design. The hole just wasn't big enough. And there was no escape now. I felt as though I had been watching a distant train for months and only now, when it was approaching, did I realise I was tied to the tracks.

My father says, quite wisely, that we should have been marsupials, pregnant up to six months, with the last three in a pouch. The disproportion was terrible. This could not be what nature intended, humans must be overbred. I couldn't walk for more than twenty minutes. Everything hurt. Somehow, I blamed the bump and not the child for the obstruction in my gut and the vile acid that was pushed up into my throat. We weren't to take antacids, because they would make us anaemic, the midwife said. I said, 'What's so bad about anaemia?' thinking that it couldn't be worse than this. I sat and surfed the Net like some terrible turnip, gagging and leaning back in my chair. My shoes didn't fit. I became clumsy, and not just because of the weight out front – dishes dropped for no reason out of my hands. At thirty-five weeks, just like all the other women on the About.com pregnancy notice-board, I started fighting with Martin: even this was predetermined, as the hormonal conveyor belt ground on. Oh, the stupidity of it, the blankness, the senseless days and the terrible, interrupted nights. Somewhere in there, I forgot entirely that I was having a child. Nothing wonderful could come of this.

I was bored to madness, and there was nothing I, or any-one else, could do about it because I had the concentration span of a gnat. A very fat gnat.

The streets, that had been full of babies in their bug-gies, now became full of the old and the infirm, people who couldn't manage the step on to the bus, or who failed to reach the queue before the till closed. Was it possible that pregnancy was turning me into a nicer person? I thought of the women I knew when I was young who were pregnant all the time. I did sums: the mother of a school friend who had had twenty-two pregnancies, eleven of which had come to term. She would look up from her plate, surrounded by bottles of pills, and say, 'Oh . . . Hello . . .' as though trying to figure out if you had come out of her or someone else. Her husband was mad about her, you could still see it, and her children, with the excep-tion of the eldest boys, were complete strangers.

Even my own much discussed, often caressed, high-focus bump was filled with someone I did not know. And perhaps never would. Pregnancy is as old-fashioned as religion, and it never ends. Every moment of my preg-nancy lasted for ever. I was pregnant in the autumn, and I was pregnant in the spring. I was pregnant as summer came. I lived like a plant on the window-sill, taking its time, starting to bud. Nothing could hurry this. There was no technology for it: I was the technology – increasingly stupid, increasingly kind, a mystery to myself, to Martin, and to everyone who passed me by.

Birth

AMNIOTIC FLUID SMELLS like tea. When I say this to Martin, he says, 'I thought that was just tea.' Of course a hospital should smell of tea: a hospital should smell of bleach. Unit C smells of tea and a little bit of ammonia, whether human or industrial is hard to tell. There is a lot of amniotic fluid in Unit C. At least three of the women have had their waters broken that afternoon, and as the evening approaches we sit draining into strips of unbleached cotton and watching each other, jealously, for signs of pain.

There is a little something extra in there, sharp and herbal – green tea maybe, or gunpowder tea. Pregnancy smelt like grass. Sort of. It certainly smelt of something growing; a distinctive and lovely smell that belongs to that family of grass, and ironed cotton, and asparagus pee. But the smell of tea is beginning to get to me. There are pints of it. I'm like some Burco Boiler with the tap left open. It flows slowly, but it will not stop. For hours I have been waiting for it to stop, and the mess of the bed is upsetting me. It upsets the housekeeper in me and it upsets the schoolgirl in me. The sanitary pads they hand you are school-issue and all the nurses are turning into nuns.

The breaking of the waters was fine. The nurse did whatever magic makes sheets appear under you while other things are folded back, and the obstetrician did something deft with a crochet hook. There was the sense of pressure against a membrane, and then pop – a bit tougher but not much different from bursting a bubble on plastic bubble wrap. It felt quite satisfying, and the rush of hot liquid that followed made me laugh. I don't think a lot of women laugh at this stage in Unit C, but why not? We were on our way.

After which, there is nothing to do but wait. As the afternoon wears on, the pink curtains are pulled around the beds. The ward is full of breathing; the sharp intake of breath and the groaning exhalation, as though we are all asleep, or having sex in our sleep. One woman sobs behind her curtain. From the bed beside me the submarine sound of the Doppler looking for a foetal heartbeat and endlessly failing – a sonic rip as it is pulled away, then bleeping, breathing; the sigh and rush of an unseen woman's electronic blood.

Then there is tea. Actual tea. The men are sent out, for some reason, and the women sit around the long table in the middle of the ward. It's a school tea. There is a woman with high blood pressure, a couple of diabetics, one barely pregnant woman who has such bad nausea she has to be put on a drip. There are at least three other women on the brink, but they stay in bed and will not eat. I am all excited and want to talk. I am very keen to compare dressing-gowns – it took me so long to find this one, and I am quite pleased with it, but when I get up after the meal, the back of it is stained a watery red. I am beginning to hate Unit C.

After tea is the football. Portugal are playing France and, when a goal is scored, the men all come out from behind the curtains to watch the replay. Then they go back in again to their groaning, sighing women. I keep the curtain open and watch Martin while he watches the game. I am keeping track of my contractions, if they are contractions. At 9.35, Martin looks at me over the back of his chair. He gives me a thumbs-up as if to say, 'Isn't this a blast? And there's football on the telly!' At 9.35 and 20 seconds I am, for the first time, in serious pain. I am in a rage with him for missing it, and call to him quietly over the sound of the game.

A woman in a dressing-gown comes to talk to me. She is very big. I ask her if she is due tonight but she says she is not due until September, which is three months away. She is the woman from the next bed, the one with the Doppler machine. They couldn't find the foetal heartbeat because of the fat. She stands at the end of the bed and lists her symptoms, which are many. She has come up from Tipperary. She is going to have a Caesarean at thirty-one weeks. I am trying to be sympathetic, but I think I hate her. She is weakness in the room.

When I have a contraction I lurch out of bed, endlessly convinced that I have to go to the toilet – endlessly, stupidly convinced, every five minutes, that there is a crap I have to take, new and surprising as the first crap Adam took on his second day in the world. This journey to the toilet is full of obstacles, the first one being Martin, whose patience is endless and whose feet are huge. When I get into the cubicle at the end of the ward, I sit uselessly on the toilet, try to mop up the mess, and listen to the woman on the other side of the partition, who is louder than me, and who doesn't seem to bother going back to her bed any more.

This has been happening, on and off, for a week. There is nothing inside me by way of food; there hasn't been for days. I am in what Americans call pre-labour, what the Irish are too macho to call anything at all. 'If you can talk through it, then it's not a contraction,' my obstetrician said when I came in a week ago, convinced that I was on my way. This week, she says, she will induce me because my blood pressure is up; but it may be simple charity. Ten days ago I wanted a natural birth, now I want a general anaesthetic. Fuck aromatherapy, I would do anything to make this stop – up to, and including, putting my head in the road, with my belly up on the kerb.

A woman answers her mobile, 'No, Ma, nothing yet. Stop calling! Nothing yet.' Pain overtakes the woman two beds down and the curtains are drawn. When they are pulled back, you can tell she is delighted. Oh, this is it. This *must* be it. Oh, oh, I'm going to have a baby. Then more pain – agony, it looks like. 'Oh, good girl! Good girl!' shouts the midwife, as the man collects her things and she is helped out of the Ante-Room to Hell that is Unit C. I am jealous, but I wish her well. The room is full of miracles waiting to happen, whether months or hours away. Another bed is empty – the woman on the other side of the toilet partition, is she in labour too? 'She went out, any-way,' says Martin. 'Hanging on to the wall.'

It is a theatre of pain. It is a pain competition (and I am losing). Martin says that Beckett would have loved Unit C. We wonder whether this is the worst place we have ever been, but decide that the prize still goes to the bus station in Nasca, the time we went to Peru and didn't bring any jumpers. All the paper pants I brought have torn and I sit knickerless on the unbleached sheet, which I have rolled up into a huge wad under me. My bump has shrunk a little, and gone slack. When I put my hand on it, there is the baby; very close now under the skin. I just know it is a girl. I feel her shoulder and an arm. For some reason I think of a skinned rabbit. I wonder are her eyes open, and if she is waiting, like me. I have loved this child in a drowsy sort of way, but now I feel a big want in me for her, for this particular baby – the one that I am touching through my skin. 'Oh, when will I see you?' I say.

This could be the phrase of the night, but instead it is

a song that repeats in my head. 'What sends her home hanging on to the wall? Boozin'! Bloody well boo-oozin'.' I stop getting out of bed every five minutes and start breathing, the way they told us to in the antenatal class. I count backwards from five when the pain hits, and then from five again. Was I in labour yet? Was this enough pain? 'If you can talk, then it's not labour.' So I try to keep talking, but by 11.00 the lights are switched off, I am lurching into sleep between my (non-)contractions for three or five minutes at a time, and Martin is nodding off in the chair.

My cervix has to do five things: it has to come forward, it has to shorten, it has to soften, it has to thin out, it has to open. A week earlier the obstetrician recited this list and told me that it had already done three of them. In the reaches of the night I try to remember which ones I have left to do, but I can't recall the order they come in, and there is always, as I press my counting fingers into the sheet, one that I have forgotten. My cervix, my cervix. Is it soft but not short? Is it soft and thin, but not yet forward? Is it short and hard, but open anyway? I have no sense that this is not a list but a sequence. I have lost my grasp of cause and effect. My cervix, my cervix: it will open as the clouds open, to let the sun come shining through. It will open like the iris of an eye, like the iris when you open the back of a camera. I could see it thinning; the tiny veins stretching and breaking. I could see it opening like something out of *Alien*. I could see it open as simply as a door that you don't know you've opened, until you are halfway across the room. I could see all this, but my cervix stayed shut.

At 2.30 a.m. I give in and Martin goes off to ask for some Pethidine. I know I will only be allowed two doses of this stuff, so it had better last a long time. I want to save the second for the birth, but in my heart of hearts I know I'm on my way to an epidural now. I don't know why I wanted to do without one, I suppose it was that Irishwoman machismo again. *Mná na hEireann. MNÁ na hEireann.* FIVE four three two . . . one. Fiiiive four three two one. Five. Four. Three. Two. One.

Once I give in and start to whimper, the (non-)contractions are unbearable. The Pethidine does not come. At 3 a.m. there is a shrieking from down the corridor, and I realise how close we are to the labour ward. The noise is ghastly, Victorian: it tears through the hospital dark. Someone is really giving it soprano. I think nothing of it. I do not wonder if the woman is mad, or if the baby has died, but that is what I wonder as I write this now.

Footsteps approach but they are not for me, they are for the woman from Tipperary who has started crying, with a great expenditure of snot, in the bed next door. The nurse comforts her. 'I'm just frikened,' the woman says. 'She just frikened me.' I want to shout that it's all right for her, she's going to have a fucking Caesarean, but it has been forty-five minutes since I realised that I could not do this any more, that the pain I had been riding was about to ride over me, and I needed something to get me back on top, or I would be destroyed by it, I would go under – in some spiritual and very real sense, I would die.

The footsteps go away again. They do not return. I look at Martin who is listening, as I am listening, and he disappears silently through the curtain. At 3.30 a.m., I get the Pethidine.

After this, I do not count through the (non-)contractions, or try to manage my breathing. I moan, with my mouth a little open. I *low*. I almost enjoy it. I sleep all the time now, between times. I have given in. I have untied my little boat and gone floating downstream.

At 5.00 a.m. a new woman comes along and tells Martin he must go home. There follows a complicated and slow conversation as I stand up to her (we are, after all, back in school). I say that I need him here, and she smiles, 'What for? What do you need him for?' (For saving me from women like you, *Missus*.) In the end, she tells us that there are mattresses he can sleep on in a room down the hall. Oh. Why didn't she say so? Maybe she's mad. It's 5 a.m., I'm tripping on Pethidine, at the raw end of a sleepless week, and this woman is a little old-fashioned, in a mad sort of way. Wow. We kiss. He goes. From now on, I stay under, not even opening my eyes when the pain comes.

I think I low through breakfast. They promise me a bed in the labour ward at 10.30, so I can stop lowing and start screaming, but that doesn't seem to be happening really.

I am sitting up and smiling for the ward round, which is nice, but I am afraid that they will notice that the contractions are fading, and I'll have to start all over again, somehow. Then the contractions come back again, and by now my body is all out of Pethidine. I spend the minutes after 10.30 amused by my rage; astonished by how bad I feel. Are these the worst hundred seconds I have ever been through? How about the next hundred seconds – let's give them a go.

At 12.00, I nip into the cubicle for one last contraction, and we are out of Unit C. The whole ward lifts as we leave, wishing us well – another one on her way. I realise I have been lowing all night, keeping these women from sleep.

The room on the labour ward is extremely posh, with its own bathroom and a high-tech bed. I like the look of the midwife; she is the kind of woman you'd want to go for a few pints with. She is tired. She asks if I have a birth plan and I say I want to do everything as naturally as possible. She says, 'Well, you've made a good start, anyway,' which I think is possibly sarcastic, given the crochet hook, and the Pethidine, and the oxytocin drip they've just ordered up. Martin goes back to pack up our stuff, and I start to talk. She keeps a half-ironic silence. For months, I had the idea that if I could do a bit of research, get a bit of chat out of the midwife, then that would take my mind off things – what is the worst thing that anyone ever said? or the weirdest? – but she won't play ball. I run out of natter and have a little cry. She says, 'Are you all right?' I say, 'I just didn't think I would ever get this far, that's all.' And I feel her soften behind me.

I don't remember everything that followed, but I do remember the white, fresh light. I also remember the feelings in the room. I could sense a shift in mood, or intention, in the women who tended me, with great clarity. It was like being in a painting. Every smile mattered; the way people were arranged in the space, the gestures they made.

I have stopped talking. The midwife is behind me, arranging things on a stand. Martin is gone, there is silence in the room. She is thinking about something. She isn't happy. It is very peaceful.

Or: She tries to put in the needle for the drip. Martin is on my right-hand side. I seem to cooperate but I won't turn my hand around. The stain from the missed vein starts to spread and she tries again. I am completely uninterested in the pain from the needle.

Or: A woman walks in, looks at me, glances between my legs. 'Well done!' she says, and walks back out again. Perhaps she just walked into the wrong room.

Even at a low dose, the oxytocin works fast. It is bucking through my system, the contractions gathering speed: the donkey who is kicking me is getting really, really annoyed. The midwife goes to turn up the drip and I say, 'You're not touching that until I get my epidural.' A joke.

A woman puts her head round the door, then edges into the room. She says something to the midwife, but they are really talking about something else. She half-turns to me with a smile. There is something wrong with one of the blood tests. She tells me this, then she tells the midwife that we can go ahead anyway. The midwife relaxes. I realise that, sometimes, they don't give you an epidural. Even if you want one. They just can't. Then everyone has a bad morning.

The midwife goes to the phone. Martin helps to turn me on my side. The contractions now are almost continuous. Within minutes, a woman in surgical greens walks in. 'Hi!' she says. 'I'm your pain-relief consultant.' She reaches over my bare backside to shake my hand. This is a woman who loves her job. Martin cups my heels and pushes my knees up towards my chest, while she sticks the needle in my spine, speaking clearly and loudly, and working at speed. I am bellowing by now, pretty much. FIVE, I roar (which seems to surprise them – five what?) FOUR. THREE. (Oh, good woman! That's it!) TWO. One. FIVE. They hold me like an animal that is trying to kick free, but I am not – I am doing this, I am getting this done. When it is over, the anaesthetist breaks it to me that it might be another ten minutes before I feel the full effect. I do not have ten minutes to spare, I want to tell her this, but fortunately, the pain has already begun to dull.

The room turns to me. The anaesthetist pats down her gown and smiles. She is used to the most abject gratitude, but I thank the midwife instead, for getting the timing spot on. The woman who talked about my blood tests has come back and the midwife tells me that she is finishing up now, Sally will see me through. This is a minor sort of betrayal, but I feel it quite keenly. Everyone leaves. Martin goes for a sandwich and Sally runs ice-cubes up my belly to check the line of the epidural. There is no more pain.

Sally is lovely: sweetness itself. She is the kind of woman who is good all the way through. It is perhaps 1.30 and in the white light, with no pain, I am having the time of my life. Literally. Karen, the obstetrician, tells me my cervix has gone from practically 0 to 8 centimetres, in no time flat. The heavens have opened, the sun has come shining through. Martin is called back from the canteen. He watches the machines as they register the pain that I cannot feel any more. He says the contractions are off the scale now. We chat a bit and have a laugh, and quite soon Sally says it is time to push. Already.

For twenty hours women have been telling me I am wonderful, but I did not believe them until now. I know how to do this, I have done it in my dreams. I ask to sit up a bit and the bed rises with a whirr. Martin is invited to 'take a leg' and he politely accepts, 'Oh, thank you.' Sally takes the other one, and braces it – my shin against her ribs. Push! They both lean into me. I wait for the top of the contraction, catch it, and ride the wave. I can feel the head, deliciously large under my pubic bone. I can feel it as it eases further down. I look at Martin, all the while – here is a present for you, mister, this one is for you – but he is busy watching the business end. Karen is back, and they are all willing me on like football hooligans, Go on! Go on! One more now, and Push! Good woman! Good girl! I can hear the knocking of the baby's heartbeat on the foetal monitor, and the dreadful silence as I push. Then, long before I expect it, Sally says, 'I want you to pant through this one. Pant.' The child has come down, the child is there. Karen says, Yes, you can see the head. I send Martin down to check the colour of the hair. (A joke?) Another push. I ask may I touch, and there is the top of the head, slimy and hot and – what is most terrifying – soft. Bizarrely, I pick up Martin's finger to check that it is clean, then tell him he must feel how soft it is. So he does. After which – enough nonsense now – it is back to pushing. Sally reaches in with her flat-bladed scissors and Martin, watching, lets my leg go suddenly slack. We are mid-push. I kick out, and he braces against me again. Karen, delighted, commands me to, 'Look down now, and see your baby being born.' I tilt my head to the maximum; and there is the back of the baby's head, easing out beyond my belly's horizon line. It is black and red, and wet. On the next push, machine perfect, it slowly turns. And here it comes – my child; my child's particular profile. A look of intense concentration, the nose tilted up, mouth and eyes tentatively shut. A blind man's face, vivid with sensation. On the next push, Sally catches the shoulders and lifts the baby out and up – in the middle of which movement the mouth opens, quite simply, for a first breath. It simply starts to breathe.

'It's a girl!'

Sally says afterwards that we were very quiet when she came out. But I didn't want to say the first thing that came to mind – which was, 'Is it? Are you sure?' A newborn's genitals are swollen and red and a bit peculiar looking, and the cord was surprisingly grey and twisted like a baroque pillar. Besides, I was shy. How to make the introduction? I think I eventually said, 'Oh, I knew you would be,' I think I also said, 'Oh, come here to me, darling.' She was handed to me, smeared as she was with something a bit stickier than cream cheese. I laid her on my stomach and pulled at my T-shirt to clear a place for her on my breast. She opened her eyes for the first time, looking into my face, her irises cloudy. She blinked and found my eyes. It was a very suspicious, grumpy look, and I was devastated.

Martin, doing the honours at a festive dinner, cut the cord. After I pushed out the placenta, Karen held it up for inspection, twirling it on her hand like a connoisseur: a bloody hairnet, though heavier and more slippy.

The baby was long. Her face looked like mine. I had not prepared myself for this: this really astonished me. 'She looks like me.' And Martin said (an old joke), 'But she's got my legs.' At some stage, she was wrapped rigid in a blue blanket, which was a mercy, because I could hardly bear the smallness of her. At some stage, they slipped out, leaving us to say, 'Oh, my God,' a lot. I put her to a nipple and she suckled. 'Oh, my *God*,' said Martin. I looked at him as if to say, 'Well, what did you expect?' I rang my mother who said, 'Welcome to the happiest day of your life,' and started to cry. I thought this was a little over the top. In a photograph taken at this time, I look pragmatic and unsurprised, as though I had just cleaned the oven and was about to tackle the fridge.

I am not stricken until they wheel us down to the ward. The child looks at the passing scene with alert pleasure. She is so clear and sharp. She is saturated with life, she is intensely alive. Her face is a little triangle and her eyes are shaped like leaves, and she looks out of them, liking the world.

Two hours later I am in the shower. When I clean between my legs I am surprised to find everything numb and mushy. I wonder why that is. Then I remember that a baby's head came out of there, actually came out. When I come to, I am sitting on a nurse. She is sitting on the toilet beside the shower. The shower is still going. I am very wet. She is saying, 'You're all right, you're all right, I've got you.' I think I am saying, 'I just had a baby. I just had a baby,' but I might be trying to say it, and not saying anything at all.

Milk

THE MILK SURPRISES me. It does not disgust me as much as I thought it would, unless it is not fresh. It is disturbing that a piece of you should go off so quickly. I don't think Freud ever discussed lactation, but the distinction between 'good' and 'bad' bodily products here is very fine. Women leak so much. Perhaps this is why we clean – which is to say that a man who cleans is always 'anal', a woman who cleans is just a woman.

There certainly is a lot of it, and it gets everywhere, and the laundry is a fright. But what fun! to be granted a new bodily function so late in life. As if you woke up one morning and could play the piano. From day to day the child is heavier in your arms, she plumps up from wrist to ankle, she has dimples where her knuckles were, she has fat on her toes. I thought we might trade weight, pound for pound, but she is gaining more than I am losing. I am faced with bizarre and difficult calculations – the weight of the groceries in a bag versus the weight of her nappies in a bag. Or my weight, plus a pint of water, minus four ounces of milk, versus her weight, plus four ounces, divided by yesterday. When I was at school, a big-chested friend put her breasts on the scales and figured that they weighed 2 pounds each. I don't know how she did it, but I still think that she was wrong. Heavier. Much heavier.

It is quite pleasant when a part of your body makes sense, after many years. A man can fancy your backside, but you still get to sit on it; breasts, on the other hand, were always just there. Even so, the anxiety of pregnancy is the anxiety of puberty all over again. I am thirty-seven. I don't want my body to start 'doing' things, like some kind of axolotl. I do not believe people when they say these things will be wonderful, that they are 'meant'. I am suspicious of the gleam in women's eyes, that pack of believers, and listen instead to the voice of a friend who breast-fed her children until they were twenty-eight years old, and who now says, 'They're like ticks.'

So I feed the child because I should, and resign myself to staying home. I never liked being around nursing women – there was always too much love, too much need in the room. I also suspected it to be sexually gratifying. For whom? Oh, for everyone: for the mother, the child, the father, the father-in-law. Everyone's voice that little bit nervy, as though it weren't happening: everyone taking pleasure in a perv-lite middle-class sort of way. Ick. 'The only women who breast-feed are doctors' wives and tinkers,' a friend's mother was told forty years ago, by the

nurse who delivered her. I thought I sensed a similar distaste in the midwives, a couple of months ago, who were
obliged by hospital and government policy to prod the
child and pinch my nipple, though perhaps – let's face it,
sisters – not quite that hard. It is probably easier for men,
who like breasts in general, but I have always found them
mildly disgusting, at least up close. They also often make
me jealous. Even the word 'breast' is difficult. Funny how
many people say they find public breast-feeding a bit 'in
your face'. Oh, the rage.

So, let us call it 'nursing' and let us be discreet – it is
still the best way I know to clear a room. My breast is not
the problem (left, or right, whichever is at issue), the
'problem' is the noise. Sometimes the child drinks as simply as from a cup, other times she snorts and gulps,
half-drowns, sputters and gasps; then she squawks a bit,
and starts all over again. This may be an iconised activity
made sacred by some and disgusting by others, but it is
first and foremost a meal. It is only occasionally serene. It
also takes a long time. I do smile at her and coo a bit, but
I also read a lot (she will hate books), talk, or type (this,
for example). Afterwards she throws up. People stare at
the whiteness of it, as I did at first. Look. Milk.

'It was the whiteness of the whale that above all
appalled me.' The nineteenth century took their breasts
very seriously, or so I suspect – I can't really get into a
library to check. I am thinking of those references I found
particularly exciting or unsettling as a child. The heroes

of *King Solomon's Mines*, for example, as they toil up Sheba's left Breast (a mountain) suffering from a torturing thirst. The chapter is called 'Water Water!' and comes from a time when you were allowed to be so obvious it hurt. 'Heavens, how we did drink!' These extinct volcanoes are 'inexpressibly solemn and overpowering' and difficult to describe. They are wreathed about with 'strange mists and clouds [that] gathered and increased around them, till presently we could only trace their pure and gigantic outline swelling ghostlike through the fleecy envelope'. In a desperate drama of hunger and satiation our heroes climb through lava and snow up to the hillock of the enormous, freezing nipple. There they find a cave, occupied by a dead man (what?! what?!), and in this cave one of their party also dies: Ventvogel, a 'hottentot' whose 'snub-nose' had, when he was alive, the ability to sniff out water (we don't want to know).

So far, so infantile. I watch the child's drama at the breast, and (when I am not reading, typing, or talking) cheer her along. She wakes with a shout in the middle of the night, and I wonder at her dreams; there is a dead man in a cave, perhaps, somewhere about my person. Oh, dear. When did it all get so serious? I turn to Swift for the comedy, as opposed to tragedy, of scale, but Gulliver perched on a Brobdingnagian nipple turns out, on rereading, to be part of a great disgustfest about giant women pissing. None of this seems *true* to me. I have no use for the child's disgust, as she has no use for mine. I am besotted by a being who is, at this stage, just a set of emotions arranged around a gut. Who is just a shitter, who is just a soul.

Are all mothers Manicheans? This is just one of the hundreds of questions that have never been asked about motherhood. What I am interested in is not the drama of being a child, but this new drama of being a mother (yes, there are cannibals in my dreams, yes) about which so little has been written. Can mothers not hold a pen? Or is it just the fact that we are all children, when we write?

I go to Books Upstairs in Dublin, to find a poem by Eavan Boland. The child in the stroller is ghetto fabulous in a white babygro complete with hoodie. I am inordinately, sadly proud of the fact that she is clean. We negotiate the steps, we knock over some books. The child does a spectacular crap in the silence of the shop, in front of the section marked 'Philosophy'. I say, 'Oh, look at all the books. Oh, *look* at all the books,' because I believe in talking to her, and I don't know what else to say.

The poem is called 'Night Feed' and is beautifully measured and very satisfying: 'A silt of milk. / The last suck. / And now your eyes are open, / Birth coloured and offended.'

But the poet chooses a bottle not a breast, placing the poem in the bland modernity of the suburbs. I grew up in those suburbs. I know what we were running away from. Because the unpalatable fact is that the Ireland of my childhood had the closest thing to a cow cult outside of India. When I was eleven, I won a Kodak Instamatic camera in the Milk Competition, a major annual event, when every school child in the country had to write an essay called 'The Story of Milk'. I can still remember the arrival of the Charolais cattle, which marked the beginning of Ireland's love affair with Europe. The most exciting thing about economic union, for my farming relatives, was not the promise of government grants but this big-eyed, nougat-coloured breed of bull whose semen could be used in beef or dairy herds – as good, if you will pardon the phrase, for meat as for milk. It was a romantic animal, as hopeful as the moon shot. There were cuff-links made in the shape of the Charolais and men wore them to Mass and to the mart. And the romance lingers on. A couple of years ago, a media personality of my acquaintance bought four of them, to match her curtains.

The country was awash with milk. Kitchens and bedrooms were hung with pictures of the Madonna and child. After the arrival of infant formula in the fifties, breast-feeding became more of a chosen, middle-class activity, but it was still common in the countryside, and was everywhere practised as a fairly optimistic form of contraception. Still, though general all over Ireland, breast-feeding was absolutely hidden. The closest the culture came to an image of actual nursing was in the icon of the Sacred Heart, endlessly offering his male breast, open and glowing, and crowned with thorns.

Actually, you know, breast-feeding hurts. Certainly, at first, it really fucking hurts. On the third night of my daughter's life I was left with a human being the size of a cat and nothing to sustain her with but this *stub*. Madwomen (apparently) think that their babies are possessed. And they are. They look at you, possessed by their own astonishing selves. You say, Where did that come from? You say, Where did YOU come from? This baby is pure need – a need you never knew you had. And all you have to offer is a mute part of your body which, you are told, will somehow start 'expressing', as though it might start singing 'Summertime'. You feed your child, it seems, on hope alone. There is nothing to see. You do not believe the milk exists until she throws it back up, and when she does, you want to cry. What is not quite yours as it leaves you, is definitely yours as it comes back.

So there we were in the hospital dark; me and my white Dracula, her chin running with milk and her eyes black. What I remember is how fully human her gaze was, even though it was so new. She seemed to say that this was a serious business, that we were in it together. Tiny babies have such emotional complexity. I am amazed that 'bravery' is one of the feelings she has already experienced, that she should be born so intrepid and easily affronted, that she should be born so much herself.

She is also, at this early stage, almost gender free. This is useful. The statistics on how much less girl babies are breast-fed, as opposed to boys, are shocking. There are probably a number of reasons for this, but one of them surely is the degree to which our society has sexualised the breast. All in all, sex has ruined breast-feeding. It is a moral business these days – a slightly dirty, slightly won-derful, always unsettling, duty. It has no comic aspects. No one has told the child this: she seems to find it, finally, quite amusing – as indeed do I.

We turn to Sterne to find glee, envy, all those ravening eighteenth-century emotions, transmuted by language into delight. Shandy quotes Ambrose Paraeus on the stunting effect of the nursing breast on a child's nose, par-ticularly those 'organs of nutrition' that have 'firmness and elastic repulsion'. These were 'the undoing of the child, inasmuch as his nose was so snubb'd, so rebuff'd, so rebated, and so refrigerated thereby, as never to arrive ad mensuram suam legitimam'. What was needed was a soft, flaccid breast so that, 'by sinking into it . . . as into so much butter, the nose was comforted, nourish'd, plump'd up, refresh'd, refocillated, and set a growing for ever'.

This was still when 'breast' was a common, easy word. Men placed their hands on their breasts, had pistols pointed at them, and were in general so set to a-swelling and a-glowing as to put the girls to shame. There is a dis-tinction between 'breast' and 'breasts', of course, but it is still charming to think that this seat of honesty and senti-ment is the singular of a plural that provoked desire. As if, in modern terms, we got horny watching someone's eyes fill with tears. As, indeed, sometimes, we do.

No. The milk surprises me, above all, because it hurts as it is let down, and this foolish pain hits me at quite the wrong times. The reflex is designed to work at the sight, sound, or thought of your baby – which is spooky enough – but the brain doesn't seem to know what a baby *is*, exactly, and so tries to make you feed anything helpless, or wonderful, or small. So I have let down milk for Russian submariners and German tourists dying on Concorde. Loneliness and technology get me every time, get my milk every time. Desire, also, stabs me not in the heart but on either side of the heart – but I had expected this. What I had not expected was that there should be some things that do not move me, that move my milk. Or that, sometimes, I only realise that I am moved when I feel the pain. I find myself lapsed into a memory I cannot catch, I find myself trying to figure out what it is in the room that is sad or lovely – was it that combination of words, or the look on his face? – what it is that has such a call on my unconscious attention, or my pituitary, or my alveolar cells.

There is a part of me, I have realised, that wants to nurse the stranger on the bus. Or perhaps it wants to nurse the bus itself, or the tree I see through the window of the bus, or the child I once was, paying my fare on the way home from school. This occasional incontinence is terrifying. It makes me want to shout – I am not sure what. Either, Take it! or, Stop! If the world would stop needing then my body would come back to me. My body would come home.

I could ask (in a disingenuous fashion) if this is what it is like to be bothered by erections. Is this what it is like to be bothered by tears? Whatever – I think we can safely say that when we are moved, it is some liquid that starts moving: blood, or milk, or salt water. I did not have a very tearful pregnancy, mostly because we don't have a television. Pregnant women cry at ads for toilet tissue: some say it is the hormones, but I think we have undertaken such a great work of imagining, we are prone to wobble on the high wire. Of course, the telly has always been a provoker of second-hand tears as well as second-hand desire. Stories, no matter how fake, produce a real biological response in us, and we are used to this. But the questions my nursing body raises are more testing to me. Do we need stories in order to produce emotion, or is an emotion already a story? What is the connection, in other words, between narrative and my alveolar cells?

I suspect, as I search the room for the hunger by the fireplace, or the hunger in her cry, that I have found a place before stories start. Or the precise place where stories start. How else can I explain the shift from language that has happened in my brain? This is why mothers do not write, because motherhood happens in the body, as much as the mind. I thought childbirth was a sort of journey that you could send dispatches home from, but of course it is not – it *is* home. Everywhere else now, is 'abroad'.

A child came out of me. I cannot understand this, or try to explain it. Except to say that my past life has become foreign to me. Except to say that I am prey, for the rest of my life, to every small thing.

Damn.

Nine Months

Day One: Ah

Development (*the baby*)

I WAKE UP to the sound of my baby saying, 'Ah.' It is the morning after she was born. 'Ah.' She says it clear and true. This is her voice. It sounds slightly surprised at itself. It certainly surprises me. 'Ah.' There she goes again.

Perhaps it is a reflex, the way this baby will stride across the sheet when you set her feet on the bed. She already knows how to talk, but it will be some months before she stops teasing me, and does it again.

We are born knowing everything.

Regression (*me*)

I wake up to the sound of my baby saying, 'Ah.' It is the morning after she was born. 'Ah.' She says it clear and true. This is her voice. It sounds slightly surprised at itself. It certainly surprises me. 'Ah.' There she goes again.

She should be crying, but she is talking instead; experimenting with this sound that comes out of her mouth. The womb is so silent. And of course. Of course! It is obvious! I have given birth to a perfect child.

I look into the cot and watch for a while. Then I decide that I must have another baby immediately.

You see, I never believed, until just this moment, that I could do this, that it could be done. Now I know that it is true – something as simple as sex can make something as complicated as a baby, a real one, and I think, What a great trick! and I wonder, How soon? How soon can we do the impossible again?

It is now the end of June. With a bit of luck we can start again in the middle of August. We could have another one by . . . next May. Allow three months for trying and failing – latest, I'll be in labour again by August of next year. Which means that I'll have to write that novel in five months, proofs at Christmas, to rush for publication late spring, and then, pop, another baby! Perfect. It all fits. I have to ring Martin and tell him this. I pick up the mobile phone he has left for me by the bedside and I dial a three. I cancel and try a six. I cancel again. I can't remember our phone number.

Usually, it takes me three years to write a book, but that's no problem: I can make babies, for heaven's sake, novels are a doddle. Look, it is all there in my head. I can flick through the pages and know the shape of it: I can relish the tone.

Usually, it takes me three years to write a book, but that's no problem: I can make babies, for heaven's sake, novels are a doddle

The novel is in my head but the phone number is not in my head. I look around the room and have a think. It's in my file – of course it is. There: just under my name. I follow the numbers with my finger and dial.

I used to be good at numbers. My brain must have been reconfigured during the night, somehow. I had heard that motherhood makes you stupid, maybe this is what they meant. Never mind, I can always use a phone book. I can do anything. I can conceive a child in the middle of November, say the 12th or 13th – Is that mid-week? It would probably be more relaxed if I ovulated at a weekend. I must ask Martin to get down the calendar.

He answers the phone.

The First Month: Dream-time

Development (*the baby*)

We dream, in our first weeks, more than at any other time in our lives. More than all the rest of our dreams over the whole span of our days. Constant dreaming. I wonder if she knows that she is awake. She opens her eyes and the world is there, she closes them and it is still there – or something very like it: the long shift of light and darkness that is week one, week two, week three. The landscape of her mother's breast. The earthquake of her mother's rising out of bed. The noise of it all.

Two faces. Two people grinning, singing, cooing, calling to her. They gaze into her eyes – but *deep* into her eyes and they do not look away. They smile – a massive break in the O of the face. Hello. Yes. Hello. Something blanks out in her head and she turns away.

Overload. Shut-down.

Regression (*me*)

I never feel her skin. She is always dressed – another vest, another babygro, always snowy white, then yellowing at the neck from crusted milk. I change her all the time, but bit by bit. I change the nappy and then the vest. Nothing will persuade me to give her a bath. She has no fat yet, under this skin of hers. So much of what we think of as skin, the pleasure of it, the way it runs under our fingers, is actually fat. Merciful, sweet fat.

I was looking forward to the softness of her, and I thought her skin would look so new. But it looks as though it belongs to someone who has been in the bath too long. It is too thin. Seven layers of cells, that is what I remember from school – our surface is seven cells thick. But I think she has only three or four. I think she has only one. It is not so much a skin, as a glaze.

At the weekend, in my parents' house, my mother quite tactfully clears the room. Just in time. I weep like someone who has been in a car crash. I weep like someone who has woken up from a dream, to find that it is all true, after all.

'Have a good cry,' says my mother, for the first time in twenty-five years. She too, at last, on home ground.

The Second Month

Development (*the baby*)

The books (the books!) say that her hands will uncurl this month, but they have always been open. Open and large and long. On the day she was born, her father looked at them and said, in a deeply regretful way, 'You know we're going to have to get a piano, now.'

She lies on her back on the white bed, wearing a white babygro, and she twists her hands slowly in front of her face; utterly graceful. She does it when there is music playing, looking very ancient, and centred, and Chinese.

She still sleeps, most of the time.

THE BABY WAKES with a yelp of hunger, and she goes for the breast like a salty old dog. 'Aaarh,' goes her mouth, as she roots to one side. 'Aaarh.' She turns away from it to fill a nappy – which is serious work, of permanently uncertain outcome, or so it seems to her; always surprising, and bravely undertaken.

'Oh, good girl!'

We squeak toys on her tummy and smile, before she blanks out, or closes her eyes to sleep again. And then one day, she does not blank out. She smiles.

Regression (me)

I am still not walking so well and the blood is an absolute nuisance. I look up the Internet to try and find someone who knows when this is supposed to stop, but it's all about joy and despair, it's all feeding and postnatal depression and not a single thing about leakage, seepage, anaemia. Never mind.

In the first weeks, some book tells me, I am supposed to take three baths a day. Hah! I run a bath and the water goes cold before I have a chance to get into it. I sit in a bath and then lurch like a big wet cow out of the bath, carefully, carefully over the tiles, to run to the baby. What does the baby want? We are all agreed that this is a very contented baby, but it seems, all the same, that ten minutes away from this contented baby is one minute too many. Here, darling, here's your big, wet Ma.

Actually I don't mind the bath so much, a quick dip is fine, I don't really need clean hair. I can't go out anyway, because my feet are still too big for all my shoes, except for one pair of floppy, disgusting sneakers. I don't mind that either. If I made a list of the things I cannot do, it would start and finish with going to the toilet. I never thought of going to the toilet as a fundamental human right, but I do now. It should be in some UN Charter, the opportunity and the privacy, the biological ability to go to the toilet. No one mentions this on the Internet. They talk about sex instead. Sex. Crikey.

At the recommended time, we try a bit of sex. It's a

wasteland down there. Women are awful liars. I do not think of all the women who gave birth in pain any more, I think of all the women who conceived in pain; the Irish families with eleven months between one child and the next. Did they feel the way I do, now – and then get pregnant again? No wonder they didn't tell us anything – those lowered voices in the kitchen when I was a child. Welcome to the big secret – it hurts.

But I really cannot believe that it hurts like this for everyone. Maybe I am too old. Maybe it is the fact that I have very loose joints. I think it isn't the tissue that hurts so much as the bones.

I don't know. I have never heard anyone discussing how long the pain is supposed to last. So I draw upon however many ghastly generations of suffering have preceded me and when I go back for my check-up, I smile hugely and say that everything is fine, wonderful, marvellous. I don't want to piss on the parade, and besides, it is true: I am extravagantly happy – messy, creaky, bewildered, exhausted, and in pain, but happy, hopeful, and immensely refreshed by it all.

Meanwhile, Martin is still on paternity leave and I can sleep. I have a talent for it. I doze, I nap, I snooze. I have no problem doing this. For the first time in months, I have an easy dream life – it seems my unconscious has relaxed. If the baby cries, on the other hand, I shoot up in the bed like an electrocuted corpse. Never mind the empty husk of your discarded body – pregnancy doesn't stop once they are out. I am still attached to this baby, I still feed myself in order to feed her. The only difference is the distance between us, now – all that space and air to get through. Air that she can suck in, and then exhale.

The baby cries. She cries on Saturday and also on Sunday. She does not take a break on Sunday night. And on Monday morning she cries again. We become acquainted with the long reaches of the night.

There are two, exactly opposite, ways to describe all this, and so I start to train myself in. The baby is a happy baby, I say, and lo! it is true. If I said the opposite, then this would become true instead. The baby is cranky, we will never sleep again – I would spiral downwards and the baby (the family! the house!) would be dragged down with me. So the baby is a happy baby because we have no other option, and the more we say it, the more true it becomes.

Besides. Look.

Such a beautiful, beautiful baby.

Once, maybe twice a day, I get an image of terrible violence against the baby. Like a flicker in the corner of my eye, it lasts for a quarter of a second, maybe less. Sometimes it is me who inflicts this violence, sometimes it is someone else. Martin says it is all right – it is just her astonishing vulnerability that works strange things in my head. But I know it is also because I am trapped, not just by her endless needs, but also by the endless, mindless love I have for her. It is important to stay on the right side of a love like this. For once, I am glad I am an older mother. I don't panic. I put a limit on the images that flash across my mind's eye. I am allowed two per day, maybe three. If I get more than that, then it's off to the doctor for the happy pills. Shoes or no shoes.

The Third Month

Development (*the baby*)

The baby cries for three days, on and off, and then she does something new, or she does a number of new things, all at once. She starts to grab and she also discovers her mouth, running her tongue around her lips. Or she finds her toes and starts to babble, both at the same time. The crying stops.

I wonder what was happening, for those three days? Waking up and crying, or turning and crying – seeing, reaching, scrabbling and suddenly setting up a wail. Brain fever. Hints and premonitions. Her mind is pulling itself up by its own bootstraps. There is something she must do, and she does not know what it is. Something is within reach, and she does not know what it might be. She has never done any of this before, and yet she knows that she has to do it. The shift and pressure of it must be huge. And then, all of a sudden, she breaks through. Not only 'habwabwa' but also toes! Not only this, but the other thing!

So that's what it was. What a relief.

Babies always know they have achieved something. They are naturally proud of themselves. She has a new expression every day now. Her worried look is more worried, her smile is slow, and complex, and huge.

Regression (*me*)

Somewhere in this month I realise that the baby will live, that when I wake up she will still be breathing.

From one day to the next, she changes from a tiny, mewling creature into the proper baby she is. All those old-fashioned words now apply: bonny, dandle, gurgle, dimple, posset. I give in to my stubbornly large feet, and buy new shoes.

I walk the streets of Dublin with the baby in a sling and everyone smiles at me and at my child. 'Isn't he lovely?' they say, assuming, for some reason, it is a boy. A man leans towards me on the bus. 'It's very hot,' he says. 'I have some water, ma'am, if you'd like to sponge the baby down.'

At home, Martin puts on her babygro, limb by tiny limb. 'Where did Napoleon put his armies?' he says. 'In his sleevies!'

I watch them and think how impossible it all is. I cannot see how this baby will grow into a person, any old person – a person like you, or me, or your boss, or that middle-aged woman in the street. I cannot see where it all goes.

The Fourth Month

Development (the baby)

The baby is becoming herself. Every day she is more present to us. A personality rises to the surface of her face, like a slowly developing Polaroid. She frowns for the first time, and it looks quite comical – the deliberate, frowny nature of her frown.

Or maybe she is disappearing. There was something so essential about her when she was just a tiny scrap: something astonishing and tenacious and altogether herself.

The baby disappears into her own personality. She gets rounder. Her features begin to look strangely confined, like a too-small mask in the middle of her big, round face.

It is now that babies look like Queen Victoria or Winston Churchill, or anyone fat, and British, and in charge. She is most imperious when her father picks her up. She sits in his arms and looks over at me as if to say, So who are you?

Regression (me)

The baby sits in her father's arms and looks over at me, like I am a stranger, walked in off the street. Oh, that blank stare. It makes me laugh, and go over to her, and take her back from him.

Silly baba.

When I have her safe, I look at Martin, and sometimes

I recognise the wan feeling that men get, after a baby is born.

I spend the next while renegotiating this new, triangular love, with its lines of affection and exclusion. I try to make it whole. The thing I have to remember is that love is, in general, a good thing (though it often feels terrible, to me). I can see why people panic about all this: they panic about their partners being lost to them, or they panic about their babies being lost to them. Men, mostly – but not just men. Whoever is most the child in the relationship is the one who is most displaced.

I think that means me.

So, for a while I try to be, and am, that 'Mother' thing – the one who holds everyone, even myself, and keeps us safe. The container (the old bag, my dear, the old bag).

The Fifth Month

Development (the baby)

The baby looks, not at her fluffy toys' faces, eyes, ears or bits of ribbon, but at the label stitched into a seam. They all have one – a big disproportional loop of washing instructions and warnings about flammability. She likes the intricacy of the writing, but perhaps in an endlessly variable world, she is attracted to something constant and small. So much for her blue heffalump with the red feet, so much for her squeaky pink mouse – let's stick to Surface Wash Only, and the importance of 40 degrees.

Regression (me)
We bring the baby to America, on a book tour. Feeding her in a coffee shop, changing her nappy on the side of the road. Everywhere I travel, I think of refugees, and all the millions of women with babies in their arms, desperate for the next safe place. There is a sixteen-year-old girl in Bosnia who lives in my head, and she is doing this job just as well as I am, with as much tenderness and as much fear.

The book tour goes all right. I think.

I FLY TO Toronto and the baby goes home with her father. It doesn't occur to me to feel guilty. I drink my head off. I lactate a little mournfully into hotel sinks and make jokes about Baileys Irish Cream. I have a brilliant time (and I walk back in the door shaking like a lover).

Finished feeding, I go back on the cigarettes. I am addicted to nicotine, but I am also addicted to slipping away for two minutes every hour, and being alone. Just two minutes, maybe three. The cigarettes are in a closed room, and the ashtray is beside my computer. When she is asleep, I work. I think I am becoming addicted to working, too.

I am amazed at how much I have done. The baby sleeps for hours at a time, and I can't exactly leave the flat. So I might as well sit and type. All kinds of stuff. It doesn't look stupid to me – maybe that comes later, after you spend a few thousand hours saying, 'Look at the BLUE balloon.' So I write even faster, to outrun my fate.

The baby sleeps, and I am free. I have not so much left the human race, as just left the *race* – which suits my kind of work very well. I feel sorry for all the parents who earn their money in the real world and have to go back out there again. If you spend a few months away from the game – the shopping, shagging, striving game – then it must be hard to see the point of it, quite.

I start a short story, a woman who says, *'There is a lull, a sort of hopelessness that comes over women just before they have children, or so it was with me. I did not know where it came from. Perhaps it came from my body, perhaps it came from my life, but I had the feeling that what I was doing was no good, or that I was no good at it. I have seen other women sink suddenly like this, they lose confidence, they dither, and then, shortly afterwards, they have children.'*

Is this true?

The child sleeps. I write about a woman on a ship, with a baby in her belly. Travelling on.

The Sixth Month

Development (*the baby*)

The baby has discovered locomotion (and frustration), propelling herself on her nappied bum, on her back, across the room. I experience dread. I cannot bring the toy to her, I cannot help her to the toy. There is a lot of grunting. I wait until it reaches a certain pitch, and give in.

She is no sooner in my arms than she is scrabbling around to reach whatever thing I have not noticed was there in the first place. The world is chock-full of ignored objects, for which the baby has no filter. A discarded CD case, a packet of seeds, a tweezers, a notebook. I am worn out and amazed by her constant ambient, grazing attention, as she flings herself from me to get at one thing or another, obliging me to catch her, time and again. The world is a circus and I am her trapeze, her stilts, her net. Not just mother, also platform and prosthesis. I'm not sure I feel like a person, any more.

I think I feel a little used.

Regression (me)

In the run-up to Christmas we take the baby out, and everyone says she is the image of her father. 'I'm not a woman,' I say, 'I'm a photocopier.' But Martin is delighted to have a little version of himself, spookily female, in his arms. When I complain, he laughs and says, 'You were just the venue.'

I am a cheap drunk. Two glasses of mulled wine and I am completely squiffy, going around the room asking, 'When does the sex thing, you know . . . get back on track?' I am conducting a straw poll. I ask the men, because they are the ones who classically complain about such things. But instead of answers, I get a pained, melancholic silence. One guy just gives me a hollow look and turns away.

No one wants to talk about sex, but they all will talk about shit. Endlessly. The shit that came out both ends at once, the shit that came out the neck of the babygro, the hard round shit and the shit that is soft and green. There is nothing new parents don't know about this substance. It makes me wonder why human beings bother with disgust, and whether we will ever be disgusted again.

ON CHRISTMAS DAY, the baby likes the wrapping paper, like every baby who has been in this house, and sat on this carpet and thrown the presents over their shoulder to eat the big, loud, crinkly pictures. Such glorious repetition. Her besotted grandmother, her uncles, cousins and aunts. And I think there is a deal of grief in all this – the family renewing itself in hope, time after time.

The Seventh Month

Development (the baby)
The baby's eyes change colour. They are blue, edged with navy, they are green with a smoky blue ring and, one day, amber spreads through the iris. Is this you? Are these your final eyes?

I LIFT THE baby over the threshold and carry her around the new house. She loves the way one room unfolds into another, and greets each space with delight. She leans forward, greedy for the fact that corners exist and there is always something else around them. She sits on the floor and likes the echo, and shouts.

Regression (*me*)

I cannot remember this month. We have bought a house and we are selling our flat. Or we haven't. There is a lot of talk about bridging finance. Martin sits up late, night after night, doing sums on scraps of paper. I cry a fair amount. Or stop myself from crying.

I won't spend a night in the new house. It is cold, I say. It is too far away. There is nowhere for the baby to sleep. I am obsessed with her sleep. She will sleep in the car on the way out to the house, but then we must leave the house, so she can sleep on the way home.

Every day I bump the buggy down four flights of stairs to let people view the flat, then pull it back up four flights with the shopping hung off the handles. I look around the flat and I think that we are selling her entire world.

Meanwhile, I have to earn some money, and the baby won't sleep. When Martin walks in, I hand her over, or even push her towards him, and go to the computer, and will not be spoken to. He must be home in the evening. I must be home in the evening. We are both frozen. No one moves.

It is all too much.

The Eighth Month

Development (*the baby*)

The baby is in flying form, lying on her back and just laughing and kicking for no reason. I don't know what she is laughing at. Is this a memory? Is she imagining, for the first time, tickles, even though there are no tickles there?

She may be the only truly happy person on the planet. I look at her and hope she isn't bonkers.

Regression (*me*)

I close the door on the flat, busy with removals men. I don't say goodbye.

On the way to the new house, the clutch cable snaps in the fast lane of the dual carriageway as I gear down to stop at some traffic lights. I break the lights and crawl across the road to find the kerb in a slow swerve. I ring Martin, whose mobile is on answering machine. I ring my mother and father. I run down to a local pub with the baby in my arms and ask does anyone know a local garage. That fella over there owns one, they say. I get to the garage in first gear. And so on, and so forth.

Behind me, the removals men have left the washing-machine connection leaking into the flat, a fact we do not hear about until two days later, when the water spills into the hall. We still have no car. Martin stays late after work in order to dry out the flat while I unpack cardboard boxes – or try to, while looking after the baby – and complain, complain, complain. I have no time to work, I say. I don't even have time to unpack. How does it always, always, fucking end up like this, with the woman climbing a domestic Everest while the man walks out the door? I would go out and look for a nursery, but I have to start earning before I can pay for a nursery. I have to start earning to pay for the house.

There is a freak snowstorm. We have no milk. I put the baby in the buggy and, slithering along the path, I push her through the gale.

The Ninth Month

*Development (**the baby**)*

Spring. The child looks out into the garden at the changing light. There is something about this scene that she understands and I don't know what it is. I don't know if it is the tree – the fact that the tree is there, or that it is green, or that it is made of so many leaves. I do not know if it is the wind she likes, the way the tree moves when it blows. She raises her hand and starts to shout. It is a long, complicated shout, 'Aah aaah bleeh oh. Ahh nyha mang bwah!' She is making a speech. Her hand is lifted high; the palm reaches towards the sky as she declaims. As far as I can tell there is nothing she wants in the garden, she just wants to say that it is there, and that it is good. She wants to say this loudly and at length.

The baba bears witness. The baba testifies.

Regression (*me*)

I have no notes for this month.

I unpack boxes. I hold the baby and love her, like a tragic event. She loves me like the best joke out.

On the day she is nine months old, I think that she has been outside of me, now, for just as long as she was inside. She is twice as old.

I am the mirror and the hinge. There she is. She is just as old as herself.

Time

My earliest memory is of a pot stand. It is set into a corner with a cupboard on one side and, on the other, a shallow step. This is where my head begins. The step leads to another room, and far on the other side of the room, there is a white-haired woman sitting in a chair.

Discussions with my mother lead to just one pot stand, in a seaside cottage the summer I was eighteen months old. It was, she says, made of black iron and it stood beside a real step and the white-haired woman must be her own mother who died when I was six. This image of her is all that I have, and even then it is not so much an image as a sense. She may have been asleep, but I think she was reading. And there was something very quiet and covert about the pot stand, which was a pyramid affair with shelves for four pots. I can remember a little saucepan on the top shelf. I am tempted to say that there was a big saucepan on the bottom one, but this is pushing things a bit. I would give anything to remember what the lino was like.

At nine months, the baby puts her head in a pot and says, Aaah Aaah Aaah. She says it very gently and listens to the echo. She has discovered this all by herself. By way of celebration, I put my own head into the pot and say, Aaah Aaah Aaah. Then she does it again. Then I do it again. And so on.

The rest of my family don't believe that I remember the pot stand, on the grounds that it is a stupid memory and, anyway, I was far too young. It is the job of families to reject each other's memories, even the pleasant ones, and being the youngest I am sometimes forced to fight for the contents of my own head. But my brother broke his elbow that summer. My mother had to take him to hospital in Dublin and my grandmother looked after us while she was away. This was the first time in my life that I was without my mother for any length of time. If she had stayed, then I am certain that I would not have remembered anything at all of that house – not the pot stand, and not my grandmother either.

We pilfer our own memories, we steal them from the world and salt them away.

I first left the baby when she was four months old. Some of the days when I was away, she spent with my mother. I wonder what image might remain with her from that time: a colour, a smell, a combination of shapes perhaps, affectless and still – and in the distance, someone. Just that. Someone.

And in the foreground? The carpet perhaps. I hope she

remembers my parents' carpet, the one I remember as a child, with a pattern of green leaves like stepping-stones all the way down the hall.

I have another, possibly earlier, memory of pulling the wallpaper off the wall from between the bars of my cot. My mother is absent from this scene too, but though the Pot Stand Memory is neither happy nor unhappy, this one is quite thrilling. I almost certainly ate the paper. The plaster underneath it was pink and powdery, and I imagine now that I can remember the shivery taste of it. I also remember the shape of the tear on the wall, or I think I do. At any rate, I see it in my mind's eye – a seam on the left, stunningly straight, with four gammy strips pulled away, like a fat raggedy set of fingers, on the right.

I know this memory is, in some sense, true, but when I try to chase it, it disappears. It exists in peripheral vision, and presents itself only when I focus on something else – like typing, for example. When I stop writing this sentence and look up from the screen to try to see the pattern of the wallpaper – a blank. Memories, by their nature, may not be examined, and the mind's eye is not the eye we use, for example, to cross the road.

I wonder if this is the way that the baby sees things: vaguely and all at once. I imagine it to be a very emotional way to exist in the world. Perhaps I am being romantic – but the visual world yields nothing but delight to her. There are (it seems) no horrors, no frights. Tiny babies see only in monochrome. I imagine colour leaking into her head like a slowly adjusted screen – tremendously slow, like a vegetable television growing silently in the corner of the room. I imagine her focus becoming sharper and deeper, like some infinitely stoned cameraman adjusting his lens. 'Oh,' she says – or something that is the precursor to 'Oh', a shallow inhalation, a stillness as she is caught by something, and begins to stalk it: careful, rapt – the most beautiful sound in the world: the sound of a baby's wondering breath.

Something pulls in me when she is caught like this. For months I am a slave to her attention. The world is all colour, light and texture and I am her proud companion. I have no choice. None of us do. In a café, three women look over to smile at her, and then, as one, they look up. 'Oh, she likes the light,' says one, and this fact pleases us all. Immensely.

The light, of course, is horrible, and this is one of the reasons mothers think they are losing their minds: this pride in the baby looking at the light, this pride in the light as they introduce it to the baby, 'Yes, the light!' There is a certain zen to it; the world simple and new as we all stop to admire the baby admiring a wrought-iron candelabra with peculiar dangly bits and five – yes, five! – glowing, tulip-shaped bulbs.

She is years away from knowing what 'five' might be, but maybe she already gets the 'fiveness' of it. This is the way her eyes move: One, one more! Another one! All of them! The other two. The first one again, another one! Something else.

Sometimes she holds her hand up like the baby Christ, and looks as though she contains everything, and understands it all. I do not ask to be forgiven, but still I feel redemption in the completeness of her gaze. And I feel the redemption in her fat baby wrists and her infinitely fine, fat baby's hand. The baby is a blessing, but sometimes she does, she *must*, also bless, which is to say that she simply sees, and lifts her hand, as a sign.

I pick the baby up and we look in the wardrobe mirror, which has always been for her a complicated delight: What is it? It's a baby! She smiles, it smiles back! (Complication upon complication! It's me! It's me! she says, and all her synapses, as I imagine, going ping! ping! ping!) She sees me smiling at her in the mirror; she sees her mother turning to smile at her in the room, and oh, it's too much, she lunges forwards to examine the knob on the wardrobe door.

There are actually two knobs on the wardrobe. One is wooden and the other, for some reason, is an amber-coloured plastic. The baby goes from one to the other and back again. One of the first confusions in her young life was when myself and Martin both looked at her at the same time: 'Oh no, there's two of them.' It almost felt unfair.

As she grew older, there was nothing she liked more than to be held by one of us and to look at the other, in a somewhat haughty way. Older still, she is completely content when the two of us are with her, quietly in a room. She has travelled from one, to two, perhaps to many. I think of this as she goes from the wooden knob to the amber one – a fairy tale of sameness and difference. This one. That one.

Of course, the first difference between this and the other is not between mother and father, or even between baby and 'baby in the mirror', but between one breast and . . . the other! If women had five teats, then mankind might, by now, be living on the moon.

Yesterday, it was warm, and I took off her socks and stood her on the grass. She loved this, but maybe not so much as I did – her first experience of grass. For her, this green stuff was just as different and as delicious as everything else – the 'first' was all mine. Sometimes, I feel as though I am introducing her to my own nostalgia for the world.

In the meantime, grass is green and springy and amazingly multiple and just itself. It might even be edible. Everything goes into her mouth. This is the taste of yellow. This is the taste of blue. Since she started moving about she has also experienced the taste of turf, of yesterday's toast, and probably of mouse droppings, because it was weeks before I realised we were not alone in the house. Paper remains her ultimate goal, and she looks over her shoulder now to check if I am around. That wallpaper looks nice.

I really do wish I could remember my own wallpaper, instead of just the tear I made in it. The baby sleeps in my cot now – the one my father made over forty years ago with some half-inch dowel, and a fairly ingenious sliding mechanism for the side to be let down. I sat beside it one night, feeding her, and I tried to remember what it was like to be inside; the view between the bars and the ripped wallpaper on the wall. Someone, over the years, had painted it nursery blue, but I remembered a green colour, I could almost recall chewing the cross bar at the top. The baby sucked, her eyelashes batting slowly over a drunken, surrendered gaze, and as my attention wandered I saw, under a chip in the blue paint, the very green I ate as a child. A strong and distant emotion washed briefly over me and was gone.

My mother, or someone, pulled the cot away from the wall and, in time, the wallpaper I do not remember was replaced with wallpaper that I do remember (flowers of blue, block-printed on white). Babies love pattern so much I have begun to regret my own attempts at tastefulness. Not a single curlicued carpet for her to crawl over, not a single flower on the wall. Even her toys are in primary colours and her mobile is from the Tate, cut-out shapes, like a Mondrian floating free.

Once I stop trying, I seem to remember my mother giving out to me about the ripped-up wall. She would have been upset about the wallpaper. Perhaps this is why I remember it. It was my first real experience of 'NO!'

My own child thinks No! is a game. I say it once and she pauses. I say it twice and she looks at me. I say it three times and she laughs. The punch-line!

Tasteful as it is, she loves the mobile. It has a big red circle that spins slowly to blue, and a little square that goes from black to white. There are various rectangles that don't particularly obsess her but, taken all in all, it is the thing she likes most in the world.

We moved when she was nearly eight months old, and it was another two weeks before I got round to stringing up the mobile for her again. When it was done, she shuddered with delight. It happened to her all in spasm. She realised, not only that the mobile was there, but also that it had once been gone. She remembered it. In order to do this she needed to see three things: the mobile in the old flat, the new room without the mobile, the new room with the mobile. Memory is not a single thing.

Martin says that his first memory, which is of one brother breaking a blue plastic jug over another brother's head, is false. His mother tells him that they never did have a slender, pale blue plastic jug. He thinks he dreamt about the jug, and that the dream also contained the idea that this was his first memory, as he dreamt a subsequent 'first memory' of people waving to him from a plane while he stood in the garden below. He was convinced for years that this was real. This makes me think that we are very young when we search for our first memory – that single moment when we entered the stream of time.

My own mother, who is curator and container of many things, among them the memory of my pot stand, worries that she is getting forgetful. The distant past is closer all the time, she says. If this is true, then the memory of her own mother is getting stronger now; sitting in a house by the sea, surrounded by children who are variously delighted, or worried, or concentrating on other things.

When you think about it, the pots can't have stayed there for long. I would have pulled them down. There would have been noise, though my memory of them is notably, and utterly, silent. Perhaps what I remember is the calm before a chaos of sound and recrimination. That delicious, slow moment, when a baby goes very, very quiet, knowing it is about to be found out.

The other morning, the baby (silently) reached the seedlings I have under the window, and she filled her mouth with a handful of hardy annuals and potting compost. I tried to prise her mouth open to get the stuff out. She clamped it shut. She bit me (by accident). She started to cry. When she cried, her mouth opened. She was undone by her own distress and this seemed so unfair to me that I left her to it. I hadn't the heart. Besides, it said on the pack that the compost was sterilised.

But she will not let my finger into her mouth, now, even to check for a tooth (she is very proud of her teeth), and when she clamps it shut and turns away she is saying, 'Me,' loud and clear. 'Oh,' a friend said, when she started to crawl, 'it's the beginning of the end,' and I knew what she meant. It is the beginning of the end of a romance between a woman who has forgotten who she is and a child who does not yet know.

Until one day there will come a moment, delightful or banal, ordinary or strange, that she will remember for the rest of her life.

Advice

It is the middle of the morning – an ordinary morning of undressing, dressing, sterilising, mixing, spooning, wiping, squawking, smiling, banging, reaching for the bread knife, falling down, climbing up, in the middle of which – a crisis! which is dealt with in the military style: change nappy, remove shitty vest, wash hands, find clean vest, pull baby away from stairs, comfort baby when she cries for stairs, dress baby, lift shitty vest, soak shitty vest, wash hands, and finally we are out the door and into the car seat, off to the supermarket, me singing 'Twinkle Twinkle Little Star' and remembering I have left the back door wide open. I am driving carefully. The sun is shining. I think, What will I tell her when she grows up? Actually I think, What if I die? What if I die, now, soon, or even later on? I am in the throes of car accidents and chemotherapy, between the first twinkle twinkle and the second twinkle twinkle. By the fourth repetition, she is trying to dress herself for school and wandering out of the house alone.

Her father has disappeared from this fantasy. She is facing the wide world, and there is nothing I can do to help her. I cannot reach her, I cannot speak. I should write her a letter, but what could it say?

Park, take the baby out of car seat, try to find keys, put the baby back in car seat, find keys, take the baby out of car seat, lock car, and so on, all the way through the coin for the trolley (leave baby down on the ground? Is that dog shit? Who would have thought there could be so much shit in the world?), I am banishing foolish thoughts. They are just the big metaphysics, swooping over our small, lovely life. I must try to live in the middle, think in a middling way, and so, as we sail along the aisles, as I keep hold of her arm while ducking down, over and over again, to pick up the half-chewed, as yet unpaid-for banana that she enjoys throwing out of the trolley, I concentrate on a simpler task. Advice. What advice can you give a child to arm and protect them in the world? I am not thinking of *Don't talk to strangers*, but of the things that only I would say. This is the perk that every mother demands, somewhere along the line – to exercise her own, particular personality. Usually, let's admit it, with disastrous results.

Smile at the checkout, apologise for the banana, sing, 'Do You Love an Apple,' to keep her still in the paused trolley, search busily through my empty head, only one nugget comes to mind. *Beware of modest people. They are the worst megalomaniacs of all.*

For the rest of the day (scrub out the shitty vest? No,

throw out the shitty vest. Don't tell anyone), this is the only wisdom I can find, the only sentence, *Beware of modest people . . .* of course it is true: Einstein, Mother Teresa, some women I know, many many nuns, a couple of poets – all so lovely, all so monstrous. You have to have a very big ego to wrestle it down to something so small. I know, I've tried. *Beware the tender smile, my daughter, the love that saddens, the crinkly eyes . . .*

But it isn't exactly useful, as advice goes. Not as useful as *Don't touch the oven, it is hot!* which is what I spend my day saying, now. *Hot! Hot!* I would also say, *Dirty! Dirty!* but I can't be bothered. I concentrate on *Careful!* or *Gently!* or plain *NO!* And so it will be, for years yet. The first thousand days of her life, the whole remarkable world around her, and all that I have to say could be reduced to one phrase, *Proceed . . . with caution.* And for the thousand days after that? *Don't talk to strangers*, of course, which is the same thing again, in a way.

There must be more. I just can't think of anything. I open my mouth and . . . my own mother comes falling out of it. But of course.

She takes advice very seriously, my mother. She still doles it out on a regular basis. She is not afraid to repeat herself. She is often right – when, for example, she says to me, *You should flatter people a little. You should at least try.*

I never listened to a word of it; except maybe for, *If Joyce was worried about what his Mammy might say, he would never have written* Ulysses (a piece of advice which she has paid for, many times since), or the excellent, *Never use a big word where a small word will do*. What about, *Cheer up, we'll soon be dead*? Did she really say that? Of course she would deny it, now – though I still find it giddily bleak and quite useful. *Cheer up, we'll soon be dead*, just one of her variations on the mother's mantra of, *All this will pass*. Having the wrong pencil-case, being forced to share a desk with Brenda Dunne, losing the boy you love, *In fifty years' time you might even laugh about it* (but what happens, Ma, when you run out of time?)

Never laugh at someone's religion, that's a good one. Actually, what she said was, 'If someone worships a stone in the road and you laugh at them, they will pick it up and hit you with it.' Fair enough.

I didn't start arguing with her until it came to men. *Never humiliate a man in public* – intriguing, this one. What were you to do in private? And then again, some men are very easily humiliated. They are humiliated when you are clever, and it is hard work being stupid. They are humiliated if you flirt, or if you don't flirt. You could spend your life tending to some man's pride, but, *There is no excuse for marrying a bastard*, she said, or something like it, as if falling for the wrong man was just a lazy way to go about your life, when there were so many good men in the world. In those days, a Good Man was someone who allowed the household the use of his pay-packet, who wasn't a drunk, and who didn't hit you. Actually, this is probably still a good baseline. Maybe this is something I could pass on to my daughter. I could translate it as:

Never sleep with someone who has more problems than you – 50 per cent of people fail to follow this advice, and it is vital to be in the other half. What else?

Never trust someone beyond their strength, because – oh, my darling girl, and the million things that could hurt her; not strangers, but friends, because these are the ones who break your heart – she must arm herself against the weak more than the strong . . .

'Oh, get a grip, Mother.'

All advice is useless. *Don't wear patterns next to your face. Never plant camellias facing east. Have sex before you go out for the night, not after you come home. The things that make you fat are booze and biscuits – nothing else.* What about, *Earn money* – my mother used to tell me to do this all the time. All right. *Earn money* – you must overcome the natural distaste you might feel for cash. If you dislike the system, then find a crack in it, and live there. And the simplest way to earn money is to go out and earn it. That is what is called the (middle-class) Tao of money.

I didn't listen to that either.

And look at this baby, just look at her – with her steady baby's gaze; her serious baby's eyes that have some joke in them all the same, as she putters towards the plastic shopping bags.

'No!' I shout, and when she cries I say, 'It's all right. It's all right.'

Proceed with caution.

Actually, most of the time I don't know what 'No' is for. Mind the door, mind the books don't fall, mind your fingers, hot!, careful of the cup, don't touch the dirt. After one particularly long day, I decided against it. It was making me depressed. So I left her to her own devices for a while, and we all cheered up.

The Sioux, Martin tells me, let their babies learn everything for themselves: fall into the river, fall into the fire, anything. But children are quite careful, really.

And what does she say to me?

'Burr!' says the baby, pointing at the sky.

Look at the bird, Mama. This is my baby's advice to me. *Look at the bird!*

Being Two

'I'M TWO,' SHE says, standing on the bathroom scales. And indeed there it is on the dial, the nice, round-topped, swoop and swan of '2'. She is fond of being two. She is nearly three. Her new little brother is only zero with a few silly bits added on. He is not even a proper number yet.

'So how's it all going?'

I want to tell people about her, but I want to tell them *everything* about her, because there is nothing else. The proper maternal mode is gabble. The proper maternal instrument is the phone. We are all a Jewish joke.

'She can read! She read her name on her birthday card!'

'And what about the number?'

'No problem. Twenty-one.'

And I want to tell them nothing about her. She is a child, she must not be described. She must be kept fluid and open; not labelled or marked. I could say that she is playful, open, stubborn, bossy, winsome, serious, giddy, boisterous, clinging, gorgeous – but these are words that describe every single two-year-old on the planet, they are not the essence of herself, the thing that will always be there. Describing a child is a matter of prediction or nostalgia. There is no present moment. You are always trying to grasp something that changes even as you look at it. Besides, all children are the same, somehow. And still I know she is different from the general run of toddlers. How do I know? I just do. And if you think I am biased, this is what other people have said about her:

'There's no doubt about it, she is a fabulous child.'
Donal Enright, Grandfather.

'I have to say I never met a more interesting, or nicer, two-year-old.'
Theo Dombrowski, a friend.

'She is very advanced for two, and I should know – I am an educational psychologist.'
Stranger (possibly mad), in the foyer of a West Cork hotel.

'Oh, all her geese are swans,' my mother used to say about boastful mothers.

In the old days – as we call the 1970s, in Ireland – a mother would dispraise her child automatically. I understand this urge: you don't want a toddler to get the edge on you, especially when you are trying to get them past a shop full of sweets; so 'She's a monkey,' a mother might say, or 'Street angel, home devil,' or even my favourite, 'She'll have me in an early grave.'

It was all part of growing up in a country where praise of any sort was taboo. Of course we are nicer now, we are more confident and positive and relaxed – which does not explain the strange urge I had when a man looked at her photograph. 'Such lovely eyes,' he said, and I said, 'Oh, they're all right,' or something even worse. It is true that I felt acutely, burningly praised, but I also felt the deep hiss of a mother who reaches out her hand to say, *Give me back my baby.*

People don't write much about their children. Sometimes they say it is to protect the child's privacy – but I am not sure how private a ten-year-old feels, for example, about a picture of his two-year-old self, or how connected. I think it is simpler than that. I think people don't want to write about their children because they think that, if they do, their children might die. And that's just for starters. I think they do not want to surrender any part of their children, certainly not for money, and particularly not to a crowd.

So this is just a mock-up. It is not the real girl at all.

'You have a smelly bum.'

'Go away. Go smell your own bum.'

'I can't smell my bum. I can't get my face around.'

She already loves a paradox, and most of them are

anatomical. 'A shark has a long nose so he can't see his mouth,' she says (well, you know what she means). Which reminds me, I must get her *Alice in Wonderland*, though:

'That's me,' she said, a while ago.

'Where?'

'In that car.'

'Oh. You're in that car?'

'Yes.'

'Where are you going?'

'I going to my house.'

'Where is your house? What kind of house?'

'It has a yellow door.'

'Oh.'

After a while, I say, 'And what is your name?'

'Alice,' she says.

This spooked me no end. She is not called Alice, and we do not have a yellow (or lello) door. I thought she was having a past-life regression, there in the back of the car – well, I didn't really, but sometimes I wish I was that bit more credulous. Then later, in the bath, she was all talk of rabbits and my-ears-and-whiskers, and I realised that she had heard, or seen, her first ever *Alice in Wonderland*.

Fantastic. The rabbit went down the plug hole, in the end.

Her father must have been away if I was giving her a bath – these more intriguing dialogues happen when her ordinary life is unbalanced in some way.

'I love him,' she says, pointing at the picture of the

author on the back of one of her books. Colin McNaughton, he is called – a very pleasant, handsome-looking guy. I have to admire her taste, though the writer thing is a bit unsettling. Never fall for a writer, I want to say. Never, ever, ever make that mistake.

Instead I say, 'Oh.'

'Yes. Because my Dada is away.'

This is nothing (I flatter myself) to the anxiety she feels when her mother is away. Endlessly recounted is the story of the witch in the supermarket, last Hallowe'en. A woman in a mask who came up and, I presume, cackled at her while she was sitting in the trolley and then, when the child started to cry, took off the witch's mask to show that she was only a nice person underneath. Silly bitch. I think taking the mask off made it worse, but there you go; I suppose it's too late to sue. Later that evening, she stood with her father in the dark, watching the local fireworks from an upstairs window. When I came home, there were spent rockets in the flower-beds.

A hundred renditions of the witch-in-the-supermarket story later, I hit on the key. I was away at the time – does she remember? She certainly does. She remembers that I was in Paris. What was I doing in there? she suddenly asks, Was I frightened? Was I watching the fireworks, too?

'I was,' I say, and once I am placed in the picture – somewhere on the other side of the fireworks – the story is allowed to fade. But she is still obsessed by witches, which is presumably, somehow, my fault – also bad fairies and wicked stepmothers. There are no nice women in the old stories. Though one morning she announces a dream – a good dream. What was it about?

'Barbie,' she says, looking very coy.

'Oh? And what was Barbie doing?'

'She was reading me a book.'

Which is one of the things that I do, of course – my tendency to interpret the child mocked by an image of myself as a six-foot plastic toy. And maybe it is not all a drama of good mother / bad mother, maybe she was just angling for a Barbie and knows how much I'd love to know what happens in her dreams. She is two. She has – perhaps they all have – a delicious mind.

She has a quality, sometimes, when she is tired. Her eyes become distant, and slightly blissed. She looks at you strangely, as though she has been here before.

I am heavily pregnant and under the shower. We are alone in the house, and I think, What would happen if I fell? Would she be able to fetch the phone? I can see it all: the gravid woman, wedged into the bath, the water playing on her senseless belly, the toddler bereft, the time passing; all this flashing through my mind in a moment, while she tilts her face up to me, and says, 'Don't fall.'

Or I am going up the stairs with her in my arms. I think, I must ring my mother and she says, 'Does Granny have stairs?'

They are so tiny and inconsequential, these coincidences of mind. They always surprise me, even though they are not so surprising – after all, for most of the time we live the same life – and I begin to build a little wall against my Midwich Cuckoo. Some of my thoughts are so unbecoming. I catch myself and think, 'I hope she didn't get that one.'

All of this is very slight, you understand, and nothing you could absolutely put a finger on. It never involves a future event, but when she talks about someone, I might ring them, just to check that they are still alive. They always are.

I tell her about her Granny and Granda, how they met at a dance, in a hotel by the sea. She says, 'Was I watching?'

I am tempted to say, 'I don't know.'

What else?

She is very bossy about the world. She is always putting it in its place and sometimes there is very little difference between ordering it, and ordering it around. 'Cars don't go into houses, they are too big.' 'That car [a convertible] has no lid.' 'Cars have roofs and motor bikes have helmets.'

Yes,' I say to all this. I have to say, Yes, or she will repeat it ad infinitum. 'Yes. Yes, absolutely. Yes.'

For months we were trapped in a kind of Beckettian rhapsody, as she tried to make the world safe. From the back seat:

'Mama, cars don't go into houses, do they?'

'No, they don't.'

'Do they?'

'No, they certainly don't, they're too big.'

'And they don't go on the path.'

'No.'

'They go on the road.'

'Yes.'

'People go on the path.'

'Yes. Absolutely.'

'Where's it gone?'

'Where's what gone?'

'Where's the street light gone?'

'It's behind us.'

'But where's it gone?'

'We'll see another one.'

'But where's it gone?'

'Oh, take it easy.'

It happens on the same stretch of road – she always grieves the disappearing street lights: the way they keep coming, only to flick away.

It was around here that I once said, 'I used to work over there, before you were born.'

'When I was a baby.'

'No, before that. Before you were born.'

'When I was just a teeny-tiny baby?'

'No, before you were even here. Before you were in my tummy.'

'I was . . . Where.'

'You were just a twinkle in your Daddy's eye.'

'I not a twinkle. I NOT a twinkle!!!' And she started to

kick and squawk. I suppose I did sound a little smug; a little complacent about the idea that she was once non-existent. Too tough, really, for any age, but especially tough for two.

Her favourite story is *Sleeping Beauty*. But only recently. Fairy tales happened in the last few weeks, at the end of 'two' and the beginning of 'nearly three', because 'two' is a very long place. She started the year obsessed by gender, moved into a long toilet phase, and ended with witches, princesses, and sleep. But also in there were numbers, which gave her huge pleasure, as did all kinds of repetition and ritual and make-believe. There was also the endless amusement to be got from ordering her parents around and giving them grief.

'Not the blue cup with the straw.'

'I thought you wanted a straw.'

'I don't want a straw.'

'Do you want the blue cup?'

'I don't want a straw.'

'OK.'

'I don't want a straw!'

And so on, all the way to wails, screams, tears. Of course the dialogue is edited to make me look like a saint, which I am not. ('The cup goes in the bin. All right? The cup – see this cup? – it's going in the bin.') Months of attrition later I realise that the best thing to do is to become benignly invisible. If I can manage simply not to exist, there is no escalation.

She started the year obsessed by gender, moved into a long toilet phase, and ended with witches, princesses, and sleep

She is only two.

Though sometimes, I am two, too.

And when she has done every single, possible thing to provoke, thwart, whine, refuse, baulk, delay, complicate and annoy, I wonder how the human race survived.

'I'll swing for you,' I heard myself saying once. Which is Irish for 'I will kill you and take the consequences.'

She is two. She is *only* two.

There is nothing better than watching her play shopping. When she walks across the room to the 'shops' she does not so much walk as 'walk' with an exaggeration of hip and heel that says, 'Here I am "walking" to the shops.' She hums to the rhythm of it. Hum. Hum. Hum. Hum. Walk. Walk. Walk. Walk.

All her inverted commas are huge, and even in ordinary conversation she will sometimes use an 'other' voice; fake wise, or fake grown-up, with much use of the word 'actually'. As in, 'That looks like a duck, actually.'

There is a place on the wall where she gets things, like broccoli, or sweets, or water. She runs over to the wall and goes, 'Ssszzsst,' rolling and twiddling her hands in a 'complicated' way. Then she runs back from the wall with my imaginary cup of tea.

'Oh, *thank* you.'

Her anxiety about the baby that is on the way brings back all kinds of eating games. 'Gobble gobble nyum nyum,' she says, 'I am eating your arm.' She does not like it so much when I eat her back. 'Nyum nyum, scarf scarf gobble nyum.' She runs to her special place on the wall and takes down bits of herself, which she sticks along her arm, and pats back into place. She is getting her real arm back, she says. I have just eaten her pretend one.

'Yes,' I say, thinking, as I often do, that she is an outrageously wonderful child. Sometimes, of course, she is just outrageous.

She is two.

'Can I be two?' I say, and have a pretend tantrum on the floor. Just a small one. I lie on my back and drum my heels. She doesn't like the look of this at all.

It is a very long year. When November comes I miss the child October gave us, that paradise, when I was only moderately pregnant and potty training had not yet begun. And I miss the baby, just walking, who looked at the black and yellow stripes of the Kilkenny hurling team and said, 'Bees! Bees!'

This is the girl who was entranced by every flying thing, who followed a plane across the sky in her Granny's back garden and never took her eyes away once, whose first or second word may have been 'bird', whose first big word was 'helicopter', who can already tell a hoverfly from a bee (but not a bee from a wasp), and a tweet-tweet birdie from one that goes caw-caw. This is the girl who got 'a moth' from Santa Claus for Christmas. She is also, of course, fond of woodlice, but give her a glider, a kite, a cloud, a woman under a parachute, a fairy, or a balloon, and she will choose them over a slug or snail any day. She is close to the ground, which might be the reason that she is always looking up, but the reason she loves butterflies is the reason she likes the mirror and also the reason that she likes hands: it is that one side is the same as the other side, and nothing has given her greater joy, I think, than folding a piece of paper over some splashes of paint, and opening a Rorschach of complete delight. It is always a butterfly, because this is the best thing it could be, and other things that mirror and match are butterflies too.

'A bum is like a butterfly,' she said once.

'Yes. Yes.'

The first play she ever went to was about bees and, when the actors gave her a set of paper wings, she declared into the stillness of the audience, 'I can fly.'

Of Christ on the Cross she says, 'Are they wings?' and I say, 'No, darling, those are His arms.'

'WHEN I WAS a little baby,' she says, wrestling with the idea of growing up, now that there is another baby in Mammy's tummy.

'When I was a little baby,' she says (because these things are always said twice), 'I used to say "pine-a-cacket".'

'And what do you say now?'

'I say, "pineapple".'

We are both amused by this. We are both fond of her former self. Now she is a big girl, she looks with tenderness at a picture of herself newborn. 'Look how pleased your Dada is to see you,' I say. She looks at this for a while, and then walks over to embrace him, properly and formally. Sometimes she has astonishing emotional clarity; and I have to catch my breath at the rightness of her.

She is nearly three. She is learning, she told me, not to cry at things. I said she could still cry at some things but she shook her head. No, she would not cry. And when she is three, she says, she will not be scared of the witch in the supermarket. It is a serious business, growing up; a heavy responsibility.

On the Friday before her birthday, I bring a (pink!) cake into the crèche, and she asks, 'I'm going to have a cake, even though I am still two?' and I realise that it is not the cake, or the candles, or the party, or the presents that matter to her, so much as *being three*. It is a different place.

© Hugh Chaloner

ANNE ENRIGHT is one of Ireland's most celebrated writers and the current Laureate for Irish Fiction. She was born and raised in Dublin, the city where she now lives. She writes articles, essays and short stories but is most famous for her novels, in particular *The Gathering*, which won the Man Booker Prize in 2007, and her most recent, the critically acclaimed, *The Green Road*.

Anne Enright's novels are interested in the difference between romance and biology, between the love we choose, and the love to which we are helpless. She writes of family life in all its maddening, ordinary glory. *Making Babies*, from which this short book is drawn, is her only work of memoir, written before Anne Enright became an internationally renowned novelist. It was lauded for its humour and honesty. Ian Sansom wrote of it: '*Making Babies* is not just a good book, it's a good thing. It induces hope. It creates an appetite for life. It is also a very effective contraceptive'.

RECOMMENDED BOOKS BY ANNE ENRIGHT:

The Green Road
The Gathering
Making Babies

Still in love with Babies?

Fatherhood
KARL OVE KNAUSGAARD

VINTAGE MINIS

Motherhood
HELEN SIMPSON

VINTAGE MINIS

Drinking
JOHN CHEEVER

VINTAGE MINIS

Sisters
LOUISA MAY ALCOTT

VINTAGE MINIS

VINTAGE MINIS

The Vintage Minis bring you the world's greatest writers on the experiences that make us human. These stylish, entertaining little books explore the whole spectrum of life – from birth to death, and everything in between. Which means there's something here for everyone, whatever your story.

vintageminis.co.uk

1 3 5 7 9 10 8 6 4 2

Vintage
20 Vauxhall Bridge Road,
London SW1V 2SA

Vintage Classics is part of the Penguin Random House
group of companies whose addresses can be found at
global.penguinrandomhouse.com

 Penguin
Random House
UK

Extract from *In Search of Lost Time, Volume V* translation
copyright © Chatto & Windus and Random House Inc. 1981
Copyright in revisions to translation © D. J. Enright 1992

First published in Great Britain in 1992 by Chatto & Windus
First published by Vintage in 1996
This short edition published by Vintage in 2017

penguin.co.uk/vintage

A CIP catalogue record for this book is available from the British Library

ISBN 9781784872694

Typeset in 9.5/14.5 pt FreightText Pro
by Jouve (UK), Milton Keynes
Printed and bound by Clays Ltd, St Ives plc

Penguin Random House is committed to a sustainable future for
our business, our readers and our planet. This book is made from
Forest Stewardship Council® certified paper.

MIX
Paper from
responsible sources
FSC
www.fsc.org
FSC® C018179

Jealousy
MARCEL PROUST

Translated from the French by C. K. Scott Moncrieff
and Terence Kilmartin
Revised by D. J. Enright

VINTAGE MINIS

No doubt, in the first days at Balbec, Albertine seemed to exist on a parallel plane to that on which I was living, but one that had converged on it (after my visit to Elstir) and had finally joined it, as my relations with her, at Balbec, in Paris, then at Balbec again, grew more intimate. Moreover, what a difference there was between the two pictures of Balbec, on my first visit and on my second, pictures composed of the same villas from which the same girls emerged by the same sea! In Albertine's friends at the time of my second visit, whom I knew so well, whose good and bad qualities were so clearly engraved on their features, how could I recapture those fresh, mysterious strangers who once could not thrust open the doors of their chalets with a screech over the sand or brush past the quivering tamarisks without making my heart beat? Their huge eyes had sunk into their faces since then, doubtless because they had ceased to be children, but also because those ravishing strangers, those actresses of that first romantic year, about whom I had gone ceaselessly in quest of information, no longer held any mystery for me. They had become for me, obedient to my whims, a mere grove of budding girls, from among whom I was not a little proud of having plucked, and hidden away from the rest of the world, the fairest rose.

Between the two Balbec settings, so different one from the other, there was the interval of several years in Paris, the long expanse of which was dotted with all the visits that Albertine had paid me. I saw her in the different years of my life occupying, in relation to myself, different positions which made me feel the beauty of the intervening spaces, that long lapse of time during which I had remained without seeing her and in the diaphanous depths of which the roseate figure that I saw before me was carved with mysterious shadows and in bold relief. This was due also to the superimposition not merely of the successive images which Albertine had been for me, but also of the great qualities of intelligence and heart, and of the defects of character, all alike unsuspected by me, which Albertine, in a germination, a multiplication of herself, a fleshy efflorescence in sombre colours, had added to a nature that formerly could scarcely have been said to exist, but was now difficult to plumb. For other people, even those of whom we have dreamed so much that they have come to seem no more than pictures, figures by Benozzo Gozzoli against a greenish background, of whom we were inclined to believe that they varied only according to the point of vantage from which we looked at them, their distance from us, the effect of light and shade, such people, while they change in relation to ourselves, change also in themselves, and there had been an enrichment, a solidification and an increase of volume in the figure once simply outlined against the sea.

Moreover, it was not only the sea at the close of day that existed for me in Albertine, but at times the drowsy murmur of the sea upon the shore on moonlit nights. For sometimes, when I got up to fetch a book from my father's study, my mistress, having asked my permission to lie down while I was out of the room, was so tired after her long outing in the morning and afternoon in the open air that, even if I had been away for a moment only, when I returned I found her asleep and did not wake her. Stretched out at full length on my bed, in an attitude so natural that no art could have devised it, she reminded me of a long blossoming stem that had been laid there; and so in a sense she was: the faculty of dreaming, which I possessed only in her absence, I recovered at such moments in her presence, as though by falling asleep she had become a plant. In this way, her sleep realised to a certain extent the possibility of love: alone, I could think of her, but I missed her, I did not possess her; when she was present, I spoke to her, but was too absent from myself to be able to think of her; when she was asleep, I no longer had to talk, I knew that I was no longer observed by her, I no longer needed to live on the surface of myself.

By shutting her eyes, by losing consciousness, Albertine had stripped off, one after another, the different human personalities with which she had deceived me ever since the day when I had first made her acquaintance. She was animated now only by the unconscious life of plants, of trees, a life more different from my own, more alien, and yet one that belonged more to me. Her personality was not constantly escaping, as when we talked, by the outlets of her unacknowledged thoughts and of her eyes. She had called back into herself everything of her that lay outside, had withdrawn, enclosed, reabsorbed herself into her body. In keeping her in front of my eyes, in my hands, I had an impression of possessing her entirely which I never had when she was awake. Her life was submitted to me, exhaled towards me its gentle breath.

I listened to this murmuring, mysterious emanation, soft as a sea breeze, magical as a gleam of moonlight, that was her sleep. So long as it lasted, I was free to dream about her and yet at the same time to look at her, and, when that sleep grew deeper, to touch, to kiss her. What I felt then was a love as pure, as immaterial, as mysterious, as if I had been in the presence of those inanimate creatures which are the beauties of nature. And indeed, as soon as her sleep became at all deep, she ceased to be merely the plant that she had been; her sleep, on the margin of which I remained musing, with a fresh delight of which I never tired, which I could have gone on enjoying indefinitely, was to me a whole landscape. Her sleep brought within my

In keeping her in front of my eyes, my hands, I had an impression of possessing her entirely which I never had when she was awake

reach something as serene, as sensually delicious as those nights of full moon on the bay of Balbec, calm as a lake over which the branches barely stir, where, stretched out upon the sand, one could listen for hours on end to the surf breaking and receding.

On entering the room, I would remain standing in the doorway, not venturing to make a sound, and hearing none but that of her breath rising to expire upon her lips at regular intervals, like the reflux of the sea, but drowsier and softer. And at the moment when my ear absorbed that divine sound, I felt that there was condensed in it the whole person, the whole life of the charming captive outstretched there before my eyes. Carriages went rattling past in the street, but her brow remained as smooth and untroubled, her breath as light, reduced to the simple expulsion of the necessary quantity of air. Then, seeing that her sleep would not be disturbed, I would advance cautiously, sit down on the chair that stood by the bedside, then on the bed itself.

I spent many a charming evening talking and playing with Albertine, but none so sweet as when I was watching her sleep. Granted that she had, as she chatted with me, or played cards, a naturalness that no actress could have imitated; it was a more profound naturalness, as it were at one remove, that was offered me by her sleep. Her hair, falling along her pink cheek, was spread out beside her on the bed, and here and there an isolated straight tress gave the same effect of perspective as those moonlit trees, lank and

pale, which one sees standing erect and stiff in the backgrounds of Elstir's Raphaelesque pictures. If Albertine's
lips were closed, her eyelids, on the other hand, seen from
where I was placed, seemed so loosely joined that I might
almost have questioned whether she really was asleep. At
the same time those lowered lids gave her face that perfect
continuity which is unbroken by the eyes. There are people
whose faces assume an unaccustomed beauty and majesty
the moment they cease to look out of their eyes.

I would run my eyes over her, stretched out below me.
From time to time a slight, unaccountable tremor ran
through her, as the leaves of a tree are shaken for a few
moments by a sudden breath of wind. She would touch her
hair and then, not having arranged it to her liking, would
raise her hand to it again with motions so consecutive, so
deliberate, that I was convinced that she was about to
wake. Not at all; she grew calm again in the sleep from
which she had not emerged. Thereafter she lay motionless.
She had laid her hand on her breast, the limpness of the
arm so artlessly childlike that I was obliged, as I gazed at
her, to suppress the smile that is provoked in us by the
solemnity, the innocence and the grace of little children.

I, who was acquainted with many Albertines in one person, seemed now to see many more again reposing by my
side. Her eyebrows, arched as I had never noticed them,
encircled the globes of her eyelids like a halcyon's downy
nest. Races, atavisms, vices reposed upon her face. Whenever she moved her head, she created a different woman,

often one whose existence I had never suspected. I seemed to possess not one but countless girls. Her breathing, as it became gradually deeper, made her breast rise and fall in a regular rhythm, and above it her folded hands and her pearls, displaced in a different way by the same movement, like boats and mooring chains set swaying by the movement of the tide. Then, feeling that the tide of her sleep was full, that I should not run aground on reefs of consciousness covered now by the high water of profound slumber, I would climb deliberately and noiselessly on to the bed, lie down by her side, clasp her waist in one arm, and place my lips upon her cheek and my free hand on her heart and then on every part of her body in turn, so that it too was raised, like the pearls, by her breathing; I myself was gently rocked by its regular motion: I had embarked upon the tide of Albertine's sleep.

Sometimes it afforded me a pleasure that was less pure. For this I had no need to make any movement, but allowed my leg to dangle against hers, like an oar which one trails in the water, imparting to it now and again a gentle oscillation like the intermittent wing-beat of a bird asleep in the air. I chose, in gazing at her, the aspect of her face which one never saw and which was so beautiful. It is I suppose comprehensible that the letters which we receive from a person should be more or less similar to one another and combine to trace an image of the writer sufficiently different from the person we know to constitute a second personality. But how much stranger is it that a woman should be conjoined, like Radica with Doodica, with another woman whose different beauty makes us infer another character, and that in order to see them we must look at one of them in profile and the other in full face. The sound of her breathing, which had grown louder, might have given the illusion of the panting of sexual pleasure, and when mine was at its climax, I could kiss her without having interrupted her sleep. I felt at such moments that I had possessed her more completely, like an unconscious and unresisting object of dumb nature. I was not troubled by the words that she murmured from time to time in her sleep; their meaning was closed to me, and besides, whoever the unknown person to whom they referred, it was upon my hand, upon my cheek that her hand, stirred by an occasional faint tremor, tightened for an instant. I savoured her sleep with a disinterested, soothing love, just as I would remain for hours listening to the unfurling of the waves.

Perhaps people must be capable of making us suffer intensely before they can procure for us, in the hours of remission, the same soothing calm as nature does. I did not have to answer her as when we were engaged in conversation, and even if I could have remained silent, as for that matter I did when it was she who was talking, still while listening to her I did not penetrate so far into the depths of her being. As I continued to hear, to capture from moment to moment, the murmur, soothing as a barely perceptible breeze, of her pure breath, it was a whole physiological existence that was spread out before me, at my disposal; just as I used to remain for hours lying on the beach, in the moonlight, so long could I have remained there gazing at her, listening to her. Sometimes it was as though the sea was beginning to swell, as though the storm was making itself felt even inside the bay, and I would press myself against her and listen to the gathering roar of her breath.

Sometimes, when she was too warm, she would take off her kimono while she was already almost asleep and fling it over an armchair. As she slept I would tell myself that all her letters were in the inner pocket of this kimono, into which she always thrust them. A signature, an assignation, would have sufficed to prove a lie or to dispel a suspicion. When I could see that Albertine was sound asleep, leaving the foot of the bed where I had been standing motionless in contemplation of her, I would take a step forward, seized by a burning curiosity, feeling that the secret of this other life lay offering itself to me, flaccid and defenceless, in that armchair. Perhaps I took this step forward also because to stand perfectly still and watch her sleeping became tiring after a while. And so, on tiptoe, constantly turning round to make sure that Albertine was not waking, I would advance towards the armchair. There I would stop short, and stand for a long time gazing at the kimono, as I had stood for a long time gazing at Albertine. But (and here perhaps I was wrong) never once did I touch the kimono, put my hand in the pocket, examine the letters. In the end, realising that I would never make up my mind, I would creep back to the bedside and begin again to watch the sleeping Albertine, who would tell me nothing, whereas I could see lying across an arm of the chair that kimono which would perhaps have told me much.

And just as people pay a hundred francs a day for a room at the Grand Hotel at Balbec in order to breathe the sea air, I felt it to be quite natural that I should spend more than that on her, since I had her breath upon my cheek, between my lips which I laid half-open upon hers, through which her life flowed against my tongue.

But this pleasure of seeing her sleep, which was as sweet to me as that of feeling her live, was cut short by another pleasure, that of seeing her wake. It was, carried to a more profound and more mysterious degree, the same pleasure as I felt in having her under my roof. It was gratifying to me, of course, that when she alighted from the car in the afternoon, it should be to my house that she was returning. It was even more so to me that when, from the underworld of sleep, she climbed the last steps of the staircase of dreams, it was in my room that she was reborn to consciousness and life, that she wondered for an instant: 'Where am I?' and, seeing the objects by which she was surrounded, and the lamp whose light scarcely made her blink her eyes, was able to assure herself that she was at home on realising that she was waking in *my* home. In that first delicious moment of uncertainty, it seemed to me that once again I was taking possession of her more completely, since, instead of her returning to her own room after an outing, it was my room that, as soon as Albertine should have recognised it, was about to enclose, to contain her, without there being any sign of misgiving in her eyes, which remained as calm as if she had never slept at all. The uncertainty of awakening, revealed by her silence, was not at all revealed in her eyes.

Then she would find her tongue and say: 'My—' or 'My darling —' followed by my first name, which, if we give the narrator the same name as the author of this book, would be 'My Marcel,' or 'My darling Marcel.' After this I would never allow a member of my family, by calling me 'darling,' to rob of their precious uniqueness the delicious words that Albertine uttered to me. As she uttered them, she pursed her lips in a little pout which she spontaneously transformed into a kiss. As quickly as she had earlier fallen asleep, she had awoken.

NO MORE THAN my own progression in time, no more than the fact of looking at a girl sitting near me beneath a lamp that shed upon her a very different light from that of the sun when I used to see her striding along the seashore, was this material enrichment, this autonomous progress of Albertine, the determining cause of the difference between my present view of her and my original impression of her at Balbec. A longer term of years might have separated the two images without effecting so complete a change; it had come about, this sudden and fundamental change, when I had learned that Albertine had been virtually brought up by Mlle Vinteuil's friend. If at one time I had been overcome with excitement when I thought I detected mystery in Albertine's eyes, now I was happy only at times when from those eyes, from those cheeks even, as revealing as the eyes, at one moment so gentle but quickly turning sullen, I succeeded in expelling every trace of mystery. The image which I sought, upon which I relied, for which I would have been prepared to die, was no longer that of Albertine leading an unknown life, it was that of an Albertine as known to me as it was possible for her to be (and it was for this reason that my love could not be lasting unless it remained unhappy, for by definition it did not satisfy the need for mystery), an Albertine who did not reflect a distant world, but desired nothing else—there were moments when this did indeed appear to be the case—than to be with me, to be exactly like me, an Albertine who was the image precisely of what was mine and not of the unknown.

When it is thus from an hour of anguish in relation to another person that love is born, when it is from uncertainty whether we shall keep or lose that person, such a love bears the mark of the revolution that has created it, it recalls very little of what we had previously seen when we thought of the person in question. And although my first impressions of Albertine, silhouetted against the sea, might to some small extent persist in my love for her, in reality, these earlier impressions occupy but a tiny place in a love of this sort, in its strength, in its agony, in its need of comfort and its resort to a calm and soothing memory with which we would prefer to abide and to learn nothing more of the beloved, even if there were something horrible to be known. Even if the previous impressions are retained, such a love is made of very different stuff!

Sometimes I would put out the light before she came in. It was in the darkness, barely guided by the glow of a smouldering log, that she would lie down by my side. My hands and my cheeks alone identified her without my eyes seeing her, my eyes that were often afraid of finding her changed; so that, by virtue of these blind caresses, she may perhaps have felt bathed in a warmer tenderness than usual.

On other evenings, I undressed and went to bed, and, with Albertine perched on the side of the bed, we would resume our game or our conversation interrupted by kisses; and in the physical desire that alone makes us take an interest in the existence and character of another person, we remain so true to our own nature (even if, on the other hand, we abandon successively the different persons whom we have loved in turn) that on one occasion, catching sight of myself in the mirror at the moment when I was kissing Albertine and calling her 'my little girl,' the sorrowful, passionate expression on my own face, similar to the expression it would have worn long ago with Gilberte whom I no longer remembered, and would perhaps assume one day with another if I were ever to forget

Albertine, made me think that, over and above any personal considerations (instinct requiring that we consider the person of the moment as the only real one), I was performing the duties of an ardent and painful devotion dedicated as an oblation to the youth and beauty of Woman. And yet with this desire by which I was honouring youth with a votive offering, with my memories too of Balbec, there was blended, in my need to keep Albertine thus every evening by my side, something that had hitherto been foreign to my amorous existence at least, if it was not entirely new in my life. It was a soothing power the like of which I had not experienced since the evenings at Combray long ago when my mother, stooping over my bed, brought me repose in a kiss. To be sure, I should have been greatly astonished at that time had anyone told me that I was not extremely kind and especially that I would ever seek to deprive someone else of a pleasure. I must have known myself very imperfectly then, for my pleasure in having Albertine to live with me was much less a positive pleasure than the pleasure of having withdrawn from the world, where everyone was free to enjoy her in turn, the blossoming girl who, if she did not bring me any great joy, was at least withholding joy from others. Ambition and fame would have left me unmoved. Even more was I incapable of feeling hatred. And yet to love carnally was none the less, for me, to enjoy a triumph over countless rivals. I can never repeat it often enough: it was more than anything else an appeasement.

For all that I might, before Albertine returned, have doubted her, have imagined her in the room at Montjouvain, once she was in her dressing-gown and seated facing my chair or (if, as was more frequent, I had remained in bed) at the foot of my bed, I would deposit my doubts in her, hand them over for her to relieve me of them, with the abnegation of a worshipper uttering a prayer. All through the evening she might have been there, curled up in a mischievous ball on my bed, playing with me like a cat; her little pink nose, the tip of which she made even tinier with a coquettish glance which gave it a daintiness characteristic of certain women who are inclined to be plump, might have given her an inflamed and provocative air, she might have allowed a tress of her long, dark hair to fall over her pale-pink waxen cheek and, half shutting her eyes, unfolding her arms, have seemed to be saying to me: 'Do what you like with me'—but when the time came for her to leave me, and she drew close to me to say good-night, it was a softness that had become almost familial that I kissed on either side of her sturdy neck which then never seemed to me brown or freckled enough, as though these solid qualities were associated with a certain frank good nature in Albertine.

'Are you coming with us tomorrow, old crosspatch?' she would ask before leaving me.

'Where are you going?'

'That will depend on the weather and on you. But have you written anything today, my little darling? No? Then it was hardly worth your while not coming with us. Tell me, by the way, when I came in this evening, you knew my step, you guessed at once who it was?'

'Of course. Could I possibly be mistaken? Couldn't I tell my little goose's footstep among a thousand? She must let me take her shoes off before she goes to bed, it will give me such pleasure. You're so nice and pink in all that white lace.'

Such was my answer, amid the sensual expressions, others will be recognised that were peculiar to my grandmother and my mother. For, little by little, I was beginning to resemble all my relations: my father who—in a very different fashion from myself, no doubt, for if things repeat themselves, it is with great variations—took so keen an interest in the weather; and not my father only, but, more and more, my aunt Léonie. Otherwise Albertine could not but have been a reason for my going out, so as not to leave her on her own, beyond my control. Although every day I found an excuse in some particular indisposition, what made me so often remain in bed was a person—not Albertine, not a person I loved but a person with more power over me than any beloved—who had transmigrated into me, a person despotic to the point of silencing at times my jealous suspicions or at least of preventing me from going to verify whether they had any foundation, and that person was my aunt Léonie—my aunt Léonie, who was entirely steeped in piety and with whom I could have sworn that I had not a single point in common, I who was so passionately fond of pleasure, apparently worlds apart from that maniac who had never known any pleasure in her life and lay telling her beads all day long, I who suffered from my inability to actualise a literary career whereas she had been the one person in the family who could never understand that reading was anything other than a means of whiling away the time, of 'amusing oneself,' which made it, even at Eastertide, permissible on Sundays, when every serious occupation is forbidden in order that the whole day may be hallowed by prayer. And as if it were not enough that I should bear an exaggerated resemblance to my father, to the extent of not being satisfied like him with consulting the barometer, but becoming an animated barometer myself, as if it were not enough that I should allow myself to be ordered by my aunt Léonie to stay at home and watch the weather, from my bedroom window or even from my bed, here I was talking now to Albertine, at one moment as the child that I had been at Combray used to talk to my mother, at another as my grandmother used to talk to me. When we have passed a certain age, the soul of the child that we were and the souls of the dead from whom we sprang come and shower upon us their riches and their spells, asking to be allowed to contribute to the new emotions which we feel and in which, erasing their former image, we recast them in an original creation. Thus my whole past from my earliest years, and, beyond these, the past of my parents and relations, blended with my impure love for Albertine the tender charm of an affection

at once filial and maternal. We have to give hospitality, at
a certain stage in our lives, to all our relatives who have
journeyed so far and gathered round us.

Before Albertine obeyed and took off her shoes, I would
open her chemise. Her two little uplifted breasts were so
round that they seemed not so much to be an integral part
of her body as to have ripened there like fruit; and her belly
(concealing the place where a man's is disfigured as though
by an iron clamp left sticking in a statue that has been
taken down from its niche) was closed, at the junction of
her thighs, by two valves with a curve as languid, as repose-
ful, as cloistral as that of the horizon after the sun has set.
She would take off her shoes, and lie down by my side.

O mighty attitudes of Man and Woman, in which there
seeks to be united, in the innocence of the world's first
days and with the humility of clay, what the Creation made
separate, in which Eve is astonished and submissive before
Man by whose side she awakens, as he himself, alone still,
before God who has fashioned him! Albertine would fold
her arms behind her dark hair, her hip swelling, her leg
drooping with the inflexion of a swan's neck that stretches
upwards and then curves back on itself. When she was
lying completely on her side, there was a certain aspect of
her face (so sweet and so beautiful from in front) which I
could not endure, hook-nosed as in one of Leonardo's caricatures, seeming to betray the malice, the greed for gain,
the deceitfulness of a spy whose presence in my house
would have filled me with horror and whom that profile

seemed to unmask. At once I took Albertine's face in my hands and altered its position.

'Be a good boy and promise me that if you don't come out tomorrow you'll work,' she would say as she slipped her chemise on again.

'Yes, but don't put on your dressing-gown yet.'

Sometimes I ended by falling asleep by her side. The room would grow cold, more wood would be wanted. I would try to find the bell above my head, but fail to do so, after fingering all the copper rods in turn save those between which it hung, and would say to Albertine who had sprung from the bed so that Françoise should not find us lying side by side: 'No, come back for a moment, I can't find the bell.'

Sweet, gay, innocent moments to all appearance, and yet moments in which there gathers the unsuspected possibility of disaster, which makes the amorous life the most precarious of all, that in which the unpredictable rain of sulphur and brimstone falls after the most radiant moments, whereupon, without having the heart or the will to draw a lesson from our misfortune, we set to work at once to rebuild upon the slopes of the crater from which nothing but catastrophe can emerge. I was as carefree as those who imagine their happiness will last. It is precisely because this tenderness has been necessary to give birth to pain—and will return moreover at intervals to calm it—that men can be sincere with each other, and even with themselves, when they pride themselves on a woman's lovingness, although, taking things all in all, at the heart of their intimacy there lurks continuously and secretly, unavowed to the rest of the world, or revealed unintentionally by questions and inquiries, a painful disquiet. But this could not have come to birth without the preliminary tenderness, which even afterwards is intermittently necessary to make the pain bearable and to avoid ruptures; and concealment of the secret hell that a life shared with the woman in question really is, to the point of parading an allegedly tender intimacy, expresses a genuine point of view, a universal process of cause and effect, one of the modes whereby the production of grief and pain is rendered possible.

It no longer surprised me that Albertine should be in the house, and would not be going out tomorrow except with myself or in the custody of Andrée. These habits of shared life, these broad lines by which my existence was demarcated and within which nobody might penetrate but Albertine, and also (in the future plan, of which I was still unaware, of my life to come, like the plan drawn up by an architect for monuments which will not be erected until long afterwards) the remoter lines, parallel to these and broader still, by which, like an isolated hermitage, the somewhat rigid and monotonous prescription of my future loves was adumbrated, had in reality been traced that night at Balbec when, in the little train, after Albertine had revealed to me who it was that had brought her up, I had decided at all costs to remove her from certain influences and to prevent her from straying out of my sight for some days. Day after day had gone by, and these habits had become mechanical, but, like those rites the meaning of which History seeks to discover, I could have said (though I would not have wished to say) to anybody who asked me to explain the meaning of this life of seclusion which I carried so far as no longer to go to the theatre, that its origin lay in the anxiety of an evening and my need to prove to myself, during the days that followed, that the girl of whose unfortunate childhood I had learned should have no possibility, whether she wished to or not, of exposing herself to similar temptations. I no longer thought, except very rarely, of these possibilities, but they were nevertheless to remain vaguely present in my consciousness. The fact that I was destroying them—or trying to do so—day by day was doubtless the reason why I took such pleasure in kissing those cheeks which were no more beautiful than many others; beneath any carnal attraction at all deep, there is the permanent possibility of danger.

I HAD PROMISED Albertine that, if I did not go out with her, I would settle down to work. But in the morning, just as if, taking advantage of our being asleep, the house had miraculously flown, I awoke in different weather beneath another clime. We do not begin to work as soon as we disembark in a strange country to the conditions of which we have to adapt ourselves. And each day was for me a different country. How could I even recognise my indolence itself, under the novel forms which it assumed? Sometimes, on days when the weather was beyond redemption, mere residence in the house, situated in the midst of a steady and continuous rain, had all the gliding ease, the soothing silence, the interest of a sea voyage; another time, on a bright day, to lie still in bed was to let the lights and shadows play around me as round a tree-trunk. Or yet again, at the first strokes of the bell of a neighbouring convent, rare as the early morning worshippers, barely whitening the dark sky with their hesitant hail-showers, melted and scattered by the warm breeze, I would discern one of those tempestuous, disordered, delightful days, when the roofs, soaked by an intermittent downpour and dried by a gust of wind or a ray of sunshine, let fall a gurgling raindrop and, as they wait for the wind to turn again, preen their iridescent pigeon's-breast slates in the momentary sunshine; one of those days filled with so many changes of weather, atmospheric incidents, storms, that the idle man does not feel that he has wasted them because he has been taking an interest in the activity which, in default of himself, the atmosphere, acting as it were in his stead, has displayed; days similar to those times of revolution or war which do not seem empty to the schoolboy playing truant, because by loitering outside the Law Courts or by reading the newspapers he has the illusion of deriving from the events that have occurred, failing the work which he has neglected, an intellectual profit and an excuse for his idleness; days, finally, to which one may compare those on which some exceptional crisis has occurred in one's life from which the man who has never done anything imagines that he will acquire industrious habits if it is happily resolved: for instance, the morning on which he sets out for a duel which is to be fought under particularly dangerous conditions, and he is suddenly made aware, at the moment when it is perhaps about to be taken from him, of the value of a life of which he might have made use to begin some important work, or merely to enjoy a few pleasures, and of which he has failed to make any use at all. 'If only I'm not killed,' he says to himself, 'how I shall settle down to work the very minute, and how I shall enjoy myself too!' Life has in fact suddenly acquired a higher value in his eyes, because he puts into life everything that it seems to him capable of giving, instead of the little that he normally demands of it. He sees it in the light of his desire, not as his experience has taught him that he was apt to make it, that is to say so tawdry. It has, at that moment, become filled with work, travel, mountain-climbing, all the splendid things which, he tells himself, the fatal outcome of the duel may render impossible, without thinking that they were already impossible before there was any question of a duel, owing to the bad habits which, even had there been no duel, would have persisted. He returns home without even a scratch, but he continues to find the same obstacles to pleasures, excursions, travel, to everything which for a moment he had feared that death would deprive him of; life is sufficient for that. As for work—exceptional circumstances having the effect of intensifying what previously existed in a man, work in the industrious, idleness in the lazy—he takes a holiday from it.

I followed his example, and did as I had always done since my first resolution to become a writer, which I had made long ago, but which seemed to me to date from yesterday, because I had regarded each intervening day as non-existent. I treated this day in a similar fashion, allowing its showers of rain and bursts of sunshine to pass without doing anything, and vowing that I would begin to work next day. But then I was no longer the same man beneath a cloudless sky; the golden note of the bells contained, like honey, not only light but the sensation of light (and also the sickly savour of preserved fruits, because at Combray it had often loitered like a wasp over our cleared dinner-table). On this day of dazzling sunshine, to remain until nightfall with my eyes shut was a thing permitted, customary, health-giving, pleasant, seasonable, like keeping the outside shutters closed against the heat. It was in such weather as this that at the beginning of my second visit to Balbec I used to hear the violins of the orchestra amid the blue-green surge of the rising tide. How much more fully did I possess Albertine today! There were days when the sound of a bell striking the hour bore upon the sphere of its sonority a plaque so spread with moisture or with light that it was like a transcription for the blind or, if you like, a musical interpretation of the charm of rain or the charm of sunlight. So much so that, at the moment, as I lay in bed with my eyes shut, I said to myself that everything is capable of transposition and that a universe that was exclusively audible might be as full of variety as the other. Travelling lazily upstream from day to day as in a boat, and seeing an endlessly changing succession of enchanted scenes appear before my eyes, scenes which I did not choose, which a moment earlier had been invisible to me, and which my memory presented to me one after another without my being free to choose them, I idly pursued over that smooth expanse my stroll in the sunshine.

Those morning concerts at Balbec were not long past. And yet, at that comparatively recent time, I had given but little thought to Albertine. Indeed, on the very first days after my arrival, I had not known that she was at Balbec. From whom then had I learned it? Oh, yes, from Aimé. It was a fine sunny day like this. The worthy Aimé! He was glad to see me again. But he does not like Albertine. Not everybody can like her. Yes, it was he who told me that she was at Balbec. But how did he know? Ah! he had met her, had thought that she was badly-behaved. At that moment, as I approached Aimé's story by a different facet from the one it had presented when he had told it to me, my thoughts, which hitherto had been sailing blissfully over these untroubled waters, exploded suddenly, as though they had struck an invisible and perilous mine, treacherously moored at this point in my memory. He had told me that he had met her, that he had thought her badly-behaved. What had he meant by bad behaviour? I had understood him to mean vulgar behaviour, because, to contradict him in advance, I had declared that she was most refined. But no, perhaps he had meant Gomorrhan behaviour. She was with another girl, perhaps their arms were round one another's waists, perhaps they were staring at other women, were indeed behaving in a manner which I had never seen Albertine adopt in my presence. Who was the other girl? Where had Aimé met her, this odious Albertine?

I tried to recall exactly what Aimé had said to me, in order to see whether it could be related to what I imagined, or whether he had meant nothing more than common manners. But in vain might I ask the question, the person who put it and the person who could supply the recollection were, alas, one and the same person, myself, who was momentarily duplicated but without any additional insight. Question as I might, it was myself who answered, I learned nothing more. I no longer gave a thought to Mlle Vinteuil. Born of a new suspicion, the fit of jealousy from which I was suffering was new too, or rather it was only the prolongation, the extension of that suspicion; it had the same theatre, which was no longer Montjouvain but the road upon which Aimé had met Albertine, and for its object one or other of the various friends who might have been with Albertine that day. It was perhaps a certain Elisabeth, or else perhaps those two girls whom Albertine had watched in the mirror at the Casino, while appearing not to see them. She had doubtless been having relations with them, and also with Esther, Bloch's cousin. Such relations, had they been revealed to me by a third person, would have been enough almost to kill me, but since it was I who imagined them, I took care to add sufficient uncertainty to deaden the pain. We succeed in absorbing daily in enormous doses, under the guise of suspicions, this same idea that we are being betrayed, a quite small quantity of which might prove fatal if injected by the needle of a shattering word. And it is no doubt for that reason, and as a by-product of the instinct of self-preservation, that the same jealous man does not hesitate to form the most terrible suspicions upon a basis of innocuous facts, provided that, whenever any proof is brought to him, he refuses to accept the irrefutable evidence. Besides, love is an incurable malady, like those diathetic states in which rheumatism affords the sufferer a brief respite only to be replaced by epileptiform headaches. If my jealous suspicion was calmed, I then felt a grudge against Albertine for not having been tender enough, perhaps for having made fun of me with Andrée. I thought with alarm of the idea that she must have formed if Andrée had repeated all our conversations; the future loomed black and menacing. This mood of depression left me only if a new jealous suspicion drove me to further inquiries or if, on the other hand, Albertine's displays of affection made my happiness seem to me insignificant. Who could this girl be? I must write to Aimé, try to see him, and then check his statement by talking to Albertine, making her confess. In the meantime, convinced that it must be Bloch's cousin, I asked Bloch himself, who had not the remotest idea of my purpose, simply to let me see her photograph, or, better still, to arrange for me to meet her.

How many persons, cities, roads jealousy makes us eager thus to know! It is a thirst for knowledge thanks to which, with regard to various isolated points, we end by acquiring every possible notion in turn except the one that we require. One can never tell whether a suspicion will not arise, for, all of a sudden, one recalls a remark that was not clear, an alibi that cannot have been given without a purpose. One has not seen the person again, but there is such a thing as a retrospective jealousy, that is born only after we have left the person, a delayed-action jealousy. Perhaps the habit that I had acquired of nursing within me certain desires, the desire for a young girl of good family such as those I used to see pass beneath my window escorted by their governesses, and especially for the girl whom Saint-Loup had mentioned to me, the one who frequented houses of ill fame, the desire for handsome lady's-maids, and especially for Mme Putbus's, the desire to go to the country in early spring to see once again hawthorns, apple-trees in blossom, storms, the desire for Venice, the desire to settle down to work, the desire to live like other people—perhaps the habit of storing up all these desires, without assuaging any of them, contenting myself with a promise to myself not to forget to satisfy them one

How many persons, cities, roads jealousy makes us eager thus to know!

day—perhaps this habit, so many years old already, of perpetual postponement, of what M. de Charlus used to castigate under the name of procrastination, had become so prevalent in me that it took hold of my jealous suspicions also and, while encouraging me to make a mental note that I would not fail, some day, to have things out with Albertine as regards the girl, or possibly girls (this part of the story was confused and blurred in my memory and to all intents and purposes indecipherable) with whom Aimé had met her, made me also postpone this inquest. In any case, I would not mention the subject to my mistress this evening, for fear of making her think me jealous and so offending her.

And yet when, on the following day, Bloch sent me the photograph of his cousin Esther, I made haste to forward it to Aimé. And at the same moment I remembered that Albertine had that morning refused me a pleasure which might indeed have tired her. Was that in order to reserve it for someone else, this afternoon, perhaps? For whom? Jealousy is thus endless, for even if the beloved, by dying for instance, can no longer provoke it by her actions, it may happen that memories subsequent to any event suddenly materialise and behave in our minds as though they too were events, memories which hitherto we had never explored, which had seemed to us unimportant, and to which our own reflexion upon them is sufficient, without any external factors, to give a new and terrible meaning. There is no need for there to be two of you, it is enough to be alone in your room, thinking, for fresh betrayals by your mistress to come to light, even though she is dead. And so we ought not to fear in love, as in everyday life, the future alone, but even the past, which often comes to life for us only when the future has come and gone—and not only the past which we discover after the event but the past which we have long kept stored within ourselves and suddenly learn how to interpret.

No matter, I was only too happy, as afternoon turned to evening, that the hour was not far off when I should be able to look to Albertine's presence for the appeasement which I needed. Unfortunately, the evening that followed was one of those when this appeasement was not forthcoming, when the kiss that Albertine would give me when she left me for the night, very different from her usual kiss, would no more soothe me than my mother's kiss had soothed me long ago, on days when she was vexed with me and I dared not call her back although I knew that I should be unable to sleep. Such evenings were now those on which Albertine had formed for the next day some plan about which she did not wish me to know. Had she confided it to me, I would have shown an eagerness to ensure its realisation that no one but Albertine could have inspired in me. But she told me nothing, and she had no need to tell me anything; as soon as she came in, before she had even crossed the threshold of my room, while she was still wearing her hat or toque, I had already detected the unknown, restive, desperate, uncontrollable desire. These were often the

evenings when I had awaited her return with the most loving thoughts, and looked forward to throwing my arms
round her neck with the warmest affection. Alas, misun-
derstandings such as I had often had with my parents,
whom I would find cold or irritable when I ran to embrace
them, overflowing with love, are as nothing in comparison
with those that occur between lovers. The anguish then is
far less superficial, far harder to endure; it has its seat in a
deeper layer of the heart.

On this particular evening, however, Albertine was
obliged to mention the plan that she had in mind; I gathered at once that she wished to go next day to pay a visit to
Mme Verdurin, a visit to which in itself I would have seen
no objection. But evidently her object was to meet someone there, to prepare some future pleasure. Otherwise she
would not have attached so much importance to this visit.
That is to say, she would not have kept on assuring me that
it was of no importance. I had in the course of my life followed a progression which was the opposite of that
adopted by peoples who make use of phonetic writing only
after having considered the characters as a set of symbols;
having, for so many years, looked for the real life and
thought of other people only in the direct statements
about them which they supplied me with of their own free
will, in the absence of these I had come to attach importance, on the contrary, only to disclosures that are not a
rational and analytical expression of the truth; the words
themselves did not enlighten me unless they were

interpreted in the same way as a rush of blood to the cheeks of a person who is embarrassed, or as a sudden silence. Such and such an adverb (for instance that used by M. de Cambremer when he understood that I was 'literary' and, not having yet spoken to me, as he was describing a visit he had paid to the Verdurins, turned to me with: '*Incidentally*, Borelli was there!') bursting into flames through the involuntary, sometimes perilous contact of two ideas which the speaker has not expressed but which, by applying the appropriate methods of analysis or electrolysis, I was able to extract from it, told me more than a long speech. Albertine sometimes let fall in her conversation one or other of these precious amalgams which I made haste to 'treat' so as to transform them into lucid ideas.

It is in fact one of the most terrible things for the lover that whereas particular details—which only experiment or espionage, among so many possible realisations, would ever make known to him—are so difficult to discover, the truth on the other hand is so easy to detect or merely to sense. Often, at Balbec, I had seen her fasten on girls who came past us a sudden lingering stare, like a physical contact, after which, if I knew the girls, she would say to me: 'Suppose we asked them to join us? I should so enjoy insulting them.' And now, for some time past, doubtless since she had succeeded in reading my mind, no request to me to invite anyone, not a word, not even a sidelong glance from her eyes, which had become objectless and mute, and, with the abstracted, vacant expression that

accompanied them, as revealing as had been their magnetic swerve before. Yet it was impossible for me to
reproach her, or to ply her with questions about things
which she would have declared to be so petty, so trivial,
stored up by me simply for the pleasure of 'nit-picking.' It
is hard enough to say: 'Why did you stare at that girl who
went past?' but a great deal harder to say: 'Why did you not
stare at her?' And yet I knew quite well—or at least I should
have known if I had not chosen instead to believe those
affirmations of hers—what Albertine's demeanour com-
prehended and proved, like such and such a contradiction
in the course of conversation which often I did not perceive until long after I had left her, which kept me in
anguish all night long, which I never dared mention to her
again, but which nevertheless continued to honour my
memory from time to time with its periodical visits. Even
in the case of these furtive or sidelong glances on the
beach at Balbec or in the streets of Paris, I might sometimes wonder whether the person who provoked them was
not only an object of desire at the moment when she
passed, but an old acquaintance, or else some girl who had
simply been mentioned to her and whom, when I heard
about it, I was astonished that anybody could have mentioned to her, so remote was she from what one would
have guessed Albertine's range of acquaintance to be. But
the Gomorrah of today is a jigsaw puzzle made up of pieces
that come from places where one least expected to find
them. Thus I once saw at Rivebelle a big dinner-party of

ten women, all of whom I happened to know, at least by name, and who, though as dissimilar as could be, were none the less perfectly united, so much so that I never saw a party so homogeneous, albeit so composite.

To return to the girls whom we passed in the street, never would Albertine stare at an old person, man or woman, with such fixity, or on the other hand with such reserve and as though she saw nothing. Cuckolded husbands who know nothing in fact know perfectly well. But it requires more accurate and abundant evidence to create a scene of jealousy. Besides, if jealousy helps us to discover a certain tendency to falsehood in the woman we love, it multiplies this tendency a hundredfold when the woman has discovered that we are jealous. She lies (to an extent to which she has never lied to us before), whether from pity, or from fear, or because she instinctively shies away in a flight that is symmetrical with our investigations. True, there are love affairs in which from the start a woman of easy virtue has posed as virtue incarnate in the eyes of the man who is in love with her. But how many others consist of two diametrically opposite periods! In the first, the woman speaks almost freely, with slight modifications, of her zest for pleasure and of the amorous life which it has made her lead, all of which she will deny later on with the utmost vigour to the same man when she senses that he is jealous of her and spying on her. He comes to regret the days of those first confidences, the memory of which torments him nevertheless. If the woman continued to make them, she would furnish him almost unaided with the secret of her conduct which he has been vainly pursuing day after day. And besides, what abandon those early confidences proved, what trust, what friendship! If she cannot live without being unfaithful to him, at least she would be doing so as a friend, telling him of her pleasures, associating him with them. And he thinks with regret of the sort of life which the early stages of their love seemed to promise, which the sequel has rendered impossible, turning that love into something agonisingly painful, which will make a final parting, according to circumstances, either inevitable or impossible.

Sometimes the script from which I deciphered Albertine's lies, without being ideographic, needed simply to be read backwards; thus this evening she had tossed at me casually the message, intended to pass almost unnoticed: 'I may go and see the Verdurins tomorrow. I don't really know whether I will go, I don't particularly want to.' A childish anagram of the admission: 'I shall go to the Verdurins' tomorrow, it's absolutely certain, I attach the utmost importance to it.' This apparent hesitation indicated a firm resolution and was intended to diminish the importance of the visit while informing me of it. Albertine always adopted a dubitative tone for irrevocable decisions. Mine was no less irrevocable: I would see that this visit to Mme Verdurin did not take place. Jealousy is often only an anxious need to be tyrannical applied to matters of love. I had doubtless inherited from my father this abrupt, arbitrary desire to threaten the people I loved best in the hopes with which they were lulling themselves with a sense of security which I wanted to expose to them as false; when I saw that Albertine had planned without my knowledge, behind my back, an expedition which I would have done everything in the world to make easier and more pleasant for her had she taken me into her confidence, I said casually, in order to make her tremble, that I expected to go out the next day myself.

I began to suggest to Albertine other expeditions in directions which would have made the visit to the Verdurins impossible, in words stamped with a feigned indifference beneath which I strove to conceal my agitation. But she had detected it. It encountered in her the electric power of a contrary will which violently repulsed it; I could see the sparks flash from Albertine's pupils. What use was it, though, to pay attention to what her eyes were saying at that moment? How had I failed to observe long ago that Albertine's eyes belonged to the category which even in a quite ordinary person seems to be composed of a number of fragments because of all the places in which the person wishes to be—and to conceal the desire to be—on that particular day? Eyes mendaciously kept always immobile and passive, but none the less dynamic, measurable in the yards or miles to be traversed before they reach the desired, the implacably desired meeting-place, eyes that are not so much smiling at the pleasure which tempts them as shadowed with melancholy and discouragement because there may be a difficulty in their getting there. Even when you hold them in your hands, such persons are fugitives. To understand the emotions which they arouse, and which others, even better-looking, do not, we must recognise that they are not immobile but in motion, and add to their person a sign corresponding to that which in physics denotes speed.

If you upset their plans for the day, they confess to you the pleasure they had concealed from you: 'I did so want to go and have tea with so and so who I'm fond of.' And then, six months later, if you come to know the person in question, you will learn that the girl whose plans you had upset, who, trapped, in order that you might set her free had confessed to you that she was thus in the habit of taking tea with a dear friend every day at the hour at which you did not see her, has never once been inside this person's house, that they have never had tea together, since the girl used to explain that her whole time was taken up by none other than yourself. And so the person with whom she confessed that she was going to tea, with whom she begged you to allow her to go to tea, that person, a reason admitted by necessity, it was not her, it was somebody else, it was something else still! What something else? Which somebody else?

Alas, the multifaceted eyes, far-ranging and melancholy, might enable us perhaps to measure distance, but do not indicate direction. The boundless field of possibilities extends before us, and if by any chance the reality presented itself to our eyes, it would be so far outside the limits of the possible that, knocking suddenly against this looming wall, we should fall over backwards in a daze. It is not even essential that we should have proof of her movement and flight, it is enough that we should guess them. She had promised us a letter; we were calm, we were no longer in love. The letter has not come; each mail fails to bring it; what can have happened? Anxiety is born afresh, and love. It is such people more than any others who inspire love in us, to our desolation. For every new anxiety that we feel on their account strips them in our eyes of some of their personality. We were resigned to suffering, thinking that we loved outside ourselves, and we perceive that our love is a function of our sorrow, that our love perhaps is our sorrow, and that its object is only to a very small extent the girl with the raven hair. But, when all is said, it is such people more than any others who inspire love.

More often than not, a body becomes the object of love only when an emotion, fear of losing it, uncertainty of getting it back, melts into it. Now this sort of anxiety has a great affinity for bodies. It adds to them a quality which surpasses beauty itself, which is one of the reasons why we see men who are indifferent to the most beautiful women fall passionately in love with others who appear to us ugly. To such beings, such fugitive beings, their own nature and our anxiety fasten wings. And even when they are with us the look in their eyes seems to warn us that they are about to take flight. The proof of this beauty, surpassing beauty itself, that wings add is that often, for us, the same person is alternately winged and wingless. Afraid of losing her, we forget all the others. Sure of keeping her, we compare her with those others whom at once we prefer to her. And as these fears and these certainties may vary from week to week, a person may one week see everything that gave us pleasure sacrificed to her, in the following week be sacrificed herself, and so on for months on end. All of which would be incomprehensible did we not know (from the experience, which every man shares, of having at least once in a lifetime ceased to love a woman, forgotten her) how very insignificant in herself a woman is when she is no longer—or is not yet—permeable to our emotions. And, of course, if we speak of fugitive beings it is equally true of imprisoned ones, of captive women whom we think we shall never be able to possess. Hence men detest procuresses, because they facilitate flight and dangle temptations, but if on the other hand we are in love with a cloistered woman, we willingly have recourse to a procuress to snatch her from her prison and bring her to us. In so far as relations with women whom we abduct are less permanent than others, the reason is that the fear of not succeeding in procuring them or the dread of seeing them escape is the whole of our love for them and that once they have been carried off from their husbands, torn from their footlights, cured of the temptation to leave us, dissociated in short from our emotion whatever it may be, they are only themselves, that is to say next to nothing, and, so long desired, are soon forsaken by the very man who was so afraid of their forsaking him.

I have said: 'How could I have failed to guess?' But had I not guessed it from the first day at Balbec? Had I not detected in Albertine one of those girls beneath whose envelope of flesh more hidden persons stir, I will not say than in a pack of cards still in its box, a closed cathedral or a theatre before we enter it, but than in the whole vast ever-changing crowd? Not only all these persons, but the desire, the voluptuous memory, the restless searching of so many persons. At Balbec I had not been troubled because I had never even supposed that one day I should be following a trail, even a false trail. Nevertheless, it had given Albertine, in my eyes, the plenitude of someone filled to the brim by the superimposition of so many persons, of so many desires and voluptuous memories of persons. And now that she had one day let fall the name 'Mlle Vinteuil,' I should have liked, not to tear off her dress to see her body, but through her body to see and read the whole diary of her memories and her future passionate assignations.

Strange how the things that are probably most insignificant suddenly assume an extraordinary value when a person whom we love (or who has lacked only this duplicity to make us love her) conceals them from us! In itself, suffering does not of necessity inspire in us sentiments of love or hatred towards the person who causes it: a surgeon can hurt us without arousing any personal emotion in us. But with a woman who has continued for some time to assure us that we are everything in the world to her, without being herself everything in the world to us, a woman whom we enjoy seeing, kissing, taking on our knee, we are astonished if we merely sense from a sudden resistance that she is not at our entire disposal. Disappointment may then revive in us the forgotten memory of an old anguish, which we nevertheless know to have been provoked not by this woman but by others whose betrayals stretch back like milestones through our past. And indeed, how have we the heart to go on living, how can we move a finger to preserve ourselves from death, in a world in which love is provoked only by lies and consists solely in our need to see our sufferings appeased by the person who has made us suffer? To escape from the depths of despondency that follow the discovery of this lying and this resistance, there is the sad remedy of endeavouring to act, against her will, with the help of people whom we feel to be more closely involved than we are in her life, upon her who is resisting us and lying to us, to play the cheat in turn, to make ourselves loathed. But the suffering caused by such a love is of the kind which must inevitably lead the sufferer to seek an illusory comfort in a change of position. These means of action are not wanting, alas! And the horror of the kind of love which anxiety alone has engendered lies in the fact that we turn over and over incessantly in our cage the most trivial utterances; not to mention that rarely do the people for whom we feel this love appeal to us physically to any great extent, since it is not our deliberate preference, but the accident of a moment's anguish (a moment indefinitely prolonged by our weakness of character, which repeats its experiments every evening until it yields to sedatives) that has chosen for us.

No doubt my love for Albertine was not the most barren of those to which, through lack of will-power, a man may descend, for it was not entirely platonic; she did give me some carnal satisfaction, and moreover she was intelligent. But all this was supererogatory. What occupied my mind was not something intelligent that she might have said, but a chance remark that had aroused in me a doubt as to her actions; I tried to remember whether she had said this or that, in what tone, at what moment, in response to what words, to reconstruct the whole scene of her dialogue with me, to recall at what moment she had expressed a desire to visit the Verdurins, what word of mine had brought that look of vexation to her face. The most important event might have been at issue without my going to so much trouble to establish the truth of it, to reconstitute its precise atmosphere and colour. No doubt, after these anxieties have intensified to a degree which we find unbearable, we sometimes manage to calm them altogether for an evening. We too are invited to the party which the woman we love was to attend and the true nature of which has been obsessing us for days; she has neither looks nor words for anyone but us; we take her home and then, all our anxieties dispelled, we enjoy a repose as complete and as healing as the deep sleep that comes after a long walk. And no doubt such repose is worth a high price. But would it not have been simpler not to buy ourselves, deliberately, the preceding anxiety, and at an even higher price? Besides, we know all too well that however profound these temporary respites may be, anxiety will still prevail. Often, indeed, it is revived by a remark that was intended to set our mind at rest. The demands of our jealousy and the blindness of our credulity are greater than the woman we love could ever suppose. When, spontaneously, she swears to us that such and such a man is no more to her than a friend, she shatters us by informing us—something we never suspected—that he has been her friend. While she is telling us, in proof of her sincerity, how they had tea together that very afternoon, at each word that she utters the invisible, the unsuspected, takes shape before our eyes. She admits that he has asked her to be his mistress, and we suffer agonies at the thought that she can have listened to his overtures. She refused them, she says. But presently, when we recall her story, we wonder whether that refusal is really genuine, for there is wanting, between the different things that she said to us, that logical and necessary connexion which, more than the facts related, is the sign of truth. Besides, there was that frightening note of scorn in her voice: 'I said to him no, categorically,' which is to be found in every class of society when a woman is lying. We must nevertheless thank her for having refused, encourage

The demands of our jealousy and the blindness of our credulity are greater than the woman we love could ever suppose

her by our kindness to repeat these painful confidences in the future. At the most, we may remark: 'But if he had already made advances to you, why did you accept his invitation to tea?' 'So that he should not hold it against me and say that I hadn't been nice to him.' And we dare not reply that by refusing she would perhaps have been nicer to us.

Albertine alarmed me further when she said that I was quite right to say, out of regard for her reputation, that I was not her lover, since 'for that matter,' she went on, 'it's perfectly true that you aren't.' I was not perhaps her lover in the full sense of the word, but then, was I to suppose that all the things that we did together she did also with all the other men whose mistress she swore to me that she had never been? The desire to know at all costs what Albertine was thinking, whom she saw, whom she loved—how strange that I should sacrifice everything to this need, since I had felt the same need to know in the case of Gilberte names and facts which now meant nothing to me! I was perfectly well aware that in themselves Albertine's actions were of no greater interest. It is curious that a first love, if by the fragile state in which it leaves one's heart it paves the way for subsequent loves, does not at least provide one, in view of the identity of symptoms and sufferings, with the means of curing them. Besides, is there any need to know a fact? Are we not aware beforehand, in a general way, of the mendacity and even the discretion of those women who have something to conceal? Is there any possibility of error? They make a virtue of their silence, when we would give anything to make them speak. And we feel certain that they have assured their accomplice: 'I never say anything. It won't be through me that anybody will hear about it, I never say anything.'

A man may give his fortune and even his life for a woman, and yet know quite well that in ten years' time, more or less, he would refuse her the fortune, prefer to keep his life. For then that woman would be detached from him, alone, that is to say non-existent. What attaches us to people are the countless roots, the innumerable threads which are our memories of last night, our hopes for tomorrow morning, the continuous weft of habit from which we can never free ourselves. Just as there are misers who hoard from generosity, so we are spendthrifts who spend from avarice, and it is not so much to a person that we sacrifice our life as to everything of ours that may have become attached to that person, all those hours and days, all those things compared with which the life we have not yet lived, our life in the relative future, seems to us more remote, more detached, less intimate, less our own. What we need is to extricate ourselves from these bonds which are so much more important than the person, but they have the effect of creating in us temporary obligations which mean that we dare not leave the person for fear of being badly thought of, whereas later on we would so dare, for, detached from us, that person would no longer be part of us, and because in reality we create obligations (even if, by an apparent contradiction, they should lead to suicide) towards ourselves alone.

If I was not in love with Albertine (and of this I could not be sure) then there was nothing extraordinary in the place that she occupied in my life: we live only with what we do not love, with what we have brought to live with us only in order to kill the intolerable love, whether it be for a woman, for a place, or again for a woman embodying a place. Indeed we should be terrified of beginning to love again if a new separation were to occur. I had not yet reached this stage with Albertine. Her lies, her admissions, left me to complete the task of elucidating the truth: her innumerable lies, because she was not content with merely lying, like everyone who imagines that he or she is loved, but was by nature, quite apart from this, a liar (and so inconsistent moreover that, even if she told me the truth every time about, for instance, what she thought of other people, she would say something different every time); her admissions, because, being so rare, so quickly cut short, they left between them, in so far as they concerned the past, huge blanks over the whole expanse of which I was obliged to retrace—and for that first of all to discover—her life.

As for the present, so far as I could interpret the sibylline utterances of Françoise, it was not only on particular points but over a whole area that Albertine lied to me, and 'one fine day' I would see what Françoise pretended to know, what she refused to tell me, what I dared not ask her.

It was no doubt with the same jealousy that she had shown in the past with regard to Eulalie that Françoise would speak of the most unlikely things, but so vaguely that at most one could deduce therefrom the highly improbable insinuation that the poor captive (who was a lover of women) preferred marriage with somebody who did not appear to be me. If this had been so, how, in spite of her telepathic powers, could Françoise have come to hear of it? Certainly, Albertine's statements could give me no definite enlightenment, for they were as different day by day as the colours of a spinning-top that has almost come to a standstill. However, it seemed that it was hatred more than anything else that impelled Françoise to speak. Not a day went by without her addressing to me, and I in my mother's absence enduring, such speeches as:

'To be sure, you're very nice, and I shall never forget the debt of gratitude that I owe you' (this probably so that I might establish fresh claims upon her gratitude) 'but the house has become infected ever since niceness brought in deceitfulness, ever since cleverness has been protecting the stupidest person that ever was seen, ever since refinement, good manners, wit, dignity in all things, the appearance and the reality of a prince, allow themselves to be dictated to and plotted against and me to be humiliated—me who've been forty years in the family—by vice, by everything that's most vulgar and base.'

What Françoise resented most about Albertine was having to take orders from somebody who was not one of ourselves, and also the strain of the additional housework which, affecting the health of our old servant (who would not, for all that, accept any help in the house, not being a 'good for nothing'), in itself would have accounted for her irritability and her furious hatred. Certainly, she would have liked to see Albertine-Esther banished from the house. This was Françoise's dearest wish. And, by consoling her, its fulfilment would in itself have given our old servant some rest. But to my mind there was more to it than this. So violent a hatred could have originated only in an over-strained body. And, more even than of consideration, Françoise was in need of sleep.

ALBERTINE WENT TO take off her things and, to lose no time in finding out what I wanted to know, I seized the telephone receiver and invoked the implacable deities, but succeeded only in arousing their fury which expressed itself in the single word 'Engaged.' Andrée was in fact engaged in talking to someone else. As I waited for her to finish her conversation, I wondered why it was—now that so many of our painters are seeking to revive the feminine portraits of the eighteenth century, in which the cleverly devised setting is a pretext for portraying expressions of expectation, sulkiness, interest, reverie—why it was that none of our modern Bouchers or Fragonards had yet painted, instead of 'The Letter' or 'The Harpsichord,' this scene which might be entitled 'At the telephone,' in which there would come spontaneously to the lips of the listener a smile that is all the more genuine because it is conscious of being unobserved.

Finally I got through to Andrée: 'Are you coming to call for Albertine tomorrow?' I asked, and as I uttered Albertine's name, I thought of the envy Swann had aroused in me when he had said to me, on the day of the Princesse de Guermantes's party: 'Come and see Odette,' and I had thought how potent, when all was said, was a Christian name which, in the eyes of the whole world including Odette herself, had on Swann's lips alone this entirely possessive sense. Such a monopoly—summed up in a single word—over the whole existence of another person had appeared to me, whenever I was in love, to be sweet indeed! But in fact, when we are in a position to say it, either we no longer care, or else habit, while not blunting its tenderness, has changed its sweetness to bitterness. I knew that I alone was in a position to say 'Albertine' in that tone to Andrée. And yet, to Albertine, to Andrée, and to myself, I felt that I was nothing. And I realised the impossibility which love comes up against. We imagine that it has as its object a being that can be laid down in front of us, enclosed within a body. Alas, it is the extension of that being to all the points in space and time that it has occupied and will occupy. If we do not possess its contact with this or that place, this or that hour, we do not possess that being. But we cannot touch all these points. If only they were indicated to us, we might perhaps contrive to reach out to them. But we grope for them without finding them.

Hence mistrust, jealousy, persecutions. We waste precious time on absurd clues and pass by the truth without suspecting it.

But already one of the irascible deities with the breathtakingly agile handmaidens was becoming irritated, not because I was speaking but because I was saying nothing.

'Come along, I've been holding the line for you all this time; I shall cut you off.'

However, she did nothing of the sort but, evoking Andrée's presence, enveloped it, like the great poet that a damsel of the telephone always is, in the atmosphere peculiar to the home, the district, the very life itself of Albertine's friend.

'Is that you?' asked Andrée, whose voice was projected towards me with an instantaneous speed by the goddess whose privilege it is to make sound more swift than light.

'Listen,' I replied, 'go wherever you like, anywhere, except to Mme Verdurin's. You must at all cost keep Albertine away from there tomorrow.'

'But that's just where she's supposed to be going.'

'Ah!'

But I was obliged to break off the conversation for a moment and to make menacing gestures, for if Françoise continued—as though it were something as unpleasant as vaccination or as dangerous as the aeroplane—to refuse to learn to use the telephone, whereby she would have spared us the trouble of conversations which she might intercept without any harm, on the other hand she would at once come into the room whenever I was engaged in a conversation so private that I was particularly anxious to keep it from her ears. When she had left the room at last, not without lingering to take away various objects that had been lying there since the previous day and might perfectly well have been left there for an hour longer, and to put on to the fire a log made quite superfluous by the burning heat generated in me by the intruder's presence and my fear of finding myself 'cut off' by the operator, 'I'm sorry,' I said to Andrée, 'I was interrupted. Is it absolutely certain that she has to go to the Verdurins' tomorrow?'

'Absolutely, but I can tell her that you don't want her to.'

'No, not at all, but I might possibly come with you.'

'Ah!' said Andrée, in a voice that sounded annoyed and somehow alarmed by my audacity, which was incidentally fortified as a result.

'Well then, good-night, and please forgive me for disturbing you for nothing.'

'Not at all,' said Andrée, and (since, now that the telephone has come into general use, a decorative ritual of polite phrases has grown up round it, as round the tea-tables of the past) she added: 'It's been a great pleasure to hear your voice.'

I might have said the same, and with greater truth than Andrée, for I had been deeply affected by the sound of her voice, having never noticed before that it was so different from the voices of other people. Then I recalled other voices still, women's voices especially, some of them slowed down by the precision of a question and by mental concentration, others made breathless, even interrupted at moments, by the lyrical flow of what they were relating; I recalled one by one the voices of all the girls I had known at Balbec, then Gilberte's, then my grandmother's, then Mme de Guermantes's; I found them all dissimilar, moulded by a speech peculiar to each of them, each playing on a different instrument, and I thought to myself how thin must be the concert performed in paradise by the three or four angel musicians of the old painters, when I saw, mounting to the throne of God by tens, by hundreds, by thousands, the harmonious and multiphonic salutation of all the Voices. I did not leave the telephone without thanking, in a few propitiatory words, the goddess who reigns over the speed of sound for having kindly exercised on behalf of my humble words a power which made them a hundred times more rapid than thunder. But my thanksgiving received no other response than that of being cut off.

When Albertine came back to my room, she was wearing a black satin dress which had the effect of making her seem paler, of turning her into the pallid, intense Parisian woman, etiolated by lack of fresh air, by the atmosphere of crowds and perhaps by the practice of vice, whose eyes seemed the more uneasy because they were not brightened by any colour in her cheeks.

'Guess,' I said to her, 'who I've just been talking to on the telephone. Andrée!'

'Andrée?' exclaimed Albertine in a loud, astonished, excited voice that so simple a piece of intelligence hardly seemed to call for. 'I hope she remembered to tell you that we met Mme Verdurin the other day.'

'Mme Verdurin? I don't remember,' I replied as though I were thinking of something else, in order to appear indifferent to this meeting and not to betray Andrée who had told me where Albertine was going next day. But how could I tell whether Andrée was not herself betraying me, whether she would not tell Albertine tomorrow that I had asked her to prevent her at all costs from going to the Verdurins', and whether she had not already revealed to her that I had on several occasions made similar recommendations? She had assured me that she had never repeated anything, but the value of this assertion was counterbalanced in my mind by the impression that for some time past Albertine's face had ceased to show the trust that she had placed in me for so long.

Suffering, when we are in love, ceases from time to time, but only to resume in a different form. We weep to see the beloved no longer respond to us with those bursts of affection, those amorous advances of earlier days; we suffer even more when, having relinquished them with us, she resumes them with others; then, from this suffering, we are distracted by a new and still more agonising pang, the suspicion that she has lied to us about how she spent the previous evening, when she was no doubt unfaithful to us; this suspicion in turn is dispelled, and we are soothed by our mistress's affectionate kindness; but then a forgotten word comes back to us; we had been told that she was ardent in moments of pleasure, whereas we have always found her calm; we try to picture to ourselves these passionate frenzies with others, we feel how very little we are to her, we observe an air of boredom, longing, melancholy while we are talking, we observe like a black sky the slovenly clothes she puts on when she is with us, keeping for other people the dresses with which she used to flatter us. If, on the contrary, she is affectionate, what joy for a moment! But when we see that little tongue stuck out as though in invitation, we think of those to whom that invitation was so often addressed that even perhaps with me, without her thinking of those others, it had remained for Albertine, by force of long habit, an automatic signal. Then the feeling that she is bored by us returns. But suddenly this pain is reduced to nothing when we think of the unknown evil element in her life, of the places, impossible to identify, where she has been, where she still goes perhaps during the hours when we are not with her, if indeed she is not planning to live there altogether, those places in which she is separated from us, does not belong to us, is happier than when she is with us. Such are the revolving searchlights of jealousy.

Jealousy is moreover a demon that cannot be exorcised, but constantly reappears in new incarnations. Even if we could succeed in exterminating them all, in keeping the beloved for ever, the Spirit of Evil would then adopt

But when we see that little tongue stuck out as though in invitation, we think of those to whom that invitation was so often addressed another form, more pathetic still, despair at having obtained fidelity only by force, despair at not being loved.

Tender and sweet though Albertine was on certain evenings, she no longer had any of those spontaneous impulses which I remembered from Balbec when she used to say 'How very nice you are, really!' and her whole heart seemed to go out to me unrestrained by any of those grievances which she now felt and which she kept to herself because she doubtless considered them irremediable, impossible to forget, unavowable, but which nevertheless created between us a significant verbal prudence on her part or an impassable barrier of silence.

'And may one be allowed to know why you telephoned to Andrée?'

'To ask whether she had any objection to my joining you tomorrow and paying the Verdurins the visit I've been promising them since La Raspelière.'

'Just as you like. But I warn you, there's an appalling fog this evening, and it's sure to last over tomorrow. I mention it because I shouldn't like you to make yourself ill. Personally, I need hardly say that I'd love you to come with us. However,' she added with a thoughtful air, 'I'm not at all sure that I'll go to the Verdurins'. They've been so kind to me that I ought, really . . . Next to you, they've been nicer to me than anybody, but there are some things about them that I don't quite like. I simply must go to the Bon Marché or the Trois-Quartiers and get a white bodice to wear with this dress which is really too black.'

To allow Albertine to go by herself into a big shop crowded with people perpetually brushing against one, provided with so many exits that a woman can always say that when she came out she could not find her carriage which was waiting further along the street, was something that I was quite determined never to consent to, but the thought of it made me extremely unhappy. And yet it did not occur to me that I ought long ago to have ceased to see Albertine, for she had entered, for me, upon that lamentable period in which a person, scattered in space and time, is no longer a woman but a series of events on which we can throw no light, a series of insoluble problems, a sea which, like Xerxes, we scourge with rods in an absurd attempt to punish it for what it has engulfed. Once this period has begun, we are perforce vanquished. Happy are they who understand this in time not to prolong unduly a futile, exhausting struggle, hemmed in on every side by the limits of the imagination, a struggle in which jealousy plays so sorry a part that the same man who, once upon a time, if the eyes of the woman who was always by his side rested for an instant upon another man, imagined an intrigue and suffered endless torments, now resigns himself to allowing her to go out by herself, sometimes with the man whom he knows to be her lover, preferring to the unknowable this torture which at least he knows! It is a question of the rhythm to be adopted, which afterwards one follows from force of habit. Neurotics who could never stay away from a dinner-party will eventually take rest cures which never seem to them to last long enough; women who recently were still of easy virtue live in penitence. Jealous lovers who, to keep an eye on the woman they loved, cut short their hours of sleep, deprived themselves of rest, now feeling that her desires, the world so vast and secret, and time are too much for them, allow her to go out without them, then to travel, and finally separate from her. Jealousy thus perishes for want of nourishment and has survived so long only by clamouring incessantly for fresh food. I was still a long way from this state.

I was now at liberty to go out with Albertine as often as I wished. As there had recently sprung up round Paris a number of aerodromes, which are to aeroplanes what harbours are to ships, and as, ever since the day when, on the way to La Raspelière, that almost mythological encounter with an airman, at whose passage overhead my horse had reared, had been to me like a symbol of liberty, I often chose to end our day's excursion—with the ready approval of Albertine, a passionate lover of every form of sport—at one of these aerodromes. We went there, she and I, attracted by that incessant stir of departure and arrival which gives so much charm to a stroll along a jetty, or merely along a beach, to those who love the sea, and to loitering about an 'aviation centre' to those who love the sky. From time to time, amid the repose of the machines that lay inert and as though at anchor, we would see one being laboriously pulled by a number of mechanics, as a boat is dragged across the sand at the bidding of a tourist

who wishes to go for an outing on the sea. Then the engine
was started, the machine ran along the ground, gathered
speed, until finally, all of a sudden, at right angles, it rose
slowly, in the braced and as it were static ecstasy of a horizontal speed suddenly transformed into a majestic, vertical
ascent. Albertine could not contain her joy, and would
demand explanations of the mechanics who, now that the
machine was in the air, were strolling back to the sheds.
The passenger, meanwhile, was covering mile after mile;
the huge skiff, upon which our eyes remained fixed, was
now no more than a barely visible dot in the sky, a dot
which, however, would gradually recover its solidity, its
size, its volume, when, as the time allowed for the excursion drew to an end, the moment came for landing. And we
watched with envy, Albertine and I, as he sprang to earth,
the passenger who had gone up like that to enjoy in the
solitary expanses of the open sky the calm and limpidity of
evening. Then, whether from the aerodrome or from some
museum or church that we had been visiting, we would
return home together for dinner. And yet I did not return
home calmed, as I used to be at Balbec by less frequent
excursions which I rejoiced to see extend over a whole
afternoon and would afterwards contemplate, standing
out like clustering flowers, against the rest of Albertine's
life as against an empty sky beneath which one muses
pleasantly, without thinking. Albertine's time did not
belong to me then in such ample quantities as today. Yet it
had seemed to me then to belong to me much more,

because I then took into account—my love rejoicing in them as in the bestowal of a favour—only the hours that she spent with me, whereas now—my jealousy searching anxiously among them for the possibility of a betrayal—it was only those hours that she spent apart from me.

Tomorrow, evidently, she was looking forward to a few such hours. I must choose to cease from suffering or to cease from loving. For, just as in the beginning it is formed by desire, so afterwards love is kept in existence only by painful anxiety. I felt that part of Albertine's life eluded me. Love, in the pain of anxiety as in the bliss of desire, is a demand for a whole. It is born, and it survives, only if some part remains for it to conquer. We love only what we do not wholly possess. Albertine was lying when she told me that she probably would not go to see the Verdurins, as I was lying when I said that I wished to go. She was seeking merely to dissuade me from going out with her, and I, by my abrupt announcement of this plan which I had no intention of putting into practice, to touch what I felt to be her most sensitive spot, to track down the desire that she was concealing and to force her to admit that my company next day would prevent her from gratifying it. She had virtually made this admission by ceasing suddenly to wish to go to see the Verdurins.

'If you don't want to go to the Verdurins',' I told her, 'there is a splendid charity show at the Trocadéro.' She listened to my exhortations to attend it with a doleful air. I began to be harsh with her as at Balbec, at the time of my first fit of jealousy. Her face reflected her disappointment, and in reproaching her I used the same arguments that had been so often advanced against me by my parents when I was small, and that had appeared so unintelligent and cruel to my misunderstood childhood. 'No, in spite of your gloomy look,' I said to Albertine, 'I can't feel sorry for you; I should feel sorry for you if you were ill, if you were in trouble, if you had suffered some bereavement; not that you would mind in the least, I dare say, considering your expenditure of false sensibility over nothing. Besides, I'm not very impressed by the sensibility of people who pretend to be so fond of us and are quite incapable of doing us the smallest favour, and whose minds wander so that they forget to deliver the letter we have entrusted to them on which our whole future depends.'

A great part of what we say being no more than a recitation from memory, I had often heard these words uttered by my mother, who (always ready to explain to me that one ought not to confuse genuine sensibility with sentimentality, what the Germans, whose language she greatly admired despite my grandfather's loathing for that nation, called *Empfindung* and *Empfindelei*) once, when I was in tears, had gone so far as to tell me that Nero was probably highly-strung and was none the better for that. Indeed, like those plants which bifurcate as they grow, side by side with the sensitive boy which was all that I had been, there was now a man of the opposite sort, full of common sense, of severity towards the morbid sensibility of others, a man resembling what my parents had been to me. No doubt, as each of us is obliged to continue in himself the life of his forebears, the level-headed, caustic individual who did not exist in me at the start had joined forces with the sensitive one, and it was natural that I should become in my turn what my parents had been to me. What is more, at the moment when this new personality took shape in me, he found his language ready made in the memory of the sarcastic, scolding things that had been said to me, that I must now say to others, and that came so naturally to my lips, either because I evoked them through mimicry and association of memories, or because the delicate and mysterious incrustations of genetic energy had traced in me unawares, as upon the leaf of a plant, the same intonations, the same gestures, the same attitudes as had been characteristic of those from whom I sprang. Sometimes, playing the sage when talking to Albertine, I seemed to be hearing my grandmother. Indeed it often happened to my mother (so many obscure unconscious currents caused everything in me even down to the tiniest movements of my fingers to be drawn into the same cycles as my parents) to imagine that it was my father at the door, so similar was my knock to his.

Moreover the coupling of contrary elements is the law of life, the principle of fertilisation, and, as we shall see, the cause of many misfortunes. As a rule we detest what resembles ourselves, and our own faults when observed in another person exasperate us. How much the more does a man who has passed the age at which one instinctively displays them, a man who, for instance, has maintained an expression of icy calm through the most aggravating moments, execrate those same faults if it is another man, younger or simpler or stupider, who displays them! There are sensitive people for whom merely to see in other people's eyes the tears which they themselves have held back is infuriating. It is excessive similarity that, in spite of affection, and sometimes all the more the greater the affection, causes division to reign in families.

Possibly in myself, as in many other people, the second man that I had become was simply another aspect of the first, excitable and sensitive where he himself was concerned, a sage mentor to others. Perhaps it was so also with my parents according to whether they were considered in relation to me or in themselves. In the case of my grandmother and mother it was only too clear that their severity towards me was deliberate on their part and indeed cost them dear, but perhaps even my father's coldness too was only an external aspect of his sensibility. For it was perhaps the human truth of this twofold aspect—the one concerned with the inner life, the other with social relations—that was expressed in a remark which seemed to me at the time as false in substance as it was commonplace in form, when someone said of my father: 'Beneath his icy exterior, he conceals an extraordinary sensibility; the truth is that he's ashamed of his feelings.' Did it not in fact conceal incessant secret storms, that calm of his, interspersed at times with sententious reflections and ironical comments on the awkward manifestations of sensibility, which now I too affected in my relations with everyone and above all never swerved from, in certain circumstances, with Albertine?

I really believe that I came near that day to making up my mind to break with her and to set out for Venice. What bound me anew in my chains had to do with Normandy, not that she showed any inclination to go to that region where I had been jealous of her (for it was my good fortune that her plans never impinged upon the painful zones in my memory), but because when I happened to say to her: 'It's as though I were speaking to you about your aunt's friend who lived at Infreville,' she replied angrily, delighted—like everyone in an argument who is anxious to muster as many points as possible on his side—to show me that I was in the wrong and herself in the right: 'But my aunt never knew anybody at Infreville, and I've never been near the place.' She had forgotten the lie that she had told me one afternoon about the touchy lady with whom she simply must go and have tea, even if by visiting this lady she were to forfeit my friendship and shorten her own life. I did not remind her of her lie. But it shattered me. And once again I postponed our rupture to another day. A person has no need of sincerity, nor even of skill in lying, in order to be loved. Here I mean by love reciprocal torture.

I saw nothing reprehensible that evening in speaking to her as my grandmother—that mirror of perfection—used to speak to me, nor, when I told her that I would escort her to the Verdurins', in having adopted the brusque manner of my father, who would never inform us of any decision except in a manner calculated to cause us the maximum of agitation, out of all proportion to the decision itself. So that it was easy for him to call us absurd for appearing so distressed by so small a matter, our distress corresponding in reality to the perturbation that he had aroused in us. And if—like the inflexible wisdom of my grandmother—these arbitrary whims of my father's had been passed on to me to complement the sensitive nature to which they had so long remained alien and, throughout my whole childhood, had caused so much suffering, that sensitive nature informed them very exactly as to the points at which they could most effectively be aimed: there is no better informer than a reformed thief, or a subject of the nation one is fighting. In certain untruthful families, a brother who has come to call without any apparent reason and makes some casual inquiry on the doorstep as he leaves, appearing scarcely to listen to the answer, indicates thereby to his brother that this inquiry was the sole object of his visit, for the brother is quite familiar with that air of detachment, those words uttered as though in parentheses and at the last moment, having frequently had recourse to them himself. Similarly, there are pathological families, kindred sensibilities, fraternal temperaments, initiated into that mute language which enables the members of a family to understand each other without speaking. Thus who can be more nerve-racking than a neurotic? And then there may have been a deeper and more general cause for my behaviour in these cases. In those brief but inevitable moments when we hate someone we love—moments which last sometimes for a whole lifetime in the case of people we do not love—we do not wish to appear kind in order not to be pitied, but at once as unpleasant and as happy as possible so that our happiness may be truly hateful and wound to the very soul the occasional or permanent enemy. To how many people have I not untruthfully maligned myself, simply in order that my 'successes' might seem to them the more immoral and infuriate them the more! The proper thing to do would be to take the opposite course, to show without arrogance that we have generous feelings, instead of taking such pains to hide them. And this would be easy if we were capable of never hating, of always loving. For then we should be so happy to say only the things that can make other people happy, melt their hearts, make them love us.

True, I felt some remorse at being so insufferable to Albertine, and said to myself: 'If I didn't love her, she would be more grateful to me, for I wouldn't be nasty to her; but no, it would be the same in the end, for I should also be less nice.' And I might, in order to justify myself, have told her that I loved her. But the avowal of that love, apart from the fact that it would have told Albertine nothing new, would perhaps have made her colder towards me than the harshness and deceit for which love was the sole excuse. To be harsh and deceitful to the person whom we love is so natural! If the interest that we show towards other people does not prevent us from being gentle towards them and complying with their wishes, it is because our interest is not sincere. Other people leave us indifferent, and indifference does not prompt us to unkindness.

The evening was drawing to a close. Before Albertine went to bed, there was no time to lose if we wished to make peace, to renew our embraces. Neither of us had yet taken the initiative.

Meanwhile, feeling that in any case she was angry with me, I took the opportunity of mentioning Esther Lévy. 'Bloch tells me,' I said untruthfully, 'that you're a great friend of his cousin Esther.'

'I shouldn't know her if I saw her,' said Albertine with a vague look.

'I've seen her photograph,' I continued angrily. I did not look at Albertine as I said this, so that I did not see her expression, which would have been her sole reply, for she said nothing.

It was no longer the peace of my mother's kiss at Combray that I felt when I was with Albertine on these evenings, but, on the contrary, the anguish of those on which my mother scarcely bade me good-night, or even did not come up to my room at all, either because she was cross with me or was kept downstairs by guests. This anguish— not merely its transposition into love but this anguish itself—which for a time had specialised in love and which, when the separation, the division of the passions occurred, had been assigned to love alone, now seemed once more to be extending to them all, to have become indivisible again as in my childhood, as though all my feelings, which trembled at the thought of my not being able to keep Albertine by my bedside, at once as a mistress, a sister, a daughter, and as a mother too, of whose regular good-night kiss I was beginning once more to feel the childish need, had begun to coalesce, to become unified in the premature evening of my life which seemed fated to be as short as a winter day. But if I felt the same anguish as in my childhood, the different person who caused me to feel it, the difference in the feeling she inspired in me, the very transformation in my character, made it impossible for me to demand its appeasement from Albertine as in the old days from my mother. I could no longer say: 'I'm unhappy.' I confined myself, with a heavy heart, to speaking of inconsequential matters that took me no further towards a happy solution. I waded knee-deep in painful platitudes. And with that intellectual egoism which, if some insignificant fact happens to have a bearing on our love, makes us pay great respect to the person who has discovered it, as fortuitously perhaps as the fortune-teller who has foretold some trivial event which has afterwards come to pass, I came near to regarding Françoise as more inspired than Bergotte and Elstir because she had said to me at Balbec: 'That girl will bring you nothing but trouble.'

Every minute brought me nearer to Albertine's good-night, which at length she said. But that evening her kiss, from which she herself was absent and which made no impression on me, left me so anxious that, with a throbbing heart, I watched her make her way to the door, thinking: 'If I'm to find a pretext for calling her back, keeping her here, making peace with her, I must be quick; only a few steps and she will be out of the room, only two, now one, she's turning the handle; she's opening the door, it's too late, she has shut it behind her!' But perhaps it was not too late after all. As in the old days at Combray when my mother had left me without soothing me with her kiss, I wanted to rush after Albertine, I felt that there would be no peace for me until I had seen her again, that this renewed encounter would turn into something tremendous which it had not been before and that—if I did not succeed by my own efforts in ridding myself of this misery—I might perhaps acquire the shameful habit of going to beg from Albertine. I sprang out of bed when she was already in her room, I paced up and down the corridor, hoping that she would come out of her room and call me; I stood stock-still outside her door for fear of failing to hear some faint summons, I returned for a moment to my own room to see whether she might not by some lucky chance have forgotten her handkerchief, her bag, something which I might have appeared to be afraid of her needing during the night, and which would have given me an excuse for going to her room. No, there was nothing. I returned to my station outside her door, but the crack beneath it no longer showed any light. Albertine had put out the light, she was in bed; I remained there motionless, hoping for some lucky accident which did not occur; and long afterwards, frozen, I returned to bestow myself between my own sheets and cried for the rest of the night.

But on certain such evenings I had recourse to a ruse which won me Albertine's kiss. Knowing how quickly sleep came to her as soon as she lay down (she knew it also, for, instinctively, before lying down, she would take off the slippers which I had given her, and her ring which she placed by the bedside, as she did in her own room when she went to bed), knowing how heavy her sleep was, how affectionate her awakening, I would find an excuse for going to look for something and make her lie down on my bed. When I returned she would be asleep and I saw before me the other woman that she became whenever one saw her full-face. But her personality quickly changed when I lay down beside her and saw her again in profile. I could take her head, lift it up, press her face to my lips, put her arms round my neck, and she would continue to sleep, like a watch that never stops, like an animal that stays in whatever position you put it in, like a climbing plant, a convolvulus which continues to thrust out its tendrils whatever support you give it. Only her breathing was altered by each touch of my fingers, as though she were an instrument on which I was playing and from which I extracted modulations by drawing different notes from one after another of its strings. My jealousy subsided, for I felt that Albertine had become a creature that breathes and is nothing else besides, as was indicated by the regular suspiration in which is expressed that pure physiological function which, wholly fluid, has the solidity neither of speech nor of silence; and, in its ignorance of all evil, drawn seemingly rather from a hollowed reed than from a human being, that breath, truly paradisiacal to me who at such moments felt Albertine to be withdrawn from everything, not only physically but morally, was the pure song of the angels. And yet, in that breathing, I thought to myself of a sudden that perhaps many names of people, borne on the stream of memory, must be revolving.

Sometimes indeed the human voice was added to that music. Albertine would murmur a few words. How I longed to catch their meaning! It would happen that the name of a person of whom we had been speaking and who had aroused my jealousy would come to her lips, but without making me unhappy, for the memory that it brought with it seemed to be only that of the conversations that she had had with me on the subject. One evening, however, when with her eyes still shut she half awoke, she said tenderly, addressing me: 'Andrée.' I concealed my emotion. 'You're dreaming, I'm not Andrée,' I said to her, smiling. She smiled also: 'Of course not, I wanted to ask you what Andrée said to you this evening.' 'I assumed that you used to lie beside her like that.' 'Oh no, never,' she said. But, before making this reply, she had hidden her face for a moment in her hands. So her silences were merely screens, her surface affection merely kept beneath the surface a thousand memories which would have rent my heart, her life was full of those incidents the good-natured, bantering account of which forms one's daily gossip at the expense of other people, people who do not matter, but which, so long as a woman remains buried in the depths of one's heart, seem to us so precious a revelation of her life that, for the privilege of exploring that underlying world, we would gladly sacrifice our own. Then her sleep would seem to me a marvellous and magic world in which at certain moments there rises from the depths of the barely translucent element the avowal of a secret which we shall not understand. But as a rule, when Albertine was asleep, she seemed to have recaptured her innocence. In the attitude which I had imposed upon her, but which in her sleep she had speedily made her own, she seemed to trust herself to me. Her face had lost any expression of cunning or vulgarity, and between herself and me, towards whom she raised her arm, on whom she rested her hand, there seemed to be an absolute surrender, an indissoluble attachment. Her sleep moreover did not separate her from me and allowed her to retain the consciousness of our affection; its effect was rather to abolish everything else; I would kiss her, tell her that I was going to take a turn outside, and she would half-open her eyes and say to me with a look of surprise—for the hour was indeed late—'But where are you off to, my darling———'(calling me by my Christian name), and at

once fall asleep again. Her sleep was no more than a sort
of blotting out of the rest of her life, an even silence over
which from time to time familiar words of tenderness
would pass in their flight. By putting these words together,
one might have arrived at the unalloyed conversation, the
secret intimacy of a pure love. This calm slumber delighted
me, as a mother, reckoning it a virtue, is delighted by her
child's sound sleep. And her sleep was indeed that of a
child. Her awakening also, so natural and so loving, before
she even knew where she was, that I sometimes asked
myself with dread whether she had been in the habit,
before coming to live with me, of not sleeping alone but of
finding, when she opened her eyes, someone lying by her
side. But her childlike grace was more striking. Like a
mother again, I marvelled that she should always awake in
such a good humour. After a few moments she would
recover consciousness, would utter charming words,
unconnected with one another, mere twitterings. By a sort
of reversal of roles, her throat, which as a rule one seldom
remarked, now almost startlingly beautiful, had acquired
the immense importance which her eyes, by being closed
in sleep, had lost, her eyes, my regular interlocutors to
which I could no longer address myself after the lids had
closed over them. Just as the closed lids impart an innocent, grave beauty to the face by suppressing all that the
eyes express only too plainly, there was in the words, not
devoid of meaning but interrupted by moments of silence,
which Albertine uttered as she awoke, a pure beauty of a

kind that is not constantly tarnished, as is conversation, by habits of speech, stale repetitions, traces of familiar defects. Moreover, when I had decided to wake Albertine, I would have been able to do so without fear, knowing that her awakening would bear no relation to the evening that we had passed together, but would emerge from her sleep as morning emerges from night. As soon as she had begun to open her eyes with a smile, she would have offered me her lips, and before she had even said a word, I would have savoured their freshness, as soothing as that of a garden still silent before the break of day.

MARCEL PROUST was a French novelist and critic who is frequently named as the most important writer of the twentieth century. A socialite amongst France's fading aristocracy, he published essays on art and literary criticism before embarking on one of modern literature's most ambitious and influential projects, his multi-volume novel, *In Search of Lost Time*.

Although Proust's work is best known for madeleines and its exploration of memory, jealousy is an ever-present force through-out. Volume V of *In Search of Lost Time* (from which this book is taken) has at its heart the ill-fated love affair between the novel's narrator and his childhood sweetheart, Albertine. The depiction of jealousy that eventually consumes them is said to be closely modelled on Proust's own failed romances.

Plagued by ill health, Proust retreated from Parisian society for the last years of his life. He died in 1922.

RECOMMENDED BOOKS BY MARCEL PROUST:

In Search of Lost Time, Volumes I–VI

Is there more to love than Jealousy?

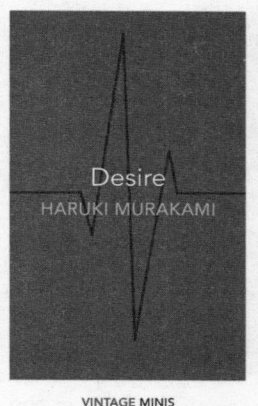

Desire
HARUKI MURAKAMI

VINTAGE MINIS

Eating
NIGELLA LAWSON

VINTAGE MINIS

Home
SALMAN RUSHDIE

VINTAGE MINIS

Babies
ANNE ENRIGHT

VINTAGE MINIS

VINTAGE MINIS

The Vintage Minis bring you the world's greatest writers on the experiences that make us human. These stylish, entertaining little books explore the whole spectrum of life – from birth to death, and everything in between. Which means there's something here for everyone, whatever your story.

Desire	Haruki Murakami
Love	Jeanette Winterson
Babies	Anne Enright
Language	Xiaolu Guo
Motherhood	Helen Simpson
Fatherhood	Karl Ove Knausgaard
Summer	Laurie Lee
Jealousy	Marcel Proust
Sisters	Louisa May Alcott
Home	Salman Rushdie
Race	Toni Morrison
Liberty	Virginia Woolf
Swimming	Roger Deakin
Work	Joseph Heller
Depression	William Styron
Drinking	John Cheever
Eating	Nigella Lawson
Psychedelics	Aldous Huxley
Calm	Tim Parks
Death	Julian Barnes

vintageminis.co.uk

3 5 7 9 10 8 6 4

Vintage
20 Vauxhall Bridge Road,
London SW1V 2SA

Vintage Classics is part of the Penguin Random House
group of companies whose addresses can be found at
global.penguinrandomhouse.com.

Penguin
Random House
UK

How To Eat was first published in Great Britain by Chatto & Windus in 1998
Kitchen was first published in Great Britain by Chatto & Windus in 2010

This edition published by Vintage in 2017

www.vintage-books.co.uk

A CIP catalogue record for this book is available from the British Library

ISBN 9781784872656

Typeset in 9.5/14.5 pt FreightText Pro
by Jouve (UK), Milton Keynes
Printed and bound by Clays Ltd, St Ives plc

Penguin Random House is committed to a sustainable future for
our business, our readers and our planet. This book is made from
Forest Stewardship Council® certified paper.

MIX
Paper from
responsible sources
FSC® C018179

Eating
NIGELLA LAWSON

VINTAGE MINIS

Contents

Preface

COOKING IS NOT about just joining the dots, following one recipe slavishly and then moving on to the next. It's about developing an understanding of food, a sense of assurance in the kitchen, about the simple desire to make yourself something to eat. And in cooking, as in writing, you must please yourself to please others. Strangely it can take enormous confidence to trust your own palate, follow your own instincts. Without habit, which itself is just trial and error, this can be harder than following the most elaborate of recipes. But it's what works, what's important.

There is a reason why this volume is called Eating rather than Cooking. It's a simple one: although it's possible to love eating without being able to cook, I don't believe you can ever really cook unless you love eating. Such love, of course, is not something which can be taught, but it can be conveyed – and maybe that's the point. In writing this book, I wanted to make food and my slavering passion for it the starting point; indeed for me it *was* the starting point. I have nothing to declare but my greed.

The French, who've lost something of their culinary confidence in recent years, remain solid on this front. Some years ago in France, in response to the gastronomic apathy and consequent lowering of standards nationally – what is known as *la crise* – Jack Lang, then Minister of Culture, initiated *la semaine du goût*. He set up a body expressly to go into schools and other institutions not to teach anyone how to cook, but how to eat. This group might take with it a perfect baguette, an exquisite cheese, some local speciality cooked *comme il faut*, some fruit and vegetables grown properly and picked when ripe, in the belief that if the pupils, if people generally, tasted what was good, what was right, they would respect these traditions; by eating good food, they would want to cook it. And so the cycle continues.

I suppose you could say that we, over here, have had our own unofficial version of this. Our gastronomic awakening – or however, and with whatever degree of irony, you want to describe it – has been to a huge extent restaurant-led. It is, you might argue, by tasting food that we have become interested in cooking it. I do not necessarily disparage the influence of the restaurant: I spent twelve years as a restaurant critic, after all. But restaurant food and home food are not the same thing. Or, more accurately, eating in restaurants is not the same thing as eating at home. Which is not to say, of course, that you can't

borrow from restaurant menus and adapt their chefs'
recipes – and I do. This leads me to the other reason this
book is about How to Eat.

I am not a chef. I am not even a trained or professional
cook. My qualification is as an eater. I cook what I want to
eat – within limits. I have a job – another job, that is, as an
ordinary working journalist – and two children, one of
whom was born during the writing of this book. And during the book's gestation, I would sometimes plan to cook
some wonderful something or other, then work out a
recipe, apply myself in anticipatory fantasy to it, write out
the shopping list, plan the dinner – and then find that
when it came down to it I just didn't have the energy. Anything that was too hard, too fiddly, filled me with dread and
panic or, even if attempted, didn't work or was unreasonably demanding, has not found its way in here. And the
recipes I do include have all been cooked in what television people call Real Time: menus have been made with all
their component parts, together; that way, I know whether
the oven settings correspond, whether you'll have enough
hob space, how to make the timings work and how not to
have a nervous breakdown about it. I wanted food that can
be made and eaten in a real life, not in perfect, isolated
laboratory conditions.

Much of this is touched upon throughout the book, but
I want to make it clear, here and now, that you need to
acquire your own individual sense of what food is about,
rather than just a vast collection of recipes.

What I am not talking about, however, is strenuous originality. The innovative in cooking all too often turns out to be inedible. The great Modernist dictum, Make It New, is not a helpful precept in the kitchen. 'Too often,' wrote the great society hostess and arch foodwriter Ruth Lowinsky, as early as 1935, 'the inexperienced think that if food is odd it must be a success. An indifferently roasted leg of mutton is not transformed by a sauce of hot raspberry jam, nor a plate of watery consommé improved by the addition of three glacé cherries.' With food, authenticity is not the same thing as originality; indeed they are often at odds. So while much is my own here – insofar as anything can be – many of the recipes included are derived from other writers. From the outset I wanted this book to be, in part, an anthology of the food I love eating and a way of paying my respects to the foodwriters I've loved reading. Throughout I've wanted, on principle as well as to show my gratitude, to credit honestly wherever appropriate, but I certainly wish to signal my thanks here as well. And if at any time a recipe has found its way onto these pages without having its source properly documented, I assure you and the putative unnamed originator that this is due to ignorance rather than villainy.

But if I question the tyranny of the recipe, that isn't to say I take a cavalier attitude. A recipe has to work. Even the great abstract painters have first to learn figure drawing. If many of my recipes seem to stretch out for a daunting number of pages, it is because brevity is no guarantee of simplicity. The easiest way to learn how to cook is by watching; and bearing that in mind I have tried more to talk you through a recipe than bark out instructions. As much as possible, I have wanted to make you feel that I'm there with you, in the kitchen, as you cook. The book that follows is the conversation we might be having.

Basics etc.

THE GREAT CULINARY Renaissance we hear so much about has done many things – given us extra virgin olive oil, better restaurants and gastroporn – but it hasn't taught us how to cook.

Of course standards have improved. Better ingredients are available to us now, and more people know about them. Food and cookery have become more than respectable: they are fashionable. But the renaissance of British cookery, as it was relentlessly tagged in the late 1980s, started in the restaurant and filtered its way into the home. This is the wrong way round. Cooking is best learned at your own stove: you learn by watching and by doing. Chefs themselves know this. The great chefs of France and Italy learn about food at home: what they do later, in the restaurants that make them famous, is use what they have learnt. They build on it, they start elaborating. They take home cooking to the restaurant, not the restaurant school of cookery to the home. Inverting the process is like learning a vocabulary without any grammar. The analogy is pertinent. In years as a restaurant critic, I couldn't help noticing that however fine the menu, some chefs, for all that they seem to have mastered the idiom, have no authentic language of their own. We are at risk, here, of becoming a land of culinary mimics. There are some things you just cannot learn from a professional chef. I am not talking of home economics – the rules that govern what food does when you apply heat or introduce air or whatever – but of home cooking, and of how experience builds organically. For there is more to cooking than being able to put on a good show. Of course there are advantages in an increased awareness of and enthusiasm for food, but the danger is that it excites an appetite for new recipes, new ingredients: follow a recipe once and then – on to the next. Cooking isn't like that. The point about real-life cooking is that your proficiency grows exponentially. You cook something once, then again, and again. Each time you add something different (leftovers from the fridge, whatever might be in the kitchen or in season) and what you end up with differs also.

You can learn how to cook fancy food from the colour supplements, but you need the basics. And anyway, it is better to be able to roast a chicken than to be a dab hand with focaccia. I would be exhausted if the cooking I did every day was recipe-index food. I don't want to cook like that all the time, and I certainly don't want to eat like that.

Nor do I want to go back to some notional golden age

of nursery food. I wasn't brought up on shepherd's pie and bread-and-butter pudding and I'm not going to start living on them now. It is interesting, though, that these homely foods have not been revived in our homes – they have been rediscovered by restaurants. And, even if I don't wish to eat this sort of thing all the time, isn't it more appropriate to learn how to cook it at home than to have to go to a restaurant to eat it?

By invoking the basics I certainly don't mean to evoke a grim, puritanical self-sufficiency, with austere recipes for home-made bread and stern admonishments against buying any form of food ready cooked. I have no wish to go on a crusade. I doubt I will ever become someone who habitually bakes her own bread – after all, shopping for good food is just as much of a pleasure as cooking it can be. But there is something between grinding your own flour and cooking only for special occasions. Cooking has become too much of a device by which to impress people rather than simply to feed them pleasurably.

IN LITERATURE, TEACHERS talk about key texts: they exist, too, in cooking. That's what I mean by basics.

Everyone's list of basics is, of course, different. Your idea of home cooking, your whole experience of eating, colours your sense of what foods should be included in the culinary canon. Cooking, indeed, is not so very different from literature: what you have read previously shapes how you read now. And so we eat; and so we cook.

If I don't include your nostalgic favourite in this chapter, you may find a recipe for it in *How to Eat*. And it is impossible to write a list without being painfully aware of what has been missed out: cooking is not an exclusive art, whatever its grander exponents might lead you to think. Being familiar with making certain dishes – so familiar that you don't need to look in a book to make them (and much of this chapter should eventually make itself redundant) – doesn't preclude you from cooking other things.

So what are basic dishes? Everyone has to know how to roast chicken, pork, beef, game, lamb: what to do with slabs of meat. This is not abstruse knowledge, but general information so basic that many books don't bother to mention it. I am often telephoned by friends at whose houses I have eaten something more elaborate than I would ever cook, to be asked how long their leg of lamb needs to be in the oven and at what temperature.

The key texts constitute the framework of your repertoire: stews, roasts, white sauce, mayonnaise, stocks, soups. You might also think of tackling pastry.

Because the English don't any longer have a firmly based culinary tradition – and, even at its solid best, English cookery never had anything like the range and variation of, say, regional French cooking – we tend to lack an enduring respect for particular dishes. It's not so much that we hunger to eat whatever is fashionable as that we drop anything that is no longer of the moment. The tendency is not exclusively English – if you were to go to a grand dinner party in France or Italy, you might be served whatever was considered the culinary *dernier cri* – but what makes our behaviour more emphatic, more ultimately sterile, is that we don't seem to cook any food other than style-conscious dinner-party food.

I think it is true, too, that we are quick to despise what once we looked at so breathlessly in colour supplements and delicatessens. Just because a food is no longer flavour of the month, it shouldn't follow that it is evermore to be spoken of as a shameful aberration. It is important always to judge honestly and independently. This can be harder than it sounds. Fashion has a curious but compelling urgency. Even those of us who feel we are free of fashion's diktats are, despite ourselves, influenced by them. As what is seemingly desirable changes, so our eye changes. It doesn't have to be wholesale conversion for this effect to take place: we just begin to look at things differently.

Of course, fashion may lead us to excesses. It is easy to ascribe the one-time popularity of nouvelle cuisine – which fashion decrees we must now treat as hootingly risible – to just such an excess. And to some extent that would be correct. But what some people forget is that the most ludicrous excesses of nouvelle cuisine were not follies committed by its most talented exponents but by the second and third rank. It is important to distinguish between what is fashionable and good and what is fashionable and bad.

With food it should be easier to maintain your integrity: you must, after all, always know whether you enjoy the taste of something or not. And in cooking as in eating, you just have to let your real likes and desires guide you.

MY LIST OF basics – and the recipes that constitute it – are dotted throughout this book. The list is eclectic. And in this chapter I have tried, in the main, to stay with the sort of food most of us anyway presume we can cook; it's only when we get started that we realise we need to look something up, check times, remind ourselves of the quantities. I want to satisfy those very basic demands without in any way wishing to make you feel as if there were some actual list of recipes which you needed to master before acquiring some notional and wholly goal-oriented culinary expertise. My aim is not to promote notions of uniformity or consistency – or even to imply that either might be desirable – but to suggest a way of cooking which isn't simply notching up recipes. In short, cooking in context.

First, you have to know how to do certain things, things that years ago it was taken for granted would be learned at home. These are ordinary kitchen skills, such as how to make pastry or a white sauce.

I learned some of these things with my mother in the kitchen when I was a child, but not all of them. So I understand the fearfulness that grips you just as you anticipate rolling out some shortcrust, say. We ate no puddings at home, my mother didn't bake and nor did my grandmothers. I didn't acquire early in life that lazy confidence, that instinct. When I cook a stew I have a sense, automatically, of whether I want to use red or white wine, of what will happen if I add anchovies or bacon. But when I bake I feel I lack that instinct, though I hope I am beginning to acquire it.

And of course I have faltered, made mistakes, cooked disasters. I know what it's like to panic in the kitchen, to feel flustered by a recipe which lists too many ingredients or takes for granted too much expertise or dexterity.

I don't think the answer, though, is to avoid anything that seems, on first view, complicated or involves elaborate procedures. That just makes you feel more fearful. But what is extraordinarily liberating is trying something – say, pastry – and finding out that, left quietly to your own devices, you can actually do it. What once seemed an arcane skill becomes second nature. It does happen.

And how it happens is by repetition. If you haven't made pastry before, follow the recipe for shortcrust on page 30. Make a flan. Don't leave it too long to make another one. Or a pie or a savoury tart. The point is to get used gradually to cooking something in the ordinary run of things. I concede that it might mean having to make more of a conscious effort in the beginning, but the time and concentration needed will recede naturally, and the effort will soon cease altogether to be conscious. It will just become part of what you do.

Basic roast chicken

You could probably get through life without knowing how to roast a chicken, but the question is, would you want to?

When I was a child we had roast chicken at Saturday lunch, and probably one evening a week, too. Even when there were only a few of us, my mother never roasted just one chicken; she cooked two, one to keep in the fridge, cold and whole, for picking at during the week. It's partly for that reason that a roast chicken, to me, smells of home, of family, of food that carries some important, extra-culinary weight.

My basic roast chicken is the same as my mother's: I stick half a lemon up its bottom, smear some oil or butter on its breast, sprinkle it with a little salt, and put it in a gas mark 6/200°C oven for about 20 minutes per 500g plus 30 minutes.

My mother could make the stringiest, toughest flesh – a bird that had been intensively farmed and frozen since the last Ice Age – taste as if it were a lovingly reared poulet de Bresse. She, you see, was a product of her age, which believed that cooking lay in what you did to inferior products (and I expect she did no more in this case than use much more butter than anyone would now); I, however, am a product of mine, which believes that you always use the best, the freshest produce of the highest quality you can afford – and then do as little as possible to it. So I buy organic free-range chickens and anoint them with the tiniest amount of extra virgin olive oil or butter – as if I were

You could probably get through life without knowing how to roast a chicken, but the question is, would you want to?

putting on very expensive handcream – before putting them in the oven. I retain the lemon out of habit – and to make my kitchen smell like my mother's, with its aromatic, oily-sharp fug.

I can't honestly say that my roast chicken tastes better than hers, but I don't like eating intensively farmed, battery-reared meat. However, if you know you've got an inferior bird in front of you, cook it for the first hour breast side down. This means you don't, at the end, have quite that glorious effect of the swelling, burnished breast – the chicken will have more of a flapper's bosom, flat but fleshy – but the white meat will be more tender because all the fats and juices will have oozed their way into it.

If you want to make a good gravy – and I use the term to indicate a meat-thick golden juice or, risking pretentiousness here, *jus* – then put 1 tablespoon of olive oil in the roasting dish when you anoint the bird before putting it in the oven, and about half an hour before the end add another tablespoon of oil and a spritz from the lemon half that isn't stuffed up the chicken. By all means use butter if you prefer, but make sure there's some oil in the pan, too, to stop the butter from burning.

When you remove the chicken, let it stand for 5 or 10 minutes before carving it, and make gravy by putting the roasting dish on the hob (remove, if you want, any excess fat with a spoon, though I tend to leave it as it is). Add a little white wine and boiling water or chicken stock, letting it all bubble away till it's syrupy and chickeny. If you don't have to hand any home-made stock a stock cube, or portion thereof, would be fine. In fact, Italians sometimes put a stock cube inside the chicken along with or instead of the lemon half before roasting it.

My basic chicken recipe also includes garlic and shallots; this is the easy way to have dinner on the table without doing much. About 50 minutes before the end of the cooking time, pour 2 tablespoons olive oil either into the same pan or another one and add the unpeeled cloves of 2 heads of garlic and about 20 unpeeled shallots. They don't roast, really, but steam inside their skins, which on the garlic are like boiled-sweet wrappers, on the shallots like twists of brown paper. Eat them by pressing on them with a fork, and letting the soft, mild – that's to say intensely flavoured and yet wholly without pungency – creamy interior squeeze out on to your plate. Put some plates on the table for the discarded skins, and if not finger bowls then napkins or a roll of paper towel. My children adore garlic and shallots cooked like this, and sometimes, when I don't want to cook a whole chicken for them, I roast a poussin instead and put the shallots and garlic and poussin in all at the same time. And if you want to make this basic recipe feel a little less basic, then you can sprinkle some toasted pine nuts and flat-leaf parsley, chopped at the last minute, over the food before serving.

If you've managed to fit the garlic and shallots in the tray with the chicken, you can roast a tray of potatoes in the same oven at the same time. Dice the potatoes, also unpeeled, into approximately 1cm cubes, or just cut new potatoes in half lengthways, and anoint them with oil (or melted lard, which fries them fabulously crisp). Sprinkle them with a little dried thyme (or freshly chopped rosemary) before cooking them for 1 hour to 1 hour 10 minutes.

All of which leads us to the next basic recipe:

Stock

Do not throw away the chicken carcass after eating the chicken. Go so far, I'd say, as to scavenge from everyone's plate, picking up the bones they've left. I'm afraid I even do this in other people's houses. You don't need to make stock now – and indeed you couldn't make anything very useful from the amount of bones from one bird – but freeze them. Indeed freeze whatever bones you can, whenever you can, in order to make stock at some later date (see page 47 for further, passionate, adumbration of this thesis).

   An actual recipe for stock would be hard to give with a straight face; boiling remains up to make stock is as far from being a precise art as you can get. There are recipes in *How to Eat* for broth and consommé if you want something highfalutin', but if you're looking for what I call chicken stock (but which classically trained French chefs, who would use fresh meat and raw bones, boiled up specifically to make stock, would most definitely not), then follow my general instructions. At home, I would use the carcasses of 3 medium, cooked chickens.

Break the bones up roughly and put them in a big pan. Add a stick of celery broken in two or a few lovage leaves, 1 or 2 carrots, depending on size, peeled and halved, 1 onion stuck with a clove, 5 peppercorns, a bouquet garni, some parsley stalks and the white of a leek. Often I have more or less everything to hand without trying, except for that leek; in which case I just leave it out. (At the time of writing, it is still permitted to buy veal shin, and I sometimes add a couple of discs if I want a deeper-toned broth of almost unctuous mellowness.) Cover with cold water, add 1 teaspoon of salt and bring to the boil, skimming off the froth and scum that rises to the surface. Lower the heat and let the stock bubble very, very gently, uncovered, for about 3 hours. Allow to cool a little, then strain into a wide, large bowl or another pan. When cold, put in the fridge without decanting yet. I like to let it chill in the fridge so that I can remove any fat that rises to the surface, and the wider that surface is, the easier.

When I've removed the fat, I taste the stock and consider whether I'd prefer it stronger flavoured. If so, I put it back in a pan on the hob and boil it down till I've got a smaller amount of rich, intensely flavoured stock.

I then store it in differing quantities in the freezer. On the whole, the amount of stock I find most useful is in packages of 150ml and 300ml. For the smaller amount, I just ladle ten tablespoons into a freezer bag or small tub with a lid; for the larger, I line a measuring jug with a freezer bag and pour it in till I've got, give or take, 300ml (it's difficult, because of the baggy lining, to judge with super-calibrated accuracy). I then twist on the tie-up and put the whole thing, jug and all, into the freezer. This is why I own so many plastic measuring jugs. I am constantly forgetting about them once they're buried in the freezer. But, in principle, what you should do is leave the stock till solid, then whisk away the jug, leaving the jug-shaped cylinder of frozen liquid, which you slot back into the deep-freeze. You may need to run hot water over the jug for a minute in order to let the stock in its bag just slip out. This is a useful way to freeze any liquid. Although it's a bore, it pays to measure accurately and to label clearly at the time of freezing. Later you can take out exactly the quantity you need.

Poussins make wonderful, strong, easily jellied stock; it must be the amount of zip and gelatin in their poor young bones. So if ever you need to make a stock from scratch, with fresh meat, not cooked bones (in other words the way you're supposed to), and you can't find a boiling fowl, then buy some poussins, about 4, cut each in half, use vegetables as above, cover with cold water and proceed as normal.

And I do not disapprove of stock cubes, if they're good.

ONE OF THE most useful things an Italian friend once showed me was how important even half a stick of celery is in providing base-note flavour, not just to stocks, but to tomato and meat sauces, to pies, in fact to almost anything savoury. The taste is not boorishly celery-like; it just provides an essential floor of flavour.

In Italy, when you buy vegetables from the greengrocer you can ask for a bunch of *odori*, which is a bunch of those herbs which breathe their essential scent into sauces and is given, gratis. Included in it will be one stick of celery. And I wish we could buy, let alone get for free, celery by the single stick in Britain. You need so little of it when cooking, and most of what's on sale anyway – white, limp and waterlogged – scarcely repays the eating. If I can get huge, leafy, green Spanish or Italian celery, I mind less about having to buy a whole bunch; apart from anything else it looks beautiful in a vase in the kitchen. But those leaf-stripped, bendy-stalked clumps of waxy-white celery that are normally on sale, especially in the supermarkets, are the saddest of dismal forced-hand purchases.

You should grow your own herbs if you can and want to, but don't spread yourself, or your plants, too thinly. It is counter-productive if you have so little of each herb that you never pick much of it for fear of totally denuding your stock. In my own garden, I stick to rosemary, flat-leaf parsley, rocket and sorrel. I like to grow lots of parsley – at least two rows, the length of the whole bed – and even more rocket. Some years I've planted garlic so that I can use the gloriously infused leaves, as they grow, cut up freshly in a salad. In pots I keep bay, marjoram and mint. This year I'm going to try some angelica – to flavour custards – and Thai basil, so that I don't have to go to the Thai shop to buy huge bunches of the stuff, wonderfully aromatic though it is, only to see it go off before I've had a chance to use it all. I have never had any success with coriander (from seed). I can manage basil easily, but then I suddenly feel overrun. And I have to say, I find watering pots excruciatingly effortful.

As with so much to do with food, a lot of a little rather than a little of a lot is the best, most comforting and most useful rule. You can always buy herbs growing in pots, in season, at good supermarkets and garden centres, and herbs cut in big bunches in specialist shops and good greengrocers.

Mayonnaise

Stock is what you may make out of the bones of your roasted chicken, but mayonnaise, real mayonnaise, is what you might make to eat with the cold, leftover meat. There is one drawback: when you actually make mayonnaise you realise, beyond the point of insistent denial, how much oil goes into it. But since even the best bottled mayonnaise bears little or no relation to real mayonnaise, you may as well know how to make it. And it really isn't difficult.

When I was in my teens, I loved Henry James. I read him with uncorrupted pleasure. Then, when I was eighteen or so, and had just started *The Golden Bowl*, someone – older, cleverer, whose opinions were offered gravely – asked me whether I didn't find James very difficult, as she always did. Until then, I had no idea that I might, and I didn't. From that moment, I couldn't read him but self-consciously; from then on, I did find him difficult. I do not wish to insult by the comparison, but I had a similar, Jamesian mayonnaise experience. My mother used to make mayonnaise weekly, twice weekly; we children would help. I had no idea it was meant to be difficult, or that it was thought to be such a nerve-racking ordeal. Then someone asked how I managed to be so breezy about it, how I stopped it from curdling. From then on, I scarcely made a mayonnaise which didn't split. It's not surprising: when confidence is undermined or ruptured, it can be difficult to do the simplest things, or to take any enjoyment even in trying.

I don't deny that mayonnaises can split, but please don't jinx yourself. Anyway, it's not a catastrophe if it does. A small drop of boiling water can fix things, and if it doesn't, you can start again with an egg yolk in a bowl. Beat it and slowly beat in the curdled mess of mayo you were previously working on. Later add more oil and a little lemon juice. You should, this way, end up with the smoothly amalgamated yellow ointment you were after in the first place. I hate to say it, but you may have to do this twice. You may end up with rather more mayonnaise than you need, but getting it right in the end restores your confidence, and this is the important thing.

I make mayonnaise the way my mother did: I warm the eggs in the bowl (as explained more fully later) then beat and add oil just from the bottle, not measuring, until the texture feels right, feels like mayonnaise. I squeeze in lemon juice, also freehand, until the look and taste feel right. If you make a habit of making mayonnaise, you will inevitably come to judge it instinctively too. I don't like too much olive oil in it: if it's too strong it rasps the back of the throat, becomes too invasive. I use a little over two-thirds groundnut oil and a little under one-third olive oil, preferably that lovely mild stuff from Liguria. If you prefer, do use half and half and a mild French olive oil, which is probably more correct, anyway, than the Italian variety.

By habit, and maternal instruction, I always used to use an ordinary whisk. This takes a long time (and I can see why my mother used us, her children, as *commis* chefs). Now I use my KitchenAid (similar to a Kenwood Chef, but American) with the wire whip in place. You can equally well use one of those electric hand-held whisks, which are cheap and useful. Please, whatever you do, don't use a food processor: if you do, your finished product tastes just like the gluey bought stuff. And then, hell, you might as well just go out and buy it.

2 egg yolks (but wait to separate the eggs, and see below)
225ml groundnut or sunflower oil

75ml extra virgin olive oil
juice of ½ lemon

Put the eggs, in their shells, in a large bowl. Fill it with warm water from the tap and leave for 10 minutes. (This brings eggs and bowl comfortably to room temperature, which will help stop the eggs from curdling, but is optional, as long as you remember to take the eggs out of the fridge well before you need them.) Then remove the eggs, get rid of the water and dry the bowl thoroughly. Wet and then wring out a tea towel and set the bowl on it; this stops it slipping and jumping about on the worksurface.

Separate the eggs. Put aside the whites and freeze them for another use, and let the yolks plop into the dried bowl. Start whisking the yolks with a pinch of salt. After a few minutes very, very gradually and drop by mean drop, add the groundnut oil. You must not rush this. It's easier to let the oil seep in gradually if you pour from a height, holding the measuring jug (or bottle with a spout attached, if you're not actually using measured quantities) well above the bowl. Keep going until you see a thick mayonnaise form, about 2–3 tablespoons' worth, then you can relax and let the oil drip in small glugs. When both oils have been incorporated (first the groundnut, then the olive oil) and you have a thick, smooth, firm mayonnaise, add a few squeezes of lemon juice, whisking all the time. Taste to see if you need to add more. Add salt and pepper as you like; my mother used white pepper, so she didn't end up with black specks.

Vinaigrette

ONE OF THE hangovers of the hostess-trolley age is the idea that the clever cook has a secret vinaigrette recipe which can transform the dullest lettuce into a Sensational Salad. I'm not sure I even have a regular vinaigrette recipe, let alone one with a winning, magic ingredient. But we all panic in the kitchen from time to time, so here is a useful, broad-brush reminder of how to compose a salad.

Plain salad dressing

I sometimes think the best way of dressing salad is to use just oil and lemon juice. The trick is to use the best possible olive oil – and as little of it as possible – and toss it far longer than you'd believe possible. Use your hands for this. Start off with 1 tablespoon of oil for a whole bowl of lettuce and keep tossing, adding more oil only when you are convinced the leaves need it. When all the leaves are barely covered with the thinnest film of oil, sprinkle over a scant ½ teaspoon sea salt. Toss again. Then squeeze over some lemon juice. Give a final fillip, then taste and adjust as necessary. Instead of lemon juice you can substitute wine vinegar (and I use red wine vinegar rather than white generally), but be sparing. Just as the perfect martini, it was always said, was made merely by tilting the vermouth bottle in the direction of the gin, so when making the perfect dressing you should merely point the cork of the vinegar bottle towards the oil.

As important is the composition of the salad itself. Keep it simple: there's a green salad, which is green; or there's a red salad, of tomatoes (and maybe onions). First-course salads may be granted a little extra leeway – the addition of something warm and sautéed – but I would never let a tomato find its way into anything leafy. For more detailed explanations (genetic as much as aesthetic) of this prejudice, please see page 95. When you're using those already-mixed packets of designer leaves, you should add one crunchy lettuce – cos or Webb – which you buy, radically and separately, as a lettuce and then tear up yourself at the last minute. Herbs – parsley, chives, chervil, lovage – are a good idea in a green salad (and you can add them either to the salad or the dressing), but, except on certain, rare, occasions, I think garlic is better left out.

Bread

BREAD IS BASIC in the staff-of-life sense, but making it is hardly a fundamental activity for most of us. I don't get the urge that often, but every time I have, and have consulted a suitable book, I have been directed to make wholemeal bread. You may as well bake hessian. Why should it be thought that only those who want wholemeal bread are the sort to bake their own? Good wholemeal bread is very hard to make, and I suspect needs heavy machinery or enormous practice and muscularity.

Anyway, I give you this recipe for old-fashioned white bread, really good white bread, the sort you eat with unsalted butter and jam – one loaf in a sitting, no trouble. The recipe comes from Foster's Bakery in Barnsley, South

Yorkshire, and found its way to me at a breadmaking work-shop given at the Flour Advisory Board in London by John Foster. He was an exceptional teacher, and completely turned me, a lifelong sceptic of the breadmaking tendency, into a would-be baker.

Basic white loaf

For a good white loaf such as even I can make convincingly – a small one, so double the quantities if you want a big loaf or a couple – you need:

300g strong flour

10g fresh yeast

10g salt (1 heaped teaspoon)

5g sugar (½ 1 teaspoon)

170ml tepid water

10g fat

Buy the best flour you can (and there are plenty of good mills in this country, most of which sell their flours through health stores) and use real yeast, not dried. Before you get put off, you should know two things. The first is that you can buy real yeast at any baker's, including the in-store bakeries of supermarkets; the second is that you use the real yeast here as you would easy-blend instant yeast – there's no frothing or blending or anything, you just add it to the mound of flour.

So: tip the flour onto a worktop and add the yeast, salt and sugar. Pour over the water and bring together, working with one hand, clawing at the floury mess rather as if your hand were a spider and your fingers the spider's legs. The spider analogy is apposite: you do have to be a bit 'If at first you don't suceed, try,

try again' about bread-making. As the dough starts to come together, add the fat – which can be lard (my favourite here), vegetable short-ening or oil – and keep squishing with your hands. When the dough has come together, begin kneading. Do this by stretching the dough away from you and working it into the worktop. Rub a little flour into your hands to remove any bits of dough that stick.

Keep kneading, pressing the heel of your hand into the dough, pushing the dough away, bringing it back and down against the work surface, for at least 10 minutes. John Foster warns that after 5 minutes you'll want to give up, and he's right. He suggests sing-ing a song to keep yourself going; I prefer listening to the radio or talking to someone, but maybe that's just the difference between northerner and southerner.

When the dough's properly mixed – after about 10 minutes – you can tell the difference; it suddenly feels smoother and less sticky. Bring it to a ball, flour the worktop and the piece of dough lightly, and cover with a plastic bag or sheet of clingfilm and a tea-towel and leave for 30 minutes.

Then knead again for 3 minutes. Flour the worktop and dough ball again, cover as before, and leave for another 30 minutes.

Flatten the dough to expel the gas bubbles. Fold it in half, then in half again, and again, and keep folding the dough over itself until it feels as if you can fold no longer, as if the dough itself resists it (rather than you can't bear it) and then shape it into a ball again. Flour the worktop and so forth, cover the dough and leave, this time for 10 minutes.

Then shape the dough as you want: either round or oval and smooth, or you can slash the top with a knife, or put in a greased

450g loaf tin. Now, place on the baking tray (or in its tin) and put it in a warm place, under a plastic bag, for an hour, before baking for 35 minutes in a preheated gas mark 8/220°C oven. The trick is to lift the bread up and knock the base; if it sounds hollow, it's cooked. Try to let the bread cool before eating it.

You can do the final proving in the fridge overnight (technically this is known as retarding). This doesn't cut out any work, but I find it makes things easier because I can do all the kneading when the children are in bed and before I go to bed (incidentally, it is, if not exactly calming, certainly very stress-relieving) and then bake the bread when I get up.

You do, however, need to increase the amount of yeast for this. Exactly how much you need to increase it by will depend on your fridge and the nature of your yeast. This may not be helpful, but it's true. Try doubling the yeast to 20g, then if the bread bolts when it's in the oven, you'll know to use 15g next time. When you get up in the morning preheat the oven, taking the bread out of the fridge on its baking tray as you do so. Leave it for 10 minutes or so, and then bake as above, maybe giving it an extra couple of minutes.

Pastry

ON THE SUBJECT of pastry, I am positively evangelical. Until fairly recently I practised heavy avoidance techniques, hastily, anxiously turning away from any recipe which included pastry, as if the cookbook's pages themselves were burning: I was hot with fear; could feel the flush rise in my panicky cheeks. I take strength from that, and so should you. Because if I can do the culinary equivalent, for me, of Learning to Love the Bomb, so can you.

It came upon me gradually. I made some plain shortcrust pastry, alone and in silence, apart from the comforting wall of voices emanating from Radio 4: it worked; I made some more. Then I tried some pâte sucrée: it worked; I made some more; it didn't. But the next time, it did; or rather, I dealt better with its difficulties. But shortcrust, or even rich shortcrust, is really easy, and that's all you need to know.

Shortcrust

At its simplest, pastry is just a quantity of flour mixed with half its weight in fat and bound with water.

So, to make enough plain shortcrust to line and cover a 23cm pie dish (in other words for a double-crust pie), you would mix 240g flour with 120g cold, diced fat (half lard or vegetable shortening and half butter for preference), rubbing the fat in with your fingertips until you have a bowl of floury breadcrumb or oatmeal-sized flakes. Then you add iced water until the flour and fat turn into a ball of dough; a few tablespoons should do it. But as simple as that is, I can make it simpler; or rather, I can make it easier, as easy as it can be.

The first way to do this is not to use our ordinary plain flour but Italian oo flour. This is the flour Italians at home, rather than in factories, use for pasta and it's certainly true that it seems to give pastry an almost pasta-like elasticity.

The second part of my facilitation programme is as follows.

Measure the flour into a bowl and add the cold fat, cut into 1cm dice. You then put this, as is, in the freezer for 10 minutes. Then you put it in the food processor with the double blade attached or into a food mixer with the paddle attached, and switch on (at slow to medium speed if you're using the mixer) until the mixture resembles oatmeal. Then you add, tablespoon by cautious tablespoon, the iced water, to which you've added a squeeze of lemon and a pinch of salt. I find you need a little more liquid when making pastry by this method than you do when the flour and fat haven't had that chilling burst in the deep-freeze.

When the dough looks as if it's about to come together, but just before it actually does, you turn off all machinery, remove the dough, divide into two and form each half into a ball, flatten the balls into fat discs, and cover these discs with clingfilm or put them each inside a freezer bag, and shove them in the fridge for 20 minutes. This makes pastry anyone could roll out, even if you add too much liquid by mistake.

Now, this method relies on a machine to make the pastry. To tell the truth, I culled and simplified the technique from a fascinating book, *Cookwise*, by an American food scientist called Shirley O. Corriher, and she does all sorts of strenuous things, including making the pastry by tipping out the freezer-chilled flour and fat onto a cold surface and battering it with a rolling pin until it looks like 'paint-flakes that have fallen off a wall'. She does, however, sanction the use of a mixer bowl (well-chilled) and paddle (set on slowest speed) and I have found, as described above, that it works well in the processor too. I know that I am not up to her hand-rolling method, or not yet at any rate.

Foods in Season

DON'T BELIEVE EVERYTHING you're told about the greater good of eating foods only when they are in season. The purists may be right, but being right isn't everything. If you live in the Tuscan hills, you may find different lovely things to eat every month of the year, but for us it would mean having to subsist half the time on a diet of tubers and cabbage, so why shouldn't we be grateful that we live in the age of jet transport and extensive culinary imports? More smug guff is spoken on this subject than almost anything else.

There is no doubt that there are concomitant drawbacks: the food is out of kilter with the climate in which it is eaten; it's picked underripe and transported in the wrong conditions; the intense pleasure of eating something when it comes into its own season is lost; the relative merits, the particular properties of individual fruits and vegetables are submerged in the greedy zeal of the tan-trumming adult who must Have It Now. There's no point in eating flown-in asparagus which tastes of nothing (though not all of it does), or peaches in December, ripe-looking but jade-fleshed. But my life is improved considerably by the fact that I can go to my greengrocer's and routinely buy stuff I would otherwise have to go to Italy to find.

I love fresh peas, but they aren't the high point of our culinary year for me. Once they get to the shops, all that pearly sugariness has pretty well turned to starch anyway. As far as I'm concerned, the foods whose short season it would be criminal to ignore are:

rhubarb, the forced, best and pinkest: January–February
Seville oranges: January–February
purple-sprouting broccoli: February–March
home-grown asparagus: May–June
elderflowers: June
grouse: 12 August–10 December
damsons: August–September
quinces: November–December
white truffles: November–January

Rhubarb

I know many people are put off rhubarb because of vile experiences in childhood. I have faith, however, or rather passionate hope, that I can overcome this prejudice. And since my own childhood contained little traditional nursery food, it takes on, for me, something of the exotic. My adult love affair with rhubarb is heady illustration of this.

Seville oranges

You can now buy Seville oranges in supermarkets, but they are regarded almost exclusively as for making marmalade. This is such a waste. Seville oranges have the fragrance and taste of oranges but the sourness of lemons. Try them, then, wherever you'd use lemons – to squirt over fish, to squeeze into salad dressings, to use in a buttery hollandaise-like sauce or in mayonnaise to eat with cold duck. A squeeze of Seville orange is pretty divine in black tea, too. And although you can only buy them in January or early February, they freeze well.

Traditionally, oranges go with duck: real canard à l'orange should be made with bitter and not sweet oranges; you shouldn't end up with jam. Put half a Seville orange up the bottom of a mallard and squeeze the other half, mixed with 1 teaspoon honey or sesame oil, as you wish, over the breast before you cook it. Roast in a hot gas mark 7/210°C oven for 40 minutes. You won't even need to deglaze the pan to make a sauce to go with the mallard: the juices there will be good enough just as they are, though if you wish you can add more Seville orange juice, sweetened with honey to taste or left sharp. If you want something more sauce-like, thicken with 1 teaspoon cornflour, made first into a paste with some of the juice.

Scallops have been cooked with bitter oranges since the eighteenth century. You can do a modern turn on the same theme simply by sautéing each glorious white disc (remove the coral for the time being) in bacon fat, butter or olive oil, 1 minute or so each side, before removing and deglazing the pan with a good squirt of Seville orange juice. Make sure you've also got enough juices in the pan to make a dressing for the watercress with which you're going to line the plate.

If they make up supper in its entirety, I'd get about 5 scallops per head. If you want to eat the corals with the scallops, then fry them for about thirty seconds after you've removed the fleshy rounds, or freeze them to fry up later with a lot of minced garlic to eat, alone and greedily, spread on toast.

Purple-sprouting broccoli

Purple-sprouting broccoli is avoided by those who think that good food has to be fancy. Clearly they don't deserve it.

Steam or lightly boil it and eat as you would asparagus, dipped into hollandaise, into plain melted butter (with or without breadcrumbs fried with it) or into a sharp, semi-emulsified sauce made by warming through some finely chopped anchovy fillets in wonderful olive oil. There can't be a wrong way to eat broccoli; just with soy sauce is fine enough.

I like a plate of sprouting broccoli mixed with asparagus (imported – it has to be). They make a good couple.

Asparagus

English asparagus is expensive in restaurants and easy to cook well at home. Don't worry about special asparagus pans, just cook the asparagus in abundant boiling salted water in a pan or couple of pans which are wide and big enough for the whole spears, stem, tip and all, to be submerged. Cook for 3–5 minutes (test and taste regularly – it's better to waste some spears than for them to be either woody or soggy) and drain thoroughly, first in the colander and then lying flat on the draining board, but do it gently, too: you want the spears to stay beautiful and remain intact.

The usual accompaniment, and always a successful one, is hollandaise, but often I like to do something more homey and give each person a boiled egg in an eggcup for them to dip their asparagus into, like bread-and-butter soldiers. The eggs have to be perfectly soft-boiled; there is no room whatsoever for error. I don't wish to frighten you, but it's the truth. Provide 2 per person and smash or cut the tops off each as soon as they're cooked.

If you feel safer with a non-traditional method, then roll the asparagus in a little olive oil, then roast it, laid out on a tray, in a seriously preheated gas mark 8/220°C oven for 15–20 minutes. When cooked, the spears should be wilted and turning sweet and brown at the tips. Sprinkle over some coarse salt, arrange on a big plate and line another big plate with thin slices of prosciutto (San Daniele or Parma). Let people pick up the hot, soft, blistered spears using the ham to wrap around the asparagus like the finest rosy silk-damask napkins.

Elderflowers

You don't need to have a vast estate with elderflowers springing lacily to flower from that avenue of trees lining the drive; just pick them roadside whenever you see them.

I don't normally go in for individual puddings, each precious darling to be ceremoniously unmoulded from its ramekin. But I make an exception here, would have to. This is, in effect, *panna cotta*, and as with the Italian pudding, this very English-tasting cream needs to be set with as little gelatine as possible. I've tried with big moulds and just can't set it enough without turning it half-way into rubber. These are perfection as they are, and anyway, I use a mixture of teacups, sticky-toffee-pudding moulds and ramekins, feeling that the pleasurable lack of uniformity makes up for any potential dinkiness. Line the moulds, cups and so on with clingfilm, pushing it well against the corners and over the rim so you've got a tuggable edge; it may make for the odd wrinkle or crease on the surface of the set cream, but that doesn't matter; what does is that you will be able to unmould them easily.

900ml double cream	6 tablespoons caster sugar
18 heads of elderflower	9.5g leaf gelatine

Heat cream over low heat in saucepan with the elderflowers. When it comes bubbling to a simmering near-boil, turn it off, remove from the heat and cover. Leave for up to a couple of hours, but not less than ½ hour, to infuse. Then stir in the sugar and bring back to boiling point. Taste to see if more sugar is needed and then sieve into a jug. While the last of the headily aromatic cream is dripping off the elderflowers, soak the leaves of gelatine in cold water. In 5 minutes or so, when the gelatine is softened, squeeze the leaves out and then beat into the warm cream in the jug. Make sure they are dissolved and dispersed and pour into the clingfilm-lined moulds. Cool and then put in the fridge overnight.

With these serve a contrastingly lumpy bowl of gooseberries: the Victorians knew well, and invoked often, the muscatty aptness of the combination of elderflower and gooseberry; about many things they were wrong; about this they were right. Put 750g gooseberries in a pan with 350ml water and 6 tablespoons of sugar. Bring it all to the boil and simmer for a couple of minutes. Drain, reserving syrup, then put the fruit in a bowl and return the lightly syrupy juices to the pan. Bring it to the boil again and let boil for 5 minutes. Pour it into a bowl or jug to cool, while the fruit cools separately in its bowl, then when you're about it eat, put the gooseberries in a shallow dish and cover with the syrup.

Grouse

Grouse should either be roasted plain, first smeared thickly with butter, in a gas mark 6/200°C oven for 30–45 minutes (the size of the birds varies, but you want the flesh to be rubied and juicy, but not underdone to the point of tough quiveriness) and eaten with bread sauce, or stuffed with thyme and mascarpone (yes, really).

Damsons

Damsons are a glorious fruit. They can't be eaten raw and are a chore to prepare and cook, but it's only once a year . . .

I sometimes make damson ice-cream, but damson fool is the recipe for which I wait most greedily. This fool is not difficult to make, but it is stunning, utterly distinctive: you can taste in it both the almost metallic depth of the sour fruit and billowy sweetness of the bulky cream. And it's wonderful after grouse.

500g damsons

2 teaspoons each dark muscovado, light muscovado and caster sugar

¼ teaspoon mixed ground spice

300ml double cream, whipped with 2 tablespoons icing sugar

Put the whole damsons (try to stone them now and you'll go really mad) in a pan with 125ml water and the sugars, bring to the boil and cook till soft. Push through a sieve or food mill to get rid of the stones and add the spice and more sugar to taste if you think it's needed.

When cool, stir into the sugar-whipped cream and pour either into individual pots or into a bowl. This will fill 6 glasses of the sort you'd eat pudding from, but if you're putting the fool in a bowl then count on feeding only 4.

Quinces

Quince, the apple which Paris presented to Helen and maybe even the one which grew in the garden of Eden (although there is, it's argued, a more convincing academic case to be made for the pomegranate here) is a ravishing mixture of *One Thousand and One Nights* exotic and Victorian kitchen homeliness. It looks like a mixture between apple and pear, but tastes like neither. And actually the taste is not the point: what this fruit is all about is heady, perfect fragrance. I have something of an obsession for quinces, although they are in the shops only for a scant eight weeks, aren't at all easy to deal with and can't be eaten raw. In the old days, quinces were kept in airing cupboards to perfume the linen, pervading the house with their honeyed but sharp aroma, so you needn't feel bad if you buy a bowlful and then just watch them rot in a kitchen or wherever.

You should add a quince, peeled, cored and sliced or chunked to apple pie or crumble. Poach them in muscat or make mostarda. Although I am not someone who goes in for preserve-making, I do make mostarda.

There's mostarda di Cremona, which has become modishly familiar over here, those stained-glass-window-coloured gleaming pots of fruits glossily preserved in mustard oil: no one, even in Italy apparently, makes their own. But mostarda di Venezia is different. You can't buy it and it's easy to make. It's just quinces boiled up with white wine, with the addition of sugar, candied peel and mustard powder. It's wonderful with any cold meat (which makes it very useful for Christmas and, since you have to leave it a month or so before eating, rather well timed for it, too). I also risk a culinary culture-clash by eating it alongside couscous and curries. Or you can eat it with a dollop of mascarpone, sweetened and flavoured with rum, as pudding.

This recipe is adapted from the one in Anna Del Conte's *The Classic Food of Northern Italy* which, as these things do, has a mixed parentage of its own. I have changed it a little. I simplify the procedure (see below) and also make it hotter and with almost double the amount of candied peel. Now, I loathe and detest commercial candied peel, but it's different here, not least because you must not use the ready-diced, bitter and oversweet at the same time, vile stuff in tubs. Seach out the good candied peel, whole, in large jars.

The second time I made mostarda di Venezia I didn't peel and core the quinces. It's such hard work. Instead I just roughly chopped the fruit and then, when cooked, pushed the lot through a fine food mill. Laziness prompted this modification, but since the peel and core help the set and intensify the flavour, you should have no qualms. If you don't own a mouli-légumes I suppose you could just push the fruit through a sieve, but that's strenuous too. So if you don't own this cheap and useful piece of equipment, it would be easier to peel, quarter and core to start with.

1.8kg quinces	**sugar (1–1.2kg, see below)**
1 bottle (750ml) white wine	**8 tablespoons English**
grated rind and juice of	**mustard powder**
1 unwaxed lemon	**250g candied peel (see above), cut into small cubes**

Roughly chop the quinces, put them in a pan and cover them with the wine. Add the lemon rind and juice and cook until soft, about 40 minutes. Purée the mixture by pushing it through a food mill, weigh and add the same weight in sugar. Return to the pan. Dissolve the mustard powder in a little hot water and add to the purée with 1 teaspoon salt and the candied peel. Cook gently until the liquid is reduced and the mostarda becomes dense and, normally, deeper-coloured, about 20–30 minutes.

Sterilise some jars (I find the dishwasher's performance adequate) and fill with the mostarda. When it is cool, cover, seal and store away. Keep for about a month before you use it.

What you should also know about quinces is that for all their hardness, they bruise very easily. Whenever I have got a batch of quinces, at least a third of them have been riddled within with speckles, or worse, of what looks like rust. I just ignore it, unless of course it's obviously rotten. Anyway, quinces darken as they cook, going from glassy-yellow to coral to deepest, burnt terracotta; the odd bit of bruising really won't show.

White truffles

No greedy person's mention of foods in season could ignore the white truffle. I don't really understand the fuss about black truffles, but a white truffle – called by Rossini the Mozart of funghi – is something else. You don't do anything to it. You just shave it. And if you're buying a truffle you may as well go the whole hog and buy the thing with which to shave it over a plate of buttery egg pasta or into an equally rich risotto made with good broth. It is instant culinary nirvana. And although expensive, so much less so, unbelievably less so, than eating it in a restaurant.

Freezer

I LIVED FOR YEARS without a freezer without ever minding very much. Certainly this allowed me the luxury of dreaming of all the goods things I would cook and put by should I ever have one: I imagined with pleasure the efficient domestic angel I would then become. Now that I do have a freezer, and a big American one to boot, it is indeed full. And, yet, I feel faintly resentful of its fullness.

The difficulty I find with stuffing a freezer full of food to eat at some future date is that when that future date comes I probably won't want to eat it. This is not because the food will spoil or disappoint, but because every time I open my freezer I see the same efficiently-stowed-away packets of coq au vin or beef stew or whatever it may be, and I get bored with them. I begin to feel as if I've eaten them as many times as I've opened the freezer door.

The freezer can easily become a culinary graveyard, a place where good food goes to die.

If you're someone who is meticulous about cooking, freezing, filing and then thawing in an orderly fashion, you need no advice from me as to how best to use your freezer. But you must be honest with yourself. There is no point in stowing away stews and soups if you are going to let them linger so long in its depths that finally all you can do is chuck them out. You'll probably find you stand more chance of eating the food you cook in advance if – when you put it in the freezer – you do so with some particular occasion in mind rather than just stashing it away for some unspecified future time. Obviously, if you know people are coming for dinner on Friday but the only time you can get any cooking done is on the weekend before, then the freezer will be useful (see Cooking in Advance). But unless you have an astonishingly capacious freezer and a mania for planning in advance, I wouldn't advise stocking up for more than one or two such occasions at any one time. However, there are occasions in which even I am ruthlessly efficient about freezing and then using food: cooking for children is unimaginably easier if you create a form of culinary database in the deep freeze.

Leftovers are obviously better put away in the freezer if the alternative destination is several days lingering in the fridge and then the bin. On the other hand, beware against using the freezer as a less guilt-inducing way of binning food you know you don't want. If no one, including you, liked the soup the first time round (and that's why you've got so much left over) there is no point in freezing it for some hopeful future date when, miraculously, it will taste delicious. But bagging leftovers – say stews – in single portions can be useful for those evenings when you're eating alone. Take the little packet out of the deep-freeze before you go to work in the morning and heat it up for supper when you get back at night. Immensely cheering.

The freezer really comes into its own not so much when you don't have time for cooking as when you don't have time for shopping. In other words, the best use for the freezer is as a store cupboard.

As with a store cupboard, you must be on your guard against overstocking. In fact having far too much in the freezer can be very much worse than a mouldering store cupboard, because food so easily gets buried and really forgotten about rather than simply ignored. But a solid supply of ingredients with which to cook, rather than just wholly prepared dishes, can really help you make good simple things to eat without exhausting last-minute trawls around the supermarket.

You should always have in your freezer some raw prawns. Cooking with raw prawns rather than cooked ones makes such a difference, and the raw ones anyway seem to be sold only in their frozen state, so you just transplant them from the fishmonger's freezer to yours. You can cook them from frozen (which means you don't need to think about defrosting in advance) by plunging them, unthawed, into boiling water, salted and maybe spiked with a little vinegar. Peel them and pile them on top of garlicky puy lentils or mix them, cooled, into a fennel salad. When I was in Los Angeles some years back, I ate at Joachim Splichal's Patina the most wonderful starter of mashed potatoes and truffles with warm Santa Barbara shrimp on top. The combination works. Purée some potatoes (they need to be whipped as well as mashed) with butter and white pepper, put a small, or maybe not so small, mound on a plate, add some barely cooked prawns, then drizzle over some truffle oil if you have some, or some Liguarian olive oil if you haven't.

Bacon is another ingredient any cook should keep in store. (And I like to keep some pancetta there too.) I always freeze bacon in pairs of rashers, so that they defrost in minutes. The point about bacon is that everywhere, even the corner shop, sells it, but the good stuff is hard to find. I get my bacon from my butcher, and I know when I cook it that 1) white froth won't seep out of it, and 2) it will taste of bacon.

Nothing is as good as a bacon sandwich made with white bread. There are times when you just need to have that salty-sweet curl of seared flesh pressed between fat-softened, rind-stained spongy slices. My guiding rule is that I always have the wherewithal for a bacon sandwich in the house. I aim to keep all the ingredients for spaghetti carbonara to hand, too.

Bread is worth keeping in the freezer. It freezes well, and I keep good bread in loaves and plastic white bread (such as is needed for bacon sandwiches) in pairs of slices. It's when I have to go shopping for basics such as bread and milk that I come back having spent far too much on absolute unnecessities. Many varieties of milk now freeze all right, too: just check the labels first. For various reasons, all of them good ones, I try to keep visits to a supermarket to a minimum: I use my freezer to help keep me away.

You must keep stock in your freezer, and also the bones you have saved up to make it. Turn your freezer into your very own Golgotha, by throwing in lamb bones, chicken carcasses and any other bones that, these days, you are allowed to boil up. I have been known to take home the carcasses with me after a dinner party once I've found out that a) they have come from a butcher and b) they were going to be thrown away. Keep ham bones or leftover trimmings from gammon joints, too, to flavour pea and bean soups at some later date. It may make your freezer look like Dennis Nilsen's, but that is a small price to pay.

Freeze your own, consequent, home-made stock in manageable portions (see page 18). I also keep a couple of tubs of good fresh stock in my freezer. Certainly, fresh stock is very useful to have on hand: making a good fish fumet is rather more serious work than making a chicken stock, and I feel guiltless about having someone else do it for me, especially if it's done better than I would myself.

Parmesan rinds can be stowed away for future use. Every time you come to the end of a wedge of parmesan, or if you've left it out unwrapped for so long that it has become rebarbatively hard, don't throw the piece away, but chuck it in the freezer (preferably in a marked bag) to use whenever you make a minestrone or other soup which would benefit from that smoky, salty depth of flavouring.

As for puddings, other than the obvious ones that are meant to be frozen, such as ice-cream, you don't need to do more than keep a packet or so of frozen summer fruits, which can be made to serve in most eventualities. Remember that defrosted strawberries take on the texture of soft, cold slugs. Remove them from the packets of mixed fruits, and chuck them out.

If, like me, you're not much of a drinker, then you can stop yourself from wasting leftover wine after dinner parties by measuring out glassfuls and freezing them, well labelled (or you'll mistake white wine for egg whites, and see below), to use for cooking later on. And as for egg whites: I've got so many frozen, my freezer is beginning to look like a sperm bank.

Store Cupboard

UNLESS YOU WANT to spend your every waking free hour buying food, you need to have at home basic ingredients that you can use to make something good when you haven't had time to shop or plan for a particular meal. But don't believe what you are told about essentials: all it means is that you'll have a larder full of lost bottles of Indonesian soy sauce with a use-by date of November 1994. There is a compromise. Buy those few ingredients which really do provide a meal quickly and easily, and don't weigh yourself down with various tempting bits and pieces that you think you may get round to using one day.

I don't want to be too dictatorial, though. Apart from anything else, so much depends on the amount of space you've got. I am the Imelda Marcos – she who had a cushion with Nouveau Riche is Better than No Riche At All embroidered on it – of the foodshop world. I am not safe in delicatessens. No wonder I can't move for food I've bankrupted myself to buy. You have to avoid finding yourself in the same position. For there is no such thing as having food to cover most eventualities which doesn't also involve regularly throwing away food that goes off before you eat it.

It's not easy to hold back. Nothing is as good as buying food. Buying store-cupboard food is highly seductive: you don't have the stress of actual, imminent here-and-now cooking. It's fantasy shopping – and that's why it gets out of hand. Food bought on these expeditions lingers on for years, untouched. Partly this is because items you buy to store away are so often expensive, rarefied delicacies which, having bought, you then feel you have to save for something special. If you can get out of that frame of mind – which is the same mind-set that leads you to buy an extremely expensive piece of clothing which you then leave hanging in the wardrobe rather than allow it to be sullied by being worn around the house – then food shopping isn't quite such a dangerous pastime.

But it isn't the pattern of extravagance followed by austerity, nor the habit of saving things for best, which argues against intensive stockpiling. There is a hard-headed practical reason for being modest in your supplies: the food that people buy packets and packets of – flour, spices, rice, lentils – doesn't actually keep for ever. The chances are that you will end up with a larder full of stale pulses. It's not that this food goes off, necessarily, but it becomes less good to eat. It's comforting to know that you've got a bag of chick peas, but you must be strict with yourself and use it, not just keep it there for some rainy day when you fondly think you'll stay in and cook *pasta e ceci*. After a few years, they won't be dried, they'll be fossilised – and tasteless.

Anyway, unless you live in a very remote part of the country, the chances are that it won't be too difficult to go shopping for any special items you need for a specific recipe. A store cupboard is much more useful for keeping stuff in that you know you'll want regularly. This sort of food is likely to be the food you eat alone, or with your family. You want to be able to cook something in the evening after work without having to go shopping, and you don't want to have to start thinking about it before you get home. (I always want to think about what I'm going to eat, not in any elaborate organisational way, but because the speculation gives me pleasure. But there are many times when idly, greedily speculating is indeed the most energetic thing I can manage to do in advance. So what I need to know is that I have some food at home that won't take long to cook and won't demand too much of me.)

The most important ingredient to keep in your larder, or food cupboard, or whatever it might be, is pasta. Stick to a few different shapes only: if you try and cover too many bases, you will simply end up with about 10 opened, almost finished, packets and you will never be able to make a decent plateful of any of them. It's useful to have rather a lot of spaghetti, so that you can suddenly cook a huge plateful of something for a kitchen-load of people if need be. Linguine are sufficiently different to be worth having as well. Short pasta is quick and easier to cook for chidren; choose fusilli or penne, for example. Some kinds of eggy pasta need little cooking, and are therefore wonderful for when you feel like Elizabeth Taylor shouting 'Hurry!' to the microwave, as Joan Rivers' cruel joke had it.

I know I said that flour and so forth doesn't keep for ever, but I do keep a modest and restrained selection, including flours, especially Italian oo, sugars, salt, spices, oil, vinegar, tinned tomatoes, vanilla extract, stock cubes and vegetable stock powders. I also make up a jar of vanilla sugar – simply by filling a Kilner jar with caster sugar and chopping a couple of vanilla pods into about 5cm lengths to go in it. This takes very little effort, makes one feel positively holy and also gives one gloriously scented sugar to use in cakes, puddings, custards and so forth whenever needed. The pods give out their sweet and fleshy scent for ages; just pour over fresh sugar as you use it.

Naturally, what I want to keep in my kitchen cupboards might not be what you want to have in yours. But I couldn't live without Marsala, Noilly Prat (or Chambéry), dry sherry and sake pretty close to hand. I don't drink much, and so don't tend to have bottles of wine open; so if I need alcohol for cooking, I need to have it in the sort of bottles that come with a screw-top. Most often, I use Marsala in recipes which specify red wine, vermouth where white's required. Other drinks have their part to play: as ever, follow your own impulses; go with your own palate.

Any time I let myself run out of garlic or onions, I curse. The base-note ingredients should be a given in your kitchen, or you always feel you're scrabbling around before you can make *anything*. And for me, fresh nutmeg is crucial, too. You don't have to get a special little nutmeg grater (you could just shave off bits with a sharp knife) but it's not expensive, and it is useful.

Fridge

I KEEP A MODEST but restrained selection in my fridge, including butter, eggs, milk, salad leaves, some herbs and blocks of parmesan cheese. That's in theory; in reality it's a constant culinary clutter. I have either too much or not enough. But that's life.

Not everything in my kitchen is organic, but it seems to be going that way. Eggs, I've already mentioned: though make sure the box says organic and free-range as free-range alone doesn't signify anything very edifying. I want my meat free-range, traceable – the buzzword in organic farming – and not pumped full of revolting things. And now that supermarkets have got wise to the ever-more-widespread lure of organic produce it's easier to find vegetables from organic farms that aren't utterly covered in mud just to show their virtuous credentials. I worry about the chemicals in non-organic reared fruit and vegetables, but to tell the truth it's the improved taste of the organic stuff that's the clincher. If you can't muster the energy or interest to go wholly organic, just buy organic carrots. A few years back the government advised us to peel carrots because of the potentially harmful residues of chemicals which had been used in their cultivation. This is enough to make me feel that the real truth must be very much worse. Besides, organically grown carrots taste so much better. You should know that the difference in taste between organically and non-organically farmed potatoes is also pronounced. And it's worth buying organic oranges and lemons just because they're unwaxed and therefore better for zesting. But without the wax, they don't keep as long – there is a trade-off here – so just store them in the fridge if your turnover's slow.

Cooking in Advance

QUICK COOKING HAS become so implanted in people's minds as the way to eat well without having a nervous breakdown that everyone ignores the real way to make life easier for yourself: cooking in advance. Knocking up a meal in fifteen minutes is good for everyday cooking, when there's just one or two of you, or if you're one of those people who feels uncomfortable with too much planning. But when you're having people to dinner, life is made so much simpler if you don't have to do everything at the last minute. If you feel flustered at the very idea of cooking, indeed hate it, doing it in advance takes away some of the stress: if you enjoy it, you'll enjoy it more if you don't put yourself under pressure; that's for the professionals, who thrive on it. I love the feeling of pottering about the kitchen, cooking slowly, stirring and chopping and getting everything done when I'm feeling well-disposed and not utterly exhausted. When I cook with too much of an audience I immediately worry about what'll happen if something goes wrong, and then, of course, something does.

Cook in advance and, if the worst comes to the worst, you can ditch it. No one but you will know that it tasted disgusting, or failed to set, or curdled or whatever. That may sound a rather negative approach, but in fact it's liberating; moreover, because you're not stressed out or desperately working against the clock, there's less chance of disaster. And if something does go wrong, you have the time calmly to find a way of rectifying it.

And things do go wrong in cooking. Indeed, it's one of the ways you learn and eventually find your own style. Some of the best food I've cooked has been as a result of trying to make up for some fault, some blip. It's when you're exploring and trying out, not simply following a recipe, that you feel what the food needs, what will make it taste how you want it to taste. Without the pressure of having to perform, you can concentrate on the food. This is not to say that cooking has to be a solitary pursuit. In a way, there's nothing better than cooking with someone to talk to while you do it. But I am someone who panics if there's too much commotion or if I've got too little time to think.

Perhaps this is a temperamental thing, but cooking is about temperament, and so, I think, is eating. You have to find a way of cooking that suits you, and that isn't just about your life, your working hours, your environment, though these, of course, matter. But what counts, too, is whether you're the sort of person who's soothed or cramped by list-making, whether you're impatient or tidy, whether spontaneity makes you feel creative or panic-stricken. Most of us like eating, but many people feel flustered and a sense of panic and, frankly, boredom when it comes to cooking. It's difficult to be good at something you aren't really interested in. But some people don't like cooking simply because they've never given themselves the chance to do it calmly and quietly and in the right mood. Obligation can be a useful prompt to activity, but it can be a terrible blight, too. Cooking in advance is a good way to learn confidence, to learn what works and why and how, and from that you can then teach yourself to trust your intuition, to be spontaneous: in short, to cook.

Cooking is about working towards a goal, towards something you have decided upon in advance. But any creative work (however cringe-makingly pretentious it sounds, cooking *is* creative, has to be) needs to liberate itself from the end product during the act of producing. This can be very difficult. There are practical constraints, which are what make the form, in cooking as in poetry. You have to learn to use these constraints to your advantage. Get over economic constraints by buying ingredients you can afford rather than making do with inferior versions of expensive produce. Make the best of the equipment you happen to have in your kitchen. Be ready to adapt to what you've got. But some other constraints – such as lack of time – merely add to your obstacles, and to the risk that if your dinner is inedible you and your guests will just have to live with it.

Some food actually benefits from being cooked in advance. Stews, for example, are always best cooked, left to get cold and hang around for a while, and then reheated. Puddings can need time to set or for their flavours to settle and deepen. Soups mellow. That's why I love this sort of cooking: the rhythms are so reassuring; I no longer feel I'm snatching at food, at life. It's not exactly that I'm constructing a domestic idyll, but as I work in the kitchen at night, or at the weekend, filling the house with the smells of baking and roasting and filling the fridge with good things to eat, it feels, corny as it sounds, as if I'm making a home.

Soup

SOUPS ARE THE obvious place to start for those thus in domestic goddess mode. Soups, of course, are some of the quickest meals that you can make. Somehow the home-made soup, lovingly prepared in advance, is no longer popular. I think it comes down to stock: our disinclination to make it from scratch, together with our disdain for cubes. It is important to stress that even though the better a stock the better a soup, it does not follow that no good soup, no superlatively good soup, can be made with stock cubes. Naturally, it depends on the kind of soup: no consommé or delicate broth should be made with anything but home-made stock; but a hearty vegetable soup can, frankly, be made with water; and in between these two extremes, use stock cubes.

If you haven't already got a supply of home-made stock in the freezer, you'll need a good day's grace: time to make the stock, to cool it, to skim the fat off it. A ham stock (just the liquid in which a gammon's been cooked) makes all the difference to a pea soup; a chicken stock, light though it may be, gives instant depth and velvety swell to a very basic parsnip soup. Grate fresh parmesan over the pea soup; drop chilli oil into the pale sweetness of the parsnip to add a probing fierceness. To both you could add some bacon, fried, grilled or baked in a hot oven, and crumbled into salty shards; marjoram, too, would work equally well with either.

This soup can be made in advance and kept in the fridge for reheating throughout the week, whether on the hob or in the microwave.

The soups that you really have to cook in advance are the ones made from pulses. Most legumes need a good day's soaking. I tend to put beans into soak as I go to bed even if I won't actually be cooking with them until the next evening. Chick peas need 24 hours, and I don't mind if I give them 36. And they need a lot of cooking, much longer than you are usually told. There seems to be a conspiracy to misinform you about chick peas: I cannot believe the number of times I've read that 45 minutes will do, when it takes double that time to cook them. Anna Del Conte is realistic about this, admitting that some chick peas can take as long as 4 hours. I use her technique for preparing chick peas. Put them in a bowl and cover them with cold water. Then mix together 1 teaspoon bicarbonate of soda and 1 tablespoon each of salt and flour – or those ingredients in that ratio: a very large quantity of peas will need more of this tenderising mixture – add water to form a runny paste and stir this paste into the soaking chick peas. Leave for a good 24 hours. Then, when cooking the chick peas (drained and rinsed), don't lift the lid off the pan for the first hour or so or the peas will harden. (Curiosity often gets the better of me.) Broad beans similarly need longer soaking than, say, cannellini or borlotti (both of which are fine with 12 hours), and all are better if you leave the salting till the last moments of the cooking time. If you're cooking in advance, it doesn't matter how long it all takes: and good though canned chick peas are, dried, soaked and cooked ones are so much better. You can taste the full, grainy, chestnutty roundness of them.

Chick pea and pasta soup is my favourite soup of all. You can cook it days before you actually want to eat it. Obviously it can't all be done in advance because the pasta must be cooked at the last minute, but since you have to reheat the soup anyway, what does it matter to you if, when reheating, you keep it simmering for 20 minutes or so extra while the ditalini swell and soften.

I cook this soup so often – just for us, at home, for

supper, in great big greedy bowlfuls; for a first course when I've got people coming for dinner; or, if they're coming for a Saturday lunch, for a main course, with a salad and cheese after – that I don't follow a recipe any more. But this is the recipe that started me off. It is Anna Del Conte's, adapted from her *Entertaining all'Italiana*. I have several copies of this book: one in the kitchen, where, eccentrically perhaps, I tend not to keep my cookery books; one in my study, where all books on food notionally live (in practice they are dotted on floors, in lavatories, throughout the house); and one in the bedroom, for late-night soothing reading and midnight-feast fantasising.

Anna's chick pea and pasta soup

This will make enough soup for 8. I sometimes add a glass of white wine or any stock to hand, from whatever animal it emanates, but the soup has quite enough taste with simply water. If you want a vegetable stock, choose a low-salt bouillon powder. You can make the soup (bar the pasta) up to 3 days in advance, or longer if you want to freeze it.

400g dried chick peas	3 litres vegetable stock
2 teaspoons bicarbonate of soda	(or meat stock or white wine and water)
2 tablespoons flour	3 sprigs rosemary
2 tablespoons salt	

8 cloves garlic, peeled and
   bruised

120ml extra virgin olive oil

400g fresh tomatoes,
   skinned and seeded

270g small tubular pasta
   such as ditalini

parmesan for grating over

chilli oil and flat-leaf parsley
   if you want

Put the chick peas in a bowl and cover with plenty of water. Mix together the bicarbonate of soda, flour and salt and add enough water to make a thin paste. Stir this mixture into the bowl with the chick peas and leave to soak for at least 12 hours, preferably 24.

When the chick peas have doubled their size (you don't have to get your ruler out: trust your eyes) they are ready to be cooked. Drain and then rinse them. Put them in a large pot and add the vegetable stock, meat stock or white wine and water or the same quantity of water.

Tie the rosemary sprigs in a muslin bag and add to the pot. This will make it possible to remove the rosemary without leaving any needles to float in the soup. This might sound pernickety, but when I ignored the advice I found the sharp and, by now, bitter needles an unpleasant intrusion. If you feel intimidated by the idea of muslin then use, disgusting though it sounds, a popsock or stocking and tie a knot at the open end, or a tea-infuser. Frankly, it doesn't matter what you use providing it does the job, although I imagine untreated muslin is better. You can get muslin or cheesecloth in any kitchen shop or haberdashery department and, come to think of it, in a baby department selling muslin nap-kins; one of those posset-catching squares you wear over your shoulder to catch infant regurgitations would do.

Add the garlic and pour in half the oil. Cover the pan tightly and bring to the boil. You will have to gauge this by ear without peeping in. Lower the heat and cook over the lowest simmer until the chick peas are tender, which can take 2–4 hours. Take a look after 1½ hours. Do not add any salt until the chick peas are nearly ready. If you put it in too soon, they'll harden.

When the chick peas are tender, remove the garlic and the rosemary bundle, which should be floating on the surface. Purée the tomatoes through a food mill or in a food processor and add to the soup with their juice. Stir well, add salt and pepper to taste and cook for a further 10 minutes or so. This is the point at which you should stop when you're cooking the soup in advance.

When you want to eat it, put it back on the hob and reheat it, so that you can proceed to the final step, which is to cook the pasta. Before you add the pasta, check that there is enough liquid in the pan. You may have to add some boiling water. Now, to the boiling soup, add the pasta and cook till al dente. I like to add some freshly chopped flat-leaf parsley, but the glory of this soup will be undiminished if you prefer not to. But do pour some of the remaining oil into the pot of soup, and drizzle some more into each bowl after you've ladled the soup in. Or just pour some into the big pot and let people add what they want as they eat. I would put good extra virgin olive oil on the table as well as a bottle of chilli oil for those who like some heat: and it does work. Serve, too, the parmesan, put on a plate with a grater, so people can add their own.

Kafka-esque or soft and crispy duck

You'd think, wouldn't you, that a roast could never ever be done in advance. Yes, we all know that any joint needs to rest after it's come out of the oven and before it goes on the table, but I now do a roast duck – the best roast duck I have ever eaten, let alone cooked – that can be started a good few days before you want to eat it. This is semi-cooking in advance and I'm blazingly evangelical about it. A method of doing the perfect roast duck which leaves you with just three-quarters of an hour's cooking on the night – and all in the oven, no basting, no faffing, nothing – has to be a good thing. I let the duck sit around in the fridge in a state of semi-cookedness for up to 3 days; but if you feel at all nervous about this, don't leave it as long. But actually, before we get on to it, it isn't that new an idea: Apicius – he of the first cookery book – likewise instructed his readers: 'lavas, ornas et in olla elixabis cum aqua, sale et aneto dimidia coctura'. Admittedly, even if he suggested boiling the duck in water (with dill as well as salt) until half-cooked, the second half's cooking would not be exactly by roasting; it would have been more like pot-roasting. Nevertheless, it reminds us pointedly that there is nothing new in cooking. That's if it's to taste good.

But this is the story: when I was last in New York I bought a copy of Barbara Kafka's *Roasting*, the premise of which is that roasting at very high temperatures makes for the most succulent, fleshily yielding and crispy skinned birds and joints. The drawback is that you need a clean oven, otherwise all that roasting at very high temperatures gives you a smoky kitchen, burning eyes and an acrid glaze on the putative pièce de résistance. I noticed that there was a recipe for roast duck which involved poaching the bird first in stock for about three-quarters of an hour and then blitzing it in the oven for half an hour. The result: tender flesh and crisp skin. And it's true, if you're not careful when you roast a duck in the more usual way you often find that the desirably crunchy carapace comes at the cost of overcooked and thus stringy meat. Everyone has an answer to this one: covering the bird with boiling water, hanging it up on a clothes line on a blustery (but dry) day, suspending it on high by means of a clothes hanger then getting a stiff wrist by aiming a hair-dryer, at full though icy blast, at it for hours.

The *echt* Kafka-esque technique involves poaching the duck, upright, in a thin, tall pot in duck stock. I couldn't quite see why you needed to poach the bird in stock, since the flesh is rich itself. More to the point, I had none. So the first time I tried it, I put the water into the requisite tall thin pot (the bottom half of my couscoussier), added the giblets, brought it to the boil, added salt, and lowered in the duck. Then, as directed, I made sure the bird was submerged for the whole 40 minutes. I did this in the morning, let the duck get cool, put it in the fridge and then brought it out in the evening, letting it get to room temperature before roasting it for the 30 minutes as recommended.

The next time I tried it, I made some changes. For one

thing, duck doesn't yield much flesh, and cooking a single, lone, duck is no use unless there are only 2 or 3 of you eating. But I couldn't get 2 ducks into my couscoussier, and getting even one out, from an upright position, tore its skin. So I decided to be even more disobedient. Figuring that the ducks would stay moist if they were steamed, not necessarily submerged, I put one duck, breast down, in a large, oblong casserole and the other in a large, deep, all-purpose frying pan. Both pans were filled with boiling salted water. The casserole had its own lid, and for the frying pan I made a tent of tin foil. I wasn't sure it would work, but there's only ever one way of finding out.

I had decided anyway – on the evidence produced by my first stab – to swap around cooking times: that's to say, poach the birds for the ½ hour and roast them for ¾ hour. The ducks weren't exactly the same size (one was about 1½ kg, the other perhaps 300g heavier) but I didn't alter the poaching times to suit: I merely took the lighter one out of its water first. And it is very much easier taking the ducks out when they are flat rather than upright. Use wooden paddle-spoons or rubber spatulas to make sure you don't rip the flesh. It would be even easier to steam the birds breast up, and frankly I doubt it matters which way up they are. I noticed some slight scalding to a patch on both ducks where the breast had come into contact with the hot base of the pan, but this didn't seem to make any difference either.

Boiling ducks produces a rather pongy fug which can

linger in the kitchen, so open a window; but I was going away for the weekend and had promised to cook something. I knew I wouldn't have time to poach the birds on the Friday so did them on Thursday at about six in the evening, let them cool on a baking tray with a wire-mesh grill arrangement set over it, and then put them in the fridge before going to bed.

For travelling on Friday evening I just put them in a plastic bag and put that plastic bag in a picnic coolbag. On arrival, I put the ducks, uncovered, on a large plate in my friends' fridge. When I got around to cooking them – which turned out to be Sunday lunch – it transpired that their Aga had died. I put the birds, anyway, into the supposedly hot oven, which turned out to be a rapidly cooling sooty box, and left them there for a hopeless 20 minutes. The ducks just got greasy, not even hot, and I got more teary and mutinous by the minute. But someone living in a neighbouring farm set her oven to high for me (she was doubtful about having ducks at top whack so we compromised on gas mark 8/220°C): the ducks were driven over to her, roasted for 45 minutes and came back, after the brief car journey, bronze and crisp and perfect.

I don't think it is possible to try out a recipe more conclusively than that.

I LOVE HAVING someone in the kitchen just to talk to as I chop, and weigh, and stir, and generally get things ready. I love cooking with other people, too. I do it rarely, though

I love having someone
in the kitchen just
to talk to as I chop,
and weigh, and stir,
and generally get
things ready

used to often with my sister Thomasina. There's something about that industrious intimacy that is both
cushioning and comforting, but also hugely confidence-
building. I love that sense of companionable bustle, of
linked activity and joint enterprise. It makes it easier to
attempt food that normally you would shrink from, not
because you rely on another's superior capabilities or
experience necessarily, but because you aren't isolated in
the attempt. Everything doesn't feel geared towards the
end product because it is a shared activity – and that itself
is pleasurable. You feel a sense of satisfaction about the
process. It isn't drudgery.

Claudia Roden, writing about her memories of childhood in Egypt, recollected kitchenfuls of women kneading
and pummelling pastries, stuffing them, wrapping them,
baking them together. But I suppose those Middle Eastern
delicacies, meticulous confections with their elaborate
farces, could have sprung only from a culture in which the
cooking was carried out by posses, by armies, of sisters and
female relatives. It doesn't do to get too lyrical about this
culinary companionship, though: which of us now would
want our lives to be spent in such service, companionable
though it might have been?

Still, it's a pity to lose all of it, never to become immersed
in that female kitchen bustle. For me, so much of cooking
in advance is tied up with that image, that idea: that's when
cooking feels like the making of provisions, the bolstering
up of a life. I don't see it as a form of subjection (unless the

position is a forced one) and I don't see it as a secondary role, either. Some people hate domesticity, I know. I'm glad I don't: I love the absorbing satisfactions of the kitchen. For me, the pleasure to be got from cooking, from food – in the shop, on the chopping board, on the plate or in the pan – is aesthetic. I think it's that I find food beautiful, intensely so.

Proper English trifle

When I say proper I mean proper: lots of sponge, lots of jam, lots of custard and lots of cream. This is not a timid construction, nor should it be. Of course, the ingredients must be good, but you don't want to end up with a trifle so upmarket it's inappropriately, posturingly elegant. A degree of vulgarity is requisite.

I soak the sponge in orange-flavoured alcohol (I loathe the acrid dustiness of standard-issue sherry), infuse the custard with orange, and make an orange caramel to sprinkle over the top; this seems to bring out the fruity, egginess of it all, even if you are reduced to using frozen fruit. I've specified raspberries but you could substitute blackberries (maybe sprinkling with a little sugar and using blackberry jam with the sponge), and I have used, too, those packets of frozen mixed berries. They're fine, but they definitely bring a sponge-sousing reminder of summer pudding with them. You can use trifle sponges here, and I do, but for those who cannot countenance such an un-chic thing, I suggest some brioche or challah, sliced; indeed, loaf-shaped supermarket brioche or challah, which have a denser crumb than the boulangerie-edition or *echt* article, are both perfect here.

In a way it is meaningless, or certainly unhelpful, to give exact measurements; as ever it so depends on the bowl you're using. Think rather of layers: one of jam-sandwiched sponge, one of custard, one of cream, and then the nutty, toffee-ish topping. So use the quantities below – which will fill a bowl of about 1½ litre capacity – as a guide only.

600ml single cream	500g raspberries
zest and juice of 1 orange	8 egg yolks
100ml Grand Marnier	75g caster sugar
50ml Marsala	450ml double cream
5 trifle sponges or 4–5 slices of brioche or challah	50g flaked almonds
	1 orange
approx. 10 heaped teaspoons best quality raspberry or boysonberry jam	approx. 100g sugar

Pour the single cream into a wide, heavy-based saucepan, add the orange zest – reserving the juice, separately, for the moment – and bring to the boil without actually letting it boil. Take off the heat and set aside for the orange flavour to infuse while you get on with the bottom layer of the trifle.

Mix together the Grand Marnier, Marsala and the reserved orange juice and pour about half of it into a shallow soup bowl, keeping the rest for replenishing halfway through. If you're using the trifle sponges, split them horizontally, if the challah or brioche slices, take the crusts off and cut them each into two equal slices. Make little sandwiches with the jam, and dunk each sandwich, first one side, then the other, into the booze in the bowl and then arrange the alcohol-sodden sandwiches at the bottom of the trifle bowl. If you're using the challah or brioche, you might need to make up more of your alcoholic mixture, as the bread seems to soak it all in much more quickly and thirstily.

When the bottom of the bowl's covered, top with the fruit and put in the fridge to settle while you get on with the custard. Bring the orange-zested cream back to the boil, while you whisk together the egg yolks and sugar in a bowl large enough to take the cream, too, in a moment. When the yolks and sugar are thick and frothy, pour the about-to-bubble cream into them, whisking as you do so. Wash out the pan, dry it well and return the custard mixture, making sure you disentangle every whisk-attached string of orange zest; you will be sieving later, but for now you want to hold on to all of it.

Fill the sink with enough cold water to come about halfway up the custard pan. On medium to low heat cook the custard, stirring all the time with a wooden spoon or spatula. With so many egg yolks, the custard should take hardly any time to thicken (and remember it will continue to thicken further as it cools) so don't overcook it. If it looks as if it might be about to boil or split, quickly plunge the pan into the sink of cold water, beating furiously until danger is averted. But I find this yolk-rich custard uneventful to make: about 7 minutes, if that, does it; it's unlikely to need cooking for more than 10. When it's cooked and thickened, take the pan over to the sink of cold water and beat robustly but calmly for a minute or so. When the custard's smooth and cooled, strain it over the fruit-topped sponge and put the bowl back in the fridge for 24 hours.

Not long before you want to eat it, whip the double cream till thick and, preferably with one of those bendy rubber spatulas, smear it thickly over the top of the custard. Put it back in the fridge. Toast the flaked almonds by tossing them in a hot, dry frying pan for a couple of minutes and then remove to a plate till cool. Squeeze the orange, pour it into a measuring jug and then measure out an equal quantity – gram for millilitre – of sugar; I reckon on getting 100ml of juice out of the average orange. Pour the orange juice into a saucepan and stir in sugar to help it dissolve. Bring to the boil and let bubble away until you have a thick but still runny toffee: if you let it boil too much until you have, almost, toffee (and I often do) it's not the end of the world, but you're aiming for a densely syrupy, sticky caramel. Remove from heat, and when cooled slightly, dribble over the whipped cream; you may find this easier to do teaspoon by slow-drizzling teaspoon. You can do this an hour or so before you want to eat it. Scatter the toasted almonds over before serving.

This is certainly enough for 10, and maybe even more, though it certainly wouldn't swamp 8.

One & Two

DON'T KNOCK MASTURBATION,' Woody Allen once said: 'it's sex with someone I love.' Most people can't help finding something embarrassingly onanistic about taking pleasure in eating alone. Even those who claim to love food think that cooking just for yourself is either extravagantly self-indulgent or a plain waste of time and effort. But you don't have to belong to the drearily narcissistic learn-to-love-yourself school of thought to grasp that it might be a good thing to consider yourself worth cooking for. And the sort of food you cook for yourself will be different from the food you might lay on for tablefuls of people: it will be better.

I don't say that for effect. You'll feel less nervous about cooking it and that translates to the food itself. It'll be simpler, more straightforward, the sort of food *you* want to eat.

I don't deny that food, its preparation as much as its consumption, is about sharing, about connectedness. But that's not all that it's about. There seems to me to be something robustly affirmative about taking trouble to feed yourself; enjoying life on purpose, rather than by default.

Even in culinary terms alone there are grounds for satisfaction. Real cooking, if it is to have any authenticity, any integrity, has to be part of how you are, a function of your personality, your temperament. There's too much culinary ventriloquism about as it is: cooking for yourself is a way of countering that. It's how you're going to find your own voice. One of the greatest hindrances to enjoying cooking is that tense-necked desire to impress others. It's virtually impossible to be innocent of this. Even if this is not your motivation, it's hard, if you're being honest, to be insensible to the reactions of others. Since cooking for other people is about trying to please them, it would be strange to be indifferent to their pleasure, and I don't think you should be. But you can try too hard. When you're cooking for yourself, the stakes simply aren't as high. You don't mind as much. Consequently, it's much less likely to go wrong. And the process is more enjoyable in itself.

When I cook for myself I find it easier to trust my instinct – I am sufficiently relaxed to listen to it in the first place – and, contrariwise, I feel freer to overturn a judgement, to take a risk. If I want to see what will happen if I add yoghurt, or stir in some chopped tarragon instead of parsley, I can do so without worrying that I am about to ruin everything. If the sauce splits or the tarragon infuses everything with an invasive farmyard grassiness, I can live with it. I might feel cross with myself, but I won't be panicked. It could be that the yoghurt makes the sauce, or that the tarragon revitalises it. I'm not saying that cooking for seven other people would make it impossible for me to respond spontaneously, but I do think it's cooking for myself that has made it possible.

Far too much cooking now is about the tyranny of the recipe on the one hand and the absence of slowly acquired experience on the other. Cooking for yourself is a way of finding out what *you* want to cook and eat, rather than simply joining up the dots. Crucially, it's a way of seeing which things work, which don't, and how ingredients, heat, implements, vessels, all have their part to play. When I feel like a bowl of thick, jellied white rice noodles, not soupy but barely bound in a sweet and salty sauce, I'm not going to look up a recipe for them. I know that if I soak the noodles in boiling water until they dislodge themselves from the solid wodge I've bought them in, fry 2 cloves of garlic with some knife-flattened spring onions and tiny square beads of chopped red chilli in a pan before wilting some greens and adding the noodles with a steam-provoking gush of soy and mirin, with maybe a teaspoon of black bean sauce grittily dissolved in it, it will taste wonderful, comforting, with or without chopped coriander or a slow-oozing drop or two of sesame oil. I can pay attention to texture and to taste. I know what sort of thing I'm going to end up with, but I'm not aiming to replicate any particular dish. Sometimes it goes wrong: I'm too heavy-handed with the soy and drench everything in brown brine, so that the sweet stickiness of the rice sticks is done for, and there's no contrast; I might feel, when eating, that the chilli interrupts too much when I'm in the mood to eat something altogether gentler. These aren't tragedies, however. And frankly most often I get satisfaction simply from the quiet putting together of a meal. It calms me, which in turn makes me enjoy eating it more.

But cooking for yourself isn't simply therapy and training. It also happens to be a pleasure in itself. Since most women don't have lives now whereby we're plunged into three family meals a day from the age of nineteen, we're not forced to learn how to cook from the ground up. I don't complain. Nor do I wish to make it sound as if cooking for yourself were some sort of checklisted culinary foundation course. The reason why you learn so much from the sort of food you casually throw together for yourself, is that you're learning by accident, by osmosis. This has nothing to do with the culinary supremacism of the great chefs, or those who'd ape them. Too many people cook only when they're giving a dinner party. And it's very hard to go from nought to a hundred miles an hour. How can you learn to feel at ease around food, relaxed about cooking, if every time you go into the kitchen it's to cook at competition level?

I love the open-ended freedom of just pottering about

in the kitchen, of opening the fridge door and deciding what to cook. But I like, too, the smaller special project, the sort of indulgent eating that has something almost ceremonial about it when done alone. I'm not saying I don't often end up with that au pair special, a bowl of cereal, or its street-princess equivalent, the phone-in pizza. But I believe in the rule of 'Tonight Lucullus is dining with Lucullus.'

EATING ALONE, FOR me, is most often a prompt to shop. This is where self-absorption and consumerism meet: a rapt, satisfyingly convoluted pleasure. The food I want most to buy is the food I most often try not to eat: a swollen-bellied tranche of cheese, a loaf of bread. These constitute the perfect meal. A slither of gorgonzola or coulommiers sacrificed on the intrusive and unyielding surface of a Bath Oliver at the end of dinner is food out of kilter. Just bread and cheese is fine to give others if you've shown the consideration of providing variety. But I want for myself the obsessive focus of the one huge, heady *baveuse* soft cheese, or else a wedge of the palate-burning hard stuff: too much, too strong. If I'm eating a salty blue cheese, its texture somewhere between creamy and crumbly, I want baguette or a bitter, fudge-coloured *pain au levain*; with cheddar, real cheddar, I want doughier English white bread: whichever, it must be a whole loaf. I might eat tomatoes with the bread and cheese, but the tomatoes mustn't be in a salad, but left whole on the plate, to be sliced or chopped, *à la minute*. But, then, I love the delicatessen-garnered equivalent of the TV supper.

I am pretty keen on the culinary ethos of the Greasy Spoon, too: bacon sandwiches, fried-egg sandwiches, egg *and* bacon sandwiches, sausage sandwiches; none requires much in the way of attention, and certainly nothing in the way of expertise. Even easier is a sandwich that on paper sounds fancier, a fab merging of caff and deli culture: get a large flat field mushroom, put it in a preheated gas mark 6/200°C oven covered with butter, chopped garlic and parsley for about 20 minutes; when ready, and garlicky, buttery juices are oozing with black, cut open a soft roll, small ciabatta or bap, or chunk of baguette even, and wipe the cut side all over the pan to soak up the pungent juices. Smear with Dijon mustard, top with the mushroom, squeeze with lemon juice, sprinkle some salt and add some chopped lettuce or parsley as you like; think of this as a fungoid – but strangely hardly less meaty – version of steak sandwich. Bite in, with the juices dripping down your arm as you eat.

There are other memorable more or less non-cooking solitary suppers: one is a bowl of Heinz tomato soup with some pale, undercooked but overbuttered toast (crusts off for full nostalgic effect); another, microwave-zapped, mustard-dunked frankfurters (proper frankfurters, from a delicatessen, not those flabby, mousse-textured things out of a tin). The difficulty is that if I have them in the house, I end up eating them while I wait for whatever I'm actually cooking for dinner to be ready. And my portions are not small to start off with. Two defences, other than pure greed: I hate meagreness, the scant, sensible serving; and if I long to eat a particular thing, I want lots of it. I don't want course upon course, and I don't want excess every day. But when it comes to a feast, I don't know the meaning of enough.

Cooking for two is just an amplification of cooking for one (rather than the former being a diminution of the latter). To tell the truth, with my cooking and portion-size, there isn't often a lot to choose between them. Many of the impulses that inform or inspire this sort of cooking are the same: the desire to eat food that is relaxed but at times culinarily elevated without loss of spontaneity; the pleasures of fiddling about with what happens to be in the fridge; and, as with any form of eating, the need to make food part of the civilised context in which we live.

Linguine with clams

My absolutely favourite dinner to cook for myself is linguine with clams. I have a purely personal reason for thinking of fish, of any sort, as the ideal solitary food because I live with someone who's allergic to it. But my principle has wider application: fish doesn't take long to cook and tastes best dealt with simply, but because it has to be bought fresh needs enough planning to have something of the ceremonial about it. I don't know why spaghetti alle vongole (I use linguine because I prefer, here, the more substantial, more resistant and at the same time more sauce-absorbent tangle they make in the mouth) is thought of as restaurant food, especially since most restaurants in this country ruin it by adding tomatoes. I have to have my sauce *bianco*.

The whole dish is easy to make. It is, for me, along with a steak béarnaise, unchallengeable contender for that great, fantasy Last Meal on Earth.

You can use venus clams, but palourdes or vongole are what you're after; at a good fishmonger's, you shouldn't have any trouble finding them. If you've got venus clams, add 1 tablespoon of bicarbonate of soda to the soaking water. If you've got the bigger palourdes, you may not need to soak them at all, a brisk wash may be enough: ask your fishmonger.

200g clams	½ dried red chilli pepper
150g linguine	80ml white wine or vermouth
1 clove garlic	(Noilly Prat)
2 tablespoons olive oil	1–2 tablespoons fresh parsley,
	chopped

Put the clams to soak in a sinkful of cold water, if necessary, while you heat the water for the pasta. When the water comes to the boil, add salt and then the linguine. Cook the linguine until nearly but not quite ready: you're going to give them a fractional amount more cooking with the clams and their winey juices. Try and time this so that the pasta's ready at the time you want to plunge it into the clams. Otherwise drain and douse with a few drops of olive oil.

Mince or finely slice the garlic and, in a pan with a lid into which you can fit the pasta later, fry it gently (it mustn't burn) in the olive oil and then crumble in the red chilli pepper. Drain the clams, discarding those that remain open, and add them to the garlic pan. Pour over the wine or vermouth and cover. In 2 minutes, the clams should be open. Add the pasta, put the lid on again and swirl about. In another minute or so everything should have finished cooking and come together: the pasta will have cooked to the requisite tough tenderness and absorbed the salty, garlicky winey clam juices, and be bound in a wonderful almost-pungent sea-syrup. But if the pasta needs more cooking, clamp on the lid and give it more time. Chuck out any clams which have failed to open.

Add half the parsley, shake the pan to distribute evenly, and turn onto a plate or into a bowl and sprinkle over the rest of the parsley. Cheese is not grated over any pasta with fish in it in Italy (nor indeed where garlic is the predominant ingredient, either) and the rule holds good. You need add nothing. It's perfect already.

THE ESSENCE OF eating for two exists in just one word: steak. I'm not saying I wouldn't cook it just for me, but there's something solid, old-fashioned and comforting about the two of you sitting down and eating steak. Too often when I'm at home alone I waft along, as you do, in a tangle of noodles, lemon grass and suchlike. Steak béarnaise is my dream. Fry a steak as a steak is fried, on a hot pan and for a short time. I don't do frites. Green salad made bloody with the steak's juices, and some real baguette, more than make up, in my book, for my chip deficiency; but then I live practically next door to a chip shop, so if I'm eating with someone who takes a less tolerant line, I'm safe. Just as I think that roast chicken is so good that I need a lot of persuading to cook it any other way, so I feel about steak that it is perfect simply grilled or fried. But steak au poivre, aux poivres, peppered steak, whichever handle you like to put on it, is, in shorn form, a forceful contender. For me it's better without the addition of cream; I like my steak butch, brown and meaty. This is hardly the orthodox approach, and I can see that you might feel a culinary classic ought to be respected. Sometimes I'd even agree. Just go cautiously. You don't want to feel you're having pudding at the same time.

Steak au poivre

I use either black peppercorns, half black, half white or, more often, a many-berried pepper mixture: some of the mixture isn't strictly speaking pepper at all, but I like its warm aromatic quality, rather mellower than the heat of pepper alone. I have been meaning for years now to buy a coffee grinder especially for spices, but still haven't managed to do so and use a pestle and mortar.

2 middle-cut rump steaks (or
    sirloin if you prefer), about
    3cm thick
scant tablespoon olive oil

3 tablespoons peppercorns,
    ground coarsely (see above)
3 tablespoons butter, plus
    more if liked
3 tablespoons brandy

Using a pastry brush if you've got one, paint the steaks on both sides with oil; you should need not more than a teaspoon on each side. Then dredge the oily steaks in the mashed peppercorns: you want a good crusty coat. If the corns are too coarse, they'll just fall off; if they're too fine, you won't stop coughing when you eat them.

In a heavy-bottomed pan, put the remaining oil to heat up. Add the steaks, and sear on each side, then, over moderate heat, add the butter and another drop of olive oil and cook the steaks for about another 3 minutes a side or to requisite bloodiness. Remove to warmed plates. Turn the heat up to high again, then pour in the brandy, stirring well all the time to deglaze the pan. When you've got a thick syrupy glaze, taste it: you may want to add salt, and you may want to whisk in a little butter just to help it all taste and look smooth and amalgamated. This, too, is where you could add your dollop of cream if you wanted. I've also, instead of the brandy, used Marsala, without which I'm pathologically incapable of existing, and it was dee-licious.

Serves 2.

EVERY DAY I thank God, or his supermarket stand-in, for frozen peas. For me, they are a leading ingredient, a green meat, almost. I don't eat them that much, straight, as a vegetable, but I'd hate to have to cook without them. The almost instant soup – a handful of peas, a jugful of stock, a rind of cheese, whatever's to hand – makes for a sweetly restoring supper. The pea risotto that follows is another regular. Risotto is best suited to two. I like relative peace in which to cook it, and I prefer handling small quantities. It is also the world's best comfort food.

The quantities I use might be nearer those ordinarily specified for four; but when I cook risotto I don't want to eat anything else after. And I feel a pang if there's only enough for one middling-sized flat puddle of the stuff.

Pea risotto

I specify frozen petits pois, simply because that's what I always use. I have used real peas, just podded, to make *risi e bisi*, the fabulously named Venetian slurpily soft risotto, or thick rice soup, however you like to think of it, complete with pea-pod stock. But to be frank, if you don't grow peas yourself, then there is (as I may have mentioned, and I do, often) not a huge advantage in using fresh ones. By the time they're in the shops, they're big and starchy and without that extraordinary, almost floral, scent; that heady but contained sweetness of peas just picked from the garden.

On the whole, I take the peas out and let them thaw before using them. But I don't see that it makes much difference.

Every day I thank God, or his supermarket stand-in, for frozen peas

As for stock: I haven't specified any in particular. When I can, I use ham stock which, because of my stock-making obsession, I usually have in the freezer; otherwise I make up some with vegetable stock granules. I wouldn't use a dark beef stock here, but any chicken, veal or light broth would be fine.

60g butter

150g frozen petits pois

approx. 1 litre stock

2 tablespoons freshly grated parmesan, plus more for the table

grated nutmeg

1 small onion or, even better, banana shallot

drop of oil

200g arborio or Canaroli rice

80ml white wine or vermouth

Put about a third of the butter in a pan and when it's melted add the peas, and cook, stirring every now and again, for 2 minutes. Remove half the peas and to the remaining half in the pan add a ladleful of the stock. Put a lid on the pan and let cook gently for about 5 minutes or so till soft. Purée this mixture – I use the mini electric chopper I used to use for baby food – with 1 tablespoon each of grated parmesan and butter and a grating each of pepper and fresh nutmeg.

Meanwhile, chop the onion or shallot very finely, and melt another tablespoon of butter, with a drop of oil in it, in a pan. Cook the onion, stirring with your wooden prodder, for about 4 minutes, then add the rice and stir till every grain glistens with the oniony fat. Pour in the wine or vermouth (last time I did this

I used Chambéry and it was fabulous: it seemed to add to the grassy freshness of the peas) and let it bubble away and absorb. Then add a ladleful of the hot stock (I keep it on low on the neighbouring hob) and stir until this too is absorbed. Carry on in this vein, patiently, for another 10 minutes, then add the whole, just sautéed peas, and then start again, a ladleful of stock at a time. In about another 8 minutes or so the rice should be cooked and the risotto creamy. Taste to see if you need any more time or liquid. It's hard to be precise: sometimes you'll find you have stock left over; at others you'll need to add water from the kettle.

When you're happy with it, add the buttery pea and parmesan purée and beat it in well. Taste, season as needed, then beat in the remaining tablespoon of parmesan and any butter you may have left. You can sprinkle over some chopped flat-leaf parsley (and since I've got it growing in the garden I have no reason not to), but the lack of it won't give you any grief.

Serves 2.

Weekend Lunch

ALTHOUGH THE DINNER party remains the symbol of social eating, most eating in company among my friends actually takes place at weekend lunch. After a long day at work many of us are, frankly, too tired to go out and eat dinner, let alone cook it. And there is, as well, the baby factor. For many people of my generation, having to get food ready after the children have gone to bed explains the popularity of the Marks & Spencer menu. And even those who haven't got children are affected by the babysitting arrangements of their friends who have. When I was younger we stayed in bed at weekends until two in the afternoon: now that most of us are woken at six in the morning, there is a gap in the day where lunch can go. We have got into the habit of filling it.

Lunch is more forgiving than dinner: there isn't the dread engendered by perceived but not-quite-formulated expectations: there's no agenda, no aspirational model to follow, no socio-culinary challenge to which to rise; in short, no pressure. Lunch is just lunch.

And if you don't want to cook it, you don't have to. Saturday lunch can be at its most relaxed and pleasurable when it is just an indoor picnic. What matters, then, is what you buy. These days shopping is nobly recast as 'sourcing' – and clever you for finding the best chilli-marinaded olives, French sourdough bread or air-dried beef: certainly no shame for not clattering about with your own pots and pans instead.

Shopping is not necessarily the easy option. It's certainly not the cheap one. But discerning extravagance (rather than mere feckless vulgarity) can be immensely pleasurable. Indeed, I can find it positively uplifting: not for nothing is shopping known as retail therapy. Shopping for food is better than any other form of shopping. There's no trying-on for a start. Choosing the right cheese, the best and ripest tomato, the pinkest, sweetest ham can be intensely gratifying. And in shopping for food which you are then going to prepare (even if that preparation involves no more than de-bagging and unwrapping) there is also the glorious self-indulgence of knowing that you are giving pleasure to others.

Shopping is not a quick activity: you need to be prepared to proceed slowly, haltingly. Compromise can be ruinous. Of course, some of the time we all eat food that is less than perfect, less than enjoyable even, but you can't set out to buy inferior produce – what would be the point?

Good food doesn't have to be difficult to cook, and it

certainly doesn't need to be difficult to buy. But you must know what you're after. The important thing is to be greedy enough to get what's good, but not so restlessly greedy that you get too much of it. Restrict your choices, so that you provide lots of a few things rather than small amounts of many. This is partly an aesthetic dictate, partly a practical one. If you buy 100g slices of six different cheeses, everyone is going to feel inhibited about cutting some off; however generous you have been, it is only the meagreness of each portion that will be apparent. Provide, instead, a semblance – indeed the reality – of voluptuous abundance. You don't need to buy more than three different cheeses, but get great big fat wodges of each. You want munificence, you want plenty, you want people to feel they can eat as much as they want and there'll still be some left over afterwards. Start by thinking along the lines of one hard cheese, one soft cheese and maybe a blue cheese or chèvre. You needn't stick to this rigidly: sometimes it's good just to be seduced by the particular cheeses spread out in front of you on a cheese counter. Keep your head, though: without ruling out whim entirely, don't be immoderately ensnared by fanciful names or the provocatively unfamiliar. One type of cheese no one has heard of might well be interesting, but not three. Anyway, the desire to be interesting is possibly the most damaging impulse in cooking. Never worry about what your guests will think of you. Just think of the food. What will taste good?

And you don't have to go through the ridiculous

pantomime of pretending everything is homespun. If you're still getting your shopping out and unwrapping your packages when everyone arrives, who cares? Your kitchen doesn't have to look like a set from a 1950s American sitcom. It is curiously relaxing to be slowly creating the canvas – arranging the table, putting flowers in a vase, chopping up herbs and putting water on for potatoes – while talking and drinking unhurriedly with friends.

The shops nearest you will probably govern what sort of food you buy. I stick to the plainest basics: meat, cheese, bread; with tomatoes, a green salad, maybe some robustly salted, herb-speckled potatoes, the waxy fleshed, puce-skinned ones, cooked till sweet and soft then doused in oil, scarcely dribbled with vinegar or spritzed with lemon, and with a few feathery pieces of chopped zest on them, left to sit around to be eaten at room temperature.

If you're buying ham, get enough to cover a huge great plate with densely meaty pink slices. I sometimes buy both English ham, cut off the bone in the shop, and the cured Italian stuff. I like prosciutto di San Daniele better than prosciutto di Parma (the glorious, requisite, honeyed saltiness is more intense), but as long as it's well cut – and obviously freshly cut – so that each white-rimmed silky slice can be removed without sticking or tearing, that's fine: more than fine.

There is internal pressure in my home to buy bresaola, too, but although I like eating it well enough, I never mind if I don't. I'd rather buy a big, unpacketed, butcher-made pork pie, one which has a short, short flaky crust lined with clear salty jelly and then, within, densely packed smooth and peppery pork. Salame, too, is good. I don't think you need both salame and pie, so choose which you prefer. If you buy a whole little salame, as with the large pork pie, you can introduce an all-important DIY element into the proceedings: put it on a wooden board with a sharp knife and let people carve off for themselves thick, fat-pearled slices of spicy sausage. This way, the individual act of cutting, slicing, serving yourself, becomes almost a conversational tool. It makes people feel at home when they're around your kitchen table. Allow yourself a few saucer-sized plates of extras – maybe some fresh, marinated anchovies, olives steeped with shards of garlic and crumbled red chillies, astringent little cornichons, those ones that look like cartoon crocodiles in embryo, a soft, moussy slab of pâté – but, again, don't go overboard. I sometimes succumb to one of those Italian jars of olive-oil-soused blackened globes of chargrilled onions, sweet and smoky and wonderful with meat or cheese or a plain plate of bitter leaves.

If you prefer fish to meat, go for the old-fashioned traditional option: a huge plate of London-cure smoked salmon – mild, satiny and softly fleshy – with cornichons, lemon and maybe a pile of blinis, potato pancakes, a loaf or two of sandy soda bread, or thinly sliced and already buttered brown. If you have a delicatessen or fishmonger near you that sells a good enough version of the stuff, then maybe you should get a tentacled mess of Italianish seafood salad. I quite like, too, that old-fashioned pairing of tuna and beans. My Great-Aunt Myra, who was a wonderful cook, always used butter beans (just out of the tin, as was, of course, the olive-oil preserved tuna) and would gently mix the two, squeeze lemon over and cover with a fine net of wafer-thin onion rings. Yes, proper dried then soaked and cooked and drained real beans are always better, but there's something comforting and familiar for me in that quick and effort-free assembly. It tastes of my childhood.

Smoked salmon calls for brown bread, but there's something reassuring about a thick wedge of white bread, heavy with cold unsalted butter and curved over a tranche of quickly grabbed ham to make a casual sandwich. But all that matters is that the bread is good: sweet, sunflower-seed-studded brown, English bloomer or French bread – which could be a just-bought baguette or, my favourite, the slender ficelle. I sometimes think if I see another ciabatta I'll scream.

Frankly, if you can get good enough tomatoes, I'd just leave them as they are, whole, with a knife near by (a good, sharp, serrated one, suitable for the job) so that people can eat them in juicy red wedges with their bread and cheese, or cut them thinly and sprinkle with oil and salt to make their own private pools of tomato salad.

A green salad needn't comprise anything other than lettuce. All you need for dressing is good oil, a quick squeeze of lemon and a confident hand with the salt, tossed with your own bare hands. You can, of course, supplement the torn leaves (and let's be frank, most of us will be opening one of those cellophane packets) with some thin tongues of courgette (the slivers stripped off with the vegetable peeler), chopped spring onions or a handful of not-even-blanched sugar-snap peas or whatever you want. There's one proviso: keep it green. There is something depressingly institutional about cheerfully mixed salads. I was brought up like this: my mother was fanatical, and her aesthetic has seeped into my bloodstream; my father takes the same line. Do not even think of adding your tomatoes: keep them separate. Cucumber tends to make the salad weepy. Give it its own plate, and dress with peppery, mint-thick or dill-soused yoghurt or an old-fashioned sweet-sour vinaigrette.

In the same way, I am fanatical about keeping fruit separate. There is, for me, something so boarding-housey about the capacious bowl filled with waxy, dusty bananas, a few oranges, some pears and the odd shrunken apple. I want a plate of oranges, another of bananas, of apples, of pears. I even put black and white grapes on separate plates.

An unfussy lunch sprawled out on a Saturday definitely doesn't demand culinary high jinks. Don't worry about pudding. You just need some tubs of good ice-cream – there is a dangerously tempting large stock of them out there now – whichever make you like most. Or buy a tart from a good French pâtisserie.

Sunday lunch

PROPER SUNDAY LUNCH is everything contemporary cook-ing is not. Meat-heavy, hostile to innovation, resolutely formalised, it is as much ritual as meal, and an almost extinct ritual at that. Contemporary trends, it is true, have hastened a reappraisal of traditional cooking. But neither nostalgia for nursery foods nor an interest in ponderous culinary Victoriana is what Sunday lunch – Sunday dinner – is all about. It doesn't change, is impervious to considerations of health or fashion; it is about solidity, the family, the home.

One of the silent, inner promises I made myself on hav-ing children was to provide a home that made a reassuring, all-comers-welcome tradition of Sunday lunch. It hasn't materialised quite yet, but few of my generation lead meat-and-two-veg lives any more. We are generally more mobile, the weekend is no longer home-bound. Nor do we want to be kitchen-bound (and those with small children hardly have the time on their hands for involved cooking). The fact is that Sunday lunch is impossible to pull off with-out putting in at least a couple of hours by the sink and the stove. And it is far from being the sort of cooking anyway that finds favour now: the relaxed, let's throw this with that and come up with something simple and pictur-esquely rustic approach will not put a joint, Yorkshire pudding and roast potatoes on the table. To cook a decent Sunday lunch needs discipline and strict timekeeping.

But with modest organisation, there can be something strangely reassuring about cooking a traditional meal. It is about choreography, about timetabling, and has its own pleasures. We are so accustomed to being invited to consider cooking an art that we forget just how rewarding and satisfying it is as pure craft. My Latin teacher, Miss Plummer, who had the misfortune to teach at one of the less academic schools I frequented, used, with a sort of elegiac condescension, to remark that none of us could know the simple yet substantial pleasures of the carpenter in making a chair. But cooking does give that pleasure, and there are particular satisfactions peculiar to the making of Sunday lunch.

I love the solidity of it all: I don't mean by that the robust nature of the food alone, so much as the weighty texture of hospitality, of plain food warmly given. But it would be wrong to dwell too much on some notional and universally shared longing for a family group assembled around a big table, sharing food. There is that, maybe, but I think people tend to be frightened of cooking Sunday lunch themselves because of a fear or dread that is, frankly, family-induced. The still-remembered tensions of Sunday lunches of the past must be the underlying deterrent, rather than the cooking itself, in the present.

But it is possible to have a family lunch which dispenses, in any literal sense, with family (not that this is necessarily desirable). In the past, connections were familial; the boundaries were of blood. Today, people get their sense of extended family from their friends. I tend to find myself surrounded by people with small children. Others are differently bound.

Now, there is no reason on earth why you should feel it incumbent on yourself to get into a frenzy of batter-making and parsnip-peeling just because it is Sunday. And it's true that I might well have people over for Sunday lunch and give them pasta. The rule – if rule there can ever be – is the same rule that applies in any form of cooking: be honest; cook what you want to eat, not what you want to be seen eating.

Whenever I cook for people I find it easier to have scribbled down in front of me the times at which I'm meant to do any key thing – put things in the oven, take them out – just because once I start talking or drinking I tend to lose track. I haven't suggested this alongside any menus elsewhere because I can't know what time you'll be eating and anyway have tried not to be too bossy. With full-on Sunday lunch, I have no such compunction. It has to be planned as efficiently as a military campaign.

Traditional Sunday lunch does, of course, mean beef. As for cuts: it helps here as well to go to a butcher rather than the supermarket. You can explain what you want, or ask what you think you should want, for how many people, how you want to carve it and so on. Rib of beef gives the best flavour, but it is very difficult to carve. I am a hopeless carver and believe that in cooking especially, though in everything really, it is better to play to your strengths than your weaknesses. Besides, if you can't do much more than hack at it, it's a waste. I am resigned to buying a boned joint. I have recently become very extravagant and gone for contrefilet; a boned sirloin would be good, too, though.

I have always found gravy problematic, but for beef I don't think you can casually deglaze the roasting dish with some red wine and hope it'll be all right. Nor does that mean the opposite extreme: the thick, floury, school gloop. Banish instant gravy powders and granules from your thoughts and your store cupboards. Instead, start caramelising your onions early, and cook them slowly. This may be difficult when you're trying to orchestrate everything else for lunch, but you can easily do the gravy the day before and then just reheat and add meat juices at the last minute.

Roast potatoes are another fraught area. I have, in the past, got frantic with despair as the time for the meat to be ready drew closer and the potatoes were still blond and untroubled in their roasting pan. The key here is to get the fat hotter than you would believe necessary before you start and to continue to cook the potatoes at a higher heat and for longer than you might believe possible. And you must roughen them up after parboiling.

The heat of the fat is again the crucial element in making a Yorkshire pudding rise. There's no doubt this is easier if you have two ovens (one for the beef, one for the Yorkshire pudding), but the beef can either be cooked at a very high temperature for a quick blast and then at a moderate one for a while or at a highish one all the time. You can always blast the Yorkshire pudding on a high heat while the beef is resting on its carving board.

Roast root vegetables are traditional, but I tend not to bother. With the roast potatoes and Yorkshire pudding, you hardly need more starch, though if I'm cooking roast pork, or roast beef without the Yorkshire pudding, or the usual roast chicken, I might do parsnips, either roasted alongside the potatoes, or anointed with honey in another pan and put in the oven to grow sweet and burnished.

As for other vegetables, I think you need two sorts. This can make life difficult, but not insurmountably so. It's just a matter, again, of time management: the important thing is not suddenly to need about 6 pans on a 4-hob stove. And there doesn't need to be too much chopping. Choose, for example, frozen peas and something to provide fresh, green crunch: beans, Savoy cabbage, pak choi. I love broccoli, but it is very sweet, and with the peas you don't really need any more sweetness. It's unconventional, but I do rather like a tomato salad somewhere too, especially if it's still warm outside.

I don't often make my own horseradish sauce – I buy a good bottled one and add a bit of crème fraîche, ordinary cream or Greek yoghurt – but mustard must, for me, be English and made up at the last minute. I don't mind having other mustards on the table but, for me, the whole meal is ruined without proper English mustard.

Traditionalists will insist on a sturdy pie or crumble for pudding, but really, after all that carbohydrate, have you got room? I am immensely greedy, but I don't like that invasive and uncomfortable feeling of bloatedness that can make you regret eating much more than a hangover can ever make you regret drinking.

Now that you seem to be able to get blueberries all the year round, I often serve them with a large, shallow bowl of Barbados cream. This – yoghurt and double cream stirred together, fudgy brown sugar sprinkled on top – has the advantage of having to be done the day before. I love lemon ice-cream after this (and it's good with blueberries, or indeed any berries, too) and I sometimes make one that doesn't need fiddling about with while freezing – you just bung it in the freezer. Nothing is quite as good as proper ice-cream, made with a custard base and then churned until solid, but home cooking is based on compromises, and a simple pudding is a compromise I am often grateful to make. You could consider a crumble if only because the crumble mixture can be made up earlier and just sprinkled on the fruit as you sit down and cooked while you eat the beef. Remember: you are not trying to produce the definitive Sunday lunch to end all Sunday lunches. Nor are you a performance artist. The idea is to make a lunch which you want to eat and can imagine sitting down to do so without bursting into tears.

I'M SORRY TO sound bossy, but Sunday lunch, as I've said, has to be run like a military campaign. I find it easier to decide when I want to eat and then work backwards, writing every move down on a pad which I keep in a fixed place in the kitchen. This timetable is engineered towards having lunch ready to eat at 2pm exactly. I take it for granted that pudding's been made already.

All quantities and timings have in mind a lunch for about 6 adults and perhaps some children and are based on having a 2¼kg joint to cook.

11.20	Start gravy
11.30	Take beef out of fridge
11.50	Peel potatoes
12.05	Put the potatoes in their water in the pan, bring to the boil and parboil. Preheat oven to gas mark 7/210°C
12.15	Put roasting pan in oven with a knob of dripping for beef
12.20	Put beef in
12.35	Prepare any veg that need chopping or cleaning, etc.
12.40	Put pan with dripping for potatoes in oven
12.50	Make Yorkshire pudding
1.00	Put potatoes in
1.05	Prepare veg. Turn on plate warmer or hot cupboard
1.25	Put veg water on
1.35	Put pan with dripping for Yorkshire pudding in oven
1.40	Take out beef and put in Yorkshire pudding, turning oven up to gas mark 8/220°C as you do so. Let beef stand
1.45	Cook vegetables
2.00	Take out Yorkshire pudding and potatoes

The roast beef

I think many people underplay how much meat you need. For 6 people, I wouldn't consider getting under 2¼kg (or

5lb), which, in other words, is about 375g per person. A joint is a sad prospect without the possibility of leftovers. For a rib you should add on about 1kg extra here.

For rare meat you can either cook the beef at the highest possible temperature for 15 minutes and then turn it down to gas mark 4/180°C and cook for 15 minutes per lb (I still find it easier to calculate the cooking time per lb) or at gas mark 7/210°C throughout for 15 minutes per lb, which is what I did here. Think of 15 minutes per lb as about 33 minutes per kg. I usually do 15 minutes per lb and then add on an extra 5 minutes so that those who don't like rare meat have a bit of slightly more cooked beef from the ends. Those who don't like blood don't have to get it: the rest of us gratifyingly do.

All I do to the beef is to massage it with dry mustard powder after I've taken it out of the fridge. I use a knob of dripping for the pan, but you could use whatever fat you have to hand.

The gravy

Gravy is one of my weaknesses, which is to say I find it hard to make a convincing light and thin juice. To overcome my deficiencies I took to following Jane Grigson's recipe for onion gravy (indeed most of my Sunday is Grigson-based), adding a drop of Marsala to it. You don't need to – you could use some Madeira or even some sweet sherry or just add a little bit more sugar – but the Marsala brings a wonderful aromatic muskiness to the gravy. If I don't have any real beef stock, I use a tub of good fresh beef stock. You can use a stock cube (try an Italian one), in which case use it well diluted and taste before putting in any more salt.

You can start the gravy the day before if you want, just reheating and adding meat juices at the last minute.

15g butter, and a dribble of oil or dripping	**pinch brown sugar**
1 onion, sliced very thinly in the food processor	**2 tablespoons Marsala**
	1 teaspoon flour
	300ml beef stock

Melt the butter (with the oil or dripping to stop it burning) in a saucepan and cook the onion in it at a very low temperature, stirring often. When the onion is soft add the sugar and Marsala and let it caramelise. Cover with foil, putting the foil as near to the bottom of the pan as possible and continue to cook, still on a very low flame, for about 10 minutes. Then stir in the flour and cook, stirring, for about 2 minutes. Stir in the stock, bring to the boil (you can turn the heat up here) then reduce the heat to very low again and simmer gently for about 20 minutes. Purée in the food processor (or you can strain it, pushing the soft onion through the sieve). Pour back into the saucepan. At the last minute, reheat and add meat juices from roasting pan. This gravy is wonderfully stress-free, since you don't have to be doing furious deglazing at the last minute.

The roast potatoes

I like roast potatoes fairly small, so I cut a medium-to-large one into about 3. For 6 people, I suppose, that's about

1¾kg. Well, that may be over-generous, but nothing is worse than too few.

Peel the potatoes and cut them into large chunks. Put them in cold salted water, bring to the boil and parboil for 4–5 minutes. Drain, put back in the saucepan, put on the lid and bang the whole thing about a bit so that the edges of the potatoes get blurred: the rough edges help them catch in the fat and so get crisp. Add 1 tablespoon or so of semolina and give the pan, with its lid on, another good shake. The semolina gives the potatoes a divinely sweet edge: not at all cloying or inappropriate, just an intensified caughtness, as it were. When my mother and aunts were young, they had an Italian au pair, Antonia, who, when required to make a British Sunday lunch (having never cooked anything other than Italian food), adopted, or rather invented, this practice. If you're unconvinced, or don't have any semolina to hand, just use flour and shake the warm potatoes around in it. The flour doesn't give the same honey-toned depth as semolina, but helps the potatoes catch and brown wonderfully.

It's essential that the fat's hot before the potatoes go in. I use 2 tablespoon-sized lumps of goose fat or some truly superb grass-fed beef dripping. If you can lay your hands on neither, of course you can use oil or even vegetable fat. The potatoes must not be taken out of the oven until you are absolutely ready to eat them. They will take approximately an hour to cook.

The Yorkshire pudding

I always use Jane Grigson's *English Food* for the Chinese York-shire pudding recipe, which is not as odd as it sounds. The story is that when a big competition was held in Leeds for the best Yorkshire pudding, the winner was a Chinese cook called Tin Sung Yang. For years it was held to have a mystery ingredient – tai luk sauce – until, Jane Grigson reports, a niece of hers found that this was a Chinese joke. Nevertheless, the recipe is different from normal: it works backwards. That's to say, you mix the eggs and milk and then stir in the flour, rather than making a well in the flour and adding the eggs and milk: and it works triumphantly; it billows up into a gloriously copper crown of a cushion. I am able to cook this for the most die-hard, pudding-proud northerners without inhibition or anxiety. I prefer Yorkshire pudding to be in one dish rather than in those depressing, canteen-style individual portions, so for this amount, I use an enamel dish about 30cm by 19cm and 7cm deep. Cook it on the top shelf of the oven but make sure the shelf isn't too high up as the Yorkshire pudding really does rise. I have had to prise it off the ceiling of the oven, which slightly dented its magnificence and my glory.

300ml milk	**250g plain flour, sifted**
4 eggs	

Mix all the ingredients, except the flour, with pepper and a scant ½ teaspoon of salt, beating them well together. I use my free-standing mixer, the fabulous American KitchenAid, but anything – hand-held electric mixer, rotary or balloon whisk – would do. Let these ingredients stand for 15 minutes and then whisk in the flour. Meanwhile put the pan with 1 tablespoon or so of dripping or whatever other fat you're using in a very high oven. Into this intensely hot pan you should pour the batter, when you're ready for it, and cook for 20 minutes. Bring it, triumphant, to the table.

Calming winter lunch for 6

Roast pork loin with roast leeks
Clapshot with burnt onions
Custard tart

MUCH AS I LOVE proper roast leg of pork with its carapace of amber-glazed crackling, I don't cook it that much: roast boned and rolled loin is my more regular pig-out. I feel at ease with it, even though the flesh can tend to dry stringiness. Ask the butcher for rib-end of loin (hard to carve, but wonderful tasting). And put a little liquid in the roasting pan so the meat grows tender in its own small pool of odoriferous steam. Anything will do: a glass of wine or cider, some stock, water mixed with apple juice, the leftover liquid you've cooked carrots in.

Cooking boned and rolled pork loin bears almost any interpretation or elaboration. By elaboration, I mean not to imply complexity of culinary arrangement but wide-rangingness. If you want, at other times, to add a modern, fusiony note, make a paste of garlic and root ginger and smear that over, rubbing ground ginger into the prepared and removed rind for hot crackling; if you want something altogether less vibrant, then pulverise some dried bay leaves, and press these against the soft covering of white fat. Or rub in ground cloves, cinnamon and cardamom to produce an almost – if inappropriate – Middle Eastern waft. Neither of these requires crackling; here you would be after altogether less strenuous eating.

Get the butcher to remove the bones and give them to you, so you can cook them around the joint, which will make the gravy. And while you're about it, ask him to chop them up small. As for the rind: if you want crackling, ask him to remove the rind, score it and give it back to you; and, even if you don't want crackling, the loin should be left elegantly wrapped in its pearly coating of fat. If there's not enough fat on the joint, it will end up too dry.

Roast loin of pork

You will need about 1.8kg boned, derinded weight, which means a joint, before butchering, in the region of 2½kg. If you're a good carver, don't bother with boning. Either way, the crackling should be cooked separately.

Preheat the oven to gas mark 7/210°C. Work out how long the loin needs – and at roughly 45 minutes per kg, for a 1.8kg joint that's about 70 minutes – and cook the loin in its pan on one shelf, and, putting it in about 45 minutes before you want to eat, the crackling on a rack over a roasting tray on another shelf. About halfway through the pork's cooking time throw a glass of wine (or whatever you're using; cider would be very good here) into the pan.

Some people simply get the rind removed and then drape it over the loin as it cooks. The reason I don't do this is because then you have to do a real number to rid the juices in the meat dish of fat. I am not one of nature's gravy makers, and therefore I do everything to make life easier for myself – and frankly suggest you do too. As for this gravy: all you need to do – having cooked the crackling in a separate pan – is pour the winey juices from the meat dish into a sauceboat or bowl, removing fat if you can and if you need to. Taste it: you may need to add a little bit of water, you may just want to use it as is. I am not on the whole a thick-gravy person: you may be.

Roast leeks

For 6 people, get about 8 not too fat leeks (although one each would probably be enough, I'd always rather have over). Once you've made sure they're clean, cut them on the diagonal into logs about 8cm long. Pour some olive oil in a roasting tray and turn the leeks in them so they're glossy all over. Sprinkle over some coarse sea salt and roast for about 30 minutes at gas mark 7/210°C, I usually roast them at a higher temperature and for slightly less time, but it would be absurd to complicate matters since you're going to have the oven at mark 7 anyway.

I love these leeks blistered sweet on the outside, suggestively oniony within their slithery centre. I know that there are going to be onions themselves with the clapshot, but the pork can take the double helping of allium. If you feel otherwise, make a large, iron-dark bowl of butter-drenched kale. Kale, indeed, is a feature of traditional clapshot; this recipe makes do without and it is tempting to make up the shortfall. If you wanted to add a slightly more modern touch, then simply get some pak choi or choi sum (which most supermarkets seem to stock now) and steam or stir-fry it with or without lacily grated ginger.

Clapshot with burnt onions

I got the idea for this in the *Tesco Recipe Collection* of October 1996 in an article written by Catherine Brown. It is a modern take on a traditional dish, which was a hodge-podge of various vegetables cooked and mushed together. This is something not so stylish as to be self-conscious, but not so hearty as to be indigestible.

1kg swede, peeled and diced	*for the burnt onions*
1kg floury potatoes, such as golden wonder, King Edward or Kerr's Pink, peeled and quartered	4 tablespoons olive oil
	2 large strong onions, very thinly sliced
100g butter	2 tablespoons caster sugar
fresh nutmeg	

First, make the clapshot: put the swede in a pan of boiling, salted water, and simmer for about 5 minutes. Add the potatoes and simmer for about 25–30 more minutes until both are just cooked. Don't overcook or they will disintegrate into potato soup. Drain thoroughly.

Dry the swede and potato slightly by putting them back in the saucepan (which you've wiped dry) and placing it over a low heat. Then mash – with a potato ricer or mouli – with the butter. Season to taste, adding a good grating of fresh nutmeg.

While the potatoes and swede are cooking, get started with the onion-burning. Heat the oil in a heavy-based frying pan over low heat. Slice the onions very finely (I use the processor for this), add to the oil and cook slowly for about 30 minutes until crisp and golden brown, stirring and scraping from time to time. Turn heat to high and sprinkle with sugar and stir continuously for a further 3 minutes or so until the sugar caramelises and the onion darkens.

Put the clapshot in a serving bowl and top with the burnt onions.

Custard tart

I adore custard tart: I love its barely-vanilla-scented, nutmeggy softness, the silky texture of that buttermilk-coloured eggy cream, solidified just enough to be carved into trembling wedges on the plate. It isn't hard to make, but I botch it often out of sheer clumsiness. But now I have learnt my lessons, and pass them on to you. One: pour the custard into the pastry case while the pastry case is in the oven, so that you don't end up leaving a trail from kitchen counter to cooker, soaking the pastry case in the process. And two: don't be so keen to use up every last scrap of that custard, filling the case right to the very brim so that it's bound – as you knew it was – to spill, making it soggy and ruining the contrast between crisp crust and tender filling. If you can manage not to do both those things, then you can make a perfect custard pie. I won't promise it's an easy exercise, though.

If you want to eat it cold, this makes life easier as you can arrange to have free play with the oven the day before. But, at its best, the custard should still have a memory of heat about it. Make it before you put the pork in the oven and let it sit for 1½ hours or thereabouts, gently subsiding into muted warmth in the kitchen.

If you can't be bothered to make the pastry yourself you have a choice: either you can use bought shortcrust or don't bother with a crust at all and make a baked custard. For a baked custard, make double quantities of custard, then pour it into a pie dish (with a capacity of just over 1 litre), stand the pie dish in a roasting tin filled with hot water and bake in a gas mark 2/150°C oven for about 1 hour.

If you don't keep vanilla sugar – although I do recommend it, see page 52 – then just add a few drops of real vanilla extract to the mixture. Of course you can always add an actual vanilla pod to the milk and cream when you warm them, but actually I don't like baked custard with too much vanilla: I like the merest musky suggestion of it.

for the pastry

120g plain flour, preferably Italian 00

30g icing sugar

80g cold butter

1 egg yolk

1/2 teaspoon pure vanilla extract

1 egg white (leftover from yolk for custard) to seal

for the custard

3 eggs	150ml milk
1 egg yolk	pinch ground mace
2 tablespoons vanilla sugar	freshly grated nutmeg
300ml single cream	

To make the pastry sift the flour and icing sugar into a dish and add the cold butter, cut into small cubes. Put this dish, just as it is, in the deep-freeze for 10 minutes. In a small bowl beat the egg yolk with the vanilla extract, a tablespoon of iced water and a pinch of salt. Put this bowl in the fridge. When the 10 minutes are up, put the flour and butter in a processor with the double blade fitted or in a mixer with the flat paddle on slow and turn on. After barely a minute, the mixture will begin to resemble oatmeal or flattened breadcrumbs, and this is when you add the yolk mixture. Be prepared to add more iced water, drop by cautious drop, until you have a nearly coherent dough. Then scoop it out, still just crumbly, push it into a fat disc, cover with clingfilm and stick in the fridge for 20 minutes. Preheat the oven to gas mark 6/200°C.

Roll out the pastry fairly thinly. Line a deep flan or quiche case with the pastry and bake blind for about 20 minutes. Take out of the oven and remove the beans and paper or foil. Beat the egg white lightly, brush the bottom and sides of the cooked pastry case with it (the idea being to seal the pastry so the custard won't make it soggy later on) and put back in the oven for 5 minutes. Turn down the oven to gas mark 3/160°C.

Put the eggs, egg yolks and sugar in a bowl and whisk together. Warm the cream and milk in a saucepan with the mace and pour into the egg and sugar mixture. Stir to mix and then strain into the pastry case, as it sits in the pulled-out rack in the oven. Grate over some nutmeg. Push the shelf back in carefully but confidently (tense hesitation can be disastrous: far too jerky), shut the door and leave the custard pie in the oven to bake for about 45 minutes. Take a look though, after about 35 minutes. The custard, when it's ready, should look more or less solid but still with a tremble at its centre.

Take out of the oven, grate some more nutmeg over and leave until it reaches tepid heaven.

Dinner

I'M NOT SURE I like the connotations of the term Dinner Party, but I think we're stuck with it. Kitchen Suppers – which is perhaps what this chapter should be called – sounds altogether too twee, even if it evokes more accurately the culinary environment most of us now inhabit. So let's just call it dinner, which is what it is. The modern dinner party was the invention of the post-war, post-Elizabeth David brigade of socially aware operators: this was the age of Entertaining-with-a-capital-E. Not only was the food distinctly not home food, it wasn't even restaurant food: what was evoked was the great ambassadorial dinner. But *autres temps, autres moeurs*: most of us don't even have dining-rooms any more. Yet people still think they should be following the old culinary agenda: they feel it is incumbent on them not so much to cook as to slave, to strive, to sweat, to *perform*. Life doesn't have to be like that. As far as I'm concerned, moreover, it shouldn't be like that. I find formality constraining. I don't like fancy, arranged napkins and I don't like fancy, arranged food.

That's not to say that I feel everything should be artfully casual: the this-is-just-something-I've-thrown-together school of cookery can be just as pretentious. What I feel passionately is that home food is home food, even when you invite other people to eat it with you. It shouldn't be laboriously executed, daintily arranged, individually portioned. It's relaxed, expansive, authentic: it should reflect your personality not your aspirations. Professional chefs have to innovate, to elaborate, to impress the paying customer. But the home cook is under no such constraints. (Indeed, you don't have to cook much at all if you are prepared to shop well.) I once went to a dinner party a good friend of mine gave, and she was so anxious, she'd been up till three in the morning the night before making stocks. She said scarcely a word to any of us after opening the door, since she was in the middle of the first of about five courses. The food was spectacular: but she spent most of the evening ever-more hysterical in the kitchen. At one point we could, as we stiltedly made conversation between ourselves, hear her crying. The fault wasn't her competence, but her conception: she felt that her dinner party must be a showcase for her culinary talents and that we must all be judging her. Some cooks, indeed, seem to resent their guests for interrupting the cooking, rather as doctors and nurses resent patients for interrupting the nice, efficient running of their hospitals.

Restaurants need to be able to produce food in short order. But unless you want to stand in your kitchen handing hot plates out to your friends at the table, you need not and should not. Avoid small portions of tender-fleshed fish that have to be conjured up at the last minute and *à point*, and anything that will wilt, grow soggy or lose character or hope as it sits, sideboard-bound and dished up. Don't make life harder on yourself. I am working on banishing the starter from my dinner-partying life. (Truth to tell, I don't have much of a dinner-partying life: but, in theory, I do invite friends for dinner.) This is not so much because cooking the starter is difficult – in fact it is the easiest course of any of them – but because clearing the table, timetabling the whole meal, keeping the main course warm, can all add to the general tension of the evening.

Besides, our lives are so different now. Because working hours are longer, we eat dinner later. And if dinner doesn't start till nine or nine-thirty, then it is going to be a very late evening if you sit down to three courses. And you don't want to miss out on the general hanging around with a drink beforehand. I am more of an eater than a drinker and tend to get unbearably anxious if the drinking goes on for hours with no sign of the eating to come, so I try to amalgamate the two. I am, in effect, not really banishing the starter, but relocating it, refashioning it. Now, I can't pretend that serving bits with drinks is an original idea, but I suggest that you think of them as the starter. There is no dinner party I would give where I couldn't just make a plate of crostini to eat as a first course.

Normally, I make a couple of different sorts. I don't assemble the crostini in advance, but I often make the mixture with which they're going to be spread days ahead and keep slices for toast, ready-carved from baguette or ficelle, bagged up in the freezer.

Indian-summer dinner for 6

Pea and lettuce soup

Lamb with chick peas

Couscous salad

Turkish delight figs with pistachio crescents

THIS IS THE SORT of food to eat when the days are unexpectedly warm, but the nights are nevertheless beginning to get cooler. You're still in the mood for summer food, but you need ballast too. This food is as suited for eating on a table in the garden as it is for a windows-shut, curtains-closed dinner inside.

Pea and lettuce soup

Shell the fresh peas. Then make a stock with the pods, some parsley stalks, peppercorns, onion, half a carrot and a stick of celery and, of course, water. If I don't feel like tackling fresh peas, or they're not available, I use frozen petits pois and either chicken stock or vegetable stock powder. I find it easier to start the soup off with thawed peas, but if they're still frozen it couldn't matter less. If you've got any basil-infused oil you can use that for softening the vegetables at the beginning. I know mint is the usual herb here, but basil seems to enhance the fruity sweetness of the peas.

2 tablespoons olive oil
4 spring onions, sliced finely
zest of ½ lemon
1 ½ kg fresh peas, podded or
  500g packet frozen petits
  pois
1 English round lettuce,
  roughly chopped

1 ¼ litres light stock (see
  above)
1 teaspoon sugar
1 tablespoon dry sherry
3–4 tablespoons double
  cream
small plant or large handful
  basil

Put the oil in the pan and when it's warm add the very finely sliced spring onions and lemon zest, stir a bit and then add the peas. Turn well in the oil and then add the lettuce and cook till it wilts and then collapses into the peas. Pour over the stock, sprinkle over the sugar and bring to the boil. Turn down to a simmer and cook gently and uncovered till the peas are soft, about 10 minutes. Purée in batches, in a blender if possible. You don't get that velvety emulsion with a processor, though you can sieve it after processing, which will do it. Or just use the mouli.

Pour back into the saucepan, add the sherry and cook for a minute or so before tasting to see what else the soup needs, bearing in mind you'll be adding some cream and eating it cold. Let it

cool a little, then stir in the cream and let it cool properly before
putting it in a tureen and into the fridge.

Just as you're about to eat, taste for more salt or pepper, add
more cream if wanted, and then shred the basil and add a good bit
to each bowlful after ladling it out from the tureen.

Lamb with chick peas

It's up to you whether you use whole noisette rolls, which
you roast and then slice, or individual noisette discs, which
you grill, griddle or fry; the former taste better, but the latter look better. I can never carve from the entire rolled
joint without it unfurling all over the place, but of course
you do get the tender, uncharred sides from the middle of
the roll. When you cook the individual noisettes, you're
sealing each slice in the heat. But the marinade will help to
make it tender. Make sure that you're using the best lamb
you can afford.

If you're going for the whole-roll option, think along
the lines of getting 3 x 400g noisettes (although I might
well get 4), and then roast them in a gas mark 7/210°C oven
for 20–40 minutes, depending on your oven and the age
and thickness of the meat.

As for the individual noisettes, I work on the assumption that you have to give each person 2, and then allow for
half of those present to have more.

I think it's easier to cook the chick peas in advance and
do the lamb on the evening itself, having put it in its marinade the night before or the morning of your dinner.

SOAK 500G CHICK peas in abundant water, and with a paste made from 3 tablespoons flour, 3 tablespoons salt and 1 tablespoon bicarbonate of soda (as on page 62). Leave for 24 hours. Drain, running the cold tap over them in the colander as you do so, then put them in a pan with 5 cloves of garlic, peeled and bashed, 2 bay leaves, 2 small onions, peeled but left whole (makes them easier to remove later) and the needles from a large sprig of rosemary. The bitter, boiled shards of rosemary will get in everyone's teeth, and ruin the creamy sweetness of the cooked chick peas, so put them in a bag or tea infuser.

Cover again with abundant water, add 1 tablespoon olive oil, put the lid on and bring to the boil, but do not open the pan; you'll have to listen closely to hear when it's starting to boil. Turn down slightly, and let the chick peas cook at a simmer for about 2 hours. You can check them after 1½ hours, but keep the lid on till then. When tender, drain, reserving a mugful of the cooking liquid. Leave, even up to a couple of days, till you want to eat. It would be better to remove the skins around each butterscotch-coloured pea, and I often start doing this, but have never yet completed the task.

To reheat, put 8 tablespoons olive oil and 6 cloves garlic, peeled and chopped, in a large, wide pan on moderate heat. I like to use a terracotta pot for this. Add to this 1–2 fresh red chillies, seeded and finely chopped, or crumble in a dried chilli pepper. Add the drained chick peas and turn well. Meanwhile, take 3 good-sized tomatoes, blanched, peeled, deseeded, roughly chopped and add to the chick peas. Salt very generously, stir well and taste; you may need to add some of the cooking liquid. You don't want this mushy exactly, but you want a degree of fusion, of fuzziness around the edges. Take off the heat, and cover until you've dealt with the lamb.

FOR 15 NOISETTES of lamb, make a marinade out of 10 tablespoons olive oil, 4 cloves garlic, crushed, 1 red onion, peeled and chopped, and 1 small fresh red chilli pepper, seeded and sliced. I find the easiest, most efficient way of doing this is by dividing everything between 2 plastic bags. Leave overnight or for as long as you can.

Just before you're about to sit down for your first course, take the lamb out of its marinade. You can drain the marinade and use that in place of the olive oil for sauté-ing the chick peas, above; in which case use a smaller amount of chilli. Cook the lamb either by frying in a cast-iron pan on a griddle, or giving it a few minutes each side under a very hot grill, or sear the meat in a pan then give them about 10 minutes in a gas mark 7/210°C oven. To keep the lamb pieces warm, leave them in a low oven on a dish covered with foil while you eat your soup.

When you serve, arrange the chick peas on a big, flattish bowl (again a terracotta one is perfect) or a couple of big plates and place the lamb over them. Chop over some fresh, flat-leaf parsley, or coriander if you feel infused with the mood of late-summer headiness.

Couscous salad

Sometimes I provide just a couple of small bowls filled with well-chopped red onion for people to sprinkle over the lamb and chick peas as they like. The alternative is a couscous salad, which in effect is panzanella, only using couscous in place of the bread. I often put basil in it, but this dinner has enough going on as it is without introducing another forceful character, so I suggest parsley.

200g couscous	½–1 small red onion, to taste
6 tablespoons olive oil	1 cucumber
2–3 tablespoons best red wine vinegar	1 bunch parsley, to yield approx. 8
6 good tomatoes	tablespoons chopped

Put the couscous into a bowl with 1 teaspoon salt and pour over 250ml boiling water. Cover and leave for 15 minutes. Fluff up with a fork and add the olive oil, 2 tablespoons of the vinegar and some pepper and put in another bowl (or leave in the same one if you're in no hurry) to cool. Prepare the tomatoes by blanching, peeling, deseeding and dicing, only make sure you don't leave them in the hot water too long. Cut the flesh into neat small dice. Chop the red onion up small. You can leave these, separately, until you want to eat. The rest I'd do at the last minute.

That's to say, when you're about to put the main course on the table, dice the cucumber and stir, along with the tomatoes, onion and 7 tablespoons of parsley, into the couscous with a fork. Add salt and more vinegar if you think it needs it.

Arrange on a plate and sprinkle on the remaining parsley.

Turkish delight figs

With thanks to Pat Harrison and Masterchef

How to say this without sounding ungracious? But I would never have expected to find such an easy, straightforward recipe on *Masterchef*. They're beautiful but not in an art-directed way: the purple-blue figs are cut to reveal the gaping red within, so that they sit in their bowl like plump little open-mouthed birds. When they're slicked with the flower-scented syrup, they become imbued with Middle Eastern sugariness, and the aromatic liquid itself absorbs and takes on a glassy pink from the figs. Perfect symbiosis.

Two figs a head should do it – they are very sweet, very intense – but if you can find only small figs, increase this to 3 per person. They're wonderful, anyway, the next day.

175g sugar

30ml/2 tablespoons rosewater

30ml/2 tablespoons orange-
   flower water

juice of 1 lemon

12 ripe, black figs

Dissolve the sugar in 175ml water in a small, heavy-based saucepan over a low heat. Increase the heat, bring to the boil and boil rapidly for 5 minutes. Add the rosewater, orange-flower water and lemon juice. Bring back to the boil and simmer for 2 minutes.

Carefully cut the figs vertically into quarters, leaving them intact at the base. Arrange on a flat, heatproof dish and spoon the hot syrup over them. Set aside to cool, basting with the syrup occasionally. Serve at room temperature, with Greek yoghurt and pistachio crescent biscuits (below).

The accompanying biscuits with the original recipe were sesame seed and cinnamon scented. I make instead these pistachio crescents, rich and tender, almost soft and definitely friable. But not hard to do. And the aromatic grittiness and moon-curled shapes give a one-thousand-and-one-nights feel, which is just right with the rosewater scent of the fig-basting syrup.

Pistachio crescents

These are rather like the hazelnut-smoky Middle-European Kipferln sold in expensive late-night supermarkets: densely powdery within, compounded by the blanket of icing sugar with which they are thickly, mufflingly covered. The amount below will make 12 biscuits.

75g pistachios (shelled weight)
60g soft unsalted butter
15g icing sugar, sifted

45g plain flour, preferably Italian 00, sifted
pinch salt

Preheat the oven to gas mark 3/160°C. Grease 2–3 baking sheets or, better still, cover them with Bake-o-Glide.

Toast the pistachios by frying them in a thick-bottomed frying pan with no fat for a few minutes so that their rich, waxy aroma is released. Pour into the bowl of the food processor and blitz until pulverised. You can buy ground pistachios from Middle Eastern shops – and I often do – but the varied, both nubbly and dusty, texture of the home-pulverised ones is good here.

With a wooden spoon, beat the butter until creamy – you are getting it ready to absorb the sugar with hardly any additional beating – and then duly add the icing sugar. I just spoon it into a tea strainer suspended over the bowl with the butter and push it through. Beat a while longer, until butter and sugar are light and incorporated, almost liquid-soft, and then add the sifted flour and salt. Keep stirring composedly and then add the ground pistachios, beating until just mixed. The dough will be sticky but firm enough to mould with your hands. If it feels too mushy, put it in the fridge for 10–20 minutes. To make the half-moons, flour your hands lightly and then take out small lumps of the dough – about 1 scant tablespoon at a time if you were measuring it, but I don't suggest you do: this is for guidance only – and roll them between your hands into sausages about 6cm long. Slightly flatten the sausage as you curl it round to form a little bulging snake of a crescent and put on the prepared baking sheet. Carry on until all the dough mixture is used up. And, by the way, don't be alarmed at how green these snakes look: cooked and dredged with icing sugar the intense lichen-coloured glow will fade.

Bake in the preheated oven for about 25 minutes, though start checking after 15. The softness should be just below the surface: take them out when the tops are firm and beginning to go blondly brown. Let the crescents sit on their baking sheets out of the oven for a few minutes and then remove to a wire rack. Go carefully: they are, as I said earlier, intensely friable. Dredge them with icing sugar very thickly indeed (again, I use a teaspoon to push the powder through a tea strainer) and leave to cool. You can do these ahead, and just dust over a little more icing sugar as you serve them.

Afterword

WHAT I'VE DISCOVERED, after what feels like a lifetime's cooking, is that anything which holds true in the kitchen, is just as true out of the kitchen. This is one of my mantras and I fear it won't be the last time you hear me chant it. And I'm sorry if it reeks of homespun philosophy, but that's just what it is. So, while it may be the case that occasionally – at the end of a long day or when I'm so exhausted that just staying upright seems a challenge – I approach cooking with something less than my usual gusto, I nearly always find that just getting on with it can make me wonder what I was dreading in the first place, and why. But then, the same applies to so many obligations and undertakings that loom over us in life, outside of the kitchen, too. Fear – of disappointment, inadequacy, failure – seems to make fools of us, causing us to forget what we all unfailingly learn from experience: that not doing what frightens us makes us fear it more rather than less. Perhaps some day I'll write a book called 'Feel the Fear and Cook it Anyway', although to some extent I suspect that this is, indeed, the subliminal message of every book I've ever written.

I understand why cooking can hold so much terror and the kitchen seem a place of stress not solace. I'm sure this is partly to do with the contemporary cult of the chef, and is further fuelled by the hysterical pursuit of perfection that defines the age we live in. I am not a chef, am horrified when thus defined and resist, without a shred of disingenuousness, the miscast role of expert. Again and again, I say and can never seem to say enough: if we really needed qualifications and expertise before we stepped into the kitchen, human beings would have fallen out of the evolutionary loop a long time ago.

I don't believe that cooking holds any inherent moral qualities or reveals essential purity of purpose and congratulation-worthy virtue. Certainly not: it wouldn't occur to me to feel guilty about eating food I hadn't cooked – so long as I enjoyed it – any more than I ever have or would feel guilty about buying clothes rather than sewing something to wear myself. The born-again fervour and judgemental outlook of the status-conscious cook seem to me positively to preclude a happy life in the kitchen – or, indeed, out of it. I don't cook because I feel I ought to, but because I want to. And, of course, there are times when I don't want to. That's life. Sometimes reality has the edge over romance: albeit I have said before, and hand-on-heart declare again, that for me the kitchen is not a place I want to escape from, but to escape *to*.

The kitchen is not a place I want to escape from but to escape to

© MasterChef Australia

NIGELLA LAWSON IS one of the world's best-loved food writers. She learned to cook in her mother's kitchen as a child, balancing on a rickety stool pushed up against the stove.

Nigella was Deputy Literary Editor of the *Sunday Times* and wrote a food column for *Vogue* before becoming a food writer full-time.

Her first book *How to Eat* (on which this book was based) was published in 1998, bringing with it a refreshing new voice to food writing and an honest and empowering attitude to cooking.

Nigella was prompted to write *How to Eat* out of a need to celebrate home cooking and give it the focus it deserves. She has since written nine books, as well as making several television series.

RECOMMENDED BOOKS BY NIGELLA LAWSON:

How to be a Domestic Goddess
Kitchen
Simply Nigella

What goes well with Eating?

Drinking
JOHN CHEEVER

VINTAGE MINIS

Home
SALMAN RUSHDIE

VINTAGE MINIS

Summer
LAURIE LEE

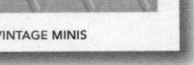

VINTAGE MINIS

Liberty
VIRGINIA WOOLF

VINTAGE MINIS

VINTAGE MINIS

The Vintage Minis bring you the world's greatest writers on the experiences that make us human. These stylish, entertaining little books explore the whole spectrum of life – from birth to death, and everything in between. Which means there's something here for everyone, whatever your story.

Desire	Haruki Murakami
Love	Jeanette Winterson
Babies	Anne Enright
Language	Xiaolu Guo
Motherhood	Helen Simpson
Fatherhood	Karl Ove Knausgaard
Summer	Laurie Lee
Jealousy	Marcel Proust
Sisters	Louisa May Alcott
Home	Salman Rushdie
Race	Toni Morrison
Liberty	Virginia Woolf
Swimming	Roger Deakin
Work	Joseph Heller
Depression	William Styron
Drinking	John Cheever
Eating	Nigella Lawson
Psychedelics	Aldous Huxley
Calm	Tim Parks
Death	Julian Barnes

vintageminis.co.uk

1 3 5 7 9 10 8 6 4 2

Vintage
20 Vauxhall Bridge Road,
London SW1V 2SA

Vintage Classics is part of the Penguin Random House
group of companies whose addresses can be found at
global.penguinrandomhouse.com.

Penguin
Random House
UK

Joseph Anton was first published in the United Kingdom by Jonathan
Cape in 2012
Shame was first published in the United Kingdom by Jonathan Cape in 1983
Imaginary Homelands was first published in the United Kingdom by Granta
Books in association with Penguin Books Ltd in 1991
East, West was first published in the United Kingdom by Jonathan Cape in 1994
This short edition published by Vintage in 2017

penguin.co.uk/vintage

A CIP catalogue record for this book is available from the British Library

ISBN 9781784872687

Typeset in 9.5/14.5 pt FreightText Pro by Jouve (UK), Milton Keynes
Printed and bound by Clays Ltd, St Ives plc

Penguin Random House is committed to a sustainable future for
our business, our readers and our planet. This book is made from
Forest Stewardship Council® certified paper.

Home

SALMAN RUSHDIE

VINTAGE MINIS

From Salman Rushdie's memoir,
Joseph Anton

WHEN HE TURNED away from his father, wearing the blue-and- white-striped cap of Bradley House and the serge mackintosh, and plunged into his English life, the sin of *foreignness* was the first thing that was made plain to him. Until that point he had not thought of himself as anyone's Other. After Rugby School he never forgot the lesson he learned there: that there would always be people who just didn't like you, to whom you seemed as alien as little green men or the Slime from Outer Space, and there was no point trying to change their minds. Alienation: it was a lesson he relearned in more dramatic circumstances later on.

At an English boarding school in the early 1960s, he quickly discovered, there were three bad mistakes you could make, but if you made only two of the three you could be forgiven. The mistakes were: to be foreign; to be clever; and to be bad at games. At Rugby the foreign, clever boys who had a good time were also elegant cricketers or, in the case of one of his contemporaries, the Pakistani Zia Mahmood, so good at cards that he grew up to become one of the world's finest bridge players. The boys who had no sporting ability had to be careful not to be too clever and, if possible, not too foreign, which was the worst of the three mistakes.

He made all three mistakes. He was foreign, clever, non-*sportif*. And as a result his years were, for the most part, unhappy, though he did well academically and left Rugby with the abiding feeling of having been wonderfully well taught – with that nourishing memory of great teachers that, if we are lucky, we can carry with us for the rest of our lives. There was P. G. Lewis, known, inevitably, as 'Pig', who so inspired him with the love of French that he rose in the course of one term from the bottom to the top of the class, and there were his history teachers J. B. Hope-Simpson, aka 'Hope Stimulus', and J. W. 'Gut' Hele, thanks to whose skilled tutelage he was able to go on to win an exhibition, a minor scholarship, to read history at his father's old alma mater, King's College, Cambridge, where he would meet E. M. Forster and discover sex, though not at the same time. (Less valuably, perhaps, 'Hope Stimulus' was also the person who introduced him to Tolkien's *The Lord of the Rings*, which entered his consciousness like a disease, an infection he never managed to shake off.) His old English teacher Geoffrey Helliwell would be seen on British television on the day after the fatwa, ruefully shaking his head and asking, in sweet, vague, daffy tones,

'Who'd have thought such a nice, quiet boy could get into so much trouble?'

Nobody had forced him to go to boarding school in England. Negin had been against the idea of sending her only son away across oceans and continents. Anis had offered him the opportunity and encouraged him to take the Common Entrance exam, but, even after he came through that with some distinction and the place at Rugby was his, the final decision to go or stay was left entirely to him. In later life he would wonder at the choice made by this thirteen-year-old self, a boy rooted in his city, happy in his friends, having a good time at school (apart from a little local difficulty with the Marathi language), the apple of his parents' eye. Why did that boy decide to leave it all behind and travel halfway across the world into the unknown, far from everyone who loved him and everything he knew? Was it the fault, perhaps, of literature (for he was certainly a bookworm)? In which case the guilty parties might have been his beloved Jeeves and Bertie, or possibly the Earl of Emsworth and his mighty sow, the Empress of Blandings. Or might it have been the dubious attractions of the world of Agatha Christie that persuaded him, even if Christie's Miss Marple made her home in the most murderous village in England, the lethal St Mary Mead? Then there was Arthur Ransome's *Swallows and Amazons* series telling of children messing about in boats in the Lake District, and, much, much worse, the terrible literary escapades of Billy Bunter, the 'Owl of the Remove',

Why did that boy decide to leave it all behind and travel halfway across the world into the unknown?

the fat boy at Frank Richards's ridiculous Greyfriars School, where, among Bunter's classmates, there was at least one Indian, Hurree Jamset Ram Singh, the 'dusky nabob of Bhanipur', who spoke a bizarre, grand, syntactically contorted English ('the contortfulness', as the dusky nabob might well have put it, 'was terrific'). Was it, in other words, a *childish* decision, to venture forth into an imaginary England that only existed in books? Or was it, alternatively, an indication that beneath the surface of the 'nice, quiet boy' there lurked a stranger being, a fellow with an unusually adventurous heart, possessed of enough gumption to take a leap in the dark exactly *because* it was a step into the unknown – a youth who intuited his future adult self's ability to survive, even to thrive, wherever in the world his wanderings might take him, and who was able, too easily, even a little ruthlessly, to follow the dream of 'away', breaking away from the lure, which was also, of course, the tedium, of 'home', leaving his sorrowing mother and sisters behind without too much regret? Perhaps a little of each. At any rate, he took the leap, and the forking paths of time bifurcated at his feet. He took the westward road and ceased to be who he might have been if he had stayed at home.

A pink stone set into the Doctor's Wall, named for the legendary headmaster Dr Arnold and overlooking the stor-eyed playing fields of the Close, bore an inscription that purported to celebrate an act of revolutionary iconoclasm. 'This is to commemorate the exploit of William Webb

Ellis,' it read, 'who, with a fine disregard for the rules of football as played in his time, first picked up the ball and ran with it, thus originating the distinctive feature of the rugby game.' But the Webb Ellis story was apocryphal, and the school was anything but iconoclastic. The sons of stockbrokers and solicitors were being educated here and 'a fine disregard for the rules' was not on the curriculum. Putting both your hands in your pockets was against the rules. So was 'running in the corridors'. However, fagging – acting as an older boy's unpaid servant – and beating were still permitted. Corporal punishment could be administered by the housemaster or even by the boy named as Head of House. In his first term the Head of House was a certain R. A. C. Williamson who kept his cane hanging in full view over the door of his study. There were notches in it, one for each thrashing Williamson had handed out.

He was never beaten. He was a 'nice, quiet boy'. He learned the rules and observed them scrupulously. He learned the school slang, *dics* for bedtime prayers in the dormitories (from the Latin *dicere*, to speak), *topos* for the toilets (from the Greek word for *place*), and, rudely, *oiks* for non-Rugby School inhabitants of the town, a place best known for the manufacture of cement. Though the Three Mistakes were never forgiven, he did his best to fit in. In the sixth form he won the Queen's Medal for a history essay about Napoleon's foreign minister, the clubfooted, cynical, amoral libertine Talleyrand, whom he vigorously defended. He became secretary of the school's debating society and spoke eloquently in favour of fagging, which was abolished not long after his schooldays ended. He came from a conservative Indian family and was in no sense a radical. But racism was something he quickly understood. When he returned to his little study, he more than once found an essay he had written torn to pieces, which were scattered on the seat of his red armchair. Once somebody wrote the words WOGS GO HOME on his wall. He gritted his teeth, swallowed the insults and did his work. He did not tell his parents what school had been like until after he left it (and when he did tell them they were horrified that he had kept so much pain to himself). His mother was suffering because of his absence, his father was paying a fortune for him to be there, and it would not be right, he told himself, to complain. So in his letters home he created his first fictions, about idyllic schooldays of sunshine and cricket. In fact he was no good at cricket and Rugby in winter was bitterly cold, doubly so for a boy from the tropics who had never slept under heavy blankets and found it hard to go to sleep when so weighed down. But if he cast them off, then he shivered. He had to get used to this weight also, and he did. At night in the dormitories, after lights out, the metal-frame beds began to shake as the boys relieved their adolescent urges, and the banging of the beds against the heating pipes running around the walls filled the large dark rooms with the night music of inexpressible desire. In this matter, as in all else, he strove to be like the others, and join in. Again: he was not, by nature, rebellious. In those early days, he preferred the Rolling Stones to the Beatles, and, after one of his friendlier housemates, a serious, cherubic boy named Richard Shearer, made him sit down and listen to *The Free-wheelin' Bob Dylan*, he became an enthusiastic Dylan worshipper; but he was, at heart, a conformist.

Still: almost as soon as he came to Rugby he did rebel. The school insisted that all boys should enrol in the CCF, or Combined Cadet Force, and then climb into full military khaki on Wednesday afternoons to play war games in the mud. He was not the sort of boy who thought that might be fun – indeed, it struck him as a kind of torture – and in the first week of his school career he went to see his housemaster, Dr George Dazeley, a mild-natured mad-scientist type with a glittering, mirthless smile, to explain to him that he did not wish to join. Dr Dazeley stiffened, glittered and pointed out, just a little icily, that boys did not have the right to opt out. The boy from Bombay, suddenly possessed by an unaccustomed stubbornness, drew himself up straight. 'Sir,' he said, 'my parents' generation have only recently fought a war of liberation against the British Empire, and therefore I cannot possibly agree to join its armed forces.' This unexpected burst of post-colonial passion stymied Dr Dazeley, who limply gave in and said, 'Oh, very well, then you'd better stay in your study and read instead.' As the young conscientious objector left his office Dazeley pointed to a picture on the wall. 'That is Major William Hodson,' he said. 'Hodson of Hodson's Horse. He was a Bradley boy.' William Hodson was the British cavalry officer who, after the suppression of the Indian Uprising of 1857 (at Rugby it was called *the Indian Mutiny*), captured the last Mughal emperor, the poet Bahadur Shah Zafar, and murdered his three sons, stripping them naked, shooting them dead, taking their jewellery, and throwing their bodies down in the dirt at one of the gates of Delhi, which was thereafter known as the Khooni Darvaza, the gate of blood. That Hodson was a former Bradley House resident made the young Indian rebel even prouder of having refused to join the army in which the executioner of the Mughal princes had served. Dr Dazeley added, vaguely, and perhaps incorrectly, that he believed Hodson had been one of the models for the character of Flashman, the school bully in Thomas Hughes's novel of Rugby, *Tom Brown's Schooldays*. There was a statue of Hughes on the lawn outside the school library, but here at Bradley House the presiding old-timer was the alleged real-life original version of the most famous bully in English literature. That seemed just about right.

The lessons one learns at school are not always the ones the school thinks it's teaching.

For the next four years he spent Wednesday afternoons reading yellow-jacketed science-fiction novels borrowed from the town library, while eating egg-salad sandwiches and crisps, drinking Coca-Cola and listening to *Two-Way Family Favourites* on the transistor radio. He became an expert on the so-called golden age of science fiction, devouring such masterworks as Isaac Asimov's *I, Robot*, wherein the Three Laws of Robotics were enshrined, Philip K. Dick's *The Three Stigmata of Palmer Eldritch*, Zenna Henderson's *Pilgrimage* novels, the wild fantasies of L. Sprague de Camp, and, above all, Arthur C. Clarke's haunting short story 'The Nine Billion Names of God', about the world quietly coming to an end once its secret purpose, the listing of all God's names, had been fulfilled by a bunch of Buddhist monks with a supercomputer. (Like his father, he was fascinated by God, even if religion held little appeal.) It might not have been the greatest revolution in history, this four-and-a-half-year fall towards the fantastic fuelled by tuckshop snack foods, but every time he saw his schoolfellows come lurching in from their war games, exhausted, muddy and bruised, he was reminded that standing up for oneself could sometimes be well worth it.

In the matter of God: the last traces of belief were erased from his mind by his powerful dislike of the architecture of Rugby Chapel. Many years later, when by chance he passed through the town, he was shocked to find that Herbert Butterfield's neo-Gothic building was in fact extremely beautiful. As a schoolboy he thought it hideous, deciding, in that science-fiction-heavy time of his life, that it resembled nothing so much as a brick rocket ship ready for take-off; and one day when he was staring at it through the window of a classroom in the New Big School during a Latin lesson, a question occurred. 'What kind of God,' he wondered, 'would live in a house as ugly as that?' An instant later the answer presented itself: obviously no self-respecting God would live there – in fact, obviously, there *was* no God, not even a God with bad taste in architecture. By the end of the Latin lesson he was a hard-line atheist, and to prove it, he marched determinedly into the school tuckshop during break and bought himself a ham sandwich. The flesh of the swine passed his lips for the first time that day, and the failure of the Almighty to strike him dead with a thunderbolt proved to him what he had long suspected: that there was nobody up there with thunderbolts to hurl.

Inside Rugby Chapel he joined the rest of the school, one term, in rehearsing and singing the Hallelujah Chorus as part of a performance of the full *Messiah* with professional soloists. He took part in compulsory matins and evensong – having attended the Cathedral School in Bombay, he had no leg to stand on if he wanted to make an argument that would excuse him from mumbling his way through Christian prayers – and he couldn't deny that he liked the hymns, whose music lifted his heart. Not all the hymns; he didn't, for example, need to *survey the wondrous cross / on which the prince of glory died*; but a lonely boy could not help but be touched when he was asked to sing *The night is dark and I am far from home / Lead Thou me on*. He liked singing 'O Come, All Ye Faithful' in Latin, which somehow took the religious sting out of it: *venite, venite in Bethlehem*. He liked 'Abide with Me' because it was sung by the whole 100,000-strong crowd at Wembley Stadium before the FA Cup Final, and what he thought of as the 'geography hymn', 'The Day Thou Gavest, Lord, Is Ended', made him sweetly homesick: *The sun that bids us rest is waking / our brethren 'neath the western* [here he would substitute *eastern*] *sky*. The language of unbelief was distinctly poorer than that of belief. But at least the music of unbelief was becoming fully the equal of the songs of the faithful, and as he moved through his teenage years and the golden age of rock music filled his ears with its pet sounds, its I-can't-get-no and hard rain and try-to-see-it-my-way and da doo ron ron, even the hymns lost some of their power to move him. But there were still things in Rugby Chapel to touch a bookish unbeliever's heart: the memorials to Matthew Arnold and his ignorant armies clashing by night, and Rupert Brooke, killed by a mosquito bite while fighting just such an army, lying in some corner of a foreign field that was forever England; and, above all, the stone in memory of Lewis Carroll, with its Tenniel silhouettes dancing around the edges in black-and-white marble in a – why, a kind of – yes! – quadrille. 'Would not, could not, would not, could not, would not join the dance,' he sang softly to himself. 'Would not, could not, would not, could not, could not join the dance.' It was his private hymn to himself.

Before he left Rugby he did a terrible thing. All school leavers were allowed to hold a 'study sale', which allowed them to pass on their old desks, lamps and other bric-a-brac to younger boys in return for small amounts of cash. He posted an auction sheet on the inside of his study door, stipulated modest starting prices for his redundant possessions, and waited. Most study-sale items were heavily worn; he, however, had his red armchair, which had been new when his father bought it for him. An armchair with only one user was a high-quality, sought-after rarity in the study-sales and the red chair attracted some serious bidding. In the end there were two energetic bidders: one of his fags, a certain P. A. F. Reed-Herbert, known as 'Weed Herbert', a small, bespectacled little worm of a fellow who hero-worshipped him a little, and an older boy named John Tallon, whose home was on The Bishop's Avenue, the millionaires' row of north London, and who could presumably afford to bid high.

When the bidding slowed down – the top bid was Reed-Herbert's offer of around five pounds – he had his terrible idea. He secretly asked John Tallon to post a seriously high bid, something like *eight pounds*, and promised him that he would not hold him to it if that ended up as the highest offer. Then, at *dics*, he told Weed Herbert solemnly that he knew for a fact that his wealthy rival, Tallon, was prepared to go even higher, perhaps even as high as twelve whole pounds. He saw Weed Herbert's face fall, noted his crushed expression and went in for the kill. 'Now, if you were to offer me, say, ten quid right away, I could close the auction and declare the chair sold.' Weed Herbert looked nervous. 'That's a lot of money, Rushdie,' he said. 'Think about it,' said Rushdie magnanimously, 'while you say your prayers.'

When *dics* were over, Weed Herbert took the bait. The Machiavellian Rushdie smiled reassuringly. 'Excellent decision, Reed-Herbert.' He had cold-bloodedly persuaded the boy to bid against himself, doubling his own top bid. The red armchair had a new owner. Such was the power of prayer.

This happened in the spring of 1965. Nine and a half years later, during the general election campaign of October 1974, he turned on his television set and saw the end of a speech by the candidate for the far-right, racist, fascist, vehemently anti-immigrant British National Front. The candidate's name was titled on the screen. *Anthony Reed-Herbert.* 'Weed Herbert!' he cried aloud in horror. 'My God, I've invented a Nazi!' It all instantly became plain. Weed Herbert, tricked into spending too much of his own money by a conniving, godless wog, had nursed his bitter rage through wormy childhood into wormier adulthood and had become a racist politician so that he could be revenged upon all wogs, with or without overpriced red armchairs to sell. (But was it the same Weed Herbert? Could there possibly have been two of them? No, he thought, it had to be little P. A. F., little no more.) In the 1974 election Weed Herbert received 6 per cent of the vote in the Leicester East constituency, 2,967 votes in all. In August 1977 he ran again, in the Birmingham Ladywood by-election, and came in third, ahead of the Liberal candidate. Mercifully that was his last significant appearance on the national scene.

Mea culpa, thought the vendor of the red armchair. *Mea maxima culpa.* In the true story of his schooldays there would always be much loneliness and some sadness. But there would also be this stain on his character; this unrecorded, unexpiated crime.

ON HIS SECOND day at Cambridge he went to a gathering of freshmen in King's College Hall and gazed for the first time upon the great Brunelleschian dome of Noel Annan's head. Lord Annan, provost of King's, the sonorous cathedral of a man whose dome that was, stood before him in all his cold-eyed, plump-lipped glory. 'You are here,' Annan told the assembled freshmen, 'for three reasons: Intellect! Intellect! Intellect!' One, two, three fingers stabbed the air as he counted off the three reasons. Later in his speech he surpassed even that aperçu. 'The most important part of your education here will not take place in the lecture rooms or libraries or supervisions,' he intoned. 'It will happen when you sit in one another's rooms, late at night, fertilising one another.'

He had left home in the middle of a war, the pointless India–Pakistan conflict of September 1965. The eternal bone of contention, Kashmir, had triggered a five-week war in which almost seven thousand soldiers died, and at the end of which India had acquired an extra seven hundred square miles of Pakistani territory, while Pakistan had seized two hundred square miles of Indian land, and nothing, less than nothing, had been achieved. (In *Midnight's*

Children, this would be the war in which most of Saleem's family is killed by falling bombs.) For some days he had stayed with distant relatives in London in a room without a window. It was impossible to get through to his family on the telephone, and telegrams from home, he was told, were taking three weeks to get through. He had no way of knowing how everyone was. All he could do was to catch the train to Cambridge, and hope. He arrived at King's College's Market Hostel in bad shape, exacerbated by his fear that the university years ahead would be a repeat of the largely wretched Rugby years. He had pleaded with his father not to send him to Cambridge, even though he had already won his place. He didn't want to go back to England, he said, to spend more years of his life among all those cold, unfriendly fish. Couldn't he stay home and go to college among warmer-blooded creatures? But Anis persuaded him to go. And then told him he had to change his subject of study. History was a useless thing to waste three years on. He had to tell the college he wanted to switch to economics. There was even a threat: if he didn't do that, Anis would not pay his fees.

Burdened by three fears of unfriendly English youth, of economics and of war – he found, on his first day up at King's, that he couldn't get out of bed. His body felt heavier than usual, as if gravity itself were trying to hold him back. More down than up, he ignored several knocks on the door of his somewhat Scandinavian-modern room. (It was the year of the Beatles' *Rubber Soul*, and he spent a good deal of it humming 'Norwegian Wood'.) But in the early evening a particularly insistent pounding forced him out of bed. At the door wearing a huge Old Etonian grin and Rupert Brooke's wavy blond hair was the tall, relentlessly friendly figure of 'Jan Pilkington-Miksa – I'm half-Polish, you know', the welcoming angel at the gateway to the future, who brought him forth on a tide of loud bonhomie into his new life.

Jan Pilkington-Miksa, the very platonic form of the English public schoolboy, looked exactly like all the creatures at Rugby who had made his life so unpleasant, but he was the sweetest-natured of young men, and seemed to have been sent as a sign that things were going to be different this time round. And so they were; Cambridge largely healed the wounds that Rugby had inflicted, and showed him that there were other, more attractive Englands to inhabit, in which he could easily feel at home.

So much for the first burden. As for economics, he was rescued by a second welcoming angel, the director of studies, Dr John Broadbent, an Eng. Lit. don so magnificently groovy that he could easily have been (though he was not) one of the models for the supercool and ultra-permissive Dr Howard Kirk, hero of Malcolm Bradbury's novel *The History Man*. Dr Broadbent asked him, when he gloomily said that he was supposed to change subjects because his father insisted on it, 'And what do *you* want to do?' Well, he didn't want to read economics, obviously; he had a history exhibition and he wanted to read history. 'Leave it to me,'

Dr Broadbent said, and wrote Anis Rushdie a gentle but fierce letter stating that in the opinion of the college Anis's son Salman was not qualified to read economics and that if he continued to insist upon doing so it would be better to remove him from the university to make room for someone else. Anis Rushdie never mentioned economics again.

The third burden, too, was soon lifted. The war in the subcontinent ended, and everyone he loved was safe. His university life began.

He did the usual things: made friends, lost his virginity, learned how to play the mysterious matchstick game featured in *L'année dernière à Marienbad*, played a melancholy game of croquet with E. M. Forster on the day Evelyn Waugh died, slowly understood the meaning of the word 'Vietnam', became less conservative, and was elected to the Footlights, became a minor bulb in that dazzling group of illuminati – Clive James, Rob Buckman, Germaine Greer – and watched Germaine perform her Stripping Nun routine, bumping and grinding her way out of her sisterly habit to reveal a full frogman's outfit beneath, on the tiny club stage in Petty Cury on the floor below the office of the Chinese Red Guards where Chairman Mao's Little Red Book was on sale. He also inhaled, saw one friend die of bad acid in the room across the hall, saw another succumb to drug-induced brain damage, was introduced to Captain Beefheart and the Velvet Underground by a third friend who died soon after they graduated; enjoyed miniskirts and see-through blouses; wrote briefly for the student paper *Varsity* until it decided it didn't need his services; acted in Brecht, Ionesco and Ben Jonson; and crashed Trinity May Ball with the future art critic of *The Times* to listen to Françoise Hardy sing the anthem of young love-less anguish, 'Tous les garçons et les filles'.

In later life he often spoke of the happiness of his Cambridge years, and agreed with himself to forget the hours of howling loneliness when he sat alone in a room and wept, even if King's Chapel was right outside his window blazing with beauty (this was in his final year, when he was living on the ground floor of S staircase in the college itself, in a room with a view, if ever there was one – chapel, lawn, river, punts – a cliché of gorgeousness). In that final year he had returned from the holidays in low spirits. That was at the end of the summer of 1967, the Summer of Love, when, if you were going to San Francisco, you had to be sure to wear some flowers in your hair. He, unfortunately, had been in London with nobody to love. By chance he had found himself at the very heart of 'where', in the parlance of those days, 'it was at', staying in a rented room above the coolest boutique of all, Granny Takes a Trip, at the World's End end of the King's Road. John Lennon's wife Cynthia wore the frocks. *Mick Jagger* was rumoured to wear the frocks.

Here, too, there was an education to be had. He learned not to say 'fab' or 'groovy'. At Granny's, you said 'beautiful' to express mild approval, and, when you wanted to call something beautiful, you said 'really nice'. He got used to nodding his head a lot, wisely. In the quest for cool, it helped that he was Indian. 'India, man,' people said. 'Far out.' 'Yeah,' he said, nodding. 'Yeah.' 'The Maharishi, man,' people said. 'Beautiful.' 'Ravi Shankar, man,' he replied. At this point people usually ran out of Indians to talk about and everyone just went on nodding, beatifically. 'Right, right,' everyone said. 'Right.'

He learned an even more profound lesson from the girl who ran the shop, an ethereal presence sitting in that fashionably darkened, patchouli-oil-scented space heavy with sitar music, in which, after a time, he became aware of a low purple glow, in which he could make out a few motionless shapes. These were probably clothes, probably for sale. He didn't like to ask. Granny's was frightening. But one day he plucked up his courage and went downstairs to introduce himself, *Hi, I'm living upstairs, I'm Salman.* The girl in the shop came close, so that he could see the contempt on her face. Then slowly, fashionably, she shrugged.

'Conversation's dead, man,' she said.

Up and down the King's Road walked the most beautiful girls in the world, ridiculously underdressed, accompanied by peacocking men who were equally ridiculously overdressed, in high-collared frock coats and frilly shirts and flared crushed velvet trousers and fake-snakeskin boots. He seemed to be the only one who didn't know what it was to be happy.

He returned to Cambridge feeling, at the ripe old age of

twenty, that life was passing him by. (Others had the final-year blues, too. Even the invariably cheerful Jan Pilkington-Miksa was deeply depressed; though happily he did recover to declare that he had decided to be a film director, and intended to head for the south of France as soon as he was done with Cambridge, 'because', he said airily, 'they probably need film directors down there'.) He took refuge in work, just as he had at Rugby. *The intellect of man is forced to choose / Perfection of the life or of the work*, Yeats said, and since the perfect life was plainly beyond him he had better look to the work instead.

That was the year he found out about the satanic verses. In Part Two of the History Tripos he was expected to choose three 'special subjects' from a wide selection on offer, and concentrate on those. He chose to work on Indian history during the period of the independence struggle against the British, from the 1857 uprising to Independence Day in August 1947; and the extraordinary first century or so of the history of the United States, 1776–1877, from the Declaration of Independence to the end of the post-Civil War period known as Reconstruction; and a third subject, offered, that year, for the first time, titled 'Muhammad, the Rise of Islam and the Early Caliphate'. In 1967 few history students at Cambridge were interested in the Prophet of Islam – so few, in fact, that the course's designated lecturer cancelled his proposed lectures and declined to supervise the few students who had chosen the course. This was a way of saying that the subject was no longer available, and another choice should be made. All the other students did indeed abandon the Muhammad paper and go elsewhere. He, however, felt an old stubbornness rise in him. If the subject was offered, it could not be cancelled as long as there was a single student who wished to study it; that was the rule. Well, he did want to study it. He was his father's son, godless, but fascinated by gods and prophets. He was also a product, at least in part, of the deep-rooted Muslim culture of South Asia, the inheritor of the artistic, literary and architectural riches of the Mughals and their predecessors. He was determined to study this subject. All he needed was a historian who was willing to supervise him.

Of the three great historians who were fellows of King's at that time, Christopher Morris was the most published, with the most established reputation, historian of Tudor political thought, ecclesiastical history and the Enlightenment, while John Saltmarsh was one of the grand eccentrics of the university with his wild white hair, muttonchop side whiskers, long-john underwear poking out at his trouser cuffs above his sockless, sandalled feet, the unrivalled expert in the history of the college and chapel, and, more broadly, in the local history of the region, often seen tramping the country lanes around Cambridge with a rucksack on his back. Both Morris and Saltmarsh were disciples of Sir John Clapham, the scholar who established economic history as a serious field of study, and both conceded that the third member of the King's history trinity,

Arthur Hibbert, a medievalist, was the most brilliant of them all, a genius who, according to college legend, had answered the questions he knew least about in his own history finals exams, so that he could complete the answers in the time allotted. Hibbert, it was decided, was the most appropriate person to deal with the matter in hand; and he agreed to do so without a moment's fuss. 'I'm not a specialist in this field,' he said modestly, 'but I know a little about it, so if you will accept me as your supervisor, I am willing to supervise you.'

This offer was gratefully accepted by the stubborn young undergraduate standing in his study sipping a glass of sherry. So came about a strange state of affairs. The special subject about Muhammad, the rise of Islam and the early caliphate had not been offered before; and in that academic year, 1967–8, only this one, obdurate student took it; and the following year, owing to lack of interest, it was not offered again. For that single student, the course was his father's vision made real. It studied the life of the Prophet and the birth of the religion as events inside history, analytically, judiciously, *properly*. It might have been designed especially for him.

At the beginning of their work together Arthur Hibbert gave him a piece of advice he never forgot. 'You must never write history,' Hibbert said, 'until you can hear the people speak.' He thought about that for years, and in the end it came to feel like a valuable guiding principle for fiction as well. If you didn't have a sense of how people spoke, you didn't know them well enough, and so you couldn't – you *shouldn't* – tell their story. The way people spoke, in short, clipped phrases, or long, flowing rambles, revealed so much about them: their place of origin, their social class, their temperament, whether calm or angry, warm-hearted or cold-blooded, foul-mouthed or clean-spoken, polite or rude; and beneath their temperament, their true nature, intellectual or earthy, plain-spoken or devious, and, yes, good or bad. If that had been all he learned at Arthur's feet, it would have been enough. But he gained much more than that. He learned a world. And in that world one of the world's great religions was being born.

From the novel *Shame*

I KNOW SOMETHING of this immigrant business. I am an emigrant from one country (India) and a newcomer in two (England, where I live, and Pakistan, to which my family moved against my will). And I have a theory that the resentments we *mohajirs* engender have something to do with our conquest of the force of gravity. We have performed the act of which all men anciently dream, the thing for which they envy the birds; that is to say, we have flown.

I am comparing gravity with belonging. Both phenomena observably exist: my feet stay on the ground, and I have never been angrier than I was on the day my father told me he had sold my childhood home in Bombay. But neither is understood. We know the force of gravity, but not its origins; and to explain why we become attached to our birthplaces we pretend that we are trees and speak of roots. Look under your feet. You will not find gnarled growths sprouting through the soles. Roots, I sometimes think, are a conservative myth, designed to keep us in our places.

The anti-myths of gravity and of belonging bear the same name: flight. *Migration, n., moving, for instance in flight, from one place to another*. To fly and to flee: both are ways of seeking freedom ... an odd thing about gravity, incidentally, is that while it remains uncomprehended everybody seems to find it easy to comprehend the notion of its theoretical counter-force: anti-gravity. But anti-belonging is not accepted by modern science ... suppose ICI or Ciba-Geigy or Pfizer or Roche or even, I guess, NASA came up with an anti-gravity pill. The world's airlines would go broke overnight, of course. Pill-poppers would come unstuck from the ground and float upwards until they sank into the clouds. It would be necessary to devise special waterproof flying garments. And when the effects of the pill wore off one would simply sink gently down to earth again, but in a different place, because of prevailing windspeeds and planetary rotation. Personalized international travel could be made possible by manufacturing pills of different strengths for different lengths of journey. Some kind of directional booster-engine would have to be constructed, perhaps in back-pack form. Mass production could bring this within the reach of every household. You see the connection between gravity and 'roots': the pill would make migrants of us all. We would float upwards, use our boosters to get ourselves to the right latitude, and let the rotating planet do the rest.

When individuals come unstuck from their native land, they are called migrants. When nations do the same thing

(Bangladesh), the act is called secession. What is the best thing about migrant peoples and seceded nations? I think it is their hopefulness. Look into the eyes of such folk in old photographs. Hope blazes undimmed through the fading sepia tints. And what's the worst thing? It is the emptiness of one's luggage. I'm speaking of invisible suitcases, not the physical, perhaps cardboard, variety containing a few meaning-drained mementoes: we have come unstuck from more than land. We have floated upwards from history, from memory, from Time.

I may be such a person. Pakistan may be such a country.

It is well known that the term 'Pakistan', an acronym, was originally thought up in England by a group of Muslim intellectuals. P for the Punjabis, A for the Afghans, K for the Kashmiris, S for Sind and the 'tan', they say, for Baluchistan. (No mention of the East Wing, you notice; Bangladesh never got its name in the title, and so, eventually, it took the hint and seceded from the secessionists. Imagine what such a double secession does to people!) – So it was a word born in exile which then went East, was borne-across or trans-lated, and imposed itself on history; a returning migrant, settling down on partitioned land, forming a pal-impsest on the past. A palimpsest obscures what lies beneath. To build Pakistan it was necessary to cover up Indian history, to deny that Indian centuries lay just beneath the surface of Pakistani Standard Time. The past was rewritten; there was nothing else to be done.

Who commandeered the job of rewriting history? – The

immigrants, the *mohajirs*. In what languages? – Urdu and English, both imported tongues, although one travelled less distance than the other. It is possible to see the subsequent history of Pakistan as a duel between two layers of time, the obscured world forcing its way back through what-had-been-imposed. It is the true desire of every artist to impose his or her vision on the world; and Pakistan, the peeling, fragmenting palimpsest, increasingly at war with itself, may be described as a failure of the dreaming mind. Perhaps the pigments used were the wrong ones, impermanent, like Leonardo's; or perhaps the place was just *insufficiently imagined*, a picture full of irreconcilable elements, midriffbaring immigrant saris versus demure, indigenous Sindhi shalwar-kurtas, Urdu versus Punjabi, now versus then: a miracle that went wrong.

As for me: I, too, like all migrants, am a fantasist. I build imaginary countries and try to impose them on the ones that exist. I, too, face the problem of history: what to retain, what to dump, how to hold on to what memory insists on relinquishing, how to deal with change. And to come back to the 'roots' idea, I should say that I haven't managed to shake myself free of it completely. Sometimes I do see myself as a tree, even, rather grandly, as the ash Yggdrasil, the mythical world-tree of Norse legend. The ash Yggdrasil has three roots. One falls into the pool of knowledge by Valhalla, where Odin comes to drink. A second is being slowly consumed in the undying fire of Muspellheim, realm of the flame-god Surtur. The third is

I, like all migrants, am a fantasist. I build imaginary countries gradually being gnawed through by a fearsome beast called the Nidhögg. And when fire and monster have destroyed two of the three, the ash will fall, and darkness will descend. The twilight of the gods: a tree's dream of death.

My story's palimpsest-country has, I repeat, no name of its own. The exiled Czech writer Kundera once wrote: 'A name means continuity with the past and people without a past are people without a name.' But I am dealing with a past that refuses to be suppressed, that is daily doing battle with the present; so it is perhaps unduly harsh of me to deny my fairyland a title.

There's an apocryphal story that Napier, after a successful campaign in what is now the south of Pakistan, sent back to England the guilty, one-word message, 'Peccavi'. *I have Sind.* I'm tempted to name my looking-glass Pakistan in honour of this bilingual (and fictional, because never really uttered) pun. Let it be *Peccavistan*.

An essay from *Imaginary Homelands*

AN OLD PHOTOGRAPH in a cheap frame hangs on a wall of the room where I work. It's a picture dating from 1946 of a house into which, at the time of its taking, I had not yet been born. The house is rather peculiar – a three-storeyed gabled affair with tiled roofs and round towers in two corners, each wearing a pointy tiled hat. 'The past is a foreign country,' goes the famous opening sentence of L. P. Hartley's novel *The Go-Between*, 'they do things differently there.' But the photograph tells me to invert this idea; it reminds me that it's my present that is foreign, and that the past is home, albeit a lost home in a lost city in the mists of lost time.

A few years ago I revisited Bombay, which is my lost city, after an absence of something like half my life. Shortly after arriving, acting on an impulse, I opened the telephone directory and looked for my father's name. And, amazingly, there it was; his name, our old address, the unchanged telephone number, as if we had never gone away to the unmentionable country across the border. It was an eerie discovery. I felt as if I were being claimed, or informed that the facts of my faraway life were illusions, and that this continuity was the reality. Then I went to visit the house in the photograph and stood outside it, neither daring nor wishing to announce myself to its new owners. (I didn't want to see how they'd ruined the interior.) I was overwhelmed. The photograph had naturally been taken in black and white; and my memory, feeding on such images as this, had begun to see my childhood in the same way, monochromatically. The colours of my history had seeped out of my mind's eye; now my other two eyes were assaulted by colours, by the vividness of the red tiles, the yellow-edged green of cactus-leaves, the brilliance of bougainvillaea creeper. It is probably not too romantic to say that that was when my novel *Midnight's Children* was really born; when I realized how much I wanted to restore the past to myself, not in the faded greys of old family-album snapshots, but whole, in CinemaScope and glorious Technicolor.

Bombay is a city built by foreigners upon reclaimed land; I, who had been away so long that I almost qualified for the title, was gripped by the conviction that I, too, had a city and a history to reclaim.

It may be that writers in my position, exiles or emigrants or expatriates, are haunted by some sense of loss, some urge to reclaim, to look back, even at the risk of being mutated into pillars of salt. But if we do look back, we must also do so in the knowledge – which gives rise to profound uncertainties – that our physical alienation from India almost inevitably means that we will not be capable of reclaiming precisely the thing that was lost; that we will, in short, create fictions, not actual cities or villages, but invisible ones, imaginary homelands, Indias of the mind.

Writing my book in North London, looking out through my window on to a city scene totally unlike the ones I was imagining on to paper, I was constantly plagued by this problem, until I felt obliged to face it in the text, to make clear that (in spite of my original and I suppose somewhat Proustian ambition to unlock the gates of lost time so that the past reappeared as it actually had been, unaffected by the distortions of memory) what I was actually doing was a novel of memory and about memory, so that my India was just that: 'my' India, a version and no more than one version of all the hundreds of millions of possible versions. I tried to make it as imaginatively true as I could, but imaginative truth is simultaneously honourable and suspect, and I knew that my India may only have been one to which I (who am no longer what I was, and who by quitting Bombay never became what perhaps I was meant to be) was, let us say, willing to admit I belonged.

This is why I made my narrator, Saleem, suspect in his narration; his mistakes are the mistakes of a fallible memory compounded by quirks of character and of circumstance, and his vision is fragmentary. It may be that when the Indian writer who writes from outside India tries to reflect that world, he is obliged to deal in broken mirrors, some of whose fragments have been irretrievably lost.

BUT THERE IS a paradox here. The broken mirror may actually be as valuable as the one which is supposedly unflawed. Let me again try and explain this from my own experience. Before beginning *Midnight's Children*, I spent many months trying simply to recall as much of the Bombay of the 1950s and 1960s as I could; and not only Bombay – Kashmir, too, and Delhi and Aligarh, which, in my book, I've moved to Agra to heighten a certain joke about the Taj Mahal. I was genuinely amazed by how much came back to me. I found myself remembering what clothes people had worn on certain days, and school scenes, and whole passages of Bombay dialogue verbatim, or so it seemed; I even remembered advertisements, film-posters, the neon Jeep sign on Marine Drive, toothpaste ads for Binaca and for Kolynos, and a footbridge over the local railway line which bore, on one side, the legend 'Esso puts a tiger in your tank' and, on the other, the curiously contradictory admonition: 'Drive like Hell and you will get there.' Old songs came back to me from nowhere: a street entertainer's version of 'Good Night, Ladies', and, from the film *Mr 420* (a very appropriate source for my narrator to have used), the hit number

'Mera Joota Hai Japani',* which could almost be Saleem's theme song.

I knew that I had tapped a rich seam; but the point I want to make is that of course I'm not gifted with total recall, and it was precisely the partial nature of these memories, their fragmentation, that made them so evocative for me. The shards of memory acquired greater status, greater resonance, because they were *remains*; fragmentation made trivial things seem like symbols, and the mundane acquired numinous qualities. There is an obvious parallel here with archaeology. The broken pots of antiquity, from which the past can sometimes, but always provisionally, be reconstructed, are exciting to discover, even if they are pieces of the most quotidian objects.

It may be argued that the past is a country from which we have all emigrated, that its loss is part of our common

*Mera joota hai Japani
Yé patloon Inglistani
Sar pé lal topi Rusi—
Phir bhi dil hai Hindustani
—which translates roughly as:
O, my shoes are Japanese
These trousers English, if you please
On my head, red Russian hat—
My heart's Indian for all that.
[This is also the song sung by Gibreel Farishta as he tumbles from the heavens at the beginning of *The Satanic Verses*.]

humanity. Which seems to me self-evidently true; but I suggest that the writer who is out-of-country and even out-of-language may experience this loss in an intensified form. It is made more concrete for him by the physical fact of discontinuity, of his present being in a different place from his past, of his being 'elsewhere'. This may enable him to speak properly and concretely on a subject of universal significance and appeal.

But let me go further. The broken glass is not merely a mirror of nostalgia. It is also, I believe, a useful tool with which to work in the present.

John Fowles begins *Daniel Martin* with the words: 'Whole sight: or all the rest is desolation.' But human beings do not perceive things whole; we are not gods but wounded creatures, cracked lenses, capable only of fractured perceptions. Partial beings, in all the senses of that phrase. Meaning is a shaky edifice we build out of scraps, dogmas, childhood injuries, newspaper articles, chance remarks, old films, small victories, people hated, people loved; perhaps it is because our sense of what is the case is constructed from such inadequate materials that we defend it so fiercely, even to the death. The Fowles position seems to me a way of succumbing to the guru-illusion. Writers are no longer sages, dispensing the wisdom of the centuries. And those of us who have been forced by cultural displacement to accept the provisional nature of all truths, all certainties, have perhaps had modernism forced upon us. We can't lay claim to Olympus, and are thus released to describe our worlds in the way in which all of us, whether writers or not, perceive it from day to day.

In *Midnight's Children*, my narrator Saleem uses, at one point, the metaphor of a cinema screen to discuss this business of perception: 'Suppose yourself in a large cinema, sitting at first in the back row, and gradually moving up, . . . until your nose is almost pressed against the screen. Gradually the stars' faces dissolve into dancing grain; tiny details assume grotesque proportions; . . . it becomes clear that the illusion itself is reality.' The movement towards the cinema screen is a metaphor for the narrative's movement through time towards the present, and the book itself, as it nears contemporary events, quite deliberately loses deep perspective, becomes more 'partial'. I wasn't trying to write about (for instance) the Emergency in the same way as I wrote about events half a century earlier. I felt it would be dishonest to pretend, when writing about the day before yesterday, that it was possible to see the whole picture. I showed certain blobs and slabs of the scene.

I ONCE TOOK part in a conference on modern writing at New College, Oxford. Various novelists, myself included, were talking earnestly of such matters as the need for new ways of describing the world. Then the playwright Howard Brenton suggested that this might be a somewhat limited aim: does literature seek to do no more than to describe? Flustered, all the novelists at once began talking about politics.

Let me apply Brenton's question to the specific case of Indian writers, in England, writing about India. Can they do no more than describe, from a distance, the world that they have left? Or does the distance open any other doors?

These are of course political questions, and must be answered at least partly in political terms. I must say first of all that description is itself a political act. The black American writer Richard Wright once wrote that black and white Americans were engaged in a war over the nature of reality. Their descriptions were incompatible. So it is clear that redescribing a world is the necessary first step towards changing it. And particularly at times when the State takes reality into its own hands, and sets about distorting it, altering the past to fit its present needs, then the making of the alternative realities of art, including the novel of memory, becomes politicized. 'The struggle of man against power,' Milan Kundera has written, 'is the struggle of memory against forgetting.' Writers and politicians are natural rivals. Both groups try to make the world in their own images; they fight for the same territory. And the novel is one way of denying the official, politicians' version of truth.

The 'State truth' about the war in Bangladesh, for instance, is that no atrocities were committed by the Pakistani army in what was then the East Wing. This version is sanctified by many persons who would describe themselves as intellectuals. And the official version of the Emergency in India was well expressed by Mrs Gandhi in a recent BBC interview. She said that there were some people around who claimed that bad things had happened during the Emergency, forced sterilizations, things like that; but, she stated, this was all false. Nothing of this type had ever occurred. The interviewer, Mr Robert Kee, did not probe this statement at all. Instead he told Mrs Gandhi and the *Panorama* audience that she had proved, many times over, her right to be called a democrat.

So literature can, and perhaps must, give the lie to official facts. But is this a proper function of those of us who write from outside India? Or are we just dilettantes in such affairs, because we are not involved in their day-to-day unfolding, because by speaking out we take no risks, because our personal safety is not threatened? What right do we have to speak at all?

My answer is very simple. Literature is self-validating. That is to say, a book is not justified by its author's worthiness to write it, but by the quality of what has been written. There are terrible books that arise directly out of experience, and extraordinary imaginative feats dealing with themes which the author has been obliged to approach from the outside.

Literature is not in the business of copyrighting certain themes for certain groups. And as for risk: the real risks of any artist are taken in the work, in pushing the work to the limits of what is possible, in the attempt to increase the sum of what it is possible to think. Books become good when they go to this edge and risk falling over it – when they endanger the artist by reason of what he has, or has not, *artistically* dared.

So if I am to speak for Indian writers in England I would say this, paraphrasing G. V. Desani's H. Hatterr: The migrations of the fifties and sixties happened. 'We are. We are here.' And we are not willing to be excluded from any part of our heritage; which heritage includes both a Bradford-born Indian kid's right to be treated as a full member of British society, and also the right of any member of this post-diaspora community to draw on its roots for its art, just as all the world's community of displaced writers has always done. (I'm thinking, for instance, of Grass's Danzig-become-Gdansk, of Joyce's abandoned Dublin, of Isaac Bashevis Singer and Maxine Hong Kingston and Milan Kundera and many others. It's a long list.)

Let me override at once the faintly defensive note that has crept into these last few remarks. The Indian writer, looking back at India, does so through guilt-tinted spectacles. (I am of course, once more, talking about myself.) I am speaking now of those of us who emigrated . . . and I suspect that there are times when the move seems wrong to us all, when we seem, to ourselves, post-lapsarian men and women. We are Hindus who have crossed the black water; we are Muslims who eat pork. And as a result – as my use of the Christian notion of the Fall indicates – we are now partly of the West. Our identity is at once plural and partial. Sometimes we feel that we straddle two cultures; at other times, that we fall between two stools. But however ambiguous and shifting this ground may be, it is not an infertile territory for a writer to occupy. If literature is in part the business of finding new angles at which to enter reality, then once again our distance, our long geographical perspective, may provide us with such angles. Or it may be that that is simply what we must think in order to do our work.

Midnight's Children enters its subject from the point of view of a secular man. I am a member of that generation of Indians who were sold the secular ideal. One of the things I liked, and still like, about India is that it is based on a non-sectarian philosophy. I was not raised in a narrowly Muslim environment; I do not consider Hindu culture to be either alien from me or more important than the Islamic heritage. I believe this has something to do with the nature of Bombay, a metropolis in which the multiplicity of commingled faiths and cultures curiously creates a remarkably secular ambience. Saleem Sinai makes use, eclectically, of whatever elements from whatever sources he chooses. It may have been easier for his author to do this from outside modern India than inside it.

I want to make one last point about the description of India that *Midnight's Children* attempts. It is a point about pessimism. The book has been criticised in India for its allegedly despairing tone. And the despair of the writer-from-outside may indeed look a little easy, a little pat. But I do not see the book as despairing or nihilistic. The point of view of the narrator is not entirely that of the author.

What I tried to do was to set up a tension in the text, a paradoxical opposition between the form and content of the narrative. The story of Saleem does indeed lead him to despair. But the story is told in a manner designed to echo, as closely as my abilities allowed, the Indian talent for non-stop self-regeneration. This is why the narrative constantly throws up new stories, why it 'teems'. The form – multitudinous, hinting at the infinite possibilities of the country – is the optimistic counterweight to Saleem's personal tragedy. I do not think that a book written in such a manner can really be called a despairing work.

ENGLAND'S INDIAN WRITERS are by no means all the same type of animal. Some of us, for instance, are Pakistani. Others Bangladeshi. Others West, or East, or even South African. And V. S. Naipaul, by now, is something else entirely. This word 'Indian' is getting to be a pretty scattered concept. Indian writers in England include political exiles, first-generation migrants, affluent expatriates whose residence here is frequently temporary, naturalized Britons, and people born here who may never have laid eyes on the subcontinent. Clearly, nothing that I say can apply across all these categories. But one of the interesting things about this diverse community is that, as far as Indo-British fiction is concerned, its existence changes the ball game, because that fiction is in future going to come as much from addresses in London, Birmingham and Yorkshire as from Delhi or Bombay.

One of the changes has to do with attitudes towards the use of English. Many have referred to the argument about the appropriateness of this language to Indian themes. And I hope all of us share the view that we can't simply use the language in the way the British did; that it needs remaking for our own purposes. Those of us who do use English do so in spite of our ambiguity towards it, or perhaps because of that, perhaps because we can find in that linguistic struggle a reflection of other struggles taking place in the real world, struggles between the cultures within ourselves and the influences at work upon our societies. To conquer English may be to complete the process of making ourselves free.

But the British Indian writer simply does not have the option of rejecting English, anyway. His children, her children, will grow up speaking it, probably as a first language; and in the forging of a British Indian identity the English language is of central importance. It must, in spite of everything, be embraced. (The word 'translation' comes, etymologically, from the Latin for 'bearing across'. Having been borne across the world, we are translated men. It is normally supposed that something always gets lost in translation; I cling, obstinately, to the notion that something can also be gained.)

To be an Indian writer in this society is to face, every day, problems of definition. What does it mean to be 'Indian' outside India? How can culture be preserved without becoming ossified? How should we discuss the need for change within ourselves and our community without seeming to play into the hands of our racial enemies? What are the consequences, both spiritual and practical, of refusing to make any concessions to Western ideas and practices? What are the consequences of embracing those ideas and practices and turning away from the ones that came here with us? These questions are all a single, existential question: How are we to live in the world?

I do not propose to offer, prescriptively, any answers to these questions; only to state that these are some of the issues with which each of us will have to come to terms.

TO TURN MY eyes outwards now, and to say a little about the relationship between the Indian writer and the majority white culture in whose midst he lives, and with which his work will sooner or later have to deal:

In common with many Bombay-raised middle-class children of my generation, I grew up with an intimate knowledge of, and even sense of friendship with, a certain kind of England: a dream-England composed of Test Matches at Lord's presided over by the voice of John Arlott, at which Freddie Trueman bowled unceasingly and without success at Polly Umrigar; of Enid Blyton and Billy Bunter, in which we were even prepared to smile indulgently at portraits such as 'Hurree Jamset Ram Singh', 'the dusky nabob of Bhanipur'. I wanted to come to England. I couldn't wait. And to be fair, England has done all right by me; but I find it a little difficult to be properly grateful. I can't escape the view that my relatively easy ride is not the result of the dream-England's famous sense of tolerance and fair play, but of my social class, my freak fair skin and my 'English' English accent. Take away any of these, and the story would have been very different. Because of course the dream-England is no more than a dream.

Sadly, it's a dream from which too many white Britons refuse to awake. Recently, on a live radio programme, a professional humorist asked me, in all seriousness, why I objected to being called a wog. He said he had always thought it a rather charming word, a term of endearment. 'I was at the zoo the other day,' he revealed, 'and a zoo keeper told me that the wogs were best with the animals; they stuck their fingers in their ears and wiggled them about and the animals felt at home.' The ghost of Hurree Jamset Ram Singh walks among us still.

As Richard Wright found long ago in America, black and white descriptions of society are no longer compatible. Fantasy, or the mingling of fantasy and naturalism, is one way of dealing with these problems. It offers a way of echoing in the form of our work the issues faced by all of us: how to build a new, 'modern' world out of an old, legend-haunted civilization, an old culture which we have brought into the heart of a newer one. But whatever technical solutions we may find, Indian writers in these islands, like others who have migrated into the north from the south, are capable of writing from a kind of double perspective: because they, we, are at one and the same time insiders and outsiders in this society. This stereoscopic vision is perhaps what we can offer in place of 'whole sight'.

THERE IS ONE last idea that I should like to explore, even though it may, on first hearing, seem to contradict much of what I've so far said. It is this: of all the many elephant traps lying ahead of us, the largest and most dangerous pitfall would be the adoption of a ghetto mentality. To forget that there is a world beyond the community to which we belong, to confine ourselves within narrowly defined cultural frontiers, would be, I believe, to go voluntarily into that form of internal exile which in South Africa is called the 'homeland'. We must guard against creating, for the most virtuous of reasons, British–Indian literary equivalents of Bophuthatswana or the Transkei.

This raises immediately the question of whom one is writing 'for'. My own, short, answer is that I have never had a reader in mind. I have ideas, people, events, shapes, and I write 'for' those things, and hope that the completed work will be of interest to others. But which others? In the case of *Midnight's Children* I certainly felt that if its subcontinental readers had rejected the work, I should have thought it a failure, no matter what the reaction in the West. So I would say that I write 'for' people who feel part of the things I write 'about', but also for everyone else whom I can reach. In this I am of the same opinion as the black American writer Ralph Ellison, who, in his collection

The largest and most dangerous pitfall would be the adoption of a ghetto mentality

of essays *Shadow and Act*, says that he finds something precious in being black in America at this time; but that he is also reaching for more than that. 'I was taken very early,' he writes, 'with a passion to link together all I loved within the Negro community and all those things I felt in the world which lay beyond.'

Art is a passion of the mind. And the imagination works best when it is most free. Western writers have always felt free to be eclectic in their selection of theme, setting, form; Western visual artists have, in this century, been happily raiding the visual storehouses of Africa, Asia, the Philippines. I am sure that we must grant ourselves an equal freedom.

Let me suggest that Indian writers in England have access to a second tradition, quite apart from their own racial history. It is the culture and political history of the phenomenon of migration, displacement, life in a minority group. We can quite legitimately claim as our ancestors the Huguenots, the Irish, the Jews; the past to which we belong is an English past, the history of immigrant Britain. Swift, Conrad, Marx are as much our literary forebears as Tagore or Ram Mohan Roy. America, a nation of immigrants, has created great literature out of the phenomenon of cultural transplantation, out of examining the ways in which people cope with a new world; it may be that by discovering what we have in common with those who preceded us into this country, we can begin to do the same.

I stress this is only one of many possible strategies. But

we are inescapably international writers at a time when the novel has never been a more international form (a writer like Borges speaks of the influence of Robert Louis Stevenson on his work; Heinrich Boll acknowledges the influence of Irish literature; cross-pollination is everywhere); and it is perhaps one of the more pleasant freedoms of the literary migrant to be able to choose his parents. My own – selected half consciously, half not – include Gogol, Cervantes, Kafka, Melville, Machado de Assis; a polyglot family tree, against which I measure myself, and to which I would be honoured to belong.

There's a beautiful image in Saul Bellow's latest novel, *The Dean's December*. The central character, the Dean, Corde, hears a dog barking wildly somewhere. He imagines that the barking is the dog's protest against the limit of dog experience. 'For God's sake,' the dog is saying, 'open the universe a little more!' And because Bellow is, of course, not really talking about dogs, or not only about dogs, I have the feeling that the dog's rage, and its desire, is also mine, ours, everyone's. 'For God's sake, open the universe a little more!'

The Courter
A story from *East, West*

1

CERTAINLY-MARY WAS THE smallest woman Mixed-Up the hall porter had come across, dwarfs excepted, a tiny sixty-year-old Indian lady with her greying hair tied behind her head in a neat bun, hitching up her red-hemmed white sari in the front and negotiating the apartment block's front steps as if they were Alps. 'No,' he said aloud, furrowing his brow. What would be the right peaks. Ah, good, that was the name. 'Ghats,' he said proudly. Word from a schoolboy atlas long ago, when India felt as far away as Paradise. (Nowadays Paradise seemed even further away but India, and Hell, had come a good bit closer.) 'Western Ghats, Eastern Ghats, and now Kensington Ghats,' he said, giggling. 'Mountains.'

She stopped in front of him in the oak-panelled lobby. 'But ghats in India are also stairs,' she said. 'Yes yes certainly. For instance in Hindu holy city of Varanasi, where the Brahmins sit taking the filgrims' money is called Dasashwamedh-ghat. Broad-broad staircase down to River Ganga. O, most certainly! Also Manikarnika-ghat. They buy fire from a house with a tiger leaping from the roof – yes certainly, a statue tiger, coloured by Technicolor, what are you thinking? – and they bring it in a box to set fire to their loved ones' bodies. Funeral fires are of sandal. Photographs not allowed; no, certainly not.'

HE BEGAN THINKING of her as Certainly-Mary because she never said plain yes or no; always this O-yes-certainly or no-certainly-not. In the confused circumstances that had prevailed ever since his brain, his one sure thing, had let him down, he could hardly be certain of anything any more; so he was stunned by her sureness, first into nostalgia, then envy, then attraction. And attraction was a thing so long forgotten that when the churning started he thought for a long time it must be the Chinese dumplings he had brought home from the High Street carry-out.

ENGLISH WAS HARD for Certainly-Mary, and this was a part of what drew damaged old Mixed-Up towards her. The letter p was a particular problem, often turning into an f or a c; when she proceeded through the lobby with a wheeled wicker shopping basket, she would say, 'Going shocking,' and when, on her return, he offered to help lift the basket up the front ghats, she would answer, 'Yes, fleas.' As the elevator lifted her away, she called through the grille: 'Oé, courter! Thank you, courter. O, yes, certainly.' (In Hindi and Konkani, however, her p's knew their place.)

So: thanks to her unexpected, somehow stomach-churning magic, he was no longer porter but courter. 'Courter,' he repeated to the mirror when she had gone. His breath made a little dwindling picture of the word on the glass. 'Courter courter caught.' Okay. People called him many things, he did not mind. But this name, this courter, this he would try to be.

2

FOR YEARS NOW I've been meaning to write down the story of Certainly-Mary, our ayah, the woman who did as much as my mother to raise my sisters and me, and her great adventure with her 'courter' in London, where we all lived for a time in the early Sixties in a block called Waverley House; but what with one thing and another I never got round to it.

Then recently I heard from Certainly-Mary after a long-ish silence. She wrote to say that she was ninety-one, had had a serious operation, and would I kindly send her some money, because she was embarrassed that her niece, with whom she was now living in the Kurla district of Bombay, was so badly out of pocket.

I sent the money, and soon afterwards received a pleasant letter from the niece, Stella, written in the same hand as the letter from 'Aya' – as we had always called Mary, palindromically dropping the 'h'. Aya had been so touched, the niece wrote, that I remembered her after all these years. 'I have been hearing the stories about you folks all my life,' the letter went on, 'and I think of you a little bit as family. Maybe you recall my mother Mary's sister. She unfortunately passed on. Now it is I who write Mary's letters for her. We all wish you the best.'

This message from an intimate stranger reached out to me in my enforced exile from the beloved country of my birth and moved me, stirring things that had been buried very deep. Of course it also made me feel guilty about having done so little for Mary over the years. For whatever reason, it has become more important than ever to set down the story I've been carrying around unwritten for so long, the story of Aya and the gentle man whom she renamed – with unintentional but prophetic overtones of romance – 'the courter'. I see now that it is not just their story, but ours, mine, as well.

3

HIS REAL NAME was Mecir: you were supposed to say Mishirsh because it had invisible accents on it in some Iron Curtain language in which the accents had to be invisible, my sister Durré said solemnly, in case somebody spied on them or rubbed them out or something. His first name also began with an m but it was so full of what we called Communist consonants, all those z's and c's and w's walled up together without vowels to give them breathing space, that I never even tried to learn it.

At first we thought of nicknaming him after a mischievous little comic-book character, Mr Mxyztplk from the Fifth Dimension, who looked a bit like Elmer Fudd and used to make Superman's life hell until ole Supe could trick him into saying his name backwards, Klptzyxm, whereupon he disappeared back into the Fifth Dimension; but because we weren't too sure how to say Mxyztplk (not to mention Klptzyxm) we dropped that idea. 'We'll just call you Mixed-Up,' I told him in the end, to simplify life. 'Mishter Mikshed-Up Mishirsh.' I was fifteen then and bursting with unemployed cock and it meant I could say things like that right into people's faces, even people less accommodating than Mr Mecir with his stroke.

WHAT I REMEMBER most vividly are his pink rubber washing-up gloves, which he seemed never to remove, at least not until he came calling for Certainly-Mary . . . At any rate, when I insulted him, with my sisters Durré and Muneeza cackling in the lift, Mecir just grinned an empty good-natured grin, nodded, 'You call me what you like, okay,' and went back to buffing and polishing the brasswork. There was no point teasing him if he was going to be like that, so I got into the lift and all the way to the fourth floor we sang *I Can't Stop Loving You* at the top of our best Ray Charles voices, which were pretty awful. But we were wearing our dark glasses, so it didn't matter.

4

IT WAS THE summer of 1962, and school was out. My baby sister Scheherazade was just one year old. Durré was a bee-hived fourteen; Muneeza was ten, and already quite a handful. The three of us – or rather Durré and me, with Muneeza trying desperately and unsuccessfully to be included in our gang – would stand over Scheherazade's cot and sing to her. 'No nursery rhymes,' Durré had decreed, and so there were none, for though she was a year my junior she was a natural leader. The infant Scheherazade's lulla-bies were our cover versions of recent hits by Chubby Checker, Neil Sedaka, Elvis and Pat Boone.

'Why don't you come home, Speedy Gonzales?' we bel-lowed in sweet disharmony: but most of all, and with actions, we would jump down, turn around and pick a bale of cotton. We would have jumped down, turned around and picked those bales all day except that the Maharaja of B— in the flat below complained, and Aya Mary came in to plead with us to be quiet.

'Look, see, it's Jumble-Aya who's fallen for Mixed-Up,' Durré shouted, and Mary blushed a truly immense blush. So naturally we segued right into a quick me-oh-my-oh; son of a gun, we had big fun. But then the baby began to yell, my father came in with his head down bull-fashion and steaming from both ears, and we needed all the good luck charms we could find.

I HAD BEEN at boarding school in England for a year or so when Abba took the decision to bring the family over. Like all his decisions, it was neither explained to nor discussed with anyone, not even my mother. When they first arrived he rented two adjacent flats in a seedy Bayswater mansion block called Graham Court, which lurked furtively in a nothing street that crawled along the side of the ABC Queensway cinema towards the Porchester Baths. He commandeered one of these flats for himself and put my mother, three sisters and Aya in the other; also, on school holidays, me. England, where liquor was freely available, did little for my father's *bonhomie*, so in a way it was a relief to have a flat to ourselves.

Most nights he emptied a bottle of Johnnie Walker Red Label and a soda-siphon. My mother did not dare to go across to 'his place' in the evenings. She said: 'He makes faces at me.'

Aya Mary took Abba his dinner and answered all his calls (if he wanted anything, he would phone us up and ask for it). I am not sure why Mary was spared his drunken rages. She said it was because she was nine years his senior so she could tell him to show due respect.

AFTER A FEW months, however, my father leased a three-bedroom fourth-floor apartment with a fancy address. This was Waverley House in Kensington Court, W8. Among its other residents were not one but two Indian Maharajas, the sporting Prince P— as well as the old B— who has already been mentioned. Now we were jammed in together, my parents and Baby Scare-zade (as her siblings had affectionately begun to call her) in the master bedroom, the three of us in a much smaller room, and Mary, I regret to admit, on a straw mat laid on the fitted carpet in the hall. The third bedroom became my father's office, where he made phone-calls and kept his *Encyclopaedia Britannica*, his *Reader's Digests*, and (under lock and key) the television cabinet. We entered it at our peril. It was the Minotaur's lair.

ONE MORNING HE was persuaded to drop in at the corner pharmacy and pick up some supplies for the baby. When he returned there was a hurt, schoolboyish look on his face that I had never seen before, and he was pressing his hand against his cheek.

'She hit me,' he said plaintively.

'Hai! Allah-tobah! Darling!' cried my mother, fussing. 'Who hit you? Are you injured? Show me, let me see.'

'I did nothing,' he said, standing there in the hall with the pharmacy bag in his other hand and a face as pink as Mecir's rubber gloves. 'I just went in with your list. The girl seemed very helpful. I asked for baby compound, Johnson's powder, teething jelly, and she brought them out. Then I asked did she have any nipples, and she slapped my face.'

My mother was appalled. 'Just for that?' And Certainly-Mary backed her up. 'What is this nonsense?' she wanted to know. 'I have been in that chemist's shock, and they have flenty nickels, different sizes, all on view.'

Durré and Muneeza could not contain themselves. They were rolling round on the floor, laughing and kicking their legs in the air.

'You both shut your face at once,' my mother ordered. 'A madwoman has hit your father. Where is the comedy?'

'I don't believe it,' Durré gasped. 'You just went up to that girl and said,' and here she fell apart again, stamping her feet and holding her stomach, '"*have you got any nipples?*"'

My father grew thunderous, empurpled. Durré controlled herself. 'But Abba,' she said, at length, 'here they call them teats.'

Now my mother's and Mary's hands flew to their mouths, and even my father looked shocked. 'But how shameless!' my mother said. 'The same word as for what's on your bosoms?' She coloured, and stuck out her tongue for shame.

'These English,' sighed Certainly-Mary. 'But aren't they the limit? Certainly-yes; they are.'

I REMEMBER THIS story with delight, because it was the only time I ever saw my father so discomfited, and the incident became legendary and the girl in the pharmacy was installed as the object of our great veneration. (Durré and

I went in there just to take a look at her – she was a plain, short girl of about seventeen, with large, unavoidable breasts – but she caught us whispering and glared so fiercely that we fled.) And also because in the general hilarity I was able to conceal the shaming truth that I, who had been in England for so long, would have made the same mistake as Abba did.

It wasn't just Certainly-Mary and my parents who had trouble with the English language. My schoolfellows tittered when in my Bombay way I said 'brought-up' for upbringing (as in 'where was your brought-up?') and 'thrice' for three times and 'quarter-plate' for side-plate and 'macaroni' for pasta in general. As for learning the difference between nipples and teats, I really hadn't had any opportunities to increase my word power in that area at all.

5

So I was a little jealous of Certainly-Mary when Mixed-Up came to call. He rang our bell, his body quivering with deference in an old suit grown too loose, the trousers tightly gathered by a belt; he had taken off his rubber gloves and there were roses in his hand. My father opened the door and gave him a withering look. Being a snob, Abba was not pleased that the flat lacked a separate service entrance, so that even a porter had to be treated as a member of the same universe as himself.

'Mary,' Mixed-Up managed, licking his lips and pushing back his floppy white hair. 'I, to see Miss Mary, come, am.'

'Wait on,' Abba said, and shut the door in his face.

CERTAINLY-MARY SPENT ALL her afternoons off with old Mixed-Up from then on, even though that first date was not a complete success. He took her 'up West' to show her the visitors' London she had never seen, but at the top of an up escalator at Piccadilly Circus, while Mecir was painfully enunciating the words on the posters she couldn't read – *Unzip a banana*, and *Idris when I's dri* – she got her sari stuck in the jaws of the machine, and as the escalator pulled at the garment it began to unwind. She was forced to spin round and round like a top, and screamed at the top of her voice, 'O BAAP! BAAPU-RÉ! BAAP-RÉ-BAAP-RÉ-BAAP!' It was Mixed-Up who saved her by pushing the emergency stop button before the sari was completely unwound and she was exposed in her petticoat for all the world to see.

'O, courter!' she wept on his shoulder. 'O, no more escaleater, courter, nevermore, surely not!'

MY OWN AMOROUS longings were aimed at Durré's best friend, a Polish girl called Rozalia, who had a holiday job at Faiman's shoe shop on Oxford Street. I pursued her pathetically throughout the holidays and, on and off, for the next two years. She would let me have lunch with her sometimes and buy her a Coke and a sandwich, and once she came with me to stand on the terraces at White Hart Lane to watch Jimmy Greaves's first game for the Spurs. 'Come on you whoi-oites,' we both shouted dutifully. 'Come on you *Lily-whoites*.' After that she even invited me into the back room at Faiman's, where she kissed me twice and let me touch her breast, but that was as far as I got.

AND THEN THERE was my sort-of-cousin Chandni, whose mother's sister had married my mother's brother though they had since split up. Chandni was eighteen months older than me, and so sexy it made you sick. She was training to be an Indian classical dancer, Odissi as well as Natyam, but in the meantime she dressed in tight black jeans and a clinging black polo-neck jumper and took me, now and then, to hang out at Bunjie's, where she knew most of the folk-music crowd that frequented the place, and where she answered to the name of Moonlight, which is what *chandni* means. I chain-smoked with the folkies and then went to the toilet to throw up.

Chandni was the stuff of obsessions. She was a teenage dream, the Moon River come to Earth like the Goddess Ganga, dolled up in slinky black. But for her I was just the young greenhorn cousin to whom she was being nice because he hadn't learned his way around.

SHE-E-RRY, WON'T YOU *come out tonight?* yodelled the Four Seasons. I knew exactly how they felt. *Come, come, come out toni-yi-yight*. And while you're at it, love me do.

6

THEY WENT FOR walks in Kensington Gardens. 'Pan,' Mixed-Up said, pointing at a statue. 'Los' boy. Nev' grew up.' They went to Barkers and Pontings and Derry & Toms and picked out furniture and curtains for imaginary homes. They cruised supermarkets and chose little delicacies to eat. In Mecir's cramped lounge they sipped what he called 'chimpanzee tea' and toasted crumpets in front of an electric bar fire.

THANKS TO MIXED-UP, Mary was at last able to watch television. She liked children's programmes best, especially *The Flintstones*. Once, giggling at her daring, Mary confided to Mixed-Up that Fred and Wilma reminded her of her Sahib and Begum Sahiba upstairs; at which the courter, matching her audaciousness, pointed first at Certainly-Mary and then at himself, grinned a wide gappy smile and said, 'Rubble.'

Later, on the news, a vulpine Englishman with a thin moustache and mad eyes declaimed a warning about immigrants, and Certainly-Mary flapped her hand at the set: 'Khali-pili bom marta,' she objected, and then, for her host's benefit translated: 'For nothing he is shouting shouting. Bad life! Switch it off.'

THEY WERE OFTEN interrupted by the Maharajas of B— and P—, who came downstairs to escape their wives and ring other women from the call-box in the porter's room.

'Oh, baby, forget that guy,' said sporty Prince P—, who seemed to spend all his days in tennis whites, and whose plump gold Rolex was almost lost in the thick hair on his arm. 'I'll show you a better time than him, baby; step into my world.'

The Maharaja of B— was older, uglier; more matter-of-fact. 'Yes, bring all appliances. Room is booked in name of Mr Douglas Home. Six forty-five to seven fifteen. You have printed rate card? Please. Also a two-foot ruler, must be wooden. Frilly apron, plus.'

THIS IS WHAT has lasted in my memory of Waverley House, this seething mass of bad marriages, booze, philanderers and unfulfilled young lusts; of the Maharaja of P— roaring away towards London's casinoland every night, in a red sports car with fitted blondes, and of the Maharaja of B— skulking off to Kensington High Street wearing dark glasses in the dark, and a coat with the collar turned up even though it was high summer; and at the heart of our little universe were Certainly-Mary and her courter, drinking chimpanzee tea and singing along with the national anthem of Bedrock.

But they were not really like Barney and Betty Rubble at all. They were formal, polite. They were . . . courtly. He courted her, and, like a coy, ringleted ingénue with a fan, she inclined her head, and entertained his suit.

7

I SPENT ONE half-term weekend in 1963 at the home in Beccles, Suffolk of Field Marshal Sir Charles Lutwidge-Dodgson, an old India hand and a family friend who was supporting my application for British citizenship. 'The Dodo', as he was known, invited me down by myself, saying he wanted to get to know me better.

He was a huge man whose skin had started hanging too loosely on his face, a giant living in a tiny thatched cottage and forever bumping his head. No wonder he was irascible at times; he was in Hell, a Gulliver trapped in that rose-garden Lilliput of croquet hoops, church bells, sepia photographs and old battle-trumpets.

The weekend was fitful and awkward until the Dodo asked if I played chess. Slightly awestruck at the prospect of playing a Field Marshal, I nodded; and ninety minutes later, to my amazement, won the game.

I went into the kitchen, strutting somewhat, planning to boast a little to the old soldier's long-time housekeeper, Mrs Liddell. But as soon as I entered she said: 'Don't tell me. You never went and won?'

'Yes,' I said, affecting nonchalance. 'As a matter of fact, yes, I did.'

'Gawd,' said Mrs Liddell. 'Now there'll be hell to pay. You go back in there and ask him for another game, and this time make sure you lose.'

I did as I was told, but was never invited to Beccles again.

STILL, THE DEFEAT of the Dodo gave me new confidence at the chessboard, so when I returned to Waverley House after finishing my O levels, and was at once invited to play a game by Mixed-Up (Mary had told him about my victory in the Battle of Beccles with great pride and some hyperbole), I said: 'Sure, I don't mind.' How long could it take to thrash the old duffer, after all?

There followed a massacre royal. Mixed-Up did not just beat me; he had me for breakfast, over easy. I couldn't believe it – the canny opening, the fluency of his combination play, the force of his attacks, my own impossibly cramped, strangled positions – and asked for a second game. This time he tucked into me even more heartily. I sat broken in my chair at the end, close to tears. *Big girls don't cry*, I reminded myself, but the song went on playing in my head: *That's just an alibi.*

'Who are you?' I demanded, humiliation weighing down every syllable. 'The devil in disguise?'

Mixed-Up gave his big, silly grin. 'Grand Master,' he said. 'Long time. Before head.'

'YOU'RE A GRAND Master,' I repeated, still in a daze. Then in a moment of horror I remembered that I had seen the name Mecir in books of classic games. 'Nimzo-Indian,' I said aloud. He beamed and nodded furiously.

'That Mecir?' I asked wonderingly.

'That,' he said. There was saliva dribbling out of a corner of his sloppy old mouth. This ruined old man was in the books. He was in the books. And even with his mind turned to rubble he could still wipe the floor with me.

'Now play lady,' he grinned. I didn't get it. 'Mary lady,' he said. 'Yes yes certainly.'

She was pouring tea, waiting for my answer. 'Aya, you can't play,' I said, bewildered.

'Learning, baba,' she said. 'What is it, na? Only a game.'

And then she, too, beat me senseless, and with the black pieces, at that. It was not the greatest day of my life.

8

FROM 100 MOST *Instructive Chess Games* by Robert Reshevsky, 1961:

> *M. Mecir – M. Najdorf*
> *Dallas 1950, Nimzo-Indian Defense*
> The attack of a tactician can be troublesome to meet – that of a strategist even more so. Whereas the tactician's threats may be unmistakable, the strategist confuses the issue by keeping things in abeyance. He threatens to threaten!
>
> Take this game for instance: Mecir posts a Knight at Q6 to get a grip on the center. Then he establishes a passed Pawn on one wing to occupy his opponent on

the Queen side. Finally he stirs up the position on the King-side. What does the poor bewildered opponent do? How can he defend everything at once? Where will the blow fall?

Watch Mecir keep Najdorf on the run, as he shifts the attack from side to side!

Chess had become their private language. Old Mixed-Up, lost as he was for words, retained, on the chessboard, much of the articulacy and subtlety which had vanished from his speech. As Certainly-Mary gained in skill – and she had learned with astonishing speed, I thought bitterly, for someone who couldn't read or write or pronounce the letter p – she was better able to understand, and respond to, the wit of the reduced maestro with whom she had so unexpectedly forged a bond.

He taught her with great patience, showing-not-telling, repeating openings and combinations and endgame tech-niques over and over until she began to see the meaning in the patterns. When they played, he handicapped himself, he told her her best moves and demonstrated their conse-quences, drawing her, step by step, into the infinite possibilities of the game.

SUCH WAS THEIR courtship. 'It is like an adventure, baba,' Mary once tried to explain to me. 'It is like going with him to his country, you know? What a place, baap-ré! Beautiful and dangerous and funny and full of fuzzles. For me it is a big-big discovery. What to tell you? I go for the game. It is a wonder.'

I understood, then, how far things had gone between them. Certainly-Mary had never married, and had made it clear to old Mixed-Up that it was too late to start any of that monkey business at her age. The courter was a widower, and had grown-up children somewhere, lost long ago behind the ever-higher walls of Eastern Europe. But in the game of chess they had found a form of flirtation, an endless renewal that precluded the possibility of boredom, a courtly wonderland of the ageing heart.

What would the Dodo have made of it all? No doubt it would have scandalised him to see chess, chess of all games, the great formalisation of war, transformed into an art of love.

As for me: my defeats by Certainly-Mary and her courter ushered in further humiliations. Durré and Muneeza went down with the mumps, and so, finally, in spite of my mother's efforts to segregate us, did I. I lay terrified in bed while the doctor warned me not to stand up and move around if I could possibly help it. 'If you do,' he said, 'your parents won't need to punish you. You will have punished yourself quite enough.'

I spent the following few weeks tormented day and night by visions of grotesquely swollen testicles and a subsequent life of limp impotence – finished before I'd even started, it wasn't fair! – which were made much worse by my sisters' quick recovery and incessant gibes. But in the end I was lucky; the illness didn't spread to the deep South. 'Think how happy your hundred and one girlfriends will be, bhai,' sneered Durré, who knew all about my continued failures in the Rozalia and Chandni departments.

On the radio, people were always singing about the joys of being sixteen years old. I wondered where they were, all those boys and girls of my age having the time of their lives. Were they driving around America in Studebaker convertibles? They certainly weren't in my neighbourhood. London, W8 was Sam Cooke country that summer. *Another Saturday night* ... There might be a mop-top love-song stuck at number one, but I was down with lonely Sam in the lower depths of the charts, how-I-wishing I had someone, etc., and generally feeling in a pretty goddamn dreadful way.

9

'BABA, COME QUICK.'

It was late at night when Aya Mary shook me awake. After many urgent hisses, she managed to drag me out of sleep and pull me, pajama'ed and yawning, down the hall. On the landing outside our flat was Mixed-Up the courter, huddled up against a wall, weeping. He had a black eye and there was dried blood on his mouth.

'What happened?' I asked Mary, shocked.

'Men,' wailed Mixed-Up. 'Threaten. Beat.'

He had been in his lounge earlier that evening when the

sporting Maharaja of P— burst in to say, 'If anybody comes looking for me, okay, any tough-guy type guys, okay, I am out, okay? Oh you tea. Don't let them go upstairs, okay? Big tip, okay?'

A short time later, the old Maharaja of B— also arrived in Mecir's lounge, looking distressed.

'Suno, listen on,' said the Maharaja of B—. 'You don't know where I am, samajh liya? Understood? Some low persons may inquire. You don't know. I am abroad, achha? On extended travels abroad. Do your job, porter. Handsome recompense.'

Late at night two tough-guy types did indeed turn up. It seemed the hairy Prince P— had gambling debts. 'Out,' Mixed-Up grinned in his sweetest way. The tough-guy types nodded, slowly. They had long hair and thick lips like Mick Jagger's. 'He's a busy gent. We should of made an appointment,' said the first type to the second. 'Didn't I tell you we should of called?'

'You did,' agreed the second type. 'Got to do these things right, you said, he's royalty. And you was right, my son, I put my hand up, I was dead wrong. I put my hand up to that.'

'Let's leave our card,' said the first type. 'Then he'll know to expect us.'

'Ideal,' said the second type, and smashed his fist into old Mixed-Up's mouth. 'You tell him,' the second type said, and struck the old man in the eye. 'When he's in. You mention it.'

He had locked the front door after that; but much later,

well after midnight, there was a hammering. Mixed-Up
called out, 'Who?'

'We are close friends of the Maharaja of B—' said a
voice. 'No, I tell a lie. Acquaintances.'

'He calls upon a lady of our acquaintance,' said a second
voice. 'To be precise.'

'It is in that connection that we crave audience,' said
the first voice.

'Gone,' said Mecir. 'Jet plane. Gone.'

There was a silence. Then the second voice said, 'Can't
be in the jet set if you never jump on a jet, eh? Biarritz,
Monte, all of that.'

'Be sure and let His Highness know', said the first voice,
'that we eagerly await his return.'

'With regard to our mutual friend,' said the second
voice. 'Eagerly.'

WHAT DOES THE *poor bewildered opponent do?* The words
from the chess book popped unbidden into my head. *How
can he defend everything at once? Where will the blow fall?
Watch Mecir keep Najdorf on the run, as he shifts the attack
from side to side!*

Mixed-Up returned to his lounge and on this occasion,
even though there had been no use of force, he began to
weep. After a time he took the elevator up to the fourth
floor and whispered through our letterbox to Certainly-
Mary sleeping on her mat.

'I didn't want to wake Sahib,' Mary said. 'You know his

trouble, na? And Begum Sahiba is so tired at end of the day. So now you tell, baba, what to do?'

What did she expect me to come up with? I was sixteen years old. 'Mixed-Up must call the police,' I unoriginally offered.

'No, no, baba,' said Certainly-Mary emphatically. 'If the courter makes a scandal for Maharaja-log, then in the end it is the courter only who will be out on his ear.' I had no other ideas. I stood before them feeling like a fool, while they both turned upon me their frightened, supplicant eyes.

'Go to sleep,' I said. 'We'll think about it in the morning.' *The first pair of thugs were tacticians*, I was thinking. *They were troublesome to meet. But the second pair were scarier; they were strategists. They threatened to threaten.*

NOTHING HAPPENED IN the morning, and the sky was clear. It was almost impossible to believe in fists, and menacing voices at the door. During the course of the day both Maharajas visited the porter's lounge and stuck five-pound notes in Mixed-Up's waistcoat pocket. 'Held the fort, good man,' said Prince P—, and the Maharaja of B— echoed those sentiments: 'Spot on. All handled now, achha? Problem over.'

The three of us – Aya Mary, her courter, and me – held a council of war that afternoon and decided that no further action was necessary. The hall porter was the front line in any such situation, I argued, and the front line had held.

And now the risks were past. Assurances had been given. End of story.

'End of story,' repeated Certainly-Mary doubtfully, but then, seeking to reassure Mecir, she brightened. 'Correct,' she said. 'Most certainly! All-done, finis.' She slapped her hands against each other for emphasis. She asked Mixed-Up if he wanted a game of chess; but for once the courter didn't want to play.

10

AFTER THAT I was distracted, for a time, from the story of Mixed-Up and Certainly-Mary by violence nearer home.

My middle sister Muneeza, now eleven, was entering her delinquent phase a little early. She was the true inheritor of my father's black rage, and when she lost control it was terrible to behold. That summer she seemed to pick fights with my father on purpose; seemed prepared, at her young age, to test her strength against his. (I intervened in her rows with Abba only once, in the kitchen. She grabbed the kitchen scissors and flung them at me. They cut me on the thigh. After that I kept my distance.)

As I witnessed their wars I felt myself coming unstuck from the idea of family itself. I looked at my screaming sister and thought how brilliantly self-destructive she was, how triumphantly she was ruining her relations with the people she needed most.

And I looked at my choleric, face-pulling father and

thought about British citizenship. My existing Indian passport permitted me to travel only to a very few countries, which were carefully listed on the second right-hand page. But I might soon have a British passport and then, by hook or by crook, I would get away from him. I would not have this face-pulling in my life.

At sixteen, you still think you can escape from your father. You aren't listening to his voice speaking through your mouth, you don't see how your gestures already mirror his; you don't see him in the way you hold your body, in the way you sign your name. You don't hear his whisper in your blood.

On the day I have to tell you about, my two-year-old sister Chhoti Scheherazade, Little Scare-zade, started crying as she often did during one of our family rows. Amma and Aya Mary loaded her into her push-chair and made a rapid getaway. They pushed her to Kensington Square and then sat on the grass, turned Scheherazade loose and made philosophical remarks while she tired herself out. Finally, she fell asleep, and they made their way home in the fading light of the evening. Outside Waverley House they were approached by two well-turned-out young men with Beatle haircuts and the buttoned-up, collarless jackets made popular by the band. The first of these young men asked my mother, very politely, if she might be the Maharani of B—.

'No,' my mother answered, flattered.

'Oh, but you are, madam,' said the second Beatle,

equally politely. 'For you are heading for Waverley House and that is the Maharaja's place of residence.'

'No, no,' my mother said, still blushing with pleasure. 'We are a different Indian family.'

'Quite so,' the first Beatle nodded understandingly, and then, to my mother's great surprise, placed a finger alongside his nose, and winked. 'Incognito, eh. Mum's the word.'

'Now excuse us,' my mother said, losing patience. 'We are not the ladies you seek.'

The second Beatle tapped a foot lightly against a wheel of the push-chair. 'Your husband seeks ladies, madam, were you aware of that fact? Yes, he does. Most assiduously, may I add.'

'Too assiduously,' said the first Beatle, his face darkening.

'I tell you I am not the Maharani Begum,' my mother said, growing suddenly alarmed. 'Her business is not my business. Kindly let me pass.'

The second Beatle stepped closer to her. She could feel his breath, which was minty. 'One of the ladies he sought out was our ward, as you might say,' he explained. 'That would be the term. Under our protection, you follow. Us, therefore, being responsible for her welfare.'

'Your husband', said the first Beatle, showing his teeth in a frightening way, and raising his voice one notch, 'damaged the goods. Do you hear me, Queenie? He damaged the fucking goods.'

'Mistaken identity, fleas,' said Certainly-Mary. 'Many Indian residents in Waverley House. We are decent ladies; *fleas.*'

The second Beatle had taken out something from an inside pocket. A blade caught the light. 'Fucking wogs,' he said. 'You fucking come over here, you don't fucking know how to fucking behave. Why don't you fucking fuck off to fucking Wogistan? Fuck your fucking wog arses. Now then,' he added in a quiet voice, holding up the knife, 'unbutton your blouses.'

JUST THEN A loud noise emanated from the doorway of Waverley House. The two women and the two men turned to look, and out came Mixed-Up, yelling at the top of his voice and windmilling his arms like a mad old loon.

'Hullo,' said the Beatle with the knife, looking amused. 'Who's this, then? Oh oh fucking seven?'

Mixed-Up was trying to speak, he was in a mighty agony of effort, but all that was coming out of his mouth was raw, unshaped noise. Scheherazade woke up and joined in. The two Beatles looked displeased. But then something happened inside old Mixed-Up; something popped, and in a great rush he gabbled, 'Sirs sirs no sirs these not B— women sirs B— women upstairs on floor three sirs Maharaja of B— also sirs God's truth mother's grave swear.'

It was the longest sentence he had spoken since the stroke that had broken his tongue long ago.

And what with his torrent and Scheherazade's squalls there were suddenly heads poking out from doorways, attention was being paid, and the two Beatles nodded gravely. 'Honest mistake,' the first of them said apologetically to my mother, and actually bowed from the waist. 'Could happen to anyone,' the knife-man added, ruefully. They turned and began to walk quickly away. As they passed Mecir, however, they paused. 'I know you, though,' said the knife-man. '"*Jet plane. Gone.*"' He made a short movement of the arm, and then Mixed-Up the courter was lying on the pavement with blood leaking from a wound in his stomach. 'All okay now,' he gasped, and passed out.

II

HE WAS ON the road to recovery by Christmas; my mother's letter to the landlords, in which she called him a 'knight in shining armour', ensured that he was well looked after, and his job was kept open for him. He continued to live in his little ground-floor cubby-hole, while the hall porter's duties were carried out by shift-duty staff. 'Nothing but the best for our very own hero,' the landlords assured my mother in their reply.

The two Maharajas and their retinues had moved out before I came home for the Christmas holidays, so we had no further visits from the Beatles or the Rolling Stones. Certainly-Mary spent as much time as she could with Mecir; but it was the look of my old Aya that worried me more than poor Mixed-Up. She looked older, and powdery, as if she might crumble away at any moment into dust.

'We didn't want to worry you at school,' my mother said. 'She has been having heart trouble. Palpitations. Not all the time, but.'

Mary's health problems had sobered up the whole family. Muneeza's tantrums had stopped, and even my father was making an effort. They had put up a Christmas tree in the sitting-room and decorated it with all sorts of baubles. It was so odd to see a Christmas tree at our place that I realised things must be fairly serious.

On Christmas Eve my mother suggested that Mary might like it if we all sang some carols. Amma had made song-sheets, six copies, by hand. When we did O *come, all ye faithful* I showed off by singing from memory in Latin. Everybody behaved perfectly. When Muneeza suggested that we should try *Swinging on a Star* or *I Wanna Hold Your Hand* instead of this boring stuff, she wasn't really being serious. So this is family life, I thought. This is it.

But we were only play-acting.

A FEW WEEKS earlier, at school, I'd come across an American boy, the star of the school's Rugby football team, crying in the Chapel cloisters. I asked him what the matter was and he told me that President Kennedy had been assassinated. 'I don't believe you,' I said, but I could see that it was true. The football star sobbed and sobbed. I took his hand.

'When the President dies, the nation is orphaned,' he eventually said, broken-heartedly parroting a piece of cracker-barrel wisdom he'd probably heard on Voice of America.

'I know how you feel,' I lied. 'My father just died, too.'

MARY'S HEART TROUBLE turned out to be a mystery; unpredictably, it came and went. She was subjected to all sorts of tests during the next six months, but each time the doctors ended up by shaking their heads: they couldn't find anything wrong with her. Physically, she was right as rain; except that there were these periods when her heart kicked and bucked in her chest like the wild horses in *The Misfits*, the ones whose roping and tying made Marilyn Monroe so mad.

Mecir went back to work in the spring, but his experience had knocked the stuffing out of him. He was slower to smile, duller of eye, more inward. Mary, too, had turned in upon herself. They still met for tea, crumpets and *The Flintstones*, but something was no longer quite right.

At the beginning of the summer Mary made an announcement.

'I know what is wrong with me,' she told my parents, out of the blue, 'I need to go home.'

'But, Aya,' my mother argued, 'homesickness is not a real disease.'

'God knows for what-all we came over to this country,' Mary said. 'But I can no longer stay. No. Certainly not.' Her determination was absolute.

So it was England that was breaking her heart, breaking it by not being India. London was killing her, by not being Bombay. And Mixed-Up? I wondered. Was the courter killing her, too, because he was no longer himself? Or was it that her heart, roped by two different loves, was being pulled both East and West, whinnying and rearing, like those movie horses being yanked this way by Clark Gable and that way by Montgomery Clift, and she knew that to live she would have to choose?

'I must go,' said Certainly-Mary. 'Yes, certainly. *Bas*. Enough.'

THAT SUMMER, THE summer of '64, I turned seventeen. Chandni went back to India. Durré's Polish friend Rozalia informed me over a sandwich in Oxford Street that she was getting engaged to a 'real man', so I could forget about seeing her again, because this Zbigniew was the jealous type. Roy Orbison sang *It's Over* in my ears as I walked away to the Tube, but the truth was that nothing had really begun.

Certainly-Mary left us in mid-July. My father bought her a one-way ticket to Bombay, and that last morning was heavy with the pain of ending. When we took her bags down to the car, Mecir the hall porter was nowhere to be seen. Mary did not knock on the door of his lounge, but walked straight out through the freshly polished oak-panelled lobby, whose mirrors and brasses were sparkling brightly; she climbed into the back seat of our Ford Zodiac and sat there stiffly with her carry-on grip on her lap,

So it was England that was breaking her heart, breaking it by not being India

staring straight ahead. I had known and loved her all my life. *Never mind your damned courter*, I wanted to shout at her, *what about me?*

AS IT HAPPENED, she was right about the homesickness. After her return to Bombay, she never had a day's heart trouble again; and, as the letter from her niece Stella confirmed, at ninety-one she was still going strong.

Soon after she left, my father told us he had decided to 'shift location' to Pakistan. As usual, there were no discussions, no explanations, just the simple fiat. He gave up the lease on the flat in Waverley House at the end of the summer holidays, and they all went off to Karachi, while I went back to school.

I became a British citizen that year. I was one of the lucky ones, I guess, because in spite of that chess game I had the Dodo on my side. And the passport did, in many ways, set me free. It allowed me to come and go, to make choices that were not the ones my father would have wished. But I, too, have ropes around my neck, I have them to this day, pulling me this way and that, East and West, the nooses tightening, commanding, *choose, choose.*

I buck, I snort, I whinny, I rear, I kick. Ropes, I do not choose between you. Lassoes, lariats, I choose neither of you, and both. Do you hear? I refuse to choose.

A YEAR OR SO after we moved out I was in the area and dropped in at Waverley House to see how the old courter was doing. Maybe, I thought, we could have a game of chess, and he could beat me to a pulp. The lobby was empty, so I knocked on the door of his little lounge. A stranger answered.

'Where's Mixed-Up?' I cried, taken by surprise. I apologised at once, embarrassed. 'Mr Mecir, I meant, the porter.'

'I'm the porter, sir,' the man said. 'I don't know anything about any mix-up.'

Acknowledgments

In 'THE COURTER', the author wishes to thank the following sources for permission to quote material: Buddy Kaye, Ethel Lee and David Hill for lyrics from 'Speedy Gonzales' copyright © 1962, copyright renewed 1990. International copyright secured. All rights reserved. Also © David Hess Music Co. (⅓rd). By permission of Memory Lane Music Ltd. Lyric reproduction of 'Speedy Gonzales' by kind permission of Carlin Music Corp., UK administrator.

'Jambalaya (On the Bayou)', words and music by Hank Williams © copyright 1951 renewed 1980 Acuff-Rose Music Incorporated, USA. Acuff-Rose Opryland Music Limited, London W1. Reproduced by permission of Music Sales Ltd. All rights reserved. International copyright secured.

'Big Girls Don't Cry' (words and music by Bob Crewe and Bob Gaudio) and 'Sherry' (words and music by Bob Gaudio) © 1962, Claridge Music Inc., USA. Reproduced by permission of Ardmore & Beechwood Ltd, London WC2H 0EA.

The passage quoted on pages 66–7 is in fact an account of a game between S. Reshevsky and M. Najdorf, played in 1957 and described in *The Most Instructive Games of Chess Ever Played*, by Irving Chernev (Faber and Faber, 1966).

© Beowulf Sheehan 2015

SIR SALMAN RUSHDIE was born in Mumbai, on the eve of India's Independence, and was educated in England. After graduating from Cambridge University he worked as an advertising copywriter in London before becoming a full-time author.

He is the author of twelve novels, four works of non-fiction and one book of stories. He is the recipient of many prizes and honours including the 'Booker of Bookers' for *Midnight's Children* – the best novel to have won the Booker Prize.

He is a Fellow of the Royal Society of Literature and Commandeur de l'Ordre des Arts et des Lettres. In 2007 he received a knighthood in the Queen's Birthday Honours. He lives primarily in New York.

RECOMMENDED BOOKS BY SALMAN RUSHDIE:

Shame
Imaginary Homelands
East, West

What do we mean by Home?

Love
JEANETTE WINTERSON

VINTAGE MINIS

Liberty
VIRGINIA WOOLF

VINTAGE MINIS

Race
TONI MORRISON

VINTAGE MINIS

Sisters
LOUISA MAY ALCOTT

VINTAGE MINIS

VINTAGE MINIS

The Vintage Minis bring you the world's greatest writers on the
experiences that make us human. These stylish, entertaining little
books explore the whole spectrum of life – from birth to death,
and everything in between. Which means there's something
here for everyone, whatever your story.

Desire	Haruki Murakami
Love	Jeanette Winterson
Babies	Anne Enright
Language	Xiaolu Guo
Motherhood	Helen Simpson
Fatherhood	Karl Ove Knausgaard
Summer	Laurie Lee
Jealousy	Marcel Proust
Sisters	Louisa May Alcott
Home	Salman Rushdie
Race	Toni Morrison
Liberty	Virginia Woolf
Swimming	Roger Deakin
Work	Joseph Heller
Depression	William Styron
Drinking	John Cheever
Eating	Nigella Lawson
Psychedelics	Aldous Huxley
Calm	Tim Parks
Death	Julian Barnes

vintageminis.co.uk

1 3 5 7 9 10 8 6 4 2

Vintage
20 Vauxhall Bridge Road,
London SW1V 2SA

Vintage Classics is part of the Penguin Random House
group of companies whose addresses can be found at
global.penguinrandomhouse.com.

 Penguin
Random House
UK

First published in Great Britain by The Hogarth Press in 1959
This short edition published by Vintage in 2017

penguin.co.uk/vintage

A CIP catalogue record for this book is available from the British Library

ISBN 9781784872922

Typeset in 9.5/14.5 pt FreightText Pro
by Jouve (UK), Milton Keynes
Printed and bound by Clays Ltd, St Ives plc

Penguin Random House is committed to a sustainable future for
our business, our readers and our planet. This book is made from
Forest Stewardship Council® certified paper.

Summer
LAURIE LEE

VINTAGE MINIS

I was set down from the carrier's cart at the age of three; and there with a sense of bewilderment and terror my life in the village began.

The June grass, amongst which I stood, was taller than I was, and I wept. I had never been so close to grass before. It towered above me and all around me, each blade tattooed with tiger-skins of sunlight. It was knife-edged, dark, and a wicked green, thick as a forest and alive with grasshoppers that chirped and chattered and leapt through the air like monkeys.

I was lost and didn't know where to move. A tropic heat oozed up from the ground, rank with sharp odours of roots and nettles. Snow-clouds of elder-blossom banked in the sky, showering upon me the fumes and flakes of their sweet and giddy suffocation. High overhead ran frenzied larks, screaming, as though the sky were tearing apart.

For the first time in my life I was out of the sight of humans. For the first time in my life I was alone in a world whose behaviour I could neither predict nor fathom: a world of birds that squealed, of plants that stank, of insects that sprang about without warning. I was lost and I did not expect to be found again. I put back my head and howled, and the sun hit me smartly on the face, like a bully.

From this daylight nightmare I was awakened, as from many another, by the appearance of my sisters. They came scrambling and calling up the steep rough bank, and parting the long grass found me. Faces of rose, familiar, living; huge shining faces hung up like shields between me and the sky; faces with grins and white teeth (some broken) to be conjured up like genii with a howl, brushing off terror with their broad scoldings and affection. They leaned over me – one, two, three – their mouths smeared with red currants and their hands dripping with juice.

'There, there, it's all right, don't you wail any more. Come down 'ome and we'll stuff you with currants.'

And Marjorie, the eldest, lifted me into her long brown hair, and ran me jogging down the path and through the steep rose-filled garden, and set me down on the cottage doorstep, which was our home, though I couldn't believe it.

That was the day we came to the village, in the summer of the last year of the First World War. To a cottage that stood in a half-acre of garden on a steep bank above a lake; a cottage with three floors and a cellar and a treasure in the walls, with a pump and apple trees, syringa and strawberries, rooks in the chimneys, frogs in the cellar, mushrooms on the ceiling, and all for three and sixpence a week.

I don't know where I lived before then. My life began on the carrier's cart which brought me up the long slow hills to the village, and dumped me in the high grass, and lost me. I had ridden wrapped up in a Union Jack to protect me from the sun, and when I rolled out of it, and stood piping loud among the buzzing jungle of that summer bank, then, I feel, was I born. And to all the rest of us, the whole family of eight, it was the beginning of a life.

But on that first day we were all lost. Chaos was come in cartloads of furniture, and I crawled the kitchen floor through forests of upturned chair-legs and crystal fields of glass. We were washed up in a new land, and began to spread out searching its springs and treasures. The sisters spent the light of that first day stripping the fruit bushes in the garden. The currants were at their prime, clusters of red, black, and yellow berries all tangled up with wild roses. Here was bounty the girls had never known before, and they darted squawking from bush to bush, clawing the fruit like sparrows.

Our Mother too was distracted from duty, seduced by the rich wilderness of the garden so long abandoned. All day she trotted to and fro, flushed and garrulous, pouring flowers into every pot and jug she could find on the kitchen floor. Flowers from the garden, daisies from the bank, cow-parsley, grasses, ferns, and leaves – they flowed in armfuls through the cottage door until its dim interior seemed entirely possessed by the world outside – a still green pool flooding with honeyed tides of summer.

I sat on the floor on a raft of muddles and gazed through

the green window which was full of the rising garden. I saw the long black stockings of the girls, gaping with white flesh, kicking among the currant bushes. Every so often one of them would dart into the kitchen, cram my great mouth with handfuls of squashed berries, and run out again. And the more I got, the more I called for more. It was like feeding a fat young cuckoo.

The long day crowed and chirped and rang. Nobody did any work, and there was nothing to eat save berries and bread. I crawled about among the ornaments on the unfamiliar floor – the glass fishes, china dogs, shepherds and shepherdesses, bronze horsemen, stopped clocks, barometers, and photographs of bearded men. I called on them each in turn, for they were the shrines and faces of a half-remembered landscape. But as I watched the sun move around the walls, drawing rainbows from the cut-glass jars in the corner, I longed for a return of order.

Then, suddenly, the day was at an end, and the house was furnished. Each stick and cup and picture was nailed immovably in place; the beds were sheeted, the windows curtained, the straw mats laid, and the house was home. I don't remember seeing it happen, but suddenly the inexorable tradition of the house, with its smell, chaos, and complete logic, occurred as though it had never been otherwise. The furnishing and founding of the house came like the nightfall of that first day. From that uneasy loneliness of objects strewn on the kitchen floor, everything flew to its place and was never again questioned.

And from that day we grew up. The domestic arrangement of the house was shaken many times, like a snow-storm toy, so that beds and chairs and ornaments swirled from room to room, pursued by the gusty energies of Mother and the girls. But always these things resettled within the pattern of the walls, nothing escaped or changed, and so it remained for twenty years.

Now I MEASURED that first growing year by the widening fields that became visible to me, the new tricks of dressing and getting about with which I became gradually endowed. I could open the kitchen door by screwing myself into a ball and leaping and banging the latch with my fist. I could climb into the high bed by using the ironwork as a ladder. I could whistle, but I couldn't lace my shoes. Life became a series of experiments which brought grief or the rewards of accomplishment: a pondering of patterns and mysteries in the house, while time hung golden and suspended, and one's body, from leaping and climbing, took on the rigid insanity of an insect, petrified as it were for hours together, breathing and watching. Watching the grains of dust fall in the sunny room, following an ant from its cradle to the grave, going over the knots in the bedroom ceiling – knots that ran like Negroes in the dusk of dawn, or moved stealthily from board to board, but which settled again in the wax light of day no more monstrous than fossils in coal.

These knots on the bedroom ceiling were the whole range of a world, and over them my eyes went endlessly voyaging in that long primeval light of waking to which a child is condemned. They were archipelagos in a sea of blood-coloured varnish, they were armies grouped and united against me, they were the alphabet of a macabre tongue, the first book I ever learned to read.

Radiating from that house, with its crumbling walls, its thumps and shadows, its fancied foxes under the floor, I moved along paths that lengthened inch by inch with my mounting strength of days. From stone to stone in the trackless yard I sent forth my acorn shell of senses, moving through unfathomable oceans like a South Sea savage island-hopping across the Pacific. Antennae of eyes and nose and grubbing fingers captured a new tuft of grass, a fern, a slug, the skull of a bird, a grotto of bright snails. Through the long summer ages of those first few days I enlarged my world and mapped it in my mind, its secure havens, its dust-deserts and puddles, its peaks of dirt and flag-flying bushes. Returning too, dry-throated, over and over again, to its several well-prodded horrors: the bird's gaping bones in its cage of old sticks; the black flies in the corner, slimy dead; dry rags of snakes; and the crowded, rotting, silent-roaring city of a cat's grub-captured carcass.

Once seen, these relics passed within the frontiers of the known lands, to be remembered with a buzzing in the ears, to be revisited when the stomach was strong. They were the first tangible victims of that destroying force whose job I knew went on both night and day, though I could never catch him at it. Nevertheless I was grateful for them. Though they haunted my eyes and stuck in my dreams, they reduced for me the first infinite possibilities of horror. They chastened the imagination with the proof of a limited frightfulness.

From the harbour mouth of the scullery door I learned the rocks and reefs and the channels where safety lay. I discovered the physical pyramid of the cottage, its stores and labyrinths, its centres of magic, and of the green, spouting island-garden upon which it stood. My Mother and sisters sailed past me like galleons in their busy dresses, and I learned the smells and sounds which followed in their wakes, the surge of breath, air of carbolic, song and grumble, and smashing of crockery.

How magnificent they appeared, full-rigged, those towering girls, with their flying hair and billowing blouses, their white-mast arms stripped for work or washing. At any moment one was boarded by them, bussed and buttoned, or swung up high like a wriggling fish to be hooked and held in their lacy linen.

The scullery was a mine of all the minerals of living. Here I discovered water – a very different element from the green crawling scum that stank in the garden tub. You could pump it in pure blue gulps out of the ground, you could swing on the pump handle and it came out sparkling like liquid sky. And it broke and ran and shone on the tiled floor, or quivered in a jug, or weighted your clothes with cold. You could drink it, draw with it, froth it with soap, swim beetles across it, or fly it in bubbles in the air. You

could put your head in it, and open your eyes, and see the
sides of the bucket buckle, and hear your caught breath
roar, and work your mouth like a fish, and smell the lime
from the ground. Substance of magic – which you could
tear or wear, confine or scatter, or send down holes, but
never burn or break or destroy.

The scullery was water, where the old pump stood. And
it had everything else that was related to water: thick
steam of Mondays edgy with starch; soapsuds boiling,
bellying and popping, creaking and whispering, rainbowed
with light and winking with a million windows. Bubble
bubble, toil and grumble, rinsing and slapping of sheets
and shirts, and panting Mother rowing her red arms like
oars in the steaming waves. Then the linen came up on a
stick out of the pot, like pastry, or woven suds, or sheets of
moulded snow.

Here, too, was the scrubbing of floors and boots, of
arms and necks, of red and white vegetables. Walk in to the
morning disorder of this room and all the garden was laid
out dripping on the table. Chopped carrots like copper
pennies, radishes and chives, potatoes dipped and stripped
clean from their coats of mud, the snapping of tight
pea-pods, long shells of green pearls, and the tearing of
glutinous beans from their nests of wool.

Grown stealthy, marauding among these preparations,
one nibbled one's way like a rat through roots and leaves.
Peas rolled under the tongue, fresh cold, like solid water;
teeth chewed green peel of apples, acid sharp, and the sweet

white starch of swedes. Beaten away by wet hands gloved with flour, one returned in a morose and speechless lust. Slivers of raw pastry, moulded, warm, went down in the shapes of men and women – heads and arms of unsalted flesh seasoned with nothing but a dream of cannibalism.

Large meals were prepared in this room, cauldrons of stew for the insatiate hunger of eight. Stews of all that grew on these rich banks, flavoured with sage, coloured with Oxo, and laced with a few bones of lamb. There was, it is true, little meat at those times; sometimes a pound of bare ribs for boiling, or an occasional rabbit dumped at the door by a neighbour. But there was green food of great weight in season, and lentils and bread for ballast. Eight to ten loaves came to the house every day, and they never grew dry. We tore them to pieces with their crusts still warm, and their monotony was brightened by the objects we found in them – string, nails, paper, and once a mouse; for those were days of happy-go-lucky baking. The lentils were cooked in a great pot which also heated the water for the Saturday-night baths. Our small wood-fire could heat sufficient water to fill one bath only, and this we shared in turn. Being the youngest but one, my water was always the dirtiest but one, and the implications of this privilege remain with me to this day.

WAKING ONE MORNING in the white-washed bedroom, I opened my eyes and found them blind. Though I stretched them and stared where the room should be, nothing was visible but a glare of gold, flat on my throbbing eyelids. I groped for my body and found it there. I heard the singing of birds. Yet there was nothing at all to be seen of the world save this quivering yellow light. Was I dead, I wondered? Was I in heaven? Whatever it was I hated it. I had wakened too soon from a dream of crocodiles and I was not ready for this further outrage. Then I heard the girls' steps on the stairs.

'Our Marge!' I shouted, 'I can't see nothing!' And I began to give out my howl.

A slap of bare feet slithered across the floor, and I heard sister Marjorie's giggle.

'Just look at him,' she said. 'Pop and fetch a flannel, Doth –'is eyes've got stuck down again.'

The cold edge of the flannel passed over my face showered me with water, and I was back in the world. Bed and beams, and the sun-square window, and the girls bending over me grinning.

''Oo did it?' I yelled.

'Nobody, silly. Your eyes got bunged up, that's all.'

The sweet glue of sleep; it had happened before, but somehow I always forgot. So I threatened the girls I'd bung theirs up too: I was awake, I could see, I was happy. I lay looking out of the small green window. The world outside was crimson and on fire. I had never seen it looking like that before.

'Doth?' I said, 'what's happening to them trees?'

Dorothy was dressing. She leaned out of the window,

slow and sleepy, and the light came through her nightdress like sand through a sieve.

'Nothing's happening,' she said.

'Yes it is then,' I said. 'They're falling to bits.'

Dorothy scratched her dark head, yawning wide, and white feathers floated out of her hair.

'It's only the leaves droppin'. We're in autumn now. The leaves always drop in autumn.'

Autumn? In autumn. Was that where we were? Where the leaves always dropped and there was always this smell. I imagined it continuing, with no change, for ever, these wet flames of woods burning on and on like the bush of Moses, as natural a part of this new found land as the eternal snows of the poles. Why had we come to such a place?

IN THE LONG hot summer of 1921 a serious drought hit the country. Springs dried up, the wells filled with frogs, and the usually sweet water from our scullery pump turned brown and tasted of nails. Although this drought was a relief to my family, it was a scourge to the rest of the village. For weeks the sky hung hot and blue, trees shrivelled, crops burned in the fields, and the old folk said the sun had slipped in its course and that we should all of us very soon die. There were prayers for rain; but my family didn't go, because it was rain we feared most of all.

As the drought continued, prayer was abandoned and more devilish steps adopted. Finally soldiers with rifles marched to the tops of the hills and began shooting at passing clouds. When I heard their dry volleys, breaking like sticks in the stillness, I knew our long armistice was over. And sure enough – whether from prayers or the shooting, or by a simple return of nature – the drought broke soon after and it began to rain as it had never rained before.

I remember waking in the night to the screams of our Mother, and to rousing alarms of a howling darkness and the storm-battered trees outside. Terror, the old terror, had come again, and as always in the middle of the night.

'Get up!' cried Mother. 'It's coming in! Get up or we'll all be drowned!'

I heard her banging about and beating the walls in accents of final doom. When Mother gave her alarms one didn't lie back and think, one didn't use reason at all; one just erected one's hair and leapt out of bed and scrambled downstairs with the others.

Our predicament was such that we lived at nature's mercy; for the cottage, stuck on its steep bank, stood directly in the path of the floods. All the spouts of the heavens seemed to lead to our door, and there was only one small drain to swallow them. When this drain blocked up, as it did in an instant, the floods poured into our kitchen – and as there was no back door to let them out again I felt it natural at the time we should drown.

'Hell in Heaven!' wailed Mother. 'Damn it and cuss! Jesus have mercy on us!'

We grizzled and darted about for brooms, then ran out to tackle the storm. We found the drain blocked already and the yard full of water. The noise of the rain drowned our cries and whimpers, and there was nothing to do but sweep.

What panic those middle-night rousings were, those trumpet-calls murdering sleep; with darkness, whirlwind, and invisible rain, trees roaring, clouds bursting, thunder crashing, lightning crackling, floods rising, and our Mother demented. The girls in their nightdresses held spitting candles while we boys swept away at the drain. Hot rods of rain struck straight through our shirts; we shivered with panic and cold.

'More brooms!' shouted Mother, jumping up and down. 'Run, someone, in the name of goodness! Sweep harder, boys! Sweet saints above, it's up to the doorstep already!'

The flood-water gurgled and moved thickly around us, breeding fat yellow bubbles like scum, skipping and frothing where the bullet rain hit it, and inching slowly towards the door. The drain was now hidden beneath the water and we swept at it for our lives, the wet candles hissed and went out one by one, Mother lit torches of newspapers, while we fought knee-deep in cries and thunder, splashing about, wet-through, half-weeping, overwhelmed by gigantic fears.

Sometimes, in fact, the water did get in; two or three inches of it. It slid down the steps like a thick cream custard and spread all over the floor. When that happened, Mother's lamentations reached elegiac proportions, and all the world was subpoenaed to witness. Dramatic apostrophes rang through the night; the Gods were arraigned, the Saints called to order, and the Fates severely ticked off.

There would be a horrible mess in the kitchen next morning, mud and slime all over the matting, followed by the long depressed drudgery of scraping it up and carrying it away in buckets. Mother, on her knees, would wring her hands and roll her eyes about.

'I can't *think* what I've done to be so troubled and tried. And just when I got the house straight. Neither saints nor angels would keep their patience if they had such things to put up with ... My poor, poor children, my precious darlings – you could die in this filthy hole. No one would care – not a bell-essed soul. Look out with that damn-and-cuss bucket!' ...

Apart from the noise and the tears and the dirt, these inundations were really not much. But I can't pretend they didn't scare me stiff. The thought that the flood-waters should actually break into our house seemed to me something worse than a fire. At the mid-hour of night, when the storms really blew, I used to lie aghast in my bed, hearing the rain claw the window and the wind slap the walls, and imagining the family, the house, and all the furniture, being sucked down the eternal drain.

It was not till much later that I reasoned things out: that our position on the hillside made it unlikely we should drown, that Mother's frenzies and scares belonged to something else altogether, and that it was possible after all to sleep through rain in peace. Even so, to this day, when the skies suddenly darken, and a storm builds up in the west, and I smell rain on the wind and hear the first growl of thunder, I grow uneasy, and start looking for brooms.

WAKING UP IN the morning I saw squirrels in the yew trees nibbling at the moist red berries. Between the trees and the window hung a cloud of gold air composed of floating seeds and spiders. Farmers called to their cows on the other side of the valley and moorhens piped from the ponds. Brother Jack, as always, was the first to move, while I pulled on my boots in bed. We both stood at last on the bare-wood floor, scratching and saying our prayers. Too stiff and manly to say them out loud, we stood back to back and muttered them, and if an audible plea should slip out by chance, one just burst into song to cover it.

Singing and whistling were useful face-savers, especially when confounded by argument. We used the trick readily, one might say monotonously, and this morning it was Jack who began it.

'What's the name of the king, then?' he said, groping for his trousers.

'Albert.'

'No, it's not. It's George.'

'That's what I said you, didn't I? George.'

'No you never. You don't know. You're feeble.'

'Not so feeble as you be, any road.'

'You're balmy. You got brains of a bed-bug.'

'Da-da-di-da-da.'

'I said you're brainless. You can't even count.'

'Turrelee-turrelee . . . Didn't hear you.'

'Yes you did then, blockhead. Fat and lazy. Big faa—'

'Dum-di-dah! . . . Can't hear . . . Hey nonnie! . . .'

Well, that was all right; honours even, as usual. We broke the sleep from our eyes and dressed quickly.

Walking downstairs there was a smell of floorboards, of rags, sour lemons, old spices. The smoky kitchen was in its morning muddle, from which breakfast would presently emerge. Mother stirred the porridge in a soot-black pot. Tony was carving bread with a ruler, the girls in their mackintoshes were laying the table, and the cats were eating the butter. I cleaned some boots and pumped up some fresh water; Jack went for a jug of skimmed milk.

'I'm all behind,' Mother said to the fire. 'This wretched coal's all slack.'

She snatched up an oil-can and threw it all on the fire. A belch of flame roared up the chimney. Mother gave a loud scream, as she always did, and went on stirring the porridge.

'If I had a proper stove,' she said. 'It's a trial getting you off each day.'

I sprinkled some sugar on a slice of bread and bolted it down while I could. How different again looked the kitchen this morning, swirling with smoke and sunlight. Some cut-glass vases threw jagged rainbows across the piano's field of dust, while Father in his pince-nez up on the wall looked down like a scandalized god.

At last the porridge was dabbed on our plates from a thick and steaming spoon. I covered the smoky lumps with treacle and began to eat from the sides to the middle. The girls round the table chewed moonishly, wrapped in their morning stupor. Still sick with sleep, their mouths moved slow, hung slack while their spoon came up; then they paused for a moment, spoon to lip, collected their wits, and ate. Their vacant eyes stared straight before them, glazed at the sight of the day. Pink and glowing from their dreamy beds, from who knows what arms of heroes, they seemed like mute spirits hauled back to the earth after paradise feasts of love.

'Golly!' cried Doth. 'Have you seen the time?'

They began to jump to their feet.

'Goodness, it's late.'

'I got to be off.'

'Me too.'

'Lord, where's my things?'

'Well, ta-ta Ma; ta boys – be good.'

'Anything you want up from the Stores . . . ?'

They hitched up their stockings, patted their hats, and went running up the bank. This was the hour when walkers and bicyclists flowed down the long hills to Stroud, when the hooters called through the morning dews and factories puffed out their plumes. From each crooked corner of Stroud's five valleys girls were running to shops and looms, with sleep in their eyes, and eggy cheeks, and in their ears night voices fading. Marjorie was off to her Milliners' Store, Phyllis to her Boots-and-Shoes, Dorothy to her job as junior clerk in a decayed cloth-mill by a stream. As for Harold, he'd started work already, his day began at six, when he'd leave the house with an angry shout for the lathe-work he really loved.

But what should we boys do, now they had all gone? If it was school-time, we pushed off next. If not, we dodged up the bank to play, ran snail races along the walls, or dug in the garden and found potatoes and cooked them in tins on the rubbish heap. We were always hungry, always calling for food, always seeking it in cupboards and hedges. But holiday mornings were a time of risk, there might be housework or errands to do. Mother would be ironing, or tidying-up, or reading books on the floor. So if we hung around the yard we kept our ears cocked; if she caught us, the game was up.

'Ah, there you are, son. I'm needing some salt. Pop to Vick's for a lump, there's a dear.'

Or: 'See if Granny Trill's got a screw of tea – only ask her nicely, mind.'

Or: 'Run up to Miss Turk and try to borrow half-crown; I didn't know I'd got so low.'

'Ask our Jack, our Mother! I borrowed the bacon. It's blummin'-well his turn now.'

But Jack had slid off like an eel through the grass, making his sly get-away as usual. He was jumpy, shifty, and quick-off-the-mark, an electric flex of nerves, skinny compared with the rest of us, or what farmers might call a 'poor doer'. If they had, in fact, they would have been quite wrong, for Jack did himself very well. He had developed a mealtime strategy which ensured that he ate for two. Speed and guile were the keys to his success, and we hungry ones called him The Slider.

Jack ate against time, that was really his secret; and in our house you had to do it. Imagine us all sitting down to dinner; eight round a pot of stew. It was lentil-stew usually, a heavy brown mash made apparently of plastic studs. Though it smelt of hot stables, we were used to it, and it was filling enough – could you get it. But the size of our family out-stripped the size of the pot, so there was never quite enough to go round.

When it came to serving, Mother had no method, not even the law of chance – a dab on each plate in any old order and then every man for himself. No grace, no warning, no starting-gun; but the first to finish what he'd had on his plate could claim what was left in the pot. Mother's swooping spoon was breathlessly watched – let the lentils fall where they may. But starving Jack had worked it all out, he followed the spoon with his plate. Absentmindedly Mother would give him first dollop, and very often a second, and as soon as he got it he swallowed it whole, not using his teeth at all. 'More please, I've finished' – the bare plate proved it, so he got the pot-scrapings too. Many the race I've lost to him thus, being just that second slower. But it left me marked with an ugly scar, a twisted, food-crazed nature, so that still I am calling for whole rice puddings and big pots of stew in the night.

THE DAY WAS over and we had used it, running errands or prowling the fields. When evening came we returned to the kitchen, back to its smoky comfort, in from the rapidly cooling air to its wrappings of warmth and cooking. We boys came first, scuffling down the bank, singly, like homing crows. Long tongues of shadows licked the curves of the fields and the trees turned plump and still. I had been off to Painswick to pay the rates, running fast through the long wet grass, and now I was back, panting hard, the job finished, with hay seeds stuck to my legs. A plate of blue smoke hung above our chimney, flat in the motionless air, and every stone in the path as I ran down home shook my bones with arriving joy.

We chopped wood for the night and carried it in; dry beech sticks as brittle as candy. The baker came down with a basket of bread slung carelessly over his shoulder. Eight quartern loaves, cottage-size, black-crusted, were handed in at the door. A few crisp flakes of pungent crust still clung to his empty basket, so we scooped them up on our spit-wet fingers and laid them upon our tongues. The twilight gathered, the baker shouted goodnight, and whistled his way up the bank. Up in the road his black horse waited, the cart lamps smoking red.

Indoors, our Mother was cooking pancakes, her face aglow from the fire. There was a smell of sharp lemon and salty batter, and a burning hiss of oil. The kitchen was dark and convulsive with shadows, no lights had yet been lit. Flames leapt, subsided, corners woke and died, fires burned in a thousand brasses.

'Poke around for the matches, dear boy,' said Mother. 'Damn me if I know where they got to.'

We lit the candles and set them about, each in its proper order: two on the mantelpiece, one on the piano, and one on a plate in the window. Each candle suspended a ball of light, a luminous fragile glow, which swelled and contracted to the spluttering wick or leaned to the moving air. Their flames pushed weakly against the red of the fire, too tenuous to make much headway, revealing our faces more by casts of darkness than by any clear light they threw.

Next we filled and lit the tall iron lamp and placed it on the table. When the wick had warmed and was drawing properly, we turned it up full strength. The flame in the funnel then sprang alive and rose like a pointed flower, began to sing and shudder and grow more radiant, throwing pools of light on the ceiling. Even so, the kitchen remained mostly in shadow, its walls a voluptuous gloom.

The time had come for my violin practice. I began twanging the strings with relish. Mother was still frying and rolling up pancakes; my brothers lowered their heads and sighed. I propped my music on the mantelpiece and sliced through a Russian Dance while sweet smells of resin mixed with lemon and fat as the dust flew in clouds from my bow. Now and then I got a note just right, and then Mother would throw me a glance. A glance of piercing, anxious encouragement as she side-stepped my swinging arm. Plump in her slippers, one hand to her cheek, her pan beating time in the other, her hair falling down about her ears, mouth working to help out the tune – old and tired though she was, her eyes were a girl's, and it was for looks such as these that I played.

'Splendid!' she cried. 'Top-hole! Clap-clap! Now give us another, me lad.'

So I slashed away at 'William Tell', and when I did that, plates jumped; and Mother skipped gaily around the hearthrug, and even Tony rocked a bit in his chair.

Meanwhile Jack had cleared some boots from the table, and started his inscrutable homework. Tony, in his corner, began to talk to the cat and play with some fragments of cloth. So with the curtains drawn close and the pancakes coming, we settled down to the evening. When the kettle boiled and the toast was made, we gathered and had our tea. We grabbed and dodged and passed and snatched, and packed our mouths like pelicans.

Mother ate always standing up, tearing crusts off the loaf with her fingers, a hand-to-mouth feeding that expressed her vigilance, like that of a wireless-operator at sea. For most of Mother's attention was fixed on the grate, whose fire must never go out. When it threatened to do so she became seized with hysteria, wailing and wringing her hands, pouring on oil and chopping up chairs in a frenzy to keep it alive. In fact it seldom went out completely, though it was very often ill. But Mother nursed it with skill, banking it up every night and blowing hard on the bars every morning. The state of our fire became as important to us as it must have been to a primitive tribe. When it sulked and sank we were filled with dismay; when it blazed all was well with the world; but if – God save us – it went out altogether, then we were clutched by primeval chills. Then it seemed that the very sun had died, that winter had come for ever, that the wolves of the wilderness were gathering near, and that there was no more hope to look for . . .

But tonight the firelight snapped and crackled, and Mother was in full control. She ruled the range and all its equipment with a tireless, nervous touch. Eating with one hand, she threw on wood with the other, raked the ashes, and heated the oven, put on a kettle, stirred the pot, and spread out some more shirts on the guard. As soon as we boys had finished our tea, we pushed all the crockery aside, piled it up roughly at the far end of the table, and settled down under the lamp. Its light was warm and live around us, a kind of puddle of fire of its own. I set up my book and began to draw. Jack worked at his notes and figures. Tony was playing with some cotton reels, pushing them slowly round the table.

All was silent except Tony's voice, softly muttering his cotton reel story.

'. . . So they come out of this big hole see, and the big chap say Fie and said we'll kill 'em see, and the pirates was waiting up 'ere, and they had this gurt cannon and they went bang fire and the big chap fell down wheeee! and rolled back in the 'ole and I said we got 'em and I run up the 'ill and this boat see was comin' and I jumped on board woosh cruump and I said now I'm captain see and they said fie and I took me 'atchet 'ack 'ack and they all fell plop in the sea wallop and I sailed the boat round 'ere and round 'ere and up 'ere and round 'ere and down 'ere and up 'ere and round 'ere and down 'ere . . .'

OUR HOUSE WAS seventeenth-century Cotswold, and was handsome as they go. It was built of stone, had hand-carved windows, golden surfaces, moss-flaked tiles, and walls so thick they kept a damp chill inside them whatever the season or weather. Its attics and passages were full of walled-up doors which our fingers longed to open – doors that led to certain echoing chambers now sealed off from us for ever. The place had once been a small country manor, and later a public beerhouse; but it had decayed even further by the time we got to it, and was now three poor cottages in one. The house was shaped like a T, and we lived in the down-stroke. The top-stroke – which bore into the side of the bank like a rusty expended shell – was divided separately among two old ladies, one's portion lying above the other's.

Granny Trill and Granny Wallon were rival ancients and lived on each other's nerves, and their perpetual enmity was like mice in the walls and absorbed much of my early days. With their sickle-bent bodies, pale pink eyes, and wild wisps of hedgerow hair, they looked to me the very images of witches and they were also much alike. In all their time as such close neighbours they never exchanged a word. They communicated instead by means of boots and brooms – jumping on floors and knocking on ceilings. They referred to each other as ''Er-Down-Under' and ''Er-Up-Atop, the Varmint'; for each to the other was an airy nothing, a local habitation not fit to be named.

'Er-Down-Under, who lived on our level, was perhaps the smaller of the two, a tiny white shrew who came nibbling through her garden, who clawed squeaking with gossip at our kitchen window, or sat sucking bread in the sun; always mysterious and self-contained and feather-soft in her movements. She had two names, which she changed at will according to the mood of her day. Granny Wallon was her best, and stemmed, we were told, from some distinguished alliance of the past. Behind this crisp and trotting body were certainly rumours of noble blood. But she never spoke of them herself. She was known to have raised a score of children. And she was known to be very poor. She lived on cabbage, bread, and potatoes – but she also made excellent wines.

Granny Wallon's wines were famous in the village, and she spent a large part of her year preparing them. The gathering of the ingredients was the first of the mysteries. At the beginning of April she would go off with her baskets and work round the fields and hedges, and every fine day till the end of summer would find her somewhere out in the valley. One saw her come hobbling home in the evening, bearing her cargoes of crusted flowers, till she had buckets of cowslips, dandelions, elder-blossom crammed into every corner of the house. The elder-flower, drying on her kitchen floor, seemed to cover it with a rancid carpet, a crumbling rime of grey-green blossom fading fast in a dust of summer. Later the tiny grape-cluster of the elderberry itself would be seething in purple vats, with daisies and orchids thrown in to join it, even strands of the dog-rose bush.

What seasons fermented in Granny Wallon's kitchen, what summers were brought to the boil, with limp flower-heads piled around the floor holding fast to their clotted juices – the sharp spiced honey of those cowslips first, then the coppery reeking dandelion, the bitter poppy's whiff of powder, the cat's-breath, death-green elder. Gleanings of days and a dozen pastures, strippings of lanes and hedges – she bore them home to her flag-tiled kitchen, sorted them each from each, built up her fires and loaded her pots, and added her sugar and yeast. The vats boiled daily in suds of sugar, revolving petals in throbbing water, while the air, aromatic, steamy, embalmed, distilled the hot dews and flowery soups and ran the wine down the dripping walls.

And not only flower-heads went into these brews; the old lady used parsnips, too, potatoes, sloes, crab-apples, quinces, in fact anything she could lay her hands on.

What seasons fermented in Granny Wallon's kitchen, what summers were brought to the boil

Granny Wallon made wine as though demented, out of anything at all; and no doubt, if given enough sugar and yeast, could have made a drink out of a box of old matches.

She never hurried or hoarded her wines, but led them gently through their natural stages. After the boiling they were allowed to settle and to work in the cool of the vats. For several months, using pieces of toast, she scooped off their yeasty sediments. Then she bottled and labelled each liquor in turn and put them away for a year.

At last one was ready, then came the day of distribution. A squeak and a rattle would shake our window, and we'd see the old lady, wispily grinning, waving a large white jug in her hand.

'Hey there, missus! Try this'n, then. It's the first of my last year's cowslip.'

Through the kitchen window she'd fill up our cups and watch us, head cocked, while we drank. The wine in the cups was still and golden, transparent as a pale spring morning. It smelt of ripe grass in some far-away field and its taste was as delicate as air. It seemed so innocent, we would swig away happily and even the youngest guzzled it down. Then a curious rocking would seize the head; tides rose from our feet like a fever, the kitchen walls began to shudder and shift, and we all fell in love with each other.

Very soon we'd be wedged, tight-crammed, in the window, waving our cups for more, while our Mother, bright-eyed, would be mumbling gaily:

'Lord bless you, Granny. Fancy cowsnips and parsney. You must give me the receipt, my dear.'

Granny Wallon would empty the jug in our cups, shake out the last drops on the flowers, then trot off tittering down the garden path, leaving us hugging ourselves in the window.

THE SEASONS OF my childhood seemed (of course) so violent, so intense and true to their nature, that they have become for me ever since a reference of perfection whenever such names are mentioned. They possessed us so completely they seemed to change our nationality; and when I look back to the valley it cannot be one place I see, but village-winter or village-summer, both separate. It becomes increasingly easy in urban life to ignore their extreme humours, but in those days winter and summer dominated our every action, broke into our houses, conscripted our thoughts, ruled our games, and ordered our lives.

Winter was no more typical of our valley than summer, it was not even summer's opposite; it was merely that other place. And somehow one never remembered the journey towards it; one arrived, and winter was here. The day came suddenly when all details were different and the village had to be rediscovered. One's nose went dead so that it hurt to breathe, and there were jigsaws of frost on the

Winter and summer dominated our every action, broke into our houses, conscripted our thoughts, ruled our games, and ordered our lives

window. The light filled the house with a green polar glow; while outside – in the invisible world – there was a strange hard silence, or a metallic creaking, a faint throbbing of twigs and wires.

SUMMER, JUNE SUMMER, with the green back on earth and the whole world unlocked and seething – like winter, it came suddenly and one knew it in bed, almost before waking up; with cuckoos and pigeons hollowing the woods since day-light and the chipping of tits in the pear-blossom.

On the bedroom ceiling, seen first through sleep, was a pool of expanding sunlight – the lake's reflection thrown up through the trees by the rapidly climbing sun. Still drowsy, I watched on the ceiling above me its glittering image reversed, saw every motion of its somnambulant waves and projections of the life upon it. Arrows ran across it from time to time, followed by the far call of a moorhen; I saw ripples of light around each root of the bulrushes, every detail of the lake seemed there. Then suddenly the whole picture would break into pieces, would be smashed like a molten mirror and run amok in tiny globules of gold, frantic and shivering; and I would hear the great slapping of wings on water, building up a steady crescendo, while across the ceiling passed the shadows of swans taking off into the heavy morning. I would hear their cries pass over the house and watch the chaos of light above me, till it slowly settled and re-collected its stars and resumed the lake's still image.

Watching swans take off from my bedroom ceiling was a regular summer wakening. So I woke and looked out through the open window to a morning of cows and cockerels. The beech trees framing the lake and valley seemed to call for a Royal Hunt; but they served equally well for climbing into, and even in June you could still eat their leaves, a tight-folded salad of juices.

Outdoors, one scarcely knew what had happened or remembered any other time. There had never been rain, or frost, or cloud; it had always been like this. The heat from the ground climbed up one's legs and smote one under the chin. The garden, dizzy with scent and bees, burned all over with hot white flowers, each one so blinding an incandescence that it hurt the eyes to look at them.

The villagers took summer like a kind of punishment. The women never got used to it. Buckets of water were being sluiced down paths, the dust was being laid with grumbles, blankets and mattresses hung like tongues from the windows, panting dogs crouched under the rain-tubs. A man went by and asked 'Hot enough for 'ee?' and was answered by a worn-out shriek.

In the builder's stable, well out of the sun, we helped to groom Brown's horse. We smelt the burning of his coat, the horn of his hooves, his hot leather harness, and dung. We fed him on bran, dry as a desert wind, till both we and the horse half-choked. Mr Brown and his family were going for a drive, so we wheeled the trap into the road, backed the blinkered horse between the shafts, and buckled his jingling straps. The road lay deserted in its layer of dust and not a thing seemed to move in the valley. Mr Brown and his best-dressed wife and daughter, followed by his bowler-hatted son-in-law, climbed one by one into the high sprung trap and sat there with ritual stiffness.

'Where we goin' then, Father?'

'Up the hill, for some air.'

'Up the hill? He'll drop down dead.'

'Bide quiet,' said Mr Brown, already dripping with sweat, 'Another word, and you'll go back 'ome.'

He jerked the reins and gave a flick of the whip and the horse broke into a saunter. The women clutched their hats at the unexpected movement, and we watched them till they were out of sight.

When they were gone there was nothing else to look at, the village slipped back into silence. The untarred road wound away up the valley, innocent as yet of motor-cars, wound empty away to other villages, which lay empty too, the hot day long, waiting for the sight of a stranger.

We sat by the roadside and scooped the dust with our hands and made little piles in the gutters. Then we slid through the grass and lay on our backs and just stared at the empty sky. There was nothing to do. Nothing moved or happened, nothing happened at all except summer. Small heated winds blew over our faces, dandelion seeds floated by, burnt sap and roast nettles tingled our nostrils together with the dull rust smell of dry ground. The grass was June high and had come up with a rush, a massed entanglement of species, crested with flowers and spears of wild wheat, and coiled with clambering vetches, the whole of it humming with blundering bees and flickering with scarlet butterflies. Chewing grass on our backs, the grass scaffolding the sky, the summer was all we heard; cuckoos crossed distances on chains of cries, flies buzzed and choked in the ears, and the saw-toothed chatter of mowing-machines drifted on waves of air from the fields.

We moved. We went to the shop and bought sherbet and sucked it through sticks of liquorice. Sucked gently, the sherbet merely dusted the tongue; too hard, and you choked with sweet powders; or if you blew back through the tube the sherbet-bag burst and you disappeared in a blizzard of sugar. Sucking and blowing, coughing and weeping, we scuffled our way down the lane. We drank at the spring to clean our mouths, then threw water at each other and made rainbows. Mr Jones's pond was bubbling with life, and covered with great white lilies – they poured from their leaves like candle-fat, ran molten, then cooled on the water. Moorhens plopped, and dabchicks scooted, insects rowed and skated. New-hatched frogs hopped about like flies, lizards gulped in the grass. The lane itself was crusted with cow-dung, hard baked and smelling good.

We met Sixpence Robinson among the bulrushes, and he said, 'Come and have some fun.' He lived along the lane just past the sheepwash in a farm cottage near a bog. There were five in his family, two girls and three boys, and their names all began with S. There was Sis and Sloppy, Stosher and Sammy, and our good friend Sixpence the Tanner. Sis and Sloppy were both beautiful girls and used to hide from us boys in the gooseberries. It was the brothers we played with: and Sammy, though a cripple, was one of the most agile lads in the village.

Theirs was a good place to be at any time, and they were good to be with. (Like us, they had no father; unlike ours, he was dead.) So today, in the spicy heat of their bog, we sat round on logs and whistled, peeled sticks, played mouth-organs, dammed up the stream, and cut harbours in the cool clay banks. Then we took all the pigeons out of their dovecots and ducked them in the water-butt, held them under till their beaks started bubbling then threw them up in the air. Splashing spray from their wings they flew round the house, then came back to roost like fools. (Sixpence had a one-eyed pigeon called Spike who he boasted could stay under longest, but one day the poor bird, having broken all records, crashed for ever among the cabbages.)

When all this was over, we retired to the paddock and played cricket under the trees. Sammy, in his leg-irons, charged up and down. Hens and guinea-fowl took to the trees. Sammy hopped and bowled like murder at us, and we defended our stumps with our lives. The cracked bat clouting; the cries in the reeds; the smells of fowls and water; the long afternoon with the steep hills around us watched by Sloppy still hid in the gooseberries – it seemed down here that no disasters could happen, that nothing

could ever touch us. This was Sammy's and Sixpence's; the
place past the sheepwash, the hide-out unspoiled by
authority, where drowned pigeons flew and cripples ran
free; where it was summer, in some ways, always.

SUMMER WAS ALSO the time of these: of sudden plenty, of
slow hours and actions, of diamond haze and dust on the
eyes, of the valley in post-vernal slumber; of burying birds
out of seething corruption; of Mother sleeping heavily at
noon; of jazzing wasps and dragonflies, haystooks and
thistle-seeds, snows of white butterflies, skylarks' eggs,
bee-orchids, and frantic ants; of wolf-cub parades, and boy
scouts' bugles; of sweat running down the legs; of boiling
potatoes on bramble fires, of flames glass-blue in the sun;
of lying naked in the hill-cold stream; begging pennies for
bottles of pop; of girls' bare arms and unripe cherries,
green apples and liquid walnuts; of fights and falls and
new-scabbed knees, sobbing pursuits and flights; of picnics high up in the crumbling quarries, of butter running
like oil, of sunstroke, fever, and cucumber peel stuck cool
to one's burning brow. All this, and the feeling that it
would never end, that such days had come for ever, with
the pump drying up and the water-butt crawling, and the
chalk ground hard as the moon. All sights twice-brilliant
and smells twice-sharp, all game-days twice as long. Double charged as we were, like the meadow ants, with the
frenzy of the sun, we used up the light to its last violet
drop, and even then couldn't go to bed.

We used up the light to its last violet drop, and even then we couldn't go to bed

When darkness fell, and the huge moon rose, we stirred to a second life. Then boys went calling along the roads, wild slit-eyed animal calls, Walt Kerry's naked nasal yodel, Boney's jackal scream. As soon as we heard them we crept outdoors, out of our stifling bedrooms, stepped out into moonlight warm as the sun to join our chalk-white, moon-masked gang.

Games in the moon. Games of pursuit and capture. Games that the night demanded. Best of all, Fox and Hounds – go where you like, and the whole of the valley to hunt through. Two chosen boys loped away through the trees and were immediately swallowed in shadow. We gave them five minutes, then set off after them. They had churchyard, farmyard, barns, quarries, hilltops, and woods to run to. They had all night, and the whole of the moon, and five miles of country to hide in . . .

Padding softly, we ran under the melting stars, through sharp garlic woods, through blue blazed fields, following the scent by the game's one rule, the question and answer cry. Every so often, panting for breath, we paused to check on our quarry. Bullet heads lifted, teeth shone in the moon. 'Whistle-or-'OLLER! Or-we-shall-not-FOLLER!' It was a cry on two notes, prolonged. From the other side of the hill, above white fields of mist, the faint fox-cry came back. We were off again then, through the waking night, among sleepless owls and badgers, while our quarry slipped off into another parish and would not be found for hours.

Round about midnight we ran them to earth, exhausted

under a haystack. Until then we had chased them through all the world, through jungles, swamps, and tundras, across pampas plains and steppes of wheat and plateaux of shooting stars, while hares made love in the silver grasses, and the large hot moon climbed over us, raising tides in my head of night and summer that move there even yet.

THE YEAR REVOLVED around the village, the festivals round the year, the church round the festivals, the Squire round the church, and the village round the Squire. The Squire was our centre, a crumbling moot tree; and few indeed of our local celebrations could take place without his shade. On the greater occasions he let us loose in his gardens, on the smaller gave us buns and speeches; and at historic moments of national rejoicing – when kings were born, enemies vanquished, or the Conservatives won an election – he ransacked his boxrooms for fancy-dresses that we might rejoice in a proper manner.

The first big festival that I can remember was Peace Day in 1919. It was a day of magical transformations, of tears and dusty sunlight, of bands, processions, and buns by the cartload; and I was so young I thought it normal . . .

We had all been provided with fancy-dress, and that seemed normal too. Apart from the Squire's contribution Marjorie had been busy for weeks stitching up glories for ourselves and the neighbours. No makeshift, rag-bag cobbling either; Marjorie had worked as though for a wedding.

On the morning of the feast Poppy Green came to the house to try on her angel's dress. She was five years old and about my size. She had russet curls like apple peelings, a polished pumpkin face, a fruity air of exploding puddings, and a perpetual cheeky squint. I loved her, she was like a portable sweet-shop. This morning I watched my sisters dress her. She was supposed to represent a spirit. They'd made her a short frilly frock, a tinfoil helmet, cardboard wings, and a wand with a star. When they'd clothed her they stood her up on the mantelpiece and had a good look at her. Then they went off awhile on some other business and left us alone together.

'Fly!' I commanded. 'You got wings, ain't you?'

Poppy squirmed and wiggled her shoulders.

I grew impatient and pushed her off the mantelpiece, and she fell with a howl into the fireplace. Looking down at her, smudged with coal and tears, her wand and wings all crumpled, I felt nothing but rage and astonishment. She should have been fluttering round the room.

They sponged and soothed her, and Poppy trotted home, her bent wand clutched in her hand. Then shapes and phantoms began to run through the village, and we started to get ready ourselves. Marge appeared as Queen Elizabeth, with Phyllis her lady-in-waiting. Marjorie, who was sixteen and at her most beautiful, wore a gown of ermine, a brocaded bodice, and a black cap studded with pearls. She filled the kitchen with such a glow of grace that we just stood and gaped at her. It was the first time I had seen Queen Elizabeth, but this was no sharp-faced Tudor. Tender and proud in her majestic robes, she was the Queen of Heaven, risen from the dust, unrecognizable as Marge till she spoke, and her eyes shone down on us from her veils of ermine like emeralds laid in snow. Thirteen-year-old Phyllis, with finery of her own, skipped like a magpie around her, wearing a long chequered dress of black and white velvet, and a hat full of feathers and moths.

The rest of us, whom Marjorie had dressed, were the result of homespun inspirations. Dorothy, as 'Night', was perhaps the most arresting; an apparition of unearthly beauty, a flash of darkness, a strip of nocturnal sky, mysteriously cloaked in veils of black netting entangled with silver paper. A crescent moon lay across her breast, a comet across her brow, and her long dark curls fell in coils of midnight and were sprinkled with tinsel dust. I smelt frost when I saw her and heard a crackling of stars; familiar Dorothy had grown far and disturbing.

Brother Jack had refused to be dressed up at all, unless in some aspect of recognized valour. So they hung him in green, gave him a bow and arrow, and he called himself Robin Hood. Little Tony was dressed as a market-girl, curly-headed and pretty as love, bare-armed and bonneted, carrying a basket of flowers, but so proud we forgave him his frock.

As for me, a squat neck and solid carriage made the part I should play inevitable. I was John Bull – whoever he was – but I quickly surmised his importance. I remember the girls stuffing me into my clothes with many odd squeals and giggles. Gravely I offered an arm or leg, but remained dignified and aloof. Marjorie had assembled the ritual garments with her usual flair and cunning. I wore a top-hat and choker, a union-jack waistcoat, a frock-coat, and pillowcase breeches. But I'd been finished off hurriedly with gaiters of cardboard fastened loosely together with pins – a slovenly makeshift which offended my taste, and which I was never able to forgive.

This Peace Day I remember as a blur of colour, leading from fury to triumph. There was a procession with a band. I walked alone solemnly. Fantastic disguises surrounded me; every single person seemed covered with beards, false-noses, bootblack, and wigs. We had not marched far when my boots fell off, followed by my cardboard gaiters. As I stopped to find them, the procession swept over me. I sat down by the roadside and howled. I howled because I could hear the band disappearing, because I was John Bull and it should not have happened. I was picked up by a carriage, restored to the procession, then placed on a trolley and pulled. Cross-legged on the trolley, bare-footed and gaiterless, I rode like a prince through the village.

Dusty, sweating from its long route-march, the procession snaked round the houses. The old and infirm stood and cheered from the gutters; I nodded back from my trolley. At last we entered the cool beech wood through which the Squire's drive twisted. The brass-band's thunder bounced back from the boughs. Owls hooted and flapped away.

We came out of the wood into the Big House gardens, and the sun returned in strength. Doves and pigeons flew out of the cedars. The swans took off from the lake. On the steps of the Manor stood the wet-eyed Squire, already in tears at the sight of us. His mother, in a speech from a basket-chair, mentioned the glory of God, the Empire, us; and said we wasn't to touch the flowers.

With the procession dispersed, I was tipped off the trolley, and I wandered away through the grounds. Flags and roses moved against the sky, bright figures among the bushes. Japanese girls and soot-faced savages grew strangely from banks of lilac. I saw Charlie Chaplin, Peter the Pieman, a collection of upright tigers, a wounded soldier about my age, and a bride on the arm of a monkey.

Later I was given a prize by the Squire and was photographed in a group by a rockery. I still have that picture, all sepia shadows, a leaf ripped from that summer day. Surrounded by girls in butter muslin, by druids and eastern kings, I am a figure rooted in unshakeable confidence, oval, substantial, and proud. About two feet high and two feet broad, my breeches like slack balloons, I stand, top-hatted, with a tilted face as severe as on a Roman coin. Others I recognize are gathered round me, all marked by that day's white dust. Tony has lost his basket of flowers, Jack his bow and arrow. Poppy Green has had her wings torn off and is grasping a broken lily. She stands beside me, squinting fiercely, ruffled a bit by the heat, and the silver letters across her helmet – which I couldn't read then – say PEACE.

OUR VILLAGE OUTINGS were both sacred and secular, and were also far between. One seldom, in those days, strayed beyond the parish boundaries, except for the annual Choir Outing. In the meantime we had our own tribal wanderings, unsanctified though they were, when a sudden fine morning would send us forth in families for a day's nutting or blackberrying. So up we'd go to the wilder end of the valley, to the bramble-entangled Scrubs, bearing baskets and buckets and flasks of cold tea, like a file of foraging Indians. Blackberries clustered against the sky, heavy and dark as thunder, which we plucked and gobbled, hour after hour, lips purple, hands stained to the wrists. Or later, mushrooms, appearing like manna, buttoning the shaggy grass, found in the mists of September mornings with the wet threads of spiders on them. They came in the night from nowhere, rootless, like a scattering of rubber balls. Their suckers clung to the roots of grass and broke off with a rubbery snap. The skin rubbed away like the bark of a birch tree, the flesh tasted of something unknown . . . At other times there would be wild green damsons, tiny plums, black sloes, pink crab-apples – the free waste of the woods, an unpoliced bounty, which we'd carry back home in bucketfuls. Whether we used them for jam or jellies or pies, or just left them to rot, didn't matter.

Then sometimes there'd be a whole day's outing, perhaps to Sheepscombe to visit relations – a four-mile walk, which to our short legs seemed further, so that we needed all day to do it. We would start out early, with the sun just rising and the valley wrapped in mist . . .

'It's going to be hot,' says our Mother brightly, and usually she is right. We climb up slowly towards Bulls Cross, picking at the bushes for birds'-nests. Or we stop to dig holes or to swing on gates while Mother looks back at the view. 'What a picture,' she murmurs. 'Green as green . . . And those poppies, red as red.' The mist drags the tree-tops, flies away in the sky, and there is suddenly blue air all round us.

Painswick sprawls white in the other valley, like the skeleton of a foundered mammoth. But active sounds of its working morning – carts and buzz-saws, shouts and hammering – come drifting in gusts towards us. The narrow lane that leads to Sheepscombe bends steeply away on our right. 'Step out, young men!' our Mother says crisply. She begins to teach us a hymn; the kind that cries for some lost land of paradise, and goes well with a tambourine. I've not heard it before (nor ever since), but it entirely enshrines our outing – the remote, shaggy valley in which we find ourselves, the smell of hot straw on the air, dog-roses and distances, dust and spring waters, and the long day's journey, by easy stages, to the sheep-folds of our wild relations.

They are waiting for us with warm ginger-beer, and a

dinner of broad beans and bacon. Aunty Fan says, 'Annie, come in out of the sun. You must be ready to drop.' We go indoors and find our Uncle Charlie hacking at the bacon with a bill-hook. Young cousin Edie and her cautious brothers seem to be pondering whether to punch our heads. Our Gramp comes in from his cottage next door, dressed in mould-green corduroy suiting. We sit down and eat, and the cousins kick us under the table, from excitement rather than spite. Then we play with their ferrets, spit down their well, have a fight, and break down a wall. Later we are called for and given a beating, then we climb up the tree by the earth closet. Edie climbs highest, till we bite her legs, then she hangs upside down and screams. It has been a full, far-flung, and satisfactory day; dusk falls, and we say good-bye.

Back down the lane in the thick hot darkness we walk drowsily, heavy with boots. Night odours come drifting from woods and gardens; sweet musks and sharp green acids. In the sky the fat stars bounce up and down, rhythmically, as we trudge along. Glow-worms, brighter than lamps or candles, spike the fields with their lemon fires, while huge horned beetles stumble out of the dark and buzz blindly around our heads.

Then Painswick appears – a starfish of light dilating in a pool of distance. We hurry across the haunted common and come at last to the top of our valley. The village water-fall, still a mile away, lifts its cool, familiar murmur. We are nearing home, we are almost there: Mother starts to recite a poem. 'I remember, I remember, the house where I was born . . .' She says it right through, and I tag beside her watching the trees walk past in the sky . . .

THE FIRST CHOIR OUTING we ever had was a jaunt in a farm-wagon to Gloucester. Only the tenors and basses and the treble boys were included in that particular treat. Later, with the coming of the horse-brake and charabanc, the whole village took part as well. With the help of the powerful new charabanc we even got out of the district altogether, rattling away to the ends of the earth, to Bristol or even further.

One year the Outing was to Weston-super-Mare, and we had saved up for months to be worthy of it. We spent the night before preparing our linen, and the girls got up at dawn to make sandwiches. The first thing I did when I came down that morning was to go out and look at the weather. The sky was black, and Tony was behind the lavatory praying hard through his folded hands. When he saw that I'd seen him he began to scratch and whistle, but the whole thing was a very bad sign.

We couldn't eat breakfast, the porridge was like gravel; so Jack and I ran up the bank to see what was going on. Families were already gathering for the charabancs, so we ran back down again. The girls were ready, and Tony was ready. Mother was raking under the piano with a broom-stick.

'Come on, our Mother! They'll go without us!'

'I've just got to find my corsets.'

She found them; then started very slowly to wash, like a duck with all summer to do it. We stood round and nagged her, rigid with nerves.

'Run along – you're under my feet.'

So we left her, and scampered along to the Woolpack. The whole village was waiting by now; mothers with pig-buckets stuffed with picnics, children with cocoa-tin spades, fathers with bulging overcoats lined entirely with clinking bottles. There was little Mrs Tulley collecting the fares and plucking at her nervous cheeks; Mr Vick, the shopkeeper, carrying his keys in a basket; the two dress-makers in unclaimed gowns; and Lily Nelson, a fugitive from her brother, whispering, 'You mustn't tell Arnold – he'd kill me.' The Squire's old gardener had brought a basket of pigeons which he planned to release from the pier. And the postman, having nobody to deliver his letters to, had dumped them, and was coming along too.

Faces looked pale in the early light. Men sniffed and peered at the sky. 'Don't look too good, do it?' 'Can't say it do.' 'Bloody black over Stroud.' 'Might clear though . . .' Teeth were sucked in, heads doubtfully shaken; I felt the doom of storm-sickness on me.

The vicar arrived to see us off – his pyjamas peeping out from his raincoat. 'There's a very nice church near the Promenade . . . I trust you will all spare a moment . . .' He issued each choirboy with his shilling for dinner, then dodged back home to bed. The last to turn up was Herbert the gravedigger, with something queer in a sack. The last, that is, except our Mother, of whom there was still no sign.

Then the charabancs arrived and everyone clambered aboard, fighting each other for seats. We abandoned our Mother and climbed aboard too, feeling guilty and miserable. The charabancs were high, with broad open seats and with folded tarpaulins at the rear, upon which, as choirboys, we were privileged to perch and to fall off and break our necks. We all took our places, people wrapped themselves in blankets, horns sounded, and we were ready. 'Is everyone present?' piped the choirmaster. Shamefully, Jack and I kept silent.

Our Mother, as usual, appeared at that moment, a distant trotting figure, calling and waving her handbags gaily to disarm what impatience there might be. 'Come on, Mother Lee! We near went without you!' Beaming, she climbed aboard. 'I just had to wash out my scarf,' she said, and tied it on the windscreen to dry. And there it blew like a streaming pennant as we finally drove out of the village.

In our file of five charabancs, a charioted army, we swept down the thundering hills. At the speed and height of our vehicles the whole valley took on new dimensions; woods rushed beneath us, and fields and flies were devoured in a gulp of air. We were windborne now by motion and pride, we cheered everything, beast and fowl, and taunted with heavy ironical shouts those unfortunates still working in the fields. We kept this up till we had roared through Stroud, then we entered the stranger's country. It was no longer so easy to impress pedestrians that we were the Annual Slad Choir Outing. So we settled down, and opened our sandwiches, and began to criticize the farming we passed through.

The flatness of the Severn Valley now seemed dull after our swooping hills, the salmon-red sandstone of the Clifton Gorges too florid compared with our chalk. Everything began to appear strange and comic, we hooted at the shapes of the hayricks, laughed at the pitiful condition of the cattle – 'He won't last long – just look at 'is knees.' We began to look round fondly at our familiar selves, drawn close by this alien country. Waves of affection and loyalty embraced us. We started shouting across the seats. 'Harry! Hey, Harry! Say whatcher, Harry! Bit of all right, ain't it, you? Hey, Bert! 'Ow's Bert? 'Ow you doin', ole sparrer? Where's Walt? Hey there, Walt! Watcher!'

Mile after rattling mile we went, under the racing sky, flying neckties and paper kites from the back, eyes screwed in the weeping wind. The elders, protected in front by the windscreen, chewed strips of bacon, or slept. Mother pointed out landmarks and lectured the sleepers on points of historical interest. Then a crawling boy found the basket of pigeons and the coach exploded with screams and wings . . .

The weather cleared as we drove into Weston, and we halted on the Promenade. 'The seaside,' they said: we gazed around us, but we saw no sign of the sea. We saw a vast blue sky and an infinity of mud stretching away to the shadows of Wales. But rousing smells of an invisible ocean astonished our land-locked nostrils: salt, and wet weeds, and fishy oozes; a sharp difference in every breath. Our deep-ditched valley had not been prepared for this, for we had never seen such openness, the blue windy world seemed to have blown quite flat, bringing the sky to the level of our eyebrows. Canvas booths flapped on the edge of the Prom, mouths crammed with shellfish and vinegar; there were rows of prim boarding-houses (each the size of our Vicarage); bath-chairs, carriages, and donkeys; and stilted far out on the rippled mud a white pier like a sleeping dragon.

The blue day was ours; we rattled our money and divided up into groups. 'Hey, Jake, Steve; let's go have a wet' – and the men shuffled off down a side street. 'I'm beat after that, Mrs Jones, ain't you? – there's a clean place down by the bandstand.' The old women nodded, and went seeking their comforts; the young ones to stare at the policemen.

Meanwhile, we boys just picked up and ran; we had a world of mud to deal with. The shops and streets ended suddenly, a frontier to the works of man; and beyond – the mud, salt winds, and birds, a kind of double ration of light, a breathless space neither fenced nor claimed, and far out a horizon of water. We whinnied like horses and charged up and down, every hoof-mark written behind us. If you stamped in this mud, you brought it alive, the footprint began to speak, it sucked and sighed and filled with water, became a foot cut out of the sky. I dug my fingers into a stretch of mud to see how deep it was, felt a hard flat pebble and drew it out and examined it in the palm of my hand. Suddenly, it cracked, and put out two claws; I dropped it in horror, and ran . . .

Half the village now had hired themselves chairs and were bravely facing the wind. Mrs Jones was complaining about Weston tea: 'It's made from the drains, I reckon.' The Squire's old gardener, having lost his pigeons, was trying to catch gulls in a basket; and the gravedigger (who appeared to have brought his spade) was out on the mud digging holes. Then the tide came in like a thick red sludge, and we all went on the pier.

Magic construction striding the waves, loaded with freaks and fancies, water-chutes and crumpled mirrors, and a whole series of nightmares for a penny. One glided secretly to one's favourite machine, the hot coin burning one's hand, to command a murder, a drunk's delirium, a haunted grave, or a Newgate hanging. This last, of course, was my favourite; what dread power one's penny purchased – the painted gallows, the nodding priest, the felon with his face of doom. At a touch they jerked through their ghastly dance, the priest, hangman, and the convict, joined together by rods and each one condemned as it were to perpetual torment. Their ritual motions led to the jerk of the corpse; the figures froze and the lights went out. Another penny restored the lights, brought back life to the cataleptic trio, and dragged the poor felon once more to the gallows to be strangled all over again.

That white pier shining upon the waves seemed a festive charnel house. With our mouths hanging open, sucking gory sticks of rock, we groped hungrily from horror to horror. For there were sideshows too, as well as the machines with hair-raising freaks under glass – including a two-headed Indian, a seven-legged sheep, and a girl's eye with a child coiled inside it.

We spent more time on that turgid pier than anywhere else in Weston. Then the tide went out, and evening fell, and we returned to the waiting charabancs. People came wandering from all directions, with bags full of whelks and seaweed, the gravedigger was dragged from his holes in the sand, and our numbers were checked and counted. Then we were all in our seats, the tarpaulin pulled over us, and with a blast of horns we left.

A long homeward drive through the red twilight, through landscapes already relinquished, the engines humming, the small children sleeping, and the young girls gobbling shrimps. At sunset we stopped at a gaslit pub for the men to have one more drink. This lasted till all of them turned bright pink and started embracing their wives. Then we repacked the charabancs, everyone grew drowsy, and we drove through the darkness beyond Bristol. The last home stretch: someone played a harmonica; we boys groped for women to sleep on, and slept, to the sway and sad roar of the coach and the men's thick boozy singing.

We passed Stroud at last and climbed the valley road, whose every curve our bodies recognized, whose every slant we leaned to, though still half asleep, till we woke to the smell of our houses. We were home, met by lanterns – and the Outing was over. With subdued 'Goodnights' we collected into families, then separated towards our beds. Where soon I lay, my head ringing with sleep, my ears full of motors and organs, my shut eyes printed with the images of the day – mud, and red rock, and hangmen . . .

THE DAY ROSIE Burdock decided to take me in hand was a motionless day of summer, creamy, hazy, and amber-coloured, with the beech trees standing in heavy sunlight as though clogged with wild wet honey. It was the time of hay-making, so when we came out of school Jack and I went to the farm to help.

The whirr of the mower met us across the stubble, rabbits jumped like firecrackers about the fields, and the hay smelt crisp and sweet. The farmer's men were all hard at work, raking, turning, and loading. Tall, whiskered fellows forked the grass, their chests like bramble patches. The air swung with their forks and the swathes took wing and rose like eagles to the tops of the wagons. The farmer gave us a short fork each and we both pitched in with the rest . . .

I stumbled on Rosie behind a haycock, and she grinned up at me with the sly, glittering eyes of her mother. She wore her tartan frock and cheap brass necklace, and her bare legs were brown with hay-dust.

'Get out a there,' I said. 'Go on.'

Rosie had grown and was hefty now, and I was terrified of her. In her cat-like eyes and curling mouth I saw unnatural wisdoms more threatening than anything I could imagine. The last time we'd met I'd hit her with a cabbage stump. She bore me no grudge, just grinned.

'I got sommat to show ya.'

'You push off,' I said.

I felt dry and dripping, icy hot. Her eyes glinted, and I stood rooted. Her face was wrapped in a pulsating haze and her body seemed to flicker with lightning.

'You thirsty?' she said.

'I ain't, so there.'

'You be,' she said. 'C'mon.'

So I stuck the fork into the ringing ground and followed her, like doom.

We went a long way, to the bottom of the field, where a wagon stood half-loaded. Festoons of untrimmed grass hung down like curtains all around it. We crawled underneath, between the wheels, into a herb-scented cave of darkness. Rosie scratched about, turned over a sack, and revealed a stone jar of cider.

'It's cider,' she said. 'You ain't to drink it though. Not much of it, any rate.'

Huge and squat, the jar lay on the grass like an unexploded bomb. We lifted it up, unscrewed the stopper, and smelt the whiff of fermented apples. I held the jar to my mouth and rolled my eyes sideways, like a beast at a water-hole. 'Go on,' said Rosie. I took a deep breath . . .

Never to be forgotten, that first long secret drink of golden fire, juice of those valleys and of that time, wine of wild orchards, of russet summer, of plump red apples, and Rosie's burning cheeks. Never to be forgotten, or ever tasted again . . .

I put down the jar with a gulp and a gasp. Then I turned to look at Rosie. She was yellow and dusty with buttercups and seemed to be purring in the gloom; her hair was rich as a wild bee's nest and her eyes were full of stings. I did not know what to do about her, nor did I know what not to do. She looked smooth and precious, a thing of unplumbable mysteries, and perilous as quicksand.

'Rosie . . .' I said, on my knees, and shaking.

She crawled with a rustle of grass towards me, quick and superbly assured. Her hand in mine was like a small wet flame which I could neither hold nor throw away. Then Rosie, with a remorseless, reedy strength, pulled me down from my tottering perch, pulled me down, down into her wide green smile and into the deep subaqueous grass.

Then I remember little, and that little, vaguely. Skin drums beat in my head. Rosie was close-up, salty, an invisible touch, too near to be seen or measured. And it seemed that the wagon under which we lay went floating away like a barge, out over the valley where we rocked unseen, swinging on motionless tides.

Then she took off her boots and stuffed them with

Never to be forgotten, that first long secret drink of golden fire, juice of those valleys and of that time, wine of wild orchards

flowers. She did the same with mine. Her parched voice crackled like flames in my ears. More fires were started. I drank more cider. Rosie told me outrageous fantasies. She liked me, she said, better than Walt, or Ken, Boney Harris, or even the curate. And I admitted to her, in a loud, rough voice, that she was even prettier than Betty Gleed. For a long time we sat with our mouths very close, breathing the same hot air. We kissed, once only, so dry and shy, it was like two leaves colliding in air.

At last the cuckoos stopped singing and slid into the woods. The mowers went home and left us. I heard Jack calling as he went down the lane, calling my name till I heard him no more. And still we lay in our wagon of grass tugging at each other's hands, while her husky, perilous whisper drugged me and the cider beat gongs in my head . . .

Night came at last, and we crawled out from the wagon and stumbled together towards home. Bright dew and glow-worms shone over the grass, and the heat of the day grew softer. I felt like a giant; I swung from the trees and plunged my arms into nettles just to show her. Whatever I did seemed valiant and easy. Rosie carried her boots, and smiled.

There was something about that evening which dilates the memory, even now. The long hills slavered like Chinese dragons, crimson in the setting sun. The shifting lane lassoed my feet and tried to trip me up. And the lake, as we passed it, rose hissing with waves and tried to drown us among its cannibal fish.

Perhaps I fell in – though I don't remember. But here I lost Rosie for good. I found myself wandering home alone, wet through, and possessed by miracles. I discovered extraordinary tricks of sight. I could make trees move and leap-frog each other, and turn bushes into roaring trains. I could lick up the stars like acid drops and fall flat on my face without pain. I felt magnificent, fateful, and for the first time in my life, invulnerable to the perils of night.

When at last I reached home, still dripping wet, I was bursting with power and pleasure. I sat on the chopping-block and sang 'Fierce Raged the Tempest' and several other hymns of that nature. I went on singing till long after supper-time, bawling alone in the dark. Then Harold and Jack came and frog-marched me to bed. I was never the same again . . .

THE LAST DAYS of my childhood were also the last days of the village. I belonged to that generation which saw, by chance, the end of a thousand years' life. The change came late to our Cotswold valley, didn't really show itself till the late 1920s; I was twelve by then, but during that handful of years I witnessed the whole thing happen.

Myself, my family, my generation, were born in a world of silence; a world of hard work and necessary patience, of backs bent to the ground, hands massaging the crops, of waiting on weather and growth; of villages like ships in the empty landscapes and the long walking distances between them; of white narrow roads, rutted by hooves and cart-wheels, innocent of oil or petrol, down which people passed rarely, and almost never for pleasure, and the horse was the fastest thing moving. Man and horse were all the power we had – abetted by levers and pulleys. But the horse was king, and almost everything grew around him: fodder, smithies, stables, paddocks, distances, and the rhythm of our days. His eight miles an hour was the limit of our movements, as it had been since the days of the Romans. That eight miles an hour was life and death, the size of our world, our prison.

This was what we were born to, and all we knew at first. Then, to the scream of the horse, the change began. The brass-lamped motor-car came coughing up the road, followed by the clamorous charabanc; the solid-tyred bus climbed the dusty hills and more people came and went. Chickens and dogs were the early sacrifices, falling demented beneath the wheels. The old folk, too, had strokes and seizures, faced by speeds beyond comprehension. Then scarlet motor-bikes, the size of five-barred gates, began to appear in the village, on which our youths roared like rockets up the two-minute hills, then spent weeks making repairs and adjustments.

These appearances did not immediately alter our lives; the cars were freaks and rarely seen, the motor-bikes mostly in pieces, we used the charabancs only once a year, and our buses at first were experiments. Meanwhile Lew Ayres, wearing a bowler-hat, ran his wagonette to Stroud twice a week. The carriage held six, and the fare was twopence, but most people preferred to walk. Mr West, from Sheepscombe, ran a cart every day, and would carry your parcels for a penny. But most of us still did the journey on foot, heads down to the wet Welsh winds, ignoring the carters – whom we thought extortionate – and spending a long hard day at our shopping.

But the car-shying horses with their rolling eyes gave signs of the hysteria to come. Soon the village would break, dissolve, and scatter, become no more than a place for pensioners. It had a few years left, the last of its thousand, and they passed almost without our knowing. They passed quickly, painlessly, in motor-bike jaunts, in the shadows of the new picture-palace, in quick trips to Gloucester (once a foreign city) to gape at the jazzy shops. Yet right to the end, like the false strength that precedes death, the old life seemed as lusty as ever.

The church, for instance, had never appeared more powerful. Its confident bell rang out each Sunday; the village heard it, asked no questions, put on satin and serge, filed into the pews, bobbed and nodded, frowned at its children, crouched and prayed, bawled or quavered through hymns, and sat in blank rows or jerkily slept while the curate reeled off those literary sermons which he had hired from the ecclesiastical library.

Sunday, far from being a day of rest, was in some ways tougher than a weekday; it was never torpid and it gave one a lift, being a combination of both indulgence and discipline. On that one day in seven – having bathed the night before – we were clean, wore our best, and ate meat. The discipline was Sunday School, learning the Collect, and worship both morning and evening. Neither mood nor inclination had any say in the matter, nor had doubt occurred to us yet.

Sunday mornings at home were the usual rush – chaos

in the kitchen, shrill orders to wash, and everyone's eyes on the clock. We polished our hair with grease and water, and scrubbed ourselves under the pump. Being Sunday, there was a pound of large sausages for breakfast, fried black and bursting with fat. One dipped them in pepper and ate them in haste, an open prayer-book propped up by the plate.

'Heavens alive, you'll be late, our lad.'

Gobble, mumble, and choke.

'What *are* you up to? Get a move on do.'

'Leave off – I'm learning the Collect.'

'What's that you say?'

'I-Gotta-Learn-Me-Collect!'

'Hurry up and learn it then.'

'I can't hurry up! Not if you keep on! . . .'

But it was really not difficult at all; ten inscrutable lines absorbed between mouthfuls, and usually on the run. Up the bank, down the road, the greasy prayer-book in one hand, the remains of the sausage in the other: 'Almighty and Most Merciful Father, who alone worketh Great Marvels . . .' In five minutes it was all in my head.

At Sunday School Miss Bagnall, polishing her nose, said: 'The Collect – now who will oblige . . .' I would jump to my feet and gabble, word perfect, the half page of sonorous syllables. It came in through the eyes and out through the mouth, and left no trace of its passing. Except that I can never read a Collect today without tasting a crisp burnt sausage . . .

After an hour of Sunday School we all went to the church, the choir going straight to the vestry. Here we huddled ourselves into our grimy robes, which only got washed at Easter. The parson lined us up and gave us a short, sharp prayer; then we filed into the stalls, took our privileged places, and studied the congregation. The Sunday School infants packed the bleak north wing, heads fuzzy as frosted flowers. The rest of the church was black with adults, solemn in cat's-fur and feathers. Most were arranged in family groups, but here and there a young couple, newly engaged, sat red in the neck and hands. The leading benches contained our gentry, their pews marked with visiting cards: the Lords of the Manor, Squire Jones and the Croomes; then the Army, the Carvossos and Dovetons; the rich and settled spinsters, the Misses Abels and Bagnalls; and finally the wealthier farmers. All were neatly arranged by protocol, with the Squire up front by the pulpit. Through prayers and psalms and rackety hymns he slept like a beaming child, save when a visiting preacher took some rhetorical flight, when he'd wake with a loud, 'God damn!'

Morning service began with an organ voluntary, perhaps a Strauss waltz played very slow. The organ was old, and its creaks and sighs were often louder than the music itself. The organ was blown by an ordinary pump-handle which made the process equally rowdy; and Rex Brown, the blower, hidden away in his box – and only visible to us in the choir – enlivened the service by parodying it in mime or by carving girls' names on the woodwork.

But in the packed congregation solemnity ruled. There was power, lamentation, full-throated singing, heavy prayers, and public repentance. No one in the village stayed away without reason, and no one yet wished to do so. We had come to the church because it was Sunday, just as we washed our clothes on Monday. There was also God taking terrible notes – a kind of Squire-archical rent-collector, ever ready to record the tenants' backsliding and to evict them if their dues weren't paid.

This morning service was also something else. It was a return to the Ark of all our species in the face of the ever-threatening flood. We are free of that need now and when the flood does come shall drown proud and alone, no doubt. As it was, the lion knelt down with the lamb, the dove perched on the neck of the hawk, sheep nuzzled wolf, we drew warmth from each other and knew ourselves beasts of one kingdom . . .

That was Sunday morning. With the service over, there was gossip among the gravestones, a slow walk home to roasted dinners, then a nap with the *News of the World*. The elders dozed sexily through the fat afternoon, while the young went again to Sunday School. Later came Even-song, which was as different from Matins as a tryst from a Trafalgar Square rally. The atmosphere was gentler, moonier, more private; the service was considered to be voluntary. We choirboys, of course, were compelled to go, but for the rest they went who would.

The church at night, in the dark of the churchyard, was

just a strip of red-fired windows. Inside, the oil-lamps and motionless candles narrowed the place with shadows. The display of the morning was absent now; the nave was intimate, and sleepy. Only a few solitary worshippers were present this time, each cloaked in a separate absorption: a Miss Bagnall, Widow White, the church-cleaning woman, a widower, and the postman at the back. The service was almost a reverie, our hymns nocturnal and quiet, the psalms traditional and never varying so that one could sing them without a book. The scattered faithful, half-obscured by darkness, sang them as though to themselves. 'Lord, now lettest Thou Thy servant depart in peace . . .' It was sung, eyes closed, in trembling tones. It could not have been sung in the morning.

From our seats in the choir we watched the year turn: Christmas, Easter and Whitsun, Rogation Sunday and prayers for rain, the Church following the plough very close. Harvest Festival perhaps was the one we liked best, the one that came nearest home. Then how heavily and abundantly was our small church loaded; the cream of the valley was used to decorate it. Everyone brought of his best from field and garden; and to enter the church on Harvest morning was like crawling head first into a horn of plenty, a bursting granary, a vegetable stall, a grotto of bright flowers. The normally bare walls sprouted leaves and fruits, the altar great stooks of wheat, and ornamental loaves as big as cartwheels stood parked by the communion rails. Bunches of grapes, from the Squire's own vines, hung blue from the lips of the pulpit. Gigantic and useless marrows abounded, leeks and onions festooned the pews, there were eggs and butter on the lectern shelves, the windows were heaped with apples, and the fat round pillars which divided the church were skirted with oats and barley.

Almost everyone in the congregation had some hand in these things. Square-rumped farmers and ploughmen in chokers, old gardeners and poultry-keepers, they nodded and pointed and prodded each other to draw attention to what they had brought. The Church was older than its one foundation, was as old as man's life on earth. The seed of these fruits, and the seed of these men, still came from the same one bowl; confined to this valley and renewing itself here, it went back to the days of the Ice. Pride, placation, and the continuity of growth were what we had come to praise. And even where we sang, 'All is safely gathered in', knowing full well that some of Farmer Lusty's oats still lay rotting in the fields, the discrepancy didn't seem important.

I remember one particular Harvest Festival which perfectly summed up this feeling. I was not old enough then to be in the choir, and I was sitting beside Tony, who was three. It was his first Harvest Festival, but he'd heard much about it and his expectations were huge. The choir, with banners, was fidgeting in the doorway, ready to start its procession. Tony gazed with glittering eyes around him, sniffing the juicy splendours. Then, in a moment of silence, just before the organ crashed into the hymn, he asked loudly, 'Is there going to be drums?'

It was a natural question, innocent and true. For neither drums, nor cymbals, nor trumpets of brass would have seemed out of place at that time.

THE DEATH OF the Squire was not the death of the church, though they drew to their end together. He died, and the Big House was sold by auction and became a Home for Invalids. The lake silted up, the swans flew away, and the great pike choked in the reeds. With the Squire's hand removed, we fell apart – though we were about to do so anyway. His servants dispersed and went into the factories. His nephew broke up the estate.

Fragmentation, free thought, and new excitements, came now to intrigue and perplex us. The first young couple to get married in a registry office were roundly denounced from the pulpit. 'They who play with fire shall be consumed by fire!' stormed the vicar. 'Ye mark my words!' Later he caught me reading *Sons and Lovers* and took it away and destroyed it. This may well have been one of his last authoritative gestures. A young apologist succeeded him soon.

Meanwhile the old people just dropped away – the white-whiskered, gaitered, booted and bonneted, ancient-tongued last of their world, who thee'd and thou'd both man and beast, called young girls 'damsels', young boys 'squires', old men 'masters', the Squire himself 'He', and who remembered the Birdlip stagecoach. Kicker Harris, the old coachman, with his top-hat and leggings, blew away like a torn-out page. Lottie Escourt, peasant shoot of a Norman lord, curled up in her relics and died. Others departed with hardly a sound. There was old Mrs Clissold, who sometimes called us for errands: 'Thee come up our court a minute, squire; I wants thee to do I a mission.' One ran to the shop to buy her a packet of bull's-eyes and was rewarded in the customary way. Bull's-eye in cheek, she'd sink back in her chair and dismiss one with a sleepy nod. 'I ain't nurn a aypence about I just now – but Mrs Crissole'll recollect 'ee . . .' We wrote her off as the day's good deed, and she died still recollecting us.

Now the last days of my family, too, drew near, beginning with the courting of the girls.

I remember very clearly how it started. It was summer, and we boys were sitting on the bank watching a great cloud of smoke in the sky.

A man jumped off his bike and cried, 'It's the boiler-works!' and we ran up the hill to see it.

There was a fire at the boiler-works almost every year. When we got there we found it a particularly good one. The warehouse, as usual, was sheathed in flame, ceilings and floors fell in, firemen shouted, windows melted like icicles, and from inside the building one heard thundering booms as the boilers started crashing about. We used up a lot of the day at this, cheering each toppling chimney.

When we got back to the village, much later in the evening, we saw a strange man down in our garden. We studied him from a distance with some feeling of shock. No one but neighbours and visiting relations had ever walked there before. Yet this ominous stranger was not only wandering free, he was being accompanied by all our women.

We rushed down the bank and burst roughly upon them, to find everyone crack-jawed with politeness. Our sisters cried La! when they saw us coming, and made us welcome as though we'd been round the world. Marjorie was particularly soft and loving, the others beamed anxiously at us; Mother, though not smart, was in her best black dress, and the stranger was twisting his hat.

'These are our brothers,' said Marjorie, grabbing two of us close to her bosom. 'This is Jackie and Loll, and that one's Tone. They're all of them terrible bad.'

There was nervous laughter and relief at this, as though several dark ghosts had been laid. We smirked and wriggled, aped and showed off, but couldn't think what was going on. In fact, the day of that boiler-works fire marked a beacon in the life of our girls. It was the day when their first young man came courting, and this stranger was he, and he was Marjorie's, and he opened a path through the garden.

He was handsome, curly-haired, a builder of barges, very strong, and entirely acceptable. His name was Maurice, and we boys soon approved him and gave him the run of the place. He was followed quite quickly by two other young men, one each for Dorothy and Phyllis. Dorothy got Leslie, who was a shy local scoutmaster, at least until he met her; Phyllis in turn produced Harold the Bootmaker, who had fine Latin looks, played the piano by ear, and sang songs about old-fashioned mothers. Then Harold, our brother, got the infection too, mended our chairs, re-upholstered the furniture, and brought home a girl for himself.

At these strokes our home life changed forever; new manners and notions crept in; instead of eight in the kitchen there were now a round dozen, and so it stayed till the girls started marrying. The young men called nightly, with candles in jars, falling headlong down our precipitous bank; or came pushing their bikes on summer evenings, loitering with the girls in the lanes; or sat round the fire talking slowly of work; or sat silent, just being there; while the sewing-machine hummed, and Mother rambled, and warm ripples of nothing lapped round them. They were wary of Mother, unsure of her temper, though her outbursts were at the world, not people. Leslie was tactful and diffident, giving short sharp laughs at her jokes. Maurice often lectured her on 'The Working Man Today', which robbed her of all understanding. Phyl's Harold would sometimes draw up to the piano, strike the keys with the strength of ten, then charm us all by bawling 'Because' or 'An Old Lady Passing By'.

Then there was cheese and cocoa, and 'Goodnight all', and the first one got up to leave. There followed long farewells by the back-kitchen door, each couple taking their turn. Those waiting inside had to bide their time. 'Our Doth! Ain't you finished yet?' 'Shan't be a minute.' Yum-yum, kiss-kiss. 'Well, hurry up do! You're awful.' Five more minutes of silence outside, then Marge shakes the latch on the door. 'How much longer, our Doth? You been there all night. There's some got to work tomorrow.' 'All right, don't get ratty. He's just off now. Night-night, my beautiful bab.' One by one they departed; we turned down the lights, and the girls heaved themselves to bed.

Sundays, or Bank Holidays, were day-long courtships, and then the lovers were all over us. When it rained it was hopeless and we just played cards, or the boy friends modelled for dress-making. When fine perhaps Mother would plan a small treat, like a picnic in the woods.

I remember a sweltering August Sunday. Mother said it would be nice to go out. We would walk a short mile to a nice green spot and boil a kettle under the trees. It sounded simple enough, but we knew better. For Mother's picnics were planned on a tribal scale, with huge preparations beforehand. She flew round the kitchen issuing orders and the young men stood appalled at the work. There were sliced cucumbers and pots of paste, radishes, pepper and salt, cakes and buns and macaroons, soup-plates of bread and butter, jam, treacle, jugs of milk, and several fresh-made jellies.

The young men didn't approve of this at all, and muttered it was blooming mad. But with a 'You carry that now, there's a dear boy', each of us carried something. So we set off at last like a frieze of Greeks bearing gifts to some woodland god – Mother, with a tea-cloth over her head, gathering flowers as she went along, the sisters following with cakes and bread, Jack with the kettle, Tony with the salt, myself with a jug of milk; then the scowling youths in their blue serge suits carrying the jellies in open basins – jellies which rapidly melted in the sun and splashed them with yellow and rose. The young men swapped curses under their breath, brother Harold hung back in shame, while Mother led the way with prattling songs determined to make the thing go.

She knew soon enough when people turned sour and moved mountains to charm them out of it, and showed that she knew by a desperate gaiety and by noisy attacks on silence.

'Now come along, Maurice, best foot forward, mind how you go, tee-hee. Leslie! just look at those pretty what-d'you-call'ems – those what's-is – *aren't* they a picture? I said Leslie, look, aren't they pretty, my dear? Funny you don't know the name. Oh, isn't it a scrumptious day, tra-la? Boys, isn't it a scrumptious day?'

Wordy, flustered, but undefeated, she got us to the woods at last. We were ordered to scatter and gather sticks and to build a fire for the kettle. The fire smoked glumly and stung our eyes, the young men sat round like martyrs, the milk turned sour, the butter fried on the bread, cake-crumbs got stuck to the cucumber, wasps seized the treacle, the kettle wouldn't boil, and we ended by drinking the jellies.

As we boys would eat anything, anywhere, none of this bothered us much. But the young courting men sat on their spread silk-handkerchiefs and gazed at the meal in horror. 'No thanks, Mrs Lee. I don't think I could. I've just had me dinner, ta.'

They were none of them used to such disorder, didn't care much for open-air picnics – but most of all they were wishing to be away with their girls, away in some field or gully, where summer and love would be food enough, and an absence of us entirely.

LAURIE LEE was born in Gloucestershire in 1914 and raised in the village of Slad. At the age of nineteen he said goodbye to his mother and left home to walk to London. Over the years that followed he worked as an office clerk, labourer, poet, journalist and documentary film-maker. He also wrote and travelled extensively in Spain.

Cider With Rosie, from which this Mini is taken, was first published in 1959. It was an instant bestseller and became a beloved memoir of childhood and the English countryside for millions of people worldwide. Laurie Lee wrote the book over ten years and it changed his life. He was able to become a full-time writer and to buy a cottage in his home village of Slad.

RECOMMENDED BOOKS BY LAURIE LEE:

Cider With Rosie
A Rose for Winter
As I Walked Out One Midsummer Morning

Still having dreams of Summer?

Liberty
VIRGINIA WOOLF

VINTAGE MINIS

Eating
NIGELLA LAWSON

VINTAGE MINIS

Swimming
ROGER DEAKIN

VINTAGE MINIS

Drinking
JOHN CHEEVER

VINTAGE MINIS

VINTAGE MINIS

The Vintage Minis bring you the world's greatest writers on the experiences that make us human. These stylish, entertaining little books explore the whole spectrum of life – from birth to death, and everything in between. Which means there's something here for everyone, whatever your story.

Desire	Haruki Murakami
Love	Jeanette Winterson
Babies	Anne Enright
Language	Xiaolu Guo
Motherhood	Helen Simpson
Fatherhood	Karl Ove Knausgaard
Summer	Laurie Lee
Jealousy	Marcel Proust
Sisters	Louisa May Alcott
Home	Salman Rushdie
Race	Toni Morrison
Liberty	Virginia Woolf
Swimming	Roger Deakin
Work	Joseph Heller
Depression	William Styron
Drinking	John Cheever
Eating	Nigella Lawson
Psychedelics	Aldous Huxley
Calm	Tim Parks
Death	Julian Barnes

vintageminis.co.uk

1 3 5 7 9 10 8 6 4 2

Vintage
20 Vauxhall Bridge Road,
London SW1V 2SA

Vintage Classics is part of the Penguin Random House
group of companies whose addresses can be found at
global.penguinrandomhouse.com.

 Penguin
Random House
UK

The stories in this edition previously appeared in the *New Yorker*

First published in Great Britain by Jonathan Cape, by arrangement with Alfred
A. Knopf, Inc in 1979
First published by Vintage in 1990
This short edition published by Vintage in 2017

penguin.co.uk/vintage

A CIP catalogue record for this book is available from the British Library

ISBN 9781784872649

Typeset in 9.5/14.5 pt FreightText Pro
by Jouve (UK), Milton Keynes
Printed and bound by Clays Ltd, St Ives plc

Penguin Random House is committed to a sustainable future for
our business, our readers and our planet. This book is made from
Forest Stewardship Council® certified paper.

Drinking
JOHN CHEEVER

VINTAGE MINIS

The Sorrows of Gin

IT WAS SUNDAY afternoon, and from her bedroom Amy could hear the Beardens coming in, followed a little while later by the Farquarsons and the Parminters. She went on reading *Black Beauty* until she felt in her bones that they might be eating something good. Then she closed her book and went down the stairs. The living room door was shut, but through it she could hear the noise of loud talk and laughter. They must have been gossiping or worse, because they all stopped talking when she entered the room.

'Hi, Amy,' Mr Farquarson said.

'Mr Farquarson spoke to you, Amy,' her father said.

'Hello, Mr Farquarson,' she said. By standing outside the group for a minute, until they had resumed their conversation, and then by slipping past Mrs Farquarson, she was able to swoop down on the nut dish and take a handful.

'Amy!' Mr Lawton said.

'I'm sorry, Daddy,' she said, retreating out of the circle, toward the piano.

'Put those nuts back,' he said.

'I've handled them, Daddy,' she said.

'Well, pass the nuts, dear,' her mother said sweetly. 'Perhaps someone else would like nuts.'

Amy filled her mouth with the nuts she had taken, returned to the coffee table, and passed the nut dish.

'Thank you, Amy,' they said, taking a peanut or two.

'How do you like your new school, Amy?' Mrs Bearden asked.

'I like it,' Amy said. 'I like private schools better than public schools. It isn't so much like a factory.'

'What grade are you in?' Mr Bearden asked.

'Fourth,' she said.

Her father took Mr Parminter's glass and his own, and got up to go into the dining room and refill them. She fell into the chair he had left vacant.

'Don't sit in your father's chair, Amy,' her mother said, not realizing that Amy's legs were worn out from riding a bicycle, while her father had done nothing but sit down all day.

As she walked toward the French doors, she heard her mother beginning to talk about the new cook. It was a good example of the interesting things they found to talk about.

'You'd better put your bicycle in the garage,' her father said, returning with the fresh drinks. 'It looks like rain.'

Amy went out onto the terrace and looked at the sky, but it was not very cloudy, it wouldn't rain, and his advice, like all the advice he gave her, was superfluous. They were always at her. 'Put your bicycle away.' 'Open the door for Grandmother, Amy.' 'Feed the cat.' 'Do your homework.' 'Pass the nuts.' 'Help Mrs Bearden with her parcels.' 'Amy, please try and take more pains with your appearance.'

They all stood, and her father came to the door and called her. 'We're going over to the Parminters' for supper,' he said. 'Cook's here, so you won't be alone. Be sure and go to bed at eight like a good girl. And come and kiss me good night.'

After their cars had driven off, Amy wandered through the kitchen to the cook's bedroom beyond it and knocked on the door. 'Come in,' a voice said, and when Amy entered, she found the cook, whose name was Rosemary, in her bathrobe, reading the Bible. Rosemary smiled at Amy. Her smile was sweet and her old eyes were blue. 'Your parents have gone out again?' she asked. Amy said that they had, and the old woman invited her to sit down. 'They do seem to enjoy themselves, don't they? During the four days I've been here, they've been out every night, or had people in.' She put the Bible face down on her lap and smiled, but not at Amy. 'Of course, the drinking that goes on here is all sociable, and what your parents do is none of my business, is it? I worry about drink more than most people, because of my poor sister. My poor sister drank too much. For ten years, I went to visit her on Sunday afternoons, and most of the time she was *non compos mentis*. Sometimes I'd find her huddled up on the floor with one or two sherry bottles empty beside her. Sometimes she'd seem sober enough to a stranger, but I could tell in a second by the way she spoke her words that she'd drunk enough not to be herself any more. Now my poor sister is gone, I don't have anyone to visit at all.'

'What happened to your sister?' Amy asked.

'She was a lovely person, with a peaches-and-cream complexion and fair hair,' Rosemary said. 'Gin makes some people gay – it makes them laugh and cry – but with my sister it only made her sullen and withdrawn. When she was drinking, she would retreat into herself. Drink made her contrary. If I'd say the weather was fine, she'd tell me I was wrong. If I'd say it was raining, she'd say it was clearing. She'd correct me about everything I said, however small it was. She died in Bellevue Hospital one summer while I was working in Maine. She was the only family I had.'

The directness with which Rosemary spoke had the effect on Amy of making her feel grown, and for once politeness came to her easily. 'You must miss your sister a great deal,' she said.

'I was just sitting here now thinking about her. She was in service, like me, and it's lonely work. You're always surrounded by a family, and yet you're never a part of it. Your pride is often hurt. The Madams seem condescending and inconsiderate. I'm not blaming the ladies I've worked for. It's just the nature of the relationship. They order chicken salad, and you get up before dawn to get ahead of yourself, and just as you've finished the chicken salad, they change their minds and want crab-meat soup.'

'My mother changes her mind all the time,' Amy said.

'Sometimes you're in a country place with nobody else in help. You're tired, but not too tired to feel lonely. You go out onto the servants' porch when the pots and pans are done, planning to enjoy God's creation, and although the front of the house may have a fine view of the lake or the mountains, the view from the back is never much. But there is the sky and the trees and the stars and the birds singing and the pleasure of resting your feet. But then you hear them in the front of the house, laughing and talking with their guests and their sons and daughters. If you're new and they whisper, you can be sure they're talking about you. That takes all the pleasure out of the evening.'

'Oh,' Amy said.

'I've worked all kinds of places – places where there were eight or nine in help and places where I was expected to burn the rubbish myself, on winter nights, and shovel the snow. In a house where there's a lot of help, there's usually some devil among them – some old butler or parlormaid – who tries to make your life miserable from the beginning. 'The Madam doesn't like it this way,' and 'The Madam doesn't like it that way,' and 'I've been with the Madam for twenty years,' they tell you. It takes a diplomat to get along. Then there is the rooms they give you, and every one of them I've ever seen is cheerless. If you have a bottle in your suitcase, it's a terrible temptation in the beginning not to take a drink to raise your spirits. But I have a strong character. It was different with my poor sister. She used to complain about nervousness, but, sitting here thinking about her tonight, I wonder if she suffered from nervousness at all. I wonder if she didn't make it all up. I wonder if she just wasn't meant to be in service. Toward the end, the only work she could get was out in the country, where nobody else would go, and she never lasted much more than a week or two. She'd take a little gin for her nervousness, then a little for her tiredness, and when she'd drunk her own bottle and everything she could steal, they'd hear about it in the front part of the house. There was usually a scene, and my poor sister always liked to have the last word. Oh, if I had had my way, they'd be a law against it! It's not my business to advise you to take anything from your father, but I'd be proud of you if you'd empty his gin bottle into the sink now and then – the filthy stuff! But it's made me feel better to talk with you, sweetheart. It's made me not miss my poor sister so much. Now I'll read a little more in my Bible, and then I'll get you some supper.'

THE LAWTONS HAD had a bad year with cooks – there had been five of them. The arrival of Rosemary had made Marcia Lawton think back to a vague theory of dispensations; she had suffered, and now she was being rewarded. Rosemary was clean, industrious, and cheerful, and her table – as the Lawtons said – was just like the Chambord. On Wednesday night after dinner, she took the train to

New York, promising to return on the evening train Thursday. Thursday morning, Marcia went into the cook's room. It was a distasteful but a habitual precaution. The absence of anything personal in the room – a package of cigarettes, a fountain pen, an alarm clock, a radio, or anything else that could tie the old woman to the place – gave her the uneasy feeling that she was being deceived, as she had so often been deceived by cooks in the past. She opened the closet door and saw a single uniform hanging there and, on the closet floor, Rosemary's old suitcase and the white shoes she wore in the kitchen. The suitcase was locked, but when Marcia lifted it, it seemed to be nearly empty.

Mr Lawton and Amy drove to the station after dinner on Thursday to meet the eight-sixteen train. The top of the car was down, and the brisk air, the starlight, and the company of her father made the little girl feel kindly toward the world. The railroad station in Shady Hill resembled the railroad stations in old movies she had seen on television, where detectives and spies, bluebeards and their trusting victims, were met to be driven off to remote country estates. Amy liked the station, particularly toward dark. She imagined that the people who traveled on the locals were engaged on errands that were more urgent and sinister than commuting. Except when there was a heavy fog or a snowstorm, the club car that her father traveled on seemed to have the gloss and the monotony of the rest of his life. The locals that ran at odd hours belonged to a world of deeper contrasts, where she would like to live.

They were a few minutes early, and Amy got out of the car and stood on the platform. She wondered what the fringe of string that hung above the tracks at either end of the station was for, but she knew enough not to ask her father, because he wouldn't be able to tell her. She could hear the train before it came into view, and the noise excited her and made her happy. When the train drew in to the station and stopped, she looked in the lighted windows for Rosemary and didn't see her. Mr Lawton got out of the car and joined Amy on the platform. They could see the conductor bending over someone in a seat, and finally the cook arose. She clung to the conductor as he led her out to the platform of the car, and she was crying. 'Like peaches and cream,' Amy heard her sob. "A lovely, lovely person.' The conductor spoke to her kindly, put his arm around her shoulders, and eased her down the steps. Then the train pulled out, and she stood there drying her tears. 'Don't say a word, Mr Lawton,' she said, 'and I won't say anything.' She held out a small paper bag. 'Here's a present for you, little girl.'

'Thank you, Rosemary,' Amy said. She looked into the paper bag and saw that it contained several packets of Japanese water flowers.

Rosemary walked toward the car with the caution of someone who can hardly find her way in the dim light. A sour smell came from her. Her best coat was spotted with mud and ripped in the back. Mr Lawton told Amy to get in the back seat of the car, and made the cook sit in front, beside him. He slammed the car door shut after her angrily, and then went around to the driver's seat and drove home. Rosemary reached into her handbag and took out a Coca-Cola bottle with a cork stopper and took a drink. Amy could tell by the smell that the Coca-Cola bottle was filled with gin.

'Rosemary!' Mr Lawton said.

'I'm lonely,' the cook said. 'I'm lonely, and I'm afraid, and it's all I've got.'

He said nothing more until he had turned into their drive and brought the car around to the back door. 'Go and get your suitcase, Rosemary,' he said. 'I'll wait here in the car.'

As soon as the cook had staggered into the house, he told Amy to go in by the front door. 'Go upstairs to your room and get ready for bed.'

Her mother called down the stairs when Amy came in, to ask if Rosemary had returned. Amy didn't answer. She went to the bar, took an open gin bottle, and emptied it into the pantry sink. She was nearly crying when she encountered her mother in the living room, and told her that her father was taking the cook back to the station.

When Amy came home from school the next day, she found a heavy, black-haired woman cleaning the living room. The car Mr Lawton usually drove to the station was at the garage for a checkup, and Amy drove to the station with her mother to meet him. As he came across the station platform, she could tell by the lack of color in his face that he had had a hard day. He kissed her mother, touched Amy on the head, and got behind the wheel.

'You know,' her mother said, 'there's something terribly wrong with the guest-room shower.'

'Damn it, Marcia,' he said, 'I wish you wouldn't always greet me with bad news!'

His grating voice oppressed Amy, and she began to fiddle with the button that raised and lowered the window.

'Stop that, Amy!' he said.

'Oh, well, the shower isn't important,' her mother said. She laughed weakly.

'When I got back from San Francisco last week,' he said, 'you couldn't wait to tell me that we need a new oil burner.'

'Well, I've got a part-time cook. That's good news.'

'Is she a lush?' her father asked.

'Don't be disagreeable, dear. She'll get us some dinner and wash the dishes and take the bus home. We're going to the Farquarsons'.'

'I'm really too tired to go anywhere,' he said.

'Who's going to take care of me?' Amy asked.

'You always have a good time at the Farquarsons',' her mother said.

'Well, let's leave early,' he said.

'Who's going to take care of me?' Amy asked.

'Mrs Henlein,' her mother said.

When they got home, Amy went over to the piano.

Her father washed his hands in the bathroom off the hall and then went to the bar. He came into the living room holding the empty gin bottle. 'What's her name?' he asked.

'Ruby,' her mother said.

'She's exceptional. She's drunk a quart of gin on her first day.'

'Oh dear!' her mother said. 'Well, let's not make any trouble now.'

'Everybody is drinking my liquor,' her father shouted, 'and I am God-damned sick and tired of it!'

'There's plenty of gin in the closet,' her mother said. 'Open another bottle.'

'We paid that gardener three dollars an hour and all he did was sneak in here and drink up my Scotch. The sitter we had before we got Mrs Henlein used to water my bourbon, and I don't have to remind you about Rosemary. The cook before Rosemary not only drank everything in my liquor cabinet but she drank all the rum, kirsch, sherry, and wine that we had in the kitchen for cooking. Then, there's that Polish woman we had last summer. Even that old laundress. *And* the painters. I think they must have put some kind of a mark on my door. I think the agency must have checked me off as an easy touch.'

'Well, let's get through dinner, and then you can speak to her.'

'The hell with that!' he said. 'I'm not going to encourage people to rob me. *Ruby!*' He shouted her name several times, but she didn't answer. Then she appeared in the dining-room doorway anyway, wearing her hat and coat.

'I'm sick,' she said. Amy could see that she was frightened.

'I should think that you would be,' her father said.

'I'm sick,' the cook mumbled, 'and I can't find anything around here, and I'm going home.'

'Good,' he said. 'Good! I'm through with paying people to come in here and drink my liquor.'

The cook started out the front way, and Marcia Lawton followed her into the front hall to pay her something. Amy had watched this scene from the piano bench, a position that was withdrawn but that still gave her a good view. She saw her father get a fresh bottle of gin and make a shaker of Martinis. He looked very unhappy.

'Well,' her mother said when she came back into the room. 'You know, she didn't look drunk.'

'Please don't argue with me, Marcia,' her father said. He poured two cocktails, said 'Cheers,' and drank a little. 'We can get some dinner at Orpheo's,' he said.

'I suppose so,' her mother said. 'I'll rustle up something for Amy.' She went into the kitchen, and Amy opened her music to 'Reflets d'Automne.' 'COUNT,' her music teacher had written. 'COUNT and lightly, lightly . . .' Amy began to play. Whenever she made a mistake, she said 'Darn it!' and started at the beginning again. In the middle of 'Reflets d'Automne' it struck her that *she* was the one who had emptied the gin bottle. Her perplexity was so intense that she stopped playing, but her feelings did not go beyond perplexity, although she did not have the strength to continue playing the piano. Her mother relieved her. 'Your supper's in the kitchen, dear,' she said. 'And you can take a popsicle out of the deep freeze for dessert. Just one.'

Marcia Lawton held her empty glass toward her husband, who filled it from the shaker. Then she went upstairs. Mr Lawton remained in the room, and, studying her father closely, Amy saw that his tense look had begun to soften. He did not seem so unhappy any more, and as she passed him on her way to the kitchen, he smiled at her tenderly and patted her on the top of the head.

When Amy had finished her supper, eaten her popsicle, and exploded the bag it came in, she returned to the piano and played 'Chopsticks' for a while. Her father came downstairs in his evening clothes, put his drink on the mantelpiece, and went to the French doors to look at his terrace and his garden. Amy noticed that the transformation that had begun with a softening of his features was even more advanced. At last, he seemed happy. Amy wondered if he was drunk, although his walk was not unsteady. If anything, it was more steady.

Her parents never achieved the kind of rolling, swinging gait that she saw impersonated by a tightrope walker in the circus each year while the band struck up 'Show Me the Way to Go Home' and that she liked to imitate herself sometimes. She liked to turn round and round and round on the lawn, until, staggering and a little sick, she would whoop, 'I'm drunk! I'm a drunken man!' and reel over the grass, righting herself as she was about to fall and finding

At last, he seemed happy. Amy wondered if he was drunk

herself not unhappy at having lost for a second her ability
to see the world. But she had never seen her parents like
that. She had never seen them hanging on to a lamppost
and singing and reeling, but she had seen them fall down.
They were never indecorous – they seemed to get more
decorous and formal the more they drank – but sometimes
her father would get up to fill everybody's glass and he
would walk straight enough but his shoes would seem to
stick to the carpet. And sometimes, when he got to the
dining-room door, he would miss it by a foot or more.
Once, she had seen him walk into the wall with such
force that he collapsed onto the floor and broke most of
the glasses he was carrying. One or two people laughed,
but the laughter was not general or hearty, and most of
them pretended that he had not fallen down at all. When
her father got to his feet, he went right on to the bar as if
nothing had happened. Amy had once seen Mrs Farquarson miss the chair she was about to sit in, by a foot, and
thump down onto the floor, but nobody laughed then, and
they pretended that Mrs Farquarson hadn't fallen down at
all. They seemed like actors in a play. In the school play,
when you knocked over a paper tree you were supposed to
pick it up without showing what you were doing, so that
you would not spoil the illusion of being in a deep forest,
and that was the way *they* were when somebody fell down.

Now her father had that stiff, funny walk that was so
different from the way he tramped up and down the station platform in the morning, and she could see that he

was looking for something. He was looking for his drink. It
was right on the mantelpiece, but he didn't look there. He
looked on all the tables in the living room. Then he went
out onto the terrace and looked there, and then he came
back into the living room and looked on all the tables
again. Then he went back onto the terrace, and then back
over the living room tables, looking three times in the
same place, although he was always telling her to look
intelligently when she lost her sneakers or her raincoat.
'Look for it, Amy,' he was always saying. 'Try and remember where you left it. I can't buy you a new raincoat every
time it rains.' Finally he gave up and poured himself
a cocktail in another glass. 'I'm going to get Mrs Henlein,'
he told Amy, as if this were an important piece of
information.

Amy's only feeling for Mrs Henlein was indifference,
and when her father returned with the sitter, Amy thought
of the nights, stretching into weeks – the years, almost –
when she had been cooped up with Mrs Henlein. Mrs
Henlein was very polite and was always telling Amy what
was ladylike and what was not. Mrs Henlein also wanted to
know where Amy's parents were going and what kind of a
party it was, although it was none of her business. She
always sat down on the sofa as if she owned the place, and
talked about people she had never even been introduced
to, and asked Amy to bring her the newspaper, although
she had no authority at all.

When Marcia Lawton came down, Mrs Henlein wished

her good evening. 'Have a lovely party,' she called after the Lawtons as they went out the door. Then she turned to Amy. 'Where are your parents going, sweetheart?

'But you must know, sweetheart. Put on your thinking cap and try and remember. Are they going to the club?'

'No,' Amy said.

'I wonder if they could be going to the Trenchers',' Mrs Henlein said. 'The Trenchers' house was lighted up when we came by.'

'They're not going to the Trenchers',' Amy said. 'They hate the Trenchers.'

'Well, where are they going, sweetheart?' Mrs Henlein asked.

'They're going to the Farquarsons',' Amy said.

'Well, that's all I wanted to know, sweetheart,' Mrs Henlein said. 'Now get me the newspaper and hand it to me politely. *Politely*,' she said, as Amy approached her with the paper. 'It doesn't mean anything when you do things for your elders unless you do them politely.' She put on her glasses and began to read the paper.

Amy went upstairs to her room. In a glass on her table were the Japanese flowers that Rosemary had brought her, blooming stalely in water that was colored pink from the dyes. Amy went down the back stairs and through the kitchen into the dining room. Her father's cocktail things were spread over the bar. She emptied the gin bottle into the pantry sink and then put it back where she had found it. It was too late to ride her bicycle and too early to go to bed, and she knew that if she got anything interesting on the television, like a murder, Mrs Henlein would make her turn it off. Then she remembered that her father had brought her home from his trip West a book about horses, and she ran cheerfully up the back stairs to read her new book.

It was after two when the Lawtons returned. Mrs Henlein, asleep on the living-room sofa dreaming about a dusty attic, was awakened by their voices in the hall. Marcia Lawton paid her, and thanked her, and asked if anyone had called, and then went upstairs. Mr Lawton was in the dining room, rattling the bottles around. Mrs Henlein, anxious to get into her own bed and back to sleep, prayed that he wasn't going to pour himself another drink, as they so often did. She was driven home night after night by drunken gentlemen. He stood in the door of the dining room, holding an empty bottle in his hand. 'You must be stinking, Mrs Henlein,' he said.

'Hmm,' she said. She didn't understand.

'You drank a full quart of gin,' he said.

The lackluster old woman – half between wakefulness and sleep – gathered together her bones and groped for her gray hair. It was in her nature to collect stray cats, pile the bathroom up to the ceiling with interesting and valuable newspapers, rouge, talk to herself, sleep in her underwear in case of fire, quarrel over the price of soup bones, and have it circulated around the neighborhood that when she finally died in her dusty junk heap, the mattress would be full of bankbooks and the pillow stuffed with hundred-dollar bills. She had resisted all these rich temptations in order to appear a lady, and she was repaid by being called a common thief. She began to scream at him.

'You take that back, Mr Lawton! You take back every one of those words you just said! I never stole anything in my whole life, and nobody in my family ever stole anything, and I don't have to stand here and be insulted by a drunk man. Why, as for drinking, I haven't drunk enough to fill an eyeglass for twenty-five years. Mr Henlein took me to a place of refreshment twenty-five years ago, and I drank two Manhattan cocktails that made me so sick and dizzy that I've never liked the stuff ever since. How dare you speak to me like this! Calling me a thief and a drunken woman! Oh, you disgust me – you disgust me in your ignorance of all the trouble I've had. Do you know what I had for Christmas dinner last year? I had a bacon sandwich. Son of a bitch!' She began to weep. 'I'm glad I said it!' she screamed. 'It's the first time I've used a dirty word in my whole life and I'm glad I said it. Son of a bitch!' A sense of liberation, as if she stood at the bow of a great ship, came over her. 'I lived in this neighborhood my whole life. I can remember when it was full of good farming people and there was fish in the rivers. My father had four acres of sweet meadowland and a name that was known far and wide, and on my mother's side I'm descended from patroons, Dutch nobility. My mother was the spit and image of Queen Wilhelmina. You think you can get away with insulting me, but you're very, very, very much mistaken.' She went to the telephone and, picking up the receiver, screamed, 'Police! Police! Police! This is Mrs Henlein, and I'm over at the Lawtons'. He's drunk, and he's calling me insulting names, and I want you to come over here and arrest him!'

The voices woke Amy, and, lying in her bed, she perceived vaguely the pitiful corruption of the adult world; how crude and frail it was, like a piece of worn burlap, patched with stupidities and mistakes, useless and ugly, and yet they never saw its worthlessness, and when you pointed it out to them, they were indignant. But as the voices went on and she heard the cry 'Police! Police!' she was frightened. She did not see how they could arrest her, although they could find her fingerprints on the empty bottle, but it was not her own danger that frightened her but the collapse, in the middle of the night, of her father's house. It was all her fault, and when she heard her father speaking into the extension telephone in the library, she felt sunk in guilt. Her father tried to be good and kind – and, remembering the expensive illustrated book about horses that he had brought her from the West, she had to set her teeth to keep from crying. She covered her head with a pillow and realized miserably that she would have to go away. She had plenty of friends from the time when they used to live in New York, or she could spend the night in the Park or hide in a museum. She would have to go away.

———

'GOOD MORNING,' HER father said at breakfast. 'Ready for a good day!' Cheered by the swelling light in the sky, by the recollection of the manner in which he had handled Mrs Henlein and kept the police from coming, refreshed by his sleep, and pleased at the thought of playing golf, Mr Lawton spoke with feeling, but the words seemed to Amy offensive and fatuous; they took away her appetite, and she slumped over her cereal bowl, stirring it with a spoon. 'Don't slump, Amy,' he said. Then she remembered the night, the screaming, the resolve to go. His cheerfulness refreshed her memory. Her decision was settled. She had a ballet lesson at ten, and she was going to have lunch with Lillian Towele. Then she would leave.

Children prepare for a sea voyage with a toothbrush and a Teddy bear; they equip themselves for a trip around the world with a pair of odd socks, a conch shell, and a thermometer; books and stones and peacock feathers, candy bars, tennis balls, soiled handkerchiefs, and skeins of old string appear to them to be the necessities of travel, and Amy packed, that afternoon, with the impulsiveness of her kind. She was late coming home from lunch, and her gateway was delayed, but she didn't mind. She could catch one of the late-afternoon locals; one of the cooks' trains. Her father was playing golf and her mother was off somewhere. A part-time worker was cleaning the living room. When Amy had finished packing, she went into her parents' bedroom and flushed the toilet. While the water murmured, she took a twenty-dollar bill from her mother's desk. Then she went downstairs and left the house and walked around Blenhollow Circle and down Alewives Lane to the station. No regrets or goodbyes formed in her mind. She went over the names of the friends she had in the city, in case she decided not to spend the night in a museum. When she opened the door of the waiting room, Mr Flanagan, the stationmaster, was poking his coal fire.

'I want to buy a ticket to New York,' Amy said.

'One-way or round-trip?'

'One-way, please.'

Mr Flanagan went through the door into the ticket office and raised the glass window. 'I'm afraid I haven't got a half-fare ticket for you, Amy,' he said. 'I'll have to write one.'

'That's all right,' she said. She put the twenty-dollar bill on the counter.

'And in order to change that,' he said, 'I'll have to go over to the other side. Here's the four-thirty-two coming in now, but you'll be able to get the five-ten.' She didn't protest, and went and sat beside her cardboard suitcase, which was printed with European hotel and place names. When the local had come and gone, Mr Flanagan shut his glass window and walked over the footbridge to the north-bound platform and called the Lawtons'. Mr Lawton had just come in from his game and was mixing himself a cock-tail. 'I think your daughter's planning to take some kind of a trip,' Mr Flanagan said.

It was dark by the time Mr Lawton got down to the

station. He saw his daughter through the station window. The girl sitting on the bench, the rich names on her paper suitcase, touched him as it was in her power to touch him only when she seemed helpless or when she was very sick. Someone had walked over his grave! He shivered with longing, he felt his skin coarsen as when, driving home late and alone, a shower of leaves on the wind crossed the beam of his headlights, liberating him for a second at the most from the literal symbols of his life – the buttonless shirts, the vouchers and bank statements, the order blanks, and the empty glasses. He seemed to listen – God knows for what. Commands, drums, the crackle of signal fires, the music of the glockenspiel – how sweet it sounds on the Alpine air – singing from a tavern in the pass, the honking of wild swans; he seemed to smell the salt air in the churches of Venice. Then, as it was with the leaves, the power of her figure to trouble him was ended; his goose-flesh vanished. He was himself. Oh, why should she want to run away? Travel – and who knew better than a man who spent three days of every fortnight on the road – was a world of overheated plane cabins and repetitious magazines, where even the coffee, even the champagne, tasted of plastics. How could he teach her that home sweet home was the best place of all?

Goodbye, My Brother

WE ARE A family that has always been very close in spirit. Our father was drowned in a sailing accident when we were young, and our mother has always stressed the fact that our familial relationships have a kind of permanence that we will never meet with again. I don't think about the family much, but when I remember its members and the coast where they lived and the sea salt that I think is in our blood, I am happy to recall that I am a Pommeroy – that I have the nose, the coloring, and the promise of longevity – and that while we are not a distinguished family, we enjoy the illusion, when we are together, that the Pommeroys are unique. I don't say any of this because I'm interested in family history or because this sense of uniqueness is deep or important to me but in order to advance the point that we are loyal to one another in spite of our differences, and that any rupture in this loyalty is a source of confusion and pain.

We are four children; there is my sister Diana and the

three men – Chaddy, Lawrence, and myself. Like most families in which the children are out of their twenties, we have been separated by business, marriage, and war. Helen and I live on Long Island now, with our four children. I teach in a secondary school, and I am past the age where I expect to be made headmaster – or principal, as we say – but I respect the work. Chaddy, who has done better than the rest of us, lives in Manhattan, with Odette and their children. Mother lives in Philadelphia, and Diana, since her divorce, has been living in France, but she comes back to the States in the summer to spend a month at Laud's Head. Laud's Head is a summer place on the shore of one of the Massachusetts islands. We used to have a cottage there, and in the twenties our father built the big house. It stands on a cliff above the sea and, excepting St Tropez and some of the Apennine villages, it is my favorite place in the world. We each have an equity in the place and we contribute some money to help keep it going.

Our youngest brother, Lawrence, who is a lawyer, got a job with a Cleveland firm after the war, and none of us saw him for four years. When he decided to leave Cleveland and go to work for a firm in Albany, he wrote Mother that he would, between jobs, spend ten days at Laud's Head, with his wife and their two children. This was when I had planned to take my vacation – I had been teaching summer school – and Helen and Chaddy and Odette and Diana were all going to be there, so the family would be together. Lawrence is the member of the family with whom the rest of us have least in common. We have never seen a great deal of him, and I suppose that's why we still call him Tifty – a nickname he was given when he was a child, because when he came down the hall toward the dining room for breakfast, his slippers made a noise that sounded like 'Tifty, tifty, tifty.' That's what Father called him, and so did everyone else. When he grew older, Diana sometimes used to call him Little Jesus, and Mother often called him the Croaker. We had disliked Lawrence, but we looked forward to his return with a mixture of apprehension and loyalty, and with some of the joy and delight of reclaiming a brother.

LAWRENCE CROSSED OVER from the mainland on the four-o'clock boat one afternoon late in the summer, and Chaddy and I went down to meet him. The arrivals and departures of the summer ferry have all the outward signs that suggest a voyage – whistles, bells, hand trucks, reunions, and the smell of brine – but it is a voyage of no import, and when I watched the boat come into the blue harbor that afternoon and thought that it was completing a voyage of no import, I realized that I had hit on exactly the kind of observation that Lawrence would have made. We looked for his face behind the windshields as the cars drove off the boat, and we had no trouble in recognizing him. And we ran over and shook his hand and clumsily kissed his wife and the children. 'Tifty!' Chaddy shouted. 'Tifty!' It is difficult to judge changes in the appearance of a brother, but both Chaddy and I agreed, as we drove back to Laud's Head, that Lawrence still looked very young. He got to the house first, and we took the suitcases out of his car. When I came in, he was standing in the living room, talking with Mother and Diana. They were in their best clothes and all their jewelry, and they were welcoming him extravagantly, but even then, when everyone was endeavoring to seem most affectionate and at a time when these endeavors come easiest, I was aware of a faint tension in the room. Thinking about this as I carried Lawrence's heavy suitcases up the stairs, I realized that our dislikes are as deeply ingrained as our better passions, and I remembered that once, twenty-five years ago, when I had hit Lawrence on the head with a rock, he had picked himself up and gone directly to our father to complain.

I carried the suitcases up to the third floor, where Ruth, Lawrence's wife, had begun to settle her family. She is a thin girl, and she seemed very tired from the journey, but when I asked her if she didn't want me to bring a drink upstairs to her, she said she didn't think she did.

When I got downstairs, Lawrence wasn't around, but the others were all ready for cocktails, and we decided to go ahead. Lawrence is the only member of the family who has never enjoyed drinking. We took our cocktails onto the terrace, so that we could see the bluffs and the sea and the islands in the east, and the return of Lawrence and his wife, their presence in the house, seemed to refresh our responses to the familiar view; it was as if the pleasure they would take in the sweep and the color of that coast, after such a long absence, had been imparted to us. While we were there, Lawrence came up the path from the beach.

'Isn't the beach fabulous, Tifty?' Mother asked. 'Isn't it fabulous to be back? Will you have a Martini?'

'I don't care,' Lawrence said. 'Whiskey, gin – I don't care what I drink. Give me a little rum.'

'We don't have any *rum*,' Mother said. It was the first note of asperity. She had taught us never to be indecisive, never to reply as Lawrence had. Beyond this, she is deeply concerned with the propriety of her house, and anything irregular by her standards, like drinking straight rum or bringing a beer can to the dinner table, excites in her a conflict that she cannot, even with her capacious sense of humor, surmount. She sensed the asperity and worked to repair it. 'Would you like some Irish, Tifty dear?' she said. 'Isn't Irish what you've always liked? There's some Irish on the sideboard. Why don't you get yourself some Irish?' Lawrence said that he didn't care. He poured himself a Martini, and then Ruth came down and we went in to dinner.

In spite of the fact that we had, through waiting for Lawrence, drunk too much before dinner, we were all anxious to put our best foot forward and to enjoy a peaceful time. Mother is a small woman whose face is still a striking reminder of how pretty she must have been, and whose conversation is unusually light, but she talked that evening about a soil-reclamation project that is going on up-island.

Diana is as pretty as Mother must have been; she is an animated and lovely woman who likes to talk about the
dissolute friends that she has made in France, but she
talked that night about the school in Switzerland where
she had left her two children. I could see that the dinner
had been planned to please Lawrence. It was not too
rich, and there was nothing to make him worry about
extravagance.

After supper, when we went back onto the terrace, the
clouds held that kind of light that looks like blood, and I
was glad that Lawrence had such a lurid sunset for his
homecoming. When we had been out there a few minutes,
a man named Edward Chester came to get Diana. She had
met him in France, or on the boat home, and he was staying for ten days at the inn in the village. He was introduced
to Lawrence and Ruth, and then he and Diana left.

'Is that the one she's sleeping with now?' Lawrence
asked.

'What a horrid thing to say!' Helen said.

'You ought to apologize for that, Tifty,' Chaddy said.

'I don't know,' Mother said tiredly. 'I don't know, Tifty.
Diana is in a position to do whatever she wants, and I don't
ask sordid questions. She's my only daughter. I don't see
her often.'

'Is she going back to France?'

'She's going back the week after next.'

Lawrence and Ruth were sitting at the edge of the terrace, not in the chairs, not in the circle of chairs. With his

mouth set, my brother looked to me then like a Puritan cleric. Sometimes, when I try to understand his frame of mind, I think of the beginnings of our family in this country, and his disapproval of Diana and her lover reminded me of this. The branch of the Pommeroys to which we belong was founded by a minister who was eulogized by Cotton Mather for his untiring abjuration of the Devil. The Pommeroys were ministers until the middle of the nineteenth century, and the harshness of their thought – man is full of misery, and all earthly beauty is lustful and corrupt – has been preserved in books and sermons. The temper of our family changed somewhat and became more lighthearted, but when I was of school age, I can remember a cousinage of old men and women who seemed to hark back to the dark days of the ministry and to be animated by perpetual guilt and the deification of the scourge. If you are raised in this atmosphere – and in a sense we were – I think it is a trial of the spirit to reject its habits of guilt, self-denial, taciturnity, and penitence, and it seemed to me to have been a trial of the spirit in which Lawrence had succumbed.

'Is that Cassiopeia?' Odette asked.

'No, dear,' Chaddy said. 'That isn't Cassiopeia.'

'Who was Cassiopeia?' Odette said.

'She was the wife of Cepheus and the mother of Andromeda,' I said.

'The cook is a Giants fan,' Chaddy said. 'She'll give you even money that they win the pennant.'

It had grown so dark that we could see the passage of light through the sky from the lighthouse at Cape Heron. In the dark below the cliff, the continual detonations of the surf sounded. And then, as she often does when it is getting dark and she has drunk too much before dinner, Mother began to talk about the improvements and additions that would someday be made on the house, the wings and bathrooms and gardens.

'This house will be in the sea in five years,' Lawrence said.

'Tifty the Croaker,' Chaddy said.

'Don't call me Tifty,' Lawrence said.

'Little Jesus,' Chaddy said.

'The sea wall is badly cracked,' Lawrence said. 'I looked at it this afternoon. You had it repaired four years ago, and it cost eight thousand dollars. You can't do that every four years.'

'Please, Tifty,' Mother said.

'Facts are facts,' Lawrence said, 'and it's a damned-fool idea to build a house at the edge of the cliff on a sinking coastline. In my lifetime, half the garden has washed away and there's four feet of water where we used to have a bathhouse.'

'Let's have a very *general* conversation,' Mother said bitterly. 'Let's talk about politics or the boat-club dance.'

'As a matter of fact,' Lawrence said, 'the house is probably in some danger now. If you had an unusually high sea, a hurricane sea, the wall would crumble and the house would go. We could all be drowned.'

'I can't *bear* it,' Mother said. She went into the pantry and came back with a full glass of gin.

I have grown too old now to think that I can judge the sentiments of others, but I was conscious of the tension between Lawrence and Mother, and I knew some of the history of it. Lawrence couldn't have been more than sixteen years old when he decided that Mother was frivolous, mischievous, destructive, and overly strong. When he had determined this, he decided to separate himself from her. He was at boarding school then, and I remember that he did not come home for Christmas. He spent Christmas with a friend. He came home very seldom after he had made his unfavorable judgment on Mother, and when he did come home, he always tried, in his conversation, to remind her of his estrangement. When he married Ruth, he did not tell Mother. He did not tell her when his children were born. But in spite of these principled and lengthy exertions he seemed, unlike the rest of us, never to have enjoyed any separation, and when they are together, you feel at once a tension, an unclearness.

And it was unfortunate, in a way, that Mother should have picked that night to get drunk. It's her privilege, and she doesn't get drunk often, and fortunately she wasn't bellicose, but we were all conscious of what was happening. As she quietly drank her gin, she seemed sadly to be parting from us; she seemed to be in the throes of travel. Then her mood changed from travel to injury, and the few remarks she made were petulant and irrelevant. When her glass was nearly empty, she stared angrily at the dark air in front of her nose, moving her head a little, like a fighter. I knew that there was not room in her mind then for all the injuries that were crowding into it. Her children were stupid, her husband was drowned, her servants were thieves, and the chair she sat in was uncomfortable. Suddenly she put down her empty glass and interrupted Chaddy, who was talking about baseball. 'I know one *thing*,' she said hoarsely. 'I know that if there is an afterlife, I'm going to have a very different kind of family. I'm going to have nothing but fabulously rich, witty, and enchanting children.' She got up and, starting for the door, nearly fell. Chaddy caught her and helped her up the stairs. I could hear their tender good nights, and then Chaddy came back. I thought that Lawrence by now would be tired from his journey and his return, but he remained on the terrace, as if he were waiting to see the final malfeasance, and the rest of us left him there and went swimming in the dark.

WHEN I WOKE the next morning, or half woke, I could hear the sound of someone rolling the tennis court. It is a fainter and a deeper sound than the iron buoy bells off the point – an unrhythmic iron chiming – that belongs in my mind to the beginnings of a summer day, a good portent. When I went downstairs, Lawrence's two kids were in the living room, dressed in ornate cowboy suits. They are frightened and skinny children. They told me their father was rolling the tennis court but that they did not want to go out because they had seen a snake under the doorstep. I explained to them that their cousins – all the other children – ate breakfast in the kitchen and that they'd better run along in there. At this announcement, the boy began to cry. Then his sister joined him. They cried as if to go in the kitchen and eat would destroy their most precious rights. I told them to sit down with me. Lawrence came in, and I asked him if he wanted to play some tennis. He said no, thanks, although he thought he might play some singles with Chaddy. He was in the right here, because both he and Chaddy play better tennis than I, and he did play some singles with Chaddy after breakfast, but later on, when the others came down to play family doubles, Lawrence disappeared. This made me cross – unreasonably so, I suppose – but we play darned interesting family doubles and he could have played in a set for the sake of courtesy.

Late in the morning, when I came up from the court alone, I saw Tifty on the terrace, prying up a shingle from the wall with his jack-knife. 'What's the matter, Lawrence?' I said. 'Termites?' There are termites in the wood and they've given us a lot of trouble.

He pointed out to me, at the base of each row of shingles, a faint blue line of carpenter's chalk. 'This house is about twenty-two years old,' he said. 'These shingles are about two hundred years old. Dad must have bought shingles from all the farms around here when he built the place, to make it look venerable. You can still see the carpenter's chalk put down where these antiques were nailed into place.'

It was true about the shingles, although I had forgotten it. When the house was built, our father, or his architect, had ordered it covered with lichened and weather-beaten shingles. I didn't follow Lawrence's reasons for thinking that this was scandalous.

'And look at these doors,' Lawrence said. 'Look at these doors and window frames.' I followed him over to a big Dutch door that opens onto the terrace and looked at it. It was a relatively new door, but someone had worked hard to conceal its newness. The surface had been deeply scored with some metal implement, and white paint had been rubbed into the incisions to imitate brine, lichen, and weather rot. 'Imagine spending thousands of dollars to make a sound house look like a wreck,' Lawrence said. 'Imagine the frame of mind this implies. Imagine wanting to live so much in the past that you'll pay men carpenters' wages to disfigure your front door.' Then I remembered Lawrence's sensitivity to time and his sentiments and opinions about our feelings for the past. I had heard him say, years ago, that we and our friends and our part of the nation, finding ourselves unable to cope with the problems of the present, had, like a wretched adult, turned back to what we supposed was a happier and a simpler time, and that our taste for reconstruction and candlelight was a measure of this irremediable failure. The faint blue line of chalk had reminded him of these ideas, the scarified door had reinforced them, and now clue after clue presented itself to him – the stern light at the door, the bulk of the chimney, the width of the floorboards and the pieces set into them to resemble pegs. While Lawrence was lecturing me on these frailties, the others came up from the court. As soon as Mother saw Lawrence, she responded, and I saw that there was little hope of any rapport between the matriarch and the changeling. She took Chaddy's arm. 'Let's go swimming and have Martinis on the beach,' she said. 'Let's have a *fabulous* morning.'

The sea that morning was a solid color, like verd stone. Everyone went to the beach but Tifty and Ruth. 'I don't mind *him*,' Mother said. She was excited, and she tipped her glass and spilled some gin into the sand. 'I don't mind *him*. It doesn't matter to me how *rude* and *horrid* and *gloomy* he is, but what I can't bear are the faces of his wretched little children, those fabulously unhappy little children.' With the height of the cliff between us, everyone talked wrathfully about Lawrence; about how he had grown worse instead of better, how unlike the rest of us he was, how he endeavored to spoil every pleasure. We drank our gin; the abuse seemed to reach a crescendo, and then, one by one, we went swimming in the solid green water. But when we came out no one mentioned Lawrence unkindly; the line of abusive conversation had been cut, as if swimming had the cleansing force claimed for baptism. We dried our hands and lighted cigarettes, and if Lawrence was mentioned, it was only to suggest, kindly, something that might please him. Wouldn't he like to sail to Barin's cove, or go fishing?

And now I remember that while Lawrence was visiting us, we went swimming oftener than we usually do, and I think there was a reason for this. When the irritability that accumulated as a result of his company began to lessen our patience, not only with Lawrence but with one another, we would all go swimming and shed our animus in the cold water. I can see the family now, smarting from Lawrence's rebukes as they sat on the sand, and I can see them wading and diving and surface-diving and hear in their voices the restoration of patience and the rediscovery of inexhaustible good will. If Lawrence noticed this change – this illusion of purification – I suppose that he would have found in the vocabulary of psychiatry, or the mythology of the Atlantic, some circumspect name for it, but I don't think he noticed the change. He neglected to name the curative powers of the open sea, but it was one of the few chances for diminution that he missed.

The cook we had that year was a Polish woman named Anna Ostrovick, a summer cook. She was first-rate – a big, fat, hearty, industrious woman who took her work seriously. She liked to cook and to have the food she cooked appreciated and eaten, and whenever we saw her, she always urged us to eat. She cooked hot bread – crescents and brioches – for breakfast two or three times a week, and she would bring these into the dining room herself and say, 'Eat, eat, eat!' When the maid took the serving dishes back into the pantry, we could sometimes hear Anna, who was standing there, say, 'Good! They eat.' She fed the garbage man, the milkman, and the gardener. 'Eat!' she told them. 'Eat, eat!' On Thursday afternoons, she went to the movies with the maid, but she didn't enjoy the movies, because the actors were all so thin. She would sit in the dark theater for an hour and a half watching the screen anxiously for the appearance of someone who had enjoyed his food. Bette Davis merely left with Anna the impression of a woman who has not eaten well. 'They are all so skinny,' she would say when she left the movies. In the evenings, after she had gorged all of us, and washed the pots and pans, she would collect the table scraps and go out to feed the creation. We had a few chickens that year, and although they would have roosted by then, she would dump food into their troughs and urge the sleeping fowl to eat. She fed the songbirds in the orchard and the chipmunks in the yard. Her appearance at the edge of the garden and her urgent voice – we could hear her calling 'Eat, eat, eat' – had become, like the sunset gun at the boat club and the passage of light from Cape Heron, attached to that hour. 'Eat, eat, eat,' we could hear Anna say. 'Eat, eat . . .' Then it would be dark.

When Lawrence had been there three days, Anna called me into the kitchen. 'You tell your mother,' she said, 'that *he* doesn't come into my kitchen. If *he* comes into my kitchen all the time, I go. *He* is always coming into my kitchen to tell me what a sad woman I am. He is always telling me that I work too hard and that I don't get paid enough and that I should belong to a union with vacations. Ha! He is so skinny but he is always coming into my kitchen when I am busy to pity me, but I am as good as him, I am as good as *anybody*, and I do not have to have people like that getting into my way all the time and feeling sorry for me. I am a famous and a wonderful cook and I have jobs everywhere and the only reason I come here to work this summer is because I was never before on an island, but I can have other jobs tomorrow, and if he is always coming into my kitchen to pity me, you tell your mother I am going. I am as good as *anybody* and I do not have to have that skinny all the time telling how poor I am.'

I was pleased to find that the cook was on our side, but I felt that the situation was delicate. If Mother asked Lawrence to stay out of the kitchen, he would make a grievance out of the request. He could make a grievance out of anything, and it sometimes seemed that as he sat darkly at the dinner table, every word of disparagement, wherever it was aimed, came home to him. I didn't mention the cook's complaint to anyone, but somehow there wasn't any more trouble from that quarter.

The next cause for contention that I had from Lawrence came over our backgammon games.

When we are at Laud's Head, we play a lot of backgammon. At eight o'clock, after we have drunk our coffee, we usually get out the board. In a way, it is one of our pleasantest hours. The lamps in the room are still unlighted, Anna can be seen in the dark garden, and in the sky above her head there are continents of shadow and fire. Mother turns on the light and rattles the dice as a signal. We usually play three games apiece, each with the others. We play for money, and you can win or lose a hundred dollars on a game, but the stakes are usually much lower. I think that Lawrence used to play – I can't remember – but he doesn't play any more. He doesn't gamble. This is not because he is poor or because he has any principles about gambling but because he thinks the game is foolish and a waste of time. He was ready enough, however, to waste his time watching the rest of us play. Night after night, when the game began, he pulled a chair up beside the board, and watched the checkers and the dice. His expression was scornful, and yet he watched carefully. I wondered why he watched us night after night, and, through watching his face, I think that I may have found out.

Lawrence doesn't gamble, so he can't understand the excitement of winning and losing money. He has forgotten how to play the game, I think, so that its complex odds can't interest him. His observations were bound to include the facts that backgammon is an idle game and a game of chance, and that the board, marked with points, was a symbol of our worthlessness. And since he doesn't understand gambling or the odds of the game, I thought that what interested him must be the members of his family. One night when I was playing with Odette – I had won thirty-seven dollars from Mother and Chaddy – I think I saw what was going on in his mind.

Odette has black hair and black eyes. She is careful never to expose her white skin to the sun for long, so the striking contrast of blackness and pallor is not changed in the summer. She needs and deserves admiration – it is the element that contents her – and she will flirt, unseriously, with any man. Her shoulders were bare that night, her dress was cut to show the division of her breasts and to show her breasts when she leaned over the board to play. She kept losing and flirting and making her losses seem like a part of the flirtation. Chaddy was in the other room. She lost three games, and when the third game ended, she fell back on the sofa and, looking at me squarely, said something about going out on the dunes to settle the score. Lawrence heard her. I looked at Lawrence. He seemed shocked and gratified at the same time, as if he had suspected all along that we were not playing for anything so insubstantial as money. I may be wrong, of course, but I think that Lawrence felt that in watching our backgammon he was observing the progress of a mordant tragedy in which the money we won and lost served as a symbol for more vital forfeits. It is like Lawrence to try to read significance and finality into every gesture that we make, and it is certain of Lawrence that when he finds the inner logic to our conduct, it will be sordid.

Chaddy came in to play with me. Chaddy and I have never liked to lose to each other. When we were younger, we used to be forbidden to play games together, because they always ended in a fight. We think we know each other's mettle intimately. I think he is prudent; he thinks I am foolish. There is always bad blood when we play anything – tennis or backgammon or softball or bridge – and it does seem at times as if we were playing for the possession of each other's liberties. When I lose to Chaddy, I can't sleep. All this is only half the truth of our competitive relationship, but it was the half-truth that would be discernible to Lawrence, and his presence at the table made me so self-conscious that I lost two games. I tried not to seem angry when I got up from the board. Lawrence was watching me. I went out onto the terrace to suffer there in the dark the anger I always feel when I lose to Chaddy.

When I came back into the room, Chaddy and Mother were playing. Lawrence was still watching. By his lights, Odette had lost her virtue to me, I had lost my self-esteem to Chaddy, and now I wondered what he saw in the present match. He watched raptly, as if the opaque checkers and the marked board served for an exchange of critical power. How dramatic the board, in its ring of light, and the quiet players and the crash of the sea outside must have seemed to him! Here was spiritual cannibalism made visible; here, under his nose, were the symbols of the rapacious use human beings make of one another.

Mother plays a shrewd, an ardent, and an interfering game. She always has her hands in her opponent's board. When she plays with Chaddy, who is her favorite, she plays intently. Lawrence would have noticed this. Mother is a sentimental woman. Her heart is good and easily moved

by tears and frailty, a characteristic that, like her handsome nose, has not been changed at all by age. Grief in
another provokes her deeply, and she seems at times to be
trying to divine in Chaddy some grief, some loss, that she
can succor and redress, and so re-establish the relationship that she enjoyed with him when he was sickly and
young. She loves defending the weak and the childlike, and
now that we are old, she misses it. The world of debts
and business, men and war, hunting and fishing has on her
an exacerbating effect. (When Father drowned, she threw
away his fly rods and his guns.) She has lectured us all endlessly on self-reliance, but when we come back to her for
comfort and for help – particularly Chaddy – she seems to
feel most like herself. I suppose Lawrence thought that the
old woman and her son were playing for each other's soul.

She lost. 'Oh *dear*,' she said. She looked stricken and
bereaved, as she always does when she loses. 'Get me my
glasses, get me my checkbook, get me something to drink.'
Lawrence got up at last and stretched his legs. He looked
at us all bleakly. The wind and the sea had risen, and I
thought that if he heard the waves, he must hear them only
as a dark answer to all his dark questions; that he would
think that the tide had expunged the embers of our picnic
fires. The company of a lie is unbearable, and he seemed
like the embodiment of a lie. I couldn't explain to him the
simple and intense pleasures of playing for money, and it
seemed to me hideously wrong that he should have sat at
the edge of the board and concluded that we were playing

for one another's soul. He walked restlessly around the room two or three times and then, as usual, gave us a parting shot. 'I should think you'd go crazy,' he said, 'cooped up with one another like this, night after night. Come on, Ruth. I'm going to bed.'

THAT NIGHT, I dreamed about Lawrence. I saw his plain face magnified into ugliness, and when I woke in the morning, I felt sick, as if I had suffered a great spiritual loss while I slept, like the loss of courage and heart. It was foolish to let myself be troubled by my brother. I needed a vacation. I needed to relax. At school, we live in one of the dormitories, we eat at the house table, and we never get away. I not only teach English winter and summer but I work in the principal's office and fire the pistol at track meets. I needed to get away from this and from every other form of anxiety, and I decided to avoid my brother. Early that day, I took Helen and the children sailing, and we stayed out until suppertime. The next day, we went on a picnic. Then I had to go to New York for a day, and when I got back, there was the costume dance at the boat club. Lawrence wasn't going to this, and it's a party where I always have a wonderful time.

The invitations that year said to come as you wish you were. After several conversations, Helen and I had decided what to wear. The thing she most wanted to be again, she said, was a bride, and so she decided to wear her wedding dress. I thought this was a good choice – sincere, lighthearted, and inexpensive. Her choice influenced mine, and I decided to wear an old football uniform. Mother decided to go as Jenny Lind, because there was an old Jenny Lind costume in the attic. The others decided to rent costumes, and when I went to New York, I got the clothes. Lawrence and Ruth didn't enter into any of this.

Helen was on the dance committee, and she spent most of Friday decorating the club. Diana and Chaddy and I went sailing. Most of the sailing that I do these days is in Manhasset, and I am used to setting a homeward course by the gasoline barge and the tin roofs of the boat shed, and it was a pleasure that afternoon, as we returned, to keep the bow on a white church spire in the village and to find even the inshore water green and clear. At the end of our sail, we stopped at the club to get Helen. The committee had been trying to give a submarine appearance to the ballroom, and the fact that they had nearly succeeded in accomplishing this illusion made Helen very happy. We drove back to Laud's Head. It had been a brilliant afternoon, but on the way home we could smell the east wind – the dark wind, as Lawrence would have said – coming in from the sea.

My wife, Helen, is thirty-eight, and her hair would be gray, I guess, if it were not dyed, but it is dyed an unobtrusive yellow – a faded color – and I think it becomes her. I mixed cocktails that night while she was dressing, and when I took a glass upstairs to her, I saw her for the first time since our marriage in her wedding dress. There would be no point in saying that she looked to me more beautiful than she did on our wedding day, but because I have grown older and have, I think, a greater depth of feeling, and because I could see in her face that night both youth and age, both her devotion to the young woman that she had been and the positions that she had yielded graciously to time, I think I have never been so deeply moved. I had already put on the football uniform, and the weight of it, the heaviness of the pants and the shoulder guards, had worked a change in me, as if in putting on these old clothes I had put off the reasonable anxieties and troubles of my life. It felt as if we had both returned to the years before our marriage, the years before the war.

The Collards had a big dinner party before the dance, and our family – excepting Lawrence and Ruth – went to this. We drove over to the club, through the fog, at about half past nine. The orchestra was playing a waltz. While I was checking my raincoat, someone hit me on the back. It was Chucky Ewing, and the funny thing was that Chucky had on a football uniform. This seemed comical as hell to both of us. We were laughing when we went down the hall to the dance floor. I stopped at the door to look at the party, and it was beautiful. The committee had hung fish nets around the sides and over the high ceiling. The nets on the ceiling were filled with colored balloons. The light was soft and uneven, and the people – our friends and neighbors – dancing in the soft light to 'Three O'Clock in the Morning' made a pretty picture. Then I noticed the number of women dressed in white, and I realized that they, like Helen, were wearing wedding dresses. Patsy Hewitt and Mrs Gear and the Lackland girl waltzed by, dressed as brides. Then Pep Talcott came over to where Chucky and I were standing. He was dressed to be Henry VIII, but he told us that the Auerbach twins and Henry Barrett and Dwight MacGregor were all wearing football uniforms, and that by the last count there were ten brides on the floor.

This coincidence, this funny coincidence, kept everybody laughing, and made this one of the most lighthearted parties we've ever had at the club. At first I thought that the women had planned with one another to wear wedding dresses, but the ones that I danced with said it was a coincidence and I'm sure that Helen had made her decision alone. Everything went smoothly for me until a little before midnight. I saw Ruth standing at the edge of the floor. She was wearing a long red dress. It was all wrong. It wasn't the spirit of the party at all. I danced with her, but no one cut in, and I was darned if I'd spend the rest of the night dancing with her and I asked her where Lawrence was. She said he was out on the dock, and I took her over to the bar and left her and went out to get Lawrence.

The east fog was thick and wet, and he was alone on the dock. He was not in costume. He had not even bothered to get himself up as a fisherman or a sailor. He looked particularly saturnine. The fog blew around us like a cold smoke. I wished that it had been a clear night, because the

easterly fog seemed to play into my misanthropic brother's hands. And I knew that the buoys – the groaners and
bells that we could hear then – would sound to him like
half-human, half-drowned cries, although every sailor
knows that buoys are necessary and reliable fixtures, and I
knew that the foghorn at the lighthouse would mean wanderings and losses to him and that he could misconstrue
the vivacity of the dance music. 'Come on in, Tifty,' I said,
'and dance with your wife or get her some partners.'

'Why should I?' he said. 'Why should I?' And he walked
to the window and looked in at the party. 'Look at it,' he
said. 'Look at that . . .'

Chucky Ewing had got hold of a balloon and was trying
to organize a scrimmage line in the middle of the floor. The
others were dancing a samba. And I knew that Lawrence
was looking bleakly at the party as he had looked at the
weather-beaten shingles on our house, as if he saw here an
abuse and a distortion of time; as if in wanting to be brides
and football players we exposed the fact that, the lights of
youth having been put out in us, we had been unable to
find other lights to go by and, destitute of faith and principle, had become foolish and sad. And that he was thinking
this about so many kind and happy and generous people
made me angry, made me feel for him such an unnatural
abhorrence that I was ashamed, for he is my brother and a
Pommeroy. I put my arm around his shoulders and tried to
force him to come in, but he wouldn't.

I got back in time for the Grand March, and after the

prizes had been given out for the best costumes, they let the balloons down. The room was hot, and someone opened the big doors onto the dock, and the easterly wind circled the room and went out, carrying across the dock and out onto the water most of the balloons. Chucky Ewing went running out after the balloons, and when he saw them pass the dock and settle on the water, he took off his football uniform and dove in. Then Eric Auerbach dove in and Lew Phillips dove in and I dove in, and you know how it is at a party after midnight when people start jumping into the water. We recovered most of the balloons and dried off and went on dancing, and we didn't get home until morning.

THE NEXT DAY was the day of the flower show. Mother and Helen and Odette all had entries. We had a pickup lunch, and Chaddy drove the women and children over to the show. I took a nap, and in the middle of the afternoon I got some trunks and a towel and, on leaving the house, passed Ruth in the laundry. She was washing clothes. I don't know why she should seem to have so much more work to do than anyone else, but she is always washing or ironing or mending clothes. She may have been taught, when she was young, to spend her time like this, or she may be at the mercy of an expiatory passion. She seems to scrub and iron with a penitential fervor, although I can't imagine what it is that she thinks she's done wrong. Her children were with her in the laundry. I offered to take them to the beach, but they didn't want to go.

It was late in August, and the wild grapes that grow pro-
fusely all over the island made the land wind smell of wine.
There is a little grove of holly at the end of the path, and
then you climb the dunes, where nothing grows but that
coarse grass. I could hear the sea, and I remember thinking
how Chaddy and I used to talk mystically about the sea.
When we were young, we had decided that we could never
live in the West because we would miss the sea. 'It is very
nice here,' we used to say politely when we visited people
in the mountains, 'but we miss the Atlantic.' We used to
look down our noses at people from Iowa and Colorado
who had been denied this revelation, and we scorned the
Pacific. Now I could hear the waves, whose heaviness
sounded like a reverberation, like a tumult, and it pleased
me as it had pleased me when I was young, and it seemed
to have a purgative force, as if it had cleared my memory
of, among other things, the penitential image of Ruth in
the laundry.

But Lawrence was on the beach. There he sat. I went in
without speaking. The water was cold, and when I came
out, I put on a shirt. I told him that I was going to walk up
to Tanners Point, and he said that he would come with me.
I tried to walk beside him. His legs are no longer than
mine, but he always likes to stay a little ahead of his companion. Walking along behind him, looking at his bent
head and his shoulders, I wondered what he could make of
that landscape.

There were the dunes and cliffs, and then, where they

declined, there were some fields that had begun to turn from green to brown and yellow. The fields were used for pasturing sheep, and I guess Lawrence would have noticed that the soil was eroded and that the sheep would accelerate this decay. Beyond the fields there are a few coastal farms, with square and pleasant buildings, but Lawrence could have pointed out the hard lot of an island farmer. The sea, at our other side, was the open sea. We always tell guests that there, to the east, lies the coast of Portugal, and for Lawrence it would be an easy step from the coast of Portugal to the tyranny in Spain. The waves broke with a noise like a 'hurrah, hurrah, hurrah,' but to Lawrence they would say '*Vale, vale.*' I suppose it would have occurred to his baleful and incisive mind that the coast was terminal moraine, the edge of the prehistoric world, and it must have occurred to him that we walked along the edge of the known world in spirit as much as in fact. If he should otherwise have overlooked this, there were some Navy planes bombing an uninhabited island to remind him.

That beach is a vast and preternaturally clean and simple landscape. It is like a piece of the moon. The surf had pounded the floor solid, so it was easy walking, and everything left on the sand had been twice changed by the waves. There was the spine of a shell, a broomstick, part of a bottle and part of a brick, both of them milled and broken until they were nearly unrecognizable, and I suppose Lawrence's sad frame of mind – for he kept his head down – went from one broken thing to another. The company of his pessimism began to infuriate me, and I caught up with him and put a hand on his shoulder. 'It's only a summer day, Tifty,' I said. 'It's only a summer day. What's the matter? Don't you like it here?'

'I don't like it here,' he said blandly, without raising his eyes. 'I'm going to sell my equity in the house to Chaddy. I didn't expect to have a good time. The only reason I came back was to say goodbye.'

I let him get ahead again and I walked behind him, looking at his shoulders and thinking of all the goodbyes he had made. When Father drowned, he went to church and said goodbye to Father. It was only three years later that he concluded that Mother was frivolous and said goodbye to her. In his freshman year at college, he had been very good friends with his roommate, but the man drank too much, and at the beginning of the spring term Lawrence changed roommates and said goodbye to his friend. When he had been in college for two years, he concluded that the atmosphere was too sequestered and he said goodbye to Yale. He enrolled at Columbia and got his law degree there, but he found his first employer dishonest, and at the end of six months he said goodbye to a good job. He married Ruth in City Hall and said goodbye to the Protestant Episcopal Church; they went to live on a back street in Tuckahoe and said goodbye to the middle class. In 1938, he went to Washington to work as a government lawyer, saying goodbye to private enterprise, but after eight months in Washington he concluded that the Roosevelt administration was sentimental and he said goodbye to it. They left Washington for a suburb of Chicago, where he said goodbye to his neighbors, one by one, on counts of drunkenness, boorishness, and stupidity. He said goodbye to Chicago and went to Kansas; he said goodbye to Kansas and went to Cleveland. Now he had said goodbye to Cleveland and come East again, stopping at Laud's Head long enough to say goodbye to the sea.

It was elegiac and it was bigoted and narrow, it mistook circumspection for character, and I wanted to help him. 'Come out of it,' I said. 'Come out of it, Tifty.'

'Come out of what?'

'Come out of this gloominess. Come out of it. It's only a summer day. You're spoiling your own good time and you're spoiling everyone else's. We need a vacation, Tifty. I need one. I need to rest. We all do. And you've made everything tense and unpleasant. I only have two weeks in the year. Two weeks. I need to have a good time and so do all the others. We need to rest. You think that your pessimism is an advantage, but it's nothing but an unwillingness to grasp realities.'

'What are the realities?' he said. 'Diana is a foolish and a promiscuous woman. So is Odette. Mother is an alcoholic. If she doesn't discipline herself, she'll be in a hospital in a year or two. Chaddy is dishonest. He always has been. The house is going to fall into the sea.' He looked at me and added, as an afterthought, 'You're a fool.'

'You're a gloomy son of a bitch,' I said. 'You're a gloomy son of a bitch.'

'Get your fat face out of mine,' he said. He walked along.

Then I picked up a root and, coming at his back – although I have never hit a man from the back before – I swung the root, heavy with sea water, behind me, and the momentum sped my arm and I gave him, my brother, a blow on the head that forced him to his knees on the sand, and I saw the blood come out and begin to darken his hair. Then I wished that he was dead, dead and about to be buried, not buried but about to be buried, because I did not want to be denied ceremony and decorum in putting him away, in putting him out of my consciousness, and I saw the rest of us – Chaddy and Mother and Diana and Helen – in mourning in the house on Belvedere Street that was torn down twenty years ago, greeting our guests and our relatives at the door and answering their mannerly condolences with mannerly grief. Nothing decorous was lacking so that even if he had been murdered on a beach, one would feel before the tiresome ceremony ended that he had come into the winter of his life and that it was a law of nature, and a beautiful one, that Tifty should be buried in the cold, cold ground.

He was still on his knees. I looked up and down. No one had seen us. The naked beach, like a piece of the moon, reached to invisibility. The spill of a wave, in a glancing run, shot up to where he knelt. I would still have liked to end him, but now I had begun to act like two men, the murderer and the Samaritan. With a swift roar, like hollowness made sound, a white wave reached him and encircled him, boiling over his shoulders, and I held him against the undertow. Then I led him to a higher place. The blood had spread all through his hair, so that it looked black. I took off my shirt and tore it to bind up his head. He was conscious, and I didn't think he was badly hurt. He didn't speak. Neither did I. Then I left him there.

I walked a little way down the beach and turned to watch him, and I was thinking of my own skin then. He had got to his feet and he seemed steady. The daylight was still clear, but on the sea wind fumes of brine were blowing in like a light fog, and when I had walked a little way from him, I could hardly see his dark figure in this obscurity. All down the beach I could see the heavy salt air blowing in. Then I turned my back on him, and as I got near to the house, I went swimming again, as I seem to have done after every encounter with Lawrence that summer.

When I got back to the house, I lay down on the terrace. The others came back. I could hear Mother defaming the flower arrangements that had won prizes. None of ours had won anything. Then the house quieted, as it always does at that hour. The children went into the kitchen to get supper and the others went upstairs to bathe. Then I heard Chaddy making cocktails, and the conversation about the flower-show judges was resumed. Then Mother cried, 'Tifty! Tifty! Oh, Tifty!'

He stood in the door, looking half dead. He had taken off the bloody bandage and he held it in his hand. 'My brother did this,' he said. 'My brother did it. He hit me with a stone – something – on the beach.' His voice broke with self-pity. I thought he was going to cry. No one else spoke. 'Where's Ruth?' he cried. 'Where's Ruth? Where in hell is Ruth? I want her to start packing. I don't have any more time to waste here. I have important things to do. I have *important* things to do.' And he went up the stairs.

THEY LEFT FOR the mainland the next morning, taking the six o'clock boat. Mother got up to say goodbye, but she was the only one, and it is a harsh and an easy scene to imagine – the matriarch and the changeling, looking at each other with a dismay that would seem like the powers of love reversed. I heard the children's voices and the car go down the drive, and I got up and went to the window, and what a morning that was! Jesus, what a morning! The wind was northerly. The air was clear. In the early heat, the roses in the garden smelled like strawberry jam. While I was dressing, I heard the boat whistle, first the warning signal and then the double blast, and I could see the good people on the top deck drinking coffee out of fragile paper cups, and Lawrence at the bow, saying to the sea, '*Thalassa, thalassa*,' while his timid and unhappy children watched the creation from the encirclement of their mother's arms. The buoys would toll mournfully for Lawrence, and while the grace of the light would make it an exertion not to throw out your arms and swear exultantly, Lawrence's eyes would trace the black sea as it fell astern;

he would think of the bottom, dark and strange, where full fathom five our father lies.

Oh, what can you do with a man like that? What can you do? How can you dissuade his eye in a crowd from seeking out the cheek with acne, the infirm hand; how can you teach him to respond to the inestimable greatness of the race, the harsh surface beauty of life; how can you put his finger for him on the obdurate truths before which fear and horror are powerless? The sea that morning was iridescent and dark. My wife and my sister were swimming – Diana and Helen – and I saw their uncovered heads, black and gold in the dark water. I saw them come out and I saw that they were naked, unshy, beautiful, and full of grace, and I watched the naked women walk out of the sea.

Reunion

THE LAST TIME I saw my father was in Grand Central Station. I was going from my grandmother's in the Adirondacks to a cottage on the Cape that my mother had rented, and I wrote my father that I would be in New York between trains for an hour and a half, and asked if we could have lunch together. His secretary wrote to say that he would meet me at the information booth at noon, and at twelve o'clock sharp I saw him coming through the crowd. He was a stranger to me – my mother divorced him three years ago and I hadn't been with him since – but as soon as I saw him I felt that he was my father, my flesh and blood, my future and my doom. I knew that when I was grown I would be something like him; I would have to plan my campaigns within his limitations. He was a big, good-looking man, and I was terribly happy to see him again. He struck me on the back and shook my hand. 'Hi, Charlie,' he said. 'Hi, boy. I'd like to take you up to my club, but it's in the Sixties, and if you have to catch an early train I guess we'd better get something to eat around here.' He put his arm around me, and I smelled my father the way my mother sniffs a rose. It was a rich compound of whiskey, after-shave lotion, shoe polish, woolens, and the rankness of a mature male. I hoped that someone would see us together. I wished that we could be photographed. I wanted some record of our having been together.

We went out of the station and up a side street to a restaurant. It was still early, and the place was empty. The bartender was quarreling with a delivery boy, and there was one very old waiter in a red coat down by the kitchen door. We sat down, and my father hailed the waiter in a loud voice. '*Kellner!*' he shouted. '*Garçon! Cameriere! You!*' His boisterousness in the empty restaurant seemed out of place. 'Could we have a little service here!' he shouted. 'Chop-chop.' Then he clapped his hands. This caught the waiter's attention, and he shuffled over to our table.

'Were you clapping your hands at me?' he asked.

'Calm down, calm down, *sommelier*,' my father said. 'If it isn't too much to ask of you – if it wouldn't be too much above and beyond the call of duty, we would like a couple of Beefeater Gibsons.'

'I don't like to be clapped at,' the waiter said.

'I should have brought my whistle,' my father said. 'I have a whistle that is audible only to the ears of old waiters. Now, take out your little pad and your little pencil and see if you can get this straight: two Beefeater Gibsons. Repeat after me: two Beefeater Gibsons.'

'I think you'd better go somewhere else,' the waiter said quietly.

'That,' said my father, 'is one of the most brilliant suggestions I have ever heard. Come on, Charlie, let's get the hell out of here.'

I followed my father out of that restaurant into another. He was not so boisterous this time. Our drinks came, and he cross-questioned me about the baseball season. He then struck the edge of his empty glass with his knife and began shouting again. '*Garçon! Kellner! Cameriere! You!* Could we trouble you to bring us two more of the same.'

'How old is the boy?' the waiter asked.

'That,' my father said, 'is none of your God-damned business.'

'I'm sorry, sir,' the waiter said, 'but I won't serve the boy another drink.'

'Well, I have some news for you,' my father said. 'I have some very interesting news for you. This doesn't happen to be the only restaurant in New York. They've opened another on the corner. Come on, Charlie.'

He paid the bill, and I followed him out of that restaurant into another. Here the waiters wore pink jackets like hunting coats, and there was a lot of horse tack on the walls. We sat down, and my father began to shout again. 'Master of the hounds! Tallyhoo and all that sort of thing. We'd like a little something in the way of a stirrup cup. Namely, two Bibson Geefeaters.'

We'd like a little something in the way of a stirrup cup. Namely, two Bibson Geefeaters

'Two Bibson Geefeaters?' the waiter asked, smiling.

'You know damned well what I want,' my father said angrily. 'I want two Beefeater Gibsons, and make it snappy. Things have changed in jolly old England. So my friend the duke tells me. Let's see what England can produce in the way of a cocktail.'

'This isn't England,' the waiter said.

'Don't argue with me,' my father said. 'Just do as you're told.'

'I just thought you might like to know where you are,' the waiter said.

'If there is one thing I cannot tolerate,' my father said, 'it is an impudent domestic. Come on, Charlie.'

The fourth place we went to was Italian. '*Buon giorno,*' my father said. '*Per favore, possiamo avere due cocktail americani, forti, forti. Molto gin, poco vermut.*'

'I don't understand Italian,' the waiter said.

'Oh, come off it,' my father said. 'You understand Italian, and you know damned well you do. *Vogliamo due cocktail americani. Subito.*'

The waiter left us and spoke with the captain, who came over to our table and said, 'I'm sorry, sir, but this table is reserved.'

'All right,' my father said. 'Get us another table.'

'All the tables are reserved,' the captain said.

'I get it,' my father said. 'You don't desire our patronage. Is that it? Well, the hell with you. *Vada all' inferno.* Let's go, Charlie.'

'I have to get my train,' I said.

'I'm sorry, sonny,' my father said. 'I'm terribly sorry.' He put his arm around me and pressed me against him. 'I'll walk you back to the station. If there had only been time to go up to my club.'

'That's all right, Daddy,' I said.

'I'll get you a paper,' he said. 'I'll get you a paper to read on the train.'

Then he went up to a newsstand and said, 'Kind sir, will you be good enough to favor me with one of your God-damned, no-good, ten-cent afternoon papers?' The clerk turned away from him and stared at a magazine cover. 'Is it asking too much, kind sir,' my father said, 'is it asking too much for you to sell me one of your disgusting specimens of yellow journalism?'

'I have to go, Daddy,' I said. 'It's late.'

'Now, just wait a second, sonny,' he said. 'Just wait a second. I want to get a rise out of this chap.'

'Goodbye, Daddy,' I said, and I went down the stairs and got my train, and that was the last time I saw my father.

The Swimmer

IT WAS ONE of those midsummer Sundays when everyone sits around saying, 'I *drank* too much last night.' You might have heard it whispered by the parishioners leaving church, heard it from the lips of the priest himself, struggling with his cassock in the *vestiarium*, heard it from the golf links and the tennis courts, heard it from the wildlife preserve where the leader of the Audubon group was suffering from a terrible hangover. 'I *drank* too much,' said Donald Westerhazy. 'We all *drank* too much,' said Lucinda Merrill. 'It must have been the wine,' said Helen Westerhazy. 'I *drank* too much of that claret.'

This was at the edge of the Westerhazys' pool. The pool, fed by an artesian well with a high iron content, was a pale shade of green. It was a fine day. In the west there was a massive stand of cumulus cloud so like a city seen from a distance – from the bow of an approaching ship – that it might have had a name. Lisbon. Hackensack. The sun was hot. Neddy Merrill sat by the green water, one hand in it, one around a glass of gin. He was a slender man – he seemed to have the especial slenderness of youth – and while he was far from young he had slid down his banister that morning and given the bronze backside of Aphrodite on the hall table a smack, as he jogged toward the smell of coffee in his dining room. He might have been compared to a summer's day, particularly the last hours of one, and while he lacked a tennis racket or a sail bag the impression was definitely one of youth, sport, and clement weather. He had been swimming and now he was breathing deeply, stertorously as if he could gulp into his lungs the components of that moment, the heat of the sun, the intenseness of his pleasure. It all seemed to flow into his chest. His own house stood in Bullet Park, eight miles to the south, where his four beautiful daughters would have had their lunch and might be playing tennis. Then it occurred to him that by taking a dogleg to the southwest he could reach his home by water.

His life was not confining and the delight he took in this observation could not be explained by its suggestion of escape. He seemed to see, with a cartographer's eye, that string of swimming pools, that quasi-subterranean stream that curved across the county. He had made a discovery, a contribution to modern geography; he would name the stream Lucinda after his wife. He was not a practical joker nor was he a fool but he was determinedly original and had a vague and modest idea of himself as a legendary figure. The day was beautiful and it seemed to him that a long swim might enlarge and celebrate its beauty.

He took off a sweater that was hung over his shoulders and dove in. He had an inexplicable contempt for men who did not hurl themselves into pools. He swam a choppy crawl, breathing either with every stroke or every fourth stroke and counting somewhere well in the back of his mind the one-two one-two of a flutter kick. It was not a serviceable stroke for long distances but the domestication of swimming had saddled the sport with some customs and in his part of the world a crawl was customary. To be embraced and sustained by the light green water was less a pleasure, it seemed, than the resumption of a natural condition, and he would have liked to swim without trunks, but this was not possible, considering his project. He hoisted himself up on the far curb – he never used the ladder – and started across the lawn. When Lucinda asked where he was going he said he was going to swim home.

The only maps and charts he had to go by were remembered or imaginary but these were clear enough. First there were the Grahams, the Hammers, the Lears, the Howlands, and the Crosscups. He would cross Ditmar Street to the Bunkers and come, after a short portage, to the Levys, the Welchers, and the public pool in Lancaster. Then there were the Hallorans, the Sachses, the Biswangers, Shirley Adams, the Gilmartins, and the Clydes. The day was lovely, and that he lived in a world so generously supplied with water seemed like a clemency, a beneficence. His heart was high and he ran across the grass. Making his way home by an uncommon route gave him the feeling that he was a pilgrim, an explorer, a man with a destiny, and he knew that he would find friends all along the way; friends would line the banks of the Lucinda River.

He went through a hedge that separated the Westerhazys' land from the Grahams', walked under some flowering apple trees, passed the shed that housed their pump and filter, and came out at the Grahams' pool. 'Why, Neddy,' Mrs Graham said, 'what a marvelous surprise. I've been trying to get you on the phone all morning. Here, let me get you a drink.' He saw then, like any explorer, that the hospitable customs and traditions of the natives would have to be handled with diplomacy if he was ever going to reach his destination. He did not want to mystify or seem rude to the Grahams nor did he have the time to linger there. He swam the length of their pool and joined them in the sun and was rescued, a few minutes later, by the arrival of two carloads of friends from Connecticut. During the uproarious reunions he was able to slip away. He went down by the front of the Grahams' house, stepped over a thorny hedge, and crossed a vacant lot to the Hammers'. Mrs Hammer, looking up from her roses, saw him swim by although she wasn't quite sure who it was. The Lears heard him splashing past the open windows of their living room. The Howlands and the Crosscups were away. After leaving the Howlands' he crossed Ditmar Street and started for the Bunkers', where he could hear, even at that distance, the noise of a party.

The water refracted the sound of voices and laughter

and seemed to suspend it in midair. The Bunkers' pool was on a rise and he climbed some stairs to a terrace where twenty-five or thirty men and women were drinking. The only person in the water was Rusty Towers, who floated there on a rubber raft. Oh, how bonny and lush were the banks of the Lucinda River! Prosperous men and women gathered by the sapphire-colored waters while caterer's men in white coats passed them cold gin. Overhead a red de Haviland trainer was circling around and around and around in the sky with something like the glee of a child in a swing. Ned felt a passing affection for the scene, a tenderness for the gathering, as if it was something he might touch. In the distance he heard thunder. As soon as Enid Bunker saw him she began to scream: 'Oh, look who's here! What a marvelous surprise! When Lucinda said that you couldn't come I thought I'd *die*.' She made her way to him through the crowd, and when they had finished kissing she led him to the bar, a progress that was slowed by the fact that he stopped to kiss eight or ten other women and shake the hands of as many men. A smiling bartender he had seen at a hundred parties gave him a gin and tonic and he stood by the bar for a moment, anxious not to get stuck in any conversation that would delay his voyage. When he seemed about to be surrounded he dove in and swam close to the side to avoid colliding with Rusty's raft. At the far end of the pool he bypassed the Tomlinsons with a broad smile and jogged up the garden path. The gravel cut his feet but this was the only unpleasantness. The party was confined to the pool, and as he went toward the house he heard the brilliant, watery sound of voices fade, heard the noise of a radio from the Bunkers' kitchen, where someone was listening to a ball game. Sunday afternoon. He made his way through the parked cars and down the grassy border of their driveway to Alewives Lane. He did not want to be seen on the road in his bathing trunks but there was no traffic and he made the short distance to the Levys' driveway, marked with a PRIVATE PROPERTY sign and a green tube for *The New York Times*. All the doors and windows of the big house were open but there were no signs of life; not even a dog barked. He went around the side of the house to the pool and saw that the Levys had only recently left. Glasses and bottles and dishes of nuts were on a table at the deep end, where there was a bathhouse or gazebo, hung with Japanese lanterns. After swimming the pool he got himself a glass and poured a drink. It was his fourth or fifth drink and he had swum nearly half the length of the Lucinda River. He felt tired, clean, and pleased at that moment to be alone; pleased with everything.

It would storm. The stand of cumulus cloud – that city – had risen and darkened, and while he sat there he heard the percussiveness of thunder again. The de Haviland trainer was still circling overhead and it seemed to Ned that he could almost hear the pilot laugh with pleasure in the afternoon; but when there was another peal of thunder he took off for home. A train whistle blew and he wondered what time it had gotten to be. Four? Five? He thought of the provincial station at that hour, where a waiter, his tuxedo concealed by a raincoat, a dwarf with some flowers wrapped in newspaper, and a woman who had been crying would be waiting for the local. It was suddenly growing dark; it was that moment when the pin-headed birds seem to organize their song into some acute and knowledgeable recognition of the storm's approach. Then there was a fine noise of rushing water from the crown of an oak at his back, as if a spigot there had been turned. Then the noise of fountains came from the crowns of all the tall trees. Why did he love storms, what was the meaning of his excitement when the door sprang open and the rain wind fled rudely up the stairs, why had the simple task of shutting the windows of an old house seemed fitting and urgent, why did the first watery notes of a storm wind have for him the unmistakable sound of good news, cheer, glad tidings? Then there was an explosion, a smell of cordite, and rain lashed the Japanese lanterns that Mrs Levy had bought in Kyoto the year before last, or was it the year before that?

He stayed in the Levys' gazebo until the storm had passed. The rain had cooled the air and he shivered. The force of the wind had stripped a maple of its red and yellow leaves and scattered them over the grass and the water. Since it was midsummer the tree must be blighted, and yet he felt a peculiar sadness at this sign of autumn. He braced his shoulders, emptied his glass, and started for the Welchers' pool. This meant crossing the Lindleys' riding ring and he was surprised to find it overgrown with grass and all the jumps dismantled. He wondered if the Lindleys had sold their horses or gone away for the summer and put them out to board. He seemed to remember having heard something about the Lindleys and their horses but the memory was unclear. On he went, barefoot through the wet grass, to the Welchers', where he found their pool was dry.

This breach in his chain of water disappointed him absurdly, and he felt like some explorer who seeks a torrential headwater and finds a dead stream. He was disappointed and mystified. It was common enough to go away for the summer but no one ever drained his pool. The Welchers had definitely gone away. The pool furniture was folded, stacked, and covered with a tarpaulin. The bathhouse was locked. All the windows of the house were shut, and when he went around to the driveway in front he saw a FOR SALE sign nailed to a tree. When had he last heard from the Welchers – when, that is, had he and Lucinda last regretted an invitation to dine with them? It seemed only a week or so ago. Was his memory failing or had he so disciplined it in the repression of unpleasant facts that he had damaged his sense of the truth? Then in the distance he heard the sound of a tennis game. This cheered him, cleared away all his apprehensions and let him regard the overcast sky and the cold air with indifference. This was the day that Neddy Merrill swam across the county. That was the day! He started off then for his most difficult portage.

HAD YOU GONE for a Sunday afternoon ride that day you might have seen him, close to naked, standing on the shoulders of Route 424, waiting for a chance to cross. You might have wondered if he was the victim of foul play, had his car broken down, or was he merely a fool. Standing barefoot in the deposits of the highway – beer cans, rags, and blowout patches – exposed to all kinds of ridicule, he seemed pitiful. He had known when he started that this was a part of his journey – it had been on his maps – but confronted with the lines of traffic, worming through the summery light, he found himself unprepared. He was laughed at, jeered at, a beer can was thrown at him, and he had no dignity or humor to bring to the situation. He could have gone back, back to the Westerhazys', where Lucinda would still be sitting in the sun. He had signed nothing, vowed nothing, pledged nothing, not even to himself. Why, believing as he did, that all human obduracy was susceptible to common sense, was he unable to turn back? Why was he determined to complete his journey even if it meant putting his life in danger? At what point had this prank, this joke, this piece of horseplay become serious? He could not go back, he could not even recall with any clearness the green water at the Westerhazys', the sense of inhaling the day's components, the friendly and relaxed voices saying that they had *drunk* too much. In the space of an hour, more or less, he had covered a distance that made his return impossible.

An old man, tooling down the highway at fifteen miles

an hour, let him get to the middle of the road, where there was a grass divider. Here he was exposed to the ridicule of the northbound traffic, but after ten or fifteen minutes he was able to cross. From here he had only a short walk to the Recreation Center at the edge of the village of Lancaster, where there were some handball courts and a public pool.

The effect of the water on voices, the illusion of brilliance and suspense, was the same here as it had been at the Bunkers' but the sounds here were louder, harsher, and more shrill, and as soon as he entered the crowded enclosure he was confronted with regimentation. 'ALL SWIMMERS MUST TAKE A SHOWER BEFORE USING THE POOL. ALL SWIMMERS MUST USE THE FOOTBATH. ALL SWIMMERS MUST WEAR THEIR IDENTIFICATION DISKS.' He took a shower, washed his feet in a cloudy and bitter solution, and made his way to the edge of the water. It stank of chlorine and looked to him like a sink. A pair of lifeguards in a pair of towers blew police whistles at what seemed to be regular intervals and abused the swimmers through a public address system. Neddy remembered the sapphire water at the Bunkers' with longing and thought that he might contaminate himself – damage his own prosperousness and charm – by swimming in this murk, but he reminded himself that he was an explorer, a pilgrim, and that this was merely a stagnant bend in the Lucinda River. He dove, scowling with distaste, into the chlorine and had to swim with his head above water to avoid collisions, but even so he was bumped into, splashed, and jostled. When he got to the shallow end both lifeguards were shouting at him: 'Hey, you, you without the identification disk, get outa the water.' He did, but they had no way of pursuing him and he went through the reek of suntan oil and chlorine out through the hurricane fence and passed the handball courts. By crossing the road he entered the wooded part of the Halloran estate. The woods were not cleared and the footing was treacherous and difficult until he reached the lawn and the clipped beech hedge that encircled their pool.

The Hallorans were friends, an elderly couple of enormous wealth who seemed to bask in the suspicion that they might be Communists. They were zealous reformers but they were not Communists, and yet when they were accused, as they sometimes were, of subversion, it seemed to gratify and excite them. Their beech hedge was yellow and he guessed this had been blighted like the Levys' maple. He called hullo, hullo, to warn the Hallorans of his approach, to palliate his invasion of their privacy. The Hallorans, for reasons that had never been explained to him, did not wear bathing suits. No explanations were in order, really. Their nakedness was a detail in their uncompromising zeal for reform and he stepped politely out of his trunks before he went through the opening in the hedge.

Mrs Halloran, a stout woman with white hair and a serene face, was reading the *Times*. Mr Halloran was taking beech leaves out of the water with a scoop. They seemed not surprised or displeased to see him. Their pool was perhaps the oldest in the country, a fieldstone rectangle, fed by a brook. It had no filter or pump and its waters were the opaque gold of the stream.

'I'm swimming across the county,' Ned said.

'Why, I didn't know one could,' exclaimed Mrs Halloran.

'Well, I've made it from the Westerhazys',' Ned said. 'That must be about four miles.'

He left his trunks at the deep end, walked to the shallow end, and swam this stretch. As he was pulling himself out of the water he heard Mrs Halloran say, 'We've been *terribly* sorry to hear about all your misfortunes, Neddy.'

'My misfortunes?' Ned asked. 'I don't know what you mean.'

'Why, we heard that you'd sold the house and that your poor children . . .'

'I don't recall having sold the house,' Ned said, 'and the girls are at home.'

'Yes,' Mrs Halloran sighed. 'Yes . . .' Her voice filled the air with an unseasonable melancholy and Ned spoke briskly. 'Thank you for the swim.'

'Well, have a nice trip,' said Mrs Halloran.

Beyond the hedge he pulled on his trunks and fastened them. They were loose and he wondered if, during the space of an afternoon, he could have lost some weight. He was cold and he was tired and the naked Hallorans and their dark water had depressed him. The swim was too much for his strength but how could he have guessed this, sliding down the banister that morning and sitting in the Westerhazys' sun? His arms were lame. His legs felt rubbery and ached at the joints. The worst of it was the cold in his bones and the feeling that he might never be warm again. Leaves were falling down around him and he smelled wood smoke on the wind. Who would be burning wood at this time of year?

He needed a drink. Whiskey would warm him, pick him up, carry him through the last of his journey, refresh his feeling that it was original and valorous to swim across the county. Channel swimmers took brandy. He needed a stimulant. He crossed the lawn in front of the Hallorans' house and went down a little path to where they had built a house for their only daughter, Helen, and her husband, Eric Sachs. The Sachses' pool was small and he found Helen and her husband there.

'Oh, *Neddy*,' Helen said. 'Did you lunch at Mother's?'

'Not *really*,' Ned said. 'I *did* stop to see your parents.' This seemed to be explanation enough. 'I'm terribly sorry to break in on you like this but I've taken a chill and I wonder if you'd give me a drink.'

'Why, I'd *love* to,' Helen said, 'but there hasn't been anything in this house to drink since Eric's operation. That was three years ago.'

Was he losing his memory, had his gift for concealing painful facts let him forget that he had sold his house, that his children were in trouble, and that his friend had been ill? His eyes slipped from Eric's face to his abdomen, where he saw three pale, sutured scars, two of them at least a foot long. Gone was his navel, and what, Neddy thought, would the roving hand, bed-checking one's gifts at 3 A.M., make of a belly with no navel, no link to birth, this breach in the succession?

'I'm sure you can get a drink at the Biswangers',' Helen said. 'They're having an enormous do. You can hear it from here. Listen!'

She raised her head and from across the road, the lawns, the gardens, the woods, the fields, he heard again the brilliant noise of voices over water. 'Well, I'll get wet,' he said, still feeling that he had no freedom of choice about his means of travel. He dove into the Sachses' cold water and, gasping, close to drowning, made his way from one end of the pool to the other. 'Lucinda and I want *terribly* to see you,' he said over his shoulder, his face set toward the Biswangers'. 'We're sorry it's been so long and we'll call you *very* soon.'

He crossed some fields to the Biswangers' and the sounds of revelry there. They would be honored to give him a drink, they would be happy to give him a drink. The Biswangers invited him and Lucinda for dinner four times a year, six weeks in advance. They were always rebuffed and yet they continued to send out their invitations, unwilling to comprehend the rigid and undemocratic realities of their society. They were the sort of people who discussed the price of things at cocktails, exchanged market tips during dinner, and after dinner told dirty stories to mixed company. They did not belong to Neddy's set – they were not even on Lucinda's Christmas-card list. He went toward their pool with feelings of indifference, charity, and some unease, since it seemed to be getting dark and these were the longest days of the year. The party when he joined it was noisy and large. Grace Biswanger was the kind of hostess who asked the optometrist, the veterinarian, the real-estate dealer, and the dentist. No one was swimming and the twilight, reflected on the water of the pool, had a wintry gleam. There was a bar and he started for this. When Grace Biswanger saw him she came toward him, not affectionately as he had every right to expect, but bellicosely.

'Why, this party has everything,' she said loudly, 'including a gate crasher.'

She could not deal him a social blow – there was no question about this and he did not flinch. 'As a gate crasher,' he asked politely, 'do I rate a drink?'

'Suit yourself,' she said. 'You don't seem to pay much attention to invitations.'

She turned her back on him and joined some guests, and he went to the bar and ordered a whiskey. The bartender served him but he served him rudely. His was a world in which the caterer's men kept the social score, and to be rebuffed by a part-time barkeep meant that he had suffered some loss of social esteem. Or perhaps the man was new and uninformed. Then he heard Grace at his back

say: 'They went for broke overnight – nothing but income –
and he showed up drunk one Sunday and asked us to loan
him five thousand dollars . . .' She was always talking about
money. It was worse than eating your peas off a knife. He
dove into the pool, swam its length and went away.

The next pool on his list, the last but two, belonged to
his old mistress, Shirley Adams. If he had suffered any
injuries at the Biswangers' they would be cured here.
Love – sexual roughhouse in fact – was the supreme elixir,
the pain killer, the brightly colored pill that would put the
spring back into his step, the joy of life in his heart. They
had had an affair last week, last month, last year. He
couldn't remember. It was he who had broken it off, his
was the upper hand, and he stepped through the gate of
the wall that surrounded her pool with nothing so considered as self-confidence. It seemed in a way to be his pool,
as the lover, particularly the illicit lover, enjoys the possessions of his mistress with an authority unknown to holy
matrimony. She was there, her hair the color of brass, but
her figure, at the edge of the lighted, cerulean water,
excited in him no profound memories. It had been, he
thought, a lighthearted affair, although she had wept when
he broke it off. She seemed confused to see him and he
wondered if she was still wounded. Would she, God forbid,
weep again?

'What do you want?' she asked.

'I'm swimming across the county.'

'Good Christ. Will you ever grow up?'

'What's the matter?'

'If you've come here for money,' she said, 'I won't give you another cent.'

'You could give me a drink.'

'I could but I won't. I'm not alone.'

'Well, I'm on my way.'

He dove in and swam the pool, but when he tried to haul himself up onto the curb he found that the strength in his arms and shoulders had gone, and he paddled to the ladder and climbed out. Looking over his shoulder he saw, in the lighted bathhouse, a young man. Going out onto the dark lawn he smelled chrysanthemums or marigolds – some stubborn autumnal fragrance – on the night air, strong as gas. Looking overhead he saw that the stars had come out, but why should he seem to see Andromeda, Cepheus, and Cassiopeia? What had become of the constellations of midsummer? He began to cry.

It was probably the first time in his adult life that he had ever cried, certainly the first time in his life that he had ever felt so miserable, cold, tired, and bewildered. He could not understand the rudeness of the caterer's barkeep or the rudeness of a mistress who had come to him on her knees and showered his trousers with tears. He had swam too long, he had been immersed too long, and his nose and his throat were sore from the water. What he needed then was a drink, some company, and some clean, dry clothes, and while he could have cut directly across the road to his home he went on to the Gilmartins' pool. Here,

He had swam too long, he had been immersed too long, and his nose and throat were sore

for the first time in his life, he did not dive but went down the steps into the icy water and swam a hobbled sidestroke that he might have learned as a youth. He staggered with fatigue on his way to the Clydes' and paddled the length of their pool, stopping again and again with his hand on the curb to rest. He climbed up the ladder and wondered if he had the strength to get home. He had done what he wanted, he had swum the county, but he was so stupefied with exhaustion that his triumph seemed vague. Stooped, holding on to the gateposts for support, he turned up the driveway of his own house.

The place was dark. Was it so late that they had all gone to bed? Had Lucinda stayed at the Westerhazys' for supper? Had the girls joined her there or gone someplace else? Hadn't they agreed, as they usually did on Sunday, to regret all their invitations and stay at home? He tried the garage doors to see what cars were in but the doors were locked and rust came off the handles onto his hands. Going toward the house, he saw that the force of the thunderstorm had knocked one of the rain gutters loose. It hung down over the front door like an umbrella rib, but it could be fixed in the morning. The house was locked, and he thought that the stupid cook or the stupid maid must have locked the place up until he remembered that it had been some time since they had employed a maid or a cook. He shouted, pounded on the door, tried to force it with his shoulder, and then, looking in at the windows, saw that the place was empty.

The Scarlet Moving Van

GOODBYE TO THE mortal boredom of distributing a skinny chicken to a family of seven and all the other rites of the hill towns. I don't mean the real hill towns – Assisi or Perugia or Saracinesco, perched on a three-thousand-foot crag, with walls the dispiriting gray of shirt cardboards and mustard lichen blooming on the crooked roofs. The land, in fact, was flat, the houses frame. This was in the eastern United States, and the kind of place where most of us live. It was the unincorporated township of B_____, with a population of perhaps two hundred married couples, all of them with dogs and children, and many of them with servants; it resembled a hill town only in a manner of speaking, in that the ailing, the disheartened, and the poor could not ascend the steep moral path that formed is natural defense, and the moment any of the inhabitants became infected with unhappiness or discontent, they sensed the hopelessness of existing on such a high spiritual altitude, and went to live in the plain. Life was unprecedentedly comfortable and tranquil. B_____ was exclusively for the felicitous. The housewives kissed their husbands tenderly in the morning and passionately at nightfall. In nearly every house there were love, graciousness, and high hopes. The schools were excellent, the roads were smooth, the drains and other services were ideal, and one spring evening at dusk an immense scarlet moving van with gold lettering on its sides came up the street and stopped in the front of the Marple house, which had been empty then for three months.

The gilt and scarlet of the van, bright even in the twilight, was an inspired attempt to disguise the true sorrowfulness of wandering. 'We Carry Loads and Part Loads to All Far-Distant Places,' said the gold letters on the sides, and this legend had the effect of a distant train whistle. Martha Folkestone, who lived next door, watched through a window as the portables of her new neighbors were carried across the porch. 'That looks like real Chippendale,' she said, 'although it's hard to tell in this light. They have two children. They seem like nice people. Oh, I wish there was something I could bring them to make them feel at home. Do you think they'd like flowers? I suppose we could ask them for a drink. Do you think they'd like a drink? Would you want to go over and ask them if they'd like a drink?'

Later, when the furniture was all indoors and the van had gone, Charlie Folkestone crossed the lawn between the two houses and introduced himself to Peaches and

Gee-Gee. This is what he saw. Peaches was peaches – blond and warm, with a low-cut dress and a luminous front. Gee-Gee had been a handsome man, and perhaps still was, although his yellow curls were thin. His face seemed both angelic and menacing. He had never (Charlie learned later) been a boxer, but his eyes were slightly squinted and his square, handsome forehead had the conformation of layers of scar tissue. You might have said that his look was thoughtful until you realized that he was not a thoughtful man. It was the earnest and contained look of those who are a little hard of hearing or a little stupid.

They would be delighted to have a drink. They would be right over. Peaches wanted to put on some lipstick and say good night to the children, and then they would be right over. They came right over, and what seemed to be an un-usually pleasant evening began. The Folkestones had been worried about who their new neighbors would be, and to find a couple as sympathetic as Gee-Gee and Peaches made them very high-spirited. Like everyone else, they loved to express an opinion about their neighbors, and Gee-Gee and Peaches were, naturally, interested. It was the beginning of a friendship, and the Folkestones over-looked their usual concern with time and sobriety. It got late – it was past midnight – and Charlie did not notice how much whiskey was being poured or that Gee-Gee seemed to be getting drunk. Gee-Gee became very quiet – he dropped out of the conversation – and then he suddenly interrupted Martha in a flat, unpleasant drawl.

'God, but you're stuffy people,' he said.

'Oh, no, Gee-Gee!' Peaches said. 'Not on our first night!'

'You've had too much to drink, Gee-Gee,' Charlie said.

'Like hell I have,' said Gee-Gee. He bent over and began to unlace his shoes. 'I haven't had half enough.'

'Please, Gee-Gee, please,' Peaches said.

'I have to teach them, honey,' Gee-Gee said. 'They've got to learn.'

Then he stood up and, with the cunning and dexterity of a drunk, got out of most of his clothing before anyone could stop him.

'Get out of here,' Charlie said.

'The pleasure's all mine, neighbor,' said Gee-Gee. He kicked over a hammered-brass umbrella stand on his way out the door.

'Oh, I'm frightfully sorry!' Peaches said. 'I feel terribly about this!'

'Don't worry, my dear,' Martha said. 'He's probably very tired, and we've all had too much to drink.'

'Oh, no,' Peaches said. 'It always happens. Everywhere. We've moved eight times in the last eight years, and there's never been anyone to say goodbye to us. Not a soul. Oh, he was a beautiful man when I first knew him! You never saw anyone so fine and strong and generous. They called him the Greek God at college. That's why he's called Gee-Gee. He was All-America twice, but he was never a money player – he always played straight out of his heart. Everybody loved him. Now it's all gone, but I tell myself that I once had the love of a good man. I don't think many women have known that kind of love. Oh, I wish he'd come back. I wish he'd be the way he was. The night before last, when we were packing up the dishes in the old house, he got drunk and I slapped him in the face, and I shouted at him, "Come back! Come back! Come back to me, Gee-Gee!" But he didn't listen. He didn't hear me. He doesn't hear anyone any more – not even the voices of his children. I ask myself every day what I've done to be punished so cruelly.'

'I'm sorry, my dear!' Martha said.

'You won't be around to say goodbye when we go,' Peaches said. 'We'll last a year. You wait and see. Some people have tender farewell parties, but even the garbage man in the last place was glad to see us go.' With a grace and resignation that transcended the ruined evening, she began to gather up the clothing that her husband had scattered on the rug. 'Each time we move, I think that the change will be good for him,' she said. 'When we got here tonight, it all looked so pretty and quiet that I thought he might change. Well, you don't have to ask us again. You know what it's like.'

A FEW DAYS or perhaps a week later, Charlie saw Gee-Gee on the station platform in the morning and saw how completely personable his neighbor was when he was sober. B_____ was not an easy place to conquer, but Gee-Gee seemed already to have won the affectionate respect of his neighbors. Charlie could see, as he watched him standing in the sun among the other commuters, that he would be asked to join everything. Gee-Gee greeted Charlie heartily, and there was no trace of the ugliness he had shown that night. Indeed, it was impossible to believe that this charming and handsome man had been so offensive. In the morning light, and surrounded by new friends, he seemed to challenge the memory. He seemed almost able to transfer the blame onto Charlie.

Arrangements for the social initiation of the new couple were unusually rapid and elaborate, and began with a dinner party at the Watermans'. Charlie was already at the party when Gee-Gee and Peaches came in, and they came in like royalty. Arm in arm, radiant and beautiful, they seemed, at the moment of their entrance, to make the evening. It was a large party, and Charlie hardly saw them until they went in to dinner. He sat close to Peaches, but Gee-Gee was at the other end of the table. They were halfway through dessert when Gee-Gee's flat and unpleasant drawl sounded, like a parade command, over the general conversation.

'What a God-damned bunch of stuffed shirts!' he said. 'Let's put a little vitality into the conversation, shall we?' He sprang onto the center of the table and began to sing a dirty song and dance a jig. Women screamed. Dishes were upset and broken. Dresses were ruined. Peaches pled to her wayward husband. The effect of this outrageous performance was to empty the dining room of everyone but Gee-Gee and Charlie.

'Get down off there, Gee-Gee,' Charlie said.

'I have to teach them,' Gee-Gee said. 'I've got to teach them.'

'You're not teaching anybody anything but the fact that you're rotten drunk.'

'They've got to learn,' Gee-Gee said. 'I've got to teach them.' He got down off the table, breaking a few more dishes, and wandered out into the kitchen, where he embraced the cook, and then went on out into the night.

ONE MIGHT HAVE thought that this was warning enough to a worldly community, but unusual amounts of forgiveness were extended to Gee-Gee. One liked him, and there was always the chance that he might not misbehave. There was always his charming figure in the morning light to confound his enemies, but it began to seem more and more like a lure that would let him into houses where he could break the crockery. Forgiveness was not what he wanted, and if he seemed to have failed at offending the sensibilities of his hostess he would increase and complicate his outrageousness. No one had ever seen anything like it. He undressed at the Bilkers'. At the Levys' he drop-kicked a bowl of soft cheese onto the ceiling. He danced the Highland fling in his underpants, set fire to wastebaskets, and swung on the Townsends' chandelier – that famous chandelier. Inside of six weeks, there was not a house in B_____ where he was welcome.

The Folkestones still saw him, of course – saw him in

You're not teaching anybody anything but the fact that you're rotten drunk

his garden in the evening and talked to him across the hedge. Charlie was greatly troubled at the spectacle of someone falling so swiftly from grace, and he would have liked to help. He and Martha talked with Peaches, but Peaches was without hope. She did not understand what had happened to her Adonis, and that was as far as her intelligence took her. Now and then some innocent stranger from the next town or perhaps some newcomer would be taken with Gee-Gee and ask him to dinner. The performance was always the same, the dishes were always broken. The Folkestones were neighbors – there was this ancient bond – and Charlie may have thought that he could save the man. When Gee-Gee and Peaches quarreled, sometimes she telephoned Charlie and asked his protection. He went there one summer evening after she had telephoned. The quarrel was over; Peaches was reading a comic book in the living room, and Gee-Gee was sitting at the dining-room table with a drink in his hand. Charlie stood over his friend.

'Gee-Gee.'

'Yes.'

'Will you go on the wagon?'

'No.'

'Will you go on the wagon if I go on the wagon?'

'No.'

'Will you go to a psychiatrist?'

'Why? I know myself. I only have to play it out.'

'Will you go to a psychiatrist if I go with you?'

'No.'

'Will you do anything to help yourself?'

'I have to teach them.' Then he threw back his head and sobbed, 'Oh, Jesus . . .'

Charlie turned away. It seemed, at that instant, that Gee-Gee had heard, from some wilderness of his own, the noise of a distant horn that prophesied the manner and the hour of his death. There seemed to be some tremendous validity to the drunken man. Folkestone felt an upheaval in his spirit. He felt he understood the drunken man's message; he had always sensed it. It was at the bottom of their friendship. Gee-Gee was an advocate for the lame, the diseased, the poor, for those who through no fault of their own live out their lives in misery and pain. To the happy and the wellborn and the rich he had this to say – that for all their affection, their comforts, and their privileges, they would not be spared the pangs of anger and lust and the agonies of death. He only meant for them to be prepared for the blow when the blow fell. But was it not possible to accept this truth without having him dance a jig in your living room? He spoke from some vision of the suffering in life, but was it necessary to suffer oneself in order to accept his message? It seemed so.

'Gee-Gee?' Charlie asked.

'Yes.'

'*What* are you trying to teach them?'

'You'll never know. You're too God-damned stuffy.'

THEY DIDN'T EVEN last a year. In November, someone
made them a decent offer for the house and they sold it.
The gold-and-scarlet moving van returned, and they
crossed the state line, into the town of Y____, where they
bought another house. The Folkestones were glad to see
them go. A well-behaved young couple took their place,
and everything was as it had been. They were seldom
remembered. But through a string of friends Charlie
learned, the following winter, that Gee-Gee had broken his
hip playing football a day or two before Christmas. This
fact, for some reason, remained with him, and one Sunday
afternoon when he had nothing much better to do he got
Gee-Gee's telephone number from Information and called
his old neighbor to say that he was coming over for a drink.
Gee-Gee roared with enthusiasm and gave Charlie directions for getting to the house.

It was a long drive, and halfway there Charlie wondered
why he had undertaken it. Y____ was several cuts below
B____. The house was in a development, and the builder
had not stopped at mere ugliness; he had constructed a
community that looked, with its rectilinear windows, like
a penal colony. The streets were named after universities –
Princeton Street, Yale Street, Rutgers Street, and so forth.
Only a few of the houses had been sold, and Gee-Gee's
house was surrounded by empty dwellings. Charlie rang
the bell and heard Gee-Gee shouting for him to come in.
The house was a mess, and as he was taking his coat off,
Gee-Gee came slowly down the hall half riding in a child's

wagon, which he propelled by pushing a crutch. His right hip and leg were encased in a massive cast.

'Where's Peaches?' Charlie asked.

'She's in Nassau. She and the children went to Nassau for Christmas.'

'And left you alone?'

'I wanted them to go. I made them go. Nothing can be done for me. I get along all right on this wagon. When I'm hungry, I make a sandwich. I wanted them to go. I made them go. Peaches needed a vacation, and I like being alone. Come on into the living room and make me a drink. I can't get the ice trays out – that's about the only thing I can't do. I can shave and get into bed and so forth, but I can't get the ice trays out.'

Charlie got some ice. He was glad to have something to do. The image of Gee-Gee in his wagon had shocked him, and he felt a terrifying stillness over the place. Out of the kitchen window he could see row upon row of ugly, empty houses. He felt as if some hideous melodrama were approaching its climax. But in the living room Gee-Gee was his most charming, and his smile and his voice gave the afternoon a momentary equilibrium. Charlie asked if Gee-Gee couldn't get a nurse to stay with him. Couldn't someone be found to stay with him? Couldn't he at least rent a wheelchair? Gee-Gee laughed away all these suggestions. He was contented. Peaches had written him from Nassau. They were having a marvelous time.

Charlie believed that Gee-Gee had made them go. It

was this detail, above everything else, that gave the situation its horror. Peaches would have liked, naturally enough, to go to Nassau, but she never would have insisted. She was much too innocent to have any envious dreams of travel. Gee-Gee would have insisted that she go; he would have made the trip so tempting that she could not, in her innocence, resist it. Did he wish to be left alone, drunken and crippled, in an isolated house? Did he need to feel abused? It seemed so. The disorder of the house and the image of his wife and children running, running, running on some coral beach seemed like a successful contrivance – a kind of triumph.

Gee-Gee lit a cigarette and, forgetting about it, lit another, and fumbled so clumsily with the matches that Charlie saw that he might easily burn to death. Hoisting himself from the wagon to the chair, he nearly fell, and, if he were alone and fell, he could easily die of hunger and thirst on his own rug. But there might be some drunken cunning in his clumsiness, his playing with fire. He smiled slyly when he saw the look on Charlie's face. 'Don't worry about me,' he said. 'I'll be all right. I have my guardian angel.'

'That's what everybody thinks,' Charlie said.

'Oh, but I have.'

Outside, it had begun to snow. The winter sky was overcast, and it would soon be dark. Charlie said that he had to go. 'Sit down,' Gee-Gee said. 'Sit down and have another drink.' Charlie's conscience held him there a few moments longer. How could he openly abandon a friend – a neighbor, at least – to the peril of death? But he had no choice; his family was waiting and he had to go. 'Don't worry about me,' Gee-Gee said when Charlie was putting on his coat. 'I have my angel.'

It was later than Charlie had realized. The snow was heavy now, and he had a two-hour drive, on winding back roads. There was a little rise going out of Y_____, and the new snow was so slick that he had trouble making the hill. There were steeper hills ahead of him. Only one of his windshield wipers worked, and the snow quickly covered the glass and left him with one small aperture onto the world. The snow sped into the headlights at a dizzying rate, and at one place where the road was narrow the car slid off onto the shoulder and he had to race the motor for ten minutes in order to get back onto the hard surface. It was a lonely stretch there – miles from any house – and he would have had a sloppy walk in his loafers. The car skidded and weaved up every hill, and it seemed that he reached the top by the thinnest margin of luck.

After driving for two hours, he was still far from home. The snow was so deep that guiding the car was like the trickiest kind of navigation. It took him three hours to get back, and he was tired when he drove into the darkness and peace of his own garage – tired and infinitely grateful. Martha and the children had eaten their supper, and she wanted to go over to the Lissoms' and discuss some school-board business. He told her that the driving was bad, and since it was such a short distance, she decided to walk. He lit a fire and made a drink, and the children sat at the table with him while he ate his supper. After supper on Sunday nights, the Folkestones played, or tried to play, trios. Charlie played the clarinet, his daughter played the piano, and his older son had a tenor recorder. The baby wandered around underfoot. This Sunday night they played simple arrangements of eighteenth-century music in the pleasantest family atmosphere – complimenting themselves when they squeezed through a difficult passage, and extending into the music what was best in their relationship. They were playing a Vivaldi sonata when the telephone rang. Charlie knew immediately who it was.

'Charlie, Charlie,' Gee-Gee said. 'Jesus. I'm in hot water. Right after you left I fell out of the God-damned wagon. It took me two hours to get to the telephone. You've got to get over. There's nobody else. You're my only friend. You've got to get over here. Charlie? You hear me?'

It must have been the strangeness of the look on Charlie's face that made the baby scream. The little girl picked him up in her arms, and stared, as did the other boy, at their father. They seemed to know the whole picture, every detail of it, and they looked at him calmly, as if they were expecting him to make some decision that had nothing to do with the continuing of a pleasant evening in a snow-bound house – but a decision that would have a profound effect on their knowledge of him and on their final happiness. Their looks were, he thought, clear and appealing, and whatever he did would be final.

'You hear me, Charlie? You hear me?' Gee-Gee asked. 'It took me damned near two hours to crawl over to the telephone. You've got to help me. No one else will come.'

Charlie hung up. Gee-Gee must have heard the sound of his breathing and the baby crying, but Charlie had said nothing. He gave no explanation to the children, and they asked for none. They knew. His daughter went back to the piano, and when the telephone rang again and he did not answer it, no one questioned the ringing of the phone. They seemed happy and relieved when it stopped ringing, and they played Vivaldi until nine o'clock, when he sent them up to bed.

He made a drink to diminish the feeling that some emotional explosion had taken place, that some violence had shaken the air. He did not know what he had done or how to cope with his conscience. He would tell Martha about it when she came in, he thought. That would be a step toward comprehension. But when she returned he said nothing. He was afraid that if she brought her intelligence to the problem it would only confirm his guilt. 'But why didn't you telephone me at the Lissoms'?' she might have asked. 'I could have come home and you could have gone over.' She was too compassionate a woman to accept passively, as he was doing, the thought of a friend, a neighbor, lying in agony. She went on upstairs. He poured some whiskey into his glass. If he had called the Lissoms', if she had returned to care for the children and left him free to help Gee-Gee, would he have been able to make the return trip in the heavy snow? He could have put on chains, but where were the chains? Were they in the car or in the cellar? He didn't know. He hadn't used them that year. But perhaps by now the roads would have been plowed. Perhaps the storm was over. This last, distressing possibility made him feel sick. Had the sky betrayed him? He switched on the outside light and went hesitantly, unwillingly, toward the window.

The clean snow gave off an ingratiating sparkle, and the beam of light shone into empty and peaceful air. The snow must have stopped a few minutes after he had entered the house. But how could he have known? How could he be expected to take into consideration the caprices of the weather? And what about that look the children had given him – so stern, so clear, so like a declaration that his place at that hour was with them, and not with the succoring of drunkards who had forfeited the chance to be taken seriously?

Then the image of Gee-Gee returned, crushing in its misery, and he remembered Peaches standing in the hall-way at the Watermans' calling, 'Come back! Come back!' She was calling back the youth that Charlie had never known, but it was easy to imagine what Gee-Gee must have been – fair, high-spirited, generous, and strong – and why had it all come to ruin? *Come back! Come back!* She seemed to call after the sweetness of a summer's day – roses in bloom and all the doors and windows open on the garden. It was all there in her voice; it was like the illusion of an abandoned house in the last rays of the sun. A large place, falling to pieces, haunted for children and a headache for the police and fire departments, but, seeing it with its windows blazing in the sunset, one thinks that they have all come back. Cook is in the kitchen rolling pastry. The smell of chicken rises up the back stairs. The front rooms are ready for the children and their many friends. A coal fire burns in the grate. Then as the light goes off the windows, the true ugliness of the place scowls into the dusk with redoubled force, as, when the notes of that long-ago summer left Peaches' voice, one saw the finality and confusion of despair in her innocent face. *Come back! Come back!* He poured himself some more whiskey, and as he raised the glass to his mouth he heard the wind change and saw – the outside light was still on – the snow begin to spin down again, with the vindictive swirl of a blizzard. The road was impassable; he could not have made the trip. The change in the weather had given him sweet absolution, and he watched the snow with a smile of love, but he stayed up until three in the morning with the bottle.

He was red-eyed and shaken the next morning, and ducked out of his office at eleven and drank two Martinis. He had two more before lunch and another at four and two on the train, and came reeling home for supper. The clinical details of heavy drinking are familiar to all of us; it is only the human picture that concerns us here, and Martha was finally driven to speak to him. She spoke most gently.

'You're drinking too much, darling,' she said. 'You've been drinking too much for three weeks.'

'My drinking,' he said, 'is my own God-damned business. You mind your business and I'll mind mine.'

It got worse and worse, and she had to do something. She finally went to their rector – a good-looking young bachelor who practiced both psychology and liturgy – for advice. He listened sympathetically. 'I stopped at the rectory this afternoon,' she said when she got home that night, 'and I talked with Father Hemming. He wonders why you haven't been in church, and he wants to talk to you. He's such a good-looking man,' she added, trying to make what she had just said sound less like a planned speech, 'that I wonder why he's never married.' Charlie – drunk, as usual – went to the telephone and called the rectory. 'Look, Father,' he said. 'My wife tells me that you've been entertaining her in the afternoons. Well, I don't like it. You keep your hands off my wife. You hear me? That damned black suit you wear doesn't cut any ice with me. You keep your hands off my wife or I'll bust your pretty little nose.'

In the end, he lost his job, and they had to move, and began their wanderings, like Gee-Gee and Peaches, in the scarlet-and-gold van.

AND WHAT HAPPENED to Gee-Gee – what ever became of him? That boozy guardian angel, her hair disheveled and the strings of her harp broken, still seemed to hover over where he lay. After telephoning Charlie that night, he telephoned the fire department. They were there in eight minutes flat, with bells ringing and sirens blowing. They got him into bed, made him a fresh drink, and one of the firemen, who had nothing better to do, stayed on until Peaches got back from Nassau. They had a fine time, eating all the steaks in the deep freeze and drinking a quart of bourbon every day. Gee-Gee could walk by the time Peaches and the children got back, and he took up that disorderly life for which he seemed so much better equipped than his neighbor, but they had to move at the end of the year, and, like the Folkestones, vanished from the hill towns.

O Youth and Beauty!

AT THE TAG end of nearly every long, large Saturday-night party in the suburb of Shady Hill, when almost everybody who was going to play golf or tennis in the morning had gone home hours ago and the ten or twelve people remaining seemed powerless to bring the evening to an end although the gin and whiskey were running low, and here and there a woman who was sitting out her husband would have begun to drink milk; when everybody had lost track of time, and the baby-sitters who were waiting at home for these diehards would have long since stretched out on the sofa and fallen into a deep sleep, to dream about cooking-contest prizes, ocean voyages, and romance; when the bellicose drunk, the crapshooter, the pianist, and the woman faced with the expiration of her hopes had all expressed themselves; when every proposal – to go to the Farquarsons' for breakfast, to go swimming, to go and wake up the Townsends, to go here and go there – died as soon as it was made, then Trace Bearden would begin to chide Cash Bentley about his age and thinning hair. The chiding was preliminary to moving the living-room furniture. Trace and Cash moved the tables and the chairs, the sofas and the fire screen, the woodbox and the footstool; and when they had finished, you wouldn't know the place. Then if the host had a revolver, he would be asked to produce it. Cash would take off his shoes and assume a starting crouch behind a sofa. Trace would fire the weapon out of an open window, and if you were new to the community and had not understood what the preparations were about, you would then realize that you were watching a hurdle race. Over the sofa went Cash, over the tables, over the fire screen and the woodbox. It was not exactly a race, since Cash ran it alone, but it was extraordinary to see this man of forty surmount so many obstacles so gracefully. There was not a piece of furniture in Shady Hill that Cash could not take in his stride. The race ended with cheers, and presently the party would break up.

Cash was, of course, an old track star, but he was never aggressive or tiresome about his brilliant past. The college where he had spent his youth had offered him a paying job on the alumni council, but he had refused it, realizing that that part of his life was ended. Cash and his wife, Louise, had two children, and they lived in a medium-cost ranch house on Alewives Lane. They belonged to the country club, although they could not afford it, but in the case of the Bentleys nobody ever pointed this out, and Cash was one of the best-liked men in Shady Hill. He was still slender – he was careful about his weight – and he walked to the train in the morning with a light and vigorous step that marked him as an athlete. His hair was thin, and there were mornings when his eyes looked bloodshot, but this did not detract much from a charming quality of stubborn youthfulness.

In business Cash had suffered reverses and disappointments, and the Bentleys had many money worries. They were always late with their tax payments and their mortgage payments, and the drawer of the hall table was stuffed with unpaid bills; it was always touch and go with the Bentleys and the bank. Louise looked pretty enough on Saturday night, but her life was exacting and monotonous. In the pockets of her suits, coats, and dresses there were little wads and scraps of paper on which was written: 'Oleomargarine, frozen spinach, Kleenex, dog biscuit, hamburger, pepper, lard . . .' When she was still half awake in the morning, she was putting on the water for coffee and diluting the frozen orange juice. Then she would be wanted by the children. She would crawl under the bureau on her hands and knees to find a sock for Toby. She would lie flat on her belly and wiggle under the bed (getting dust up her nose) to find a shoe for Rachel. Then there were the housework, the laundry, and the cooking, as well as the demands of the children. There always seemed to be shoes to put on and shoes to take off, snowsuits to be zipped and unzipped, bottoms to be wiped, tears to be dried, and when the sun went down (she saw it set from the kitchen window) there was the supper to be cooked, the baths, the bedtime story, and the Lord's Prayer. With the sonorous words of the Our Father in a darkened room the children's day was over, but the day was far from over for Louise Bentley. There were the darning, the mending, and some ironing to do, and after sixteen years of housework she did not seem able to escape her chores even while she slept. Snowsuits, shoes, baths, and groceries seemed to have permeated her subconscious. Now and then she would speak in her sleep – so loudly that she woke her husband. 'I can't *afford* veal cutlets,' she said one night. Then she sighed uneasily and was quiet again.

By the standards of Shady Hill, the Bentleys were a happily married couple, but they had their ups and downs. Cash could be very touchy at times. When he came home after a bad day at the office and found that Louise, for some good reason, had not started supper, he would be ugly. 'Oh, for Christ sake!' he would say, and go into the kitchen and heat up some frozen food. He drank some whiskey to relax himself during this ordeal, but it never seemed to relax him, and he usually burned the bottom out of a pan, and when they sat down for supper the dining space would be full of smoke. It was only a question of time before they were plunged into a bitter quarrel. Louise would run upstairs, throw herself onto the bed and sob. Cash would grab the whiskey bottle and dose himself. These rows, in spite of the vigor with which Cash and Louise entered into them, were the source of a great deal of pain for both of them. Cash would sleep downstairs on the sofa, but sleep never repaired the damage, once the trouble had begun, and if they met in the morning, they would be at one another's throats in a second. Then Cash would leave for the train, and, as soon as the children had been taken to nursery school, Louise would put on her coat and cross the grass to the Beardens' house. She would cry into a cup of warmed-up coffee and tell Lucy Bearden her troubles. What was the meaning of marriage? What was the meaning of love? Lucy always suggested that Louise get a job. It would give her emotional and financial independence, and that, Lucy said, was what she needed.

The next night, things would get worse. Cash would not come home for dinner at all, but would stumble in at about eleven, and the whole sordid wrangle would be repeated, with Louise going to bed in tears upstairs and Cash again stretching out on the living-room sofa. After a few days and nights of this, Louise would decide that she was at the end of her rope. She would decide to go and stay with her married sister in Mamaroneck. She usually chose a Saturday, when Cash would be at home, for her departure. She would pack a suitcase and get her War Bonds from the desk. Then she would take a bath and put on her best slip. Cash, passing the bedroom door, would see her. Her slip was transparent, and suddenly he was all repentance, tenderness, charm, wisdom, and love. 'Oh, my darling!' he would groan, and when they went downstairs to get a bite to eat about an hour later, they would be sighing and making cow eyes at one another; they would be the happiest married couple in the whole eastern United States. It was usually at about this time that Lucy Bearden turned up with the good news that she had found a job for Louise. Lucy would ring the doorbell, and Cash, wearing a bathrobe, would let her in. She would be brief with Cash, naturally, and hurry into the dining room to tell poor Louise the good news. 'Well, that's very nice of you to have looked,' Louise would say wanly, 'but I don't think that I want a job any more. I don't think that Cash wants me to work, do you, sweetheart?' Then she would turn her big dark eyes on Cash, and you could practically smell smoke. Lucy would excuse herself hurriedly from this scene of depravity, but never left with any hard feelings, because she had been married for nineteen years herself and she knew that every union has its ups and downs. She didn't seem to leave any wiser, either; the next time the Bentleys quarreled she would be just as intent as ever on getting Louise a job. But these quarrels and reunions, like the hurdle race, didn't seem to lose their interest through repetition.

ON A SATURDAY night in the spring, the Farquarsons gave the Bentleys an anniversary party. It was their seventeenth anniversary. Saturday afternoon, Louise Bentley put herself through preparations nearly as arduous as the Monday wash. She rested for an hour, by the clock, with her feet high in the air, her chin in a sling, and her eyes bathed in

some astringent solution. The clay packs, the too tight gir-
dle, and the plucking and curling and painting that went
on were all aimed at rejuvenation. Feeling in the end that
she had not been entirely successful, she tied a piece of
veiling over her eyes – but she was a lovely woman, and all
the cosmetics that she had struggled with seemed, like her
veil, to be drawn transparently over a face where mature
beauty and a capacity for wit and passion were undisguis-
able. The Farquarsons' party was nifty, and the Bentleys
had a wonderful time. The only person who drank too
much was Trace Bearden. Late in the party, he began to
chide Cash about his thinning hair and Cash good-
naturedly began to move the furniture around. Harry
Farquarson had a pistol, and Trace went out onto the terrace to fire it up at the sky. Over the sofa went Cash, over
the end table, over the arms of the wing chair and the fire
screen. It was a piece of carving on a chest that brought
him down, and down he came like a ton of bricks.

Louise screamed and ran to where he lay. He had cut a
gash in his forehead, and someone made a bandage to stop
the flow of blood. When he tried to get up, he stumbled
and fell again, and his face turned a terrible green. Harry
telephoned Dr Parminter, Dr Hopewell, Dr Altman, and Dr
Barnstable, but it was two in the morning and none of
them answered. Finally, a Dr Yerkes – a total stranger –
agreed to come. Yerkes was a young man – he did not seem
old enough to be a doctor – and he looked around at the
disordered room and the anxious company as if there was

something weird about the scene. He got off on the wrong foot with Cash. 'What seems to be the matter, old-timer?' he asked.

Cash's leg was broken. The doctor put a splint on it, and Harry and Trace carried the injured man out to the doctor's car. Louise followed them in her own car to the hospital, where Cash was bedded down in a ward. The doctor gave Cash a sedative, and Louise kissed him and drove home in the dawn.

CASH WAS IN the hospital for two weeks, and when he came home he walked with a crutch and his broken leg was in a heavy cast. It was another ten days before he could limp to the morning train. 'I won't be able to run the hurdle race any more, sweetheart,' he told Louise sadly. She said that it didn't matter, but while it didn't matter to her, it seemed to matter to Cash. He had lost weight in the hospital. His spirits were low. He seemed discontented. He did not himself understand what had happened. He, or everything around him, seemed subtly to have changed for the worse. Even his senses seemed to conspire to damage the ingenuous world that he had enjoyed for so many years. He went into the kitchen late one night to make himself a sandwich, and when he opened the icebox door he noticed a rank smell. He dumped the spoiled meat into the garbage, but the smell clung to his nostrils. A few days later he was in the attic, looking for his varsity sweater. There were no windows in the attic and his flashlight was dim. Kneeling on the floor to unlock a trunk, he broke a spider web with his lips. The frail web covered his mouth as if a hand had been put over it. He wiped it impatiently, but also with the feeling of having been gagged. A few nights later, he was walking down a New York side street in the rain and saw an old whore standing in a doorway. She was so sluttish and ugly that she looked like a cartoon of Death, but before he could appraise her – the instant his eyes took an impression of her crooked figure – his lips swelled, his breathing quickened, and he experienced all the other symptoms of erotic excitement. A few nights later, while he was reading *Time* in the living room, he noticed that the faded roses Louise had brought in from the garden smelled more of earth than of anything else. It was a putrid, compelling smell. He dropped the roses into a wastebasket, but not before they had reminded him of the spoiled meat, the whore, and the spider web.

He had started going to parties again, but without the hurdle race to run, the parties of his friends and neighbors seemed to him interminable and stale. He listened to their dirty jokes with an irritability that was hard for him to conceal. Even their countenances discouraged him, and, slumped in a chair, he could regard their skin and their teeth narrowly, as if he were himself a much younger man.

The brunt of his irritability fell on Louise, and it seemed to her that Cash, in losing the hurdle race, had lost the thing that had preserved his equilibrium. He was rude to his friends when they stopped in for a drink. He was rude and gloomy when he and Louise went out. When Louise asked him what was the matter, he only murmured, 'Nothing, nothing, nothing,' and poured himself some bourbon. May and June passed, and then the first part of July, without his showing any improvement.

THEN IT IS a summer night, a wonderful summer night. The passengers on the eight-fifteen see Shady Hill – if they notice it at all – in a bath of placid golden light. The noise of the train is muffled in the heavy foliage, and the long car windows look like a string of lighted aquarium tanks before they flicker out of sight. Up on the hill, the ladies say to one another, 'Smell the grass! Smell the trees!' The Farquarsons are giving another party, and Harry has hung a sign, WHISKEY GULCH, from the rose arbor, and is wearing a chef's white hat and an apron. His guests are still drinking, and the smoke from his meat fire rises, on this windless evening, straight up into the trees.

In the clubhouse on the hill, the first of the formal dances for the young people begins around nine. On Alewives Lane sprinklers continue to play after dark. You can smell the water. The air seems as fragrant as it is dark – it is a delicious element to walk through – and most of the windows on Alewives Lane are open to it. You can see Mr and Mrs Bearden, as you pass, looking at their television. Joe Lockwood, the young lawyer who lives on the corner, is practicing a speech to the jury before his wife. 'I intend to show you,' he says, 'that a man of probity, a man whose reputation for honesty and reliability . . .' He waves his bare arms as he speaks. His wife goes on knitting. Mrs Carver – Harry Farquarson's mother-in-law – glances up at the sky and asks, '*Where* did all the stars come from?' She is old and foolish, and yet she is right: Last night's stars seem to have drawn to themselves a new range of galaxies, and the night sky is not dark at all, except where there is a tear in the membrane of light. In the unsold house lots near the track a hermit thrush is singing.

The Bentleys are at home. Poor Cash has been so rude and gloomy that the Farquarsons have not asked him to their party. He sits on the sofa beside Louise, who is sewing elastic into the children's underpants. Through the open window he can hear the pleasant sounds of the summer night. There is another party, in the Rogerses' garden, behind the Bentleys'. The music from the dance drifts down the hill. The band is sketchy – saxophone, drums, and piano – and all the selections are twenty years old. The band plays 'Valencia,' and Cash looks tenderly toward Louise, but Louise, tonight, is a discouraging figure. The lamp picks out the gray in her hair. Her apron is stained. Her face seems colorless and drawn. Suddenly, Cash begins frenziedly to beat his feet in time to the music. He sings some gibberish – Jabajabajabajaba – to the distant saxophone. He sighs and goes into the kitchen.

Here a faint, stale smell of cooking clings to the dark. From the kitchen window Cash can see the lights and figures of the Rogerses' party. It is a young people's party.

The Rogers girl has asked some friends in for dinner before the dance, and now they seem to be leaving. Cars are driving away. 'I'm covered with grass stains,' a girl says. 'I hope the old man remembered to buy gasoline,' a boy says, and a girl laughs. There is nothing on their minds but the passing summer nights. Taxes and the elastic in underpants – all the unbeautiful facts of life that threaten to crush the breath out of Cash – have not touched a single figure in this garden. Then jealousy seizes him – such savage and bitter jealousy that he feels ill.

He does not understand what separates him from these children in the garden next door. He has been a young man. He has been a hero. He has been adored and happy and full of animal spirits, and now he stands in a dark kitchen, deprived of his athletic prowess, his impetuousness, his good looks – of everything that means anything to him. He feels as if the figures in the next yard are the specters from some party in that past where all his tastes and desires lie, and from which he has been cruelly removed. He feels like a ghost of the summer evening. He is sick with longing. Then he hears voices in the front of the house. Louise turns on the kitchen light. 'Oh, here you are,' she says. 'The Beardens stopped in. I think they'd like a drink.'

Cash went to the front of the house to greet the Beardens. They wanted to go up to the club, for one dance. They saw, at a glance, that Cash was at loose ends, and they urged the Bentleys to come. Louise got someone to stay with the children and then went upstairs to change.

When they got to the club, they found a few friends of their age hanging around the bar, but Cash did not stay in the bar. He seemed restless and perhaps drunk. He banged into a table on his way through the lounge to the ballroom. He cut in on a young girl. He seized her too vehemently and jigged her off in an ancient two-step. She signaled openly for help to a boy in the stag line, and Cash was cut out. He walked angrily off the dance floor onto the terrace. Some young couples there withdrew from one another's arms as he pushed open the screen door. He walked to the end of the terrace, where he hoped to be alone, but here he surprised another young couple, who got up from the lawn, where they seemed to have been lying, and walked off in the dark toward the pool.

Louise remained in the bar with the Beardens. 'Poor Cash is tight,' she said. And then, 'He told me this afternoon that he was going to paint the storm windows,' she said. 'Well, he mixed the paint and washed the brushes and put on some old fatigues and went into the cellar. There was a telephone call for him at around five, and when I went down to tell him, do you know what he was doing? He was just sitting there in the dark with a cocktail shaker. He hadn't touched the storm windows. He was just sitting there in the dark, drinking Martinis.'

'Poor Cash,' Trace said.

'You ought to get a job,' Lucy said. 'That would give you emotional and financial independence.' As she spoke, they all heard the noise of furniture being moved around in the lounge.

'Oh, my God!' Louise said. 'He's going to run the race. Stop him, Trace, stop him! He'll hurt himself. He'll kill himself!'

They all went to the door of the lounge. Louise again asked Trace to interfere, but she could see by Cash's face that he was way beyond remonstrating with. A few couples left the dance floor and stood watching the preparations. Trace didn't try to stop Cash – he helped him. There was no pistol, so he slammed a couple of books together for the start.

Over the sofa went Cash, over the coffee table, the lamp table, the fire screen, and the hassock. All his grace and strength seemed to have returned to him. He cleared the big sofa at the end of the room and instead of stopping there, he turned and started back over the course. His face was strained. His mouth hung open. The tendons of his neck protruded hideously. He made the hassock, the fire screen, the lamp table, and the coffee table. People held their breath when he approached the final sofa, but he cleared it and landed on his feet. There was some applause. Then he groaned and fell. Louise ran to his side. His clothes were soaked with sweat and he gasped for breath. She knelt down beside him and took his head in her lap and stroked his thin hair.

CASH HAD A terrible hangover on Sunday, and Louise let him sleep until it was nearly time for church. The family went off to Christ Church together at eleven, as they always did. Cash sang, prayed, and got to his knees, but the most he ever felt in church was that he stood outside the realm of God's infinite mercy, and, to tell the truth, he no more believed in the Father, the Son, and the Holy Ghost than does my bull terrier. They returned home at one to eat the overcooked meat and stony potatoes that were their customary Sunday lunch. At around five, the Parminters called up and asked them over for a drink. Louise didn't want to go, so Cash went alone. (Oh, those suburban Sunday nights, those Sunday-night blues! Those departing weekend guests, those stale cocktails, those half-dead flowers, those trips to Harmon to catch the Century, those postmortems and pickup suppers!) It was sultry and overcast. The dog days were beginning. He drank gin with the Parminters for an hour or two and then went over to the Townsends' for a drink. The Farquarsons called up the Townsends and asked them to come over and bring Cash with them, and at the Farquarsons' they had some more drinks and ate the leftover party food. The Farquarsons were glad to see that Cash seemed like himself again. It was half past ten or eleven when he got home. Louise was upstairs, cutting out of the current copy of *Life* those scenes of mayhem, disaster, and violent death that she felt might corrupt her children. She always did this. Cash came upstairs and spoke to her and then went down again. In a little while, she heard him moving the living-room furniture around. Then he called to her, and when she went down, he was standing at the foot of the stairs in his stocking feet, holding the pistol out to her. She had never fired it before, and the directions he gave her were not much help.

'Hurry up,' he said, 'I can't wait all night.'

He had forgotten to tell her about the safety, and when she pulled the trigger nothing happened.

'It's that little lever,' he said. 'Press that little lever.' Then, in his impatience, he hurdled the sofa anyhow.

The pistol went off and Louise got him in midair. She shot him dead.

JOHN CHEEVER WAS born in 1912. The son of a shoe salesman, Cheever enjoyed a somewhat idyllic childhood in the suburbs of Massachusetts before his father lost his fortune and fell to drinking. Frequently referred to as the Chekhov of these suburbs, Cheever published seven collections of stories and five novels throughout his lifetime, and was awarded the National Medal for Literature and the Pulitzer Prize, among others.

Cheever's own struggle with alcoholism is reflected in much of his writing. 'The Swimmer', which went on to become a major Hollywood movie featuring Burt Lancaster, portrays the grinding toll of suburban-ite socialising, while 'Goodbye, My Brother' and 'O Youth and Beauty!' depict the blind destruction that mindless drinking inflicts on families.

Cheever finally quit drinking in 1975. He died seven years later.

RECOMMENDED BOOKS BY JOHN CHEEVER:

Collected Stories
Falconer
The Wapshot Chronicle

How to detox after Drinking?

Swimming
ROGER DEAKIN

VINTAGE MINIS

Eating
NIGELLA LAWSON

VINTAGE MINIS

Calm
TIM PARKS

VINTAGE MINIS

Love
JEANETTE WINTERSON

VINTAGE MINIS

VINTAGE MINIS

The Vintage Minis bring you the world's greatest writers on the experiences that make us human. These stylish, entertaining little books explore the whole spectrum of life – from birth to death, and everything in between. Which means there's something here for everyone, whatever your story.

vintageminis.co.uk

1 3 5 7 9 10 8 6 4 2

Vintage
20 Vauxhall Bridge Road,
London SW1V 2SA

Vintage Classics is part of the Penguin Random House
group of companies whose addresses can be found at
global.penguinrandomhouse.com.

Penguin
Random House
UK

Song of Solomon first published in Great Britain by Chatto & Windus in 1978
The Bluest Eye first published in Great Britain by Chatto & Windus in 1979
Beloved first published in Great Britain by Chatto & Windus in 1987
'Recitatif' first published in *Confirmation: An Anthology of
African American Women* in 1983
'Make America White Again' originally published in the *New Yorker*, 2016
This short edition published by Vintage in 2017

penguin.co.uk/vintage

A CIP catalogue record for this book is available from the British Library

ISBN 9781784872779

Typeset in 9.5/14.5 pt FreightText Pro
by Jouve (UK), Milton Keynes
Printed and bound by Clays Ltd, St Ives plc

Penguin Random House is committed to a sustainable future for
our business, our readers and our planet. This book is made from
Forest Stewardship Council® certified paper.

Race

TONI MORRISON

VINTAGE MINIS

From the novel *Song of Solomon*

AT FIFTY-TWO, MACON Dead was as imposing a man as he had been at forty-two, when Milkman thought he was the biggest thing in the world. Bigger even than the house they lived in. But today he had seen a woman who was just as tall and who had made him feel tall too.

'I know I'm the youngest one in this family, but I ain't no baby. You treat me like I was a baby. You keep saying you don't have to explain nothing to me. How do you think that makes me feel? Like a baby, that's what. Like a twelve-year-old baby!'

'Don't you raise your voice to me.'

'Is that the way your father treated you when you were twelve?'

'Watch your mouth!' Macon roared. He took his hands out of his pockets but didn't know what to do with them. He was momentarily confused. His son's question had shifted the scenery. He was seeing himself at twelve, standing in Milkman's shoes and feeling what he himself had felt for his own father. The numbness that had settled on him when he saw the man he loved and admired fall off the fence; something wild ran through him when he watched the body twitching in the dirt. His father had sat for five nights on a split-rail fence cradling a shotgun and in the end died protecting his property. Was that what this boy felt for him? Maybe it was time to tell him things.

'Well, did he?'

'I worked right alongside my father. Right alongside him. From the time I was four or five we worked together. Just the two of us. Our mother was dead. Died when Pilate was born. Pilate was just a baby. She stayed over at another farm in the daytime. I carried her over there myself in my arms every morning. Then I'd go back across the fields and meet my father. We'd hitch President Lincoln to the plow and . . . That's what we called her: President Lincoln. Papa said Lincoln was a good plow hand before he was President and you shouldn't take a good plow hand away from his work. He called our farm Lincoln's Heaven. It was a little bit a place. But it looked big to me then. I know now it must a been a little bit a place, maybe a hundred and fifty acres. We tilled fifty. About eighty of it was woods. Must of been a fortune in oak and pine; maybe that's what they wanted – the lumber, the oak and the pine. We had a pond that was four acres. And a stream, full of fish. Right down in the heart of a valley. Prettiest mountain you ever saw, Montour Ridge. We lived in Montour County. Just north of the Susquehanna. We had a four-stall hog pen. The big barn was forty feet by a hundred and forty – hip-roofed too. And all around in the mountains was deer and wild turkey. You ain't tasted nothing till you taste wild turkey the way Papa cooked it. He'd burn it real fast in the fire. Burn it black all over. That sealed it. Sealed the juices in. Then he'd let it roast on a spit for twenty-four hours. When you cut the black burnt part off, the meat underneath was tender, sweet, juicy. And we had fruit trees. Apple, cherry. Pilate tried to make me a cherry pie once.'

Macon paused and let the smile come on. He had not said any of this for years. Had not even reminisced much about it recently. When he was first married he used to talk about Lincoln's Heaven to Ruth. Sitting on the porch swing in the dark, he would re-create the land that was to have been his. Or when he was just starting out in the business of buying houses, he would lounge around the barbershop and swap stories with the men there. But for years he hadn't had that kind of time, or interest. But now he was doing it again, with his son, and every detail of that land was clear in his mind: the well, the apple orchard, President Lincoln; her foal, Mary Todd; Ulysses S. Grant, their cow; General Lee, their hog. That was the way he knew what history he remembered. His father couldn't read, couldn't write; knew only what he saw and heard tell of. But he had etched in Macon's mind certain historical figures, and as a boy in school, Macon thought of the personalities of his horse, his hog, when he read about these people. His father may have called their plow horse President Lincoln as a joke, but Macon always thought of Lincoln with fondness since he had loved him first as a strong, steady, gentle, and obedient horse. He even liked General Lee, for one spring they slaughtered him and ate the best pork outside Virginia, 'from the butt to the smoked ham to the ribs to the sausage to the jowl to the feet to the tail to the head cheese' – for eight months. And there was cracklin in November.

'General Lee was all right by me,' he told Milkman, smiling. 'Finest general I ever knew. Even his balls was tasty. Circe made up the best pot of maws she ever cooked. Huh! I'd forgotten that woman's name. That was it, Circe. Worked at a big farm some white people owned in Danville, Pennsylvania. Funny how things get away from you. For years you can't remember nothing. Then just like that, it all comes back to you. Had a dog run, they did. That was the big sport back then. Dog races. White people did love their dogs. Kill a nigger and comb their hair at the same time. But I've seen grown white men cry about their dogs.'

His voice sounded different to Milkman. Less hard, and his speech was different. More southern and comfortable and soft. Milkman spoke softly too. 'Pilate said somebody shot your father. Five feet into the air.'

'Took him sixteen years to get that farm to where it was paying. It's all dairy country up there now. Then it wasn't. Then it was . . . nice.'

'Who shot him, Daddy?'

Macon focused his eyes on his son. 'Papa couldn't read, couldn't even sign his name. Had a mark he used. They tricked him. He signed something, I don't know what, and they told him they owned his property. He never read nothing. I tried to teach him, but he said he couldn't remember those little marks from one day to the next. Wrote one word in his life – Pilate's name; copied it out of the Bible. That's what she got folded up in that earring. He should have let me teach him. Everything bad that ever happened to him happened because he couldn't read. Got his name messed up cause he couldn't read.'

'His name? How?'

'When freedom came. All the colored people in the state had to register with the Freedmen's Bureau.'

'Your father was a slave?'

'What kind of foolish question is that? Course he was. Who hadn't been in 1869? They all had to register. Free and not free. Free and used-to-be-slaves. Papa was in his teens and went to sign up, but the man behind the desk was drunk. He asked Papa where he was born. Papa said Macon. Then he asked him who his father was. Papa said, "He's dead." Asked him who owned him, Papa said, "I'm free." Well, the Yankee wrote it all down, but in the wrong spaces. Had him born in Dunfrie, wherever the hell that is, and in the space for his name the fool wrote, "Dead" comma "Macon." But Papa couldn't read so he never found out what he was registered as till Mama told him.

They met on a wagon going North. Started talking about one thing and another, told her about being a freedman and showed off his papers to her. When she looked at his paper she read him out what it said.'

'He didn't have to keep the name, did he? He could have used his real name, couldn't he?'

'Mama liked it. Liked the name. Said it was new and would wipe out the past. Wipe it all out.'

'What was his real name?'

'I don't remember my mother too well. She died when I was four. Light-skinned, pretty. Looked like a white woman to me. Me and Pilate don't take nothing after her. If you ever have a doubt we from Africa, look at Pilate. She look just like Papa and he looked like all them pictures you ever see of Africans. A Pennsylvania African. Acted like one too. Close his face up like a door.'

'I saw Pilate's face like that.' Milkman felt close and confidential now that his father had talked to him in a relaxed and intimate way.

'I haven't changed my mind, Macon. I don't want you over there.'

'Why? You still haven't said why.'

'Just listen to what I say. That woman's no good. She's a snake, and can charm you like a snake, but still a snake.'

'You talking about your own sister, the one you carried in your arms to the fields every morning.'

'That was a long time ago. You seen her. What she look like to you? Somebody nice? Somebody normal?'

'Well, she . . .'

'Or somebody cut your throat?'

'She didn't look like that, Daddy.'

'Well she *is* like that.'

'What'd she do?'

'It ain't what she did; it's what she is.'

'What is she?'

'A snake, I told you. Ever hear the story about the snake? The man who saw a little baby snake on the ground? Well, the man saw this baby snake bleeding and hurt. Lying there in the dirt. And the man felt sorry for it and picked it up and put it in his basket and took it home. And he fed it and took care of it till it was big and strong. Fed it the same thing he ate. Then one day, the snake turned on him and bit him. Stuck his poison tongue right in the man's heart. And while he was laying there dying, he turned to the snake and asked him, "What'd you do that for?" He said, "Didn't I take good care of you? Didn't I save your life?" The snake said, "Yes." "Then what'd you do it for? What'd you kill me for?" Know what the snake said? Said, "But you knew I was a snake, didn't you?" Now, I mean for you to stay out of that wine house and as far away from Pilate as you can.'

Milkman lowered his head. His father had explained nothing to him.

'Boy, you got better things to do with your time. Besides, it's time you started learning how to work. You start Monday. After school come to my office; work a couple of hours there and learn what's real. Pilate can't teach you a thing you can use in this world. Maybe the next, but not this one. Let me tell you right now the one important thing you'll ever need to know: Own things. And let the things you own own other things. Then you'll own yourself and other people too. Starting Monday, I'm going to teach you how.'

THEY WERE SITTING in Mary's Place on a Sunday afternoon a few days after Hagar's latest attempt on his life.

'You're not smoking?' asked Milkman.

'No. I quit. Feel a hell of a lot better too.' There was another pause before Guitar continued. 'You ought to stop yourself.'

Milkman nodded. 'Yeah. If I stay around you I will. I'll stop smoking, fucking, drinking – everything. I'll take up a secret life and hanging out with Empire State.'

Guitar frowned. 'Now who's meddling?'

Milkman sighed and looked straight at his friend. 'I am. I want to know why you were running around with Empire State last Christmas.'

'He was in trouble. I helped him.'

'That's all?'

'What else?'

'I don't know what else. But I know there is something else. Now, if it's something I can't know, okay, say so. But something's going on with you. And I'd like to know what it is.'

Guitar didn't answer.

'We've been friends a long time, Guitar. There's nothing you don't know about me. I can tell you anything – whatever our differences, I know I can trust you. But for some time now it's been a one-way street. You know what I mean? I talk to you, but you don't talk to me. You don't think I can be trusted?'

'I don't know if you can or not.'

'Try me.'

'I can't. Other people are involved.'

'Then don't tell me about other people; tell me about you.'

Guitar looked at him for a long time. Maybe, he thought. Maybe I can trust you. Maybe not, but I'll risk it anyway because one day . . .

'Okay,' he said aloud, 'but you have to know that what I tell you can't go any further. And if it does, you'll be dropping a rope around my neck. Now do you still want to know it?'

'Yeah.'

'You sure?'

'I'm sure.'

Guitar poured some more hot water over his tea. He looked into his cup for a minute while the leaves settled slowly to the bottom. 'I suppose you know that white people kill black people from time to time, and most folks shake their heads and say, "Eh, eh, eh, ain't that a shame?"'

Milkman raised his eyebrows. He thought Guitar was

going to let him in on some deal he had going. But he was slipping into his race bag. He was speaking slowly, as though each word had to count, and as though he were listening carefully to his own words. 'I can't suck my teeth or say "Eh, eh, eh." I had to do something. And the only thing left to do is balance it; keep things on an even keel. Any man, any woman, or any child is good for five to seven generations of heirs before they're bred out. So every death is the death of five to seven generations. You can't stop them from killing us, from trying to get rid of us. And each time they succeed, they get rid of five to seven generations. I help keep the numbers the same.

'There is a society. It's made up of a few men who are willing to take some risks. They don't initiate anything; they don't even choose. They are as indifferent as rain. But when a Negro child, Negro woman, or Negro man is killed by whites and nothing is done about it by *their* law and *their* courts, this society selects a similar victim at random, and they execute him or her in a similar manner if they can. If the Negro was hanged, they hang; if a Negro was burnt, they burn; raped and murdered, they rape and murder. If they can. If they can't do it precisely in the same manner, they do it any way they can, but they do it. They call themselves the Seven Days. They are made up of seven men. Always seven and only seven. If one of them dies or leaves or is no longer effective, another is chosen. Not right away, because that kind of choosing takes time. But they don't seem to be in a hurry. Their secret is

time. To take the time, to last. Not to grow; that's dangerous because you might become known. They don't write
their names in toilet stalls or brag to women. Time and
silence. Those are their weapons, and they go on forever.

'It got started in 1920, when that private from Georgia
was killed after his balls were cut off and after that vet-
eran was blinded when he came home from France in
World War I. And it's been operating ever since. I am one
of them now.'

Milkman had held himself very still all the time Guitar
spoke. Now he felt tight, shriveled, and cold.

'You? You're going to kill people?'

'Not people. White people.'

'But why?'

'I just told you. It's necessary; it's got to be done. To
keep the ratio the same.'

'And if it isn't done? If it just goes on the way it has?'

'Then the world is a zoo, and I can't live in it.'

'Why don't you just hunt down the ones who did the
killing? Why kill innocent people? Why not just those who
did it?'

'It doesn't matter who did it. Each and every one of
them could do it. So you just get any one of them. There
are no innocent white people, because every one of them
is a potential nigger-killer, if not an actual one. You think
Hitler surprised them? You think just because they went
to war they thought he was a freak? Hitler's the most natural white man in the world. He killed Jews and Gypsies

because he didn't have us. Can you see those Klansmen shocked by him? No, you can't.'

'But people who lynch and slice off people's balls – they're crazy, Guitar, crazy.'

'Every time somebody does a thing like that to one of us, they say the people who did it were crazy or ignorant. That's like saying they were drunk. Or constipated. Why isn't cutting a man's eyes out, cutting his nuts off, the kind of thing you never get too drunk or ignorant to do? Too crazy to do? Too constipated to do? And more to the point, how come Negroes, the craziest, most ignorant people in America, don't get that crazy and that ignorant? No. White people are unnatural. As a race they are unnatural. And it takes a strong effort of the will to overcome an unnatural enemy.'

'What about the nice ones? Some whites made sacrifices for Negroes. Real sacrifices.'

'That just means there are one or two natural ones. But they haven't been able to stop the killing either. They are outraged, but that doesn't stop it. They might even speak out, but that doesn't stop it either. They might even inconvenience themselves, but the killing goes on and on. So will we.'

'You're missing the point. There're not just one or two. There're a lot.'

'Are there? Milkman, if Kennedy got drunk and bored and was sitting around a potbellied stove in Mississippi, he might join a lynching party just for the hell of it. Under those circumstances his unnaturalness would surface. But I know I wouldn't join one no matter how drunk I was or how bored, and I know you wouldn't either, nor any black man I know or ever heard tell of. Ever. In any world, at any time, just get up and go find somebody white to slice up. But they *can* do it. And they don't even do it for profit, which is why they do most things. They do it for fun. Unnatural.'

'What about . . .' Milkman searched his memory for some white person who had shown himself unequivocally supportive of Negroes. 'Schweitzer. Albert Schweitzer. Would he do it?'

'In a minute. He didn't care anything about those Africans. They could have been rats. He was in a laboratory testing *himself* – proving he could work on human dogs.'

'What about Eleanor Roosevelt?'

'I don't know about the women. I can't say what their women would do, but I do remember that picture of those white mothers holding up their babies so they could get a good look at some black men burning on a tree. So I have my suspicions about Eleanor Roosevelt. But *none* about Mr Roosevelt. You could've taken him and his wheelchair and put him in a small dusty town in Alabama and given him some tobacco, a checkerboard, some whiskey, and a rope and he'd have done it too. What I'm saying is, under certain conditions they would *all* do it. And under the same circumstances we would not. So it doesn't matter that some of them *haven't* done it. I listen. I read. And now

I know that they know it too. They know they are unnatural. Their writers and artists have been saying it for years. Telling them they are unnatural, telling them they are depraved. They call it tragedy. In the movies they call it adventure. It's just depravity that they try to make glorious, natural. But it ain't. The disease they have is in their blood, in the structure of their chromosomes.'

'You can prove this, I guess. Scientifically?'

'No.'

'Shouldn't you be able to prove it before you act on something like that?'

'Did they prove anything scientifically about us before they killed us? No. They killed us first and then tried to get some scientific proof about why we should die.'

'Wait a minute, Guitar. If they are as bad, as unnatural, as you say, why do you want to be like them? Don't you want to be better than they are?'

'I am better.'

'But now you're doing what the worst of them do.'

'Yes, but I am reasonable.'

'Reasonable? How?'

'I am not, one, having fun; two, trying to gain power or public attention or money or land; three, angry at anybody.'

'You're not angry? You must be!'

'Not at all. I hate doing it. I'm afraid to do it. It's hard to do it when you aren't angry or drunk or doped up or don't have a personal grudge against the person.'

'I can't see how it helps. I can't see how it helps anybody.'

'I told you. Numbers. Balance. Ratio. And the earth, the land.'

'I'm not understanding you.'

'The earth is soggy with black people's blood. And before us Indian blood. Nothing can cure them, and if it keeps on there won't be any of us left and there won't be any land for those who are left. So the numbers have to remain static.'

'But there are more of them than us.'

'Only in the West. But still the ratio can't widen in their favor.'

'But you should want everybody to know that the society exists. Then maybe that would help stop it. What's the secrecy for?'

'To keep from getting caught.'

'Can't you even let other Negroes know about it? I mean to give us hope?'

'No.'

'Why not?'

'Betrayal. The possibility of betrayal.'

'Well, let *them* know. Let white people know. Like the Mafia or the Klan; frighten them into behaving.'

'You're talking foolishness. How can you let one group know and not the other? Besides, we are not like them. The Mafia is unnatural. So is the Klan. One kills for money, the other kills for fun. And they have huge profits and protection at their disposal. We don't. But it's not about other people knowing. We don't even tell the victims. We just whisper to him, "Your Day has come." The beauty of what we do is its secrecy, its smallness. The fact that nobody needs the unnatural satisfaction of talking about it. Telling about it. We don't discuss it among ourselves, the details. We just get an assignment. If the Negro was killed on a Wednesday, the Wednesday man takes it; if he was killed on Monday, the Monday man takes that one. And we just notify one another when it's completed, not how or who. And if it ever gets to be too much, like it was for Robert Smith, we do *that* rather than crack and tell somebody. Like Porter. It was getting him down. They thought somebody would have to take over his day. He just needed a rest and he's okay now.'

Milkman stared at his friend and then let the spasm he had been holding back run through him. 'I can't buy it, Guitar.'

'I know that.'

'There's too much wrong with it.'

'Tell me.'

'Well, for one thing, you'll get caught eventually.'

'Maybe. But if I'm caught I'll just die earlier than I'm supposed to – not better than I'm supposed to. And how I die or when doesn't interest me. What I die *for* does. It's the same as what I live for. Besides, if I'm caught they'll accuse me and kill me for one crime, maybe two, never for all. And there are still six other days in the week. We've been around for a long long time. And believe me, we'll be around for a long long time to come.'

'You can't marry.'

'No.'

'Have children.'

'No.'

'What kind of life is that?'

'Very satisfying.'

'There's no love in it.'

'No love? No love? Didn't you hear me? What I'm doing ain't about hating white people. It's about loving us. About loving you. My whole life is love.'

'Man, you're confused.'

'Am I? When those concentration camp Jews hunt down Nazis, are they hating Nazis or loving dead Jews?'

'It's not the same thing.'

'Only because they have money and publicity.'

'No; because they turn them over to the courts. You kill and you don't kill the killers. You kill innocent people.'

'I told you there are no –'

'And you don't correct a thing by –'

'We poor people, Milkman. I work at an auto plant. The rest of us barely eke out a living. Where's the money, the state, the country to finance our justice? You say Jews try their catches in a court. Do we have a court? Is there one courthouse in one city in the country where a jury would convict them? There are places right now where a Negro still can't testify against a white man. Where the judge, the jury, the court, are legally bound to ignore anything a Negro has to say. What that means is that a black man is a victim of a crime only when a white man says he is. Only then. If there was anything like or near justice or courts when a cracker kills a Negro, there wouldn't have to be no Seven Days. But there ain't; so we are. And we do it without money, without support, without costumes, without newspapers, without senators, without lobbyists, and without illusions!'

'You sound like that red-headed Negro named X. Why don't you join him and call yourself Guitar X?'

'X, Bains – what difference does it make? I don't give a damn about names.'

'You miss his point. His point is to let white people know you don't accept your slave name.'

'I don't give a shit what white people know or even think. Besides, I do accept it. It's part of who I am. Guitar is *my* name. Bains is the slave master's name. And I'm all of that. Slave names don't bother me; but slave status does.'

'And knocking off white folks changes your slave status?'

'Believe it.'

'Does it do anything for my slave status?'

Guitar smiled. 'Well, doesn't it?'

'Hell, no.' Milkman frowned. 'Am I going to live any longer because you all read the newspaper and then ambush some poor old white man?'

'It's not about you living longer. It's about how you live and why. It's about whether your children can make other children. It's about trying to make a world where one day white people will think before they lynch.'

'Guitar, none of that shit is going to change how I live or how any other Negro lives. What you're doing is crazy. And something else: it's a habit. If you do it enough, you can do it to anybody. You know what I mean? A torpedo is a torpedo, I don't care what his reasons. You can off anybody you don't like. You can off me.'

'We don't off Negroes.'

'You hear what you said? *Negroes.* Not Milkman. Not "No, I can't touch *you*, Milkman," but "We don't off Negroes." Shit, man, suppose you all change your parliamentary rules?'

'The Days are the Days. It's been that way a long time.'

Milkman thought about that. 'Any other young dudes in it? Are all the others older? You the only young one?'

'Why?'

''Cause young dudes are subject to change the rules.'

'You worried about yourself, Milkman?' Guitar looked amused.

'No. Not really.' Milkman put his cigarette out and reached for another one. 'Tell me, what's your day?'

'Sunday. I'm the Sunday man.'

Milkman rubbed the ankle of his short leg. 'I'm scared for you, man.'

'That's funny. I'm scared for you too.'

GUITAR WAS WATCHING him carefully. 'What's the matter?' he asked. 'Why you so low? You don't act like a man on his way to the end of the rainbow.'

Milkman turned around and sat on the sill. 'I hope it *is* a rainbow, and nobody has run off with the pot, cause I need it.'

'Everybody needs it.'

'Not as bad as me.'

Guitar smiled. 'Look like you really got the itch now. More than before.'

'Yeah, well, everything's worse than before, or maybe it's the same as before. I don't know. I just know that I want to live my own life. I don't want to be my old man's office boy no more. And as long as I'm in this place I will be. Unless I have my own money. I have to get out of that house and I don't want to owe anybody when I go. My family's driving me crazy. Daddy wants me to be like him and hate my mother. My mother wants me to think like her and hate my father. Corinthians won't speak to me; Lena wants me out. And Hagar wants me chained to her bed or dead. Everybody wants something from me, you know what I mean? Something they think they can't get anywhere else. Something they think I got. I don't know what it is – I mean what it is they really want.'

Guitar stretched his legs. 'They want your life, man.'

'My life?'

'What else?'

'No. Hagar wants my life. My family . . . they want –'

'I don't mean that way. I don't mean they want your dead life; they want your living life.'

'You're losing me,' said Milkman.

'Look. It's the condition our condition is in. Everybody wants the life of a black man. Everybody. White men want us dead or quiet – which is the same thing as dead. White women, same thing. They want us, you know, "universal," human, no "race consciousness." Tame, except in bed. They like a little racial loincloth in the bed. But outside the bed they want us to be individuals. You tell them, "But they lynched my papa," and they say, "Yeah, but you're better than the lynchers are, so forget it." And black women, they want your whole self. Love, they call it, and understanding. "Why don't you *understand* me?" What they mean is, Don't love anything on earth except me. They say, "Be responsible," but what they mean is, Don't go anywhere where I ain't. You try to climb Mount Everest, they'll tie up your ropes. Tell them you want to go to the bottom of the sea – just for a look – they'll hide your oxygen tank. Or you don't even have to go that far. Buy a horn and say you want to play. Oh, they love the music, but only after you pull eight at the post office. Even if you make it, even if you stubborn and mean and you get to the top of Mount Everest, or you do play and you good, real good – that still ain't enough. You blow your lungs out on the horn and they want what breath you got left to hear about how you love them. They want your full attention. Take a risk and they say you not for real. That you don't love them. They won't even let you risk your own life, man, your *own* life – unless it's over them. You can't even die unless it's about them. What good is a man's life if he can't even choose what to die for?'

'Nobody can choose what to die for.'

'Yes you can, and if you can't, you can damn well try to.'

'You sound bitter. If that's what you feel, why are you playing your numbers game? Keeping the racial ratio the same and all? Every time I ask you what you doing it for, you talk about love. Loving Negroes. Now you say –'

'It *is* about love. What else but love? Can't I love what I criticize?'

'Yeah, but except for skin color, I can't tell the difference between what the white women want from us and what the colored women want. You say they all want our life, our living life. So if a colored woman is raped and killed, why do the Days rape and kill a white woman? Why worry about the colored woman at all?'

Guitar cocked his head and looked sideways at Milkman. His nostrils flared a little. 'Because she's *mine*.'

'Yeah. Sure.' Milkman didn't try to keep disbelief out of his voice. 'So everybody wants to kill us, except black men, right?'

'Right.'

'Then why did my father – who is a very black man – try to kill me before I was even born?'

'Maybe he thought you were a little girl; I don't know. But I don't have to tell you that your father is a very strange Negro. He'll reap the benefits of what we sow, and there's nothing we can do about that. He behaves like a

What good is a man's life if he can't even choose what to die for?

white man, thinks like a white man. As a matter of fact, I'm glad you brought him up. Maybe you can tell me how, after losing everything his own father worked for to some crackers, after *seeing* his father shot down by them, how can he keep his knees bent? Why does he love them so? And Pilate. She's worse. She saw it too and, first, goes back to get a cracker's bones for some kind of crazy self-punishment, and second, leaves the cracker's gold right where it was! Now, is that voluntary slavery or not? She slipped into those Jemima shoes cause they fit.'

'Look, Guitar. First of all, my father doesn't care whether a white man lives or swallows lye. He just wants what they have. And Pilate is a little nuts, but she wanted us out of there. If she hadn't been smart, both our asses would be cooling in the joint right now.'

'My ass. Not yours. She wanted you out, not me.'

'Come on. That ain't even fair.'

'No. Fair is one more thing I've given up.'

'But to Pilate? What for? She knew what we did and still she bailed us out. Went down for us, clowned and crawled for us. You saw her face. You ever see anything like it in your life?'

'Once. Just once,' said Guitar. And he remembered anew how his mother smiled when the white man handed her the four ten-dollar bills. More than gratitude was showing in her eyes. More than that. Not love, but a willingness to love. Her husband was sliced in half and boxed backward. He'd heard the mill men tell how the two halves, not even fitted together, were placed cut side down, skin side up, in the coffin. Facing each other. Each eye looking deep into its mate. Each nostril inhaling the breath the other nostril had expelled. The right cheek facing the left. The right elbow crossed over the left elbow. And he had worried then, as a child, that when his father was wakened on Judgment Day his first sight would not be glory or the magnificent head of God – or even the rainbow. It would be his own other eye.

Even so, his mother had smiled and shown that willingness to love the man who was responsible for dividing his father up throughout eternity. It wasn't the divinity from the foreman's wife that made him sick. That came later. It was the fact that instead of life insurance, the sawmill owner gave his mother forty dollars 'to tide you and them kids over,' and she took it happily and bought each of them a big peppermint stick on the very day of the funeral. Guitar's two sisters and baby brother sucked away at the bone-white and blood-red stick, but Guitar couldn't. He held it in his hand until it stuck there. All day he held it. At the graveside, at the funeral supper, all the sleepless night. The others made fun of what they believed was his miserliness, but he could not eat it or throw it away, until finally, in the outhouse, he let it fall into the earth's stinking hole.

'Once,' he said. 'Just once.' And felt the nausea all over again. 'The crunch is here,' he said. 'The big crunch. Don't let them Kennedys fool you. And I'll tell you the truth: I hope your daddy's right about what's in that cave. And I sure hope you don't have no second thoughts about getting it back here.'

'What's that supposed to mean?'

'It means I'm nervous. Real nervous. I need the bread.'

'If you're in a hurt, I can let you have –'

'Not *me*. *Us*. We have work to do, man. And just recently' – Guitar squinted his eyes at Milkman – 'just recently one of us was put out in the streets, by somebody I don't have to name. And his wages were garnisheed cause this somebody said two months rent was owing. This somebody needs two months rent on a twelve-by-twelve hole in the wall like a fish needs side pockets. Now we have to take care of this man, get him a place to stay, pay the so-called back rent, and –'

'That was my fault. Let me tell you what happened . . .'

'No. Don't tell me nothing. You ain't the landlord and you didn't put him out. You may have handed him the gun, but you didn't pull the trigger. I'm not blaming you.'

'Why not? You talk about my father, my father's sister, and you'll talk about my sister too if I let you. Why you trust me?'

'Baby, I hope I never have to ask myself that question.'

It ended all right, that gloomy conversation. There was no real anger and nothing irrevocable was said. When Milkman left, Guitar opened his palm as usual and

Milkman slapped it. Maybe it was fatigue, but the touching of palms seemed a little weak.

MILKMAN TURNED IN his seat and tried to stretch his legs. It was morning. He'd changed buses three times and was now speeding home on the last leg of his trip. He looked out the window. Far away from Virginia, fall had already come. Ohio, Indiana, Michigan were dressed up like the Indian warriors from whom their names came. Blood red and yellow, ocher and ice blue.

He read the road signs with interest now, wondering what lay beneath the names. The Algonquins had named the territory he lived in Great Water, *michi gami*. How many dead lives and fading memories were buried in and beneath the names of the places in this country. Under the recorded names were other names, just as 'Macon Dead,' recorded for all time in some dusty file, hid from view the real names of people, places, and things. Names that had meaning. No wonder Pilate put hers in her ear. When you know your name, you should hang on to it, for unless it is noted down and remembered, it will die when you do. Like the street he lived on, recorded as Mains Avenue, but called Not Doctor Street by the Negroes in memory of his grandfather, who was the first colored man of consequence in that city. Never mind that he probably didn't deserve their honor – they knew what kind of man he was: arrogant, color-struck, snobbish. They didn't care about that. They were paying their respect to whatever it was that made him *be* a doctor in the first place, when the odds were that he'd be a yardman all of his life. So they named a street after him. Pilate had taken a rock from every state she had lived in – because she *had* lived there. And having lived there, it was hers – and his, and his father's, his grandfather's, his grandmother's. Not Doctor Street, Solomon's Leap, Ryna's Gulch, Shalimar, Virginia.

He closed his eyes and thought of the black men in Shalimar, Roanoke, Petersburg, Newport News, Danville, in the Blood Bank, on Darling Street, in the pool halls, the barbershops. Their names. Names they got from yearnings, gestures, flaws, events, mistakes, weaknesses. Names that bore witness. Macon Dead, Sing Byrd, Crowell Byrd, Pilate, Reba, Hagar, Magdalene, First Corinthians, Milkman, Guitar, Railroad Tommy, Hospital Tommy, Empire State (he just stood around and swayed), Small Boy, Sweet, Circe, Moon, Nero, Humpty-Dumpty, Blue Boy, Scandinavia, Quack-Quack, Jericho, Spoonbread, Ice Man, Dough Belly, Rocky River, Gray Eye, Cock-a-Doodle-Doo, Cool Breeze, Muddy Waters, Pinetop, Jelly Roll, Fats, Lead-belly, Bo Diddley, Cat-Iron, Peg-Leg, Son, Shortstuff, Smoky Babe, Funny Papa, Bukka, Pink, Bull Moose, B. B., T-Bone, Black Ace, Lemon, Washboard, Gatemouth, Cleanhead, Tampa Red, Juke Boy, Shine, Staggerlee, Jim the Devil, Fuck-Up, and *Dat* Nigger.

Angling out from these thoughts of names was one

more – the one that whispered in the spinning wheels of the bus: 'Guitar is biding his time. Guitar is biding his time. Your day has come. Your day has come. Guitar is biding his time. Guitar is a very good Day. Guitar is a very good Day. A very good Day, a very good Day, and biding, biding his time.'

In the seventy-five-dollar car, and here on the big Greyhound, Milkman felt safe. But there were days and days ahead. Maybe if Guitar was back in the city now, among familiar surroundings, Milkman could defuse him. And certainly, in time, he would discover his foolishness. There was no gold. And although things would never be the same between them, at least the man-hunt would be over.

Even as he phrased the thought in his mind, Milkman knew it was not so. Either Guitar's disappointment with the gold that was not there was so deep it had deranged him, or his 'work' had done it. Or maybe he simply allowed himself to feel about Milkman what he had always felt about Macon Dead and the Honoré crowd. In any case, he had snatched the first straw, limp and wet as it was, to prove to himself the need to kill Milkman. The Sunday-school girls deserved better than to be avenged by that hawk-headed raven-skinned Sunday man who included in his blood sweep four innocent white girls and one innocent black man.

Perhaps that's what all human relationships boiled down to: Would you save my life? or would you take it?

'Everybody wants a black man's life.'

Yeah. And black men were not excluded. With two exceptions, everybody he was close to seemed to prefer him out of this life. And the two exceptions were both women, both black, both old. From the beginning, his mother and Pilate had fought for his life, and he had never so much as made either of them a cup of tea.

Would you save my life or would you take it? Guitar was exceptional. To both questions he could answer yes.

From the novel *The Bluest Eye*

1.

SHE SLEPT IN the bed with us. Frieda on the outside because she is brave – it never occurs to her that if in her sleep her hand hangs over the edge of the bed 'something' will crawl out from under it and bite her fingers off. I sleep near the wall because that thought *has* occurred to me. Pecola, therefore, had to sleep in the middle.

Mama had told us two days earlier that a 'case' was coming – a girl who had no place to go. The county had placed her in our house for a few days until they could decide what to do, or, more precisely, until the family was reunited. We were to be nice to her and not fight. Mama didn't know 'what got into people,' but that old Dog Breedlove had burned up his house, gone upside his wife's head, and everybody, as a result, was outdoors.

Outdoors, we knew, was the real terror of life. The threat of being outdoors surfaced frequently in those days. Every possibility of excess was curtailed with it. If somebody ate too much, he could end up outdoors. If somebody used too much coal, he could end up outdoors. People could gamble themselves outdoors, drink themselves outdoors. Sometimes mothers put their sons outdoors, and when that happened, regardless of what the son had done, all sympathy was with him. He was outdoors, and his own flesh had done it. To be put outdoors by a landlord was one thing – unfortunate, but an aspect of life over which you had no control, since you could not control your income. But to be slack enough to put oneself outdoors, or heartless enough to put one's own kin outdoors – that was criminal.

There is a difference between being put *out* and being put out*doors*. If you are put out, you go somewhere else; if you are outdoors, there is no place to go. The distinction was subtle but final. Outdoors was the end of something, an irrevocable, physical fact, defining and complementing our metaphysical condition. Being a minority in both caste and class, we moved about anyway on the hem of life, struggling to consolidate our weaknesses and hang on, or to creep singly up into the major folds of the garment. Our peripheral existence, however, was something we had learned to deal with – probably because it was abstract. But the concreteness of being outdoors was another matter – like the difference between the concept of death and being, in fact, dead. Dead doesn't change, and outdoors is here to stay.

Knowing that there was such a thing as outdoors bred

in us a hunger for property, for ownership. The firm possession of a yard, a porch, a grape arbor. Propertied black people spent all their energies, all their love, on their nests. Like frenzied, desperate birds, they overdecorated everything; fussed and fidgeted over their hard-won homes; canned, jellied, and preserved all summer to fill the cupboards and shelves; they painted, picked, and poked at every corner of their houses. And these houses loomed like hothouse sunflowers among the rows of weeds that were the rented houses. Renting blacks cast furtive glances at these owned yards and porches, and made firmer commitments to buy themselves 'some nice little old place.' In the meantime, they saved, and scratched, and piled away what they could in the rented hovels, looking forward to the day of property.

Cholly Breedlove, then, a renting black, having put his family outdoors, had catapulted himself beyond the reaches of human consideration. He had joined the animals; was, indeed, an old dog, a snake, a ratty nigger. Mrs Breedlove was staying with the woman she worked for; the boy, Sammy, was with some other family; and Pecola was to stay with us. Cholly was in jail.

She came with nothing. No little paper bag with the other dress, or a nightgown, or two pair of whitish cotton bloomers. She just appeared with a white woman and sat down.

We had fun in those few days Pecola was with us. Frieda and I stopped fighting each other and concentrated on our guest, trying hard to keep her from feeling outdoors.

When we discovered that she clearly did not want to dominate us, we liked her. She laughed when I clowned for her, and smiled and accepted gracefully the food gifts my sister gave her.

'Would you like some graham crackers?'

'I don't care.'

Frieda brought her four graham crackers on a saucer and some milk in a blue-and-white Shirley Temple cup. She was a long time with the milk, and gazed fondly at the silhouette of Shirley Temple's dimpled face. Frieda and she had a loving conversation about how cu-ute Shirley Temple was. I couldn't join them in their adoration because I hated Shirley. Not because she was cute, but because she danced with Bojangles, who was *my* friend, *my* uncle, *my* daddy, and who ought to have been soft-shoeing it and chuckling with me. Instead he was enjoying, sharing, giving a lovely dance thing with one of those little white girls whose socks never slid down under their heels. So I said, 'I like Jane Withers.'

They gave me a puzzled look, decided I was incomprehensible, and continued their reminiscing about old squint-eyed Shirley.

Younger than both Frieda and Pecola, I had not yet arrived at the turning point in the development of my psyche which would allow me to love her. What I felt at that time was unsullied hatred. But before that I had felt a stranger, more frightening thing than hatred for all the Shirley Temples of the world.

It had begun with Christmas and the gift of dolls. The big, the special, the loving gift was always a big, blue-eyed Baby Doll. From the clucking sounds of adults I knew that the doll represented what they thought was my fondest wish. I was bemused with the thing itself, and the way it looked. What was I supposed to do with it? Pretend I was its mother? I had no interest in babies or the concept of motherhood. I was interested only in humans my own age and size, and could not generate any enthusiasm at the prospect of being a mother. Motherhood was old age, and other remote possibilities. I learned quickly, however, what I was expected to do with the doll: rock it, fabricate storied situations around it, even sleep with it. Picture books were full of little girls sleeping with their dolls. Raggedy Ann dolls usually, but they were out of the question. I was physically revolted by and secretly frightened of those round moronic eyes, the pancake face, and orangeworms hair.

The other dolls, which were supposed to bring me great pleasure, succeeded in doing quite the opposite. When I took it to bed, its hard unyielding limbs resisted my flesh – the tapered fingertips on those dimpled hands scratched. If, in sleep, I turned, the bone-cold head collided with my own. It was a most uncomfortable, patently aggressive sleeping companion. To hold it was no more rewarding. The starched gauze or lace on the cotton dress irritated any embrace. I had only one desire: to dismember it. To see of what it was made, to discover the dearness, to find the beauty, the desirability that had escaped me, but apparently only me. Adults, older girls, shops, magazines, newspapers, window signs – all the world had agreed that a blue-eyed, yellow-haired, pink-skinned doll was what every girl child treasured. 'Here,' they said, 'this is beautiful, and if you are on this day "worthy" you may have it.' I fingered the face, wondering at the single-stroke eyebrows; picked at the pearly teeth stuck like two piano keys between red bowline lips. Traced the turned-up nose, poked the glassy blue eyeballs, twisted the yellow hair. I could not love it. But I could examine it to see what it was that all the world said was lovable. Break off the tiny fingers, bend the flat feet, loosen the hair, twist the head around, and the thing made one sound – a sound they said was the sweet and plaintive cry 'Mama,' but which sounded to me like the bleat of a dying lamb, or, more precisely, our icebox door opening on rusty hinges in July. Remove the cold and stupid eyeball, it would bleat still, 'Ahhhhhh,' take off the head, shake out the sawdust, crack the back against the brass bed rail, it would bleat still. The gauze back would split, and I could see the disk with six holes, the secret of the sound. A mere metal roundness.

Grown people frowned and fussed: 'You-don't-know-how-to-take-care-of-nothing. I-never-had-a-baby-doll-in-my-whole-life-and-used-to-cry-my-eyes-out-for-them. Now-you-got-one-a-beautiful-one-and-you-tear-it-up-what's-the-matter-with-you?'

How strong was their outrage. Tears threatened to erase the aloofness of their authority. The emotion of years of unfulfilled longing preened in their voices. I did not know why I destroyed those dolls. But I did know that nobody ever asked me what I wanted for Christmas. Had any adult with the power to fulfill my desires taken me seriously and asked me what I wanted, they would have known that I did not want to have anything to own, or to possess any object. I wanted rather to feel something on Christmas day. The real question would have been, 'Dear Claudia, what experience would you like on Christmas?' I could have spoken up, 'I want to sit on the low stool in Big Mama's kitchen with my lap full of lilacs and listen to Big Papa play his violin for me alone.' The lowness of the stool made for my body, the security and warmth of Big Mama's kitchen, the smell of the lilacs, the sound of the music, and, since it would be good to have all of my senses engaged, the taste of a peach, perhaps, afterward.

Instead I tasted and smelled the acridness of tin plates and cups designed for tea parties that bored me. Instead I looked with loathing on new dresses that required a hateful bath in a galvanized zinc tub before wearing. Slipping around on the zinc, no time to play or soak, for the water chilled too fast, no time to enjoy one's nakedness, only time to make curtains of soapy water careen down between the legs. Then the scratchy towels and the dreadful and humiliating absence of dirt. The irritable, unimaginative cleanliness. Gone the ink marks from legs and face, all my creations and accumulations of the day gone, and replaced by goose pimples.

I destroyed white baby dolls.

But the dismembering of dolls was not the true horror. The truly horrifying thing was the transference of the same impulses to little white girls. The indifference with which I could have axed them was shaken only by my desire to do so. To discover what eluded me: the secret of the magic they weaved on others. What made people look at them and say, 'Awwwww,' but not for me? The eye slide of black women as they approached them on the street, and the possessive gentleness of their touch as they handled them.

If I pinched them, their eyes – unlike the crazed glint of the baby doll's eyes – would fold in pain, and their cry would not be the sound of an icebox door, but a fascinating cry of pain. When I learned how repulsive this disinterested violence was, that it was repulsive because it was disinterested, my shame floundered about for refuge. The best hiding place was love. Thus the conversion from pristine sadism to fabricated hatred, to fraudulent love. It was a small step to Shirley Temple. I learned much later to worship her, just as I learned to delight in cleanliness, knowing, even as I learned, that the change was adjustment without improvement.

LETTING HERSELF BREATHE easy now, Pecola covered her head with the quilt. The sick feeling, which she had tried to prevent by holding in her stomach, came quickly in spite of her precaution. There surged in her the desire to heave, but as always, she knew she would not.

'Please, God,' she whispered into the palm of her hand. 'Please make me disappear.' She squeezed her eyes shut. Little parts of her body faded away. Now slowly, now with a rush. Slowly again. Her fingers went, one by one; then her arms disappeared all the way to the elbow. Her feet now. Yes, that was good. The legs all at once. It was hardest above the thighs. She had to be real still and pull. Her stomach would not go. But finally it, too, went away. Then her chest, her neck. The face was hard, too. Almost done, almost. Only her tight, tight eyes were left. They were always left.

Try as she might, she could never get her eyes to disappear. So what was the point? They were everything. Everything was there, in them. All of those pictures, all of those faces. She had long ago given up the idea of running away to see new pictures, new faces, as Sammy had so often done. He never took her, and he never thought about his going ahead of time, so it was never planned. It wouldn't have worked anyway. As long as she looked the way she did, as long as she was ugly, she would have to stay with these people. Somehow she belonged to them. Long hours she sat looking in the mirror, trying to discover the secret of the ugliness, the ugliness that made her ignored or despised at school, by teachers and classmates alike. She was the only member of her class who sat alone at a double desk. The first letter of her last name forced her to sit in the front of the room always. But what about Marie Appolonaire? Marie was in front of her, but she shared a desk with Luke Angelino. Her teachers had always treated her this way. They tried never to glance at her, and called on her only when everyone was required to respond. She also knew that when one of the girls at school wanted to be particularly insulting to a boy, or wanted to get an immediate response from him, she could say. 'Bobby loves Pecola Breedlove! Bobby loves Pecola Breedlove!' and never fail to get peals of laughter from those in earshot, and mock anger from the accused.

It had occurred to Pecola some time ago that if her eyes, those eyes that held the pictures, and knew the sights – if those eyes of hers were different, that is to say, beautiful, she herself would be different. Her teeth were good, and at least her nose was not big and flat like some of those who were thought so cute. If she looked different, beautiful, maybe Cholly would be different, and Mrs Breedlove too. Maybe they'd say, 'Why, look at pretty-eyed Pecola. We mustn't do bad things in front of those pretty eyes.'

> *Pretty eyes. Pretty blue eyes. Big blue pretty eyes.*
> *Run, Jip, run. Jip runs, Alice runs. Alice has blue eyes.*
> *Jerry has blue eyes. Jerry runs. Alice runs. They run*
> *with their blue eyes. Four blue eyes. Four pretty*
> *blue eyes. Blue-sky eyes. Blue-like Mrs Forrest's*

blue blouse eyes. Morning-glory-blue-eyes.
Alice-and-Jerry-blue-storybook-eyes.

Each night, without fail, she prayed for blue eyes. Fervently, for a year she had prayed. Although somewhat discouraged, she was not without hope. To have something as wonderful as that happen would take a long, long time.

Thrown, in this way, into the binding conviction that only a miracle could relieve her, she would never know her beauty. She would see only what there was to see: the eyes of other people.

She walks down Garden Avenue to a small grocery store which sells penny candy. Three pennies are in her shoe – slipping back and forth between the sock and the inner sole. With each step she feels the painful press of the coins against her foot. A sweet, endurable, even cherished irritation, full of promise and delicate security. There is plenty of time to consider what to buy. Now, however, she moves down an avenue gently buffeted by the familiar and therefore loved images. The dandelions at the base of the telephone pole. Why, she wonders, do people call them weeds? She thought they were pretty. But grown-ups say, 'Miss Dunion keeps her yard so nice. Not a dandelion anywhere.' Hunkie women in black babushkas go into the fields with baskets to pull them up. But they do not want the yellow heads – only the jagged leaves. They make dandelion soup. Dandelion wine.

Nobody loves the head of a dandelion. Maybe because they are so many, strong, and soon.

There was the sidewalk crack shaped like a Y, and the other one that lifted the concrete up from the dirt floor. Frequently her sloughing step had made her trip over that one. Skates would go well over this sidewalk – old it was, and smooth; it made the wheels glide evenly, with a mild whirr. The newly paved walks were bumpy and uncomfortable, and the sound of skate wheels on new walks was grating.

These and other inanimate things she saw and experienced. They were real to her. She knew them. They were the codes and touchstones of the world, capable of translation and possession. She owned the crack that made her stumble; she owned the clumps of dandelions whose white heads, last fall, she had blown away; whose yellow heads, this fall, she peered into. And owning them made her part of the world, and the world a part of her.

She climbs four wooden steps to the door of Yacobowski's Fresh Veg. Meat and Sundries Store. A bell tinkles as she opens it. Standing before the counter, she looks at the array of candies. All Mary Janes, she decides. Three for a penny. The resistant sweetness that breaks open at last to deliver peanut butter – the oil and salt which complement the sweet pull of caramel. A peal of anticipation unsettles her stomach.

She pulls off her shoe and takes out the three pennies. The gray head of Mr Yacobowski looms up over the counter. He urges his eyes out of his thoughts to encounter her. Blue eyes. Blear-dropped. Slowly, like Indian summer moving imperceptibly toward fall, he looks toward her. Somewhere between retina and object, between vision and view, his eyes draw back, hesitate, and hover. At some fixed point in time and space he senses that he need not waste the effort of a glance. He does not see her, because for him there is nothing to see. How can a fifty-two-year-old white immigrant storekeeper with the taste of potatoes and beer in his mouth, his mind honed on the doe-eyed Virgin Mary, his sensibilities blunted by a permanent awareness of loss, *see* a little black girl? Nothing in his life even suggested that the feat was possible, not to say desirable or necessary.

'Yeah?'

She looks up at him and sees the vacuum where curiosity ought to lodge. And something more. The total absence of human recognition – the glazed separateness. She does not know what keeps his glance suspended. Perhaps because he is grown, or a man, and she a little girl. But she has seen interest, disgust, even anger in grown male eyes. Yet this vacuum is not new to her. It has an edge; somewhere in the bottom lid is the distaste. She has seen it lurking in the eyes of all white people. So. The distaste must be for her, her blackness. All things in her are flux and anticipation. But her blackness is static and dread. And it is the blackness that accounts for, that creates, the vacuum edged with distaste in white eyes.

He does not see her, because for him there is nothing to see

She points her finger at the Mary Janes – a little black shaft of finger, its tip pressed on the display window. The quietly inoffensive assertion of a black child's attempt to communicate with a white adult.

'Them.' The word is more sigh than sense.

'What? These? These?' Phlegm and impatience mingle in his voice.

She shakes her head, her fingertip fixed on the spot which, in her view, at any rate, identifies the Mary Janes. He cannot see her view – the angle of his vision, the slant of her finger, makes it incomprehensible to him. His lumpy red hand plops around in the glass casing like the agitated head of a chicken outraged by the loss of its body.

'Christ. Kantcha talk?'

His fingers brush the Mary Janes.

She nods.

'Well, why'nt you say so? One? How many?'

Pecola unfolds her fist, showing the three pennies. He scoots three Mary Janes toward her – three yellow rectangles in each packet. She holds the money toward him. He hesitates, not wanting to touch her hand. She does not know how to move the finger of her right hand from the display counter or how to get the coins out of her left hand. Finally he reaches over and takes the pennies from her hand. His nails graze her damp palm.

Outside, Pecola feels the inexplicable shame ebb.

Dandelions. A dart of affection leaps out from her to them. But they do not look at her and do not send love back. She thinks, 'They *are* ugly. They *are* weeds.' Pre-occupied with that revelation, she trips on the sidewalk crack. Anger stirs and wakes in her; it opens its mouth, and like a hot-mouthed puppy, laps up the dredges of her shame.

Anger is better. There is a sense of being in anger. A reality and presence. An awareness of worth. It is a lovely surging. Her thoughts fall back to Mr Yacobowski's eyes, his phlegmy voice. The anger will not hold; the puppy is too easily surfeited. Its thirst too quickly quenched, it sleeps. The shame wells up again, its muddy rivulets seeping into her eyes. What to do before the tears come. She remembers the Mary Janes.

Each pale yellow wrapper has a picture on it. A picture of little Mary Jane, for whom the candy is named. Smiling white face. Blond hair in gentle disarray, blue eyes looking at her out of a world of clean comfort. The eyes are petulant, mischievous. To Pecola they are simply pretty. She eats the candy, and its sweetness is good. To eat the candy is somehow to eat the eyes, eat Mary Jane. Love Mary Jane. Be Mary Jane.

Three pennies had bought her nine lovely orgasms with Mary Jane. Lovely Mary Jane, for whom a candy is named.

2.

THEY COME FROM Mobile. Aiken. From Newport News. From Marietta. From Meridian. And the sound of these places in their mouths make you think of love. When you ask them where they are from, they tilt their heads and say 'Mobile' and you think you've been kissed. They say 'Aiken' and you see a white butterfly glance off a fence with a torn wing. They say 'Nagadoches' and you want to say 'Yes, I will.' You don't know what these towns are like, but you love what happens to the air when they open their lips and let the names ease out.

Meridian. The sound of it opens the windows of a room like the first four notes of a hymn. Few people can say the names of their home towns with such sly affection. Perhaps because they don't have home towns, just places where they were born. But these girls soak up the juice of their home towns, and it never leaves them. They are thin brown girls who have looked long at hollyhocks in the backyards of Meridian, Mobile, Aiken, and Baton Rouge. And like hollyhocks they are narrow, tall, and still. Their roots are deep, their stalks are firm, and only the top blossom nods in the wind. They have the eyes of people who can tell what time it is by the color of the sky. Such girls live in quiet black neighborhoods where everybody is gainfully employed. Where there are porch swings hanging from chains. Where the grass is cut with a scythe, where rooster combs and sunflowers grow in the yards, and pots of bleeding heart, ivy, and mother-in-law tongue line the steps and windowsills. Such girls have bought watermelon and snapbeans from the fruit man's wagon. They have put in the window the cardboard sign that has a pound measure printed on each of three edges – 10 lbs., 25 lbs., 50 lbs. – and NO ICE on the fourth. These particular brown girls from Mobile and Aiken are not like some of their sisters. They are not fretful, nervous, or shrill; they do not have lovely black necks that stretch as though against an invisible collar; their eyes do not bite. These sugar-brown Mobile girls move through the streets without a stir. They are as sweet and plain as butter-cake. Slim ankles; long, narrow feet. They wash themselves with orange-colored Lifebuoy soap, dust themselves with Cashmere Bouquet talc, clean their teeth with salt on a piece of rag, soften their skin with Jergens Lotion. They smell like wood, newspapers, and vanilla. They straighten their hair with Dixie Peach, and part it on the side. At night they curl it in paper from brown bags, tie a print scarf around their heads, and sleep with hands folded across their stomachs. They do not drink, smoke, or swear, and they still call sex 'nookey.' They sing second soprano in the choir, and although their voices are clear and steady, they are never picked to solo. They are in the second row, white blouses starched, blue skirts almost purple from ironing.

They go to land-grant colleges, normal schools, and learn how to do the white man's work with refinement: home economics to prepare his food; teacher education to instruct black children in obedience; music to soothe the weary master and entertain his blunted soul. Here they learn the rest of the lesson begun in those soft houses with porch swings and pots of bleeding heart: how to behave. The careful development of thrift, patience, high morals, and good manners. In short, how to get rid of the funkiness. The dreadful funkiness of passion, the funkiness of nature, the funkiness of the wide range of human emotions.

Wherever it erupts, this Funk, they wipe it away; where it crusts, they dissolve it; wherever it drips, flowers, or clings, they find it and fight it until it dies. They fight this battle all the way to the grave. The laugh that is a little too loud; the enunciation a little too round; the gesture a little too generous. They hold their behind in for fear of a sway too free; when they wear lipstick, they never cover the entire mouth for fear of lips too thick, and they worry, worry, worry about the edges of their hair.

They never seem to have boyfriends, but they always marry. Certain men watch them, without seeming to, and know that if such a girl is in his house, he will sleep on sheets boiled white, hung out to dry on juniper bushes, and pressed flat with a heavy iron. There will be pretty paper flowers decorating the picture of his mother, a large Bible in the front room. They feel secure. They know their work clothes will be mended, washed, and ironed on Monday, that their Sunday shirts will billow on hangers from the door jamb, stiffly starched and white. They look at her hands and know what she will do with biscuit dough; they smell the coffee and the fried ham; see the white, smoky grits with a dollop of butter on top. Her hips assure them that she will bear children easily and painlessly. And they are right.

What they do not know is that this plain brown girl will build her nest stick by stick, make it her own inviolable world, and stand guard over its every plant, weed, and doily, even against him. In silence will she return the lamp to where she put it in the first place; remove the dishes from the table as soon as the last bite is taken; wipe the doorknob after a greasy hand has touched it. A sidelong look will be enough to tell him to smoke on the back porch. Children will sense instantly that they cannot come into her yard to retrieve a ball. But the men do not know these things. Nor do they know that she will give him her body sparingly and partially. He must enter her surreptitiously, lifting the hem of her nightgown only to her navel. He must rest his weight on his elbows when they make love, ostensibly to avoid hurting her breasts but actually to keep her from having to touch or feel too much of him.

While he moves inside her, she will wonder why they didn't put the necessary but private parts of the body in some more convenient place – like the armpit, for example, or the palm of the hand. Someplace one could get to easily, and quickly, without undressing. She stiffens when she feels one of her paper curlers coming undone from the activity of love; imprints in her mind which one it is that is coming loose so she can quickly secure it once he is through. She hopes he will not sweat – the damp may get into her hair; and that she will remain dry between her legs – she hates the glucking sound they make when she is moist. When she senses some spasm about to grip him, she will make rapid movements with her hips, press her fingernails into his back, suck in her breath, and pretend she is having an orgasm. She might wonder again, for the six hundredth time, what it would be like to have *that* feeling while her husband's penis is inside her. The closest thing to it was the time she was walking down the street and her napkin slipped free of her sanitary belt. It moved gently between her legs as she walked. Gently, ever so gently. And then a slight and distinctly delicious sensation collected in her crotch. As the delight grew, she had to stop in the street, hold her thighs together to contain it. That must be what it is like, she thinks, but it never happens while he is inside her. When he withdraws, she pulls her nightgown down, slips out of the bed and into the bathroom with relief.

Occasionally some living thing will engage her affections. A cat, perhaps, who will love her order, precision, and constancy; who will be as clean and quiet as she is. The cat will settle quietly on the windowsill and caress her with his eyes. She can hold him in her arms, letting his back paws struggle for footing on her breast and his forepaws cling to her shoulder. She can rub the smooth fur and feel the unresisting flesh underneath. At her gentlest touch he will preen, stretch, and open his mouth. And she will accept the strangely pleasant sensation that comes when he writhes beneath her hand and flattens his eyes with a surfeit of sensual delight. When she stands cooking at the table, he will circle about her shanks, and the trill of his fur spirals up her legs to her thighs, to make her fingers tremble a little in the pie dough.

Or, as she sits reading the 'Uplifting Thoughts' in *The Liberty Magazine*, the cat will jump into her lap. She will fondle that soft hill of hair and let the warmth of the animal's body seep over and into the deeply private areas of her lap. Sometimes the magazine drops, and she opens her legs just a little, and the two of them will be still together, perhaps shifting a little together, sleeping a little together, until four o'clock, when the intruder comes home from work vaguely anxious about what's for dinner.

The cat will always know that he is first in her affections. Even after she bears a child. For she does bear a child – easily, and painlessly. But only one. A son. Named Junior.

One such girl from Mobile, or Meridian, or Aiken who did not sweat in her armpits nor between her thighs, who smelled of wood and vanilla, who had made soufflés in the Home Economics Department, moved with her husband, Louis, to Lorain, Ohio. Her name was Geraldine. There she built her nest, ironed shirts, potted bleeding hearts, played with her cat, and birthed Louis Junior.

Geraldine did not allow her baby, Junior, to cry. As long as his needs were physical, she could meet them – comfort and satiety. He was always brushed, bathed, oiled, and shod. Geraldine did not talk to him, coo to him, or indulge him in kissing bouts, but she saw that every other desire was fulfilled. It was not long before the child discovered the difference in his mother's behavior to himself and the cat. As he grew older, he learned how to direct his hatred of his mother to the cat, and spent some happy moments watching it suffer. The cat survived, because Geraldine was seldom away from home, and could effectively soothe the animal when Junior abused him.

Geraldine, Louis, Junior, and the cat lived next to the playground of Washington Irving School. Junior considered the playground his own, and the schoolchildren coveted his freedom to sleep late, go home for lunch, and dominate the playground after school. He hated to see the swings, slides, monkey bars, and seesaws empty and tried to get kids to stick around as long as possible. White kids; his mother did not like him to play with niggers. She had explained to him the difference between colored people and niggers. They were easily identifiable. Colored people were neat and quiet; niggers were dirty and loud. He belonged to the former group: he wore white shirts and blue trousers; his hair was cut as close to his scalp as possible to avoid any suggestion of wool, the part was etched into his hair by the barber. In winter his mother put Jergens Lotion on his face to keep the skin from becoming ashen. Even though he was light-skinned, it was possible to ash. The line between colored and nigger was not always clear; subtle and telltale signs threatened to erode it, and the watch had to be constant.

Junior used to long to play with the black boys. More than anything in the world he wanted to play King of the Mountain and have them push him down the mound of dirt and roll over him. He wanted to feel their hardness pressing on him, smell their wild blackness, and say 'Fuck you' with that lovely casualness. He wanted to sit with them on curbstones and compare the sharpness of jackknives, the distance and arcs of spitting. In the toilet he wanted to share with them the laurels of being able to pee far and long. Bay Boy and P. L. had at one time been his idols. Gradually he came to agree with his mother that neither Bay Boy nor P. L. was good enough for him. He played only with Ralph Nisensky, who was two years younger, wore glasses, and didn't want to *do* anything. More and more Junior enjoyed bullying girls. It was easy making them scream and run. How he laughed when they fell down and their bloomers showed. When they got up, their faces red and crinkled, it made him feel good. The nigger girls he did not pick on very much. They usually traveled in packs, and once when he threw a stone at some of them, they chased, caught, and beat him witless. He lied to his mother, saying Bay Boy did it. His mother was very upset. His father just kept on reading the Lorain *Journal*.

When the mood struck him, he would call a child passing by to come play on the swings or the seesaw. If the child wouldn't, or did and left too soon, Junior threw gravel at him. He became a very good shot.

Alternately bored and frightened at home, the playground was his joy. On a day when he had been especially idle, he saw a very black girl taking a shortcut through the playground. She kept her head down as she walked. He had seen her many times before, standing alone, always alone, at recess. Nobody ever played with her. Probably, he thought, because she was ugly.

Now Junior called to her. 'Hey! What are you doing walking through my yard?'

The girl stopped.

'Nobody can come through this yard 'less I say so.'

'This ain't your yard. It's the school's.'

'But I'm in charge of it.'

The girl started to walk away.

'Wait.' Junior walked toward her. 'You can play in it if you want to. What's your name?'

'Pecola. I don't want to play.'

'Come on. I'm not going to bother you.'

'I got to go home.'

'Say, you want to see something? I got something to show you.'

'No. What is it?'

'Come on in my house. See, I live right there. Come on. I'll show you.'

'Show me what?'

'Some kittens. We got some kittens. You can have one if you want.'

'Real kittens?'

'Yeah. Come on.'

He pulled gently at her dress. Pecola began to move toward his house. When he knew she had agreed, Junior ran ahead excitedly, stopping only to yell back at her to come on. He held the door open for her, smiling his encouragement. Pecola climbed the porch stairs and hesitated there, afraid to follow him. The house looked dark. Junior said, 'There's nobody here. My ma's gone out, and my father's at work. Don't you want to see the kittens?'

Junior turned on the lights. Pecola stepped inside the door.

How beautiful, she thought. What a beautiful house. There was a big red-and-gold Bible on the dining-room table. Little lace doilies were everywhere – on arms and backs of chairs, in the center of a large dining table, on little tables. Potted plants were on all the windowsills. A color picture of Jesus Christ hung on a wall with the prettiest paper flowers fastened on the frame. She wanted to see everything slowly, slowly. But Junior kept saying, 'Hey, you. Come on. Come on.' He pulled her into another room, even more beautiful than the first. More doilies, a big lamp with green-and-gold base and white shade. There was even a rug on the floor, with enormous dark-red flowers. She was deep in admiration of the flowers when Junior said, 'Here!' Pecola turned. 'Here is your kitten!' he screeched. And he threw a big black cat right in her face. She sucked in her breath in fear and surprise and felt fur in her mouth. The cat clawed her face and chest in an effort to right itself, then leaped nimbly to the floor.

Junior was laughing and running around the room clutching his stomach delightedly. Pecola touched the scratched place on her face and felt tears coming. When she started toward the doorway, Junior leaped in front of her.

'You can't get out. You're my prisoner,' he said. His eyes were merry but hard.

'You let me go.'

'No!' He pushed her down, ran out the door that separated the rooms, and held it shut with his hands. Pecola's banging on the door increased his gasping, high-pitched laughter.

The tears came fast, and she held her face in her hands. When something soft and furry moved around her ankles, she jumped, and saw it was the cat. He wound himself in and about her legs. Momentarily distracted from her fear, she squatted down to touch him, her hands wet from the tears. The cat rubbed up against her knee. He was black all over, deep silky black, and his eyes, pointing down toward his nose, were bluish green. The light made them shine like blue ice. Pecola rubbed the cat's head; he whined, his tongue flicking with pleasure. The blue eyes in the black face held her.

Junior, curious at not hearing her sobs, opened the door, and saw her squatting down rubbing the cat's back. He saw the cat stretching its head and flattening its eyes. He had seen that expression many times as the animal responded to his mother's touch.

'Gimme my cat!' His voice broke. With a movement both awkward and sure he snatched the cat by one of its hind legs and began to swing it around his head in a circle.

'Stop that!' Pecola was screaming. The cat's free paws were stiffened, ready to grab anything to restore balance, its mouth wide, its eyes blue streaks of horror.

Still screaming, Pecola reached for Junior's hand. She heard her dress rip under her arm. Junior tried to push her away, but she grabbed the arm which was swinging the cat. They both fell, and in falling, Junior let go the cat, which, having been released in mid-motion, was thrown full force against the window. It slithered down and fell on the radiator behind the sofa. Except for a few shudders, it was still. There was only the slightest smell of singed fur.

Geraldine opened the door.

'What is this?' Her voice was mild, as though asking a perfectly reasonable question. 'Who is this girl?'

'She killed our cat,' said Junior. 'Look.' He pointed to the radiator, where the cat lay, its blue eyes closed, leaving only an empty, black, and helpless face.

Geraldine went to the radiator and picked up the cat. He was limp in her arms, but she rubbed her face in his fur. She looked at Pecola. Saw the dirty torn dress, the plaits sticking out on her head, hair matted where the plaits had come undone, the muddy shoes with the wad of gum peeping out from between the cheap soles, the soiled socks, one of which had been walked down into the heel of the shoe. She saw the safety pin holding the hem of the dress up. Up over the hump of the cat's back she looked at her. She had seen this little girl all of her life. Hanging out of windows over saloons in Mobile, crawling over the porches of shotgun houses on the edge of town, sitting in bus stations holding paper bags and crying to mothers who kept saying 'Shet up!' Hair uncombed, dresses falling apart, shoes untied and caked with dirt. They had stared at her with great uncomprehending eyes. Eyes that questioned nothing and asked everything. Unblinking and unabashed, they stared up at her. The end of the world lay in their eyes, and the beginning, and all the waste in between.

They were everywhere. They slept six in a bed, all their pee mixing together in the night as they wet their beds each in his own candy-and-potato-chip dream. In the long, hot days, they idled away, picking plaster from the walls and digging into the earth with sticks. They sat in little rows on street curbs, crowded into pews at church, taking space from the nice, neat, colored children; they clowned on the playgrounds, broke things in dime stores, ran in front of you on the street, made ice slides on the sloped sidewalks in winter. The girls grew up knowing nothing of girdles, and the boys announced their manhood by turning the bills of their caps backward. Grass wouldn't grow where they lived. Flowers died. Shades fell down. Tin cans and tires blossomed where they lived. They lived on cold black-eyed peas and orange pop. Like flies they hovered; like flies they settled. And this one had settled in her house. Up over the hump of the cat's back she looked.

'Get out,' she said, her voice quiet. 'You nasty little black bitch. Get out of my house.'

The cat shuddered and flicked his tail.

Pecola backed out of the room, staring at the pretty milk-brown lady in the pretty gold-and-green house who was talking to her through the cat's fur. The pretty lady's words made the cat fur move; the breath of each word parted the fur. Pecola turned to find the front door and saw Jesus looking down at her with sad and unsurprised eyes, his long brown hair parted in the middle, the gay paper flowers twisted around his face.

Outside, the March wind blew into the rip in her dress. She held her head down against the cold. But she could not hold it low enough to avoid seeing the snowflakes falling and dying on the pavement.

Foreword to *Beloved*

IN 1983 I lost my job – or left it. One, the other, or both. In any case, I had been part-time for a while, coming into the publishing house one day a week to do the correspondence-telephoning-meetings that were part of the job; editing manuscripts at home.

Leaving was a good idea for two reasons. One, I had written four novels and it seemed clear to everyone that writing was my central work. The question of priorities – how can you edit and write at the same time – seemed to me both queer and predictable; it sounded like 'How can you both teach and create?' 'How can a painter or a sculptor or an actor do her work and guide others?' But to many this edit–write combination was conflicting.

The second reason was less ambiguous. The books I had edited were not earning scads of money, even when 'scads' didn't mean what it means now. My list was to me spectacular: writers with outrageous talent (Toni Cade Bambara, June Jordan, Gayle Jones, Lucille Clifton, Henry

Dumas, Leon Forrest); scholars with original ideas and hands-on research (William Hinton's *Shen Fan*, Ivan Van Sertima's *They Came Before Columbus*, Karen DeCrow's *Sexist Justice*, Chinweizu's *The West and the Rest of Us*); public figures eager to set the record straight (Angela Davis, Muhammad Ali, Huey Newton). And when there was a book that I thought needed doing, I found an author to write it. My enthusiasm, shared by some, was muted by others, reflecting the indifferent sales figures. I may be wrong about this, but even in the late seventies, acquiring authors who were certain sellers outranked editing manuscripts or supporting emerging or aging authors through their careers. Suffice it to say, I convinced myself that it was time for me to live like a grown-up writer: off royalties and writing only. I don't know what comic book that notion came from, but I grabbed it.

A few days after my last day at work, sitting in front of my house on the pier jutting out into the Hudson River, I began to feel an edginess instead of the calm I had expected. I ran through my index of problem areas and found nothing new or pressing. I couldn't fathom what was so unexpectedly troubling on a day that perfect, watching a river that serene. I had no agenda and couldn't hear the telephone if it rang. I heard my heart, though, stomping away in my chest like a colt. I went back to the house to examine this apprehension, even panic. I knew what fear felt like; this was different. Then it slapped me: I was happy, free in a way I had never been, ever. It was the oddest sensation. Not ecstasy, not satisfaction, not a surfeit of pleasure or accomplishment. It was a purer delight, a rogue anticipation with certainty. Enter *Beloved*.

I think now it was the shock of liberation that drew my thoughts to what 'free' could possibly mean to women. In the eighties, the debate was still roiling: equal pay, equal treatment, access to professions, schools . . . and choice without stigma. To marry or not. To have children or not. Inevitably these thoughts led me to the different history of black women in this country – a history in which marriage was discouraged, impossible, or illegal; in which birthing children was required, but 'having' them, being responsible for them – being, in other words, their parent – was as out of the question as freedom. Assertions of parenthood under conditions peculiar to the logic of institutional enslavement were criminal.

The idea was riveting, but the canvas overwhelmed me. Summoning characters who could manifest the intellect and the ferocity such logic would provoke proved beyond my imagination until I remembered one of the books I had published back when I had a job. A newspaper clipping in *The Black Book* summarized the story of Margaret Garner, a young mother who, having escaped slavery, was arrested for killing one of her children (and trying to kill the others) rather than let them be returned to the owner's plantation. She became a cause célèbre in the fight against the Fugitive Slave laws, which mandated the return of escapees to their owners. Her sanity and lack of repentance caught the attention of Abolitionists as well as newspapers. She was certainly single-minded and, judging by her comments, she had the intellect, the ferocity, and the willingness to risk everything for what was to her the necessity of freedom.

The historical Margaret Garner is fascinating, but, to a novelist, confining. Too little imaginative space there for my purposes. So I would invent her thoughts, plumb them for a subtext that was historically true in essence, but not strictly factual in order to relate her history to contemporary issues about freedom, responsibility, and women's 'place.' The heroine would represent the unapologetic acceptance of shame and terror; assume the consequences of choosing infanticide; claim her own freedom. The terrain, slavery, was formidable and pathless. To invite readers (and myself) into the repellant landscape (hidden, but not completely; deliberately buried, but not forgotten) was to pitch a tent in a cemetery inhabited by highly vocal ghosts.

I sat on the porch, rocking in a swing, looking at giant stones piled up to take the river's occasional fist. Above the stones is a path through the lawn, but interrupted by an ironwood gazebo situated under a cluster of trees and in deep shade.

She walked out of the water, climbed the rocks, and leaned against the gazebo. Nice hat.

So she was there from the beginning, and except for me, everybody (the characters) knew it – a sentence that later became 'The women in the house knew it.' The figure most central to the story would have to be her, the murdered, not the murderer, the one who lost everything and had no say in any of it. She could not linger outside; she would have to enter the house. A real house, not a cabin. One with an address, one where former slaves lived on their own. There would be no lobby into this house, and there would be no 'introduction' into it or into the novel. I wanted the reader to be kidnapped, thrown ruthlessly into an alien environment as the first step into a shared experience with the book's population – just as the characters were snatched from one place to another, from any place to any other, without preparation or defense.

It was important to name this house, but not the way 'Sweet Home' or other plantations were named. There would be no adjectives suggesting coziness or grandeur or the laying claim to an instant, aristocratic past. Only numbers here to identify the house while simultaneously separating it from a street or city – marking its difference from the houses of other blacks in the neighborhood; allowing it a hint of the superiority, the pride, former slaves would take in having an address of their own. Yet a house that has, literally, a personality – which we call 'haunted' when that personality is blatant.

In trying to make the slave experience intimate, I hoped the sense of things being both under control and out of control would be persuasive throughout; that the order and quietude of everyday life would be violently

disrupted by the chaos of the needy dead; that the hercu-
lean effort to forget would be threatened by memory
desperate to stay alive. To render enslavement as a personal experience, language must get out of the way.

I husband that moment on the pier, the deceptive river,
the instant awareness of possibility, the loud heart kicking, the solitude, the danger. And the girl with the nice
hat. Then the focus.

From the novel *Beloved*

UNFORTUNATELY HER BRAIN was devious. She might be hurrying across a field, running practically, to get to the pump quickly and rinse the chamomile sap from her legs. Nothing else would be in her mind. The picture of the men coming to nurse her was as lifeless as the nerves in her back where the skin buckled like a washboard. Nor was there the faintest scent of ink or the cherry gum and oak bark from which it was made. Nothing. Just the breeze cooling her face as she rushed toward water. And then sopping the chamomile away with pump water and rags, her mind fixed on getting every last bit of sap off – on her carelessness in taking a shortcut across the field just to save a half mile, and not noticing how high the weeds had grown until the itching was all the way to her knees. Then something. The plash of water, the sight of her shoes and stockings awry on the path where she had flung them; or Here Boy lapping in the puddle near her feet, and suddenly there was Sweet Home rolling,

rolling, rolling out before her eyes, and although there was not a leaf on that farm that did not make her want to scream, it rolled itself out before her in shameless beauty. It never looked as terrible as it was and it made her wonder if hell was a pretty place too. Fire and brimstone all right, but hidden in lacy groves. Boys hanging from the most beautiful sycamores in the world. It shamed her – remembering the wonderful soughing trees rather than the boys. Try as she might to make it otherwise, the sycamores beat out the children every time and she could not forgive her memory for that.

When the last of the chamomile was gone, she went around to the front of the house, collecting her shoes and stockings on the way. As if to punish her further for her terrible memory, sitting on the porch not forty feet away was Paul D, the last of the Sweet Home men. And although she could never mistake his face for another's, she said, 'Is that you?'

'What's left.' He stood up and smiled. 'How you been, girl, besides barefoot?'

When she laughed it came out loose and young. 'Messed up my legs back yonder. Chamomile.'

He made a face as though tasting a teaspoon of something bitter. 'I don't want to even hear 'bout it. Always did hate that stuff.'

Sethe balled up her stockings and jammed them into her pocket. 'Come on in.'

'Porch is fine, Sethe. Cool out here.' He sat back down

and looked at the meadow on the other side of the road, knowing the eagerness he felt would be in his eyes.

'Eighteen years,' she said softly.

'Eighteen,' he repeated. 'And I swear I been walking every one of em. Mind if I join you?' He nodded toward her feet and began unlacing his shoes.

'You want to soak them? Let me get you a basin of water.' She moved closer to him to enter the house.

'No, uh uh. Can't baby feet. A whole lot more tramping they got to do yet.'

'You can't leave right away, Paul D. You got to stay awhile.'

'Well, long enough to see Baby Suggs, anyway. Where is she?'

'Dead.'

'Aw no. When?'

'Eight years now. Almost nine.'

'Was it hard? I hope she didn't die hard.'

Sethe shook her head. 'Soft as cream. Being alive was the hard part. Sorry you missed her though. Is that what you came by for?'

'That's some of what I came for. The rest is you. But if all the truth be known, I go anywhere these days. Anywhere they let me sit down.'

'You looking good.'

'Devil's confusion. He lets me look good long as I feel bad.' He looked at her and the word 'bad' took on another meaning.

Sethe smiled. This is the way they were – had been. All of the Sweet Home men, before and after Halle, treated her to a mild brotherly flirtation, so subtle you had to scratch for it.

Except for a heap more hair and some waiting in his eyes, he looked the way he had in Kentucky. Peachstone skin; straight-backed. For a man with an immobile face it was amazing how ready it was to smile, or blaze or be sorry with you. As though all you had to do was get his attention and right away he produced the feeling you were feeling. With less than a blink, his face seemed to change – underneath it lay the activity.

'I wouldn't have to ask about him, would I? You'd tell me if there was anything to tell, wouldn't you?' Sethe looked down at her feet and saw again the sycamores.

'I'd tell you. Sure I'd tell you. I don't know any more now than I did then.' Except for the churn, he thought, and you don't need to know that. 'You must think he's still alive.'

'No. I think he's dead. It's not being sure that keeps him alive.'

'What did Baby Suggs think?'

'Same, but to listen to her, all her children is dead. Claimed she felt each one go the very day and hour.'

'When she say Halle went?'

'Eighteen fifty-five. The day my baby was born.'

'You had that baby, did you? Never thought you'd make it.' He chuckled. 'Running off pregnant.'

'Had to. Couldn't be no waiting.' She lowered her head and thought, as he did, how unlikely it was that she had made it. And if it hadn't been for that girl looking for velvet, she never would have.

'All by yourself too.' He was proud of her and annoyed by her. Proud she had done it; annoyed that she had not needed Halle or him in the doing.

'Almost by myself. Not all by myself. A whitegirl helped me.'

'Then she helped herself too, God bless her.'

'You could stay the night, Paul D.'

'You don't sound too steady in the offer.'

Sethe glanced beyond his shoulder toward the closed door. 'Oh it's truly meant. I just hope you'll pardon my house. Come on in. Talk to Denver while I cook you something.'

Paul D tied his shoes together, hung them over his shoulder and followed her through the door straight into a pool of red and undulating light that locked him where he stood.

'You got company?' he whispered, frowning.

'Off and on,' said Sethe.

'Good God.' He backed out the door onto the porch. 'What kind of evil you got in here?'

'It's not evil, just sad. Come on. Just step through.'

He looked at her then, closely. Closer than he had when she first rounded the house on wet and shining legs, holding her shoes and stockings up in one hand, her skirts in the other. Halle's girl – the one with iron eyes and back-bone to match. He had never seen her hair in Kentucky. And though her face was eighteen years older than when last he saw her, it was softer now. Because of the hair. A face too still for comfort; irises the same color as her skin, which, in that still face, used to make him think of a mask with mercifully punched-out eyes. Halle's woman. Pregnant every year including the year she sat by the fire telling him she was going to run. Her three children she had already packed into a wagonload of others in a cara-van of Negroes crossing the river. They were to be left with Halle's mother near Cincinnati. Even in that tiny shack, leaning so close to the fire you could smell the heat in her dress, her eyes did not pick up a flicker of light. They were like two wells into which he had trouble gazing. Even punched out they needed to be covered, lidded, marked with some sign to warn folks of what that emptiness held. So he looked instead at the fire while she told him, because her husband was not there for the telling. Mr Garner was dead and his wife had a lump in her neck the size of a sweet potato and unable to speak to anyone. She leaned as close to the fire as her pregnant belly allowed and told him, Paul D, the last of the Sweet Home men.

There had been six of them who belonged to the farm, Sethe the only female. Mrs Garner, crying like a baby, had sold his brother to pay off the debts that surfaced the minute she was widowed. Then schoolteacher arrived to put things in order. But what he did broke three more

Sweet Home men and punched the glittering iron out of Sethe's eyes, leaving two open wells that did not reflect firelight.

Now the iron was back but the face, softened by hair, made him trust her enough to step inside her door smack into a pool of pulsing red light.

She was right. It was sad. Walking through it, a wave of grief soaked him so thoroughly he wanted to cry. It seemed a long way to the normal light surrounding the table, but he made it – dry-eyed and lucky.

'You said she died soft. Soft as cream,' he reminded her.

'That's not Baby Suggs,' she said.

'Who then?'

'My daughter. The one I sent ahead with the boys.'

'She didn't live?'

'No. The one I was carrying when I run away is all I got left. Boys gone too. Both of em walked off just before Baby Suggs died.'

Paul D looked at the spot where the grief had soaked him. The red was gone but a kind of weeping clung to the air where it had been.

Probably best, he thought. If a Negro got legs he ought to use them. Sit down too long, somebody will figure out a way to tie them up. Still . . . if her boys were gone . . .

'No man? You here by yourself?'

'Me and Denver,' she said.

'That all right by you?'

'That's all right by me.'

She saw his skepticism and went on. 'I cook at a restaurant in town. And I sew a little on the sly.'

Paul D smiled then, remembering the bedding dress. Sethe was thirteen when she came to Sweet Home and already iron-eyed. She was a timely present for Mrs Garner who had lost Baby Suggs to her husband's high principles. The five Sweet Home men looked at the new girl and decided to let her be. They were young and so sick with the absence of women they had taken to calves. Yet they let the iron-eyed girl be, so she could choose in spite of the fact that each one would have beaten the others to mush to have her. It took her a year to choose – a long, tough year of thrashing on pallets eaten up with dreams of her. A year of yearning, when rape seemed the solitary gift of life. The restraint they had exercised possible only because they were Sweet Home men – the ones Mr Garner bragged about while other farmers shook their heads in warning at the phrase.

'Y'all got boys,' he told them. 'Young boys, old boys, picky boys, stroppin boys. Now at Sweet Home, my niggers is men every one of em. Bought em thataway, raised em thataway. Men every one.'

'Beg to differ, Garner. Ain't no nigger men.'

'Not if you scared, they ain't.' Garner's smile was wide. 'But if you a man yourself, you'll want your niggers to be men too.'

'I wouldn't have no nigger men round my wife.'

It was the reaction Garner loved and waited for.

'Neither would I,' he said. 'Neither would I,' and there was always a pause before the neighbor, or stranger, or peddler, or brother-in-law or whoever it was got the meaning. Then a fierce argument, sometimes a fight, and Garner came home bruised and pleased, having demonstrated one more time what a real Kentuckian was: one tough enough and smart enough to make and call his own niggers men.

And so they were: Paul D Garner, Paul F Garner, Paul A Garner, Halle Suggs and Sixo, the wild man. All in their twenties, minus women, fucking cows, dreaming of rape, thrashing on pallets, rubbing their thighs and waiting for the new girl – the one who took Baby Suggs' place after Halle bought her with five years of Sundays. Maybe that was why she chose him. A twenty-year-old man so in love with his mother he gave up five years of Sabbaths just to see her sit down for a change was a serious recommendation.

She waited a year. And the Sweet Home men abused cows while they waited with her. She chose Halle and for their first bedding she sewed herself a dress on the sly.

'Won't you stay on awhile? Can't nobody catch up on eighteen years in a day.'

Out of the dimness of the room in which they sat, a white staircase climbed toward the blue-and-white wallpaper of the second floor. Paul D could see just the beginning of the paper; discreet flecks of yellow sprinkled among a blizzard of snowdrops all backed by blue. The luminous white of the railing and steps kept him glancing toward it. Every sense he had told him the air above the stairwell was charmed and very thin. But the girl who walked down out of that air was round and brown with the face of an alert doll.

Paul D looked at the girl and then at Sethe who smiled saying, 'Here she is my Denver. This is Paul D, honey, from Sweet Home.'

'Good morning, Mr D.'

'Garner, baby. Paul D Garner.'

'Yes sir.'

'Glad to get a look at you. Last time I saw your mama, you were pushing out the front of her dress.'

'Still is,' Sethe smiled, 'provided she can get in it.'

Denver stood on the bottom step and was suddenly hot and shy. It had been a long time since anybody (good-willed whitewoman, preacher, speaker or newspaperman) sat at their table, their sympathetic voices called liar by the revulsion in their eyes. For twelve years, long before Grandma Baby died, there had been no visitors of any sort and certainly no friends. No coloredpeople. Certainly no hazelnut man with too long hair and no notebook, no charcoal, no oranges, no questions. Someone her mother wanted to talk to and would even consider talking to while barefoot. Looking, in fact acting, like a girl instead of the quiet, queenly woman Denver had known all her life. The one who never looked away, who when a man got stomped to death by a mare right in front of Sawyer's restaurant did not look away; and when a sow began eating her own litter did not look away then either. And when the baby's spirit picked up Here Boy and slammed him into the wall hard enough to break two of his legs and dislocate his eye, so hard he went into convulsions and chewed up his tongue, still her mother had not looked away. She had taken a hammer, knocked the dog unconscious, wiped away the blood and saliva, pushed his eye back in his head and set his leg bones. He recovered, mute and off-balance, more because of his untrustworthy eye than his bent legs, and winter, summer, drizzle or dry, nothing could persuade him to enter the house again.

Now here was this woman with the presence of mind to repair a dog gone savage with pain rocking her crossed ankles and looking away from her own daughter's body. As though the size of it was more than vision could bear. And neither she nor he had on shoes. Hot, shy, now Denver was lonely. All that leaving: first her brothers, then her grandmother – serious losses since there were no children willing to circle her in a game or hang by their knees from her porch railing. None of that had mattered as long as her mother did not look away as she was doing now, making Denver long, downright *long*, for a sign of spite from the baby ghost.

'She's a fine-looking young lady,' said Paul D. 'Fine-looking. Got her daddy's sweet face.'

'You know my father?'

'Knew him. Knew him well.'

'Did he, Ma'am?' Denver fought an urge to realign her affection.

'Of course he knew your daddy. I told you, he's from Sweet Home.'

Denver sat down on the bottom step. There was nowhere else gracefully to go. They were a twosome, saying 'Your daddy' and 'Sweet Home' in a way that made it clear both belonged to them and not to her. That her own father's absence was not hers. Once the absence had belonged to Grandma Baby – a son, deeply mourned because he was the one who had bought her out of there. Then it was her mother's absent husband. Now it was this hazelnut stranger's absent friend. Only those who knew him ('knew him well') could claim his absence for themselves. Just as only those who lived in Sweet Home could remember it, whisper it and glance sideways at one another while they did. Again she wished for the baby ghost – its anger thrilling her now where it used to wear her out. Wear her out.

'We have a ghost in here,' she said, and it worked. They were not a twosome anymore. Her mother left off swinging her feet and being girlish. Memory of Sweet Home dropped away from the eyes of the man she was being girlish for. He looked quickly up the lightning-white stairs behind her.

'So I hear,' he said. 'But sad, your mama said. Not evil.'

'No sir,' said Denver, 'not evil. But not sad either.'

'What then?'

'Rebuked. Lonely and rebuked.'

'Is that right?' Paul D turned to Sethe.

'I don't know about lonely,' said Denver's mother. 'Mad, maybe, but I don't see how it could be lonely spending every minute with us like it does.'

'Must be something you got it wants.'

Sethe shrugged. 'It's just a baby.'

'My sister,' said Denver. 'She died in this house.'

Paul D scratched the hair under his jaw. 'Reminds me of that headless bride back behind Sweet Home. Remember that, Sethe? Used to roam them woods regular.'

'How could I forget? Worrisome . . .'

'How come everybody run off from Sweet Home can't stop talking about it? Look like if it was so sweet you would have stayed.'

'Girl, who you talking to?'

Paul D laughed. 'True, true. She's right, Sethe. It wasn't sweet and it sure wasn't home.' He shook his head.

'But it's where we were,' said Sethe. 'All together. Comes back whether we want it to or not.' She shivered a little. A light ripple of skin on her arm, which she caressed back into sleep. 'Denver,' she said, 'start up that stove. Can't have a friend stop by and don't feed him.'

'Don't go to any trouble on my account,' Paul D said.

'Bread ain't trouble. The rest I brought back from where I work. Least I can do, cooking from dawn to noon, is bring dinner home. You got any objections to pike?'

'If he don't object to me I don't object to him.'

At it again, thought Denver. Her back to them, she jostled the kindlin and almost lost the fire. 'Why don't you spend the night, Mr Garner? You and Ma'am can talk about Sweet Home all night long.'

Sethe took two swift steps to the stove, but before she could yank Denver's collar, the girl leaned forward and began to cry.

'What is the matter with you? I never knew you to behave this way.'

'Leave her be,' said Paul D. 'I'm a stranger to her.'

'That's just it. She got no cause to act up with a stranger. Oh baby, what is it? Did something happen?'

But Denver was shaking now and sobbing so she could not speak. The tears she had not shed for nine years wetting her far too womanly breasts.

'I can't no more. I can't no more.'

'Can't what? What can't you?'

'I can't live here. I don't know where to go or what to do, but I can't live here. Nobody speaks to us. Nobody comes by. Boys don't like me. Girls don't either.'

'Honey, honey.'

'What's she talking 'bout nobody speaks to you?' asked Paul D.

'It's the house. People don't –'

'It's not! It's not the house. It's us! And it's you!'

'Denver!'

'Leave off, Sethe. It's hard for a young girl living in a haunted house. That can't be easy.'

'It's easier than some other things.'

'Think, Sethe. I'm a grown man with nothing new left to see or do and I'm telling you it ain't easy. Maybe you all ought to move. Who owns this house?'

Over Denver's shoulder Sethe shot Paul D a look of snow. 'What you care?'

'They won't let you leave?'

'No.'

'Sethe.'

'No moving. No leaving. It's all right the way it is.'

'You going to tell me it's all right with this child half out of her mind?'

Something in the house braced, and in the listening quiet that followed Sethe spoke.

'I got a tree on my back and a haint in my house, and nothing in between but the daughter I am holding in my arms. No more running – from nothing. I will never run from another thing on this earth. I took one journey and I paid for the ticket, but let me tell you something, Paul D Garner: it cost too much! Do you hear me? It cost too much. Now sit down and eat with us or leave us be.'

Paul D fished in his vest for a little pouch of tobacco – concentrating on its contents and the knot of its string while Sethe led Denver into the keeping room that opened off the large room he was sitting in. He had no smoking papers, so he fiddled with the pouch and listened through the open door to Sethe quieting her daughter. When she came back she avoided his look and went straight to a

No more running – from nothing. I will never run from another thing on this earth

small table next to the stove. Her back was to him and he could see all the hair he wanted without the distraction of her face.

'What tree on your back?'

'Huh.' Sethe put a bowl on the table and reached under it for flour.

'What tree on your back? Is something growing on your back? I don't see nothing growing on your back.'

'It's there all the same.'

'Who told you that?'

'Whitegirl. That's what she called it. I've never seen it and never will. But that's what she said it looked like. A chokecherry tree. Trunk, branches, and even leaves. Tiny little chokecherry leaves. But that was eighteen years ago. Could have cherries too now for all I know.'

Sethe took a little spit from the tip of her tongue with her forefinger. Quickly, lightly she touched the stove. Then she trailed her fingers through the flour, parting, separating small hills and ridges of it, looking for mites. Finding none, she poured soda and salt into the crease of her folded hand and tossed both into the flour. Then she reached into a can and scooped half a handful of lard. Deftly she squeezed the flour through it, then with her left hand sprinkling water, she formed the dough.

'I had milk,' she said. 'I was pregnant with Denver but I had milk for my baby girl. I hadn't stopped nursing her when I sent her on ahead with Howard and Buglar.'

Now she rolled the dough out with a wooden pin.

'Anybody could smell me long before he saw me. And when he saw me he'd see the drops of it on the front of my dress. Nothing I could do about that. All I knew was I had to get my milk to my baby girl. Nobody was going to nurse her like me. Nobody was going to get it to her fast enough, or take it away when she had enough and didn't know it. Nobody knew that she couldn't pass her air if you held her up on your shoulder, only if she was lying on my knees. Nobody knew that but me and nobody had her milk but me. I told that to the women in the wagon. Told them to put sugar water in cloth to suck from so when I got there in a few days she wouldn't have forgot me. The milk would be there and I would be there with it.'

'Men don't know nothing much,' said Paul D, tucking his pouch back into his vest pocket, 'but they do know a suckling can't be away from its mother for long.'

'Then they know what it's like to send your children off when your breasts are full.'

'We was talking 'bout a tree, Sethe.'

'After I left you, those boys came in there and took my milk. That's what they came in there for. Held me down and took it. I told Mrs Garner on em. She had that lump and couldn't speak but her eyes rolled out tears. Them boys found out I told on em. Schoolteacher made one open up my back, and when it closed it made a tree. It grows there still.'

'They used cowhide on you?'

'And they took my milk.'

'They beat you and you was pregnant?'

'And they took my milk!'

The fat white circles of dough lined the pan in rows. Once more Sethe touched a wet forefinger to the stove. She opened the oven door and slid the pan of biscuits in. As she raised up from the heat she felt Paul D behind her and his hands under her breasts. She straightened up and knew, but could not feel, that his cheek was pressing into the branches of her chokecherry tree.

Not even trying, he had become the kind of man who could walk into a house and make the women cry. Because with him, in his presence, they could. There was something blessed in his manner. Women saw him and wanted to weep – to tell him that their chest hurt and their knees did too. Strong women and wise saw him and told him things they only told each other: that way past the Change of Life, desire in them had suddenly become enormous, greedy, more savage than when they were fifteen, and that it embarrassed them and made them sad; that secretly they longed to die – to be quit of it – that sleep was more precious to them than any waking day. Young girls sidled up to him to confess or describe how well-dressed the visitations were that had followed them straight from their dreams. Therefore, although he did not understand why this was so, he was not surprised when Denver dripped tears into the stovefire. Nor, fifteen minutes later, after telling him about her stolen milk, her mother wept as well. Behind her, bending down, his body an arc of kindness, he held her breasts in the palms of his hands. He rubbed his cheek on her back and learned that way her sorrow, the roots of it; its wide trunk and intricate branches. Raising his fingers to the hooks of her dress, he knew without seeing them or hearing any sigh that the tears were coming fast. And when the top of her dress was around her hips and he saw the sculpture her back had become, like the decorative work of an ironsmith too passionate for display, he could think but not say, 'Aw, Lord, girl.' And he would tolerate no peace until he had touched every ridge and leaf of it with his mouth, none of which Sethe could feel because her back skin had been dead for years. What she knew was that the responsibility for her breasts, at last, was in somebody else's hands.

Would there be a little space, she wondered, a little time, some way to hold off eventfulness, to push busyness into the corners of the room and just stand there a minute or two, naked from shoulder blade to waist, relieved of the weight of her breasts, smelling the stolen milk again and the pleasure of baking bread? Maybe this one time she could stop dead still in the middle of a cooking meal – not even leave the stove – and feel the hurt her back ought to. Trust things and remember things because the last of the Sweet Home men was there to catch her if she sank?

WHEN DENVER LOOKED in, she saw her mother on her knees in prayer, which was not unusual. What was unusual (even for a girl who had lived all her life in a house peopled

by the living activity of the dead) was that a white dress
knelt down next to her mother and had its sleeve around
her mother's waist. And it was the tender embrace of the
dress sleeve that made Denver remember the details of
her birth – that and the thin, whipping snow she was
standing in, like the fruit of common flowers. The dress
and her mother together looked like two friendly
grown-up women – one (the dress) helping out the other.
And the magic of her birth, its miracle in fact, testified to
that friendliness as did her own name.

Easily she stepped into the told story that lay before
her eyes on the path she followed away from the window.
There was only one door to the house and to get to it from
the back you had to walk all the way around to the front
of 124, past the storeroom, past the cold house, the privy,
the shed, on around to the porch. And to get to the part
of the story she liked best, she had to start way back:
hear the birds in the thick woods, the crunch of leaves
underfoot; see her mother making her way up into the
hills where no houses were likely to be. How Sethe was
walking on two feet meant for standing still. How they
were so swollen she could not see her arch or feel her
ankles. Her leg shaft ended in a loaf of flesh scalloped by
five toenails. But she could not, would not, stop, for when
she did the little antelope rammed her with horns and
pawed the ground of her womb with impatient hooves.
While she was walking, it seemed to graze, quietly – so
she walked, on two feet meant, in this sixth month of

pregnancy, for standing still. Still, near a kettle; still, at the churn; still, at the tub and ironing board. Milk, sticky and sour on her dress, attracted every small flying thing from gnats to grasshoppers. By the time she reached the hill skirt she had long ago stopped waving them off. The clanging in her head, begun as a churchbell heard from a distance, was by then a tight cap of pealing bells around her ears. She sank and had to look down to see whether she was in a hole or kneeling. Nothing was alive but her nipples and the little antelope. Finally, she was horizontal – or must have been because blades of wild onion were scratching her temple and her cheek. Concerned as she was for the life of her children's mother, Sethe told Denver, she remembered thinking: Well, at least I don't have to take another step. A dying thought if ever there was one, and she waited for the little antelope to protest, and why she thought of an antelope Sethe could not imagine since she had never seen one. She guessed it must have been an invention held on to from before Sweet Home, when she was very young. Of that place where she was born (Carolina maybe? or was it Louisiana?) she remembered only song and dance. Not even her own mother, who was pointed out to her by the eight-year-old child who watched over the young ones – pointed out as the one among many backs turned away from her, stooping in a watery field. Patiently Sethe waited for this particular back to gain the row's end and stand. What she saw was a cloth hat as opposed to a straw one, singularity enough in that world of cooing women each of whom was called Ma'am.

'Seth-thuh.'

'Ma'am.'

'Hold on to the baby.'

'Yes, Ma'am.'

'Seth-thuh.'

'Ma'am.'

'Get some kindlin in here.'

'Yes, Ma'am.'

Oh but when they sang. And oh but when they danced and sometimes they danced the antelope. The men as well as the ma'ams, one of whom was certainly her own. They shifted shapes and became something other. Some unchained, demanding other whose feet knew her pulse better than she did. Just like this one in her stomach.

'I believe this baby's ma'am is gonna die in wild onions on the bloody side of the Ohio River.' That's what was on her mind and what she told Denver. Her exact words. And it didn't seem such a bad idea, all in all, in view of the step she would not have to take, but the thought of herself stretched out dead while the little antelope lived on – an hour? a day? a day and a night? – in her lifeless body grieved her so she made the groan that made the person walking on a path not ten yards away halt and stand right still. Sethe had not heard the walking, but suddenly she heard the standing still and then she smelled the hair. The voice, saying, 'Who's in there?' was all she needed to know that she was about to be discovered by a whiteboy. That he too had mossy teeth, an appetite. That on a ridge of pine near the Ohio River, trying to get to her three children, one of whom was starving for the food she carried; that after her husband had disappeared; that after her milk had been stolen, her back pulped, her children orphaned, she was not to have an easeful death. No.

She told Denver that a *something* came up out of the earth into her – like a freezing, but moving too, like jaws inside. 'Look like I was just cold jaws grinding,' she said. Suddenly she was eager for his eyes, to bite into them; to gnaw his cheek.

'I was hungry,' she told Denver, 'just as hungry as I could be for his eyes. I couldn't wait.'

So she raised up on her elbow and dragged herself, one pull, two, three, four, toward the young white voice talking about 'Who that back in there?'

'"Come see," I was thinking. "Be the last thing you behold," and sure enough here come the feet so I thought well that's where I'll have to start God do what He would, I'm gonna eat his feet off. I'm laughing now, but it's true. I wasn't just set to do it. I was hungry to do it. Like a snake. All jaws and hungry.

'It wasn't no whiteboy at all. Was a girl. The raggediest-looking trash you ever saw saying, "Look there. A nigger. If that don't beat all."'

And now the part Denver loved the best:

Her name was Amy and she needed beef and pot liquor

like nobody in this world. Arms like cane stalks and enough hair for four or five heads. Slow-moving eyes. She didn't look at anything quick. Talked so much it wasn't clear how she could breathe at the same time. And those cane-stalk arms, as it turned out, were as strong as iron.

'You 'bout the scariest-looking something I ever seen. What you doing back up in here?'

Down in the grass, like the snake she believed she was, Sethe opened her mouth, and instead of fangs and a split tongue, out shot the truth.

'Running,' Sethe told her. It was the first word she had spoken all day and it came out thick because of her tender tongue.

'Them the feet you running on? My Jesus my.' She squatted down and stared at Sethe's feet. 'You got anything on you, gal, pass for food?'

'No.' Sethe tried to shift to a sitting position but couldn't.

'I like to die I'm so hungry.' The girl moved her eyes slowly, examining the greenery around her. 'Thought there'd be huckleberries. Look like it. That's why I come up in here. Didn't expect to find no nigger woman. If they was any, birds ate em. You like huckleberries?'

'I'm having a baby, miss.'

Amy looked at her. 'That mean you don't have no appetite? Well I got to eat me something.'

Combing her hair with her fingers, she carefully surveyed the landscape once more. Satisfied nothing edible was around, she stood up to go and Sethe's heart stood up too at the thought of being left alone in the grass without a fang in her head.

'Where you on your way to, miss?'

She turned and looked at Sethe with freshly lit eyes. 'Boston. Get me some velvet. It's a store there called Wilson. I seen the pictures of it and they have the prettiest velvet. They don't believe I'm a get it, but I am.'

Sethe nodded and shifted her elbow. 'Your ma'am know you on the lookout for velvet?'

The girl shook her hair out of her face. 'My mama worked for these here people to pay for her passage. But then she had me and since she died right after, well, they said I had to work for em to pay it off. I did, but now I want me some velvet.'

They did not look directly at each other, not straight into the eyes anyway. Yet they slipped effortlessly into yard chat about nothing in particular – except one lay on the ground.

'Boston,' said Sethe. 'Is that far?'

'Ooooh, yeah. A hundred miles. Maybe more.'

'Must be velvet closer by.'

'Not like in Boston. Boston got the best. Be so pretty on me. You ever touch it?'

'No, miss. I never touched no velvet.' Sethe didn't know if it was the voice, or Boston or velvet, but while the white-girl talked, the baby slept. Not one butt or kick, so she guessed her luck had turned.

'Ever see any?' she asked Sethe. 'I bet you never even seen any.'

'If I did I didn't know it. What's it like, velvet?'

Amy dragged her eyes over Sethe's face as though she would never give out so confidential a piece of information as that to a perfect stranger.

'What they call you?' she asked.

However far she was from Sweet Home, there was no point in giving out her real name to the first person she saw. 'Lu,' said Sethe. 'They call me Lu.'

'Well, Lu, velvet is like the world was just born. Clean and new and so smooth. The velvet I seen was brown, but in Boston they got all colors. Carmine. That means red but when you talk about velvet you got to say "carmine."' She raised her eyes to the sky and then, as though she had wasted enough time away from Boston, she moved off saying, 'I gotta go.'

Picking her way through the brush she hollered back to Sethe, 'What you gonna do, just lay there and foal?'

'I can't get up from here,' said Sethe.

'What?' She stopped and turned to hear.

'I said I can't get up.'

Amy drew her arm across her nose and came slowly back to where Sethe lay. 'It's a house back yonder,' she said.

'A house?'

'Mmmmm. I passed it. Ain't no regular house with people in it though. A lean-to, kinda.'

'How far?'

'Make a difference, does it? You stay the night here snake get you.'

'Well he may as well come on. I can't stand up let alone walk and God help me, miss, I can't crawl.'

'Sure you can, Lu. Come on,' said Amy and, with a toss of hair enough for five heads, she moved toward the path.

So she crawled and Amy walked alongside her, and when Sethe needed to rest, Amy stopped too and talked some more about Boston and velvet and good things to eat. The sound of that voice, like a sixteen-year-old boy's, going on and on and on, kept the little antelope quiet and grazing. During the whole hateful crawl to the lean-to, it never bucked once.

Nothing of Sethe's was intact by the time they reached it except the cloth that covered her hair. Below her bloody knees, there was no feeling at all; her chest was two cushions of pins. It was the voice full of velvet and Boston and good things to eat that urged her along and made her think that maybe she wasn't, after all, just a crawling graveyard for a six-month baby's last hours.

The lean-to was full of leaves, which Amy pushed into a pile for Sethe to lie on. Then she gathered rocks, covered them with more leaves and made Sethe put her feet on them, saying: 'I know a woman had her feet cut off they was so swole.' And she made sawing gestures with the blade of her hand across Sethe's ankles. 'Zzz Zzz Zzz Zzz.'

'I used to be a good size. Nice arms and everything. Wouldn't think it, would you? That was before they put me in the root cellar. I was fishing off the Beaver once. Catfish in Beaver River sweet as chicken. Well I was just fishing there and a nigger floated right by me. I don't like drowned people, you? Your feet remind me of him. All swole like.'

Then she did the magic: lifted Sethe's feet and legs and massaged them until she cried salt tears.

'It's gonna hurt, now,' said Amy. 'Anything dead coming back to life hurts.'

'Recitatif', a short story

MY MOTHER DANCED all night and Roberta's was sick. That's why we were taken to St Bonny's. People want to put their arms around you when you tell them you were in a shelter, but it really wasn't bad. No big long room with one hundred beds like Bellevue. There were four to a room, and when Roberta and me came, there was a shortage of state kids, so we were the only ones assigned to 406 and could go from bed to bed if we wanted to. And we wanted to, too. We changed beds every night and for the whole four months we were there we never picked one out as our own permanent bed.

It didn't start out that way. The minute I walked in and the Big Bozo introduced us, I got sick to my stomach. It was one thing to be taken out of your own bed early in the morning – it was something else to be stuck in a strange place with a girl from a whole other race. And Mary, that's my mother, she was right. Every now and then she would stop dancing long enough to tell me something important and one of the things she said was that they never washed their hair and they smelled funny. Roberta sure did. Smell funny, I mean. So when the Big Bozo (nobody ever called her Mrs Itkin, just like nobody every said St Bonaventure) – when she said, 'Twyla, this is Roberta. Roberta, this is Twyla. Make each other welcome,' I said, 'My mother won't like you putting me in here.'

'Good,' said Bozo. 'Maybe then she'll come and take you home.'

How's that for mean? If Roberta had laughed I would have killed her, but she didn't. She just walked over to the window and stood with her back to us.

'Turn around,' said the Bozo. 'Don't be rude. Now Twyla. Roberta. When you hear a loud buzzer, that's the call for dinner. Come down to the first floor. Any fights and no movie.' And then, just to make sure we knew what we would be missing, '*The Wizard of Oz*.'

Roberta must have thought I meant that my mother would be mad about my being put in the shelter. Not about rooming with her, because as soon as Bozo left she came over to me and said, 'Is your mother sick too?'

'No,' I said. 'She just likes to dance all night.'

'Oh,' she nodded her head and I liked the way she understood things so fast. So for the moment it didn't matter that we looked like salt and pepper standing there and that's what the other kids called us sometimes. We were eight years old and got F's all the time. Me because I couldn't remember what I read or what the teacher said.

And Roberta because she couldn't read at all and didn't even listen to the teacher. She wasn't good at anything except jacks, at which she was a killer: pow scoop pow scoop pow scoop.

We didn't like each other all that much at first, but nobody else wanted to play with us because we weren't real orphans with beautiful dead parents in the sky. We were dumped. Even the New York City Puerto Ricans and the upstate Indians ignored us. All kinds of kids were in there, black ones, white ones, even two Koreans. The food was good, though. At least I thought so. Roberta hated it and left whole pieces of things on her plate: Spam, Salisbury steak – even jello with fruit cocktail in it, and she didn't care if I ate what she wouldn't. Mary's idea of supper was popcorn and a can of Yoo-Hoo. Hot mashed potatoes and two weenies was like Thanksgiving for me.

It really wasn't bad, St Bonny's. The big girls on the second floor pushed us around now and then. But that was all. They wore lipstick and eyebrow pencil and wobbled their knees while they watched TV. Fifteen, sixteen, even, some of them were. They were put-out girls, scared runaways most of them. Poor little girls who fought their uncles off but looked tough to us, and mean. God did they look mean. The staff tried to keep them separate from the younger children, but sometimes they caught us watching them in the orchard where they played radios and danced with each other. They'd light out after us and pull our hair or twist our arms. We were scared of them, Roberta and me, but neither of us wanted the other one to know it. So we got a good list of dirty names we could shout back when we ran from them through the orchard. I used to dream a lot and almost always the orchard was there. Two acres, four maybe, of these little apple trees. Hundreds of them. Empty and crooked like beggar women when I first came to St Bonny's but fat with flowers when I left. I don't know why I dreamt about that orchard so much. Nothing really happened there. Nothing all that important, I mean. Just the big girls dancing and playing the radio. Roberta and me watching. Maggie fell down there once. The kitchen woman with legs like parentheses. And the big girls laughed at her. We should have helped her up, I know, but we were scared of those girls with lipstick and eyebrow pencil. Maggie couldn't talk. The kids said she had her tongue cut out, but I think she was just born that way: mute. She was old and sandy-colored and she worked in the kitchen. I don't know if she was nice or not. I just remember her legs like parentheses and how she rocked when she walked. She worked from early in the morning till two o'clock, and if she was late, if she had too much cleaning and didn't get out till two-fifteen or so, she'd cut through the orchard so she wouldn't miss her bus and have to wait another hour. She wore this really stupid little hat – a kid's hat with ear flaps – and she wasn't much taller than we were. A really awful little hat. Even for a mute, it was dumb – dressing like a kid and never saying anything at all.

'But what about if somebody tries to kill her?' I used to wonder about that. 'Or what if she wants to cry? Can she cry?'

'Sure,' Roberta said. 'But just tears. No sounds come out.'

'She can't scream?'

'Nope. Nothing.'

'Can she hear?'

'I guess.'

'Let's call her,' I said. And we did.

'Dummy! Dummy!' She never turned her head.

'Bow legs! Bow legs!' Nothing. She just rocked on, the chin straps of her baby-boy hat swaying from side to side. I think we were wrong. I think she could hear and didn't let on. And it shames me even now to think there was somebody in there after all who heard us call her those names and couldn't tell on us.

We got along all right, Roberta and me. Changed beds every night, got F's in civics and communication skills and gym. The Bozo was disappointed in us, she said. Out of 130 of us state cases, 90 were under twelve. Almost all were real orphans with beautiful dead parents in the sky. We were the only ones dumped and the only ones with F's in three classes including gym. So we got along – what with her leaving whole pieces of things on her plate and being nice about not asking questions.

I think it was the day before Maggie fell down that we found out our mothers were coming to visit us on the same Sunday. We had been at the shelter twenty-eight days (Roberta twenty-eight and a half) and this was their first visit with us. Our mothers would come at ten o'clock in time for chapel, then lunch with us in the teachers' lounge. I thought if my dancing mother met her sick mother it might be good for her. And Roberta thought her sick mother would get a big bang out of a dancing one. We got excited about it and curled each other's hair. After breakfast we sat on the bed watching the road from the window. Roberta's socks were still wet. She washed them the night before and put them on the radiator to dry. They hadn't, but she put them on anyway because their tops were so pretty – scalloped in pink. Each of us had a purple construction-paper basket that we had made in craft class. Mine had a yellow crayon rabbit on it. Roberta's had eggs with wiggly lines of color. Inside were cellophane grass and just the jelly beans because I'd eaten the two marshmallow eggs they gave us. The Big Bozo came her-self to get us. Smiling she told us we looked very nice and to come downstairs. We were so surprised by the smile we'd never seen before, neither of us moved.

'Don't you want to see your mommies?'

I stood up first and spilled the jelly beans all over the floor. Bozo's smile disappeared while we scrambled to get the candy up off the floor and put it back in the grass.

She escorted us downstairs to the first floor, where the other girls were lining up to file into the chapel. A bunch of grown-ups stood to one side. Viewers mostly. The old biddies who wanted servants and the fags who wanted company looking for children they might want to adopt. Once in a while a grandmother. Almost never anybody young or anybody whose face wouldn't scare you in the night. Because if any of the real orphans had young relatives they wouldn't be real orphans. I saw Mary right away. She had on those green slacks I hated and hated even more now because didn't she know we were going to chapel? And that fur jacket with the pocket linings so ripped she had to pull to get her hands out of them. But her face was pretty – like always, and she smiled and waved like she was the little girl looking for her mother – not me.

I walked slowly, trying not to drop the jelly beans and hoping the paper handle would hold. I had to use my last Chiclet because by the time I finished cutting everything out, all the Elmer's was gone. I am left-handed and the scissors never worked for me. It didn't matter, though; I might just as well have chewed the gum. Mary dropped to her knees and grabbed me, mashing the basket, the jelly beans, and the grass into her ratty fur jacket.

'Twyla, baby. Twyla, baby!'

I could have killed her. Already I heard the big girls in the orchard the next time saying, 'Twyyyyyla, baby!' But I couldn't stay mad at Mary while she was smiling and hugging me and smelling of Lady Esther dusting powder. I wanted to stay buried in her fur all day.

To tell the truth I forgot about Roberta. Mary and I got in line for the traipse into chapel and I was feeling proud because she looked so beautiful even in those ugly green slacks that made her behind stick out. A pretty mother on earth is better than a beautiful dead one in the sky even if she did leave you all alone to go dancing.

I felt a tap on my shoulder, turned, and saw Roberta smiling. I smiled back, but not too much lest somebody think this visit was the biggest thing that ever happened in my life. Then Roberta said, 'Mother, I want you to meet my roommate, Twyla. And that's Twyla's mother.'

I looked up it seemed for miles. She was big. Bigger than any man and on her chest was the biggest cross I'd ever seen. I swear it was six inches long each way. And in the crook of her arm was the biggest Bible ever made.

Mary, simple-minded as ever, grinned and tried to yank her hand out of the pocket with the raggedy lining – to shake hands, I guess. Roberta's mother looked down at me and then looked down at Mary too. She didn't say anything, just grabbed Roberta with her Bible-free hand and stepped out of line, walking quickly to the rear of it. Mary was still grinning because she's not too swift when it comes to what's really going on. Then this light bulb goes off in her head and she says 'That bitch!' really loud and us almost in the chapel now. Organ music whining; the Bonny Angels singing sweetly. Everybody in the world turned around to look. And Mary would have kept it up – kept calling names if I hadn't squeezed her hand as hard as I could. That helped a little, but she still twitched and crossed and uncrossed her legs all through service.

Even groaned a couple of times. Why did I think she would come there and act right? Slacks. No hat like the grandmothers and viewers, and groaning all the while. When we stood for hymns she kept her mouth shut. Wouldn't even look at the words on the page. She actually reached in her purse for a mirror to check her lipstick. All I could think of was that she really needed to be killed. The sermon lasted a year, and I knew the real orphans were looking smug again.

We were supposed to have lunch in the teachers' lounge, but Mary didn't bring anything, so we picked fur and cellophane grass off the mashed jelly beans and ate them. I could have killed her. I sneaked a look at Roberta. Her mother had brought chicken legs and ham sandwiches and oranges and a whole box of chocolate-covered grahams. Roberta drank milk from a thermos while her mother read the Bible to her.

Things are not right. The wrong food is always with the wrong people. Maybe that's why I got into waitress work later – to match up the right people with the right food. Roberta just let those chicken legs sit there, but she did bring a stack of grahams up to me later when the visit was over. I think she was sorry that her mother would not shake my mother's hand. And I liked that and I liked the fact that she didn't say a word about Mary groaning all the way through the service and not bringing any lunch.

Roberta left in May when the apple trees were heavy and white. On her last day we went to the orchard to watch the big girls smoke and dance by the radio. It didn't matter that they said, 'Twyyyyyla, baby.' We sat on the ground and breathed. Lady Esther. Apple blossoms. I still go soft when I smell one or the other. Roberta was going home. The big cross and the big Bible was coming to get her and she seemed sort of glad and sort of not. I thought I would die in that room of four beds without her and I knew Bozo had plans to move some other dumped kid in there with me. Roberta promised to write every day, which was really sweet of her because she couldn't read a lick so how could she write anybody. I would have drawn pictures and sent them to her but she never gave me her address. Little by little she faded. Her wet socks with the pink scalloped tops and her big serious-looking eyes – that's all I could catch when I tried to bring her to mind.

I WAS WORKING behind the counter at the Howard Johnson's on the Thruway just before the Kingston exit. Not a bad job. Kind of a long ride from Newburgh, but okay once I got there. Mine was the second night shift – eleven to seven. Very light until a Greyhound checked in for breakfast around six-thirty. At that hour the sun was all the way clear of the hills behind the restaurant. The place looked better at night – more like shelter – but I loved it when the sun broke in, even if it did show all the cracks in the vinyl and the speckled floor looked dirty no matter what the mop boy did.

It was August and a bus crowd was just unloading.

They would stand around a long while: going to the john, and looking at gifts and junk-for-sale machines, reluctant to sit down so soon. Even to eat. I was trying to fill the coffee pots and get them all situated on the electric burners when I saw her. She was sitting in a booth smoking a cigarette with two guys smothered in head and facial hair. Her own hair was so big and wild I could hardly see her face. But the eyes. I would know them anywhere. She had on a powder-blue halter and shorts outfit and earrings the size of bracelets.

Talk about lipstick and eyebrow pencil. She made the big girls look like nuns. I couldn't get off the counter until seven o'clock, but I kept watching the booth in case they got up to leave before that. My replacement was on time for a change, so I counted and stacked my receipts as fast as I could and signed off. I walked over to the booths, smiling and wondering if she would remember me. Or even if she wanted to remember me. Maybe she didn't want to be reminded of St Bonny's or to have anybody know she was ever there. I know I never talked about it to anybody.

I put my hands in my apron pockets and leaned against the back of the booth facing them.

'Roberta? Roberta Fisk?'

She looked up. 'Yeah?'

'Twyla.'

She squinted for a second and then said, 'Wow.'

'Remember me?'

'Sure. Hey. Wow.'

'It's been a while,' I said, and gave a smile to the two hairy guys.

'Yeah. Wow. You work here?'

'Yeah,' I said. 'I live in Newburgh.'

'Newburgh? No kidding?' She laughed then, a private laugh that included the guys but only the guys, and they laughed with her. What could I do but laugh too and wonder why I was standing there with my knees showing out from under that uniform. Without looking I could see the blue and white triangle on my head, my hair shapeless in a net, my ankles thick in white oxfords. Nothing could have been less sheer than my stockings. There was this silence that came down right after I laughed. A silence it was her turn to fill up. With introductions, maybe, to her boyfriends or an invitation to sit down and have a Coke. Instead she lit a cigarette off the one she'd just finished and said, 'We're on our way to the Coast. He's got an appointment with Hendrix.'

She gestured casually toward the boy next to her.

'Hendrix? Fantastic,' I said. 'Really fantastic. What's she doing now?'

Roberta coughed on her cigarette and the two guys rolled their eyes up at the ceiling.

'Hendrix. Jimi Hendrix, asshole. He's only the biggest – Oh, wow. Forget it.'

I was dismissed without anyone saying goodbye, so I thought I would do it for her.

'How's your mother?' I asked. Her grin cracked her whole face. She swallowed. 'Fine,' she said. 'How's yours?'

'Pretty as a picture,' I said and turned away. The backs of my knees were damp. Howard Johnson's really was a dump in the sunlight.

JAMES IS AS comfortable as a house slipper. He liked my cooking and I liked his big loud family. They have lived in Newburgh all of their lives and talk about it the way people do who have always known a home. His grandmother is a porch swing older than his father and when they talk about streets and avenues and buildings they call them names they no longer have. They still call the A & P Rico's because it stands on property once a mom and pop store owned by Mr Rico. And they call the new community college Town Hall because it once was. My mother-in-law puts up jelly and cucumbers and buys butter wrapped in cloth from a dairy. James and his father talk about fishing and baseball and I can see them all together on the Hudson in a raggedy skiff. Half the population of Newburgh is on welfare now, but to my husband's family it was still some upstate paradise of a time long past. A time of ice houses and vegetable wagons, coal furnaces and children weeding gardens. When our son was born my mother-in-law gave me the crib blanket that had been hers.

But the town they remembered had changed. Something quick was in the air. Magnificent old houses, so ruined they had become shelter for squatters and rent risks, were bought and renovated. Smart IBM people moved out of their suburbs back into the city and put shutters up and herb gardens in their backyards. A brochure came in the mail announcing the opening of a Food Emporium. Gourmet food it said – and listed items the rich IBM crowd would want. It was located in a new mall at the edge of town and I drove out to shop there one day – just to see. It was late in June. After the tulips were gone and the Queen Elizabeth roses were open everywhere.

I trailed my cart along the aisle tossing in smoked oysters and Robert's sauce and things I knew would sit in my cupboard for years. Only when I found some Klondike ice cream bars did I feel less guilty about spending James's fireman's salary so foolishly. My father-in-law ate them with the same gusto little Joseph did.

Waiting in the check-out line I heard a voice say, 'Twyla!'

The classical music piped over the aisles had affected me and the woman leaning toward me was dressed to kill. Diamonds on her hand, a smart white summer dress. 'I'm Mrs Benson,' I said.

'Ho. Ho. The Big Bozo,' she sang.

For a split second I didn't know what she was talking about. She had a bunch of asparagus and two cartons of fancy water.

'Roberta!'

'Right.'

'For heaven's sake. Roberta.'

'You look great,' she said.

'So do you. Where are you? Here? In Newburgh?'

'Yes. Over in Annandale.'

I was opening my mouth to say more when the cashier called my attention to her empty counter.

'Meet you outside.' Roberta pointed her finger and went into the express line.

I placed the groceries and kept myself from glancing around to check Roberta's progress. I remembered Howard Johnson's and looking for a chance to speak only to be greeted with a stingy 'wow.' But she was waiting for me and her huge hair was sleek now, smooth around a small, nicely shaped head. Shoes, dress, everything lovely and summery and rich. I was dying to know what happened to her, how she got from Jimi Hendrix to Annandale, a neighborhood full of doctors and IBM executives. Easy, I thought. Everything is so easy for them. They think they own the world.

'How long,' I asked her. 'How long have you been here?'

'A year. I got married to a man who lives here. And you, you're married too, right? Benson, you said.'

'Yeah. James Benson.'

'And is he nice?'

'Oh, is he nice?'

'Well, is he?' Roberta's eyes were steady as though she really meant the question and wanted an answer.

He's wonderful, Roberta. Wonderful.'

'So you're happy.'

'Very.'

'That's good,' she said and nodded her head. 'I always hoped you'd be happy. Any kids? I know you have kids.'

'One. A boy. How about you?'

'Four.'

'Four?'

She laughed. 'Step kids. He's a widower.'

'Oh.'

'Got a minute? Let's have a coffee.'

I thought about the Klondikes melting and the inconvenience of going all the way to my car and putting the bags in the trunk. Served me right for buying all that stuff I didn't need. Roberta was ahead of me.

'Put them in my car. It's right here.'

And then I saw the dark blue limousine.

'You married a Chinaman?'

'No,' she laughed. 'He's the driver.'

'Oh, my. If the Big Bozo could see you now.'

We both giggled. Really giggled. Suddenly, in just a pulse beat, twenty years disappeared and all of it came rushing back. The big girls (whom we called gar girls – Roberta's misheard word for the evil stone faces described in a civics class) there dancing in the orchard, the ploppy mashed potatoes, the double weenies, the Spam with pineapple. We went into the coffee shop holding onto one another and I tried to think why we were glad to see each other this time and not before. Once, twelve years ago, we passed like strangers. A black girl and a white girl meeting in a Howard Johnson's on the road and having nothing to say. One in a blue and white triangle waitress hat – the other on her way to see Hendrix. Now we were behaving like sisters separated for much too long. Those four short months were nothing in time. Maybe it was the thing itself. Just being there, together. Two little girls who knew what nobody else in the world knew – how not to ask questions. How to believe what had to be believed. There was politeness in that reluctance and generosity as well. Is your mother sick too? No, she dances all night. Oh – and an understanding nod.

We sat in a booth by the window and fell into recollection like veterans. 'Did you ever learn to read?'

'Watch.' She picked up the menu. 'Special of the day. Cream of corn soup. Entrees. Two dots and a wriggly line. Quiche. Chef salad, scallops . . .'

I was laughing and applauding when the waitress came up.

'Remember the Easter baskets?'

'And how we tried to introduce them?'

'Your mother with that cross like two telephone poles.'

'And yours with those tight slacks.'

We laughed so loudly heads turned and made the laughter harder to suppress.

'What happened to the Jimi Hendrix date?'

Roberta made a blow-out sound with her lips.

'When he died I thought about you.'

'Oh, you heard about him finally?'

'Finally. Come on, I was a small-town country waitress.'

'And I was a small-town country dropout. God, were we wild. I still don't know how I got out of there alive.'

'But you did.'

'I did. I really did. Now I'm Mrs Kenneth Norton.'

'Sounds like a mouthful.'

'It is.'

'Servants and all?'

Roberta held up two fingers.

'Ow! What does he do?'

'Computers and stuff. What do I know?'

'I don't remember a hell of a lot from those days, but Lord, St Bonny's is as clear as daylight. Remember Maggie? The day she fell down and those gar girls laughed at her?'

Roberta looked up from her salad and stared at me. 'Maggie didn't fall,' she said.

'Yes, she did. You remember.'

'No, Twyla. They knocked her down. Those girls pushed her down and tore her clothes. In the orchard.'

'I don't – that's not what happened.'

'Sure it is. In the orchard. Remember how scared we were?'

'Wait a minute. I don't remember any of that.'

'And Bozo was fired.'

'You're crazy. She was there when I left. You left before me.'

'I went back. You weren't there when they fired Bozo.'

'What?'

'Twice. Once for a year when I was about ten, another for two months when I was fourteen. That's when I ran away.'

'You ran away from St Bonny's?'

'I had to. What do you want? Me dancing in that orchard?'

'Are you sure about Maggie?'

'Of course I'm sure. You've blocked it, Twyla. It happened. Those girls had behavior problems, you know.'

'Didn't they, though. But why can't I remember the Maggie thing?'

'Believe me. It happened. And we were there.'

'Who did you room with when you went back?' I asked her as if I would know her. The Maggie thing was troubling me.

'Creeps. They tickled themselves in the night.'

My ears were itching and I wanted to go home suddenly. This was all very well but she couldn't just comb her hair, wash her face and pretend everything was hunky-dory. After the Howard Johnson's snub. And no apology. Nothing.

'Were you on dope or what that time at Howard Johnson's?' I tried to make my voice sound friendlier than I felt.

'Maybe, a little. I never did drugs much. Why?'

'I don't know; you acted sort of like you didn't want to know me then.'

'Oh, Twyla, you know how it was in those days: black-white. You know how everything was.'

But I didn't know. I thought it was just the opposite. Bus-loads of blacks and whites came into Howard Johnson's together. They roamed together then: students, musicians, lovers, protesters. You got to see everything at Howard Johnson's and blacks were very friendly with whites in those days.

But sitting there with nothing on my plate but two hard tomato wedges wondering about the melting Klondikes it seemed childish remembering the slight. We went to her car, and with the help of the driver, got my stuff into my station wagon.

'We'll keep in touch this time,' she said.

'Sure,' I said. 'Sure. Give me a call.'

'I will,' she said, and then just as I was sliding behind the wheel, she leaned into the window. 'By the way. Your mother. Did she ever stop dancing?'

I shook my head. 'No. Never.'

Roberta nodded.

'And yours? Did she ever get well?'

She smiled a tiny sad smile. 'No. She never did. Look, call me, okay?'

'Okay,' I said, but I knew I wouldn't. Roberta had messed up my past somehow with that business about Maggie. I wouldn't forget a thing like that. Would I?

STRIFE CAME TO us that fall. At least that's what the paper called it. Strife. Racial strife. The word made me think of a bird – a big shrieking bird out of 1,000,000,000 B. C. Flapping its wings and cawing. Its eye with no lid always bearing down on you. All day it screeched and at night it slept on the rooftops. It woke you in the morning and from the *Today* show to the eleven o'clock news it kept you an awful company. I couldn't figure it out from one day to the next. I knew I was supposed to feel something strong, but I didn't know what, and James wasn't any help. Joseph was on the list of kids to be transferred from the junior high school to another one at some far-out-of-the-way place and I thought it was a good thing until I heard it was a bad thing. I mean I didn't know. All the schools seemed dumps to me, and the fact that one was nicer looking didn't hold much weight. But the papers were full of it and then the kids began to get jumpy. In August, mind you. Schools weren't even open yet. I thought Joseph might be frightened to go over there, but he didn't seem scared so I forgot about it, until I found myself driving along Hudson Street out there by the school they were trying to integrate and saw a line of women marching. And who do you suppose was in line, big as life, holding a sign in front of her bigger than her mother's cross? MOTHERS HAVE RIGHTS TOO! it said.

I drove on, and then changed my mind. I circled the block, slowed down, and honked my horn.

Roberta looked over and when she saw me she waved. I didn't wave back, but I didn't move either. She handed

Racial strife. The word made me think of a bird – a big shrieking bird out of 1,000,000,000 B. C.

her sign to another woman and came over to where I was parked.

'Hi.'

'What are you doing?'

'Picketing. What's it look like?'

'What for?'

'What do you mean, "What for?" They want to take my kids and send them out of the neighborhood. They don't want to go.'

'So what if they go to another school? My boy's being bussed too, and I don't mind. Why should you?'

'It's not about us, Twyla. Me and you. It's about our kids.'

'What's more us than that?'

'Well, it is a free country.'

'Not yet, but it will be.'

'What the hell does that mean? I'm not doing anything to you.'

'You really think that?'

'I know it.'

'I wonder what made me think you were different.'

'I wonder what made me think you were different.'

'Look at them,' I said. 'Just look. Who do they think they are? Swarming all over the place like they own it. And now they think they can decide where my child goes to school. Look at them, Roberta. They're Bozos.'

Roberta turned around and looked at the women. Almost all of them were standing still now, waiting. Some were even edging toward us. Roberta looked at me out of some refrigerator behind her eyes. 'No, they're not. They're just mothers.'

'And what am I? Swiss cheese?'

'I used to curl your hair.'

'I hated your hands in my hair.'

The women were moving. Our faces looked mean to them of course and they looked as though they could not wait to throw themselves in front of a police car, or better yet, into my car and drag me away by my ankles. Now they surrounded my car and gently, gently began to rock it. I swayed back and forth like a sideways yo-yo. Automatically I reached for Roberta, like the old days in the orchard when they saw us watching them and we had to get out of there, and if one of us fell the other pulled her up and if one of us was caught the other stayed to kick and scratch, and neither would leave the other behind. My arm shot out of the car window but no receiving hand was there. Roberta was looking at me sway from side to side in the car and her face was still. My purse slid from the car seat down under the dashboard. The four policemen who had been drinking Tab in their car finally got the message and strolled over, forcing their way through the women. Quietly, firmly they spoke. 'Okay, ladies. Back in line or off the streets.'

Some of them went away willingly; others had to be urged away from the car doors and the hood. Roberta didn't move. She was looking steadily at me. I was fumbling to turn on the ignition, which wouldn't catch because the gearshift was still in drive. The seats of the car were a mess because the swaying had thrown my grocery coupons all over it and my purse was sprawled on the floor.

'Maybe I am different now, Twyla. But you're not. You're the same little state kid who kicked a poor old black lady when she was down on the ground. You kicked a black lady and you have the nerve to call me a bigot.'

The coupons were everywhere and the guts of my purse were bunched under the dashboard. What was she saying? Black? Maggie wasn't black.

'She wasn't black,' I said.

'Like hell she wasn't, and you kicked her. We both did. You kicked a black lady who couldn't even scream.'

'Liar!'

'You're the liar! Why don't you just go on home and leave us alone, huh?'

She turned away and I skidded away from the curb.

The next morning I went into the garage and cut the side out of the carton our portable TV had come in. It wasn't nearly big enough, but after a while I had a decent sign: red spray-painted letters on a white background – AND SO DO CHILDREN****. I meant just to go down to the school and tack it up somewhere so those cows on the picket line across the street could see it, but when I got there, some ten or so others had already assembled – protesting the cows across the street. Police permits and everything. I got in line and we strutted in time on our side while Roberta's group strutted on theirs. That first day we were all dignified, pretending the other side didn't exist. The second day there was name calling and finger gestures. But that was about all. People changed signs from time to time, but Roberta never did and neither did I. Actually my sign didn't make sense without Roberta's. 'And so do children what?' one of the women on my side asked me. Have rights, I said, as though it was obvious.

Roberta didn't acknowledge my presence in any way and I got to thinking maybe she didn't know I was there. I began to pace myself in the line, jostling people one minute and lagging behind the next, so Roberta and I could reach the end of our respective lines at the same time and there would be a moment in our turn when we would face each other. Still, I couldn't tell whether she saw me and knew my sign was for her. The next day I went early before we were scheduled to assemble. I waited until she got there before I exposed my new creation. As soon as she hoisted her MOTHERS HAVE RIGHTS TOO I began to wave my new one, which said, HOW WOULD YOU KNOW? I know she saw that one, but I had gotten addicted now. My signs got crazier each day, and the women on my side decided that I was a kook. They couldn't make heads or tails out of my brilliant screaming posters.

I brought a painted sign in queenly red with huge black

letters that said, IS YOUR MOTHER WELL? Roberta took her lunch break and didn't come back for the rest of the day or any day after. Two days later I stopped going too and couldn't have been missed because nobody understood my signs anyway.

It was a nasty six weeks. Classes were suspended and Joseph didn't go to anybody's school until October. The children – everybody's children – soon got bored with that extended vacation they thought was going to be so great. They looked at TV until their eyes flattened. I spent a couple of mornings tutoring my son, as the other mothers said we should. Twice I opened a text from last year that he had never turned in. Twice he yawned in my face. Other mothers organized living room sessions so the kids would keep up. None of the kids could concentrate so they drifted back to *The Price Is Right* and *The Brady Bunch*. When the school finally opened there were fights once or twice and some sirens roared through the streets every once in a while. There were a lot of photographers from Albany. And just when ABC was about to send up a news crew, the kids settled down like nothing in the world had happened. Joseph hung my HOW WOULD YOU KNOW? sign in his bedroom. I don't know what became of AND SO DO CHILDREN****. I think my father-in-law cleaned some fish on it. He was always puttering around in our garage. Each of his five children lived in Newburgh and he acted as though he had five extra homes.

I couldn't help looking for Roberta when Joseph graduated from high school, but I didn't see her. It didn't trouble me much what she had said to me in the car. I mean the kicking part. I know I didn't do that, I couldn't do that. But I was puzzled by her telling me Maggie was black. When I thought about it I actually couldn't be certain. She wasn't pitch-black, I knew, or I would have remembered that. What I remember was the kiddie hat, and the semicircle legs. I tried to reassure myself about the race thing for a long time until it dawned on me that the truth was already there, and Roberta knew it. I didn't kick her; I didn't join in with the gar girls and kick that lady, but I sure did want to. We watched and never tried to help her and never called for help. Maggie was my dancing mother. Deaf, I thought, and dumb. Nobody inside. Nobody who would hear you if you cried in the night. Nobody who could tell you anything important that you could use. Rocking, dancing, swaying as she walked. And when the gar girls pushed her down, and started roughhousing, I knew she wouldn't scream, couldn't – just like me and I was glad about that.

WE DECIDED NOT to have a tree, because Christmas would be at my mother-in-law's house, so why have a tree at both places? Joseph was at SUNY New Paltz and we had to economize, we said. But at the last minute, I changed my mind. Nothing could be that bad. So I rushed around town looking for a tree, something small but wide.

By the time I found a place, it was snowing and very late. I dawdled like it was the most important purchase in the world and the tree man was fed up with me. Finally I chose one and had it tied onto the trunk of the car. I drove away slowly because the sand trucks were not out yet and the streets could be murder at the beginning of a snowfall. Downtown the streets were wide and rather empty except for a cluster of people coming out of the Newburgh Hotel. The one hotel in town that wasn't built out of cardboard and Plexiglas. A party, probably. The men huddled in the snow were dressed in tails and the women had on furs. Shiny things glittered from underneath their coats. It made me tired to look at them. Tired, tired, tired. On the next corner was a small diner with loops and loops of paper bells in the window. I stopped the car and went in. Just for a cup of coffee and twenty minutes of peace before I went home and tried to finish everything before Christmas Eve.

'Twyla?'

There she was. In a silvery evening gown and dark fur coat. A man and another woman were with her, the man fumbling for change to put in the cigarette machine. The woman was humming and tapping on the counter with her fingernails. They all looked a little bit drunk.

'Well. It's you.'

'How are you?'

I shrugged. 'Pretty good. Frazzled. Christmas and all.'

'Regular?' called the woman from the counter.

'Fine,' Roberta called back and then, 'Wait for me in the car.'

She slipped into the booth beside me. 'I have to tell you something, Twyla. I made up my mind if I ever saw you again, I'd tell you.'

'I'd just as soon not hear anything, Roberta. It doesn't matter now, anyway.'

'No,' she said. 'Not about that.'

'Don't be long,' said the woman. She carried two regulars to go and the man peeled his cigarette pack as they left.

'It's about St Bonny's and Maggie.'

'Oh, please.'

'Listen to me. I really did think she was black. I didn't make that up. I really thought so. But now I can't be sure. I just remember her as old, so old. And because she couldn't talk – well, you know, I thought she was crazy. She'd been brought up in an institution like my mother was and like I thought I would be too. And you were right. We didn't kick her. It was the gar girls. Only them. But, well, I wanted to. I really wanted them to hurt her. I said we did it, too. You and me, but that's not true. And I don't want you to carry that around. It was just that I wanted to do it so bad that day – wanting to is doing it.'

Her eyes were watery from the drinks she'd had, I guess. I know it's that way with me. One glass of wine and I start bawling over the littlest thing.

'We were kids, Roberta.'

'Yeah. Yeah. I know, just kids.'

'Eight.'

'Eight.'

'And lonely.'

'Scared, too.'

She wiped her cheeks with the heel of her hand and smiled. 'Well that's all I wanted to say.'

I nodded and couldn't think of any way to fill the silence that went from the diner past the paper bells on out into the snow. It was heavy now. I thought I'd better wait for the sand trucks before starting home.

'Thanks, Roberta.'

'Sure.'

'Did I tell you? My mother, she never did stop dancing.'

'Yes. You told me. And mine, she never got well.' Roberta lifted her hands from the tabletop and covered her face with her palms. When she took them away she really was crying. 'Oh shit, Twyla. Shit, shit, shit. What the hell happened to Maggie?'

'Making America White Again', an essay

THIS IS A serious project. All immigrants to the United States know (and knew) that if they want to become real, authentic Americans they must reduce their fealty to their native country and regard it as secondary, subordinate, in order to emphasize their whiteness. Unlike any nation in Europe, the United States holds whiteness as the unifying force. Here, for many people, the definition of 'Americanness' is color.

Under slave laws, the necessity for color rankings was obvious, but in America today, post-civil-rights legislation, white people's conviction of their natural superiority is being lost. Rapidly lost. There are 'people of color' everywhere, threatening to erase this long-understood definition of America. And what then? Another black President? A predominantly black Senate? Three black Supreme Court Justices? The threat is frightening.

In order to limit the possibility of this untenable change, and restore whiteness to its former status as a marker of national identity, a number of white Americans are sacrificing themselves. They have begun *to do things they clearly don't really want to be doing*, and, to do so, they are (1) abandoning their sense of human dignity and (2) risking the appearance of cowardice. Much as they may hate their behavior, and know full well how craven it is, they are willing to kill small children attending Sunday school and slaughter churchgoers who invite a white boy to pray. Embarrassing as the obvious display of cowardice must be, they are willing to set fire to churches, and to start firing in them while the members are at prayer. And, shameful as such demonstrations of weakness are, they are willing to shoot black children in the street.

To keep alive the perception of white superiority, these white Americans tuck their heads under cone-shaped hats and American flags and deny themselves the dignity of face-to-face confrontation, training their guns on the unarmed, the innocent, the scared, on subjects who are running away, exposing their unthreatening backs to bullets. Surely, shooting a fleeing man in the back hurts the presumption of white strength? The sad plight of grown white men, crouching beneath their (better) selves, to slaughter the innocent during traffic stops, to push black women's faces into the dirt, to handcuff black children. Only the frightened would do that. Right?

These sacrifices, made by supposedly tough white men, who are prepared to abandon their humanity out of fear of black men and women, suggest the true horror of lost status.

It may be hard to feel pity for the men who are making these bizarre sacrifices in the name of white power and supremacy. Personal debasement is not easy for white people (especially for white men), but to retain the conviction of their superiority to others – especially to black people – they are willing to risk contempt, and to be reviled by the mature, the sophisticated, and the strong. If it weren't so ignorant and pitiful, one could mourn this collapse of dignity in service to an evil cause.

The comfort of being 'naturally better than,' of not having to struggle or demand civil treatment, is hard to give up. The confidence that you will not be watched in a department store, that you are the preferred customer in high-end restaurants – these social inflections, belonging to whiteness, are greedily relished.

So scary are the consequences of a collapse of white privilege that many Americans have flocked to a political platform that supports and translates violence against the defenseless as strength. These people are not so much angry as terrified, with the kind of terror that makes knees tremble.

On Election Day, how eagerly so many white voters – both the poorly educated and the well educated – embraced the shame and fear sowed by Donald Trump. The candidate whose company has been sued by the Justice Department for not renting apartments to black people.

The candidate who questioned whether Barack Obama was born in the United States, and who seemed to condone the beating of a Black Lives Matter protester at a campaign rally. The candidate who kept black workers off the floors of his casinos. The candidate who is beloved by David Duke and endorsed by the Ku Klux Klan.

William Faulkner understood this better than almost any other American writer. In 'Absalom, Absalom,' incest is less of a taboo for an upper-class Southern family than acknowledging the one drop of black blood that would clearly soil the family line. Rather than lose its 'whiteness' (once again), the family chooses murder.

© Toni Morrison

TONI MORRISON was born in Ohio in 1931. She began writing while teaching literature at Howard University and went on to publish her first novel, *The Bluest Eye* in 1970. She has since published eleven novels, including *Song of Solomon* and the Pulitzer-prize winning *Beloved*, as well as many non-fiction books and plays.

Morrison's writing is tirelessly engaged with issues of race and racism. *The Bluest Eye* explores what it means to be 'beautiful' in a world where whiteness monopolizes the mind, while *Beloved* plumbs the psychological pain and fracture, as well as the inconceivable sacrifices of those living under the tyranny of slavery. Her essay, 'Making America White Again' (which is also included in this book) examines the state of race relations in the Trump era.

Among the many prizes her work has been awarded, Morrison was presented with the Nobel Prize for Literature in 1993, and the Presidential Medal of Freedom in 2012.

RECOMMENDED BOOKS BY TONI MORRISON:

Beloved
Song of Solomon
The Bluest Eye

Hoping for some harmony after Race?

Sisters
LOUISA MAY ALCOTT

VINTAGE MINIS

Love
JEANETTE WINTERSON

VINTAGE MINIS

Babies
ANNE ENRIGHT

VINTAGE MINIS

Language
XIAOLU GUO

VINTAGE MINIS

VINTAGE MINIS

The Vintage Minis bring you the world's greatest writers on the experiences that make us human. These stylish, entertaining little books explore the whole spectrum of life – from birth to death, and everything in between. Which means there's something here for everyone, whatever your story.

vintageminis.co.uk

1 3 5 7 9 10 8 6 4 2

Vintage
20 Vauxhall Bridge Road,
London SW1V 2SA

Vintage Classics is part of the Penguin Random House
group of companies whose addresses can be found at
global.penguinrandomhouse.com.

Penguin
Random House
UK

The Doors of Perception was first published in Great Britain in 1954
by Chatto & Windus
This edition published by Vintage in 2017

penguin.co.uk/vintage

A CIP catalogue record for this book is available from the British Library

ISBN 9781784872748

Typeset in 9.5/14.5 pt FreightText Pro
by Jouve (UK), Milton Keynes
Printed and bound by Clays Ltd, St Ives plc

Penguin Random House is committed to a sustainable future for
our business, our readers and our planet. This book is made from
Forest Stewardship Council® certified paper.

MIX
Paper from
responsible sources
FSC® C018179

Psychedelics

ALDOUS HUXLEY

VINTAGE MINIS

The Doors of Perception

IT WAS IN 1886 that the German pharmacologist, Ludwig Lewin published the first systematic study of the cactus, to which his own name was subsequently given. *Anhalonium Lewinii* was new to science. To primitive religion and the Indians of Mexico and the American Southwest it was a friend of immemorially long standing. Indeed, it was much more than a friend. In the words of one of the early Spanish visitors to the New World, 'they eat a root which they call Peyotl, and which they venerate as though it were a deity.'

Why they should have venerated it as a deity became apparent when such eminent psychologists as Jaensch, Havelock Ellis and Weir Mitchell began their experiments with mescalin, the active principle of peyotl. True, they stopped short at a point well this side of idolatry; but all concurred in assigning to mescalin a position among drugs of unique distinction. Administered in suitable doses, it changes the quality of consciousness more profoundly and yet is less toxic than any other substance in the pharma-cologist's repertory.

Mescalin research has been going on sporadically ever since the days of Lewin and Havelock Ellis. Chemists have not merely isolated the alkaloid; they have learned how to synthesize it, so that the supply no longer depends on the sparse and intermittent crop of a desert cactus. Alienists have dosed themselves with mescalin in the hope thereby of coming to a better, a first-hand understanding of their patients' mental processes. Working unfortunately upon too few subjects within too narrow a range of circum-stances, psychologists have observed and catalogued some of the drug's more striking effects. Neurologists and physiologists have found out something about the mech-anism of its action upon the central nervous system. And at least one professional philosopher has taken mescalin for the light it may throw on such ancient unsolved riddles as the place of mind in nature and the relationship between brain and consciousness.

There matters rested until, two or three years ago, a new and perhaps highly significant fact was observed.[1] Actually

[1] See the following papers:

Schizophrenia: A New Approach. By Humphry Osmond and John Smythies. Journal of Mental Science. Vol. xcviii. April 1952.

On Being Mad. By Humphry Osmond. Saskatchewan Psychiatric Ser-vices Journal. Vol. i. No. 2. September 1952.

The Mescalin Phenomena. By John Smythies. The British Journal for the Philosophy of Science. Vol. iii. February 1953.

Schizophrenia: A New Approach. By Abram Hoffer, Humphry Osmond the fact had been staring everyone in the face for several decades; but nobody, as it happened, had noticed it until a young English psychiatrist, at present working in Canada, was struck by the close similarity, in chemical composition, between mescalin and adrenalin. Further research revealed that lysergic acid, an extremely potent hallucinogen derived from ergot, has a structural biochemical relationship to the others. Then came the discovery that adrenochrome, which is a product of the decomposition of adrenalin, can produce many of the symptoms observed in mescalin intoxication. But adrenochrome probably occurs spontaneously in the human body. In other words, each one of us may be capable of manufacturing a chemical, minute doses of which are known to cause profound changes in consciousness. Certain of these changes are similar to those which occur in that most characteristic plague of the twentieth century, schizophrenia. Is the mental disorder due to a chemical disorder? And is the chemical disorder due, in its turn, to psychological distresses affecting the adrenals? It would be rash and premature to affirm it. The most we can say is that some kind of a *prima facie* case has been made out. Meanwhile the clue is being systematically followed, the sleuths – biochemists, psychiatrists, psychologists – are on the trail.

---

and John Smythies. The Journal of Mental Science. Vol c. No. 418. January 1954.

Numerous other papers on the biochemistry, pharmacology, psychology and neurophysiology of schizophrenia and the mescalin phenomena are in preparation.

By a series of, for me, extremely fortunate circumstances I found myself, in the spring of 1953, squarely athwart that trail. One of the sleuths had come on business to California. In spite of seventy years of mescalin research, the psychological material at his disposal was still absurdly inadequate, and he was anxious to add to it. I was on the spot and willing, indeed eager, to be a guinea-pig. Thus it came about that, one bright May morning, I swallowed four-tenths of a gramme of mescalin dissolved in half a glass of water and sat down to wait for the results.

We live together, we act on, and react to, one another; but always and in all circumstances we are by ourselves. The martyrs go hand in hand into the arena; they are crucified alone. Embraced, the lovers desperately try to fuse their insulated ecstasies into a single self-transcendence; in vain. By its very nature every embodied spirit is doomed to suffer and enjoy in solitude. Sensations, feelings, insights, fancies – all these are private and, except through symbols and at second hand, incommunicable. We can pool information about experiences, but never the experiences themselves. From family to nation, every human group is a society of island universes.

Most island universes are sufficiently like one another to permit of inferential understanding or even of mutual empathy or 'feeling into.' Thus, remembering our own bereavements and humiliations, we can condole with others in analogous circumstances, can put ourselves (always, of course, in a slightly Pickwickian sense) in their

Sensations, feelings, insights, fancies – all these are private and, except through symbols and at second hand, incommunicable

places. But in certain cases communication between universes is incomplete or even non-existent. The mind is its own place, and the places inhabited by the insane and the exceptionally gifted are so different from the places where ordinary men and women live, that there is little or no common ground of memory to serve as a basis for understanding or fellow feeling. Words are uttered, but fail to enlighten. The things and events to which the symbols refer belong to mutually exclusive realms of experience.

To see ourselves as others see us is a most salutary gift. Hardly less important is the capacity to see others as they see themselves. But what if these others belong to a different species and inhabit a radically alien universe? For example, how can the sane get to know what it actually feels like to be mad? Or, short of being born again as a visionary, a medium or a musical genius, how can we ever visit the worlds which, to Blake, to Swedenborg, to Johann Sebastian Bach, were home? And how can a man at the extreme limits of ectomorphy and cerebrotonia ever put himself in the place of one at the limits of endomorphy and viscerotonia or, except within certain circumscribed areas, share the feelings of one who stands at the limits of mesomorphy and somatotonia? To the unmitigated behaviourist such questions, I suppose, are meaningless. But for those who theoretically believe what in practice they know to be true – namely, that there is an inside to experience as well as an outside – the problems posed are real problems, all the more grave for being, some completely insoluble, some soluble only in exceptional circumstances and by methods not available to everyone. Thus, it seems virtually certain that I shall never know what it feels like to be Sir John Falstaff or Joe Louis. On the other hand, it had always seemed to me possible that, through hypnosis, for example, or auto-hypnosis, by means of systematic meditation, or else by taking the appropriate drug, I might so change my ordinary mode of consciousness as to be able to know, from the inside, what the visionary, the medium, even the mystic were talking about.

From what I had read of the mescalin experience I was convinced in advance that the drug would admit me, at least for a few hours, into the kind of inner world described by Blake and Æ. But what I had expected did not happen. I had expected to lie with my eyes shut, looking at visions of many-coloured geometries, of animated architectures, rich with gems and fabulously lovely, of landscapes with heroic figures, of symbolic dramas trembling perpetually on the verge of the ultimate revelation. But I had not reckoned, it was evident, with the idiosyncrasies of my mental make-up, the facts of my temperament, training and habits.

I am and, for as long as I can remember, I have always been a poor visualizer. Words, even the pregnant words of poets, do not evoke pictures in my mind. No hypnagogic visions greet me on the verge of sleep. When I recall something, the memory does not present itself to me as a vividly seen event or object. By an effort of the will, I can evoke a not very vivid image of what happened yesterday afternoon, of how the Lungarno used to look before the bridges were destroyed, of the Bayswater Road when the only buses were green and tiny and drawn by aged horses at three and a half miles an hour. But such images have little substance and absolutely no autonomous life of their own. They stand to real, perceived objects in the same relation as Homer's ghosts stood to the men of flesh and blood, who came to visit them in the shades. Only when I have a high temperature do my mental images come to independent life. To those in whom the faculty of visualization is strong my inner world must seem curiously drab, limited and uninteresting. This was the world – a poor thing but my own – which I expected to see transformed into something completely unlike itself.

The change which actually took place in that world was in no sense revolutionary. Half an hour after swallowing the drug I became aware of a slow dance of golden lights. A little later there were sumptuous red surfaces swelling and expanding from bright nodes of energy that vibrated with a continuously changing, patterned life. At another time the closing of my eyes revealed a complex of grey structures, within which pale blueish spheres kept emerging into intense solidity and, having emerged, would slide noiselessly upwards, out of sight. But at no time were there faces or forms of men or animals. I saw no landscapes, no enormous spaces, no magical growth and metamorphosis of buildings, nothing remotely like a drama or a parable. The other world to which mescalin admitted me was not the world of visions; it existed out there, in what I could see with my eyes open. The great change was in the realm of objective fact. What had happened to my subjective universe was relatively unimportant.

I took my pill at eleven. An hour and half later I was sitting in my study, looking intently at a small glass vase. The vase contained only three flowers – a full-blown Belle of Portugal rose, shell pink with a hint at every petal's base of a hotter, flamier hue; a large magenta and cream-coloured carnation; and, pale purple at the end of its broken stalk, the bold heraldic blossom of an iris. Fortuitous and provisional, the little nosegay broke all the rules of traditional good taste. At breakfast that morning I had been struck by the lively dissonance of its colours. But that was no longer the point. I was not looking now at an unusual flower arrangement. I was seeing what Adam had seen on the morning of his creation – the miracle, moment by moment, of naked existence.

'Is it agreeable?' somebody asked. (During this part of the experiment, all conversations were recorded on a dictating machine, and it has been possible for me to refresh my memory of what was said.)

'Neither agreeable nor disagreeable,' I answered. 'It just *is*.'

Istigkeit – wasn't that the word Meister Eckhart liked to use? 'Is-ness.' The Being of Platonic philosophy – except that Plato seems to have made the enormous, the grotesque mistake of separating Being from becoming, and identifying it with the mathematical abstraction of the Idea. He could never, poor fellow, have seen a bunch of flowers shining with their own inner light and all but quivering under the pressure of the significance with which they were charged; could never have perceived that what rose and iris and carnation so intensely signified was nothing more, and nothing less, than what they were – a transience that was yet eternal life, a perpetual perishing that was at the same time pure Being, a bundle of minute, unique particulars in which, by some unspeakable and yet self-evident paradox, was to be seen the divine source of all existence.

I continued to look at the flowers, and in their living light I seemed to detect the qualitative equivalent of breathing – but of a breathing without returns to a starting-point, with no recurrent ebbs but only a repeated flow from beauty to heightened beauty, from deeper to ever deeper meaning. Words like Grace and Transfiguration came to my mind, and this of course was what, among other things, they stood for. My eyes travelled from the rose to the carnation, and from that feathery incandescence to the smooth scrolls of sentient amethyst which were the iris. The Beatific Vision, *Sat Chit Ananda*, Being-Awareness-Bliss – for the first time I understood, not on the verbal level, not by inchoate hints or at a distance, but precisely and completely what those prodigious syllables referred to. And then I remembered a passage I had read in one of Suzuki's essays. 'What is the

Dharma-Body of the Buddha?' (The Dharma-Body of the Buddha is another way of saying Mind, Suchness, the Void, the Godhead.) The question is asked in a Zen monastery by an earnest and bewildered novice. And with the prompt irrelevance of one of the Marx Brothers, the Master answers, 'The hedge at the bottom of the garden.' 'And the man who realizes this truth,' the novice dubiously enquires, 'what, may I ask, is he?' Groucho gives him a whack over the shoulders with his staff and answers, 'A golden-haired lion.'

It had been, when I read it, only a vaguely pregnant piece of nonsense. Now it was all as clear as day, as evident as Euclid. Of course the Dharma-Body of the Buddha was the hedge at the bottom of the garden. At the same time, and no less obviously, it was these flowers, it was anything that I – or rather the blessed Not-I released for a moment from my throttling embrace – cared to look at. The books, for example, with which my study walls were lined. Like the flowers, they glowed, when I looked at them, with brighter colours, a profounder significance. Red books, like rubies; emerald books; books bound in white jade; books of agate, of aquamarine, of yellow topaz; lapis lazuli books whose colour was so intense, so intrinsically meaningful, that they seemed to be on the point of leaving the shelves to thrust themselves more insistently on my attention.

'What about spatial relationships?' the investigator enquired, as I was looking at the books.

It was difficult to answer. True, the perspective looked

rather odd, and the walls of the room no longer seemed to meet in right angles. But these were not the really important facts. The really important facts were that spatial relationships had ceased to matter very much and that my mind was perceiving the world in terms of other than spatial categories. At ordinary times the eye concerns itself with such problems as *Where? – How far? – How situated in relation to what?* In the mescalin experience the implied questions to which the eye responds are of another order. Place and distance cease to be of much interest. The mind does its perceiving in terms of intensity of existence, profundity of significance, relationships within a pattern. I saw the books, but was not at all concerned with their positions in space. What I noticed, what impressed itself upon my mind was the fact that all of them glowed with living light and that in some the glory was more manifest than in others. In this context, position and the three dimensions were beside the point. Not, of course, that the category of space had been abolished. When I got up and walked about, I could do so quite normally, without misjudging the whereabouts of objects. Space was still there; but it had lost its predominance. The mind was primarily concerned, not with measures and locations, but with being and meaning.

And along with indifference to space there went an even completer indifference to time.

'There seems to be plenty of it,' was all I would answer when the investigator asked me to say what I felt about time.

Plenty of it, but exactly how much was entirely irrelevant. I could, of course, have looked at my watch; but my watch, I knew, was in another universe. My actual experience had been, was still, of an indefinite duration or alternatively of a perpetual present made up of one continually changing apocalypse.

From the books the investigator directed my attention to the furniture. A small typing-table stood in the centre of the room; beyond it, from my point of view, was a wicker chair and beyond that a desk. The three pieces formed an intricate pattern of horizontals, uprights and diagonals – a pattern all the more interesting for not being interpreted in terms of spatial relationships. Table, chair and desk came together in a composition that was like something by Braque or Juan Gris, a still life recognizably related to the objective world, but rendered without depth, without any attempt at photographic realism. I was looking at my furniture, not as the utilitarian who has to sit on chairs, to write at desks and tables, and not as the camera-man or scientific recorder, but as the pure aesthete whose concern is only with forms and their relationships within the field of vision or the picture space. But as I looked, this purely aesthetic Cubist's-eye view gave place to what I can only describe as the sacramental vision of reality. I was back where I had been when I was looking at the flowers – back in a world where everything shone with the Inner Light, and was infinite in its significance. The legs, for example, of that chair – how miraculous their tubularity, how supernatural their polished smoothness! I spent several minutes – or was it several centuries? – not merely gazing at those bamboo legs, but actually *being* them – or rather being myself in them; or, to be still more accurate (for 'I' was not involved in the case, nor in a certain sense were 'they'), being my Not-self in the Not-self which was the chair.

Reflecting on my experience, I find myself agreeing with the eminent Cambridge philosopher, Dr C. D. Broad, 'that we should do well to consider much more seriously than we have hitherto been inclined to do the type of theory which Bergson put forward in connection with memory and sense perception. The suggestion is that the function of the brain and nervous system and sense organs is in the main *eliminative* and not productive. Each person is at each moment capable of remembering all that has ever happened to him and of perceiving everything that is happening everywhere in the universe. The function of the brain and nervous system is to protect us from being overwhelmed and confused by this mass of largely useless and irrelevant knowledge, by shutting out most of what we should otherwise perceive or remember at any moment, and leaving only that very small and special selection which is likely to be practically useful.' According to such a theory, each one of us is potentially Mind at Large. But in so far as we are animals, our business is at all costs to survive. To make biological survival possible, Mind at Large has to be funnelled through the reducing valve of the brain and nervous system. What comes out at the other end is a measly trickle of the kind of consciousness which will help us to stay alive on the surface of this particular planet. To formulate and express the contents of this reduced awareness, man has invented and endlessly elaborated those symbol-systems and implicit philosophies which we call languages. Every individual is at once the beneficiary and the victim of the linguistic tradition into which he or she has been born – the beneficiary inasmuch as language gives access to the accumulated records of other people's experience, the victim in so far as it confirms him in the belief that reduced awareness is the only awareness and as it bedevils his sense of reality, so that he is all too apt to take his concepts for data, his words for actual things. That which, in the language of religion, is called 'this world' is the universe of reduced awareness, expressed and, as it were, petrified by language. The various 'other worlds' with which human beings erratically make contact are so many elements in the totality of the awareness belonging to Mind at Large. Most people, most of the time, know only what comes through the reducing valve and is consecrated as genuinely real by the local language. Certain persons, however, seem to be born with a kind of by-pass that circumvents the reducing valve. In others temporary by-passes may be acquired either spontaneously, or as the result of deliberate 'spiritual exercises,' or through hypnosis, or by means of drugs. Through these permanent or temporary by-passes there flows, not indeed the perception 'of everything that is happening everywhere in the universe' (for the by-pass does not abolish the reducing valve, which still excludes the total content of Mind at Large), but something more than, and above all something different from, the carefully selected utilitarian material which our narrowed, individual minds regard as a complete, or at least sufficient, picture of reality.

The brain is provided with a number of enzyme systems which serve to co-ordinate its workings. Some of these enzymes regulate the supply of glucose to the brain cells. Mescalin inhibits the production of these enzymes and thus lowers the amount of glucose available to an organ that is in constant need of sugar. When mescalin reduces the brain's normal ration of sugar, what happens? Too few cases have been observed, and therefore a comprehensive answer cannot yet be given. But what happens to the majority of the few who have taken mescalin under supervision can be summarized as follows.

(1) The ability to remember and to 'think straight' is little if at all reduced. (Listening to the recordings of my conversation under the influence of the drug, I cannot discover that I was then any stupider than I am at ordinary times.)

(2) Visual impressions are greatly intensified and the eye recovers some of the perceptual innocence of childhood, when the sensum was not immediately and automatically subordinated to the concept. Interest in space is diminished and interest in time falls almost to zero.

(3) Though the intellect remains unimpaired and though perception is enormously improved, the will suffers a profound change for the worse. The mescalin taker sees no reason for doing anything in particular and finds most of the causes for which, at ordinary times, he was prepared to act and suffer, profoundly uninteresting. He can't be bothered with them, for the good reason that he has better things to think about.

(4) These better things may be experienced (as I experienced them) 'out there,' or 'in here,' or in both worlds, the inner and the outer, simultaneously or successively. That they *are* better seems to be self-evident to all mescalin takers who come to the drug with a sound liver and an untroubled mind.

These effects of mescalin are the sort of effects you could expect to follow the administration of a drug having the power to impair the efficiency of the cerebral reducing valve. When the brain runs out of sugar, the undernourished ego grows weak, can't be bothered to undertake the necessary chores, and loses all interest in those spatial and temporal relationships which mean so much to an organism bent on getting on in the world. As Mind at Large seeps past the no longer watertight valve, all kinds of biologically useless things start to happen. In some cases there may be extra-sensory perceptions. Other persons discover a world of visionary beauty. To others again is revealed the glory, the infinite value and meaningfulness of naked existence, of the given, unconceptualized event. In the final stage of egolessness there is an 'obscure knowledge' that All is in all – that All is actually each. This is as near, I take it, as a finite mind can ever come to 'perceiving everything that is happening everywhere in the universe.'

In this context, how significant is the enormous heightening, under mescalin, of the perception of colour! For certain animals it is biologically very important to be able to distinguish certain hues. But beyond the limits of their utilitarian spectrum, most creatures are completely colour blind. Bees, for example, spend most of their time 'deflowering the fresh virgins of the spring'; but, as von Frisch has shown, they can recognize only a very few colours. Man's highly developed colour sense is a biological luxury – inestimably precious to him as an intellectual and spiritual being, but unnecessary to his survival as an animal. To judge by the adjectives which Homer puts into their mouths, the heroes of the Trojan War hardly excelled the bees in their capacity to distinguish colours. In this respect, at least, mankind's advance has been prodigious.

Mescalin raises all colours to a higher power and makes the percipient aware of innumerable fine shades of difference, to which, at ordinary times, he is completely blind. It would seem that, for Mind at Large, the so-called secondary characters of things are primary. Unlike Locke, it evidently feels that colours are more important, better worth attending to than masses, positions and dimensions. Like mescalin takers, many mystics perceive supernaturally brilliant colours, not only with the inward eye, but even in the objective world around them. Similar reports are made by psychics and sensitives. There are certain mediums to whom the mescalin taker's brief revelation is a matter, during long periods, of daily and hourly experience.

From this long but indispensable excursion into the realm of theory we may now return to the miraculous facts – four bamboo chair legs in the middle of a room. Like Wordsworth's daffodils, they brought all manner of wealth – the gift, beyond price, of a new direct insight into the very Nature of Things, together with a more modest treasure of understanding in the field, especially, of the arts.

A rose is a rose is a rose. But these chair legs were chair legs were St Michael and all angels. Four or five hours after the event, when the effects of a cerebral sugar shortage were wearing off, I was taken for a little tour of the city, which included a visit, towards sundown, to what is modestly claimed to be The World's Biggest Drug Store. At the Back of the W.B.D.S., among the toys, the greeting cards and comics stood a row, surprisingly enough, of art books. I picked up the first volume that came to hand. It was on Van Gogh, and the picture at which the book opened was *The Chair* – that astounding portrait of a *Ding an Sich*, which the mad painter saw, with a kind of adoring terror, and tried to render on his canvas. But it was a task to which the power even of genius proved wholly inadequate. The chair Van Gogh had seen was obviously the same in essence as the chair I had seen. But, though incomparably more real than the chair of ordinary perception, the chair in his picture remained no more than an unusually expressive symbol of the fact. The fact had been manifested Suchness; this was only an emblem. Such emblems are sources of true knowledge about the Nature of Things, and this true knowledge may serve to prepare the mind which accepts it for immediate insights on its own account. But that is all. However expressive, symbols can never be the things they stand for.

It would be interesting, in this context, to make a study of the works of art available to the great knowers of Suchness. What sort of pictures did Eckhart look at? What sculptures and paintings played a part in the religious experience of St John of the Cross, of Hakuin, of Hui-neng, of William Law? The questions are beyond my power to answer; but I strongly suspect that most of the great knowers of Suchness paid very little attention to art – some refusing to have anything to do with it at all, others being content with what a critical eye would regard as second-rate, or even tenth-rate, works. (To a person whose transfigured and transfiguring mind can see the All in every *this*, the first-rateness or tenth-rateness of even a religious painting will be a matter of the most sovereign indifference.) Art, I suppose, is only for beginners, or else for those resolute dead-enders, who have made up their minds to be content with the *ersatz* of Suchness, with symbols rather than with what they signify, with the elegantly composed recipe in lieu of actual dinner.

I returned the Van Gogh to its rack and picked up the

volume standing next to it. It was a book on Botticelli. I turned the pages. *The Birth of Venus* – never one of my favourites. *Venus and Mars*, that loveliness so passionately denounced by poor Ruskin at the height of his long-drawn-out sexual tragedy. The marvellously rich and intricate *Calumny of Apelles*. And then a somewhat less familiar and not very good picture, *Judith*. My attention was arrested and I gazed in fascination, not at the pale neurotic heroine or her attendant, not at the victim's hairy head or the vernal landscape in the background, but at the purplish silk of Judith's pleated bodice and long wind-blown skirts.

This was something I had seen before – seen that very morning, between the flowers and the furniture, when I looked down by chance, and went on passionately staring by choice, at my own crossed legs. Those folds in the trousers – what a labyrinth of endlessly significant complexity! And the texture of the grey flannel – how rich, how deeply, mysteriously sumptuous! And here they were again, in Botticelli's picture.

Civilized human beings wear clothes, therefore there can be no portraiture, no mythological or historical story telling without representations of folded textiles. But though it may account for the origins, mere tailoring can never explain the luxuriant development of drapery as a major theme of all the plastic arts. Artists, it is obvious, have always loved drapery for its own sake – or, rather, for their own. When you paint or carve drapery, you are painting or carving forms which, for all practical purposes, are

Those folds in the trousers – what a labyrinth of endlessly significant complexity!

non-representational – the kind of unconditioned forms on which artists even in the most naturalistic tradition like to let themselves go. In the average Madonna or Apostle the strictly human, fully representational element accounts for about ten per cent of the whole. All the rest consists of many coloured variations on the inexhaustible theme of crumpled wool or linen. And these non-representational nine-tenths of a Madonna or an Apostle may be just as important qualitatively as they are in quantity. Very often they set the tone of the whole work of art, they state the key in which the theme is being rendered, they express the mood, the temperament, the attitude to life of the artist. Stoical serenity reveals itself in the smooth surfaces, the broad untortured folds of Piero's draperies. Torn between fact and wish, between cynicism and idealism, Bernini tempers the all but caricatural verisimilitude of his faces with enormous sartorial abstractions, which are the embodiment, in stone or bronze, of the everlasting commonplaces of rhetoric – the heroism, the holiness, the sublimity to which mankind perpetually aspires, for the most part in vain. And here are El Greco's disquietingly visceral skirts and mantles; here are the sharp, twisting, flame-like folds in which Cosimo Tura clothes his figures: in the first, traditional spirituality breaks down into a nameless physiological yearning; in the second, there writhes an agonized sense of the world's essential strangeness and hostility. Or consider Watteau; his men and women play lutes, get ready for balls and harlequinades, embark, on velvet lawns and under noble trees, for the Cythera of every lover's dream; their enormous melancholy and the flayed, excruciating sensibility of their creator find expression, not in the actions recorded, not in the gestures and the faces portrayed, but in the relief and texture of their taffeta skirts, their satin capes and doublets. Not an inch of smooth surface here, not a moment of peace or confidence, only a silken wilderness of countless tiny pleats and wrinkles, with an incessant modulation – inner uncertainty rendered with the perfect assurance of a master hand – of tone into tone, of one indeterminate colour into another. In life, man proposes, God disposes. In the plastic arts the proposing is done by the subject matter; that which disposes is ultimately the artist's temperament, proximately (at least in portraiture, history and genre) the carved or painted drapery. Between them these two may decree that a *fête galante* shall move to tears, that a crucifixion shall be serene to the point of cheerfulness, that a stigmatization shall be almost intolerably sexy, that the likeness of a prodigy of female brainlessness (I am thinking now of Ingres' incomparable Mme Moitessier) shall express the austerest, the most uncompromising intellectuality.

But this is not the whole story. Draperies, as I had now discovered, are much more than devices for the introduction of non-representational forms into naturalistic paintings and sculptures. What the rest of us see only under the influence of mescalin, the artist is congenitally equipped to see all the time. His perception is not limited to what is biologically or socially useful. A little of the knowledge belonging to Mind at Large oozes past the reducing value of brain and ego into his consciousness. It is a knowledge of the intrinsic significance of every exist-ent. For the artist as for the mescalin taker, draperies are living hieroglyphs that stand in some peculiarly expressive way for the unfathomable mystery of pure being. More even than the chair, though less perhaps than those wholly supernatural flowers, the folds of my grey flannel trousers were charged with 'is-ness.' To what they owed this privi-leged status, I cannot say. Is it, perhaps, because the forms of folded drapery are so strange and dramatic that they catch the eye and in this way force the miraculous fact of sheer existence upon the attention? Who knows? What is important is less the reason for the experience than the experience itself. Poring over Judith's skirts, there in the World's Biggest Drug Store, I knew that Botticelli – and not Botticelli alone, but many others too – had looked at draperies with the same transfigured and transfiguring eyes as had been mine that morning. They had seen the *Istigkeit*, the Allness and Infinity of folded cloth and had done their best to render it in paint or stone. Necessarily, of course, without success. For the glory and the wonder of pure existence belong to another order, beyond the power of even the highest art to express. But in Judith's skirt I could clearly see what, if I had been a painter of genius, I might have made of my old grey flannels. Not much, heaven knows, in comparison with the reality; but

enough to delight generation after generation of behold-
ers, enough to make them understand at least a little of the
true significance of what, in our pathetic imbecility, we call
'mere things' and disregard in favour of television.

'This is how one ought to see,' I kept saying as I looked
down at my trousers, or glanced at the jewelled books in
the shelves, at the legs of my infinitely more than
Van-Goghian chair. 'This is how one ought to see, how
things really are.' And yet there were reservations. For if
one always saw like this, one would never want to do anything else. Just looking, just being the divine Not-self of
flower, of book, of chair, of flannel. That would be enough.
But in that case what about other people? What about
human relations? In the recording of that morning's conversations I find the question constantly repeated 'What
about human relations?' How could one reconcile this
timeless bliss of seeing as one ought to see with the temporal duties of doing what one ought to do and feeling as
one ought to feel? 'One ought to be able,' I said, 'to see
these trousers as infinitely important and human beings as
still more infinitely important.' One ought – but in practice it seemed to be impossible. This participation in the
manifest glory of things left no room, so to speak, for
the ordinary, the necessary concerns of human existence,
above all for concerns involving persons. For persons are
selves and, in one respect at least, I was now a Not-self,
simultaneously perceiving and being the Not-self of
the things around me. To this new-born Not-self, the

behaviour, the appearance, the very thought of the self it
had momentarily ceased to be, and of other selves, its
one-time fellows, seemed not indeed distasteful (for dis-
tastefulness was not one of the categories in terms of
which I was thinking), but enormously irrelevant. Compelled by the investigator to analyse and report on what I
was doing (and how I longed to be left alone with Eternity
in a flower, Infinity in four chair legs and the Absolute in
the folds of a pair of flannel trousers!) I realized that I was
deliberately avoiding the eyes of those who were with me
in the room, deliberately refraining from being too much
aware of them. One was my wife, the other a man I
respected and greatly liked; but both belonged to the world
from which, for the moment, mescalin had delivered me –
the world of selves, of time, of moral judgments and
utilitarian considerations, the world (and it was this aspect
of human life which I wished, above all else, to forget) of
self-assertion, of cocksureness, of over-valued words and
idolatrously worshipped notions.

At this stage of the proceedings I was handed a large
coloured reproduction of the well-known self-portrait by
Cézanne – the head and shoulders of a man in a large straw
hat, red-cheeked, red-lipped, with rich black whiskers and
a dark unfriendly eye. It is a magnificent painting; but it
was not as a painting that I now saw it. For the head
promptly took on a third dimension and came to life as a
small goblin-like man looking out through a window in the
page before me. I started to laugh. And when they asked

me why, 'What pretensions!' I kept repeating. 'Who on earth does he think he is?' The question was not addressed to Cézanne in particular, but to the human species at large. Who did they all think they were?

'It's like Arnold Bennett in the Dolomites,' I said, suddenly remembering a scene, happily immortalized in a snapshot of A. B. some four or five years before his death toddling along a wintry road at Cortina d'Ampezzo. Around him lay the virgin snow; in the background was a more than gothic aspiration of red crags. And there was dear, kind, unhappy A. B. consciously overacting the role of his favourite character in fiction, himself, the Card in person. There he went, toddling slowly in the bright Alpine sunshine, his thumbs in the arm-holes of a yellow waistcoat which bulged, a little lower down, with the graceful curve of a Regency bow window at Brighton – his head thrown back as though to aim some stammered utterance, howitzer-like, at the blue dome of heaven. What he actually said, I have forgotten; but what his whole manner, air and posture fairly shouted was, 'I'm as good as those damned mountains.' And in some ways, of course, he was infinitely better; but not, as he knew very well, in the way his favourite character in fiction liked to imagine.

Successfully (whatever that may mean) or unsuccessfully, we all overact the part of our favourite character in fiction. And the fact, the almost infinitely unlikely fact, of actually being Cézanne makes no difference. For the consummate painter, with his little pipe-line to Mind at Large by-passing the brain-valve and ego-filter, was also and just as genuinely this whiskered goblin with the unfriendly eye.

For relief I turned back to the folds in my trousers. 'This is how one ought to see,' I repeated yet again. And I might have added, 'These are the sort of things one ought to look at.' Things without pretensions, satisfied to be merely themselves, sufficient in their suchness, not acting a part, not trying, insanely, to go it alone, in isolation from the Dharma-Body, in Luciferian defiance of the grace of God.

'The nearest approach to this,' I said, 'would be a Vermeer.'

Yes, a Vermeer. For that mysterious artist was trebly gifted – with the vision that perceives the Dharma-Body as the hedge at the bottom of the garden, with the talent to render as much of the vision as the limitations of human capacity permit, and with the prudence to confine himself in his paintings to the more manageable aspects of reality; for though Vermeer represented human beings, he was always a painter of still life. Cézanne, who told his female sitters to do their best to look like apples, tried to paint portraits in the same spirit. But his pippin-like women are more nearly related to Plato's Ideas than to the Dharma-Body in the hedge. They are Eternity and Infinity seen, not in sand or flower, but in the abstractions of some very superior band of geometry. Vermeer never asked his girls to look like apples. On the contrary, he insisted on their being girls to the very limit – but always with the proviso that they refrain from behaving girlishly. They might sit or quietly stand but never giggle, never display self-consciousness, never say their prayers or pine for absent sweethearts, never gossip, never gaze enviously at other women's babies, never flirt, never love nor hate nor work. In the act of doing any of these things they would doubtless become more intensely themselves, but would cease, for that very reason, to manifest their divine essential Not-self. In Blake's phrase, the doors of Vermeer's perception were only partially cleansed. A single panel had become almost perfectly transparent; the rest of the door was still muddy. The essential Not-self could be perceived very clearly in things and in living creatures on the hither side of good and evil. In human beings it was visible only when they were in repose, their minds untroubled, their bodies motionless. In these circumstances Vermeer could see Suchness in all its heavenly beauty – could see and, in some small measure, render it in a subtle and sumptuous still life. Vermeer is undoubtedly the greatest painter of human still lives. But there have been others, for example, Vermeer's French contemporaries, the Le Nain brothers. They set out, I suppose, to be *genre* painters; but what they actually produced was a series of human still lives, in which their cleansed perception of the infinite significance of all things is rendered not, as with Vermeer, by a subtle enrichment of colour, and texture, but by a heightened clarity, an obsessive distinctness of form, within an austere, almost monochromatic tonality. In our own day we have had Vuillard, the painter, at his best, of unforgettably splendid pictures of the Dharma-Body manifested in a bourgeois bedroom, of the Absolute blazing away in the midst of some stockbroker's family in a suburban garden, taking tea.

> *Ce qui fait que l'ancien bandagiste renie*
> *Le comptoir dont le faste alléchait les passants,*
> *C'est son jardin d'Auteuil, où, veufs de tout encens,*
> *Les Zinnias ont l'air d'être en tôle vernie.*

For Laurent Taillade the spectacle was merely obscene. But if the retired rubber goods merchant had sat still enough, Vuillard would have seen in him only the Dharma-Body, would have painted, in the zinnias, the goldfish pool, the villa's Moorish tower and Chinese lanterns, a corner of Eden before the Fall.

But meanwhile my question remained unanswered. How was this cleansed perception to be reconciled with a proper concern with human relations, with the necessary chores and duties, to say nothing of charity and practical compassion? The age-old debate between the actives and the contemplatives was being renewed – renewed, so far as I was concerned, with an unprecedented poignancy. For until this morning I had known contemplation only in its humbler, its more ordinary forms – as discursive thinking; as a rapt absorption in poetry or painting or music; as a patient waiting upon those inspirations, without which even the prosiest writer cannot hope to accomplish anything; as occasional glimpses, in nature, of Wordsworth's 'something far more deeply interfused'; as systematic silence leading, sometimes, to hints of an 'obscure knowledge.' But now I knew contemplation at its height. At its height, but not yet in its fullness. For in its fullness the way of Mary includes the way of Martha and raises it, so to speak, to its own higher power. Mescalin opens up the way of Mary, but shuts the door on that of Martha. It gives access to contemplation – but to a contemplation that is incompatible with action and even with the will to action, the very thought of action. In the intervals between his revelations the mescalin taker is apt to feel that, though in one way everything is supremely as it should be, in another there is something wrong. His problem is essentially the same as that which confronts the quietist, the *arhat* and, on another level, the landscape painter and the painter of human still lives. Mescalin can never solve that problem: it can only pose it, apocalyptically, for those to whom it had never before presented itself. The full and final solution can be found only by those who are prepared to implement the right kind of *Weltanschauung* by means of the right kind of behaviour and the right kind of constant and unstrained alertness. Over against the quietist stands the active-contemplative, the saint, the man who, in Eckhart's phrase, is ready to come down from the seventh heaven in order to bring a cup of water to his sick brother. Over against the *arhat*, retreating from appearances into an entirely transcendental Nirvana, stands the

Bodhisattva, for whom Suchness and the world of contingencies are one, and for whose boundless compassion every one of those contingencies is an occasion not only for transfiguring insight, but also for the most practical charity. And in the universe of art, over against Vermeer and the other painters of human still lives, over against the masters of Chinese and Japanese landscape painting, over against Constable and Turner, against Sisley and Seurat and Cézanne stands the all-inclusive art of Rembrandt. These are enormous names, inaccessible eminences. For myself, on this memorable May morning, I could only be grateful for an experience which had shown me, more clearly than I have ever seen it before, the true nature of the challenge and the completely liberating response.

Let me add, before we leave this subject, that there is no form of contemplation, even the most quietistic, which is without its ethical values. Half at least of all morality is negative and consists in keeping out of mischief. The Lord's prayer is less than fifty words long, and six of those words are devoted to asking God not to lead us into temptation. The one-sided contemplative leaves undone many things that he ought to do; but to make up for it he refrains from doing a host of things he ought not to do. The sum of evil, Pascal remarked, would be much diminished if men could only learn to sit quietly in their rooms. The contemplative whose perception has been cleansed does not have to stay in his room. He can go about his business, so completely satisfied to see and be a part of the divine Order of

The Lord's prayer is less than fifty words long, and six of those words are devoted to asking God not to lead us into temptation

Things that he will never even be tempted to indulge in what Traherne called 'the dirty Devices of the world.' When we feel ourselves to be sole heirs of the universe, when 'the sea flows in our veins . . . and the stars are our jewels,' when all things are perceived as infinite and holy, what motive can we have for covetousness or self-assertion, for the pursuit of power or the drearier forms of pleasure? Contemplatives are not likely to become gamblers, or procurers, or drunkards; they do not as a rule preach intolerance, or make war; do not find it necessary to rob, swindle or grind the faces of the poor. And to these enormous negative virtues we may add another which, though hard to define, is both positive and important. The *arhat* and the quietist may not practise contemplation in its fullness; but if they practise it at all, they may bring back enlightening reports of another, a transcendent country of the mind; and if they practise it in the height, they will become conduits through which some beneficent influence can flow out of that other country into a world of darkened selves, chronically dying for lack of it.

Meanwhile I had turned, at the investigator's request, from the portrait of Cézanne to what was going on, inside my head, when I shut my eyes. This time, the inscape was curiously unrewarding. The field of vision was filled with brightly coloured, constantly changing structures that seemed to be made of plastic or enamelled tin.

'Cheap,' I commented. 'Trivial. Like things in a Five and Ten.'

And all this shoddiness existed in a closed, cramped universe.

'It's as though one were below decks in a ship,' I said. 'A five-and-ten-cent ship.'

And as I looked, it became very clear that this five-and-ten-cent ship was in some way connected with human pretensions. This suffocating interior of a dime-store ship was my own personal self; these gimcrack mobiles of tin and plastic were my personal contributions to the universe.

I felt the lesson to be salutary, but was sorry, none the less, that it had had to be administered at this moment and in this form. As a rule the mescalin taker discovers an inner world as manifestly a datum, as self-evidently infinite and holy, as that transfigured outer world which I had seen with my eyes open. From the first, my own case had been different. Mescalin had endowed me temporarily with the power to see things with my eyes shut; but it could not, or at least on this occasion did not, reveal an inscape remotely comparable to my flowers or chair or flannels 'out there.' What it had allowed me to perceive, inside, was not the Dharma-Body in images, but my own mind; not archetypal Suchness, but a set of symbols – in other words, a homemade substitute for Suchness.

Most visualizers are transformed by mescalin into visionaries. Some of them – and they are perhaps more numerous than is generally supposed – require no transformation; they are visionaries all the time. The mental species to which Blake belonged is fairly widely distributed even in the urban-industrial societies of the present day. The poet-artist's uniqueness does not consist in the fact that (to quote from his *Descriptive Catalogue*) he actually *saw* 'those wonderful originals called in the Sacred Scriptures the Cherubim.' It does not consist in the fact that 'these wonderful originals seen in my visions were some of them one hundred feet in height . . . all containing mythological and recondite meaning.' It consists solely in his ability to render, in words or (somewhat less successfully) in line and colour, some hint at least of a not excessively uncommon experience. The untalented visionary may perceive an inner reality no less tremendous, beautiful and significant than the world beheld by Blake; but he lacks altogether the ability to express, in literary or plastic symbols, what he has seen.

From the records of religion and the surviving monuments of poetry and the plastic arts it is very plain that, at most times and in most places, men have attached more importance to the inscape than to objective existents, have felt that what they saw with their eyes shut possessed a spiritually higher significance than what they saw with their eyes open. The reason? Familiarity breeds contempt, and how to survive is a problem ranging in urgency from the chronically tedious to the excruciating. The outer world is what we wake up to every morning of our lives, is the place where, willy-nilly, we must try to make our living. In the inner world there is neither work nor monotony. We visit it only in dreams and musings, and its strangeness is such that we never find the same world on two successive occasions. What wonder, then, if human beings in their search for the divine have generally preferred to look within! Generally, but not always. In their art no less than in their religion, the Taoists and the Zen Buddhists looked beyond visions to the Void, and through the Void at 'the ten thousand things' of objective reality. Because of their doctrine of the Word made flesh, Christians should have been able, from the first, to adopt a similar attitude towards the universe around them. But because of the doctrine of the Fall, they found it very hard to do so. As recently as three hundred years ago an expression of thorough-going world denial and even world condemnation was both orthodox and comprehensible. 'We should feel wonder at nothing at all in Nature, except only the Incarnation of Christ.' In the seventeenth century, Lallemant's phrase seemed to make sense. Today it has the ring of madness.

In China the rise of landscape painting to the rank of a major art form took place about a thousand, in Japan about six hundred and in Europe about three hundred years ago. The equation of Dharma-Body with hedge was made by those Zen Masters, who wedded Taoist naturalism with Buddhist transcendentalism. It was, therefore, only in the Far East that landscape painters consciously regarded their art as religious. In the West religious painting was a matter of portraying sacred personages, of illustrating hallowed texts. Landscape painters regarded themselves as secularists. Today we recognize in Seurat one of the supreme masters of what may be called mystical landscape painting. And yet this man who was able, more effectively than any other, to render the One in the many, became quite indignant when somebody praised him for the 'poetry' of his work. 'I merely apply the System,' he protested. In other words he was merely a *pointilliste* and, in his own eyes, nothing else. A similar anecdote is told of John Constable. One day towards the end of his life, Blake met Constable at Hampstead and was shown one of the younger artist's sketches. In spite of his contempt for naturalistic art, the old visionary knew a good thing when he saw it – except, of course, when it was by Rubens. 'This is not drawing,' he cried, 'this is inspiration!' 'I had meant it to be drawing,' was Constable's characteristic answer. Both men were right. It *was* drawing, precise and veracious, and at the same time it *was* inspiration – inspiration of an order at least as high as Blake's. The pine trees on the Heath had actually been seen as identical with the Dharma-Body. The sketch was a rendering, necessarily imperfect but still profoundly impressive, of what a cleansed perception had revealed to the open eyes of a great painter. From a contemplation, in the tradition of Wordsworth and Whitman, of the Dharma-Body as hedge, and from visions, such as Blake's, of the 'wonderful originals' within the mind, contemporary poets have retreated into an investigation of the personal, as opposed to the more than personal, subconscious and to a rendering, in highly abstract terms, not of the given, objective fact, but of mere scientific and theological notions. And something similar has happened in the field of painting. Here we have witnessed a general retreat from landscape, the predominant art form of the nineteenth century. This retreat from landscape has not been into that other, inner divine Datum, with which most of the traditional schools of the past were concerned, that Archetypal World, where men have always found the raw materials of myth and religion. No, it has been a retreat from the outward Datum into the personal subconscious, into a mental world more squalid and more tightly closed than even the world of conscious personality. These contraptions of tin and highly coloured plastic – where had I seen them before? In every picture gallery that exhibits the latest in non-representational art.

And now someone produced a phonograph and put a record on the turntable. I listened with pleasure, but experienced nothing comparable to my seen apocalypses of flowers or flannel. Would a naturally gifted musician *hear* the revelations which, for me, had been exclusively visual? It would be interesting to make the experiment. Meanwhile, though not transfigured, though retaining its normal quality and intensity, the music contributed not a little to my understanding of what had happened to me and of the wider problems which those happenings had raised.

Instrumental music, oddly enough, left me rather cold. Mozart's C-minor Piano Concerto was interrupted after the first movement, and a recording of some madrigals by Gesualdo took its place.

'These voices,' I said appreciatively, 'these voices – they're a kind of bridge back to the human world.'

And a bridge they remained even while singing the most startlingly chromatic of the mad prince's compositions. Through the uneven phrases of the madrigals, the music pursued its course, never sticking to the same key for two bars together. In Gesualdo, that fantastic character out of a Webster melodrama, psychological disintegration had exaggerated, had pushed, to the extreme limit, a tendency inherent in modal as opposed to fully tonal music. The resulting works sounded as though they might have been written by the later Schoenberg.

'And yet,' I felt myself constrained to say, as I listened to these strange products of a Counter-Reformation psychosis working upon a late mediaeval art form, 'and yet it does not matter that he's all in bits. The whole is disorganized. But each individual fragment is in order, is a representative of a Higher Order. The Higher Order prevails even in the disintegration. The totality is present even in the broken pieces. More clearly present, perhaps, than in a completely coherent work. At least you aren't lulled into a sense of false security by some merely human, merely fabricated order. You have to rely on your immediate perception of the ultimate order. So in a certain sense disintegration may have its advantages. But of course it's dangerous, horribly dangerous. Suppose you couldn't get back, out of the chaos . . .'

From Gesualdo's madrigals we jumped, across a gulf of three centuries, to Alban Berg and the *Lyric Suite*.

'This,' I announced in advance, 'is going to be hell.'

But, as it turned out, I was wrong. Actually the music sounded rather funny. Dredged up from the personal sub-conscious, agony succeeded twelve-tone agony; but what struck me was only the essential incongruity between a psychological disintegration even completer than Gesualdo's and the prodigious resources, in talent and technique, employed in its expression.

'Isn't he sorry for himself?' I commented with a derisive lack of sympathy. And then, '*Katzenmusik* – learned *Katzen-musik*.' And finally, after a few more minutes of the anguish, 'Who cares what his feelings are? Why can't he pay atten-tion to something else?'

As a criticism of what is undoubtedly a very remarkable work, it was unfair and inadequate – but not, I think, irrele-vant. I cite it for what it is worth and because that is how, in a state of pure contemplation, I reacted to the *Lyric Suite*.

When it was over, the investigator suggested a walk in the garden. I was willing; and though my body seemed to have dissociated itself almost completely from my mind – or, to be more accurate, though my awareness of the transfigured outer world was no longer accompanied by an awareness of my physical organism – found myself able to get up, open the French-window and walk out with only a minimum of hesitation. It was odd, of course, to feel that 'I' was not the same as these arms and legs 'out there,' as this wholly objective trunk and neck and even head. It was odd; but one soon got used to it. And anyhow the body seemed perfectly well able to look after itself. In reality, of course, it always does look after itself. All that the conscious ego can do is to formulate wishes, which are then carried out by forces which it controls very little and understands not at all. When it does anything more – when it tries too hard, for example, when it worries, when it becomes apprehensive about the future – it lowers the effectiveness of those forces and may even cause the devitalized body to fall ill. In my present state, awareness was not referred to an ego; it was, so to speak, on its own. This meant that the physiological intelligence controlling the body was also on its own. For the moment that interfering neurotic who, in waking hours, tries to run the show was blessedly out of the way.

From the French-window I walked out under a kind of pergola covered in part by a climbing rose tree, in part by laths, one inch wide with half an inch of space between them. The sun was shining and the shadows of the laths made a zebra-like pattern on the ground and across the seat and back of a garden chair, which was standing at this end of the pergola. That chair – shall I ever forget it? Where the shadows fell on the canvas upholstery, stripes of a deep but glowing indigo alternated with stripes of an incandescence so intensely bright that it was hard to believe that they could be made of anything but blue fire. For what seemed an immensely long time I gazed without knowing, even without wishing to know, what it was that confronted me. At any other time I would have seen a chair barred with alternate light and shade. Today the percept had swallowed up the concept. I was so completely absorbed in looking, so thunderstruck by what I actually saw, that I could not be aware of anything else. Garden furniture, laths, sunlight, shadow – these were no more than names and notions, mere verbalizations, for utilitarian or scientific purposes, after the event. The event was this succession of azure furnace-doors separated by gulfs of unfathomable gentian. It was inexpressibly wonderful, wonderful to the point, almost, of being terrifying. And suddenly I had an inkling of what it must feel like to be mad. Schizophrenia has its heavens as well as its hells and purgatories. I remember what an old friend, dead these many years, told me about his mad wife. One day in the early stages of the disease, when she still had her lucid intervals, he had gone to the hospital to talk to her about their children. She listened for a time, then cut him short. How could he bear to waste his time on a couple of absent children, when all that really mattered, here and now, was the unspeakable beauty of the patterns he made, in this brown tweed jacket, every time he moved his arms? Alas, this paradise of cleansed perception, of pure, one-sided contemplation, was not to endure. The blissful intermissions became rarer, became briefer, until finally there were no more of them; there was only horror.

Most takers of mescalin experience only the heavenly part of schizophrenia. The drug brings hell and purgatory only to those who have had a recent case of jaundice, or who suffer from periodical depressions or a chronic anxiety. If, like the other drugs of remotely comparable power, mescalin were notoriously toxic, the taking of it would be enough, of itself, to cause anxiety. But the reasonably healthy person knows in advance that, so far as he is concerned, mescalin is completely innocuous, that its effects will pass off after eight or ten hours, leaving no hangover and consequently no craving for a renewal of the dose. Fortified by this knowledge, he embarks upon the experiment without fear – in other words, without any pre-disposition to convert an unprecedentedly strange and other than human experience into something appalling, something actually diabolical.

Confronted by a chair which looked like the Last Judgment – or, to be more accurate, by a Last Judgment which, after a long time and with considerable difficulty, I recognized as a chair – I found myself all at once on the brink of panic. This, I suddenly felt, was going too far. Too far, even though the going was into intenser beauty, deeper significance. The fear, as I analyse it in retrospect, was of being overwhelmed, of disintegrating under a pressure of reality greater than a mind, accustomed to living most of the time in a cosy world of symbols, could possibly bear. The literature of religious experience abounds in references to the pains and terrors overwhelming those who have come, too suddenly, face to face with some manifestation of the *Mysterium tremendum*. In theological language, this fear is due to the incompatibility between man's egotism and the divine purity, between man's self-aggravated separateness and the infinity of God. Following Boehme and William Law, we may say that, by unregenerate souls, the divine Light at its full blaze can be apprehended only as a burning, purgatorial fire. An almost identical doctrine is to be found in *The Tibetan Book of the Dead*, where the departed soul is described as shrinking in agony from the Clear Light of the Void, and even from the lesser, tempered Lights, in order to rush headlong into the comforting darkness of self-hood as a reborn human being, or even as a beast, an unhappy ghost, a denizen of hell. Anything rather than the burning brightness of unmitigated Reality – anything!

The schizophrenic is a soul not merely unregenerate, but desperately sick into the bargain. His sickness consists in the inability to take refuge from inner and outer reality (as the sane person habitually does) in the homemade universe of common sense – the strictly human world of useful notions, shared symbols and socially acceptable conventions. The schizophrenic is like a man permanently under the influence of mescalin, and therefore unable to shut off the experience of a reality which he is not holy enough to live with, which he cannot explain away because it is the most stubborn of primary facts, and which, because it never permits him to look at the world with merely human eyes, scares him into interpreting its unremitting strangeness, its burning intensity of significance, as the manifestations of human or even cosmic malevolence, calling for the most desperate counter-measures, from murderous violence at one end of the scale to catatonia, or psychological suicide, at the other. And once embarked upon the downward, the infernal road, one would never be able to stop. That, now, was only too obvious.

'If you started in the wrong way,' I said in answer to the investigator's questions, 'everything that happened would be a proof of the conspiracy against you. It would all be self-validating. You couldn't draw a breath without knowing it was part of the plot.'

'So you think you know where madness lies?'

My answer was a convinced and heartfelt, 'Yes.'

'And you couldn't control it?'

'No, I couldn't control it. If one began with fear and hate as the major premiss, one would have to go on to the conclusion.'

'Would you be able,' my wife asked, 'to fix your attention on what *The Tibetan Book of the Dead* calls the Clear Light?'

I was doubtful.

'Would it keep the evil away, if you could hold it? Or would you not be able to hold it?'

I considered the question for some time.

'Perhaps,' I answered at last, 'perhaps I could – but only if there were somebody there to tell me about the Clear Light. One couldn't do it by oneself. That's the point, I suppose, of the Tibetan ritual – someone sitting there all the time and telling you what's what.'

After listening to the record of this part of the

experiment, I took down my copy of Evans-Wentz's edition of *The Tibetan Book of the Dead*, and opened at random. 'O nobly born, let not thy mind be distracted.' That was the problem – to remain undistracted. Undistracted by the memory of past sins, by imagined pleasure, by the bitter aftertaste of old wrongs and humiliations, by all the fears and hates and cravings that ordinarily eclipse the Light. What those Buddhist monks did for the dying and the dead, might not the modern psychiatrist do for the insane? Let there be a voice to assure them, by day and even while they are asleep, that in spite of all the terror, all the bewilderment and confusion, the ultimate Reality remains unshakably itself and is of the same substance as the inner light of even the most cruelly tormented mind. By means of such devices as recorders, clock-controlled switches, public address systems and pillow speakers it should be very easy to keep the inmates of even an understaffed institution constantly reminded of this primordial fact. Perhaps a few of the lost souls might in this way be helped to win some measure of control over the universe – at once beautiful and appalling, but always other than human, always totally incomprehensible – in which they find themselves condemned to live.

None too soon, I was steered away from the disquieting splendours of my garden chair. Drooping in green parabolas from the hedge, the ivy fronds shone with a kind of glassy, jade-like radiance. A moment later a clump of Red Hot Pokers, in full bloom, had exploded into my field of vision. So passionately alive that they seemed to be standing on the very brink of utterance, the flowers strained upwards into the blue. Like the chair under the laths, they protested too much. I looked down at the leaves and discovered a cavernous intricacy of the most delicate green lights and shadows, pulsing with undecipherable mystery.

> Roses:
> The flowers are easy to paint,
> The leaves difficult.

Shiki's *haiku* (which I quote in F. H. Blyth's translation) expresses, by indirection, exactly what I then felt – the excessive, the too obvious glory of the flowers, as contrasted with the subtler miracle of their foliage.

We walked out into the street. A large pale blue automobile was standing at the kerb. At the sight of it, I was suddenly overcome by enormous merriment. What complacency, what an absurd self-satisfaction beamed from those bulging surfaces of glossiest enamel! Man had created the thing in his own image – or rather in the image of his favourite character in fiction. I laughed till the tears ran down my cheeks.

We re-entered the house. A meal had been prepared. Somebody, who was not yet identical with myself, fell to with ravenous appetite. From a considerable distance and without much interest, I looked on.

When the meal had been eaten, we got into the car and went for a drive. The effects of the mescalin were already on the decline: but the flowers in the gardens still trembled on the brink of being supernatural, the pepper trees and carobs along the side streets still manifestly belonged to some sacred grove. Eden alternated with Dodona, Yggdrasil with the mystic Rose. And then, abruptly, we were at an intersection, waiting to cross Sunset Boulevard. Before us the cars were rolling by in a steady stream – thousands of them, all bright and shiny like an advertiser's dream and each more ludicrous than the last. Once again I was convulsed with laughter.

The Red Sea of traffic parted at last, and we crossed into another oasis of trees and lawns and roses. In a few minutes we had climbed to a vantage point in the hills, and there was the city spread out beneath us. Rather disappointingly, it looked very like the city I had seen on other occasions. So far as I was concerned, transfiguration was proportional to distance. The nearer, the more divinely other. This vast, dim panorama was hardly different from itself.

We drove on, and so long as we remained in the hills, with view succeeding distant view, significance was at its everyday level, well below transfiguration point. The magic began to work again only when we turned down into a new suburb and were gliding between two rows of houses. Here, in spite of the peculiar hideousness of the architecture, there were renewals of transcendental otherness, hints of the morning's heaven. Brick chimneys and green composition roofs glowed in the sunshine, like fragments of the New Jerusalem. And all at once I saw what Guardi had seen and (with what incomparable skill!) had so often rendered in his paintings – a stucco wall with a shadow slanting across it, blank but unforgettably beautiful, empty but charged with all the meaning and the mystery of existence. The Revelation dawned and was gone again within a fraction of a second. The car had moved on; time was uncovering another manifestation of the eternal Suchness. 'Within sameness there is difference. But that difference should be different from sameness is in no wise the intention of all the Buddhas. Their intention is both totality and differentiation.' This bank of red and white geraniums, for example – it was entirely different from that stucco wall a hundred yards up the road. But the 'is-ness' of both was the same, the eternal quality of their transience was the same.

An hour later, with ten more miles and the visit to the World's Biggest Drug Store safely behind us, we were back at home, and I had returned to that reassuring but profoundly unsatisfactory state known as 'being in one's right mind.'

———

THAT HUMANITY AT large will ever be able to dispense with Artificial Paradises seems very unlikely. Most men and women lead lives at the worst so painful, at the best so monotonous, poor and limited that the urge to escape, the longing to transcend themselves if only for a few moments, is and has always been one of the principal appetites of the soul. Art and religion, carnivals and saturnalia, dancing and listening to oratory – all these have served, in H. G. Wells' phrase, as Doors in the Wall. And for private, for everyday use there have always been chemical intoxicants. All the vegetable sedatives and narcotics, all the euphorics that grow on trees, the hallucinogens that ripen in berries or can be squeezed from roots – all, without exception, have been known and systematically used by human beings from time immemorial. And to these natural modifiers of consciousness modern science has added its quota of synthetics – chloral, for example, and benzedrine, the bromides and the barbiturates.

Most of these modifiers of consciousness cannot now be taken except under doctor's orders, or else illegally and at considerable risk. For unrestricted use the West has permitted only alcohol and tobacco. All the other chemical Doors in the Wall are labelled Dope, and their unauthorized takers are Fiends.

We now spend a good deal more on drink and smoke than we spend on education. This, of course, is not surprising. The urge to escape from selfhood and the environment is in almost everyone almost all the time. The urge to do something for the young is strong only in parents, and in them only for the few years during which their children go to school. Equally unsurprising is the current attitude towards drink and smoke. In spite of the growing army of hopeless alcoholics, in spite of the hundreds of thousands of persons annually maimed or killed by drunken drivers, popular comedians still crack jokes about alcohol and its addicts. And in spite of the evidence linking cigarettes with lung cancer, practically everybody regards tobacco smoking as being hardly less normal and natural than eating. From the point of view of the rationalist utilitarian this may seem odd. For the historian, it is exactly what you would expect. A firm conviction of the material reality of Hell never prevented mediaeval Christians from doing what their ambition, lust or covetousness suggested. Lung cancer, traffic accidents and the millions of miserable and misery-creating alcoholics are facts even more certain than was, in Dante's day, the fact of the Inferno. But all such facts are remote and unsubstantial compared with the near, felt fact of a craving, here and now, for release or sedation, for a drink or a smoke.

Ours is the age, among other things, of the automobile and of rocketing population. Alcohol is incompatible with safety on the roads, and its production, like that of tobacco, condemns to virtual sterility many millions of acres of the most fertile soil. The problems raised by alcohol and tobacco cannot, it goes without saying, be solved by prohibition. The universal and ever-present urge to self-transcendence is not to be abolished by slamming the currently popular Doors in the Wall. The only reasonable policy is to open other, better doors in the hope of inducing men and women to exchange their old bad habits for new and less harmful ones. Some of these other, better doors will be social and technological in nature, others religious or psychological, others dietetic, educational, athletic. But the need for frequent chemical vacations from intolerable selfhood and repulsive surroundings will undoubtedly remain. What is needed is a new drug which will relieve and console our suffering species without doing more harm in the long run than it does good in the short. Such a drug must be potent in minute doses and synthesizable. If it does not possess these qualities, its production, like that of wine, beer, spirits and tobacco, will interfere with the raising of indispensable food and fibres. It must be less toxic than opium or cocaine, less likely to produce undesirable social consequences than alcohol or the barbiturates, less inimical to heart and lungs than the tars and nicotine of cigarettes. And, on the positive side, it should produce changes in consciousness more interesting, more intrinsically valuable than mere sedation or dreaminess, delusions of omnipotence or release from inhibition.

To most people, mescalin is almost completely innocuous. Unlike alcohol, it does not drive the taker into the kind of uninhibited action which results in brawls, crimes of violence and traffic accidents. A man under the influence of mescalin quietly minds his own business. Moreover, the business he minds is an experience of the most enlightening kind, which does not have to be paid for (and this is surely important) by a compensatory hangover. Of the long-range consequences of regular mescalin taking we know very little. The Indians who consume peyote buttons do not

What is needed is a new drug which will relieve and console our suffering species

seem to be physically or morally degraded by the habit. However, the available evidence is still scarce and sketchy.[1]

Although obviously superior to cocaine, opium, alcohol and tobacco, mescalin is not yet the ideal drug. Along with the happily transfigured majority of mescalin takers there is a minority that finds in the drug only hell or purgatory. Moreover, for a drug that is to be used, like alcohol, for general consumption, its effects last for an inconveniently long time. But chemistry and physiology are capable nowadays of practically anything. If the psychologists and sociologists will define the ideal, the neurologists and

---

[1] In his monograph *Menomini Peyotism*, published (December 1952) in the Transactions of the American Philosophical Society, Professor J. S. Slotkin has written that 'the habitual use of Peyote does not seem to produce any increased tolerance or dependence. I know many people who have been Peyotists for forty to fifty years. The amount of Peyote they use depends upon the solemnity of the occasion; in general they do not take any more Peyote now than they did years ago. Also, there is sometimes an interval of a month or more between rites, and they go without Peyote during this period without feeling any craving for it. Personally, even after a series of rites occurring on four successive weekends, I neither increased the amount of Peyote consumed nor felt any continued need for it.' It is evidently with good reason that 'Peyote has never been legally declared a narcotic, or its use prohibited by the federal government.' However, 'during the long history of Indian–white contact, white officials have usually tried to suppress the use of Peyote, because it has been conceived to violate their own mores. But these attempts have always failed.' In a footnote Dr Slotkin adds that it is amazing to hear the fantastic stories about the effects of Peyote and the nature of the ritual, which are told by the white and Catholic Indian officials in the Menomini Reservation. 'None of them have had the slightest first-hand experience with the plant or with the religion, yet some fancy themselves to be authorities and write official reports on the subject.'

pharmacologists can be relied upon to discover the means whereby that ideal can be realized or at least (for perhaps this kind of ideal can never, in the very nature of things, be fully realized) more nearly approached than in the wine-bibbing past, the whisky-drinking, marijuana-smoking and barbiturate-swallowing present.

The urge to transcend self-conscious selfhood is, as I have said, a principal appetite of the soul. When, for whatever reason, men and women fail to transcend themselves by means of worship, good works and spiritual exercises, they are apt to resort to religion's chemical surrogates – alcohol and 'goof-pills' in the modern West, alcohol and opium in the East, hashish in the Mohammedan world, alcohol and marijuana in Central America, alcohol and coca in the Andes, alcohol and the barbiturates in the more up-to-date regions of South America. In *Poisons Sacrés, Ivresses Divines* Philippe de Félice has written at length and with a wealth of documentation on the immemorial connection between religion and the taking of drugs. Here, in summary or in direct quotation, are his conclusions. The employment for religious purposes of toxic substances is 'extraordinarily widespread . . . The practices studied in this volume can be observed in every region of the earth, among primitives no less than among those who have reached a high pitch of civilization. We are therefore dealing not with exceptional facts, which might justifiably be overlooked, but with a general and, in the widest sense of the word, a human phenomenon, the kind of phenomenon which cannot be disregarded by anyone who is trying to discover what religion is, and what are the deep needs which it must satisfy.'

Ideally, everyone should be able to find self-transcendence in some form of pure or applied religion. In practice it seems very unlikely that this hoped for consummation will ever be realized. There are, and doubtless there always will be, good churchmen and good churchwomen for whom, unfortunately, piety is not enough. The late G.K. Chesterton, who wrote at least as lyrically of drink as of devotion, may serve as their eloquent spokesman.

The modern Churches, with some exceptions among the Protestant denominations, tolerate alcohol; but even the most tolerant have made no attempt to convert the drug to Christianity, or to sacramentalize its use. The pious drinker is forced to take his religion in one compartment, his religion-surrogate in another. And perhaps this is inevitable. Drinking cannot be sacramentalized except in religions which set no store on decorum. The worship of Dionysos or the Celtic god of beer was a loud and disorderly affair. The rites of Christianity are incompatible with even religious drunkenness. This does no harm to the distillers, but is very bad for Christianity. Countless persons desire self-transcendence and would be glad to find it in church. But, alas, 'the hungry sheep look up and are not fed.' They take part in rites, they listen to sermons, they repeat prayers; but their thirst remains unassuaged. Disappointed, they turn to the bottle. For a time at least and in a kind of way, it works. Church may still be attended; but it is no more than the Musical Bank of Butler's *Erewhon*. God may still be acknowledged; but He is God only on the verbal level, only in a strictly Pickwickian sense. The effective object of worship is the bottle and the sole religious experience is that state of uninhibited and belligerent euphoria which follows the ingestion of the third cocktail.

We see, then, that Christianity and alcohol do not and cannot mix. Christianity and mescalin seem to be much more compatible. This has been demonstrated by many tribes of Indians, from Texas to as far north as Wisconsin. Among these tribes are to be found groups affiliated with the Native American Church, a sect whose principal rite is a kind of Early Christian Agape, or Love-Feast, where slices of peyote take the place of the sacramental bread and wine. These Native Americans regard the cactus as God's special gift to the Indians, and equate its effects with the workings of the divine Spirit.

Professor J. S. Slotkin – one of the very few white men ever to have participated in the rites of a Peyotist congregation – says of his fellow worshippers that they are 'certainly not stupefied or drunk . . . They never get out of rhythm or fumble their words, as a drunken or stupefied man would do . . . They are all quiet, courteous and considerate of one another. I have never been in any white man's house of worship where there is either so much religious feeling or decorum.' And what, we may ask, are these devout and well-behaved Peyotists experiencing? Not the mild sense of virtue which sustains the average Sunday churchgoer through ninety minutes of boredom. Not even those high feelings, inspired by thoughts of the Creator and the Redeemer, the Judge and the Comforter, which animate the pious. For these Native Americans, religious experience is something more direct and illuminating, more spontaneous, less the homemade product of the superficial, self-conscious mind. Sometimes (according to the reports collected by Dr Slotkin) they see visions, which may be of Christ Himself. Sometimes they hear the voice of the Great Spirit. Sometimes they become aware of the presence of God and of those personal shortcomings which must be corrected if they are to do His will. The practical consequences of these chemical openings of doors into the Other World seem to be wholly good. Dr Slotkin reports that habitual Peyotists are on the whole more industrious, more temperate (many of them abstain altogether from alcohol), more peaceable than non-Peyotists. A tree with such satisfactory fruits cannot be condemned out of hand as evil.

In sacramentalizing the use of peyote, the Indians of the Native American Church have done something which is at once psychologically sound and historically respectable. In the early centuries of Christianity many pagan rites and festivals were baptized, so to say, and made to serve the purposes of the Church. These jollifications were not particularly edifying; but they assuaged a certain psychological hunger and, instead of trying to suppress them, the earlier missionaries had the sense to accept them for what they were, soul-satisfying expressions of fundamental urges, and to incorporate them into the fabric of the new religion. What the Native Americans have done is essentially similar. They have taken a pagan custom (a custom, incidentally, far more elevating and enlightening than most of the rather brutish carousals and mummeries adopted from European paganism) and given it a Christian significance.

Though but recently introduced into the northern United States, peyote-eating and the religion based upon it have become important symbols of the Red Man's right to spiritual independence. Some Indians have reacted to white supremacy by becoming Americanized, others by retreating into traditional Indianism. But some have tried to make the best of both worlds, indeed of all the worlds – the best of Indianism, the best of Christianity, and the best of those Other Worlds of transcendental experience, where the soul knows itself as unconditioned and of like nature with the divine. Hence the Native American Church. In it two great appetites of the soul – the urge to independence and self-determination and the urge to self-transcendence – were fused with, and interpreted in the light of, a third – the urge to worship, to justify the ways of God to man, to explain the universe by means of a coherent theology.

> Lo, the poor Indian, whose untutored mind
> Clothes him in front, but leaves him bare behind.

But actually it is we, the rich and highly educated whites, who have left ourselves bare behind. We cover our anterior nakedness with some philosophy – Christian, Marxian, Freudo-Physicalist – but abaft we remain uncovered, at the mercy of all the winds of circumstance. The poor Indian, on the other hand, has had the wit to protect his rear by supplementing the fig-leaf of a theology with the breech-clout of transcendental experience.

I am not so foolish as to equate what happens under the influence of mescalin or of any other drug, prepared or in the future preparable, with the realization of the end and ultimate purpose of human life: Enlightenment, the Beatific Vision. All I am suggesting is that the mescalin experience is what Catholic theologians call 'a gratuitous grace,' not necessary to salvation but potentially helpful and to be accepted thankfully, if made available. To be shaken out of the ruts of ordinary perception, to be shown for a few timeless hours the outer and the inner world, not as they appear to an animal obsessed with survival or to a human being obsessed with words and notions, but as they are apprehended, directly and unconditionally, by Mind at Large – thus an experience of inestimable value to everyone and especially to the intellectual. For the intellectual is by definition the man for whom, in Goethe's phrase, 'the word is essentially fruitful.' He is the man who feels that 'what we perceive by the eye is foreign to us as such and need not impress us deeply.' And yet, though himself an intellectual and one of the supreme masters of language, Goethe did not always agree with his own evaluation of the word. 'We talk,' he wrote in middle life, 'far too much. We should talk less and draw more. I personally should like to renounce speech altogether and, like organic Nature, communicate everything I have to say in sketches. That fig tree, this little snake, the cocoon on my window sill quietly awaiting its future – all these are momentous signatures. A person able to decipher their meaning properly would soon be able to dispense with the written or the spoken word altogether. The more I think of it, there is something futile, mediocre, even (I am tempted to say) foppish about speech. By contrast, how the gravity of Nature and her silence startle you, when you stand face to face with her, undistracted, before a barren ridge or in the desolation of the ancient hills.' We can never dispense with language and the other symbol systems; for it is by means of them, and only by their means, that we have raised ourselves above the brutes, to the level of human beings. But we can easily become the victims as well as the beneficiaries of these systems. We must learn how to handle words effectively; but at the same time we must preserve and, if necessary, intensify our ability to look at the world directly and not through that half-opaque medium of concepts, which distorts every given fact into the all too familiar likeness of some generic label or explanatory abstraction.

Literary or scientific, liberal or specialist, all our education is predominantly verbal and therefore fails to accomplish what it is supposed to do. Instead of transforming children into fully developed adults, it turns out students of the natural sciences who are completely unaware of Nature as the primary fact of experience, it inflicts upon the world students of the Humanities who know nothing of humanity, their own or anyone else's.

Gestalt psychologists, such as Samuel Renshaw, have devised methods for widening the range and increasing the acuity of human perceptions. But do our educators apply them? The answer is, No.

Teachers in every field of psycho-physical skill, from seeing to tennis, from tightrope walking to prayer, have discovered, by trial and error, the conditions of optimum functioning within their special fields. But have any of the great Foundations financed a project for co-ordinating these empirical findings into a general theory and practice of heightened creativeness? Again, so far as I am aware, the answer is, No.

All sorts of cultists and queer fish teach all kinds of techniques for achieving health, contentment, peace of mind; and for many of their hearers many of these techniques are demonstrably effective. But do we see respectable psychologists, philosophers and clergymen boldly descending into those odd and sometimes malodorous wells, at the bottom of which poor Truth is so often condemned to sit? Yet once more the answer is, No.

And now look at the history of mescalin research. Seventy years ago men of first-rate ability described the transcendental experiences which come to those who, in good health, under proper conditions and in the right spirit, take the drug. How many philosophers, how many theologians, how many professional educators have had the curiosity to open this Door in the Wall? The answer, for all practical purposes, is, None.

In a world where education is predominantly verbal, highly educated people find it all but impossible to pay serious attention to anything but words and notions. There is always money for, there are always doctorates in, the learned foolery of research into what, for scholars, is the all-important problem: Who influenced whom to say what when? Even in this age of technology the verbal Humanities are honoured. The non-verbal Humanities, the arts of being directly aware of the given facts of our existence, are almost completely ignored. A catalogue, a bibliography, a definitive edition of a third-rate versifier's *ipsissima verba*, a stupendous index to end all indexes – any genuinely Alexandrian project is sure of approval and financial support. But when it comes to finding out how you and I, our children and grandchildren, may become more perceptive, more intensely aware of inward and outward reality, more open to the Spirit, less apt, by psychological malpractices, to make ourselves physically ill, and more capable of controlling our own autonomic nervous system – when it comes to any form of non-verbal education more fundamental (and more likely to be of some practical use) than Swedish Drill, no really respectable person in any really respectable university or church will do anything about it. Verbalists are suspicious of the non-verbal; rationalists fear the given, non-rational fact;

intellectuals feel that 'what we perceive by the eye (or in any other way) is foreign to us as such and need not impress us deeply.' Besides, this matter of education in the non-verbal Humanities will not fit into any of the established pigeon-holes. It is not religion, not neurology, not gymnastics, not morality or civics, not even experimental psychology. This being so, the subject is, for academic and ecclesiastical purposes, non-existent and may safely be ignored altogether or left, with a patronizing smile, to those whom the Pharisees of verbal orthodoxy call cranks, quacks, charlatans and unqualified amateurs.

'I have always found,' Blake wrote rather bitterly, 'that Angels have the vanity to speak of themselves as the only wise. This they do with a confident insolence sprouting from systematic reasoning.'

Systematic reasoning is something we could not, as a species or as individuals, possibly do without. But neither, if we are to remain sane, can we possibly do without direct perception, the more unsystematic the better, of the inner and outer worlds into which we have been born. This given reality is an infinite which passes all understanding and yet admits of being directly and in some sort totally apprehended. It is a transcendence belonging to another order than the human, and yet it may be present to us as a felt immanence, an experienced participation. To be enlightened is to be aware, always, of total reality in its immanent otherness – to be aware of it and yet to remain in a condition to survive as an animal, to think and feel as a human being, to resort whenever expedient to systematic reasoning. Our goal is to discover that we have always been where we ought to be. Unhappily we make the task exceedingly difficult for ourselves. Meanwhile, however, there are gratuitous graces in the form of partial and fleeting realizations. Under a more realistic, a less exclusively verbal system of education than ours, every Angel (in Blake's sense of that word) would be permitted as a sabbatical treat, would be urged and even, if necessary, compelled to take an occasional trip through some chemical Door in the Wall into the world of transcendental experience. If it terrified him, it would be unfortunate but probably salutary. If it brought him a brief but timeless illumination, so much the better. In either case the Angel might lose a little of the confident insolence sprouting from systematic reasoning and the consciousness of having read all the books.

Near the end of his life Aquinas experienced Infused Contemplation. Thereafter he refused to go back to work on his unfinished book. Compared with *this* everything he had read and argued about and written – Aristotle and the Sentences, the Questions, the Propositions, the majestic Summas – was no better than chaff or straw. For most intellectuals such a sit-down strike would be inadvisable, even morally wrong. But the Angelic Doctor had done more systematic reasoning than any twelve ordinary Angels, and was already ripe for death. He had earned the right, in those last months of his mortality, to turn from merely symbolic straw and chaff to the bread of actual and substantial Fact. For Angels of a lower order and with better prospects of longevity, there must be a return to the straw. But the man who comes back through the Door in the Wall will never be quite the same as the man who went out. He will be wiser but less cocksure, happier but less self-satisfied, humbler in acknowledging his ignorance yet better equipped to understand the relationship of words to things, of systematic reasoning to the unfathomable Mystery which it tries, forever vainly, to comprehend.

ALDOUS HUXLEY is best known for his novel *Brave New World*, an alarmingly prophetic vision of a future human race controlled by global capitalism, now universally acclaimed as a modern classic. Before the publication of *Brave New World* in 1932, Huxley had found literary fame through his first novels; bright, brilliant satires in which Huxley wittily passed judgement on the shortcomings of contemporary society. But his talents and interests as a writer ranged far beyond fiction, into philosophy, science, and politics. After moving to California in 1937, Huxley came increasingly to believe that the key to solving the world's problems lay in changing the individual through mystical enlightenment. The exploration of the inner life through mysticism and hallucinogenic drugs remained an emphasis in his work for the rest of his life.

The Doors of Perception had widespread influence from its first publication in 1954, inspiring many in the counter-culture movement of the 1960s, and writers and artists from J. G. Ballard and Allen Ginsberg to The Beatles. Huxley's ground-breaking work even provided the name for psychedelic rock band, The Doors. According to philosopher Isaiah Berlin, Huxley 'helped to liberate a generation by shedding light in dark places.'

RECOMMENDED BOOKS BY ALDOUS HUXLEY:

Brave New World
Island
Time Must Have a Stop

And if we can't have Psychedelics?

Drinking
JOHN CHEEVER

VINTAGE MINIS

Swimming
ROGER DEAKIN

VINTAGE MINIS

Eating
NIGELLA LAWSON

VINTAGE MINIS

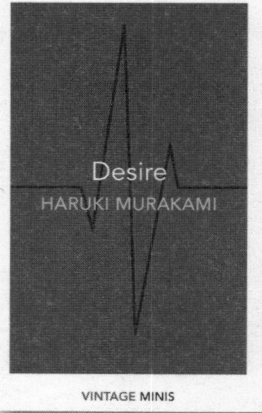

Desire
HARUKI MURAKAMI

VINTAGE MINIS

VINTAGE MINIS

The Vintage Minis bring you the world's greatest writers on the experiences that make us human. These stylish, entertaining little books explore the whole spectrum of life – from birth to death, and everything in between. Which means there's something here for everyone, whatever your story.

vintageminis.co.uk

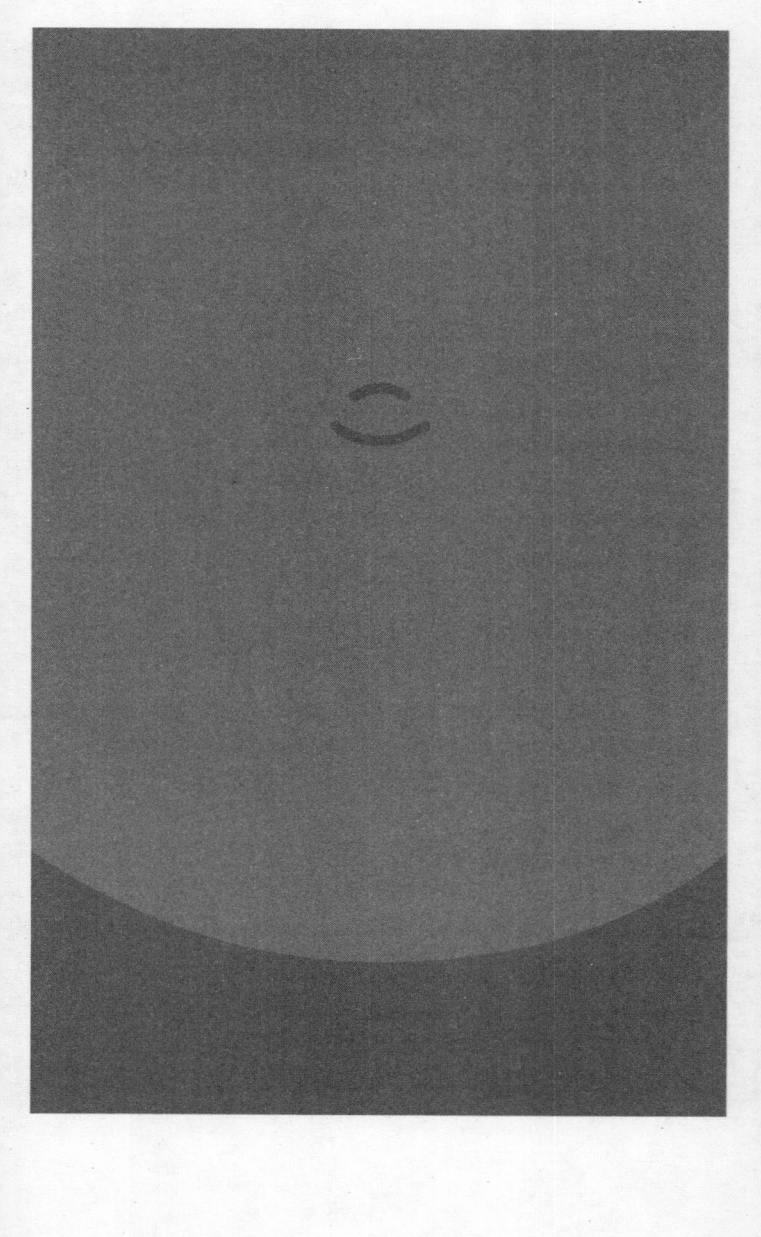

1 3 5 7 9 10 8 6 4 2

Vintage
20 Vauxhall Bridge Road,
London sw1v 2sa

Vintage Classics is part of the Penguin Random House
group of companies whose addresses can be found at
global.penguinrandomhouse.com.

Penguin
Random House
UK

A Bunch of Fives was first published in Great Britain by
Vintage Classics in 2012

This short edition published by Vintage in 2017

penguin.co.uk/vintage

A CIP catalogue record for this book is available from the British Library

ISBN 9781784872731

Typeset in 9.5/14.5 pt FreightText Pro
by Jouve (UK), Milton Keynes
Printed and bound by Clays Ltd, St Ives plc

Penguin Random House is committed to a sustainable future for
our business, our readers and our planet. This book is made from
Forest Stewardship Council® certified paper.

MIX
Paper from
responsible sources
FSC® C018179

Motherhood

HELEN SIMPSON

VINTAGE MINIS

Lentils and Lilies

JADE BEAUMONT WAS TECHNICALLY UP in her bedroom revising for the A levels which were now only weeks away. Her school gave them study days at home, after lectures on trust and idleness. She was supposed to be sorting out the differences between Wordsworth and Coleridge at the moment.

Down along the suburban pleasantness of Miniver Road the pavements were shaded by fruit trees, and the front gardens of the little Edwardian villas smiled back at her with early lilac, bushes of crimson flowering currant and the myopic blue dazzle of forget-me-nots. She felt light on her feet and clever, like a cat, snuffing the air, pinching a pungent currant leaf.

There was a belief held by Jade's set that the earlier you hardened yourself off and bared your skin, the more lasting the eventual tan; and so she had that morning pulled on a brief white skirt and T-shirt. She was on her way to an interview for a holiday job at the garden centre. Summer!

She couldn't wait. The morning was fair but chilly and the white-gold hairs on her arms and legs stood up and curved to form an invisible reticulation, trapping a layer of warm air a good centimetre deep.

> I may not hope from outward forms to win
> The passion and the life, whose fountains are within.

That was cool, but Coleridge was a minefield. Just when you thought he'd said something really brilliant, he went raving off full steam ahead into nothingness. He was a nightmare to write about. Anyway, she herself found outward forms utterly absorbing, the colour of clothes, the texture of skin, the smell of food and flowers. She couldn't see the point of extrapolation. Keats was obviously so much better than the others, but you didn't get the choice of questions with him.

She paused to inhale the sweet air around a philadelphus Belle Etoile, then noticed the host of tired daffodils at its feet.

> Shades of the prison-house begin to close
> Upon the growing boy,
> But he beholds the light, and whence it flows,
> He sees it in his joy.

She looked back down her years at school, the reined-in feeling, the stupors of boredom, the teachers in the classrooms like tired lion-tamers, and felt quite the opposite.

She was about to be let out. And every day when she left the house, there was the excitement of being noticed, the warmth of eye-beams, the unfolding consciousness of her own attractive powers. She was the focus of every film she saw, every novel she read. She was about to start careering round like a lustrous loose cannon.

> Full soon thy soul shall have her earthly freight,
> And custom lie upon thee with a weight,
> Heavy as frost, and deep almost as life!

She was never going to go dead inside or live somewhere boring like this, and she would make sure she was in charge at any work she did and not let it run her. She would never be like her mother, making rotas and lists and endless arrangements, lost forever in a forest of twitching detail with her tense talk of juggling and her self-importance about her precious job and her joyless 'running the family'. No, life was not some sort of military campaign; or, at least, *hers* would not be.

When she thought of her mother, she saw tendons and hawsers, a taut figure at the front door screaming at them all to do their music practice. She was always off out; she made them do what she said by remote control. Her trouble was, she'd forgotten how to relax. It was no wonder Dad was like he was.

And everybody said she was so amazing, what she managed to pack into twenty-four hours. Dad worked hard, they said, but she worked hard too *and* did the home shift,

She would never be like her mother, making rotas and lists and endless arrangements

whatever that was. Not really so very amazing though; she'd forgotten to get petrol a couple of weeks ago, and the school run had ground to a halt. In fact some people might say downright inefficient.

On the opposite side of the road, a tall girl trailed past with a double buggy of grizzling babies, a Walkman's shrunken tinkling at her ears. Au pair, remarked Jade expertly to herself, scrutinising the girl's shoes, cerise plastic jellies set with glitter. She wanted some just like that, but without the purple edging.

She herself had been dragged up by a string of au pairs. Her mother hated it when she said that. After all, she *was* supposed to take delight in us! thought Jade viciously, standing stock-still, outraged; like, *be* there with us. For us. Fair seed-time had my soul I *don't* think.

Above her the cherry trees were fleecy and packed with a foam of white petals. Light warm rays of the sun reached her upturned face like kisses, refracted as a fizzy dazzle through the fringing of her eyelashes. She turned to the garden beside her and stared straight into a magnolia tree, the skin of its flowers' stiff curves streaked with a sexual crimson. She was transported by the light and the trees, and just as her child self had once played the miniature warrior heroine down green alleys, so she saw her self now floating in this soft sunshine, moving like a panther into the long jewelled narrative which was her future.

Choice landscapes and triumphs and adventures quivered, quaintly framed there in the zigzag light like pendant crystals on a chandelier. There was the asterisk trail of a shooting star, on and on for years until it petered out at about thirty-three or thirty-four, leaving her at some point of self-apotheosis, high and nobly invulnerable, one of Tiepolo's ceiling princesses looking down in beautiful amusement from a movie-star cloud. This was about as far as any of the novels and films took her too.

A pleasurable sigh escaped her as the vision faded, and she started walking again, on past the tranquil houses, the coloured glass in a hall window staining the domestic light, a child's bicycle propped against the trunk of a standard rose. She sensed babies breathing in cots in upstairs rooms, and solitary women becalmed somewhere downstairs, chopping fruit or on the telephone organising some toddler tea. It really was suburban purdah round here. They were like battery hens, weren't they, rows of identical hutches, so neat and tidy and narrow-minded. Imagine staying in all day, stewing in your own juices. Weren't they bored out of their skulls? It was beyond her comprehension.

And so materialistic, she scoffed, observing the pelmetted strawberry-thief curtains framing a front room window; so bourgeois. Whereas her gap-year cousin had just been all over India for under £200.

> The world is too much with us; late and soon,
> Getting and spending, we lay waste our powers.
> Little we see in Nature that is ours;
> We have given our hearts away, a sordid boon!

Although after a good patch of freedom she fully intended to pursue a successful career, the way ahead paved by her future degree in Business Studies. But she would never end up anywhere like here. No! It would be a converted warehouse with semi-astral views and no furniture. Except perhaps for the ultimate sofa.

Jade rounded the corner into the next road, and suddenly there on the pavement ahead of her was trouble. A child was lying flat down on its back screaming while a man in a boilersuit crouched over it, his anti-dust mask lifted to his forehead like a frogman. Above them both stood a broad fair woman, urgently advising the child to calm down.

'You'll be better with a child than I am,' said the workman gratefully as Jade approached, and before she could agree – or disagree – he had shot off back to his sand-blasting.

'She's stuck a lentil up her nose,' said the woman crossly, worriedly. 'She's done it before. More than once. I've got to get it out.'

She waved a pair of eyebrow tweezers in the air. Jade glanced down at the chubby blubbering child, her small squat nose and mess of tears and mucus, and moved away uneasily.

'We're always down at Casualty,' said the mother, as rapidly desperate as a talentless stand-up comedian. 'Last week she swallowed a penny. Casualty said, a penny's OK, wait for it to come out the other end. Which it did. But they'd have had to open her up if it had been a five-pence piece, something to do with the serration or the size. Then she pushed a drawing pin up her nose. They were worried it might get into her brain. But she sneezed it out. One time she even pushed a chip up her nostril, really far, and it needed extracting from the sinus tubes.'

Jade gasped fastidiously and stepped back.

'Maybe we should get her indoors,' suggested the woman, her hand on Jade's arm. 'It's that house there across the road.'

'I don't think . . .' started Jade.

'The baby, oh the baby!' yelped the woman. 'He's in the car. I forgot. I'll have to . . .'

Before Jade could escape, the woman was running like an ostrich across the road towards a blue Volvo, its passenger door open onto the pavement, where from inside came the sobbing of the strapped-in baby. Jade tutted, glancing down at her immaculate clothes, but she had no option really but to pick up the wailing child and follow the mother. She did not want to be implicated in the flabby womany-ness of the proceedings, and stared crossly at this overweight figure ahead of her, ludicrously top-heavy in its bulky stained sweatshirt and sagging leggings.

Closer up, in the hallway, her hyperaesthetic teenage eyes observed the mother's ragged cuticles, the graceless way her heels stuck out from the backs of her sandals like hunks of Parmesan, and the eyes which had dwindled to dull pinheads. The baby in her arms was dark red as a crab apple from bellowing, but calmed down when a bottle was plugged into its mouth.

It was worse in the front room. Jade lowered her snuffling burden to the carpet and looked around her with undisguised disdain. The furniture was all boring and ugly while the pictures, well the pictures were like a propaganda campaign for family values – endless groupings on walls and ledges and shelves of wedding pictures and baby photos, a fluttery white suffocation of clichés.

The coffee table held a flashing ansaphone and a hideous orange Amaryllis lily on its last legs, red-gold anthers shedding pollen. Jade sat down beside it and traced her initials in this yolk-yellow dust with her fingertip.

'I used to love gardening,' said the woman, seeing this. 'But there's no time now. I've got an Apple up in the spare room, I try to keep a bit of part-time going during their naps. Freelance PR. Typing CVs.'

She waved the tweezers again and knelt above her daughter on the carpet.

I wouldn't let you loose on my CV, thought Jade, recoiling. Not in a million years. It'd come back with jam all over it.

The little girl was quite a solid child and tried to control her crying, allowing herself to be comforted in between the probings inside her face. But she was growing hotter, and when, at the woman's request, Jade unwillingly held her, she was like a small combustion engine, full of distress.

'See, if I hold her down, you have a try,' said the woman, handing her the tweezers.

Jade was appalled and fascinated. She peered up the child's nose and could see a grey-green disc at the top of one fleshy nostril. Tentatively she waved the silver tongs. Sensibly the child began to howl. The mother clamped her head and shoulders down with tired violence.

'I don't think I'd better do this,' said Jade. She was frightened that metal inside the warm young face combined with sudden fierce movement could be a disastrous combination.

The woman tried again and the walls rang with her daughter's screams.

'Oh God,' she said. 'What can I do?'

'Ring your husband?' suggested Jade.

'He's in Leeds,' said the woman. 'Or is it Manchester. Oh dear.'

'Ha,' said Jade. You'd think it was the fifties, men roaming the world while the women stayed indoors. The personal was the political, hadn't she heard?

'I've got to make a phone call to say I'll be late,' said the woman, distracted yet listless. She seemed unable to think beyond the next few minutes or to formulate a plan of action, as though in a state of terminal exhaustion. Jade felt obscurely resentful. If she ever found herself in this sort of situation, a man, babies, etcetera; when the time came; IF. Well, he would be responsible for half the childcare and half the housework. At least. She believed in justice, unlike this useless great lump.

'Why don't you ring Casualty?' she suggested. 'See what the queues are like?'

'I did that before,' said the woman dully. 'They said, try to get it out yourself.'

'I'm sorry,' said Jade, standing up. 'I'm on my way to an interview. I'll be late if I stay.' People should deal with their own problems, she wanted to say; you shouldn't get yourself into situations you can't handle then slop all over everybody else.

'Yes,' said the woman. 'Thank you anyway.'

'You could ring the doctor,' said Jade on the way to the front door. 'Ask for an emergency appointment.'

'I'll do that next,' said the woman, brightening a little; then added suddenly, 'This year has been the hardest of my life. The two of them.'

'My mother's got four,' said Jade censoriously. '*And* a job. Goodbye.'

She turned with relief back into the shining spring morning and started to sprint, fast and light, as quick off the blocks as Atalanta.

Café Society

TWO SHATTERED WOMEN AND A bright-eyed child have just sat down at the window table in the café. Both women hope to talk, for their minds to meet; at the same time they are aware that the odds against this happening are about fifty to one. Still they have decided to back that dark horse Intimacy, somewhere out there muffledly galloping. They order coffee, and toast for the boy, who seizes a teaspoon and starts to bash away at the cracked ice marbling of the formica table.

'No, Ben,' says his mother, prising the spoon from his fingers and diverting his attention to the basket of sugar sachets. She flings discreet glances at the surrounding tables, gauging the degrees of irritability of those nearest. There are several other places they could have chosen, but this sandwich bar is where they came.

They might have gone to McDonald's, so cheap and tolerant, packed with flat light and fat smells and unofficial crèche clamour. There they could have slumped like the old punchbags they are while Ben screeched and flew around with the other children. McDonald's is essentially a wordless experience, though, and they both want to see if they can for a wonder exchange some words. Then there is Pete's Café on the main road, a lovely steamy unbuttoned room where men sit in their work clothes in a friendly fug of bonhomie and banter, smoking, stirring silver streams of sugar into mugs of bright brown tea. But it would not be fair to take this child in there and spoil that Edenic all-day-breakfast fun. It would take the insensitivity of an ox. Unthinkable.

Here is all right. They get all sorts here. Here is used to women walking in with that look on their faces – 'What hit me?' Even now there is a confused-looking specimen up there ordering a decaffeinated coffee, takeaway, at the counter.

'Every now and then I think *I* might give it up, see if that helps,' says Frances. 'Caffeine. But then I reckon it's just a drop in the ocean.'

Ben rocks backwards in his chair a few times, seeing how far he can go. He is making a resonant zooming noise behind his teeth, but not very loudly yet. Sally keeps her baggy eye on him and says, 'Sometimes I think I'm just pathetic but then other times I think, I'm not a tank.'

'Cannonfodder,' observes Frances.

'It's all right if you're the sort who can manage on four hours,' says Sally. 'Churchill. Thatcher. Bugger.'

Ben, having tipped his chair to the point of no return, carries on down towards the floor in slow motion. Frances dives in and with quiet skill prevents infant skull from hitting lino-clad concrete.

'Reflexes,' says Sally gratefully. 'Shot to pieces.'

She clasps the shaken child to her coat with absent fervour. He is drawing breath for a blare of delayed shock when the arrival of the toast deflects him.

'The camel's back,' says Sally obscurely.

'Not funny,' comments Frances, who understands that she is referring to sleep, or its absence.

Ben takes the buttery knife from the side of his plate and waves it in the air, then drops it onto his mother's coat sleeve. From there it falls to her lap and then, noisily, to the floor. She dabs at the butter stains with a tissue and bangs her forehead as she reaches beneath the table for the knife. Ben laughs and sandpapers his chin with a square of toast.

This woman Sally has a drinker's face, but her lustreless grey skin and saurian eye come not from alcohol but from prolonged lack of sleep.

As a former research student it has often occurred to her that a medical or sociology post-graduate might profitably study the phenomenon in society of a large number of professional women in their thirties suffering from exhaustion. Her third child, this bouncing boy, has woken at least four times a night since he was born. Most mornings he won't go back to sleep after five, so she has him in with her jumping and playing and singing. She hasn't shared a bedroom with her husband for eighteen months now. She'd carried on full-time through the first and second. They slept. Luck of the draw. Yes of course she has talked to her health visitor about this, she has taken the boy to a sleep clinic, she has rung Cry-sis and listened to unseen mothers in the same foundering boat. The health visitor booked her into a sleep counselling course which involved her taking an afternoon every week off work, driving an hour's round trip on the North Circular, only to listen to some well-meaning woman tell her what damage this sleep pattern was causing to the family unit, to her health, to her marriage, to the boy's less demanding siblings. Well she knew all that anyway, didn't she? After the third session she said, what's the point? Not every problem has a solution, she decided, and here it is obviously a brutally simple question of survival, of whether she cracks before he starts sleeping through. It's years now.

THESE THOUGHTS FLASH through her mind, vivid and open, but must remain unspoken as Ben's presence precludes anything much in the way of communication beyond blinking in Morse. The few words she has exchanged with this woman Frances, known only by sight after all from the nursery school queue, are the merest tips of icebergs. Such thoughts are dangerous to articulate anyway, bringing up into the air what has been submerged. Nearly all faces close in censorship at the merest hint of such talk. Put up and shut up is the rule, except with fellow mothers. Even then it can be taken as letting the side down. She yawns uncontrollably so that her eyes water, leaving her with the face of a bloodhound.

Put up and shut up is the rule, except with fellow mothers

From her handbag this tired woman Sally takes a pad and felt tips and places them in front of her son Ben, who is rolling his eyes and braying like a donkey.

'Shush, Ben,' she says. 'You're not a donkey.'

He looks at her with beautiful affectless eyes. He sucks in air and starts up a series of guttural snorts.

'You're not a piggy, Ben, stop it,' says Sally.

'Piggy,' says Ben, laughing with lunatic fervour.

'They were brilliant at work, they bent over backwards,' says Sally, rapidly, anyway. 'It was me that resigned, I thought it wasn't fair on them. I was going into work for a rest. Ben!'

'That's hard,' says Frances, watching as Sally straightens the boy in his chair and tries to engage him in colouring a picture of a rabbit in police uniform.

'Do you work then?' asks Sally, filling in one long furry ear with pink.

'Yes. No,' says Frances. 'I shouldn't be here! You know, round the edges at the moment. I mean, I must. I have. Always. Unthinkable! But, erm. You know. Freelance at the moment.'

Ben pushes the paper away from him and grasps at a handful of felt tips. He throws them against the window and cheers at the clatter they make on impact.

'No, Ben!' growls Sally through clenched teeth. 'Naughty.'

The two women grovel under the table picking up pens. Ben throws a few more after them.

WHAT FRANCES WOULD *have said had there been a quiet patch of more than five seconds was that she had worked full-time all through the babyhood of her first child, Emma, and also until her second, Rose, was three, as well as running the domestic circus, functioning as the beating heart of the family while deferring to the demands of her partner's job in that it was always her rather than him who took a day off sick when one of the girls sprained a wrist or starred in a concert, and her too of course who was responsible for finding, organising and paying for childcare and for the necessary expenditure of countless megavolts of the vicarious emotional and practical energy involved in having someone else look after your babies while you are outside the house all day, all the deeply unrestful habits of vigilance masquerading as 'every confidence' in the girl who would, perfectly reasonably, really rather be an aerobics instructor working on Legs Tums 'n Bums.*

Then there was one childcare-based strappado too many; and she cracked. After all those years. She had come home unexpectedly in the afternoon to find the girl fast asleep on the sofa, clubbed out as she later put it, while Emma and Rose played on the stairs with needles and matches or some such. Could be worse, her sensible woman-in-the-workplace voice said; she's young, she likes a good time and why shouldn't she; nothing happened, did it? To hell with that, her mother-in-the-house voice said; I could be the one on the sofa rather than out there busting a gut and barely breaking even.

She needed work, she loved work, she was educated for it. Didn't she, Sally, feel the same way? She'd never asked her partner for money; no, they were equals, pulling together. Well, work was fabulous while you were there, it was what you had to do before and after work that was the killer. It was good for the girls to see their mother out working in the real world, he said when she talked of feeling torn apart; a role model. There's no need to feel guilty, he would begin, with God-like compassion. It's not guilt, you fool. It's the unwelcome awareness that being daily ripped in half is not good, not even ultimately. I agree with all the reasons. 'I'm sorry, they've got to realise that you are a person in your own right and have work to do.' I couldn't agree more. 'Women have always worked, except for that brief sinister time in the fifties.' Yes. But had they always had to work a ten-hour day at a full hour's commuting distance from their babies while not showing by a murmur or a flicker what this was doing to them?

So here she was after all these years 'gone freelance', that coy phrase, cramming a full-time job into their school hours and also the evenings once they'd gone to bed. She had a large envelope of sweets pinned to the wall by the telephone so that she could receive work calls to the noise of lollipop-sucking rather than shrilling and howls. And now, of course, she had no sick pay, paid holiday, pension or maternity leave should she be so foolish as to find herself pregnant again. Just as the Welfare State she'd been raised to lean on was packing up.

UNFORTUNATELY NOT ONE word of this makes it into the light of day, as Ben is creating.

'It was more fun at work,' Frances bursts out, watching

Sally wipe the child's buttery jawline with another of the inexhaustible supply of tissues from her bag. 'You get some *respect* at work.'

'My last childminder,' says Sally. She flinches.

'Snap,' says Frances.

The two women sip their powerless cappuccinos.

'In a couple of years' time, when this one starts school,' says Sally, 'I could probably get back, get by with an au pair in term-time. Someone to collect them from school, get their tea. But then there's the holidays.'

'Very long, the holidays,' agrees Frances.

'Not fair on the poor girl,' says Sally. 'Not when she doesn't speak English. Now if it was just Leo he'd be fine,' she continues, off on another tack, thinking aloud about her two eldest children. 'But Gemma is different.'

The child Ben slides off his chair and runs over to the glass-fronted display of sandwich fillings, the metal trays of damp cheese, dead ham and tired old tuna mixed with sweetcorn kernels. He starts to hit the glass with the flat of his hand. There is a collective intake of breath and everyone turns to stare. As she lurches over to apologise and expostulate, Sally's mind continues to follow her train of thought, silently addressing Frances even if all that Frances can see of her is a bumbling, clucking blur.

CHILDREN ARE ALL *different, Sally thinks on, and they are different from birth. Her own son Leo has a robust nature, a level temperament and the valuable ability to amuse himself, which is what makes him so easy to care for. He has smilingly greeted more than half a dozen childminders in his time, and waved them goodbye with equal cheeriness. Gemma, however, was born more anxious, less spirited. She cries easily and when her mother used to leave for work would abandon herself to despair. She is crushingly jealous of this youngest child Ben. She wants to sit on Sally's lap all the time when she is there, and nags and whines like a neglected wife, and clings so hard that all around are uncomfortably filled with irritation. She has formed fervid attachments to the aforementioned childminders, and has wept bitterly at their various departures. Well, Gemma may thrive better now her mother is at home, or she may not; the same could be said of her mother. Time will tell, but by then of course it will be then and not now, and Sally will be unemployable whichever way it has turned out.*

'OOF,' GRUNTS SALLY, returning with her son, who leaps within her arms like a young dolphin. She sits him firmly on his chair again.

'My neighbour's au pair wrote their car off last week,' says Frances. 'Nobody hurt, luckily.'

They both shudder.

'We're so lucky,' they agree, po-faced, glum, gazing at zany Ben as he stabs holes into the police rabbit with a sharp red pen. Sally yawns uncontrollably, then Frances starts up where she leaves off.

After all, they're getting nowhere fast.

An elderly woman pauses as she edges past their table on the way to the till. She cocks her head on one side and smiles brightly at Ben, whose mouth drops open. He stares at her, transfixed, with the expression of a seraph who has understood the mystery of the sixth pair of wings. His mother Sally knows that he is in fact temporarily dumbstruck by the woman's tremendous wart, which sits at the corner of her mouth with several black hairs sprouting from it.

'What a handsome little fellow,' says the woman fondly. 'Make the most of it, dear,' she continues, smiling at Sally. 'It goes so fast.' Sally tenses as she smiles brightly back, willing her son not to produce one of his devastating monosyllables. Surely he does not know the word for wart yet.

'Such a short time,' repeats the woman, damp-eyed.

WELL, NOT REALLY, *thinks Frances. Sometimes it takes an hour to go a hundred yards. Now she knows what she knows she puts it at three and a half years per child, the time spent exhausted, absorbed, used up; and, what's more, if not, then something's wrong. That's a whole decade if you have three! This is accurate, wouldn't you agree, she wants to ask Sally; this is surely true for all but those women with Olympic physical stamina, cast-iron immune systems, steel-clad nerves and sensitivities. Extraordinary women; heroines, in fact. But what about the strugglers? The ordinary mother strugglers? Why do they educate us, Sally, only to make it so hard for us to work afterwards? Why don't they insist on hysterectomies for girls who want further education and have done with it? Of course none of this will get said. There is simply no airspace.*

BEN'S EYES HAVE sharpened and focused on his admirer's huge side-of-the-mouth wart.

'Witch,' he says, loud and distinct.

'Ben,' says Sally. She looks ready to cry, and so does the older woman, who smiles with a hurt face and says, 'Don't worry, dear, he didn't mean anything,' and moves off.

'WITCH,' shouts Ben, following her with his eyes.

At this point, Sally and Frances give up. With a scraping of chairs and a flailing of coats, they wordlessly heave themselves and Ben and his paraphernalia up to the counter, and pay, and go. They won't try that again in a hurry. They smile briefly at each other as they say goodbye, wry and guarded. They have exchanged little more than two hundred words inside this hour, and how much friendship can you base on that?

After all, it's important to put up a decent apologia for your life; well, it is to other people, mostly; to come up with a convincing defence, to argue your corner. It's nothing but healthy, the way the sanguine mind does leap around looking for the advantages of any new shift in situation. And if you can't, or won't, you will be shunned. You will appear to be a whiner, or a malcontent. Frances knows this, and so does Sally.

Even so they pause and turn and give each other a brief, gruff, foolish hug, with the child safely sandwiched between them.

Hey Yeah Right Get a Life

DORRIE STOOD AT THE EDGE of the early-morning garden and inhaled a column of chilly air. After the mulch of soft sheets and stumbling down through the domestic rubble and crumbs and sleeping bodies, it made her gasp with delight, outside, the rough half-light of March and its menthol coldness.

The only other creature apart from herself was next door's cat which sauntered the length of the fence's top edge stately as a *fin de siècle* roué returning from a night of pleasure. That was what she was after, the old feline assurance that she had a place here. Of course you couldn't expect to remain inviolate; but surely there had to be some part of yourself you could call your own without causing trouble. It couldn't *all* be spoken for. She watched the cat hunch its shoulders and soundlessly pour itself from the fence onto the path.

Nowadays those few who continued to see Dorrie at all registered her as a gloomy, timid woman who had grown rather fat and over-protective of her three infants. They sighed with impatient pity to observe how easily small anxieties took possession of her, how her sense of proportion appeared to have receded along with her horizons. She was never still, she was always available, a conciliatory twittering fusspot. Since the arrival of the children, one, two and then three, in the space of four years, she had broken herself into little pieces like a biscuit and was now scattered all over the place. The urge – indeed, the necessity – to give everything, to throw herself on the bonfire, had been shocking; but now it was starting to wear off.

Back in the warmth of her side of the bed she lay listening to Max's breathing, and the clink and wheezing protest of a milk float, then the first front doors slamming as the trainee accountants and solicitors set off for the station. There was a light pattering across the carpet and a small round figure stood by the bed. She could see the gleam of his eyes and teeth smiling conspiratorially in the blanching dark.

'Come on then,' she whispered. 'Don't wake Daddy.'

He climbed into bed and curled into her, his head on her shoulder, his face a few inches from hers, gazed into her eyes and heaved a happy sigh. They lay looking at each other, breathing in each other's sleepy scent; his eyes were guileless, unguarded and intent, and he gave a little occasional beatific smile.

'Where's your pyjama top?' she whispered.

'Took it *off*,' he whispered back. 'Too itchy.'

Since the arrival of the children she had broken herself into little pieces like a biscuit and was now scattered all over the place

'It's *not* itchy,' she tutted. 'I'll put some special oil in your bath tonight.'

His chest was like a huge warm baroque pearl. She satined the side of her face against it for a moment.

'When are you going to stop wearing nappies at night?' she scolded in a whisper.

'When I'm four,' he chuckled, and shifted his pumpkin padding squarely onto her lap.

Max stirred and muttered something.

'Ssssh,' said Robin, placing a forefinger against his mother's lips and widening his eyes for emphasis.

They watched Max's dark bearded face break into a yawn, a seadog or a seagod about to rally his crew. He was waking up. Robin wriggled under the bedclothes to hide. Last night it had been her under the bedclothes and Max's hands on her head while she brought him off with her mouth. Then she had curled into him, her head on his shoulder, until he fell into a dense sleep, and she basked like a lioness in the sun. Next, gently unwinding herself from his knotty embrace she had glided along to the next room and plucked this heavy boy from his bed, standing him, sleep-dazed, in front of the lavatory, pointing the shrimp of his penis for him, whispering encouragement as the water hissed, before closing in on him with the midnight nappy.

Max's eyes flickered awake and he smiled at Dorrie.

'Mmmm,' he said. 'Come here.' He reached over and grabbed her, buried his face in her neck, and then as he reached downwards his hands encountered his son.

'No! No!' screeched Robin, laughing hectically. 'Get *away*, Daddy!'

This brought his siblings, Martin and Maxine, running from their bedroom and they hurled themselves into the heap of bodies. Max struggled out of it growling, and was gone.

The three children shoved and biffed their way into shares of her supine body. Robin clung to his central stake, arms round her neck, head between her breasts, kicking out at attempts to supplant him. Martin hooked his legs round her waist and lay under her left arm gnawing his nails and complaining it wasn't fair. Maxine burrowed at her right side, all elbows and knees, until she settled in the crook of her other arm, her head beside Dorrie's on the pillow.

'Mummy. A good heart is never proud. Is that true?' said Maxine.

'What?'

'It was on my *Little Mermaid* tape. I can make my eyes squelch, listen.'

'Oof, careful, Robin,' said Dorrie, as Robin brought his head up under her chin and crashed her teeth together.

'Goodbye,' said Max from the doorway.

'Don't forget we're going out tonight,' said Dorrie from the pillows.

'Oh yes,' said Max. He looked at the heap of bodies on the bed. 'Your mother and I were married eight years ago today,' he said into the air, piously.

'Where was *I*?' said Maxine.

'*Not* going out,' hissed Robin, gripping Dorrie more tightly. 'Stay inner house, Mummy.'

'And I'm not going to stand for any nonsense like that,' growled Max. He glared at his youngest son. 'Get off your mother, she can't move. It's ridiculous.'

'It's all right, Max,' said Dorrie. 'Don't make yourself late.'

'Go away, Daddy,' shouted Robin.

'Yeah,' joined in Martin and Maxine. 'Go away, Daddy.'

Max glared at them impotently, then turned on his heel like a pantomime villain. A moment later they heard the front door slam.

'Yesss!' said Robin, punching the air with his dimpled fist. The bed heaved with cheers and chuckles.

'You shouldn't talk to Daddy like that,' said Dorrie.

'Horble Daddy,' said Robin dismissively.

'He's not horble,' huffed Dorrie. 'Horrible. Time to get up.'

They all squealed and clutched her harder, staking her down with sharp elbows and knees wherever they could.

'You're hurting me,' complained Dorrie. 'Come on, it really is time to get up.' And at last she extracted herself like a slow giantess from the cluster of children, gently detaching their fingers from her limbs and nightdress.

When she turned back from drawing the curtains, Martin was painting his shins with a stick of deodorant while Maxine sat on the floor, galloping her round bare heels in the cups of a discarded bra, pulling on the straps like a jockey, with shouts of 'Ya! Ya! Giddy up, boy!' Robin ran round and round his mother's legs, wrapping and rewrapping her nightdress. Then he rolled on the carpet with both hands round her ankle, a lively leg-iron, singing alleluia, alleluia, alleluia.

'Don't do that, Martin,' said Dorrie as she climbed into yesterday's jeans and sweatshirt. But he was already on to something else, crossing the floor with a bow-legged rocking gait, a pillow across his shoulders, groaning under its imaginary weight and bulk.

'I'm Robin Hood carrying a deer,' he grinned back over his shoulder. Maxine roared with laughter, hearty as a Tudor despot.

'Come on, darlings,' Dorrie expostulated feebly. 'Help me get you dressed.'

They ran around her and across the landing, ignoring her, screeching, singing, bellowing insults and roaring into the stairwell. She pulled vests and socks and jumpers from various drawers, stepping around them like a slave during a palace orgy. Their separate energies whizzed through the air, colliding constantly, as random as the weather. She grabbed Martin as he shot past and started to strip off his nightclothes.

'No!' he yelled and tore himself free, running off trouserless. He was as quick as she was slow. It was like wading through mud after dragonflies.

'I hate you!' he was screaming at Maxine now for some reason. 'I wish you were dead!'

'Now now,' said Dorrie. 'That's not very nice, is it.'

Then there were pinches and thumps and full-chested bellows of rage. By the time she had herded them down for the cornflakes stage, they had lived through as many variants of passion as occur in the average Shakespeare play. She looked at their momentarily woebegone faces streaked with tears of fury over whichever was the most recent hair-pulling or jealousy or bruising, she had lost track, and said with deliberate cheer, 'Goodness, if we could save all the tears from getting ready in the mornings, if we could collect them in a bucket, I could use them to do the washing up.'

All three faces broke into wreathed smiles and appreciative laughter at this sally, and then the row started up again. They did not take turns to talk, but cut across each other's words with reckless thoughtlessness. She was trying to think through the hairbrushing, shoe-hunting, tooth-cleaning, packed lunch for Martin, empty toilet roll cylinder for Maxine's Miss Atkinson, with an eye on the clock, but it was a non-starter.

'SHUSH,' she shouted. 'I can't hear myself THINK.'

'Are you thinking?' asked Maxine curiously.

'No,' she said. 'Hurry UP.'

It was not in fact possible to think under these conditions; no train of thought could ever quite leave the platform, let alone arrive at any sort of destination. This was what the mothers at the school gates meant when they said they were brain-dead, when they told the joke about the secret of childcare being a frontal lobotomy or a bottle

in front of me. This was why she had started waking in the
small hours, she realised, even though heaven knew she
was tired enough without that, even though she was still
being woken once or twice a night by one or the other of
them; not Max because he had to be fresh for work and
anyway they wouldn't want him. They wanted *her*. But
when they were all safe, breathing regularly, asleep, quiet,
she was able at last to wait for herself to grow still, to grow
still and alive so that the sediment settled and things grew
clearer. So that she could *think*.

'Mrs Piper said Jonathan had nits and she sent him
home,' said Martin, lifting his face up. She was brushing his
hair, and pushed his brow back down against her breastbone. Then, more muffled, came, '*Don't* make me look like
Elvis de Presto.'

'What I want to know, Mum,' he said as she pushed him
back and knelt at Maxine's feet to struggle with her shoe
buckles. 'What I *need* to know, nobody will tell me,' he continued crossly, 'is, is God there, *can* he hold the whole
world in his hand – or is he like the Borrowers? I mean,
what is he? Is he a man? Is he a cow?'

She was working grimly against the clock now. Her
hands shook. She was shot to hell. Maxine was complaining of a blister on her little toe. Dorrie ran off upstairs like
a heifer for the plaster roll and cut a strip and carefully
fitted it round the pea-sized top joint of the toe. Maxine
moaned and screamed, tears squirted from her eyes, her
face became a mask of grief as she felt the plaster

arrangement inside her sock even more uncomfortable once strapped into her shoe. It all had to be removed again and a square quarter inch of plaster carefully applied like a miniature postage stamp to the reddened area.

'We're late,' hissed Dorrie, but even in the middle of this felt a great sick thud of relief that it was not two years ago when she had been racing against the clock to get to work pretending to them there that all this had not just happened. When at last she had caved in, when she had given in her notice, it felt like giving up the world, the flesh and the devil. It had been terrible at first, the loss of breadth, the loss of adult company. There were the minutes at various school gates with the other mothers, but you couldn't really call that proper talk, not with all the babies and toddlers on at them. After all she had not managed to keep both worlds up in the air. She knew she had failed.

She picked Robin up and jammed him into the buggy.

'Teeth!' said Martin, baring his own at her. 'You've forgotten about teeth!'

'Never mind,' she said through hers, gritted, manoeuvring the buggy across the front doorstep. 'Come on.'

'Why?' asked Martin, pulling his school jumper up to his eyes and goggling at himself in front of the hall mirror. 'Burglars don't show their noses, Mum. Look. Mum.'

THESE DAYS MARTIN flew off towards the playground as soon as they reached the school gate, for which she was profoundly grateful. For his first five years he had been full of complaints, fault-finding and irritability. He still flew into towering rages and hit her and screamed until he was pink or blue in the face, often several times a day. As he was her first child this had come as a shock. She even asked the doctor about it, and the doctor had smiled and said his sounded a fiery little nature but he would no doubt learn to control himself in time. 'Also, all behaviour is *learned* behaviour,' said the doctor reprovingly. 'Never shout back or you'll just encourage him.' Plenty of the other mothers had children who behaved similarly, she noticed after a while. You just had to take it, and wait for time to pass. It could take years. It did. He was loud, waspish, frequently agitated and a constant prey to boredom. When she saw him nibbling his nails, tired and white as a cross elf, she would draw him onto her lap and make a basket of her arms around him. She saw his lack of ease in the world, and grieved for him, and knew it was her fault because she was his mother.

Maxine was less irritable but more manipulative. Her memory was terrifyingly precise and long – yesterday, for example, she had raged at Dorrie for stealing a fruit pastille, having remembered the colour of the top one from several hours before. She relished experiments and emotional mayhem. Her new trick this week was to fix you with her pale pretty eye, and say, quite coolly, 'I hate you.' This poleaxed Dorrie. And yet this little girl was also utterly unglazed against experience, as fresh and easily hurt as one of those new daffodil shoots.

Only when Robin was born had she realised what it was to have what is commonly known as an easy child. No rhyme nor reason to it. Same treatment, completely different. They were as they were as soon as they were born, utterly different from each other. That was something at least. It couldn't *all* be her fault.

Now it was halfway through Martin's first school year and he had settled in well. It was wonderful. She glanced in passing at other less fortunate mothers talking low and urgent with their infants, entwined and unlinking, like lovers, bargaining with furtive tears, sobs, clinging arms, angry rejections, pettishness and red eyes.

It was the same when she dropped Maxine off at nursery school half an hour later. On the way out she and Robin passed a little girl of three or so saying to her mother, 'But Mummy, I *miss* you'; and the mother, smartly dressed, a briefcase by her, rather tightly reasoning with her, murmuring, glancing at her watch. Dorrie felt herself break into a light sympathetic sweat.

The little scene brought back Robin's trial morning there last week. He had refused to walk through the nursery school's entrance and was shouting and struggling as she carried him in. She had set him down by a low table of jigsaw puzzles and told him sternly that she would sit over there in that corner for five minutes, that his sister was just over there in the Wendy house, and that he must let her go quietly. From the toy kitchen he had brought her a plastic cupcake with a fat ingratiating smile.

'Here y'are,' he'd said.

'Save it for when I come to pick you up,' Dorrie had said, handing it back to him, pity and coldness battling through her like warring blood corpuscles. At last he had given her a resigned kiss on the cheek and gone off to the painting table without another look. (Two hours alone, for the first time in months. Wait till he's at school, said the mothers; you won't know yourself.) She dashed a tear away, sneering at her own babyishness.

Now, today, there was this precious time with Robin. He liked to be around her, within a few yards of her, to keep her in his sight, but he did not pull the stuffing out of her as the other two did. He did not demand her thoughts and full attention like Maxine; nor that she should identify and change colour like litmus paper with his every modulation of emotion as it occurred, which was what Martin seemed to need. Sometimes those two were so extravagantly exacting, they levied such a fantastic rate of slavish fealty that they left her gasping for air.

No, Robin talked to his allies and foes, *sotto voce*, in the subterranean fields which ran alongside the privet-hedged landscape in which they moved together. He sent out smiles or little waves while Dorrie was working, and took breaks for a hug or to pause and drink squash, him on her lap like a stalwart beanbag.

She sorted the dirty whites from the coloured wash up on the landing, and he put them into the washing basket for her. Up and down the stairs she went with round baskets of washing, the smell of feet and bottoms, five sets, fresh and smelly, all different. Robin stuffed the garments into the washing machine one by one, shutting the door smartly and saying 'There!' and smiling with satisfaction. She did some handwashing at the sink, and he pushed a chair over across the floor to stand on, and squeezed the garments, then took handfuls of the soap bubbles that wouldn't drain away and trotted to and from the bucket on the mat with them.

'What a helpful boy you are!' she said. He beamed.

'Now I'm going to iron some things including Daddy's shirt for tonight,' she said. 'So you must sit over there because the iron is dangerous.'

'Hot,' he agreed, with a sharp camp intake of breath.

He sat down on the floor with some toys in a corner of the kitchen and as she ironed she looked over now and then at his soft thoughtfully frowning face as he tried to put a brick into a toy car, the curve of his big soft cheek like a mushroom somehow, and his lovely close-to-the-head small ears. He gave an unconscious sigh of concentration; his frequent sighs came right from deep in the diaphragm. Squab or chub or dab had been the words which best expressed him until recently, but now he was growing taller and fining down, his limbs had lost their chubbiness and his body had become his own.

No longer could she kiss his eyelids whenever she wished, nor pretend to bite his fingers, nor even stroke his hair with impunity. He was a child now, not a baby, and must be accorded his own dignity. The baby was gone, almost.

Abruptly she put the iron on its heel and swooped down on him, scooped him up and buried her nose in his neck with throaty growling noises. He huffed and shouted and laughed as they swayed struggling by the vegetable rack. She tickled him and they sank down to the lino laughing and shouting, then he rubbed his barely there velvet nose against hers like an Eskimo, his eyes close and dark and merry, inches from hers, gazing in without shame or constraint.

It was going to be a long series of leave-takings from now on, she thought; goodbye and goodbye and goodbye; that had been the case with the others, and now this boy was three and a half. Unless she had another. But then Max would leave. Or so he said. This treacherous brainless greed for more of the same, it would finish her off if she wasn't careful. If she wasn't already.

She took Max's shirt upstairs on a hanger and put the rest of the ironing away. What would she wear tonight? She looked at her side of the wardrobe. Everything that wasn't made of T-shirt or sweatshirt fabric was too tight for her now. Unenthusiastically she took down an old red shirt-dress, looser than the rest, and held it up against her reflection in the full-length mirror. She used to know what she looked like, she used to be interested. Now she barely recognised herself. She peeled off her sweatshirt and jeans and pulled the dress on. She looked enormous. The dress was straining at the seams. She looked away fast, round the bedroom, the unmade bed like a dog basket, the mess everywhere, the shelves of books on the wall loaded with forbidden fruit, impossible to broach, sealed off by the laws of necessity from her maternal eyes. During the past five years, reading a book had become for her an activity engaged in at somebody else's expense.

The doorbell rang and she answered it dressed as she was. Robin hid behind her.

'Gemma's got to be a crocodile tomorrow,' said Sally, who lived two roads away. 'We're desperate for green tights, I've tried Mothercare and Boots and then I thought of Maxine. I don't suppose?'

'Sorry,' said Dorrie. 'Only red or blue.'

'Worth a try,' said Sally, hopeless. 'You look dressed up.'

'I look fat,' said Dorrie. 'Wedding anniversary,' she added tersely.

'Ah,' said Sally. 'How many years?'

'Eight,' said Dorrie. 'Bronze. Sally, can you remember that feeling before all the family stuff kicked in, I know it's marvellous but. You know, that spark, that feeling of fun and – and lightness, somehow.'

Immediately Sally replied, 'It's still there in me but I don't know for how much longer.'

'You could try Verity,' said Dorrie. 'I seem to remember she put Hannah in green tights last winter to go with that holly berry outfit.'

'So she did!' said Sally. 'I'll give her a ring.'

'Kill,' whispered Robin, edging past the women into the

tiny front garden; 'Die, megazord,' and he crushed a snail shell beneath his shoe. Half hidden beneath the windowsill he crouched in a hero's cave. Across the dangerous river of the front path he had to save his mother, who was chatting to a wicked witch. He started round the grape hyacinths as though they were on fire and squeezed his way along behind the lilac bush, past cobwebs and worms, until he burst out fiercely into the space behind the hedge. She was being forced to walk the plank. He leaped into the ocean and cantered sternly across the waves.

THEY WERE LATE coming out of nursery school, and Dorrie stood with the other mothers and au pairs in the queue. Some were chatting, some were sagging and gazing into the middle distance.

In front of her, two women were discussing a third just out of earshot.

'Look at her nails,' said the one directly in front of Dorrie. 'You can always tell. Painted fingernails mean a rubbish mother.'

'I sometimes put nail polish on if I'm going out in the evening,' said the other.

'If,' scoffed the first. 'Once in a blue moon. And then you make a mess of it, I bet. You lose your touch. Anyway, you've got better things to do with your time, you give your time to your children, not to primping yourself up.'

Robin pushed his head between Dorrie's knees and clutched her thighs, a mini Atlas supporting the world.

Dorrie saw it was Patricia from Hawthornden Avenue.

'*I* was thinking of doing my nails today,' said Dorrie.

'What on earth *for?*' laughed Patricia. She was broad in the beam, clever but narrow-minded.

'Wedding anniversary,' said Dorrie. 'Out for a meal.'

'There you are then,' said Patricia triumphantly, as though she had proved some point.

'I had a blazing row with *my* husband last night,' said Patricia's friend. 'And I was just saying to myself, Right that's it, I was dusting myself down ready for the off, when I thought, No, hang on a minute, I *can't* go. I've got three little children, I've *got* to stay.'

Patricia's eyebrows were out of sight, she reeled from side to side laughing. They all laughed, looking sideways at each other, uneasy.

'Have you noticed what happens now that everyone's splitting up,' snorted Patricia's friend. 'I've got friends, their divorce comes through and do you know they say it's amazing! They lose weight and take up smoking and have all the weekends to themselves to do *whatever they want* in because the men take the children off out then.'

'Divorce,' said Dorrie ruminatively. 'Yes. You get to thirty-seven, married, three kids, and you look in the mirror, at least I did this morning, and you realise – it's a shock – you realise nothing else is supposed to happen until you die. Or you spoil the pattern.'

The nursery school doors opened at last. Dorrie held her arms out and Maxine ran into them. Maxine had woken screaming at five that morning, clutching her ear, but then the pain had stopped and she had gone back to sleep again. Dorrie had not. That was when she had gone downstairs and into the garden.

'The doctor's going to fit us in after her morning surgery, so I must run,' said Dorrie, scooping Maxine up to kiss her, strapping Robin into the buggy.

'Mum,' called Maxine, as they galloped slowly along the pavement, 'Mum, Gemma says I must only play with her or she won't be my friend. But I told her Suzanne was my best friend. Gemma's only second best.'

'Yes,' said Dorrie. 'Mind that old lady coming towards us.'

'Suzanne and me really wanted Gemma to play Sour Lemons but Shoshaya wanted her to play rabbits,' panted Maxine. 'Then Shoshaya cried and she told Miss Atkinson. And Miss Atkinson told us to let her play. But Gemma wanted to play Sour Lemons with me and Suzanne and she did.'

'Yes,' said Dorrie. She must get some milk, and extra cheese for lunch. She ought to pick up Max's jacket from the cleaners. Had she got the ticket? Had she got enough cash? Then there was Max's mother's birthday present to be bought and packed up and posted off to Salcombe, and a card. She had to be thinking of other people all the time or the whole thing fell apart. It was like being bitten all over by soldier ants without being able to work up enough interest to deal with them. Sometimes she found herself holding her breath for no reason at all.

'Why do you always say yes?' said Maxine.

'What?' said Dorrie. They stood at the kerb waiting to cross. She looked up at the top deck of the bus passing on the other side and saw a young man sitting alone up there. He happened to meet her eye for a moment as she stood with the children, and the way he looked at her, through her, as though she were a greengrocer's display or a parked car, made her feel less than useless. She was a rock or stone or tree. She was nothing.

'Why do you always say yes?' said Maxine.

'What?' said Dorrie.

'Why do you always say YES!' screamed Maxine in a rage.

'Cross *now*,' said Dorrie, grabbing her arm and hauling her howling across the road as she pushed the buggy.

They turned the corner into the road where the surgery was and saw a small boy running towards them trip and go flying, smack down onto the pavement.

'Oof,' said Maxine and Robin simultaneously.

The child held up his grazed hands in grief and started to split the air with his screams. His mother came lumbering up with an angry face.

'I told you, didn't I? I told you! You see? God was looking down and he saw you were getting out of control. You wouldn't do what I said, would you. And God said, *right*, and He made you fall down like that and that's what happens when you're like that. So now maybe you'll listen the next time!'

Dorrie looked away, blinking. That was another thing, it

had turned her completely soft. The boy's mother yanked him up by the arm, and dragged him past, moralising greedily over his sobs.

'She should have hugged him, Mummy, shouldn't she,' said Maxine astutely.

'Yes,' said Dorrie, stopping to blow her nose.

THE TATTERED COVERS of the waiting room magazines smiled over at them in a congregation of female brightness and intimacy. The women I see in the course of a day, thought Dorrie, and it's women only (except Max at the end of the day), we can't really exchange more than a sentence or two of any interest because of our children. At this age they need us all the time; and anyway we often have little in common except femaleness and being in the same boat. Why should we? She scanned the lead lines while Robin and Maxine chose a book from the scruffy pile – 'How to dump him: twenty ways that work'; 'Your hair: what does it say about you?', 'Countdown to your best orgasm'. Those were the magazines for the under-thirties, the free-standing feisty girls who had not yet crossed the ego line. And of course some girls never did cross the ego line. Like men, they stayed the stars of their own lives. Then there was this lot, this lot here with words like juggle and struggle across their covers, these were for her and her like – 'Modern motherhood: how do you measure up?'; 'Is your husband getting enough: time management and you'; 'Doormat etiquette: are you too nice?'

Am I too *nice*? thought Dorrie. They even took *that* away. Nice here meant weak and feeble, *she* knew what it meant. Nice was now an insult, whereas self had been the dirty word when she was growing up. For girls, anyway. She had been trained to think of her mother and not be a nuisance. She couldn't remember ever saying (let alone being asked) what she wanted. To the point of thinking she didn't really mind what she wanted as long as other people were happy. It wasn't long ago.

The doctor inspected Maxine's eardrum with her pointed torch, and offered a choice.

'You can leave it and hope it goes away. That's what they'd do on the Continent.'

'But then it might flare up in the night and burst the eardrum. That happened to Martin. Blood on the pillow. Two sets of grommets since then.'

'Well, *tant pis*, they'd say. They're tough on the Continent. Or it's the usual amoxcyllin.'

'I don't like to keep giving them that. But perhaps I could have some in case it gets very painful later. And not give it otherwise.'

'That's what I'd do,' said the doctor, scribbling out a prescription.

'How are you finding it, being back at work?' asked Dorrie timidly but with great interest. The doctor had just returned after her second baby and second five-month maternity leave.

'Fine, fine,' smiled the doctor, rubbing her eyes briefly,

tired blue eyes kind in her worn face. 'In fact of course it's easier. I mean, it's hard in terms of organisation, hours, being at full stretch. But it's still easier than being at home. With tiny children you really have to be so . . . selfless.'

'Yes,' said Dorrie, encouraged. 'It gets to be a habit. In the end you really do lose yourself. Lost. But then they start to be not tiny.'

'Lost!' said Maxine. 'Who's lost? What you talking about, Mum? *Who's* lost?'

The doctor glanced involuntarily at her watch.

'I'm sorry,' said Dorrie, bustling the children over to the door.

'Not at all,' said the doctor. She did look tired. 'Look after yourself.'

Look after yourself, thought Dorrie as she walked the children home, holding her daughter's hand as she skipped and pulled at her. She glanced down at her hand holding Maxine's, plastic shopping bags of vegetables over her wrist, and her nails looked uneven, not very clean. According to the nursery school queue, that meant she was a good mother. She did nothing for herself. She was a vanity-free zone. Broken nails against that tight red dress wouldn't be very alluring, but all that was quite beyond her now. By schooling herself to harmlessness, constant usefulness to others, she had become a big fat zero.

By the time they got home Dorrie was carrying Robin straddled African-style across her front, and he was alternately sagging down protesting, then straightening his back and climbing her like a tree. He had rebelled against the buggy, so she had folded it and trailed it behind her, but when he walked one of his shoes hurt him; she knew the big toenail needed cutting but whenever his feet were approached he set up a herd-of-elephants roar. She made a mental note to creep up with the scissors while he slept. I can't see how the family would work if I let myself start wanting things again, thought Dorrie; give me an inch and I'd run a mile, that's what I'm afraid of.

INDOORS, SHE PEELED vegetables while they squabbled and played around her legs. She wiped the surfaces while answering long strings of zany questions which led up a spiral staircase into the wild blue nowhere.

'I know when you're having a thought, Mummy,' said Maxine. 'Because when I start to say something then you close your eyes.'

'Can I have my Superman suit?' said Robin.

'In a minute,' said Dorrie, who was tying up a plastic sack of rubbish.

'Not in a minute,' said Robin. '*Now*.'

The thing about small children was that they needed things all day long. They wanted games set up and tears wiped away and a thousand small attentions. This was all fine until you started to do something else round them, or something that wasn't just a basic menial chore, she thought, dragging the hoover out after burrowing in the stacking boxes for the Superman suit. You had to be infinitely elastic and adaptable; all very laudable but this had the concomitant effect of slowly but surely strangling your powers of concentration.

Then Superman needed help in blowing his nose, and next he wanted his cowboys and Indians reached down from the top of the cupboard. She forgot what she was thinking about.

Now she was chopping onions finely as thread so that Martin would not be able to distinguish their texture in the meatballs and so spit them out. (Onions were good for their immune systems, for their blood.) She added these to the minced lamb and mixed in eggs and breadcrumbs then shaped the mixture into forty tiny globes, these to bubble away in a tomato sauce, one of her half-dozen flesh-concealing ruses against Maxine's incipient vegetarianism. (She knew it was technically possible to provide enough protein for young children from beans as long as these were eaten in various careful conjunctions with other beans – all to do with amino acids – but she was not want-ing to plan and prepare even more separate meals – Max had his dinner later in the evening – not just yet anyway – or she'd be simmering and peeling till midnight.)

The whole pattern of family life hung for a vivid moment above the chopping board as a seamless cycle of nourish-ment and devoural. And after all, children were not teeth extracted from you. Perhaps it was necessary to be devoured.

Dorrie felt sick and faint as she often did at this point

in the day, so she ate a pile of tepid left-over mashed potato and some biscuits while she finished clearing up and peace-keeping. The minutes crawled by. She wanted to lie down on the lino and pass out.

Maxine's nursery school crony, Suzanne, came to play after lunch. Dorrie helped them make a shop and set up tins of food and jars of dried fruit, but they lost interest after five minutes and wanted to do colouring in with felt tips. Then they had a fight over the yellow. Then they played with the Polly Pockets, and screamed, and hit each other. Now, now, said Dorrie, patient but intensely bored, as she pulled them apart and calmed them down and cheered them up.

At last it was time to drop Suzanne off and collect Martin. Inside the school gates they joined the other mothers, many of whom Dorrie now knew by name or by their child's name, and waited at the edge of the playground for the release of their offspring.

'I can't tell you anything about Wednesday until Monday,' said Thomas' mother to a woman named Marion. A note had been sent back in each child's reading folder the previous day, announcing that the last day before half term would finish at twelve. The women who had part-time jobs now started grumbling about this, and making convoluted webs of arrangements. 'If you drop Neil off at two then my neighbour will be there, you remember, he got on with her last time all right, that business with the spacehopper; then Verity can drop Kirsty by after Tumbletots and I'll be back with Michael and Susan just after three-thirty. Hell! It's ballet. Half an hour later. Are you *sure* that's all right with you?'

'They're late,' said Thomas' mother, glancing at her watch.

'So your youngest will be starting nursery after Easter,' said Marion to Dorrie. 'You won't know yourself.'

'No,' said Dorrie. She reached down to ruffle Robin's feathery hair; he was playing around her legs.

'Will you get a job then?' asked Marion.

'Um, I thought just for those weeks before summer I'd get the house straight, it's only two hours in the morning. And a half,' said Dorrie in a defensive rush. 'Collect my thoughts. If there are any.'

'Anyway, you do your husband's paperwork in the evenings, don't you?' said Thomas' mother. 'The accounts and that. VAT.'

'You get so you can't see the wood for the trees, don't you,' said Dorrie. 'You get so good at fitting things round everything else. Everybody else.'

'I used to be in accounts,' said Marion. 'B.C. But I couldn't go back now. I've lost touch. I couldn't get into my suits any more, I tried the other day. I couldn't do it! I'd hardly cover the cost of the childcare. I've lost my nerve.'

'My husband says he'll back me up one hundred per cent when the youngest starts school,' said Thomas' mother pensively. 'Whatever job I want to do. But no way would he be able to support change which would end by making his working life more difficult, he said.'

'That's not really on, then, is it?' said Marion. 'Unless

you get some nursery school work to fit round school hours. Or turn into a freelance something.'

'Some people seem to manage it,' said Thomas' mother. 'Susan Gloverall.'

'I didn't know she was back at work.'

'Sort of. She's hot-desking somewhere off the A3, leaves the kids with a childminder over Tooting way. Shocking journey, but the devil drives.'

'Keith still not found anything, then? That's almost a year now.'

'I know. Dreadful really. I don't think it makes things any, you know, easier between them. And of course she can't leave the kids with him while he's looking. Though she said he's watching a lot of TV.'

'What about Nicola Beaumont, then?' said Dorrie.

'Oh her,' said Marion. 'Wall-to-wall nannies. No thank you.'

'I could never make enough to pay a nanny,' said Thomas' mother. 'I never earned that much to start with. And then you have to pay their tax on top, out of your own taxed income. You'd have to earn eighteen thousand at least before you broke even if you weren't on the fiddle. I've worked it out.'

'Nearer twenty-two these days,' said Marion. 'In London. Surely.'

'Nicola's nice though,' said Dorrie. 'Her daughter Jade, the teenage one, she's babysitting for us tonight.'

'Well she never seems to have much time for me,' said Marion.

'I think she just doesn't have much time full stop,' said Dorrie.

'Nor do any of us, dear,' said Thomas' mother. 'Not *proper* time.'

'Not time to yourself,' said Marion.

'I bet she gets more of that than I do. She commutes, doesn't she? There you are then!'

They were all laughing again when the bell went.

'HARRY SWALLOWED HIS tooth today,' said Martin. 'Mrs Tyrone said it didn't matter, it would melt inside him.' He wiggled his own front tooth, an enamel tag, tipping it forward with his fingernail. Soon there would be the growing looseness, the gradual twisting of it into a spiral, hanging on by a thread, and the final silent snap.

'He won't get any money from the Tooth Fairy, will he, Mum,' said Martin. 'Will he, Mum? Will he, Mum? Mum. Mum!'

'Yes,' said Dorrie. 'What? I expect so, dear.' She was peeling carrots and cutting them into sticks.

'And Kosenia scratched her bandage off today, and she's got eczema, and she scratched off, you know, that stuff on top, like the cheese on Shepherd's Pie, she just lifted it off,' Martin went on.

'Crust,' said Dorrie.

'Yes, crust,' said Martin. 'I'm not eating those carrots. No way.'

'Carrots are very good for you,' said Dorrie. 'And tomorrow I'm going to pack some carrot sticks in your lunch box and I want you to eat them.'

'Hey yeah right,' gabbled Martin. 'Hey yeah right get a life!'

And he marched off to where the other two were watching a story about a mouse who ate magic berries and grew as big as a lion. Television was nothing but good and hopeful and stimulating compared with the rest of life so far as she could see. Certainly it had been the high point of her own childhood. Her mother thought she spoiled her children, but then most of her friends said their mothers thought the same about them. She was trying to be more tender with them – she and her contemporaries – to offer them choices rather than just tell them what to do; to be more patient and to hug them when they cried rather than briskly talk of being brave; never to hit them. They felt, they all felt they were trying harder than their parents had ever done, to love well. And one of the side effects of this was that their children were incredibly quick to castigate any shortfall in the quality of attention paid to them.

Now they were fighting again. Martin was screaming and chattering of injustice like an angry ape. Maxine shrilled back at him with her ear-splitting screech. Robin sat on the ground, hands to his ears, sobbing deep-chested sobs of dismay.

She groaned with boredom and frustration. Really she could not afford to let them out of her sight yet; not for another six months, anyway; not in another room, even with television.

'Let's all look at pictures of Mummy and Daddy getting married,' she shouted above the din, skilfully deflecting the furies. Sniffing and shuddering they eventually allowed themselves to be gathered round the album she had dug out, while she wiped their eyes and noses and clucked mild reproaches. The thing was, it did not do simply to turn off. She was not a part of the action but her involved presence was required as it was necessary for her to be ready at any point to step in as adjudicator. What did not work was when she carried on round them, uninvolved, doing the chores, thinking her own thoughts and making placatory noises when the din grew earsplitting. Then the jaws of anarchy opened wide.

Soon they were laughing at the unfamiliar images of their parents in the trappings of romance, the bright spirited faces and trim figures.

'Was it the best day in your life?' asked Maxine.

There was me, she thought, looking at the photographs; there used to be me. She was the one who'd put on two stone; he still looked pretty fit. The whole process would have been easier, she might have been able to retain some self-respect, if at some point there had been a formal handing over like Hong Kong.

At the end of some days, by the time each child was

breathing regularly, asleep, she would stand and wait for herself to grow still, and the image was of an ancient vase, crackle-glazed, still in one piece but finely crazed all over its surface. I'm shattered, she would groan to Max on his return, hale and whole, from the outside world.

Now, AT THE end of just such a day, Dorrie was putting the children down while Max had a bath after his day at work. It was getting late. She had booked a table at L'Horizon and arranged for Jade to come round and baby-sit at eight. They had not been out together for several months, but Dorrie had not forgotten how awful it always was.

It was twenty to eight, and Robin clung to her.

'Don't go, Mummy, don't go,' he sobbed, jets of water spouting from his eyes, his mouth a square buckle of anguish.

'Don't be silly,' said Dorrie, with her arms round him. 'I've got to go and change, darling. I'll come straight back.'

'No you won't,' he bellowed. Martin watched with interest, nibbling his nails.

'He's making me feel sad, Mum,' commented Maxine. 'I feel like crying now too.'

'So do I,' said Dorrie grimly.

'What's all the noise?' demanded Max, striding into the room drubbing his hair with a towel. 'Why aren't you children asleep yet?'

Robin took a wild look at his father and, howling with

fresh strength, tightened his grip on Dorrie with arms, legs and fingers.

'Let go of your mother this minute,' snarled Max in a rage, starting to prise away the desperate fingers one by one. Robin's sobs became screams, and Maxine started to cry.

'Please, Max,' said Dorrie. 'Please don't.'

'This is ridiculous,' hissed Max, wrenching him from her body. Dorrie watched the child move across the line into hysteria, and groaned.

'Stop it, Daddy!' screamed Martin, joining in, and downstairs the doorbell rang.

'Go and answer it then!' said Max, pinning his frantic three-year-old son to the bed.

'Oh God,' said Dorrie as she stumbled downstairs to open the door to the babysitter.

'Hello, Jade!' she said with a wild fake smile. 'Come in!'

'Sounds like I'm a bit early,' said Jade, stepping into the hall, tall and slender and dressed in snowy-white shirt and jeans.

'No, no, let me show you how to work the video, that's just the noise they make on their way to sleep,' said Dorrie, feeling herself bustle around like a fat dwarf. It seemed pathetic that she should be going out and this lovely girl staying in. The same thought had crossed Jade's mind, but she had her whole life ahead of her, as everyone kept saying.

'Any problems, anything at all, if one of them wakes and

asks for me, please ring and I'll come back, it's only a few minutes away.'

'Everything'll be *fine*,' said Jade, as if to a fussy infant. 'You shouldn't worry so much.'

'I'll swing for that child,' they heard Max growl from the landing, then a thundering patter of feet, and febrile shrieks.

'EIGHT YEARS, EH,' said Max across the candlelit damask. 'My Old Dutch. No need to look so tragic.'

Dorrie was still trying to quiet her body's alarm system, the waves of miserable heat, the klaxons of distress blaring in her bloodstream from Robin's screams.

'You've got to go out sometimes,' said Max. 'It's getting ridiculous.'

'I'm sorry I didn't manage to make myself look nice,' said Dorrie. '*You* look nice. Anyway, it's four pounds an hour. It's like sitting in a taxi.'

Max was big and warm, sitting relaxed like a sportsman after the game, but his eyes were flinty.

'It's just arrogant, thinking that nobody else can look after them as well as you,' he said.

'They can't,' mumbled Dorrie, under her breath.

'You're a dreadful worrier,' said Max. 'You're always worrying.'

'Well,' said Dorrie. 'Somebody's got to.'

'Everything would carry on all right, you know, if you stopped worrying.'

'No it wouldn't. I wish it would. But it wouldn't.'

Lean and sexually luminous young waiting staff glided gracefully around them.

'Have you chosen,' he said, and while she studied the menu he appraised her worn face, free of make-up except for an unaccustomed and unflattering application of lipstick, and the flat frizz of her untended hair. She was starting to get a double chin, he reflected wrathfully; she had allowed herself to put on more weight. Here he was on his wedding anniversary sitting opposite a fat woman. And if he ever said anything, *she* said, the children. It showed a total lack of respect; for herself; for him.

'I just never seem to get any time to myself,' muttered Dorrie. She felt uneasy complaining. Once she'd stopped bringing in money she knew she'd lost the right to object. So did he.

'It's a matter of discipline,' said Max, sternly.

He felt a terrible restlessness at this time of year, particularly since his fortieth. The birthday cards had all been about being past it. Mine's a pint of Horlicks, jokes about bad backs, expanding waistlines, better in candlelight. There it stretched, all mapped out for him; a long or not-so-long march to the grave; and he was forbidden from looking to left or right. He had to hold himself woodenly impervious, it would seem, since every waking moment was supposed to be a married one. All right for her, she could stun herself with children. But he needed a romantic motive or life wasn't worth living.

He could see the food and drink and television waiting for him at each day's end, and the thickening of middle age, but he was buggered if he was going to let himself go down that route. He watched Dorrie unwisely helping herself to sautéed potatoes. Her body had become like a car to her, he thought, it got her around, it accommodated people at various intervals, but she herself seemed to have nothing to do with it any more. She just couldn't be bothered.

What had originally drawn him to her was the balance between them, a certain tranquil buoyancy she had which had gone well with his own more explosive style. These days she was not so much tranquil as stagnant, while all the buoyancy had been bounced off. He wished he could put a bomb under her. She seemed so apathetic except when she was loving the children. It made him want to boot her broad bottom whenever she meandered past him in the house, just to speed her up.

The children had taken it out of her, he had to admit. She'd had pneumonia after Maxine, her hair had fallen out in handfuls after Robin, there had been two caesareans, plus that operation to remove an ovarian cyst. The saga of her health since babies was like a seaside postcard joke, along with the mothers-in-law and the fat-wife harridans. After that childminder incident involving Martin breaking his leg at the age of two, she'd done bits of part-time but even that had fizzled out soon after Robin, so now she wasn't bringing in any money at all. When he married her, she'd had an interesting job, she'd earned a bit, she was lively and sparky; back in the mists of time. Now he had the whole pack of them on his back and he was supposed to be as philosophical about this as some old leech-gatherer.

He didn't want to hurt her, that was the trouble. He did not want the house to fly apart in weeping and wailing and children who would plead with him not to go, Daddy. He did not want to seem disloyal, either. But, he thought wildly, neither could he bear being sentenced to living death. Things were going to have to be different. She couldn't carry on malingering round the house like this. It wasn't fair. She shouldn't expect. He felt a shocking contraction of pity twist his guts. Why couldn't she bloody well look after herself better? He took a deep breath.

'Did I mention about Naomi,' he said casually, spearing a floret of broccoli.

Naomi was Max's right-hand woman at the builder's yard. She oversaw the stock, manned the till when necessary, sorted the receipts and paperwork for Dorrie to deal with at home and doled out advice about undercoats to the customers. She had been working for them for almost two years.

'Is she well?' asked Dorrie. 'I thought she was looking very white when I saw her last Wednesday.'

'Not only is she not well, she's throwing up all over the place,' said Max heavily. 'She's pregnant,' he added in a muffled voice, stuffing more vegetables into his mouth.

'Pregnant?' said Dorrie. 'Oh!' Tears came to her eyes and she turned to scrabble under the table as if for a dropped napkin. So far she had managed to hide from him her insane lusting after yet another.

'That's what I thought,' sighed Max, misinterpreting her reaction.

'I'm so pleased for her, they've been wanting a baby for ages,' said Dorrie, and this time it was her voice that was muffled.

'So of course I've had to let her go,' said Max, looking at his watch.

'You've *what*?' said Dorrie.

'It's a great shame, of course. I'll have to go through all that with someone else now, showing them the ropes and so on.'

'How *could* you, Max?'

'Look, I knew you'd be like this. I *know*. It's a shame isn't it, yes; but there it is. That's life. It's lucky it happened when it did. Another few weeks and she'd have been able to nail me to the wall, unfair dismissal, the works.'

'But they need the money,' said Dorrie, horrified. 'How are they going to manage the mortgage now?'

'He should pull his finger out then, shouldn't he,' shrugged Max. 'He's public sector anyway, they'll be all right. Look, Dorrie, I've got a wife and children to support.'

'Get her back,' said Dorrie. 'Naomi will be fine. She's not like me, she'll have the baby easily, she won't get ill afterwards, nor will the baby. We were unlucky. She's very capable, she's not soft about things like childminders. You'd be mad to lose her.'

'Actually,' said Max, 'I've offered her a part-time job when she is ready to come back, and I rather think that might suit us better too. If I keep her below a certain number of hours.'

'What did Naomi say to *that*?'

'She was still a bit peeved about being let go,' said Max. 'But she said she'd think about it. If she could combine it with another part-time job. Beggars can't be choosers. I mean, if she chooses to have a baby, that's her choice.'

'I see,' said Dorrie carefully. 'So who will take over her work at the yard meanwhile?'

'Well, you, of course,' said Max, swallowing a big forkful of chop, his eyes bulging. He hurried on. 'Robin starts at nursery after Easter, Maxine's nearly finished there, and Martin's doing fine at school full-time now. So you can work the mornings, then you can collect Robin and Maxine and bring them along for a sandwich and work round them from then till it's time to pick up Martin. We can leave the paperwork till the evening. We'll save all ways like that. He's a big boy now, he can potter around.'

'He's only three and a half,' she said breathlessly. 'And when would I do the meals and the ironing and the cleaning and the shopping in all this?'

'Fit it in round the edges,' said Max. 'Other women do. It'll be good for you, get you out of the house. Come on, Dorrie, I can't carry passengers forever. You'll have to start pulling your weight again.'

It was towards the end of the main course and they

had both drunk enough house white to be up near the surface.

'They're hard work, young children, you know,' she said.

'You said yourself they're getting easier every day. You said so yourself. It's not like when they were all at home all day screaming their heads off.'

'It is when they're on holiday,' she said. 'That's nearly twenty weeks a year, you know. What happens *then*?'

'You're off at a tangent again,' he said, sighing, then demanded, 'What *do* you want out of life?'

'It's not some sort of anaconda you've got to wrestle with,' said Dorrie. She realised that this latest sequestration of her hours would send her beside herself. Loss of inner life, that's what it was; lack of any purchase in the outside world, and loss of all respect; continuous unavoidable Lilliputian demands; numbness, apathy and biscuits. She was at the end of her rope.

'We can't just wait for things to fall into our laps though,' said Max, thinking about his own life.

'We're doing all right,' said Dorrie.

'That doesn't mean to say we couldn't do better. We need to expand.'

'We're managing the mortgage,' said Dorrie. 'I think we should be grateful.'

'That's the spirit,' said Max. 'That's the spirit that made this island great. Stand and stare, eh. Stand and stare.'

'What would you prefer?' said Dorrie. 'Life's a route march, then you die?'

'But then *you've* got what you wanted, haven't you – the children.'

'You are horrible,' said Dorrie. She took a great gulp of wine and drained her glass. 'It's about how well you've loved and how well you've been loved.' She didn't sound very convincing, she realised, in fact she sounded like Thought for the Day. She sounded like some big sheep bleating.

'I don't know what it is, Dorrie,' he said sadly. 'But you're all damped down. You've lost your spirit. You're not there any more.'

'I know. I know. But that's what I'm trying to say. You think I've just turned into a boring saint. But I'm still there. If you could just take them for a few hours now and then and be *nice* to them, if I just had a bit of quiet time . . .'

'I'm not exactly flourishing either, you know. You're getting to me.'

'Sorry. Sorry. I seem to be so dreary these days. But . . .'

'That's what I mean. Such a victim. Makes me want to kick you.'

'Don't, Max. Please don't. We've got to go back to that girl and pay her first.'

'Just being miserable and long-suffering, you think that'll make me sorry for you.'

'Max . . .'

'But it makes me hate you, if you must know.'

BACK AT THE house, Max handed Dorrie his wallet and went off upstairs. He was tired as he brushed his teeth, and angry at the way the evening had gone; nor did he like his bad-tempered reflection in the bathroom mirror. Soon he was asleep, frowning in release like a captive hero.

Dorrie meanwhile was fumbling with five-pound notes, enquiring brightly as to whether Jade had had a quiet evening.

'Oh yes, there wasn't a sound out of them once you'd gone,' said Jade, not strictly truthfully, still mesmerised by the beautiful eyes of the sex murderer with the razor on the screen. There had actually been a noise from the boys' bedroom and when she had put her head around the door sure enough the younger one was lying in a pool of sick. But he was breathing fine so she left him to it, it wasn't bothering him and no way was she going to volunteer for that sort of thing. She was getting paid to babysit, not to do stuff like that. That would have been right out of order.

'Would you like to stay and finish your video?' asked Dorrie politely, flinching as she watched the razor slit through filmstar flesh.

'No, that's all right,' said Jade reluctantly. She flicked the remote control and the bloody image disappeared. She sighed.

'Well, thank you again,' said Dorrie. 'It's lovely to know I can leave them with someone I can trust.'

'That's OK,' said Jade. 'No problem.' And with a royal yawn she made her exit.

IT TOOK DORRIE half an hour or so to bathe the dazed
Robin, to wash the acrid curds holding kernels of sweetcorn and discs of peas from his feathery hair and wrap him
in clean pyjamas and lay him down in the big bed beside
his noble-looking father, where he fell instantly asleep,
slumbering on a cloud of beauty.

She kissed his warm face and turned back, her body
creaking in protest, to the job in hand. Downstairs in the
midnight kitchen she scraped the duvet cover and pillow
case with the knife kept specifically for this purpose,
dumping the half-digested chyme into the sink, running
water to clear it away, then scraping again, gazing out of
the window into the blackness of the wild garden, yearning
at the spatter of rain on the glass and the big free trees out
there with their branches in the sky.

Their needs were what was set. Surely that was the logic
of it. It was for *her* to adapt, accommodate, modify in order
to allow the familial organism to flourish. Here she was
weeping over her own egotism like a novice nun, for goodness sake, except it was the family instead of God. But still
it was necessary, selflessness, for a while, even if it made
you spat on by the world. By your husband. By your children. By yourself.

She wanted to smash the kitchen window. She wanted
to hurt herself. Her ghost was out there in the garden, the
ghost from her free-standing past. If she kept up this business of reunion, it would catch hold of her hands and saw
her wrists to and fro across the jagged glass. It would tear

her from the bosom of this family she had breastfed. No. She must stay this side of the glass from now on, thickening and cooling like some old planet until at last she killed the demands of that self-regarding girl out there.

She twisted and squeezed water from the bedlinen she had just rinsed. If she were to let herself be angry about this obliteration, of her particular mind, of her own relish for things, then it would devour the family. Instead she must let it gnaw at her entrails like some resident tiger. This was not sanctimony speaking but necessity. All this she knew but could not explain. She was wringing the sheet with such force that it creaked.

'Fresh air,' she said aloud, and tried to open the window in front of her. It was locked, clamped tight with one of the antiburglar fastenings which they had fitted on all the windows last summer. She felt around in the cupboard above the refrigerator for the key, but it wasn't in its usual place. She hunted through the rows of mugs, the tins of tuna and tomatoes, the bags of rice and flour and pasta, and found it at last inside the glass measuring jug.

Leaning across the sink she unlocked the window and opened it onto the night. A spray of rain fell across her face and she gasped. There was the cold fresh smell of wet earth. It occurred to her that this might not necessarily be killer pain she was feeling, not terrible goodbyeforever pain as she had assumed; and she felt light-headed with the shock of relief.

Perhaps this was not the pain of wrist-cutting after all.

Instead, the thought came to her, it might be the start of that intense outlandish sensation that comes after protracted sleep; the feeling in a limb that has gone numb, when blood starts to flow again, sluggishly at first, reviving; until after a long dormant while that limb is teeming again, tingling into life.

Out in the garden, out in the cold black air, she could see the big trees waving their wild bud-bearing branches at her.

Heavy Weather

'YOU SHOULD NEVER HAVE MARRIED ME.'

'I haven't regretted it for an instant.'

'Not *you*, you fool! *Me!* You shouldn't have got me to marry you if you loved me. Why *did* you, when you knew it would let me in for all *this*. It's not *fair*!'

'I didn't know. I know it's not. But what can I do about it?'

'I'm being mashed up and eaten alive.'

'I know. I'm sorry.'

'It's not your fault. But what can I do?'

'I don't know.'

So the conversation had gone last night in bed, followed by platonic embraces. They were on ice at the moment, so far as anything further was concerned. The smoothness and sweet smell of their children, the baby's densely packed pearly limbs, the freshness of the little girl's breath when she yawned, these combined to accentuate the grossness of their own bodies. They eyed each other's mooching adult bulk with mutual lack of enthusiasm, and fell asleep.

At four in the morning, the baby was punching and shouting in his Moses basket. Frances forced herself awake, lying for the first moments like a flattened boxer in the ring trying to rise while the count was made. She got up and fell over, got up again and scooped Matthew from the basket. He was huffing with eagerness, and scrabbled crazily at her breasts like a drowning man until she lay down with him. A few seconds more and he had abandoned himself to rhythmic gulping. She stroked his soft head and drifted off. When she woke again, it was six o'clock and he was sleeping between her and Jonathan.

For once, nobody was touching her. Like Holland she lay, aware of a heavy ocean at her seawall, its weight poised to race across the low country.

The baby was now three months old, and she had not had more than half an hour alone in the twenty-four since his birth in February. He was big and hungry and needed her there constantly on tap. Also, his two-year-old sister Lorna was, unwillingly, murderously jealous, which made everything much more difficult. This time round was harder, too, because when one was asleep the other would be awake and vice versa. If only she could get them to nap at the same time, Frances started fretting, then she might be able to sleep for some minutes during the day and that would get her through. But they wouldn't, and she couldn't. She had taken to muttering I can't bear it, I can't bear it, without realising she was doing so until she heard Lorna chanting I can't bear it! I can't bear it! as she skipped along beside the pram, and this made her blush with shame at her own weediness.

Now they were all four in Dorset for a week's holiday. The thought of having to organise all the food, sheets, milk, baths and nappies made her want to vomit.

In her next chunk of sleep came that recent nightmare, where men with knives and scissors advanced on the felled trunk which was her body.

'How would you like it?' she said to Jonathan. 'It's like a doctor saying, now we're just going to snip your scrotum in half, but don't worry, it mends very well down there, we'll stitch you up and you'll be fine.'

It was gone seven by now, and Lorna was leaning on the bars of her cot like Farmer Giles, sucking her thumb in a ruminative pipe-smoking way. The room stank like a lion house. She beamed as her mother came in, and lifted her arms up. Frances hoisted her into the bath, stripped her down and detached the dense brown nappy from between her knees. Lorna carolled, 'I can sing a *rain*bow,' raising her faint fine eyebrows at the high note, graceful and perfect, as her mother sluiced her down with jugs of water.

'Why does everything take so *long*?' moaned Jonathan. 'It only takes *me* five minutes to get ready.'

Frances did not bother to answer. She was sagging with

the effortful boredom of assembling the paraphernalia needed for a morning out in the car. Juice. Beaker with screw-on lid. Flannels. Towels. Changes of clothes in case of car sickness. Nappies. Rattle. Clean muslins to catch Matthew's curdy regurgitations. There was more. What was it?

'Oh, come on, Jonathan, think,' she said. 'I'm fed up with having to plan it all.'

'What do you think I've been doing for the last hour?' he shouted. 'Who was it that changed Matthew's nappy just now? Eh?'

'Congratulations,' she said. 'Don't shout or I'll cry.'

Lorna burst into tears.

'Why is everywhere always such a *mess*,' said Jonathan, picking up plastic spiders, dinosaurs, telephones, beads and bears, his grim scowl over the mound of primary colours like a traitor's head on a platter of fruit.

'I *want* dat spider, Daddy!' screamed Lorna. 'Give it to me!'

During the ensuing struggle, Frances pondered her tiredness. Her muscles twitched as though they had been tenderised with a steak bat. There was a bar of iron in the back of her neck, and she felt unpleasantly weightless in the cranium, a gin-drinking side effect without the previous fun. The year following the arrival of the first baby had gone in pure astonishment at the loss of freedom, but second time round it was spinning away in exhaustion. Matthew woke at one a.m. and four a.m., and Lorna at

six-thirty a.m. During the days, fatigue came at her in concentrated doses, like a series of time bombs.

'Are we ready at last?' said Jonathan, breathing heavily.
'Are we ready to go?'

'Um, nearly,' said Frances. 'Matthew's making noises. I
think I'd better feed him, or else I'll end up doing it in a
lay-by.'

'Right,' said Jonathan. 'Right.'

Frances picked up the baby. 'What a nice fat parcel
you are,' she murmured in his delighted ear. 'Come on, my
love.'

'Matthew's not your love,' said Lorna. '*I'm* your love.
You say, C'mon love, to *me*.'

'You're *both* my loves,' said Frances.

The baby was shaking with eagerness, and pouted his
mouth as she pulled her shirt up. The little girl sat down
beside her, pulled up her own teeshirt and applied a teddy
bear to her nipple. She grinned at her mother.

Frances looked down at Matthew's head, which was
shaped like a brick or a small wholemeal loaf, and remembered again how it had come down through the middle of
her. She was trying very hard to lose her awareness of this
fact, but it would keep re-presenting itself.

'D'you know,' said Lorna, free hand held palm upwards,
hyphen eyebrows lifting, 'd'you know, I was sucking my
thumb when I was coming downstairs, mum, mum, then
my foot slipped and my thumb came out of my mouth.'

'Well, that's very interesting, Lorna,' said Frances.

Two minutes later, Lorna caught the baby's head a ringing smack and ran off. Jonathan watched as Frances lunged clumsily after her, the baby jouncing at her breast, her stained and crumpled shirt undone, her hair a bird's nest, her face craggy with fatigue, and found himself dubbing the tableau, Portrait of rural squalor in the manner of William Hogarth. He bent to put on his shoes, stuck his right foot in first then pulled it out as though bitten.

'What's *that*,' he said in tones of profound disgust. He held his shoe in front of Frances' face.

'It looks like baby sick,' she said. 'Don't look at me. It's not my fault.'

'It's all so bloody *basic*,' said Jonathan, breathing hard, hopping off towards the kitchen.

'If you think that's basic, try being me,' muttered Frances. 'You don't know what basic *means*.'

'Daddy put his foot in Matthew's sick,' commented Lorna, laughing heartily.

AT CERNE ABBAS they stood and stared across at the chalky white outline of the Iron-Age giant cut into the green hill.

'It's enormous, isn't it,' said Frances.

'Do you remember when we went to stand on it?' said Jonathan. 'On that holiday in Child Okeford five years ago?'

'Of course,' said Frances. She saw the ghosts of their frisky former selves running around the giant's limbs and up onto his phallus. Nostalgia filled her eyes and stabbed her smartly in the guts.

'The woman riding high above with bright hair flapping free,' quoted Jonathan. 'Will you be able to grow *your* hair again?'

'Yes, yes. Don't look at me like that, though. I know I look like hell.'

A month before this boy was born, Frances had had her hair cut short. Her head had looked like a pea on a drum. It still did. With each pregnancy, her looks had hurtled five years on. She had started using sentences beginning, 'When I was young.' Ah, youth! Idleness! Sleep! How pleasant it had been to play the centre of her own stage. And how disorientating was this overnight demotion from Brünnhilde to spear-carrier.

'What's that,' said Lorna. 'That *thing*.'

'It's a giant,' said Frances.

'Like in Jacknabeanstork?'

'Yes.'

'But what's that *thing*. That thing on the giant.'

'It's the giant's thing.'

'Is it his stick thing?'

'Yes.'

'My baby budder's got a stick thing.'

'Yes.'

'But I haven't got a stick thing.'

'No.'

'Daddy's got a stick thing.'

'Yes.'

'But *Mummy* hasn't got a stick thing. We're the same, Mummy.'

She beamed and put her warm paw in Frances'.

'YOU CAN'T SEE round without an appointment,' said the keeper of Hardy's cottage. 'You should have telephoned.'

'We did,' bluffed Jonathan. 'There was no answer.'

'When was that?'

'Twenty to ten this morning.'

'Hmph. I was over sorting out some trouble at Clouds Hill. T. E. Lawrence's place. All right, you can go through. But keep them under control, won't you.'

They moved slowly through the low-ceilinged rooms, whispering to impress the importance of good behaviour on Lorna.

'This is the room where he was born,' said Jonathan, at the head of the stairs.

'Do you remember from when we visited last time?' said Frances slowly. 'It's coming back to me. He was his mother's first child, she nearly died in labour, then the doctor thought the baby was dead and threw him into a basket while he looked after the mother. But the midwife noticed he was breathing.'

'Then he carried on till he was eighty-seven,' said Jonathan.

They clattered across the old chestnut floorboards, on into another little bedroom with deep thick-walled windowseats.

'Which one's your favourite now?' asked Frances.

'Oh, still *Jude the Obscure*, I think,' said Jonathan. 'The tragedy of unfulfilled aims. Same for anyone first generation at university.'

'Poor Jude, laid low by pregnancy,' said Frances. 'Another victim of biology as destiny.'

'Don't *talk*, you two,' said Lorna.

'At least Sue and Jude aimed for friendship as well as all the other stuff,' said Jonathan.

'Unfortunately, all the other stuff made friendship impossible, didn't it,' said Frances.

'Don't *talk*!' shouted Lorna.

'Don't shout!' said Jonathan. Lorna fixed him with a calculating blue eye and produced an ear-splitting scream. The baby jerked in his arms and started to howl.

'Hardy didn't have children, did he,' said Jonathan above the din. 'I'll take them outside, I've seen enough. You stay up here a bit longer if you want to.'

Frances stood alone in the luxury of the empty room and shuddered. She moved around the furniture and thought fond savage thoughts of silence in the cloisters of a convent, a blessed place where all was monochrome and non-viscous. Sidling up unprepared to a mirror on the wall she gave a yelp at her reflection. The skin was the colour and texture of pumice stone, the grim jaw set like a lion's muzzle. And the eyes, the eyes far back in the skull were those of a herring three days dead.

Jonathan was sitting with the baby on his lap by a row of lupins and marigolds, reading to Lorna from a newly acquired guide book.

'When Thomas was a little boy he knelt down one day in a field and began eating grass to see what it was like to be a sheep.'

'What did the sheep say?' asked Lorna.

'The sheep said, er, so now you know.'

'And what else?'

'Nothing else.'

'Why?'

'What do you mean, why?'

'*Why?*'

'Look,' he said when he saw Frances. 'I've bought a copy of *Jude the Obscure* too, so we can read to each other when we've got a spare moment.'

'Spare moment!' said Frances. 'But how lovely you look with the children at your knees, the roses round the cottage door. How I would like to be the one coming back from work to find you all bathed and brushed, and a hot meal in the oven and me unwinding with a glass of beer in a hard-earned crusty glow of righteousness.'

'*I don't get that,*' Jonathan reminded her.

'That's because I can't do it properly yet,' said Frances. 'But, still, I wish it could be the other way round. Or at least, half and half. And I was thinking, what a cheesy business Eng. Lit. is, all those old men peddling us lies about life and love. They never get as far as this bit, do they.'

'Thomas 1840, Mary 1842, Henry 1851, Kate 1856,' read Jonathan. 'Perhaps we could have two more.'

'I'd kill myself,' said Frances.

'What's the matter with you?' said Jonathan to Matthew, who was grizzling and struggling in his arms.

'I think I'll have to feed him again,' said Frances.

'What, already?'

'It's nearly two hours.'

'Hey, you can't do that here,' said the custodian, appearing at their bench like a bad fairy. 'We have visitors from all over the world here. Particularly from Japan. The Japanese are a very modest people. And they don't come all this way to see THAT sort of thing.'

'It's a perfectly natural function,' said Jonathan.

'So's going to the lavatory!' said the custodian.

'Is it all right if I take him over behind those holly-hocks?' asked Frances. 'Nobody could possibly see me there. It's just, in this heat he won't feed if I try to do it in the car.'

The custodian snorted and stumped back to his lair.

Above the thatched roof the huge and gentle trees rustled hundreds of years' worth of leaves in the pre-storm stir. Frances shrugged, heaved Matthew up so that his socks dangled on her hastily covered breast, and retreated to the hollyhock screen. As he fed, she observed the green-tinged light in the garden, the crouching cat over in a bed of limp snapdragons, and registered the way things look before an onslaught, defenceless and excited, tense and passive. She thought of Bathsheba Everdene at bay, crouching in the bed of ferns.

When would she be able to read a book again? In life before the children, she had read books on the bus, in the bathroom, in bed, while eating, through television, under radio noise, in cafés. Now, if she picked one up, Lorna shouted, 'Stop reading, Mummy,' and pulled her by the nose until she was looking into her small cross face.

Jonathan meandered among the flowerbeds flicking through *Jude the Obscure*, Lorna snapping and shouting at his heels. He was ignoring her, and Frances could see he had already bought a tantrum since Lorna was now entered into one of the stretches of the day when her self-control flagged and fled. She sighed like Cassandra but didn't have the energy to nag as he came towards her.

'Listen to this,' Jonathan said, reading from *Jude the Obscure*. '"Time and circumstance, which enlarge the views of most men, narrow the views of women almost invariably."'

'Is it any bloody wonder,' said Frances.

'I want you to *play* with me, Daddy,' whined Lorna.

'Bit of a sexist remark, though, eh?' said Jonathan.

'Bit of a sexist process, you twit,' said Frances.

Lorna gave Matthew a tug which almost had him on the ground. Torn from his milky trance, he quavered, horror-struck, for a moment, then, as Frances braced herself, squared his mouth and started to bellow.

Jonathan seized Lorna, who became as rigid as a steel girder, and swung her high up above his head. The air was split with screams.

'Give her to me,' mouthed Frances across the awe-inspiring noise.

'She's a noise terrorist,' shouted Jonathan.

'Oh, please let me have her,' said Frances.

'You shouldn't give in to her,' said po-faced Jonathan, handing over the flailing parcel of limbs.

'Lorna, sweetheart, look at me,' said Frances.

'Naaoow!' screamed Lorna.

'Shshush,' said Frances. 'Tell me what's the matter.'

Lorna poured out a flood of incomprehensible complaint, raving like a chimpanzee. At one point, Frances deciphered, 'You always feed MATTHEW.'

'You should *love* your baby brother,' interposed Jonathan.

'You can't tell her she *ought* to love anybody,' snapped Frances. 'You can tell her she must behave properly, but you can't tell her what to feel. Look, Lorna,' she continued, exercising her favourite distraction technique. 'The old man is coming back. He's cross with us. Let's run away.'

Lorna turned her streaming eyes and nose in the direction of the custodian, who was indeed hotfooting it across the lawn towards them, and tugged her mother's hand.

The two of them lurched off, Frances buttoning herself up as she went.

THEY FOUND THEMSELVES corralled into a cement area at the back of the Smuggler's Arms, a separate space where young family pariahs like themselves could bicker over fish fingers. Waiting at the bar, Jonathan observed the comfortable tables inside, with their noisy laughing groups of the energetic elderly tucking into plates of gammon and plaice and profiteroles.

'Just look at them,' said the crumpled man beside him, who was paying for a trayload of Fanta and baked beans. 'Skipped the war. Nil unemployment, home in time for tea.' He took a great gulp of lager. 'Left us to scream in our prams, screwed us up good and proper. When our kids come along, what happens? You don't see the grandparents for dust, that's what happens. They're all off out enjoying themselves, kicking the prams out the way with their Hush Puppies, spending the money like there's no tomorrow.'

Jonathan grunted uneasily. He still could not get used to the way he found himself involved in intricate conversations with complete strangers, incisive, frank, frequently desperate, whenever he was out with Frances and the children. It used to be only women who talked like that, but now, among parents of young children, it seemed to have spread across the board.

Frances was trying to allow the baby to finish his recent

interrupted feed as discreetly as she could, while watching Lorna move inquisitively among the various family groups. She saw her go up to a haggard woman changing a nappy beside a trough of geraniums.

'Your baby's got a stick thing like my baby budder.' Lorna's piercing voice soared above the babble. 'I haven't got a stick thing cos I'm a little gel. My mummy's got fur on her potim.'

Frances abandoned their table and made her way over to the geranium trough.

'Sorry if she's been getting in your way,' she said to the woman.

'Chatty, isn't she,' commented the woman unenthusiastically. 'How many have you got?'

'Two. I'm shattered.'

'The third's the killer.'

'That's my baby budder,' said Lorna, pointing at Matthew.

'He's a big boy,' said the woman. 'What did he weigh when he came out?'

'Ten pounds.'

'Just like a turkey,' she said, disgustingly, and added, 'Mine were whoppers too. They all had to be cut out of me, one way or the other.'

BY THE TIME they returned to the cottage, the air was weighing on them like blankets. Each little room was an envelope of pressure. Jonathan watched Frances collapse into a chair with children all over her. Before babies, they had been well matched. Then, with the arrival of their first child, it had been a case of Woman Overboard. He'd watched, ineffectual but sympathetic, trying to keep her cheerful as she clung on to the edge of the raft, holding out weevil-free biscuits for her to nibble, and all the time she gazed at him with appalled eyes. Just as they had grown used to this state, difficult but tenable, and were even managing to start hauling her on board again an inch at a time, just as she had her elbows up on the raft and they were congratulating themselves with a kiss, well, along came the second baby in a great slap of a wave that drove her off the raft altogether. Now she was out there in the sea while he bobbed up and down, forlorn but more or less dry, and watched her face between its two satellites dwindling to the size of a fist, then to a plum, and at last to a mere speck of plankton. He dismissed it from his mind.

'I'll see if I can get the shopping before the rain starts,' he said, dashing out to the car again, knee-deep in cow parsley.

'You really should keep an eye on how much bread we've got left,' he called earnestly as he unlocked the car. 'It won't be *my* fault if I'm struck by lightning.'

There was the crumpling noise of thunder, and silver cracked the sky. Frances stood in the doorway holding the baby, while Lorna clawed and clamoured at her to be held in her free arm.

'Oh, Lorna,' said Frances, hit by a wave of bone-aching

fatigue. 'You're too heavy, my sweet.' She closed the cottage door as Lorna started to scream, and stood looking down at her with something like fear. She saw a miniature fee-fi-fo-fum creature working its way through a pack of adults, chewing them up and spitting their bones out.

'Come into the back room, Lorna, and I'll read you a book while I feed Matthew.'

'I don't want to.'

'Why don't you want to?'

'I just don't want to.'

'Can't you tell me why?'

'Do you know, I just don't WANT to!'

'All right, *dear*. I'll feed him on my own then.'

'NO!' screamed Lorna. 'PUT HIM IN DA BIN! HE'S RUBBISH!'

'Don't scream, you little beast,' said Frances hopelessly, while the baby squared his mouth and joined in the noise.

Lorna turned the volume up and waited for her to crack. Frances walked off to the kitchen with the baby and quickly closed the door. Lorna gave a howl of rage from the other side and started to smash at it with fists and toys. Children were petal-skinned ogres, Frances realised, callous and whimsical, holding autocratic sway over lower, larger vassals like herself.

There followed a punishing stint of ricochet work, where Frances let the baby cry while she comforted Lorna; let Lorna shriek while she soothed the baby; put Lorna down for her nap and was called back three times before she gave up and let her follow her destructively around; bathed the baby after he had sprayed himself, Lorna and the bathroom with urine during the nappy-changing process; sat on the closed lavatory seat and fed the baby while Lorna chattered in the bath which she had demanded in the wake of the baby's bath.

She stared at Lorna's slim silver body, exquisite in the water, graceful as a Renaissance statuette.

'Shall we see if you'd like a little nap after your bath?' she suggested hopelessly, for only if Lorna rested would she be able to rest, and then only if Matthew was asleep or at least not ready for a feed.

'No,' said Lorna, off-hand but firm.

'Oh thank God,' said Frances as she heard the car door slam outside. Jonathan was back. It was like the arrival of the cavalry. She wrapped Lorna in a towel and they scrambled downstairs. Jonathan stood puffing on the doormat. Outside was a mid-afternoon twilight, the rain as thick as turf and drenching so that it seemed to leave no room for air between its stalks.

'You're wet, Daddy,' said Lorna, fascinated.

'There were lumps of ice coming down like tennis balls,' he marvelled.

'Here, have this towel,' said Frances, and Lorna span off naked as a sprite from its folds to dance among the chairs and tables while thunder crashed in the sky with the cumbersomeness of heavy furniture falling down uncarpeted stairs.

'*S'il vous plaît,*' said Frances to Jonathan. '*Dansez, jouez avec le petit diable, cette fille. Il faut que je* get Matthew down for a nap, she just wouldn't let me. *Je suis tellement* shattered.'

'Mummymummymummy,' Lorna chanted as she caught some inkling of this, but Jonathan threw the towel over her and they started to play ghosts.

'MY LITTLE FAT boy,' she whispered at last, squeezing his strong thighs. '*Hey*, fatty boomboom, *sweet* sugar dumpling. It's not fair, is it? I'm never alone with you. You're getting the rough end of the stick just now, aren't you.'

She punctuated this speech with growling kisses, and his hands and feet waved like warm pink roses. She sat him up and stroked the fine duck tail of hair on his baby bull neck. Whenever she tried to fix his essence, he wriggled off into mixed metaphor. And so she clapped his cloud cheeks and revelled in his nest of smiles; she blew raspberries into the crease of his neck and onto his astounded hardening stomach, forcing lion-deep chuckles from him.

She was dismayed at how she had to treat him like some sort of fancy man to spare her daughter's feelings, affecting nonchalance when Lorna was around. She would fall on him for a quick mad embrace if the little girl left the room for a moment, only to spring apart guiltily at the sound of the returning Start-rites.

The serrated teeth of remorse bit into her. In late pregnancy she had been so sandbagged that she had had barely

And so she clapped his cloud cheeks and revelled in his nest of smiles

enough energy to crawl through the day, let alone reciprocate Lorna's incandescent two-year-old passion.

'She thought I'd come back to her as before once the baby arrived,' she said aloud. 'But I haven't.'

The baby was making the wrangling noise which led to unconsciousness. Then he fell asleep like a door closing. She carried him carefully to his basket, a limp solid parcel against her bosom, the lashes long and wet on his cheeks, lower lip out in a soft semicircle. She put him down and he lay, limbs thrown wide, spatchcocked.

AFTER THE HOLIDAY, Jonathan would be back at the office with his broad quiet desk and filter coffee while she, she would have to submit to a fate worse than death, drudging round the flat to Lorna's screams and the baby's regurgitations and her own sore eyes and body aching to the throb of next door's Heavy Metal.

The trouble with prolonged sleep deprivation was that it produced the same coarsening side effects as alcoholism. She was rotten with self-pity, swarming with irritability and despair.

When she heard Jonathan's step on the stairs, she realised that he must have coaxed Lorna to sleep at last. She looked forward to his face, but when he came into the room and she opened her mouth to speak, all that came out were toads and vipers.

'I'm smashed up,' she said. 'I'm never alone. The baby guzzles me and Lorna eats me up. I can't ever go out because I've always got to be there for the children, but you flit in and out like a humming bird. You need me to be always there, to peck at and pull at and answer the door. I even have to feed the cat.'

'I take them out for a walk on Sunday afternoons,' he protested.

'But it's like a favour, and it's only a couple of hours, and I can't use the time to read, I always have to change the sheets or make a meatloaf.'

'For pity's sake. I'm tired too.'

'Sorry,' she muttered. 'Sorry. Sorry. But I don't feel like me any more. I've turned into some sort of oven.'

They lay on the bed and held each other.

'Did you know what Hardy called *Jude the Obscure* to begin with?' he whispered in her ear. '*The Simpletons*. And the Bishop of Wakefield burnt it on a bonfire when it was published.'

'You've been reading!' said Frances accusingly. '*When* did you read!'

'I just pulled in by the side of the road for five minutes. Only for five minutes. It's such a good book. I'd completely forgotten that Jude had three children.'

'*Three?*' said Frances. 'Are you sure?'

'Don't you remember Jude's little boy who comes back from Australia?' said Jonathan. 'Don't you remember little Father Time?'

'Yes,' said Frances. 'Something very nasty happens to him, doesn't it?'

She took the book and flicked through until she reached the page where little Time and his siblings are discovered by their mother hanging from a hook inside a cupboard door, the note at their feet reading, 'Done because we are too menny.'

'What a wicked old man Hardy was!' she said, incredulous. 'How *dare* he!' She started to cry.

'You're too close to them,' murmured Jonathan. 'You should cut off from them a bit.'

'How *can* I?' sniffed Frances. '*Somebody*'s got to be devoted to them. And it's not going to be you because you know I'll do it for you.'

'They're yours, though, aren't they, because of that,' said Jonathan. 'They'll love you best.'

'They're *not* mine. They belong to themselves. But I'm not allowed to belong to *my* self any more.'

'It's not easy for me either.'

'I know it isn't, sweetheart. But at least you're still allowed to be your own man.'

They fell on each other's necks and mingled maudlin tears.

'It's so awful,' sniffed Frances. 'We may never have another.'

They fell asleep.

WHEN THEY WOKE, the landscape was quite different. Not only had the rain stopped, but it had rinsed the air free of oppression. Drops of water hung like lively glass on every leaf and blade. On their way down to the beach, the path was hedged with wet hawthorn, the fiercely spiked branches glittering with green-white flowers.

The late sun was surprisingly strong. It turned the distant moving strokes of the waves to gold bars, and dried salt patterns onto the semi-precious stones which littered the shore. As Frances unbuckled Lorna's sandals, she pointed out to her translucent pieces of chrysoprase and rose quartz in amongst the more ordinary egg-shaped pebbles. Then she kicked off her own shoes and walked wincingly to the water's edge. The sea was casting lacy white shawls onto the stones, and drawing them back with a sigh.

She looked behind her and saw Lorna building a pile of pebbles while Jonathan made the baby more comfortable in his pushchair. A little way ahead was a dinghy, and she could see the flickering gold veins on its white shell thrown up by the sun through moving seawater, and the man standing in it stripped to the waist. She walked towards it, then past it, and as she walked on, she looked out to sea and was aware of her eyeballs making internal adjustments to the new distance which was being demanded of them, as though they had forgotten how to focus on a long view. She felt an excited bubble of pleasure expanding her ribcage, so that she had to take little sighs of breath, warm and fresh and salted, and prevent herself from laughing aloud.

After some while she reached the far end of the beach.

Slowly she wheeled, like a hero on the cusp of anagnorisis, narrowing her eyes to make out the little group round the pushchair. Of course it was satisfying and delightful to see Jonathan – she supposed it *was* Jonathan? – lying with the fat mild baby on his stomach while their slender elf of a daughter skipped around him. It was part of it. But not the point of it. The concentrated delight was there to start with. She had not needed babies and their pleased-to-be-aliveness to tell her this.

She started to walk back, this time higher up the beach in the shade of cliffs which held prehistoric snails and traces of dinosaur. I've done it, she thought, and I'm still alive. She took her time, dawdling with deliberate pleasure, as though she were carrying a full glass of milk and might not spill a drop.

'I thought you'd done a Sergeant Troy,' said Jonathan. 'Disappeared out to sea and abandoned us.'

'Would I do a thing like that,' she said, and kissed him lightly beside his mouth.

Matthew reached up from his arms and tugged her hair.

'When I saw you over there by the rock pools you looked just as you used to,' said Jonathan. 'Just the same girl.'

'I am not just as I was, however,' said Frances. 'I am no longer the same girl.'

The sky, which had been growing more dramatic by the minute, was now a florid stagey empyrean, the sea a soundless blaze beneath it. Frances glanced at the baby, and saw how the sun made an electric fleece of the down on his head. She touched it lightly with the flat of her hand as though it might burn her.

'Isn't it mind-boggling,' said Jonathan. 'Isn't it impossible to take in that when we were last on this beach, these two were thin air. Or less. They're so solid now that I almost can't believe there was a time before them, and it's only been a couple of years.'

'What?' said Lorna. '*What* did you say?'

'Daddy was just commenting on the mystery of human existence,' said Frances, scooping her up and letting her perch on her hip. She felt the internal chassis, her skeleton and musculature, adjust to the extra weight with practised efficiency. To think, she marvelled routinely, to think that this great heavy child grew in the centre of my body. But the surprise of the idea had started to grow blunt, worn down by its own regular self-contemplation.

'Look, Lorna,' she said. 'Do you see how the sun is making our faces orange?'

In the flood of flame-coloured light their flesh turned to coral.

Early One Morning

SOMETIMES THEY WERE QUIET IN the car and sometimes they talked.

'Mum.'

'Yes?'

'Can I swear one time in the day? If I don't swear in the others?'

'Why?'

'In the morning. When you come and wake me. Can I say, "Bollocks"?'

'No.'

He's the only person in the world who listens to me and does what I tell him, thought Zoe. That morning when she had gone to wake him he had groaned, unconscious, spontaneous – 'Already?' Then he had reached up from his pillow to put strong sleepy arms round her neck.

For these years of her life she was spending more time alone with her boy, side by side in the car, than with anybody else, certainly far more than with her husband, thirty times more, unless you counted the hours asleep. There was the daily business of showing herself to him and to no one else; thinking aloud, urging each other on in the hunt for swimming things, car keys, maths books; yawning like cats, as they had to leave soon after seven if they were going to get to school on time. Then they might tell each other the remains of a dream during the first twenty-five minutes on the way to Freda's house, or they might sit in comfortable silence, or sometimes they would talk.

This morning when she had pointed out the sun rising in the east to hit the windscreen and blind them with its flood of flashy light, her nine-year-old boy had scoffed at her and said the earth twizzled on its axis and went round the sun, and how she, his mother, was as bad as the ancient Egyptians, how they sacrificed someone to Ra if the sun went in and finished off everybody when there was an eclipse. It's running out, this hidden time (thought Zoe). You're on your own at eleven, goes the current unwritten transport protocol, but until then you need a minder. Less than two years to go.

'I remember when I was at school,' she'd said that morning while they waited for the Caedmon Hill lights. 'It seemed to go on forever. Time goes by slowly at school. Slowly. Slowly. Then, after you're about thirty, it goes faster and faster.'

'Why?' asked George.

'I don't know,' she said. 'Maybe it's because after that you somehow know that there'll be a moment for you when there isn't any more.'

'Ooh-ah!'

Then he looked at a passing cyclist and commented, 'Big arse.'

'George!' she said, shocked.

'It just slipped out,' he said, apologetic, adult. 'You know, like when that man in the white van wouldn't let you in and you said, "Bastard."'

SOMETIMES THIS DAILY struggle and inching along through filthy air thick with the thwarted rage of ten thousand drivers gave her, Zoe, pause. It took forty-five minutes to travel the two and three-quarter miles to George's school (Sacred Heart thanks to his father's faith springing anew, rather than Hereward the Wake half a mile along), and forty-five minutes for her to come back alone in the empty car. In the afternoons it was the same, but the other way round of course, setting off a little after two-thirty and arriving back well after four. There was no train. To do the journey by bus, they would have had to catch a 63A then change and wait for a 119 at Sollers Junction. They had tried this, and it had doubled the journey time. Why couldn't there be school buses for everyone as there were in America, the mothers asked each other. Nobody knew why not, but apparently there couldn't. They were just about able to walk it in the same time as it took in the car, and they had tried this too, carrying rucksacks of homework and packed lunch and sports equipment through the soup of fumes pumped out by crawling cars. Add wind and

rain, and the whole idea of pavement travel looked positively quixotic.

'I'll get it, Mum,' said George, as her mobile beeped its
receipt of a text.

It was from her friend Amy, whose husband had recently
left her for one of his students.

– If I say anything, he gets very angry (Amy had told her
on their last phone call); he doesn't allow me to be angry.

– But he was the one to leave you.

– Yes. But now he's furious with me, he hates me.

– Do you still love him?

– I don't recognise him. I can't believe this man I ate
with and slept beside for fifteen years is capable of being
so cold and so, yes, cruel.

Is it true, then, that women can take grief as grief
(thought Zoe), but men refuse to do that, they have to convert it into diesel in order to deal with it, all the loss and
pain converted into rage?

Her husband had looked around and said, Why don't
you do like Sally and Chitra and Mo, organise an au pair,
pay for a few driving lessons if necessary, hand it over to
someone who'll be glad of the job. She, Zoe, had thought
about this, but she'd already been through it all once
before, with Joe and Theresa, who were both now at secondary school. She'd done the sums, gone through the
interviews in her imagination, considered the no-claims
bonus; she'd counted the years for which her work time
would be cut in half, she'd set off the loss of potential

income against the cost of childcare, and she'd bitten the bullet. 'It's your choice,' said Patrick. And it was.

'You're a loser, Mum,' her daughter Theresa had told her on her return from a recent careers convention. But she wasn't. She'd done it all now – she'd been through the whole process of hanging on to her old self, carving out patches of time, not relinquishing her work, then partly letting go in order to be more with the children, his work taking precedence over hers as generally seemed to be the case when the parents were still together. Unless the woman earned more, which opened up a whole new can of modern worms. Those long-forgotten hours and days were now like nourishing leaf mould round their roots. Let the past go (sang Zoe beneath her breath), time to move on; her own built-in obsolescence could make her feel lively rather than sad. And perhaps the shape of life would be like an hour-glass, clear and wide to begin with, narrowing down to the tunnel of the middle years, then flaring wide again before the sands ran out.

'Mum, can you test me on my words?' asked George. He was doing a French taster term, taking it seriously because he wanted to outstrip his friend Mick who was better than him at maths.

'Well I'm not supposed to,' said Zoe. 'But we're not moving. Here, put it on my lap and keep your eye open for when the car in front starts to move.'

When I was starting out, leaving babies till after thirty was seen as leaving it late (thought Zoe). Over thirty was the time of fade for women, loss of bloom and all that. Now you're expected to be still a girl at forty-two – slim, active, up for it. But if I hadn't done it, had Joe at twenty-six and Theresa at twenty-eight, hammered away at work and sweated blood in pursuit of good childminders, nurseries, au pairs, you name it, and finally, five years later when George came along, slowed down for a while at least; then I wouldn't know why so many women are the way they are. Stymied at some point; silenced somewhere. Stalled. Or, merely delayed?

'It's who, when, where, how and all that sort of thing,' said George. 'I'll tell you how I remember *quand*. I think of the Sorcerer's Apprentice, because you know he had a WAND, rhymes with *quand*, and then he goes away with all those buckets of water and then WHEN he comes back . . . Get it? WHEN he comes back! That's how it stays in my mind. And *qui* is the KEY in a door and you answer it and who is there? WHO! I thought of all that myself, yeah. Course. And *où* is monkeys in the rainforest. Oo oo oo. Hey look, it's moving.'

They crawled forward, even getting into second gear for a few seconds, then settled again into stasis.

'Why the rainforest?' asked Zoe. 'Monkeys in the rainforest?'

'Because, WHERE are they?' he asked. 'Where *are* they, the trees in the rainforest. That's what the monkeys want to know, oo oo oo. Cos they aren't there any more, the trees in the rainforest.'

'You remember everything they teach you at school, don't you,' said Zoe admiringly.

'Just about,' said George with a pleased smile. 'Mum, I don't want you to die until I'm grown up.'

There was a pause.

'But I don't want to die *before* you,' he added.

'No, I don't want that either,' said Zoe.

This boy remembers every detail of every unremarkable day (thought Zoe); he's not been alive that long and he's got acres of lovely empty space in his memory bank. Whereas I've been alive for ages and it's got to the point where my mind is saying it already has enough on its shelves, it just can't be bothered to store something new unless it's *really* worth remembering.

I climb the stairs and forget what I'm looking for. I forgot to pick up Natasha last week when I'd promised her mother, and I had to do a three-point turn in the middle of Ivanhoe Avenue and go back for her and just hope that none of the children already in the car would snitch on me. But that's nothing new. I can't remember a thing about the last decade or so, she told other mothers, and they agreed, it was a blur, a blank; they had photographs to prove it had happened, but they couldn't remember it themselves. She, Zoe, saw her memory banks as having shrivelled for lack of sleep's welcome rain; she brooded over the return of those refreshing showers and the rehydration of her pot-noodle bundles of memories, and how (one day) the past would plump into action, swelling with import, newly alive.

When she was old and free and in her second adolescence, she would sleep in royally, till midday or one. Yet old people cannot revisit that country, they report; they wake and listen to the dawn chorus after four or five threadbare hours, and long for the old three-ply youth-giving slumber.

They had reached Freda's house, and Zoe stopped the car to let George out. He went off to ring the bell and wait while Freda and also Harry, who was in on this lift, gathered their bags and shoes and coats. It was too narrow a road to hover in, or rather Zoe did not have the nerve to make other people queue behind her while she waited for her passengers to arrive. This morning she shoehorned the car into a minute space three hundred yards away, proudly parking on a sixpence.

What's truly radical now though (thought Zoe, rereading the text from Amy as she waited) is to imagine a man and woman having children and living happily together, justice and love prevailing, self-respect on both sides, each making sure the other flourishes as well as the children. The windscreen blurred as it started to rain. If not constantly, she modified, then taking turns. Where *are* they?

But this wave of divorces (she thought), the couples who'd had ten or fifteen years or more of being together, her feeling was that often it wasn't as corny as it seemed to be in Amy's case – being left for youth. When she, Zoe, looked closely, it was more to do with the mercurial resentment quotient present in every marriage having risen to the top of the thermometer. It was more to do with how

When she was old and free and in her second adolescence, she would sleep in royally, till midday or one the marriage had turned out, now it was this far down the line. Was one of the couple thriving and satisfied, with the other restless or foundering? Or perhaps the years had spawned a marital Black Dog, where one of them dragged the other down with endless gloom or bad temper or censoriousness and refused to be comforted, ever, and also held the other responsible for their misery.

There had been a scattering of bust-ups during the first two or three years of having babies, and then things seemed to settle down. This was the second wave, a decade or so on, a wild tsunami of divorce as children reached adolescence and parents left youth behind. The third big wave was set to come when the children left home. She, Zoe, had grown familiar with the process simply by listening. First came the shock, the vulnerability and hurt; then the nastiness (particularly about money) with accompanying baffled incredulity; down on to indignation at the exposure of unsuspected talents for treachery, secretiveness, two-faced liardom; falling last of all into scalding grief or adamantine hatred. Only last week her next door neighbour, forced to put the house on the market, had hissed at her over the fence, 'I hope he gets cancer and dies.' Though when it came to showing round prospective purchasers, the estate agents always murmured the word 'amicable' as reassurance; purchasers wanted to hear it was amicable rather than that other divorce word, acrimonious.

She peered into the driver's mirror and saw them trudging towards her with their usual heaps of school luggage. It was still well before eight and, judging herself more bleached and craggy than usual, she added some colour just as they got to the car.

'Lipstick, hey,' said George, taking the front seat. The other two shuffled themselves and their bags into the back.

'I used to wear make-up,' said Zoe. 'Well, a bit. When I was younger. I really enjoyed it.'

'Why don't you now?' asked Freda. Freda's mother did, of course. Her mother was thirty-eight rather than forty-two. It made a difference, this slide over to the other side, reflected Zoe, and also one was tireder.

'Well, I still do if I feel like it,' she said, starting the car and indicating. She waited for a removal van to lumber along and shave past. 'But I don't do it every day like brushing my teeth. It's just another thing.' Also, nobody but you lot is going to see me so why would I, she added silently, churlishly.

She was aware of the children thinking, what? *Why* not? Women *should* wear make-up. Freda in particular would be on the side of glamour and looking one's best at all times.

'We had a Mexican student staying with us once,' she told them, edging onto the main road. 'And at first she would spend ages looking after her long glossy hair, and more ages brushing make-up onto her eyelids and applying that gorgeous glassy lipgloss. But after a while she stopped, and she looked just like the rest of us – she said to me that it was a lovely holiday after Mexico City, where she really couldn't go outside without the full works or everybody would stare at her. So she kept it for parties or times when she felt like putting it on, after that.'

'Women look better with make-up,' commented Harry from the back. Harry's mother dropped him off at Freda's on Tuesday and Thursday mornings, and, in the spirit of hawk-eyed reciprocity on which the whole fragile school-run ecosystem was founded, Zoe collected George from Harry's house on Monday and Wednesday afternoons, which cut *that* journey in half.

'Well I'm always going to wear make-up when I'm older,' said Freda.

'Women used to set their alarm clocks an hour early so they could put on their false eyelashes and lid liner and all that,' said Zoe. 'Imagine being frightened of your husband seeing your bare face!'

There was silence as they considered this, grudging assent, even. But the old advice was still doing the rounds, Zoe had noticed, for women to listen admiringly to men and not to laugh at them if they wanted to snare one of their very own. Give a man respect for being higher caste than you, freer, more powerful. And men, what was it men wanted? Was it true they only wanted a cipher? That a woman should not expect admiration from a man for any other qualities than physical beauty or selflessness? Surely not. If this were the case, why live with such a poor sap if you could scrape your own living?

'Do you like Alex?' asked Harry. 'I don't. I hate Alex, he whines and he's mean and he cries and he whinges all the time. But I pretend I like him, because I want him to like me.'

There was no comment from the other three. They were sunk in early-morning torpor, staring at the static traffic around them.

'I despite him,' said Harry.

'You can't say that,' said Freda. 'It's despise.'

'That's what I said,' said Harry.

George snorted.

It was nothing short of dangerous and misguided (thought Zoe) not to keep earning, even if it wasn't very much and you were doing all the domestic and emotional work as well, for the sake of keeping the marital Black Dog at bay. Otherwise if you spoke up it would be like biting the hand that fed you. Yes you wanted to be around (thought Zoe), to be an armoire, to make them safe as houses. But surrendering your autonomy for too long, subsumption without promise of future release, those weren't good for the health.

'I hate that feeling in the playground when I've bullied someone and then they start crying,' said Harry with candour.

'I don't like it if someone cries because of something I've said,' said Freda.

'I don't like it when there's a group of people and they're making someone cry,' said George over his shoulder. 'That makes me feel bad.'

'Oh I don't mind that,' said Harry. 'If it wasn't me that

made them cry. If it was other people, that's nothing to do with me.'

'No, but don't you feel bad when you see one person like that,' replied George, 'and everyone picking on them, if you don't, like, say something?'

'No,' said Harry. 'I don't care. As long as I'*m* not being nasty to them I don't feel bad at what's happening.'

'Oh,' said George, considering. 'I do.'

'Look at that car's number plate,' said Freda. 'The letters say XAN. XAN! XAN!'

'FWMM!' joined in Harry. 'FWMMFWMM! FWMMFWMMFWMM!'

'BGA,' growled George. 'BGA. Can you touch your nose with your tongue?'

Zoe stared out from the static car at the line of people waiting in the rain at a bus stop, and studied their faces. Time sinks into flesh (she mused), gradually sinks it. A look of distant bruising arrives, and also for some reason asymmetry. One eye sits higher than the other and the mouth looks crooked. We start to resemble cartoons or caricatures of ourselves. On cold days like today the effect can be quite trollish.

'Who would you choose to push off a cliff or send to prison or give a big hug?' George threw over his shoulder. 'Out of three – Peter Vallings—'

'Ugh, not Peter Vallings!' shrieked Freda in an ecstasy of disgust.

'Mrs Campbell. And – Mr Starling!'

'Mr Starling! Oh my God, Mr Starling,' said Harry, caught between spasms of distaste and delight. 'Yesterday he was wearing this top, yeah, he lets you see how many ripples he's got.'

Your skin won't stay with your flesh as it used to (thought Zoe); it won't move and follow muscle the way it did before. You turn, and there is a fan of creases however trim you are; yet once you were one of these young things at the bus stop, these over-eleven secondary school pupils. Why do we smile at adolescent boys, so unfinished, so lumpy (she wondered) but feel disturbed by this early beauty of the girls, who gleam with benefit, their hair smooth as glass or in rich ringlets, smiling big smiles and speaking up and nobody these days saying, 'Who do you think you are?' or 'You look like a prostitute.' It's not as if the boys won't catch up with a vengeance.

'I love my dog,' said Harry fiercely.

'Yes, he's a nice dog,' agreed Freda.

'I love my dog so much,' continued Harry, 'I would rather die than see my dog die.'

'*You* would rather die than your *dog*?' said George in disbelief.

'Yes! I love my dog! Don't you love *your* dog?'

'Yes. But . . .'

'You don't really love your dog. If you wouldn't die instead of him.'

Zoe bit her tongue. Her rule was, never join in. That way they could pretend she wasn't there. The sort of internal monologue she enjoyed these days came from being round older children, at their disposal but silent. She was able to dip in and out of her thoughts now with the freedom of a bird. Whereas it was true enough that no thought could take wing round the under-fives; what they needed was too constant and minute and demanding, you had to be out of the room in order to think and they needed you *in* the room.

When George walked beside her he liked to hold on to what he called her elbow flab. He pinched it till it held a separate shape. He was going to be tall. As high as my heart, she used to say last year, but he had grown since then; he came up to her shoulder now, this nine-year-old.

'Teenagers!' he'd said to her not long ago. 'When I turn thirteen I'll be horrible in one night. Covered in spots and rude to you and not talking. Jus' grunting.'

Where did he get all that from? The most difficult age for girls was fourteen, they now claimed, the parenting experts, while for boys it was nineteen. Ten more years then. Good.

'Would you like to be tall?' she'd asked him that time.

'Not very,' he'd said decisively. 'But I wouldn't like just to be five eight or something. I'd want to be taller than my wife.'

His *wife*! Some way down the corridor of the years, she saw his wife against the fading sun, her face in shade. Would his wife mind if she, Zoe, hugged him when they met? She might, she might well. More than the father giving away his daughter, the mother must hand over her son. Perhaps his *wife* would only allow them to shake hands. When he was little his hands had been like velvet, without knuckles or veins; he used to put his small warm hands up her cardigan sleeves when he was wheedling for something.

They were inching their way down Mordred Hill, some sort of delay having been caused by a juggernaut trying to back into an eighteenth-century alley centimetres too narrow for it. Zoe sighed with disbelief, then practised her deep breathing. Nothing you could do about it, no point in road rage, the country was stuffed to the gills with cars and that was all there was to it. She had taken the Civil Service exams after college and one of the questions had been, 'How would you arrange the transport system of this country?' At the time, being utterly wrapped up in cliometrics and dendrochronology, she had been quite unable to answer; but now, a couple of decades down the line, she felt fully qualified to write several thousand impassioned words, if not a thesis, on the subject.

But then if you believe in wives and steadfastness and heroic monogamy (thought Zoe, as the lorry cleared the space and the traffic began to flow again), how can you admit change? Her sister Valerie had described how she was making her husband read aloud each night in bed from *How to Rescue a Relationship*. When he protested, she pointed out that it was instead of going to a marriage guidance counsellor. Whoever wants to live must forget, Valerie had told her drily; that was the gist of it. She, Zoe,

wasn't sure that she would be able to take marriage guidance counselling seriously either, as she suspected it was
probably done mainly by women who were no longer
needed on the school run. It all seemed to be about
women needed and wanted, then not needed and not
wanted. She moved off in second gear.

No wonder there were gaggles of mothers sitting over
milky lattes all over the place from 8.40 a.m. They were
recovering from driving exclusively in the first two gears
for the last hour; they had met the school deadline and
now wanted some pleasure on the return run. Zoe preferred her own company at this time of the morning, and
also did not relish the conversation of such groups, which
tended to be fault-finding sessions on how Miss Scantle-
bury taught long division or post-mortems on reported
classroom injustices, bubblings-up of indignation and the
urge to interfere, still to be the main moving force in their
child's day. She needed a coffee though – a double mac-
chiato, to be precise – and she liked the café sensation of
being alone but in company, surrounded by tables of
huddled intimacies each hived off from the other, scraps of
conversation drifting in the air. Yesterday, she remembered, there had been those two women in baggy velour
tracksuits at the table nearest to her, very solemn.

'I feel rather protective towards him. The girls are very
provocative the way they dress now. He's thirteen.'

'Especially when you're surrounded by all these images.
Everywhere you go.'

'It's not a very nice culture.'

'No, it's not.'

And all around there had been that steady self-justificatory hum of women telling each other the latest version of themselves, their lives, punctuated with the occasional righteous cry as yet another patch of moral high ground was claimed. That's a real weakness (she thought, shaking her head), and an enemy of, of – whatever it is we're after. Amity, would you call it?

'Last year when we were in Cornwall we went out in a boat and we saw sharks,' said Harry.

'Sharks!' scoffed George. 'Ho yes. In *Cornwall*.'

'No, really,' insisted Harry.

'It's eels as well,' said Freda. 'I don't like them either.'

'Ooh no,' Harry agreed, shuddering.

'What about sea-snakes,' said George. 'They can swim into any hole in your body.'

The car fell silent as they absorbed this information.

'Where did you hear this?' asked Zoe suspiciously; she had her own reservations about Mr Starling.

'Mr Starling told us,' smirked George. 'If it goes in at your ear, you're dead because it sneaks into your brain. But if it goes up your . . .'

'What happens if it gets in up there?' asked Harry.

'If it gets in there, up inside you,' said George, 'you don't die but they have to take you to hospital and cut you open and pull it out.'

The talk progressed naturally from here to tapeworms.

'They hang on to you by hooks all the way down,' said Harry. 'You have to poison them, by giving the person enough to kill the worm but not them. Then the worm dies and the hooks get loose and the worm comes out. Either of your bottom or somehow they pull it through your mouth.'

'That's enough of that,' said Zoe at last. 'It's too early in the morning.'

They reached the road where the school was with five minutes to spare, and Zoe drew in to the kerb some way off while they decanted their bags and shoes and morning selves. Would George kiss her? She only got a kiss when they arrived if none of the boys in his class was around. He knew she wanted a kiss, and gave her a warning look. No, there was Sean McIlroy – no chance today.

They were gone. The car was suddenly empty, she sat unkissed, redundant, cast off like an old boot. 'Boohoo,' she murmured, her eyes blurring for a moment, and carefully adjusted her wing mirror for something to do.

Then George reappeared, tapping at the window, looking stern and furtive.

'I said I'd forgotten my maths book,' he muttered when she opened the car door, and, leaning across as though to pick up something from the seat beside her, smudged her cheek with a hurried – but (thought Zoe) unsurpassable – kiss.

© Celia Clark

HELEN SIMPSON writes sharply funny, brilliantly observed short stories, and with each of her six collections, one published every five years since *Four Bare Legs in a Bed* in 1990, she has been hailed as a 'contemporary maestro of the short story' (*Sunday Times*) and 'a wry, humane and brilliant observer of our peculiar condition' (*Independent*). In the introduction to the Vintage Classics selection of her work, *A Bunch of Fives*, Simpson addresses the fact that many of her stories deal with 'baby stuff', pointing out there was very little in print about it when her earliest collections were published – another example of how her stories are ground-breaking while remaining rooted in every-day life. She has also said she is 'interested in how men and women (and children) live together. Or don't.'

Before writing her first stories, Helen Simpson was a staff writer at *Vogue* and published two cookery books. She lives in London, and her latest collection is *Cockfosters* (2015).

RECOMMENDED BOOKS BY HELEN SIMPSON:

Dear George
Hey Yeah Right Get a Life
Constitutional
A Bunch of Fives
In-Flight Entertainment

How do we survive Motherhood?

Language
XIAOLU GUO

VINTAGE MINIS

Fatherhood
KARL OVE KNAUSGAARD

VINTAGE MINIS

Eating
NIGELLA LAWSON

VINTAGE MINIS

Drinking
JOHN CHEEVER

VINTAGE MINIS

VINTAGE MINIS

The Vintage Minis bring you the world's greatest writers on the experiences that make us human. These stylish, entertaining little books explore the whole spectrum of life – from birth to death, and everything in between. Which means there's something here for everyone, whatever your story.

vintageminis.co.uk

1 3 5 7 9 10 8 6 4 2

Vintage
20 Vauxhall Bridge Road,
London SW1V 2SA

Vintage Classics is part of the Penguin Random House
group of companies whose addresses can be found at
global.penguinrandomhouse.com.

 Penguin
Random House
UK

Extracts from *Teach Us to Sit Still* copyright © Tim Parks 2010

Tim Parks has asserted his right to be identified as the author of this
Work in accordance with the Copyright, Designs and Patents Act 1988

First published in Great Britain in 2010 by Harvill Secker
This short edition published by Vintage in 2017

penguin.co.uk/vintage

A CIP catalogue record for this book is available from the British Library

ISBN 9781784872595

Typeset in 9.5/14.5 pt FreightText Pro
by Jouve (UK), Milton Keynes
Printed and bound by Clays Ltd, St Ives plc

Penguin Random House is committed to a sustainable future for
our business, our readers and our planet. This book is made from
Forest Stewardship Council® certified paper.

MIX
Paper from
responsible sources
FSC® C018179
FSC
www.fsc.org

Calm

TIM PARKS

VINTAGE MINIS

Author's Note

How did I come to be where the reader will find me at the beginning of these pages? Not by careful planning, nor any deep wish of mine, and certainly not in order to report back this experience to the world. Quite the contrary. If there was one thing in my life I never imagined myself doing, it was a Buddhist meditation retreat. Brought up in an evangelical household with parents who spoke in tongues and occasionally performed exorcisms, I had vowed to spend my life as far as possible from anything that smacked of spirituality. Then, in midlife, chronic pain struck. I won't describe the details, but they were embarrassing. Let's say my lower abdomen felt like a lump of molten lava. There were urinary issues. The doctors let me down. They filled me with drugs and offered surgery while admitting they didn't understand what was up. Nothing worked. Finally, I had the good luck to discover a book called *A Headache in the Pelvis* by a certain Dr Wise. It advised a series of breathing exercises, oddly described as paradoxical relaxation, which proved an immense help but had the unexpected side effect of leading me to understand that I must change my life. Then an old friend who gave shiatsu massages told me, if you want to learn to relax through breathing, you should go to a Vipassana retreat. So after a year's prevaricating, I did.

The Gong

VIPASSANA MEDITATION IS done sitting cross-legged like
a Buddha. Before confirming my booking, I phoned the
meditation centre to warn them that I had never been able
to sit cross-legged; I wasn't a flexible guy. They reassured
me I could always use a chair. Lying down, however, was
not permitted. The back must be upright.

I was anxious.

'The position is not the problem,' a man with a haggard,
monkish face announced.

On arrival, I was surprised to find people talking. I had
assumed the whole retreat took place in silence. Sitting on
the front doorstep of the farmhouse, looking out over an
Alpine panorama of peaks and stone and misty cloud, a girl
in her mid-twenties had been expressing her concern (and
mine) about spending ten to twelve hours a day with her
butt on a low cushion.

'The position is not the problem,' this gloomy, handsome man repeated. From the way he spoke it appeared

that there was a problem, perhaps a very considerable one, just that it wasn't 'the position'.

What then?

Before departing I had looked up 'Vipassana meditation' on the net:

> **Vipassana** *means seeing things as they really are. It is the process of self-purification by self-observation. It is a universal remedy for universal problems.*

'Universal' and 'remedy', I thought, are two words that when put together can only epitomise wishful thinking, unless we are talking about a bullet in the brain. Purification, on the other hand, was a concept I couldn't begin to understand and hence a goal I could hardly desire. As for seeing things as they are, I knew that meditation was done with the eyes closed.

'Vipassana helps you to start feeling your body,' Ruggero, my shiatsu friend, said. Lots of his fellow shiatsu practitioners did it; it enabled them to explore the meridians. He suggested I look on the retreat as a *merely physical therapy*.

What could that mean from a man who didn't believe in the separation of mind and body?

In the early evening we gathered in the meditation room and were invited to take a vow of silence. Seventeen of us. From now on we wouldn't be able to compare notes. Since the centre advertised itself as a lay Buddhist, non-religious organisation, I was surprised by the liturgical solemnity of the language and the moral seriousness of some of the avowals. For the space of our stay: we mustn't speak or communicate in any way; we mustn't kill, or harm any living creature; we mustn't steal or use what was not ours; we mustn't ingest intoxicants or any mind-altering medicines; we mustn't indulge in any sexual activity; we mustn't disturb those around us; we mustn't read or write; we mustn't engage in any other religious or meditative practice; we mustn't leave the grounds; we mustn't wear shoes in the meeting room; we mustn't lie down in the meeting room; we mustn't sit with our feet pointing towards the teacher.

I had no problem with any of this.

There was one positive instruction: we must ask the teacher, a certain Edoardo Parisi, to teach us Vipassana. He was not proselytising. We must seek him out.

Repeating a formula that was read out to us, we asked. We wanted to be taught.

There was then a 'guided meditation'.

The meeting room was a modern wood-and-glass extension built onto the side of the renovated farmhouse, itself perched on the steep slope of the mountain. Outside, rain fell steadily through the darkness. Inside, the only light came from burning logs behind the glass door of a stove and a dim lamp on the floor. The participants, men to one side, women to the other, sat cross-legged on cushions facing the teacher who was slightly raised on a low dais. Just one elderly lady had chosen a chair. Was it vanity, then, made me choose to sit cross-legged? Looking around as we removed our shoes and entered the room, I had simply copied the others. Against the wall there was a stack of cushions, hard and soft. I put two under my butt and pillows each side of my feet to support the knees. My ankles had to be yanked into position.

There was a long silence. The outside of the feet pressing against the mat would be the first to complain, I thought.

'May all beings live in peace,' the meditation began.

'May all beings be free from all attachment and all sorrow.

'May all beings be happy and enlightened.'

'Sadhu Sadhu Sadhu,' the more experienced meditators replied.

I was taken aback by the religious feel of this – the mumbo-jumbo 'sadhu' in particular – but accepted that it was a rigmarole that must be gone through if I was to enjoy the benefits of the days ahead. There was no assent in my mind. The idea that all beings might ever be free from sorrow was impossible and hence it was impossible for me to wish it. I remembered Emil Cioran dismissing utopian ideas that 'do honour to the heart and disqualify the intellect' and simultaneously warned myself that if I had come to pit my 'superior' intelligence against ancient formulas I might as well have stayed at home.

After another long silence we were invited to concentrate on the sensation of the breath crossing the upper lip as it enters and leaves the nostrils. Already the pressure of my left ankle bearing down on my right was painful. Already the straight back I had forced myself to assume was collapsing into a hunch. How could I concentrate on something so nebulous as breath on the lip in this state of discomfort? Lying down, I might have done it. Lying down I had learned to dispel the tension in my body. Thanks to Dr Wise's relaxation exercises. Cross-legged, tension was intensifying rapidly. Everything went rigid.

I wriggled. Perhaps I had got the position of the cushions wrong. They should have been tipped forward a bit.

I tried to adjust them, tried to sit still. This was hard work.

'If thoughts should arise,' the teacher at last intoned, 'don't worry, it doesn't matter, just say to yourself: thoughts, fantasies, not *my* thoughts, not *my* fantasies, and bring your attention gently back to the breath crossing the lip beneath the nose. The in-breath crossing the lip' – pause – 'the out-breath crossing the lip.'

The voice was soft and reassuring and I tried to follow its instructions. At the same time it was now evident that I had made a mistake coming here. I would never sit through an hour in this position. It had definitely been a big mistake not putting a third cushion under my butt, plus something to ease the pressure where my crossed legs touched. 'Not *my* thoughts,' I repeated, disbelieving. When, for a moment, I felt a light breath on my lip, I clutched at it as a man falling into a fiery pit might clutch at a thread. It snapped. The fiery pit was my legs where pins and needles were advancing rapidly. Amid a turmoil of angry reflections, I

remembered something I had translated once from a book
on pre-Vedic philosophy: 'So as not to be hurt, before coming
near the fire, the wise man wraps himself in the meters.' The
arcane instruction had impressed, I remembered it, and I
had a vague idea it might now be appropriate in some way,
but it also sounded like something from Indiana Jones.

'Thoughts, fantasies,' I repeated determinedly and went
looking for my breath again. It eluded me.

'If pains should arise,' came the teacher's quiet voice,
'don't worry, it doesn't matter, just say to yourself: aches,
pains, not *my* aches, not *my* pains, and bring your attention
gently back to the air crossing the lip beneath the nose.
The in-breath crossing the lip' – pause – 'the out-breath
crossing the lip.'

Saying 'pain, not *my* pain' worked even less than saying
'thoughts, not *my* thoughts'. Whose pain, if not mine?
After twenty minutes the pins and needles had crept up
from my crushed ankles to my cramped calves. My thighs
were simultaneously burning and numb. My curved shoulders were a rigid block. There would be no warm wave of
relaxation tonight. Angrily, I hung on. When the hour mercifully ended, I couldn't stand up.

So why did you come? I demanded of myself in bed.
Surely you didn't really believe this experiment would help
you stand up straight. Who cared about standing up
straight, anyway? Why had I chosen to give the business of
posture such symbolic force?

Oddly, it now appeared that there was a gap between my actually being here, in this remote valley, sharing a room with two younger men (one snoring steadily), and some moment in the past when, presumably, I had had my good reasons for signing up to five days of Vipassana meditation.

Had I thought of it as penitence?

No. Since age fifteen I have refused to think of myself as a sinner.

I stayed awake for some time, got up to go to the bathroom, returned, listened to the man snoring, put in my earplugs, turned to the wall.

'You were looking for a showdown with yourself,' I muttered. That was it. A showdown with this tangled self, these tussling selves. You decided that without that showdown the pains would soon be back. Or other pains.

What form would the showdown take? I had no idea. But I had been told that, sitting in silence for days, people do come to a new knowledge of themselves. That was the goal. Knowledge, confrontation. To plumb the source of my tensions and defuse them once and for all. Settle *once and for all* that 'tussle in the mind'.

Of course, I had no more believed I would be successful in this project than a knight setting out to find the Holy Grail supposes he will be the one chosen to recover it. At some deep level, I wasn't even surprised to have spent a miserable hour merely verifying the fact that my hips, legs and thighs were too stiff for me to sit cross-legged. What else had I expected? Yet the following morning, after a tedious night taking care not to wake my room-mates as I padded back and forth to the bathroom, I went once more to the cushions, not to a chair. And I went *without hesitation*. I went cheerfully, *expectantly*.

In the end, I no longer believe that it is given to us to understand why we behave as we do. I should stop trying.

I say 'the following morning'. In fact the gong sounded at four a.m. Dead of night. It was a rather beautiful gong, a sort of auditory moonlight rippling through the deep silence of the house, promising calm and clarity. I was already awake and went downstairs at once. In the kitchen were flasks of herb tea. I poured something minty and went outside to drink it under the eaves of the house looking out into cloud and fog. A woman about my own age came and lit a cigarette beside me. It wasn't unpleasant, standing silently there together, listening to trees and gutter as they dripped, smelling her cigarette smoke in the damp air. I remember she shifted from one foot to the other. The not-talking actually made us more aware of each other's presence.

At four thirty the gong sounded again and the meditation began. Unguided, two hours. Seventeen people breathing, sniffling, coughing. Some wore hoods or swathed head and shoulders in blankets against the chill, which gave the scene a monkish feel. I had built my seat a little higher and brought a T-shirt to fold between my ankles. I did not expect these small expedients would bring comfort, nor did they. After half an hour toes, feet, ankles, knees, thighs and hips welded together in a scorching pyre from which my curved trunk rose like the torso of some broken martyr. Round this carnage, thoughts flitted and circled like bats in smoke. It would be impossible to convey how many thoughts arose, or how ferociously they blocked all attempts to focus on my breath. There had been nothing of comparable intensity when I had begun the paradoxical relaxation at home with Dr Wise. If, for three seconds, I did focus wordlessly on the sensation of breathing, immediately a yell of self-congratulation was raised, followed by a pertinent reflection on the inappropriateness of such a yell, then another reflection, equally pertinent, that this verbalised statement of inappropriateness only compounded the problem, then another reflection that such pertinent reflections were stealing away the experience that I had come for, the experience of wordlessness. Reflection comes at the expense of being, I told myself. Perhaps especially when pertinent. I was pleased that I had framed the idea so succinctly. And ironically. Would I be able to remember these words at the end of the session? How could I make myself remember, without pen and paper? Oh, but what is the point, Tim, of trying to meditate if you are only interested in describing the perversity of everything that prevents you from doing so?

So it went on. A mental seething. A stampede of cows, flies buzzing round shit, rats at a corpse. By some cruel stroke of irony, our farmhouse was situated in a valley with at least three churches whose mixture of clocks chiming the hours and bells summoning the faithful kept one constantly aware of time passing, and thus hopeful of an end, but also constantly confused as to how much time had passed, and thus despairing when no end came. If I opened my eyes and turned a little I could see the watch which the companion to my left had placed on the floor beside him. But what was the sense of checking the time? What was the point of being here if I was merely yearning for the two hours to be over, my mind projected into the future when I was supposed to be savouring the present – 'the present where there is no conflict' the teacher had said in yesterday's guided session? What did that mean? On the other hand, how savour the present when the present was pain, pain that I knew would dissolve the moment I made up my mind to move? But when I did move, swaying my trunk back and forth, for example, or, more radically, uncrossing and re-crossing my legs, then, after a moment's relief, the hot pain returned stronger still. It was worse.

Accepting defeat, I opened my eyes. There was no sign of dawn. The dark windows were a glossy mirror. The fire glowed red. Raised on a low platform, the teacher, in his early sixties, balding, blond, with a fine, pointed nose, sat in perfect stillness, swathed in a thin white blanket. Around me, others too sat perfectly still. One young man in particular had a wonderfully straight back, a marvellously smooth face. The woman to my right sat in a half lotus, unflinching, motionless, her breast rising and falling very slowly and gently. I envied them. And I held on *because* of them. Something about that young man, at once virile and serene, focused and silent, seemed to rebut my sophisticated objections. Closing my eyes again, I struggled once more to find this elusive point where breath and skin met. Perhaps for a whole minute then, I had the impression that the air coming in and out of my nostrils was a silver thread passing through transparent water. All around me was dark still transparent water and this delicate, mercurial thread of air ran gleaming across it connecting me to some distant point beyond my ken.

HAD I LEFT the retreat after lunch on day three, I would never have 'meditated' again. On the evening of the second day two young men disappeared. I heard angry voices from the garden during the afternoon break and at the evening session they were gone. If I had left with them, I could have read a book, or gone running, or canoeing, or for a walk with my wife, Rita, and the dog. Halfway through the third morning, another place was empty. The maestro spoke calmly of 'right effort, right concentration, right awareness'. 'If you experience pleasure in your meditation,' he said, 'do not attach to it with yearning. If you experience pain, do not attach to it with aversion.'

Attachment with aversion was a new idea to me. But I sensed at once what he meant. It was like when I read an author I despised *because* I despised him, because I enjoyed thinking what a scandal it was that this man was a celebrity.

Or when I kept complaining about a colleague at the university because my identity was intensified by my opposition to him. Or when I listened to the radio outside Ruggero's study *in order* to loathe it. Did I attach to pain in the same way? Scratching sores. Was it possible that this grand showdown with myself that I had planned and been denied actually had to do with the pain I was now experiencing? The showdown was taking place without my realising it *was* the showdown. Why else would I continue to sit cross-legged, without a break, when others had chosen to remove to chairs from time to time?

This form of meditation where you concentrate entirely on the breath was called Anapana, we were told, and merely preparatory to Vipassana, which was something quite different and more challenging. Only when the mind had been tamed and tied down to the breath crossing the lip, like a dog to a chain, could we progress. That would be the fourth day. I knew I wouldn't be ready. But on the third evening, towards the end of the last session, something happened. In the midst of the usual fierce pains, with a strange naturalness and inevitability, my consciousness at last fused with my upper lip: the breath, the lip, the mind, these apparently incompatible entities did, in fact, fit together, flow together, were one. I was my lip bathed in soft breath. At once the breathing that had been irregular and forced subsided to a light caress passing back and forth across the skin, a soft rising and falling breathed, not by me it seemed, but by my whole body, by the air outside my body, by everything around me. Then, as if at the touch of a switch, the scalding rigidity tensing thighs and hips dissolved. In a moment, the lower body sank into suppleness. Where there had been formless pain, I became aware of thighs, knees, calves, ankles, feet. A strange heat was being forced downward through them. My bare feet were cold but a hot pain was passing out pleasantly through the soles.

The experience could not have been more unexpected. Or more welcome. I was immediately anxious it must end at once, anxious that some malignant thought would rise up to cancel it out. Don't think, Tim. Do *not* think! Do not give yourself commands not to think! Silence! I focused on that breath that now seemed so strangely detached from me, or rather that I was just a small part of, as if the boundaries that routinely separated me from the world that was not me had blurred. And after perhaps a minute – but there is no measuring time in these circumstances – like a prisoner released from a yoke, my back, which had been cramped and bent, rose gently upright and was straight. As it did so, I was aware of each of the muscles that quietly lifted it. I felt how natural the erect position was. I felt blessed.

A few moments later and things were back to normal: the pain, the frustration, the waiting for the gong that would bring release.

Don't think, Tim. Do *not* think! Do not give yourself commands not to think! Silence!

Surprise Party

ON THE FOURTH DAY, I wept. It is more embarrassing to talk about this than about my urinary troubles, but to miss it out would be to lose a turning point.

I had got through the two-hour early-morning session. There had been no repeat of the previous evening's brief beatitude, but a corner had been turned nevertheless, for I discovered that the more I let go, without worrying when each session would end or what I was thinking or feeling, then the less the pain of sitting like this bothered me. Rather, it was now as if this cross-legged pain were helping me to discover a movement of the mind that I had never really made before: unquestioning acceptance, letting go. It had been hard work getting to this point and it was not until I discovered that movement, or rather until it simply happened to me, that I even appreciated it was possible. Words can describe a mental experience, after the event, but had the same words been spoken to me a thousand times before the experience, I would no more have understood them than a child born in the tropics would understand sleet and snow. That gloomy man had been right: the position was not the problem. The problem was in my head.

So I sat, still in some pain but no longer angry. And the less I was angry the less I was in pain. At times the position began to feel comfortable, even beautiful, the way it invited stillness: the legs locked, the back anchored, the hands quietly joined, and the mind too seemed to have been quietened *by the position*. Everything came from having accepted that one really was here for the whole five days, from truly *not* wishing for the time to hurry by, truly *not* wanting to be back at one's computer writing it all down.

How right they had been to forbid us pens and paper!

After the morning session, at six thirty, we went to breakfast. We picked up plates, queued at a small table stacked with food, then sat together in silence. I had not expected what a pleasure this would be. The long hours spent wrestling, eyes closed, with wayward thoughts seemed to have heightened our sense of taste. Everybody ate slowly and with relish. A piece of fresh white bread seemed as good as any cake. And each face took on a calm and dignity that made one feel unusually happy to be part of the human race. There was no competition for attention, no flirting or coteries, no exhibitionism, no privileged partnerships. In short, nothing for a story. If you needed milk or water or tea, people understood and offered at once, with a faint smile. Afterwards, each person went to the sink and washed his plate and cup. No wonder they called it the Noble Silence.

But this morning I didn't make it to the food. Leaving the meditation room, you stepped into the small garden, whence it was a few yards to the door into the house and the dining room. On the threshold, I felt a sob rising from chest to throat.

The novelty of the experience was that I was not feeling unhappy in any way. Rather the contrary. Also unusual was my immediate appreciation that what was happening was beyond the usual social controls. My body had decided to sob, the way when it's ill, it decides to vomit.

I stepped aside to let the others pass and, to hide my face, turned to look out over the low garden parapet across the broad valley with its shreds of cloud and shafts of sunlight, its villages and churches, and then, beyond the valley, the great chain of mountain peaks: woods, scree, snow.

The weeping burst on me like a storm. I shook.

This crisis lasted half an hour. On two occasions I tried to go in to eat – I was hungry – but each time the emotion surged up with renewed force. My throat ached. So I sat on a stone table under a pergola and continued to gaze through my tears across the valley which seemed intensely part of the experience, as if, again, there were nothing separating self and outside – I was truly *in* this huge panorama, mind and body, weeping.

Then, as though a voice were calling a class register, name after name was announced to my mind, people I knew or had known; and together with the names came faces, bodies, vivid expressions and gestures. One after another, faster and faster, these folk were crowding into consciousness. It was as if, at some carefully engineered surprise party, a door had been thrown open and I was confronted with everyone who ever mattered to me: my wife principally and throughout – we had been together thirty years – then my son, my daughters, my mother and my father, my brother and sister, my friends, lovers, everybody precious, but colleagues too, old acquaintances, neighbours even, they were all here beside me on the terrace under the pergola looking out over the valley, not summoned by myself, not expecting to see me, but glad nevertheless to be here at this impromptu gathering – and solemn too, solemnly aware of our shared mortality, aware that some had already passed on, while others of us were well on our way through life's journey. Then I saw that the long valley we were gazing over *was* the journey. I was one with the group, the living and the dead, and we were one with the landscape. And slowly, between fits of bewildered tears, it dawned on me, at long last, that the roads to health and to death were one: to recover my health, fully, I must accept death as I had accepted the pain sitting cross-legged in the meditation room. I couldn't do that. I just couldn't. But I knew that if I did, this was what they meant by purification.

I have never wept so deeply. Like most people, I have sometimes been very unhappy, and sometimes very happy.

But there had never been this outpouring, nor this feeling simply of being present, a mere witness, while something necessary unfolded. Had I wanted to resist, I could not have done so.

Finally, when it really was over and I could go to the bathroom to wash my face, I was struck, glancing in the mirror, by this obvious thought: that the two selves that had shouted their separateness on waking that morning almost a year ago were my daily life on the one hand and the ambitions that had always taken precedence over that life on the other. I had always made a very sharp distinction between the business of being here in the flesh, and the project of achieving something, becoming someone, writing books, winning prizes, accruing respect. The second had always taken precedence over the first. How else can one ever get anywhere in life? That was why I had been so challenged when Dr Wise warned me that I must put my painful and embarrassing condition at the centre of my 'project'. What he had meant, I saw now, was that the real project was always mortality.

THE NEXT MEDITATION session was not till eight a.m., and, retiring to my bed in the meantime, I called up a thousand bookish references to get a fix on what had just happened to me, to turn it, as always, into words. 'Life presents itself first and foremost as a task. We take no pleasure in it except when we are striving after something.' I remembered reading that, but couldn't remember where.

It had sounded a warning, I had made a mental note. But over the years I had read a hundred warnings and made a thousand mental notes and none had carried the conviction of the ugly bellyache that had stopped me sitting at my computer.

'We go to novels for life.' I had read those words, or words to that effect, quite recently, in James Wood's book *How Fiction Works*. But they might easily have been spoken by D. H. Lawrence or F. R. Leavis. And I understood now with absolute certainty that this claim was a false and self-regarding piety. Life is *not* in novels. The novels that most compellingly keep us away from life are those that most accurately, intensely and wonderfully imagine it and replace it for us, the novels of Dostoevsky and, yes, of Lawrence, of the truly great writers. But the novels themselves are *not* life and we don't go to them for life. If it's life we want, we put the book down. There were some dumb lines from O-level Browning:

> And you, great sculptor – so, you gave
> A score of years to Art, her slave,
> And that's your Venus, whence we turn
> To yonder girl that fords the burn!

'Yonder', 'fords' and 'burn' were awful, I thought. Why had such poor poetry stuck in my head?

Or there was Poe's story about the painter who so obsessively has his young wife sit for her portrait, that only when the absolutely life-like painting is finished does he notice the girl is dead. Art at life's expense.

Then I remembered – the weeping experience had set my brain racing – Robert Walser and the Benjamenta Institute of his novel *Jakob von Gunten*. Yes. Jakob, the narrator, is sent to a school where he must 'learn to think of nothing', something he at first finds absurd, but that eventually wins him over. 'One must go courageously into the inevitable,' was a line I remembered.

But why seek to tie down the intensity of what had happened to me with all these literary references? First the emotion, then the excited reflection on emotion, attempting to divert it from its initial function, to enrol it in my career project, to turn it into smartness and writing. First the illness to warn you away from monomania and back to life and then the reflection on that process, moving you away from life and back to monomania, back to writing and books. Was that what Wordsworth meant by 'Emotion recollected in tranquillity.' The formula sounded so innocuous, but the next logical step was to seek the emotion *in order* to recall it in tranquillity, to care more about the recollection than the emotion, because it was the sophisticated recollection that brought recognition and celebrity and self-esteem. 'Who can ever feel at ease when he cares about the world's praise and admiration?' *Jakob von Gunten* again. I had remembered that line too. More warnings. Jakob comes to appreciate the school's curriculum of thinking about nothing because he is disturbed by the power and ugliness of the instinct to achieve. I remembered an anecdote about Walser. One day his admirer, Carl Seelig, went to visit him in the mental home where he lived. You know, Robert, Seelig told him, you are perhaps the greatest writer in the German language at this time. Walser was upset. If you ever say such a thing again, he told Seelig, I will never speak to you.

I lay on my bed, leafing through the pages of my literary memory. As I did so I knew that it was foolish. The thing to do was to get back to the silence. Go to the meditation room now, I told myself, even *before* the next session. Go and sit in silence. At once a quotation rose to possess even this decision.

> The important thing is not to learn, but to undergo
> an emotion, and to be in a certain state.

That was Aristotle. I laughed and discovered something that has served me well since: the more we threaten thought and language with silence, or simply seek to demote them in our lives from the ludicrous pedestal on which our culture and background have placed them, then the more fertile, in their need to justify and assert themselves, they become. Reflection is never more exciting than when reflecting on the damage reflection does, language never more seductive than when acknowledging its unreality.

This is the territory of Beckett, I thought. 'Of it goes

on!' *The Unnameable*. The mind's mindless chatter. Beckett too had spoken of being brought to an awareness of his sick psychological state by an array of inexplicable pains.

I stopped myself and went downstairs for the first session of Vipassana.

Anicca

Wordless wakefulness, lively stillness, meditation resists description. When, at the beginning, words
and images fizz in resistance to our attempt to put them
aside, the writer can have fun. But when thought at last
relents, when eyes close behind closed eyes and the mind
sinks silent into the flesh, then it's hard to describe that
strange state of alertness, oneness, quiet. Moreover, the
meditator loses all desire to do so.

To what end?

Vipassana, however, does offer a few fireworks on the
way to composure which all practitioners recognise.
Something can be told, though the experience lies beyond
any verification. Above all, you can't see it. There is nothing you can copy, the way we might all copy the movements
of a tennis player, or the way Eugen Herrigel copied his
Zen master of archery.

'Now,' our teacher says, 'take your concentration away
from the breath crossing the lip, and raise it to the top

When thought at last
relents, when eyes close
behind closed eyes and
the mind sinks silent
into the flesh, then it's
hard to describe that
strange state of
alertness, oneness, quiet

centre of the head, a small area, about the size of a coin, corresponding, in an infant, to the fontanel. Focus your attention there. Take note of any sensations that arise, without seeking to induce sensations where there are none, without resisting or altering sensations when they occur.'

So, at each of the retreats I have been to, whether of five days or ten, of twenty people or of sixty, on the fourth morning, it begins. Never, at first attempt, do I find any sensation in this neglected area of my anatomy: the bald spot. I can't even locate it. What does happen is that a headache flares as the mind detaches from the breath and moves out to explore the body. The tension swells into the skull for a few seconds, then fades.

Superficially, the Vipassana process is not unlike Dr Wise's paradoxical relaxation. One is to contemplate sensation as it flows and ebbs throughout the body. The difference lies in the intensity and thoroughness of the exploration and the attitude with which it is undertaken. One renounces any objective beyond the contemplation itself. You are not here *in order* to relax, or to overcome pain, or to resolve a health problem – the experience is not subordinated to a higher goal – you are here to be here, side by side with the infinitely nuanced flux of sensation in the body.

First the fontanel, then the forehead, then the temples (left and right), the back of the head, the ears (left and right), the eyes (left and right), the nose, the nostrils (left and right), the cheeks (left and right), the lips (upper and lower), the gums (all), the teeth (every one), the tongue (above and below), the pallet, the jowls (left and right), the throat, the jaw, the neck.

And we have only just begun. The body is a universe. It has many parts. It is made up of many materials. The skin, the muscle, the nerves, the tendons, the blood, the bone . . .

But what does it mean that the mind, or the attention, *moves* around the body? The body is absolutely still (you are not flexing muscles to feel, as you did in the early days of paradoxical relaxation), yet, within the three-dimensional stillness of limbs, head, trunk, you have the impression of the mind shifting, exploring, travelling up and down, left and right, as if, with the body parts that are usually in movement now firmly anchored, the usually anchored mind can move at will. And this is not the movement of the schoolboy's eye over diagrams of anatomy. It is not the movement of looking. Rather it is like a man wandering through the rooms of a house, in the dark, knocking on this door and that, perhaps after a long absence, checking if anyone is home, if anyone wants to talk, or gripe, or rejoice, or simply turn on a light for him.

For a while, perhaps, there will be no response. The doors are closed, perhaps locked. You must be patient. Nobody has passed this way for some time and it would be impolite of you to start rattling the handles. This is not a police raid.

The forehead doesn't respond.

The ears don't respond.

The nape of the neck never responds.

In another part of the house, on a lower floor perhaps, a noisy melodrama demands your attention. A fierce cramp is shouting in the calves. An ache hammers at the back. These people want an argument. They are protesting. But those are not the doors you are knocking on now. Their turn will come. For the moment you tap politely at the nose. You listen politely to the skin at the bridge of the nose.

No response.

But you have time! Hours of time. You are not in a hurry. There are many doors to try.

Attention attends, unrequited.

Then, all at once, the temples!

I remember distinctly, my first session of Vipassana, it was in my temples that it began. First one, then the other: singing, buzzing, dancing. Had I wished to induce a sensation in this part of the body, I would never have imagined such mayhem, as though insect eggs had hatched, or breath on ashes found a nest of live embers. Yet it wasn't creepy. And it wasn't hot. It was the lively sparkle of freshly poured soda water.

In my temples.

At this point you realise that focusing the mind – eyes closed – on a part of the body is quite different from focusing on something outside yourself, a ball, say, or a bottle, or a boat. In that case the object remains an object, however long we look at it. But like light through a lens, or through a glass of still water perhaps, the mind sets the body alight, or the body the mind. It is hard to say which; the skin glows in the mind and the mind fizzes in the skin. Together, neither flesh nor fleshless, or both flesh *and* fleshless, they burn.

This is the beginning of Vipassana.

The inclination now is to enjoy this novel sensation. It's such a relief, after twenty minutes perhaps, to get a response from the body at last, to understand at long last what the teacher was leading you to. So relax now and enjoy. As you relaxed with Dr Wise. This song in the temples, this temple song, is such a pleasurable sensation.

But the teacher is moving on. We must not attach to pleasures as we must not attach to pain.

Nose now.

Lips now.

Tongue now.

The encouraging thing is that once one part of the body has answered your polite enquiry, others too seem more willing to respond: here a band of heat, there a patch of coldness, here a dull throb, now a tingling current. The whole house is waking up and as you pass from door to door each occupant acknowledges your presence by turning something on: now a blue light, now a red, here a coffee grinder, there a TV. The tower block starts to hum.

These varied sensations, our teacher now tells us, are manifestations of *anicca*, which is to say, the constant instability of all things. He invites us to contemplate *anicca*. To know *anicca*, the eternal flux, in our hands, our chests. To recognise that nothing is fixed. Ego, identity, they have no permanence.

Immediately, my thinking mind rebels. My determined self resists. Who needs this mumbo-jumbo – I'm angry – these mystifying foreign words? *Anicca!* Who needs this *theory*? The body may indeed be subject to constant change, but it is also true that it remains largely the same for many years. I recognise my friends year in year out. In childhood photographs, my face is already essentially me, *Tim Parks*.

As I think these thoughts, the temple dance fades, the lights dim, the pain-mongers on the lower floors increase their clamour.

Damn and damn.

I choose to forget the debate and concentrate on sensation. I remember Ruggero: treat it as an entirely physical thing.

The thud of the beating heart, the rise and fall of the diaphragm, a burning hoop around the waist, a warm tremor in the belly – very slowly, part by ageing part, the body was put together. The book I had translated on early Indian philosophy, Roberto Calasso's *Ka*, told the story of the so-called altar of fire. Blessed with longevity, but nevertheless mortal, the lesser gods sought out the first god, Prajapati, whose broken body was dispersed throughout the world, *was* the world, to ask if there was any way they might be 'saved'. 'You must reconstruct my lost wholeness,' Prajapati told them. 'How?' 'Take three hundred and sixty boundary stones and ten thousand eight hundred bricks . . .' The numbers corresponded to the days and hours of the Vedic year. Every brick was an 'intense concentration'.

The altar was built from the outside inward, focusing the mind. Its shape was that of the eagle, bird of eternal wakefulness. If ever you managed to complete the construction, a fire would kindle and the eagle would take flight to the paradise of immortality.

Well, there comes a moment in Vipassana, if you are lucky, if you stay focused, patient, if you learn not to want such a moment, when the entire body links up and ignites. Once, I remember, it began in my wrists. Pulsing waves accelerated into whirling orbits of bright electrons, pure energy, without substance. Contemplating this marvel, it did seem the ego was bleeding away into the hectic flow. If they wanted to call it *anicca*, let them.

But more often, for me at least, it begins when contemplating pain. It is hard to sit with pain in stillness, allowing it to be there, uncomplaining. A knife blade thrust between the vertebrae, for example. But if you do, then, perhaps, just perhaps, for one can never command these things, a sudden intensification will invade the spine, a rush of fierce heat flushes through the chest and dissolves away through arms and legs. The pain is gone. The hunched back straightens, the lungs fill, and the body is one, as if all the doors in a house had been taken away allowing free movement throughout. You are feeling *everything*, simultaneously, or rather, you *are* everything, from toes to fingertips to the hairs on your head. You dance through the rooms, you who never learned to dance.

The first time this happened to me, on the last session of that first retreat, the experience came together with three warm showers. Implausible as science fiction, that small area at the top centre of the head had begun to buzz, to glow, then overflowed in three drenching floods of warmth. A baptism. When the hour ended I jumped to my feet.

IN THE CAR to the station at Maroggia the young man driving was furious. The whole five days had been an utter waste of time. The teacher was a charlatan, a fool. We had been taken for a ride. *Anicca, Anicca, Anicca!* The Buddha was rubbish. Nirvana was rubbish. Reincarnation was rubbish. There is no way anyone can feel the breath crossing his lip. Bullshit. He had been through the pains of hell trying to sit in that dumb cross-legged position when he could have been skiing. He could have been playing tennis.

I believed in nothing, I said, least of all reincarnation, but it had been an important experience for me.

The other man in the car was the gloomy, handsomely haggard fellow who had told us the position was not the problem. Session after session he had sat two places to my left on a cylindrical cushion in granitic stillness. He did not respond to the angry boy who dropped us at the station, but on the train to Milan he told me he ran a very busy car insurance agency. He had been to a dozen such retreats. These were the only days in the year that were truly his own. It was a rule of his, he said, never to speak of his experiences during meditation. However, one aspect of Vipassana still bothered him, indeed had come to bother him more and more, to the point where he was now ready to stop meditating. 'What does it mean,' he asked, 'when they say the thoughts are not *my* thoughts? What can that mean? How can the thoughts not be *my* thoughts?'

The Booker Speech

NO LONGER MUCH interested in standing up straight, I found my back pulling upright by itself. It happened over the spring. Taking my familiar run across the hills, I was surprised to find myself aware of muscles at the base of the spine. How odd. Days later I could feel my shoulders. A slight warm presence. Finally my neck. It was as if skeletal spaces had been very lightly pencilled in. Becoming aware of the muscles turned out to be one with straightening them. Or letting them straighten me. I didn't do anything. I just had to pay attention. The only difficult thing was getting used to seeing the world from a different angle.

'*Complimenti*,' Ruggero grinned. He insisted I looked ten centimetres taller.

No longer interested in prostates, pelvic floors and plumbing problems, I found my pains were gone. Truly gone. I had stopped watching out for them and they had slouched off. The ease and lightness in my stomach and back made walking a pleasure that was at once a powerful sense of nowness and a memory of childhood. I walked very slowly, savouring my body walking. On my way to the café in the morning I nodded at the moustachioed man in the white cowboy hat who had once demanded that I stand up straight. He nodded back, with new respect, I hoped. It became genuinely hard to believe the state I'd been in two years ago. Had it really been *that* painful?

Only the night-time trips to the bathroom remained, three or four. Irreducible to any pathology, they had stayed, I decided, to prevent me from growing too pleased with myself, or to keep the night present.

With varying results, I continued the meditation at home. Paradoxical relaxation was behind me. It had been directly addressed to the symptom and the symptom was gone. I fixed up a mat and a few cushions in a corner of the bedroom and tried to meditate an hour a day. It was at once more comfortable than at the retreat, and less intense. The warm showers did not return. Nor the fierce pains. It was liturgy after revelation.

Knowing that I had scarcely scratched the surface, I signed up to a ten-day retreat in August. This time there would be a famous teacher, an ageing American, John Coleman. I made no attempt to find out about the man or to look up the philosophy that underpinned Vipassana. The last thing I needed was to turn Buddhist. I just wanted the quiet sitting, the increased perception of the body, the Noble Silence. I went confident that there would be no pain this time. I had sorted that out at home. I knew how to sit cross-legged. At times I even experimented with the Burmese position. It's so hard not to feel pleased with oneself.

Since there were sixty participants, the retreat was in an ex-monastery, in the Tuscan hills. Less chic than you would imagine. On arrival, in the fervour of conversation that precedes the vow of silence, all the talk was of Coleman and what a fantastic teacher he was. '*My* teacher,' someone said. '*Il mio maestro.*' 'I switched to Coleman from Goenka,' said another. There was a general rush to place one's mat and cushion towards the front of the meditation room, near the charismatic guru. May all beings be free from all attachment, I remembered, but, not wanting to be left out, I hurried along with them. I got a good place.

Coleman was on his last legs, shuffling, pushing eighty, fat, sometimes fatuous. He spoke slowly in a sonorous voice between heavy sighs, sprawled in a deep armchair, wearing loose jeans and sloppy sweater. A bland smile suggested he too was pleased with himself. Sitting on a table beside him, a young man with only one leg translated his words into Italian in a grating, high-pitched voice. At once this translation business irritated me. It hadn't occurred to me that language would be an issue. Much of the translation was inaccurate and all of it expressionless. There were occasions when it was hard not to shout out better solutions.

Coleman talked about the three refuges, the four truths, the five precepts, the seven stages of purification, the eightfold path to enlightenment, the ten perfections, the Buddha, the Dhamma, the Sangha, karma, anicca, anatta, samsara, dukkha, suffering, the root of all suffering, the remedy for all suffering, the bodhi tree.

What drivel this was, I thought. And why do all faiths – because this clearly wasn't science – share this mad appetite for numeration? The Trinity, the seven sacraments, the ten commandments. It wasn't *worth* translating properly. On the other hand, I always tell my students that translating accurately is a pleasure *in itself* regardless of the inanity of the original. Certainly I was suffering more for the poor translation than the mystical content.

Every few minutes the man behind me – and he was very close behind me – sniffed three times in rapid succession, then cleared his throat, then coughed. To my dismay, when the meditation proper began, fat old Coleman had someone fetch a large kitchen clock and place it at his feet. It was the kind of clock I could have heard ticking about ten miles away. Immediately I thought of all the guestrooms, classrooms, university offices and rented apartments, where the first thing I'd done on arrival was remove the battery from a ticking clock. What a satisfaction that is, killing the sound that constantly returns you to the passing moment, that stops you being elsewhere in your head. Here I was helpless. This will be hell, I decided.

And I hadn't conquered the pain at all. Twenty minutes into the first session I was in agony.

Nor had I learned to sit up straight. My back collapsed, doubled even. My nose was at my feet (my aching feet).

Why? This was *worse* than Maroggia. I should never have come.

The meditation room was narrow and very long and I was about four rows from the front in ripple and cross-ripple of fidgeting and buttock shifting. Every time I thought I might at last be getting a hold on my breathing, every time the pain began to ease up as the mind focused on the skin of the lip, from behind, came, Sniff, sniff, sniff, er er hemmmm! At once the clock ticked more loudly. Sniff, sniff, sniff, er er *hemmmm*! Tick tick TOCK **TOCK**! The volcano that was my haunches threatened to erupt.

'If there are feelings of pain,' the would-be hypnotic Coleman crooned for the nth time, 'just make an objective note, pain pain . . .'

So what would a subjective note be, Mr Coleman? Or a note that was neither subjective nor objective, for that matter? Why pretend there is anything *reasonable* about all this?

For the nth time the one-legged man on the table translated – *fare una nota obiettiva* (does anyone say, '*fare una nota*?') – his voice as bored and mechanical as Coleman's was sonorous and rhythmic.

I now felt homicidal.

From the corridor came the din of someone wheeling a trolley full of plates and cutlery along the monastery's uneven, unending, stone-flagged corridor. First you heard it approach for a minute or more. At the crescendo, it stopped, right outside the meditation-room door. Now I was waiting for it to start again. Was it going to go away or wasn't it? It was teasing us. I couldn't meditate until it moved off, or until I knew it was staying. Then just when you thought it was staying, off it went with a long-drawn-out squeal followed by a great clatter of plates, knives, spoons and pans, like a goods train at dead of night, the rattle, bang and boom sustained for another minute and more before the din began to fade at what I judged must be the turn of the corridor. How many clock ticks before it is gone completely, I wondered? Twenty? I counted. Tick tock. Tick tock. No, ten ticks more. Still the clatter echoed faintly off the stone surfaces. And the rattle. Fainter and fainter, but still faintly there. Tick . . . tick . . . tick. The guy was *deliberately* going slowly! And a jingle of teaspoons. Tick tick tick. Still ever so faintly. Perhaps he was taking a step back for every two steps forward. He was *deliberately* choosing the uneven flagstones, he was rattling the cutlery trays!

Gone, it was suddenly gone. But now the clock's ticking had got into my skin and was stitching my lips together, each tick was a stitch, up and down, through my lips. How could I feel my breath with a needle sewing up my lips? I imagined the first major massacre at a meditation retreat. 'The assailant was a man in his fifties known to be searching for inner peace. It is not clear why he came to the monastery armed with a Kalashnikov.'

At the same time I recognised this package of feelings all too well. This is me, I thought, me of old. Unredeemed TP. Old resentments, dramatisations, would-be black comedy.

You are getting off on being angry now. You're enjoying it, imagining yourself *imaginatively* angry. À la Geoff Dyer who himself wanted to be à la D. H. Lawrence. Gritting my teeth, I hung on to the end of the session and stumbled over a fizz of pins and needles to collapse on the lawn in the garden.

The monastery was supposedly in a secluded area, high on a steep hot hill and surrounded by an impressive stone wall, but the village immediately beneath the hill had arranged its summer fête for this week. At eight in the evening rock music began, as poorly played as Coleman's meditations were poorly translated. The summer air filtered out most of the treble leaving only a dull beat of drum and bass and the lament of a direly strained voice.

Added to which the Olympics were now under way. From the windows of the convent located directly across the courtyard from our meditation room came the sound of nuns cheering on Italian athletes. In China. If there is one thing I loathe it's the Olympic Games, festival of empty pieties, crass patriotism and sophisticated performance drugs. It was extraordinary how excited and patriotic those old nuns were. Apparently it did not occur to them they might be disturbing us. What a terrible, terrible farce all this was. Ten days of my precious and very busy life wasted!

Still I hung on. I had no idea why. My diligence was a mystery to me. One day I wondered if they had deliberately arranged for us to be assailed by these noises to test our meditative stamina.

The routine at these retreats is that you eat breakfast at

six thirty, after the wonderfully quiet early session, lunch
at eleven, then just a piece of fruit late afternoon and nothing till the following morning. 'A little hunger in the
evening will do no harm,' fat Coleman smiled. The food, all
strictly vegetarian, was not as good as the homemade fare
at the smaller retreat in Maroggia. Brought in from outside, the pimply caterers grinned at us as if we were
picturesque eccentrics. They seemed to take special pleasure in banging down the knives and forks when they laid
the table and then shaking them vigorously in their metal
trays when they collected them again, as if panning for
gold. The fruit in the evening was chiefly kiwis. I'm not
fond of kiwis. How can you peel a kiwi without getting
sticky fingers? Fifty people queued around two kettles for
tea. I had the distinct impression that old Coleman was
enjoying little natters with the prettiest woman on the
course. I had caught them three times at the turn of
the staircase. Talking.

Where was the Noble Silence?

Every other afternoon, for an hour, there was a
so-called 'check-up'. In alphabetical order people were
invited, four by four, to bring their cushions to the front,
sit before the teacher and report on their progress. On the
second day, almost everyone spoke of their pain with the
sitting position, their difficulty eliminating their thoughts;
many complained of a film playing out before their closed
eyes, some old drama rehearsed a thousand times with no
solution, as when a ghost appears again and again in the

same place in the same clothes – an ex-husband, a dead sister – makes the same gestures and is gone, then back. Never there, never not there.

'I'm in a loop,' one man said. He found it distressing.

'I have a big decision to take when I get home, I just can't get it out of my mind, I see the conversation over and over.'

People couldn't identify the place on their lips where breath met skin. When they did identify it, they couldn't focus their attention there, they lost it. 'It must be my moustache,' one man thought. He would shave it. Perhaps they felt the breath going out, but not the breath coming in. Or they could feel it in their nose, but not on their lip. Why was it so important to feel the breath on the upper lip?

'I have a pain in my shoulder, from an accident a few years ago.'

'I keep getting this fierce headache right behind my eyes, it won't go away.'

'My feet are on fire.'

'I've got period cramps.'

To all these people, sitting cross-legged on their cushions before him, Coleman, enthroned in his armchair, gave the same advice. 'You must say, doesn't matter, pain, pain, not *my* pain. You must say thoughts, thoughts, doesn't matter, not *my* thoughts.'

He smiled and settled his bulk.

I felt rage.

Given my place in the alphabet, I knew I wouldn't be

invited to present myself to the grand old man until the third day. Try as I might to eliminate the mental chatter from my mind, I began to go over and over what I planned to say. I would mention my surprise that while I had no problem meditating at home, here I was experiencing all kinds of pains. Why? I sat up straight at home, here my back collapsed. Did he have any advice beyond, pain, pain, not *my* pain?

I thought of all kinds of attractive ways of phrasing this little speech, ways that would make it clear that I was neither an absolute beginner nor a practised meditator. I would say something different from the others. And of course I would speak in English, rather than going through the translator, the lousy translator. Perhaps I could take the opportunity to offer my own translation services.

Then I was angry with myself. What was this, a theatre? A TV show? I remembered how, on being told I was on the Booker Prize shortlist, I had been unable to stop a modest acceptance speech from playing itself over and over in my mind for weeks before the event. Literally for weeks this acceptance speech had driven me crazy. From the moment of the phone call telling me I was on the list to the moment of the announcement that someone else had won, my acceptance speech refused to stop accepting the prize in my head. Each time with some tiny addition, some precious new flourish. The experience was simultaneously infuriating and immensely gratifying. It really was such a clever, ironic, modest speech. People would not be impressed immediately, I thought. They would just think what a nice ordinary guy I was. Only later would they see what a clever speech it had been. Then they would think me doubly clever, and doubly modest for not having wished to impose my full cleverness on them immediately, but with delayed effect, like those fertiliser sticks you put in the ground that dissolve slowly for months.

On and on this speech performed itself for me, on and on and on. And now I was doing the same thing *for Coleman*. At every new pain and ache and itch that arose, every sound that irritated and interrupted, I revised my little speech. I polished my speech, shortened my speech, lengthened my speech. Which was insane. At least for the Booker there was an audience. Would have been an audience. TV! If I'd won. Here there were just sixty people living in silence, trying in silence to achieve some better relationship with themselves, with existence. *What could it possibly matter how I came across to them?* They didn't care about me. I didn't care about them. And then, how can it *ever* truly matter how one comes across? What on earth could anyone care about a Booker acceptance speech? For Christ's sake! And then, I had known from the beginning that I couldn't win the Booker with the novel I had written. My chances were not six to one but six million to one. It was a miracle they had put me on the list with such an angry book that had sentences more than two pages long. They'd never let it win. So preparing my acceptance speech was doubly ridiculous. At least here I was bound to get a hearing. From sixty people. The speech would happen.

Or maybe not. Because now it occurred to me that what I must do was ask to be excused from saying anything. That was the solution. Then I could stop playing the speech over and over in my mind. I might simply announce: 'Please, Mr Coleman, I would rather say nothing.' Or, 'Teacher, I wish to take refuge in the Noble Silence.' That was good. Then people would know that I *did not want* to draw attention to myself. Perhaps I would speak in Italian, so they weren't obliged to marvel at my being English. Except there was my accent, of course. There is always something that gives you away. Then they would be obliged to marvel how well I spoke Italian. Despite the slight accent. And of course I would immediately translate what I had said into English so that Coleman wouldn't have to hear my carefully chosen words from this incompetent one-legged wonder who disturbed us all from time to time by dragging himself in and out of the room on his crutches. Presumably to go to the bathroom.

'I would rather say nothing, if that's allowed,' I would say, in Italian. Or even better, I could approach Coleman in the corridor before tomorrow and, murmuring softly, ask if he could avoid calling me out to the front. Certainly people could hardly say I was looking for attention if I stayed sitting when the others went up to talk.

Or could they?

It was simply maddening how insistently this

meaningless chatter ground away in my head those first three days of the retreat. Perhaps I should confess, I thought, when I was called out to the front, that I had wasted hours and hours of this precious meditation time with self-regarding thoughts about what I should say when called out to the front, thoughts entirely directed to the effect of my performance on the audience rather than an honest comment on the way my meditation was going. Badly, needless to say. Should I be confessional? Or would that have even more *effect*?

Of course I then imagined *writing* about this meaningless chatter and how brilliantly I could deconstruct myself, or someone like me (very like me), in a novel perhaps. I could very cleverly show how useless I was. Should I write a novel or should I make it non-fiction? Which would seem more *necessary*? And if I wrote non-fiction, should I perhaps use a third person, as Coetzee had in *Boyhood* and *Youth*, or accept the slithery candour of the first person like everyone else? Those are strange books that Coetzee wrote. They make you feel uneasy.

It went on and on. I hated it. I couldn't find a way out. After the first retreat I had read Coetzee's essay on Robert Walser and been astonished by a curious fact and by Coetzee's response to it, a fact that now came back to my mind as being extremely pertinent to this speech madness. In his mid-thirties Walser suddenly found that he could no longer hold a pen. His hand became painfully cramped every time he picked one up. He couldn't write. But of course he had to write, otherwise who was he, where were his old ambitions? So he fell to writing with a pencil. And his handwriting changed drastically. Instead of the generously rounded calligraphy of the well-educated young man from the provinces, he now wrote in a script so minuscule that to the naked eye it looked like some indecipherable code. Even experts, Coetzee remarked, cannot be sure they have got it right.

Why could Walser work with a pencil but not a pen? I wondered now, partly as an antidote to playing this idiotic speech over and over in my head and partly because I suspected that, however self-aggrandising it might seem, Walser's problem and my own were not unrelated. And why, in particular, did he talk about his 'pencil method'? Here comes Coetzee's bizarre interpretation. Like an artist using charcoal, the Nobel winner claimed, Walser needed 'to get a steady rhythmic hand movement going before he could slip into the frame of mind in which reverie, composition, and the flow of the writing tool became the same thing'. That is, he needed the rhythmic movement of the pencil to overcome some obstacle which Coetzee wasn't eager to identify.

But why is a pencil more rhythmic than a pen? Is the charcoal analogy pertinent? Painters do not try to execute miniatures in charcoal, do they? Surely if Walser's script had now shrunk to the indecipherably microscopic, the hand movements would have been *more cramped* and not free and rhythmic at all. Isn't it more likely that Walser's problem lay with the egotism and exhibitionism inherent in writing and publication? That was what was cramping his hand. 'Writers do not know what they lost when they sacrificed anonymity,' Walser had written somewhere. Words to that effect. His novels were all glaringly autobiographical, with an alter ego at the centre of each story. Was it possible that the switch to pencil, which, unlike ink, can be erased, gave him a feeling that what he was doing was provisional, could be reversed? And that writing in such a tiny script he was in a way *hiding* his work from others? He was doing it and not doing it. For a while Walser would copy out his pencil manuscripts in a fair hand for the publishers, using a pen. Detached from the moment of creation, or self-revelation, self-affirmation, the pen was mysteriously useable again. But later he left his work in pencil without trying to publish it, and later still he *stopped writing altogether*.

I kept thinking about Walser in relation to this conundrum of self-presentation, of simultaneously wanting to take the stage and truly not wanting to take it, above all not wanting to want to take it, or not wanting to be seen to want to take it. And wasn't there something of the same conundrum in Coetzee's disquieting decision to write his autobiography in the third person? As if he wasn't writing about himself, but someone else. And no one is harder on that someone else than Coetzee in *Boyhood* and *Youth*, that person responsible for his committing the unforgivable indiscretion of writing these books. He was hard on himself because he was writing books about himself. And everyone knew it. Even though he pretended it wasn't himself. That was what he hated. Writing about himself, he wrote against himself. Himself being a writer writing himself. 'Not I,' Beckett proclaimed. Or had a mouth proclaim. A mouth without a face. Without an I, without an eye. 'Shall I never be able to lie upon any subject other than myself?' wonders Malone, or Beckett, in *Malone Dies*. A rhetorical question. No. Pain, pain, not *my* pain. Please. And when Deirdre Bair went to interview Beckett for the biography the first thing he said was, 'So you've come to demonstrate that it was all, after all, autobiographical.'

And it was!

And I was in deep trouble. I couldn't go on. For long periods, as the hours ticked by, I felt I was swaying from side to side and must sooner or later crash to the floor. I began to look forward to it. Or fall on my nose. I was so hunched. It would be such a relief when I crashed on my nose and everyone would see how much I was suffering and then I could stop and take a rest, take a walk, go to bed, go home perhaps. There was now a stabbing pain right between the shoulders. It was ferocious. Stab, stab, stab. Bizarre lights and burning heat radiated out from it. How could I be in so much pain when I knew there was nothing at all wrong with me? What was I learning from all this, I wondered? Nothing. Nothing except that *every single thought* that rose to my mind was in some way *self-regarding*. No, in *every* way self-regarding. Every thought. My analysis of Walser's problem was no doubt accurate, I complimented myself, and fitted in with many other elements in Walser's biography. My sense that Coetzee actually needed to miss the point was in line with his own obvious conflict when it came to presenting himself. But what is there to present, in writing, if not oneself? Even if I wrote about the man on the moon it would be self-presentation. *Especially* if I wrote about the man on the moon. What I must say when I am finally called to the front, I decided, is that these three days of meditation have revealed to me that every thought I think is, in one way or another, an ugly, fatuous form of self-congratulation. Even what appears to be the most searing self-criticism is in fact self-congratulation. A man capable of seeing his worst side, you congratulate yourself. Coetzee is pleased to have been so hard on himself. Nice observation, Tim. Was there no way out of this? How could I stop it, really stop it, *forever*? Without blowing my brains out.

'Gently return your attention to the breath crossing the point on the upper lip. The in-breath crossing the point, the out-breath crossing the point. Nama and Rupa, mind and material. Everything in the world, mind and material. Without identity.'

Tom Pax was called to the front with three other names.

So much for identity. The translator was misreading from his list of names. Pax I'm used to, but I hate it when I'm called Tom.

Knowing that Coleman always proceeded from left to right, I put down my cushion on the far right.

The first man admitted to panic attacks.

Coleman was silent. 'Just concentrate on the breath,' he told him eventually. 'And make an objective note of the fear.'

The second man confessed he kept falling asleep then waking himself up as his body slipped and slumped.

Like the disciples at Gethsemane, I thought, and thinking this was simultaneous with congratulating myself for the pertinent allusion, then wearily ticking myself off for another manifestation of self-regard.

'One does tend to get sleepy the first three days,' Coleman told him. 'It will stop as we go on. Don't be angry with yourself. Make an objective mental note – sleepiness – then return your concentration to the breath on your lips.'

In a late change of plan I decided I would simply say I was having a lot of pain and was finding it hard to concentrate. Nothing else. The most bland summary of what everyone else had said. I hoped that wouldn't sound provocative. I hoped it wouldn't sound anything at all.

I would say it in Italian. Speak in Italian, as if you were one of them.

What was the 'as if' about?

Then the third man confessed that his main difficulty these last two days had been that he had kept thinking about what he would say, now, when he was called to the front. And Coleman laughed. Coleman laughed deep in his fat belly, a really hearty, rumbly, fat laugh, and said he had been wondering when somebody was going to own up to that. He was evidently much amused.

We had been set up.

'And now I'm saying something completely different from what I planned to say,' my companion lamented.

Coleman smiled. 'So you lost the present for a future moment that didn't even happen.'

That was my Booker story exactly.

'We never say what we plan to say, do we?' Coleman added kindly. 'So why not just leave the words till the moment itself? Nothing is at stake here. You're not being interviewed for a job.'

My turn next. Stay to plan, I decided. The new plan, that is. There is nothing worse than the penalty taker who decides at the last second to go for the other corner.

The fat man turned to me. There was a charisma about him. There was a merriment in his heavy features. Sunk in the flesh, the eyes were bright and young.

'Well, Tom Pax?'

I opened my mouth and nothing came out. It's an experience I've had a thousand times in dreams, but never till now in life. I was voiceless. I was supposed to speak and I couldn't say a word. Three or four times I tried. Nothing but air and pain in my throat.

Shaking his head, Coleman looked down on me from his armchair throne with a mixture of condescension and sympathy.

'I don't know what's happening,' I finally croaked. The words were barely audible.

He leaned slightly towards me. 'Why don't you go back to your place?' he said.

Personally Of Course I Regret Everything

OVER THE NEXT four days I decided I must stop writing. I had just gathered some concentration, tuned my mind to the breathing, allowed the ticking clock to enter my unresisting pulse, to run across my cheeks and lips and up and down my arms, dissolve in my chest and belly, just got myself settled, in short, into the sitting position, into the meditation room, into the company of my fellow meditators, when the time came to switch from Anapana to Vipassana, from breathing to exploration. Then it was like stepping from a darkened bedroom into a burning house. Or coming out of anaesthetic after surgery. First a prolonged explosion deep in the skull, then, one after another, in the dark landscape behind closed eyes, not so much fires as burning rocks, great boulders of obstruction and pain.

After the first hour of this I hurried outside into the afternoon sunshine, overwhelmed by déjà vu. Had I been writing these experiences as a novel, I thought, then the crisis on the mountain terrace that rainy dawn in Maroggia would have been the obvious place for the story to end, with a life-changing breakthrough. But it had not been life-changing. Here I was five months later, back at square one, back with my old self, back with a sense of something that would never budge, with a body that seemed to resist me, didn't want my company.

Back with my bent back.

I watched the others bringing tea and kiwis out into the garden. On day one, day two, day three, people had walked vigorously up and down, or lain on the grass to do sit-ups and stretching exercises. It was a flat, symmetrical renaissance-style garden, a lawn split by a cross of paths. Now on day four everybody was moving in slow motion. People would take a few steps then stop, standing absolutely motionless for five minutes, even ten, transfixed. They sipped their tea slowly, peeled their kiwis as if it didn't matter whether they ever actually ate the fruit or not. Nobody was exercising. I too had lost any desire to exercise. And I had the impression that I wasn't the only one to have been caught out by the Vipassana. There was a shell-shocked look to the young man passing back and forth in front of me, placing one foot in front of another, heel to toe, as if walking a tightrope over an abyss.

Then it seemed to me that the only way to force an irreversible change in my life would be to dump the project that had been driving me, goading me, making me ill, I decided, for as long as I could remember: the *WORD*

PROJECT. If illness is a sign of election in an author, I thought – where had I read that? – then renouncing writing might be a necessary step to being well. Not that I was actually *ill* any more. But I certainly wasn't *healed* either. Otherwise, what was I doing in this crazy place?

Pulling my ankles into place for the next cross-legged hour, I remembered it had been V. S. Naipaul who had said that to me. We were eating lunch together at a conference many years ago. 'A writer must undergo a serious illness,' Naipaul had confided solemnly. This was some years before his Nobel. 'To awaken his conscience.' Which of course was only Naipaul's way of saying that *he* had undergone a serious illness and *he* was one of the elect. The man was nothing if not vain. How could I have fallen for such nonsense? Because he had indeed written some great novels, of course. Then I recalled that moment in *The Information* when one literary author wonders why a rival literary author bothers to keep on writing. And you know at once that the question is really Amis's question. He calculates the man's earnings. Less per hour than a taxi driver makes. Why does he do it? *To avoid facing up to naked, unmitigated, unmediated reality*, the author (and no doubt Amis) decides. Perhaps it was time, then, for me to face up to that: the simply being here, instead of taking refuge in writing about being here. I must go speechless. The moment of aphony at the check-up had shown me the way.

Guru Coleman, I felt, was trying to tell us something similar in his evening talks. The most immediate reality, the *only* reality to which we had access at every moment of our lives, the fat man said, was the breath, this breath, this instant, crossing our upper lip as it went in and out of our lungs. *The* breath, not *our* breath. Everything else was empty imagining.

These evening talks – from six p.m. to seven – were remarkable for their combination of blandness and pessimism. Sprawled in his chair, vapid smile on slack cheeks, ham hands on chubby knees, Coleman lurched into the sort of wet, preacherly parables my father would not have stooped to with a Sunday School class. 'So you want to have a red Ferrari?' Coleman almost crooned to the Italian crowd. He paused at every rest point. 'All your life you have dreamed of a red Ferrari' – pause – 'you *have* to have that red Ferrari' – pause, smile – 'and when you get it?' – pause, deep sigh – 'When you *get* it?'

He didn't bother to say, what then?

Please, I thought, while the translator trundled through his deadpan approximation for the benefit of the very few Italians who hadn't already grasped the idea, please, do me the favour of finding an object of desire that it would be genuinely hard to relinquish.

I must have a certain woman.

I must win the Nobel Prize.

It irritated me immensely that he drivelled on about this red Ferrari. People on meditation retreats are hardly of a kind to sell their souls for a sports car.

I supposed.

Sometimes Coleman felt too tired to talk and had his translator read us something directly in Italian, while he looked on with the same bland smile on his face.

'There are ten levels of awareness in Vipassana meditation,' the translator read swinging his one leg from the table top.

Sammasana, theoretical recognition of *Anicca*, *Dukkha* and *Anatta* (change, dissatisfaction, emptiness), through observation and analysis;

Udayabbaya, awareness of the appearance and dissolution of *Nama* and *Rupa*, mind and material, through observation and analysis;

Bangha, awareness of the rapid change of *Nama* and *Rupa*, like a swift current or a flow of energy; intense awareness of things dissolving;

Bhaya, awareness that this existence is terrible;

Adinava, awareness that this existence is full of misery;

Nibbida, awareness that this existence is disgusting;

Muncitukamyata, awareness of the urgent need and desire to flee this existence;

Patisankha, awareness that the time has come to work for complete liberation, through *Anicca*;

Sankarupekkha, awareness that the time has come to detach ourselves from all contingent phenomena (*sankhara*) and to break with our ego-centred lives;

Anuloma, awareness that speeds up our attempt to achieve liberation.

When he reached *Adinava* I began to smile and by *Munci*-whatever-it-was I was laughing. I couldn't help it. It was so *Beckett*, so like Arsene's great speech in *Watt* that I always use with my second-year students, and that always sets me chuckling:

> Personally of course I regret everything. Not a word, not a deed, not a thought, not a need, not a grief, not a joy, not a girl, not a boy, not a doubt, not a trust, not a scorn, not a lust, not a hope, not a fear, not a smile, not a tear, not a name, not a face, no time, no place, that I do not regret, exceedingly. An ordure from beginning to end.

And it goes on:

> The Tuesday scowls, the Wednesday growls, the Thursday curses, the Friday howls, the Saturday snores, the Sunday yawns, the Monday mourns, the Monday morns. The whacks, the moans, the cracks, the groans, the welts, the squeaks, the belts, the shrieks, the pricks, the prayers, the kicks, the tears, the skelps, and the yelps . . .

But why did these lines of Beckett make me laugh, I wondered, the way I was laughing now at *Bhaya, Adinava, Nibbida* – this existence terrible, this existence full of misery, this existence disgusting? Because they were so over the top, I suppose, because the trite rhythms and rhymes showed how misleading language can be, making everything sound hunky-dory while in fact what we were talking about was deep despair, as if I'd recounted my own months of pain as a nursery rhyme.

But it was more than that. I had been laughing at Beckett, I realised, ever since I was an adolescent, because these ideas were *forbidden*. My Anglican parents would never have countenanced such a vision of life. The blandness of the Anglican sermon always ended in optimism: the risen Christ, redemption, renewed commitment, the promise of glory. All my life I had associated blandness with Christian conformity, socialist optimism, complacency; and hence, vice versa, pessimism with non-conformity, intellectual acuity, liberation from coercive fairy tale into unpleasant truth.

My parents hated Beckett, hated it when I started reading Beckett. 'You've been led astray by your brother!' they yelled. They hated Beckett's *nihilism*, his defeatism. 'And if I could begin it all over again,' Arsene goes on,

knowing what I know now, the result would be the same. And if I could begin again a third time, knowing what I would know then, the result would be the same. And if I could begin it all over again a hundred times, knowing each time a little more than the time before, the result would always be the same, and the hundredth life as the first, and the hundred lives as one. A cat's flux.

A hundred lives as one. A cat's flux! I loved that. And now I discovered that it was the essence of Buddhism, and that I was supposed to be arriving at an awareness of this awfulness while meditating. So many people see reincarnation as reassuring, even wishful thinking – you don't die, you get another shot at it – but Beckett, like Buddha, knew better. Every existence plumps you right back on the rollercoaster of desire and disappointment, scratching yourself out of one itch into another. Best out of it! And too bad that suicide only thrusts you deeper into the *samsara* shit.

Nihilism was evil, my parents insisted. Just the way my mother said 'nihilism' gave it a dangerous foreign sound, like an Italian stiletto. Or like Nietzsche. Foreign names, evil foreign words. Nothing sensible and Anglo-Saxon about nihilism. Nihilism was of the devil, it was the beginning of all criminal behaviour. Who would ever behave if life was meaningless? Even worse, nihilism was the beginning of *not trying*, not making a wholesome Anglican effort to improve the world. God had created us in his image, life was good; if the Fall had left the world less than perfect, that was our fault and it was up to us to make it better. Not to bellyache. Nor to bail out like a wimp. Buddhist fatalism was evil and led people to corruption and despondency which was why millions were dying of hunger and disease in Asia. 'We know because we've been there,' my parents would say, referring to missionary trips to Malaysia, India, Pakistan.

All this when I was sixteen, seventeen.

Now, listening to the complacent, pessimistic Coleman, it occurred to me that Buddhism framed things differently. To perceive the emptiness at the heart of existence, you must *first* achieve purity. Far from being a plunge into criminal behaviour, such a vision was – how odd! – the *reward* for good behaviour, and a key in the first door that would get you out of gaol. It was impurities and ignorance that prevented you from seeing things as they really were (awful) and hence prompted you to grow attached to life and suffer. The person who perceives deeply that life is empty, must be morally admirable otherwise he could never have arrived at the concentration required to grasp this. Certainly, I thought, I had always had an impression of Beckett as somehow saintly, or at least hermit-like in his pessimism, hardly a man plagued by the desire for this world's goods.

On the other hand, and this was where it all grew complicated, there was no way I personally thought of life as a veil of misery. No way could I accept Coleman's vision. Or Beckett's, for that matter. Precisely the problem for me is that life is *so beautiful*. I am very attached to it. My misery when I was ill was only in part the pain. More important was losing beauty, being unable to enjoy. But I have never imagined joy was impossible.

Thus my confused reflections in the old monastery garden after that evening's talk, with the air now silvering to twilight and that grating music striking up in the valley below. It was beautiful being here, I decided, in this balmy air beneath the cypresses high on the Tuscan hills. The fairground noise had ceased to bother me. It was beautiful watching my fellow meditators cloaked in their thoughts at dusk, noble in their silence. There was a young woman, I remember, six or seven months pregnant, standing at the low parapet gazing down into the valley. Her fingers, just meeting on her belly, were relaxed and slender, and from time to time she turned her head this way and that, twisting her long neck, as if to relieve some stiffness there. Life is *too* beautiful, I decided. Not disgusting at all. There was a shadow of a smile on her lips. And the act of meditation was making it *more* beautiful, causing me to experience it more calmly. Simply eating had become an intense, slow pleasure, feeling a rough crust of bread on the roof of your mouth, a crisp carrot between your teeth, a forkful of rice melting in saliva on the tongue, slithering down the throat, then the cool cleanness of the water that washed it all away, the quiet sense of repletion. Sitting silently at table with the others was also an intense pleasure, watching their silent faces as they ate, watching their concentration. Breathing the evening air was beautiful.

I should definitely stop writing, I decided. How could I possess this deep calm day by day if I went on writing, hoping, fighting? I remembered Emil Cioran saying of Beckett that, if, over dinner, someone started discussing the relative merits of contemporary writers, Beckett would be furious and turn his chair to the wall in mute disgust. He

I should definitely stop writing, I decided. How could I possess this deep calm day by day if I went on writing, hoping, fighting?

refused to be part of such conversations. Wasn't all Beckett's later writing, it occurred to me, like Walser's tiny pencil script, an attempt to stop writing while still going on writing? First the switch to French – language, language, not *my* language – then the pieces getting shorter and shorter, with each sentence appearing to cancel out the one before, the whole thing more and more resistant to the reader, more and more concentrated on simple physical movements, walking, shifting the eyes, breathing. 'All writing is a sin against speechlessness,' Beckett had said. He would have stopped, I thought, if he could.

Again I recalled the evening I was at the Booker dinner. My acceptance speech churning in my head, I nevertheless prepared myself to clap when Arundhati Roy won. I think all of us on the shortlist knew that Arundhati Roy would win: the book was charming, it was already a bestseller, it was from India, it was about poor children who suffer abuse but make good, the author was beautiful without being too young, sophisticated without being a member of the English upper classes. How could she not win? I prepared myself to clap, and I *did* clap, damn it! And Arundhati Roy went to the podium and stood there smiling, beautifully – she was wearing a beautiful dress – and said she was lost for words, quite lost, because she had *never imagined* she could win, she hadn't prepared anything to say. And I knew this was false because I had been to lunch with her the day before and she seemed more than prepared to win. If nothing else, the bookmakers were giving her as odds-on favourite. So this speech, like the one I never delivered, had been carefully prepared, I realised, and prepared, like mine, to seem modest and unprepared, hence doubly false.

Then Salman Rushdie walked over to me and frowned and said if it was him he would be furious; he would be throwing chairs round and complaining that he should have won. I smiled and said I *was* furious, but not in this particular moment, just generally. Generally in a fury. If I threw chairs around all the time there would be nowhere for anyone to sit.

How can one lead such a life without running into an ulcer or two?

Stop.

I suppose it has taken me an hour and more to write down these last few reflections, but it only takes a second or two for them to flash through the mind as you try to focus on the breathing on your lips. How many times did these ideas race through my head in the following days, in the long silent dawns, in the guided sessions as Guru Coleman invited us to explore our bodies, in the twilight hour with the cackling nuns and the clashing music and the strong cries of children playing outside the monastery walls? Stop writing, I told myself. Enough. Enough.

Uncalled for, unwanted, the thoughts flew across my mental space, back and forth, hither and thither, like birds in the evening sky, chasing and losing and finding each other, racing, wheeling, dispersing, gathering, gliding a while then flapping in hard flight, always moving, through each other and across each other, at different altitudes, different speeds, as the light fails and the breeze comes up and the rain spatters on rustling leaves. Then one by one, at last, they begin to settle, they drop from view. With a last flutter, a thought settles on its perch and is quiet. On a rooftop perhaps, or in your wrist, in your throat. Another joins the first, and another. Thoughts fluffing their feathers before falling still. Perhaps one last squawk – *Rushdie was right! I should have hurled a chair!* – then silence. Until, huddled together on their wire, between your ears, they lose definition, merge into each other, become a single pool of feathery shadow, deep shadow in the darkness, one layer beneath another, beneath others, as eyes close behind closed eyelids, watched by still deeper eyes, and the mind at last discovers itself transparent.

It was on the sixth or seventh evening that I came to myself in the meditation room and found I was alone: the others had gone. I was late for bed.

Coleman

ITCH BY ITCH, ache by ache, pulse by pulse, the body was explored. There was the first time I felt the roots of my teeth, a deep vibration in the gums, the first time the tongue throbbed and twitched and was truly present in my mouth, the first time a ball of fire rose slowly from stomach to chest. Pains flared, burned, petered out. Then returned.

Meantime one's personality was being stripped apart. It was a complicated demolition job where work had to proceed in a certain order: first this certainty came down, then that, then the one on the floor beneath. Not a sudden collapse but a steady dismantling. Or perhaps it was simply that without the people each side of you who make you who you are – wife, family, colleagues, friends – without work, TV, radio, without newspapers and books, phone and email, without a keyboard or paper to write on, the construct that was me was falling apart, rather as though a ship held together by the water it sailed in had been lifted into dry dock. Bits fell off. There was a day of tears, a day of confusion, a day of panic, a day of optimism.

'May all beings be free from all attachment,' Coleman intoned and he explained the pains we were experiencing thus: the body was an asbestos-clad stove full of burning coals. The coals were the smouldering accumulation of our past thoughts and actions. If we felt no heat in the ordinary way it was because the constant stimulation of our senses, the interminable churning of our mental activity, were powerful insulators: always moving, thinking, doing, we didn't notice. But by taking the five precepts and practising Anapana we had stripped off the asbestos and cracked open the stove. Then we felt our karma's painful heat. Now, day by day, with Vipassana, we would go into every corner of the stove, we would turn the coals so that they glowed and scorched. It was hard, he said. But slowly, surely, they would burn themselves out and all would be calm. Our minds would be pure and empty.

I thought: So they wait until the seventh day to tell you that the whole thing is based on pain, experiencing pain, accepting pain, something that, had you been informed beforehand, would most likely have deterred you from coming.

'Attachment to self,' Coleman said, 'is so strong that we will never be rid of it unless the suffering we feel within is stronger.' I remembered Beckett's *Endgame*. 'You must learn to suffer better than that, Clov, if you want them to weary of punishing you – one day.'

I had developed a curious state of mind during these evening talks. I believed nothing. I found the ideas ridiculous and contradictory: if life was utterly empty, how could you ascribe a value to purity, how could there be rules governing reincarnation based on your behaviour? etc, etc. At the same time I listened attentively, I enjoyed listening, and I saw that there were indeed ways in which Coleman's words could be applied to my experiences. I felt I knew what he meant when he spoke of everything flowing, mind and material dissolving into energy. Nor was it unthinkable that the strange pains I had been feeling had in some way to do with all those years sitting tensely, racking my brains over sheets of empty paper, building up hopes, rejoicing over some small achievement, over-reacting to setbacks and disappointments. And it was true that if you placed yourself, or your attention, as it were *beside* these pains, if you just sat together with them and let them be, not reacting or wishing them away, they did in the end subside. Likewise the thoughts: if you let them bubble up without judging them, or engaging them in any way, they gradually fizzled out. What's more, you felt that a certain serenity had been acquired in this process, an understanding that much of the pain we feel comes from our reaction to pain, much of our agitation from our excitement with agitation.

Above all, and more generally, I did sense the first hints of that famous equanimity Coleman was constantly speaking of. I had learned to put up with the lazy translation. I forgave our one-legged interpreter. In the end the guy seemed extremely pleasant, and now I was getting some perspective, not at all as incompetent as I had supposed. Some remarks he made in answer to people's questions were extremely helpful. I even forgave *myself* when, from time to time, I still grew irritated with him. Of the two, forgiving myself was harder. It came to me now that I'd always risen to the bait of yelling at myself, I'd always been determined to savour just how humiliating failure can be, and to make an exhibition of it. So this was progress, of a kind; paradoxically, letting go, you actually gained control, albeit of a different kind from the control you'd spent your life seeking. Distance, rather than grip. All you have to do now is stop writing, I decided, and you'll have clinched it. You'll have changed for ever.

But if I stopped writing, what would I do for a living? It was a false question. I had my teaching. I would be a teacher, a sort of servant. Robert Walser had been obsessed by the idea of service, of burying the ego in service. He dreamed of being a butler and actually worked as one for a while. I knew that this was a bridge too far for me. But teaching is an honest job. I enjoy teaching. With the writing behind me, the tussle in the mind would be over, likewise the gap between experience and fabricating a written account of experience, plus the foolish yearning for praise and success. All over. My health could only improve.

On the eighth morning I had an appointment to see Coleman. The afternoon check-ups had been suspended from day four. I wondered if this was because they were concerned that some of the more negative, aggressive participants might start a rebellion (one woman had used the word gulag when complaining about the rule against leaving the grounds); or because, with sixty people, they felt it was too much of a waste of time, too distracting to have everyone listen to everyone else. If you needed advice, they said, you could sign up for a fifteen-minute appointment with Coleman during the unguided meditation sessions on the seventh, eighth and ninth days.

My first thought was not to sign up. I had nothing to ask Coleman, or to tell him. If I wanted to know more about Buddhism, I could read about it, though I couldn't really see the point of pursuing notions so whimsical that I would never be able to accept them; those born in a rich, beautiful, peaceful country like Italy, Coleman had told us, could congratulate themselves on having scored highly in their previous lives. Ergo, those born in the Sudan had behaved badly. Nor did I imagine the guru would be interested in my views or reflections. Why should he be? Why should I want him to be? No, the only reason for my going to see Coleman would be curiosity, meaning, in my case, the possibility of collecting an interesting conversation to put in a book at some later date. Or in an article. I could write to the *New York Review* and ask them if they would be interested in an article on Vipassana meditation. Or to the *Guardian*.

But if you don't want to go on writing, what is the point of collecting things to write? Don't do it.

On the other hand, I *was* curious about Coleman. He was a type I'd never encountered before, a strange mix of blandness, serenity and shrewdness. He had spoken of an earlier life, in the 1950s and '60s, working for the CIA in Thailand before his search for a more tranquil state of mind led him to Burma, Buddhism and Vipassana. The anecdotes in his evening talks were infantile, deliberately so I had begun to sense, and delivered with a childish take-it-or-leave-it enthusiasm. He was deliberately insulting the intelligence, attempting to put that pesky faculty in its place. On the plus side, he had none of the sanctimoniousness that fatally attaches itself to every Christian clergyman. Nor did he wear any item of clothing that smacked of robe or ritual, or New Age vogue, for that matter. It was always: old slippers, shapeless pants, a colourless T-shirt. 'I had to have these pants made for me,' he announced apropos of nothing. 'Because I'm so fat.'

My immediate impression, then, was that the man was harmless. He wouldn't harm a fly, which was just as well, being a Buddhist. But once we shifted from the monotony of Anapana, to the more taxing adventure of Vipassana, I began to sense how powerful Coleman's charisma could be. He would wait until we were all settled in the meditation room before making his entrance. We would take off our shoes at the door, go to our places, reorganise our cushions, drag our ankles into place, arrange our hands in laps or on knees, close our eyes and settle. Only when we had been there for some minutes would we pick up the sound of slippers shuffling along the corridor. Outside, the guru would pause, as if he hadn't quite made up his mind whether to come in. Then the door clicked, creaked open, swung to and clicked shut again. Again he paused, standing at the threshold, and I remember having the impression that he liked to hold on to things for support, the door handle, the table where the translator sat. Or perhaps just to touch them. He liked to touch things. We listened to his footsteps, teasingly slow, as he made his way to his shabby armchair. He sighed heavily, slumped into the upholstery and was silent.

Behind our closed eyes, his presence filled the room, his laboured breathing became our breathing. The clock ticked. Sometimes, in the far distance, you might hear a train hooting, or, on one afternoon, very faintly, an ambulance. More often dogs barked, a chained dog barking at others passing by, I thought. Thoughts, thoughts. I made my objective note. The minutes passed. Coleman was silent. There was no hurry. At the same time a fine tension began to creep around the room, a collective waiting for his voice; when at last it did ring out, we started. It seemed to speak from inside us.

'May all beings live in peace.'

Guiding the meditations, Coleman had a deeper, more measured, sonorous voice than the one he used in his talks. 'May all beings be free from all attachment and all sorrow. May all beings be filled with happiness and sympathetic joy.'

'Sadhu Sadhu Sadhu.'

I didn't say the words myself, but I assented.

He began tamely. He had us focus on the breath for some minutes, the breath crossing the lip. When he didn't speak for a while, you wondered if he mightn't have fallen asleep. Then the voice boomed out again. No doubt because our eyes were closed and because we were sitting so still for so long, sounds became physical things. The clock ticked in fingers and toes. The gong that began and ended each session tingled in my cheeks. A door slamming was a slap. Coleman's voice clanged a bell in your chest. Your body rang.

'Now we will take our attention away from the breath,' he said calmly, 'and move it upwards to the top of the skull.' He began to lead us through our bodies, and when Coleman named a part of the body it really was easier for you to get in contact with it, easier than if you were meditating alone. Naming a part of the body, his voice touched it, but without using any mystical formulas. 'Now move your attention to your cheeks. To the left cheek. To the right cheek. To both cheeks. Pay attention. Take note of any sensation that arises in this part of the body.'

His timing was impressive. He would have you concentrate on a wrist, thigh, or shoulder to the point that it became an agony to be so focused. I had never imagined that this combination of emptying the mind of thought and concentrating it on physical sensation could be such hard work. 'Feel how the sensation changes, in your hands, the back of the hands, the fingers, the fingertips, constantly changes, infinitely nuanced, infinitely delicate; *anicca*, know *anicca*.'

Then after a long pause, just when it seemed you couldn't maintain this focus a moment longer, he would say: 'And now, let go. Not holding on to the sensation if it's pleasurable. Not fighting the sensation if it's painful. Just . . . let . . . go.'

And I did. It was as if Coleman, Coleman's voice, were able to command the same waves of release that had initially so surprised me when practising paradoxical relaxation. He commanded and I let go; a strange fluid rushed in, rigidity dissolved.

'Deeper,' Coleman insisted. 'Deeper and deeper, into the muscle, into the bone. Feel the sensation in the very bone. Feel that even the bone is subject to change. *Anicca*.'

We were concentrating on the arms, the elbows, and now it seemed I really was feeling the two bones in my right forearm. The ulna and the radius were present to me, their shape and consistency. It was the first time Coleman had invited us to go into the bone and, sceptical as I always am, I wondered if this was hypnotism. Was I the object of some clever hypnotic suggestion? But if it was hypnotism, would I be able to wonder if it was hypnotism?

'Let go,' Coleman said softly, 'just let go,' and another barrier went. I began to look forward to him saying the words. I was disappointed when he didn't. I realised that in the future, meditating alone at home, I would say this formula to myself – let go – imagining Coleman saying it, imagining his voice and the particular cadence he used, and I would feel how much more effective the words would have been if he were there in person to say them.

I decided I would, after all, make an appointment to see Coleman and signed myself in on the morning of the eighth day. Standing outside his door, I felt unexpectedly emotional. I had made a considerable effort over the last day or so not to plan a speech, or imagine the conversation, or even make a list of things to say. All the same, the meeting had begun to loom in my mind as something special. Outside his door I felt agitated. Something important was at stake. The feeling irritated me. I was an adult, canny, experienced and illusion-free. Why on earth was I going to talk to a guru?

With impressive punctuality, the woman before me came out of the room together with the translator and I went in and sat down. Coleman smiled and asked me if I had got my voice back and I said, 'Now we'll see.'

'Bravo!' he laughed.

It was a small sitting room with two armchairs arranged face to face and the shutters half closed against the August sun. I asked him how come he was limping so badly and he explained that they had been moving him around a conference complex in Malaysia on an open golf buggy when the driver braked hard and he had fallen out of the buggy and broken his hip.

Coleman spent some minutes describing the accident and the hospital. He seemed oddly enthusiastic about it all. 'The Malaysian nurses were wonderful!' Then he asked, 'But how are you getting on?'

I told him the retreat had stirred up a lot of emotions and reflections.

He waited.

I looked at him. He smiled at me. Not inviting, just waiting. The problem was, I said, that I didn't see how one could go on living the same way one always had and incorporate Vipassana into that. I felt this discipline was demanding pride of place, demanding that my whole life change.

Even as I said these portentous things I appreciated that had someone like myself made this kind of declaration, this admission of weakness, to my mother and father in their evangelical heyday, they would have had him on his knees giving his heart to Jesus in no time at all. There would have been tears and prayers and rivers of emotion. Coleman raised a bushy eyebrow. After a long pause he said: 'A lot of people get that idea into their heads.'

I was a little thrown. I waited but nothing more was forthcoming.

'Well,' I eventually said, 'I'm being asked to look on life as an affliction, a source of suffering, and to learn not to want it, whereas, the truth is I find the whole thing very beautiful. Living. These hills, the people here. I'm very attached to it all. Perhaps that's why I don't see how Vipassana is compatible. With the way I live, I mean. I keep feeling I'm being asked to say goodbye to life.'

Coleman was attentive, pleasant, distant. Again, after a pause, he said, 'Concentrate on *anicca*, get to know *anicca*.'

This did begin to sound like, 'Get to know our Lord

Jesus.' I felt annoyed. I could play mute as well as anyone, I decided. I wouldn't say anything else till he started taking the interview seriously.

We watched each other. He seemed to understand my decision and instead of prolonging the silence asked, 'What do you do for a living?'

'I teach translation. And write books.'

'How interesting. What kind of books?'

'Novels, essays.'

He sat smiling at me. I waited. Then I realised he was smiling because he knew I was waiting for him to ask another question about my books, so that I could talk about them. And he wasn't going to.

'I mean,' I said hurriedly, 'I wonder how one can square writing, desiring success, with Vipassana. I've been wondering if I should stop.'

'Vipassana?'

'No, writing.'

'Oh.' He frowned and sighed. 'You know, lots of people come to these retreats and get it into their heads they should retire to a monastery or something. I can't see why.'

I was beginning to find the encounter galling. 'Well, monks don't write books, do they? The two things are evidently incompatible.'

Again the slow smile. 'Monks don't do lots of things. Who said you have to be a monk?'

'The fact is, more than anything else, words seem to take me away from the present moment. I'm never really here. Always word-mongering. I feel a lot of what's wrong with my life comes from words.'

He always waited a while before replying.

'We're speaking now,' he eventually said. 'We're using words now. It's quite pleasant, isn't it? Maybe useful.'

'It's different with books.'

The way he watched made you feel that despite his eighty and more years, he was focused on you, he cared. Then the answers were offhand.

'But books are wonderful things.' He chuckled. 'I even wrote one myself way back.'

'*The Tranquil Mind.*'

'That's right.'

I had seen a copy on the table outside the meditation room.

'It's not a very good book, I don't think, but an effective way of communicating a lot of information to a large number of people.'

Realising I would get nowhere, I said abruptly, 'Mr Coleman, perhaps you could help me with a smaller thing. I have trouble sitting up straight when I'm meditating. Especially here. At home I seem to manage. Here my back just collapses. I keep feeling I'm going to keel over.'

Coleman reflected, or appeared to. Perhaps it was the merest performance.

'I used to have a lot of problems sitting up straight,' he said.

'But what can I do?'

He breathed deeply. 'I wonder why you want to sit up straight.'

'Well, because it would be more comfortable, for a start, better for my back. I'd breathe better.'

He seemed unconvinced. 'I wouldn't do anything about it.'

'It does seem a fair thing to want, though.'

He looked out of the window. Perhaps he was going senile. He was losing touch.

'Sure.' He turned back to me. 'Everybody would prefer to sit up straight, yes.' He waited. 'You know, sometimes, when things don't happen for us, it's because we want them too much.'

I was silent.

'*Anicca*,' he said. 'Concentrate on *anicca*.' He leaned forward and offered me his hand. 'It would be interesting to go on talking, but I only have fifteen minutes per person.'

So that was it! I shook his hand, smiled daggers and went to the door in a fury. I had demeaned myself coming to talk to a guru and he had barely acknowledged my existence. So much for acquiring wisdom. As I left, an elderly man was waiting to come in. Coleman was running to schedule.

I stood in the stone corridor. It had recently been renovated and whitewashed but the Gothic arches round the doorways still kept their antique feel. The window at the far end was a square of brilliant light around the dark candle of a cypress outside. I went to look. The hills were ablaze with dusty sunshine. Down on the lawn, smoking and sunning herself on a deckchair, was the pretty young woman I'd caught Coleman talking to the first days of the retreat. She was taking time out. Join her, I decided. The hell with it.

Downstairs, approaching the main entrance, I stopped. The old bastard had called my bluff. He had seen through me. I was that simple. I shook my head, hesitated, and turned back down the corridor.

I had never entered the meditation room in the middle of a session. I closed the door as quietly as I could, and even so, as it clicked, a tremor ran through the bodies around me. The door was at the back of the room where three or four people sat on chairs. I passed them and padded barefoot up the narrow space between the men, two by two on mats to the left, and the women, two by two to the right. The four windows along the right-hand wall were open and a soft summeriness drifted in. Nevertheless I was aware of an intense, still calm, a hum almost. There was a collective mental energy around me that seemed tangible, as though I were wading through a warm sea of mind.

Having reached my place, I stood still to take a last look. Rows and rows of seated and kneeling figures. A fat man on a mountain of cushions. A gaunt Arab-looking boy who used nothing more than a low block of wood for a seat. Some sat straight-backed, some bowed. There were smooth, untroubled faces, frowning faces, faces smiling faintly. Some had all the gear, the oriental shawls, the cushions with esoteric symbols; some wore washed-out shorts, shapeless T-shirts. The pregnant woman was serene in a half lotus. One man rested his hands on his knees, the palms turned up, forefinger and thumb just touching. Another let his arms drop in his lap. Then I saw that the elderly woman to my right had a fly on her cheek. A black blowfly. It was walking up from her neck to her cheek. She didn't flinch. The clock ticked. The fly followed her hairline above an ear. She had greying hair tied in a bun. Was she aware of the creature or not?

I sat down. I was glad I had come back. I felt privileged to have seen the room when everyone was so still and concentrated. I settled down as quietly as I could and closed my eyes. My anger with Coleman had abated. He had been right to suspect my reasons for wanting to sit up straight. I wanted to prove I could do it, to myself and others. Exhibitionism. Perhaps he was right about the writing too. Maybe the real change would be to stop trying to impress myself with all this talk of drastic changes. 'A lot of people get that idea into their heads,' he had said. And: 'I used to have problems sitting up straight myself.' You and I are alike and like the others too, he was saying. Don't look for some special relationship with me because you're a tortured writer. He'd been very polite, I thought. He wasn't proselytising, he wasn't out to recruit disciples. I closed my eyes and waited for the breath to declare itself on my upper lip.

Charity

THINGS AS THEY ARE. This bowl. The table. White yoghurt. At the last breakfast I was overwhelmed by the sheer presence of it all. This bread, this square of butter. Things as they are. My hand. The blemished skin, a scarred knuckle, a dirty fingernail. Everything was intensely itself, source at once of fascination and indifference. Scattered crumbs, splashed milk. I gazed at them. As in a Cézanne, each object had been set free from the mesh of human interpretation. A cup beside a slice of melon. Absolutely themselves. I say the words now – cup, melon – but my mind at the time was wordless. The cup, the melon, were things without words, not in relation, not part of a sentence or a story. And there was no distance between us. I was in the cup, I was sticky with melon. Raising my eyes, I looked at the young man across the table, cheeks freshly shaven, a red T-shirt, a tattoo on his middle finger. The tattoo mimicked a ring, etched into his skin. I watched. He was holding a biscuit, using a knife to smear it with pink jam. It was too intense.

The jam was too pink. The strong fingers too present. I was touching them. The fingers were touching me. Watching was touching. Words protect us perhaps. Words keep the world at bay. I say that now. The thought didn't occur to me then. I was tongue-tied, there, in the middle of it all. I really was right there.

In slow motion we went to the meditation room. The man behind me took his place, eyes closed, lips pressed together. I hadn't heard him cough for days. The man in front was a sack of coal, bulk settling into bulk. The woman to my right perched electrically still; she was a bird, a parrot. She could fly off at any moment.

I closed my eyes and waited. Sure enough, other eyes opened in the dark. I was in the pitch dark putting out to sea. Mine was a frail craft, an oarless skiff. I wasn't concerned. I had put out to sea before without coming back. It wasn't a problem. The keel grated on the stones and bobbed free, free as the breath floating on my lip.

How quickly I'd got going!

Time passed. Despite sitting still, my body was twisting; my face had detached itself from my head, it was drifting away: lips, nose and eyes stretched and skewed like a gargoyle's. It didn't matter. The sea has its tides and currents. Looking across the space between skull and skin, I saw coils of grey smoke under my nostrils. I watched the smoke turn. It seemed extraordinarily delicate. The coils were very tight and fluffy among the hairs poking from my nostrils.

'May all beings,' Coleman's voice boomed out, 'be free from all attachment.' A tremor stiffened my back. I hadn't heard him come in. He sighed heavily and said, 'Today, our last day, the Metta bhavana. Today, the sharing of merits.' Raising his voice to its most vatic and hypnotic, Coleman began to read:

Though I speak with the tongues of men and of angels, and have not charity, I am become as sounding brass, or a tinkling cymbal.

Damn. The wave that swept across me now was the exact opposite of a wave of relaxation. Nothing could have jerked me more sharply out of my tranced focus on the present moment than these words, nothing could have thrust me more forcibly back into history and narrative. 1 Corinthians 13 was Dad's favourite passage from St Paul. For a moment my father's voice and Coleman's were one. My little boat sank like a stone.

And though I have the gift of prophecy, and understand all mysteries, and all knowledge; and though I have all faith, so that I could remove mountains, and have not charity, I am nothing.

Charity! My mind raced. Why was Coleman reading *this*? Did he know my past? I saw my father in the pulpit, robes gleaming in the sunlight that fell through the rose window on summer mornings, bald head gleaming. These were the words, he believed, that more than any other established Christianity's superiority. St Paul's great hymn to charity. Being read by a Buddhist.

And though I bestow all my goods to feed the poor, and though I give my body to be burned, and have not charity, it profiteth me nothing.

As Coleman read each verse so the one-legged translator read the Italian version. Knowing both languages, each blow struck twice.

Se distribuissi anche tutti i miei beni ai poveri, e dessi il mio corpo ad essere bruciato, se non ho la carità, tutto questo non mi giova nulla.

What did it mean 'though I give my body to be burned'? Why would anyone do that? I was right back in the world of words and angry questions, the world of my young self pitted against my dad's preaching, against every form of proselytising and coercion and mystery-mongering.

Charity suffereth long, and is kind; charity envieth not; charity vaunteth not itself, is not puffed up.

It was odd. I was furious with Coleman for reading this passage, for bringing back my father, my embattled

adolescence, furious with him for ruining what I had supposed would be another long, peaceful emptying of the
mind into the spell of the present. At the same time, how
could I not assent to these words? How could I not see that
they were in line with all I had been thinking? Charity vaunteth not itself. It is not forever preparing prize acceptance
speeches. Ergo, self-regard is uncharitable. How right that
was! And though I sell a billion copies of my next novel,
though I win the Nobel twice over and join the holy canon
of literary greats, and have not charity, I am nothing.

Charity doth not behave itself unseemly, seeketh not
her own, is not easily provoked, thinketh no evil;
rejoiceth not in iniquity, but rejoiceth in the truth;
beareth all things, believeth all things, hopeth all
things, endureth all things.

This was mad. How can you believe all things, hope all
things? For some reason I was on the brink of tears. I tried
to remember a sermon where my father had explained the
different words for love in the Bible, told his congregation
why the word here had been translated as charity rather
than love. I couldn't. I couldn't recall it. I must swallow
down these emotions. The storm had blown up so quickly.
There had been no warning.

Charity never faileth: but whether there be prophe-
cies, they shall fail; whether there be tongues, they

shall cease; whether there be knowledge, it shall vanish away.

Right, all this was so right! Whether there be novels,
they shall disappear from the shelves. Only a month after
publication most likely. And essays and articles and newspapers and websites and even the most beautiful poems.
Though your book last a thousand years, though it last a
hundred thousand, it will vanish. You are nothing.

But wouldn't charity vanish too? a cool voice remarked.
What did it mean, charity never faileth? That was empty
piety.

For we know in part, and we prophesy in part. But
when that which is perfect is come, then that which
is in part shall be done away.

Listening to Coleman's deep voice, listening to the
translator's lame echo, I realised I had never really taken
in this passage before. It had always been one of those irri-
tating parts of the Bible that obliged you to acknowledge
that Christianity wasn't all silly, that St Paul wasn't just an
anal retentive. Here we know 'in part'. That was exactly
the problem. Knowledge comes in parts. The urologist, the
neurologist, the psychologist. And the mathematician,
the linguist, the climatologist. Even in daily conversation,
every word divides the world in parts. But when that which
is perfect is come . . .

What? What is perfect? And when?

I opened my eyes and watched Coleman read. Like my father, he knew the text so well he barely needed to look at it.

When I was a child, I spake as a child, I understood as a child, I thought as a child: but when I became a man, I put away childish things. For now we see through a glass, darkly; but then face to face: now I know in part; but then shall I know even as also I am known.

Did I ever become a man? I wondered. And what would it mean, to know as one was known? Who really knows me anyway? Nobody. Despite all your novels and half confessions, nobody knows you. There was something very fine about the words 'through a glass darkly', so fine that you hardly wanted to know things any other way. Through a glass darkly was OK by me.

Coleman paused and launched into the last great verse:

For now abideth faith, hope, charity, these three; but the greatest of these is charity.

Why, I demanded – my head shaking slowly from side to side – why why why wasn't it possible for me to have the benefits I had no doubt obtained from this retreat, from this meditative practice, the mindful breathing, the

exploration of the body, the growing awareness and equanimity, without bringing in these religious imponderables
that always shake me up so badly? Why couldn't Coleman
have done one last session of Vipassana and sent us off happily home?

The guru was talking now. By the end of our ten-day
retreat, he was saying, we should have reached the stage
known as *sotapanna*, 'he who has entered the stream',
sometimes also called *sotapatti*, 'stream-winner'. He smiled
blandly. He hoped it would be clear how these words
related to the discipline we had been following. We had
been learning to enter the stream. *Anicca*. But we hadn't
done this exclusively for our own benefit. We weren't here
to gaze at our navels. The very hard work we had done, he
said, had accumulated for each of us a large number of
merits. Every moment's escape from the confines of our
narrow egos was transformed into a wealth of merits.
Now, if we shared these merits with others, we could help
them, we could improve the world.

How beautiful St Paul was, I thought. At least in that
one passage on charity. At least in the King James version.
And what drivel Coleman was talking.

There followed one of those strange half-hours where
the intellect is hopelessly at war with the emotions. Our
guru rambled on about merits and how, by sharing them
with others, they actually multiplied for you too, so the
more you shared your merits the more merits you had to
share. We would embark now, he said, on the Metta

bhavana, or meditation of loving kindness, which involved thinking intensely first of those closest to us, wishing them well, then the wider family, then, gradually, those we knew less well, those we didn't know at all, those who suffered in every corner of the globe, and those who killed and tortured and raped, even those who pushed destruction's buttons in the Pentagon, the Kremlin. We would share our merits with them and improve their lives and ours.

Crap. If one could save the world thinking good thoughts, it would have been done time ago.

While Coleman spoke, people fidgeted, nodding their heads, or shaking them, swaying from side to side, shifting their weight here and there. It was interesting that the moment you lost the concentration of Anapana and Vipassana it became impossible to maintain the meditation position. You had to move. I wondered if the others felt as embarrassed as I did by all this.

Coleman invited us to think of our parents. We were to close our eyes again, to concentrate on our parents, to recall their faces, to recall all they had done for us, to share our merits with our father and mother, to wish them well. 'May they be free from all attachment. May their lives be full of happiness and sympathetic joy. I gladly share all my merits with them.'

I thought of my dead father, my ageing, sick, but still sprightly mother. Naturally I couldn't wish my father well, because he was dead.

Could I?

Crap. If one could save the world thinking good thoughts, it would have been done time ago

Or could I?

I mean logically I couldn't, but what if I did wish him well anyway? What harm could it do for me to wish my father well? It was meaningless because Dad was beyond harm and beyond being well. He was beyond being. On the other hand, it couldn't harm, could it, for Christ's sake? Is it such a problem to do something meaningless?

Why was this bothering me so much?

I wished my mother well.

Wish your father well, a voice said. I resisted. It makes no fucking sense to wish my father well. He's dead. I won't have anything to do with this mumbo-jumbo and he wouldn't want me to, or rather, wouldn't have wanted me to. In fact, he would have been the first person to tell me to get up and walk out of this pagan bullshit right away. I smiled. Anglican through and through, Dad loathed the Catholic practice of praying for the dead. 'Paganism!' he would shake his head. 'Sheer, unadulterated paganism!' If I couldn't remember his face clearly, I had his voice spot on.

I wish my mother well because I always wish my mother well. I won't share my merits with her because I can't possibly believe in the claptrap of metaphysical accountancy. Next we'll be selling indulgences. Next we'll be lighting candles by photos of the dear departed.

Jesus!

I was stuck. Why? Why was all this emotional stuff happening? Why couldn't I just have sorted out my bellyaches and peeing problems and got right back to work?

I wish my father well, I thought.

How strange it seemed to say those words in my head! Dad has been dead so long. We argued before he died. I wish him well. We argued because I would not say, standing beside his bed, his deathbed, I would not say that I believed in God, that I was a Christian, to please him. 'I'm sure you do believe, Timothy,' he said. His face was grey, spectral. 'Tell me you do.' His lips barely moved. It was two days before he died. He stank. 'No.' I stood my ground. I wouldn't say the words for him because they weren't true. I wasn't a Christian. 'You shouldn't ask me to say such things.' I had been furious. It was the most underhand coercion.

Dad, I wish you well.

Then I sensed a stirring of the mind, a deep well-wishing in the mind, in the belly, in the bowels, that wasn't the words I was rehearsing, but that had been awakened or revealed by those words. Light had fallen on a dark place. I really did wish my father well, *enormously*. I was *bursting* with well-wishing for my father. There was a rolling ocean of well-wishing in me. Where had it come from?

'Maybe we have issues with those close to us. They have made us suffer. How we have suffered for the way they have behaved! And we have made them suffer. No doubt they too have suffered a great deal.' Coleman paused and sighed. 'All the same, I willingly share my merits with them. I share my merits with them gladly. May their lives be full of happiness and sympathetic joy.'

It was really too bad I couldn't believe in this merits claptrap. There was such a deep ring of sincerity in Coleman's voice. I began to have a little respect for him, even though it was intellectually disqualifying to hold such nutty points of view. I fell to thinking of my wife. How we had made each other suffer!

Don't go there.

Our children. Our three children. My brother. My sister.

Faces appeared. I remembered those moments on the terrace at Maroggia. It was the same story, more controlled now, but the same. Something in this business of sitting still, emptying the mind of self-regard, settling into your flesh and blood, something in the soft breathing and the long hours just being there, just accepting that you really were here, here today and gone tomorrow that is; at some point it opened your heart.

There. I have used words that normally make me cringe. It opened your heart to the people around you. Suddenly you wished them well. Even people you really did not wish well. Now you did. However briefly. It brought down barriers and blurred boundaries. In your muscles, first, and your mind. Inside you. Rigidities, routines. They broke down. The mind melted in the flesh. The gap between you and the breakfast utensils shrank, between you and the landscape, between you and the people sitting beside you. We were all on a level. On the eighth or ninth day I had found myself sitting on a bench in the garden, a cup of herb tea in my hand, when the man who had talked about shaving his moustache to feel the breath on his lip came and sat down beside me. It was the only bench in the shade. He was a big athletic man in his early forties, I suppose. The sun was hot. We were sitting a foot or two apart, on the bench, and did not look at each other. We observed the Noble Silence. Yet at once there was an uncanny communion between us. I felt it instantly, intensely, and I knew he was feeling it too. We both knew, without having looked for it or wanted it, that the other was feeling a deep sympathy, a knowledge, but devoid of content. A knowledge of each other. We were both surprised and knew we were surprised. We were both glad, quietly. It must have lasted some minutes. I didn't know him from Adam.

Was this charity?

How can you, I wondered, as Coleman shared his merits now with American generals and Iraqi suicide bombers, how can you pretend to escape from the compartmentalisation of Western medicine and then complain when people go the whole hog and talk spirituality and aura and reincarnation?

How can you? Where draw the line?

Believeth all things. Hopeth all things.

Perhaps it's impossible to integrate mind and body without integrating both with everything.

Would it have been charity to tell my father I believed in God, even if I didn't? I don't.

Suffereth long, and is kind.

I wish you well, Dad.

I couldn't listen to Coleman. 'How they must suffer for

their crimes,' he was saying of Bush and Blair and Putin and bin Laden. 'I gladly share all my merits with them.' Coleman was mad. I went back to St Paul, to Dad's first love. If I have all those wonderful skills, he says, which are just a part, or parts, and have not charity, then I am nothing. It profiteth nothing. Because incomplete, transitory. The part is nothing. Charity is beyond parts, beyond boundaries, beyond time. Hence beyond words. Defined by negatives. It vaunteth not. It faileth not. Or by the absence of exclusions. Beareth believeth hopeth endureth all things. Perhaps it was charity, then, that I had been learning through Vipassana. The knowledge that you are one with the whole. Perhaps the day will come, I thought, when the water snakes rise beside my little boat and I will bless them with all my heart.

'Your vow of silence is lifted,' Coleman said. 'You may talk.'

At once there was movement in the meditation room, there was noise, commotion. I was astonished how eager everyone was to speak, to know each other, how loudly they cried out their names. People jumped from their mats and were shaking hands, saying hello, introducing themselves. Shrill voices, deep voices. Eye contact, gestures, multiplicity. A camera flashed.

In a daze I had just reached the door when a young woman danced up to me, barefoot, beaming.

'Are you, by any chance,' this pretty woman asked, 'Tim Parks, the writer?'

TIM PARKS is an author, translator, critic and teacher. Born in Manchester to deeply religious parents, he grew up in London and studied at Cambridge and Harvard before moving to Italy where he has lived ever since.

He is the author of fourteen novels which have brought him the Somerset Maugham, Llewellyn Rhys and Betty Trask awards and a shortlisting for the Booker Prize. He has also written non-fiction about Italy, football, reading, translation, the Medicis and trains. His one hobby is white-water kayaking, which he hopes to pursue into extreme old age.

Tim Parks now meditates every day and claims to have remained absolutely calm the mornings after both the Brexit referendum and the election of Donald Trump.

RECOMMENDED BOOKS BY TIM PARKS:

Teach Us to Sit Still
Europa
Italian Ways
Where I'm Reading From

How do we find Calm in our modern world?

Swimming
ROGER DEAKIN

VINTAGE MINIS

Motherhood
HELEN SIMPSON

VINTAGE MINIS

Work
JOSEPH HELLER

VINTAGE MINIS

Liberty
VIRGINIA WOOLF

VINTAGE MINIS

VINTAGE MINIS

The Vintage Minis bring you the world's greatest writers on the experiences that make us human. These stylish, entertaining little books explore the whole spectrum of life – from birth to death, and everything in between. Which means there's something here for everyone, whatever your story.

vintageminis.co.uk